27-50 ✓

Developing
JAVA
Software

Edition

WORLDWIDE SERIES IN COMPUTER SCIENCE

Series Editors   **Professor David Barron,** *Southampton University, UK*
Professor Peter Wegner, *Brown University, USA*

The Worldwide Series in Computer Science has been created to publish textbooks which both address and anticipate the needs of an ever evolving curriculum thereby shaping its future. It is designed for undergraduates majoring in Computer Science and practitioners who need to reskill. Its philosophy derives from the conviction that the discipline of computing needs to produce technically skilled engineers who will inevitably face, and possibly invent, radically new technologies throughout their future careers. New media will be used innovatively to support high quality texts written by leaders in the field.

Developing JAVA Software

Second Edition

Russel Winder
King's College London, UK

and

Graham Roberts
University College London, UK

JOHN WILEY & SONS, LTD
Chichester • New York • Weinheim • Brisbane • Singapore • Toronto

Other Wiley Editorial Offices

John Wiley & Sons, Inc., 605 Third Avenue,
New York, NY 10158-0012, USA

Weinheim • Brisbane • Singapore • Toronto

A catalogue record for this book is available from the British Library.

ISBN 0 471 60696 0

Cover image: Paul Gaugin — At the Bottom of the Mountain. Reproduced with permission from SuperStock.

Designed by Mark and Sally Spedding, Salisbury, Wiltshire, UK.

Produced from PostScript files supplied by Russel Winder.

Printed and bound by Biddles Ltd, Guildford and King's Lynn, UK.

This book is printed on acid-free paper responsibly manufactured from sustainable forestry, for which at least two trees are planted for each one used for paper production.

V

Contents

3 Adding Structure   51

4 Drawing Pictures   91

5 Introducing Containers   113

6 Classes and Objects   145

8 Introducing Exceptions and Threads   225

9 The Programming Process   245

Part 2 Building Class Libraries

20 Sorting — Comparative Methods   569

21 Sorting — Distributive Methods   593

22 Sorting — External Methods   603

Part 3 Case Studies in Developing Programs

Part 4 The Java Programming Language in Detail

27 A Java Language Reference   761

33 Threads and Concurrency 921

Part 5 Endmatter

Preface

Java is now a well established programming system — not just a programming language but also a large collection of libraries and tools. It is being widely used for developing innovative network-based applications, notably those running on servers, and is seeing success elsewhere. Java has also become a popular language for teaching programming at universities and other further and higher education institutes. It is this aspect in particular that prompted us to write the first edition of this book, and then update it to deliver the second edition you are reading now.

This new edition incorporates a great deal of knowledge and feedback obtained from readers of the first edition, and also from us using the book as the course text for the programming courses we teach. The Computer Science Departments at both King's College London (KCL) and University College London (UCL) now use Java as a first language for all undergraduates, and at UCL it is also taught to conversion MSc students and used for advanced MSc courses. The experience of teaching Java and using the first edition has led us to retain the core structure of the book, with some reordering of material, but to rewrite and expand Part 1 which introduces programming to the beginner. In particular, we have taken a more rigorous early approach to using classes and objects, and provided many more example Java programs.

Throughout the second edition, we emphasize both good programming practice and, in particular, testing. If a program is to be useful it must work reliably, so testing must done, not as an unwelcome final stage after the programming is done, but as an integral part of the programming process. Applied effectively, testing is an important tool, saving much effort in the long run that would otherwise be spent trying to find and fix bugs. Learners should be taught how to test, so that it becomes part of their standard tool set.

Having taught Java as a first language we know it works very well and is very motivating to students. A good example of the motivation is the ease with which graphics and graphical user interfaces can be incorporated into programs allowing for interesting but straightforward programs to be written by those new to programming. In the Part 1 of the book we have added two chapters to support this, the first dealing with program to create simple drawings, the second providing an introduction to graphical user interface construction using the Swing library.

In our courses, we place great emphasis on students doing lots of programming. This motivated us to provide exercise questions at the end of each chapter. Reading a book and attending lectures or seminars must be supported by the learner spending significant amounts of time writing programs and solving programming problems. Ideally this is done in labs where there is plenty of expert help, and more particularly advice, available. Learners are encouraged to experiment, explore all the features of Java, and make lots of mistakes — good programmers become good programmers by making mistakes, recognizing that they have made mistakes, correcting those mistakes and learning how to avoid making the same mistake again.

Learning to Program

People who intend to program, either professionally or as amateurs, need to know how to use Java. This book is support material for learning how to program using Java but is not just about the Java programming language. There are a large number of books on the market that describe the specific features of Java, some of those that we have seen and liked are listed in the bibliography of this book. We are not trying to compete with these books, we are trying to complement them. Thus, we rarely worry about covering all the minute details of the Java language. Whilst we do cover many aspects of the language, it is in the context of examining how the features contribute to learning how to program.

The most important thing about Java is that it is object-oriented which means that objects are the most important thing in Java. We think that this means that objects should be introduced as soon as practical in the lifetime of a Java programmer. Many people think that you need to learn about the infrastructure and technology for constructing objects before actually dealing with objects. The argument goes "you have to be able to construct objects before you can construct applications and you need all the base technology in order to construct objects, so let us start at the bottom and show you all the features of the language so you will then be able to program". This is essentially the 'traditional' bottom-up approach, with each topic being covered in full detail before moving onto the next topic. We do not believe that this is the correct philosophy for learning the skill of programming. We believe that a more holistic approach is needed, where you spiral through the topics adding more of the details each time around. We believe this book supports teaching and learning using this philosophy.

One of the major drives behind languages like Java is reuse: programmers should construct applications by reusing as much previously generated material as possible. This is a good philosophy and one we want to apply to learning the language as well as using the language. We believe that showing how to construct applications using partially pre-constructed software and then deconstructing that pre-constructed software as part of the learning process, is the best way of engendering this approach.

There are other reasons why we do not subscribe to the traditional teaching programme but instead believe that you should cover object concepts early. There is no single linear learning path that is suitable for everyone: the standard bottom-up approach to learning programming is authoritarian in this respect. As indicated above, we believe learning programming is a more holistic activity. People learn bits here and bits there, integrating them for themselves. Learning any practical craft, and programming is no exception, is a matter of learning how to do it for oneself. Moreover, it is an human reasoning activity and no-one yet knows exactly how people do that. There are hypotheses and models but no full proven theories.

Programming has been taught bottom-up for many years, following the history of the various programming constructs. We believe many educators use this approach because this was how they learnt. There may be a more insidious factor at work. Experienced practitioners and educators tend to know a number of languages and learn a new language of the same paradigm by comparing the new language with the languages they already know and relating the new language to the way that they already program. This can be a very efficient technique of learning for the experienced — they already have a massive armoury of knowledge about programming, programming techniques and languages and learning a new language is just augmenting this knowledge. The problem arises when educators assume that people new to programming learn in the same way they do and this is patently not true.

The issue of programming paradigms (imperative, procedural, declarative, functional, etc.) also has an impact. When changing paradigms, for example moving from the procedural world to the object-oriented world, many experienced programmers think it is hard simply because they are having to construct a new way of thinking about computations. Educators often tend to think that students will have difficulties because they did, reasoning that is self-centred and fundamentally flawed.

Our position, therefore, is that people new to programming will not be worried about object-orientation if they are *not told* it is hard and *not taught* it as an hard extension to the traditional procedural view of imperative programming. We believe that the approach that we have developed as a consequence of this view is also useful to people who are already experienced in programming.

In this book we present what we think is the best linear read of the material. However, the reader is free to follow the links and cross-references as and when they want. We do not guarantee that all Java language features are explained before being used. In fact we know that this is definitely not the case. However, the level of use-before-explanation is appropriate for the holistic learning model we are following. The cross-references and indexing should allow anyone who wants to find out about a feature.

Our linear read of the material starts with the basic question "What is programming?" and presents the conceptual material that acts as a foundation for the understanding of objects. This is followed by a systematic introduction to classes and objects before moving on to object-oriented programming. The programming exercises provided in these early chapters encourage students to practice programming by writing lots of small programs. This way syntax and usage is understood even if the details are not yet totally clear. We like to think of this approach as the middle-out approach to learning programming. Objects early, as this is what really matters. Syntax and control statements are the easily learnt filling — and represent the downward learning thread. The upward thread is the combining of objects and classes and constructing applications

In support of this approach, we have split the work into five parts. We start in Part 1, as noted above, by presenting conceptual material about programming and in particular programming with objects and classes, supported by plenty of example programs. Part 2 builds on Part 1 by looking at the development of libraries of Java classes, focusing on data structures and algorithms. This is the bottom-up development of abstractions that augment Java and can be used to construct applications. Part 3, the case studies, looks at the development of actual applications, by describing the design and implementation of three larger programs, illustrating the kind of activities and thought processes that take place when non-trivial programs are written. Throughout Parts 1, 2 and 3 we emphasize code testing, giving examples and advice about what to test and how to test.

In Part 4 we provide a Java language reference that systematically describes the Java language, providing many further example programs. Part 5, the appendices, separates out the bits and pieces of information that don't actually fit anywhere else!

The sixth part of this five part book is the support material on the Web site:

http://www.dcs.kcl.ac.uk/DevJavaSoft/

We have put up supplementary material on this site: lecture slides, extra notes, exercise sheets and answers to exercises in the book — the sort of material associated with presenting this material as the first programming course of an undergraduate degree. At Wiley's behest, we will be using this site to add future material and case studies: the plan is that the book will undergo as much continuous evolution as it is possible to have.

Using this Book

This book is designed both as a support text for those teaching object-oriented programming using Java and as a self-learning text. The division into distinct parts is quite deliberate and is based on over a decade of experience of teaching object-oriented programming, using C++ and more recently Java, and object-oriented analysis and design.

The contents of the book more than provides support for one full academic year, or 24 weeks, of programming teaching or learning (this being equivalent to two semesters or two terms, depending on where you are in the world). Part 1, supported by Part 4, is meant for the first half (12 weeks), Parts 2 and 3 are for the second half. Alternatively, Part 1 could be the basis of a first year course, while Parts 2 and 3 are used for a second year course. By providing a language reference in Part 4, along with good depth and discussion of the programming process in the earlier Parts, we also see the book as being useful throughout a degree or learning programme. This is not a book that the reader will grow out of and discard after the basic skills have been learnt.

Nearly all chapters in Parts 1, 2 and 3 finish with a collection of exercise questions. The questions are split into three categories. The first are self review questions that can be answered directly by the reader to check their understanding of the chapter, but would also make good questions for tutorial sessions or formative written work. The second category provide programming questions which require some thought and a program to be written. These can be used as the basis of lab exercises as illustrated on the book's web site. The third category of questions provide challenges, where the reader not only has to deal with a more difficult programming problem but also has to do some supplementary research to understand and address the issues raised in the question. Such challenges are important as they stretch the capabilities of the reader and go beyond the immediate issues raised in the current chapter.

Part 1 presents material on which lectures can be based and works through all the key concepts and ideas of both object-oriented programming with Java and the object-oriented development process. The ideas presented here need to be effectively communicated so the new programmer isn't diverted by misconceptions and bad practice. The kind of material in Part 1 is well suited for lecture based presentation and provides plenty of scope for moving outside the rigid confines of simply describing Java. Don't forget that, although in the end Java is just a programming language, the ideas and concepts behind it are applicable across much wider areas.

Part 2 provides extensive lecturing material, while Part 3 provides self-study case studies. There is, however, plenty of scope for organizing class discussions and tutorial sessions around the material in Part 3, as well as providing the basis for project work by extending the programs developed. As with Part 1, as much programming practice as possible should be undertaken, backed up by working on program design.

Part 4, the reference, is intended as a self-study guide to the Java language. The reading of Part 4 should be backed up by extensive programming practice, ideally organized around supported lab classes. To properly learn a programming language you have to write programs using it and get them reviewed by experts. There is no alternative to this. As a result (and especially as the result of teaching C++), we don't advocate spending much lecture time on teaching the specifics of the Java language.

Acknowledgements

Whilst the authors have done all the work of writing the material contained herein, more people than just the named authors contribute to the construction of a book of this sort and it is only fair and just that they get named somewhere and here is that somewhere.

Peter Wood, Alex Poulovassilis, Nigel Chapman, Al Sutton, Nahed Stokes, Malcolm Bird and Richard Overill are past or current colleagues of RW whose input has resulted in features of both the first and second editions. Vasa Curcin, Jitesh Vassa, Dan Alderman and Ross Burton were students at KCL and were particularly helpful to RW in evolving the material from the first edition to the second edition. In fact, all the students on all the courses RW has taught at KCL over the last two years deserve credit (for surviving as well as helping to evolve the material) but they are, unfortunately, too numerous (about 600) to mention individually. Joshua Bloch, the author of the Collections Framework has had a number of email communications with RW that contributed to the evolution of the ADS package. Doug Lea also provided contributions on this that proved very helpful. Perhaps the most significant input though came from Joe Bergin who provided a most constructive critique of the worst parts of the original ADS package.

GR would like to thank various colleagues at UCL who have supported the development of Java teaching, and to the students who pioneered to use of Java for coursework and projects, giving valuable feedback about what learners really need to know. Also thanks to the students that have taken the courses based on the book and survived!

Gaynor Redvers-Mutton from John Wiley & Sons cajoled and bullied us brilliantly (again!) from the very outset. She phoned and met with us (and occasional bought lunch) at exactly the right moments in the process to maximize delivery throughput. Dawn Booth, also from John Wiley & Sons, helped massively with the production of the PostScript files which were sent to the printers. Without both of their support and efforts we would never have got this tome finished and certainly not in the timescale we did. We would also like to thank Mark Spedding for his design of this tome. Hopefully you like it as much as we do.

The support of the people you live with is incredibly important in managing to create works like this. Geri Winder kept her spouse (RW) going even in the depths of depression caused by trying to eradicate all the bugs he kept on putting into the programs, not to mention helping to find the right phrases when the words would not come. GR was ably supported by family and pets, not least the helping beak of Billy the Cockatoo.

Russel Winder

Department of Computer Science, King's College London,
Strand, London WC2R 2LS
russel@dcs.kcl.ac.uk

Graham Roberts

Department of Computer Science, University College London,
Gower Street, London WC1E 6BT.
G.Roberts@cs.ucl.ac.uk

1

Programming with Objects and Classes

Part 1

Objectives

This part of the book explains what object-oriented programming with Java is all about, starting from first principles. It closes with a description of how Java programs are designed and implemented, supported by an example design exercise.

Contents

Introduction

Objectives

This chapter sets the scene by introducing the background concepts needed to begin programming using Java.

Keywords

history

jargon

abstraction

humour

1.1   The Start

This book, as may be inferred from the title, is about programming with Java. We assume the reader is basically computer literate, being familiar with using a computer for tasks such as word processing, World Wide Web browsing, possibly even some programming, but has little or no *object-oriented programming* experience. Object-oriented? It's the technical term for the kind of programming method that Java embodies and any competent programmer needs to know about. This book is all about object-oriented programming using Java.

In this chapter, we are going to set out the background information needed to give context. In the following chapters, in the five parts of the book, we will proceed through not just a description of what Java is but, rather more importantly, how to use it properly and effectively. By the end of the book, you, the reader, should be ready to write some serious and useful programs. That is one of the key reasons we wrote this book: we want to leave the reader ready to tackle real problems and get professional results. This book is not simply a Java language primer but is a full description of the object-oriented approach to programming.

To set the scene for those new to programming, we first need to define some basic terms. A *program* is a (usually long and complex) series of instructions that are carried out (or *executed*, or *run*) by a computer. The instructions define what the program does, whether it is a word-processor, spreadsheet, game or any other kind of program. The role of the *programmer* is to create, or write, programs which is usually done using a *programming language*, one of which is called Java. *Application programming* or development is the process of programming in order to create a program (the *application*) to be used by people (*end users*) in order to get something useful done. *Systems programming*, on the other hand, is the activity of writing, amending or extending the *operating system* which is the program that manages a computer's resources in order to allow applications to be run.

As can be seen from the last paragraph, talking about programming and Java involves becoming familiar with lots of technical terms and jargon. We try to explain the jargon as we begin to use it but if you find some that you don't understand try looking in the glossary (see Appendix A, Page 939).

1.2   A (Very!) Short History of Java

"Java is this new language that allows you to do things with Web pages…" (Anon)

Possibly. Java has certainly not been around for that long and it is often described as the World Wide Web programming language. However, whilst Java may have a short history, it is built on some very solid foundations, especially those laid by the object-oriented revolution of the last decade. Moreover, whilst Java certainly has strong Web connections, it is a powerful application programming system, not just a programming language for Web *applets*.

1.2 A (Very!) Short History of Java

5

Given such claims, the actual origins of Java are, perhaps, interesting. The development of what we now call Java started out as work on a programming language called Oak, designed during the early 1990s by a team of developers at Sun Microsystems (the name Oak being inspired by a large oak tree visible from an office window). Oak was meant to be used for programming the embedded systems in consumer electronics devices, with a particular emphasis on areas such as interactive cable TV control devices and electronic home management systems. Among other features, these applications needed new kinds of user interface, easy networking and a programming system to support system development.

As it turned out, the consumer market for programmable control devices didn't develop on anything like the scale or time anticipated. However, as work on Oak continued, the Internet and, in particular, the Web exploded into widespread use. In early 1994, a decision was made to adapt the Oak language to the needs of the Internet and provide an Internet programming language for Web-based applications. This decision was made because Oak included many features that were relevant for the Internet environment, including the idea of being *architecturally neutral*, meaning that the same program can run on a wide variety of different machines without having to be re-written.

In January 1995, Oak was renamed Java (because the name Oak was already in commercial use elsewhere), having been developed into a robust programming language suitable for building Web-based applications. In May 1995 Sun released the initial Java Development Kit (usually referred to as the JDK) via the Internet which allowed developers all over the world to download it and start using Java. The JDK was supported by the release of a Web browser called HotJava which was capable of running Java programs in the form of *applets* embedded in Web pages, a feature since taken up by browsers from Microsoft and Netscape. From these beginnings, Java has become increasingly popular and is now widely supported by commercial developers and software companies, who are busy providing development tools and many other facilities.

Late in 1998, the Java 2 Platform was released along with Sun's implementation of it, Java 2 SDK, Standard Edition (J2SDK). Sun continues to develop Java by enhancing the basic J2SDK and adding many additional features to extend the environment. Some of these features are concerned with new ways of constructing programs while others come in the form of *class libraries*, or as they are often referred to, APIs (Application Programmer Interfaces). APIs provide the programmer with a wide range of additional facilities in a ready to use form, saving much time and effort. Two of these APIs are so important that they are now an integral part of J2SDK:

JFC — the Java Foundation Classes. A set of components that includes the Swing library for building graphical user interfaces (using windows, menus, buttons, and so on).

Java2D — providing 2D graphics drawing capabilities.

Perhaps the most prominent APIs that can be used with the standard J2SDK are:

JavaBeans — the Java object component technology. This is a key technology that allows pre-built program fragments (the components) to be combined together quickly and easily to create programs.

note

For a detailed history of the development of Java, visit Sun's Java Web site at http://java.sun.com/.

note

SDK stands for System Development Kit.

Servlets — an efficient way of using Java programs in conjunction with a Web server.

JDBC — the Java Database Connectivity package, providing a Java-based interface to SQL databases.

Java Advanced Imaging Framework — an extension of Java2D and releasing a full set of codecs and a wide range of image file formats.

Java Media Framework (JMF) — providing for video and audio playback.

Java3D — providing 3D graphics drawing capabilities.

Java Accessibility — providing mechanisms to give easy access to Java programs for people with disabilities.

JavaMail — for constructing programs to work with electronic mail.

JavaSound — for working with high quality sound.

JavaHelp — for creating help systems to support the use of applications.

And also many more. Visit Sun's Web pages to see the full list — which is frequently extended. There are also various complete applications that have been developed entirely in Java itself:

JavaServer — a complete Web server written in Java, supporting servlets.

Java Workshop — a Java programming environment for developing Java programs which is itself written in Java.

HotJava — a Web browser completely written in Java.

An important consequence of the evolution of Java is that it has grown into a full-scale, general development system, quite capable of being used for developing large applications that exist outside of the browser-based Web environment. In fact, it can potentially be used to create all kinds of programs, with a particular emphasis on those that make extensive use of networking and communications. At the time of writing, Java is having its greatest success as a language for developing what are known as *middleware* applications, which form the core component of distributed applications running on networks. Java is also being widely adopted in universities as a language for teaching programming.

1.3   Being at the Right Place at the Right Time

One of the most notable features of Java is that it has become very popular in a short space of time. The growth in interest has been spectacular and has taken many by surprise. It's worth asking why.

Java is not a perfect language but it does exploit a number of recent, but nonetheless well established, ideas about programming languages and programming methods. Although this is important, there are a number of other factors which have enabled Java to achieve mega-stardom:

- It looks familiar to users of other popular languages, notably C, C++ and Smalltalk. Familiarity avoids potential users seeing a new language as 'too different' and, therefore, not worth the time to learn.
- It's closely connected to the Web which is very popular. How important this connection will continue to be in the future is not entirely clear but it was the right thing to get a big kick start.
- Programming 'gurus' liked it. Gurus are early adopters of new programming languages, even if they (the languages, not the gurus) are still immature, and can have a big impact on how quickly information about the language is disseminated.
- You can get it for free! Very important this, as it allows potential users to try out a new language with very little start-up cost (at least, in direct financial terms).

Interestingly, this list shows that the most important thing about a new language is the social aspect — people must want to use it because it does something they want to do *now*. Technical considerations often come a distant second!

Overall, Java was launched in the right place (on the Web), at the right time (just as the Web was getting really popular), with the right features (it is object-oriented) and at the right cost (free).

1.4   What is Java?

The name Java is typically used as a generic label encompassing the Java programming language, the tools and environment of the development kit and all the class libraries and APIs that are delivered as standard. To a large extent all these elements are inseparable, so learning about Java is learning about them all. Sometimes you hear references to the 'Java Programming System', emphasizing that Java is not just a programming language on its own.

Java provides an *object-oriented programming language*. The chapters in Part 1 will describe what this means. For now we need to know that a programming language allows you to express programs in a textual form, and that object-oriented development is *the* modern approach to designing and building systems, best supported by programming languages that embody directly the key object-oriented concepts.

Object-oriented development is now widely used as it addresses a large number of the problems that arise during software development, providing viable and practical solutions. This is of enormous significance as the track record for successful software development is perceived to be very poor. This is actually something of a misconception. Whilst there is a lot of software that is written but never used, and there have been some very high profile failures of software development projects and there is a lot of software that is delivered very late and of very poor quality, there is a large amount of very good and very reliable software in the world. Don't assume, though, that 'going object-oriented' will be like waving a magic wand to solve all your software development problems.

What it will give you is a conceptual framework and an approach to software development that is based on a great deal of experience of what works best. Java embodies much of this experience and this book aims to put that across while you learn how to use Java. In the end, though, you have to do the hard work to learn to use Java efficiently and effectively.

So, Java is a programming language based on a particular way of doing software development. As must be the case with any programming language, Java is properly defined so that programmers can write programs and understand what they mean. The written form of a programming language is specified by its *syntax*, whereas the meaning of what has been written (i.e. what the program does) is specified by its *semantics*. Parts 1–3 of this book will introduce much of the syntax and semantics of the Java programming language in the context of actually developing software while Part 4 presents more detailed information in a reference-like style.

Programming is a learnt skill. Practice is essential.

Object-oriented programming centres on identifying and working with *abstractions*. An abstraction allows a concept or idea to be expressed and then repeatedly used without all the detail getting in the way. As an analogy consider describing a chair. There are all sorts of different kinds of chair but people learn to recognize the range of properties of what makes a chair — 'chairness' if you like — allowing them to deal with chairs without having to continually describe all the detail of a chair. Java supports the use of abstraction via the object-oriented mechanism of *class*, where a class allows an abstraction to be expressed once and then re-used many times without getting side-tracked by all the detail.

Abstraction *is **THE** key concept in computing.*

Many basic abstractions are widely and repeatedly used, so there is no point in having to continually recreate them. As noted earlier, the Java system comes with an integral library of basic abstractions in the form of a large class library. This library is intimately inter-connected with the programming language to the extent that neither can be used without the other. Hence, the Java programmer must not only learn a programming language but must also become familiar with a large collection of classes. The advantage of making this commitment comes from having a large number of ready made building blocks available when writing programs. Instead of having to describe everything in full detail, abstractions can be substituted, saving much time and effort.

There is an infinite amount of knowledge. However much is known, there is always more to learn.

The use of abstractions does not stop with those that come from the standard Java library, the programmer needs to find, learn and use other appropriate class libraries that can added to the development environment (e.g. the Java Generic Library — JGL) or build new ones themselves. Finding and building abstractions is the key to the successful systems development, particularly object-oriented development. Failure to use and build abstractions really misses the point and is going to lead to poorly designed, unstable programs.

Abstractions are built up in layers. At the bottom is the programming language, next the abstractions from the standard library, then one or more layers of abstractions provided by the programmer. Each layer of abstraction provides a higher level point of view of the system being implemented as a program. For any non-trivial program, matching the level of abstraction with the way people think and reason about systems is critical. If the programmer is forced to deal with too much detail at any one time, mistakes will be made and progress will grind to a halt. Following the chair analogy, say we are trying to find the right location in a room for the chair. Using abstraction, we treat the chair as a whole and just name a spot. Without abstraction we must take the collection of parts (legs, seat, back, etc.) and specify exactly where each part must go, hoping that we have placed things in such a way that they make a complete chair. Clearly not a sensible thing to do.

Unsurprisingly then, most of this book is about abstraction. Part 1 introduces class-based abstraction whereas Part 2 demonstrates how to go about creating new abstractions. All the while, of course, we advocate using pre-constructed abstractions whenever possible to save both time and effort.

Beyond creating abstractions, the programmer needs, ultimately, to create whole programs. This involves designing the overall structure of the program, building and putting together the pieces, and then testing the program to see that it actually works. Part 3 of the book provides case studies showing the design and implementation of several programs, demonstrating the process that was followed to create them.

1.5 The Java 2 Platform

To use Java and get some programming done, development tools are needed. Java is distributed by Sun Microsystems as the Java 2 Platform System Development Kit (J2SDK) which can be obtained from Sun's Java Web site. This is a set of command line tools. A number of vendors offer full graphical environments, all of which are wrappers around Sun's J2SDK.

At the time of writing this book, the current version of Sun's Java system is J2SDK v1.2.2, though v1.3 is due out very soon. The original version of Sun's Java system was called the Java Development Kit (JDK) 1.0. It went through several revisions and stabilized with version 1.0.2. The next major version of the JDK was 1.1. This also went through a number of revisions, ending up at 1.1.8. Early releases of the J2SDK were labelled JDK 1.2 but for various reasons Sun changed the labelling so we have J2SDK v1.2.2. Although every attempt is made for Java to be backwardly compatible so that existing programs can still be used, there is a policy of allowing deprecation (i.e. removal) of out-dated features. Thus, programmers will occasionally, during compilation of Java code, encounter warnings about 'deprecated' features, most of which are replaced with new features. Since a deprecated feature can be removed in the next release of the J2SDK, it is wise to change code to remove the deprecated features immediately: the good programmer never leaves deprecated features in their code.

To use the J2SDK, it must first be installed on your computer — following the instructions provided. J2SDK comes with an extensive set of tools and features. The core elements are:

- The Java development tools.
- The Java class libraries, organized into a collection of *packages*.

- A number of demonstration programs.

- Various supporting tools and components, including the *source code* of the classes in the libraries.

A full set of documentation is available separately from the main J2SDK and should be installed as a matter of priority when the J2SDK is installed. In particular, the documentation describes all the classes in the class libraries, providing essential information for the programmer. The documentation is supplied in the form of Web pages so it is easy to browse when using a computer.

A first priority of the Java programmer, is to become familiar with the main development tools. Programs, written by the programmer in textual form, need to be transformed into a format that can be executed by a computer. This is done by a tool called a *compiler*. The Java compiler is named `javac`.

To execute or run a Java program, a *run-time environment* containing a Java *interpreter* is needed and this is provided by a tool called `java`. Another tool called a *debugger* is provided for *debugging* programs. Debugging is the process of locating and fixing errors in programs, something programmers tend to spend a lot of time doing, even the good ones!

The basic J2SDK provides the tools as command line versions, meaning that they are generally used by typing in commands to a command interpreter (in an MSDOS window if using Windows95/NT; an xterm or equivalent if using UNIX). Many vendors are now also supplying Java development environments, usually with the tools integrated into sophisticated graphical programming environments. This book will assume the use of the standard J2SDK but any J2SDK compatible programming environment can be used.

note

IBM have released a Java compiler called jikes which is well worth looking at. Like javac, it is free. Look at http://www.ibm.com/developerworks/opensource/.

1.6   Applications and Applets

Java programs come in two forms — *applications* and *applets*. Java applications are no different from the ordinary, mainstream applications you run on your computer whereas applets provide mini-applications that are embedded in Web pages.

Applets are downloaded to a browser and contain one or more small Java programs which will start executing when the Web page is displayed. As applets are obtained from a remote site to run on your local computer, they are not trusted and are subject to a number of security restrictions. For example, an applet cannot access your local files or printer —after all you don't want to download an applet that prints several hundred pages of adverts while you are browsing Web pages. These restrictions mean that there are many kinds of program that cannot be written as an applet.

Applications, in contrast to applets, are not restricted in what they can do. An application can access local files and can print. Applications allow the programmer to write any kind of program that is possible with Java.

This book is almost entirely about Java applications, with only a few references to applets appearing. The rationale here is that applets are just special forms of application: in order to write applets, you need to know how to write applications.

1.7 Java is Architecture Neutral

Java is a *compiled language* but rather than producing instructions for a specific hardware processor, the Java compiler generates Java *bytecodes* which are interpreted by a *Java Virtual Machine (JVM)*. The JVM is a program that implements an idealized computer optimized to run Java programs. Providing a computer or workstation has an implementation of the JVM program, any Java program can be run on that machine. Hence, a Java program is run by another program, the JVM, which is in turn running on a real processor.

A consequence of this is that a Java program can be compiled once, stored on a server, transferred across the network to a client machine and then executed on that machine without worrying about what kind of machine it is. A Java program is said to be *architecture neutral* as its executable representation is independent of both the physical architecture of a machine and the operating system it is running.

These portability issues have important commercial considerations. Since a Java program can be executed on any machine with any operating system (such as Windows95/NT or UNIX), as long as it has a JVM, there is no longer any need to be concerned about which operating system a machine is running: operating systems become less important. Developers will no longer have to worry about targeting a particular operating system since the JVM will be the architecture everyone writes programs for.

Figure 1.1 presents an overview of the JVM environment. The Peer interface is used to adapt Java graphics so they can adopt the style of the local machine, and Just in Time Compilers (JITs) optimize and speed up bytecode execution for specific machine architectures.

A further feature of the JVM is that it can provide a safe execution environment (often referred to as the Sandbox). Particularly in the case of applets, this is used to enforce security, as every time Java code is loaded it is verified to check that it has not been tampered with. In addition, Java programs can run with a security manager which verifies that the program has permission to access resources such as files and network connections. Even with Java applications, rather than applets, this is becoming increasingly important as networking and the Internet become more and more widely used, allowing un-trusted programs to be downloaded and executed very easily.

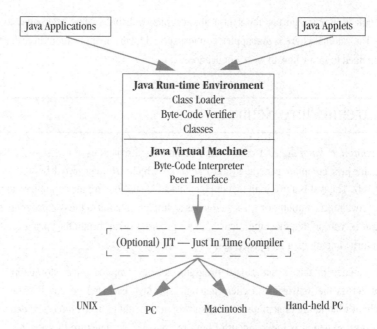

Figure 1.1 Overview of the Java environment.

1.8   Java is No Joke

It is reputed that the name Java is an acronym for Just Another Virtual Architecture. It is certainly the name of an island in the Indian Ocean that is (at the time of writing anyway) part of Indonesia. Java is famous for having Bali to the east and a small volcano (Krakatau) to the west — well, it is small compared to what it used to be before the 1883 explosion that gave us the song Blue Moon (allegedly) and the previous larger (!) explosion of 416. Java is also famous for having revealed Homo Erectus (Java Man) in 1890.

Having said all this, most people have heard of Java because it grows a shrub, coffee, which can be used to create a drink, coffee, that contains a substance, caffeine, copious quantities of which are supposedly required for programmers to be able to function.

So legendary are the stories of programmers' use and abuse of coffee, that the arrival of Java as a programming language has enabled vendors, authors, everyone, to construct huge humorous edifices and indeed some jokes. The originators of Java, or someone associated with their publishing activity, created the coffee cup logo that appears on all of Sun's Java products, amongst other icons now an integral part of the culture of Java (the programming system anyway).

Many authors make use of the coffee theme, extending it to include related food imagery. In fact, so extreme has some of the coffee related humour become, from vendors in particular, that many authors have gone for a backlash and completely eschewed any reference to coffee. Indeed, going so far as to invent anti-coffee allegories.

All of this is good natured and, at least for the moment, very humorous. However, amidst all this we must not forget that Java has the potential to be used for real, large scale application development. Do not let any of the humour of presentation detract from the very non-humorous purpose of Java.

1.9 Summary

We have argued in this chapter that Java is a modern programming system and is very much the 'right thing at the right time'. We believe that Java is also very suitable for teaching and for learning to work with object-oriented development.

This chapter has really just set the scene by providing necessary background. We are now ready to start exploring what programming is all about and how it can be done with Java.

Programming Fundamentals

Objectives

This chapter begins the examination of what programming is, and how a programming language like Java works, starting with a look at the concepts of *sequence*, *selection*, *iteration* and *state*. The following chapters will develop these basic ideas and lead on to an explanation of object-oriented programming.

Keywords

sequence

iteration

loops

selection

variables

process

comments

initialization

input–output

interaction

testing

2.1   Introduction

Programming is the activity of designing and writing programs. Programs, in turn, instruct a computer what to do. Much of programming is all about good communication. We, the human beings, have to tell a computer how to perform a task, by breaking the task down into a long sequence of simple instructions. We have to do this very precisely as the computer will literally do anything we instruct it to, sensible or not. The instructions forming a program are written by humans in a textual form using a *programming language*. In programming jargon the textual representation is the *source code*; the source of the code, or instructions, the computer executes.

Once the source code of a program has been written, the step of communicating the program to a computer is a relatively minor, and largely automated, task. The hard work lies in creating the source code in the first place and that is a job done by people. Most of the real communication involved takes place between people who have to talk about the design of their programs, and by their actions of reading and writing program source code. Like working with any text, program code has to be carefully presented and structured in order to be understandable and accurately convey our intent. Moreover, we need an agreed understanding of how to interpret the meaning of what we write, and that meaning has to be consistent with the way the computer works. In this chapter we will start looking at how Java programs work and how they are represented.

To construct any computer program, we must use some process to translate the idea for the use of the computer into lines of source code that can be *compiled* (translated into instructions the computer understands) and *executed* (get the computer to carry out the instructions). This process typically includes the tasks of: *requirements gathering,* what we would like the program to do; *analysis,* finding out how the program should behave; *design*, deciding the structure of the program to be constructed; *implementation*, writing the source code; and *testing, verification* and *validation*, making sure the program does what we claim. The tasks of implementation and testing also include the task of *debugging*, which is the finding and removing of errors discovered by testing (usually called bugs, hence the term debugging).

Measured in terms of the quantity of source code required to implement them, programs come in varying sizes from the very small (tens of lines of source code) to the very large (millions of lines of source code). This book deals with designing and writing smaller-sized programs, an activity that is often simply referred to as *programming*. Larger programs require considerably more design effort, with the use of *software engineering* methods becoming important, and programming primarily being the sub-task of writing the source code. The use of software engineering methods is beyond the scope of this book, but the programming principles introduced are applicable on all scales of development.

The principal tool for programming is the programming language, with the Java programming language being the focus of this book. The design of a language like Java is based on principles that are the result of both many years of research and the practical use of earlier generations of

note

The Concise Oxford Dictionary defines execute *(definition truncated): 1. carry out a sentence of death 2. carry into effect, perform 3. make (a legal document) valid by signing. In computing, the term is usually used with meaning 2.*

programming languages. The research addresses not only the best ways of making the computer behave as we want it to, but also how best to avoid the errors that human beings, being imperfect, introduce into the systems they are developing. The practical experience of using programming languages highlights those features that provide useful solutions to real problems and work effectively in the social environment of the development team.

Underlying all of this we need an understanding of how a program works, described by the *execution model*. This knowledge is essential so that we can reason about how our programs will work once on the computer. The mental execution of a program is an integral part of the way in which people construct programs and hence is an important skill any programmer requires.

So what execution model does Java have? Slipping into the vocabulary of programming language design, Java can be categorized as an *imperative object-oriented programming language* with a model of computation based on interacting *objects* that combine state and behaviour. We use *object-oriented analysis and design methods* to determine how to give structure to the implementation of a Java program and use imperative programming concepts to fill in the details. Then, when a computer runs the program, the execution model is in turnn built on top of fundamental ideas such as instruction sequences and memory.

But what does all this jargon really mean? This and the other chapters of this part of the book will explore these ideas and show how they are supported by Java. Let us start with some of the most basic ideas.

2.2 Statement Sequences

A program written using an imperative programming language consists of an *ordered sequence* of instructions; in programming languages such as Java these instructions are usually termed *statements*. Following from this, a program may be designed by decomposing a problem into a sequence of statements and then having them executed in the order they are written down.

As an example, let us consider moving around a two-dimensional space such as a chessboard. From a given square, it is possible to go `forward`, `left`, `right` or `backward` (we will ignore diagonal movement for the moment) and so these four actions will form our basic set of instructions. These actions need to be associated with the thing that will actually be moving around, and which we will call `piece` (as in chess piece). The association is done by writing a statement such as:

```
piece.forward();
```

This means "tell `piece` to move `forward`". The dot connects the action with the thing performing the action, while the parentheses — the () brackets — cause the action to take place. The semicolon acts simply as punctuation and marks the end of the statement.

`piece` is an example of what is known as an *object*. It is an entity that represents some concept (a chess piece), maintains information about itself (what the piece's legal moves are, for example) and can perform actions (such as moving). The actions are normally referred to as *methods*. Objects are a core feature of Java and we will be seeing many examples.

Given this, the following is a reasonable program:

```
piece.forward() ;
piece.left() ;
piece.forward() ;
piece.right() ;
piece.forward() ;
```

This will move the `piece` object around the board, following the sequence of moves given. In order to be able to decide the exact outcome of the execution of this program, we need to know several more things: What actually happens when a movement statement is executed (the *semantics* of the statement) and where is the starting position?

Determining the semantics of a movement statement requires two bits of information:

1. How many squares constitute a single move?

2. Are the directions of movement fixed relative to the board or relative to the direction of travel?

Supplying answers to these questions allows us to determine what the program as a whole actually does, and where the piece ends up. Since it is the simplest solution, indeed the most basic, let us assume the piece moves one square at a time. This then leaves deciding how the direction of movement is specified.

If the directions are fixed relative to the board and each statement causes a one square move in the given direction, then, assuming the piece starts from a square somewhere in the middle of the board, the above program gives the following behaviour:

In fact, with this interpretation, any ordering of this set of statements will take the piece through different squares but always leave it at the *same place*; a different ordering of the statements results in different movement behaviour but the same result. For example, the sequence:

```
piece.forward() ;
piece.forward() ;
piece.right() ;
piece.forward() ;
piece.left() ;
```

results in the following path:

The piece has taken a different route to the same place, the square 3 forward — in effect the left and right moves cancel each other out.

If the directions are determined with respect to the direction of travel, we have a very different situation. The original program now does this:

whereas the second program does this:

Not only is the sequence of squares visited different but also the destination square is different. With this execution model, the order of statements matters much more than it did with the previous model.

A completely different execution model using the same statements is where `forward` is the only movement statement, with `left` and `right` being orientation-changing statements only. With these semantics, the first program produces the behaviour:

whereas the second program produces the behaviour:

Again, the different ordering of the statements results in a different behaviour (squares visited) and a different final square.

So, we have seen that not only does changing the order of statements change the behaviour of a program, it can, and usually does, mean that the final result is different. Moreover, we have to know exactly how the meaning of each statement is to be interpreted. If our interpretation differs from that of the computer, we will end up writing programs that will not produce the results we expect.

We have also seen that a statement sequence comprises two or more statements written one after the other, with semicolons at the end of each statement. The semicolons can be thought of as markers showing exactly where a statement ends. They are primarily needed so that the Java compiler (the tool that converts the program source code into an executable program) can always accurately determine where statements end. Compilers are not as clever as humans in reading and understanding text, so they need help. Having said this, semicolons also help us humans read our own programs, so they are doubly useful.

2.3   Iteration

The ideas of statements, statement sequences and their correct interpretation constitute a useful starting point. However, writing programs consisting of one long list of statements, with a fixed order, is not only uninteresting, it also severely limits the kinds of program that can be created.

For example, suppose we want to write a program to move the piece to a specific square on the chess board, having decided that `forward` is the movement command, with `left` and `right` used to change orientation. If we know exactly where the piece starts from, and it is facing in the right direction, then a simple sequence of statements will get the right result, for example:

```
piece.forward() ;
piece.forward() ;
piece.forward() ;
piece.forward() ;
```

giving:

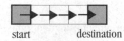

start   destination

However, if the piece starts from a different square the program will fail:

start   destination

To get the program working again we need to modify it to:

```
piece.forward() ;
piece.forward() ;
piece.forward() ;
piece.forward() ;
piece.forward() ;
```

so as to get:

start   destination

While this gives a solution, it does mean we have to modify the program for every problem we need to solve, even if each version has a basically similar solution: keep moving forward until the destination is reached.

A more desirable, and more general-purpose, solution is to write a single program that can solve a variety of similar problems. If we assume that the problem is to move a piece from one square to another square on the same line, then the following *algorithm*, which we have expressed in *psuedocode* is a general solution to the problem:

> *while (piece not at destination)*
> *piece moves forward*

An algorithm is a sequence of steps used to solve a problem. Pseudocode is a way of writing down an algorithm in semi-formal English that looks a lot like program code but does not represent a specific programming language.

To express the algorithm above we had to draw on an additional concept called *iteration,* in the form of a *while statement.* Iteration allows the execution of a sub-sequence of statements to be repeated, depending on the value of some condition. In this case the condition *piece not at destination* is a test to see if the destination has been reached, generating a *boolean* result. The condition has been written as a sequence of words connected by underscores to emphasize it is a single action. As we are working with pseudocode we do not have to be specific about how the condition works, just that it does.

Java supports three kinds of iteration statement, the *while statement,* the *do statement* and the *for statement,* each being suited to a particular kind of use. These statements are commonly referred to as *loop* statements or just *loops,* in that they cause program execution to loop back on itself. Programmers often talk about "going round the loop", or "looping", when referring to the repeated execution of the loop. The looping or repetition may either be bounded (repeated a fixed number of times), or unbounded (repeated some arbitrary number of times depending on the current state of the program).

2.3.1 The Java While Statement and Compound Statement

The *while loop* will continually execute one or more statements while some condition is true. For example:

```
while (piece.notAtDestination()) {
  piece.forward() ;
}
```

This loop will repeatedly execute the `piece.forward();` statement while the method `piece.notAtDestination()` returns `true`, i.e. the piece is not at the destination square. When the destination is reached the method `piece.notAtDestination()` will return `false`, the loop will *terminate* and program execution continues with the statement following the loop.

The word `while` marks the start of the while statement and is an example of a *keyword*. A keyword is part of the syntax of a programming language and is recognized as having a specific meaning. The loop condition appears in parentheses following the while keyword and uses another action or method belonging to the piece object. This method differs from the movement methods in that it returns a result of either `true` or `false`, depending on where the piece is. The condition, in turn, is followed by the *loop body*, comprising the statements to be repeatedly executed.

note

Booleans represent truth values. A `boolean` *can either have the value* `true` *or* `false`.

The loop body is a sequence of one or more statements bracketed together using braces ({ and }). Such a bracketed sequence is known as a *compound statement,* which, as the name implies, is actually a kind of statement in its own right. One consequence of this is that a compound statement can contain other compound statements, a concept often referred to as *nesting.* Compound statements appear in various roles in Java, as we shall see in the following chapters. We will also see that compound statements have other properties which give important structuring mechanisms to program code.

A loop body does not have to be a compound statement, it can consist of just a single statement:

```
while (piece.notAtDestination())
  piece.forward() ;
```

For safety, always use a compound statement as the loop body.

However, it is good practice to always use a compound statement when writing a loop, even if only one statement is to be repeated. This helps avoid problems later if the the loop body is modified by adding additional statements to the loop (and forgetting to add the braces to create a compound statement).

An important property of the while loop is that the test is performed every time before the loop body is executed. If the test evaluates to `false` the first time the loop is reached, the loop body is never executed. Hence, a while loop body will be executed zero or more times.

2.3.2   The Java Do Statement

Closely related to the while loop is the do or do-while loop. This kind of loop starts with the `do` keyword and finishes with a while clause. For example:

```
do {
  piece.forward() ;
} while (piece.notAtDestination()) ;
```

Here, the test follows the loop body, so it is performed every time after the body has been executed (and note the location of the semicolon). As a consequence, the do loop body is always executed at least once.

Always check loop conditions and loop bodies very careful to ensure that loops terminate.

Both the while and do loops require their test to eventually evaluate to `false` so that the loop terminates. A general rule is that one or more statements in the loop body must do something that causes the test to evaluate to `false`. If the test never evaluates to `false`, the loop will carry on executing forever and we label it an *infinite loop.* Infinite loops usually occur due to programmer mistakes. However, loops that appear at first sight to be infinite loops can have legitimate uses: sometimes there is a need for loops that test in the middle of the loop body rather than at the beginning or end. Section 2.4.2, Page 25, will introduce this idea more fully.

The remaining kind of loop is the for-loop. However, to understand this kind of loop we first need to introduce some additional concepts, so we will leave it until later. A full explanation of all three kinds of loop can be found in Part 4 of the book, which provides a detailed reference to the Java programming language (see Chapter 29, Page 805).

2.4 Selection

Returning to the program for moving a piece on a chess board, we have been able to write something more general purpose, but it is, of course, still limited to moving in a straight line. Given the situation below, the program will fail:

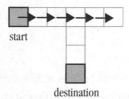

The general problem is still the same — move to the destination square — but the solution needs to be more sophisticated, as at some point the piece needs to turn right:

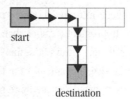

Taking this situation as a starting point, and by thinking through similar examples, we can try to write a pseudocode algorithm expressing a solution to the more general problem. In doing so, we find ourselves using another new kind of statement, the *if statement*:

> *while (piece is not at destination)*
> > *if (destination is to the left)*
> > > *piece moves left*
> > *else*
> > > *if (destination is to the right)*
> > > > *piece moves right*
> > *piece moves forward*

This is noticeably more complicated and makes use of *selection*; making a choice between doing one thing or another. However, it does give a reasonable, and more general purpose, solution for the problem we have been looking at.

We should note that two more tests have been invented to see if a left or right turn is needed, further expanding the set of features required by our system. An important element of program design (and also programming language design) is to identify the core set of features needed to write well-structured programs. With too few features useful programs can't be written at all, while with too many the system or programming language becomes over complex and confusing.

In reading the text of the new algorithm you may find it ambiguous, although the indentation hopefully makes the meaning obvious. When writing a program, however, we must make sure that there are no possible ambiguities and the program only has one meaning. Any confusion will lead to programs that don't work as expected and general frustration. The intent of the algorithm can be made more obvious by using braces to form compound statements, as well as using indentation:

```
while ( piece is not at destination ) {
    if ( destination is to the left ) {
        piece moves left
    } else {
        if ( destination is to the right ) {
            piece moves right
        }
    }
    piece moves forward
}
```

A good programmer always writes code so that it is as easy to read as possible, exploiting the layout of the text on the page or screen, and making effective use of blank lines and spaces. A common mistake made by those learning to program is to try to fit as much program text as possible into the minimum amount of space; avoid all such temptations!

An important principle has also been introduced: where possible provide a general-purpose solution that solves a range of similar problems, rather than lots of specialized solutions each solving a single problem. Good programmers always have this in mind as they work, as they know that general purpose solutions not only save time and effort in the long run, but they are also more robust and reliable. Above all, they try to avoid repeatedly re-solving the same problem if a good solution already exists.

2.4.1   The Java If Statement

The *if statement* has two variations. The first allows conditional execution of a statement sequence, for example:

```
if (piece.canMoveToTheRight()) {
  piece.right() ;
  piece.forward() ;
}
```

The keyword `if` marks the start of the if statement and is followed by a condition (a boolean expression) in parentheses. If the condition evaluates to `true` when the program runs, the if statement body is executed. The body is usually a compound statement, as in the example above, but can be just a single statement. If the condition evaluates to `false`, the body is skipped over and execution continues with the next statement following the if statement.

The second variation of the if statement is known as *if-then-else* or *if-else* and selects between two statements (or sequences using compound statements) for execution. One or other of the statements must be executed but not both (the semantics are do this *else* do that). For example:

```
if (piece.canMoveToTheRight()) {
  piece.right() ;
} else {
  piece.forward() ;
}
```

tip

Spacing and alignment is important for the readability of any text, especially source code. Use spacing and alignment to reflect the meaning of the code.

note

A general solution to a problem is invariably better than a specialized solution.

tip

For safety, always use a compound statement as the statement body.

Note that the entire section of code above comprises the if statement, starting with the keyword `if` and ending with the closing brace on the second compound statement. There is no need to follow the if statement with a semicolon as the final close brace marks the end of the statement sufficiently well. Once one of the statements (actually compound statements in the example above) has been executed, the program continues with the statement following the if statement.

2.4.2 The Java Break Statement

Using an if statement in conjunction with a *break statement* in a loop body provides an alternative way of terminating a loop. This allows us to add the idea of 'test in the middle' to the ideas of 'test at the beginning' (while statement) and 'test at the end' (do statement). Consider the following (possibly artificial) situation: a piece normally moves forwards two squares at a time until it reaches the edge of the board but if it can only move one square, it will. Clearly, we could solve this with:

```
while (piece.canMoveForwardTwoSpaces()) {
  piece.forward() ;
  piece.forward() ;
}
if (piece.canMoveForward()) {
  piece.forward() ;
}
```

but this seems a little clumsy. An alternative using the idea of 'test in the middle' is:

```
while (piece.canMoveForward()) {
  piece.forward() ;
  if (! piece.canMoveForward()) // ! means not, i.e. invert the test
    break ;
  piece.forward() ;
}
```

The break statement causes the loop to terminate immediately and the program execution to jump to the statement following the loop. This turns out to be a useful strategy and can often simplify the structure of loops.

2.5 Variables

In general, statements are only useful if they are able to manipulate *stored values*. To see why, think of trying to do some simple arithmetic, for example doing the sum:

$$33 + 72 + 111 + 132$$

without the ability to remember intermediate results. Normally, a typical strategy would be to start with $33 + 72$ and remember the result 105. Then the 105 would be added to 111, giving a new result of 216 to be remembered for the next step, and so on. However, if the intermediate results cannot be remembered then the strategy falls apart and the only way to do the calculation is to somehow do it all in one step. Even then, this leaves the question of what to do with the final result.

Programming languages use the concept of *state* in order to remember things: the state provides a set of values that can be manipulated by statements. The execution of a program can be described in terms of a *state machine model*, where each statement causes the program to change from one state to the next. The initial state holds the set of starting values (the input) while the final state holds the set of result values (the output). The statements in the program are responsible for transforming the initial state to the final state.

The state of a Java program is represented by:

- the Java Virtual Machine that defines how Java programs are executed; and
- a collection of *variables* to hold the values that are manipulated by the program.

A variable is a *container* which is able to hold a *representation* that denotes a *value*. For example:

$$\boxed{1}$$

Here the box represents a variable (the container), holding a binary number (the representation) that denotes the value one. This may seem like an unnecessarily fussy description of what a variable is but, as we shall see, this detail does matter.

Values, for example the integer value one, are abstract things that cannot be manipulated directly — how can you pick up "the value one"? In order to be manipulated, we must use a representation of the value. The same abstract value can be represented in many different ways; for example, one can be represented on paper by '1', 'i', 'I', 'one' and 'ONE'. Different representations have different properties. For example, consider the roman and arabic representation of numbers. The number nineteen hundred and ninety nine can be represented in words (as we just have), in its roman number representation, MCMLXXXXIX, or in its arabic number representation, 1999. Doing arithmetic with the arabic representation is relatively easy, using the roman representation makes it very hard. The arabic representation system is therefore the one we normally make use of.

Computer hardware represents integer values using a binary representation, which the Java Virtual Machine makes direct use of when a Java program executes. Fortunately, programmers do not have to worry about this representation most of the time since the Java programming language shields us from it. When writing Java programs we can make use of representations employing arabic style numbers.

It is crucially important to distinguish between the variable, the representation it holds and the value that is represented. A variable is just a container. The representation, on the other hand, is some representation of an *abstract value*. This is not an artificial distinction. Consider integers (positive or negative whole numbers); there are an infinite number of them. If we wished to store *any* integer value we would need to have a variable that could hold a representation of infinite size. This is not very practical (to say the least!), so the representation is limited to a range of integers between a fixed maximum and minimum value; a finite range. As a programmer you need to know what that range is and be aware that integers outside that range cannot be represented even though they are otherwise normal values.

note

Most computers use a representation called "2's complement binary" for integer numbers. We are not going to present the details of the representation in this book; the interested reader is referred to any good book on computer architecture.

2.5.1 Variable Names

Variables are given names, allowing statements in a program to refer to them. For example, the variable holding the result of a calculation can be called `result`. Naming a variable is equivalent to sticking a name onto the variable container.

The rules of the Java language allow lots of flexibility in what can be used as a variable name but there are a number of rules to observe. Names should start with an upper or lower case letter (e.g. `cost`, `size`, `Length`) but cannot start with a digit (e.g. `3things`). Each variable should have a different name (although we shall see in later chapters this statement is not very accurate; for now it is good enough).

Variable names, and indeed all text in a Java program, are case sensitive. This means that for two names to be the same, they must have exactly the same characters, with the letters being in the same case. Following from this, `Result` and `result` are different names, as the former starts with a capital `R` while the latter starts with lowercase `r`. Mismatching the case of letters in a name is a common programming mistake, so check carefully.

Perhaps the most important thing about a variable name is that it should be pronounceable and make clear what the role of the variable is. For example, the name `width` implies a variable holds a measurement of size, whereas `value` would be more vague and `sdfbsdf` rather meaningless. Single letter names, such as `x` or `r`, are acceptable for variables that have temporary roles, otherwise recognizable names are best.

The full details of what makes a valid variable name can be seen in Section 28.3, Page 772.

tip

Make all variable names meaningful so that code is as self-commenting as possible.

2.5.2 Assignment

Variables are *updateable*: the contents of the variable container can be overwritten, by replacing the current representation with a new one. The execution of an imperative program relies on variables being updated in order to change its state and produce the end result. A typical Java program will have many variables, which are constantly updated as the program executes.

The act of changing a variable is known as *assignment*. A variable may be assigned a new value, meaning that the contents of the container changes. Assignment does not change the name of a variable, only the representation held in the variable container.

An example of assignment is the Java statement:

```
x = 1 ;
```

The = symbol is the *assignment operator* and the semicolon marks the end of the statement. The result of the execution of this statement is that the variable named `x` is assigned a representation of the value one. When programmers talk about assignment they often use phrases like "assign the variable `x` the value one". The representation and value are both referred to as "the value". However, as noted above, it is important to distinguish the two, something which can really only be done by appreciating the context in which the term is being used.

Interestingly, assignment allows you to write the statement:

```
x = x + 1 ;
```

This is a valid statement in an imperative language like Java — it means fetch the value in x, add one to it, and save the result back into x. If we were to think of this as a mathematical expression, it would only be valid for the value infinity (∞) or in a very strange algebra!

2.5.3   Variable Types

An abstract value has a *type*. A type defines the set of possible values that are members of the type and the operations that can be applied to those values. For example, in mathematics the value one is of type integer, has a representation such as '1' and can be manipulated using the mathematical operations normally associated with integer numbers: addition, subtraction, multiplication, division, and so on.

As abstract values can be given types, so can representations of them and also the variables that hold the representations. This allows the programmer to specify that a variable can hold values of a particular type and no others. In Java, this is done by specifying a type when a variable is first named, or *declared,* to use the technical term. For example:

```
int j ;
```

Java has roots in the older programming languages C and C++. These languages used the name int *as a label for the integer type. Many of the other syntactic conventions of Java are derived from C and C++ which explains some of the more cryptic elements which appear.*

declares a variable called j of type int, where int stands for type integer. In fact, variables must be declared and given a type before they can be used, so the programmer always has to decide on the variable type as well as a variable name. If the variable j is used in an assignment statement such as j = 1; without having been declared, the Java compiler would report an error, as it would not know what kind of thing j is naming. You might argue that the compiler should be able to work out that j is of type int by looking at the value being assigned to it. In principle this is true but it would make the compiler much more complicated and slower. In addition, it would probably lead to more programmer mistakes since the programmer's intention is not expressed explicitly in the source code.

Other commonly used Java types are:

- double — to represent real numbers like 4.253 (often referred to as floating point numbers).
- char — to represent characters, such as 'a', 'B' or '3'.
- boolean — to represent the boolean values of true and false.

These are known as *primitive types* as they are represented in a binary form directly supported by computer hardware. As later chapters will demonstrate, primitive types can be used to construct more complex *class types*. Values of class types are objects, like the piece object introduced in earlier sections.

One commonly used class type is String. String objects are used to represent text such as "this is a string". Programs that display or manipulate text make use of 'string variables', or simply 'strings', which is how variables declared as type `String` are often referred to. Just as integers can be represented directly in a program, so can strings:

```
String s ;
s = "this is a string" ;
```

Here the text of the string is written directly into the program, with double quotes used to mark the start and end.

2.5.4 Initializing Variables

The rules of the Java language demand that all variables be *initialized* to a known and valid value before any other use is made of them. Newly declared variables (for example, `int n;`) cannot be left to take on some random value. Enforcing initialization is an important safety feature as it prevents a range of errors where the programmer mistakenly assumes that a new variable has a certain value but in reality it does not.

It is good practice always to initialize a new variable explicitly using an *initialization expression*. For example:

```
int j = 0 ;
double pi = 3.141 ;
String string = "Hello" ;
```

This makes the initial value of the variable obvious and should be considered the preferred way of declaring a variable. The alternative is to declare a variable without explicit initialization but then use assignment to assign to it before it is used for anything else. For example:

```
double pi;
...
pi = 3.141;
```

This should be considered poor practice. Failure to initialize or assign a value to a variable before it is used is considered an error and the program will be rejected by the Java compiler. Having said this, we should note that the Java system provides default initialization for all variables. For example, `int` variables are initialized to `0` and `double` variables to `0.0`. However, the Java compiler still checks for the cases where default initialization is relied on and will complain in cases where it matters, so it is always better practice to use explicit initialization. See Section 28.8.2, Page 783, for the full details on variable initialization.

2.5.5 Variables and Type Checking

Types are an important way of accurately specifying how a program is to work and of verifying that a program is properly constructed. Java is a *strongly typed language*, meaning that each variable *must* have a type associated with it determining what kind of representation (and hence value) the variable is able to hold. The Java compiler uses types to do *type checking* which means that it checks that any representation assigned to a variable is of the right type to put in that variable. For example, the following code:

```
int j = 3.0 ;
```

note

People often use the term value to mean representation. It is usually clear from the context what is meant.

tip

*It is **always** best to explicitly initialize all variables.*

will cause the Java compiler to notice that an attempt is being made to assign a real number value to an integer number variable. However, `doubles` and `ints` are different representations, they have different storage formats in the computer, they are different types. So, as the types don't match, the assignment is not allowed and an error is reported. The error prevents an executable program from being created, forcing the programmer to correct the problem.

Strong typing should not be seen as something the programmer must fight with. Quite the contrary, in fact, it is there as a support tool for avoiding avoidable errors. The principle being used here is that if the programmer is required to specify exactly the types of all the representations and variables used throughout the program, then any violation of strong type checking indicates either a trivial error on the part of the programmer (which can be corrected trivially) or that there is a more serious error of analysis or design. In all cases, the programmer, in correcting the problem, must reason carefully about the program and why it is being rejected by the compiler. Strong typing is a support tool to help the programmer in this reasoning activity. Again, it is the issue of making intention explicit in the course code.

2.5.6 Comparing Variables

The values of variables often need to be compared to see if they are the same, different, less than or greater than each other. Such comparisons are frequently used as the conditions in `if while` or `do` statements. Variables and values of the primitive types can be compared using *boolean operators*. These are:

!

Because of the way the real number representations work, there is an error factor associated with them. Thus, it is dangerous to rely on equality and inequality when using `doubles`.

- `==` — equals: test whether two values are the same.
  ```
  if (a == b) ...
  ```

- `!=` — not equals: test whether two values are different.
  ```
  if (a != 42) ...
  ```

- `>` — greater than: test whether the left is greater than the right.
  ```
  if (a > b) ...
  ```

- `>=` — greater than or equal to: test whether the left is greater than or equal to the right.
  ```
  if (a >= b) ...
  ```

- `<` — less than: test whether the left is less than the right.
  ```
  if (d < 3.1415926) ...
  ```

- `<=` — less than or equal to: test whether the left is less than or equal to the right.
  ```
  if (d <= 3.1415926) ...
  ```

These operations work as expected for primitive types. However, there are complications for variables of class type. Thus, variables of class type, such as `String`, are not usually compared using these boolean operators. Instead, a comparison method is provided, as we will see later.

2.6 Writing a Simple Java Program

We have now seen a range of core imperative programming features, along with examples of their Java representation, but not yet a complete Java program. Let's take that next step.

First we need to know what program to write; we need a statement of the problem. Here is a very simple example: "*Write a program to display the numbers 1 to 5*".

Statement of Problem

Next we need to develop a design for a program that meets the specification presented in the Statement of Problem. The first thing to do is to decide a strategy for displaying the numbers. We could simply have five statements in sequence that display the five numbers. However, that would be a program with a poor design, for all the same reasons discussed previously (see Section 2.3, Page 20), i.e. that the program is special purpose and unmaintainable against an altered problem statement. Instead it is better to make use of a loop and an integer variable. The following pseudocode outlines a proposed design:

Design

```
initialize counter
while (counter < 6) {
    display the counter value
    increment counter by one
}
```

Here the variable `counter` is used to determine which number to display each time the loop body is executed. The loop test also makes use of the variable and is written using the *expression* `counter < 6`. We use the term expression to describe a combination of operators and operands and talk about *evaluating* the expression to determine its value. In this case the expression has a boolean value and is evaluated by testing to see if the value of the variable `counter` is less than 6.

Having produced a potential design for the program, a short review is useful to confirm that the end result is likely to work and that it is of good quality. Checking that a program will work is, in general, difficult, as it will contain many statements and variables. This program, however, is simple enough that the checking can be done by 'mentally executing' the pseudocode above and informally confirming it does the right thing. Unfortunately, things will not be so straightforward as programs get larger.

Design Review

Reviewing the quality of the design involves asking a range of questions, including:

- Is the pseudocode properly presented and laid out?
- Have sensible variable names been used?
- Is the program going to be easy to modify and extend in the future?

These questions will, of course, also apply to the source code.

As you continue to read this book and as your programming experience increases, you will find more questions to ask. The idea is not to have to ask them explicitly but for them to be second nature: they should be questions that are automatically asked without prompting. Moreover, you will begin to develop an appreciation for what makes a well-designed program.

Implementation

The design presented above appears to be sound, so the next step is to translate the pseudocode into source code. This will give the following Java program, which we have called `Program1`:

```
public class Program1 {
  public static void main(final String[] args) {
    int counter = 1 ;
    while (counter < 6) {
      System.out.println(counter) ;
      counter = counter + 1 ;
    }
  }
}
```

note

See Appendix E, Page 959, for information about compiling and running a Java program.

When the program is run, the numbers 1 through 5 should appear in the terminal window, like this:

```
1
2
3
4
5
```

Looking at `Program1` it is immediately clear that it has a lot of source code features that we have not yet discussed. Notably, the program includes the lines:

```
public class Program1 {
  public static void main(final String[] args) {
    ...
  }
}
```

where the ellipsis is used to indicate that other code is present here: the three dots are not a feature of Java.

These lines of code must be present in order to have a complete and syntactically correct Java program (if you are doubtful, try compiling the program without these lines present to see the error messages produced by the compiler). The phrase `public class Program1` not only names the program but declares a new *class*; this language feature will be dealt with in Chapter 6. The line `public static void main(final String[] args)` is declaring a *method*, an important concept that will be described in the next chapter. For now we ask you to live with the fact that these lines are required but that you may not fully understand them.

A further difference is that the statement:

```
System.out.println(counter) ;
```

has been used to implement the pseudocode line:

> *display the counter value*

While the pseudocode expresses the intention, we must use valid Java code to actually output the numbers, and this statement does exactly that: it requests the system to display to the screen a representation of the variable counter. Section 2.8 will expand on what this statement means.

Testing

With the program written and apparently working, we need to test it against the problem statement to verify whether it really does do what was requested. For `Program1` the testing is essentially trivial. Our *test plan* consists of one test; run the program and check that it displays the numbers 1 to 5. There is no input and only one expected output: the test plan in this case is rather trivial.

In general, however, testing a program is hard, as there are a very large number of possible statement sequences that might be executed when the program is run. Trying to identify and run each possible sequence is effectively impossible and, even if it were undertaken, could take a very long time — literally many, many years for larger programs. Hence, the role of testing is to try to find errors by running and using the program in ways which are most likely to cause them. Testing continues until the rate at which errors are found falls below our acceptance threshold. However, except for trivial programs, we can never be entirely sure that all the errors have been found: testing can only prove the presence of errors, not their absence.

With the program apparently finished, it is a good idea to have a final review. A good programmer always spends time evaluating their own work and looking for ways to improve it.

Looking at the program, we can be pleased that it seems to have no errors that we can find and is neatly presented on the page. Also we can note that by changing the initial value of the variable `counter` or the loop test we could make the program display different ranges of numbers, without having to make major changes to the design.

On the negative side we could be critical of several things. While we can make small edits to the program to display different numbers, we still have to alter the program source code and recompile it. It would be better to have one program that requires no alteration to display different ranges of numbers, by asking the user of the program what range to display. Further, we might want to add some explanations of the program within the program to provide additional information to anyone who reads the source code in the future.

> *!*
>
> *The aim of testing is to find the errors that we put into the programs we write. A successful test is one that finds an error.*

Review

2.7 Using Comments

It is important to keep accurate descriptions of the design and implementation of a program. Typically these descriptions are referred to as the program *documentation*. Many programs are complex and without good documentation can be difficult or impossible to develop and maintain. Documentation comes in two major forms; the program source code and separate written descriptions of the design, structure and behaviour of the program. Ideally, both should be consistent and up to date.

A *comment* allows additional textual information to be included in the source code of a program. For example:

```
int width ; // Width of the widget in millimetres
```

The comment is written in plain text following the `//` characters. The two `/` characters must have no space between them in order for the compiler to recognize them as the "start a one line comment" sequence. Any text following // on the same line will be considered part of the comment and not part of the program source code, allowing the comment to contain any characters or words.

In fact, Java supports several types of comment, each suited to a particular role. The // style is best for short comments that fit neatly onto the current line. An alternative, the bracketing pair /* ... */, can be used to surround a comment that may extend across several lines, for example:

```
/*  Volume of the widget stored in
    cubic centimetres, measured at
    the default temperature. */
int volume ;
```

The comment starts with the /* and finishes only when a */ is reached. As with the // form, the characters /* and */ must be consecutive, i.e. no spaces between them, to be recognized as the comment start and comment stop sequences. Any text can appear within the comment.

The third kind of Java comment, starting with /** and finishing with */, is a special form of the bracketing pair comment, the *documentation comment*. The end comment sequence is the same but the start comment sequence is the three character sequence /**. This kind of comment is used to automatically generate documentation from source code. The Java environment includes a tool, javadoc, which reads through source code and generates Web pages detailing the features present in the code. Documentation comments are described in detail in Section 28.2, Page 768 and also used extensively in the programs in Parts 2 and 4 of this book, but here is a brief example to show what one looks like:

```
/**
 * This is a documentation comment
 *
 * @see Integer
 * @version 1.1 1999.12.04
 * @author Graham Roberts
 */
```

Documentation comments have a structure to allow them to be processed automatically. The first sentence of the comment is assumed to be a summary and the rest of the comment the main body of information. Within these comments you can embed HTML tags, for example to add emphasis or other typesetting features. The @see, @version and @author elements are special javadoc tags that allow the programmer to mark information as having a particular meaning and be treated accordingly when the documentation is created.

Comments should always be used to add information to source code, not to repeat what is obvious by reading the source code. The key to good commenting is balance. Too few comments may require too much study of the source code to work out what is going on, while too many comments will hide the source code and be laborious to read.

Program1 is short and simple, so does not need much in the way of comments; the source code is largely self-documenting. However, for every program it is useful to have some preliminary comments that state things such as the purpose of the program, who wrote it and when, and a revision history summarising changes made to the program. These are all useful bits of information that cannot be determined from the source code alone.

A commented version of `Program1` would then look like this:

```
// A program to display the numbers 1 to 5.
// Written by Graham Roberts, 11th July 1999.
// Revision history:
// 11.7.99 - added comments
public class Program1 {
  public static void main(final String[] args) {
    int counter = 1 ;
    while (counter < 6) {
      System.out.println(counter) ;
      ccunter = counter + 1 ;
    }
  }
}
```

`Program1` is sufficiently simple that documentation comments are not really useful but we could have used them.

Comments that state the obvious, such as:

```
int counter = 1 ; // This is a variable called counter
```

are not useful. Similarly, comments describing the language level details of a section of code are not useful (unless, of course, the sequence is a particularly tricky one — not true in this case). The following is a particularly useless comment:

```
/*   This is a loop that iterates while the variable counter
     has a value less than six. The loop body displays the value
     of counter and then increments it by one.
*/
```

since it is probably easier to read the code than the comment!

As code becomes more complex, it does become appropriate to start adding comments to sections of code but always with the goal of improving understandability of the code not just repeating what is obvious from the code. So, for example, we could add comments detailing the intention of the code but not descending to explaining the detailed semantics. We believe that the code presented in this book uses comments in a sensible way and acts as a paradigm of good use.

tip

Get into the habit of writing the comments whilst programming. Use the comments as tools for development, not as something added on after a program is complete.

2.8 Output Statements

`Program1` uses the statement:

```
System.out.println(counter) ;
```

to display the value of the variable `counter`. A full explanation of the structure and meaning of this statement must wait until various concepts from later chapters have been introduced. For now, though, we can make the following observations to provide some understanding. The expression `System.out` identifies an object that has the capability of displaying text on the computer screen. In the same way that earlier in the chapter we moved a chess piece object around a board by asking it to perform movement actions (e.g. `piece.forward();`), we can ask the `System.out` object to display things. In this case `println` is the method we ask the object to execute. The *method parameter*, which appears in parentheses after the method name, is what we want to display. Asking the object to perform the method is usually referred to as *calling the method*.

The `System.out` object has a number of display methods but most fall into two categories: variants of `print` and `println`. Using these methods most types of values can be displayed in a readable form, including all the types we have seen so far. The only difference between `print` and `println` is that `println` always follows what is displayed by a newline, so that the next item to be displayed appears on the next line of the display. So, for example, the sequence:

```
System.out.print("Hello ") ;
System.out.print("World") ;
```

displays:

```
Hello World
```

whereas:

```
System.out.println("Hello ");
System.out.println("World");
```

displays:

```
Hello
World
```

The statement:

```
System.out.println("") ;
```

can be used to start a new line on the display (it displays nothing followed by a newline). This is equivalent to:

```
System.out.print("\n") ;
```

as the `\n` stands for newline. `\` is known as an *escape character* and provides a way (using a sequence of two consecutive characters) of representing an otherwise invisible character on the screen. See Section 28.5, Page 774, for more information about escape characters.

Statements that display information are typically known as *output statements* (hence, the title of this section). Programmers also talk about the "output of a program" or "performing output".

---

note

On a computer, newline is represented as a character, just like visible characters such as a, b or c. When displayed, newline is invisible but you see the side-effect of its presence as characters following the newline appear on the next line of the display.

2.9   Input Statements

Essentially as important as getting information out of a program is getting information in, or "doing input". A program becomes interactive if it requests information from a user and waits for something to be typed in from the keyboard. Input is harder to deal with than output, though, as the program has cope with unexpected as well as expected input — users make mistakes or sometimes deliberately enter the wrong information.

The standard Java environment provides a number of ways of reading input from the keyboard but these require a greater depth of knowledge than we have covered so far. Hence, we provide a simplified and packaged up version of input in the form of a class `KeyboardInput`. This is used to create an input object, which has methods that can be called to read input typed in from the keyboard. The full source code of `KeyboardInput` can be seen in Appendix F, Page 963.

`KeyboardInput` provides methods for reading types such an `int`, `double`, `char` and `String`, and is used by first creating an input object and then calling the input methods. For example:

```
KeyboardInput input = new KeyboardInput () ; // Create object
String s = input.readString() ; // Read a string
char c = input.readCharacter() ; // Read a single character
double d = input.readDouble() ; // Read a double
int i = input.readInteger() ; // Read an integer
```

The full meaning of the first line of code will be explained in later chapters. For now we just need to know that the keyword `new` is used to create the input object, while the variable `input` is used to name and manipulate the object. The methods, such as `readInteger`, return the value typed in at the keyboard. They can appear in initialization statements since they result in a representation of the correct type being available to act as the initial value. If input fails, typically because the user has typed the wrong thing, the input methods return appropriate default values, such as 0 for `int` or an empty string (one that contains no characters) for `String`.

When an input method is executed, the program stops and waits for the user to type something in (the input). Before the program will resume, the user must signal the end of the input by pressing the 'return' or 'enter' key. If the key is not pressed, the program continues to wait and nothing will happen.

note

See Appendix E, Page 959, for information about compiling the `KeyboardInput` *class.*

2.10 Interactive Programs

Now that basic input and output has been introduced, it is possible to write some interactive programs.

.10.1 Program2 — Basic Input and Ouput

"Write a program which asks for and then inputs your name and a message of greeting and then display both on the screen."

Statement of Problem

The sequence of statements needed is essentially straightforward, so the source code of the program can be written down directly:

Design and Implementation

```
// A program to input a name and message and then display them.
// Written by Graham Roberts, July 1999.
// Revision history:
// none
public class Program2 {
  public static void main(final String[] args) {
    KeyboardInput in = new KeyboardInput () ;
    System.out.print("Type your name: ") ;
    String name = in.readString() ;
    System.out.print("Type in a message: ") ;
    String message = in.readString() ;
```

```
        System.out.println("\n\nHello, you are: " + name) ;
        System.out.println("And your message is: " + message) ;
    }
}
```

For a more complicated program, a more rigorous design stage would be appropriate rather than rushing directly into Java code. The only new feature to note is the + *operator* that appears in the last two statements:

```
System.out.println("\n\nHello, you are: " + name) ;
System.out.println("And your message is: " + message) ;
```

This operator performs string concatenation or, in other words, appends one string on to the end of another. In the lines above this saves having to use two extra statements and outputting the text and the variable in separate statements.

Testing

The testing of `Program2` is a little more interesting than that for `Program1`, as the exact behaviour of the program depends upon what the user types in. The basic test strategy is to find out what inputs cause the program to fail or behave improperly and also to check that it displays output as expected for all sensible input. The test plan should include a small set of example input that can be used to check non-error behaviour and as many unusual conditions as can be thought of to try and find the input that the program cannot handle. A few examples of possible inputs that might cause error spring to mind immediately but there are bound to be many more:

1. The user types 'return' immediately without typing any other characters for the first and/or second inputs.

2. The user types Cntl-Z (Control key and Z key simultaneously) or Cntl-D (Control key and D key simultaneously) immediately without typing any other characters. (The Cntl-Z and Cntl-D keys are special keys for both the Windows and UNIX. Cntl-Z mean 'end of file' for Windows and suspend to UNIX whereas Cntl-D means end of file to UNIX.)

3. The user holds down a key and doesn't let go when inputting.

We suggest that you enter, compile and test the program yourself at this point.

In our testing of this program, all correct input results in expected output. Typing 'return' immediately results in sensible behaviour. Use of Cntl-Z and Cntl-D also results in sensible behaviour. Pressing and holding a key was tested for about 1000 characters under Windows95 and the program seemed to work fine but under Solaris 2.6, after about 256 characters, the system refused to take further input and execution had to be terminated. We claim that this behaviour is a feature in Solaris 2.6 and not a fault in our program. We believe that whilst it is possible that the program has bugs, it is as bug free as it is possible to make any program.

2.10.2   Program3 — Using Strings

Statement of Problem   "*Write a program to keep reading in* `String` *values until the word* stop *is entered.*"

The problem statement requires the the program to "keep reading…", so a loop of some sort is clearly going to be needed in order that statements (in the loop body) can repeatedly ask for input until the word "stop" is typed in. Perhaps the main question is: Is it a while loop or a do loop? Using pseudocode, this issue is: which of the following is better?

> *while (input is not "stop") {*
> > *display input prompt*
> > *read input*
> *}*

or:

> *do {*
> > *display input prompt*
> > *read input*
> *} while (input is not "stop")*

The while loop appears to need to test string values before any input has happened, whilst the do loop assumes that string input and output are possible without any tests having been done. This doesn't really give us any way of disambiguation, so we must either make an arbitrary choice or try both. In a case like this (small), it is probably sensible to actually try both to see if there is anything we can learn that enables us to say if one approach is better than the other.

The other main issue is to find out how to actually compare two strings. In Section 2.5.6, Page 30, we stated that `String`s were not usually compared by using the boolean operators but that a method was used instead. In fact, there are several methods available for comparing strings, but for now we shall focus on the one called `compareTo`.

Comparing string values is more complicated than comparing integer or real number values. A string is made up of a sequence of characters, so a comparison means looking at each character in turn so as to determine the order relationship between two strings. This leads to the question of which character comes before (or is "less than", or is ordered before) another character. For example, it is accepted that 'a' comes before 'b', but does 'A' come before 'a' or '2' come before 'b'? Only with the answers to these questions can we say whether "Hello" come before or after "hello".

These questions are answered by considering the way characters are represented in the computer as binary numbers. Each character is allocated a unique number or code, and this allows characters to be compared as if they were numbers. The code for each character is defined by the *Unicode* standard which determines the basic ordering as 0–9, A–Z, a–z. So, 'A' does come before 'a', '2' before 'b' and so "Hello" comes before before "hello". The necessary ordering knowledge is coded up within the `compareTo` method of class `String`. Here is an example code sequence that shows this method in use:

```
String s = "Hello" ;
String t = "hello" ;
int result = s.compareTo(t) ;
```

Strings are compared by calling the `compareTo` method for one string (using the '.' to separate the object name from the method name) and giving the other string as the parameter value. The method returns an integer value that encodes the result of the comparison, which in the example is stored in the variable `result`. The return value will be less than zero if string s comes before t, zero if s and t represent strings of equal value, and greater than zero if s comes after t. For the example above, `result` should be initialized to an integer less than zero, as "Hello" comes before "hello".

We now have enough information to present two versions of the code, first using a while loop:

```
// Program to input strings until stop is typed.
// Written by Graham Roberts, July 1999.
// Revision history:
// none
public class Program3a {
  public static void main(final String[] args) {
    KeyboardInput in = new KeyboardInput() ;
    String s = "" ;
    while (s.compareTo("stop") != 0) {
      System.out.print("Type a String: ") ;
      s = in.readString() ;
    }
  }
}
```

Notice how we use the expression `s.compareTo("stop") != 0` to ask the question whether the string s has the same representation as `"stop"`. The boolean expression is evaluated by first calling the method and then comparing the integer result with 0 using the not equal operator (`!=`). Note also that we have initialized the `String` s to the empty string. This is essential so that s has a value when we make the test against the value `"stop"` prior to outputting the prompt and reading the user input.

Now for the version using a do loop:

```
// Program to input strings until stop is typed.
// Written by Russel Winder August 1999.
// Revision history:
// none
public class Program3b {
  public static void main(final String[] args) {
    KeyboardInput in = new KeyboardInput() ;
    String s  = "" ;
    do  {
      System.out.print("Type a String: ") ;
      s = in.readString() ;
    } while (s.compareTo("stop") != 0) ;
  }
}
```

The comparison expression is the same since the termination condition is unchanged. Again, the `String` s is initialized but this is more out of (good) habit than any actual need. The reason why initialization is not actually essential here is that we can trace how the code is executed and show that s must be given a value by assignment from user input before the value is used in the test clause. Safety determines, though, that initializing is safer, so we do it.

So which is better?

The only difference between the two loops is that the latter does one fewer comparisons, so in some sense it is more efficient. However, the difference in this case is quite minor, so it is really up to which is deemed to be better on aesthetic grounds.

As ever, the testing strategy must be to try and find (and eradicate) bugs in the program in order to show to the best of our abilities that there are none. The test plan should show that the program will only terminate when the user types in the word 'stop' and that all other input is read and ignored: the program should not stop when any other word, words or random characters are typed in. However, we cannot hope to demonstrate this by typing in every possible input other than 'stop' to see what happens. There is an infinite number of possible inputs and we cannot enter them all. In fact, because computers can only deal with strings of a finite length (since the computers are of finite size), we can only test a very small proportion of the infinity of possible strings anyway. Unfortunately, this still leaves a very large number of strings and it would take an inordinately long time to try them all. Thus, exhaustive testing is just not feasible — it would take too many years to accomplish. Instead we have to rely on doing enough testing to gain enough confidence that the program is bug free. We can try to spot potential problem inputs, such as 'Stop' or just pressing newline, to help though. As before, it is the bizarre situations that are the most fruitful area for trying to find test data that cause the program to perform erroneously.

Testing

In our testing of this program, we found the following:

- Correct input resulted in expected output.
- Inputting very long strings had the same effect as that observed with `Program2`.
- Typing Cntl-Z at Windows and Cntl-D at UNIX does not cause any difficulties. It is a moot point whether typing the 'end of file' character ought, in fact, to terminate the execution of the program.

The program proved straightforward to write once string comparison was understood. Care was taken to get the loop correct, making sure that things are done in the right order, every time round the loop. Note that the program was not written like this:

Review

```
KeyboardInput in = new KeyboardInput() ;
System.out.print("Type a String: ") ;
String s = in.readString() ;
while (s.compareTo("stop") != 0) {
  System.out.print("Type a String: ") ;
  s = in.readString() ;
}
```

This version reads in a string before the loop but in doing so duplicates two lines of code. Whenever this kind of situation occurs, the code should be restructured to remove the duplicate lines. In this case, the do loop version above is what would be written instead of this code.

2.10.3 Program4 — Using Expressions

"Write program to input the lengths of the sides of a triangle, and output the area and perimeter of the triangle."

Statement of Problem

Background Knowledge

Clearly there are concepts in the problem statement that require knowledge outside the field of programming. In particular, we need to know what a triangle is and how to calculate the area and perimeter of it. Consulting any good book on basic geometry will result in finding the following knowledge:

If a, b and c are the sides of the triangle then the perimeter is the sum of the lengths of the sides:

$$perimeter = a + b + c$$

and the area is given by the equation:

$$area = \sqrt{s(s-a)(s-b)(s-c)}$$

where s is the *semiperimeter*:

$$s = \frac{1}{2}(a + b + c)$$

We are now in a position to proceed with the computing issues.

Design and Implementation

This program requires some planning before trying to write Java code, unlike the earlier simpler examples. Inputting the lengths of the three sides is straightforward and implies that three variables will be needed to store the values. The type of the variables could be `int` but that would unnecessarily restrict the program to working with lengths expressed as a whole number. Type `double` provides more flexibility, so it will be chosen instead. We note, though, that whilst `int`s are guaranteed to be stored exactly, `double`s are prone to rounding errors.

The next issue is ensuring that the three values input by the user do actually represent a triangle. The problem statement offers no suggestions on how to do this, so we need to do some thinking to work out what to do. The simplest approach seems to be to check that the sum of the length of each pair of sides is not less than the length of the third size. The source code presented below shows how that can be done in Java code. As a side issue, the problem statement gives no specification regarding what is to happen in the case of faulty input by the user. Clearly the calculation cannot be performed, so we will have to output some sort of useful error message to the user.

The calculations of the perimeter, semiperimeter and area require the formulas to be translated into Java statements, using variables and arithmetic operators. The only potentially tricky part is performing the square root but this turns out to be easy as the J2SDK provides a square root method already implemented. Note, though, that we had to know this. This can be done by extensive prior study or by judicious use of the J2SDK online documentation — which has a method index that can prove exceptionally useful.

Jotting down some pseudocode gives an outline to the overall program, following the obvious order of steps inferred from the problem statement:

> *input the lengths*
> *if (the input is not a valid triangle) {*
>   *display an error message*
> *} else {*
>   *calculate the perimeter*
>   *calculate the semiperimeter*
>   *calculate the area*

?

Information about using the J2SDK documentation can be found in Appendix C, Page 953.

tip

Spend time browsing the J2SDK to become familiar with what is available.

display the results
}

As this seems to be reasonable, the next stage is to write the Java code from the pseudocode, giving the following program:

```
// Program to input the lengths of the sides of a triangle
// and output the area and perimeter of the triangle.
// Written by Graham Roberts, July 1999.
// Revision history:
// none
public class Program4 {
  public static void main(final String[] args) {
    // Obtain data from the user.
    KeyboardInput in = new KeyboardInput () ;
    System.out.print("Enter length of first side: ") ;
    double side1 = in.readDouble() ;
    System.out.print("Enter length of second side: ") ;
    double side2 = in.readDouble() ;
    System.out.print("Enter length of third side: ") ;
    double side3 = in.readDouble() ;
    // Now test to see if the input describes an invalid
    // triangle by seeing if the sum of the lengths of
    // any two sides is less than the length of the third.
    if ( ((side1 + side2) < side3) ||
         ((side2 + side3) < side1) ||
         ((side3 + side1) < side2)
       ) {
      System.out.println("The input does not describe a triangle.") ;
    } else {
      // Now do the calculations...
      double perimeter = side1 + side2 + side3 ;
      double semiperimeter = 0.5 * perimeter ;
      double temp = semiperimeter *
        (semiperimeter - side1) *
        (semiperimeter - side2) *
        (semiperimeter - side3) ;
      double area = Math.sqrt(temp) ;
      // ...and output the results.
      System.out.println("Perimeter is: " + perimeter) ;
      System.out.println("Area is: " + area) ;
    }
  }
}
```

An inspection of the code reveals several new Java features. The first is the structure of the test in the if statement:

```
((side1 + side2) < side3) ||
((side2 + side3) < side1) ||
((side3 + side1) < side2)
```

This is an example of a boolean expression formed from various sub-expressions and boolean operators. The '||' symbol is the *or operator* that, when used in an expression such as 'A || B', returns true if either or both of A or B is true. (Not used here is the *and operator*, denoted by '&&', which returns true if, and only if, both A and B are true.) Given this, the overall structure of the boolean expression that is the if test is 'A or B or C'. Each of the A, B or C is then a sub-expression which tests to see if the length of the sum of two sides is less than the third. Parentheses are used to make clear how the sub-expression should be evaluated just as they are in mathematical expressions. In fact, these parentheses could be left out since the way in which the expression is evaluated is unchanged by the inclusion of them. However, for safety we have them in. Not only do they protect against the impossible, they are also a good code documentation feature.

The calculation of the semiperimeter is another expression that uses parentheses:

```
double temp = semiperimeter *
    (semiperimeter - side1) *
    (semiperimeter - side2) *
    (semiperimeter - side3) ;
```

In this case, the parentheses are actually essential and not just for precision and clarity of expression. Without the parentheses the wrong order of evaluation would occur since multiplication is done before subtraction. Just as with mathematical expressions, we talk about *operator precedence*: multiplication has a higher precedence than subtraction. Analysing the if test, addition has a higher precedence than less than which has a higher precedence than or, so in that case the parentheses just re-confirm the order of evaluation that would happen anyway.

As noted earlier, as well as ensuring that expressions are evaluated correctly, parentheses can and should be used to aid readability. Providing that they are inserted correctly, parentheses can be used as frequently as needed to show intention. A common source of errors made by programmers is to leave out parentheses, leaving an expression that is interpreted differently by the Java system than was assumed by the programmer. Don't let that happen to you.

The final point to note in `Program4` is the statement:

```
double area = Math.sqrt(temp) ;
```

This is where the square root is calculated using the `sqrt` method. The sub-expression `Math.sqrt` identifies a method included as part of extensive Java *class libraries,* that contain many features for use by Java programs.

As you do more Java programming you will need to become familiar with the contents of the Java class libraries. They are fully documented in the J2SDK documentation. We suggest you locate your copy now and look up `class Math` to see more information about the `sqrt` method so as to become familiar with how to use this exceptionally useful resource as well as to find out information about the `sqrt` method.

Testing

Testing this program is more demanding than the previous ones and we need to devise a more rigorous test plan. A single test will consist of three input values and the expected results. Running the program, supplying the input and comparing the output with the expected results will determine if the test is passed or failed. To be confident the program has no findable bugs, we need to run a good number of tests, but what should the inputs be? We need to analyse the problem domain so as to try and find inputs that have the best chance of finding bugs in our program.

The tests needed fall into three categories:

- Those with valid input, used to check the program can actually calculate the right answer.
- Those with invalid input, to check that the input is rejected correctly.
- Those with valid input that might cause an error when the calculations are done.

The last category is the hardest to define. The goal is to try and predict where the program could fail unexpectedly. For example, there is potentially input that creates calculations that cause arithmetic overflow in the JVM. This would occur when an addition or multiplication generates a result which is too large to represent and store in a variable. If such a case is found, the program must either be modified or the valid range of input redefined.

So what might a useful initial test data set comprise?

The following table lists the beginnings of a test data set. Within the Valid input category we try and use values that have obscure properties to see if we can find any bugs in the calculations, similarly with the Invalid input category. For the Error Creating category we try and find any variety of input that does damage! The tuples in the Test Data column are of the form:

(user input 1, user input 2, user input 3, expected perimeter, expected area)

where a dash in the expected perimeter and/or expected area slot means that no output is expected for that value.

Input Category	Test Data
Valid Input	(0.0, 0.0, 0.0, 0.0, 0.0)
	(0.0, 1.0, 1.0, 2.0, 0.0)
	(1.0, 1.0, 2.0, 4.0, 0.0)
	(1.0, 1.0, 1.0, 3.0, 0.433)
	(3.0, 4.0, 5.0, 12.0, 6.0)
Invalid Input	(-1.0, -1.0, -1.0, –, –)
	(1.0, 1.0, 3.0, –, –)
Error Creating Input	(Cntl-Z, Cntl-Z, Cntl-Z, 0.0, 0.0)
	(Cntl-D, Cntl-D, Cntl-D, 0.0, 0.0)

`Program4` passes all the tests, so we can have fairly good confidence in our program.

Review

This has been the largest program presented so far, but with some careful planning has proved easy to implement. It has demonstrated the use of expressions, showing how they are built up from operators, variables and parentheses. By dint of doing sufficient testing, we are confident that the program produces the correct answer as required but note that devising a full set of tests is going to be hard work and will take time. The above is only a start; further testing is essential if the program is to be relied upon.

The quality of the program code is reasonable. It is laid out neatly on the page (or screen), makes appropriate use of comments and has sensible variable names. So is there anything to criticize? The program is specialized to doing one thing and this could well be an issue if we want to extend it, or want to take out the triangle area calculating code and use it in another program. The next chapter will examine ways to more readily enable such activities but for now we can be satisfied that we have a straightforward program providing a solution to a straightforward problem.

There is one final issue to raise. Given some example input, say 5, 3, 5, the value displayed for the area is: 7.1545440106270926. How many decimal places should the answer be displayed with and does this affect testing? The answers are probably 2–3 decimal places are sufficient and, yes, it does affect testing because small errors tend to accumulate when doing arithmetic with real numbers, so the decimal places towards the end of the number are likely to be inaccurate.

2.11   Summary

This chapter has introduced a number of basic ideas about programming and shown some examples of simple Java programs. The next chapter will build on this and begin the process of showing how larger programs are structured.

Key points in this chapter:

- A program is written as an ordered sequence of statements.
- The meaning of each statement must be completely defined.
- While and do statements allow repetition.
- The if statement allows selection.
- Variables store representations of the values used by a program.
- Assignment is used to change the value of a variable.
- A type defines a set of values and the operations on those values.
- All variables must have a type and can only store values of that type.
- Variables must be initialized when declared.
- Programs should be commented effectively.
- Objects are entities that provide services in the form of methods.
- Input and output objects allow a program to be interactive.
- Programs should be carefully tested and reviewed to ensure they work and are of good quality.

Self-review Questions

Self-review 2.1 Explain the meaning of `piece.forward();`. Why is the semicolon present?

Self-review 2.2 How many different interpretations of the following statement sequence are there?

```
piece.forward() ;
piece.forward() ;
piece.right() ;
piece.forward() ;
piece.left() ;
```

Self-review 2.3 Write down a sequence of statements that describes making a telephone call. Can it be done without using control statements?

Self-review 2.4 Does the pseudocode below (from Section 2.4, Page 23) describe a general-purpose solution to starting from and moving to any square on a chess board?

```
while (not at destination) {
    if ( destination is to the left ) {
        piece moves left
    } else {
        if (destination is to the right)
            piece moves right;
    }
    piece moves forward
}
```

Self-review 2.5 Write in pseudocode a program to move from one corner of a chess board to the corner diagonally opposite, assuming that some of the squares are blocked and cannot be used. Note that additional test conditions will be needed, possibly something like "is the square ahead blocked". Does allowing diagonal moves make the program easier to write?

Self-review 2.6 How might a real number be stored in a variable. How does the fixed size of a variable affect the storage of real numbers?

Self-review 2.7 Why can't a value of type `int` be stored in a variable of type `double`?

Self-review 2.8 Compare the idea of types with the units used for measuring size or weight. Are such units actually types?

Self-review 2.9 How would the following strings be ordered if compared using the `compareTo` method: program, proGram, PROGRAM, Program, ProGram, programs, program3.

Self-review 2.10 Find the list of Java keywords and familiarize yourself with them. What happens if a keyword is used as a variable name?

Self-review 2.11 Why is each of these variable declarations invalid?

```
int i = 1.2 ;
double d = 1,200.46 ;
char c = "hello" ;
double j = 2.3x10⁴
String s = "word;"
```

Self-review 2.12 What are the values of these expressions:

```
true || false && true
true && false || true
```

Programming Exercises

Note that all these exercises require you to develop a program. This means you should, therefore, construct a test plan as well, even if that plan is very trivial — it is good to get into the habit. Moreover, you should actually run the tests and document the results to create a *test log*. Again a good habit to get into.

Exercise 2.1 Type in and run `Program1` and `Program2` on your computer system.

Exercise 2.2 Write a program to keep inputting integer values until −1 is entered.

Exercise 2.3 Write a program using a `while` loop to display a message 10 times. Each message should be on a separate line using this format:

```
1: A message
2: A message
3: A message
. . .
```

Numbering should start from 1.

Exercise 2.4 Repeat question 3 using a `do` loop.

Exercise 2.5 Write a program using loops to display the following:

```
****
****
****
****
```

You may only output one character at a time.

Exercise 2.6 Write a program using loops to display the following:

```
*
**
***
****
*****
******
```

You may only output one character at a time.

Exercise 2.7 Write a program to input 10 integers, add them up and display their sum and average.

Exercise 2.8 Repeat Exercise 2.6 but first ask the user how many integers will be typed in and then input that number.

Exercise 2.9 Write a program to confirm that your answer to Self-review 2.9 is correct.

Exercise 2.10 Modify `Program4` so that it repeatedly asks for input until the user wants to stop.

Exercise 2.11 Write a program to input 10 words and then display the words that are first and last in alphabetical order.

Exercise 2.12 Write a program that inputs the radius of a circle and displays its circumference and area.

Exercise 2.13 Write a program that determines the height of a building, given the angle of the top of the building and the distance from the building at which the angle was measured.

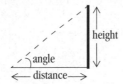

Hint: the methods `Math.sin` and `Math.cos` are available but they work in radians. The method `Math.toRadians` will convert from degress to radians.

Challenges

We shall assume you are already in the habit of constructing test plans and running them to create test logs , so we won't labour the point any more.

Challenge 2.1 Modify `Program4` so that it tests itself against a reasonable sized collection of tests. Do this by putting together the tests, complete with the expected correct answers. Then perform each test and compare the results with the expected answers.

Challenge 2.2 Write a program to read in a line of text as a `String` and output the number of characters and words it contains. Spaces and tabs should not be counted as characters.

Hint: Look in the J2SDK documentation for information about methods provided by the `String` class.

Challenge 2.3 Write a program to read in a day, month and year, create a `Date` object and output the result.

Hint: You can't create a `Date` directly. Look at the J2SDK documentation for the `GregorianCalendar` class first.

3

Adding Structure

Objectives

Programs need to be structured properly in order to be manageable. This is done by exploiting the ideas of abstraction (hiding the detail while focusing on the essential issues) and encapsulation (localizing features behind an interface). This chapter examines method-based abstraction, as the first step in giving programs structure, and looks at how the scope and lifetime of variables provides the basic facilities of encapsulation. To complete the chapter, more features of the Java language are introduced, including the switch statement and for-loop.

Keywords

abstraction

encapsulation

method

parameter

return

recursion

scope

lifetime

switch

for-loop

3.1   Introduction

The preceding chapter introduced the basic concepts of imperative programming on which Java is built. We have seen the ideas of sequence, iteration, selection and variables, and know that by using these features a programmer can express algorithms — step-by-step descriptions of how to go about things. With these basic building blocks it is possible to build useful small programs, but the approach does not scale up. Writing larger programs this way becomes tedious and error prone, to the point where it is no longer worth proceeding. We therefore need further infrastructure in order to allow arbitrarily complex programs to be written in such a way that we can hope to deal with them, i.e. be able to understand and reason about them.

Let us consider the problems of using only sequence, iteration and selection in a little more detail, to give ourselves an insight into the new features that we need. The following diagram shows, abstractly, the sort of situation we are thinking of:

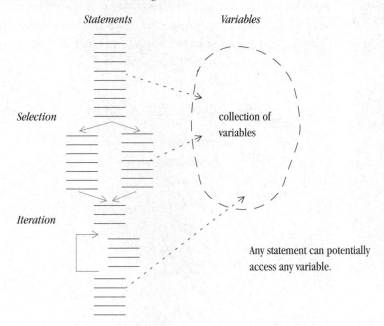

- There is little structure to this sort of program beyond that provided by iteration and selection statements. A program consists of one long list of statements, with execution starting at the first and moving sequentially through the rest, following the written order. Statements are placed according to their execution order, not according to a higher-level structure for the program.

- Everything has to be built from the basic elements. Statements are able to manipulate variables, control iteration and make selections but there is no way of creating larger building blocks. We need a way to group related blocks of statements together so they only need to be written once and used many times.

- There is little control over access to a variable and how that variable is used. One group of statements may use a variable for one purpose, while another uses the same variable for a different purpose. Access to a variable should be limited to only those statements that are supposed to be making use of it.

- It is very difficult for people to read and maintain such programs. Just like reading a book with no paragraph or chapter structure, reading a long list of instructions is difficult and frustrating. Mistakes can be easily made.

We need to start imposing some further order and structure on our programs. To be able to do this, we must examine some additional basic principles. First we need to consider *abstraction* and the *encapsulation* of instructions and data, and then ideas about *scope* and *lifetime*.

3.2 Abstraction and Encapsulation

Abstraction is the process of capturing the essential or distinguishing features of something while suppressing or ignoring the detail. Abstraction provides a crucial mechanism to enable people to understand, communicate and reason about complex systems. Without abstraction, the level of detail required to understand a system becomes so overwhelming that people are unable to build their mental models of how the system is structured and how it works. In fact, abstraction is a mechanism that people use all the time to understand and interact with the real world usually without noticing that it occurs. For example, a conversation about how to drive from A to B can take place without ever having to discuss all the details of how a car works or how every road on the route is constructed: we abstract away the details of road surface construction, the internal combustion engine and all the rest of the technology, discussing only the abstractions of turning right, travelling one block, and so on.

As dealing with long complicated sequences of statements is hard for people, even programmers, exploiting abstraction is essential if any non-trivial program is to be constructed. We want to be able to hide away the full detail of parts of a program behind a simpler, more abstract, interface; we want to be able to collect parts of the statement sequence together into abstractions of the statement sequence. This will allow the programmer to conceptualize the program in terms of a smaller number of abstractions, rather than a much larger number of individual statements.

Abstraction in programming is intimately associated with the concept of *encapsulation*. Encapsulation is a mechanism for ensuring that things have a definite inside and outside. The inside is protected from anything on the outside, offering a guarantee that some outside agent cannot arbitrarily change anything on the inside.

Once protected by encapsulation an abstraction can only be accessed via a well-defined interface visible from the outside. The inner workings are hidden and do not have to be known about to make use of the abstraction. Hence, the outside view and the interface present the abstraction, hiding away the internal details. Encapsulation is often referred to as being an *information hiding* mechanism, for fairly obvious reasons.

Defining and using the various kinds of abstractions that provide encapsulation is a key part of programming using any modern programming language and is most especially important in Java programming. Java provides abstractions over state (variables and types) as well as abstractions over statements. The abstractions over state are the objects that give rise to the label object-oriented. First, though, we must look at abstractions over statements.

3.3   Methods

ref

Section 30.2.5, Page 840.

To reason sensibly about even relatively small programs, we need to break up long lists of statements into smaller chunks. Each chunk is given a name, and from then on can be referred to and used by name without having to worry what the list of statements in the chunk actually are. Abstraction allows us to focus on the name of the chunk and what it does, without needing the detail of how it does whatever it does.

In languages preceding Java, this idea is known as *procedural abstraction,* and the chunks of code referred to as *procedures* or sometimes *functions*. In object-oriented languages like Java, however, this form of abstraction is termed *method-based abstraction*, and the chunks of code are called *methods*. In fact, the term method should already be familiar as we made use of it in the last chapter, although we didn't go into much detail about what they are then.

note

A method declaration introduces a method.

A *method declaration* consists of a named sequence of statements that appear within a compound statement. The rules for composing method names are the same as those for variables. An example method declaration is:

```
void sayHello() {
   System.out.println("Hello!") ;
   System.out.println("This is a method called hello") ;
   System.out.println("It contains 3 statements") ;
}
```

This method is named `sayHello`. In the *method body*, the statement sequence within the compound statement, there are three output statements. The significance of the keyword `void` preceding the method name, and the parentheses following it, will be explained shortly.

A method must always be declared within a *class*, so putting the method `sayHello` into its proper context gives:

```
class Hello {
   // Other parts of the class
   // ...

   void sayHello() {
```

```
      System.out.println("Hello!") ;
      System.out.println("This is a method called hello") ;
      System.out.println("It contains 3 statements") ;
   }
}
```

The method has been embedded in a class called `Hello`. We have touched on the idea of class several times already but we leave it until Chapter 6, Page 145, to start looking at it in real detail. For now we only need to know that the class can be used to create `Hello` objects, and those objects will have a `sayHello` method — the one declared in the class.

To invoke the method (or as it is often termed, "call the method") and execute its statements we need an object and a statement of the form:

```
anObject.sayHello();
```

This should be familiar from the example programs in the last chapter but now we have the ability to define our own methods for our own objects. The object needs to be created using the `new` operator before it can be used:

```
Hello anObject = new Hello();
```

With this information we can now go ahead and create a complete program that uses the `sayHello` method:

```
// Program to demonstrate the sayHello method.
// Written by Graham Roberts, July 1999.
// Revision history:
// none
public class Hello {
  void sayHello() {
    System.out.println("Hello!") ;
    System.out.println("This is a method called sayHello") ;
    System.out.println("It contains 3 statements") ;
  }
  public static void main(final String[] args) {
    Hello anObject = new Hello () ;
    anObject.sayHello() ;
    anObject.sayHello() ;
  }
}
```

Perhaps the most obvious thing about this program is that it actually contains two method declarations. Following `sayHello` is a second method called `main`. This method is the first one called when the program starts running. In this case, `main` contains the statements that create and use an `Hello` object.

Having created and compiled the program, it is run using the command:

```
java Hello
```

This command causes the Java run-time system to search for the executable code of the `Hello` class by locating the file `Hello.class` and then to execute the `main` method belonging to the named class. Thus, the execution of any Java program is always initiated by calling a `main` method. If no `main` method is found in the named class, the program cannot be executed and the following error message is displayed:

```
Exception in thread "main" java.lang.NoSuchMethodError: main
```

note

*A method call executes
the method's
statements.*

!

*All programs must have
a* main *method.*

ref

Public: Section 30.2.2,
Page 836.
Static: Section 30.2.4,
Page 838.

The `main` method differs from the `sayHello` method in a number of very important ways, most notably it is declared with the keywords `public` and `static`. The `public` is to do with managing the scope of the method. Discussion of this must be delayed until later. The `static` marks the method as a *static method*, meaning that, although it is part of the class, it can be called directly and not called for a specific object in the way the `sayHello` must be. A typical `main` method, including the one in `Hello`, will create an object of the class it is declared in and then call the object's methods.

Once an `Hello` object has been created, the method `sayHello` can be called as many times as needed. Crucially, we only need to write the `sayHello` method once to do this. Once written, and we are satisfied it works as required, we can simply call the `sayHello` method without having to repeatedly write its statement sequence — abstraction in action.

A final point: notice that a statement inside one method can be a method call to another method, so `main` can contain method calls to `sayHello`. Programmers often talk about one "method calling another" and this will form an important way of thinking and reasoning about how programs work.

3.3.1   Returning Values from a Method

As well as acting as an abstraction over statements, methods can be used to compute and return a value. This allows a method call to be used as though it were a value in an expression, for example:

```
int i = anObject.f() * 10;
```

This statement is evaluated by first calling the method `f` for the object `anObject`, multiplying the value returned from `f` by `10` and initializing the variable `i` with the result. The method `f` could be declared in the following way:

```
int f() {
  int returnValue = ... ;
  // Do some calculation and store the result in returnValue

  return returnValue ;
}
```

ref

Section 29.4.3, Page 829.

The method body includes a *return statement*. When executed, the value of the expression following the `return` keyword is returned as the value of the method. The method itself is declared as `int f()`, the `int` specifies that the method returns a result and it will be of type `int`. The Java compiler checks this information and makes sure that the method does actually return a result and that it is of the right type. A method can only return a single value but can contain several return statements, only one of which can be executed for any single call of the method.

3.3.2   Methods and Type Void

One type that has already been used in the example programs so far, but not yet discussed, is type `void`. For example, the `main` method in each program is declared as `static void main`, and the `sayHello` method used earlier was declared as `void sayHello()`.

Rather than having two kinds of method, one that specifies a return type and another that does not, Java requires that all methods have a return type. This necessitates having a type indicating that there is no return value from a method. This type is type `void`: `void` is effectively a place-holder for strong type checking purposes. A method declared as:

```
void f() { ... }
```

is a method with no return value. Although `void` is a perfectly valid type, there are no values of the type and hence no operations on them. It is not possible to have variables of type `void`, as there is no representation that can be stored in them. The type only makes sense associated with methods where returning `void` simply means that a method will be returning no value.

note

void *is a type that has no values.*

3.3.3   Method Arguments

Mathematical functions (for example square root, sine, cosine and factorial) are applied to a value and return a result which depends upon that value. We are familiar with using mathematical functions in expressions such as:

$$x = \sqrt{y}$$

or

$$x = \cos y$$

Methods (whether value-returning or not) need this capability so that when called they can be supplied with an initial value and so perform a computation that depends upon that initial value. Programming languages like Java provide a mechanism called *parameter passing* to enable methods to be given initial values. The values are referred to as *parameter values* (or often just *parameters* or sometimes *arguments*).

note

A method can be parameterized.

As an example of parameter passing here is a method that takes an integer value as a parameter and returns twice that value:

```
int times2 (final int x) {
   return x * 2 ;
}
```

The method name, `times2`, is preceded by the return type of `int` and followed by a *parameter declaration*. The parameter declaration appears in parentheses and looks very like a variable declaration, which in fact it is. The `int x` is declaring a *parameter variable* called x. (Parameter variables are often simply termed parameters just as parameter values are, the context invariably disambiguates.) Within the method body, x is used just like any other variable. The `final` in front of the declaration is a declaration modifier which states that the value of x will not be changed after it has been initialized. If the `final` is not present, then the value of the parameter can be changed in the method body. Neither situation is more correct, the right choice depends upon the context. However, in all situations where the parameter remains unchanged in the method it is always best to have the `final`. The compiler checks to ensure that the value is never actually assigned to supporting the intentionality of the programmer.

tip

Always make parameters final and then remove the final if the method really must amend the parameter value.

The method `times2` is called using statements such as:

```
int y = anObject.times2(10); // Initialize y to 20
```

The value 10 is supplied as the parameter value appearing within the parentheses following the method name. The parameter value is used to initialize the parameter variable x before the method body is executed, so x takes on whatever value is provided in the method call.

Given a series of method calls to `times2`:

```
int a = anObject.times2(2) ;
int b = anObject.times2(4) ;
int c = anObject.times2(6) ;
```

the parameter variable will be initialized to a different value for each call and the method returns a different result.

Parameter values are not just limited to numbers but can be given by any expression (such as a variable) that evaluates to the correct type of value. For example, the `times2` method could be called in a loop, using a variable to determine the parameter value:

```
int counter = 1 ;
int result = 0 ;
while (counter < 10) {
  result = result + anObject.times2(counter) ;
  counter = counter + 1 ;
}
```

or a more complicated expression could be used:

```
int counter = 1 ;
int result = 0 ;
while (counter < 10) {
  result = result + anObject.times2(counter + result + 10) ;
  counter = counter + 1 ;
}
```

or, indeed, the parameter value can be the value returned by a call to a method:

```
int counter = 1 ;
int result = 0 ;
while (counter < 10) {
  result = result + anObject.times2(anObject.times2(counter)) ;
  counter = counter + 1 ;
}
```

3.3.4   Multiple Method Parameters

A method can actually have any number of parameters. A *parameter list* rather than a single parameter can be declared. For example:

```
double f(final double a, final double b) {
  return (a * 10) + (b * 100) ;
}
```

The parameter list is simply a comma-separated sequence of parameter variable declarations, with modifier `final` since none of the parameters will be changed in the method. It is good practice not to have more than about six to eight arguments unless absolutely necessary since this usually leads to bulky and less comprehensible code.

A method taking a single argument is, of course, simply a parameter list of size one, while an empty parameter list is a list of size zero. This is why methods taking no arguments are still declared with parentheses (e.g. `void sayHello()`).

All parameter variables must have a type so that strong type checking of the match between arguments in method calls and parameter variables can take place. This makes sure that a method is always called with the right number and types of parameter values. A mismatch will cause a compilation error and the mistake must be corrected before an executable can be produced. This is an important safety feature — a method cannot work as expected if it is given unexpected types of data.

Finally in this section, we must note that there is a potential danger of being drawn into the assumption that all value returning methods are actually mathematical functions. Mathematical functions always return the same return value given the same parameter value; this is termed *referential transparency*. Methods that implement mathematical functions must clearly exhibit referential transparency in order to be proper implementations. However, not all methods implement mathematical functions; these other methods may, or may not, be referentially transparent — it is possible to call some methods with the same arguments several times but get different results each time.

3.3.5 Recursion

As well as being able to call other methods, a method can also call itself. This behaviour is known as *recursion*. Here is an example of a *recursive method*:

```
int sum(final int n) {
  if (n == 0) {
    return 0 ;
  } else {
    return sum(n-1) + n ;
  }
}
```

This method returns the sum of the integers from 1 to n, where n is the parameter value the method is called with. For example, the sum of 1 to 5 can be computed using:

```
obj.sum(5) ;
```

The *recursive method call* appears in the statement:

```
return sum(n-1) + n ;
```

As the call is being made to the same object as that of the method containing the call, there is no need to name an object to make this method call; simply using the method name is sufficient.

To help understand how the method works, a trace can be written:

```
call sum(5)
sum(5):   n != 0, call sum(4)
sum(4):    n != 0, call sum(3)
sum(3):     n != 0, call sum(2)
sum(2):      n != 0, call sum(1)
sum(1):       n != 0, call sum(0)
sum(0):        n == 0, return 0
```

```
sum(1):              return 0 + 1 (1)
sum(2):             return 1 + 2 (3)
sum(3):            return 3 + 3 (6)
sum(4):          return 6 + 4 (10)
sum(5):        return 10 + 5 (15)
```

The label at the start of each line shows which method call is being executed. When `sum(0)` has been reached a chain of active method calls exist, each waiting on the next to complete and return a value. Such a chain is referred to as the *call chain*. A call chain is built up whenever methods call one another and are waiting for the called methods to finish. This applies always and not just to recursion, it is just that it is more important to appreciate the details in order to understand how recursion works. (The call chain is sometimes referred to as the *call stack*. This term derives from the way that method calls are managed by the run-time system in some languages; it is not an appropriate label for the abstract concept of a call chain.)

In fact, recursion is essentially just another way of implementing iteration, as this example shows. The recursive summation method above is equivalent to:

```
int sum(int n) {
  int result = 0 ;
  while (n > 0) {
    result = result + n ;
    n = n - 1 ;
  }
  return result ;
}
```

By equivalent here we mean that they return the same return value for the same parameter value. Note that here the parameter is not final since the algorithm implemented in the method uses the parameter variable as the counter for the iteration.

tip

Recursive methods can provide very elegant solutions to problems but they can be slow and use a lot of memory — plan their use carefully.

In general, recursive methods can be re-written using explicit iteration, although the transformation may not be easy. For many algorithms, use of recursion provides a more compact and in many ways more elegant implementation. Also, recursive solutions tend to be far faster to code since there is less iteration management code to be written. However, recursion usually employs more memory resources and often this can be a barrier to its use.

tip

Beware of unintended mutual recursion.

A special case of recursion is indirect or *mutual recursion*. This occurs when method A makes a call to method B and B then makes a call back to method A before it returns the call from A. In fact, there can be an entire chain of method calls before the call back to A. Although mutual recursion can be useful, it can also be hard to manage and is best avoided unless properly justified. Mutual recursion more often happens as a result of a design or programming error, rather than being planned.

3.4   Writing Programs with Methods

We are now in a position to write some example programs consisting of several methods, including those that take a parameter and return a result.

3.4.1 Program MultiplicationTable

Statement of Problem

"Write a program that uses a method to display a multiplication table, given an integer between 2 and 12 inclusive. The program should ask the user which table to display and reject any invalid request."

Design and
Implementation

With most of the previous example programs we only really thought and planned in terms of a single statement sequence. However, now we know how to write methods, we want to update our strategy and first consider the design in terms of methods.

Obviously there will be a method that displays the multiplication table, which we will call `table`. This will take an integer parameter but does not need to return a result, so can be declared as `void table(int n)`. Equally obvious, there will be a `main` method, as all programs must have one. However, should the `main` method ask the user for input and call `table`, or should that behaviour be put into a third method?

The answer to this question lies in an important method design principle: each method should be *cohesive* — that is, it should focus on doing one, and only one, well-defined chunk of behaviour needed by the program. Following this principle, the `main` method can focus on initializing the program by creating an object and then call another method to handle the user input. The input method in turn can then focus on doing one thing before calling the method to display the table. Hence, we now have a method called `input`, and have established which method calls another.

!

Cohesive methods focus on doing one thing well.

tip

Solve problems using a 'divide and conquer' approach.

With the methods and their behaviour identified, each can now be looked at in turn to design their respective method bodies. Moreover, rather than having to consider the entire statement sequence in the program at one go, we are now concerned only with small portions at a time. This has divided a larger and more complex design problem into a collection of smaller, and more easily designed, components. Further, each component has a well-defined interface by which it connects to other components. The interface is the name of the method and its parameter list, i.e. the number and types of the parameters.

The design of each method is now straightforward. Method `table` needs a loop and output statements to display a multiplication table, while the `input` asks the user to enter a value and checks it is within the supported range. If it is then `table` is called, otherwise an error message is displayed. Here is our implementation:

```
// Program to display a multiplication table.
// Written by Graham Roberts, August 1999.
// Revision history:
// none
public class MultiplicationTable {
  // Display multiplication table for n.
  void table(final int n) {
    int counter = 1 ;
    System.out.println("The " + n + " times table") ;
    while (counter < 13) {
      System.out.print(counter + " x " + n) ;
      System.out.println(" = " + counter * n) ;
      counter = counter + 1 ;
```

```
      }
    }
    // Get table to display.
    void input() {
      KeyboardInput in = new KeyboardInput () ;
      System.out.print("Which table (2-12)? ") ;
      int x = in.readInteger() ;
      if ((x < 2) || (x > 12)) {
        System.out.println("Cannot display that table") ;
      } else {
        table(x) ;
      }
    }
    public static void main(final String[] args) {
      MultiplicationTable obj = new MultiplicationTable () ;
      obj.input() ;
    }
  }
```

Notice that each method declaration is preceded by a short comment explaining the purpose of the method. Also notice the output statements used in `table`, as they illustrate method calls with more complicated parameter value expressions.

Testing

Testing turns out to be straightforward. All twelve valid inputs can be quickly tested, followed by a range of invalid inputs (for example, 0, 13, 100, hello) to check the error handling.

Review

The implementation looks successful but it is always worth asking if anything could have been done differently and whether that would give a better design. The most obvious issue is that `input` appears to be showing poor cohesion in that it is responsible for both inputting the value from the user and causing the table to be printed. An alternative is to make `input` return the value the user inputs, and move the call to `table` into the `main` method:

```
    int input() {
      ... <code as before> ...

      if ((x < 2) || (x > 12)) {
        System.out.println("Cannot display that table") ;
        System.exit(1) ;
      }
      return x ;
    }
    public static void main(String[] args) {
      MultiplicationTable obj = new MultiplicationTable() ;
      obj.table(obj.input()) ;
    }
```

This is an equally good, if not better, solution. Responsibility is partitioned more sensibly, the methods are more cohesive: `main` is in control of the sequence of activities that are happening, `input` is responsible for delivering up a sensible value from the user. Finding out which table to display is separated from deciding when to do the display. The problem introduced is that `input` has to terminate the program if it does not get a valid input from the user. We still have an element of dispersion of responsibility. In fact, Java has a rather nice way of handling this sort of situation and that is exceptions. We shall introduce these in Section 8.1, Page 226.

Programming frequently involves comparing two or more variations of a design and trying to determine which one to use. Principles such as cohesiveness, generalization and planning ahead for future change are just some of the guidelines that can be used to make good decisions.

Notice that the call to `table` is written as:

```
obj.table(...)
```

in the revised `main` method, and as:

```
table(...)
```

in the original `input` method. The difference is explained by the fact that in `input` a method call is being made to *same* object as `input` was called for. When a call is made to the same object, the dot notation is not needed as the object is already identified. In contrast, `main` is not called for an object, so an object needs to be nominated for the call to occur on.

3.4.2 Program Palindrome

Many of the methods seen so far in this chapter have had a mathematical flavour. The next example will instead focus on using strings and characters.

"Write a program that determines whether a word or sentence is a palindrome. (A palindrome reads backwards the same way as forwards, for example: 'Able was I ere I saw Elba'.) Spaces are considered as significant."

Statement of Problem

The problem statement gives little information about designing the program, so we definitely need to do some thinking and planning before trying to write code. First of all we need an algorithm to test whether a string is a palindrome. This turns out to be easy:

Design and
Implementation

> *make a copy of the string*
> *reverse the order of the characters*
> *compare the copy with the original to see if they are the same*

Now that we know that it's possible to check for a palindrome, the next step is to consider the overall sequence of events that should take place when the program runs. This gives:

> *input string to test*
> *make a copy*
> *do the reverse*
> *check the result*
> *display answer*

Have a design strategy. Find an algorithm, allocate behaviour to methods, implement, test, review, repeat.

Next we want to determine what methods are required and allocate behaviour to them. We could bundle everything into a single method but that would violate our cohesion guidelines. Instead, we identify the following methods:

```
String getInput() // Get the input string to be tested
void testForPalindrome(String s) // Check if s is a palindrome
boolean check(String s1, String s2) // Is s2 the reverse of s1?
String reverse(String s) // Return the reverse of the argument String
```

tip

Keep methods as short as
possible.

?

Information about
using the J2SDK
documentation can be
found in Appendix C,
Page 953.

tip

The first character in a
String is at position 0.
Real Programmers
always count from 0.

tip

Always keep checking the
details of the problem to
make sure you're
working on the right
solution.

This may seem more methods than necessary. That could turn out to be true but at this stage we are deliberately breaking the overall behaviour down into minimally sized methods to get a good feel for the design. Methods can be combined and behaviour re-allocated later if it seems appropriate.

With the methods identified, each can be considered in turn to design its method body. Method `getInput` is easy as it simply requests input and returns the resulting string. `TestForPalindrome` is also straightforward, it just needs to call the `check` method with the same string for both parameter values. `Check` is a bit more interesting as the decision has been made to make it more general purpose than is strictly necessary for this version of the program. The idea for `check` is that it can actually test any two strings to see if they are the reverse of each other. `TestForPalindrome` will call it with the same string for both arguments since it checks for self-reversed strings. `Check` works by reversing one string and then doing a string comparison using the `compareTo` method in the `String` class. We knew about this `compareTo` method because we have previously studied the J2SDK documentation.

This leaves `reverse`, which requires a bit more work. The basic strategy here is to unpack the original string character by character and reassemble the characters in the reverse order to create a new string. To find out how to extract individual characters from a string, we need to return to the documentation for class `String`. This shows that there is a method declared as `char charAt(int index)`, which returns the character at position `index`, counting from 0 as the position of the first character. The `String` documentation also shows a method `int length()` that returns the number of characters in a `String`. With these methods we can construct a loop to access each character in turn:

```
// Given some String s
int position = 0;
while (position < s.length()) { // Characters run from 0 to length-1
  ...s.charAt(position) ; // Get the character and do something
  position = position + 1 ; // Move to next character
}
```

Building the new string requires further searching of the J2SDK documentation to find a method to join a `char` to a `String`. The `String` class does not provide one, so we start looking at other classes. It turns out there is a class `Character`, whose objects represent characters that can be used to create a `String` from a single `char` using an expression like:

```
// Given a char c
... new Character(c).toString() ...
```

The `toString()` method converts from a `Character` object to a `String` object. The two strings can then be concatenated using the + operator.

We now have all the pieces ready to write the program. However, a review of the problem statement to check we are still answering the right question highlights a problem: the sample palindrome is only a palindrome if the case of the letters is ignored; if the case of the letters is significant then the sample string is not a palindrome. If our current design was applied to this sample string, it would not be accepted as a palindrome. Given that the string was supplied as an example of a palindrome, it must be that case is not significant. We therefore need to address this in our design.

The answer to the problem is to convert all the characters in the input string to lower case before testing to see if it is a palindrome. A further search of the `String` class documentation provides the solution in the form of a method declared as `String toLowerCase()`, which returns a lower case version of the string it is called for. Calls to the method can be inserted appropriately to cause case to be non-significant.

Here then is the program:

```
// Program to check for a palindrome.
// Written by Graham Roberts, August 1999.
// Revision history:
// none
public class Palindrome {
  // Return a String which is the reverse of the argument String
  String reverse(final String s) {
    String result = new String() ;
    int position = 0 ;
    while (position < s.length()) {
      result = new Character(s.charAt(position)).toString() + result ;
      position = position + 1 ;
    }
    return result ;
  }
  // Check to see if the two argument Strings are the reverse of each
  // other. Return true if they are and false otherwise..
  boolean check(final String s1, final String s2) {
    String s = reverse(s2) ;
    if (s1.compareTo(s) == 0) {
      return true ;
    } else {
      return false ;
    }
  }
  // Get user to input a String.
  String getInput() {
    KeyboardInput in = new KeyboardInput () ;
    System.out.print("Enter text to check: ") ;
    return in.readString() ;
  }
  // Do the palindrome test and display the result
  void testForPalindrome(final String s) {
    if (check(s.toLowerCase(), s.toLowerCase())) {
      System.out.println("String is a palindrome.") ;
    } else {
      System.out.println("String is not a palindrome.") ;
    }
  }
  public static void main(final String[] args) {
    Palindrome obj = new Palindrome () ;
    obj.testForPalindrome(obj.getInput()) ;
  }
}
```

This is another program where exhaustive testing is not possible since there is an infinite number of strings that need testing. Thus, we must rely on doing enough tests of the 'right sort' to gain confidence that the program works and has no obvious bugs. Following the categories of tests first identified in Section 2.10.3, Page 41, we might have these kinds of test:

Testing

- Tests using a collection of sample palindromes. To save finding meaningful palindromes we can construct nonsense ones, e.g. "abc deF fed cBa".

- Tests using strings that are not palindromes to ensure we do not get false positives.

- Tests using strings that are not palindromes but which try to anticipate programming errors. For example, "abc cb" — one character missing at the end to check to see if string reversal and comparisons deal with every character correctly.

Review

tip

Browse the J2SDK documentation to become familiar with the classes and methods available.

The design process behind this program was elaborated in detail to show the kind of activities that typically go on:

- Identifying algorithms is important and can require a lot of thought and research.

- Identifying behaviour and allocating it to methods needs to be done carefully.

- The J2SDK provides many useful classes and methods that need to be found and exploited.

- Guidelines, such as writing cohesive methods, need to be applied.

- Poor design needs to be detected and repaired.

The skill of programming requires all these to be juggled to produce an acceptable result.

What about the design of our palindrome program? One argument says: It works, so leave it alone. However, the danger with that approach is that when the program is extended or modified in the future, poor design makes the work harder and more error prone. With a large program this can make change very expensive, if not impossible. As programmers we also want to take pride in our work and produce the best quality we can.

So, can the design of the palindrome be improved? Yes. In fact, the alarm bells should be ringing already over the `check` method and the `reverse` method.

The `check` method is over-simplistic, it lacks sophistication. In fact the following would be a far better implementation:

```
boolean check(final String s1, final String s2) {
  return s1.compareTo(reverse(s2)) == 0 ;
}
```

The observations here are: Firstly, that an `==` expression results in a boolean value so there is no need for a selection and then return `true` or `false` explicitly, we just return the value of the expression. Secondly, there is no need to assign to `s2`, we can use the result of the call to the method `reverse` directly as the parameter value for the `compareTo` method call. The moral of this story is that apparently simple code can actually be more complicated, certainly longer. By employing a slightly more sophisticated approach we get a shorter, more comprehensible method implementation.

Now to `reverse`. The code looks and feels awkward and it was hard work to write; we seemed to be having to tweak things unnaturally. These are warning bells. There are two main possibilities in this situation:

1. We did not do enough research with the documentation to find the right classes and methods for our algorithm.

2. The algorithm is not actually the right one for the tools we have available.

In either case, the way forward is simple: more perusing of the documentation!

Further searching of the J2SDK documentation reveals that `Strings` are intended to be immutable things; they are read-only objects. In effect, `Strings` are supposed to be constants. For string manipulation, the J2SDK has the class `StringBuffer`. Given that we want to manipulate a string, `StringBuffer` must be researched. It takes very little research in fact to find that `StringBuffer` has a method `reverse`. It seems that reversing a string is such a sufficiently common thing to do that it has been incorporated as part of a standard class. Since the method implements exactly what we want, we immediately change strategy and cease thinking about reversing algorithms and decide how best to make use of this class. The moral of this episode is "look before you leap": look in the manual before you leap into code construction. We unnecessarily spent time writing our own version when one existed already.

Analysing the episode a little more, the principle problem we were having with the first implementation was that we were over-committed to the algorithm we had come up with in the face of difficulties. We were trying to force an algorithm on classes that were not set up to handle the algorithm. In such a situation, it is a question of finding more appropriate classes and methods or finding a more appropriate algorithm.

With this new information, we can revise our program design and code, a process referred to as *refactoring*. Our method `reverse` can be eliminated and a call made to `StringBuffer` reverse in `check`. This gives:

```
boolean check(final String s1, final String s2) {
  // Create a StringBuffer from s2, reverse the string
  // and convert back to a String object
  s2 = new StringBuffer(s2).reverse().toString() ;
  return s1.compareTo(s2) == 0 ;
}
```

This change then leads to the question: Is method `check` really needed? Its behaviour could be moved into `testForPalindrome` and `check` could be deleted. We originally included `check` on the grounds that it could test any two strings to see if one is the reverse of the other, and because it might be useful in the future. However, it is really rather redundant because the J2SDK has more capability than we first thought it had.

This is actually one of the potential dangers of the decompositional approach we have employed here. In worrying about how to organize the necessary algorithms and methods, sight can be lost of what the development environment provides. All too often people end up re-inventing code that is standard because they focus too much on the problem at hand!

Here, then, is a replacement version of the program that makes maximal use of the standard classes:

```
// Program to check for a palindrome.
// Written by Graham Roberts, August 1999.
// Revision history:
// none
public class Palindrome2 {
  // Get user to input a String.
  String getInput() {
    KeyboardInput in = new KeyboardInput () ;
    System.out.print("Enter text to check: ") ;
    return in.readString() ;
  }
  // Do the palindrome test and display the result
  void testForPalindrome(final String s) {
    String reverse =
      new StringBuffer(s.toLowerCase()).reverse().toString() ;
    System.out.print("The String is ") ;
    if (s.compareTo(reverse) != 0) {
      System.out.print("not ") ;
    }
    System.out.println("a palindrome") ;
  }
  public static void main(final String[] args) {
    Palindrome2 obj = new Palindrome2 () ;
    obj.testForPalindrome(obj.getInput()) ;
  }
}
```

*Programming is all
about learning. As we
learn about the problem
we learn about the
solution which tells us
more about the
problem, and so on.*

This demonstrates that review and refactoring of programs is important and necessary. We propose and implement a first design, and in doing so learn and understand more about the problem we are working with. We use that new knowledge to evolve the design and implementation, generating a better result, which we were unlikely to have discovered the first time round. This means that an iterative approach to developing programs is the natural and right way of working.

3.5 Procedural Decomposition

With the introduction of methods, we have seen programs consisting of several methods that call each other in sequence. The `main` method is called first, it then calls other methods, those methods can call still more methods, and so on. We now have the basis of strategy that we could, but won't, employ to design and structure complete programs, known as *procedural decomposition* or *top-down refinement*.

When a program is constructed to solve a problem, the entire problem is first cast as a single procedure. This top-level procedure is then defined in terms of calls to other procedures, which are in turn defined in terms of other procedures, creating a hierarchy of procedures. This process continues until a collection of procedures is reached that do not need to be refined further since they are constructed entirely in terms of statements in the base language. Hence the use of the term 'top-down refinement'.

At this point we have a collection of procedures defining a complete program. The program is executed by calling the top-level procedure. Figure 3.1 shows an example situation in which a program has been decomposed into procedures Main, P1, P2, P3 and P4. When run, Main calls P2,

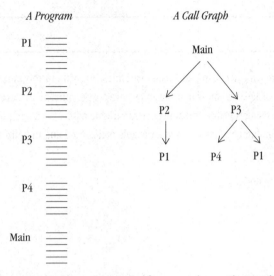

Figure 3.1 A program constructed from procedures with a possible call graph.

P2 calls P1, control then returns to Main which next calls P3, P3 calls P4 followed by P1. No classes or objects exist, as they are outside the domain of this approach.

As well as the code itself, we can construct what is termed a *call graph* of the program. A call graph is used to show which procedures are called by which other procedures. The right-hand side of Figure 3.1 shows the call graph for the program shown on the left. The usefulness of call graphs is that they show a view of the program in an immediate way that is not obtainable from perusing the source code itself. They enable the programmer to reason about their program behaviour and structure at a more abstract level.

Top-down refinement using procedures is the basis of what is known as *structured programming*. This style of programming became very popular in the late sixties and early seventies and is exemplified in programming languages like Pascal and C. The development of structured programming was a quite natural progression of programming technology and was quite rightly popular. However, since then technology has moved on, first by exploiting the concept of *abstract data types* and then moving to *object-oriented programming*. This led to programming languages like Smalltalk, C++ and Ada, and most recently Java.

Whilst it is possible to write a Java program designed using top-down refinement, the language is really not designed to support this style. Java only works properly when the full object-oriented approach is followed. One reason why Java terminology uses the label method instead of procedure or function, is to make clear that the role of procedural abstraction is to support object-oriented programming not structured programming. This does not invalidate the example programs seen so far. This is partly due to the small size of the programs but also because top-down refinement remains a useful technique at the small scale, and for designing small parts of larger object-oriented programs.

3.6   Encapsulation

We have become familiar with declaring and using variables but without too much regard to the rules which govern their usage. We know that variables have a type, must be declared correctly and have to be initialized. Choosing sensible and appropriate variable names is also important. However, we haven't addressed a fundamental issue: once a variable is declared and initialized, in what parts of a program can it be used?

Consider the following code:

```
void f() {
  int x = 0 ;
  ...
  // work with x
}
void g() {
  x = 10; // What x?
}
```

The variable x is declared and used in method f. A variable called x is assigned to in method g: is it the same variable as the one declared in f? If not, then where is it declared? Or is trying to use x in g an error that the Java compiler will reject? To answer these questions we need to start looking at the ideas underlying encapsulation.

3.6.1   Scope and Lifetime

To understand how variables are managed, we need to introduce two important concepts:

Scope — defining which parts of a program can access a variable.

Lifetime — defining when a variable is created and destroyed.

ref

Section 28.7, Page 779.

Every variable has a *scope*, that part of a program where it is declared and where it can be used. Program statements in the same scope can access the variable after its declaration, while statements outside the scope cannot access it at all.

Methods and compound statements define a *local scope*. A variable declared in a local scope can be accessed only by statements in that scope (i.e. the method or compound statement). Thus a method can have *local variables* that only statements within that method can access Similarly, a compound statement can have local variables only accessible within the statement (in fact, a method body is essentially a compound statement). Being declared within the method scope, method parameter variables are also local variables.

Scopes can be *nested*, so that one scope can exist inside another scope. For example, this occurs when compound statements are used within a method body. The inner or nested scope can access any variables declared in the enclosing scope but variables declared in the inner scope can only be accessed within that scope (or scopes nested inside it).

Using nested scopes is a way of minimizing the region of a program in which a particular variable can be used. This reduces the risk of the variable being used inappropriately in part of a program that was not really meant to have access to it, so scope is a mechanism to aid the programmer in enforcing encapsulation. A good programming principle to follow is to always limit the scope of a variable to the minimum possible.

Since variables are only accessible when they are *in scope*, they need only exist when they are in scope. Because of this property, the language can ensure that variables only get created when they are needed. Once out of scope, they can be destroyed and the memory used for the variable reclaimed. For local variables, their *lifetime* is the same as their scope.

This means that every time a method is called a new set of local and parameter variables is created and initialized. When the method call returns, the variables go out of scope and are destroyed, so that specific set of variables cannot be used or accessed again. The next time the method is called a new set of variables is created. Note that it is this mechanism that allows recursion: each call results in new variables being created. The different recursive calls do not share variables.

This principle also applies to compound statements, including those used for loop bodies. Consider the following code fragment:

```
{
    int x = 0 ;
    while (x < 10) {
        int y = x ;
        // rest of loop body
        // both x and y are in scope
        ...
    }

    // x is in scope here
    // y is not
}
```

The variable x is declared at the top of the enclosing compound statement and so is in scope for the entire fragment, allowing it to be accessed from any statement including those inside the while loop. The variable y is local to the loop body and can be accessed only within the loop. Moreover, every time the loop body is executed a new variable y is created. The lifetime of the variable is the scope because the variable is local and so a new variable is created and destroyed each time we re-enter the scope.

It is worth pointing out here that all variable names in a scope must be unique. Unlike some languages, Java does not allow *shadowing* of variables. The following code fragment is not legal Java, the compiler treats it as an error:

```
{
    int x = 0 ;
    while (x < 10) {
        int x = 3 ; // This is an error.
    }
}
```

tip

Limit the scope of all names to the minimum possible.

note

Creating a variable means allocating space for it in the computer's memory. This is dealt with automatically by the programming language.

It is also worth emphasizing that the textual ordering of variable declarations and statements matters. All variables must be declared before being used. Thus, the following is incorrect:

```
{
    x = 10 ; // This is an error.
    ...
    int x = 1 ;
    ...
}
```

The first statement attempts to assign to x but at this point x is not yet accessible as, in the textual order, the declaration statement has not been reached. So, although the first statement is in the same scope unit as x, it cannot use x since x is not actually in scope until after the declaration.

3.6.2   Names and Scope

The idea of scope is not limited to variables. In fact, all names in a program have scopes including variable and method names, as well as other kinds of names yet to be introduced.

Any name used in a program must have been declared, in either the current scope or an enclosing scope, before it can be used. If this is not the case then the Java compiler will report an error. In addition to being declared, names have to be unique within a scope. This means that the same name cannot be declared twice in the same scope, as that would create ambiguity. For example:

```
{
    int x = 0;
    ...
    double x = 10.0; // Error, x already declared
}
```

Attempting to declare the name x a second time in the same scope results in a compilation error. Further, the following situation would also cause a compilation error for the same reason:

```
{
    int x = 0 ;
    ...
    while (true) {
        int x = 1 ; // Error, x already declared in enclosing scope
        ...
    }
}
```

The second x, declared as a local variable within the loop body, will cause an error as an x has already been declared in the enclosing scope. The nested scope of the loop body includes all the declarations of its enclosing scope, so the new declaration creates an ambiguity.

On the other hand, the following is acceptable:

```
{
    while (...) {
        int i = 0 ;
    }
    ...
    while (...) {
        int i = 1 ; // OK
    }
}
```

In this case, the second declaration of `i` causes no problems, as the first is not in an enclosing scope.

3.7 More Operators

As well as the familiar arithmetic operators (`+,-,*,/`, etc.) and the assignment operator (`=`), there are a number of other operators available in the Java language. Many of these are just notational short hand for operations that can be achieved by other means. However, using these operators sensibly makes code much more comprehensible. The full list of operators can be seen in the language reference (Section 28.9, Page 788) but we take this opportunity to introduce some of them here so that we can make use them from now on.

3.7.1 Increment, Decrement and Assignment Operators

Quite frequently algorithms require numeric variables (values of types such as `int` and `double`) to be incremented or decremented by one. A number of examples have appeared in this book already. Till now we have written increment as:

```
n = n + 1 ;
```

Section 28.9, Page 788.

but Java has two other operators that can achieve the same functionality: these are the increment by one operator, `++`, and the increment by some value operator, `+=`. Increment by one can be applied in two ways; first there is the post-increment operator:

```
n++ ; // post-increment n by 1
```

and then there is the pre-increment operator:

```
++n ; // pre-increment n by 1
```

Although both operators increase the value of the operand by one, the semantics of the two are subtly but crucially different. For the moment we will gloss over this difference since, in the use we make for the moment, the difference cannot be distinguished. See Section 28.9, Page 788, for the full details.

As well as an increment by one operator, there is a decrement by one operator, `--`. It is very similar to the increment by one operator, except that it subtracts one from its argument:

```
n-- ; // post-decrement n by 1
--n ; // pre-decrement b by 1
```

As noted above, there is an increment by some amount operator, `+=`, and its partner the decrement by some amount operator, `-=`. These operators can clearly achieve what the `++` and `--` operators can:

```
n += 1; // increment by one
n -= 1; // decrement by one
```

However, these two operators can actually do much more. Unlike `++` and `--`, they are not limited to increments or decrements of one, thus:

```
n += 10; // increment by 10
n -= 8; // decrement by 8
d += 3.123; // increment by 3.123
```

Other arithmetic operators such as '*' and '/' can also be used combined with assignment in this way. So, for example:

```
n *= 2; // multiply by 2
d /= 0.5; // divide by 0.5
```

Another operator worth mentioning here is '%'. This is the *remainder operator* that returns the remainder when one value is divided by another:

```
n = 4 % 3; // 4 % 3 = 1
```

There is also an assignment operator version:

```
n %= 3; // remainder of n / 3
```

3.7.2   Arithmetic Expressions and Types

Expressions involving the arithmetic operators often need some thought regarding the types involved. This expression:

```
3 / 2
```

results in a value of type `int` (1); both operands are of type `int` so the result is of type `int`. The expression:

```
3 / 1.2
```

on the other hand, involves an `int` and a `double`, so the result will be a `double` (2.5). This means that whilst statements such as:

```
int n = 3 / 2;
```

are entirely reasonable, statements such as:

```
int n = 3 / 1.2; // Error, can't assign double to int
```

are invalid due to a type mismatch — it is not possible to initialize an `int` with a `double`. This expression would result in a compilation error since the compiler, using strong type checking, can deduce the types of the values and variable involved.

The basic rule when applying an arithmetic operator is that the type of the result is determined by taking the most general type of the operands. Most general means the type best able to represent the result without loss of accuracy, so type `double` is more general than type `int` as it can represent a greater range of values.

3.8   More Control Statements

The previous chapter introduced the if statement and the while and do loops, all examples of control statements. The Java language includes two other control statements, the for loop and the switch statement, which we will now introduce.

3.8.1 For Loops

In Section 2.3, Page 20, we introduced the while and do loops and mentioned the existence of the *for loop*. Having covered the concept of scope, we are now able to introduce for loops so that we can make use of them.

Section 29.3.3, Page 819.

The for loop is primarily for bounded or counted iteration, where a counter variable is used to control how many times the loop is repeated. An example of a for loop is:

```
for (int n = 0 ; i < 10 ; ++i) {
  // locp body
}
```

The for keyword is followed by three expressions in parentheses, separated by semicolons, that determine the loop behaviour. The first expression (int n = 0) initializes a local variable to be used as a counter to determine how many times the loop repeats. The variable is local to the loop body and goes out of scope once the loop has finished. The next expression (i < 10) determines that the loop will continue executing while i has a value less than 10. This expression is re-evaluated and tested before every execution of the loop body to check whether the execution should happen or whether the loop should terminate. The third expression (++i) determines how to change the value of i after each execution of the loop body. Thus, the loop as a whole initializes a variable n that counts from 0 to 9, and executes the loop body 10 times. As the loop variable i is a local variable, its value can be accessed inside the loop body but is out of scope and out of lifetime outside the loop body.

The following method illustrates typical usage of a for loop by generating the sum of the sequence of integers from 1 to n (compare this with the versions in Section 3.3.5, Page 59):

```
int sum(final int n) {
  int result = 0 ;
  fcr (int i = 1 ; i <= n ; ++i) {
    result += i ;
  }
  return result ;
}
```

The for loop is very flexible. We are not restricted to increments by one as shown above. The final, 'increment' section of the for loop can contain any expression. Here is an example showing a decrement by an amount other than one:

```
for (int i = 10 ; i > 0; i -= 2) {
  // loop body
}
```

Always check that the test and increment sections work together to create a finite loop.

We are not required to actually have entries in all three of the expression slots. Invariably there is a test and an increment/decrement but we don't always need a new variable. The following, which is (yet another) version of the summation method, hints at the total flexibility that the for loop gives to us. In fact, this is perhaps the most likely production version of the summation method since it is essentially minimal:

```
int sum(int n) {
  int result = 0 ;
  for ( ; n > 0 ; --n) {
```

```
        result += n ;
      }
      return result ;
   }
```

3.8.2 Program CharacterTriangle

To further illustrate the use of the `for`-loop, this section and the following section provide two example programs.

Statement of Problem   "*Write a program using loops to display the following:*

```
*
**
***
****
*****
******
```

You may display only one character at a time."

Design and Implemention

The problem statement requires us to output one character at a time. This prevents us from simply doing the obvious which is a sequence of output statements; we need to do something more sophisticated.

The shape has to be displayed line by line, with characters output left to right. This suggests two loops are needed, one to count the number of lines and the other to count the number of characters in a line as it is displayed. The loop displaying a line will need to be *nested* inside the loop counting the lines. As a loop body can contain any statement, including other loops, this presents no problem; nesting loops is a common arrangement.

Knowing this, the program is actually straightforward to write, providing care is taken to get the loop start and end conditions correct.

If this were a real system we would investigate the problem statement itself to see if it was necessary to dictate the solution strategy. Problem statements should only specify required functionality and not solution constraints. In this situation, for pedagogical reasons, we are requiring the constraints so that we are forced to use loops.

```
// Program to display a triangle using characters.
// Written by Graham Roberts, August 1999.
// Revision history:
// none
public class CharacterTriangle {
  void displayTriangle(final int height) {
    for (int m = 0 ; m < height ; ++m)  {
      for (int n = 0 ; n < m + 1 ; ++n) {
        System.out.print('*') ;
      }
      System.out.println() ;
    }
  }
  public static void main(final String[] args) {
    CharacterTriangle obj = new CharacterTriangle () ;
    obj.displayTriangle(6) ;
  }
}
```

Note the expression used to determine when to end the inner loop. This has to display the same number of stars as the line number, but lines are counted from zero so an adjustment of plus one has to be made. The `displayTriangle` method takes a parameter that actually allows it to draw triangles of any size, although this is not exploited fully in this problem as set.

Individual characters are denoted by putting the character in single quotes: `'*'`. Single characters are of type `char` not `String`, which is why single quotes rather than double quotes are used.

In this case testing is very straightforward; simply check that the correct triangle is display for a variety of parameter values. The value needed to solve the program as set is 6 but since we have written a more general method we have a responsibility to test it for the more general case. Obviously, exhaustive testing is out of the question but trying a range of values — –10, –1, 0, 1, 5, 20 might be a reasonable test data set — should give us high enough confidence in the code.

Testing

3.8.3 Program CharacterRectangle

"Write a program to display the following:

Statement of Problem

```
********
*      *
*      *
********
```

You may display only one character at a time."

The key to designing this program is to determine the algorithm for displaying the shape. There are two kinds of line to display; solid lines and lines with a star at the beginning and the end. One strategy is to have a loop counting through each line, with the loop body containing a test to see if the first or last lines are being displayed. Depending on the result of the test, the correct sort of line is displayed. This gives:

Design and Implemention

```java
// Program to display a rectangle using characters.
// Written by Graham Roberts, August 1999.
// Revision history:
// none
public class CharacterRectangle {
  void displayRectangle(final int height, final int width) {
    for (int x = 0 ; x < height ; ++x) {
      if ((x == 0) || (x == 3)) {
        for (int y = 0 ; y < width ; ++y) {
          System.out.print('*') ;
        }
      } else {
        System.out.print('*') ;
        for (int y = 0 ; y < width-2 ; ++y) {
          System.out.print(' ') ;
        }
        System.out.print('*') ;
      }
      System.out.println() ;
    }
  }
  public static void main(final String[] args) {
    CharacterRectangle obj = new CharacterRectangle () ;
    obj.displayRectangle(4, 8) ;
  }
}
```

A method `displayRectangle` has been written that does all the work of displaying the shape. It takes parameters specifying the width and height.

Again, testing is straightforward as the program has no input and displays a fixed sized shape as output. This code successfully solves the problem as set but did you notice that it has a bug?

As with the previous example, we have provided a more general solution to the problem than is absolutely required to solve the problem as set — just in case we have to solve a similar problem in the future. Because of this, as well as testing the code for the problem as set, we have a responsibility to test the code for the more general case. A sensible test data set might be $(-2, -2)$, $(0, 0)$, $(2, 2)$, $(8, 8)$, $(3, 9)$, $(20, 40)$. Running this test data, we see that the code handles negative values and 0 by displaying nothing which is reasonable but it does highlight a bug in the code: it is always the fourth line (if that line exists) that is a full row of '*' with the last line only ever having the end points.

As with any debugging, the issues are:

- Observe that the bug exists.
- Understand why the bug is a bug.
- Understand why the bug got in there.
- Decide what the correct code should be.
- Re-test the program deciding whether the test data set should be extended further.

Observation of a bug is all about design and execution of a good test data set. We seem to have done that since we have highlighted a bug. The bug exists because the end condition was incorrectly specified using a constant rather than usage of the parameter. The error is that in the `displayRectangle` method, in the if statement within the first loop, we have a 3:

```
if ((x == 0) || (x == 3))
```

This is definitely wrong. At the very least we should have had:

```
if ((x == 0) || (x == height-1))
```

The bug arose because a specific solution to a problem was extended to be more general but not all necessary changes were made. Re-running the test data with the amended statement highlights no further bugs. There seems no real need to extend the test data set any further.

Once the algorithm has been identified, writing the program presents no problems (except the ability to introduce bugs!). As always, working on the algorithm using pen and paper before trying to write the code is likely to be valuable so the details can be established without getting side-tracked by programming language details.

tip

Develop the algorithm (using pseudocode) before trying to write the code.

Although this is only a small program, it is worth asking whether the `displayRectangle` method should be split into three smaller methods. One that manages displaying the shape as a whole, one to display a solid line and one to display a line with stars at the edges. An argument in favour of having the three methods is that it is always a good idea to keep methods as short as possible and maximize their cohesion. Here is the program using this design:

```
// Program to display a rectangle using characters.
// Written by Graham Roberts, August 1999.
// Revision history:
// none
public class CharacterRectangle2 {
  void displaySolidLine(final int width) {
    for (int i = 0 ; i < width ; ++i) {
      System.out.print('*') ;
    }
  }
  void displayLineWithEndsOnly(final int width) {
    System.out.print('*') ;
    for (int i = 0 ; i < width-2 ; ++i) {
      System.out.print(' ') ;
    }
    System.out.print('*') ;
  }
  void displayRectangle(final int height, final int width) {
    for (int i = 0 ; i < height ; ++i) {
      if ((i == 0) || (i == height-1)) {
        displaySolidLine(width) ;
      } else {
        displayLineWithEndsOnly(width) ;
      }
      System.out.println() ;
    }
  }
  public static void main(final String[] args) {
    CharacterRectangle2 obj = new CharacterRectangle2 () ;
    obj.displayRectangle(4, 8) ;
  }
}
```

This program is, we believe, easier to understand. Whenever a section of code starts to get complicated and difficult to read, consider pulling out pieces to create helper methods. Make sure the helper methods are given names which clearly describe what they do. This makes the original section of code easier to read, as the method names replace more complicated pieces of code.

tip

Name methods to clearly describe what the method does.

!

Never try and patch up incomprehensible code with comments; make the code comprehensible first and then see if it still needs commenting.

3.8.4 The Switch Statement

The *switch statement* allows the selection of one or more statement sequences from among an unlimited number. This is useful when there is a need to select from a number of alternatives and using if statements becomes too cumbersome. Here is a short example switch statement to show the basic form:

ref

Section 29.3.1, Page 815.

```
switch (n) {
  case 1 : // action to take if n is 1
    break;
  case 2 : // action to take if n is 2
    break;
// more cases as required
  default : // default action if no cases match
    break ;
}
```

The switch statement starts with the `switch` keyword, followed by an expression in parentheses and then a compound statement forming the switch statement body. Inside the body there are a series of labels marked with the keyword `case`. Each *case label* is followed by an integer value then a colon and then one or more statements (including compound statements).

The switch statement is executed by first evaluating the expression in parentheses after the `switch` keyword which must yield a value of type `int`. Execution then jumps to the case label with the matching integer value, and the statement sequence associated with that label is executed. Normally, the last statement of the sequence associated with the label is a *break statement*, which causes a jump to the statement following the switch statement, i.e. it 'jumps out' of the switch statement body. If no labels are matched, then the statement sequence associated with the `default` label is executed.

The switch statement provides a mechanism for achieving a multi-way selection. Contrast this with the if statement which only allowed us to execute (or not) a statement sequence or to select between one of two sequences. A further difference lies in the way in which selection is decided upon. The if statement requires a `boolean` valued expression whereas the switch statement uses an `int` valued expression. Surprisingly, the switch statement is, in many ways, quite restrictive because of this requirement. It is, nonetheless, useful and very used despite this.

3.8.5   Program ConvertBinaryToDecimal

The following example program illustrates the use of the switch statement:

Statement of Problem

"Write a program to read in a string representing a binary integer and convert it to a decimal integer."

Design and Implementation

Perusal of the J2SDK documentation reveals that the class `Integer` has a method (`parseInt`) that could do all the hard work. The real solution to this problem is just to use it, resulting in the code:

```
// Program to convert a string representing a binary
// number to an int to be output in decimal.
// Written by Russel Winder, September 1999
// Revision history:
// none
public class ConvertBinaryToDecimal {
  public static void main(final String[] args) {
    KeyboardInput in = new KeyboardInput () ;
    System.out.print("Enter binary number: ") ;
    String s = in.readString() ;
    int result = Integer.parseInt(s, 2) ;
    System.out.println(s + " == " + result) ;
  }
}
```

However, in this case we choose to ignore this existing conversion method and write our own, to illustrate the use of a switch statement. Also, of course, someone, sometime had to write the `parseInt` method: it is often interesting and useful to investigate the implementation of standard methods.

So, the first design step is to identify an algorithm to convert from the character-based binary representation to a decimal integer. Remembering that each digit position in a binary number corresponds to a power of 2, for an eight digit number the places in the number represent $2^7, 2^6, 2^5, 2^4, 2^3, 2^2, 2^1, 2^0$. We can find the decimal equivalent by multiplying things out, for example:

$$
\begin{aligned}
10110011_2 \;=\; & 1\times 2^7 + 0\times 2^6 + 1\times 2^5 + 1\times 2^4 + 0\times 2^3 + 0\times 2^2 + 1\times 2^1 + 1\times 2^0 \\
=\; & 1\times (1\times 10^2 + 2\times 10^1 + 8\times 10^0) + \\
& 0\times (6\times 10^1 + 4\times 10^0) + \\
& 1\times (3\times 101 + 2\times 10^0) + \\
& 1\times (1\times 10^1 + 6\times 10^0) + \\
& 0\times (8\times 10^0) + \\
& 0\times (4\times 10^0) + \\
& 1\times (2\times 10^0) + \\
& 1\times 10^0 \\
=\; & (1\times 1)\times 10^2 + \\
& (1\times 2 + 0\times 6 + 1\times 3 + 1\times 1)\times 10^1 + \\
& (1\times 8 + 0\times 4 + 1\times 2 + 1\times 6 + 0\times 8 + 0\times 4 + 1\times 2 + 1\times 1)\times 10^0 \\
=\; & 1\times 10^2 + \\
& 6\times 10^1 + \\
& 1\times 10^1 + 9\times 10^0 \\
=\; & 179_{10}
\end{aligned}
$$

Of course, we would normally just ignore the columns with zero. Also, we would not normally explicitly put in all the powers of 10 but write it as:

$$
\begin{aligned}
10110011_2 \;=\; & 1\times 2^7 + 1\times 2^5 + 1\times 2^4 + 1\times 2^1 + 1\times 2^0 \\
=\; & 1\times 128 + 1\times 32 + 1\times 16 + 1\times 2 + 1 \\
=\; & 179_{10}
\end{aligned}
$$

but this is only because we are taught decimal (aka denary) arithmetic from a very early age and we make assumptions about what things mean.

Based on this, a loop can be used to iterate through the characters of the binary number string and do the appropriate calculation when a one digit is present.

As we look at each digit of the binary number there are three possible actions to take:

- it's a 1, so do the calculation;
- it's a 0, so do nothing; and
- it's not a binary digit, as the input was invalid, so do something to deal with the error condition.

In addition, the binary number might start with a minus sign, so that also needs to be dealt with. As we have multiple choices depending on the current digit in the binary number, a switch statement provides a more convenient way of handling them than using multiple if statements.

Once the conversion algorithm is understood, writing the conversion method should be straightforward, except for one issue. This is deciding what to do if an invalid binary number is input (the number contains non-binary digits, for example) and the conversion can't be completed. For this program the decision is made to simply give up and return the current, partially calculated, value. However, this gives no indication to the caller of the conversion method that anything went wrong. Unfortunately at this stage there is no truly satisfactory solution to this problem — we have to wait until Section 8.1, Page 226, to see how we should deal with this problem.

Putting all this together, a method to do the conversion can be written and put into a program to test it.

```java
// Program to convert a string representing a binary
// number to an int to be output in decimal.
// Written by Graham Roberts, August 1999.
// Revision history:
// none
public class ConvertBinaryToDecimal {
  // Attempt to convert the string argument representing a binary
  // number to a decimal integer.  If any invalid characters are found
  // in the string give up and return the partially converted value.
  int convertBinaryToDecimal(final String s) {
    int value = 0 ;
    int power = 1 ;
    for (int position = s.length() - 1 ;
         position > -1 ;
         position--, power *= 2) {
      switch (s.charAt(position)) {
        case '0' :
          break ;
        case '1' :
          value += power ;
          break ;
        case '-' :
          if (position == 0) {
            value = -value ;
            break ;
          } else {
            return value ;
          }
        default :
          return value ;
      }
    }
    return value ;
  }
  public static void main(final String[] args) {
    KeyboardInput in = new KeyboardInput () ;
    ConvertBinaryToDecimal obj = new ConvertBinaryToDecimal () ;
    System.out.print("Enter binary number: ") ;
    String s = in.readString() ;
    int result = obj.convertBinaryToDecimal(s) ;
    System.out.println(s + " == " + result) ;
  }
}
```

Testing

Testing this program follows the now familiar routine. We cannot hope to do exhaustive testing so we choose a representative set that we hope exercises the program sufficiently to highlight any bugs that there might be. Table 3.1 presents what strikes us as a not unreasonable test data set.

When the test data set is run using the program above we get the results shown in Table 3.2.

It seems that something strange is happening when there are more than 31 bits of data. The explanation for this is quite straightforward. The program stores the result of the parse of the input string in an int. An int is a representation of finite size and so there are values that cannot be stored. Java ints are 32-bit signed numbers resulting in 31 bits of value information. Thus it is of

Binary	Decimal
−00000000000000000000000000000000000000000	0
−11111111111111111111111111111111111111111	−1099511627775
−11111111111111111111111111111111	−4294967295
−1111111111111111111111111111111	−2147483647
−11111111111111111111	−1048575
−00000000000011111111111100000000	−1048320
−10110011	−179
−0	0
0	0
10110011	179
00000000000011111111111100000000	1048320
11111111111111111111	1048575
1111111111111111111111111111111	2147483647
11111111111111111111111111111111	4294967295
11111111111111111111111111111111111111111	1099511627775
00000000000000000000000000000000000000000	0

Table 3.1 A Test data set for the `ConvertBinaryToDecmial` program,

Binary	Decimal
−00000000000000000000000000000000000000000	0
−11111111111111111111111111111111111111111	1
−11111111111111111111111111111111	1
−1111111111111111111111111111111	−2147483647
−11111111111111111111	−1048575
−00000000000011111111111100000000	−1048320
−10110011	−179
−0	0
0	0
10110011	179
00000000000011111111111100000000	1048320
11111111111111111111	1048575
1111111111111111111111111111111	2147483647
11111111111111111111111111111111	−1
11111111111111111111111111111111111111111	−1
00000000000000000000000000000000000000000	0

Table 3.2 Results of running the program.

no surprise that 31 bits worked and 32 bits failed in our test. Note here that the earlier 'production' version of the program that employed the `Integer.parseInt` method also suffers from this problem since it too uses an `int` for the intermediate representation of the data value.

Actually, we knew that this was going to happen when we generated the test data — and so we should. In generating test data it is important to test values that are likely to cause problems as well as values that indicate that our program works. Understanding the properties of the program and the properties of the input domain are critical to the generation of test data. In this case, the input domain has only three types of data: negative numbers, positive numbers and zero. The program, however, has four types of representation: negative numbers, positive numbers, zero and error — i.e. values whose representation cannot be handled by the program. In selecting our test data for this program we knew that 31 bits was going to be a limiting factor so we purposefully chose values around that boundary in order to properly exercise the program.

The upshot of this testing is that the program appears to work as well as it can with the current design. If we want to achieve more correct performance we must redesign the program to remove the dependence on an `int` for the intermediate representation of the value.

Review

In reviewing the program there doesn't actually seem to be a lot to say. The basic algorithm seems to be the right one and the implementation, whilst only one of many, seems to be about as good as it gets. The major issue is, of course, whether the program is going to need to be able to deal with values that require more than 32 bits of representation. If this does become a requirement then we have to really get to work. Well, not, in fact. The problem of dealing with values that are not representable in 32 bits turns out to be quite common, so the J2SDK has a class specially for handling such numbers. There are two classes, `BigInteger` and `BigDouble`, designed for exactly the situation we find ourselves in. Here is a version of the program using these types:

```
// Program to convert a string representing a binary
// number to a BigInteger to be output in decimal.
// Written by Russel Winder, September 1999
// Revision history:
// none
import java.math.BigInteger ;
public class ConvertBinaryToDecimal {
  public static void main(final String[] args) {
    KeyboardInput in = new KeyboardInput () ;
    System.out.print("Enter binary number: ") ;
    String s = in.readString() ;
    BigInteger result = new BigInteger(s, 2) ;
    System.out.println(s + " == " + result.toString(10)) ;
  }
}
```

This program is the production code version. Again for pedagogical reasons, we could insist that we have to do the parsing ourselves, in which case we would end up with:

```
// Program to convert a string representing a binary
// number to a BigInteger to be output in decimal.
// Written by Graham Roberts, August 1999.
// Revision history:
// none
import java.math.BigInteger ;
```

```java
public class ConvertBinaryToDecimal {
  // Attempt to convert the string argument representing a binary
  // number to a decimal integer.  If any invalid characters are found
  // in the string give up and return the partially converted value.
  BigInteger convertBinaryToBigInteger(final String s) {
    BigInteger value = new BigInteger ("0") ;
    BigInteger power = new BigInteger ("1") ;
    BigInteger two = new BigInteger ("2") ;
    for (int position = s.length() - 1 ;
            position > -1 ;
            position--, power = power.multiply(two)) {
      switch (s.charAt(position)) {
        case '0' :
          break ;
        case '1' :
          value = value.add(power) ;
          break ;
        case '-' :
          if (position == 0) {
            value = value.negate() ;
            break ;
          } else {
            return value ;
          }
        default :
          return value ;
      }
    }
    return value ;
  }
  public static void main(final String[] args) {
    KeyboardInput in = new KeyboardInput () ;
    ConvertBinaryToDecimal obj = new ConvertBinaryToDecimal () ;
    System.out.print("Enter binary number: ") ;
    String s = in.readString() ;
    BigInteger result = obj.convertBinaryToBigInteger(s) ;
    System.out.println(s + " == " + result.toString(10)) ;
  }
}
```

Both of these implementations, deliver the values expected in the original test data set table. An expected problem, though, is both of these programs will fail for any value that requires more than 2^{32} bits to represent it. We believe it sufficiently unlikely that this constraint will be an issue, at least in the short term, that we will not treat this as a bug.

3.9 Summary

In this chapter, we have shown how a program can be given structure using methods. This structuring exploits the principles of abstraction, whereby a program is broken down into named units that allow details to be suppressed in favour of a higher level of abstraction, but more understandable description. Abstraction works with encapsulation, which is built on mechanisms such as scope and lifetime, and enables greater control over variables. The net result is that programs become more understandable by people, while the additional structure allows tools such as compilers to do more checking about the correctness and good behaviour of a program.

Key points in this chapter:

- A method is an abstraction over a statement sequence.
- Methods can have parameters and return results.
- A recursive method calls itself.
- Scope determines where a variable exists and can be accessed.
- Lifetime determines how long a variable exists.
- Increment, decrement and additional assignment operators are available.
- The for loop allows counted iteration.
- The switch statement allows choice between one of many statement sequences.

Self-review Questions

Self-review 3.1   Consider a television set. What abstractions does it present and how is encapsulation used?

Self-review 3.2 Which of the following are valid method names:

```
convert, 2times, add one, add_two,
time/space, AddUp, dRaawcIRCle, class
```

Self-review 3.3 Can a method return more than one value at a time?

Self-review 3.4 What type checking is done on methods?

Self-review 3.5 Why are there no values of type `void`?

Self-review 3.6 Write a summary of the scope rules for compound statements.

Self-review 3.7 What are the values of these expressions:

```
22 / 7
4 + 3 / 6.1
1.3 * 2.2
34 % 55
2.1 % 3
2147483647 + 1
```

Self-review 3.8 Is the method `times2` (see Page 57) referentially transparent?

Self-review 3.9   Devise a test plan for a modified version of program `MultiplicationTable` (see Page 61) that allows any multiplication table from 1 to 100,000,000 to be displayed.

Self-review 3.10 Execute program `ConvertBinaryToDecimal` by hand to convert the binary numbers 1001, 11100101 and 1000101010001011 to decimal.

Self-review 3.11 Convert this for loop to a while loop:

```
for (int i = 10 ; i > -2 ; i -= 2)
{
```

```
    . . .
  }
```

Programming Exercises

Exercise 3.1 Write methods to do the following:

- Convert from feet to centimetres.
- Convert from yards to metres.
- Convert from miles to kilometres.

Include the methods in an interactive program that lets the user select which conversion to perform.

Exercise 3.2 Write a program that counts the number of times a specified character appears in a line of text.

Exercise 3.3 Write a program to read in a decimal integer and print out the binary equivalent.

Exercise 3.4 Write a program that uses a method to display the following:

```
     *
    **
   ***
  ****
 *****
******
```

You may only display one character at a time.

Exercise 3.5 Write a program, using methods, that displays triangles of the following form:

```
   *
  ***
 *****
*******
```

The user should input how many lines to display. You may only display one character at a time.

Exercise 3.6 Write a method to display rectangles with the following form:

```
*****
*****
*****
*****
```

The method parameters should give the number of rows and columns of the rectangle. Use the method in a test program to display various rectangles of different sizes.

Exercise 3.7 Write a program using methods to display your name, or any other message, in the middle of a line 80 characters wide.

Exercise 3.8 Modify program `ConvertBinaryToDecimal` to create a program that converts from base 8 to base 10 numbers called `ConvertOctalToDecimal`.

Exercise 3.9 Write a program that uses a recursive method to calculate the product of a sequence of numbers specified by the user. For example, if the user specifies 4 to 8, the method calculates `4*5*6*7*8`.

Exercise 3.10 Write a program that reads in a line of text and displays the number of characters and words it contains. Spaces and tabs should not be counted as characters.

Exercise 3.11 Consider displaying a large letter formed from stars:

```
*     *
*     *
******
*     *
*     *
```

Write a method that displays one line of the large character H, where the line to display is given as a parameter (e.g. `bigH(3)` would display the third line).

Then write a program to display six large H's in a row, with one space between each H:

```
*     * *     * *     * *     * *     * *     *
*     * *     * *     * *     * *     * *     *
****** ****** ****** ****** ****** ******
*     * *     * *     * *     * *     * *     *
*     * *     * *     * *     * *     * *     *
```

Exercise 3.12 Write a method to test if an integer of type `long` is a prime number. The method should return a `boolean` value. Test your method by writing a test program that reads an integer typed at the keyboard and states whether the integer was prime. Using your prime method, write a program that finds all the prime numbers that can be represented by an integer of type `long`.

Exercise 3.13 Write a program that acts as a simple desktop calculator which allows you type in a sequence of values and operators and displays the results of your calculation. For example, the following might be typed in (<return> indicates the return key being pressed):

```
5 <return>
+ <return>
6 <return>
= <return>
11
```

Challenges

Challenge 3.1 Write a program to display the multiplication tables from 2 to 12 displayed as four rows of three tables, i.e.:

```
1 x 2 = 2        1 x 3 = 3        1 x 4 = 4
2 x 2 = 4        2 x 3 = 6        2 x 4 = 8
3 x 2 = 6        3 x 3 = 9        3 x 4 = 12
```

and so on.

Challenge 3.2 Write a program that includes a recursive method to calculate the greatest common divisor of two numbers.

Challenge 3.3 Write methods to display a large E, L and O as below. Use the methods to display HELLO in large letters in the following arrangement:

```
*       *
*       *   * * * * * *
* * * * * *   *               *
*       *   * * * *     *             *
*       *   *   *       *       *     * * * * * *
        * * * * * *   *         *         *     *
                * * * * * *   *           *     *
                        * * * * * *   *         *     *
                                * * * * * *
```

Challenge 3.4 Consider a table that shows temperature conversions from Celsius to Fahrenheit, like this:

```
        Temperature Conversion
        ----------------------
  C    F      C    F      C    F      C    F      C    F
  0    32     1    33     2    35     3    37     4    39
  5    41     6    42     7    44     8    46     9    48
 10    50    11    51    12    53    13    55    14    57
```

and so on up to 100°C.

Write a program that asks for the number of columns to display (one column is one C/F pair) and displays a conversion table. Make sure the columns of numbers line up neatly.

Hints: Write a method to convert from Celsius to Fahrenheit $\left(F = \frac{9}{5}C - 32 \right)$.

Write a method that displays one line of the table, given the line number and the number of columns.

Write a method that displays the table one line at a time.

Separate the columns of C/F pairs using tab characters. A tab is represented using \t, for example System.out.print('\t').

Challenge 3.5 Write a program that reads an integer between 0 and 99 and 'verbalizes it'. For example, if the program is given 23 it would display 'twenty three'.

Hints: Write the following methods that:

- Take a single digit and returns a string between 'zero' and 'nine'.

- Take a number between 10 and 19 and returns a string between 'ten' and 'nineteen'.

- Take a number between 0 and 99 and, using the other methods as necessary, verbalize the number.

4

Drawing Pictures

Objectives

Having covered the basics of programming, and before moving on to more advanced material, this chapter looks at writing programs to draw simple pictures. This provides a good opportunity to exercise the skills learnt in the last two chapters, and also to introduce some of the graphics facilities provided by the Java system.

Keywords

J2SDK

Graphics2D

Color

Line2D

Rectangle2D

Ellipse2D

shape

shape path

4.1   Introduction

The programs presented so far all rely on using some sort of text-based terminal window to display output and let the user enter input. Although such programs are a good vehicle when learning to program, almost all interactive programs now make use of a Graphical User Interface (GUI), with windows, menus, buttons, etc. The programming of GUIs will be examined in Chapter 11 as it requires rather more knowledge of programming than covered so far, but here we will look at some simple programs that draw pictures in a window on the screen.

The J2SDK provides considerable support for displaying *graphics* — pictures composed of line segments and shapes. In this chapter we will investigate this by using a class from the J2SDK called `Graphics2D`. This class provides a range of methods for displaying shapes. It is supported by a family of other classes that allow shapes to be created and manipulated.

The documentation for class `Graphics2D` can be found in the package `java.awt`, while the classes for representing shapes can be found in the package `java.awt.geom`. This chapter is going to make use of a number of classes from both `java.awt` and `java.awt.geom`. You may want to intersperse reading this chapter with perusing bits of the documentation for these packages.

4.2   Creating Drawings

A picture is drawn using shapes such as line segments, rectangles, ellipses, etc. The shapes are positioned on a drawing using a two dimensional coordinate system, as shown in Figure 4.1. This is rather like drawing on to a sheet of graph paper but note that the origin, point (0,0), is in the top left hand corner. The x axis goes from left to right, while the y axis goes from top to bottom.

Using the standard Java graphics classes, a drawing is actually made on a panel, which is a rectangular drawing area placed within a window which then appears on a computer display. The example programs shown in this chapter will make use of a panel class called `DrawPanel` which is displayed in a window created from a class called `DrawFrame`. These classes are ones built by us from standard J2SDK classes in order to provide a few simplifying features. The code listing for `DrawFrame` and `DrawPanel` are to be found in Appendix H, Page 969.

To create our drawing programs, the following program template has been used:

```
// A template for a drawing program.
import java.awt.* ;
import java.awt.geom.* ;
// If you want to give your class a different name, change the class
// name from Drawing to your class name in the next line and
// throughout the file.
public class Drawing extends DrawPanel {
  // Create a frame and drawing, display them on the screen.
  public static void main(final String[] args) {
```

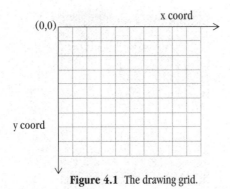

Figure 4.1 The drawing grid.

```
// Change the string "Drawing" to change the frame title
DrawFrame frame = new DrawFrame ("Drawing") ;
// Don't forget to edit the names here if you change the class
// name
Drawing drawing = new Drawing () ;
// The drawing grid size can be changed by using a statement like
// this:
// Drawing drawing = new Drawing(500, 600) ;
// This will give a 500 x 600 frame.
// Don't change these lines.
frame.add(drawing) ;
frame.pack() ;
frame.centreOnScreen() ;
frame.setVisible(true) ;
}
// If the class name is changed, then edit the names of the
// following two methods to match -- i.e. if your class is called
// MyPicture, the next method becomes:
// public MyPicture() {}
public Drawing() {}
public Drawing(final int w, final int h) {
  super(w,h) ;
}
// This method is called to do the actual drawing
public void paint(final Graphics g) {
  // Don't edit this line.
  Graphics2D g2d = (Graphics2D)g ;
  // Change anything below this line to draw a picture
}
// Other methods can be added here
}
```

If you use this template, only add code where indicated by the comments leaving the rest of the code as is. If you amend any of the bits of code provided, things will not necessarily work as expected, if they work at all.

The default name of the class is Drawing but by substituting a new name wherever Drawing appears, the program can be renamed (follow the instructions in the comments). This allows you to call your class and program whatever you like. Don't forget, however, to save your code to a file named classname.java where classname is the name you choose. The default window title that appears in the title bar at the top of the window can also be changed, by editing the string as indicated by the comment.

Figure 4.2 An example window displayed by the drawing program.

The management of the window is left to `DrawFrame` and other classes, so we do not need to be worried about the issues involved — abstraction wins again. The method `paint` in the template is the one called when a drawing needs to be displayed, so the statements to do the drawing are placed in that method. Additional helper methods can be added and called as needed, of course.

To draw a shape, such as a line segment, an object is created to represent the shape and then a `Graphics2D` object is asked to draw it. The `Graphics2D` object takes care of all the details of displaying the shape in the correct position with the correct attributes.

When one of our programs based on this template is executed, a window will appear in the middle of the screen and the drawing will appear in it. Figure 4.2 shows an example. The window is closed and the program terminates when the Quit button at the bottom of the window is clicked.

The template provides a default sized drawing grid of 300×300 pixels. This can be changed by specifying the required size when the `Drawing` object is created. So by replacing the line:

```
Drawing drawing = new Drawing () ;
```

with:

```
Drawing drawing = new Drawing (500,400) ;
```

a 500×400 pixels grid will be created and the window will increase in size accordingly.

Appendix E.4, Page 961, details the mechanics of how to create your own drawing programs based on the material in this chapter.

4.2.1   Drawing a Line Segment

An object of the class `Line2D.Double` is used to represent a line, which is specified using two coordinates; the two end points. Coordinates are specified in the usual way by giving a pair of numbers (x, y). The numbers are normally of type `int`, but if you need to specify points between the grid point they can be of type `double`. A line segment object is created in the following way:

```
Line2D aLine = new Line2D.Double(10,10,70,70) ;
```

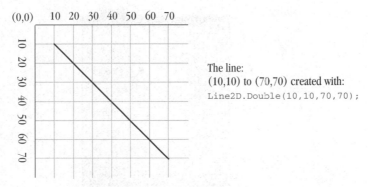

The line:
(10,10) to (70,70) created with:
`Line2D.Double(10,10,70,70);`

Figure 4.3 Drawing a line.

This will create the line segment shown in Figure 4.3. It is not a mistake that the type of the variable `aLine` is `Line2D` and the type of the object `Line2D.Double`. To explain fully why this is correct requires knowledge from later chapters, so we must gloss over this for now. For the moment we must ask you to accept that `Line2D` is a type for handling line segment objects in general, while `Line2D.Double` is a specific line segment type.

The line is drawn (the term *rendered* is often used) onto the panel which holds the drawing that appears on the screen using the statement:

```
g2d.draw(aLine) ;
```

where `g2d` is a `Graphics2D` object and `draw` is one of its methods, one that knows how to draw the shape given as a parameter.

To create a program to draw the line segment, the template shown above is copied and edited, with the line drawing code placed in the `paint` method. The code below provides an example of doing this. Compare it with the template to see what has been changed. Note that the class has been renamed to `DrawLine`.

```
// A program to demonstrate drawing a line.
// Written by Graham Roberts, July 1999
// Revision History: none
import java.awt.* ;
import java.awt.geom.* ;
public class DrawLine extends DrawPanel {
  // Create frame and drawing, display them on the screen.
  public static void main(final String[] args) {
    DrawFrame frame = new DrawFrame ("Drawing of a line") ;
    DrawLine drawing = new DrawLine () ;
    frame.add(drawing) ;
    frame.pack() ;
    frame.centreOnScreen() ;
    frame.setVisible(true) ;
  }
  public DrawLine() {}
  public DrawLine(final int w, final int h) {
    super(w, h) ;
  }
  // This method is called to do the actual drawing
  public void paint(final Graphics g) {
    Graphics2D g2d = (Graphics2D)g ;
    Line2D aLine = new Line2D.Double (10, 10, 70, 70) ;
```

Figure 4.4 The line 10,10,70,70.

```
    g2d.draw(aLine) ;
  }
}
```

When run this program displays the window seen in Figure 4.4, with the line in the top left corner.

The line segment that the `Line2D` object represents can be altered using the `setLine` method, for example:

```
    aLine.setLine(0,10,290,300) ;
```

If this statement were added to the program then, after executing it, `aLine` would cease to represent the line segment ((10, 10), (70, 70)); instead it would represent the line segment ((0, 10), (290, 300)). If we were to then draw `aLine`, a new line would appear in the new position. The line previously drawn remains on the screen since drawing to the panel is an additive process. Using the `setLine` method, the grid shown in Figure 4.2 can be drawn using a loop to repeatedly redefine and draw the line segment. The `paint` method required for this is:

```
public void paint(final Graphics g) {
  Graphics2D g2d = (Graphics2D)g ;
  // The line segment object is created here and then
  // set to the desired line segment in the loop.
  Line2D aLine = new Line2D.Double (0, 0, 0, 0) ;
  for (int i = 1 ; i < 11 ; ++i) {
    aLine.setLine(20, i*20, 200, i*20) ;
    g2d.draw(aLine) ;
    aLine.setLine(i*20, 20, i*20, 200) ;
    g2d.draw(aLine) ;
  }
}
```

4.2.2 Drawing Rectangles, Squares, Ellipses and Circles

Rectangles are represented by objects of class `Rectangle2D.Double`, and are specified by giving the position of the top left hand corner and the width and height of the rectangle (see Figure 4.5). For example:

```
    Rectangle2D r = new Rectangle2D.Double(10,10,50,60) ;
```

A rectangle can be repositioned and resized using the method `setRect`:

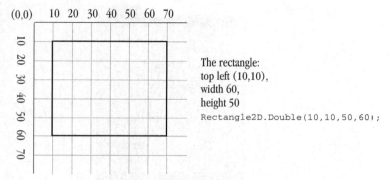

Figure 4.5 Specifying a rectangle.

The rectangle:
top left (10,10),
width 60,
height 50
`Rectangle2D.Double(10,10,50,60);`

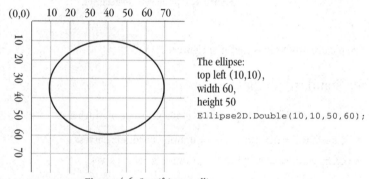

Figure 4.6 Specifying an ellipse.

The ellipse:
top left (10,10),
width 60,
height 50
`Ellipse2D.Double(10,10,50,60);`

```
// top left (20,20), width 100, height 150
r.setRect(20,20,100,150) ;
```

Since a square is just a rectangle with width and height equal, there is no need for a class to define a square. Indeed, Ockham's Razor requires us not to define such a class.

An ellipse is represented by an object of class `Ellipse2D.Double`, with its position, width and height specified by the circumscribed rectangle, i.e. the smallest rectangle that the ellipse fits into: an ellipse is defined by giving the top left corner, width and height of a rectangle (see Figure 4.6). An ellipse is repositioned and resized using the `setFrame` method.

In the same way that a square is a special form of rectangle, a circle is a special form of ellipse: a circle is an ellipse defined by a square, i.e. with width and height equal. Again, by Ockham's Razor we do not define a class to represent a circle.

The following `paint` method displays a picture composed of rectangles and ellipses:

```
public void paint(final Graphics g) {
  Graphics2D g2d = (Graphics2D)g ;
  Rectangle2D r = new Rectangle2D.Double (0, 0, 0, 0) ;
  Ellipse2D e = new Ellipse2D.Double (0, 0, 0, 0) ;
  for (int i = 0 ; i < 10 ; ++i) {
    r.setRect(i*15, i*15, 100, 50) ;
    g2d.draw(r) ;
    e.setFrame(i*10, 200-i*10, 15*i, 20*i) ;
    g2d.draw(e) ;
  }
```

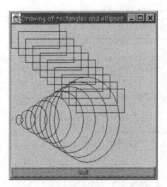

Figure 4.7 Rectangles and ellipses.

```
}
```

The picture produced is shown in Figure 4.7.

4.2.3   Other Standard Shapes

There are a variety of other shape classes available, some of which are:

- `QuadCurve2D.Double` for drawing quadratic curves.
- `CubicCurve2D.Double` for drawing cubic curves.
- `RoundRectangle2D.Double` for drawing rectangles with rounded corners.
- `Arc2D.Double` for drawing arcs.

The J2SDK documentation for these classes contains much more about them.

4.2.4   Creating New Shapes

The shape classes seen so far are provided as standard as they are frequently used and it is convenient to have them pre-defined. In fact, all these shapes are specific examples of a more general concept called a *path*. A path is simply the sequence of lines and curves that are needed to draw a shape. Using class `GeneralPath`, it is possible to create your own shapes. The following code shows how to create a triangle shape:

```
public void paint(final Graphics g) {
  Graphics2D g2d = (Graphics2D)g ;
  GeneralPath triangle = new GeneralPath () ;
  triangle.moveTo(100,150) ;
  triangle.lineTo(200,150) ;
  triangle.lineTo(150,50) ;
  triangle.lineTo(100,150) ;
  triangle.closePath() ;
  g2d.draw(triangle) ;
}
```

The triangle is created by specifying three lines in the correct positions. First a `GeneralPath` object is created and the `moveTo` method called to set the coordinate of the starting position. Next the `lineTo` method is called to specify a line starting at the current position and running to the

Figure 4.8 A triangle.

position specified by the method arguments. `lineTo` is called twice more to complete the triangle. To finish, the `closePath` method is called, denoting that the end of the shape has been reached. When the shape is drawn using the `draw` of method of the `Graphics2D` object a triangle appears, as illustrated in Figure 4.8. To draw multiple triangles of different shapes it would make sense to write a `createTriangle` method to package up the creation of the path.

Curves can also be added to a path using the `curveTo` and `quadTo` methods. See the J2SDK documentation for information on how these are used.

4.3 Properties of Drawings

4.3.1 Colour

The colour a shape is drawn in can be set by calling the `setPaint` method on the `Graphics2D` object that will render the shape. For example:

```
g2d.setPaint(Color.green) ;
```

`setPaint` takes a `Color` object as a parameter to specify the colour. Once a colour has been set, all future drawing will be done with that colour until it is changed again. The standard colours are:

Color.white	Color.black	Color.yellow
Color.lightGray	Color.red	Color.green
Color.gray	Color.pink	Color.magenta
Color.darkGray	Color.orange	Color.cyan
		Color.blue

The following method will draw a blue rectangle:

```
public void paint(final Graphics g) {
  Graphics2D g2d = (Graphics2D)g ;
  Rectangle2D r = new Rectangle2D.Double(25, 120, 150, 50) ;
  g2d.setPaint(Color.blue) ;
  g2d.draw(r) ;
}
```

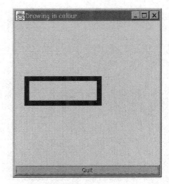

Figure 4.9 Rectangle drawn with a line width of 10.

New colours can be created using the `Color` class, as and when needed.

4.3.2   Line Thickness

The thickness of the line used to draw a shape can be changed by creating a `BasicStroke` object and passing it as an argument to the `setStroke` method. For example, the following statements set the line thickness to 10:

```
BasicStroke stroke = new BasicStroke(10) ;
g2d.setStroke(stroke) ;
```

Now when any shapes are drawn they will have thicker borders. The paint method below draws a rectangle with a border of width 10, and the result can be seen in Figure 4.9:

```
public void paint(final Graphics g) {
  Graphics2D g2d = (Graphics2D)g ;
  Rectangle2D r = new Rectangle2D.Double(25, 120, 150, 50) ;
  BasicStroke s = new BasicStroke (10) ;
  g2d.setStroke(s) ;
  g2d.draw(r) ;
}
```

Note that the thickness of the border effectively increases the overall size of the shape drawn.

4.3.3   Filled Shapes

A shape can be drawn as a filled shape. By filled we mean that rather than just drawing the border of the shape, the entire shape is drawn as a solid area of colour. The `Graphics2D` object has a method `fill` which draws a filled shape. It is called instead of `draw`:

```
g2d.fill(aRect) ;
```

The following `paint` method will draw a filled green rectangle:

```
public void paint(final Graphics g) {
  Graphics2D g2d = (Graphics2D)g ;
  Rectangle2D r = new Rectangle2D.Double(25, 120, 150, 50) ;
  g2d.setPaint(Color.green) ;
  g2d.fill(r) ;
}
```

Figure 4.10 Filled rectangle with border.

A filled shape with a border can be drawn but it needs to be done in two stages. We set up the shape, then the fill is rendered by setting the colour as desired and using the `fill` method, then the outline is rendered by setting up the border thickness and colour as desired and using the `draw` method. The following `paint` provides example code and Figure 4.10 shows the result:

```
public void paint(final Graphics g) {
   Graphics2D g2d = (Graphics2D)g ;
   Rectangle2D r = new Rectangle2D.Double(25, 120, 150, 50) ;
   g2d.setPaint(Color.cyan) ;
   g2d.fill(r) ;
   BasicStroke stroke = new BasicStroke(10) ;
   g2d.setStroke(stroke) ;
   g2d.setPaint(Color.red) ;
   g2d.draw(r) ;
}
```

4.4 Drawing Text

Text can be drawn by using the `drawString` method. This method takes three parameters, the string to be drawn and the *x* and *y* values of the position where the string will appear. For example:

```
public void paint(final Graphics g) {
   Graphics2D g2d = (Graphics2D)g ;
   g2d.drawString("Hello World!", 20, 150) ;
}
```

This will display "Hello World!" in the default font with default size, which as can be seen in Figure 4.11 is fairly small.

The font and size can be changed by creating a `Font` object and using the `setFont` method. The following `paint` method shows an example and Figure 4.12 shows the result.

```
public void paint(final Graphics g) {
   Graphics2D g2d = (Graphics2D)g ;
   Font big = new Font("Serif", Font.PLAIN, 50) ;
   g2d.setFont(big) ;
   g2d.drawString("Hello World!", 20, 150) ;
}
```

Figure 4.11 String displayed with default font.

Figure 4.12 String displayed with large font.

tip

*The full set of fonts
available change from
computer to computer.
It is invariably best to
use the standard fonts
that are guaranteed to
be available on every
machine.*

A font is created by specifying a name, appearance and size. The J2SDK documentation provides the details of what is available as standard and how to introduce non-standard capabilities.

4.5   Example Programs

There are many more drawing facilities provided in the J2SDK that are not covered here. However, we have enough to start drawing some interesting pictures. For those who are interested, spend time browsing the J2SDK documentation (as suggested a number of times earlier). One feature particularly worth looking at is the use of affine transformations which allow shapes to be translated (moved), rotated and scaled.

The following sub-sections will investigate various programs that draw what we think might be interesting shapes and diagrams.

4.5.1   Program Chessboard

Statement of Problem   *"Write a program to display a chessboard of red and green squares."*

A chessboard is basically an 8 × 8 collection of squares of alternating colour, with the colour of the square at the end of a row being the same as the square at the start of the next row. Following that observation we can put together the following algorithm:

set current colour to start colour
for each row {
    for each square in the row {
        set the current colour
        draw a filled square
        if (the current square is not at the end of a row) {
            swap current colours
        }
    }
}

This works through the 8 rows of 8 squares alternating the colour as each square is drawn.

Taking a deliberately simple approach to the implementation, most of the code can go into the `paint` method, while a supporting method deals with swapping the current colour. This gives:

```
// A program to draw a chessboard.
// Written by Graham Roberts, July 1999
// Revision History: none
import java.awt.*;
import java.awt.geom.*;
public class Chessboard extends DrawPanel {
  public static void main(final String[] args) {
    DrawFrame frame = new DrawFrame ("A Chessboard") ;
    Chessboard drawing = new Chessboard () ;
    frame.add(drawing) ;
    frame.pack() ;
    frame.centreOnScreen() ;
    frame.setVisible(true) ;
  }
  public Chessboard() {}
  public Chessboard(final int w, final int h) {
    super(w,h) ;
  }
  Color swapColour(final Color current) {
    if (current.equals(Color.red)) {
      return Color.green ;
    } else {
      return Color.red ;
    }
  }
  public void paint(final Graphics g) {
    Graphics2D g2d = (Graphics2D)g ;
    int squareSize = 35 ;
    Color colour = Color.red ;
    for (int row = 0 ; row < 8 ; ++row) {
      for (int column = 0 ; column < 8 ; ++column) {
        g.setColor(colour) ;
        g.fillRect(row * squareSize,
                   column * squareSize,
                   squareSize,
                   squareSize) ;
        if (column != 7) {
          colour = swapColour(colour) ;
        }
      }
    }
  }
}
```

Design and Implementation

Figure 4.13 A chessboard as displayed by program Chessboard.

There are two principal things to note. Firstly, it is possible to declare and use a variable of class `Color`, making control of the colour easy. Secondly, two colour values can be compared using the `equals` method, rather than the `==` operator. When run the program displays the chessboard shown in Figure 4.13.

Testing

The program is easily tested by looking at the drawing displayed, although that doesn't easily show that the squares are exactly the size specified.

Review

The implementation of the suggested algorithm presented no problems. However, the limitations of the program should be considered. The chessboard is drawn to a fixed size and position. It would be better to write a `chessboard` method that took appropriate parameters and was able to display a board of the required size in the required position. The `paint` method would then contain only a call to `chessboard`.

4.5.2   Program Spiral

Statement of Problem

"Write a program to draw a spiral."

Design and
Implementation

Not surprisingly, the key to solving this problem is to identify a spiral drawing algorithm. There is no pre-defined spiral class so we will have to try something more basic. Drawing a spiral using pen and paper highlights that a spiral can be drawn by trying to draw a circle but continually increasing the radius. We could use this observation as the basis of an algorithm and approximate the appearance of a spiral by plotting a series of points following the edge of the circle as it grows. Figure 4.14 shows the basic idea. If the points are drawn close enough together they will look like a continuous line.

From trigonometry, we know that a circle of radius r is defined by the set of points ($r \cos \theta$, $r \sin \theta$), θ being an independent variable which creates the locus as its value changes. By systematically changing r as we change θ, i.e. we make r dependent on θ rather than being a constant, we create a spiral instead of a circle. This leads us to the following program:

```
// A program to draw a spiral
// Written by Graham Roberts, July 1999
// Revision History: none
import java.awt.* ;
```

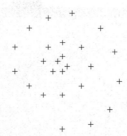

Figure 4.14 A spiral as a series of points.

Figure 4.15 Spiral drawn by program Spiral using dots.

```
import java.awt.geom.* ;
public class Spiral extends DrawPanel {
  public static void main(final String[] args) {
    DrawFrame frame = new DrawFrame ("Drawing of a spiral") ;
    Spiral drawing = new Spiral () ;
    frame.add(drawing) ;
    frame.pack() ;
    frame.centreOnScreen() ;
    frame.setVisible(true) ;
  }
  public Spiral() {}
  public Spiral(final int w, final int h) {
    super(w, h) ;
  }
  public void paint(final Graphics g) {
    Graphics2D g2d = (Graphics2D)g ;
    Rectangle2D rectangle = new Rectangle2D.Double (0, 0, 0, 0) ;
    double theta = 0.0 ;
    double increment = 2 * Math.PI/100.0 ;
    for (int n = 0 ; n < 1500 ; ++n) {
      theta += increment ;
      double radius = 75.0 * n / 1000 ;
      double x = 150 + (radius * Math.cos(theta)) ;
      double y = 150 + (radius * Math.sin(theta)) ;
      rectangle.setRect(x, y, 1, 1) ;
      g2d.draw(rectangle) ;
    }
  }
}
```

The only complication is to remember that the `cos` and `sin` methods work with radians and not degrees. The program displays the spiral shown in Figure 4.15.

Figure 4.16 Spiral drawn with more dots than Figure 4.15.

Figure 4.17 Spiral drawn with lines.

Testing

Testing is really confined to looking at the spiral and seeing if it appears acceptable and as expected.

Review

The obvious weakness with the program is that the spiral is composed of a series of dots (actually 1 by 1 rectangles). To close up the gaps we could either plot more dots or join the existing dots up with lines.

Following the first strategy of plotting more dots, the value of the variable `increment` can be decreased. If the statement:

```
double increment = 2 * Math.PI/350.0 ;
```

is used instead of the one shown in the program above, then the spiral shown in Figure 4.16 is obtained. This certainly looks better than the original, although the gaps between the lines are wider and it requires the same amount of computation as the original.

Joining up dots with lines requires more rewriting of the code but has the advantage that the points calculated on the spiral can be further apart so fewer need to be calculated. This will give a performance advantage which may be important if the spiral drawing algorithm is used in other programs. One of the issues with drawing graphics is that they can be computed and displayed fast enough, so looking for faster algorithms is a major area of activity.

The final version of the spiral algorithm can be seen in the code below, with the result shown in Figure 4.17.

```
public void paint(final Graphics g) {
  Graphics2D g2d = (Graphics2D)g ;
  Line2D line = new Line2D.Double(0, 0, 0, 0) ;
  double theta = 0.0 ;
  double increment = 2 * Math.PI/50.0 ;
  double xOffset = 150 ;
  double yOffset = 150 ;
  double lastx = xOffset ;
  double lasty = yOffset ;
  for (int n = 0 ; n < 500 ; ++n) {
    theta += increment ;
    double radius = (xOffset / 2) * n / 300 ;
    double x = xOffset + (radius * Math.cos(theta)) ;
    double y = yOffset + (radius * Math.sin(theta)) ;
    line.setLine(lastx, lasty, x, y) ;
    g2d.draw(line) ;
    lastx = x ;
    lasty = y ;
  }
}
```

4.5.3 Program Graph

Statement of Problem

"Write a program that draws the following simple graph:"

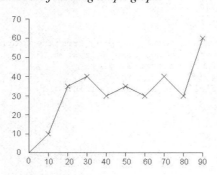

Although at first sight the drawing may seem fairly complex, it can be drawn by breaking the process down into a series of simple stages. First the x-axis can be drawn, then the y-axis, and then the points plotted and connected. This suggests three methods, one for each stage, and this gives the following program:

Design and Implementation

```
// A program to draw a graph.
// Written by Graham Roberts, July 1999
// Revision History: none
import java.awt.* ;
import java.awt.geom.* ;
public class Graph extends DrawPanel {
  public static void main(final String[] args) {
    DrawFrame frame = new DrawFrame ("Drawing of a graph") ;
    Graph drawing = new Graph (500, 400) ;
    frame.add(drawing) ;
    frame.pack() ;
    frame.centreOnScreen() ;
    frame.setVisible(true) ;
  }
  public Graph() {}
  public Graph(final int w, final int h) {
    super(w,h) ;
```

```
    }
    void drawXaxis(final Graphics2D g2d) {
      Line2D line = new Line2D.Double (50, 350, 450, 350) ;
      g2d.draw(line) ;
      for (int i = 0 ; i < 11 ; ++i) {
        if (i != 0) {
          line.setLine((i*40)+50, 350, (i*40)+50, 355) ;
          g2d.draw(line) ;
        }
        g2d.drawString(new Integer(i*10).toString(), (i*40)+42, 370) ;
      }
    }
    void drawYaxis(final Graphics2D g2d) {
      Line2D line = new Line2D.Double(50, 350, 50, 70) ;
      g2d.draw(line) ;
      for (int i = 0 ; i < 8 ; ++i) {
        if (i != 0) {
          line.setLine(50, 350-(i*40), 45, 350-(i*40)) ;
          g2d.draw(line) ;
        }
        g2d.drawString(new Integer (i*10).toString(), 24, 355-(i*40)) ;
      }
    }
    // Draw a cross where a point is plotted.
    void plotCross(final Graphics2D g2d, final int x, final int y) {
      Line2D line = new Line2D.Double (x-5, y-5, x+5, y+5) ;
      g2d.draw(line) ;
      line.setLine(x+5, y-5, x-5, y+5) ;
      g2d.draw(line) ;
    }
    // Plot an individual point, mapping from the graph
    // coordinate system to the drawing system.
    void plotPoint(final Graphics2D g2d,
                   final int x, final int y,
                   final int oldx, final int oldy) {
      int posX = 4 * x + 50 ;
      int posY = 350 - 4 * y ;
      int posOldX = 4 * oldx + 50 ;
      int posOldY = 350 - 4 * oldy ;
      plotCross(g2d,posX,posY) ;
      Line2D line = new Line2D.Double (posOldX, posOldY, posX, posY) ;
      g2d.draw(line) ;
    }
    // This method provides the set of points to display.
    // The points are given in the coordinate system of
    // the graph.
    void points(final Graphics2D g2d) {
      plotPoint(g2d, 10, 10,  0,  0) ;
      plotPoint(g2d, 20, 35, 10, 10) ;
      plotPoint(g2d, 30, 40, 20, 35) ;
      plotPoint(g2d, 40, 30, 30, 40) ;
      plotPoint(g2d, 50, 35, 40, 30) ;
      plotPoint(g2d, 60, 30, 50, 35) ;
      plotPoint(g2d, 70, 40, 60, 30) ;
      plotPoint(g2d, 80, 30, 70, 40) ;
      plotPoint(g2d, 90, 60, 80, 30) ;
    }
    public void paint(final Graphics g) {
      Graphics2D g2d = (Graphics2D)g ;
      drawXaxis(g2d) ;
      drawYaxis(g2d) ;
      points(g2d) ;
    }
  }
```

The program displays the picture seen in Figure 4.18.

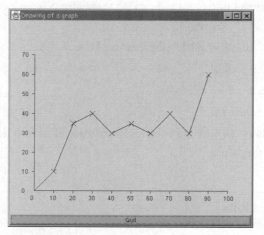

Figure 4.18 The graph drawn by program Graph.

Again, checking that the graph has the desirable appearance can be done, but in addition the positions of the points plotted need to be checked.

Testing

This program serves mainly as a demonstration of how a more complex drawing can be produced. The next stage of development might be to be allow the graph to be displayed in any position and at any size. At the moment there are too many coordinates coded directly in the program and they should be removed. Other additions might include: allowing the scale on the axes to be specified, using different colours; displaying points differently, and so on.

Review

Another important issue that should be raised is: where does the data come from? At the moment the points to be plotted are coded rather awkwardly into the program. Much more realistically they should either be generated by a computation in some other part of the program or read from a *data file*. A later chapter will revisit this program and show how it can display data from a file.

4.6 Summary

This chapter has given an introduction to the `Graphics2D` class, its associated shape classes and how they can all be used to draw pictures and diagrams. Enough ground has been covered to allow some quite sophisticated drawing to be done, but by browsing the SDK documentation and experimenting, further features can be uncovered and used. The key is to spend time exploring and trying things out — don't be deterred or overwhelmed by the amount of information and jargon, in time it will all start to make sense.

Key points in this chapter:

- Study the J2SDK documentation to find the useful classes.

- Class `Graphics2D` provides the basic support for displaying 2D graphics.

- Pictures are drawn by creating and drawing shape objects using a grid-based coordinate system.
- Attributes such as colour and line thickness can be set.
- Shape classes are available for common shapes. New shapes can be defined.
- All shapes are described by a path.
- Pictures can include text.
- Complex pictures can be drawn by creating a collection of methods, each of which draws a small part of the picture.

Self-review Questions

Self-review 4.1   Use a Web browser to find the documentation for classes: `Line2D`, `Line2D.Double`, `Graphics2D`, `BasicStroke` and `Color`.

Self-review 4.2 Find class `Arc2D.Double` in the J2SDK documentation and work out how to draw arcs.

Self-review 4.3 What needs to be done to rename class `Drawing` to class `MyPicture`?

Self-review 4.4 How can the size of the drawing grid be changed?

Self-review 4.5 Where is the origin (position $(0, 0)$) of a drawing grid?

Self-review 4.6 How is the size and shape of an ellipse specified?

Self-review 4.7 How can you draw a circle?

Self-review 4.8 What is the path of a dodecahedron?

Programming Exercises

Exercise 4.1 Write a program to draw a hexagon using lines.

Exercise 4.2 Write a program to draw a hexagon using class `GeneralPath`.

Exercise 4.3 Write a program to draw a collection of hexagons of different sizes and in different positions, using the `GeneralPath` you created in the last question.

Exercise 4.4 Write a program to draw a picture of a house.

Exercise 4.5 Write a program to that uses `drawString` to display your name and a message, using a large font.

Exercise 4.6 Write a program to draw a sine wave.

Exercise 4.7 As suggested in Section 4.2.4, Page 98, write a method called `createTriangle` that can be used to create triangles of any size at any position. Use the method in a program to demonstrate that triangle drawing works correctly.

Exercise 4.8 Repeat the last question but additionally allow the fill colour and border width of triangles to specified as well. (This will require some thinking about what actually goes in the `createTriangle` method.)

Exercise 4.9 Rewrite program Chessboard so that it can display a board of any size in any position, as suggested in the design review section.

Exercise 4.10 Write a program to display a shape like this one:

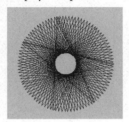

Exercise 4.11 Write a program that displays a graph showing the curves $y = \sin x$, $y = \cos x$ and $y = \tan x$.

Exercise 4.12 Rewrite program Graph along the lines suggested in the Design Review session, allowing the graph to be placed in any position and to be of any size.

Challenges

Challenge 4.1 Write a program to draw a random collection of shapes, with different fills and border widths. Browse the J2SDK documentation to find a class that generates random numbers and employ it to determine the properties of the shapes drawn.

Challenge 4.2 Write a program that draws a series of curves using the classes `CubicCurve2D.Double` and `QuadCurve2D.Double`.

Challenge 4.3 Draw a picture of a Mandelbrot set.

Challenge 4.4 Find out how to create new colours using class `Color` and draw a picture containing at least 256 different colours.

Introducing Containers

Objectives

This chapter gives an introductory overview of the concept of containers. We introduce three: the array, the ArrayList and the file. These are containers which have different properties and are used in different parts of the programs we write. Array and ArrayList are containers that are in memory, files are containers that are on disk. Files therefore allow us to store information between different runs of a program.

Keywords

array
ArrayList
container
element
file
indexing

5.1   Introduction

So far in our programs all our variables have only been able to store a single value. Until now this has not been constraining: we have never felt in need of a variable that was able to hold many values. However, there are very few problems that are of this sort; most will require us to store items of data so that we can access the values many times. Consider, for example, sorting some data. Without some form of *container*, we would have to have a separate variable for each item of data. This means we would have to know exactly how many data items were going to be in the data set so that we could declare the right number of variables. This fact alone means we do not do things this way, we need a new way since we must be able to write programs that can sort data where the number of items does not need to be known beforehand. Thus, we are going to require of our containers that not only are they objects that can hold a collection of values rather than just a single value, but that they can be accessed using a single name.

note

Containers are also known as collections. The two words are used synonymously.

Traditionally, containers held in memory (often called data structures) have been treated completely separately from containers held on disk (files). Increasingly, however, this separation is being replaced by the notion that both of these are just containers. Admittedly they are containers with very different properties, with these different properties leading to different capabilities and hence to different uses, but they are essentially the same abstraction. Indeed as various packages show, the same abstractions can be used to program using the different containers even though there are different properties involved.

5.2   Arrays

As the first example of an in-memory container, we introduce the concept of an *array*. An array is the most basic kind of container and is directly integrated into the Java programming language. In the next few sub-sections we will examine what an array is and show some example programs using arrays.

ref

Section 28.8.3, Page 785.

Before going further in explaining arrays, we feel we must say the following: the J2SDK, and also add-in libraries such as the Java Generic Library (JGL), provide a number of container types that are more advanced than arrays (these will be covered in detail in Part 2 of the book). We will introduce one such container type, `ArrayList`, taken from the J2SDK, in the next section for comparison with arrays. Whilst arrays are an integral part of the Java language, their real use is as building blocks for creating more advanced containers such as `ArrayList`. Of course, there are times when arrays are used directly in application code but the point here is that the programmer needs to be certain that the use of an array is necessary rather than using one of the more advanced containers.

5.2.1 Declaring an Array

Arrays are containers which hold a collection of values, usually referred to as *elements*. All values stored in a given array must be of the same type. So it is usual to talk of, for example, an 'array of integers' or 'array of strings'.

An array is represented as a row of variable containers. For example, an array of 10 items would be represented as:

```
name:  |   |   |   |   |   |   |   |   |   |   |

index    0   1   2   3   4   5   6   7   8   9
```

An array is a contiguous sequence of variables each of which contain a single value. The array as a whole has a name and the individual array elements are accessed via their offset from the beginning of the array rather than being given individual names. Accessing the individual elements is usually called *indexing*. Indexing works by numbering each array element, starting from zero, so that by using the combination of the array name and the index, any element can be accessed. There is a special syntax in Java based on square brackets ([ ]) to denote array indexing.

An array is declared and created using a statement such as the following:

```
int[] n = new int [10] ; // An array of 10 integers
```

This is a two stage process: declare a variable of array type and then initialize it to refer to a particular array of objects.

An array type is specified by using a type name following by a pair of square brackets ([ ]), so that int[] n, is declaring a variable n of type array of int. Any type can be used to declare an array of values of that type, so double[] d and String[] s are equally valid, declaring a variable of type array of double and array of String, respectively.

Declaring an array variable does not create an array. An array is a constructed object so the variable has to be initialized with a new expression. The new . . . expression specifies the type of the array elements, which must match the type given in the array variable declaration, and the size of the array. The size of the array gives the number of array elements the array will hold. Once an array has been created its size is fixed and cannot be changed.

Java separates *primitive data types* and *object data types* handling variables of the two sorts of type very differently. Until we started looking at arrays we had only dealt with primitive types, for example int, double. (String is special in that whilst it is actually an object data type, there is special syntactic support so that it can be used somewhat like a primitive data type.) With arrays we can no longer hide the difference between primitive types and object types. A variable of an object type does not contain a representation in the way a variable of primitive type does. Instead, it contains a *reference* to an object that is a representation. So in the declaration above, the variable n is a reference to an array object which is constructed using the new expression. It is important to separate the variable and the object for arrays and all object types.

tip

Forgetting to create the array object using new is a common source of errors. Always check the array object gets created.

!

References are covered more fully in Section 6.6, Page 159.

The size of an array does not have to be pre-determined by the programmer, it can be calculated as the program runs. For example:

```
int size = ... // Calculate size somehow
int[] n = new int [size] ; // Create array of calculated size
```

The size value specified when the array is created can be calculated by any expression that returns a positive integer result.

Arrays can be of any finite size but it should be remembered that each array element will use up memory space in the computer. This means that although it may be possible to declare an array of size 10,000, for example, it could have an undesirable effect on the performance of the computer due to the demand on memory. If an array is too big for the computer to handle, then trying to create it will cause the program to fail.

Java syntax allows array types to be declared with the square brackets following the variable name, as in:

```
int n[] = new int [10] ;
```

This, however, is simply historical baggage, a hang over from C and C++. The (very strongly) preferred Java style is to put the square brackets following the type name, as used throughout this book. The only reason we mention this historical (mis-) feature is that you might see it used in older Java code.

5.2.2   Array Indexing

Once created, an array is accessed using the index operator, with expressions such as:

```
int j = n[2] ; // Access value stored in array at position 2.
n[0] = 1 ; // Assign a value to array element 0.
```

The index operator is denoted by square brackets applied to an array variable — this is a different use of [] than that in array variable declarations. The index of the element to access appears inside the brackets and must be an expression that evaluates to type int; array indexes are integers. The expression is not limited to constant values such as 0 or 2, but can be any expression that returns an integer. For example:

```
n[x+y] = 3; // assign to element at index position x+y where
            // both x and y are integer variables.
int k = n[obj.f()+2] ;// Use a value returned from a method
                      // must be an int value.
```

Indexing allows the value of an array element to be read or assigned to, depending on which side of the assignment operator the array indexing operation is.

An array of size n is indexed from 0 to n-1 and any attempt to use an index outside of that range will result in an error when the program is run. This is known as *bounds checking* and if an out-of-bounds indexing is attempted a message similar to this is displayed:

```
java.lang.ArrayIndexOutOfBoundsException at T4.main(T4.java:6)
```

By default, the error will cause the program to terminate, requiring the problem in the code to be located, corrected and re-compiled.

One of the strengths of arrays is that indexing allows any element to be accessed at any time, in any order and without the position in the array imposing any extra performance cost: an array is a *random access container.* Frequently, an operation is applied to either a range of elements or all the elements in an array, so a for loop is used to count through the array indexes. For example, the following code will sum the elements of the array of integers declared earlier:

```
int sum = 0 ;
for (int i = 0 ; i < 10 ; ++i) {
  sum += n[i] ; // access each element of n in turn as loop counts
                // from 0 to 9
}
```

Emphasizing the point about array bounds: Particular care must be taken to check that the loop counts through the correct range of values. In the example above, the array is of size 10 but as the first index is 0, the loop must count from 0 to 9, not 0 to 10. Trying to access n[10] would cause an error as that element does not exist.

An array always knows its own size: For an array a, the expression a.length returns the number of elements in the array. This expression is not a method call so no parentheses are used. The loop presented above can be re-written as:

```
int sum = 0 ;
for (int i = 0 ; i < n.length ; ++i) {
  sum += n[i] ; // access each element of n in turn as loop counts
                // from 0 to n.length
}
```

This is actually a *much* better solution if the entire array is to be accessed by the loop, since it removes the explicit use of the constant 10. If the size of the array subsequently changes, the second version of the loop will still work, whereas the first version would have to be located and edited to replace the 10 with another number.

5.2.3   Array Parameters and Return Values

Arrays can be passed as parameters to methods and returned as the result. However, the effects of the parameter mechanism when applied to arrays are very different compared to when applied to primitive types and so requires closer examination.

An array parameter is specified in the same way as any other parameter, using a parameter variable declaration. The size of the array does not need to be included in the declaration as an array knows its own size:

```
void f(int[] array) { ... }
```

The variable is initialized with an array specified in the method call:

```
int[] n = new int[100];
obj.f(n) ;
...
```

This is essentially no different to what happened with primitive types, except that, we are passing the array reference and not the array object as a parameter: the parameter variable and parameter value are references to an array object. This means that the array object is not copied; the array object

tip

Always check loops counting through arrays carefully to see that they don't count beyond the end of the array.
AND
Avoid explicit constants in control statements.

inside the called method is the same as the one in the caller. The result of this is that if array elements are changed by assignment in the method, the array seen outside the method is also changed as it is the same array. For example:

```
void f(final int[] array) {
  array[3] = 1 ;     // Assignment to an array element here changes
                     // the array declared in method g below.
}
void g() {
  int[] n = new int [5];
  ...
  n[3] = 10 ;        // Element 3 is assigned 10 here.
  obj.f(n) ;
  int x = n[3] ;  // Now element 3 has the value 1.
  ...
}
```

Contrast passing an array to passing an int *as a method argument. The* int *is copied, so changing its value in the method has no effect outside of the method.*

The consequence of this is that care has to be taken to check that an assignment to an element of an array passed as a parameter doesn't cause an unexpected problem elsewhere in the program. Such problems can be hard to find and remove.

A method can be declared as returning an array as a result:

```
// Return a new array with size elements, all initialized
// to value.
int[] initNewArray(final int size, final int value) {
  int[] array = new int [size] ;
  for (int i = 0 ; i < array.length ; ++i)
  {
    array[i] = value ;
  }
  return array ;
}
```

This method creates an array of int object and uses it to initialize a variable, array, that is a reference to an array of int. The for loop then performs the initialization of each of the array elements. Finally, we return a reference to the array object that we just created and initialized. When called using an expression like:

```
int[] result = obj.initNewArray(10,5) ;
```

the variable result is assigned a reference to the array object created inside the method. Like parameter passing, the array object is not copied as a result of being returned.

Whilst the variable array in the method initNewArray has scope and lifetime bounded by the method, the array object has a lifetime that is not. The lifetime of the array object is not controlled by the method scope but by whether or not we are able to access it, i.e. whether or not we have a variable that has a reference to the array object. We will return to this issue later.

5.2.4   Program Average

We now have enough information about arrays to present an example program using one. Arrays are often used for numerical calculations, such as the simple one in the following program. The need to support complex calculations provided the motivation for including arrays in programming languages in the first place.

"Write a program which lets the user type in a series of numbers and then calculates the average."

The strategy followed by the program will be:

Ask the user how many numbers will be typed in
Create the array and read in each number
Iterate through the array and calculate the sum and average
Display the average

We could actually remove the array and calculate the sum as the numbers are typed in. If we were just answering this question and no more then to do so would be a better solution. However, let us assume that this is just the beginning of a larger system and that we need to store the user's input for other processing as well as calculation of the average.

Allocating the behaviour to methods, we can decide on having one method to do all the input and create the array, and a second method to calculate the average. We also assume we will be working with real numbers, so the array will be an array of `double`.

This gives the following program:

```
// A program using arrays to calculate an average.
// Written by Graham Roberts, July 1999
// Revision History: none
public class Average {
  double[] readNumbers() {
    KeyboardInput in = new KeyboardInput() ;
    System.out.print("How many numbers will be entered: ") ;
    int count = in.readInteger() ;
    double[] values = new double[count] ;
    for (int i = 0 ; i < count ; ++i) {
      System.out.print("Enter number " + i +": ") ;
      values[i] = in.readDouble() ;
    }
    return values ;
  }
  double average(final double[] values) {
    double sum = 0.0 ;
    for (int n = 0 ; n < values.length ; ++n) {
      sum += values[n] ;
    }
    return sum / values.length ;
  }
  public static void main(final String[] args) {
    Average obj = new Average () ;
    double average = obj.average(obj.readNumbers()) ;
    System.out.println("Average is: " + average) ;
  }
}
```

Testing follows the familiar pattern of checking that the program works correctly with valid input, checking what happens with invalid input and checking boundary or edge conditions where errors might occur.

Testing the boundary conditions is actually a bit more interesting with this example as it is possible that calculating the sum will cause an arithmetic overflow or underflow — though this is rather unlikely during typical use of the program. Java `double`s can only store values in either of the ranges $(1.797 \times 10^{308}, 4.94 \times 10^{-324})$ and $(-4.94 \times 10^{-324}, -1.797 \times 10^{308})$. If we calculate a value greater than 1.797×10^{308} or less than -1.797×10^{308}, then we have overflow. If we calculate a value in the range $(4.94 \times 10^{-324}, -4.94 \times 10^{-324})$ we have underflow. Overflow results in the representation `Infinity` or `-Infinity`, depending on whether we are overflowing positively or negatively. Underflow results in the representation `0`. There is another special representation associated with Java numbers and that is Not-a-Number (`NaN`). This representation is used for the result of any computation which has no other representation.

The results of our tests were:

- The program seemed to calculate correctly given valid input.
- The program correctly generated `Infinity` when a set of data whose sum overflowed positively was provided.
- The program correctly generated `-Infinity` when a set of data whose sum overflowed negatively was provided.
- The program correctly generated `NaN` when we stated that the number of data items was 0. `NaN` results since 0/0 is not a number.

5.2.5   The Class Arrays

The J2SDK provides a class `Arrays` in the package `java.util`. This provides a number of useful utility methods for working with arrays, such as those for sorting and searching. For example, if an array of integers needs to be sorted into ascending order, the following statement can be used:

```
// Assume n is an array of integers in unsorted order
Arrays.sort(n) ; // sort the array
```

The `sort` method is a static method (see Section 3.3, Page 54, and Section 6.6.6, Page 166), so does not need to be called for a specific object.

It is worth investigating the J2SDK documentation to find out what other methods are already available for working with arrays; it will save writing code for yourself that someone else has already written and *tested*.

5.2.6   Multi-Dimensional Arrays

The arrays seen so far are have all been single or 1-dimensional (1D), meaning that they store a simple row of values. Arrays can also be created with multiple dimensions, so a 2-dimensional (2D) array has rows and columns, while a 3-dimensional (3D) array can be thought of as a cube of values. Arrays with higher dimensions are possible in Java but are not used that often.

People interested in mathematical computation might start thinking about vectors and matrices at this point. We quickly note that arrays would not be used directly to represent these abstractions in user's code. Chapter 6, Page 145, will introduce the Java technology that would be used to construct types for such abstractions.

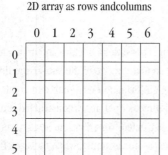

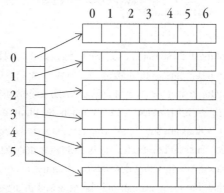

Figure 5.1 Thinking about 2D arrays.

The following examples show some multi-dimensional array declarations; additional sets of square brackets are used to add dimensions:

```
// 2D array with 10 rows of 20 columns
int[][] array2D = new int[10][20] ;

// 3D array of String of size 10x20x30
String[][][] array3D = new String[10][20][30] ;

// 4D array of double of size 5x10x5x10
double[][][][] array4D = new double[5][10][5][10] ;
```

Array indexing follows the same strategy of using additional index (square bracket) operators. The following examples use the declarations above:

```
array2D[1][2] = 2 ;
array3D[4][6][8] = "Hello" ;
array4D[1][1][1][1] = 2.34 ;
```

Computer memory is only a 1-dimensional structure so we have to have a way of mapping these multi-dimensional structures. In Java, multi-dimensional arrays are represented by multiple 1-dimensional arrays. A 2D array is, therefore, an array of arrays, with each of the column array object elements being an array holding row values (see Figure 5.1). A 3D array is an array of arrays of arrays. A consequence of this is that multi-dimensional arrays can be constructed or pulled apart following the array object structure. The following code illustrates what is possible:

```
// Declare and create a normal 1D array
int[] oned1 = new int[20] ;

// Declare an array (size 10) of integer arrays.
// Only the column array is created, not the
// individual row arrays.
int[][] twod = new int[10][] ;

// Assign an array to element zero, adding one
// of the rows.
twod[0] = oned1 ;

// An integer element can now be accessed in
// row zero, using normal 2D indexing.
int i = twod[0][2] ;

// Create another 1D array, this time of size 50.
```

Arrays with lots of dimensions can use up a lot of memory. Other kinds of container often provide a better solution.

```
int[] oned2 = new int[50] ;
// Assign the new array as element one of twod
twod[1] = oned2 ;
// Access an element in the new row.
twod[1][45] = 10 ;
```

Looking at these statements, two things stand out. Firstly, it is possible to declare and create just part of a multi-dimensional array (e.g. `new int[10][]`), so that the size of the sub-arrays does not have to be fixed or their objects created. As long as enough information is available to create at least the first array object, that is enough. Secondly, a multi-dimensional array constructed along these lines does not have to be a regular shape and can be constructed from different sized parts as required. This can be a useful way of saving memory resources, as, for example, when the size of an array-based data structure depends on circumstances when a program is run. Array indexing works as normal, but elements can only be accessed in array objects that exist, otherwise an error will occur when the program runs.

5.2.7   Array Initialization Expressions

Array declaration and use both have special Java syntax and so does array initialization. Arrays can be initialized using initialization expressions. The following are examples of fully initialized array declarations:

```
int[] j = {5, 4, 3, 2, 1} ;
String[] words = {"These","are","some","words"} ;
int[][] twod2 = {{1,2,3}, {4,5,6}, {7,8,9}} ;
```

Because of the use of initialization expressions, we have no need to use a `new` expression; the array variable is initialized to refer to an array object that is automatically created and filled with the data provided in the initializer list (the comma-separated list of values in braces). The number of values in the initializer list determines the size of the array, so array `j` above is of size 5, indexed from 0 to 4. A 2D array or higher can be initialized using nested lists of lists. The values in an initializer list do not have to be constants, they can be variables or any other expression of the expected type:

```
int[] k = {a1,b,3+4,obj.f()} ;
```

5.2.8   Program AddUpColumns

The following program provides an example of working with a 2D array.

Statement of Problem   *"Write a method that takes a 2D array of doubles as an argument and returns a 1D array containing the total of each column."*

Design and Implementation   The method and its enclosing program are primarily to demonstrate various aspects of 2D array handling, so the design can be kept very straightforward. Apart from a method to calculate the totals, it will be useful to have a helper method to display the totals. To keep things simple a 2D array will be initialized directly in the main method to allow the program to run.

The program follows:

```
// A program to add up the columns of a 2D array.
```

```
// Written by Graham Roberts, July 1999
// Revision History: none
public class AddUpColumns {
  // Add up each column in the 2D array and return
  // a 1D array of the totals.
  double[] totalColumns(final double[][] array) {
    int nColumns = array[0].length ;
    double[] totals = new double [nColumns] ;
    for (int column = 0 ; column < nColumns ; ++column) {
      totals[column] = 0.0 ;
      for (int row = 0 ; row < array.length ; ++row) {
        totals[column] += array[row][column] ;
      }
    }
    return totals ;
  }
  void displayTotals(final double[] totals) {
    System.out.print("Totals are: ") ;
    for (int column = 0 ; column < totals.length ; ++column) {
      System.out.print(totals[column] + "  ") ;
    }
    System.out.println() ;
  }
  public static void main(final String[] args) {
    AddUpColumns object = new AddUpColumns () ;
    double[][] testArray = { {2.1,3.4,5.6,9.6,5.5},
                             {4.2,3.5,6.6,1.9,3.2},
                             {1.1,5.8,8.2,4.5,2.8} } ;
    object.displayTotals(object.totalColumns(testArray)) ;
  }
}
```

The use of nested for loops, as seen in the `totalColumns` method, is typical when working with multi-dimensional arrays. In this case the outer loop counts through the columns, while the inner loop repeatedly counts through the rows. The result is that every element in the array can be visited once within the body of the inner for loop, and that is where the addition is done to find the column totals.

The `totalColumns` method is written with the assumption that the 2D array passed as an argument will be of a regular shape, with all rows the same length. The expression `array[0].length` selects the first row of the 2D array and returns its length, giving the number of columns to be added up (remember how 2D arrays are represented as an array of arrays). The expression `array.length` gives the number of rows.

For this program, testing is a matter of checking the totals displayed against the argument array. **Testing** More realistically the program might be modified to read a number of 2D arrays from a data file and total the columns of each one, providing a more thorough check.

5.2.9   Character and Byte Arrays

A character array is an array of `char`. J2SDK classes `String` and `StringBuffer`, normally used for working with text, are both constructed using `char` arrays and provide ways of converting from `char` arrays to `Strings`. For example:

```
char[] hello = {'h','e','l','l','o'} ;
String s = new String (hello) ;
```

The character array `hello`, created using an initializer list, can be used to create a string s that holds the word 'hello'. Of course, we are more used to seeing this as:

```
String s = "hello" ;
```

Although a String is a constructed type, the compiler recognizes the special syntax.

Occasionally, it can be useful to convert a `String` to a `char` array, in order to manipulate the individual characters, though using `StringBuffer` is the more usual alternative. This can be done by using the `toCharArray` method of class `String`:

```
char[] hello2 = s.toCharArray() ;
```

Type `byte` represents 8-bit binary numbers. Bytes are typically used to represent individual memory locations in a computer and also to represent the most primitive type of data stored in data files or communicated across a network. Occasionally, the Java programmer has to work with byte arrays and a number of J2SDK classes provide methods that either take or return byte arrays, including class `String`:

```
byte[] b = new byte[256] ;
// Read bytes from somewhere
...
// Convert from bytes to a String
String message = new String(b) ;
```

In this case, it might be assumed that an array of bytes representing a message has been received across a network connection. These bytes can then be easily converted to a string, but the programmer should be sure that the bytes actually represent characters, otherwise the message will end up as a garbled collection of random characters.

5.2.10   The main Method Parameter

Having introduced arrays, we can now say something more about the `main` method and, in particular, its method parameter. All `main` methods are declared as:

```
public static void main(final String[] args)
```

It is now clear that the method parameter, `args`, is an array of strings. This parameter allows values to be passed to the program when it is run. Whether from the command line or by some other method such as clicking on an icon, a command like the following:

```
java MyClass
```

is issued to start a Java program: it is possible to add *command line parameters* to the command line, for example:

```
java MyClass p1 p2
```

Traditionally, command line parameters have also been termed *command line arguments*. Hence the name `args` for the parameter variable.

When the program starts, an array of strings containing the command line arguments is created and passed as the parameter to `main`. The following simple program displays the arguments typed on the command line when the program is run:

```
// A program to display command line arguments.
// Written by Graham Roberts, August 1999
// Revision History: none
public class CommandLineParameters {
  public static void main(final String[] args) {
    for (int i = 0 ; i < args.length ; ++i) {
      System.out.println("Parameter " + i + ": " + args[i]) ;
    }
  }
}
```

If run using the command line:

```
java CommandLineParameters one two three four
```

the program displays:

```
Parameter 0: one
Parameter 1: two
Parameter 2: three
Parameter 3: four
```

The `java` command name and the program name (`CommandLineParameters`) are not included in the array that is the parameter variable.

In practice, command line parameters typically have a form such as the following:

```
java Program -d -name test hello.dat
```

Here a set of flags, conventionally beginning with a '-' character, are used to give configuration information to the program to be run. A simple flag like `-d` might turn on a particular feature, while a more complex one, such as `-name test`, has a parameter of its own. After the flags, there might possibly be other entries in the command line; in the example above we have given the name of a data file, `hello.dat`.

The following program illustrates how the command line parameters might be scanned to pick out the flags and other values. It looks for the flags `-a`, `-b` and `-c <p>` and then reads the final entry in the list. Some error checking is done but it remains possible to type invalid parameters that the program will still accept.

```
// Another program to display command line arguments.
// Written by Graham Roberts, August 1999
// Revision History: none
public class CLP {
  public static void main(final String[] args) {
    // Complain if there are no arguments at all
    if (args.length < 1) {
      error() ;
      return ;
    }
    // Variables to store the state of flags and other command line
    // arguments.
    boolean flaga = false ;
    boolean flagb = false ;
    String flagcArg = "" ;
    String fileName = "" ;
    for (int i = 0 ; i < (args.length - 1) ; ++i) {
      if (!args[i].startsWith("-")) {
        break ;
      }
      if (args[i].equals("-a")) {
        flaga = true ;
```

```
      } else
      if (args[i].equals("-b")) {
        flagb = true ;
      } else
      if (args[i].equals("-c")) {
        // Try to read flag argument.  Report an error and give up if
        // there are not enough entries on the command line.
        ++i ;
        if (i < (args.length- 1)) {
          flagcArg = args[i] ;
        } else {
          error() ;
          return ;
        }
      }
    }
    fileName = args[args.length-1] ;
    // These statements verify that the command line arguments have
    // been read correctly.  They should be removed if this code is
    // used in a non-example program.
    System.out.println("flag a: " + flaga) ;
    System.out.println("flag b: " + flagb) ;
    System.out.println("flag c parameter: " + flagcArg) ;
    System.out.println("filename: " + fileName) ;
  }
  // Helper method to display an error message.
  public static void error() {
    System.err.println("Usage: java CLP [-ab] [-c name] file") ;
  }
}
```

note

System.err *is a*
special output variable
which gives the best
guarantees that the user
will see the message. It is
used just like
System.out.

Several parts of this program are worth highlighting. The method named `error` is a helper method used to display an error message. Its declaration avoids having to scatter the same error message in different parts of the code. The method `error`, like `main`, is declared as `static`, meaning that it does not have to be called for a specific object. It uses `System.err`, the error stream, to display its message on the screen. `System.err` is similar to `System.out` except that there are stronger guarantees that any text output will appear on the screen, and will be seen by the user. Text displayed with `System.out` can appear elsewhere and be missed. The methods `equal` and `startsWith` are provided by class `String`

5.3   Container Classes

Arrays are useful but can be inflexible. For example, the size of an array cannot change. Also, without a lot of programming effort, additional elements cannot be inserted between two other elements in an array, nor can elements cannot be removed from an array. Since this extra flexibility is often required it is sensible to have more flexible array-like types in the library; this avoids everyone having to program the functionality for themselves. The J2SDK provides such container classes, classes that can behave like arrays but add additional operations and have the ability to change size. The limitation that we have to accept for these container classes is that they can only store objects and not primitive types such as `int` or `double`.

With Java versions 1.0 and 1.1 the container class of the sort required was called `Vector`. Java 2 introduced the Collections Framework that includes classes such as `ArrayList`, `HashSet` and `LinkedList`, `ArrayList` being the flexible array-like type that supersedes `Vector` (though `Vector` is still used by some despite `ArrayList` being preferred). Each of the Collections classes has different performance properties, so the programmer selects the one most suitable for the problem at hand. Part 2 of this book will explore these and other classes in detail, so here we provide only a simple introduction to `ArrayList` for comparison with arrays.

5.3.1 ArrayList

An `ArrayList` is created like any other object:

```
ArrayList a = new ArrayList () ; // Create an empty ArrayList
```

The number of values that the `ArrayList` can store does not need to be specified, as it will automatically grow as necessary. Unlike an array, an `ArrayList` starts out with no elements at all.

Before an `ArrayList` can be declared, however, an *import statement* has to appear (usually but not necessarily placed at the beginning of the source code file). This tells the Java compiler where it can find information about the named class thereby making it available for use. This is not done automatically, the import statement must appear before the first use. Once the `ArrayList` is created, values can be added to it using the `add` method. So, for example:

```
import java.util.ArrayList ; // Use ArrayList from java.util
ArrayList a = new ArrayList () ;
String s1 = "hello" ;
String s2 = "world" ;
a.add(s1) ; // add elements to end of ArrayList
a.add(s2) ;
```

Initially, the `ArrayList` has a size of zero but grows by one every time a value is added. This is in contrast to the array where all the elements are available immediately.

Values can be fetched from the `ArrayList` using the `get` method which works like array indexing. The square bracket notation used with arrays is not available for use with container classes because, unlike arrays, this class has no special relationship with the compiler. To index into the `ArrayList`:

```
String s = (String)a.get(0) ; // Get element 0
```

Getting a value from a container requires an extra piece of syntax in the form of the *cast expression*, the `(String)` in the statement above. This is needed because when an object is stored in a container, its specific type is apparently lost. The cast expression recovers the type when the object is fetched using the `get` method. So in the example above, the cast expression recovers the fact that the object fetched was a `String`. The detailed reasons for why this is needed will be covered in a later chapter.

The `set` method allows the existing value of an element to be changed and is equivalent to assignment to an array element:

```
a.set(1,"WORLD") ;
```

ref

*Cast: Section 28.9.2,
Page 790.*

The major advantage of an `ArrayList` over arrays becomes apparent when considering the next two methods. The first is a variant of the `add` method that takes two arguments:

```
a.add(1,"happy") ; // insert element at position 1
```

This will insert a new element at the position given by the first argument, shifting all the existing elements at that position and beyond forward by one, and growing the size of the `ArrayList` by one. This operation is not available directly on an array; the equivalent functionality would have to be explicitly programmed using the following algorithm:

> *To insert a value at position m in an array of size n:*
> *Create a new array of size n+1*
> *Copy the values from 0 to m-1 in the old array to the new array*
> *Assign the new value to m in the new array*
> *Copy the values from m to n-1 in the old array to m+1 to n in the new array*
> *Use the new array from now on*

Matching `add` is `remove` which will completely remove an element from an `ArrayList`, closing up the gap left and shrinking the overall size by one:

```
a.remove(1) ; // Remove element at index 1
```

Again, this operation would have to be programmed explicitly if we were using arrays.

Each array knows its own size using *arrayname*`.length`. This is not available with `ArrayList`s. Instead we make use of the method `size` to get the size of the container:

```
int theSize = a.size() ;
```

The equivalent of multi-dimensional arrays are constructed using an `ArrayList` of `ArrayList`s and so on, following the same strategy as array implementations.

5.3.2   Storing Numbers in a Container

note

Values of primitive types need putting into wrapper objects in order to be used in containers other than arrays.

Primitive types are not objects in the way that arrays are, nor as is needed for storage in `ArrayList`s. However, it is important that we can use objects that represent numbers so that we can have `ArrayList`s that can contain numbers. In the package `java.lang` of J2SDK there is a set of classes matching each of the primitive types: `Integer`, `Double`, `Boolean`, and so on, specifically for enabling this. So, for example, `Integer` and `Double` objects can be created using statements like:

```
Integer n = new Integer(10) ;
Double d = new Double(2.3) ;
```

These objects can then be stored in an `ArrayList`:

```
ArrayList numbers = new ArrayList () ;
numbers.add(n) ;
numbers.add(d) ;
```

and then fetched back — remembering to use a cast expression:

```
Integer n2 = (Integer)numbers.get(0) ;
Double d2 = (Double)numbers.get(1) ;
```

The last two statements illustrate another difference between `ArrayLists` and arrays: values of *different* types can be stored in an `ArrayList`. However, it is up to the programmer to correctly specify the correct type when a value is fetched. If a mistake is made, for example:

```
Double d3 = (Double)numbers.get(0) ; // Type error
```

then the program will fail when run, since an `Integer` (which is the type of the value stored at index 0) is not type compatible with `Double` (which is the type the statement is trying to cast to). This sort of error can only be caught at run time, it cannot be caught by the compiler, and it can lead to nasty surprises when the program unexpectedly fails at some later date. In general, avoid mixing different types of value in the same container: treat this flexibility as something that is only used if it is absolutely essential and not at all if possible.

Arithmetic cannot be performed directly on number wrapper objects. Instead the primitive value has to be retrieved using the `intValue` method for `Integers` and the `doubleValue` method for `Doubles`. For example:

```
Integer x = new Integer(10) ;
Integer y = new Integer(5) ;
int z = x.intValue() + y.intValue() ;

Double e = new Double(3.675) ;
Double f = new Double(5.234) ;
double g = e.doubleValue() + f.doubleValue() ;
```

5.3.3 Program AverageUsingArrayList

To finish this brief introduction to containers, here is a version of the program `Average`, presented earlier and implemented using arrays, re-written to use `ArrayList`.

```
// A program using ArrayList to calculate an average.
// Written by Graham Roberts, August 1999
// Revision History: re-written from Average
import java.util.ArrayList ;
public class AverageUsingArrayList {
  ArrayList readNumbers() {
    KeyboardInput in = new KeyboardInput () ;
    System.out.print("How many numbers will be entered: ") ;
    int count = in.readInteger() ;
    ArrayList values = new ArrayList () ;
    for (int i = 0 ; i < count ; ++i) {
      System.out.print("Enter number " + i +": ") ;
      values.add(new Double (in.readDouble())) ;
    }
    return values ;
  }
  double average(final ArrayList values) {
    double sum = 0.0 ;
    for (int n = 0 ; n < values.size() ; ++n) {
      sum += ((Double)values.get(n)).doubleValue() ;
    }
    return sum / values.size() ;
  }
  public static void main(final String[] args) {
    AverageUsingArrayList object = new AverageUsingArrayList () ;
    double average = object.average(object.readNumbers()) ;
    System.out.println("Average is: " + average) ;
  }
}
```

tip

When a program fails it is often when being demonstrated to an Important Person thereby causing the programmer maximum embarrassment. Avoid assumptions in your code and test it thoroughly to minimize the probability of this happening to you.

In a sense we have missed a trick with this code: with the change from array usage to `ArrayList` usage, there is actually no need to specify the number of input items at the beginning. Since the `ArrayList` can be expanded as needed, we could use a different algorithm for the data input. The only reason for specifying the size of the data seems to have been the need to have a known size for the array declaration. Given that this requirement has gone away, we should review the algorithm. Instead of a fixed number of values, we could say that we don't know how many numbers there will be but we know that the input will end with a certain value. The issue is then to select a value. If we know that all the data will be positive then we could use any negative value (-1, say) since that would not be a legal value for the input. The `readNumbers` method could be changed to:

```
ArrayList readNumbers() {
  KeyboardInput in = new KeyboardInput () ;
  System.out.println("Enter numbers, terminate with -1.") ;
  ArrayList values = new ArrayList () ;
  while (true) {
    System.out.print("Enter number " + ": ") ;
    double datum = in.readDouble() ;
    if (datum == -1)
      break ;
    values.add(new Double (datum)) ;
  }
  return values ;
}
```

This is not really satisfactory for two reasons:

1. We rely on being able to test two `doubles` for equality (`datum == -1`) which is not very safe. It should work but there are no guarantees.
2. This program does not work if the selected stop value is a legal input value.

To get round these points we really need an input value that can never be a legal part of the input. There is, in fact, such a value, called 'end of file' or EOF. This character is generated by typing Control+D under UNIX and Control+Z under Windows. Unfortunately, the class `KeyboardInput` stops us going down this route. We created this type to hide various bits of necessary complication so as to make it easy for people new to Java to do input from the keyboard. In order to implement the design of this program using EOF as the input terminator, we would have to stop using `KeyboardInput` and deal with all the complexity (exceptions) explicitly. Since we have not covered this topic, we will have to leave this design until later.

5.4   Data Files

Programs that have no output of any sort are essentially useless. So programs always need to be able to write data and more often than not need to read data as well. All our programs so far have read data from the keyboard and displayed data on the screen. This has been fine for our programs so far but such data is very transient, it is lost once a program terminates. We really want our programs to be able to store data so that it can be used by other programs and/or itself next time it runs. Moreover for testing, we had to type on the keyboard the same data many times when it would be far more sensible to use some form of permanent storage to hold the test data set. We only have to think about this issue for a very, very short time (milliseconds) to realize that we need some way of reading and writing disk store from our Java program.

This section is about *data files*, which provide a place to store data independently of the execution of any program. As the name implies, a data file is a named file stored on a disk drive or file server that contains data. The data can be in many different formats or representations but in this section we will consider data files holding data represented using text and characters. Data files can essentially be thought of as containers where the values are stored outside a program. At the lowest level of abstraction, files are essentially arrays of bytes that are held on disk rather than in memory. We shall look at the case where this lowest level of abstraction supports arrays of characters.

A program that uses data files is exposed to a new set of potential reliability problems caused by dealing with resources (the files) outside of its direct control. For example, a file server may become unavailable while a program is running, or disk space may run out. This can make the use of data files quite complicated and requires the use of Java language features not yet covered. Hence, in this section we make use of two classes that we have constructed, `FileInput` and `FileOutput`, that hide away most of the difficulties and allow us to concentrate on the basic ideas. `FileInput` is not dissimilar to `KeyboardInput`, while `FileOuptut` provides write methods rather than read methods. The source code for the classes is listed in Appendix I, Page 971, and Appendix J, Page 975.

5.4.1 Text-based Data

Text-based data is simply data that is entirely represented using characters. If a file containing such data is viewed in an editor, the data appears as normal text and can be read directly from the screen. Numbers, like values of type `int` and `double,` are represented in their written form (e.g. `123`, `4.563`). Strings and values of type char have the obvious direct representation.

The simplest kind of data file, which we will be concentrating on for the moment, has each data item on a separate line in the file. The following represents a `String`, an `int` and a `double`:

```
Hello world
123
3.434
```

An invisible newline character ends each line but is ignored except when reading individual characters. Data files can be created either by a program or by using an editor to directly type data into a file.

5.4.2 Reading Data with FileInput

A program *reads* data from an *input file*. Class `FileInput` provides a collection of methods to read different primitive data types and strings. The steps for reading data from a file are as follows:

note

Text-based data can be read by humans. Binary data can be read only by computers (or very patient humans).

1. *Open* the file. All files have a name which is determined by the underlying operating system and which the program must use to identify which file is to be opened. Opening the file establishes a connection between program and file via the operating system and makes the file ready for reading.

2. *Read* the data. Methods are called to read the data. The program has to know the structure and order of data in the file so that it can use the correct reading operations, in the correct order, to correctly extract the data from the file. Trying to read an integer when the next entry in the file is a string will result in an error.

3. *Close* the file. This releases the connection to the file and does any tidying up needed.

With `FileInput`, data items can be read only in the order they appear in a file, so for this reason the files are referred to as *sequential files* and have sequential access. A more sophisticated file class might provide *random access*, allowing data items to be accessed in any order.

The following program shows an example of reading different types of data from the following text file (with values intended to be of types `int`, `long`, `double`, `float`, `char` and `String`):

```
123
12345
1.2345
1.23
c
This is a string.
```

and the program code:

```java
// A program to read data from a data file
// using the FileInput class.
// Written by Graham Roberts, August 1999
// Revision History: none
public class FileInputExample {
  public static void main(final String[] args) {
    // Create the FileInput object using the filename
    // test1.dat. Any file name (including a full path name)
    // can be used, or a String variable holding the name
    // can be given.
    FileInput in = new FileInput("test1.dat") ;
    // Now read some data.
    int n = in.readInteger() ;
    System.out.println("Integer was: " + n) ;
    long l = in.readLong() ;
    System.out.println("Long was: " + l) ;
    double d = in.readDouble() ;
    System.out.println("Double was: " + d) ;
    float f = in.readFloat() ;
    System.out.println("float was: " + f) ;
    char c = in.readCharacter() ;
    System.out.println("char was: " + c) ;
    //============================================================
    //  NB Having read one character leaves the newline in the input
    //  buffer.  This leads to a BIG problem since there is a
    //  dependence on which operating system wrote the data file.
    //  UNIX machines represent newline with a single character,
    //  newline, whereas Windows uses two characters, carriage return
    //  and newline.  Thus, the program needs to know whether to read
    //  one or two characters to remove the newline, which means
    //  knowing which operating system wrote the data file.
    //============================================================
```

```
      //c = in.readCharacter() ;
      c = in.readCharacter() ;
      String s = in.readString() ;
      System.out.println("String was: " + s) ;
      // Finished with the file, so close it.
      in.close() ;
    }
  }
```

This shows the methods readInteger, readLong, readDouble, readFloat, readCharacter and readString, along with the creation of the FileInput object and the call of the close method at the end of the program. The string "test1.dat" is the name of the data file.

The only small complication occurs when reading characters, as the end of line character needs to be explicitly read as well. Unfortunately, UNIX and Windows systems represent the end of line differently, using one and two characters, respectively, so the number of calls to the readCharacter methods differs.

Data is often read in a while or do loop, which repeats until the end of the file is reached. A method is provided to test for 'end of file' (EOF), allowing the loop to terminate. This will be illustrated in the example programs shown later in this chapter.

5.4.3 Writing Data with FileOutput

A program *writes* data to an *output file*. Class FileOutput provides a collection of methods to write different primitive data types and strings, matching those seen in FileInput. The steps for writing data to a file are as follows:

1. *Open* the file, in the same way as with FileInput.

2. *Write* the data. Methods are called to write the data using the correct order and format you define for the content of the data file.

3. *Close* the file. This is very important when writing files as failure to close a file can result in some data not being written to the file and hence lost. Java makes best attempts to ensure that this does not happen but it is best to be safe and not rely on this. The issue here is that our program is interacting with the operating system which needs to be informed that the file is being closed so that it can ensure proper writing of all information to the file.

The following program illustrates the use of FileOutput and writes the data file used in the last sub-section:

```
// A program to write data to a data file
// using the FileOutput class.
// Written by Graham Roberts, August 1999
// Revision History: none
public class FileOutputExample {
  public static void main(final String[] args) {
    // Create and open file.
    FileOutput out = new FileOutput("test1.dat") ;
    // Write different types of value.
    // Each line must be explicitly separated
```

tip

12345L means the integer 12345 of type long. *1.2345D means 1.2345 of type* double *and 1.23F means 1.23 of type* float. *See Section 28.5, Page 774, for more information.*

```
      // with a newline.
      out.writeInteger(123) ;
      out.writeNewline() ;
      out.writeLong(12345L) ;
      out.writeNewline() ;
      out.writeDouble(1.2345D) ;
      out.writeNewline() ;
      out.writeFloat(1.23F) ;
      out.writeNewline() ;
      out.writeCharacter('c') ;
      out.writeNewline() ;
      out.writeString("This is a string.") ;
      out.close() ;
    }
  }
```

Again, the file name is `test1.dat` and the file will be in the same directory as the program. If the file already exists then its contents will be replaced by the data the program writes. Anything already stored in the file will be overwritten. The methods `writeInteger`, `writeLong`, `writeDouble`, `writeFloat`, `writeCharacter` and `writeString` write values of the corresponding data types. In addition, the method `writeNewLine` is called to explicitly write a newline character (in the correct format for the computer used) after each data value is written.

Both `FileInput` and `FileOutput` are written so that if a file error occurs, the program immediately stops and displays an error message. While this is acceptable for our purposes, production quality programs need to be much more robust and keep on running.

We are now in a position to develop some programs that use files. We therefore present some examples.

5.4.4   Program DisplayTextFile

Statement of Problem   *"Write a program to ask for the name of a text file and display its contents on the screen."*

Design and Implementation   A text file simply holds text (a document, letter, email message, note, etc.), and contains normal characters, digits, spaces, tabs and newlines. Displaying this on screen is simply a matter of reading one character at a time until the end of file is reached. The minimalist approach to this would be to have a simple sequence within `main`:

```
// A program to display the contents of a text file.
// Written by Russel Winder, September 1999
// Revision History: none
public class DisplayTextFile {
  public static void main(final String[] args) {
    KeyboardInput in = new KeyboardInput () ;
    System.out.print("Enter name of file to display: ") ;
    String fileName = in.readString() ;
    FileInput inFile = new FileInput(fileName) ;
    // Note that one character has to be read first
    // before the loop starts.
    char c = inFile.readCharacter() ;
    while (!inFile.eof()) {
      System.out.print(c) ;
      c = inFile.readCharacter() ;
    }
    inFile.close() ;
```

```
        }
    }
```

The while loop does all the work of copying the characters and uses the eof method of class
FileInput to determine when to stop work. eof returns true when all the data has been read
from the file and false while there is still data available. To trigger eof to return true an attempt
must be made to read a data value once the end of file has been reached. This explains the order of
the statements in the while loop and why a readCharacter method call precedes the loop. If
the data file is empty, the call before the loop will try to read non-existent data and eof will be
triggered to return true. In that case, the loop body is never executed.

The program should be asked to read various text files (including an empty file) and the displayed   **Testing**
contents compared with the real contents.

Reading and displaying one character at a time is usually considered to be inefficient and slow.   **Review**
Although it is very unlikely that this program will show any adverse affects, it would be better to read
one line of the text file at a time using the readString method.

The above program is sufficiently straightforward that having the entire code within the method
main is probably entirely acceptable. It does save the hassle of creating an initial object: we have
not had to define any new methods in the program so we have not needed to create an initial object
in order to make method calls. However, it is definitely the case that there are two activities going
on, getting the file name and doing the displaying, so it could be argued that we should do the
partitioning anyway.

Putting these two points together gives us:

```
// A prcgram to display the contents of a text file.
// Written by Graham Roberts & Russel Winder, September 1999
// Revision History: none
public class DisplayTextFile2 {
  public String getFileName() {
    KeyboardInput in = new KeyboardInput () ;
    System.out.print("Enter name of file to display: ") ;
    return in.readString() ;
  }
  public void display(final String fileName) {
    FileInput in = new FileInput(fileName) ;
    String s = in.readString() ;
    while (!in.eof()) {
      System.out.println(s) ;
      s = in.readString() ;
    }
    in.close() ;
  }
  public static void main(final String[] args) {
    DisplayTextFile2 obj = new DisplayTextFile2 () ;
    obj.display(obj.getFileName()) ;
  }
}
```

This program should behave identically to the earlier version. It should be tested with all the
same tests that the previous version underwent in order to have confidence that it does indeed work
indentically.

5.4.5   Program Copy

Statement of Problem

"Write a program that asks for two text file names and copies the contents of the first file to the second."

Design and Implementation

This is just a straightforward extension of the previous question. The issue is replacing the code that outputs to the screen with code that outputs to a file. The hard part is to decide whether to extend the version which had all the code in the main method, or whether to work with the version that had multiple methods.

Given the small size of this example program, we are not entirely convinced there is a clear-cut argument one way or the other. In such situations we rely on extendability as the deciding factor. The version with multiple methods may use more resources but, because of the partitioning of responsibility and code amongst the methods, it is arguably more extensible. We therefore choose to extend the multiple method version. This gives us:

```
// A program to copy a text file.
// Written by Graham Roberts, August 1999
// Revision History: none
public class Copy {
  public String getFileName(final String message) {
    KeyboardInput in = new KeyboardInput () ;
    System.out.print(message) ;
    return in.readString() ;
  }
  public void copy(final String source, final String destination) {
    FileInput in = new FileInput (source) ;
    FileOutput out = new FileOutput (destination) ;
    String s = in.readString() ;
    while (!in.eof()) {
      out.writeString(s) ;
      out.writeCharacter('\n') ;
      s = in.readString() ;
    }
    in.close() ;
    out.close() ;
  }
  public static void main(final String[] args) {
    Copy object = new Copy () ;
    String source =
     object.getFileName("Enter source filename: ") ;
    String destination =
     object.getFileName("Enter destination filename: ") ;
    object.copy(source, destination) ;
  }
}
```

Testing

The program can be tested by copying a set of example text files. Many systems provide a utility to compare files (often called `diff` or `comp`) that will make checking the results easier.

Review

Displaying prompts asking the user to type in two file names is not necessarily the ideal way of asking for user input. Sometimes it is better to type the file names on the command line and use the parameters to the main method to give the program the file names, for example:

```
java Copy sourceFile destinationFile
```

This is very much in the UNIX tradition, where considerable use is made of command lines in terminal windows. DOS under Windows also supports this same style of interaction. With other systems, which do not provide command lines, this might be considered an old-fashioned approach to interaction. This would be a short-sighted view.

Given that we are going to extend an extant program, we have an opportunity to make it a more general tool. What we could do is merge the file display program and the copy program together along with an extension to deal with command line parameters. We could extend the problem statement to be something like:

"The program is to be a file copying program that can take zero, one or two command line parameters. If there are two then the program takes these to be names of files and copies the contents of the file whose name is the first parameter to the file whose name is the second parameter. If there is one parameter then the program displays the contents of the file whose name is the parameter to the screen. If there are no parameters then the program will prompt for file names from the user. If the user types a string for the first prompt then this will be the name of the source file. If the user types EOF for the first string then the input will be from the keyboard. If the user types a string for the second name this will be the name of the destination file. If the user types EOF for the second name then output will be to the screen."

Whilst this may sound complicated, extending the previous code to achieve a program that meets the requirement is actually quite easy. It results in:

```
// A program to copy or display a text file.
// Written by Russel Winder & Graham Roberts, September 1999
// Revision History: none
public class Copy2 {
  public String getFileName(final String message) {
    KeyboardInput in = new KeyboardInput () ;
    System.out.print(message) ;
    return in.readString() ;
  }
  public void echo() {
    KeyboardInput in = new KeyboardInput () ;
    String s = in.readString() ;
    while (!s.equals("")) {
      System.out.println(s) ;
      s = in.readString() ;
    }
  }
  public void capture(final String fileName) {
    KeyboardInput in = new KeyboardInput () ;
    FileOutput out = new FileOutput (fileName) ;
    String s = in.readString() ;
    while (!s.equals("")) {
      out.writeString(s) ;
      out.writeCharacter('\n') ;
      s = in.readString() ;
    }
  }
  public void display(final String fileName) {
    FileInput in = new FileInput (fileName) ;
    String s = in.readString() ;
    while (!in.eof()) {
      System.out.println(s) ;
```

```
      s = in.readString() ;
    }
    in.close() ;
  }
  public void copy(final String source, final String destination) {
    FileInput in = new FileInput (source) ;
    FileOutput out = new FileOutput (destination) ;
    String s = in.readString() ;
    while (!in.eof()) {
      out.writeString(s) ;
      out.writeCharacter('\n') ;
      s = in.readString() ;
    }
    in.close() ;
    out.close() ;
  }
  public static void main(final String[] args) {
    Copy2 object = new Copy2 () ;
    switch (args.length) {
    case 0:
      String source =
       object.getFileName("Enter source filename: ") ;
      String destination =
       object.getFileName("Enter destination filename: ") ;
      if (source.equals("")) {
        if (destination.equals("")) {
          object.echo() ;
        } else {
          object.capture(destination) ;
        }
      } else {
        if (destination.equals("")) {
          object.display(source) ;
        } else {
          object.copy(source, destination) ;
        }
      }
      break ;
    case 1:
      object.display(args[0]) ;
      break ;
    case 2:
      object.copy(args[0], args[1]) ;
      break ;
    default:
      System.err.println("Usage: java Copy [<file1> [<file2>]]') ;
      break ;
    }
  }
}
```

Testing this code is fairly straightforward: Exercise all the five different variations of command line parameters and file name input with various different input files.

There is at least one mis-feature in this program — we don't call it a bug since it is known about and is not actually an error, more a "this is the only way we can think of implementing it". This mis-feature is that when entering data from the keyboard we have to type spaces before the newline if we want a blank line in the output. Typing a newline on its own will terminate the input.

Finally, do you feel a sense of unease about this program? We hope you do because we certainly do. The problem we see is that we have four methods, echo, capture, display and copy, all of which are fundamentally the same but because the source and/or destination are of different types we have to have separate methods. Clearly (!) there ought to be some way of parameterizing things so that all four actions can be handled with the same method. In fact, there is but not with the classes we are using here for doing input–output. We must postpone further discussion of this until Chapter 8 where we cover exception handling. We will return to this program there.

5.4.6 Program WordCount

"Write a program that asks for the name of a text file, then counts the number of characters, words and lines in the file, and then displays the results."

Statement of Problem

The challenge here is to identify an algorithm for counting the characters, words and lines. Counting characters and lines is easy, and we will assume that invisible characters such as spaces, tabs and newlines will all be counted as characters. The harder part is deciding what constitutes a word. For our purposes we will define a word as any group of visible characters bounded by non-visible characters, spaces and newlines.

Design and Implementation

A simple algorithm for counting words is to use a boolean flag which is toggled on and off as characters are read from the text file. If the current character is not a visible character then the flag is set to false. If the current character is visible and the flag is false, the flag is set to true and the word count incremented, as a new word has just started. This produces the following program:

```
// A program to count the number of characters,
// words and lines in a text file.
// Written by Graham Roberts, August 1999
// Revision History: none
public class WordCount {
  public String getFileName() {
    KeyboardInput in = new KeyboardInput () ;
    System.out.print("Enter name of file: ") ;
    return in.readString() ;
  }
  public void count(final String fileName) {
    FileInput fileIn = new FileInput (fileName) ;
    int charCount = 0 ;
    int wordCount = 0 ;
    int lineCount = 0 ;
    boolean inWord = false ;
    char c = fileIn.readCharacter() ;
    while (!fileIn.eof()) {
      charCount++ ;
      switch (c) {
      case ' ' :
      case '\t' :
        if (inWord) {
          inWord = false ;
        }
        break ;
      case '\n' :
        if (inWord) {
          inWord = false ;
        }
        lineCount++ ;
        break ;
      default :
        if (!inWord) {
```

```
                inWord = true ;
                wordCount++ ;
            }
          }
          c = fileIn.readCharacter() ;
        }
      System.out.print("\nNumber of characters: ") ;
      System.out.println(charCount) ;
      System.out.print("Number of words: ") ;
      System.out.println(wordCount) ;
      System.out.print("Number of lines: ") ;
      System.out.println(lineCount) ;
    }
    public static void main(final String[] args) {
      WordCount wc = new WordCount () ;
      wc.count(wc.getFileName());
    }
  }
```

Testing   A set of text files should be created with known character, word and line counts, and an empty file should be included. The program should then be tested against these files.

5.4.7   Program GraphFile

In Section 4.5.3, Page 107, we presented a drawing program to draw a graph given a set of data points. The coordinates of the points were included as part of the program which meant that plotting different points required the program to be edited and re-compiled. Here we revisit the program: we implement the obvious modification of reading the data points from a file. This leads to a much more satisfactory solution and eliminates two awkward-looking methods. Here is the new version of the program:

```
// A program to draw a graph with the points
// to be plotted read from a file.
// Written by Graham Roberts, August 1999
// Revision History: A modification of Graph
import java.awt.* ;
import java.awt.geom.* ;
public class GraphFile extends DrawPanel {
  public static void main(final String[] args) {
    DrawFrame frame = new DrawFrame ("Graph2") ;
    GraphFile drawing = new GraphFile (500, 400) ;
    frame.add(drawing) ;
    frame.pack() ;
    frame.centreOnScreen() ;
    frame.setVisible(true) ;
  }
  public GraphFile() {}
  public GraphFile(final int w, final int h) {
    super(w, h) ;
  }
  void drawXaxis(final Graphics2D g2d) {
    Line2D line = new Line2D.Double (50, 350, 450, 350) ;
    g2d.draw(line) ;
    for (int i = 0 ; i < 11 ; ++i) {
      if (i != 0) {
        line.setLine((i*40)+50, 350, (i*40)+50, 355) ;
        g2d.draw(line) ;
      }
      g2d.drawString(new Integer (i*10).toString(), (i*40)+42, 370) ;
    }
```

```
    }
    void drawYaxis(final Graphics2D g2d) {
      Line2D line = new Line2D.Double(50, 350, 50, 70) ;
      g2d.draw(line) ;
      for (int i = 0 ; i < 8 ; ++i) {
        if (i != 0) {
          line.setLine(50,350-(i*40),45,350-(i*40)) ;
          g2d.draw(line) ;
        }
        g2d.drawString(new Integer (i*10).toString(), 24, 355-(i*40)) ;
      }
    }
    // Draw a cross where a point is plotted.
    void plotCross(final Graphics2D g2d, final int x, final int y) {
      Line2D line = new Line2D.Double(x-5, y-5, x+5, y+5) ;
      g2d.draw(line) ;
      line.setLine(x+5, y-5, x-5, y+5) ;
      g2d.draw(line) ;
    }
    // This method reads data points from a file,
    // plots each point and connects points
    // with a line.
    public void plotPoints(final Graphics2D g2d, final String fileName){
      FileInput in = new FileInput (fileName) ;
      int oldx = 50 ;
      int oldy = 350 ;
      while (true) {
        int x = (4 * in.readInteger()) + 50 ;
        if (in.eof())
          return ;
        int y = 350 - (4 * in.readInteger()) ;
        if (in.eof())
          return ;
        plotCross(g2d,x,y) ;
        Line2D line = new Line2D.Double (oldx, oldy, x, y) ;
        g2d.draw(line) ;
        oldx = x ;
        oldy = y ;
      }
    }
    public void paint(final Graphics g) {
      Graphics2D g2d = (Graphics2D)g ;
      drawXaxis(g2d) ;
      drawYaxis(g2d) ;
      plotPoints(g2d, "points.dat") ;
    }
  }
```

The data file (`points.dat`) has one number per line, so that each pair of lines represents a point coordinate. The file used to draw the same graph as seen in Figure 4.18, Page 109, contains the following:

```
10
10
20
35
30
40
40
30
50
35
60
30
70
```

```
40
80
30
90
60
```

Different points can be plotted by loading the file into a normal text editor, changing or adding points and then running the program.

One final note on this program. The file name is made a parameter to `plotPoints`. This means that we could have more than one line plotted on the graph.

5.5   Summary

This chapter has introduced the array which is the basic container supported by Java. The array gives us the ability to store a collection of values and access them all using a single name. The size of an array can be computed, allowing some control over the amount of computer memory used, as well as allowing the number of values stored by a program to vary without having to change the program.

Arrays have some significant limitations, however, particularly if the number of elements stored in an array has to change. Container classes solve these problems by providing more flexible data structures, along with a range of methods providing common operations that would otherwise have to be programmed explicitly if needed. While arrays are an important feature of Java, container classes are more convenient and useful for everyday programming. This is one reason why Part 2 of this book examines container classes in detail.

Data files provide an essential mechanism for storing information outside of a program. Opening, reading or writing, and closing a file, form the core activities of file use. Text-based data files store everything in an easy to use textual format that can be read by people and edited if necessary.

Key points in this chapter:

- An array provides a way of storing a collection of values under a single name.
- Arrays are represented by array objects created using the `new` operator.
- Indexing allows array elements to be accessed.
- Arrays and indexing are supported directly by the Java programming language.
- Arrays are fixed in size and all elements are of the same type.
- Multi-dimensional arrays are constructed using arrays of array objects.
- Container classes, such as `ArrayList`, provide an alternative to using arrays.
- Containers include a range of methods that make insertion and removal of elements straightforward.
- Data files allow data to be stored outside of a program, so that the data has a lifetime considerably longer than the execution time of any program.

- Simple data files use a textual representation for all data.
- A file needs to be opened, read from or written to, and then closed.

Self-review Questions

Self-review 5.1 Which of the following are valid array declarations?
```
int x = new int[10] ;
int[][] = new int[][10] ;
double   []d = new double[10] ;
char[] s = "Hello" ;
```

Self-review 5.2 What is array bounds checking?

Self-review 5.3 What is the maximum index than can be used with an array of size 7?

Self-review 5.4 How is a 3D array represented in terms of array objects?

Self-review 5.5 Which of these are valid array indexing expressions for an array of size 10?
```
n[2.5]
n[0]
n[3-7]
n[2*3]
n[n[1]]
```

Self-review 5.6 When is it an advantage to use an `ArrayList` rather than an array?

Self-review 5.7 Explain how array parameters work. What happens if an element of an array passed as a parameter to a method is changed by assignment? Do `ArrayLists` behave the same or differently?

Self-review 5.8 What do opening and closing a file do?

Self-review 5.9 How does `eof` work?

Programming Exercises

Exercise 5.1 Write a program to read in 10 integers and store them in an array. Then display the contents of the array.

Exercise 5.2 Write a program to read in a sequence of integers until 'stop' is entered. Store the integers in an array. Then display the average of the numbers entered.

Exercise 5.3 Repeat Exercise 5.2 but use an `ArrayList` instead of an array.

Exercise 5.4 A matrix can be represented using a 2D array. Write methods to perform matrix addition, subtraction and multiplication. Each method should take two 2D arrays as an argument and return a new 2D array containing the result. Use the methods in a test program to verify that they work correctly.

Exercise 5.5 Re-write program `AddUpColumns` in Section 5.2.8, Page 122, to use `ArrayLists` instead of arrays.

Exercise 5.6 Re-write program `DisplayTextFile` to read and display strings instead of characters.

Exercise 5.7 Write a program to find the largest sized array you can use on your computer system.

Exercise 5.8 Create a program that writes a data file containing 1000 random integers between 1 and 25. Use the J2SDK class `Random` to create random numbers, or implement your own random number algorithm. Then write a second program that reads the integers from the file and counts how many of each integer is in the file.

Exercise 5.9 Using the data file created in the last question, write a drawing program that plots a bar chart showing how many of each integer between 1 and 25 appears in the file.

Exercise 5.10 Write a method that takes two character array arguments and returns true if the sequence of characters stored in the second array is a sub-sequence of those characters stored in the first array.

Exercise 5.11 Write a method that takes two character array parameters and returns true if both arrays contain the same characters but not necessarily in the same order.

Exercise 5.12 Write a program that reads a text file and counts the number of times a selected word appears in the file.

Exercise 5.13 Write a program that reads a text file containing Java source code and verifies that there is a matching number of opening and closing braces (curly brackets). Beware of braces appearing in comments, or in character and constants.

Challenges

Challenge 5.1 Write a program that sorts an array of integers into ascending order. Include a sort method that you write yourself, rather than using one from the J2SDK.

Challenge 5.2 Write a program to act as a simple address book, storing names and addresses in a data file.

Challenge 5.3 Write a program that reads a text file and builds an `ArrayList` containing each distinct word found in the file, in sorted order, along with a count of how many times each word appears.

Classes and Objects

Objectives

Java is an object-oriented programming language, and is used to create programs consisting of collections of interacting objects. Each kind of object used by a program is defined by a class and it is the programmer's job to identify and create the classes required. This chapter examines what classes and objects are, and how they are created.

Keywords

abstract data type

call-by-value

class

class type

constructor

instance

object

overload

public

private

reference

this

6.1   Introduction

Until now we have mostly been working with features such as selection, iteration, variables, scope, lifetime and methods, to give our programs structure. Classes and objects have been used but not explained in detail. This chapter, and indeed the rest of this part of the book, will focus on creating and using classes and objects — essentially how to go about object-oriented programming.

Well designed and properly written Java programs of any size demand that a fully object-oriented approach is taken. The strengths of object-oriented development lie in being able to design and build programs reliably, provide much better support for maintenance and extension of working programs, and being able to reuse large sections of design and code across a number of programs.

To understand the basis of object-oriented programming, various concepts need to be introduced, including: abstract data type (ADT), object, class and instantiation. In the following sections we will work through these concepts to see how they work, and provide an understanding of why they matter.

6.2   Creating New Data Types

In the history of programming language development, the concept of ADT is an important milestone on the path leading to object-oriented programming. Once the principles of procedures, variables, lifetime and scope were established in procedural languages, the desire to exploit ADTs led to the investigation of the next level of program structure.

An ADT specifies a new data type by defining the values that belong to the type and the operations that can be performed on those values. An implementation of the type specified by an ADT can be created using variables to provide a representation of the ADT values, and procedures to implement the operations. Using only these tools, however, requires the programmer to do all the hard work. Obviously, it is better if the programming language provides direct support for representing types described by an ADT and that the compiler provide support for checking proper use of the types. Following this line of reasoning, along with the belief that types and type checking are essential for reliable program development, led to the development of programming languages supporting the creation of new types, and then on to object-oriented programming languages.

note

Stacks are sometimes described using the term 'last in – first out' or LIFO; the effect is the same as FILO.

To explore the implementation of new types using an object-oriented approach, we will make use of an example, that of a *stack*. A stack is a collection of data values that is managed in a particular way: a stack is a container of values implementing a 'first in – last out' (FILO) access policy. To envisage what is meant here, consider manipulating a pile of plates. New plates are added to the pile by placing (or *pushing* in stack-speak) them on top of the pile. Plates are removed (or *popped*) by picking up the plate that is on top of the pile. You might argue that you can always add or remove plates from anywhere in the pile, and whilst this is possible for the strong, this is not the way the stack is meant to be used. In a stack, only the plate at the top of the pile can be manipulated directly. In some canteens, plates are held in 'stackers', spring-loaded containers of plates in which the access policy really is first in – last out; the stacker really does implement and enforce a stack since there is no access to any other than the top plate.

A stack of data items in a program behaves in a fairly similar way to a stack of plates. To implement a stack we need:

- a method to *push* a value onto the stack;

- a method to *pop* a value off the stack;

- a method to return the value at the *top* of the stack;

- a method to test if the stack *is empty*; and

- a container (aka *data structure*) to hold the data.

The first four of these implement the behaviour of the stack. The fifth item, a data structure, provides a representation for the value or state of the stack. However, trying to program the representation using variables raises a serious issue. If we only have local and parameter variables we quickly discover that trying to use either is pointless, as these variables would only be in scope while a stack method was being executed; the lifetime of the variables we need must outlast the lifetime of any method scope, otherwise there is no way of maintaining the state of a stack. Given this, we have to conclude that the variables forming the stack data structure need to be declared *outside* the scope of any of the methods, while still allowing the statements within the methods access. Further, the variables need a lifetime that lasts at least as long as the stack is needed, regardless of what stack methods are called.

Variables declared outside the scope of a method might be labelled *global variables*, meaning that they are accessible from any statement within a program and have a lifetime that lasts as long as the program runs. The combination of global variables and the stack methods would allow a stack to be used within a program. However, let's consider the implications of such an arrangement:

- Without a finer grain of control, any statement in any method in a program, not just those to do with stacks, could modify the stack data variables, possibly in a way that violates the way a stack is supposed to be used.

- The collection of methods defined to manipulate the stack cannot be grouped together into a coherent unit that enforces proper stack usage. We should be able to state that the only operations allowed on a stack are `push`, `pop`, `top` and `isEmpty`. However, to do this we need support from the programming language syntax and rules, and the programmer should be prevented from arbitrarily adding new operations — we need to define a type.

- The programmer has to do *all* the work of making sure any stack is used properly.

ref

Constructing robust production code for stacks will be covered in Section 14.8, Page 438.

These points are essentially saying that we have not properly encapsulated the stack abstraction. The conclusion is that we need some new program structuring concepts supported by programming language syntax and semantics.

6.2.1   A Stack Object

To overcome the difficulties listed in the last section, we need to group all the components of the stack (methods and variables) into a single unit — such a unit is called an *object*. An object is an entity which has both variables and methods, the management of which is supported directly by an object-oriented programming language. The collection of variables comprise the state of the object and the methods are the mechanisms for accessing or changing the state of the object.

Simply collecting things together into an object is not enough. The state of the object must be protected. Other parts of the program must be prevented from accessing the data variables and changing them in any way. To protect the contents of the object we must enforce encapsulation. Variables or methods inside the object must be accessible or callable only if the object gives permission. This idea is similar to that of scope but applied to an object rather than a method.

By enforcing encapsulation we can say that an object has an *interface*, which specifies the access properties of the variables and methods in the object:

- *Public* variables or methods can be accessed from outside the object.
- *Private* variables or methods cannot be accessed from outside.

This gives us the basis of what we need to implement a single stack object with full encapsulation. Providing the programming language allows us to express these features, we could write the program code and create an object implementation of the stack abstraction. However, while this is a good start, there are still limitations.

6.2.2   A Stack Class

What if we want two stacks? Or ten stacks? To have more than one stack, we need a separate data structure for each one. For any stack object, the variables for just one stack come built in, so creating another stack implies creating a new object. It is clear that we need a mechanism for creating a number of objects that have the same methods but different data. We need a template for creating objects which defines how stack objects are constructed. Using such a template, we can create as many stack objects as required, each with a different *identity* and holding different data yet *sharing* the same method code and variable declarations — since these are the same for all stacks.

ref

Chapter 30, Page 833.

Such a template is known as a *class*: a stack class declares the methods needed by stack objects and the set of variables that need to be stored inside each stack object. A process called *instantiation* creates stack objects using the description in the stack class, and once created each object has its own separate identity.

Java directly and fully supports classes, allowing new classes to be declared as required. Indeed, all of the example programs presented in earlier chapters are actually class declarations, but until now we have not used them from an object-oriented perspective.

The following is an outline *class declaration* of a stack of `ints` class — parts of the declaration are elided in order to focus on the structure:

```
class IntStack {
    // The stack public methods.
    public void push(int) { ... }
    public void pop() { ... }
    public int top() { ... }
    public boolean isEmpty() { ... }

    // The private data structure used to store the stack elements
    private ... // One or more variable declarations
    ...
}
```

note

The source code for class `IntStack` *should be saved in a file called* `IntStack.java`, *and compiled to create* `IntStack.class`.

Looking at this, we first see the words `class IntStack`, indicating that what follows is a class declaration that will enable instantiation of stack objects. The class body is bracketed by braces and contains four method declarations and one or more variable declarations. The variable declarations are within the class declaration but outside of any of the method bodies.

A stack object instantiated using the class is referred to as an '*instance object*' or '*class instance*', as it is an instance of the stack class. The methods are properly called *instance methods*, as they are methods than can be called for instance objects. Similarly, the variables are *instance variables*, as each instance object gets its own set of the variables. An instance object can only be an instance of one class: it is not possible to create an object by instantiating bits of several classes.

tip

Multi-word method names, like `isEmpty`, *are constructed by joining together the words and capitalizing the first letter of the second and subsequent words.*

The class body defines the *class scope*, so that anything declared within the body is within the class scope. The encapsulation of instance objects follows from the class scope, with everything declared within the class being 'inside', or part of, an instance object. Every method or variable is explicitly labelled as public or private, using the keywords of the same name. Public methods can be called from outside the class scope, by any statement elsewhere in a program, and together form the *public method interface*, or just *public interface*, of the class and its objects. Private methods, sometimes called *helper methods*, can be called only from methods within the same class scope.

The instance variables are accessible from statements within the instance method bodies and have a lifetime the same as that as the object. This solves the problem of providing variables accessible to a collection of methods, while at the same time limiting their scope to that of a single class. Instance variables are usually declared as private, as they should only be accessed by statements within the same class scope. While instance variables can be declared public, and therefore accessible from outside the class scope, this is almost always a sign of a serious design flaw in your program, so should not be done.

tip

Instance variables should never be public.

6.2.3 A Java Stack Class – Version 1

We now have enough information to actually write a basic but fully functional stack class in Java:

```java
// A basic stack of ints class.
// Written by Graham Roberts, August 1999
// Revision History: none
public class IntStack {
  // The data structure is an array and stores the values
  // pushed onto the stack. An int variable holds
  // the index of the element at the top of the stack
  // (or -1 if the stack is empty).
  private int[] elements = new int[100] ;
  private int top = -1 ;
  public void push(final int n) {
    ++top ;
    elements[top] = n ;
  }
  public void pop() {
    --top ;
  }
  public int top() {
    return elements[top] ;
  }
  public boolean isEmpty() {
    return top >= 0 ;
  }
  public static void main(final String[] args) {
    IntStack s = new IntStack () ;
    s.push(1) ;
    s.push(2) ;
    s.push(3) ;
    s.push(4) ;
    System.out.println("Top of stack is: " + s.top()) ;
    s.pop() ;
    System.out.println("Top of stack is now: " + s.top()) ;
    while (!s.isEmpty()) {
      s.pop() ;
    }
    System.out.println("Stack is " +
                        (s.isEmpty() ? "" : "not ") +
                        "empty.") ;
  }
}
```

Follow the Java class, method and variable naming conventions, and use them consistently.

By convention all class names in Java start with a capital letter, so this class is deliberately named `IntStack` rather than `intstack`. Method and variable names, on the other hand, follow the convention of starting with a lower case letter. Some people go further and follow a convention that instance variables names start with an underscore, followed by the name starting with a lower case letter (for example, `_top` and `_elements`). The aim here is to make instance variables stand out from local and parameter variables.

The class includes a `main` method providing testing of objects of the class. As the main method is local to the class scope, all classes can have one without there being any name clashing. This `main` here is just the beginnings of a proper *unit test* and this is what most `main` methods will be for. Of course there will be one `main` method that is the start of the application; each application needs to provide an actual starting point for execution of the program as a whole.

Always give all your classes a main method to provide for unit testing.

`IntStack` objects are created with the, now familiar, `new` operator:

```java
IntStack s = new IntStack () ;
```

The stack object will be created with its two instance variables (`elements` and `top`) initialized to the values specified with their declarations. As `elements` is an array we must make sure that the array object gets created, and the best place to do that is by directly initializing the variable when declared. A new stack object represents an empty stack and is ready to use by calling its methods, for example:

```
s.push(1) ;
s.pop() ;
int i = s.top() ;
if (s.isEmpty()) { ... }
```

Encapsulation prevents misuse of the stack object. Statements outside of the scope of the class are prevented from accessing any private instance variables. For example, the statement:

```
s.elements[1] = 2 ; // ERROR
```

would cause the Java compiler to issue an error message and force the programmer to fix the problem. The statement:

```
s.f() ;
```

would also cause the Java compiler to report an error, as the method `f` is not declared in the `IntStack` class. The same would happen if `IntStack` did include a method `f` but it was declared `private`.

This version of class `IntStack` is useable but limited. First of all, it can only be used to store values of type `int`. Secondly, it provides no runtime checking against misuse of stack objects, so it is possible to either push too many values on or pop too many off. Ways to deal with these issues and implement a better version of a stack class will be covered in later chapters — see Chapter 14, Page 407.

tip

Name your class to make its role clear.

6.3 The Relationship Between Classes and Types

Declaring a class `IntStack` allowed us to declare a variable of type `IntStack`. What is the relationship between a class and a type? Is a class a type? These are questions which are the subject of debate but the consensus is now that classes and types are distinct but intimately related concepts.

To explore the relationship between classes and types, we can look in more detail at the idea of *abstract data type* (ADT). An ADT, as the name implies, provides an abstract description of a type. By abstract we mean that it describes the properties of the type but does not say anything about how it might be represented or implemented.

A Stack ADT specification can be written as follows:

```
Name: Stack <elementType>

Operations: create -> Stack
            push(Stack,elementType) -> Stack
            pop(Stack)-> Stack
            top(Stack)-> elementType
            isEmpty(Stack)-> boolean
```

```
Axioms:        forall S : Stack and i : elementType
               isEmpty(create) = true
               isEmpty(push(S,i)) = false
               top(create) = error
               top(push(S,i)) = i
               pop(create) = error
                   pop(push(S,i)) = S
```

The ADT is presented in the form of an algebraic specification which is based on a formal (mathematically well defined) notation and reasoning system. The first line names the type and also shows that there is a *type parameter* denoted by `elementType`. `elementType` is the type of the values stored in the stack. `Stack<int>` would instantiate the parameter to define a stack of integers, with the type `int` substituted wherever `elementType` appears. Hence, the stack ADT is actually a generator of useful stack types.

The next section of the ADT, labelled Operations, lists the operations that are applicable to values of the `Stack` ADT. As well as the `push`, `pop`, `top` and `isEmpty` operations there is also a stack creation operation, needed to provide for the correct initialization of new stack values. We use the name operation rather than method, as a method is the implementation of an operation using a programming language, and is not part of an ADT.

The final section of the ADT presents a set of axioms which define how values of the `Stack` type behave when the operations are applied to them. Notice that nothing appears about how the operations might be implemented, just what they do to in terms of operations and values. The axioms of the abstract data type determine how the operations behave with respect to each other, there is no specification of how data is stored or manipulated.

Given an ADT, it is possible to write a Java class that meets the specification presented by the ADT, which is what the `IntStack` class in Section 6.2.3 more or less does. The ADT operations are implemented as public methods, while private variables provide a representation for stack values. Additional private methods, if any are needed, can be added to assist in the implementation of public methods.

note

A class defines an implementation and declares a new type.

Although Java provides no mechanism for declaring ADTs *per se*, a class declaration does declare a new type. The type name is the same as the class name and once the name has been defined it can be used to declare variables of that type. We can also use terms like '*class type*' to denote a type that has been defined using a class and can talk about a variable having a class type.

As classes let the programmer define new types, in addition to those built-in to the Java programming language, we can also say that a class allows for *user defined types*. Writing a class bundles together the act of creating a new type with creating a representation for values of that type and providing methods implementing the operations. We must, however, keep the distinction between class and type in mind as it will become important later on. In particular, we will see the idea of objects *conforming* to different types, while still being an instance of only one class.

Types are an important resource for programmers, as they are used for type checking to support ensuring the correctness of a program when it is compiled and, in some cases, also when it is running. In particular, Java compilers use types to enforce encapsulation and to make sure that objects of a given class are only used in the ways permitted by the associated type.

6.4 Method Names and Scope

A typical Java program will make use of a number of classes, some of which will be declared by the programmer, others of which will come from the J2SDK class libraries. Some thought needs to be given to the method names used in all these classes and how they all co-exist.

We have already learnt that different variables can have the same name, providing they are declared in different, disjoint, scopes. This avoids every variable in a program having to have a unique name, and explains why the same variable name can appear in different methods. The same principle applies to method names in class scope. This means that the same method names can be re-used in different classes but because they are declared in different scopes, they can happily co-exist within a single program.

If several classes each declare a method called `pop`, and a method call is made using the expression `obj.pop()`, then the version of `pop` executed is determined by the class of the object the method is called for. As the object can only be of one class, this always identifies exactly which version of `pop` is to be called.

Although method names can be reused in different classes, the most important thing to remember is that a method name should always act as a concise description of what the method does. It is far easier to read source code if the method names make clear what a method call is for. So, while `push` and `pop` are good method names to use with stacks, more cryptic names such as `f` and `g` are not.

6.4.1 Overloading Methods

In Section 3.6.2, Page 72, we stated that names should be unique within a given scope. This is certainly true for variable names but is not quite true for method names. It remains true that all variables and methods must be uniquely identifiable but methods, unlike variables, are not identified by their name alone. A method identifier is actually a combination of both the name and the number and type of the parameters and is usually known as the *method signature*. This means that there can be two or more methods with the same name but different signatures within the same scope. This ability to have two or more methods with the same name but different parameter numbers and/or types is termed *overloading*, and we call the methods involved *overloaded methods*. The return type is not taken into account, so overloaded methods can return values of different types. The ability to overload methods is important since it allows us to provide different implementations for a method depending on the types of the arguments supplied. This is a form of *polymorphism*, an

ref

Section 30.2.5, Page 840.

note

Polymorphism is the ability of one thing to have several forms, or one form to apply to several things.

important programming mechanism that reduces the dependencies, or coupling, between units of code.

The following class illustrates the use of overloaded methods. An object of the class generates formatted strings to represent data in a format suitable for some other program to process. By putting all the formatting information into one class, it avoids distributing code for doing the formatting around the rest of the program. If the formatting needs to change then only the code in this class needs to be modified, with the rest of the program continuing to use its public methods without having to be edited.

```java
// A class to demonstrate overloading.
// Written by Graham Roberts, September 1999
// Revision History: none
public class Format {
  private StringBuffer buffer = new StringBuffer () ;
  public void add(final int i) {
    buffer.append("I" + i + " ") ;
  }
  public void add(final double d) {
    buffer.append("R" + d + " ") ;
  }
  public void add(final char c) {
    buffer.append(c) ;
  }
  public void add(final String s) {
    buffer.append(s) ;
  }
  public void add(final double a, final double b) {
    add(a) ;
    add("OP ") ;
    add(b) ;
  }
  public String toString() {
    return buffer.toString() ;
  }
  public static void main(final String[] args) {
    Format formatter = new Format () ;
    formatter.add("DATASET\n") ;
    formatter.add(1) ;
    formatter.add(2.3) ;
    formatter.add(9.8,4.5) ;
    formatter.add("\nEND") ;
    System.out.println(formatter.toString()) ;
  }
}
```

!

By convention classes implement a toString *method, to return a string representation of the current value of an instance object.*

The class includes five overloaded add methods, each (necessarily) taking different parameters. The main method illustrates how an object of the class might be used. The version of add to execute is determined by looking at the types and number of parameters in each method call. Each method appends formatted data to a string stored in a StringBuffer instance variable. Once the complete set of data has been formatted, the final string is retrieved using the toString method.

The add method that takes two float arguments makes three more method calls to other overloads of add. This kind of strategy is quite common, as it avoids duplicating code and allows an overloaded method to act as a parameter type converter for calls to one of the other overloads of the method.

In fact, this strategy is often taken further so that one of the overloaded methods does all the real work, while all the other overloads call it. The major advantage of doing this is that code that manipulates the object state or does other important work can all be put into a single method. This localizes knowledge of particular actions or data structures to the minimum scope. With a small amount of rearrangement the format class can implement this strategy:

```
// A class to demonstrate overloading.
// Written by Graham Roberts, September 1999
// Revision History: none
public class Format {
  private StringBuffer buffer = new StringBuffer () ;
  public void add(final String s) {
    buffer.append(s) ;
  }
  public void add(final int i) {
    add("I" + i + " ") ;
  }
  public void add(final double d) {
    add("R" + d + " ") ;
  }
  public void add(final char c) {
    add(new String("c")) ;
  }
  public void add(final double a, final double b) {
    add(a) ;
    add("OP ") ;
    add(b) ;
  }
  public String toString() {
    return buffer.toString() ;
  }
  public static void main(final String[] args) {
    Format formatter = new Format () ;
    formatter.add("DATASET\n") ;
    formatter.add(1) ;
    formatter.add(2.3) ;
    formatter.add(9.8,4.5) ;
    formatter.add("\nEND") ;
    System.out.println(formatter.toString()) ;
  }
}
```

Now only add(final String s) manipulates the string being constructed. If a future version of the class replaces the StringBuffer instance variable with some other data structure then the number of methods to modify has been minimized.

6.5 Object Initialization

We have already seen that the proper initialization of variables is very important and the rules of the Java language insist that it is done properly. The initialization of objects is of equal importance; once created an object must be initialized to a known and valid state. The Java system ensures that all an object's instance variables get initialized but the programmer is responsible for making sure that the initial state of the object is valid with respect to the intended purpose of the object. This section looks at what happens when objects are created and how they should be properly initialized.

Creating a new object is actually a multi-stage process, triggered by the use of the `new` operator. First of all, memory has to be allocated for the object to use but this is taken care of by the Java run-time system and is not under the control of the programmer. Secondly, the new object has to be initialized. In particular, all the instance variables of the new object have to be set to some known value and there may also be other necessary activities to make the object usable, such as opening a file. The initialization activity is controlled by the programmer using three mechanisms:

- Direct instance variable initialization, as we saw in the `Format` class earlier, i.e. the declaration of the `StringBuffer` variable called `buffer`.
- Special methods called *constructor methods* or, more usually, *constructors*, which are guaranteed to be called when an object is created.
- Instance initializers, to allow instance variables to be initialized using a block of code.

6.5.1 Direct Instance Variable Initialization

Instance variables can be initialized directly using the familiar variable initialization expression:

```
class StackUser {
  private Stack s = new Stack () ;
  ...
}
```

This is the same idea as variable initialization first seen in Section 2.5.4, Page 29. Any instance variable declared with an initialization expression will be initialized immediately after a new object is created. The limitation of this kind of initialization is that only a single expression can be used to provide the initial value, and that expression cannot make use of any variables that are not yet initialized. So, for example, it is possible to do this:

```
class Test {
  private int n = 10 ;
  private int x = n * 10 ;
  ...
}
```

as initialization takes place in the order of variable declarations: in the order shown, the variable n is already initialized when it is used in the expression that calculates the value which initialized x. Reversing the order of the declarations would cause a compilation error since then the variable n would not be declared when it is used to calculate the initial value of x.

An instance variable can be declared without being explicitly initialized, in which case default initialization will take place automatically. For numerical types and `char` the variable will be default initialized to 0 or 0.0, for boolean to `false` and for class types to the special value `null` (see Section 6.6.4, Page 164). Once initialized by default, a variable can be used without having to be explicitly initialized or assigned to. It should be noted that this behaviour is in contrast to that of local variables which must always be explicitly initialized or assigned to before being used.

tip

Always initialize all variables unless it is provably not sensible.

6.5.2   Constructors

A constructor is declared within a class like any other method but has the specific purpose of being responsible for initializing the state of a new object. Statements in the method body can assign suitable values to instance variables, create other objects, open files, and do any other operation needed. When a constructor terminates, the object should be in a valid state and ready to use.

ref

Section 30.2.7, Page 845.

A constructor is subject to special rules, the most significant being that the name of the constructor is the *same* as the name of the class. For example, if we add a constructor to the `Stack` class it would be named `Stack`:

```
class Stack {
  Stack() {
    // Method body
  }
  ...
}
```

Constructors can have parameters, like any other method, and can also be overloaded. However, unlike ordinary methods, constructors do not return a result and do not have a return type, not even `void`. A constructor that has no parameters (i.e. has an empty parameter list) is called a *default constructor*.

!

Constructors are very special but they are just methods.

In a statement such as:

```
String s = new String ("Hello") ;
```

the sub-expression `String ("Hello")` serves two purposes. First, `String` identifies the class of the new object to create and, secondly, the parameter list identifies which constructor to call once the object is in existence. A constructor with a matching parameter list must have been declared in the class, otherwise the compiler will report an error. Where a class declares multiple constructors, the parameter list is used to select which one to call using the usual rules for selecting between overloaded methods, i.e. by signature not just by name. Before a constructor is called, any instance variables within the new object that have direct initialization expressions are initialized. The use of parameters in the constructor call gives the user of a class a chance to pass in values to the initialization process and gain some control over the initial state of the object.

A call to a constructor automatically takes place as part of the evaluation of any `new` expression; whenever an object is created a constructor is called. Consider the following:

```
ArrayList a = new ArrayList () ; // Use the default constructor
```

the empty constructor parameter list means that there is a call to the default constructor. As noted earlier, if the class being instantiated does not declare the constructor implied by the parameter list of the `new` expression, it is an error. If the class defines no constructors then the Java system creates a default constructor (with an empty body) so that the rule that a constructor is always called can be guaranteed.

A call to a constructor is thus an integral and unavoidable part of the `new` operation, offering a guarantee that any newly created object will be left in a well-defined state — an important principle if properly behaved programs are to be created.

A constructor body can contain any statements needed to do its work, except for return statements returning a value. Of course, care must be taken in the constructor body not to use any instance variables, or to call other instance methods that use instance variables, before the variables have been initialized or assigned a value.

The ability to overload constructors allows an object to be initialized in different ways using different parameters. For example, the `Stack` class could define two constructors, one with no parameters providing a default initialization, and the second being a constructor taking a single `int` parameter which could perhaps create a `Stack` object with a specific storage capacity:

```
class Stack {
  Stack() { ... }
  Stack(int n) { ... }
  ...
}
...
Stack s = new Stack () ; // Stack storing default number of values
Stack s = new Stack (10) ; // Stack storing a maximum of 10 values
```

6.5.3   Instance Initializers

So far we have seen direct variable initialization and we have indicated how constructors can be used to support the initialization of objects. Although it is most frequently the case that we initialize an instance variable with a single expression, and can use direct variable initialization for this, sometimes we need a statement sequence for the initialization. Clearly, we could put this sequence in a constructor but Java provides another mechanism, the *instance initializer block*, which allows the initialization code to be located with the declaration rather than being in a constructor separated from the declaration. An instance initializer associates a block of code directly with a single instance variable. The block, which is simply a compound statement, follows directly after the declaration of the variable. For example, if we have an instance variable of type `Stack` that needs to be initialized to refer to a stack object containing a particular set of values, then we could write:

```
class StackUser {
  ...
  private Stack s ; {
    s = new Stack () ;
    s.push(1) ;
    s.push(2) ;
    s.push(3) ;
  }
  ...
}
```

When a class containing an instance variable which has an instance initializer is instantiated, the instance initializer code is executed to initialize the instance variable immediately before the constructor is called. Like constructor calls, the execution of instance initializers is guaranteed to happen. The initializer block can contain any statements needed to do the initialization providing other instance variables used have already been initialized. Where there are instance initializers for several instance variables, they are executed in the order they appear in the class declaration.

6.5.4 Choosing Between the Alternatives

Object initialization is primarily concerned with ensuring that all of an object's instance variables are given an appropriate initial value. Of course in doing so, other resources may be obtained such as disk files or network connections. The set of instance variables represent the object's state and it is important that the initial state is valid so that any method called on the object can rely on that state. However, the programmer has a choice of three different ways to initialize an instance variable. How should the choice be made?

There are two main arguments that could be put forward: initialize each variable as close as possible to where it is declared or put all initialization in the same place in the constructor. In practice, both of these have merit but neither are really sufficient.

Constructors are an important part of the initialization behaviour and are the only place where initialization parameterization can be handled, giving the user of a class some control over what initialization is done. In addition, constructors provide the proper location for initialization code that is not directly connected with giving an instance variable an initial value. Hence, constructors are required and could be argued to provide a convenient location to group together all the initialization for an object.

Instance initializers and standard variable initialization (together providing direct initialization) have the advantage of locating the code doing the initialization immediately after the variable declaration. This means that it is possible to see and check that an instance variable is properly initialized, without having to search elsewhere for the initialization code — this is a potentially valuable weapon in the *defensive programming* armoury. Note, though, that whilst instance initializers can have any code, they should not be used to do anything other than initialization of the instance variable with which they are associated.

So what approach is to be recommended? The key issue is actually to define a coding standard that everyone in your programming group knows and uses. In this way you will know what to expect when you are reviewing source code and hence avoid surprises (another aspect of defensive programming). In most cases, the coding standard will be a compromise between constructors and direct initialization: use direct initialization where possible and put everything else into the constructor. If an instance variable is not directly initialized then add a comment saying where it is initialized.

6.6 Object References

We are familiar with the idea that variables act as containers holding representations of values. Until now, we haven't looked at how this principle applies to objects, although that hasn't stopped us

note

Instance initializers are executed in the order they appear in the file.

note

Defensive programming is an approach to programming centred around not allowing errors in the features provided rather than the more optimistic strategy of simply providing features.

making use of objects. While objects represent values, they are not stored directly in variables. Instead, a variable of class type holds a *reference* to an object.

A reference is like an arrow or *pointer* that points to an object:

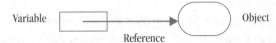

Variables (including parameter variables) of class type therefore hold as their representation a reference to an object that is stored elsewhere. The type of the variable indicates what *type* of object it can reference; a variable of type `Stack` can only reference objects of *type* `Stack`. Notice that we explain references in terms of object types, and refer to type `Stack` rather than class `Stack`, when stating what kind of object a reference can refer to. This is very deliberate, as objects can have, or *conform to*, multiple types, so the object referred to by a reference variable of type `Stack` may not be an instance of class `Stack`. The next chapter will explore this important idea further.

As arrays are represented by objects, we can now state that variables of array type are actually object references. In turn, an array of objects, such as an array of strings, is represented by an array object holding object references. Similarly, an array of arrays requires an array object holding an array of array references.

Objects are always accessed via references, regardless of what expression is being evaluated. Much of the time this is fairly transparent, so the example programs using objects presented so far have worked as expected, although behind the scenes object references are being manipulated. However, references do require extra thought for some operations such as assignment and parameter passing, as we shall see below and in Section 6.6.3, Page 162.

Assignment to a reference variable means that the current reference is replaced by another reference to an object of the same type. This has two potentially important consequences: firstly, one object may become referenced by two or more variables; secondly, an object can be left with no references referring to it. When an object has no references it can be thrown away as it is inaccessible. Section 6.6.1 explores this further.

An object with multiple references to it is said to be *shared*. References to an object can be created using assignment, initialization, parameter passing and other mechanisms, so a number of variables scattered throughout a program can refer to the same object. In itself this is not necessarily a bad thing, and it would be hard to write useful programs without this happening. However, there is a risk that one part of a program will change an object in a way that causes another part of the program to fail; the state of the object changes in a way that some part of the program cannot deal with.

It is up to the programmer to prevent this kind of situation from occurring by using good development practice, including rigorous checking and testing. This can be helped by designing classes correctly in the first place, so they are harder to misuse and prevent instance objects getting into invalid states.

note

References are called references rather than pointers as the term pointer has a long history of use in other programming languages, along with a lot of semantic baggage that does not apply to Java. Nonetheless, references are really pointers.

note

Objects can only be an instance of one class, but can conform to several types. An object conforms to a type when it has all the methods corresponding to the operations specified by the type, and those methods implement the correct behaviour.

An interesting consequence of object references is that the lifetime of a variable of class type is distinct from the lifetime of any objects it may reference. For example, a local or parameter reference variable can go out of scope without the object it is referencing also being destroyed, as that object can be referenced by other variables elsewhere. All we can say is that an object must be in existence if it is referenced by a variable, but once the variable goes out of scope or is assigned to, the continued existence of the object depends upon what other references to it exist.

6.6.1 Removing Old Objects

Once an object is no longer needed it can be removed and the memory space it was occupying reclaimed. An object is considered to be no longer needed when there are no variables holding references to it — the object becomes *unreachable*. At that point the Java run-time system is free to dispose of the object as and when it sees fit. This process is called *garbage collection*, and is done automatically without the programmer needing to do anything explicitly. Garbage collection may occur periodically while a program is running but there are no guarantees as to when it will occur, so unreachable objects can remain in memory for an unpredictable period of time. For small programs the garbage collector may never run.

Often it is possible for an object to be garbage collected without having to worry about what happens to the values held by the instance variables. If an instance variable references another object, that object will automatically be garbage collected if nothing else refers to it. However, to allow the programmer some control over how an object is removed, a method called `finalize` can be declared in the object's class, and will be called just before the object is removed from memory by the garbage collector.

Typically, the `finalize` method does all the work needed to free resources held by an object that won't be managed properly by the garbage collector. For instance, it might arrange to properly close a network connection or make sure that data held by an object is safely written to a file and not lost. `finalize` is just an ordinary instance method, and is not subject to special rules, except for the fact that the method with the signature:

```
public void finalize() ;
```

is called automatically by the garbage collector when the object is being garbage collected.

One final point to note regarding automatic garbage collection is that the default behaviour of any Java program when it terminates is *not* to perform garbage collection and not to call any outstanding `finalize` methods. This behaviour cannot be changed. However, the ability to ensure all objects are properly terminated is so important that there is a method to support the behaviour: `System.runFinalization`. This method essentially forces the calling of all pending `finalize` methods.

Garbage collection generally makes life easier for programmers as there is no need to explicitly determine when to remove unwanted objects and perform what is termed *memory management*. The Java runtime system does the work instead. The penalty for having garbage collection is a small

tip

The programmer can force garbage collection to take place by calling `System.gc()` *or* `Runtime.gc()`.

overhead when programs are running since garbage collection uses machine resources when it runs. However, experience shows that, most of the time, the advantages of automatic garbage collection easily outweigh any disadvantages.

6.6.2 Objects and Primitive Types

If variables store references to objects there are two more questions to answer:

> Where are objects stored?
>
> What is the difference between objects and primitive values?

Objects are stored in an area called the *heap*. The heap is a pool of memory which can be allocated in small units for use by objects. The Java runtime system manages this area of memory automatically, so programmers rarely, if ever, have to be concerned with it. Programmers can instead focus their concerns on objects as abstractions, and not be concerned with how those abstractions are implemented on the computer.

Apart from class objects, we have seen and used variables of the primitive types `boolean`, `char`, `byte`, `long`, `float` and `double`. We have stated already that representations of these types are stored directly in variables, and this is still a true statement. Java effectively supports two kinds of variable: variables of class type store a representation that is a reference to an object; and variables of primitive types that store a representation of the type directly. Non-object values are referred to as *primitive* as they use representations directly determined by computer hardware, not by objects. Primitive types are the basic building blocks and are not constructed from other types, while objects are directly or indirectly built entirely from primitive types and object references.

The advantage in having primitive types is efficiency. Primitive types are less expensive both in terms of memory and speed of use. However, at times it can be inconvenient not to represent things like integers as objects, so Java provides a class to match each primitive type: `Integer` corresponds to the primitive type `int`, `Boolean` to `boolean`, and so on. This means that, when required, every type of value can be represented by an object, providing complete uniformity.

6.6.3 Objects and Method Parameters

As there are two kinds of variable, we need to re-visit and re-examine the case of method arguments to see if we have missed anything in our understanding of them.

If a value of primitive type is passed as an argument then the parameter variable is initialized to be a *copy* of the value. If the method argument is a variable (rather than an expression generating a value), this results in two variables each holding a copy of the original value. Changing the parameter variable by assignment in the method body will have no effect on the other variable. For example:

```
class Test {
  void f(int x) {
    x = 10 ;
  }
```

note

A run-time system is a sub-system of the final running application that is inserted automatically when a program is run. It handles all the low-level infrastructure to enable a Java application to execute properly.

note

If object references are considered to be primitive values, then all variables store values of primitive types.

```
}
...
Test t = new Test() ;
int i = 1 ;
t.f(i) ;

// i still has the value 1.
...
```

The method f takes an int parameter, a copy of which is stored in the parameter variable x. In the method body an assignment is made to x but this does not affect the variable i given as the argument in the method call. After the method f has finished executing, the variable i still holds the value 1.

This kind of parameter passing is known as *call-by-value*, and it results in method arguments being *copied* when the parameter variables are initialized. In Java, arguments of primitive types are always passed by value and, hence, copied.

Variables of class type are also passed using call-by-value and hence the object reference is copied. However, the object being referenced is *not* copied, so the situation is more complicated. The result of this situation is what is usually termed *call-by-reference* parameter passing — we are passing a reference to an object. Consider the following example:

```
class Test2 {
  void f(final Stack s) {
    s.push(10) ; }
}

...
Test2 t2 = new Test2() ;
Stack aStack = new Stack() ;
aStack.push(2) ;

// Before calling f the stack only contains the value 2
t2.f(s) ;
// After calling f the stack now contains 2 and 10
...
```

When the method f is called, the parameter variable s is initialized to hold a copy of the Stack object reference. The Stack object itself is *not* copied. This leads to the situation where the parameter variable s and the variable aStack both refer to the same Stack object. Changing the state of the Stack object from inside the method f by pushing the value 10, results in changing the same Stack object that the 2 was pushed onto and, furthermore, the change is not undone when the method f finishes executing.

The same basic mechanism also explains what happens when objects are returned from a method. Although we commonly use a phrase like "return an object from a method", what really happens is that an object reference is returned — effectively this is return-by-reference, although, like parameter passing, values are returned by copying primitive types or references.

Reference parameters have the same implications for programmers as does assignment to a reference variable. Great care has to be taken that a method doesn't have the side-effect of changing the state of an object in an unexpected way. If a change is made then everything else referencing the

Although the effect is that objects are passed using call-by-reference, it should be noted that in Java all parameters are passed-by-value. References are the parameter values that are actually passed, and they get copied.

Array variables are references which explains the behaviour of the array parameter example shown in Section 5.2.3, Page 117.

note

Values are returned from methods using return-by-value.

object must remain unaffected by that change. For example, if a method pushes five values onto a stack and expects to be able to pop the same number off the stack, it must not call another method which pops a value off the stack thereby leaving too few for the first method to work properly.

This is a design and algorithms problem rather than a coding or Java language problem. Java provides a certain computational model that is both needed and potentially dangerous. It is the programmer's design task to ensure that their use of the features is both sensible and valid. The language implementation will help in certain places by providing error management support tools that can help with certain classes of error, and this is very useful. In the main, though, with this sort of algorithm problem, programmers are on their own.

6.6.4   Null

There is one special reference called the *null reference* or just *null*. A reference variable can have this value if it is not referring to any object, so the null reference is one that points nowhere. A reference variable can be assigned the value `null`:

```
obj = null ; // obj no longer references an object
```

Also, a class type instance variable that has not been explicitly initialized will have the value `null`.

If any mistaken attempt is made to use `null` as though it actually referenced an object, for example by trying to call a method, then a runtime error will occur. This causes an error message like the following to be displayed:

```
java.lang.NullPointerException
   at T9.<init>(T9.java:23)
   at T9.main(T9.java:5)
Exception in thread "main"
```

note

The compiler cannot detect the misuse of null references.

When you see a `NullPointerException` you immediately know that you should start looking for a null reference problem.

It is common practice to use `null` to indicate that an object value is not available, especially with method parameter variables of class type. For example:

```
String s = null ;
... // s is not assigned to
obj.f(s) ;
```

Here the method call is deliberately made with s having the value `null` (perhaps the value of s was to be read from a data file but was not found). This is acceptable providing the method f was written with the assumption that the parameter value might be `null`. The method can then check for `null` and act accordingly:

```
void f(final String s) {
   if (s == null) { // Test for null
   // use some default value
   } else {
     // Use the string value of s
   }
}
```

The drawback to using `null` like this is that code requires a lot more tests to see if a class type variable has the value `null`. This can lead to more complicated code that is more difficult to write and harder to maintain.

6.6.5   This

All instance methods, including constructors, have an automatically declared local variable called `this`. `this` is a reference to the object the method has been called for, and is of the type of that object — `this` is a special, totally polymorphic variable. There are two main uses of `this`. Firstly, it allows a reference to the current object to be passed as a parameter to another method, for example:

ref

Section 30.2.9, Page 849.

```
obj.f(this) ; // Pass reference to current object as parameter
```

Secondly, it can be used when calling other methods or accessing instance variables on the current object. For example:

```
public void f() {
  this.g() ;
  this.h(this.y) ;
}
```

The expressions `this.h` and `this.g` call the methods `h` and `g` as normal, the only difference being one of readability in that the two methods are clearly identified as being other instance methods of the same class. Hence, using `this` can be a useful documentation aid. In more complex situations than we have encountered so far, using `this` can also remove ambiguities if there are other `g` or `h` methods in scope.

The expression `this.y` names an instance variable `y` of the same class. The dot notation can be used to access instance variables as well as methods, although as instance variables are usually private such expressions are not often seen. Using `this` in this context serves the same documentation role as with methods but is also useful for using two variables of the same name in the same scope, as in this example:

```
class Test {
  private int x ;
  private int y ;

  public Test(final int x, final int y) {
    this.x = x ;
    this.y = y ;
  }
  ...
}
```

note

Within the scope of the method body, the parameter variables x and y hide the instance variables of the same name.

Here the constructor parameter variables have the same name as the instance variables. This is possible as `this` is used when naming the instance variables in the method body, removing the ambiguity. This technique avoids having to invent extra names for the parameter variables and is widely used with both constructor and normal instance methods. Many, however, eschew this in order to avoid having variables with the same name.

Another use of `this` is to allow one constructor to call another. For example:

```
class Test {
  ...
  public Test(final int x, final double y, final boolean z) {
    // Initialize object using x, y & z
  }
  public Test(final int x, final double y) {
    this(x, y, true) ; // call of constructor with three parameters
                       // giving a definite value for the third parameter
  }
  public Test() {
    this(0, 0.0, true) ; // call of three parameter constructor
                         // providing default for all parameters

  }
}
```

When this is used as though it were a method name, and is followed by a parameter list, a call is made to the constructor with a matching parameter list. Only constructors can call each other like this and the call *must* be the first statement in the constructor body. As the example above shows, this can be a useful way of providing multiple constructors with only one of them doing the actual initialization work. This can save having copies of essentially identical code.

6.6.6   Static Variables and Methods

ref

Section 30.2.6, Page 844.

Instance methods and variables belong to instance objects but Java also supports variables and methods which effectively belong to a class. These variables and methods (usually termed *class variables* and *class methods*) are declared as static in the class definition. For example:

```
class Example {
  static private int i = 0 ;
  static void f() { ... }
  ...
}
```

We are very familiar with one class method already and that is main.

Only one copy of a static variable ever exists. This one and only variable is accessible to all the instance objects of the class. One example of the proper use of a static variable is to keep a count of the number of objects instantiated from a class:

```
class CountInstances {
  private static int count = 0 ;
  public CountInstances() {
    count++ ;
    ...
  }
  public finalize() {
  --count ;
  }
  public static int getCount() {
    return count ;
  }
  ...
}
```

Every time a new instance object of this class is created, its constructor will increment the counter represented by the static variable count. As count is shared by all instance objects, the correct count will be kept.

Static variables (but not instance variables nor instance methods) are also accessible to static methods, which are declared much like instance methods but are not called for an object. Instead they are called using a class name in place of an object reference, for example:

```
int n = CountInstances.getCount() ;
```

Static variables can also be initialized using a static initializer block. See Section 30.2.8, Page 848.

would be used to call the static `getCount` method from within another class. Static methods can also be called from instance methods of the same class by using the method name only, i.e. as though it were another instance method in the class, although using the class name as well serves as useful documentation, making it clear that a static method is being called.

Static methods are frequently used to provide utility methods, which perform a useful service but don't need to be called for an object. Many J2SDK classes provide such methods, a good example being class `Math` in package `java.lang`. It consists entirely of static methods implementing mathematical functions such as `sin`, `log` and `sqrt`, which can be called using expressions like:

```
double a = Math.sin(10) ;
double b = Math.sqrt(42) ;
```

Class `Math` also demonstrates a common use of static variables, as it declares:

```
public static final double E = 2.7182818284590452354 ;
```

and:

```
public static final double PI = 3.14159265358979323846 ;
```

These provide constant values for e and π. Since they are declared `public` as well as `static`, they can be used anywhere within a program. For example:

```
double area = 2 * Math.PI * radius ;
```

This is one of the few acceptable uses of public variables. Note carefully that the variables are declared as `final` to prevent programs from changing their values.

6.7 Example Classes

This section will show some further examples of classes and their construction. The features discussed in the preceding sub-sections will also be heavily used and illustrated in Parts 2 and 3 of the book, so there will be plenty of example code to study.

6.7.1 Class Name

"*Write a class to represent a person's name.*"

Statement of Problem

For our purposes, we will consider that a name consists of a family name or surname, along with a collection of zero, one or two first names. A collection of access methods can be provided to set and get the various parts of a name.

Design and Implementation

```
// A class to represent a person's name.
// Written by Graham Roberts, August 1999
// Revision History: none
import java.util.* ;
```

```java
public class Name {
  private String surname = "" ;
  private ArrayList firstNames  ;
  // Constructors to initialize a new Name object.
  // An upper limit of three first names is allowed.
  public Name(final String firstName1,
              final String firstName2,
              final String surname) {
    this.surname = surname ;
    setFirstNames(firstName1,firstName2) ;
  }
  public Name(final String firstName1, final String surname) {
    this(firstName1,null,surname) ;
  }
  public Name(final String surname) {
    this(null,null,surname) ;
  }
  public String getSurname() {
    return surname ;
  }
  public void setSurName(final String surname) {
    this.surname = surname ;
  }
  public void setFirstNames(final String firstName1,
                            final String firstName2) {
    firstNames = new ArrayList() ;
    if (firstName1 != null) {
      firstNames.add(firstName1) ;
    }
    if (firstName2 != null) {
      firstNames.add(firstName2) ;
    }
  }
  // Position is either 1 or 2.
  // Return null if a name is not available.
  public String getFirstName(final int position) {
    if (position > firstNames.size()) {
      return null ;
    } else {
      return (String)firstNames.get(position-1) ;
    }
  }
  public static void main(String[] args) {
    Name name1 = new Name("Catherine","Janeway") ;
    System.out.println(name1.getSurname()) ;
    System.out.println(name1.getFirstName(1)) ;
    // Only one firstname, so null gets displayed.
    System.out.println(name1.getFirstName(2)) ;
    Name name2 = new Name("James","Tiberius","Kirk") ;
    System.out.println(name2.getSurname()) ;
    System.out.println(name2.getFirstName(1)) ;
    System.out.println(name2.getFirstName(2)) ;
  }
}
```

Testing

The example main method provides some basic test code. This could be extended to include more tests with different names.

Review

The main purpose of this class is to show various features of the Java syntax in use, notably the use of constructors. Whether this would be a practical class to use in a real application is open to debate. However, it does demonstrate the important principle of a class being an abstraction of some concept, in this case of a person's name. Objects of the class encapsulate name information and provide a set of access methods to allow the information to be retrieved or updated. Once a suitable public interface is established, the internal representation of names can be changed without affecting users of the name class.

There is perhaps one issue worth highlighting: The class shows a potential inefficiency in the representation storage used. The use of `ArrayList` here is possibly an incorrect decision. We know that there is a maximum number of names possible and a primitive array would be more efficient in this situation. However, the fixed number of names is an artefact of the desire to show constructors in action. If this class were being designed for production code the constructor architecture would be changed so as to deal with an indeterminate number of names, in which situation the `ArrayList` is exactly the correct representation storage.

6.7.2 Class Matrix

Statement of Problem

"*A matrix is a two-dimensional structure of values frequently used in mathematics and computing. Implement a matrix class, providing a matrix addition method. Matrices should store values of type* `double`."

Design and
Implementation

A matrix class needs to provide a data structure, a set of access operations and a set of mathematical operations (for this example only addition is needed). The obvious data structure is a two-dimensional array of doubles, along with a set of methods that allow elements to be accessed. This leads to the following class:

```java
// A basic matrix class.
// Written by Graham Roberts, September 1999
// Revision History: none
public class Matrix {
  // Use a 2D array for the data structure.
  // The array knows its own size, so we don't
  // have to record the number of rows and columns
  // separately.
  private double[][] elements ;
  public Matrix(final int rows, final int columns) {
    if ((rows < 1) || (columns < 1)) {
      elements = new double[1][1] ;
    } else {
      elements = new double[rows][columns] ;
    }
  }
  // A conversion constructor, for turning a 2D array
  // into a matrix. This is provided for convenience.
  public Matrix(final double[][] data) {
    this(data.length,data[0].length) ;
    for (int row = 0 ; row < getNumberOfRows() ; ++row) {
      for (int col = 0 ; col < getNumberOfColumns() ; ++col) {
        setElement(row, col, data[row][col]) ;
      }
    }
  }
  public int getNumberOfRows() {
    return elements.length ;
  }
  public int getNumberOfColumns() {
    return elements[0].length ;
  }
  // Return true if the selected element is actually
```

```
      // within the matrix.
      private boolean isValidElement(final int row, final int col) {
        return ( (row > -1) && (row < getNumberOfRows()) &&
                 (col > -1) && (col < getNumberOfColumns())) ;
      }
      public double getElement(final int row, final int col) {
        if (isValidElement(row,col)) {
          return elements[row][col] ;
        } else {
          return 0.0 ;
        }
      }
      public void setElement(final int row, final int col,
                             final double val) {
        if (isValidElement(row,col)) {
          elements[row][col] = val ;
        }
      }
      // Add the argument matrix to this, or return null
      // if the sizez do not match.
      public Matrix add(final Matrix m) {
        if ((getNumberOfRows() != m.getNumberOfRows()) ||
            (getNumberOfColumns() != m.getNumberOfColumns())) {
          return null ;
        }
        Matrix result =
         new Matrix(getNumberOfRows(),getNumberOfColumns()) ;
        for (int row = 0 ; row < getNumberOfRows() ; ++row) {
          for (int col = 0 ; col < getNumberOfColumns() ; ++col) {
            double value = getElement(row, col) + m.getElement(row, col) ;
            result.setElement(row, col, value) ;
          }
        }
        return result ;
      }
      // Helper static method to display a matrix.
      public static void display(Matrix m) {
        for (int row = 0 ; row < m.getNumberOfRows() ; ++row) {
          System.out.print('[') ;
          for (int col = 0 ; col < m.getNumberOfColumns() ; ++col) {
            System.out.print(m.getElement(row, col) + " ");
          }
          System.out.println(']') ;
        }
      }
      public static void main(final String[] args) {
        Matrix m1
          = new Matrix(new double[][]{{1.2,2.5,4.5}, {3.9,4.2,0.9}}) ;
        Matrix m2
          = new Matrix(new double[][]{{1.3,7.5,5.2}, {4.8,8.3,9.1}}) ;
        Matrix m3 = m1.add(m2) ;
        display(m3) ;
      }
    }
```

The coding of the class presents no significant issues once declaring classes and instance methods is understood. There is one new piece of syntax present in the `main` method, where anonymous array initializations are used for convenience. An expression like:

```
new double[][] {{1.2,3.4},{3.3,5.6}}
```

means create and initialize a 2D array of doubles, combining array creation with initialization. This works for any dimensional array and can be a useful shorthand.

The second constructor, taking a 2D array of doubles, is an example of a *conversion constructor*, so called as it converts from one type (array of array of `double`) to another (`Matrix`). Conversion constructors are often useful for streamlining the creation of new objects.

Testing

A collection of tests involving the creation of matrices and performing addition need to be assembled. As ever, we need to test some safe, sensible cases to ensure the algorithms actually do their job but we also need to test extensively near all the 'edges'. For example, we should check using a `Matrix` of zero rows and columns. There are, in fact, many error situations that can occur which complicate testing but we need to try out each one.

Review

The class is for the most part straightforward but there are a couple of issues worth pointing out. The most important is the way it deals, or rather doesn't, with error handling. The various methods do make checks for invalid matrix sizes and access operations but respond *silently* by carrying on and pretending all is well. This is a not a good strategy but we must wait until after exceptions are covered in a Section 8.1, Page 226, to see a proper solution.

tip

Write code to minimise the affects of change.

A second issue is that deliberate use has been made of *getter* and *setter* methods to return values such as the number of rows and columns, and to set and get matrix elements. These are used in preference to directly accessing the data array, even in instance methods. The idea here is to minimize the dependence of methods on the data structure — the `add` method, for example, doesn't make any direct access to the data array at all. If the data structure changes, which it might well do as this is only a first attempt at writing a matrix class, then `add` will continue to work unchanged. The advantages of this outweigh any perceived inefficiencies of the extra method calls (which are often spurious).

tip

Trying to optimize the efficiency of your code as you write it is a mistake, as you will only be guessing about where any inefficiencies lie. Only think about optimizing after the code is finished.

Of course the coding of the `add` method, using nested loops, is the most naïve algorithm for matrix addition. It can almost certainly be improved. Moreover, the constructor that takes a primitive 2D double array is also inefficient in that it uses a nested loop. In order to make them more efficient, however, some assumptions about the rest of the implementation will have to be made. The trade-off then is efficiency versus maintainability and safety.

6.7.3 Class Graph

This example will again re-visit the program for drawing a graph seen in Section 4.5.3, Page 107, and Section 5.4.7, Page 140, modifying it to produce a basic, but proper, class for drawing a graph.

Statement of Problem

"*Create a* `GraphPanel` *class, where a graph panel object can display a simple line graph, with labelled axes. The class should have a constructor that has the following arguments:*

- *the width and height of the panel in pixels;*
- *the maximum values of the axes of the graph, defining the graph coordinate system; and*
- *the increment between labels on the axes.*

Write another class to use `GraphPanel` *to display graphs.*"

Design and Implementation

tip

When developing existing code, do it in fairly small steps. Trying to do too much at one go will lead to more errors.

tip

Always avoid the temptation to make instance variables public. 'Getter' methods always should be used, even if they seem unnecessary.

This is a much more elaborate program and will consist of several classes. Firstly there is the class `GraphPanel`, which will be the next iteration of development of the existing graph drawing code. Secondly, a class will be needed to make use of `GraphPanel` and take responsibility for reading the points to plot from a data file. Thirdly, it will be useful to have a `DataPoint` class to represent individual data points.

The need for the `DataPoint` class comes from thinking through what data is needed to draw a graph and how the `GraphPanel` object gets hold of it. The constructor will take care of the size of the graph and how the axes will be labelled, so the `GraphPanel` object only needs to be given a complete collection of data points before it can draw a graph (at this stage we are not going to allow points to be individually added, that will be left to a later development iteration).

We could represent the data as two arrays of x and y coordinates. However, that would be rather primitive and miss the point of exploiting objects. Instead we want to have a single container holding a collection of data point objects. Class `DataPoint` represents a single data point, so that an `ArrayList` can be used as the container, exploiting its useful ability to grow in size on demand.

Putting all this together, we arrive at the following class:

```
// Class to represent a data point with x,y
// coordinates.
// This class creates immutable objects.
// Written by Graham Roberts, August 1999
// Revision History: none
class DataPoint {
  private final int x ;
  private final int y ;
  public DataPoint(final int xVal, final int yVal) {
    x = xVal ;
    y = yVal ;
  }
  public int getX() {
    return x ;
  }
  public int getY() {
    return y ;
  }
}
```

tip

When objects of a class can be made immutable, do so.

The interesting thing about this class is that it creates strongly encapsulated, *immutable*, objects. The objects are strongly encapsulated as the internal representation is not accessible from the outside and the methods `getX` and `getY` must be used to get the x and y coordinates. `DataPoint`s are immutable, as once an object is created, the value it represents cannot be changed — there is no way of changing the state of the object. For types like `DataPoint`, `String`, etc., immutability is a good design strategy, particularly in languages such as Java that support garbage collection.

The `GraphPanel` class can now be implemented. It is basically the next iteration of the existing code, taking care to create a properly formed class using the principles seen earlier in the chapter. Previously, we essentially had procedural code wrapped up in a class. The most obvious changes are the new constructor, as required by the problem specification, and the use of instance variables to store information such as the size of the graph and the graph panel. Using instance variables means that the instance methods don't need to be passed a large number of parameters. Another change to look out for is that all methods are declared public or private, with only those that should be called by other parts of the program being public.

Many of the 'magic number' have now be removed from the code, and the methods are no longer restricted to drawing the same graph.

```java
// This class draws a line graph,
// created from a series of points.
// Written by Graham Roberts, August 1999
// Revision History: modified from class GraphFile
import java.awt.* ;
import java.awt.geom.* ;
import java.util.* ;
public class GraphPanel extends DrawPanel {
  // The size of the graph in graph coordinates
  private int xMaximum = 0 ;
  private int yMaximum = 0 ;
  // The space between labels on the axes
  private int xIncrement = 0 ;
  private int yIncrement = 0 ;
  // The width of the border between the axes and the
  // edge of the panel. The labels for the axes are
  // drawn in the border.
  private final int border = 35 ;
  // The scaling factor between graph coordinates
  // and the size of the panel.
  private double xScaleFactor = 0.0 ;
  private double yScaleFactor = 0.0 ;
  // The points to plot when the graph is displayed.
  private ArrayList points = new ArrayList() ;
  // Create an empty graph with axes from 0 to xMaximum
  // and 0 to yMaximum, labelled at xIncrement and YIncrment
  // intervals. xMaximum and yMaximum define the coordinate
  // system of the graph.
  // The graph is drawn in a panel of
  // size width by height.
  public GraphPanel(final int width, final int height,
                    final int xMaximum, final int yMaximum,
                    final int xIncrement, final int yIncrement) {
    super(width,height) ;
    this.xMaximum = xMaximum ;
    this.yMaximum = yMaximum ;
    this.xIncrement = xIncrement ;
    this.yIncrement = yIncrement ;
    // Calculate the scaling factor between the panel size
    // and the graph coordinates. Note the the literal 2.0
    // is used to force the calculation to work with type double.
    // Using ints results in a serious loss of accuracy.
    this.xScaleFactor = (width - (2.0 * border)) / xMaximum ;
    this.yScaleFactor = (height - (2.0 * border)) / yMaximum ;
  }
  // Draw the x axis using the information stored in the
  // various instance variables.
  private void drawXaxis(final Graphics2D g2d) {
    int yCoord = getHeight() - border ;
    Line2D line = new Line2D.Double(border,yCoord,
                                    getWidth()-border,yCoord) ;
    g2d.draw(line) ;
    for (int x = 0 ; x <= xMaximum ; x += xIncrement) {
      int xCoord = (int)(border + (x * xScaleFactor)) ;
      if (x != 0) {
        line.setLine(xCoord,yCoord,xCoord,yCoord+5) ;
        g2d.draw(line) ;
      }
```

```
      g2d.drawString(new Integer(x).toString(),xCoord-7,yCoord+18) ;
    }
  }
  // Draw the y axis using the information stored in the
  // various instance variables.
  private void drawYaxis(final Graphics2D g2d) {
    Line2D line = new Line2D.Double(border,border,
                                    border,getHeight()-border) ;
    g2d.draw(line) ;
    for (int y = 0 ; y <= yMaximum ; y += yIncrement) {
      int yCoord = (int)(getHeight()-border-(y * yScaleFactor)) ;
      if (y != 0) {
        line.setLine(border,yCoord,border-5,yCoord) ;
        g2d.draw(line) ;
      }
      g2d.drawString(new Integer(y).toString(),border-30,yCoord+5) ;
    }
  }
  // Draw a cross where a point is plotted.
  // x and y are in the graph coordinate system.
  private void plotCross(final Graphics2D g2d,
                         final int x, final int y) {
    Line2D line = new Line2D.Double(x-5,y-5,x+5,y+5) ;
    g2d.draw(line) ;
    line.setLine(x+5,y-5,x-5,y+5) ;
    g2d.draw(line) ;
  }
  // Plot the points stored in the instance variable points
  // and connect them with lines.
  private void plotPoints(final Graphics2D g2d) {
    int oldx = border ;
    int oldy = getHeight() - border ;
    for (int n = 0 ; n < points.size() ; ++n) {
      DataPoint p = (DataPoint)points.get(n) ;
      int xCoord = (int)((p.getX() * xScaleFactor) + border) ;
      int yCoord = (int)(getHeight() -
                         (p.getY() * yScaleFactor) - border) ;
      plotCross(g2d,xCoord,yCoord) ;
      Line2D line = new Line2D.Double(oldx,oldy,xCoord,yCoord) ;
      g2d.draw(line) ;
      oldx = xCoord ;
      oldy = yCoord ;
    }
  }
  // Set the collection of points to plot.
  public void setPoints(final ArrayList pointsToPlot) {
    points = pointsToPlot ;
  }
  // The method that coordinate drawing a graph.
  // This is called automatically by the code
  // that manages the graph window.
  public void paint(Graphics g) {
    Graphics2D g2d = (Graphics2D)g ;
    drawXaxis(g2d) ;
    drawYaxis(g2d) ;
    plotPoints(g2d) ;
  }
}
```

note

Each class should be saved in its own `.java` *file and compiled. The program is run using the command* `java Graph`.

This leaves class `Graph` which reads the file data, creates the window and `GraphPanel` object, and then causes the graph to be drawn.

```
// This class represents reads a collection of data points
// from a file and a graph using a GraphPanel object.
// Written by Graham Roberts, September 1999
// Revision History: none
```

```
import java.util.* ;
public class Graph {
  private GraphPanel graphDrawing ;
  private ArrayList points = new ArrayList() ;
  public Graph() {
    DrawFrame frame = new DrawFrame ("Graph") ;
    graphDrawing = new GraphPanel (500, 400, 100, 70, 10, 10) ;
    frame.add(graphDrawing) ;
    frame.pack() ;
    frame.centreOnScreen() ;
    frame.setVisible(true) ;
  }
  // This method reads data points from a file,
  // and stores them in the data structure.
  private void readData(final String filename) {
    FileInput in = new FileInput (filename) ;
    while (true) {
      int x = in.readInteger() ;
      if (in.eof()) {
        return ;
      }
      int y = in.readInteger() ;
      if (in.eof()) {
        return  ;
      }
      points.add(new DataPoint (x, y)) ;
    }
  }
  // Get the graph drawn.
  private void draw() {
    graphDrawing.setPoints(points) ;
    // The repaint method forces the panel to
    // update its display.
    graphDrawing.repaint() ;
  }
  // The name of the file containing the data points
  // can be given as a command line argument, otherwise
  // the default file name is used.
  public static void main(String[] args) {
    // points.dat is the default data file name
    String filename = "points.dat" ;
    if (args.length > 0) {
      filename = args[0] ;
    }
    Graph graph = new Graph() ;
    graph.readData(filename) ;
    graph.draw() ;
  }
}
```

The same tests as used on the previous version of the graph drawing program can be re-used here. This code is a rewrite of the earlier code adding no extra functionality. There is therefore no necessity to extend the test data set beyond that already used. Of course, there is always good reason to do more tests, so don't be afraid to add more.

Testing

The classes presented represent the next iteration of the development of a graph drawing application. The emphasis has now decisively switched to creating a graph drawing class, capable of drawing a range of graphs, given the appropriate information. There are many further improvements that could be made, although we want to be clear about what they are before rushing in and making further changes.

Review

6.8   Programming with Classes and Objects

While objects combine data and methods, they are not limited to simply representing data structures such as containers like `Stack` and `ArrayList`. An object can be used to represent any entity that a program needs to work with. For example, a program to keep track of seat bookings in a theatre might make use of seat and customer objects, as well as a theatre object which keeps a collection of all the seats. Each kind of object is described by a class, giving classes `Seat`, `Customer` and `Theatre` that determines how the objects are implemented.

As we start to use classes and objects, something very crucial changes regarding the way we think about and write programs. We are heading towards a strategy where we *first* identify the objects (and hence classes) that the program will need, along with some thoughts about how the objects might interact with each other by calling on each others' services. Only after this do we think in much detail about variables, methods and lines of code.

In the case of the theatre, we might determine that we need to work with seats and people as the key entities, along with a theatre entity to collect together all the seats. These entities can then be considered as objects and thought given to the information each object needs to hold and the services it needs to provide. Services are identified by considering the tasks the program as a whole is meant to achieve, and adding services to the objects that allow each task to be performed. Just as we aim for cohesive methods, we also want cohesive objects, so the services an object provides must focus on working with the data held by the object. An object must not become an arbitrary collection of unrelated services.

This is a complete contrast to the top-down structured programming approach we briefly mentioned in Section 3.5, Page 68. The focus of attention has changed from merely thinking about statement sequences and method calls, to thinking about how a collection of objects interact and cooperate in order to achieve results. Further, the structure of a program is now determined by a set of classes and their relationships with one another, rather than a hierarchical collection of methods that call each another.

6.8.1   Objects Providing Services

This object-oriented way of thinking about program design is reinforced by talking about objects (and hence their classes) providing services. An object maintains some set of information that allows it to handle requests for services based on that information. A theatre object provides the service of checking to see if a seat is available and then booking the seat if the customer wants it. The customer object requests the booking and can then provide payment details. A seat object maintains information about the state of a seat (is its available, what price) and can respond to requests to reserve itself for a customer who is making a booking.

In object-oriented terminology, objects are often described as interacting by *message passing* — one object sends a message to another *requesting that a service* be performed. We can talk about an object sending a message, and another object receiving the message. A message consists of a message name (the name of the service being requested) and zero or more arguments. Crucially, it is up to the object receiving the message to decide which method to execute by looking at the message name and argument types and finding a method declared by its class that matches with them.

This activity is known as *dynamic binding* — a message is bound to a method which is then executed, the binding takes place when the message is received. The sender of the message does not know, or need to know, which method the receiver will execute, only that the named service requested will be fulfilled and a suitable response returned.

Why have this mechanism? For a number of reasons. Firstly, it helps *decouple* the message sender from the receiver by not requiring the sender to explicitly select which method will be executed. Secondly, it makes it possible to send the same message to a collection of objects of different types, and each object will be able to respond in its own specialized way.

In Java, calling a method is essentially message passing. A method call may be dynamically bound using the method name, the parameters and the type of the object the method was called for, to locate a method body to execute. Hence, it is possible to have a sequence where the same method call is applied to objects of different types, each resulting in a different method body being executed depending on the type of the object involved in each call. This will be valuable as it allows programmers to work with an interface rather than a specific implementation, something that experience has shown to be very desirable. The next chapter will explain how this works in programming terms.

The upshot of all this is that we should be thinking in terms of class declarations from which objects are instantiated, resulting in a program that consists of a collection of interacting objects when executed. How types are structured and behave has become more important than how programs are implemented as instruction sequences. Compared to writing programs as sequences of instructions or to top-down refinement, we have now moved to a quite different point of view.

Why this way? Experience shows that it leads to better quality programs, programs that are easier to create and, perhaps more importantly, easier to maintain.

6.8.2   Classes and Encapsulation

An important guideline to follow when designing a class is to only make the minimum necessary public, exploiting encapsulation as much as possible. Users of stack objects don't need to know how values will be stored or manipulated by the stack. Indeed as part of our drive for abstraction, users should not really be able to even find out how the values are stored and manipulated, and should only depend upon the public interface presented by the class.

The benefits of encapsulation are that the internal or private implementation of an object is protected. The addition of dynamic binding provides further benefits. Firstly, *clients* of a class (users of objects of a class) need only be concerned with the public interface presented by the class. Providing the names and behaviour of the methods are properly stated (i.e. what they are expected to do), a client does not need to know how a class is implemented. We can state that the *coupling* between the class and its client is minimized, meaning that the client is not dependent on the implementation of the class, only its type and public interface.

Following from this, we are free to change the implementation of a class providing that its public interface remains constant (or is only changed in well documented and publicized ways). Clients need not be aware of any internal changes. This not only allows the programmer to make alterations (such as efficiency improvements or changing the data structure) but also limits the scope of changes to the implementation of the class. For example, changing the name of an instance variable does not require any other class in the program to be altered as well.

Localization is an important design goal to aim for when creating object-oriented programs. Programmers should localize the affects of change by using encapsulated objects that communicate through well defined interfaces. Localization also limits the scope of bugs and errors in a program by reducing the amount of code that has to be searched when errors occur.

6.9   Summary

This chapter has introduced the ideas of object and class. An object combines variables and methods into a single unit, giving a public interface and an encapsulated private representation. A class is used to define the implementation of an object and, in doing so, introduces a new type. Objects interact by calling each others' methods and those methods are dynamically bound, so the use of an object is only concerned with its services provided by its public interface and not its implementation.

Key points in this chapter:

- A *Class* defines a user-defined data type, creating a new type and providing the implementation for objects of that class. Classes specify a *public interface* and a *private implementation*.
- An *Object* is an *instance* of a class (and only one class). From the outside an object can *only* be used according to the public interface defined by its class.
- A *Method* is a procedure or operation defined by a class and used by an object.
- An *Instance Variable* is a variable that is defined by a class and is part of an object of that class.
- An object is created by *instantiation* of a particular class and the object can be *referenced* by a variable of the class type.

- The *state* of an object is determined by the values of its instance variables. As the methods of an object are called, the object changes from one state to the next. An object should always be in a valid state.

Self-review Questions

Self-review 6.1 Why is an abstract data type abstract?

Self-review 6.2 How is the state of an object represented?

Self-review 6.3 What is object identity?

Self-review 6.4 What determines the public interface of an object?

Self-review 6.5 Define an ADT for a set data type.

Self-review 6.6 What are the rules for method overloading?

Self-review 6.7 Why should instance variables not be made public?

Self-review 6.8 How is object encapsulation enforced?

Self-review 6.9 How many ways can an instance variable be initialized?

Self-review 6.10 What would a private constructor mean?

Self-review 6.11 What is a shared object?

Self-review 6.12 What is an unreachable object?

Self-review 6.13 How do object references work when passing parameters and performing assignment?

Self-review 6.14 Why can't static methods access instance variables and instance methods?

Self-review 6.15 What is `this`?

Self-review 6.16 Devise a comprehensive test plan for class `Matrix`.

Self-review 6.17 Could class `DataPoint` used in Section 6.7.3, Page 171, be replaced by class `Point` from the J2SDK? What would the pros and cons of making the change be?

Self-review 6.18 Outline the differences between procedural and object-oriented programming.

Programming Exercises

Exercise 6.1 Complete the `Stack` class to include two or more constructors.

Exercise 6.2 Write and test a class to represent phone numbers. International and area codes should be stored separately from the rest of the number.

Exercise 6.3 Consider a Queue of integers. Integers can be added to the back of the queue and removed from the front. The adding and removing of integers can take place in any order. If the queue is full, then no more integers can be added. If the queue is empty, then no integers can be removed.

Write a class that implements a queue of integers object, along with a test code to test that your objects work. Make sure that you test all the relevant states of the queue.

Hints: Your class needs a constructor, an `add(int)` method and an `int remove()` method. Queued integers can be held in an array. In addition, two methods are needed to test the state of a queue: `boolean isFull()` and `boolean isEmpty()`, allowing code using the queue to decide if it is possible to add or remove an integer.

Exercise 6.4 Write a class Set to store a set of integers. Include code to test the class.

Exercise 6.5 Write and test a class to represent dates (don't use the J2SDK Date class).

Exercise 6.6 Write a chessboard class that can be used to create objects for drawing any reasonable sized chessboard.

Exercise 6.7 Write a pie-chart panel class to display pie-charts, following the structure shown by class `GraphPanel`.

Exercise 6.8 Implement matrix subtraction and multiplication methods for class `Matrix`.

Exercise 6.9 Write a sparse matrix class which stores only values explicitly added to a matrix. All other values are assumed to be zero. The class should not allocate any variables or objects to represent matrix elements that have not been added.

Challenges

Challenge 6.1 Write a program that can act as an interactive dictionary with the following functionality:

- The meaning of a word can be looked up. For example, entering the word "hello" will display the meaning "a greeting".
- New words and their meanings can be added.

- Words and meanings can be deleted.
- The entire collection of words and meanings can be saved to a file and read back again next time the program is run.

Lots of hints:

1. A word and its meaning can be represented as a pair of Strings. Write a class Pair, so that a Pair object can store one word and its meaning. Make sure you provide appropriate public methods and remember that instance variables must be kept private.

2. Write a class WordDictionary to provide a dictionary object. The class should have methods to look up the meaning of a word, add a word and meaning, remove a word and meaning, save the dictionary to file and load the dictionary from file. Use an array of Pairs to store the words and meanings.

3. Provide a main method (and possibly some supporting methods) that consists of a main loop which asks the user if they want to search, add, remove, load, save, or quit. Having read appropriate input values it should then call the methods of the WordDictionary object. The main loop should run until the user asks to quit.

4. The two classes need to be stored in separate .java files which are named after the classes. The main method can be included as part of the WordDictionary class (so run the program using java WordDictionary).

Challenge 6.2 Write a collection of classes to implement a theatre seat booking program.

Class Relationships

Objectives

The high-level structure of an object-oriented program is determined by the relationships between the classes it is composed of. Finding the right relationships between classes is a crucial part of creating a well designed program and is one of the key skills an object-oriented programmer needs to develop.

Keywords

abstract

association

conformance

inheritance

instanceof

interface

Object

override

package

protected

super

7.1   Introduction

As our program design process is going to revolve around identifying objects and classes, we need to be able to express *class relationships* so that we can define the structure of a program. The relationships and connections between classes become increasingly important as the size of a program increases and more classes are used. If the relationships are poorly defined and ill-thought out then the design of a program will suffer and become unstable.

There are two principal kinds of class relationship: *association* and *inheritance* (often referred to as the *has-a* and *is-a* relationships). This chapter will explore how these are used and introduce a number of related features, one of the most important of which is the Java *interface* declaration.

7.2   Association

Association is the most straightforward way of relating classes and is the general label applied to the common situation where one class 'knows' about another. In particular, a class can declare a reference instance variable, allowing the public methods of an object of another class to be called. This relationship can be seen as *has-a* or *uses-a*, as one class 'has a' or 'uses a' reference to an object of another class. A class establishes an association by making appropriate declarations, while objects of the class realise the association by holding references to other objects.

This kind of relationship appeared in the example classes presented in the last chapter. For example, the Name class declared two instance variables:

```
public class Name {
   private String surname ;
   private ArrayList firstNames ;
   ...
```

A Name object stores references to both a String and an ArrayList object to use as required when representing the name abstraction. The *clients* (other classes within the program which are users) of class Name do not depend upon the referenced objects or their types, only being concerned with the public methods presented by the Name class. We can work with the abstraction represented by Name, without needing to know the details.

Associations can be one-to-one, as between a Name and its String; one-to-many, as between an ArrayList and Strings; and many-to-many. They can also be direct or indirect (in the sense that a Name holds name strings actually contained by another object).

A variation on the association relationship is where an object obtains a reference to another object via a method argument, for example:

```
public class Example {
   public int doSomething(Stack data) {
```

```
            ...
        }
    }
```

The method doSomething, and indeed any methods called from it if the object reference is passed on, can use this parameter object in effectively the same way as if the reference was held in an instance variable, but only during the lifetime of the method call.

7.2.1 Ownership

Although association appears straightforward, and often is, the possibility and consequences of object sharing have to be considered. An association can represent ownership, implying that an object is completely controlled by another. Changes to the owned object can only be made by the owner. On the other hand, an association can represent usage, where the referenced object will be shared and used by some number of other objects.

If strict ownership is needed, then the design of a class must make sure that the owned object does not become accessible to other objects of different classes in some way that will break the ownership and make possible unexpected changes to the state of the owned object. This is a particular issue if the owned object reference is passed as a parameter or returned as a method result.

7.2.2 Using Association Effectively

The number of associations between classes can be counted and used as a measure of *coupling*. Usually this measure is applied only to references held by instance variables. The general aim is to keep the amount of coupling between classes low in order to minimise the number of *dependencies* of one class on another. The more dependent a class is on another, the more likely that changes to the other class will force changes to be made on the first class.

tip

Keep the coupling between classes low.

A common mistake made by those new to object-oriented development is to end up with one class referencing, via instance variables, most or all of the other classes in the program. This tends to happen when one class is used as a control centre and all the other classes serve purely as data structures. Counting the references will quickly show when this situation occurs. If it does occur then it is time to re-think the design.

7.3 Inheritance

There is another, very different, kind of relationship possible between classes, a relationship where one class is an *extension* of another class. This relationship is known as *inheritance* and, together with *dynamic binding*, is a key feature of object-oriented programming.

Inheritance allows a class to take on, or inherit, all the features of another class. This is often represented in a diagram like this:

Chapter 31, Page 869.

superclass

subclass

The class being inherited from is known as the *superclass*, while the class that inherits is known as the *subclass*. The subclass inherits the variables and methods declared by the superclass, except for constructors, meaning that the subclass includes the superclass variables and methods as part of itself. In addition, the subclass can add new variables and methods, or can redefine (usually termed *override*) the implementation of an inherited method so as to be able to specialize it to the needs of the subclass. A subclass can be seen as both an extension and a *specialization* of a superclass.

Inheritance can be seen as the *is-a* relationship, as the subclass is everything the superclass is, and more. For example, if we have a class `Vehicle`, a subclass `Car` can be defined as an extension of `Vehicle`. We can then say that a `Car` is-a `Vehicle`; a `Car` is everything a `Vehicle` is along with a set of additional or more specialized features. Inheritance is not limited to one level, so a subclass can have its own subclass and so on, allowing, for example, a class `SportsCar` to be a subclass of, and hence an extension of, `Car`. Further, a superclass can have multiple subclasses, with `Truck` being another subclass of `Vehicle`. The consequences of this will be explored further in Section 7.8, Page 206. There is one important limitation: a subclass can only have *one* superclass; multiple superclasses are *not* allowed.

*A sequence of subclasses
is often referred to as a
'chain', so we can talk
about a chain of
subclasses from a
specific superclass.*

In terms of objects, if an object is an instance of a subclass then the object representation will contain all the variables declared by both the subclass and the superclass. Further, any of the methods declared by either class can be called for objects of the subclass, provided they are public. Following from this, if an object is an instance of a subclass of a subclass, then it contains all the instance variables from all the superclasses and any of the superclass public methods can be called.

Inheritance is subject to some fairly complex rules, some of which will be introduced in the following sections and most of which will be described in more detail in the language reference, Chapter 31.

7.3.1   Using Inheritance

To investigate how inheritance works and is supported by the Java programming language, we will look at the implementation of some simple queue classes. A queue is a storage device that allows new items to be added at the back and removed from the front. Suppose we have a class `IntQueue`, which provides objects that can store a queue of `int`s. The class might be outlined as:

*More robust Queue
implementations are
investigated in
Chapter 14, Page 407.*

```
public class IntQueue {
    private int[] items ;
    public IntQueue(int size) { ... }
    public void addBack(int n) { ... }
    public int removeFront() { ... }
    ...
}
```

This queue comprises a data structure, an array of integers, and two methods; one to add an integer to the back of the queue and one to remove an integer from the front of the queue (we will ignore empty or full queue conditions for the moment).

Now suppose we want to implement an `IntDequeue`, which is a queue of integers that can have items added and removed from both the back and front of the queue (creating a 'double-ended queue', hence dequeue). We could implement a completely new class in the following way:

```
public class IntDequeue {
    private int[] items ;
    ...
    public IntDequeue(final int length) { ... }
    public void addBack(final int n) { ... }
    public int removeBack() { ... }
    public void addFront(final int n) { ... }
    public int removeFront() { ... }
    ...
}
```

but in doing so we notice that it shares quite a bit of similarity with the `IntQueue` class. In fact an `IntDequeue` can be seen as an extension of an `IntQueue` — a queue with additional add and remove operations. Rather than create the `IntDequeue` class from scratch, we could make it a *subclass* of `IntQueue`, inheriting the methods and variables declared by that class:

```
public class IntDequeue extends IntQueue {
    public IntDequeue(final int length) { ... }
    public int removeBack() { ... }
    public void addFront(final int x) { ... }
    ...
}
```

The line:

```
class IntDequeue extends IntQueue
```

declares that `IntDequeue` is a subclass of `IntQueue`, making use of the `extends` keyword. `IntDequeue` needs only to provide two new public methods in order to extend the `IntQueue` class and implement the public interface needed by dequeues. The inherited methods, `addBack` and `removeFront`, are also part of the public interface of `IntDequeue` but do not need to be re-declared. The constructor declared in `IntQueue` is *not* inherited and `IntDequeue` must declare its own constructor.

7.3.2 Protected

Further development of the `IntDequeue` class presents a problem that must be addressed immediately. The `IntQueue` class defines its data structure as:

```
private int[] items ;
```

This dictates that the data variable `items` is private to the `IntQueue` class and can only be accessed by methods declared in the `IntQueue` class; this is encapsulation being properly enforced — `private` states that the scope of the variable is this class alone and no others, not even subclasses. The problem, however, is that the methods added by the `IntDequeue` subclass need to access `items` but are not allowed to, even though the `IntDequeue` objects contain that

note

One role of inheritance is to enable code sharing, avoiding code duplication.

!

Constructors are not inherited.

ref

Section 31.2.2, Page 872.

variable. Inheritance does not bypass the strict encapsulation of private instance variables, or allow private methods to be called.

This situation is resolved by making the array `items` *protected,* rather than private:

```
public class IntQueue {
    protected int[] items ;
    public IntQueue(final int length) { ... }
    public void addBack(final int n) { ... }
    public int removeFront() { ... }
    ...
}
```

note

The relationship between protected and packages is explored further in Section 7.12.

The `protected` keyword, like the `private` and `public` keywords, allows the degree of encapsulation of an instance method or variable to be specified. `protected` opens up the encapsulation to allow subclasses, and any other classes in the same package, access to methods and variables, so is less strict than `private` but not as open as `public`. With this change in place we can now create a usable `IntDequeue` class, noting that the declarations in class `IntQueue` do not need to be changed further in order to do so.

This example highlights the rules of encapsulation. A private variable is only accessible to methods declared in the *same* class. Inheritance does not violate the encapsulation rules, so even though a subclass inherits private variables, none of the methods declared by a subclass can access those variables directly. If access is needed then either indirect access must be available by calling an inherited public or protected method, or the variable has to be protected, as was the case with `IntDequeue`. The same rule applies to calling inherited private methods — subclasses can't!

Clearly the rules defining a class scope are quite complicated. Not only are variables and methods declared by a given class within the scope of that class but so are any public or protected variables and methods inherited from a superclass. Private variables inherited from the superclass are not in the class scope, despite being part of an instance object. This means that determining the full membership of the scope of a class requires the superclass chain to be examined.

The last part of this bit of the jigsaw is associated with knowing what variables and methods are in scope when a method is called. For a subclass method all the variables and methods in the subclass scope are available. If the method then calls an inherited method, that method has access only to the superclass scope, despite being called for the same subclass object.

tip

Making all instance variables private and setting up accessor methods for the public and protected interface is strongly recommended.

While `protected` provides a useful mechanism, it has a cost in that it increases the coupling between classes. Classes declaring protected methods and variables now have a protected interface as well as a public interface which some subset of the other classes in the program have access to. If the protected interface changes, then classes using that interface may have to change as well. Further, while public interfaces rarely, if ever, include instance variables, protected interfaces, such as the one we have just created, often do. The effect of changing the type of a protected variable is typically more far-reaching than changing a method and may require all users of that variable in other classes to be re-written. Given this, an argument can be put forward that only protected methods should be used, even if only subclasses will be using the protected interface.

7.3.3 Inheritance and Constructors

Constructors, instance variable initialization and initializer blocks are responsible for performing the correct initialization of the objects of the class they are declared in. This is straightforward for a single class, but with inheritance both the superclass and subclass provide constructors and instance variable initializations, raising the question: How is everything coordinated?

The Java language enforces the following rules of class construction to ensure a deterministic and sensible initialization:

See Section 31.2.8, Page 886.

1. After any parameter variables have been initialized, a call is immediately made to a superclass constructor before any other statements in the constructor body are executed. This can be done explicitly with the `super` keyword (see the next sub-section), otherwise it will happen automatically.

2. All directly initialized instance variables are initialized and any initializer blocks evaluated, following the order they are declared in.

3. The statements in the subclass constructor body are executed.

With the `IntDequeue` class implemented by inheritance from `IntQueue`, creating an `IntDequeue` object using the `new` operator:

```
IntDequeue dequeue = new IntDequeue (10) ;
```

results in the `IntDequeue` constructor being called, which immediately calls the `IntQueue` constructor. Any directly initialized instance variables declared by `IntQueue` are then initialized and the statements in the `IntQueue` constructor body executed. Control then returns to the `IntDequeue` constructor where the same happens. The end result is a fully initialized empty `IntDequeue` object that is ready to use.

Thus, objects are initialized top-down, from the top-most superclass down to the subclass for which an instance object is being instantiated. Control of the initialization sequence is driven bottom-up by subclass constructor calling superclass constructor. The call to a superclass constructor *must* be the first thing that a constructor does. The language rules enforce this and the Java compiler automatically inserts a call to a superclass constructor if one is not explicitly provided. Moreover, following the superclass constructor call, the compiler inserts code to perform instance variable initialization. This explains why all classes must have a constructor and why the compiler will automatically create a default constructor if the programmer doesn't define any constructors at all.

Although a constructor can assign to any instance variable that is in scope, the following guideline should always be observed: Each class should be responsible for initializing the instance variables it declares and no other. A subclass can assume that inherited superclass variables are initialized before it initializes its own variables, so should not try to initialize any superclass variables itself.

7.3.4   Super

See Section 31.2.8,
Page 886 and
Section 31.2.9, Page 888.

The `IntDequeue` constructor has been shown as taking an `int` parameter, allowing the length of the queue to be specified. Given this, we might want to declare the full constructor as something like:

```
public IntDequeue(final int length) {
  items = new int [length] ; // bad style...see below
}
```

As noted in the previous sub-section, this would violate our rule that a constructor should not initialize instance variables from a superclass. What we want to do instead is to call the superclass constructor with `length` as the argument. This can be done by making use of the `super` keyword:

```
public IntDequeue(final int length) {
  super(length) ;
}
```

The expression `super(length)` modifies the automatic call to the superclass constructor, so that the constructor with the matching parameter list is called. This results in a call to `IntQueue(int length)` with some parameter value ensuring that the variable and the array object are initialized by the correct constructor.

The `super` call must be the first statement in the method body. Placing it anywhere else will result in a compilation error. Also, the superclass must provide a constructor with a parameter list that matches that in the `super` call. If no explicit `super` call appears then an attempt will be made to call the default constructor in the superclass. If there is no default constructor then that too will cause a compilation error — trying to compile the first constructor in this sub-section results in this error since `IntQueue` does not define a default constructor, i.e. one taking no parameters.

`Super` is actually quite similar to `this`, except that it is a reference of the type of the superclass of the current object rather than its own type. This means that it can be used as an object reference, as well as for calling superclass constructors. The full details can be seen in the language reference in Part 4 of the book.

7.3.5   IntQueue and IntDequeue Implementations

Circular arrays are
explained more in
Section 14.2.2, Page 416.

We now have enough information to write basic, but working, implementations of the `IntQueue` and `IntDequeue` classes. The contents of a queue are stored in an array which is used as a *circular array* or *ring buffer*. In this data structure, the array is treated as though the last element is followed by the first element, so that when the end of the array is reached while adding to the queue, further additions wrap round to the beginning of the array. The advantage of using this data structure is that values stored in the array do not have to be moved when other values are added or removed.

```
// A class providing a simple queue of integers. This class is not
// robust and deals with errors by ignoring them.
//
// Written by Graham Roberts, Sept 1999
```

```java
// Revision History: none
public class IntQueue {
  // The array stores the queue. It will be treated as though it were
  // a ring or circular array, so that indexing beyond the last
  // element causes a wrap around back to the beginning of the
  // array. Taking this approach avoids the need to move array
  // elements when inserting or deleting.
  protected int[] items ;
  // Size of the current queue
  protected int size = 0 ;
  // Indexes of front and back of queue in the array.
  protected int front = 1 ;
  protected int back = 0 ;

  public IntQueue(final int length) {
    items = new int[length] ;
  }
  public void addBack(final int n) {
    if (isFull()) {
      return ;
    }
    size++ ;
    back++ ;
    if (back == items.length) {
      back = 0 ;
    }
    items[back] = n ;
  }
  public int removeFront() {
    if (isEmpty()) {
      return 0 ;
    }
    size-- ;
    int result = items[front] ;
    front++ ;
    if (front == items.length) {
      front = 0 ;
    }
    return result ;
  }
  public boolean isFull() {
    return (size == items.length) ;
  }
  public boolean isEmpty() {
    return (size == 0) ;
  }
  public static void main(final String[] args) {
    IntQueue q = new IntQueue(10) ;
    for (int i = 0 ; i < 10 ; ++i) {
      q.addBack(i) ;
    }
    while (!q.isEmpty()) {
      System.out.println(q.removeFront()) ;
    }
    for (int i = 0 ; i < 10 ; ++i) {
      q.addBack(i) ;
    }
    for (int i = 0 ; i < 5 ; ++i) {
      q.removeFront() ;
    }
    for (int i = 0 ; i < 5 ; ++i) {
      q.addBack(i) ;
    }
    while (!q.isEmpty()) {
      System.out.println(q.removeFront()) ;
    }
```

```
      }
    }
```

The `IntDeque` subclass is implemented as follows:

```java
// A class providing a simple dequeue implemented as a subclass of
// Queue.
// Written by Graham Roberts, Sept 1999
// Revision History: none
public class IntDequeue extends IntQueue {
  // Dequeue of default size
  public IntDequeue() {
    super(25) ;
  }
  public IntDequeue(final int length) {
    super(length) ;
  }
  public void addFront(final int n) {
    if (isFull())
      return ;
    size++ ;
    if (front == 0) {
      front = items.length - 1 ;
    } else {
      front-- ;
    }
    items[front] = n ;
  }
  public int removeBack() {
    if (isEmpty()) {
      return 0 ;
    }
    size-- ;
    int result = items[back] ;
    if (back == 0) {
      back = items.length - 1 ;
    } else {
      back-- ;
    }
    return result ;
  }
  public static void main(String[] args) {
    IntDequeue q = new IntDequeue(10) ;
    for (int i = 0 ; i < 10 ; ++i) {
      q.addFront(i) ;
    }
    while (!q.isEmpty()) {
      System.out.println(q.removeBack()) ;
    }
    for (int i = 0 ; i < 10 ; ++i) {
      q.addFront(i) ;
    }
    for (int i = 0 ; i < 5 ; ++i) {
      q.removeBack() ;
    }
    for (int i = 0 ; i < 5 ; ++i) {
      q.addFront(i) ;
    }
    while (!q.isEmpty()) {
      System.out.println(q.removeBack()) ;
    }
  }
}
```

Note that both classes include a `main` method with some code to handle basic testing of the classes.

7.3.6 Hiding Names

It is possible to hide an inherited variable by declaring a new one with the same name in a subclass. For example:

```
public class Superclass {
  protected String s = "hello" ;
  ...
}
public class Subclass extends Superclass {
  private String s = "world" ; // Hiding the inherited s
  public void show() {
    System.out.println(s) ;
    System.out.println(super.s) ;
  }
  ...
}
```

When the show method in Subclass is called it will display:

```
world
hello
```

When the variable s is output, the show method displays the value of the instance variable declared in class Subclass, the inherited variable is hidden. However, while s is hidden it is not inaccessible and the expression super.s can be used to access it, as the second println statement shows. This is an example of super being used as a reference of the superclass type.

While hiding a superclass variable is possible, it is best not to actually do so if it can be avoided, as the result can be confusing and cause mistakes to be made when the classes are modified later on.

Like instance variables, instance methods can also be hidden and called using super. However, unlike the case with variables, there are good reasons for hiding methods and we will return to the subject in Section 7.7, Page 203.

7.3.7 Static Variables and Inheritance

To complete our coverage of initialization and inheritance we should briefly consider how static variables are managed. Both static variables and methods are inherited, but it should be noted that this does not affect the property that only one copy of a static variable ever exists within a program.

To understand how and when static variables are initialized, we need to know how classes are represented when a program is executed. The information about a class, including type information and the bytecodes for all the methods, is stored in the .class file that is generated when the class is compiled. Each class has its own .class file, and that file needs to be loaded into the computer memory by the Java Virtual Machine (JVM) when a program using the class is executed.

When a .class file is loaded it is verified and linked. Verification checks that the file is properly formed and has not been tampered with, while linking checks that the types of all methods and variables are consistent with what other classes expect. Classes are loaded on demand as a

note

Hiding is often referred to as shadowing.

tip

Avoid variable shadowing: Choose your subclass variable names so that they differ from inherited names.

ref

Static variables are discussed in detail in Chapters 30 and 31.

program runs, rather than all being loaded at once before the program starts. Loading a subclass requires any superclasses to be loaded first.

If a class has static variables, they are allocated memory space and initialized after the class has been loaded but before any use of any part of the class is made. Initialization order respects inheritance, so static variables are initialized top-down from superclass to subclass, as well as following the textual order of declarations in a class. This allows a static variable to be initialized using an inherited static variable, for example:

```
public class A {
  protected static int n = 10 ;
  ...
}
public class B extends A {
  protected static int a = n * 10 ; // a initialized using n
  ...
}
```

The idea of hiding also applies to static variables and methods, although again it is something best avoided.

7.4 Choosing Between Inheritance and Association

Looking at the IntQueue and IntDequeue classes, we can note that an IntQueue is simpler than an IntDequeue, but also that an IntDequeue is a more *specialized* extension of an IntQueue. It was exactly this observation which led us to take the decision that IntDequeue could be a subclass of IntQueue — we saw that we could make use of already written code. Perhaps more importantly, though, an IntDequeue object can do everything that an IntQueue object can do, as it has all the instance methods that IntQueue does and those methods perform the expected queuing operations (of course, given that the methods were inherited, this is unavoidable). More interestingly, this allows an IntDequeue object to be *substituted* for an IntQueue object without changing the behaviour of a program. An IntDequeue may do more than an IntQueue but, nonetheless, it can function without problem as an IntQueue: an IntDequeue 'is-a' IntQueue.

We can now see that inheritance actually serves two distinct purposes:

- A mechanism for sharing implementation by making one class an extension of another.
- A mechanism for sharing a public interface (a set of public methods) such that an object of one class can safely be substituted for an object of another class.

The sharing of implementation using inheritance seems to be a relatively straightforward issue. If two or more classes need to use the same variables or methods, a superclass can be created to contain them and inheritance used to access them. The advantage of doing this is that the variable and method declarations no longer need to be duplicated and only need to be written and tested once.

Inheritance

```
public class X {
  public void f() { ... }
  protected int a ;
}
public class Y extends X {
  ...
}
```

Association

```
public class X {
  public void f() { ... }
  private int a ;
}
public class Y {
  public void f() {
    x.f();
  }
  private X x = new X() ;
}
```

Figure 7.1 Inheritance v. Association.

However, is inheritance always the best way to share code? An alternative design approach is to use association and to put the shared methods and variables into another class but gain access via an instance variable referring to an object of that class. In terms of code, the alternatives are shown in Figure 7.1.

How do we decide which approach to take in a given situation? The answer comes by thinking about why we are relating the classes and about the public interfaces needed by the classes involved. If a class simply needs to use the implementation of another class but does not need to have (and extend) the same public interface then inheritance is not appropriate; association can, indeed should, be used. In fact, in this situation, trying to use inheritance is invariably a mistake, not least because the new subclass will end up with an inherited public method it doesn't need.

If a decision is made to use inheritance, it should be the case that both the implementation and the public interface of the proposed superclass are needed. It should be possible to substitute a subclass object for a superclass object and still expect a program to run correctly. A good rule-of-thumb when checking that inheritance is appropriate is to try and verbalize the relationship between the two classes. If you can say that a class Y *is-a* or *is-a-kind-of* class X and it makes sense, then inheritance is probably appropriate. For example, it makes sense to say that an IntDequeue is a kind of IntQueue but it does not make sense to say that an IntDequeue is a kind of Stack.

We should note here that using association for sharing is not without its drawbacks. In the example of Figure 7.1, it may be that the methods of class X require access to the variable a in class Y in order to properly complete their tasks. With inheritance and a protected, a was in the scope of X and therefore accessible. With association this is not the case. To gain access to the variable a either it has to be public (a very bad idea since this weakens encapsulation and increases the risk of misuse) or there have to be *accessor methods* to the variable a provided by class Y. If neither of these are the case then there is an insurmountable problem.

An accessor method is a method which allows access to the member variable, which can then always be private, for example:

```
public class Y {
  public void f() ;
  public void seta(int) ; // Setter function to set a
  public int geta() ;      // Getter function to get value of a
  private int a ;
}
```

tip

If a public interface is not being shared, don't use inheritance.

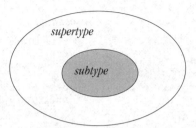

Figure 7.2 Super and subtype values.

A *setter function*, seta, is used to set the value of a, while a *getter function*, geta, is used to retrieve the value of a. At first sight this appears simply to add the inconvenience of having to call methods in order to use the variable a, meaning that operations such as direct assignment to a are no longer possible. However, it has had the affect of decoupling the details of the variable and its type from users of class X. If in the future it was decided to change the way in which the value a was stored (for example, by using a variable of a different type or even a value computed on demand rather than stored directly); the external interface of the class could remain the same and users of the class would be unaffected regardless of the internal, but private, changes.

The principle being exploited here is: Decouple classes as much as possible. This means always thinking ahead about how the implementation of a class may change and avoid any of those changes having to be propagated to all the users of the class. Ideally, once the public interface (i.e. the set of public methods) of a class has been defined and publicized, it should at most be changed infrequently and preferably never.

tip

Always minimize coupling. Use appropriate method calls and not direct variable access to support this goal.

7.5   Inheritance and Types

The previous section proposed the idea of being able to substitute a subclass (e.g. IntDequeue) object for a superclass (e.g. IntQueue) object. This is possible due to the way the type system works and the way it interacts with inheritance. We already know that a class declares a type, allowing reference variables of that type to be declared. Following on from this, a subclass also declares a type, and that type is an extension, or *subtype*, of the superclass type, or *supertype*. Hence, there is a supertype–subtype relationship between types that reflects the superclass and subclass relationships.

In terms of ADTs, which we use to more formally define what a type is, a subtype ADT has all the operations of the supertype ADT along with refinements and additions that don't violate the supertype axioms. Any supertype operation can be applied to a subtype value, and the expected result produced. Moreover, the set of subtype values is a subset of the set of supertype values; in other words, all values of the subtype are also values of the supertype (see Figure 7.2).

Following from this, one type *conforms* to another type if it supports all the operations of the first type; type *conformance* is the name used for the relationship when one type conforms to another. Clearly a subtype conforms to a supertype, but conformance can also occur when an otherwise unrelated type provides all the operations (and, strictly, supports all the axioms) of another type. Java provides a mechanism called an *interface* to support this more general form of conformance, and this will be explored in Section 7.9, Page 208.

Type conformance means that a value can have more than one type, allowing the value to be used wherever a value of one of the types it conforms to is expected. This is a powerful tool as it enables a form of *polymorphism*, where a value can be used in different locations with different types, without having to change the value in any way.

In terms of classes and objects, conformance means that an object can have several types and can be referred to by a reference variable of *any* of those types. For example, looking at the queue classes described earlier, we see that class `IntDequeue` declares type `IntDequeue`, and `IntDequeue` objects have that type. However, as `IntDequeue` is a subclass of `IntQueue`, an `IntDequeue` object also is of, or conforms to, type `IntQueue`. This allows a statement such as the following to be written:

```
IntQueue aQueue = new IntDequeue (10) ; // Valid code
```

which creates an `IntDequeue` object as expected but stores the reference to it in a variable of type `IntQueue`. A variable of superclass type can reference a subclass object. This explains why the statement:

```
Line2D aLine = new Line2D.Double(10,10,70,70) ;
```

seen back in Section 4.2.1, Page 94, is valid. `Line2D` is a superclass of `Line2D.Double`, so a reference of the superclass type is referring to an object of subclass type.

7.5.1 Object Substitutability

Type conformance allows object *substitutability*; one object can be substituted for another providing its type conforms correctly. For example, an `IntDequeue` object can be used wherever an `IntQueue` object was expected. This opens up a range of important possibilities. A method declared as:

```
void consume(IntQueue q)
```

can be passed a reference to an `IntQueue` object *or* any an object of a class that conforms to `IntQueue`, e.g. any subclass of `IntQueue`. Inside the method body any `IntQueue` instance method can be called and be expected to work as all objects referenced by the parameter variable must support the methods — the type checking system will guarantee this to be the case or the compiler will reject the code.

The same principle can apply when returning object references from a method:

```
IntQueue produce() {
  IntDequeue dequeue = new IntDequeue (10) ;
  // Use the dequeue
  ...
  return dequeue
}
```

note

*Primitive values (*int*, *double*, etc.) can only have one type under the Java type system.*

The method is declared as returning an `IntQueue` reference but the method body can safely return an `IntDequeue` reference since `IntDequeue` is a subclass of `IntQueue` and hence conforms to that type.

Substitutability comes into play when we write methods or declare variables using references of class types in the knowledge that any object with a conforming type (particularly subclasses) can be used now or in the future. As new subclasses are added, objects of those classes can be used without having to change existing code.

7.6   Class Object

For a number of reasons, it is very useful if *all* objects, of whatever class, have a core set of public methods that are always supported. For example, all objects should have a `toString` method that can be called to return a string representing the value of the object. Moreover, to implement abstractions like containers properly, a 'universal' object reference is needed that can refer to any kind of object.

ref

Class `Object` *is described in detail in the J2SDK documentation (in package java.lang).*

These features are supported by making all classes subclasses of class `Object`. Class `Object` is unique in that it alone has no superclass, and because of this, it is given special recognition by the Java programming language.

Inheriting from `Object` happens automatically, without having to explicitly use the `extends` keyword. So the declaration of `IntQueue` made earlier:

```
class IntQueue { ... }
```

is equivalent to writing:

```
class IntQueue extends Object { ... }
```

`IntQueue` is a *direct* subclass of `Object`, while `IntDequeue` being a subclass of `IntQueue` is an *indirect* subclass of `Object`.

As every class inherits from `Object` we can also see that all classes are related into a single inheritance tree with class `Object` at the top. A consequence of this is that all classes inherit the public interface and methods declared by class `Object`, giving the desired ability for all objects to have a common sub-set of methods. As well as `toString`, the common methods cover basic operations such as copying (cloning in Java-speak) an object and finding the class of an object.

Another consequence of class `Object` is that a reference variable of type `Object` can refer to an object of *any* type. This is going to be a very important factor in the way we design our systems.

7.6.1   Container Classes and Object

The classes `IntQueue` and `IntDequeue` have the major drawback of being able to store only values of type `int`. To store values of other types we would potentially have to start creating new classes, such as `StringQueue`, `DateDequeue` and so on. This would lead to a highly undesirable proliferation of largely identical classes and hence excessive duplication of code — something we are not prepared to do.

Fortunately, now that we know about class `Object`, we have a mechanism for overcoming the problem of replicating classes. We can implement classes `Queue` and `Dequeue` once, storing references of type `Object`. As an object of any type can be referenced by a variable of type `Object`, the `Queue` and `Dequeue` classes can store any object we want.

We can now declare a more realistic `Queue` class to replace `IntQueue`:

```
// A class providing a simple queue This class is not robust and deals
// with errors by ignoring them.
//
// Written by Graham Roberts, Sept 1999
// Revision History: rewrite of IntQueue
public class Queue {
  // The array stores the queue. It will be treated as though it were
  // a ring or circular array, so that indexing beyond the last
  // element causes a wrap around back to the beginning of the
  // array. Taking this approach avoids the need to move array
  // elements when inserting or deleting.
  protected Object[] items ;
  // Size of the current queue
  protected int size = 0 ;
  // Indexes of front and back of queue in the
  // array.
  protected int front = 1 ;
  protected int back = 0 ;

  public Queue(final int length) {
    items = new Object[length] ;
  }
  public void addBack(final Object obj) {
    if (isFull())
      return ;
    size++ ;
    back++ ;
    if (back == items.length) {
      back = 0 ;
    }
    items[back] = obj ;
  }
  public Object removeFront() {
    if (isEmpty()) {
      // Returning null is a stop-gap measure
      // until a later chapter presents a proper
      // solution. Don't do this!
      return null ;
    }
    size-- ;
    Object result = items[front] ;
    front++ ;
    if (front == items.length) {
      front = 0 ;
    }
    return result ;
  }
  public boolean isFull() {
    return (size == items.length) ;
  }
  public boolean isEmpty() {
```

```
      return (size == 0) ;
    }
  public static void main(final String[] args) {
    Queue q = new Queue(10) ;
    for (int i = 0 ; i < 10 ; ++i) {
      q.addBack(new Integer (i)) ;
    }
    while (!q.isEmpty()) {
      System.out.println(q.removeFront()) ;
    }
    for (int i = 0 ; i < 10 ; ++i) {
      q.addBack(new Integer(i)) ;
    }
    for (int i = 0 ; i < 5 ; ++i) {
      q.removeFront() ;
    }
    for (int i = 0 ; i < 5 ; ++i) {
      q.addBack(new Integer(i)) ;
    }
    while (!q.isEmpty()) {
      System.out.println(q.removeFront()) ;
    }
  }
}
```

The use of type `int` from `IntQueue` has been replaced with type `Object`. As the `main` method shows, the queue can no longer store type `int` directly, or any other primitive type for that matter, so `Integer` objects are used instead.

Note, however, that this class still does not deal with errors very well, most notably in the `removeFront` method where it can return `null`. This is actually a very dangerous thing to do as it would require any code calling the method to test the returned value to see if it is `null`. This is easy to forget to do and also makes the calling code more clumsy. Chapter 8 will present a proper solution to this problem, i.e. exceptions. See Chapter 14 for a more full coverage of constructing robust queue implementations.

Classes like `Queue` (or `Stack`) are known as *container* classes, as they represent data structures that store objects of other types. This `Queue` class can additionally be described as a *generic container* class, where generic means it can store items of any reference type. The Java class libraries use this approach to implement a number of container classes, such as `ArrayList` (which was introduced in Chapter 5).

There are drawbacks, however, with using type `Object` to create the *polymorphism* we are seeing here (i.e. the ability to use one kind of container to store objects of many different types). Firstly, the primitive types cannot be stored in generic container classes as they are not objects. Secondly, and more crucially, when an object is stored in the container class its exact type appears to be lost as everything in the container is assumed to be of type `Object`. This is potentially very awkward, as when an object is removed from the container to be used, its only known type is `Object`.

ref

Cast: Section 28.9.2, Page 790. Also see Chapter 5.3.1, where cast was first introduced.

All is not lost, however, as it is possible to recover the apparently lost type using a *cast* expression, examples of which have been seen a number of times in earlier chapters. A cast allows the type of an expression to be changed, providing the type rules of the Java language are not violated. This is most useful when we want to cast from type `Object` back to the actual type of the object being referenced. For example:

```
Queue q = new Queue () ;
Date d = new Date () ; // Date is a library class used to
                       // represent dates.
q.addBack(d) ;
...
Date e = (Date)q.removeFront() ;
```

Here a `Date` object is stored in a `Queue`. When the `Date` is removed from the `Queue` the cast expression `(Date)` is used to recover the type of the object returned from `removeFront` from `Object` back to `Date`. (Note that the cast acts not on the variable q but on the whole `q.removeFront()` expression and hence on the object returned.) If the cast had been absent the last assignment would be illegal as we would be trying to assign an `Object` reference to a `Date` — it is not possible to assign a superclass type where a subclass type is expected.

Casting works by changing the type of an expression, not the type of an object or primitive value. However, it is not possible to simply cast the type of an expression to any type regardless of what object or primitive value is being used in the expression. An object must be able to conform to the result type of a cast expression, while for primitive values there must be a *conversion* that can be applied to the value to get a value of the desired type. For example:

```
double d = 10 ;
int x = (int)d ;
```

is valid as the Java language provides a conversion from type `double` to type `int` that can be invoked with the `cast` expression. On the other hand, the following is not allowed:

```
double d = 10 ;
int x = d ; // Invalid
```

This will be rejected at compile time as without the cast expression no conversion will take place. All conversions involving primitive values will always be checked by the compiler.

In contrast, casting the type of object references requires both compile time *and* run-time checking. In general, the only way to tell if an object referenced by an expression will conform to the result type of a cast expression is to check at run-time. While type conformance provides a lot of flexibility, it makes the type checking task too complex for the compiler to perform completely when compiling code. For example, when checking the expression:

```
Stack e = (Stack)q.removeFront() ; // q is of type Queue
```

the compiler can check that the type of the expression on the right-hand side is compatible with the type on the left, but cannot predict what object will be returned by the `removeFront` method and whether it will conform to `Stack` when the cast is applied. Hence, a run-time check has to be performed when the cast expression is executed. If there is a problem then an error occurs, which, by default, will stop the program.

Casting is a necessary mechanism but has some dangers and needs to be used carefully. The main problem is that it relies on the programmer explicitly using cast expressions and specifying the

note

A cast from a supertype to a subtype is often known as a 'downcast'.

note

An invalid cast causes a `ClassCastException`. *Exceptions will be introduced in Section 8.1, Page 226.*

types correctly. If a mistake is made, the error will rarely be detected by the compiler (which would force the programmer to fix the problem immediately) but will normally occur when the program is run, usually causing the program to terminate. Only if a complete and thorough test of the program is undertaken will the potential run-time error be detected before the program has been delivered for use. It is unfortunate that too many programs are delivered without having undergone enough testing. Not to test properly is very unprofessional. Users dislike it as well!

7.6.2   Class Class and Instanceof

The checking of cast expressions at run-time is possible because an object knows which class it is an instance of and this information can be used to determine which types the object will conform to. When a program is run, each class (and primitive type and array) is represented by an instance of class `Class`, which is declared in the J2SDK package `java.lang`. A `Class` object stores detailed information about a class including the names and types of all methods and instance variables. This information can be accessed at run-time in order to manipulate classes and objects in sophisticated ways; the techniques are usually referred to as *reflective programming* (or just reflection).

note

The library package `java.lang.reflect` *contains classes to support reflective programming.*

The method `getClass`, inherited from class `Object`, returns an instance of class `Class` when called for any object. Class `Class` has a static method `forName` that can be used to deliver up a reference to the object that is the class object associated with the name that is the string parameter. Thus it is possible to explicitly check the class of an object. For example:

note

To use method `forName`, *exception handling is required. See Chapter 8.*

```
Queue q = new Queue (10) ;
...
if (q.getClass() == Class.forName("Queue")) {
  // The class object associated with q is the same as the
  // class object associated with the string "Queue".
  System.out.println("Instance of Queue") ;
}
```

An alternative mechanism is to ask the class object found by calling the method `getClass` to deliver up the string of the name of the class and then to test that against a literal:

```
Queue q = new Queue (10) ;
...
if (q.getClass().getName.equals("Queue")) {
  // The class object associated with q is associated with
  // the string "Queue".
  System.out.println("Instance of Queue") ;
}
```

The full power of reflection is not always needed for applications programming yet asking about the type of an object can be very important. Java provides a mechanism for asking this question without the need to make use of the full reflection system. The operator `instanceof`, can be used as in:

```
Queue q = new Queue (10) ;
...
if (q instanceof Queue) {
  System.out.println("Instance of Queue") ;
}
```

Instanceof can be used on any object reference to see if the referenced object is an instance of a class or any of its subclasses.

While it can be useful to find the class of an object, beware of writing code like the following:

```
if (obj instanceof String) { // NB This is horrendously bad code.
  ...
} else if (obj instanceof ArrayList) {
  ...
} else {
  ...
}
```

Here repeated tests are made to try to find the class of an object. This is invariably a sign of poor design and the code will be incredibly difficult to maintain, as well as being a major source of errors. If ever you find yourself wanting to write code such as the above, rethink the design of the program.

7.7 Overriding Methods

A subclass can add new methods over and above those inherited from the superclass, as we have seen with IntDequeue. Much of the time the new methods will have different names or signatures (the same name, parameter type and return type) to those in the superclass. However, there is nothing to stop us declaring in the subclass methods of the same signatures as in the superclass. This is hiding of methods which, as indicated at the end of Section 7.3.6, Page 193, can actually be a very desired thing. Because of this, rather than call it hiding, it is called *overriding* an inherited method. For example, consider the following class that might represent customers within a program that handles the on-line payment for items purchased through a Web-based shop:

ref

See Section 31.2.4, Page 875, for details of method overriding.

```
public class Customer {
  // Variable, constructor and method declarations are here.
  ...
  // This method is called when the customer makes a payment for items
  // selected. The parameter represents the amount of money and the
  // method will do what is appropriate to complete the payment for
  // that amount. The method returns false if the payment cannot be
  // made. In this class, the default is to do nothing and simply
  // return false.
  public boolean makePayment(final int amount) {
    return false ;
  }
  ...
}
```

The amount of money parameter is an integer (in cents, pence, etc.) to avoid inaccuracies that can occur when floating point numbers are used.

Subclasses of Customer might include HomeCustomer, representing a typical private consumer paying by credit card, and BusinessCustomer, representing an account which will expect to be sent an invoice to make payment via their company's payment system. Structurally, these might look like:

```
public class HomeCustomer extends Customer {
  // Get credit card details from the customer and make the payment.
  public boolean makePayment(final int amount) {
    ...
  }
}
```

```
public class BusinessCustomer extents Customer {
  // Check the customer's account status and generate an invoice.
  public boolean makePayment(final int amount) {
    ...
  }
}
```

note

*An overriding method
must have exactly the
same signature as the
version in the superclass.*

The `makePayment` method in all three classes has the same signature. The versions declared in the subclasses *override* the one inherited from `Customer`. The significance of this is that whenever `makePayment` is called, the method executed will be the one declared by the class of the object it is called for. This is particularly important when you have a situation such as:

```
Customer aCustomer = new HomeCustomer () ;
...
boolean OK = aCustomer.makePayment(amount) ;
```

note

*Dynamic binding selects
a method to execute by
looking at the class of the
object, not the type of the
reference.*

Here we have a superclass reference to a subclass object, with the reference used to make a call to `makePayment`. As the type of the reference is `Customer`, one might expect the method in class `Customer` to be called but that is not the case. Instead, *dynamic binding* takes place and the method called is determined by the class of the object referenced, rather than the type of the reference. Hence, it is the `makePayment` declared by class `HomeCustomer` that gets called.

The type of the reference does matter, however, as type checking is always performed by the compiler. The method called must exist in the scope of the class of the variable used to refer to the object in order for the method to be callable — only if this is the case does the expression pass static type checking at compile-time. At run-time, dynamic binding happens and the method of the subclass scope is the one actually called.

The combination of inheritance, overridden methods in subclasses and dynamic binding leads to some very important capabilities. All customer subclasses inherit a common interface of public methods from `Customer`. If chosen carefully, these methods represent all the operations that need to be performed on a customer, regardless of what kind of customer is being dealt with at any given moment. Overriding allows a subclass to specialize a method to deal with its particular kind of customer, while preserving the common method interface. Dynamic binding ensures that the correct method is called even if the calling code is written in terms of type `Customer`. The usefulness of this can be illustrated by a method such as the following:

```
// Method to handle the overall strategy of paying for a
// collection of items.
void buy(Customer aCustomer, ArrayList items) {
  Check customer details
  Check items and calculate total amount to pay
  Call makePayment method on aCustomer
  Send dispatch notice to packing
}
```

This method describes the entire strategy of handling the buying of items but delegates the details to objects like the customer object. Dynamic binding ensures that the correct methods to deal with each kind of customer get called. Overall the aim is to write as much of the full program as possible using superclass types such as `Customer`, with the details of how to perform specific actions contained in the methods of subclasses.

7.7.1 Applets

Although this book concentrates on writing programs which are Java applications, it is worth a quick look at a Java applet, as applets rely on inheritance to work. An applet is designed to be part of a Web page, but rather than being a complete program with a `main` method, it consists of one or more classes that are dynamically loaded into an existing Java environment running in a Web browser.

The Java class library provides a class `Applet` which implements the core infrastructure needed by an applet (allowing it to interact and be displayed by a Web browser). This class is inherited by the programmer's applet class and a key set of methods overridden. When the new applet object is loaded the overridden methods are called in a pre-determined order to get the applet to do its work. The Web browser's Java environment provides a framework into which applet objects can fit and knows which methods to call and when. The following is a basic skeleton of an `Applet` subclass:

```
public class MyApplet extends Applet {
    // This method is called to perform any initialisation needed before
    // the applet does anything else. No constructors are used.
    public void init() { ... }
    // This method is called when the applet is no longer required by
    // the browser and should release any resources held by the applet.
    public void destroy() { ... }
    // This method is called to get the applet to display its output in
    // an area of the browser window.
    public void paint(Graphics g) { ... }
}
```

As well as the methods shown above, class `Applet` provides a collection of methods which can be overridden or used by a subclass to specialize its behaviour for whatever the new applet needs to do; if the subclass chooses not to declare an overriding of a method then the 'default' method supplied by `Applet` will be used. As a subclass inherits the interface needed by applet objects, its instance objects can function fully as applets. Dynamic binding takes care of correctly calling the methods of the new applet.

The following example provides a simple, but complete, applet which displays a text message using the technique shown in Section 4.4, Page 101:

```
import java.applet.* ;
import java.awt.* ;
import java.awt.geom.* ;

public class MyApplet extends Applet {
  private Font bigFont ;

  public void init()  {
    bigFont = new Font("Serif", Font.PLAIN, 50) ;
  }
  public void paint(Graphics g)  {
    Graphics2D g2d = (Graphics2D)g ;
    g2d.setFont(bigFont) ;
    g2d.drawString("Hello World!", 20, 150) ;
  }
}
```

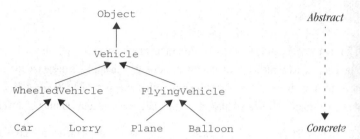

Figure 7.3 An inheritance hierarchy.

The `init` method is used to create the `Font` object needed to display the message, while the `paint` method actually displays the message. `Paint` will be called by the Java environment in the Web browser whenever the applet needs to update its display.

7.8   Inheritance Hierarchies

Inheritance is not limited to just one level which means that classes must be organized into an *hierarchy*. Hierarchies may be any number of levels deep (see Figure 7.3 for an example of a small hierarchy). A subclass can be at the end of a chain of superclasses, with each class in the chain being able to add variables and add or override methods. The immediate superclass of a class (the one which it extends) can be referred to as the *direct* superclass, while others higher up in the chain are *indirect* superclasses. Whilst it is possible to construct long chains of these relationships, it is a general guideline that there should not be too many layers of relationships otherwise it can become difficult to reason about them. Also, it shouldn't be forgotten that any hierarchy actually extends up to class `Object`.

tip

Keep inheritance hierarchies as shallow as possible.

In any inheritance hierarchy, classes should change from being *abstract* towards the top to *concrete* at the bottom. A *concrete class* is meant to have objects instantiated from it, and must therefore provide a complete implementation. An *abstract class*, on the other hand, is not meant to be instantiated, so does not need to provide a complete implementation, instead acting as a place holder for additional variables and methods to be added by subclasses.

This now gives us two kinds of classes to design; those which provide a partial implementation and are designed to be inherited from, and those which provide complete implementations that may include parts inherited from a superclass.

A particular role of an abstract class is to specify a public method interface which can be inherited by direct or indirect subclasses. This means that all the subclasses of the abstract class will share the same interface (and possibly extend it in their own way). The methods declared by the abstract class are typically overridden by the subclasses, to specialize their behaviour. The declarations of the methods in the abstract class may provide default implementations or simply have no method bodies.

7.8.1 Abstract Classes

The ideas behind abstract classes are sufficiently important that the Java language provides direct support for the concept, allowing a class to be explicitly marked as abstract. The `Customer` class seen earlier is a good candidate for marking as abstract as it doesn't make sense to create `Customer` instance objects and the primary role of the class is to define a shared public interface for superclasses. An abstract class would be declared as follows:

```
public abstract class Customer {
    // Variable, constructor and method declarations are here.
    ...
    // This method is called when the customer makes a payment for items
    // selected. The parameter represents the amount of money and the
    // method will do what is appropriate to complete the payment for
    // that amount. The method returns false is the payment cannot be
    // made. In this class, the default is to do nothing and simply
    // return false.
    public abstract boolean makePayment(final int amount) ;
    ...
}
```

The keyword `abstract` has two roles in this class. Firstly, the class itself is declared as abstract, telling the Java compiler that instances of the class cannot be created. An attempt to compile:

```
Customer aCustomer = new Customer () ;
```

will result in an error message. Secondly, the `makePayment` method is declared abstract. An abstract method has *no* method body, so there are no braces — the parameter list is followed by a semicolon. A concrete subclass must override an abstract method and provide a method body, something that is carefully checked by the Java compiler.

An abstract class still declares a type, so a statement like:

```
Customer aCustomer = new BusinessCustomer () ;
```

is completely valid and, indeed, is required if we want to retain the properties discussed in Section 7.7, Page 203. Methods can safely be called using the reference of `Customer` type, as dynamic binding takes care of calling a valid method.

Abstract classes can still declare complete methods that don't have to be overridden. For example, if `Customer` has a string variable storing the customer name, then the following method can be declared and inherited:

```
public String getName() {
    return name ;
}
```

Declaring methods like this avoids having duplicate methods in subclasses and allows the abstract class to fulfil its role as a place holder for shared implementation to be inherited by subclasses.

A class should always be declared abstract if it is not meant to have instance objects, or if it does not make sense to have instance objects. Doing this will let the language compiler help with checking that a program is properly constructed and not trying to create objects of a class that is not supposed to have instances.

ref

See Section 31.2.10, Page 889, for more details on abstract classes and Section 31.2.11, Page 890, for abstract methods.

7.9   Interfaces

ref

*For detailed information
about interfaces see
Section 31.3, Page 897.*

It is possible to envisage an abstract class comprising only abstract methods. In fact, this is such an important concept in Java that there is a special construct for it: the *interface*.

A class can declare variables, methods, method implementations and, unless abstract, can have instance objects. An interface, on the other hand, cannot define instance variables (except possibly static final variables) nor methods with method bodies, i.e. it is limited to declaring certain kinds of variables and abstract methods. An interface cannot be used to instantiate objects. So whilst a class combines the three roles of declaring a type, defining a public method interface and describing an object's implementation, an interface only performs the first two roles.

The purpose of an interface is to allow a type to be declared that is unrelated to any class (and hence free of any restrictions imposed by structure of the class hierarchy), and then exploit type conformance to make use of the type. This allows a type to be specified to which objects from a number of classes can conform without needing an inheritance relationship between the classes of those objects.

An interface is declared much like a class, with the `class` keyword replaced by the `interface` keyword. The following example declares a `Queue` interface:

```
interface Queue {
  void addBack(final Object x) ;
  Object removeFront() ;
}
```

Declarations for methods to add or remove values are present but no method bodies. The interface is used by declaring a class to *implement* the interface:

```
class QueueImpl implements Queue
{
  // The class body implements the addBack and removeFront methods,
  // along with the instance variable declarations and a main method
  // for testing.
  public void addBack(final Object x) { ... }
  public Object removeFront() { ... }
  ...
}
```

The `implements` keyword is used to denote the implementation relationship, requiring the class to provide method bodies for the methods declared by the interface, i.e. for the class to conform to the interface. The class `QueueImpl` implementation is the same as that described for class `Queue` in Section 7.6.1, Page 198.

Using the `Queue` interface and the classes implementing it, we can write statements such as:

```
Queue queue = new QueueImpl () ;
...
// Now use the queue
queue.addback("Hello") ;
...
String s = (String)queue.removeFront() ;
```

Queue is a perfectly valid type and can be used in all the ways described earlier. In particular, the parts of a program using queues can mostly be written in terms of the Queue type, without having to be concerned with the class of the objects actually providing queue implementations. The code that creates specific queue objects can be localized in one place, avoiding the need for the rest of the program to use the implementation class directly. Should a new kind of queue with a different implementation be used in the future, only the statements creating the new queue object need to be changed and the rest of the program will carry on working unchanged.

As might be expected, subclasses of a class implementing an interface also inherit the requirement to implement the interface. A DequeueImpl class could be declared as follows:

```
class DequeueImpl extends QueueImpl {
  // Implementation of a dequeue
  ...
}
```

This would allow a DequeueImpl object to be used directly or to conform to type Queue:

```
Queue queue = new DequeueImpl () ;
...
// Now use the dequeue as a queue
queue.addback("Hello") ;
...
String s = (String)queue.removeFront() ;
```

Of course, it would make sense to declare a Dequeue interface as well. This can be done either by declaring a stand-alone dequeue interface or by extending the existing Queue interface:

```
public interface Dequeue extends Queue {
  void addFront(final Object n) ;
  Object removeBack() ;
}
```

This demonstrates that interfaces can inherit from one another, allowing an interface hierarchy to be developed independently from any class hierarchy.

Using the Dequeue interface leads to the following declaration for the DequeImpl class:

```
public class DequeueImpl extends QueueImpl implements Dequeue
```

This demonstrates the ability of a class to inherit part of its implementation from one class, while implementing another interface at the same time. Further, a class can be declared as implementing two or more interfaces:

```
class StackDequeueImpl implements Stack, Dequeue
```

Here we assume the existence of a Stack interface in order to create a class that can behave as both a stack and a dequeue, though it should be noted that this is not a particularly sensible thing to do.

note

An interface can extend multiple other interfaces and is not limited to single inheritance like classes.

7.10 Copying and Comparing Objects

We know that assignment of object references copies the reference and not the object being referenced. If assignment does not actually copy an object then what do we do if we actually do want

ref

See Section 31.2.12, Page 892, for more information about cloning comparing objects.

note

Calling clone can fail and cause an exception to be thrown — exceptions will be introduced in Chapter 8, so are not shown here.

to copy the object? The answer is that objects that need to be copied must implement a method called `clone` which can be called to clone (make an exact copy of) the object, returning a reference to a new object with the same internal state as the original. The basic `clone` method is declared in class `Object` and hence inherited by all other classes. Any class can override the basic definition in order to specialize it to copy objects of that class.

For the `clone` method to work at all, a class that has a `clone` method must implement the interface `Cloneable`. Doing this marks objects of the class as being cloneable and allows the method `clone` to be called.

So for example, assuming a `clone` method has been added to class `QueueImpl`, then:

```
Queue s = new QueueImpl () ;
Queue t = s.clone() ;
```

results in `s` being a reference to a `QueueImpl` object and `t` being a reference to a different `QueueImpl` object initialized to the same *value* as that referred to by `s`.

So far, so good, but what are the semantics of the clone operation: what does copying an object actually do? On the face of it we want it to allocate space for a new object the same size as the one that is being copied and then copy the values of all the instance variables into the new object. This presents no problems for instance variables of primitive types but what happens with object references? The question is: Do just the references get copied or do the objects being referenced get copied?

The basic `clone` method declared by class `Object` makes a copy of object references but not the objects being referenced. Variables holding values of primitive types are simply copied as expected. This is known as making a *shallow copy*, resulting in a copy of the object being cloned but nothing else that the object is associated with. All associated objects are *shared* by the original and the clone.

Copying everything, the object and all objects associated with it, is known as a *deep copy*. Such an operation must copy the object and then follow all the object references cloning all objects that it finds. As you can imagine, doing a deep copy is potentially very expensive in terms of time and memory, particularly if many objects are involved. This is why the default `clone` method is a shallow copy. If a deep copy is really required then it has to be implemented explicitly by the programmer. This is not usually done by overriding the `clone` method, since this is understood to be a shallow copy. Deep copy would normally be implementing using a new method. The exception is where it makes no sense to shallow copy for whatever reason, in which case overriding `clone` may well be the right thing to do.

A variation on cloning is to make use of a *copy constructor*. This is a constructor that takes a reference to an object of the same class as a parameter. The new object is then initialized to be a copy of the object referenced by the parameter. `Clone` is not a suitable method to call in this situation as the copy already exists in the form of the new object being initialized. The constructor body must perform the copying required, which is often similar to that needed by `clone`, so putting the common code into a private helper method tends to be the done thing.

A similar situation applies to comparing objects. Again, class `Object` declares an `equals` method which does a shallow comparison. The programmer must override `equals` to do deep comparison for their classes.

Comparing objects is trickier than might appear at first sight. A common mistake is to try to compare objects using the `==` operator. However, this operator will only compare the object references not the objects that are being referenced. Hence, it can be used to check if two reference variables are referencing the *same* object but not for anything else.

The correct way to compare objects using `equals` is carefully defined in the J2SDK documentation for class `Object` and is also described in Section 31.2.12, Page 892. Essentially the programmer has to decide what it means for the values of two distinct objects to be equal. It may be sufficient to simply compare the values of the instance variables, comparing object references, which would be a shallow comparison. On the other hand, a deep comparison might be required where the values of referenced objects are also compared.

The issues to do with `clone` and `equals` will be explored further in Part 2 of this book, along with examples of their use.

tip

The operator == compares object references not objects.

7.11 Nested Classes

To complete our examination of classes in this chapter we will briefly introduce the concept of *nested* and *member* classes. These are examined in detail in the reference section of the book while there are many examples of their use in Parts 2 and 3.

Nested and member classes are declared *inside* another class and so are nested in the scope of that class. Such classes can be declared as `public`, `protected` or `private`, allowing control over their accessibility to the program as a whole. Often they are declared as private and act as a building block for the data structures used by the enclosing class.

A brief summary of the varieties of nested and member classes is as follows:

- A *nested top-level class* is declared as `static`, but is otherwise a normal class within the scope of the enclosing class.
- A *member class* is declared without using the `static` keyword and has the additional capability of having access to the full scope of the enclosing class (whereas nested top-level classes do not). An important consequence of this is that instance objects must be created by an object of the enclosing class and have full access to the state of that object.
- A *local class* is like a member class but is declared within a compound statement, and has access to the scope it is declared in as well as the scope of the enclosing class.

ref

See Section 30.4, Page 852, for detailed information about nested and member classes, including examples of their use.

- An *anonymous class* is a local class that is declared as a subclass of some other named class but has no name itself.

Member, local and anonymous classes may seem obscure at this stage but turn out to be powerful mechanisms that will be exploited in later chapters, where their use can be illustrated with useful examples.

7.12 Packages

ref

Section 30.5, Page 864.

As with any other documents held on computer, the source code of a Java program needs to be stored in files on disk. Usually, each class is stored in a separate file, although it is possible (and sometimes useful) to have several classes in the same file. Given that classes are usually in different files, there needs to be a mechanism for making the declaration of one class accessible to another. This is handled by the compilation system (in particular, the way the Java compiler locates classes) and interacts with what are known as *packages*.

Earlier chapters emphasized the need to structure programs, which led to the idea of classes as a way of grouping methods and variables together. This theme can be taken one step further by providing a way to group related classes together. Java provides the idea of a package which has a name and defines a scope containing one or more classes. Classes inside a package can be declared public, making them accessible to other classes outside the package, so the package enforces another level of encapsulation.

As we have seen a number of times, the standard Java class libraries are organized into a number of packages with names like `java.awt`, `java.util` and `java.lang`. To access a class in a package either the entire package or an individual class in a package must be *imported* using an `import` statement, for example:

```
import java.awt.* ;      // Import all the AWT classes
import java.util.Date ;  // Import the Date class
```

Import statements are usually placed at the top of source files and are used to make class declarations in other files accessible, hence the relationship between packages and files.

Of course, if a class is in a package there must be some way of specifying the package name. This is done using a package statement which is placed in a source file before any classes are declared. For example:

```
package MyPackage ;
```

More than one file can define classes in the same package, so each file would contain the package declaration. Following the package statement any class declared in the file will be in that package.

By default a class will be private to the package it is declared in, so the class can only be accessed by other classes in the same package (this is encapsulation at work). To make a class accessible to other packages using the import statement, the class must be made public. This is done be preceding the class declaration with the keyword public:

```
public class Stack { ... }
```

Note that making a class local to a package is done by omitting the public keyword, not by using the private keyword.

Any class in a file that does not include a package statement is assumed to be part of the anonymous *default package*, so classes are always members of a package.

Packages actually define another level of scope, and the fact that all classes are within a package, even if it is the default package, explains why all the classes shown so far are declared as public. As programs get larger and consist of a larger number of classes, it begins to make sense to define new packages and make some classes private to their package. A private class provides support for the implementation of other classes in the package but is not meant for use by the rest of the program.

Package scope allows classes with the same name to co-exist within the same program, as they can be declared within different packages. This is very useful if a program combines classes from different sources but which might have classes with the same names. If classes are delivered within a package then problems will be avoided (providing the package names are different).

Package names are hierarchical so a name like java.util.Date denotes the class Date in the package util which, in turn, is in package java. Moreover, the directory structure in which the .java and .class files are stored on disk must reflect the package structure. This means that Date.java and Date.class must be in a directory called util, which is in a directory called java. If the directory structure is not in place, and the directory names are not the same as the package names, then it is not possible to compile or use any classes in the package.

7.12.1 Packages and Protected

The package scope interacts with protected variable and method declarations, so that anything declared protected is accessible by other classes within the *same* package, as well as any subclasses, whether in the same package or not. This can be confusing at first and is also open to abuse if the coupling between classes in the same package is increased by indiscriminate use of protected variables and methods. While there are times when accessing protected methods and variables of another class that is not a superclass is useful, care should be taken to ensure that good design decisions are being made: always minimize coupling.

The situation is made more complex by the ability to declare methods and variables without using any of the public, protected or private keywords. These can be accessed by the class they are declared in and any other class in the same package. Again this risks an unnecessary increase in coupling between classes and should be used carefully, if at all.

tip

Always declare methods and variables using the public, protected *or* private *keywords, unless you have a very good reason not to.*

7.13   Class Matrix Revisited

To illustrate a number of the features shown in the chapter up to this point we will revisit and re-factor the matrix class example given in Section 6.7.2, Page 169.

Statement of Problem   *"Implement a standard matrix class and a sparse matrix class that can be used interchangeably and share a common interface."*

Design and Implementation   A sparse matrix only stores values that are explicitly added to it. All other values are assumed to be zero. A sparse matrix is useful if very large matrices are to be used where many of the values are zero (something that is quite common in many numerical calculations).

Looking at the design issues, if the matrix classes are to share a common interface then either an interface or an abstract class could be used. Looking at an interface first, we can declare the following:

```
// A basic matrix interface.
// Written by Graham Roberts, September 1999
// Revision History: none
public interface Matrix {
  public int getNumberOfRows() ;
  public int getNumberOfColumns() ;
  public double getElement(final int row, final int col) ;
  public void setElement(final int row, final int col,
                         final double val) ;
  public Matrix add(final Matrix m) ;
}
```

This declares the public methods used in the original matrix class (for this example, we will still only deal with matrix addition). Class `Matrix` can be renamed to `MatrixImpl` and implement the interface with a few minor changes:

```
// A basic matrix class implementing the matrix interface.
// Written by Graham Roberts, September 1999
// Revision History: none
public class MatrixImpl implements Matrix {
  // Use a 2D array for the data structure.  The array knows its own
  // size, so we don't have to record the number of rows and columns
  // separately.
  private double[][] elements ;

  public MatrixImpl(final int rows, final int columns) {
    if ((rows < 1) || (columns < 1)) {
      elements = new double[1][1] ;
    } else {
      elements = new double[rows][columns] ;
    }
  }
  // A conversion constructor, for turning a 2D array into a
  // matrix. This is provided for convenience.
  public MatrixImpl(final double[][] data) {
    this(data.length,data[0].length) ;
    for (int row = 0 ; row < getNumberOfRows() ; ++row) {
      for (int col = 0 ; col < getNumberOfColumns() ; ++col) {
        setElement(row,col,data[row][col]) ;
      }
    }
```

```java
      }
      public int getNumberOfRows() {
        return elements.length ;
      }
      public int getNumberOfColumns() {
        return elements[0].length ;
      }
      // Return true if the selected element is actually
      // within the matrix.
      private boolean isValidElement(final int row, final int col) {
        return ( (row > -1) && (row < getNumberOfRows()) &&
                 (col > -1) && (col < getNumberOfColumns()))) ;
      }
      public double getElement(final int row, final int col) {
        if (isValidElement(row,col)) {
          return elements[row][col] ;
        } else {
          return 0.0 ;
        }
      }
      public void setElement(final int row, final int col,
                             final double val) {
        if (isValidElement(row,col)) {
          elements[row][col] = val ;
        }
      }
      // Add the argument matrix to this, or return null
      // if the sizez do not match.
      public Matrix add(final Matrix m) {
        if ((getNumberOfRows() != m.getNumberOfRows()) ||
            (getNumberOfColumns() != m.getNumberOfColumns())) {
          return null ;
        }
        Matrix result =
          new MatrixImpl(getNumberOfRows(),getNumberOfColumns()) ;
        for (int row = 0 ; row < getNumberOfRows() ; ++row) {
          for (int col = 0 ; col < getNumberOfColumns() ; ++col) {
            double value = getElement(row,col) + m.getElement(row,col) ;
            result.setElement(row,col,value) ;
          }
        }
        return result ;
      }
      // Helper method to display a matrix.
      public static void display(final Matrix m) {
        for (int row = 0 ; row < m.getNumberOfRows() ; ++row) {
          System.out.print('[') ;
          for (int col = 0 ; col < m.getNumberOfColumns() ; ++col) {
            System.out.print(m.getElement(row,col) + " ");
          }
          System.out.println(']') ;
        }
      }
      public static void main(final String[] args) {
        Matrix m1
          = new MatrixImpl(new double[][]{{1.2,2.5,4.5}, {3.9,4.2,0.9}}) ;
        Matrix m2
          = new MatrixImpl(new double[][]{{1.3,7.5,5.2}, {4.8,8.3,9.1}}) ;
        Matrix m3 = m1.add(m2) ;
        display(m3) ;
      }
    }
```

The new `SpareMatrixImpl` class needs a new data structure as only values explicitly added using the `setElement` method need to be stored, everything else being zero. The data structure used here is a `HashMap` from the J2SDK, which stores values that are indexed or *keyed* using an object value, rather than integers that an array or `ArrayList` uses. Our key values will be objects of a nested class called `Index`, which represents an (x, y) matrix element coordinate.

```java
// A basic sparse matrix class.
// Written by Graham Roberts, September 1999
// Revision History: developed from class Matrix
import java.util.HashMap ;
public class SparseMatrixImpl implements Matrix {
  private class Index {
    private int x = 0 ;
    private int y = 0 ;
    // Each value (rather than object) requires a unique identifier or
    // hash value which is stored in this variable.
    private int hashvalue = 0 ;
    public Index(final int x, final int y) {
      this.x = x ;
      this.y = y ;
      hashvalue = ((new Integer(x)).toString() +
                   (new Integer(y)).toString()).hashCode() ;
    }
    // Override equals to compare to Index objects.  If used properly
    // the parameter object should always be an Index but we will
    // check anyway, to show the use of instance of.
    public boolean equals(Object obj) {
      if (obj instanceof Index) {
        Index index = (Index)obj ;
        return ((x == index.x) && (y == index.y)) ;
      } else {
        return false ;
      }
    }
    // Override the inherited method from
    // class Object.
    public int hashCode() {
      return hashvalue ;
    }
  }
  // Use hashtable for the data stucture
  private HashMap elements ;
  // Instance variables are needed to remember
  // the size of the matrix.
  private int numberRows = 0 ;
  private int numberColumns = 0 ;
  public SparseMatrixImpl(final int rows, final int columns) {
    elements = new HashMap() ;
    if ((rows > 0) && (columns > 0)) {
      numberRows = rows ;
      numberColumns = columns ;
    }
  }
  // A conversion constructor, for turning a 2D array into a
  // matrix. This is provided for convenience.
  public SparseMatrixImpl(final double[][] data) {
    this(data.length,data[0].length) ;
    for (int row = 0 ; row < getNumberOfRows() ; ++row) {
      for (int col = 0 ; col < getNumberOfColumns() ; ++col) {
        setElement(row,col,data[row][col]) ;
      }
    }
  }
  public int getNumberOfRows() {
    return numberRows ;
  }
  public int getNumberOfColumns() {
```

```java
    return numberColumns ;
}
// Return true if the selected element is actually within the
// matrix.
private boolean isValidElement(final int row, final int col) {
  return ( (row > -1) && (row < getNumberOfRows()) &&
           (col > -1) && (col < getNumberOfColumns()))) ;
}
private boolean contains(final int row, final int col) {
  return elements.containsKey(new Index(row,col)) ;
}
public double getElement(final int row, final int col) {
  if (isValidElement(row,col) && contains(row,col)) {
    return
      ((Double)elements.get(new Index(row,col))).doubleValue() ;
  } else {
    return 0.0 ;
  }
}
public void setElement(final int row, final int col,
                       final double val) {
  if (isValidElement(row,col)) {
    if (contains(row,col)) {
      elements.remove(new Index(row,col)) ;
    }
    elements.put(new Index(row,col), new Double(val)) ;
  }
}
// Add the argument matrix to this, or return null
// if the sizez do not match.
public Matrix add(final Matrix m) {
  if ((getNumberOfRows() != m.getNumberOfRows()) ||
      (getNumberOfColumns() != m.getNumberOfColumns())) {
    return null ;
  }
  Matrix result =
    new SparseMatrixImpl(getNumberOfRows(),getNumberOfColumns()) ;
  for (int row = 0 ; row < getNumberOfRows() ; ++row) {
    for (int col = 0 ; col < getNumberOfColumns() ; ++col) {
      double value = getElement(row,col) + m.getElement(row,col) ;
      result.setElement(row,col,value) ;
    }
  }
  return result ;
}
// Helper method to display a matrix.
public static void display(final Matrix m) {
  for (int row = 0 ; row < m.getNumberOfRows() ; ++row) {
    System.out.print('[') ;
    for (int col = 0 ; col < m.getNumberOfColumns() ; ++col) {
      System.out.print(m.getElement(row,col) + " ");
    }
    System.out.println(']') ;
  }
}
public static void main(final String[] args) {
  Matrix m1
    = new SparseMatrixImpl(
        new double[][]{{1.2,2.5,4.5}, {3.9,4.2,0.9}}) ;
  Matrix m2
    = new SparseMatrixImpl(
        new double[][]{{1.3,7.5,5.2}, {4.8,8.3,9.1}}) ;
  Matrix m3 = m1.add(m2) ;
  display(m3) ;
}
}
```

Testing   The testing strategy for the original matrix class can be reused for the two new classes.

Review   Although using an interface works, it has the problem that code is duplicated in both classes, notably
the add method (and in the future, other methods like multiply). This is made worse by the fact
that add has been written so it does not depend upon the data structure used to implement a
particular kind of matrix. The add method does depend upon creating a matrix of a specific class,
however, but by delegating matrix creation to another method, this dependency can be removed.

The obvious way to fix the problem of code duplication is to change the interface into an abstract
class and declare the common methods there. This gives the following abstract class:

```
// A basic matrix abstract class.
// Written by Graham Roberts, September 1999
// Revision History: none
public abstract class Matrix {
  public abstract int getNumberOfRows() ;
  public abstract int getNumberOfColumns() ;
  public abstract double getElement(final int row, final int ccl) ;
  public abstract void setElement(final int row, final int col,
                          final double val) ;
  // Helper method to create a new matrix
  protected abstract Matrix create(final int rows, final int cols) ;
  // Add argument matrix to this or return null if the addition is not
  // possible.
  public final Matrix add(final Matrix m) {
    if ((getNumberOfRows() != m.getNumberOfRows()) ||
        (getNumberOfColumns() != m.getNumberOfColumns())) {
      return null ;
    }
    // Obtain a new matrix by calling the overridden create method.
    Matrix result =
     create(getNumberOfRows(),getNumberOfColumns()) ;
    for (int row = 0 ; row < getNumberOfRows() ; ++row) {
      for (int col = 0 ; col < getNumberOfColumns() ; ++col) {
        double value = getElement(row,col) + m.getElement(row,col) ;
        result.setElement(row,col,value) ;
      }
    }
    return result ;
  }
  // Helper method to display a matrix.
  public final static void display(final Matrix m) {
    for (int row = 0 ; row < m.getNumberOfRows() ; ++row) {
      System.out.print('[') ;
      for (int col = 0 ; col < m.getNumberOfColumns() ; ++col) {
        System.out.print(m.getElement(row,col) + " ");
      }
      System.out.println(']') ;
    }
  }
}
```

note

*A final method cannot be
overridden by a subclass.*

The public methods that depend upon how a particular matrix class is implemented are
declared as abstract and must be overridden by subclasses. The create method is also
abstract but is declared as protected. Full declarations of the add method and static
display method are provided. Both have been declared as final which means they cannot be

overridden by subclasses — we are making the statement that these methods must be implemented this way and should not be changed by subclasses.

The new versions of `MatrixImpl` and `SparseMatrixImpl` are much the same as already seen, so will not be repeated in full. The methods `add` and `display` are removed, the class declaration changed to extend `Matrix` rather than implement an interface, and a protected create method added:

```
protected Matrix create(final int rows, final int cols) {
  return new MatrixImpl(rows, cols) ;
}
```

and

```
protected Matrix create(final int rows, final int cols) {
  return new SparseMatrixImpl(rows, cols) ;
}
```

The abstract class solution aims to maximize code sharing but otherwise, from the point of view of clients of the matrix classes, works much the same.

A final refinement would be to create a package to keep the matrix classes in. This would be done by creating a subdirectory with the package name — for example, `DJSMatrix` — and moving the `.java` files into that package. At the start of each file the declaration:

```
package DJSMatrix ;
```

should be added. Other classes needing to use the matrix classes would then need to import the package by placing an import statement at the start of the file:

```
import DJSMatrix.* ;
```

This would import all classes found in the package. The following class consisting of only a `main` method illustrates this and also shows how the use of the different matrix implementations can be intermixed:

```
// A text program for the matrix classes.
// Written by Graham Roberts, September 1999
// Revision History: developed from class Matrix
import DJSMatrix.* ;
public class TestMatrix {
  public static void main(final String[] args) {
    Matrix m1
      = new SparseMatrixImpl(
          new double[][]{{1.2,2.5,4.5}, {3.9,4.2,0.9}}) ;
    Matrix m2
      = new SparseMatrixImpl(
          new double[][]{{1.3,7.5,5.2}, {4.8,8.3,9.1}}) ;
    Matrix m3 = m1.add(m2) ;
    SparseMatrixImpl.display(m3) ;
    Matrix m4
      = new MatrixImpl(new double[][]{{1.2,2.5,4.5}, {3.9,4.2,0.9}}) ;
    Matrix m5
      = new MatrixImpl(new double[][]{{1.3,7.5,5.2}, {4.8,8.3,9.1}}) ;
    Matrix m6 = m4.add(m5) ;
    MatrixImpl.display(m6) ;
    Matrix m7 = m1.add(m5) ;
    MatrixImpl.display(m7) ;
  }
}
```

7.14   Reusability and Components

Abstract classes and interfaces, declaring a set of public methods, give an important extension to the way we can design programs. The core framework of a program can be designed around a set of abstract classes and interfaces. These specify the structure of a program, the core set of behaviours it should provide and the interfaces by which components in the framework fit together.

With the abstract framework in place, inheritance can be used to specialize each abstract class, creating a matching collection of concrete subclasses. The concrete classes provide detailed implementation and specific behaviour for the program.

Interfaces then provide an additional way in which objects of those classes can work with one another without their classes having to be related by inheritance. Providing a class supports a particular interface, its objects can be used wherever that interface is specified.

This gives two major advantages:

- The clear identification of the abstractions and interconnections needed to implement an application, packaged up as a set of abstract classes supported by interfaces. Experience shows that this leads to better designed and more maintainable programs.

- *Reusability* — the abstract framework can be reused for similar applications by providing a new set of concrete subclasses which provide the detail needed by the new application.

Reuse is a recurring theme with object-oriented programming. Classes form the basic building block of reuse as they provide encapsulated objects which are relatively easy to reuse in many different situations. Java fully exploits this as it comes with a large class library providing many reusable classes.

However, reuse is not limited to individual classes. Collections of classes also provide reusable units in the form of frameworks and components. Indeed, a powerful force that is driving the development of programming systems is the growing support for *pluggable* components (see Figure 7.4). A component is typically implemented by a small collection of classes, with one class acting as an interface to the component.

Rather than designing a program from scratch, it can be built out of a set of pre-defined components which are linked together with small amounts of new code. This approach is termed *component-based design*, though in the Web environment it is called *object scripting*.

The connections between components are enabled using the mechanisms of inheritance, interfaces and dynamic binding. Users of the component make use of the public interface to call the component's methods but need not be aware of the details of the component implementation.

An important feature of pluggable components is that new components can be created and added without having to change the users of the components (they carry on using the existing

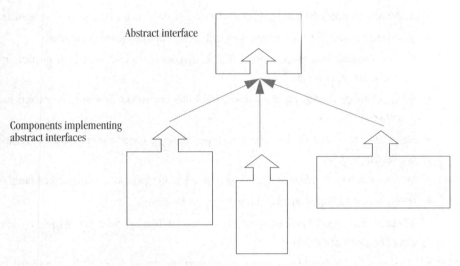

Abstract interface

Components implementing
abstract interfaces

Figure 7.4 Pluggable components.

interface). Users do not even need to know exactly what kind of component they are using, only that it supports the right interface. Note, 'the right interface' not only means the right set of operation names but also that the expected behaviours must match the requirements, so the different components must all behave in the way expected.

Java provides a standard mechanism for constructing and using components which is know as 'JavaBeans'.

7.15 Summary

This chapter has introduced three kinds of class relationship: association, inheritance and conformance. Association is where objects of one class make use of objects of another, while inheritance allows a subclass to be an extension of a superclass. Inheritance interacts with dynamic binding and type conformance to allow subclass objects to be used when a superclass type is specified, providing substitutability of objects, a form of polymorphism. Substitutability in turn relies on the use of carefully defined public interfaces described by collections of public methods. This idea is sufficiently important that Java provides interface declarations to allow interfaces to be declared independently of both classes and inheritance.

Using association and inheritance, a program can be constructed by first identifying the classes and interfaces required and then determining how they are related. The resulting set of classes, interfaces and relationships gives the structure of the program, tying all its parts together. Identifying the correct relationships is a key part of the programming process and avoiding mistakes here will be very important to the overall quality of the program.

Key points in this chapter:

- Association provides the has-a or uses-a relationship, implemented using object references.
- Inheritance provides the is-a relationship and allows one class to extend another.
- Protected variables and methods are accessible to subclasses and class in the same package, but not to any other classes.
- Subclass objects are initialized top-down, with rules controlling how the constructors are executed.
- Super is a reference of the superclass type, allowing control over which superclass constructor is called.
- Methods can be overridden by a subclass by re-declaring them with a new method body.
- Object substitutability is possible through type conformance.
- All classes are direct or indirect subclasses of class `Object`. A reference of type `Object` can refer to any type of object.
- An abstract class provides a partial object implementation that can be completed by subclasses. Abstract classes cannot have instances.
- Supertype and subtype relationships exist between types.
- An interface allows a type to be specified independently of classes.
- A package provides a scope in which a collection of classes to be grouped together.
- Classes must be imported from a package before being used.

Self-review Questions

Self-review 7.1 How is association between classes implemented?

Self-review 7.2 When is association more appropriate to use than inheritance?

Self-review 7.3 What does object ownership mean?

Self-review 7.4 How is a subclass object initialized?

Self-review 7.5 What are the advantages and disadvantages of using protected variables?

Self-review 7.6 What is `super`?

Self-review 7.7 How does a name get hidden?

Self-review 7.8 What is type conformance?

Self-review 7.9 Why can a reference of type `Object`, refer to any kind of object?

Self-review 7.10 Why is casting potentially dangerous?

Self-review 7.11 How is a method overridden?

Self-review 7.12 What are the differences between an abstract class and an interface?

Self-review 7.13 Describe how shallow and deep copying work.

Self-review 7.14 What is a nested class?

Self-review 7.15 How does a package work?

Programming Exercises

Exercise 7.1 Re-write the `Stack` class from Section 6.2.3, Page 149, to create a generic container class storing references of type `Object`.

Exercise 7.2 Write the `Dequeue` class that would be a subclass of `Queue` shown in Section 7.6.1, Page 198.

Exercise 7.3 Write a program to manage the inventory of a simple warehouse. Class `Item` defines the basic properties of an item stored in the warehouse, with subclasses representing real kinds of items. All items have a common set of properties such as size, weight, sell-by date and so on. Allow items to be added to and removed from the warehouse, and also make it possible to display a complete list of the current contents of the warehouse.

Exercise 7.4 Implement matrix multiplication for all the matrix implementation classes shown in Section 7.13, Page 214. The multiplication method should *not* depend upon how a specific kind of matrix is implemented.

Challenge

Challenge 7.1 Starting with class `GraphPanel` shown in Section 6.7.3, Page 171, create a `Graphing` interface declaring a common set of methods to be implemented by class `GraphPanel`, `PieChartPanel` and `BarChartPanel`, each of which draws a graph or chart of the appropriate form.

Introducing Exceptions and Threads

Objectives

To complete the examination of core Java programming principles, this chapter introduces exceptions and threads. Exceptions provide a way of properly dealing with unexpected errors that would otherwise cause a program to fail, while threads provide an important new kind of control mechanism.

Keywords

catch
exception
finally
synchronized
thread
throw
throws
try

8.1   Exceptions

Until now we have not seriously addressed what to do if an error occurs when a program is running. Without taking any action, an error risks either causing a program to fail immediately, or to generate spurious data leading to other errors.

A good example is the `removeFront` method declared in the `Queue` class from Section 7.6.1, Page 198. An item can only be removed from a queue if the queue is not empty. The method adopts the strategy of testing to see if the queue is empty and returning a default value if it is:

```
public Object removeFront() {
  if (isEmpty()) {
    return null ;
  }
  ...
```

This is unsatisfactory for two reasons: it attempts to cover up that a problem has occurred; and it returns a value that is likely to cause problems elsewhere unless the calling code tests to see if `null` has been returned.

An alternative approach might be to recognize that an error has occurred and deliberately stop the program:

```
public Object removeFront() {
  if (isEmpty()) {
    System.err.println("Attempting to remove item from empty queue") ;
    System.exit(0) ;
  }
  ...
```

note

`System.exit(0)`
*causes a program to
terminate immediately.
See the documentation
for class* `System` *for
further information.*

Rather than attempt to ignore the problem, this represents the other extreme in that an error message is displayed and the program is stopped. The aim is to force whoever is using the program to take notice and fix the real cause of the problem. Of course, if the user is not the programmer then this approach is going to cause great annoyance and should not be used in production code.

What is needed is a mechanism that allows an error to be detected in a way that the program itself can attempt to rectify the problem and carry on. Java provides such a mechanism in the form of exceptions and exception handing.

8.1.1   Kinds of Errors

Before looking at the Java language support for exception handling, we first need to examine the various kinds of error that can occur within a program. Errors can be put into the following categories: *syntax errors*, *type errors*, *logic errors* and *run-time errors*.

Syntax errors are relatively easily dealt with as they are caused by the source code of a program failing to conform to the *syntactic grammar* of the Java programming language. The syntactic grammar defines how the source code of a program is written down with everything in the correct order and place. Keywords must be used correctly, brackets must be in the right places, semicolons must be present, and so on. Syntax errors are often caused by typing mistakes or the failure of the programmer to remember the correct form of a Java statement. The Java compiler will find and report any and all syntax errors so they can be fixed immediately by the programmer while the program code is being written. It is not possible, nor sensible, to create something that can be run if the source code has errors in it, so the compiler will simply not allow it.

Type errors are caused by mismatches between types by, for example, trying to assign a variable a value of the wrong type, or trying to call a method that the class of an object does not provide. Many, but not all, errors of this sort can be detected by the Java compiler and are reported immediately. As with syntax errors, if the compiler detects a type error it will not generate executable code and the program will not be able to be run. However, as we saw in Section 7.6.1, Page 198, some expressions, such as cast expressions, require run-time type checking and can cause errors that the compiler will not detect.

Logic errors are very different sorts of thing. These are errors in the *algorithms* or implementations of the algorithms in a program and cannot be detected by the Java compiler. Logic errors only manifest themselves when a program is running and are noticed when the program calculates the wrong value or performs in an incorrect way. For example, attempting to pop a value off an empty stack or add an item to a queue that is full will be the result of logic errors. Dividing a number by zero is another classic logic error, caused by the failure to recognize that the implementation of an algorithm includes the possibility that division by zero can occur. Thorough code inspection and good testing strategies are the only way of finding and helping to fix errors of this variety.

Run-time errors are similar to logic errors in many ways but they are not caused by the program being wrongly constructed. Instead, they are caused by an event occurring that was either unexpected or outside the range of conditions the program was designed to work with. Handling user input is often a source of run-time errors, as users make mistakes in the data they are entering. For example, a user can provide an incorrect file name, so the program fails to open a file.

Run-time errors and some logic errors are said to cause *exceptions* — unexpected events that cause a program to fail. Exceptions that are not *handled* are undesirable as, by default, the program will terminate and not complete what it is doing. This can often result in a loss of data and is very annoying to the user of the program. Ideally, if an error occurs, we want to be able to recover the situation and enable the program to carry on. If that is not possible, the program should at least terminate in a safe and tidy way, preserving any data that would otherwise be lost.

The J2SDK library classes make extensive use of exceptions to notify a program of errors, often as a way of reporting that code calling a library class method has supplied invalid parameters or is attempting to misuse the library method.

tip

Ideally, a properly designed and tested program should never terminate unexpectedly. Even if it is not possible to carry on, important data should be saved, so that it can be recovered next time the program is run.

8.1.2   Catching Exceptions

ref

See for Chapter 32, Page 907, for a detailed description of exceptions.

Java provides an exception handling mechanism to deal with exceptions when they occur. The basic idea is to identify a sequence of statements that may cause an exception when executed and explicitly arrange to deal with any exceptions that may happen. In Java terminology, exceptions are *thrown*, so when we *try* to execute a statement and should an error occur, a piece of code can be provided to *catch* any exceptions that get thrown. The `try` and `catch` keywords are provided to support this:

```
try {
  anObject.f() ;
  anotherObject.g() ;
}
catch (SomeException e) {
  // do something to recover
}
```

This fragment of code contains a *try block* which consists of a compound statement, preceded by the keyword `try`, that will be executed as part of the usual order of execution. If an error occurs that causes an exception to be thrown, the following *catch block* will try to catch the exception. If an exception is caught, the statements in the compound statement following the `catch` keyword will be executed. These statements should attempt to rectify any problems and let the program continue, or, at worst, save any data and terminate the program gracefully. If no exceptions are thrown, or none are thrown that are caught by the catch block, the statements in the catch block are skipped over and not executed.

note

An exception represented by `Exception` *or any of its subclasses except* `RuntimeException` *(and its subclasses), must be caught otherwise the compiler will report an error.*

Exceptions are represented by objects which hold information about what happened to cause the exception. The Java class libraries provide a large number of exception classes, all of which are direct or indirect subclasses of the library class `Throwable`. Most exceptions that are handled by `try` and `catch` blocks are actually subclasses of class `Exception` which is a subclass of `Throwable`. Another small family of exceptions are the subclasses of `Error`, a further subclass of `Throwable`. Subclasses of `Error` represent conditions that are too serious to usually consider catching. Typically these are the result of being unable to load a class, a failure of the Java virtual machine or running out of memory. A program can also declare new exception subclasses to represent the errors that are specific to its needs.

Catch blocks have a parameter that specifies which type of exception object they will catch. In the example above, the catch block specifies that it will catch exceptions of the (fictitious) class `SomeException` or any of its subclasses. If the thrown exception object is of the right type, it will be caught and the exception parameter variable initialized to reference it. Although we have shown only a single catch block in the example, you can have several catch blocks, one after the other, each dealing with a different exception that might be thrown from the corresponding try block. An individual catch block can only have a single parameter.

If an exception is caught then the statements in the exception block will be executed and the program can carry on executing. Unless a statement in the catch block causes control to go elsewhere, the program will continue executing the statements following the catch block.

If an exception is not caught by the current set of catch blocks it will be passed, or *propagated*, back along the sequence of method calls that have been made to reach the current point in the program until a catch block dealing with that exception is found. Each method in the sequence containing an active try block (i.e. a try block that is waiting for a method call to return) has a chance to catch the exception if the exception type matches. If the exception is not caught anywhere and propagates all the way back along the chain of method calls, it will be dealt with by the Java run-time system and the program will be terminated. When an exception is propagated out of a method, that method is terminated and any local variables go out of scope.

note

The sequence of active method calls is called the call chain.

8.1.3 Throwing an Exception

As well as being able to catch an exception, it is necessary to be able to create and *throw* an exception. An exception needs to be thrown when an error cannot or should not be dealt with in the current method and needs to be handled by the caller of the method. To represent the exception, the programmer can define a new exception class by subclassing class `Exception` and then throwing an object of that class.

Returning to the `Queue` class, we can throw an exception to respond to an attempt to remove an item from an empty queue. The `removeFront` method is not in a position to try and correct the error in the code that is using the queue and called the method, so instead it should use the exception mechanism to force the calling code to take responsibility. This has the important effect of firmly placing the responsibility for dealing with errors on the calling code, which is entirely appropriate as that code caused the problem in the first place.

A throw statement, using the `throw` keyword, is used to throw an exception, so the `removeFront` method needs to be modified to be as follows:

```
public Object removeFront() throws EmptyQueueException {
   if (isEmpty()) {
    throw new EmptyQueueException("removeFront called on empty queue");
   }
   // Rest of method as before
   ...
}
```

Quite a lot is happening here:

- When the `isEmpty` test finds an empty queue, an exception object of type `EmptyQueueException` is created and thrown. The method immediately terminates, without returning a value, and the exception is delivered to the calling method.

- A subclass of `Exception` called `EmptyQueueException` is being used to represent exceptions thrown by the `Queue` class when an empty queue error occurs. The constructor is passed a string parameter with detailed information about the cause of the exception.

- A `throws` declaration appears following the method arguments, declaring what kind of exception the method will throw. This must be present as the method has to declare what exceptions it might throw.

!

throw *and* throws *are two distinct keywords.*

The last point is important as it tells the Java compiler that the method may throw an exception and, therefore, the exception *must* be caught by code in the calling method, or one of the methods further back in the call chain. The compiler will check that this is the case and report an error if it is not.

Assuming the method calling removeFront will catch the EmptyQueueException, it will contain try and catch blocks such as the following:

```
Queue q = new QueueImpl (10) ; // A queue to hold strings
q.addBack("Hello") ;
...
try {
  String s = (String)q.removeFront() ;
  // Process the string
  ...
}
catch (EmptyQueueException e) {
    // Either do nothing, as the subsequent code will still work if no
    // valid string is returned, or do something to prevent the absence
    // of a string from causing problems.
}
```

If the calling method does not catch the exception it must, in turn, declare that it throws an EmptyQueueException, and any exception thrown will be propagated back to its caller. The EmptyQueueException class is a straightforward subclass of Exception:

```
// A class representing the exception thrown when a queue is empty.
// Written by Graham Roberts, Sept 1999
// Revision History:
public class EmptyQueueException extends Exception {
  public EmptyQueueException() {
    super("Attempt to remove an item from an empty queue.") ;
  }
  public EmptyQueueException(final String s) {
    super(s) ;
  }
}
```

This illustrates the typical structure of an exception class, with two constructors, one taking a string argument. If necessary, additional methods and instance variables can be added to provide more information about why an exception occurred. Class Throwable provides storage for the string message along with the method getMessage to return the string. It also provides various methods for finding out more information about where the exception was thrown from. As is the case with EmptyQueueException, it is often enough to rely on the class of the exception object to identify why an exception has occurred.

You might argue that an error like trying to remove an element from an empty queue is one that should never happen given that the algorithms will be properly implemented in your program. This is too optimistic a position — a more defensive approach is needed. You might then argue that putting in place the exception handling mechanism when a queue is used is too much overhead to merit the gain in program safety. This argument has some merit. Indeed, it has sufficient merit that everyone agrees that two varieties of exception are needed, which is why Exception has the subclass RuntimeException that does require exceptions to be caught. Care is needed with this sort of exception exactly because not everything is explicit. RuntimeExceptions subvert the strict discipline of explicitly declared propagation, leaving potential execution flows implicit. Where things are implicit, experience shows that errors, when they do arise, are much harder to find.

8.1.4 The Finally Block

When an exception is caught, the current sequence of execution is interrupted and control jumps to a catch block, or may result in the current method terminating as the exception is propagated up. Whatever happens, it is sometimes desirable to always perform some specific operations or tidy-up the state of the current object, whether an exception gets thrown or not. This can be achieved by adding a finally block directly after the catch block:

Section 32.1.2, Page 910.

```
try {
  anObject.f() ;
  anotherObject.g() ;
}
catch (SomeException e) {
  // Recover from an exception conforming to SomeException
}
finally {
  // Execute this code whatever happens
}
```

A finally block is always executed, whether or not an exception occurs and even if an exception causes the current method to terminate. Although the need for a finally block does not occur that often, it is very useful when it is needed and avoids otherwise convoluted code to achieve the same result.

8.1.5 Plan to Use Exceptions

Using the exception handling mechanism, the programmer can anticipate where a program may fail and take steps to deal with the problem without the program terminating. This allows more robust and reliable programs to be created. When classes are implemented, they should throw exceptions whenever an error condition occurs that the class cannot deal with directly.

Exceptions are, therefore, an integral part of a program's internal communication. This means that using exceptions is an integral part of constructing an application, and exception handling should not be added as an afterthought. It is worth noting that the Java class library makes extensive use of exceptions and a number of library methods can only be used inside try blocks. Hence, the Java programmer needs to know about, and be confident in using, exceptions. Chapter 32 will examine the Java exception mechanism in more detail and show how it can be used effectively.

8.1.6 The Queue Class with Exceptions

"Update class Queue to throw exceptions."

A queue can fail for two reasons: it is empty and an attempt is made to remove an item; it is full and an attempt is made to add an item. We will have a separate exception class to represent each of these

Statement of Problem

Design and

Implementation

errors, `EmptyQueueException` and `FullQueueException`. This will allow the class of the exception object thrown by a queue to be used to determine what happened, as we can rely on the automatic mechanism of matching exception objects to catch blocks to choose which catch block to execute, rather than having to examine the exception object to select what action to take. With a try block containing a combination of additions and removals from a queue, this will also let separate catch blocks deal with the different exceptions.

Class `EmptyQueueException` is the class shown earlier. Class `FullQueue-Exception` is of identical structure:

```
// A class representing the exception thrown when a queue is full.
// Written by Graham Roberts, Sept 1999
// Revision History:
public class FullQueueException extends Exception {
  public FullQueueException() {
    super("Attempt to add an item to a full queue.") ;
  }
  public FullQueueException(final String s) {
    super(s) ;
  }
}
```

As is typical of many exception classes, this class simply declares two constructors, matching those of the superclasses. All other behaviour is inherited, including the ability to display the message string. Class `FullQueueException` is nearly identical, except for the obvious name changes and a different default message.

The changes to the `Queue` class involve adding the `throw` statements and the `throws` declarations. The `Queue` does not, and should not, attempt to catch any of its own exceptions. This gives the following class:

```
// A class providing a simple queue This class is not robust and deals
// with errors by ignoring them.
// Written by Graham Roberts, Sept 1999
// Revision History: Revised version of Queue class
public class Queue {
  // The array stores the queue. It will be treated as though it were
  // a ring or circular array, so that indexing beyond the last
  // element causes a wrap around back to the beginning of the
  // array. Taking this approach avoids the need to move array
  // elements when inserting or deleting.
  protected Object[] items ;
  // Size of the current queue
  protected int size = 0 ;
  // Indexes of front and back of queue in the array.
  protected int front = 1 ;
  protected int back = 0 ;
  public Queue(final int length) {
    items = new Object[length] ;
  }
  public void addBack(final Object obj) throws FullQueueException {
    if (isFull()) {
      throw new FullQueueException() ;
    }
    size++ ;
    back++ ;
    if (back == items.length) {
      back = 0 ;
```

```
    }
    items[back] = obj ;
  }
  public Object removeFront() throws EmptyQueueException {
    if (isEmpty()) {
      throw new EmptyQueueException() ;
    }
    size-- ;
    Object result = items[front] ;
    front++ ;
    if (front == items.length) {
      front = 0 ;
    }
    return result ;
  }
  public boolean isFull() {
    return (size == items.length) ;
  }
  public boolean isEmpty() {
    return (size == 0) ;
  }
}
```

The following test class shows how `try` and `catch` blocks are used in conjunction with calling the queue methods:

```
// A text program for the Queue class.
// Written by Graham Roberts, September 1999
// Revision History: none
public class TestQueue {
  public static void main(final String[] args) {
    Queue queue = new Queue(1) ;
    try {
      String s = (String)queue.removeFront() ;
    }
    catch (EmptyQueueException e) {
      System.out.println(e.getMessage()) ;
    }
    try {
      queue.addBack("one") ;
      queue.addBack("two") ;
    }
    catch (FullQueueException e) {
      System.out.println(e.getMessage()) ;
    }
  }
}
```

Testing now has to include additional tests to check that the exceptions are thrown under the correct conditions. The test program above provides some basic checks of the exceptions and should be developed further. The original tests should also be added, so that we can continue to check that the normal behaviour of the class is unaffected by the addition of exceptions.

Testing

Adding exception handling has proved straightforward. First the error conditions were identified and then exception classes provided to represent the errors. Then `throw` statements and `throws` declarations were added as required. The biggest change will be for clients of the `Queue` class; other code and classes that make use of queues. They now have to be modified to use `try` and `catch` blocks and decisions have to be made about what to be done when an exception is thrown. Ideally, the client code will be able to recover and carry on without any side-effects.

Review

The changes that need to made to client code suggest that it would be a much better strategy to include exception handling right from the beginning of the design of the Queue class. Hence, exception handling should not be treated as an afterthought but properly designed in the first place.

8.2   Threads — Doing More Than One Thing At Once

ref

Chapter 33, Page 921.

A *thread* of control is a single path of execution through a program. Many of the example programs seen so far have a thread that starts with the main method, and follows through the full sequence of statements and method calls to where the program finishes, all strictly in order. Simple programs only need this simple model of control; proceed from the first statement to be executed to the last, in order.

However, Java also supports having multiple threads of control which execute *concurrently*, meaning that a program can appear to be doing a number of different things at once. We say 'appear' as the processor running the program can only be executing one instruction from one thread at any given time. To allow multiple threads to be executing instructions they are *interleaved*, meaning that the currently executing thread is periodically switched for another one. A program that uses threads is said to be *threaded*. When it first starts running, any program begins with a single thread that can then create more threads as needed.

note

If a program is running on a multi-processor machine, then threads can run in parallel, with each processor executing a thread at the same time.

Why should a program need to use multiple threads? Until this point there has been the assumption that programs are always executed sequentially from beginning to end, with only one thing happening at any one time. This is actually just the special case of a multi-threaded program being restricted to a single thread. Hence, one reason to allow multi-threading is to remove artificial restrictions on the ways that programs and algorithms can be expressed. Doing so opens up a range of new programming and problem solving techniques.

Another, more practical, reason for using threads is that they conveniently solve common but otherwise difficult programming problems. A good example is a program that needs to read data coming from several different sources on a network. A single-threaded program would somehow have to explicitly monitor all the sources, waiting for something to arrive. This is difficult as waiting usually implies *blocking*, where the program stops until data arrives from a particular source and is unable to do anything else. If the program is blocked waiting for one data source, it could miss data arriving from another source. Such a program could use the technique of *polling* where it loops around testing each data source in turn, reacting when data arrives. However, polling is very wasteful of resources as it ties up processor time, meaning that other programs on the same computer run slower. Figure 8.1 shows an abstract model of an example situation.

Threads provide the ideal solution to the problem: they provide the control abstraction that allows us to set up monitors on all the sources without having to employ polling. The program creates a new thread to deal with each data source, leaving the main thread free to do other work. Each data source monitoring thread is only responsible for waiting for data from a single source,

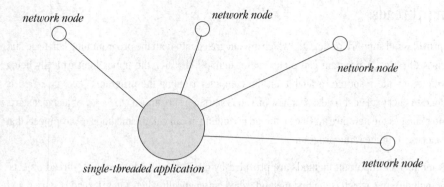

Figure 8.1 A single-threaded application with four network connections.

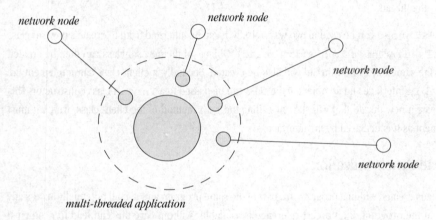

Figure 8.2 A multi-threaded application with four network connections.

which, when it arrives, the thread can read and pass on appropriately. As each of these threads is only doing one thing, reading the data from one data source, it doesn't matter if they block and hence there is no risk of missing data or having to use polling. Figure 8.2 shows an abstract model of an example situation.

Threads are also commonly used by programs that need to manage graphical user interfaces (windows, menus, buttons, graphics, etc.). A well designed program should have a responsive user interface and so it is important that it responds quickly when the user clicks a mouse button or types on the keyboard. With a single-threaded program this can be difficult to arrange, particularly if the program has to do a lot of processing, such as rendering an image. While the program is busy it either ignores the user interface, giving the user the impression that the program has crashed, or it has to use polling to check whether something has happened. A multi-threaded program can avoid these problems by having one or more threads managing the user interface while other threads perform the main processing.

8.2.1   Using Threads

ref

Use of class Thread *and the* Runnable *interface are described in more detail in Section 33.2, Page 923.*

Java provides full support for threads, which are integrated into both the programming language and the class libraries. A program can make use of multiple threads, the upper limit typically being determined by the resources available on the computer running the program. Class Thread is provided to encapsulate threads, so a new thread is started by creating a Thread object that starts up and manages the new thread. Once a thread is running, it can call the methods of any objects that it has access to in the same program.

A number of important methods are provided by class Thread for use with thread objects. These include run, which is the first method called automatically when a new thread is started and is roughly equivalent to the main method for the new thread. If the run method terminates, then so does the thread.

Class Thread can be used in two ways. Firstly, it can be inherited from to create a new subclass (e.g. class myThread extends Thread). Objects of the new subclass can then be created and at the same time a new thread will also be created. Secondly, a client class can implement the Runnable interface and an object of the class can be passed to a Thread class constructor. This will create a new thread that will start by calling the run method of the client class, which it must implement as it is declared by the interface.

8.2.2   Thread Synchronization

All threads created within a program are part of the same program and can all potentially access any object in the program, if an object reference is available. Without care this can lead to problems: what happens if two threads are both using the same object at the same time? For example, suppose two threads are both using the same Stack object and at the same time call the push method. Both threads will separately execute the push method but will be accessing the *same* data structure (the array used to store stack elements). This can lead to unpredictable results as we have not yet introduced mechanisms for the push method to coordinate threads. It may be the case that both values are successfully pushed onto the stack but it could also be the case that both threads try to write a value into the *same* location in the stack data structure. In that case one thread would store its value only to have it overwritten by the other thread. As far as both threads are concerned, no error has occurred but now one data value has been lost. This kind of error is known as a *race condition*. Both threads are racing to access resources and are interleaving in unpredictable ways.

The solution to this kind of problem used in Java is to provide *monitors*, high-level mechanisms for ensuring that only one thread at a time executes a *critical region* of code. The code comprising the critical region is guaranteed by the monitor to be executed by one and only one thread, from start to finish, at any one time. If a thread tries to enter a critical region that is already in use by another thread, it will be blocked by the monitor until the other thread leaves the section. The implementation of monitors and hence the enforcement of access to critical regions is enabled by *locks* on objects, so each critical region is associated with an object lock. When a thread enters the critical region it tries to obtain the object lock and if successful can proceed into the critical region. The lock is released when the thread leaves the critical region.

Java does not require the programmer to manipulate locks directly, the monitor abstraction is supported directly by keywords in the programming language — the locks are just the implementation model. Monitor access is supported in two ways, both of which are provided in terms of the *synchronization* of two or more threads, using the `synchronized` keyword.

The first way to manage synchronization is by declaring that an entire method is to be a critical region, i.e. the method is made a *synchronized method*. For example:

```
public synchronized void push(final int x) { ... }
```

ref

See Section 33.3, Page 929 and Section 33.4, Page 933.

To call a synchronized method, a thread must first obtain the lock on the object the method is being called for. If the lock is not available then the thread must wait until it becomes available and can do no other processing. A class can declare as many synchronized methods as is needed to ensure the correct behaviour of an instance object in the presence of multiple threads. Only one of the synchronized methods can be executed at any one time for a given object, as the same object lock is required for each synchronized method that can be called for the object. Usually, all methods that assign a value to an instance variable should be synchronized, otherwise the state of the object can be compromised. Methods that only read the values of instance variables can be left un-synchronized, providing there is no risk of an invalid value being used. Unsynchronized methods can be called at any time by other threads, even when a synchronized method is being executed.

The second way to manage synchronization is to use a *synchronized statement* which allows access to a compound statement to be monitored, giving a finer grain of control. For example:

```
synchronized (aVar) { ... }
```

In this case, the statements inside the compound statement will not be executed until the current thread obtains the lock on the object referenced by `aVar`.

When using either synchronized methods or statements it is possible to create conditions that cause a program to unexpectedly fail. One such condition, is known as *deadlock* and occurs when two or more threads are holding locks but are also waiting to obtain a lock held by one of the other threads. The other thread will not release its lock and is blocked, which in turn, causes the waiting threads to be blocked. In this situation, a program cannot make any further progress and effectively halts but does not terminate.

Some of the synchronization problems associated with thread-based programming are dealt with in Parts 2 and 3 but a detailed discussion is beyond the scope of this book. You should look at the books that deal with concurrency since the issues require careful study in order to avoid the various problems that can happen.

8.2.3   Thread Scheduling

A program using more than one thread needs to be subject to a set rules that determine which thread should be running at any one time, and when to switch between one thread and another. If threads aren't switched around, or *scheduled*, any advantages of using them will be lost as some threads will never get a chance to run (a condition known as *starvation*). To help with this, threads are given priority levels, so that a thread with a higher priority will be selected over one with a lower priority. When a program is run, the thread it uses will continually be switching between a running state and a suspended state, as they are scheduled and synchronize with one another.

The thread scheduling rules will be explored further in Chapter 33 but there are essentially three ways of switching between threads:

- The current thread is blocked or terminates, allowing another thread to take over.

- A higher priority thread becomes available and *pre-empts* the current lower priority thread.

- A scheduling event occurs and the current thread is forcibly suspended in favour of another thread. This is also known as *time-slicing* (but is not supported by all Java implementations).

Providing the programmer takes into account the scheduling rules and properly uses synchronization, threads provide a valuable addition to the range of problem solving techniques available.

Although not obvious at first sight, all Java programs use multiple threads when they are run. One of the threads is used to execute the `main` method of the program you have written. Other threads are used to manage aspects of the Java Virtual Machine, such as a thread to perform garbage collection. Programs with graphical user interfaces, such as the drawing programs seen in earlier chapters, also rely on threads to manage the input devices and update of the display. Fortunately, it is a very rare program indeed that needs to worry about these management threads — they can normally be left to themselves.

8.2.4   A Thread Example

Statement of Problem

"Write a drawing program that acts as a simple clock by displaying the date and time, updated once per second."

Design and Implementation

The current date and time can be obtained by creating an instance of the `Date` class from the package `java.util`. The default `Date` constructor will create a new `Date` object representing the time at which the object was created. The overridden `toString` method, provided by `Date`, can then be called to obtain a string representation of the date and time. Strings can be displayed by a drawing program using the technique shown in Section 4.4, Page 101, so we have a way of displaying the current date and time in the drawing program window. If the drawing window can be updated every second with a new date and time, we have a way of displaying a simple clock.

As we have seen in all the drawing program examples, a subclass of `DrawPanel` is created to display our drawing or text, so for the clock we will create a subclass called `ClockPanel` which displays the data and time following the approach described in the last paragraph.

The key to writing this program is to use a thread that updates the clock display once per second. The `run` method of the thread object can simply be a loop which waits for one second, then calls a method called `repaint` for the `ClockPanel` object. `Repaint` is an inherited method that causes the panel to be re-displayed by calling the `paint` method, which it turn displays the current time. We don't call `paint` directly as this would violate the protocol by which the display of panels is managed.

To manage the thread we will use a subclass of class `Thread` called `Timer`, declared as follows:

```java
// A subclass of class Thread that sleeps for a period specified in
// the first constructor argument and then wakes up to call repaint on
// the panel specified as the second constructor argument.
// Written by Graham Roberts, October 1999
// Revision History: none
import javax.swing.* ;
public class Timer extends Thread {
  private int waitTime ;
  private JPanel panel ;
  // The thread will keep running while this variable is true.
  private boolean active = true ;

  public Timer(int waitTime, JPanel panel) {
    this.waitTime = waitTime ;
    this.panel = panel ;
  }
  // The overridden run method. This will keep looping while the
  // thread is active.
  public void run() {
    while (active) {
      try {
        sleep(waitTime) ;
      }
      catch (InterruptedException e) {
        // Any exceptions will be caught but ignored
      }
      panel.repaint() ;
    }
  }
  // This method should be called to stop the thread by causing the
  // run method to terminate.
  public void stopTimer() {
    active = false ;
  }
}
```

As a subclass of `Thread`, `Timer` must override the `run` method, which is called when the thread is started. The `run` method consists of a loop which executes while the boolean variable `active` is true. The loop can be terminated when another thread calls the `stopTimer` method, setting `active` to false. When the `run` method terminates, after the loop stops looping, the thread will finish.

Care must be taken to terminate a thread properly. This should be done by letting the run method finish.

Inside the loop body the method `sleep` is used to suspend the thread for the number of milliseconds given by the method parameter. Sleep must be called inside a `try` block as it is declared as throwing an `InterruptedException` exception. When the thread wakes up it calls the `repaint` method on the panel object displaying the clock (although it will work for any kind of panel). The effect of the loop is to call repaint every specified number of milliseconds, giving our clock tick.

The `ClockPanel` class is declared as follows:

```
// A drawing program to display a simple text clock.
// Written by Graham Roberts, July 1999
// Revision History: none
import java.awt.* ;
import java.awt.geom.* ;
import java.util.Date ;
public class ClockPanel extends DrawPanel {
  // Create frame and drawing, display them on the screen.
  public static void main(final String[] args) {
    DrawFrame frame = new DrawFrame ("Clock") ;
    ClockPanel clockPanel = new ClockPanel (570, 75) ;
    frame.add(clockPanel) ;
    frame.pack() ;
    frame.centreOnScreen() ;
    frame.setVisible(true) ;
    // Create and start the new thread
    Timer timer = new Timer (1000, clockPanel) ;
    timer.start() ;
  }
  public ClockPanel() {
  }
  public ClockPanel(final int w, final int h) {
    super(w, h) ;
  }
  // This method is called to do the actual drawing
  public void paint(final Graphics g) {
    Graphics2D g2d = (Graphics2D)g ;
    Rectangle2D background =
      new Rectangle2D.Double (0,0,
                              getSize().getWidth(),
                              getSize().getHeight()) ;
    g2d.fill(background) ;
    Font big = new Font("Serif", Font.PLAIN, 40) ;
    g2d.setFont(big) ;
    g2d.setPaint(Color.white) ;
    g2d.drawString((new Date()).toString(), 20, 50) ;
  }
}
```

The `paint` method contains the drawing code to display the clock, which is shown in Figure 8.3. When displayed, the seconds, minutes and hours tick forward (as will the date, day and year if you are patient enough). The `main` method includes two lines of code to create a `Timer` object and start the thread by calling the `start` method.

Testing

Programs that create and use threads are generally harder to test as the scheduling of threads make their behaviour far less predictable. For this program, we must rely on observing the display of the running program and checking that it updates once per second as expected.

Figure 8.3 The clock program window.

The `Timer` class included a method called `stopTimer` that could be called to stop the timer
thread running. In the event we didn't need to call it as we only need to stop the thread when the
clock program itself terminates. However, in general, close attention should be paid as to when a
thread is no longer needed and can be shut down.

Review

The `Timer` class just presented was implemented as a subclass of `Thread` but we could have
made use of the `Runnable` interface instead, declaring `Timer` as follows:

```
// A class acting as a simple timer, implementing the Runnable
// interface.  A period specified in the first constructor argument
// and then wakes up to call repaint on the panel specified as the
// second constructor argument.
// Written by Graham Roberts, October 1999
// Revision History: Rewrite of the class implemented
// as a thread subclass.
import javax.swing.* ;
public class Timer implements Runnable {
  private int waitTime ;
  private JPanel panel ;
  // The thread will keep running while this variable is true.
  private boolean active = true ;

  public Timer(final int waitTime, final JPanel panel) {
    this.waitTime = waitTime ;
    this.panel = panel ;
  }
  // The overridden run method. This will keep looping while the
  // thread is active.
  public void run() {
    while (active) {
      try {
        Thread.sleep(waitTime) ;
      }
      catch (InterruptedException e) {
        // Any exceptions will be caught but ignored
      }
      panel.repaint() ;
    }
  }
  // This method should be called to stop the thread by causing the
  // run method to terminate.
  public void stopTimer() {
    active = false ;
  }
}
```

This version of `Timer` differs only in two aspects. Firstly, it implements the `Runnable`
interface, avoiding the need to be a `Thread` subclass. This allows the option of inheriting from a
different class, which would be ruled out if we had to subclass `Thread`. Secondly, the call to
`sleep` now has to be written as `Thread.sleep`, otherwise the method will not be found

causing a compilation error. `Sleep` is actually a static method which works on the current thread when called, which explains the syntax used to call it.

The `ClockPanel` class needs to be modified to use the `Runnable` implementation by replacing the lines that create and start the thread with:

```
Thread timer = new Thread (new Timer(1000, clockPanel)) ;
timer.start() ;
```

An instance of class `Thread` is created directly, with the constructor being given an instance of a class implementing the `Runnable` interface, in this case a `Timer`. Calling the `start` method on the thread object will start the thread and call the `run` method of the `Timer` object.

8.3   Summary

This chapter has outlined two important mechanisms that the Java programmer needs to make use of in order to create well designed programs. Both mechanisms affect the way a program is designed, exceptions by providing a way to allow programs to deal with and recover from unexpected errors, and threads by allowing several sequences of control to be active simultaneously.

Key points in this chapter:

- An exception is thrown from a method using a `throw` statement to notify the method's caller that it has encountered an error and cannot continue.

- A `try` block, containing calls to methods that may throw exceptions, allows any exceptions thrown to be caught in one or more matching `catch` blocks.

- Uncaught exceptions are propagated up the call chain until they are caught or until the exception is propagated out of `main` at which point the program terminates.

- A method uses a `throws` declaration to declare what exceptions it can throw.

- Exceptions are represented by objects, provided by subclasses of `Throwable`. Any subclass of `Exception`, except for `RuntimeException` (and its subclasses), must be caught and this will be checked by the compiler.

- Threads allow a program to have multiple paths of execution. Thread scheduling determines when a particular thread gets to run.

- A critical region is a section of code that can be executed by only one thread at a time. Object locks are used to control entry to a critical region.

- Critical regions are denoted using synchronized methods and statements, which are declared using the `synchronized` keyword.

- Thread objects can either be created using subclasses of `Thread` or by providing a class that implements the `Runnable` interface.

Self-review Questions

Self-review 8.1 Is there anything wrong with simply stopping a program when an error occurs?

Self-review 8.2 What kinds of error should the exception handling mechanism be used to catch?

Self-review 8.3 Why should methods that throw exceptions not also try to catch them?

Self-review 8.4 What happens to an uncaught exception?

Self-review 8.5 What is the purpose of a `throws` declaration?

Self-review 8.6 How does a `catch` block work?

Self-review 8.7 What does `finally` do?

Self-review 8.8 What is a thread?

Self-review 8.9 How are threads created?

Self-review 8.10 What is the purpose of a critical region?

Self-review 8.11 What is thread scheduling?

Self-review 8.12 How does a thread terminate?

Programming Exercises

Exercise 8.1 Modify class `Dequeue` so that it throws and catches exceptions appropriately. Declare any exception classes needed and write a test class.

Exercise 8.2 Update the matrix classes shown in Section 7.13, Page 214, so that they throw exceptions to deal with error conditions. Write a test class to check that the exception handling works correctly.

Exercise 8.3 Modify the clock program to display only the time, without the day, date or year.

Exercise 8.4 Rewrite class `ClockPanel` to display a graphical representation of a round clock face with hour, minute and second hands.

Exercise 8.5 Write a `Stack` class that throws exceptions and is thread safe, meaning that a stack object can be used by multiple threads. Write a test class that creates multiple threads to test your `Stack` class.

Challenge

Challenge 8.1 Extend Exercise 8.3 so that the `ClockPanel` displays four clock faces, one
updated continuously, one once per second, one once per minute and one every five minutes.

The Programming Process

Objectives

Having introduced the Java programming language, this chapter concentrates on the overall process of designing and implementing programs. Effective programming needs a process in order to have a clear framework within which a program can be reliably and systematically built.

Keywords

analysis

debugging

design

iterative development

maintenance

problem domain

prototyping

requirements

testing

UML notation

9.1   Introduction

From the previous chapters, we now have a good idea of what classes and objects are, along with many of the key issues surrounding them, such as abstraction, encapsulation and inheritance. We have also seen how these ideas are supported by the Java programming language based on implementation mechanisms such as references. So, given all this information, how do we actually go about designing and writing a non-trivial program?

At the start of Chapter 2 there was a brief overview of the things a programmer needs to do when constructing a program; requirements gathering, analysis, design, implementation and testing. This chapter will establish an overall framework into which each stage fits and examine what is done during each stage. First, though, we need some background information about the principles of designing systems using classes and objects.

9.2   Object-oriented Software Engineering

During the last decade, Object-oriented Software Engineering (OOSE), in the form of Object-oriented Analysis (OOA) and Object-oriented Design (OOD), has become an established discipline. Software Engineering is the term given to the activity of defining, designing, implementing and maintaining a software system. OOSE, as the name implies, takes an object-oriented approach to software engineering, based on the use of classes and objects.

To describe the activity of object-oriented software engineering, a number of well known practitioners have developed and publicized a variety of *object-oriented methods*. A method typically comprises a set of notations for describing the system being built and a process describing what to actually do. The process will cover analysis, design and, possibly, implementation as a series of stages, with the results of each stage being documented using the notation defined by the method.

The first generation of methods includes examples such as the Object Modelling Technique (OMT) developed by a team led by James Rumbaugh, the Booch Method developed by Grady Booch, OOA/OOD/OOP developed by Peter Coad and Edward Yourdon, the method developed by Sally Shlaer and Steven Mellor and the Object-oriented Software Engineering (OOSE) method created by Ivar Jacobson and his team. These all have their own distinct notations supported by a set of process descriptions, although many of the underlying ideas are common.

note

CASE stands for Computer-Aided Software Engineering. A CASE tool are is used to design software.

In addition to the methods named above, there are also fifteen to twenty other methods that have been proposed, usually accompanied by one or more books, some with fully fledged system development environments — usually called CASE environments. One result of this proliferation of methods has been a desire to provide a standardized modelling language for object-oriented systems, two of which have been proposed:

1. The Unified Modelling Language (UML) has been developed by Booch, Rumbaugh and Jacobson (the 'three amigos'!) and is now a standard supported by the Object Management Group (OMG).

2. The OPEN Modelling Language (OML) developed by Don Firesmith, Brian Henderson-Sellers and Ian Graham, which has been released as a de facto standard.

Both UML and OML are notations for modelling object-oriented systems, the process descriptions are separate. The Unified Software Development Process has been proposed for UML, while OPEN has its own object-based process model.

The description of any of these methods is outside the scope of this book as we are primarily concerned with small- to medium-scale programming and these methods are aimed mainly at the software engineering of medium- to very large-scale systems. Of course, once a programmer has mastered the essentials of the Java language, and especially as a move is made to developing larger programs, these methods should be studied and used. It is important to remember that there are established object-oriented analysis and design methods beyond the lower level programming concepts. The bibliography at the end of the book contains entries for several object-oriented analysis and design texts which are well worth studying.

ref

Bibliography
Appendix L, Page 981

That said, we will be using a subset of the UML notation for documenting the structure of programs in Parts 2 and 3 of the book, and will borrow on the experience gained from object-oriented methods in general to describe the process of developing programs.

9.3 Why Object-oriented?

We have already given some justification for using an object-oriented approach to development. In this sub-section we attempt to give a more definitive answer to the question "Why object-oriented?".

Preceding object-orientation there have been other well known analysis and design models, such as Structured Analysis and Design, Functional Decomposition and Logic-based Programming. These are still used but in the last few years it has been object-oriented development that has become very popular and, indeed, become the mainstream approach for much modern software development. Why?

There are a number of reasons including the use of abstraction, the benefits of encapsulation and the power of inheritance. Experience has shown that these are all effective ways of creating robust, reliable programs that are cleanly designed. Further, the emphasis on interfaces and exchangeable components allows a shift away from developing programs from scratch to developing programs by combining together components.

However, if we delve deeper there are some more important reasons for choosing classes and objects: reasons that the Java programmer needs to understand in order to get the best from the language.

9.3.1   Route Planning — An Allegory

Consider wanting to know how to travel from A to B. You could ask someone for a route plan and get a list of instructions containing statements such as "go to the end of the road, turn left, then turn right at the third turning on the left", and so on. With a basic understanding of how each statement is interpreted (i.e. how to count turnings to find the third on the left), you can follow the instructions and get to your destination.

So far so good but what if you want to travel from A to C the next day? You have to go back and ask for a new route plan to solve your new problem. The basic statements in the plan would have the same form, and in that sense be reusable, but the plan itself is essentially new. Unless there is some overlap, the old plan is no help for travelling from A to C. In fact, the first plan is only ever useful for travelling from A to B.

The consequence of using this strategy for finding out how to travel between two places is that you have to go and ask for a new list of instructions every time you want to travel. This is not only tedious but is inefficient on your part — and a good way to lose friends!

An alternative strategy for dealing with your travelling problem is to make use of a map. This will allow you to travel between any two points on the map and do your own route planning. There is a cost for using the map, you have to learn how to read and interpret it, as well as develop strategies for planning routes. However, in the longer term the benefits more than outweigh the initial learning costs. Moreover, much more of the map strategy is reusable — it is easy to transfer the solution strategy from one problem to the next.

9.3.2   Problem Domains

The key lesson of this for software developers is that solutions to specific problems tend to be fragile and short-lived. As soon as the problem requirements change (and they frequently do), the solution, your program, requires modification. If your program is not designed to be easily changed, then large parts or even all of it will have to be thrown away.

A *problem domain* is the context in which a particular problem exists. For example, the problem domain in which a specific route plan exists is that of maps, route planning, travelling and strategies for moving around. Critically, the problem domain is relatively stable, changing only slowly, while specific problems are transient and change regularly.

If you are able to capture the problem domain as the core of the design of your program, then the program code is likely to be more stable, more reusable and more easily adaptable to specific problems as they come and go. If you only capture a specific problem as the core of your design then your program code is only good for solving one problem and will, at best, require significant modification to solve a different problem.

Structured analysis and design, which leads to structured programming (see Section 3.5, Page 68), is based on a design process of top-down decomposition. This specifies that the development process is one of continual top-down refinement of a problem until no further subdivision is needed. Unfortunately, this leads to programs that are designed around a specific solution (like the route plan you get by asking someone for directions) that end up with a very rigid structure, invariably with centralized control. When the time comes to modify the program to meet new or just slightly altered requirements, it turns out to be very difficult as the necessary changes require wide ranging modifications to the code.

In particular, we get the situation where the abstractions in the program (e.g. travelling from A to B) end up depending on the details. When the details change, the abstractions have to change as well. This is a fundamentally unstable situation.

In contrast, object-oriented analysis and design is based on a process of first identifying the abstractions needed by a program and modelling them as classes. This leads to a middle-out process where in the downwards direction the details of individual classes are implemented as code and in the upwards direction the overall structure of a program is developed using association and inheritance. A key part of the process is identifying the problem domain abstractions and getting them into place first. Then the details can be filled in. Interestingly, this generates programs with decentralized control with objects each taking responsibility for a particular feature.

Good object-oriented development leads to a design where the details depend upon the abstractions, the opposite to what is typically obtained with structured design. The abstractions are stable and so the core of your design changes slowly. The details needed for a specific problem can then be added or removed in a far less destructive and more easily managed way. In implementation terms this leads to a core framework of abstract classes and interfaces representing the core abstractions, which are specialized by inheritance to provide concrete classes targeted at a specific problem. The concrete classes are only specializations of the abstractions and can be easily changed without affecting the abstractions. This leads us back to the arguments presented in Section 7.14, Page 220, about class relationships, components and reusability — the Java programming model and object-oriented design are intimately related.

ref

See the simulation developed in Chapter 26 for an example of an abstract framework specialized by inheritance.

9.4 Writing Programs

Having explored some ideas about object-oriented philosophy, and building on many ideas presented in earlier chapters, we want to outline the process of actually designing and implementing a program. This book is aimed at those learning object-oriented programming using the Java language, so we are primarily concerned with building small-scale programs, written by a single person. A small-scale program is typically under a thousand lines of source code (excluding comments). We need to distinguish small-scale from large-scale as, although the key object-oriented ideas remain just as important, large-scale programs are typically developed by a team of people and require considerably more analysis and design effort.

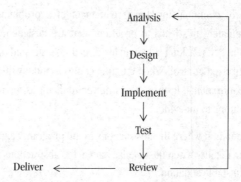

Figure 9.1 The iteration cycle of programming.

9.4.1   An Overview

The development of a program can be split into four main phases: inception, elaboration, implementation, and testing and delivery. Each phase has one or more steps:

- ***Inception***: obtaining the initial idea and inspiration
    - *User requirements gathering*: find out what the program needs to do

- ***Elaboration***: turn the requirements into a specification that can be implemented as a program
    - *Analysis*: identify the key abstractions, classes and relationships
    - *Design*: refine your class model so it can be implemented
    - *Identifying reuse*: locating what already exists that you can reuse

- ***Implementation***: write the code and construct the program
    - *Programming*: creating the classes, writing the methods
    - *Class testing*: testing each class as it is developed
    - *Integrating*: put the parts together to create a complete program
    - *Creating reuse*: making classes and components reusable in the future

- ***Testing and Delivery***: making sure the program works properly and putting it to use
    - *Overall testing*: testing the program as a whole
    - *Delivery*: giving the finished program to its users

An overall process is needed to order the steps, and determine what to do when. Although the list above could be followed strictly in order from beginning to end, this is not a good way of proceeding. Instead, we normally adopt an *iterative* approach; the process we are assuming here goes under the title *iterative prototyping*. This process is often characterized as "Analyse a little, design a little, program a little, test a lot, review and repeat until finished" (see Figure 9.1).

Iteration is important as it very hard to get the design of a program correct first time (unless the program is really very trivial!). In particular, it is difficult to identify all the key abstractions right at

Design tries to predict the future — be prepared to get it wrong.

the start. Often they only become apparent as you develop your understanding of the program with each stage of iteration.

Iteration allows the design and implementation of a program to be explored in an incremental way, making it possible to try alternatives and, more importantly, for mistakes to be corrected. A useful iterative strategy is to implement a very simple, minimal version of your program as a first step and then review what has been achieved. Based on the review, make decisions about what to do next and proceed to the next iteration, which will create a more complete version of the program. This cycle repeats until the program achieves the design goals, at which point it is delivered.

There are dangers with iteration in that it can be difficult to control the quality and scope of your program, and also it can be hard to know when it is finished (there is always a temptation to add one more 'feature'). Problems can be avoided by pausing regularly to review progress, usually after having implemented some new aspect of the program.

A further consequence of iteration and prototyping is that, although the various development stages are listed separately, they may be merged together or omitted. In particular, for small programs, analysis and design can be treated as more or less the same thing, with the design itself being developed by actually writing (and commenting) Java code.

When prototyping there are two other important activities that should be going on. First, you should be keeping regular backups of the code you are working on. Regular in this context means just before *every* time you make a new change or addition (this could literally be every few minutes). If something doesn't work out, you need to be able to quickly and easily revert to a previous version. Secondly, you want to keep notes of all important decisions, ideas and thoughts you have while working on your program. Jot these down on a note pad, or type into an editor, and regularly review and re-visit entries. Also don't forget to add all those things you need to do to complete the current version, but haven't got round to yet. The rationale for doing this is simple: anything you don't write down will get forgotten.

The following subsections will review each development stage in detail, describing what should happen and how positive results can be achieved. Throughout, we assume that small-scale programs are being written by a single programmer.

tip

Effective iteration requires constant review and testing of your code.

tip

Investigate the use of Version Management Tools to manage your code.

9.4.2   User Requirements Gathering

> **Step 1**: Accurately determine what is expected of the program, what input is needed and what output will be generated.
> **Result**: A written list of things the program is supposed to do, supported by a set of scenarios.

User requirements gathering is a somewhat grand name for finding out what the program is supposed to do and writing down a list of requirements for it. However, whatever you care to call this phase of program development, it is important to make clear what it is you expect your program to do. Large scale developments (especially those funded by governments) are notorious for failing to specify accurately what is expected of a program, ending up wasting a lot of time and money. For the single programmer there is a strong temptation to jump right in and start writing code, resulting in ending up disillusioned after a few days with the realization that there is no clear idea of what it is the code is actually meant to do.

Requirements are discovered by thinking carefully about how the program is expected to be used, what input is needed and what output should be generated and, if possible, by asking the eventual users of the system. In fact, whenever possible the end users or 'customers' of the program should not only be asked to describe what they expect it to do, they should also be involved in reviewing the requirements when they are produced. Moreover, the end users should also be involved in reviewing the working prototypes of the program as part of the reviews in each of the cycles of the prototyping process.

The goal of requirements gathering is to generate a list of what the program is expected to do. For example:

- An address book program is needed to store names, addresses and phone numbers.
- It should be possible to create new entries and edit existing ones.
- It should be possible to print out an entry.
- …

To support requirements gathering, a good tactic is to construct *scenarios*. A scenario is a sequence of steps the program will need to go through to get a particular task done, written down primarily from the point of view of the program user. Each task that can be performed by a program should have its own scenario.

A scenario typically has a title, an input stage, a processing stage and an output stage. For example, a scenario for doing a particular kind of address book query might be as follows:

Name: Look up company phone number

    i.   Select the find phone number option.

    ii. Enter the name of the company whose phone number is needed, click search.

    iii. Search the address book data structures, using the name as the search key.

    iv. Display the results.

From this scenario we can tell that the program needs a way of starting a search (perhaps by selecting a menu item or clicking a button), inputting some text, accessing an address book data structure and displaying the results. As program development proceeds, each of these will be translated into code somewhere in the program. At this stage, though, the scenario can be summarized as a single requirement:

- It should be possible to look up a phone number by entering a name.

As we are dealing with a relatively informal design process for small-scale programs, we are not too concerned that the scenario also includes steps (iii) and (iv) which talk about requirements in terms of what the program does internally, information that is of no concern to the end user. For larger-scale programs more care would be needed.

Requirements gathering continues, supported by constructing scenarios, until a comprehensive list of requirements is produced, given the understanding of the problem achieved so far. While the hope is that no major requirements will have been missed, the list may well need to be extended or modified as development continues. This is a natural consequence of the exploration of the problem as part of the "analyse a little, design a little, implement a little, test a lot" approach. It's also a good reason to adopt an iterative strategy.

So far, nothing has been said about classes or objects; these come next.

9.4.3   Analysis

> **Step 2**: Identify the classes and their relationships.
> **Step 3**: Verify the dynamic behaviour of the proposed system.
> **Result**: A class diagram and class descriptions.

Analysis is about building a model of the system using classes and class relationships. In large-scale system development "a model of the system" would mean using classes to capture the real world system that is to be at least partly replaced by software. With small-scale development we can be more focused and use analysis as the phase for identifying the classes needed by the program, while at the same time working out how objects of those classes send each other messages in order to perform the tasks identified by the requirements — the dynamic behaviour. Design will take those classes and turn them into code, with the methods determined by what messages objects need to respond to.

note

Analysis is concerned with identifying the structure and function of a program using classes and objects, but does not deal with how classes are constructed.

Although analysis and design are being presented as separate steps, they are really just phases within the single activity of building the classes needed by the program. During the first iteration of development it is worth having them as distinct steps but for later iterations they effectively merge together. Another way of differentiating between analysis and design is to consider that analysis is about *outsides* — the role of a class, its relationship with other classes and the public methods it provides — while design is about *insides* — data structures, method bodies and algorithms. As you work with classes and their implementation, your point of view is continually moving from inside to outside and back.

How are classes identified? By a process of brain-storming, applying common sense, searching the requirements, using an analysis method like CRC (which will be described below) and experience. The classes we want are those which represent the key abstractions in the program — the things, entities, roles, strategies and data structures. The classes are going to be related by association or inheritance, as introduced in Chapter 7. For each class a list of variables and public methods need to be identified. Many people prefer to use the term *attributes* to mean any of data, variables or public methods that objects of a class possess at this stage, as it is helpful to avoid making decisions about types and, in particular, whether something is a variable or a public method, too early on.

Brain-storming and common sense. Some potential classes may be obvious by simply looking at the problem. Typically, such classes represent data structures and entities. However, beware of doing a superficial job.

Searching the requirements. The requirements can be searched to pick out the names of things, entities, roles, etc. These form a list of potential classes or attributes of classes. The list can then be reviewed to firm up decisions. This approach has been criticized, particularly for large-scale development, as it can be poor at identifying abstractions. Nonetheless, it is usually adequate for small-scale programs, and provides a convenient starting point.

The CRC method. CRC stands for *Class, Responsibility, Collaboration* and is a process for identifying classes. It is actually aimed at use by small groups of developers but is still useful for the individual programmer (some of the books mentioned in the bibliography address these points in more detail). Its main advantage is the clear way that it both identifies classes and shows how objects of the classes interact by message passing.

Responsibilities comprise the knowledge that objects of a class maintain and the services they provides. For example, a bank class is responsible for maintaining a collection of bank accounts and providing a collection of access operations to use the accounts.

Collaborators are classes whose services are required to fulfil a responsibility. For example, a bank class collaborates with a bank account class in order to manipulate bank accounts. Each responsibility can be fulfilled by collaborating with zero or more collaborators. Many people use the term *association* for this.

The CRC method uses these basic ideas to find the set of classes needed to model a problem. As information about each class is discovered, it is recorded on a 'card' as either a responsibility or collaboration. CRC information is found by the developer or developers role-playing the interaction between objects and recording the results.

We present a short example of using CRC in the following chapter, and present a longer description of CRC in the appendix.

The results of analysis can be recorded in two ways, written descriptions called *class templates* and *class diagrams*.

A class template is an outline for recording information about a class as it is discovered. It has the form:

Name:
Superclass:
Subclasses:
List of Attributes:
  …
List of Methods:

note

For small-scale or prototyping based development, you can document the class by writing the Java code. This requires good discipline but can be effective.

Each entry is a short written description of the appropriate item.

A class diagram gives a pictorial view of the classes and their relationships. The pictorial view can be a very helpful way of seeing the overall picture and quickly sketching possible program structures. This book will use a subset of the UML notation for class diagrams. This notation uses rectangles to denote classes (often called class icons), with connecting lines and annotations to denote class relationships. Figure 9.2 gives a summary of the notation.

Class icons come in simple and elaborated forms. The elaborated form includes a list of attributes and a list of method names (and possibly parameters). Associations between classes can be labelled with role names indicating the role that a class plays in the association. They can also be labelled to denote one-to-many or many-to-many relationships between objects of the classes.

A stronger form of association called *aggregation* is also available, to allow the statement that an object of one class *is-composed-of* some collection of objects of another class. This is useful when objects form a data structure, rather than simply being associated in order to send messages to one another.

The triangle shape on a connecting line denotes inheritance with the point of the triangle attached to the superclass. The same thing with a dashed line denotes a class implementing an interface, with the interface represented by a class icon with the label '<<interface>>' above the interface name.

Figure 9.3 shows an example UML class diagram. This diagram captures the structure of a simple dice game, where a collection of players each take a turn to throw a cup containing dice. A scoring system is used to determine who throws the best score. There are four classes along with their associations (some of which are aggregations).

When looking at such a diagram it should be remembered that it represents the static class-based structure of a program. When the program is run, one or more objects of each class are created, as shown in Figure 9.4. An object is shown in UML notation as a rectangle with an underlined label giving the name of the object, followed by its class. The connections between objects correspond to the associations between their classes and, when the code is written, to object references. The arrow heads have been added to emphasize which object is referring to which.

Understanding the relationship between class diagrams and objects is important and something you need to visualize whenever you create or read class diagrams. It is useful to think of the class diagram as floating over the sea of objects that exist when a program is running. Each object is connected to its class, so that some classes will have many attached objects. The references between objects are determined by the corresponding associations between classes. Figure 9.5 illustrates the idea. Note that inheritance relationships don't exist as links between objects, as inheritance doesn't relate classes in the same way as associations.

So far, we have mostly looked at identifying the static structure of a program but we must also consider its *dynamic behaviour* as well. Dynamic behaviour is simply a term to cover what the

tip

UML provides a large and complex visual notation-based language for describing object systems. Most of the time the basic subset shown here is entirely adequate.

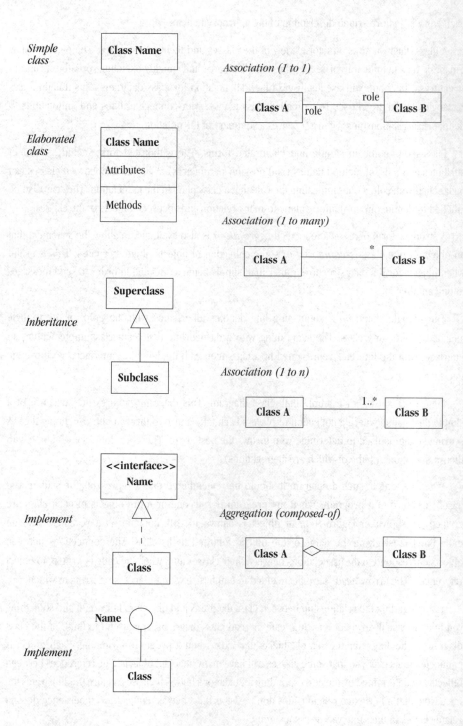

Figure 9.2 Minimal subset of UML notation.

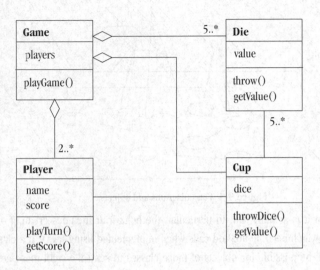

Figure 9.3 An example class diagram using elaborated class icons.

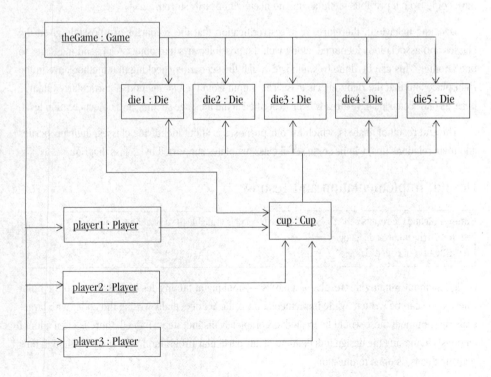

Figure 9.4 Dice game objects.

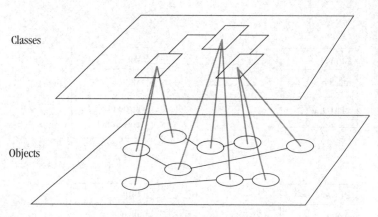

Figure 9.5 Class diagrams and objects.

program does when it is actually run. In particular, the behaviour includes creating objects and sending messages (which become method calls when implemented using Java). If a class diagram is valid then it must be possible for objects of those classes to send the right messages (i.e. call methods) to one another. If an object of class A is to send a message to an object of class B, then it must have a reference to the class B object. If the reference corresponds to a class attribute, there must be an association between classes A and B on the class diagram, otherwise the reference must have come from a previous method call and been temporarily stored.

Dynamic behaviour, therefore, requires verification that the scenarios are possible given the classes and associations identified, along with the possible ways that objects can send messages to one another. This can be done by walking through the scenarios checking that methods are in the right place and that the right objects exist. The output from the CRC method is particularly valuable here, as CRC scenarios have already been described at the message sending and object creation level.

The end result of analysis, which for our purposes is about identifying classes, their properties and their relationships, will be some set of class templates supported by a class diagram.

9.4.4   Design, Implementation and Testing

Step 4: Refine the results of analysis until enough detail is available to write code.
Step 5: Write and test the code.
Result: A set of coded classes.

note

A tool that can automatically construct a class diagram from source code can make the design task easier.

Design is about refining the results of analysis — looking at the insides of classes — to the point where code can be written, while implementation is the act of actually writing the code. With large-scale development these would be treated as completely distinct steps. Indeed, there is often a lot of emphasis in making the design independent of any particular programming language, although how realistic this is, is open to question.

However, for our purposes — building small programs — we can be somewhat more relaxed and go as far as rolling design and implementation into one step. In effect, the design is documented by writing, and commenting, Java source code. With small projects, there is not usually a need for separate design documentation; the design information can be presented in the source code documents. However, for large projects exactly the opposite is true. The process for design then becomes:

- Create a Java class for each design class.
- Determine a type for each attribute (making as much use of library types as possible) and represent them using a variable or a public accessor method.
- Add each method declaration, specifying return type and parameters.
- Fill in each method body based on the specifications obtained earlier.

As code is written, design decisions, and also implementation choices and decisions, should be commented in the code where needed or written up as part of your notes, but remember not to clutter things up with superfluous information.

Before effort is put into writing a class it is important to discover whether an existing class, either from a library or a previous program, can be reused. This is most likely if the class represents some form of container or common data type such as a `Date`. Ideally, reuse means taking the existing class and using it without modification but it could also mean inheriting from and extending an existing class or, possibly, modifying an existing class. However, beware that modification may involve more changes than are worth doing.

As well as trying to reuse classes, it is worth looking at examples of method and algorithm implementations, if not for direct reuse of the code then for inspiration about how a particular technique or design can be used to solve a programming problem. Indeed, it is worth spending time reading the code that others have written to see what it looks like, how other people go about writing code and how it works.

Classes need to be tested to make sure they behave as expected. This can often be conveniently done by giving each class a static `main` method specifically for testing the behaviour of the class. Testing should try to:

- Initialize new objects and check they have a valid state.
- Call each method with appropriate arguments and check the results.

Inspections, *walk-throughs* and *code reviews* can also play a part in checking class code. Note, however, that testing cannot 'prove' a class to be correct as it is, in general, impossible to check all combinations of object state and method calls. Testing can only discover errors but only if you happen to do the right test. Another, very important, element of the defensive programming philosophy comes out here:

> *A successful test is one that exposes an error in the class or program. A test that results in a 'correct' running of a program, showing no apparent error, gives us no new information.*

tip

Too much documentation can be as bad as too little — people have to be able to quickly understand what is going on.

tip

The J2DSK and other APIs already contain many classes you may need. Beware of re-inventing something already available.

note

Testing individual classes is usually referred to as unit testing.

When we have run all the tests that we think can highlight errors in a program then we declare the program usable, allow it to be used and await the first error reports.

Whilst this may sound like a pessimistic viewpoint, taking this humble stand over our code is to admit the (unfortunate) truth that all software has bugs in it and that we should take pleasure in expunging any error that is found for us in our software. Professionalism is taking pride in our code, pride sufficient that we are happy for others to read it, comment on it, test it and find errors in it. Of course, if the errors are too easily found or too easily fixed then perhaps the original testing was not sufficiently rigorous.

When a class has been developed to a satisfactory level it is worth asking if it could be reused in other programs. If so, are there any modifications that would be worth making to make the class easier to reuse? Beware, though, of striving for reuse just for the sake of it, as you may end up making unnecessary changes, most notably by adding variables and methods that are not entirely necessary.

After a core set of classes is in place, they can be put together to form the program. If the design and, in particular, verifying the dynamic behaviour has been done correctly, the pieces should fit and you should have a working program!

9.4.5   Review and Iterate

> **Step 6**: Review what has been achieved on the current iteration, plan the next iteration and proceed.
> **Result**: A better set of classes.

The previous sections have presented requirements gathering, analysis, design and implementation. We should not forget that these activities are taking place in the framework of iterative prototyping. The first pass through will produce a working but minimal program, while subsequent iterations will extend and improve the prototype. During the first pass it is unlikely that you will want to attempt to implement the entire program, so you should work with a subset of the full requirements. On subsequent iterations a further batch of requirements can be dealt with.

At the end of an iteration it is important to stop and review what has been discovered and achieved. It is often the case, even for experienced programmers, that the full implications of the requirements and design do not become apparent until at least one prototype has been put together. This is the time to review the key design decisions, go through your list of notes and observations and ask the question "Is this going right?" Make sure problems are given proper attention before trying to carry on.

A common pitfall, especially for those new to object-oriented development, is to end up with what is essentially a procedural design superficially partitioned into classes. This is easily done by placing too much emphasis on coding a linear sequence of events based on the scenarios identified. Instead, you should be looking to create objects that encapsulate data and provide a set of services

tip

Be proud of your code. Let others read it. When they find errors don't be upset, just fix them.

tip

Be prepared to throw away code that doesn't work or a design that's going nowhere.

based on that information (review Section 6.8, Page 176, for more about objects and services). The implementation of scenarios then comes from using the services that objects provide. This reflects the shift in thinking from 'what sequence of steps are needed?' to 'how does this collection of objects interact to achieve the required result?'.

It is important to know when to stop developing a prototype and deliver a product. Once all the requirements have been met in a satisfactory way (you can literally tick them off), the code can be tidied up, documentation completed and the program delivered. If the program is to be used by others, get them to test it and respond to their requests for changes and alterations (and bug fixes!), before considering your own changes.

For some programs you might want to try building separate prototypes in order to evaluate different ways of solving the same problem.

9.4.6 Program Testing and Delivery

When the program is ready it needs to be properly tested, hopefully building on the testing done before. Testing needs to be organized so that it is clear what a program should produce and so that testing is repeatable. For larger programs the best way to manage testing is to produce a *test plan*. A test plan describes how you intend to test that your program has no observable bugs. It should consist of a list of tests that aim to show that your program works in a well defined way. Each test should describe the required input (if any) and show the expected results.

Testing will essentially be done by experiment (i.e. decide what should happen and then see what actually happens). The limitations of this kind of testing have already been discussed but it's the best we have without resorting to much harder formal methods.

There are at least three kinds of test that can be done:

1. Tests where valid input and data is given across some range.
2. Tests where valid input and data is given at the limits of a range.
3. Tests where invalid data and input is given.

The results of running a set of tests should be a *test log* which shows the results produced by the tests described in the test plan. The log should demonstrate that each test produced the output described by the test plan. If it does not then we have clearly found an error, usually in the program, though conceivably the test plan could have been wrong. Having found a bug, it must be fixed. When we believe it is corrected and gone we must run the entire test plan again, not just the one that failed. The Principle of Maximum Paranoia requires us to believe that we may have introduced a new bug into our program during our efforts to fix the bug that was previously highlighted. Eventually, this iterative testing results in a test log with all tests meeting the expected outcomes. The program can then be deemed to be deliverable.

Delivery involves not just giving the program to the customer but also making sure that supporting documentation is complete and that the user is properly trained in using the software.

note

Testing is best done by automating the testing process. This allows tests to be repeatedly run and the results notified quickly.

note

Tests must be repeatable, always starting from a known state.

!

Always document your programs properly as the someone who has to maintain it may be you.

For the programmer this means making sure that the design has been properly documented (so you can reliably make modifications to the program in the future). It may be necessary to write a separate *system manual* to supplement the commented code, and things like the class diagram should certainly be properly recorded. For the user of the software some form of *user manual* and training will be necessary.

9.4.7 Debugging

Debugging is the sub-process of testing and fixing problems. It is worth mentioning separately as it is often a very time consuming activity! Debugging follows a mini-cycle:

1. Write some code.
2. Compile the code.
3. Test the code and detect errors.
4. Locate the cause of the error.
5. Decide on the code needed to fix the error.
6. Goto 1.

Previously (Section 8.1, Page 226), we categorized errors not caught at compile time as being either logic errors or run-time errors. Run-time errors are usually fatal whereas logic errors tend to result in the wrong behaviour or the wrong result. Fatal errors are easy to spot as the program will terminate, often due to an unexpected exception being thrown. Logic errors are harder to find as the program will typically carry on executing but will sooner or later produce the wrong result. Finding logic errors relies on a good set of test plans.

Once an error is detected, the programmer has to locate the cause. Often the observed failure is only a side-effect of the real error which could have occurred at any point in the execution of the program before it failed. In fact, localizing the code where the error actually is is usually the hardest part of debugging. Thus the real skill of debugging is locating the actual cause of the error given the symptoms. There are three principle ways to track down the causes of errors:

note

The J2SDK comes with a debugger tool, jdb, and commercial programming environments will come with an equivalent, often with a graphical user interface. Make sure you find out about the debugger on your Java system — programming life is much more worth living using one.

- Do code inspections and walk through the execution of the program manually. This involves reasoning about what each program statement does and trying to spot the problem by mentally executing the program.
- At relevant locations in the program add output statements that write messages to the console showing the current state of execution, e.g. 'executing method f, x has value 10'.
- Use a tool called a *debugger*.

Of these, the last option is usually the most helpful and efficient. A debugger is a tool that allows the programmer to control the execution of a program and inspect its state as it is running. In particular, the debugger will allow the programmer to step through a program one statement at a time and print out the values of variables and objects. It is also possible to set *breakpoints* that will stop the program close to the point where you believe an error occurs. It is very important that you become familiar with the debugger in your programming environment and use it as much as possible. Beginners are often put off learning about their debugger only to waste lots of time trying to debug their program in other ways.

In the end debugging, like programming, is a skill that has to be learnt and you will definitely get lots of practice, everyone who programs does!

9.5 Maintenance

When introducing the program development process, we listed the stages of development as inception, elaboration, implementation and testing and delivery. Actually, we should add a further stage: *Maintenance*. It's easy to forget this stage and we may well be criticized for not having including this stage in our original listing. However, we thought it was so important a stage that we should separate it out so as to indicate how important it is.

Maintenance covers all the activities following the delivery of a program. These include:

1. Fixing the bugs that we were unable to detect at testing time that come to light during use.
2. Correcting any faulty behaviour of the program (i.e. where the program does not behave as expected and as required by the user), even if this was not discovered during testing.
3. Supporting the program in new environments, such as changes to operating system software.
4. Modifications to change the behaviour of the program due to changes in requirements.
5. New features that need to be added to the program, again due to evolving requirements.

!

In principle, Java programs should be immune to changes in operating system or hardware environment. In practice, issues will always come up.

Now whilst (1), (2) and (3) are "keeping things going as they are" type maintenance, (4) and (5) are very definitely extending and evolving the system beyond that which was original planned: (4) and especially (5) are qualitatively different forms of maintenance. Indeed, many would argue that these should not be labelled 'maintenance' at all but should be considered as new developments from a pre-existing system. Such an attitude implies that (4) and (5) should be activities that involve the full "inception, elaboration, implementation and testing and delivery" process cycle. Whereas (1), (2) and (3) require activity that is really a "test, implement, test, repeat until satisfied, and deliver" cycle — in effect a sub-cycle of the full development cycle that we have presented.

Whichever sort of maintenance is being undertaken, whoever does the maintenance (and this is often not the original programmer) needs to understand the design as well as the implementation of the program in order to modify it correctly. All too often, changes are made in an ad hoc way that leads to the deterioration of the structure of the program — a phenomenon known as 'software rot'. This leads to the situation where changes to the program to address one problem can have the side-effect of breaking something somewhere else in the program. Eventually, such uncontrolled amendment leads to 'spaghetti code' with the cost of making any change outweighing any possible advantages. If a piece of software gets anywhere near to this state, it is time to consider replacing it which may mean a complete re-implementation from scratch.

Since most of the life of a program is spent in 'maintenance' and not in 'development', promoting good maintainability is clearly very important. This can be promoted in two principal ways:

1. By providing good, concise documentation that the maintainer can read in order to understand how the program is designed and how to go about modifying it.

2. By the maintainer being properly trained and understanding how to do object-oriented development and programming — by being a professional.

Of course, the maintainer must keep the documentation consistent and up to date. Change logs, which are basically lists of amendments to the code, help here, allowing the history of the program to be tracked. However, there are also the system and user manuals to consider. The system manual details design and implementation information not apparent elsewhere, and needs to be changed to reflect any changes to the design and or implementation so that it describes the current state of the system. The user manual, giving instructions to users on how to use the program, needs changing whenever any changes are made to the way the program works from the users' point of view. Again, the manual must reflect the current state of the system.

Clearly, having the bulk of the system documentation embedded in the source code supports ensuring that system documentation is kept up to date: comments should be updated as the source code itself is amended. The automatic generation of documentation from the source code (using `javadoc`) is a great boon here with its philosophy of keeping documentation in the source code files. However, not all system documentation, and certainly no user documentation, can be embedded in the source code, so a discipline is needed, perhaps supported by organizational procedures, to ensure that all the documentation and not just the source code is amended.

9.6   Practice and Experience

An important set of skills for the programmer lie in self-assessment and being able to accurately judge the quality of programs as they are developed. As you gain experience, you will learn to recognize good and bad design, and what it means to produce 'elegant' code. You will also build up your own catalogue of good solutions to design problems. This is indicative that there are elements of commonality to problems and design solutions to them.

In fact, it has been shown that all well designed object-oriented systems exploit recurring design structures that exhibit good abstraction, flexibility, modularity and elegance. Such design structures contain valuable design knowledge that needs to be remembered and reused since it is more than a personal catalogue. This idea has been formalized in terms of the idea of *design patterns*.

A design pattern captures a component of a complete design that has been seen to recur in solutions to problems and can be used not only to construct designs but also to communicate knowledge about these solutions. Design patterns can also be used as elements of a pattern language, which provides a way of communicating design level information, in the same kind of way that a programming language communicates code level information.

This is another boon for maintainability. If an application makes use of design patterns that are catalogued and known widely, it is much easier for a maintainer (who we presume is also knowledgable about design patterns) to comprehend the design of the system. This makes it easier for that person to make bug fixes or amendments to the program without violating the basic design and/or structure.

There is an increasing literature with specifications of accepted design patterns and we strongly recommended that, once you start programming, you find out about design patterns as they are an excellent way of improving your design work. It will save you having to build up you own personal catalogue from scratch!

tip

A competent software developer should spend a significant amount of time reading the literature and keeping up with current developments. Aim to read at least one text book a month along with 2–3 journals.

9.7 Summary and Questions

The core of this chapter has been about the process of designing and implementing small-scale object-oriented programs. In doing so, however, it has tackled the key questions of what object-oriented analysis and design are about. Building and expanding on these key ideas will be crucial for the programmer who wants to move on to designing and building large applications.

For small-scale programs, taking an iterative prototyping approach to development is often the most effective way of proceeding. It is always valuable to spend time planning and designing a program, so the steps of analysis, design and implementation need to be placed in an overall iterative process. The value of having such a process is found in having a reliable, repeatable and systematic way of producing software.

The next chapter will present a program design example, following the guidelines presented in this chapter.

Key points in this chapter:

- Object-oriented analysis and design methods are now well established, and are needed to design larger Java programs.
- UML (the Unified Modelling Language) is a widely used notation for documenting object-oriented systems.
- Requirements define what a program should be capable of doing.
- Analysis determines structure and function, design creates an implementable description of a program — insides and outsides.

- Key classes in a design should capture the stable problem domain.
- Testing needs to be repeatable and performed frequently.
- Iteration and prototyping provide a framework for the development of small to medium size programs.
- Debugging is the art of locating and fixing errors in a program.
- Maintenance fixes bugs and adds features to a program.
- A good programmer puts significant effort into code reviews, testing, self-assessment and keeping up to date with developments in design and programming practice.

Self-review Questions

Self-review 9.1 What is a problem domain? Why are problem domains relatively stable?

Self-review 9.2 Identify the problem domain entities for payroll systems.

Self-review 9.3 What are the strengths and weaknesses of prototyping?

Self-review 9.4 Write a collection of scenarios for an application to manage the renting of videos from a video rental store.

Self-review 9.5 What is the role of analysis?

Self-review 9.6 How can classes be identified?

Self-review 9.7 What is the role of design?

Self-review 9.8 List the properties of a well designed class.

Self-review 9.9 What is the aim of testing and what are the limitations?

Self-review 9.10 Make suggestions as to how a code review might be conducted.

Self-review 9.11 What is an appropriate amount of documentation for a program? What should it include?

Self-review 9.12 What is the key information that you require in order to effectively maintain code written by someone else?

Self-review 9.13 Summarize the strengths and weaknesses of object-oriented development.

Self-review 9.14 What is the point of reuse? What features should a reusable class have?

Programming Exercises

Exercise 9.1 Write Java classes corresponding to the classes shown in this UML diagram.

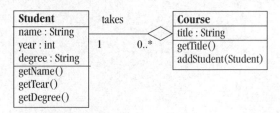

Exercise 9.2 The UML class diagram below represents a simple order system.

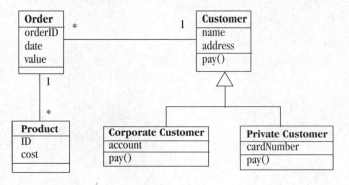

Write a Java class for each class identified in the diagram.

Challenges

Challenge 9.1 Consider the following specification:

"A program is required to run the controller of a burglar alarm system. A typical system consists of a number of sensors connected by individual circuits to a central control box containing the controller. The control box has a simple keypad and display. Sensors include switches, heat detectors and motion detectors. Each sensor has an identification code which can be read by the controller to identify the sensor.

The controller allows an operator to select which sensors are active and turn on or off the system. If a sensor is triggered when the system is active, the controller must activate the alarms (a siren and a bell) and display a message on the display panel indicating which sensor is involved. The operator must enter a security code before the system is turned on or off."

a. Identify a set of classes which might be used to model the system from an object-oriented point of view.

b. Use the classes to construct a class diagram to show the structure of the system.

c. Write a program to simulate the system, using the classes.

Challenge 9.2 Create a UML class diagram showing the classes and their relationships in the J2SDK package `java.util`.

10

A Program Design Example

Objectives

This chapter presents the first stages in the design of an object-oriented program in order
to provide an example of how the ideas of the last chapter are put into practice.

Keywords

analysis

CRC

design

iterative development

prototyping

requirements

scenario

10.1   Introduction

This chapter assumes that, as an exercise, you have been asked to write a program to simulate the account management activities of a small bank. The following requirements have been given to you:

- A bank manages a collection of customer accounts.
- There are different kinds of bank accounts, such as current accounts and savings accounts. Some kinds of account pay interest on the money saved.
- It is possible to open a new account or close an existing account.
- It is possible to deposit and withdraw money from an account, as well as ask for details of the current balance.

What we will do in the rest of the chapter is outline how these requirements can be turned into a working program. We do not intend to show a complete solution to bank account management, but just to show that there is a clear process you follow to create a reasonable program.

10.2   Requirements and Scenarios

We have already been given a short list of requirements for what the program needs to do. As the first stage of developing a solution, we review the requirements, add any which were missing and develop a set of scenarios showing what the program should do from the user's point of view. Ideally, we would then want to take the results back to the intended users of the program and ask them to review the results. However, as this is an exercise and there are no actual users, we compromise and make assumptions about what is needed.

A quick review of the requirements reveals that they are understandable and don't present any obvious inconsistencies. We can quickly identify the following scenarios:

1. Open a new account.
2. Close an existing account.
3. Check the balance of an account.
4. Deposit money in an account.
5. Withdraw money from an account.

Next, for each scenario, we write down the steps involved to complete it, looking out for new insights we can gain about what needs to happen. When developing the scenarios at this stage we are simply identifying the steps it would take to get something done. We are not yet concerned with how the program will work in any detail and are mostly focusing on what the user will do.

10.2.1   Scenario 1 — Opening a New Account

We can quickly jot down a series of steps to fulfil this scenario:

1. Select open new account option.
2. Enter contact details (e.g. name, address, phone number, etc.) of new account holder.
3. Create a new account and return the account details (i.e. account number).

Doing this, we immediately notice that a way of doing input and output is required and we can add a new requirement:

*   The program will make use of a Graphical User Interface (GUI), and the user will interact with the program using standard GUI features such as menus, buttons and dialogue boxes.

We have also identified that each account will need a set of information associated with it, notably the details (name, address, etc.) of the account holder and also an account number to uniquely identify the account. This is leading to a new requirement outlining what an account is but looking ahead we can see that there will be other account details emerging in other scenarios (such as the balance of the account), so will wait before writing the requirement down.

Checking with the initial set of requirements, an omission in the scenario can be seen; we need to know what kind of account is being opened. The requirements list two varieties of account but what is the full list? The answer we choose is interesting: the different kinds of account will change over time but for the moment there are the two kinds listed in the requirements. Moreover, the savings account accumulates interest while the current account does not.

Does this mean we need to add a requirement to allow new kinds of account to be created? This would make the program rather more complicated but also more flexible for the users. The alternative is to assume that the program code needs to be edited in order to create new kinds of account, something that cannot be done by the user and will require a programmer.

To make a choice we need to evaluate the risks. On the one hand, there is the risk of trying to design a significantly more complicated program, thereby increasing the short term costs. On the other hand, there is the risk that the program will need extensive modification after it is in use, increasing the long term costs. In addition, the decisions we make about data structures now may turn out to be inadequate when we start adding new kinds of account. However, we can look to the properties of object-oriented design to reduce this risk.

One way to attempt to make a design more future-proof is to develop a set of *change cases*, as work on the system progresses. A change case is a description of how a specific requirement may change over time, along with an assessment of its impact on the design of the system. The design should exploit encapsulation and abstraction to both minimize the scope of a change and allow the change to be easily made.

As this program is being constructed as an exercise, the decision is made to assume that new kinds of account will require modification to the program. This will allow us to build a simple first

!

Deferring the addition of features raises an aspect of professionalism: you should not choose to require the code to be edited simply to keep your job! The decision should be taken on technical and user requirements grounds only.

prototype and get a good feel for how it fits together. Later on the decision can be revisited to see if it is still justified. The iterative development process will allow changes to be made if found necessary. We must make a formal note of this decision so it won't get forgotten:

Note I — review decision on how to add new kinds of account.

10.2.2   Scenario 2 — Closing an Account

The steps to fulfil this scenario are:

1. Select close account option.
2. Enter account number.
3. Verify that the correct account is being closed.
4. Close the account and remove from bank.

This turns out to be straightforward given the existing requirements. We can, however, query two points: "What happens to the money in the account?" and "Should the bank keep an archive record of the closed account?"

If we were dealing with a real bank these would be rather important questions! However, for the exercise we can quickly decide that the money is assumed to be returned to the ex-account holder and that no archive records are needed, although we make a note to review that decision later:

Note II — are archive records needed of closed accounts?

10.2.3   Scenario 3 — Check Balance of Account

The steps are:

1. Select check balance option.
2. Enter an account number.
3. Return the balance details.

Nothing of particular note here, but notice that this confirms that the balance is part of an account.

10.2.4   Scenario 4 — Deposit Money in an Account

The steps are:

1. Select deposit option.
2. Enter an account number and the amount of money to be paid-in.
3. Add money to the account.
4. Show the results.

No surprises here, but note that (4) needs a bit more thought so that the user can verify that the right thing happened.

10.2.5 Scenario 5 — Withdraw Money from an Account

The steps are:

1. Select remove option.

2. Enter an account number and the amount of money to be removed.

3. Check that there is enough money in the account.

4. Deduct the money withdrawn from balance.

5. Show the results.

This is slightly more complicated than the last scenario as a decision has been made not to allow an account balance to go negative. With a bit more thought about what happens in that situation, a new requirement can be added to the list.

- An account balance cannot be left in a negative state when money is withdrawn. If an attempt is made to withdraw more money than available, only the current balance is withdrawn.

At this point we can also add an extra requirement about accounts, as noted earlier.

- An account should store the account holder's details (name, address, phone) and have a unique account number.

Another issue for real banks would be the questions of authentication and authorization. Does the person requesting the transaction have the authority to do so and how do we know they are who they say they are? This is not just an issue for this scenario but also for the previous one since it is a matter of obtaining account information. Interestingly, we could be less strict about this for depositing money! Perhaps a note is appropriate:

Note III — review the authorization and authentication issues if need be.

10.2.6 Scenario Results

The results of identifying scenarios and stepping through them has been to make us think more deeply about what is required. As a result, several new requirements have been identified and some notes made for future reference. As yet, we haven't really made any decisions about the program design, except for deciding that a GUI will be used, as we want to be reasonably sure of the requirements before making design decisions.

The revised requirements are summarized in Figure 10.1. This is a 'living document', though, so it is bound to be changed and added to as we progress with the project.

Working through scenarios and developing requirements can appear tedious but is vital. Too many programming projects founder due to inadequate requirements and a desire to rush in and write code for the sake of writing code. Without having a clear and concise understanding of what of program is for and what it should do, an appropriate and stable design cannot be achieved.

note

Real bank accounts typically have an overdraft option. This implies that at some point a 'grant overdraft' feature will need to be supported.

!

Think first, write code second!

- A bank manages a collection of bank accounts.

- There are different kinds of bank accounts, such as current accounts and savings accounts. Some kinds of account pay interest on the money saved.

- It is possible to open a new account or close an existing account.

- It is possible to deposit and withdraw money from an account, as well as ask for details of the current balance.

- An account balance cannot be left in a negative state when money is withdrawn. If an attempt is made to withdraw more money than available, only the current balance is withdrawn.

- An account should store the account holder's details (name, address, phone) and have a unique account number.

- The program will make use of a Graphical User Interface (GUI), and the user will interact with the program using standard GUI features such as menus, buttons and dialogue boxes.

Note I — review decision on how to add new kinds of account.
Note II — are archive records needed of closed accounts?
Note III — review the authorization and authentication issues if need be.

Figure 10.1 Summary of requirements and notes.

10.3 Object-oriented Analysis (OOA)

We are now in a position to start thinking about the problem in terms of classes and objects. There are three ways we can go about identifying classes. The first is to go for the 'obvious' things like Bank and Account, using our intuition and, as it is built up, experience. However, this approach is likely to be rather superficial and certainly informal, giving a high risk of omissions and mistakes.

The second way is to be more systematic by reviewing the requirements looking for nouns, strategies, roles and concepts that might represent classes, attributes or methods, and use those to put together a class diagram for the system. Although this approach can be rather crude (and is often criticized as such), for simple problems such as this one, it is usually enough to produce a reasonable result.

The third way is to make use of the CRC analysis method and role-play through the scenarios given above in order to identify classes. This is a valuable way of analysing systems, particularly if they are fairly complex or in an unfamiliar area. We will review this approach in a later subsection.

10.3.1 Looking for Classes

Checking the requirements quickly yields a list of potential classes, attributes and methods.

Classes: `Bank, Account, CurrentAccount, SavingsAccount, Customer, UserInterface`

Attributes: Balance, Name, Address, Phone Number

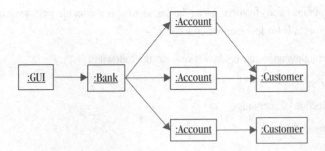

Figure 10.2 Potential objects.

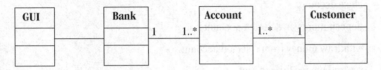

Figure 10.3 A first attempt UML class diagram.

Methods: Create Account, Close Account, Deposit, Withdraw, Check Balance

At the same time, a quick sketch of the system in terms of potential objects gives us the picture shown in Figure 10.2.

Each box represents an object, so that one `Bank` object references a collection of `Account` objects, with each `Account` object referencing one `Customer` object (which holds the information about the customer whose account it is). There is also a GUI object which, for the purposes of this example, serves as the user interface. If the program was implemented in full, this single object would expand to a number of Java Swing component objects which would implement the GUI seen on the screen. Before designing the user interface we would undertake a more detailed investigation into the Human–Computer Interaction (HCI) issues. This would involve researching the HCI literature, using HCI guidelines to support the design and using user interface prototypes and user evaluations to obtain feedback on the design and hence improve it. The bibliography contains some good books on HCI that are well worth a read.

One crucially important point here: Notice that the GUI does not directly access `Account` objects, it only makes use of the `Bank` object. This means that the GUI can change as much as we like but as long as it only uses the `Bank` public interface to interact with the rest of the program, we don't have to worry. It is important, however, to check that the `Bank` class provides sufficient functionality in its interface for the appropriate GUI to be constructed.

Figure 10.3 shows a first attempt at the class diagram, using UML notation. Next we can put together more detailed descriptions for the various classes. The attributes and methods are allocated using our common sense understanding of what banks and bank accounts are, but strongly guided by whether those attributes and methods are needed to implement the scenarios identified. One thing we don't want to do is to arbitrarily add everything to a class that might be useful, as this will

tip

Only add methods and attributes to a class if they are really needed.

clutter it up with unnecessary features. Using the CRC method is a valuable way of sorting out what is really needed, especially for less familiar concepts.

Working through what we have, Class `Bank` has the following:

- *Attributes*:
  - collection of accounts
  - name of the bank
- *Methods*:
  - open account
  - close account
  - deposit money in selected account
  - withdraw money from selected account
  - return balance for account

Notice that one attribute of the bank, the collection of accounts, is potentially an object in its own right. The bank also has a name, as a way of distinguishing one bank from another. This comes from anticipating that the program is later extended to include several banks, and also from experience showing that it is useful to give objects like a bank object a distinct identity. However, in keeping with our principle of only adding features that are needed, we keep the identity attribute to the minimum of a name.

Class `Account`:

- *Attributes*:
  - account number
  - balance (amount of money)
  - account holder information
- *Methods*:
  - deposit money
  - withdraw money
  - return current balance

What about current and savings accounts? These are both clearly *kinds-of* bank accounts with specializations needed in the case of the savings account. Being able to say that a current or savings account is a kind-of bank account very strongly suggests that inheritance should be used, so that the current and savings account classes are subclasses of the `Account` class. Further, the `Account` class can be made abstract, providing a common interface and any shared attributes and methods. This will allow the bank class to access bank accounts via the abstract `Account` interface, and, most of the time, not be concerned with specific kinds of accounts. However, the bank will have to be concerned with creating accounts, so some more specific knowledge will be needed. We should note this when working on the design and see what the affect might be.

Introducing inheritance gives two more classes; `CurrentAccount` and `SavingsAccount`. `CurrentAccount` will be a subclass of `Account` but at this stage does not need to add any additional attributes, only to implement the methods inherited from the abstract superclass.

`SavingsAccount` is a bit more complicated. It needs to have an associated rate of interest and a way of calculating the amount of interest earned. This implies an extra attribute and an extra method, `calculateInterest`. Adding the attribute is easy but the new method causes a problem as it will not be part of the interface inherited from `Account`, requiring special treatment of `SavingsAccount`, something we are trying to avoid.

The solution is to add a public method called `update` to the class `Account` interface. This will be called periodically to get account objects to update their balance and anything else that may be discovered in the future. For the `CurrentAccount` class this will be a null operation but for the `SavingsAccount` it will result in the balance being changed.

Making this change introduces a further issue: When should `update` be called? Some kind of time-based event is needed, controlled by the `Bank` class, which will also need to work with dates. A new method will be added to bank, also called `update`, the calling of which will be examined during design.

While thinking about these issues, another omission is found. The `Bank` object needs some way of identifying account objects, presumably by asking for their account number. Hence, class `Account` needs a method to return the account number.

The customer class holds information about a bank customer.

Class `Customer`:
- *Attributes*:
  - name of account holder
  - address of account holder
  - phone number of account holder
- *Methods*:
  - \<not certain yet\>

It is difficult to say which data attributes are the ones that we actually need and it is difficult to say what methods we will need other than accessor functions. We shall leave this as a pending question for the moment.

10.3.2 Revised Classes

This now gives us the following classes:

Class `Bank`

- *Attributes*:
  - a collection of accounts
  - name of the bank
- *Methods*:
  - open account
  - close account
  - deposit money in selected account
  - withdraw money from selected account
  - update accounts
  - return balance for account

Class `Account`:

- *Attributes*:
  - account number
  - balance (amount of money)
  - account holder information
- *Methods*:
  - deposit money (abstract)
  - withdraw money (abstract)
  - return current balance (defaults to returning balance)
  - update account (defaults to null operation)
  - get account number

Class `CurrentAccount` extends `Account`:

- *Attributes*:

  <no new attributes>

- *Methods*:
  - deposit money (overridden)
  - withdraw money (overridden)

Class `SavingsAccount` extends Account:

- *Attributes*:
  - Interest rate
- *Methods*:
  - deposit money (overridden)
  - withdraw money (overridden)
  - update account (overridden)

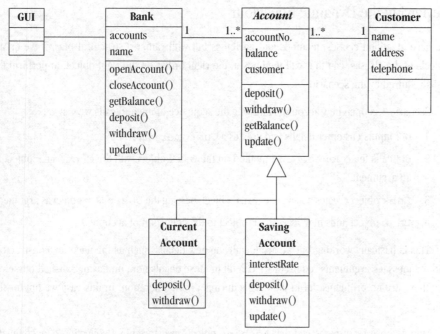

Figure 10.4 Revised UML class diagram.

Class Customer:

- *Attributes*:

  - name of account holder

  - address of account holder

  - phone number of account holder

- *Methods*:

    <not certain yet>

From this information we can now generate a revised class diagram, as seen in Figure 10.4 (we use Java style method and variable names on the diagram). As we have seen, the attribute and method lists have been determined at this stage by 'knowing' what accounts are meant to be and do. As more is understood about accounts, further new detail may be discovered and added. The role of OOA has been to identify classes and their relationships, providing each class with a list of methods and attributes. OOA is an iterative process; it takes time and experimentation to find all the attributes and operations. Moreover, the iteration may well cause us to revisit and revise requirements, as we learn more about the problem.

It is essential to understand the problem in terms of encapsulated objects and their interfaces. Although this may seem artificial for a simple example like this, it becomes very important as programs get larger. By restricting communication between objects to well known interfaces, it becomes easier to understand, alter and maintain a program.

tip

Be prepared to throw away anything that is not needed. Don't accumulate junk!

10.3.3   Reviewing the Dynamic Behaviour

We have identified classes, methods and attributes but with rather a structural bias. If we create objects of the classes, can they call methods in the right order, on the right object, to perform the tasks required by the scenarios?

Scenario 1 is open new account. Following the sequence of method calls we get:

1. GUI inputs customer details and creates a `Customer` object.
2. GUI calls the `openAccount` method on the `Bank` object with the `Customer` object as an argument.
3. `Bank` object creates a new `Account` object, passing the `Customer` object as argument.
4. `Bank` object adds new `Account` object to the collection of accounts.

This is basically working but we are identifying new details, such as the need for constructors and the message arguments required. We can fill in those details now, or, having satisfied ourselves that there are no problems, fill in the details during a design iteration. In this case we opt for the latter.

Step 4 above records the fact that `Account` objects are stored in a collection of accounts by the bank. We don't attempt to model the collection further, as we know that collections are one of the basic building blocks we already have. We might ask, however, if the `Bank` object should also have a collection of `Customer` objects — after all, a bank should know its customers, it may want to do mail shots for example. At the moment the `Bank` object has no way of accessing a customer after an account is created, although none of the scenarios require it to (account numbers being used to identify accounts).

Three options are available for immediately dealing with this situation:

a. Add a customer collection attribute to the `Bank` class.
b. Add a `getCustomer` method to the `Account` class.
c. Do nothing for now, and wait until the need for the `Bank` to use a `Customer` object arises.

Following our rule about adding only those features that are actually used, option c) will be taken up. In the longer term it is a fair guess that the `Bank` object will need use to `Customer` objects in some way (a search for customer requirement may be added, for example), but until we know how, we don't want to make any false assumptions. Options a) or b) may be useful, but there are other possibilities as well.

Scenario 2 is close account. The method sequence is:

1. GUI inputs account number, does some verification to check that the account really should be closed and calls `closeAccount` method on the `Bank` object.
2. The `Bank` object closes the account and removes the `Account` object from the collection of accounts.

There is nothing here that invalidates our classes, but also nothing new. The same questions posed in the scenario are still to be resolved. As no new information is available we will have to return to this later.

Scenario 3 is check account balance, and by inspection we can see that the work will by done by calling the `getBalance` method on `Bank`. Similarly, for scenarios 4 and 5, we can see that the `Bank` and `Account` classes provide suitable methods to be called. Until we start writing the method bodies, we won't know if additional methods will be needed.

Overall, our review of the dynamic behaviour — checking that methods are available to be called to perform the tasks — has revealed some new information and confirmed that the structure identified so far is plausible.

10.3.4 Using CRC

We could have used the CRC method to help identify classes and find the dynamic behaviour. This would be useful if we were unclear about what classes are needed or what methods (responsibilities) a class should provide. An example of how it might be used follows.

Take Scenario 1 — Open a new `Account`. Ignoring the user interface issues and assuming a `Bank` class card has already been created, talking through the scenario gives us:

1. The customer's name, address and phone number for the new account have been entered. Let's assume a current account is wanted and send a message to the `Bank` object asking for a new current account, giving the new customer details as an argument.
   Action: Add a create account responsibility to the `Bank` card.

2. The customer details entered have to be stored, the obvious place being a current account object. Create a class `CurrentAccount` CRC card. This needs an initialize responsibility that will take the account holder details.
   Action: Add a collaboration to the `Bank` card opposite the new account entry.

3. The `CurrentAccount` initialization doesn't need to collaborate with any other class so the scenario is complete.

This is showing much the same results as the review in the last sub-section, confirming that the right things are happening. CRC works very nicely when there are a group of people involved, and, as it is relatively informal, allows end-users of the proposed system to be involved. As experts in how the bank works in reality, they can check that the system being developed has the correct behaviour and produces the right results.

ref

Read through Appendix B, Page 947, if you are unsure about how the CRC method works.

10.4   Designing the Program — First Iteration

Having analysed the problem and done sufficient design to identify a set of classes, the next stage is to design the classes and the main method. At this point, the detailed issues of using Java have to be taken into account.

With an object-oriented approach, design is primarily about continued elaboration of details until we have enough to write the code. When designing a large-scale program we would have a distinct design phase before coding. However, for small-scale programs we are usually able write the Java code directly during the design phase. This is not an excuse for sloppy coding, however.

The analysis has identified a set of attributes and methods for each class. The methods become public methods in the class declaration, while attributes become private instance variables. The first stage of design is to translate the analysis classes into Java.

10.4.1   Class Bank

A first pass at the `Bank` class can be made as follows:

```
public class Bank {
   // Open account, return account number.
   public int openAccount(Customer accountHolder) { ... }
   // Close account given account number.
   public int closeAccount(int accountNumber) { ... }
   // Deposit money given account number and money in cents/pence.
   public void deposit(int accountNumber, int amount) { ... }
   // Withdraw money, given account number and money in cents/pence.
   // Return amount actually withdrawn.
   public int withdraw(int accountNumber, int amount) { ... }
   // Return balance details for given account.
   public int getBalance(int accountNumber) { ... }
   // Update state of bank and bank accounts.
   public void update() { ... }

   private ArrayList accounts ;
   private String bankName ;
}
```

tip

When prototyping a class, it is a good idea to simultaneously write the code to test the class. In fact, some would advocate writing the test code first.

Constructors have yet to be added, while various decisions have been made about method details including argument types and result types, based on what we have discovered so far. It has been decided that an `ArrayList` will be used to store the account objects, as it provides a suitably flexible data structure and comes ready made from the Java class libraries.

10.4.2   Class Account

A first pass through the `Account` class produces:

```
public abstract class Account {
   // Deposit money (in cents/pence) -- abstract so must override.
   abstract public void deposit(int) ;
   // Withdraw money, return amount withdrawn.
   // Abstract so must override.
   abstract public int withdraw(int amount) ;
   // Method called to get account to update.
```

```
    public void update() {}
    // Return current balance.
    public int getBalance() { ... }
    // Return account number.
    public int getAccountNumber() { ... }

    // Protected member variables, so subclasses can access them.
    protected int balance ;
    protected int accountNumber ;
    protected Customer accountHolder ;
}
```

The class and some of the methods are abstract, so we make sure that they are declared using the `abstract` keyword.

The attributes uncovered during analysis have to be given types. A decision has been made to represent both the balance and account number as integers. The point here is to store the number of pence/cents since that is always an integer and can be stored and manipulated exactly — to use a floating point number for the number of pounds/dollars would introduce rounding errors during computation. This keeps things simple but could cause problems if in the future we decide to represent the attributes differently, as we have also decided that the `getBalance` and `getAccountNumber` methods should return `int`s. If the representation of the balance or the account number changes, it will probably force a change of these public interfaces as well, meaning that all the users of accounts would have to be located and edited. It may be better to introduce `Money` and `AccountNumber` types, similar to the way we have introduced a `Customer` class. For the moment we will opt for simplicity and stick with integers but we note this decision so that later we can revisit it.

Some decisions have also been made about the arguments and return types of methods. These are based on judgements about what will be useful. At this stage the decisions are provisional, although we want to stabilize the types as early as possible.

10.4.3 Account Subclasses

The two subclasses of `Account` are straightforward to declare at this stage:

```
public class CurrentAccount extends Account {
    // Deposit money (in pence/cents)
    public void deposit(int amount) { ... }
    // Withdraw money, return amount withdrawn
    public int withdraw(int amount) { ... }
}
```

`CurrentAccount` only needs to override `deposit` and `withdraw`.

```
public class SavingsAccount extends Account {
    // Deposit money (in pence/cents)
    public void deposit(int amount) { ... }
    // Withdraw money, return amount withdrawn
    public int withdraw(int amount) { ... }
    // Method called to get account to update
    public void update() { ... }

    protected int interestRate ;
}
```

tip

It can take time to correctly identify inheritance relationships. If in doubt, start off with association relationships and change them to inheritance when the need becomes obvious.

`SavingsAccount` needs to additionally override `update` and declare a new instance variable, which is made protected in case this class has subclasses.

10.4.4   Class Customer

The first pass of the `Customer` class comprises the data attributes:

```
public class Customer {
   public Customer (String name, String address, String telephone) {
      ...
   }

   protected String name ;
   protected String address ;
   protected String telephone ;
}
```

Until we go further with the design, it is difficult to say what else is needed other than the constructor. We are not yet certain what actual contact information we need to store. Also, we are uncertain as to what use is to be made of the information and hence what methods are needed.

The decision to store all the contact information as `Strings` is not unreasonable for the `name` and `address` but for `telephone` it can easily be challenged. The reason is that telephone numbers have a very rigid structure and this structure needs to be enforced. We should consider introducing a `TelephoneNumber` class. Actually, it could easily be argued that name and address have rules and structure as well and so classes should be introduced to construct their representations.

10.4.5   First Review

The first pass through the design has been done by writing down the class declarations using Java syntax. The method bodies have yet to be filled in but we can see that the basic design seems to be coming together. While doing this we have been thinking about the design details quite a bit and probably started asking new questions which need answers. For example:

- Constructors have been rather neglected and we need to sort out how objects, including their member variables, get initialized.

- It has been decided to represent account numbers as `int`s but what decides which integer to allocate to each account object? It seems likely that the `Bank` is responsible for allocating account numbers — however, no extra variables or methods have yet been added to deal with this. Indeed, it may be that `int`s are an entirely inappropriate representation.

- Do the `withdraw` and `deposit` methods in `Account` need to be abstract or can a default implementation be provided?

- What does `update` do and, more particularly, how does the `SavingsAccount` calculate interest? Dates and periods of time seem to be involved.

- Where does the static `main` method go? Will it be part of the `Bank` class or in some GUI subclass when the GUI is implemented?

These kinds of questions need to be addressed in the next iteration of design work, as we start to write the method bodies. It might also be necessary to go back and do more analysis or even requirements gathering in order to find out more about interest calculations.

Notice that both `Bank` and `Account` have methods named `deposit, withdraw` and `getBalance`. However, they do different things as the bank `deposit` locates an account and calls the account `deposit` method to get the account to update itself, while the account `deposit` only deals with adjusting the balance for the account.

Most importantly, the `Bank` object only accesses `Accounts` via the public interface defined by class `Account`: on no account must the `Bank` object ever access an account balance directly; to do so would break the encapsulation of the object and ruin the structure of the program. Similarly, the `Bank` object should only be accessed via its public interface. We can use the encapsulation rules of the Java language to enforce this.

10.5 Designing the Program — Second Iteration

Writing the class declarations has gained a lot of insight into how the program will be structured and work. We now want to continue development by filling in the method bodies. We won't attempt to cover every method but will cover enough so that the rest could be filled in straightforwardly (as an exercise for the reader).

Ideally, each class should be provided with a test program and test plan, to test its behaviour and make sure that it works. This can be done by providing a static main function that includes test routines.

0.5.1 Second Design of the Bank Class

The `Bank` needs a constructor. This can take as its argument a `String` representing the name of the `Bank` and do any initialization that is needed. For this program, we could make the design decision that all object initialization will be done in the constructor body rather than by direct initialization of the member variables. In which case:

```
public Bank(String name) {
    accounts = new ArrayList() ;
    bankName = name ;
}
```

At this stage there is no need to provide a `finalize` method. An attempt to code the `openAccount` method can be started:

```
public int openAccount(Customer accountHolder) {
    // We want a new account
    Account newAccount = new ????? // Uh oh ...
    ...
}
```

A problem suddenly arises that we had previously missed. To open an account we need to know which account subclass to instantiate. We also have a conflict of interest; on the one hand, we would like the `Bank` class to avoid naming account subclasses directly; on the other hand, we have to name the subclass to get a object. Further, we would also like to avoid account objects being manipulated by anything other than the bank, ruling out the possibility of creating the account object elsewhere and passing an object reference to the `openAccount` method.

Reluctantly, we decide to add an extra parameter to the `openAccount` method, indicating what kind of account is needed, and then test that variable to determine which account subclass to instantiate. We also make a note to revisit this decision later on. Trying again:

```
public int openAccount(Customer accountHolder, String kind) {
   // We want a new account
   Account newAccount = null ;
   if (kind.equals("SavingsAccount"))
     newAccount =
       new SavingsAccount(accountHolder,accountNumber) ;
   else if (kind.equals("CurrentAccount"))
     newAccount =
       new CurrentAccount(accountHolder,accountNumber) ;
   ...
   return newAccount.getAccountNumber() ;
}
```

Beware of temporary solutions becoming permanent problems. If a quick fix is too unacceptable, replace it immediately with something better.

Better, but two more issues arise; how do we find the account number and what happens if an attempt is made to open a kind of account that doesn't exist? We also note that an assumption has been made about the form of the yet to be written account subclasses constructors.

To deal with the account numbers a counter could be used to count the number of accounts ever created. When a new account number is needed the counter is incremented and the result used as the account number. A new private variable will need to be added to the `Bank` class and initialized. This feels a bit crude and reinforces the hints that a proper account number class is needed.

Always try to anticipate what will happen if an element in the design is changed in the future and takes steps to avoid undesirable side-effects.

Prior to adopting the counter another strategy was considered. It was proposed that as the bank's data structure is an `ArrayList`, it could be asked for the number of elements it holds and then that number could be used as the new account number (remember that accounts are numbered from zero). However, that approach was recognized as seriously flawed. Firstly, when an account is removed from the vector, when the account is closed, the element count will decrease allowing a duplicate account number to be generated when the next new account is opened. Secondly, if the type of the data structure is changed, then it may not be possible to use the same strategy for getting account numbers at all. The lesson here is to be very careful about dependencies on arbitrary features of data structures. When the data structures change, so does the nature of the dependencies.

Write the main code sequence to deal with normal behaviour and use exceptions to handle the unexpected. But, don't use exceptions as an alternative control statement.

To deal with the problem of trying to open an invalid account, an exception can be thrown, which will require a new exception subclass.

The `openAccount` method can now be written as:

```
public int openAccount(Customer AccountHolder, String kind)
   throws BankException {
```

```
    int accountNumber = numberOfAccounts++ ; // Using the new counter
    Account newAccount = null ;
    if (kind.equals("SavingsAccount"))
      newAccount =
        new SavingsAccount(accountHolder,accountNumber) ;
    else if (kind.equals("CurrentAccount"))
      newAccount =
        new CurrentAccount(accountHolder,accountNumber) ;
    else
      throw new BankException("Invalid account name: " + kind) ;
    return newAccount.getAccountNumber() ;
  }
```

An attempt at the `withdraw` method can now be made:

```
  public int withdraw(int accountNumber, int amount) {
    for (int i = 0 ; accounts.size() ; i++) {
      // Recover account from the ArrayList, using cast to get
      // the correct type.
      Account account = (Account)accounts.get(i) ;
      if (account.getAccNumber() == accountNumber) {
        return account.withdraw(amount) ;
      }
    }
    return 0 ; // Temporary compromise
  }
```

The method finds the selected account object and calls its `deposit` method, returning the amount actually withdrawn. There is a problem over what to do if the account is not found. A compromise of returning zero has been used for this attempt at writing the function. This is not ideal as zero may mean the account was found but the balance was zero, or it may mean that the account did not exist.

This problem should be flagged and corrected by using exceptions. Trying to implement the method has again uncovered more detail about the problem — this is all part of the programming process. As your analysis and design skills develop, it will be easier to anticipate and avoid these kinds of problem at an earlier stage.

Another problem with this code is the search algorithm for finding the correct account; it is a simple linear search which is horrendously inefficient, searching as it does from the beginning of the `ArrayList` until the account is found or the end of accounts reached. There are far better ways of structuring the data so that searches are much more efficient. We will look at some of these algorithms and data structures in Part 2 of the book. For the moment we leave it as a problem to be solved later.

10.5.2 Second Design of the Account Classes

Having had a look at how accounts are used by `Banks`, the account classes can be revised to include a constructor. In class `Account` this will look like:

```
  public Account(Customer accountHolder, int accountNumber) {
    // Initialize variables.
    ...
  }
```

The subclass constructors need to use super to pass the arguments back to the superclass constructor:

```
public SavingsAccount(Customer accountHolder, int accountNumber) {
  super(accountHolder, accountNumber) ;
  // Initialize variables.
  ...
}
```

Apart from dealing with interest, the methods for the account classes should be straightforward. For example, class `CurrentAccount` withdraw method:

```
public int withdraw(int amount) {
  if (balance > amount) {
    balance -= amount ;
    return amount ;
  } else {
    int tmp = balance ;
    balance = 0 ;
    return tmp ;
  }
}
```

This method assumes that only an amount up to the current balance can be withdrawn. The value returned is the amount of money withdrawn. Note that different decisions about how accounts are used will lead to different implementations — it is important to think through the assumptions and details first. For example, if an attempt is made to withdraw more money than is available, another action could be taken (set up an overdraft, perhaps).

10.6   The Main Method

Ignoring the GUI issues, the `main` method for using the program as a whole turns out to be very simple. A `Bank` object is created, a reference stored in an appropriate variable and the object used by calling its methods:

```
public static void main(final String[] args) {
  // Initialisation needed by GUI
  ...
  theBank = new Bank("JavaBank") ;
  // method calls to "run" the user interface
  ...
}
```

10.7   Testing

The program needs thorough and repeated testing, so a test strategy is should be developed. The best way to test the program would be to test each class individually, and then the full program based on the assumption that the classes all work correctly — this would be a lot easier than trying to test all the classes at one go. Testing needs to be done continuously, not as a separate activity after most of the programming is believed to be complete. After any change is made to a class it should be possible to immediately test it, making sure that no existing features have been broken and that new features work as expected. This means that as new code is added to a class, new tests should be added to test that code.

A class can be tested by creating a *test harness* — a program just used to test the class (which for a simple class could be a static `main` method in the class, although this may end up adding a lot of extra code to a class that you don't want to deliver with the program). Combined with a test plan this can be used to verify the behaviour of the class. For example, for class Bank, a test program could be constructed to fill up a bank with accounts, close accounts, deposit and withdraw money, and so on. The test program would look for:

- Correct behaviour with normal data.
- Correct behaviour if all accounts are unused (i.e. depositing to an unused account, closing an unused account).
- Correct behaviour if all accounts are in use (i.e. opening new account).
- Correct behaviour if invalid account numbers are given.

By working through case by case, a complete series of tests can be developed, a test harness written and the class tested. As classes are combined then groups of classes can be tested together, and then finally the whole program tested.

Once development is complete, and all code passes all tests, the program is ready and the programmer should make sure that all documentation and code commenting is complete and accurate. This will be essential for the maintenance of the program as any changes and modifications need to be done with a thorough understanding of the design of the program.

note

Tests must be repeatable and testing repeatedly done. The purpose of testing is to check the correctness of code as it is added and as classes are integrated together.

10.8   A Critique

How well have we done in creating a program meeting the requirements at the start of the chapter?

Clear progress has been made and a program is starting to emerge. Certainly a lot more has been learnt about the nature of the problem and the detailed elaboration needed to write the code. However, we also have a growing list of notes, decisions to review, changes and additions. In particular:

- We could have done a better job of identifying the classes needed. The main ones such as `Bank`, and `Account` are reasonable but the need for others such as `AccountNumber` and `Money` has only been recognized later on. We opted for apparent simplicity in the short term which could well lead to complications and re-design in the longer term. In fact, the question is whether we should re-start the design from scratch using all the knowledge we have.
- The requirement that some accounts generate interest has been partly addressed but has really raised more questions than answers in the process. In particular, it is not clear how

or when the update method should be called — is some sort of timer needed or should the user interface provide a button to click? Nor is it clear how interest is calculated. We cannot progress further on this front with the knowledge we have; more information is needed from the client.

- The handling of customer information is vague. We have a class `Customer` and accounts that reference a `Customer` object but there is really a need for a proper collection of customer objects to be maintained by the bank.

Where does this leave us? Well actually a lot better informed. The iterative development process can be continued and the issues above can be properly addressed. We may have to make significant changes and rethink parts of the design but we are doing this at the best time — well before any program is delivered, when it is possible to make large changes without undermining lots of other work.

By adding a GUI and completing the iterative implementation work started above, we can be increasingly confident of building a well designed program. In doing so, we have learnt a lot about the problem and gained experience. Beware, however, of not declaring the program finished and forever adding new 'features'. The review stage at the end of each iteration should assess carefully what should be done next (if anything), ensuring that the priorities are dealt with first.

10.9   Summary

This chapter has outlined the kind of process that is gone through when designing a real object-oriented program and implementing it using Java.

The process is highly *iterative*. As analysis and design proceeds, the structure and behaviour of the program becomes better understood and more detail is uncovered. This requires decisions to be constantly reviewed and, if necessary, changed to fit the new information.

It is impossible to discover all the information needed in any one pass. Iteration has to be used to look forward, find out new things and then return to review old decisions.

There is no single correct solution to the problem — but it does matter that the chosen solution works. In programming there are often many ways to solve a problem — the programmer's job is to select one that works and can be judged to be appropriate both at the current time and in the future.

Selecting solutions takes account of many trade-offs between time and resources available, flexibility, speed, program size and, on occasion, the phase of the moon. What you are learning about programming will hopefully allow you to make well informed decisions.

It is important to go through a well defined analysis and design process. The solution to the bank problem outlined earlier shows one way the program could be designed and implemented. *It is not*

tip

Once you have a good working prototype, be prepared to write completely new code for the production version of the program.

the only way — it is not necessarily the best way. You may well have made different decisions if you had been implementing these classes — there is nothing wrong with that, providing you can justify what you did and have documented you decision and its justification in the source code and/ or supporting documentation.

Key points in this chapter:

- Requirements establish what a program should be able to do.
- Scenarios and the CRC method establish the expected dynamic behaviour of a program.
- Analysis identifies classes and objects, attributes and methods.
- Design creates an implementable description of a program, possibly including the program code itself.
- Development relies on prototyping and iteration to explore the analysis and design issues, and establish a feasible design.

Self-review Questions

Self-review 10.1 What are requirements and scenarios and what roles do they play?

Self-review 10.2 How can classes be identified?

Self-review 10.3 What is dynamic behaviour?

Self-review 10.4 What is the difference between analysis and design?

Self-review 10.5 What are the strengths and weaknesses of prototyping?

Self-review 10.6 What is a suitable strategy for testing a program that is composed of a number of classes?

Self-review 10.7 What should be done to review the suitability of the classes, methods and attributes that have been identified?

Programming Exercises

The bank system as described above is only the beginnings of the first draft of the prototype. You might want to think about how to take things further in order to try out some of the ideas behind object-oriented design. At each stage you should really develop a working program (following the prototyping development approach). The following is a suggested work programme:

Exercise 10.1 Complete the classes outlined in the chapter, along with a simple text-based user interface.

Exercise 10.2 Add the ability to load and save the bank data to and from a data file.

Exercise 10.3 Add the ability to update name, address and phone information for each account.

Exercise 10.4 Provide detailed reporting facilities for both accounts and the bank.

Exercise 10.5 Add a new `Account` subclass called `HighInterestSavingsAccount`. Money can only be withdrawn from the account 30 days after notification.

Challenge

Challenge 10.1 Create a GUI for the program (read ahead to Chapter 11 for information about creating GUIs).

User Interfaces

Objectives

Many programs have a Graphical User Interface (GUI) constructed from a range of user interface components. The Java Swing library provides an extensive set of such components, allowing Java programs to be easily given a graphical interface. This chapter introduces the basic ideas for constructing user interfaces with the Swing components.

Keywords

component

container

event

event handler

layout manager

listener

panel

Swing

11.1   Introduction

The user interface of a program is what the user sees and interacts with when trying to use the program. More often than not these days, programs have graphical interfaces, consisting of windows, menus, buttons and so on. Such an interface is referred to as a *Graphical User Interface* or GUI, and a simple example is illustrated in Figure 11.1.

How are GUIs constructed? The answer is, perhaps not surprisingly, out of objects. The preceding chapters have covered enough information about classes and objects to allow us to look at and understand how user interfaces can be built.

As the implementation of GUIs is a huge and complicated subject area, this chapter gives a very brief introduction to the key ideas by describing several example programs to show the ideas in practice. We don't attempt to give an exhaustive explanation of all the details but simply provide enough information to allow you to get started. Once you have read this chapter we recommend that you look for more detailed reference material, one good source being the on-line Java JFC/Swing tutorial provided at Sun's Java web site (http://java.sun.com/).

As you read this chapter, we recommend that you actively refer to the online documentation of all the classes mentioned in order to access the details of those classes and their methods..

11.1.1   Visual Components and Swing

A user interface is built up as a collection of components, many of which are *visual components* as they have a visible representation on the screen. We use the word component here, rather than object, as a typical user interface component (such as a button or scroll bar) is implemented as a collection of objects. Each object in the collection has a specific set of responsibilities, such as drawing the component's representation on the screen or maintaining the state of the component. One object from the collection acts as the interface to the component as a whole and coordinates the others. This interfacing object is public in that its public methods can be called by code using the component, whereas the other objects are private and are not directly accessed from outside the component.

From the programmer's point of view each component is represented by a class, which is the class of the interface object. An instance of the component is created by simply instantiating an instance of the component class. The other objects will be created automatically behind the scenes.

The Java 2 Platform comes with a full set of visual components which are provided as part of the Java Foundation Classes (JFC). These components are collectively referred to as the Swing Set or just Swing. The complete Swing Set consists of around two dozen components supported by many more classes and interfaces. In this book, we will focus on a commonly used sub-set of features, rather than attempt to describe everything. The bibliography has references to some books which describe Swing in full detail.

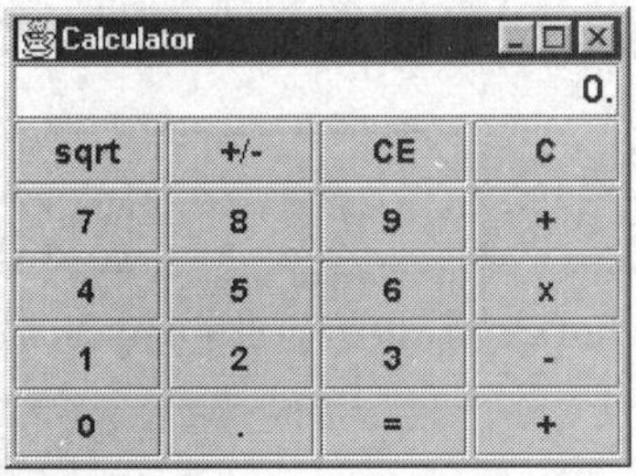

Figure 11.1 The interace to a simple calculator

11.1.2 Swing and AWT

The Swing library is implemented as an extension of the Abstract Window Toolkit (AWT) library. AWT was developed to provide a set of graphical user interface component types in versions of Java prior to Java 2. One of the most important features of the AWT library is that it interfaces to the underlying windowing system of the computer running a Java program (often referred to as the *native* windowing system). This allows a program using an AWT-based graphical interface to be displayed appropriately on any computer, regardless of which windowing system it uses. Thus when writing programs with a GUI, we use the AWT components without having to worry about the details of a particular windowing system. We can rely on the AWT to translate between AWT components and the native windowing system. This supports the aim of writing one Java program that can run, unchanged, on any computer system.

The translation between AWT components and matching native components is performed by *peer* classes, implemented using Java native methods. Apart from a few exceptional cases, we never need to use peer classes directly. AWT components implemented using peer classes are known as *heavyweight components* as they map directly to native components, requiring resources provided by the native windowing system.

Swing provides an extensive library of classes for building more sophisticated user interfaces that include many more features and facilities than the AWT one's provide. The Swing library is written entirely in Java but makes use of the AWT to get user interface components displayed on the screen. Swing components are said to be *lightweight* as they do not directly make use of peer classes.

One notable feature of Swing is its support for "pluggable look and feel", meaning that the appearance of a graphical interface implemented in Swing can be changed on demand, without having to re-write any code. This allows a Swing program to automatically adapt itself to the style and appearance conventions (the look and feel) of the machine it is running on, without the programmer having to explicitly develop the interface for that particular kind of machine. In fact, the look and feel is not limited to the normal conventions of a specific machine, as Swing allows new look and feel styles to be developed. A default style designed for Java called 'The Java Look and Feel' (also known as 'Metal') provides a Java look and feel independent of any particular windowing system, and will be the style used for examples in this chapter.

note

A native method encapsulates a call to code written in a programming language other than Java (usually C or C++), allowing the functionality of the JVM to be extended.

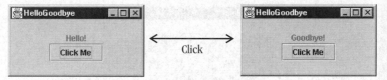

Figure 11.2 The HelloGoodbye program window

11.2   Core GUI Concepts

The construction of user interfaces builds on a number of basic concepts, including the idea of components, containers, layout managers and event handling. The next few sections will introduce these concepts by working through a small but complete example program.

11.2.1   Program HelloGoodbye

The HelloGoodbye program window is shown in Figure 11.2. When the button, labelled 'Click Me" is clicked, the text message displayed just above the button toggles between "Hello" and "Goodbye". The program listing follows, the details being explained in the following sub-sections:

The programming style of using an object as it's own listener (for the action listener in this example) is quite common but not necessarily good. There is an argument that says that listeners should always be separate classes (as with the window listener which uses an anonymous class in this example). We show both here as a pedagogical example.

```
import java.awt.* ;
import java.awt.event.* ;
import javax.swing.* ;
public class HelloGoodbye extends JFrame implements ActionListener {
  private static final String HELLO = "Hello!" ;
  private static final String GOODBYE = "Goodbye!" ;
  private String message = HELLO ;
  private JPanel counterPanel ;
  private JButton counterButton ;
  private JLabel counterLabel ;
  public HelloGoodbye() {
    super("HelloGoodbye") ;
    counterLabel = new JLabel (message, SwingConstants.CENTER) :
    counterButton = new JButton ("Click Me") ;
    counterButton.addActionListener(this) ;
    counterPanel = new JPanel () ;
    counterPanel.setBorder(
      BorderFactory.createEmptyBorder(20, 60, 20, 60));
    counterPanel.setLayout(new BorderLayout ()) ;
    counterPanel.add(counterLabel, BorderLayout.CENTER) ;
    counterPanel.add(counterButton, BorderLayout.SOUTH) ;
    getContentPane().add(counterPanel) ;
    addWindowListener(new WindowAdapter() {
      public void windowClosing(WindowEvent e) {
        System.exit(0) ;
      }
    }) ;
    pack() ;
    setVisible(true) ;
  }
  public void actionPerformed(ActionEvent e) {
    if (message.equals(HELLO)) {
      message = GOODBYE ;
    } else {
      message = HELLO ;
    }
    counterLabel.setText(message) ;
  }
```

```
    public static void main(final String[] args) {
      final HelloGoodbye app = new HelloGoodbye () ;
    }
}
```

11.2.2 Creating the Window

All Swing based programs, including the HelloGoodbye program, need at least one window to display their interface. The window acts as a container for the GUI components used by the program's interface, which will be constrained to appear inside the window. A window is created by using the Swing `JFrame` class, either by directly instantiating an instance object or, as is the case for the example program, by creating a subclass of `JFrame` and then instantiating an object of the subclass. The `HelloGoodbye` class specializes `JFrame` to display the specific interface we need and handle the event caused by the mouse button being clicked.

Hence, class `HelloGoodbye` is a subclass of `JFrame`, and, in fact, forms the entire program. The `HelloGoodbye` constructor is responsible for creating and adding GUI components to the frame, which acts as a *container*. Class `HelloGoodbye` also includes a `main` method which will be examined later.

11.2.3 Creating the Swing GUI Components

The full Swing Set implementation comprises a large number of classes spread across a collection of packages. A subset of these classes are those used to create GUI components. The HelloGoodbye program uses the following components, in addition to the `JFrame`:

- a label, an instance of class `JLabel`, to display the words "Hello" or "Goodbye",

- a button, an instance of class `JButton`, to provide a clickable button (a button that responds when the mouse cursor is over the button and a mouse button clicked).

- a panel, an instance of class `JPanel`, to contain and manage the display of the label and button placed inside it.

All the component classes have a name beginning with 'J' and are found in the package javax.swing. Swing is considered to be an extension to the core set of Java classes, hence the package name javax or Java extension. This is true even though Swing is now a standard part of the Java 2 Platform. To make use of Swing classes several import statements are needed:

```
import java.awt.* ;
import java.awt.event.* ;
import javax.swing.* ;
```

The first statement allows classes from the AWT to be used. Even though we want to build a Swing interface, we still need the AWT: Swing is an extension to the AWT, not a replacement, and we will need to use some AWT features (and all the Swing component classes are direct or indirect subclasses of the AWT classes `Component` or `Container`). The second import statement allows the use of the

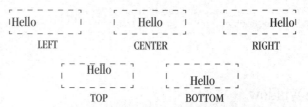

Figure 11.3 Positioning a string within a label

event classes, enabling a program to respond to the user interacting with the GUI. The final import statement allows the Swing GUI component classes to be used.

Three instance variables are declared to reference the component objects:

```
private JPanel counterPanel ;
private JButton counterButton ;
private JLabel counterLabel ;
```

They are initialized in the `HelloGoodbye` constructor method with the statements:

```
counterPanel = new JPanel() ;
counterButton = new JButton("Click Me") ;
counterLabel = new JLabel(message,SwingConstants.CENTER) ;
```

In each case, an object is created using the `new` operator and suitable constructor parameters. The `JButton` constructor parameter is a `String` giving the label to display on the button, while the `JLabel` parameters give the message to display along with its position within the space allocated to the label when it is displayed. The value `SwingConstants.CENTER` specifies that the string should appear centered (see Figure 11.3).

SwingConstants is a utility interface that declares a number of useful constant values such as CENTER, allowing the values to be referred to by name rather than more cryptic integers.

The variables could have been initialized directly where they were declared, however, the decision was made to put all the GUI building code, including component creation, within the constructor to keep it all in one place. Using instance variables to refer to component objects allows the objects to be manipulated by other methods. In this example, only the variable `counterLabel` has to be an instance variable, the other two could be local variables within the constructor. The decision was taken to widen the scope of the variables for perceived clarity of expression and in case extensions were made to the class. Only time will tell if this was a correct decision.

11.2.4   Containers and Layout Managers

Some GUI components, notably `JFrames` and `JPanels` are containers, meaning that they contain a collection of other components, which are displayed within their visible area. Each component added to a container needs a size and a position to determine how it will appear within the container. The size and position are controlled by a combination of the size a component wants to be and a *layout manger* that determines its position and actual size within the container.

The HelloGoodbye program makes use of a `JPanel` container to hold the label and button, with the `JPanel` in turn placed inside a `JFrame`. Figure 11.4 shows how the components are arranged. The `JPanel` includes a border which surrounds the area allocated to the contained

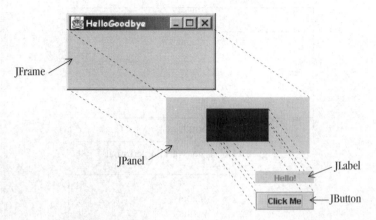

Figure 11.4 The arrangement of components forming the HelloGoodbye GUI.

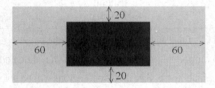

Figure 11.5 The dimensions of the border.

`JLabel` and `JButton`. This improves the appearance of the GUI and avoids the label and button from occupying the whole area of the panel. The border is set using the `setBorder` method on the `JPanel`:

```
counterPanel.setBorder(
    BorderFactory.createEmptyBorder(20, 60, 20, 60));
```

This will give the panel a border as shown in Figure 11.5. The `BorderFactory` utility class provides a number of convenience methods for creating borders, which are actually implemented by a family of classes in the package javax.swing.border. Swing supports a wide variety of kinds of border, although in this case we are using a simple plain border.

The button and label components are placed inside the panel by calling the `add` method but first the panel is given a layout manager to determine how to position or layout the components:

```
counterPanel.setLayout(new BorderLayout()) ;
```

The AWT and Swing include a number of layout managers, one of the most commonly used being the `BorderLayout`. A `BorderLayout` divides a container into 5 regions as shown in Figure 11.6. Between 1 and 5 components can be added to the container, each allocated to 1 region: North, South, East, West or Center. When the container is displayed on the screen, the layout manager determines the size of the screen area allocated to the container and subdivides the space between the contained components. Each component will be given space relative to its region and will then display itself in that space, adjusting its size to suit what is available. Ideally, each component will have enough space to display itself properly, if not then it makes a best effort but is likely to be partially obscured.

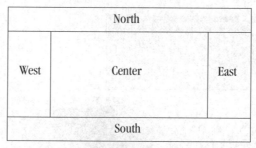

Figure 11.6 Regions of a BorderLayout.

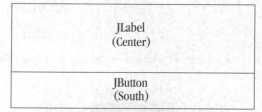

Figure 11.7 Label and button positioned by the `BorderLayout`.

As we have only two components to display, they will be allocated to the Center and South regions. The unused space of the North, East and West regions will be given to the Center rather than be left blank. When a component is added to a container using the `add` method, a parameter is used to denote which region it should be allocated to:

```
counterPanel.add(counterLabel,BorderLayout.CENTER) ;
counterPanel.add(counterButton,BorderLayout.SOUTH) ;
```

Figure 11.7 shows the result.

The `JFrame` representing the window also uses a layout manager to position its contents, and that manager is a `BorderLayout` by default. In fact, the structure of a `JFrame` is quite complex, so the role of the container is delegated to a another panel to which the manager actually belongs. The `JPanel` containing the button and label is therefore added to the `JFrame` using the following statement, which contains an extra method call to obtain the correct panel:

```
getContentPane().add(counterPanel) ;
```

We have now seen how the GUI is constructed by creating components, adding them to containers, and using layout managers to position and size components. The layering of components within panels is used to build up the structure of a GUI, and as a GUI becomes more complicated more and more layers will be added by placing containers within containers. Indeed, the way to manage complex GUIs is to fully exploit layering and avoid putting too many components within a single container.

11.2.5   The Layout Manager Advantage

The major advantage of using a layout manager is that it takes over all responsibility for positioning and sizing a collection of components. You, as the programmer, need write no more code than

Figure 11.8 Resizing the HelloGoodbye window.

shown above, or have to work out the exact positions of components yourself. This becomes obvious when a window is resized, as shown in Figure 11.8. The window on the left has been made larger and the layout manager has expanded the button to fill the increased width, while the label text remains the same size, centred in the label area. The middle window has been increased in height but decreased in width, with the button shrinking as its area is reduced. As there is no longer room to display the complete button label the word 'Me' has been replaced by '...'. The right hand window shows what happens if the size overall size is decreased further with both the button and label shrinking below the point where they are able to fully display themselves.

With a proper combination of layout managers and panels, a window and its contents will display correctly whatever size it is given, provided it is not reduced below a minimum size. The layout mangers will ensure that components have an appropriate size and remain positioned in the same relative locations. A window containing a number of layered panels requires the cooperation of all the layout managers to position the components, with the process of positioning everything being known as 'laying out'. Laying out takes place top-down starting with the `JFrame`, which determines the overall area of the GUI. Each panel is allocated a certain amount of space, depending on what other components or panels it shares space with. A panel's layout manager then allocates that space to all the contained panels and components. Layered panels repeat the process until everything is positioned.

11.2.6   Different Layout Managers

In addition to the commonly used `BorderLayout`, there are a number of other layout managers available including `FlowLayout`, `GridLayout`, `CardLayout` and `GridBagLayout`.

`FlowLayout` is the default layout manager for `JPanels`. It simply places components left-to-right, row-by-row in the space available, as illustrated in Figure 11.9. As the window changes size the components are repositioned in new rows according to the space available. Each component is displayed at its default size if possible.

A `GridLayout` divides the container area into a grid of the specified size. Components can be placed into grid rectangles for display, with each component filling the entire rectangle allocated to it as shown in Figure 11.10. If there are fewer components than grid rectangles, the unused areas are left blank. The `GridLayout` is useful when components need to be arranged in fixed rows and columns.

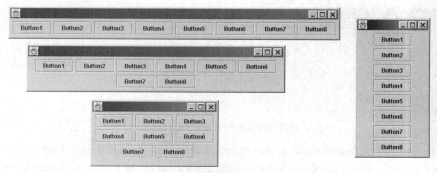

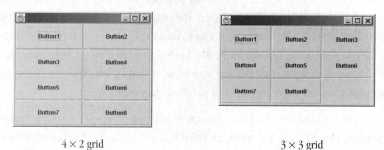

Figure 11.9 The FlowLayout.

4 × 2 grid   3 × 3 grid

Figure 11.10 The GridLayout.

Figure 11.11 The CardLayout.

A CardLayout provides a GUI that behaves somewhat like a stack of cards, where each card displays a different interface, with the interface of the top most card being the only one visible. At any time a new card can be selected to display a different interface. The example window shown in Figure 11.11 is implemented with a CardLayout and every time the Next button is clicked a new 'card' is displayed, changing the interface.

A GridBagLayout is the most complicated kind of layout manager but gives the most control over the way components are laid out. Effectively it allows components to be positioned on a grid where each grid rectangle can be of different size and the spatial relationship between components specified precisely.

11.2.7   Displaying the Window

Once a GUI has been built, the JFrame containing it needs to be displayed. By default building the GUI simply does just that and without a few extra lines of code nothing will appear on the screen. The

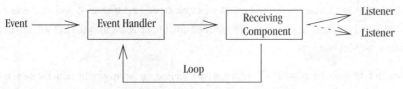

Figure 11.12 The Event Loop.

HelloGoodBye includes the following method calls to the `JFrame` object in order to cause the `JFrame` window to appear on the screen:

```
pack() ;
setVisible(true) ;
```

The `pack` method causes the size of the `JFrame` to be determined and the contents to be laid out using the layout managers. The `setVisible` method call actually causes the window to be displayed and made useable.

By default a `JFrame` will be the minimum size needed to properly display its contents, according to the sizes of the contained components. Alternatively, the `setSize` method can be used to explicitly set the size of the `JFrame`:

```
setSize(300,400) ; // Create a 300 x 400 pixel window
```

11.2.8 Events

A GUI interacts with the user by responding to *events*. An event is a trigger or signal that occurs in response to something the user of a program does, such as clicking the mouse button or typing on the keyboard. The basic behaviour of a program with a GUI is to wait for events and respond to them. This activity is managed by an Event Loop, implemented within the Swing and AWT libraries (see Figure 11.12).

When an event occurs, event handler code within the libraries determines which visual component should receive the event. For example, the user clicking on a button results in an event being sent to the button component that was clicked. The component then notifies one or more *listeners* which can respond to the event. Listeners are provided by the GUI programmer and implement code to perform whatever needs to be done in response to the event. Once the listeners have done their work, control returns or loops back to the event handler code which waits for the next event. As well as notifying listeners a component can also provide visual feedback to let the user know that the event has been received. A button, for example, will use some simple animation to give the appearance of moving up and down.

Events are represented by event objects which hold information about what event occurred (e.g. which key was typed or the coordinates of the mouse cursor). A listener are also represented by objects that include one or more methods to be called when it is required to respond to an event. The event object will be passed as a method parameter. Listener methods are implemented by the GUI programmer and can call any other method in scope in order to respond to the event. For example, the HelloGoodbye button listener responds by changing the label text being displayed. It is

!

Forgetting to call the `setVisible` method results in the frustrating experience of the program appearing to run but nothing being displayed on the screen.

note

In this chapter we are only considering events caused by user action, but events can also be triggered by other components in the program, independently of the user.

very important that a listener method does its jobs quickly and returns, as no other events can be handled while it is running. If control is not returned quickly, or at all, then the GUI will not respond to any other user interactions.

A listener is associated with a component by calling an appropriate add listener method providing a listener object as the parameter. In the HelloGoodbye program, a listener is added to the button by the following line of code:

```
counterButton.addActionListener(this) ;
```

The addActionListener method expects a listener capable of responding to button clicks. A component may be able to respond to several different kinds of event, so will have more than one add method. Further, any number of listeners can be associated with an event, and can be added or removed at any time, so the way a component responds to an event is very flexible and easily changed.

Event listener objects are provided by classes implemented by the GUI programmer, which either implement a listener interface from the Swing library or a subclass a listener utility class In either case one or more methods must be provided to respond to the types of event the listener should expect.

As can be seen above, the parameter to the addActionListener method in the HelloGoodbye program is this, the HelloGoodbye object itself. This explains why the class HelloGoodbye is declared as:

```
public class HelloGoodbye extends JFrame implements ActionListener
```

As the class implements the ActionListener interface it is required to provide a method called actionPerformed, which will be called to respond to the action events caused by clicking the button. The actionPerformed method is declared as follows:

```
public void actionPerformed(ActionEvent e) {
  if (message.equals(HELLO)) {
    message = GOODBYE ;
  } else {
    message = HELLO ;
  }
  counterLabel.setText(message) ;
}
```

An action event is represented by an ActionEvent object which is passed as the method parameter, although not actually used within the method body. The method body updates the value of the label string, toggling between "Hello" and "Goodbye", and displays the new string by calling the label's setText method.

11.2.9   Running and Terminating the HelloGoodbye Program

The main method included in class HelloGoodbye is very simple:

```
public static void main(String[] args) {
  final HelloGoodbye app = new HelloGoodbye () ;
}
```

All it does is create a `HelloGoodbye` object and then terminates. However, this raises the question of how does the program run, display a window and respond to events if the `main` method finishes — surely the program will run and then immediately terminate?

The answer lies in the fact that GUI programs are always multi-threaded, with the GUI event management code running in its own thread. When the HelloGoodbye program is run, the `main` method is called from the default thread created when the program starts. The method creates a HelloGoodBye object, causing the constructor to be executed, the GUI to be built and the window to be displayed. As a consequence of doing this a new thread is started to run the GUI event loop. This thread remains active after the default thread finishes (when `main` terminates) and keeps the program alive and running. All the event handling and the execution of the listener methods is then performed by the GUI thread. The same thread is also responsible for updating and redrawing the window as necessary.

The above explanation raises a new question: How does the program terminate? From the users point of view the quit button (or equivalent) is clicked on the window and the program stops. Internally, an event is generated for which a listener method must be provided that terminates the program. The event will be a window closing event for which a window listener must be provided. In the HelloGoodbye program this is implemented by the following piece of code:

```
addWindowListener(new WindowAdapter() {
  public void windowClosing(WindowEvent e) {
    System.exit(0) ;
  }
}) ;
```

The `addWindowListener` method is called for the HelloGoodbye object (a subclass of `JFrame`, don't forget) and given an event object that provides a `windowClosing` method. This is the exactly the same idea as for handling the button click, except it uses another commonly used way of implementing the event object for illustration.

The event object is an instance of an anonymous inner class which is declared as the `addWindowListener` method parameter. The syntax:

```
new WindowAdapter() {
  ...
}
```

declares a subclass of the utility class `WindowAdapter` without naming the subclass (so it is anonymous). The class body comprises the declaration of one listener method, `windowClosing`. The `new` operator creates an instance of the anonymous class.

When the listener method is called, the following method call is made:

```
System.exit(0) ;
```

which forces the termination of the program. Hence, responding to the window closing event leads directly to the program terminating.

ref

See Section 30.4.4, Page 861 for more information about anonymous inner classes.

Figure 11.13 GUI of a binary to decimal conversion program

11.2.10   HelloGoodbye Summary

The detailed examination of the HelloGoodbye program has taken us through an explanation of the key basic concepts needed to build a GUI. A GUI is constructed from components placed within containers and positioned by layout managers. Containers can be layered to build up the structure of a GUI, while the top-most container, a JFrame, represents the window. Events are triggered when a user interacts with a GUI and are represented as event objects which are passed, via components, to event listeners.

All GUIs have the same basic structure but are typically more complex than the simple example presented by the HelloGoodbye program. The next few sections will look at some more complicated GUIs and also show further features of Swing.

11.3   Text Input with a GUI

As well as displaying text and graphics, and providing components such as buttons to click, GUIs are often used for doing text input. Many of the example programs in the preceding chapters that do input, could, in principle, use a GUI rather than the command line. For example, a program that converts a binary number to decimal could have the GUI illustrated in Figure 11.13. The program implementation is a follows:

```
import java.awt.* ;
import java.awt.event.* ;
import javax.swing.* ;
public class Convert extends JFrame {
  private JPanel labelPanel ;
  private JPanel inputOutputPanel ;
  private JPanel displayPanel ;
  private JPanel buttonPanel ;
  private JPanel backPanel ;
  private JTextField binaryInput ;
  private JTextField decimalOutput ;
  private JButton button ;
  // Build and display the user interface
  public Convert() {
    super("Converter") ;
    labelPanel = new JPanel () ;
    labelPanel.setLayout(new GridLayout (2, 1)) ;
    labelPanel.add(new JLabel ("Binary: ")) ;
    labelPanel.add(new JLabel ("Decimal: ")) ;
    inputOutputPanel = new JPanel () ;
    inputOutputPanel.setLayout(new GridLayout (2, 1)) ;
    binaryInput = new JTextField (15) ;
    inputOutputPanel.add(binaryInput) ;
```

```
          decimalOutput = new JTextField (15) ;
          decimalOutput.setEditable(false) ;
          inputOutputPanel.add(decimalOutput) ;
          displayPanel = new JPanel () ;
          displayPanel.setLayout(new BorderLayout ()) ;
          displayPanel.add(labelPanel,BorderLayout.WEST) ;
          displayPanel.add(inputOutputPanel,BorderLayout.CENTER) ;
          button = new JButton("Convert") ;
          buttonPanel = new JPanel() ;
          buttonPanel.add(button) ;
          backPanel = new JPanel() ;
          backPanel.setLayout(new BorderLayout()) ;
          backPanel.add(displayPanel,BorderLayout.CENTER) ;
          backPanel.add(buttonPanel,BorderLayout.SOUTH) ;
          getContentPane().add(backPanel) ;
          button.addActionListener(new ActionListener () {
              public void actionPerformed(ActionEvent e) {
                doConversion() ;
              }
          }) ;
          addWindowListener(new WindowAdapter () {
              public void windowClosing(WindowEvent e) {
                System.exit(0) ;
              }
          }) ;
          pack() ;
          setResizable(false) ;
          setVisible(true) ;
      }
      private void doConversion() {
          // Get the string that is meant to represent a binary
          // number from the binaryInput component.
          String binary = binaryInput.getText() ;
          // Try to convert to decimal and display result,
          // or display an error message.
          try {
            int n = Integer.parseInt(binary, 2) ;
            decimalOutput.setText("" + n) ;
          }
          catch (NumberFormatException e) {
            decimalOutput.setText("Not binary!") ;
          }
      }
      public static void main(final String[] args) {
          final Convert convert = new Convert () ;
      }
  }
```

The interface is built up from a number of layered `JPanels` using `GridLayout` and `BorderLayout` managers. The user is prevented from resizing the window by calling the method `setResizable(false)` on the `JFrame`, as a way of keeping the GUI components in reasonable alignment.

A binary number can be typed as text in to the `JTextField` component next to the label "Binary". A `JTextField` displays a box into which one line of text can be typed, and automatically supports cursor control and basic text editing. When the button is clicked the text is read from the `JTextField` and an attempt made to convert the value represented into decimal. The output from the program is either a decimal number or an error message, and is displayed in a second `JTextField`, below the first, that has had its input ability disabled by the method call `setEditable(false)`, to avoid the user mistakenly typing into the field.

note

The method `setResizable` *is inherited by class* `JFrame` *from class* `Frame`. *GUI classes inherit many methods so always look at the superclasses to find out all the capabilities of a component.*

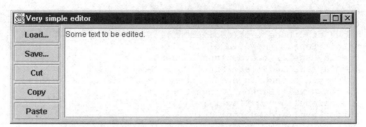

Figure 11.14 The Very Simple Editor window.

In contrast to the HelloGoodbye program, the button in this program is given a listener object provided by an anonymous class. The listener method implemented by the class calls the private method `doConversion` to actually do the binary to decimal conversion. This uses the method `getText` to get a `String` representing the current text displayed in the input `JTextField` and then the binary to decimal conversion is attempted. The result is displayed in the output text field by calling its `setText` method.

A refinement to the program would be to allow the user to type the <Return> key when entering input, resulting in the behaviour as when the button is clicked. This can be done very easily by simply adding the following code to the constructor:

```
binaryInput.addActionListener(new ActionListener() {
  public void actionPerformed(ActionEvent e) {
    doConversion() ;
  }
}) ;
```

A `JTextField` treats a press of the <Return> key in the same way as a button deals with a mouse click, so a listener can be added to the field using the same listener code. Components often respond to a number of events, so it is worth checking the documentation to see what is possible.

This example illustrates a common form of GUI-based input and shows how a number of earlier example programs could be given a GUI, with the existing code performing the computation being called from one or more listener methods. A GUI can have a number of `JTextField`s to input multiple values, the text in each field being accessed using the `getText` method. One difference between this kind of GUI input and command line based input using the `KeyboardInput` class is that all input values are of type `String` and have to be explicitly converted to other types. The code listing of `KeyboardInput` in the appendix (see Appendix F, Page 963) includes methods that illustrate how to convert strings to other types (internally `KeyboardInput` is based on reading strings from the command line).

11.4   A Very Simple Text Editor

The following program listing implements a very simple, but fully functional, text editor built from Swing components. The editor window can be seen in Figure 11.14.

```
// Example Swing program to illustrate a very simple text editor
```

```java
// Need to import classes from all these packages.
import java.awt.*;
import javax.swing.*;
import java.awt.event.*;
import javax.swing.border.*;
import java.io.* ;
public class VerySimpleEditor extends JFrame {
    // Instance variables for the GUI components used.
    // Declaring the variables here allows them to be
    // used by any instance methods in the class.
    JPanel topPanel ;
    JPanel buttonPanel ;
    JPanel editorPanel ;
    JButton loadButton ;
    JButton saveButton ;
    JButton cutButton ;
    JButton copyButton ;
    JButton pasteButton ;
    JScrollPane scroller ;
    JTextArea editor ;
    // The constructor build the window using a utility
    // method and displays it.
    public VerySimpleEditor() {
        // Create and configure the various panels
        topPanel = new JPanel () ;
        topPanel.setLayout(new BorderLayout ()) ;
        editorPanel = new JPanel () ;
        editorPanel.setLayout(new BorderLayout ()) ;
        editorPanel.setBorder(BorderFactory.createEmptyBorder(5,5,5,5));
        buttonPanel = new JPanel () ;
        buttonPanel.setBorder(BorderFactory.createEtchedBorder ()) ;
        // The panel containing the buttons uses a GridLayout of 1 column
        // and 5 rows to position the buttons in a column.
        GridLayout grid = new GridLayout () ;
        grid.setColumns(1) ;
        grid.setHgap(10) ;
        grid.setRows(5) ;   // Set a small gap between the buttons
        grid.setVgap(3) ;   // to improve the appearance.
        buttonPanel.setLayout(grid) ;
        scroller = new JScrollPane () ;
        // The editor component handles all text display and editing. It
        // is given a width of 40 characters.
        editor = new JTextArea () ;
        editor.setColumns(40) ;
        // Now create the buttons, giving each a listener to respond to
        // the button being clicked. The listener methods delagate to
        // private helper methods later in the class, to avoid the
        // constructor method becoming too long and unwieldy.
        loadButton = new JButton("Load...") ;
        loadButton.addActionListener(new java.awt.event.ActionListener() {
            public void actionPerformed(ActionEvent e) {
                loadFile();
            }
        }) ;
        saveButton = new JButton("Save...");
        saveButton.addActionListener(new java.awt.event.ActionListener() {
            public void actionPerformed(ActionEvent e) {
                saveFile() ;
            }
        }) ;
        cutButton = new JButton("Cut");
        cutButton.addActionListener(new java.awt.event.ActionListener() {
            public void actionPerformed(ActionEvent e) {
                cut() ;
            }
        }) ;
```

```
      copyButton = new JButton("Copy") ;
      copyButton.addActionListener(new java.awt.event.ActionListener() {
          public void actionPerformed(ActionEvent e) {
            copy() ;
          }
        }) ;
      pasteButton = new JButton("Paste") ;
      pasteButton.addActionListener(new java.awt.event.ActionListener(){
          public void actionPerformed(ActionEvent e) {
            paste() ;
          }
        }) ;
    // Configure the top-level JFrame
    setTitle("Very simple editor") ;
    getContentPane().add(topPanel, BorderLayout.CENTER) ;
    addWindowListener(new java.awt.event.WindowAdapter() {
        public void windowClosing(WindowEvent e) {
          System.exit(0) ;
        }
      }) ;
    // Now assemble the components
    topPanel.add(buttonPanel, BorderLayout.WEST);
    buttonPanel.add(loadButton) ;
    buttonPanel.add(saveButton) ;
    buttonPanel.add(cutButton) ;
    buttonPanel.add(copyButton) ;
    buttonPanel.add(pasteButton) ;
    topPanel.add(editorPanel, BorderLayout.CENTER) ;
    editorPanel.add(scroller, BorderLayout.CENTER) ;
    scroller.getViewport().add(editor) ;
    pack() ;
    setVisible(true) ;
  }
  // The following methods implement the button click behaviour.
  // Display a file dialog and load a file
  private void loadFile() {
    JFileChooser fc = new JFileChooser () ;
    int returnVal = fc.showOpenDialog(this) ;
    if (returnVal == JFileChooser.APPROVE_OPTION) {
      // If a file was selected, try and load it.
      File file = fc.getSelectedFile() ;
      try {
        editor.read(new FileReader(file),null) ;
      }
      catch (IOException exp) {}
    }
  }
  // Display a save file dialog and save the current file.
  private void saveFile() {
    JFileChooser fc = new JFileChooser () ;
    int returnVal = fc.showSaveDialog(this) ;
    if (returnVal == JFileChooser.APPROVE_OPTION) {
      File file = fc.getSelectedFile() ;
      try {
        editor.write(new FileWriter(file)) ;
      }
      catch (IOException exp) {}
    }
  }
  // Cut, copy and paste are implemented using methods provided by a
  // superclass of the JTextArea class, and work with the system
  // clipboard.  Very useful and makes it very easy to implement
  // cut/copy/paste!!
  //
  // The requestFocus method is used to make the JTextArea the active
  // component after a button is clicked. The component with the focus
```

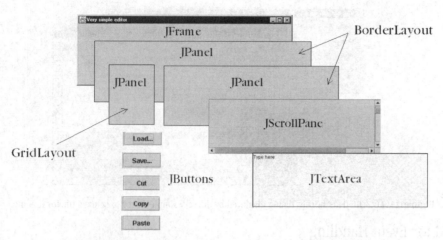

Figure 11.15 The Structure of the Very Simple Editor window.

```
// receives the input events. If focus is not returned to the
// JTextArea it remains with the button, preventing text being
// entered into the text area until it is clicked on to regain
// focus.
private void copy() {
  editor.copy() ;
  editor.requestFocus() ;
}
private void paste() {
  editor.paste() ;
  editor.requestFocus() ;
}
private void cut() {
  editor.cut() ;
  editor.requestFocus() ;
}
public static void main(final String[] args) {
  final VerySimpleEditor editor = new VerySimpleEditor () ;
}
}
```

The editor program follows much the same basic structure as the HelloGoodbye and Convert programs, with the constructor used to build and display the GUI. The GUI makes use of layered panels and components as shown in Figure 11.15. All the display and editing of text is handled by a JTextArea component, which forms the main part of the window. The JTextArea is placed inside a JScrollPane component which automatically provides scrollbars, allowing the user to scroll through the displayed text. The rest of the interface is built up using panels, one of which contains the buttons. Each panel makes use of an appropriate layout manager to display its contents.

Perhaps the most interesting feature of the editor program is how much of the behaviour is handled by the GUI components. The program code presented essentially creates the components and fits them together with some 'glue' code. Very little of the complicated activity of displaying and editing text needs to be programmed by the programmer, instead pre-built components are plugged together and a useful program quickly constructed.

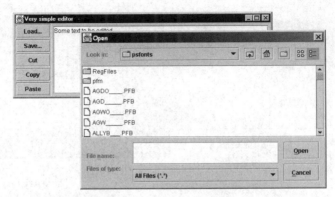

Figure 11.16 The JFileChooser dialog displayed by the very simple editor to select a file for loading.

11.4.1 Editor Event Handling

Event handling makes use of listeners implemented using anonymous inner classes, with each button having its own listener. The `JTextArea` takes care of all the events associated with text manipulation (key strokes, mouse clicks, selecting text and so on), so none of these need be dealt with explicitly by the editor program. The button event listener methods make use of private helper methods, to avoid too much code ending up in the constructor method.

A text file is loaded into the editor by using a `JFileChooser` dialog that allows a file to be selected (see Figure 11.16, the exact appearance of the dialog will vary with the windowing system running on your computer). The method call `showOpenDialog` causes the chooser to be displayed and from then on it takes control, letting the user either select a file or cancel. If a file is selected, a `FileReader` object is created to allow the contents of the file to be read and the `FileReader` passed to the `JTextArea` component when the `read` method is called. The `JTextArea` will then take care of reading and displaying the contents of the file. Saving a text file, when the save button is clicked, works in much the same way, using a `FileWriter` object to let the `JTextArea` write the text it is editing to a file. Loading and saving files again demonstrates that most of the hard work is done by Swing components, leaving the GUI programmer to connect the parts together with a relatively small amount of code.

The same theme continues when looking at the code that performs the cut, copy and paste operations. The `JTextArea` component is able to interact with the system clipboard and implements all the behaviour required to cut, copy and paste text. Copying text simply requires a call to the `copy` method and the currently selected text will be copied to the clipboard. Cutting works in a similar way using the `cut` method, while pasting copies the contents of the clipboard to the current text cursor position. The only extra code needed for the cut, copy and paste methods is the call of the `requestFocus` method. A component has the focus when it is selected (usually by clicking on it), enabling it to receive events. Clicking a button shifts the focus to the button, so the `requestFocus` method call returns the focus to the `JTextArea`, allowing the user to carry on editing text.

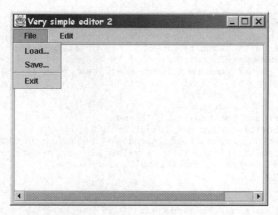

Figure 11.17 Simple editor with a menu bar and the File menu showing.

With the event handling outlined, there is little more to say about the simple editor program, other than to emphasize how straightforward it is to write useful programs using Swing. The advantage of using pre-built libraries and GUI components is the ease with which user interfaces can be developed.

11.5 Menus

The great majority of programs with a GUI include a menu bar, with pull down menus. The program listing below is for a second version of the simple editor program, with the buttons replaced by a menu bar. The editor window, with a menu displayed, is shown in Figure 11.17.

```java
// Example Swing program to illustrate a simple text editor
// with a menu bar.
import java.awt.*;
import javax.swing.*;
import java.awt.event.*;
import javax.swing.border.*;
import java.io.* ;
public class VerySimpleEditor2 extends JFrame {
  // Instance variables for the GUI components used.
  // Declaring the variables here allows them to be
  // used by any instance methods in the class.
  JPanel topPanel ;
  JPanel editorPanel ;
  JScrollPane scroller ;
  JTextArea editor ;
  JMenuBar menuBar ;
  JMenu fileMenu ;
  JMenu editMenu ;
  JMenuItem fileMenuLoad ;
  JMenuItem fileMenuSave ;
  JMenuItem fileMenuExit ;
  JMenuItem editMenuCut ;
  JMenuItem editMenuCopy ;
  JMenuItem editMenuPaste ;
  // The constructor builds the window and displays it.
  public VerySimpleEditor2() {
    // Create and configure the various panels
    topPanel = new JPanel () ;
```

```
      topPanel.setLayout(new BorderLayout ()) ;
      editorPanel = new JPanel () ;
      editorPanel.setLayout(new BorderLayout ()) ;
      editorPanel.setBorder(BorderFactory.createEmptyBorder(2,2,2,2));
      scroller = new JScrollPane () ;
      // The editor component handles all text display and editing. It
      // is given a width of 40 characters.
      editor = new JTextArea () ;
      editor.setColumns(40) ;
      // Configure the top-level JFrame
      this.setTitle("Very simple editor 2") ;
      this.getContentPane().add(topPanel, BorderLayout.CENTER) ;
      this.addWindowListener(new java.awt.event.WindowAdapter () {
          public void windowClosing(WindowEvent e) {
            System.exit(0) ;
          }
        }) ;
      // Now assemble the components
      topPanel.add(editorPanel, BorderLayout.CENTER) ;
      editorPanel.add(scroller, BorderLayout.CENTER) ;
      scroller.getViewport().add(editor) ;
      // Create the menu bar, making use of helper methods.
      menuBar = new JMenuBar () ;
      setJMenuBar(menuBar) ;
      addFileMenu() ;
      addEditMenu() ;
      pack() ;
      setSize(400,300) ;
      setVisible(true) ;
    }
    // Add the File menu to the menu bar.
    private void addFileMenu() {
      fileMenu = new JMenu ("File") ;
      fileMenuLoad = new JMenuItem ("Load...") ;
      fileMenuLoad.addActionListener(new ActionListener () {
          public void actionPerformed(ActionEvent e) {
            loadFile();
          }
        });
      fileMenu.add(fileMenuLoad) ;
      fileMenuSave = new JMenuItem ("Save...") ;
      fileMenuSave.addActionListener(new ActionListener () {
          public void actionPerformed(ActionEvent e) {
            saveFile();
          }
        });
      fileMenu.add(fileMenuSave) ;
      fileMenu.addSeparator() ;
      fileMenuExit = new JMenuItem ("Exit") ;
      fileMenuExit.addActionListener(new ActionListener () {
          public void actionPerformed(ActionEvent e) {
            System.exit(0) ;
          }
        });
      fileMenu.add(fileMenuExit) ;
      menuBar.add(fileMenu) ;
    }
    // Add the Edit menu to the menu bar.
    private void addEditMenu() {
      editMenu = new JMenu ("Edit") ;
      editMenuCut = new JMenuItem ("Cut") ;
      editMenuCut.addActionListener(new ActionListener () {
        public void actionPerformed(ActionEvent e) {
          cut();
        }
        });
```

```
        editMenu.add(editMenuCut) ;
        editMenuCopy = new JMenuItem ("Copy") ;
        editMenuCopy.addActionListener(new ActionListener () {
            public void actionPerformed(ActionEvent e) {
              copy();
            }
        });
        editMenu.add(editMenuCopy) ;
        editMenuPaste = new JMenuItem("Paste") ;
        editMenuPaste.addActionListener(new ActionListener () {
            public void actionPerformed(ActionEvent e) {
              paste() ;
            }
        });
        editMenu.add(editMenuPaste) ;
        menuBar.add(editMenu) ;
    }
    // The following methods implement the menu item bahaviour.  Display
    // a file dialog and load a file
    private void loadFile() {
      JFileChooser fc = new JFileChooser () ;
      int returnVal = fc.showOpenDialog(this) ;
      if (returnVal == JFileChooser.APPROVE_OPTION) {
        // If a file was selected, try and load it.
        File file = fc.getSelectedFile() ;
        try {
          editor.read(new FileReader(file), null) ;
        }
        catch (IOException exp) {}
      }
    }
    // Display a save file dialog and save the current file.
    private void saveFile() {
      JFileChooser fc = new JFileChooser () ;
      int returnVal = fc.showSaveDialog(this) ;
      if (returnVal == JFileChooser.APPROVE_OPTION) {
        File file = fc.getSelectedFile() ;
        try {
          editor.write(new FileWriter(file)) ;
        }
        catch (IOException exp) {}
      }
    }
    private void copy() {
      editor.copy() ;
      editor.requestFocus() ;
    }
    private void paste() {
      editor.paste() ;
      editor.requestFocus() ;
    }
    private void cut() {
      editor.cut() ;
      editor.requestFocus() ;
    }
    public static void main(final String[] args) {
      final VerySimpleEditor2 editor = new VerySimpleEditor2 () ;
    }
}
```

Not surprisingly menus are built from Swing components. A menu is represented by a JMenu object, with each item displayed on the menu represented by a JMenuItem object (see Figure 11.18). Each menu is added to the menu bar, a JMenuBar object, which in turn is added to the top-level JFrame by calling the method setJMenuBar. Each JMenuItem is given a listener

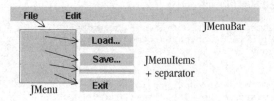

Figure 11.18 Structure of a menu.

object which provides a method to call when the menu item is selected. The method then performs the action denoted by the item. Other than building the menus component by component and providing the listeners, the management of menus is performed by Swing.

11.6 Painting

With the information presented so far it is now possible to understand most of how the classes DrawPanel and DrawFrame, used in Chapter 4, Page 91 and listed in Appendix G, Page 967 and Appendix H, Page 969, work. DrawFrame subclasses JFrame and is used to contain a panel, which is a subclass of DrawPanel programmed by the person creating a drawing program. One aspect that needs further examination, however, is the way drawing actually works.

Drawing a picture takes place by using a Graphics2D object to draw directly onto a JPanel. However, the drawing must be performed within the paint method (or a method called by paint). The explanation for this lies in the way components are displayed.

All components inherit and override the paint method, which is called whenever the component needs to displayed or updated (including when a window changes size or is uncovered having been hidden by other windows). In the case of a JPanel, the default paint behaviour is to ask its contained components to paint themselves, or if a panel contains no components, as is the case in the drawing program, the panel paints itself in the default background colour. As paint can be repeatedly called at any time, depending what is done with a window, it has to always be able to correctly draw a component. If not, then the window contents will quickly become corrupted.

A DrawPanel subclass specializes a panel to display a picture by using the paint method to draw the picture. Any drawing not performed by paint (or a method it calls) risks being destroyed as soon as paint is called. Hence, drawing programs must put their drawing code in paint. This basic mechanism can be exploited to create your own components, displaying whatever you like. It is also possible to force to window to redisplay by calling the repaint method.

11.7 Summary

This chapter has given an overview of how user interfaces are constructed using the Swing library. Once the basic principles of component, container, layout manager and event handling are understood, it becomes straightforward to construct GUIs. The major advantage of using Swing lies in the amount of functionality provided by the components, greatly reducing the time and effort needed by the programmer creating a user interface.

Key points in this chapter:

- A GUI is built from visual GUI components.
- Components are placed within containers, and positioned and sized by layout managers.
- Events are represented by objects and passed to components.
- Event listeners provide listener methods to respond to events, and are added to components to allow a program to respond to events.
- GUI programs are multi-threaded, with the GUI thread responsible for managing the interface and calling the listener methods.
- Components provide a great deal of functionality allowing interfaces to be easily constructed without the programmer having to write complex code.

Self-review Questions

Self-review 11.1 What is a GUI component?

Self-review 11.2 What does a layout manager do?

Self-review 11.3 What are the advantages of using a layout manager?

Self-review 11.4 Why are panels layered?

Self-review 11.5 What role does a `JFrame` provide?

Self-review 11.6 What does the method `setVisible` do?

Self-review 11.7 How is an event represented?

Self-review 11.8 What is a listener?

Self-review 11.9 Why are listeners implemented as objects?

Self-review 11.10 What is an aonymous class?

Self-review 11.11 How is a menu constructed?

Self-review 11.12 What does a `JTextField` component do?

Self-review 11.13 What does `paint` do?

Self-review 11.14 How is a GUI program terminated?

Self-review 11.15 Why are GUI programs multi-threaded?

Programming Exercises

Exercise 11.1 Draw a pencil and paper picture illustrating how the GUI of the Convert program in Section 11.3, Page 306 is laid out.

Exercise 11.2 Implement a program with this interface:

Clicking the buttons increments or decrements the displayed counter value.

Hint: How do you position the 2 buttons? You might try this: add a panel, using a FlowLayout, to hold the 2 buttons.

Exercise 11.3 Write a Swing program to display this window:

When the button is clicked, the text typed into the `JTextField` at the top of the window is copied into the label in the middle of the window. Note the position and size of the button.

Exercise 11.4 Modify the first version of the VerySimpleEditor so that the buttons remain a fixed size when the window is made larger.

Exercise 11.5 Implement a Swing program with this interface:

The buttons on the left are Radio Buttons (`JRadioButton` objects — see the JDSK docmentation for more information). When a number is entered in the `JTextField` on the right, and a radio button clicked, the number is converted to the new number base and displayed in place of the original. Note, only digits valid in the current number base can be typed into the `JTextField`.

Hints: Use an `EtchedBorder` on the panel holding the radio buttons, the `BorderFactory` class will create one for you. The radio buttons need to be in a `ButtonGroup`. A `JTextField` can generate a `KeyEvent` when a character is typed and accepts `KeyListeners`. Class `Integer` will do all the work of number base conversion.

Exercise 11.6 Repeat the last question but replace the radio buttons with a `JComboBox`.

Exercise 11.7 Rewrite the palindrome program presented in Section 3.4.2, Page 63, so that it has a GUI.

Challenges

Challenge 11.1 Implement a calculator program based on the GUI shown in Figure 11.1, Page 295.

Challenge 11.2 Extend the graph program shown in Section 6.7.3, Page 171 to include a complete GUI, with a menu bar. It should be possible to select and load a data file, and select and configure the kind of graph to be displayed (support at least bar graphs, line graphs and pie charts).

Challenge 11.3 Modify the second version Very Simple Editor program with the menu bar (Section 11.5, Page 313), so that it uses a `JTextPane` rather than a `JTextArea` to display and edit text. Extend the program to provide support for different fonts, and bold and italic text.

2

Building Class Libraries

Part 2

Objectives

This part investigates the issues in building new class libraries using packages. The aim is not to develop a complete library but to show how such a library could be constructed. Links are made to the Java Generic Library (JGL) and the Collections Framework as instances of real production libraries. The second aim is to introduce various data structures and algorithms as part of learning about programmin g.

Contents

Building Libraries

Objectives

Building libraries of abstractions (classes and packages of classes) is an important part of developing applications in Java. In this chapter, we look at some of the issues in constructing a library and then in the following chapters show how to put things into practice by constructing the beginnings of a library containing some abstract data types and some searching and sorting algorithms.

Keywords

architecture

Collections

iterators

Java Generic Library

JGL

order relations

sequences

12.1   Introduction

So far, we have been constructing Java programs using the features of the core programming language, enabling us to build our own classes, and by using classes from packages provided in the standard library. The library classes represent a wide range of abstractions that are often required when implementing applications and their availability removes the need for any and every programmer to re-invent them. Whilst this allows a great deal to be achieved, to construct larger applications we need the capability of building new libraries of abstractions using our own classes and packages. For example, if we were an organization involved in developing computer-based systems for the financial services sector, we would want to build abstractions such as `Customer`, `Account`, `Trade`, and so on, within a `FinancialServices` package, and have them available as reusable components for all the applications we construct.

In fact, there are many reasons why building additional libraries of abstractions is important. In particular, a library allows an organization to:

- incrementally (and bottom-up) develop, over time, a software asset that models and codifies knowledge about the organization's own activities, operations and applications portfolio;
- develop a consistent organizational system architecture, enabling large systems to be more easily comprehended and constructed, and for sub-systems to inter-work more effectively;
- impose a uniformity of implementation (i.e. an house style) so that it is easier for developers to understand, and hence work on, each other's systems;
- allow much of a system to be constructed from reusable components, avoiding wasteful re-implementation; and
- allow developers to work at higher conceptual levels when designing and implementing systems.

These points are not unrelated to each other, essentially they are different aspects of the same basic approach to system implementation. Applications tend to be analysed and designed in an 'outside-in' way with 'top-down' predominating, aiming to maximize the reuse of existing abstractions and software components. Work starts with a statement of the overall problem and requirements of the system to be built. The architecture of the system is established and broken down into manageable elements (hence, outside-in and top-down), with a goal of making as much reuse of already developed components as possible. Implementation also tends to be 'outside-in' but with 'bottom-up' playing an important role, as coding proceeds by writing code using the base programming language and 'gluing' together existing components, along with the construction of new components. Identifying the abstractions that the new components implement raises the level of thinking and modelling in developing applications.

In Java, components are implemented as classes and packages of classes so that, when placed somewhere accessible to all the developers in the organization, they become the reusable

!

Using packages other than the standard ones from the J2SDK requires the environment variable CLASSPATH to be set properly. See Appendix E.5, Page 961.

components that all can make use of to avoid replication of code and waste of time and effort re-implementing sub-systems. Although beyond the scope of this book, this idea is taken further in the form of JavaBeans, which provides a standard for constructing and interconnecting reusable Java components, allowing JavaBeans to be easily reused across many applications.

The first step on the road of developing a reusable classes and components is to recognize that the Java programming system only comes with relatively basic (but nonetheless very powerful) abstractions. These abstractions are language feature oriented (e.g. `ArrayList` and `Iterator`). This is quite rightly the first step in the abstraction construction process: extend the features of the language to make it more expressive. These new abstractions can then be used to build domain specific (i.e. more specialized) abstractions. Note the trade-off here: as the abstractions become higher level, less about programming and more about modelling the real world, they become more specific to an application domain and less generally applicable. Thus, whilst `ArrayList` is used by all Java programmers, `Customer` is only going to be used in a buying–selling context and `Trade` only in a financial services context. However, `Customer` or `Trade` will contain carefully refined sets of features that allow them to work effectively and efficiently in their appropriate context.

So, we need to be able to extend the standard library with the useful abstractions for the kind of applications we are interested in. Extending the Java system further with more abstractions is both the object-oriented philosophy and the way of making the construction of large and useful applications easier and more efficient.

Creating new abstractions and libraries of them is, in fact, such an important activity that many organizations have teams whose sole task is to develop libraries either from scratch (not the best way) or by reviewing all the applications being worked on in the organization and drawing out the common abstractions from them. The teams then create the library classes which in turn, of course, requires the applications to be evolved to use them.

A growing number of companies go further than this and exist, making a very good turnover and profit, solely by constructing high quality (i.e. well implemented, well documented, easy to understand and use) libraries of components and selling them.

Inevitably, in every domain, there is a tendency to get a little parochial and different organizations bring into being their own libraries that are essentially the same library that everyone else is busily implementing. Close to the application domain this can be a good thing, as having your own high-quality library can become a serious competitive advantage. At the lower end, where we are dealing more with language-level abstractions, replication just leads to massive confusion and wasted effort. It is often significantly cheaper to buy-in libraries than develop them in-house.

Over the last 20 years a lot of knowledge has been gained about the low-level abstractions in the data structuring and manipulation area. There are a large number of books on the market which consider, in great detail, algorithms and data structures and their properties. Indeed, the field of *algorithmics* is the branch of computer science that studies these things in great detail. However, having a large number of distinct and different implementations of the same abstractions, particularly when the abstractions are well understood and efficient implementations are similar and widely available, is the cause of most of the confusion alluded to in the previous paragraph.

The C++ programming language community has been battling with this problem and as a consequence has developed a data structures and algorithms library called the Standard Template Library (STL). The specification (though not the implementation) of the types and procedures in the library has become standardized and is now part of the C++ language. Standardization of libraries and making them part of the language definitions ensures both that the abstractions are available to all programmers in all organizations and that all programmers can use all the abstractions — making it easier for staff to change jobs and for organizations to find staff. It clears away much of the confusion.

The basic structure and content of the STL is proving to be appropriate for Java as well as C++. This should not be a surprise since Java has some of its parentage in C++. A number of implementations of the STL for Java have now appeared. One in particular, the Java Generic Library (JGL), has proved very popular. So much so that many Java program development environment vendors automatically include it in their products.

note

Because there are crucial difference between C++ and Java. STL and JGL have significant differences.

In pre-J2SDK versions of the Sun Java distribution, there was a lack of sensible implementations for the well-known data structures. This fact was one of the driving forces behind the development of JGL. Sun themselves appreciated that this was a significant lack but rather than take JGL on board, chose to develop their own abstractions. So now, as part of the J2SDK, Sun has the Java Collections Framework (usually just called Collections). Collections provides a number of *container classes* along with some sorting and searching algorithms. In effect Collections is now the de facto standard, since it come as an integral part of the standard J2SDK. However, many people continue to prefer and use the JGL.

Given the existence of these two production quality libraries of abstractions, it makes no sense to try and construct new libraries replicating the data structures and algorithms provided by them. Instead, we should choose one of these libraries and use it. So why are we, nonetheless, going to describe the design and development of a library of data structures and algorithms? There are a number of reasons:

1. Constructing such a library is an excellent example of what a library is; it brings out almost all of the issues that must be considered.

2. It allows us to describe the fundamental data structures and algorithms so that you can learn about them and, perhaps more importantly, learn about how to use them.

3. There are many implementation techniques, for example linked lists and trees, that we should study in order to increase our knowledge of programming techniques but also so that we can understand the purpose and use of Collections and JGL.

4. It allows us to compare and contrast the Collections and JGL libraries. There are both a lot of similarities and a lot of differences between the two libraries, and understanding these can only increase our knowledge and ability as programmers.

5. Neither Collections nor JGL are complete; they do not contain all the useful abstractions that, perhaps, they should. Some of the abstractions that we will develop in this part of the book ought possibly to be in these libraries.

Therefore, in this and the following chapters, we develop a small, but incomplete, library of Abstract Data Types (ADTs) and various searching and sorting algorithms, all of which will be implemented as a single package of classes. As part of the description of the development, we will:

- introduce the idea of system architectures;
- introduce the details of how to build a package, which is the key mechanism Java provides to support library construction;
- explain how to extend the toolkit of data structuring and data manipulation techniques codified in classes;
- introduce more knowledge and toolkit features to make programming easier;
- investigate the properties of some ADTs, all of which happen to be containers;
- investigate how to construct good, efficient and useful libraries of software; and
- give leaders into the way in which Collections and JGL do things.

Rather than presenting a manual or catalogue of classes and abstractions, there is a pedagogical flow to the text, focusing on discussion of how the ADTs can be implemented as classes and the design decisions involved. We will first look at abstractions that are part of the infrastructure critical to the rest of the package, followed by some more general abstractions, and along the way consider some of their properties. We next move on to examine algorithms for searching and sorting data. Before doing any of this, though, we will look at the strategy we are going to follow when implementing the package.

To illustrate one of the reasons why we need to spend time examining container classes and container abstractions, consider arrays and `ArrayLists`. Both of these, as we have seen earlier, are part of the J2SDK and are used as containers to store collections of objects. An `ArrayList` is basically an implementation of an array with more dynamic properties to do with managing objects stored within it. Although arrays provide efficient access to a collection of values, they are actually quite restrictive. There has to be a rigid upper bound on the number of items to be stored and moving data within the array is inefficient. Thus, whilst arrays are very good for storing data that is relatively static, different abstractions are needed for when the data is more dynamic, which is why `ArrayList` has been developed. `ArrayList` is built using arrays but encapsulates and abstracts the code needed to implement the dynamism on the essentially static data structure that is an array. The design of containers such as `ArrayList` has to take into account not only the abstractions but the properties of implementations of those abstractions and the properties of the package in which the abstraction is placed.

ref

Class `ArrayList` *was briefly introduced in Section 5.3.1, Page 127.*

12.2   Introducing the Package Architecture

In the following chapters, we are going to introduce a package providing implementations for a number of different ADTs but the one thing we must avoid is inconsistency. Although the types are different and distinct, they need to be implemented in a consistent way. Consistency here means having the same approach to: exceptions; threads; type conformance; inheritance; programming style; use of language features; design style; method naming; parameter ordering; use of other libraries; and internal cross-use within the package. Taken together, these sorts of issues are usually talked about as the *architecture* of the package or library.

The basic aim behind this package is for it to be the *prototype* of a usable production package. It is not intended as a pedagogical toy library, it is intended to be the basis of a real library. Thus, there are some details that other authors might miss out in order to concentrate on the core ideas. Whilst we have great sympathy with keeping things simple and making sure the core ideas are well presented, overall we feel it better to expose the full reality. There are two main reasons for this:

1. we want the book to have vocational as well as educational benefit so we deal with real-world situations; and

2. what might have been seen as detail issues in the past are increasingly becoming core issues.

Having made explicit this attitude towards the package, what is the basic architecture of the package?

First of all, we want to be clear about the labels ADT, type and class. The package will be implemented using interfaces, classes and the features of the Java programming language. Each class and interface will define a type which essentially consists of a name and a set of methods, each denoted by a name, argument types and a result type. Objects will, therefore, be an instance of a single class and be able to conform to one or more types.

Each class will also be an implementation of one or more ADTs. An ADT serves the role of defining a set of methods a class must provide *and* the behaviour of those methods in terms of how the state of objects of that class must change when the method is called (see Chapter 6.3, Page 151). Unlike classes and types, ADTs only exist as part of the design of the package and are not part of the source code or accessible to the Java compiler. Hence, the overall design of the package can be expressed in terms of ADTs, which will be implemented by interfaces and classes, that in turn provide types to be used for type checking. During the description of the package we will refer to ADTs, types and classes, so it is important to be clear about the role of each.

The package is intended to be as simple as possible. In line with the principle of Ockham's Razor, nothing has been, or should be, added to the package unless it has some definite purpose not already achievable within the package. The very worst thing to have in any system is many ways of achieving the same goal or purpose; to do this will only serve to confuse. Where there is choice, there should be clear guidelines for choosing one approach over another. This is not to say that

!

Ockham's Razor: *The philosophic rule that entities should not be multiplied unnecessarily — usually attributed to William of Ockham (sometimes spelt Occam), a philosopher of the early 14th century.*

there won't be design problems when there is only a single way of doing things, but to add unnecessary choice is to introduce further possibilities for confusion and error.

Each container in the package needs to be *polymorphic*, allowing it to contain elements of any type. Without this requirement a different container would need to be provided for every type of element that could be stored, making it impossible to create a self-contained and complete library (every time someone invented a new type, a new set of containers would have to be added). The natural approach to polymorphism in Java is to use references of type `Object`.

The package developed in this book will also have some non-container types. These types are there essentially to support the containers, but these are as few as can be — in line with the Ockham's Razor.

The above sets out some of the architecture of the package, mostly background attitude, approach and requirements. The remaining sections of this chapter introduce further aspects of the architecture and in some cases deal with different possibilities for various of the core features. First, though, let us worry about assumptions.

12.3   Avoiding Assumptions

A very important feature of the package we will design and implement, and indeed of any package of this sort, is that it must make no assumptions about how or in what context the package is to be used.

The most obvious thing about which no assumptions should be made is the input–output system, particularly that concerned with the computer screen and keyboard. In fact, the classes should do no input–output at all, all communication with the application should be using return values from the methods or using exceptions. It is the responsibility of the user interface system to undertake input–output, it is not the place of a container type to assume a certain style or approach to input–output. This has always been a strong principle for all libraries to follow, it is even more critical for a language able to construct applets for the Web.

The same principle applies to reading and writing values of the container types within the package. No assumptions can be made about the storage devices in which a program employing the types from this package has access to. J2SDK has the notion of stream and serialization which abstract the input–output activities and these should be used. The user, or *client*, of a library class provides the actual streams, the library class itself is only concerned with the abstract `Reader` or `Writer` stream interface. In this way the details of what a stream may be connected to are not relevant: it is not for the class in the package to be concerned whether the stream is or is not connected to a given file, it just uses the stream it is given. In essence we are parameterizing the class using the interface concept.

note

Threads and thread safety were introduced in Section 8.1, Page 141 and are dealt with in more detail in Chapter 35, Page 843.

Perhaps less obvious than input–output, but nonetheless equally crucial, is the issue of threads. As library designers and implementors we must ensure that we do not enforce any inappropriate constraints on the programmer. For example, we must make *no* assumptions about how many threads the application will have. All too often the temptation is to assume that only a single thread will ever be executing in our library code at any time. We cannot do this, we must either make our library *thread safe* or we must provide tools so that any parts of the library that are not thread safe can be made so. Thread safe means that if a method can be executed by more than one thread at a time then, no matter how many threads are concurrently executing that method, there is no interaction (data coupling) between the threads caused by the library code — coupling between threads caused by the application is not our problem.

Collections and JGL have very different philosophies regarding thread safety. Collections uses the strategy that the core classes are for single threaded usage only and that for multi-threaded usage, special proxy classes must be used to provide the thread safety. JGL has fully thread safe classes only. The trade off here is speed of execution versus programming safety. The Collections philosophy emphasizes programmer control and speed of execution whereas the JGL philosophy emphasizes ease of use and protection against programmer error. The JGL philosophy is founded on the idea that multi-threaded applications and applets are the norm whereas the Collections philosophy is that only the programmer of the application can know the real need for thread management. Note that the two philosophies are, effectively, mutually incompatible. It can be argued that either approach is as good as the other in some ways but there is a definite shift generally towards the view that the philosophy embodies in the Collection library is, in fact, the correct one. The main argument is that this architecture allows single threaded code to be as efficient as possible, and only requires the overhead of thread management when needed. The library should not, perhaps cannot, try and cover all possibilities of thread use but should leave it as the responsibility of the application programmer to use the right tools at the right time to ensure that an application is thread safe.

Enabling a library to support thread safe operation using the Collections philosophy is actually relatively easy but we do have to ensure that the facility is provided.

12.4   What's in a Name?

Returning to our ADTs package specifically, we need to set up some basic infrastructure to make our package and classes usable. First of all, we must give the package a name: the package we are building will be called ADS (standing for Algorithms and Data Structures) and so all files contributing to the package will include the line:

```
package ADS ;
```

with all the files being placed in the same directory called ADS, which will exist in the filestore in a directory which is on the search path of the Java compiler.

The ADS package defines a scope: the scope rules mean that we can carefully control what is accessible to users of the package, and at the same time allows a finer grain of control over the accessibility of methods and variables to other elements within the package. In particular, some variables can be made accessible anywhere within the package, making access to components of the package very much easier. This also means that we do not need `import` statements within the package in order to access other parts of the package.

Throughout the ADS library, full use is made of inner and anonymous classes wherever possible; classes are defined within the class, indeed within the methods in many cases, that defines the required scope of that class. We do this to try and limit the scope of any name (class, variable or method) used in the implementation of the package. Limiting the scope of a name to the smallest possible scope unit required is a defensive mechanism that is an attempt to avoid errors. Experience shows that limiting scope is *always* a good idea.

The containers defined in this package deal only with elements of type `Object`, which is how the container polymorphism is obtained (all objects conform to type `Object` as every class is a subclass of class `Object`). This means that a reference to an element object will be of type `Object` when it gets put into the container and has to be cast back to the original subclass when taken out. Casting of references in this way is always a manual activity with little compile-time typechecking, though because of run-time type-checking, these casting actions are relatively safe overall. If fully compile-time type-checked, type-safe containers are required (i.e. containers which can only contain specific types), then these would have to be constructed independently for each container. We will show an example of this sort of container in Section 14.5, Page 429.

It could be argued that it is a pity that Java does not (at the time of writing anyway) incorporate a mechanism supporting parameterized types, allowing the declaration of *generic* container classes that have a parameter specifying the type of the objects to be held in the container. For example, a class Stack could have a parameter specifying the type of the stack elements: Stack<String> or Stack<Date>, for example. The generic Stack class would be written once and then instantiated to automatically provide the stack classes actually used. With the additional type information, the compiler could then perform full compile time type checking, making sure that only values of the correct type are stored, and also eliminating the need for cast expressions.

12.5 How to Iterate?

Some containers in this package are *open containers* (or *glass box containers*) and some are *closed containers* (or *opaque box containers*): an open container is one we are allowed to see into and examine the contents; a closed container is one we are not supposed to be allowed to look into and hence not be able to determine the values of the elements in the container. As we shall see in later chapters, `Stack` is a closed container whereas `BinaryTree` is an open one. In general, ADTs which are containers with special access controls are closed containers.

As a sweeping generalization: open containers are simply alternative mechanisms for storing data, whereas closed containers are designed to provide specific access protocols, often making use of the various open containers. We shall pick this point up and explain it more fully in the following chapters.

An *iterator* is a mechanism for visiting each element within a container in turn, realized as an object. For every open container, an iterator over the elements in the container *must* be provided, as the elements are accessible. We can view indexing of arrays as a form of iterator. Consider the following code fragment:

Iterators are the variables used to control iteration associated with a container.

```
for (int i = 0 ; i < 30 ; ++i) {
   x += a[i] ;
}
```

or we could have the analogous thing with ArrayList:

```
for (int i = 0 ; i < 30 ; ++i) {
   x += a.get(i) ;
}
```

In both cases the loop is iterating over the elements of the array a using the int i which is, in effect, acting as an iterator: the variable i is keeping track of which is the current item of interest within the container. Now for arrays, this is the only method of iteration but for ArrayLists we can use *iterator objects*. In Collections, iterators are instances of classes that implement the interface Iterator (or, in earlier versions of Java, Enumeration). Moreover, each class provides a method called iterator, which delivers an initialized iterator over the elements in the container object. (Classes that use the Enumeration interface conventionally use the method name elements for this method.) Classes in Collections may also subclass Iterator to define more specialized forms of iterator.

Using iteration over the ArrayList a, we can write:

```
for (Iterator i = a.iterator() ; i.hasNext() ; ) {
   x += i.next() ;
}
```

The Iterator reference i is initialized using the iterator returned by the object that is to be iterated over by the method call a.iterator(). The iterator knows whether or not it has reached the end of the container, as the call i.hasNext() will return false when there is no "next" element available. In the loop body, i.next() returns a reference to the next element in the container. There is no separate move forward operation as the activity of getting the next value automatically moves the iterator forward to the next element in the container.

In JGL, things are a little more formalized. There are a number of types of iterator defined independently of specific containers. Different containers can have different properties and therefore will implement different iterators to match the capabilities of the underlying container. In effect JGL defines an abstract framework of iterators whereas Collections does not. The most used of the JGL iterators are:

InputIterator — reads an item at a time in a forward direction.

OutputIterator — writes an item at a time in a forward direction.

ForwardIterator — read or write an item at a time in a forward direction.

BidirectionalIterator — a ForwardIterator that can also read or write an item at a time in a backward direction.

RandomAccessIterator — a BidirectionalIterator that has the ability to be sensibly compared for relative position in a container with another RandomAccessIterator.

Both Collections and JGL agree that an iterator is an instance of an object that is delivered by a method call on the container object.

JGL has a type `Array` which is completely analogous to `ArrayList` in Collections. The code fragment above re-coded for JGL would look like:

```
for (ForwardIterator i = a.start() ; !i.atEnd() ; i.advance()) {
  x += i.get() ;
}
```

The `ForwardIterator` reference `i` is initialized in analogous way to an iterator in Collections by using the method call `a.start()`. The iterator knows when it has reached the end of the container as the call `i.atEnd()` will return true — note that this is the opposite condition to Collections. There are separate advancement and element access operations using the method calls `i.get()` and `i.advance()` respectively — a crucial difference between Collections and JGL iterators. Many people believe that separating the methods of iterator control from those of element access, as is done in JGL, is better than mixing the two as is done in Collections. We know from private communication that the author of the Collections Framework does not believe this.

It turns out that this difference in how to handle the control and access methods of iterators is one of the single biggest architectural difference between Collections and JGL. In all other aspects of iterators and their use, whilst there are minor differences, for example the inversion of the test for knowing when the iterator has dealt with all elements, the core approach to the library architecture is fundamentally the same. The fact that Collections is a part of the `java.util` package and that JGL is split up into a number of different packages is actually a minor organization difference, it does not really impact on the architecture.

Perhaps the single biggest real difference between Collections and JGL is not the iterators themselves but the way in which the containers interact with the iterators: Collections has an architecture of containers working with a single iterator whereas JGL has this and also the ability to work with pairs of iterators to create slices on the container. A *slice* results from taking a range of elements from the container, delineated by start and end iterators. Most people would argue that on this point the JGL has it right.

As can be seen from the above examples, an iterator is, in essence, a reference or *pointer* to an element in a container. An iterator identifies a particular element of the container and allows operations to be performed on it. Iterating using an iterator in a solely forwards direction means

note

A Collections `Iterator` *is essentially the same thing as a JGL* `ForwardIterator`.

!

Iterators are one of the most important abstractions in programming. They have far reaching, unifying and simplifying effects on the way we write programs.

moving through all items of the container in some order so that each element is visited once and only once.

In ADS, basic iterators are input iterators and conform to the following interface:

ADS is a stripped down package designed to show how real packages work. It is not intended for production use. Use Collections or JGL.

note

```
package ADS ;
/**
 *   All iterators over containers in ADS conform to this interface.
 *   This is basically just an input iterator.
 *
 *   @version 1.0 1999.09.11
 *   @author Russel Winder
 */
public interface Iterator extends Cloneable {
    /**
     *   Deliver the value we are currently referring to.
     */
    Object get() ;
    /**
     *   Move on to the next element in the container.
     */
    void advance() ;
    /**
     *   Have we reached the end of the iteration?
     */
    boolean atEnd() ;
    /**
     *   Are two iterators equal, i.e. do two iterators refer to the
     *   same item in the same data structure.
     */
    boolean equals(Iterator i) ;
    /**
     *   Return the reference to the object I am working.
     */
    Object myObject() ;
    /**
     *   Clone this <CODE>Iterator</CODE>.
     */
    Object clone() ;
}
```

the package also defines forward iterators, which conform to:

```
package ADS ;
/**
 *   All forward iterators iterators over containers in ADS conform to
 *   this interface.
 *
 *   @version 1.0 1999.09.11
 *   @author Russel Winder
 */
public interface ForwardIterator extends Iterator {
    /**
     *   Set the value at the current position.
     */
    void set(Object o) ;
}
```

bidirectional iterators which conform to:

```
package ADS ;
/**
 *   All bidirectional iterators over containers in ADS conform to this
 *   interface.
 *
```

```
 *   @version 1.0 1999.09.11
 *   @author Russel Winder
 */
public interface BiDirectionalIterator extends ForwardIterator {
  /**
   *   Move back to the previous element in the container.
   */
  void retreat() ;
  /**
   *   Have we reached the beginning of the iteration?
   */
  boolean atBegin() ;
}
```

and random access iterators which conform to:

```
package ADS ;
/**
 *   All bidirectional iterators over containers in ADS conform to this
 *   interface.
 *
 *   @version 1.0 1999.09.11
 *   @author Russel Winder
 */
public interface RandomAccessIterator extends BiDirectionalIterator {
  /**
   *   Move forward n elements in the container.
   */
  void advance(int n) ;
  /**
   *   Move back n elements in the container.
   */
  void retreat(int n) ;
  /**
   *   Calculate the distance between the two iterators.
   */
  int separation(RandomAccessIterator i) ;
}
```

Other, more specific, iterators can be defined by classes but they must all supply one conforming to `Iterator`. In order for the package to work, we must be able to make such assumptions.

This is just a brief introduction to iterators, there is much, much more to be said. As we introduce more and more containers we will see iterators in use and discover more about them. The architectural point is that all open containers must support iterators.

12.6   Making Assumptions

So that we can be sure that a specific set of behaviours are supported by all the containers in the package, all container classes implement the following methods:

`makeEmpty` — remove any elements from the container, making it empty.

`isEmpty` — return a `boolean` stating whether the container has any objects in it.

`size` — return the number of elements in the container object.

equals — determine whether the contents of this container object are the same as the contents of another container of the same type? (Note the use of 'type'. It should be possible to compare containers that are implemented using different classes but conform to the same type.) This methods overrides the equals method inherited from class Object, and provides semantic equality (comparing the values represented by objects) rather than the object identity equality that is the, quite reasonable, default meaning in Object. Of course, we still have == for object identity equality.

contains — return a boolean stating whether an object is in the container object or not.

add — add an object into the container object.

remove — remove an object from the container object.

clone — produce a shallow copy of the container, sharing the contained objects.

toString — return a string representation of the container and its contents.

iterator— deliver up an iterator (compatible with type Iterator) over the elements in the container.

We are requiring the methods clone, equals and toString to be overridden from their definitions in Object since we believe that the implementations in Object are not appropriate for the classes in the ADS package, but we do not require the method hashCode to be overridden.

Ensuring that these methods are defined for all classes in the package allows certain assumptions to be made within other parts of the package. These sort of assumptions, unlike ones about input–output systems, are reasonable but only as long as *everything* is consistent — and documented.

The guarantee that these methods are provided is ensured by requiring that all container classes implement the Container interface, allowing objects of those classes to conform to the type Container.

```
package ADS ;
/**
 *  An interface defining the necessary properties to be deemed to be
 *  a <CODE>Container</CODE>.
 *
 *  @version 1.1 1999.08.23
 *  @author Russel Winder
 */
public interface Container extends Cloneable {
  /**
   *  Remove the entire contents of the <CODE>Container</CODE>.
   */
  void makeEmpty() ;
  /**
   *  Determine whether the <CODE>Container</CODE> is an empty one.
   */
  boolean isEmpty() ;
  /**
   *  Return the number of items in the <CODE>Container</CODE>.
   */
  int size() ;
  /**
   *  Compare this <CODE>Container</CODE> with another and determine
```

```
 *   whether they represent the same value, i.e. have the same item
 *   values in the <CODE>Container</CODE>.
 *
 *   <P> <CODE>equals</CODE> is made into semantic equality
 *   rather than an object identity equality.  Equality for
 *   <CODE>Object</CODE>s is defined to be that the two
 *   <CODE>Object</CODE>s are the same <CODE>Object</CODE>.  For
 *   <CODE>Container</CODE>s, we want to define equality to be that
 *   they contain exactly the same values.
 */
boolean equals(Object o) ;
/**
 *   Determine whether the value represented by the
 *   parameter <CODE>Object</CODE> is in the <CODE>Container</CODE>.
 */
boolean contains(Object o) ;
/**
 *   Add an element to the <CODE>Container</CODE>.
 */
void add(Object o) ;
/**
 *   Remove an element of a given value from the
 *   <CODE>Container</CODE> if it is in the <CODE>Container</CODE>.
 *
 *   @return whether the item was actually in the
 *   <CODE>Container</CODE>.
 */
boolean remove(Object o) ;
/**
 *   Deliver up a complete shallow copy of the
 *   <CODE>Container</CODE>.
 */
Object clone() ;
/**
 *   Deliver up a <CODE>String</CODE> representation of the
 *   <CODE>Container</CODE>.
 */
String toString() ;
/**
 *   Deliver up an input iterator over the
 *   <CODE>Container</CODE>.
 */
Iterator iterator() ;
/**
 *   Containers can have synchronized forms provided by this class.
 */
public static class Synchronized implements Container {
  /**
   *   The <CODE>Container</CODE> that holds the data.
   */
  protected final Container theContainer ;
  /**
   *   The <CODE>Object</CODE> on which to do all locking.
   */
  protected final Object theLock ;
  /**
   *   The default constructor.  Gives an <CODE>Container</CODE> with
   *   default initial size and increment.
   */
  public Synchronized(final Container c) {
    theContainer = c ;
    theLock = this ;
  }
  /**
   *   The constructor that supplies an object to synchronize on.
   */
```

All containers have public iterators. Allowing iterators over closed containers may seem the wrong thing to do but we do it nonetheless. The issue here is that we can only enforce the existence of public methods using interfaces and we want to support iterator based activity. We could introduce ClosedContainers and OpenContainers as different interfaces in order to make the separation, or we could choose not to enforce having this method in order to be a Container. Since we need to use iterators to be able to compare ADTs of different implementations we really need to require the iterator. Thus, neither of these solutions is entirely satisfactory. The compromise is to allow closed containers to be iterated through by user code.

```java
public Synchronized(final Container c, final Object o) {
  theContainer = c ;
  theLock = o ;
}
/**
 *  Remove the entire contents of the <CODE>Container</CODE>.
 */
public final void makeEmpty() {
  synchronized (theLock) { theContainer.makeEmpty() ; }
}
/**
 *  Determine whether the <CODE>Container</CODE> is an empty one.
 */
public final boolean isEmpty() {
  synchronized (theLock) { return theContainer.isEmpty() ; }
} ;
/**
 *  Return the number of items in the <CODE>Container</CODE>.
 */
public final int size() {
  synchronized (theLock) { return theContainer.size() ; }
} ;
/**
 *  Compare this <CODE>Container</CODE> with another and determine
 *  whether they represent the same value, i.e. have the same item
 *  values in the <CODE>Container</CODE>.
 */
public final boolean equals(final Object o) {
  synchronized (theLock) { return theContainer.equals(o) ; }
} ;
/**
 *  Determine whether the value represented by the parameter
 *  <CODE>Object</CODE> is in the <CODE>Container</CODE>.
 */
public final boolean contains(final Object o) {
  synchronized (theLock) { return theContainer.contains(o) ; }
} ;
/**
 *  Add an element to the <CODE>Container</CODE>.
 */
public final void add(final Object o) {
  synchronized (theLock) { theContainer.add(o) ; }
} ;
/**
 *  Remove an element of a given value from the
 *  <CODE>Container</CODE> if it is in the <CODE>Container</CODE>.
 *
 *  @return whether the item was actually in the
 *  <CODE>Container</CODE>.
 */
public final boolean remove(final Object o) {
  synchronized (theLock) { return theContainer.remove(o) ; }
} ;
/**
 *  Deliver up a complete shallow copy of the
 *  <CODE>Container</CODE>.
 */
public final Object clone() {
  synchronized (theLock) { return theContainer.clone() ; }
} ;
/**
 *  Deliver up a <CODE>String</CODE> representation the
 *  <CODE>Container</CODE>.
 */
public final String toString() {
  synchronized (theLock) { return theContainer.toString() ; }
```

```
    } ;
    /**
     *  Deliver up an iterator over all the items in the
     *  <CODE>Container</CODE>.
     */
    public final Iterator iterator() {
      return theContainer.iterator() ;
    }
  }
}
```

This interface is somewhat longer than might have been expected. The reason for the extra length is that we have defined a nested top-level class `Synchronized` which provides a fully synchronized version of a `Container`. This is the first example of our approach to thread safety. All the classes in ADS will have no thread protection associated with them, this makes them as lightweight as possible so as to avoid any overheads when they are not needed. As pointed out in Section 12.3, Page 329, not making assumptions is an important part of good package design. The assumption we are not making here is that all programs need full protection against the problems of multi-threading. In not making this assumption, we do have the responsibility to provide the necessary tools for those cases where protection is required. The class `Synchronized` is the necessary tool for `Containers`. It can be used like this:

```
    Container c = new Container.Synchronized(new Container()) ;
```

whenever there is a need to ensure full synchronization protection.

This approach to concurrency control is very much the same as that of Collections, though we use a very different implementation technique. JGL has a very different approach; making the assumption that full concurrency control is needed at all times. We believe, as do many others, that Collections has it right on this and JGL does not.

Despite the difference of opinion regarding concurrency control both Collections and JGL take the same approach to providing a container interface as we have here for ADS. Collections has an interface `Collection` and JGL has an interface `Container` which are directly analogous to the the interface defined above. It seems there is an absolute commonality of design on this point.

12.7   Order Relations

Some of the package's container ADTs require an *order relation* to be defined for the container elements. By 'order relation' we mean one of the six relations: 'less than', 'less than or equal to', 'equal to', 'not equal to', 'greater than', and 'greater than or equal to'. These are used to compare objects stored in a container, allowing, for example, the stored objects to be stored in a sorted order. When comparing objects we are really comparing the *values* that the objects represent, so making a comparison can be quite complex depending on how an object represents its value.

For the primitive numeric types such as `ints`, the order relations are provided as the operators `<, <=, ==, !=, >, >=` but these cannot be used with objects and equivalent comparison methods

note

The operators == and != can be used to compare object references but only to determine whether two references refer to the same object. They do not compare object values.

must be provided instead. However, we must provide an architecture for the comparison methods to exist within, rather than arbitrarily adding methods when needed.

There are two basic architectures for dealing with order relations, the internal view and the external view. For the internal view, order relations are an issue for the type of the data. The class implementing the data type has to declare one (or more) methods for testing the order of two data items of the class. The external view is to make use of *method objects* for testing the order between two objects of a given class. A method object is an object that has no data, just methods, and preferably only a single method. Such an object is basically a server to the rest of the system; such an object exists just to service requests for calls to the order testing methods that the method object encapsulates. The two viewpoints are not mutually exclusive, indeed they can and should both be present since they are useful in different circumstances. Methods objects, for example, enable us to develop classes and methods that are parameterized on the relation. This is an important facility.

An important goal of both the internal and external views is to allow objects to be compared without having to know which specific class they are an instance of (although the two objects being compared are usually expected to be instance of the same class). This is achieved by separating the protocol for making a comparison, using interface types, from the implementation of the comparison operation needed for specific kinds of objects. One important consequence is that *generic* code can be written to work with different kinds of object, without that code having to be re-written or duplicated to deal with different ways of comparing different kinds of object. For example, it should be possible to sort the objects held in a container without the sorting algorithm having to know what kind of objects are actually being sorted.

The J2SDK makes use of the internal view by providing an interface called `Comparable`, which declares a method called `compareTo`. Classes representing data types can implement the interface and provide a `compareTo` method that can be called directly on an instance object, using the method argument to provide an object to make the comparison with. Class `String` and subclasses of `Number`, such as `Integer` and `Double`, implement `Comparable`, while various methods in Collections make use of it. For internal completeness the ADS package provides its own version of the `Comparable` interface that makes the same declaration as the J2SDK version:

```
package ADS ;
/**
 *  The interface conformed to by classes that represent data with a
 *  total ordering.
 *
 *  @version 1.0 1999.09.11
 *  @author Russel Winder
 */
public interface Comparable {
    /**
     *  Compare the value of this item with the value of the parameter
     *  and return:
     *
     *  <PRE>
     *  -ve if this value is less than the parameter.
     *  0 if this value is equal to the parameter.
```

```
    *   +ve if this value is greater than the parameter.
    *   </PRE>
    */
   public int compareTo(Object o) ;
}
```

Objects of classes that implement `Comparable`, such as `Integer`, can be compared in the following way:

```
Integer i1 = new Integer (3) ;
Integer i2 = new Integer (4) ;
if (i1.compareTo(i2) == 0) {
   ...
}
```

The `compareTo` method provides the order relation and delivers a negative value if `i1` is less than `i2`, 0 if the two are equal and a positive value if `i1` is greater than `i2`. `CompareTo` has also been seen for comparing `String` objects in Chapter 2 and in Chapter 3.

The external view architecture is to make use of classes providing method objects implementing the order relations. There are two ways that these classes can be defined, either as individual top-level classes or as nested top-level classes defined within the type (class or interface) they relate to. The latter is clearly preferred if we are in control of the underlying types but the former is necessary if we cannot change those types.

Both Collections and JGL support the method object approach in addition to making use of the internally provided order relations but it is far more extensively supported in JGL. The designers of JGL made a design decision to emphasize the approach since it fitted better with their library architecture. What they have done, in fact, is to formalize the whole concept of method objects. JGL defines the concepts of `UnaryFunction` and `BinaryFunction` as interfaces. These define what it means to be a method object providing one parameter and two parameter methods. These are also `UnaryPredicate` and `BinaryPredicate` which define method objects (of one and two parameters) that deliver boolean values. Order relations are clearly `BinaryPredicates`. This infrastructure is not something that Collections has gone in for. It just defines the notion of `Comparator` which is an interface for defining binary predicates that are order relations.

For ADS, we take the simpler approach and define a class `Comparator` to represent the order relations.:

```
package ADS ;
/**
 *  An interface defining the necessary properties to be deemed
 *  to be a <CODE>Comparator</CODE>.
 *
 *  @version 1.0 1997.07.02
 *  @author Russel Winder
 */
public interface Comparator {
  /**
    *  The relation that this <CODE>Comparator</CODE> represents.
    */
  boolean relation(Object a, Object b) ;
}
```

!

Any type that represents an ADT whose elements have a total ordering defined should conform to `Comparable`.

The sole method required of a type conforming to `Comparator` is `relation`, a method that compares the values of the two parameters according to the order relation the `Comparator` represents, returning a `boolean`. A `Comparator` compliant object must represent one and only one of the six possible relations. Notice that the parameters to `relation` are both of type `Object`, meaning that methods implementing `relation` will need to cast the parameter types to that needed to do the comparison required.

12.7.1 The First Implementation Approach

We now have to provide implementations of the six relations for a given data type. One way of doing this is to define a class for each of the relations. So for `Integers`, for example, we would define six classes. Since we have no access to the `Integer` implementation, we can only define top-level classes so we name them in a way that shows what their applicability is. The six classes are:

IntegerLessThan	IntegerLessThanOrEqualTo
IntegerEqualTo	IntegerNotEqualTo
IntegerGreaterThan	IntegerGreaterThanOrEqualTo

This is the implementation of the 'less than' relation:

```
package ADS ;
/**
 *  A class to represent the less than order relation between
 *  <CODE>Integer</CODE> types.
 *
 *  @see Integer
 *  @version 1.0 1997.07.02
 *  @author Russel Winder
 */
public class IntegerLessThanComparator implements Comparator {
  /**
   *  The relation that this <CODE>Comparator</CODE> represents.
   *  Compares the two parameters according to the relation.
   *
   *  @exception ComparatorParameterException if the types of
   *  the parameters are not compatible with <CODE>Integer</CODE>.
   */
  public final boolean relation(final Object a, final Object b) {
    if (! (a instanceof Integer) || ! (b instanceof Integer))
      throw new ComparatorParameterException() ;
    return execute((Integer)a, (Integer)b) ;
  }
  /**
   *  The static form of the relation that this
   *  <CODE>Comparator</CODE> represents.  Compares the two
   *  parameters according to the relation.
   */
  public static boolean execute(final Integer a, final Integer b) {
    return a.intValue() < b.intValue() ;
  }
}
```

The other five classes are essentially identical but with the operation in the `execute` method changed to the correct order relation between `int`s. In the implementations of the order relations, we have made use of an exception called `ComparatorParameterErrorException`. We need to declare it:

```
package ADS ;
/**
 *   A class to represent the exception of attempting to compare types
 *   of data that the <CODE>Comparator</CODE> was not designed for.
 *
 *   @see Comparator
 *   @version 1.0 1997.07.02
 *   @author Russel Winder
 */
public class ComparatorParameterException
  extends RuntimeException {
  /**
   *   The exception without a message.
   */
  public ComparatorParameterException() {
    super() ;
  }
  /**
   *   The exception with a message.
   */
  public ComparatorParameterException(final String s) {
    super(s) ;
  }
}
```

We should note here that we do not actually have to define separate comparator classes for `Integer`, `Double` and the other numeric classes, as it is possible to work with the methods declared by the superclass `Number` to perform the comparisons needed. Indeed this is exactly how JGL defines things. However, in order to understand how to implement things in this way, we would need a much more detailed knowledge of a number of classes from J2SDK. We don't propose to go into this detail here since, in some sense, it is peripheral to the core argument, but instead suggest that you investigate this issue at a later date.

The implementation of the order relation method object class given above clearly begs the following question: "Why have we defined things with two methods, a static method that does the work and an instance method which just calls the static method?" By having a static method we are able to make use of the order relation without having to actually create a comparator object. So for example:

```
Integer i1 = new Integer (3) ;
Integer i2 = new Integer (4) ;
if (IntegerLessThan.execute(i1, i2)) {
  ...
}
```

The static method can also be used if we do have a comparator object, so we have not lost functionality:

```
Comparator c = new IntegerLessThanComparator () ;
Integer i1 = new Integer (3) ;
Integer i2 = new Integer (4) ;
if (c.execute(i1, i2)) {
  ...
}
```

However, in order to have guarantees (i.e. be able to make assumptions), `Comparator` requires conforming classes to have a method `relation` which can be used as follows:

```
Comparator c = new IntegerLessThanComparator () ;
Integer i1 = new Integer (3) ;
Integer i2 = new Integer (4) ;
if (c.relation(i1, i2)) {
  ...
}
```

So the implementation is balancing the use of interfaces to provide guarantees and the use of both static and non-static methods to increase functionality. Comparators in Collections and JGL do not provide this extra functionality but require there to be an actual comparator object.

The following program shows the beginnings of a test program for the comparators that we have developed:

```
import ADS.Comparator ;
import ADS.IntegerLessThanComparator ;
public class testComparator {
  public static void main(final String[] argv) {
    //
    //  Create a couple of Integers to show the Comparator at
    //  work.
    //
    Integer a = new Integer (1) ;
    Integer b = new Integer (10) ;
    //
    //  Create a Comparator representing the < relation.
    //
    Comparator tester = new IntegerLessThanComparator () ;
    //
    //  Show the Comparator being used to compare two Integer
    //  values.
    //
    boolean testResult = tester.relation(a, b) ;
    System.out.println(testResult) ;
    //
    //  Show the use of the static form.
    //
    testResult = IntegerLessThanComparator.execute(b, a) ;
    System.out.println(testResult) ;
  }
}
```

Note that in the code fragments and in the program above we have made the comparator method object variable be of type `Comparator` and not an `IntegerLessThanComparator`. There are two intimately related reasons for this:

1. Semantically, we want to use type `Comparator` as much as possible to make code independent of concrete classes such as `IntegerLessThanComparator`. This avoids writing code, or creating containers, that will only work correctly with one class of object.

2. An `IntegerLessThanComparator` may have more methods available than a `Comparator` since it only conforms to `Comparator`. By giving the variables the type `Comparator`, we are ensuring that none of the extra methods are available to the application code.

Thus, we are supporting design intention by employing the polymorphism between these types. Of course this only works between types that have a conformance or inheritance relationship, but then that is exactly what we need in order to implement our container classes. The code of a container class implementation only needs to use the `Comparator` type to make comparisons and not any of the specialized classes that implement the type.

The major problem with such a design is the large number of class names and files that are required, though this is not really a serious problem.

We have, in fact, uncovered a feature here that would be part of our architecture if we choose the above function object design as an architectural feature of the ADS package. The naming of the methods — in this case using `execute` as the name of the static member of a function object — would be the standard naming convention for all function objects in the package.

12.7.2 An Alternative Implementation Approach

An alternative design, though many would say a less safe and less object-oriented one, is to define a single class responsible for managing all the relations. In this design, a `Comparator` compliant object would have to remember which relation it represented, so some state would be needed. Because of this, some constants are required to represent the different possible states. Therefore, for this design, we must extend the `Comparator` definition to provide these constants:

```
package ADS ;
/**
 *  An interface defining the necessary properties to be deemed
 *  to be a <CODE>Comparator</CODE>.
 *
 *  @version 1.0 1997.07.02
 *  @author Russel Winder
 */
public interface Comparator {
  //
  //  The constants that define the possible states that a
  //  <CODE>Comparator</CODE> can be in.
  //
  static final int lessThan              = 0 ;
  static final int lessThanOrEqualTo     = 1 ;
  static final int equalTo               = 2 ;
  static final int notEqualTo            = 3 ;
  static final int greaterThan           = 4 ;
  static final int greaterThanOrEqualTo  = 5 ;
  /**
    *  Compares the two parameters according to the relation.
    *
    *  @exception ComparatorParameterException if the type of
    *  the data is not compatible with the type expected by the
    *  <CODE>Comparator</CODE>.
    *
    *  @exception ComparatorRelationUndefinedException if the
    *  representation of the relation is not an allowed one.  Is
    *  raised at construction time if the argument is not a valid
    *  representation of a relation.  It can also be raised at
    *  runtime but this is impossible (!).
    */
  boclean relation(Object a, Object b) ;
}
```

Given this, we can construct the following as a `Comparator` of `Integer`s:

```
package ADS ;
/**
 *  A class to represent order relations between <CODE>Integer</CODE>
 *  types.
 *
 *  @see Comparator
 *  @see Integer
 *  @version 1.0 1997.07.02
 *  @author Russel Winder
 */
public class IntegerComparator implements Comparator {
  /**
   *  The variable that remembers which relation we represent.  This
   *  variable is final so that it can only be set by initialization.
   *  Since there is no initializer here, it must be assigned in the
   *  constructor.  NB <CODE>IntegerComparator</CODE>s are immutable.
   */
  private final int theRelation ;
  /**
   *  Construct a <CODE>Comparator</CODE> of <CODE>Integer</CODE>s
   *  ensuring that we represent a valid order relation.  This method
   *  ensures that the object cannot represent a non-existant
   *  relation.  I.e. it ensures that the <CODE>int</int> which
   *  determines the relation is not out of range.
   *
   *  @param c An <CODE>int</CODE> representing the desired
   *  relation.
   *
   *  @exception ComparatorRelationUndefinedException if the
   *  parameter is not a valid relation.
   */
  public IntegerComparator(final int c) {
    if ((c < lessThan) || (c > greaterThanOrEqualTo))
      throw new ComparatorRelationUndefinedException() ;
    theRelation = c ;
  }
  /**
   *  The relation that this <CODE>Comparator</CODE> represents.
   *  Compares the two parameters according to the relation.
   *
   *  @exception ComparatorParameterException if the parameters
   *  are not both <CODE>Integer</CODE>.
   *
   *  @exception ComparatorRelationUndefinedException if there is an
   *  attempt to compare with a relation whose index is out of
   *  range.  (This can never happen!)
   */
  public final boolean relation(final Object a, final Object b) {
    if (! (a instanceof Integer) || ! (b instanceof Integer))
      throw new ComparatorParameterException() ;
    switch (theRelation) {
    case lessThan:
      return ((Integer)a).intValue() < ((Integer)b).intValue() ;
    case lessThanOrEqualTo:
      return ((Integer)a).intValue() <= ((Integer)b).intValue() ;
    case equalTo:
      return ((Integer)a).intValue() == ((Integer)b).intValue() ;
    case notEqualTo:
      return ((Integer)a).intValue() != ((Integer)b).intValue() ;
    case greaterThan:
      return ((Integer)a).intValue() > ((Integer)b).intValue() ;
    case greaterThanOrEqualTo:
      return ((Integer)a).intValue() >= ((Integer)b).intValue() ;
    default: //  This can never happen.
```

```
            throw new ComparatorRelationUndefinedException() ;
        }
    }
    /**
     * Redefinition of equals so that two
     * <CODE>IntegerComparator</CODE>s are equal if they represent
     * the same order relation (as opposed to equals testing if two
     * items are the same object which is the default test).
     *
     * @param o The object to compare ourself with.
     */
    public synchronized boolean equals(Object o) {
        return (o != null) && (o instanceof IntegerComparator) &&
           (theRelation == ((IntegerComparator)o).theRelation) ;
    }
}
```

As a comparator object now needs to store which relation it represents, it is no longer possible to provide a static method that can be called to compare objects, and a comparator object must be created. We have also introduced another exception class to deal with an attempt to create an invalid relation (class `ComparatorRelationshipUndefinedException`), so it also needs to be declared. However, since it is identical in structure to the definition of the existing `ComparatorParameterErrorException` we do not show it here.

We can make use of this alternative comparator class in the following sort of way — which is essentially exactly the same as the previous test program (Page 344), except for the way in which the comparator object is created:

```
import ADS.Comparator ;
import ADS.IntegerComparator ;
class testIntegerComparator {
  public static void main(final String[] args) {
    //
    //  Create a couple of Integers to show the Comparator at
    //  work.
    //
    Integer a = new Integer (1) ;
    Integer b = new Integer (10) ;
    //
    //  Create a Comparator representing the < relation.
    //
    Comparator tester = new IntegerComparator (Comparator.lessThan) ;
    //
    //  Show the Comparator being used to compare two Integer
    //  values.
    //
    boolean testResult = tester.relation(a, b) ;
    System.out.println(testResult) ;
  }
}
```

The choice of relation that the `Comparator` compliant object represents is specified as a parameter to the constructor rather than in the name of the class.

We note that the two implementations of the order relations presented so far are in fact intimately related, though it may seem strange to say this. In the latter implementation approach, we store a datum that determines which method is executed when asked to perform a check — in essence this datum encodes the type of the order relation. In the inheritance-based approach, we are using the inheritance system and the language supported typing and dynamic method binding to encode the same order relation type information into an object: the dynamic binding determines which relation is executed whereas in the stored datum case the programmer has implemented the method dispatch manually. It is this last point in particular which is considered to undermine the principles of object-oriented design, the main reason being that introducing a new relation (if there were any) would involve editing existing finished code.

12.7.3   A Third Variant Implementation

In fact, the last design misses the opportunity for the class to be a 'server of relations', so that an instance of the class could be asked to return the value of any relation. It is still important for the architecture of the package that the `Comparator` represents a specific relation, so the constants and the state are still required. The following shows the design:

```
package ADS ;
/**
 *   A class to represent an order relation between <CODE>String</CODE>
 *   types.
 *
 *   @see Comparator
 *   @see String
 *   @version 1.1 1999.11.21
 *   @author Russel Winder
 */
public class StringComparator implements Comparator {
  /**
   *   The relation that this <CODE>Comparator</CODE> represents is
   *   determined by this stored datum.  This variable is final so that
   *   it can only be set by initialization.  Since there is no
   *   initializer here, it must be assigned in the constructor.  NB
   *   <CODE>StringComparator</CODE>s are immutable.
   */
  private final int theRelation ;
  /**
   *   The constructor method of <CODE>StringComparator</CODE>s.  This
   *   method ensures that the object cannot represent a non-existant
   *   relation, i.e. it ensures that the <CODE>int</CODE> which
   *   determines the relation is not out of range.
   *
   *   @param c An <CODE>int</CODE> representing the desired
   *   relation.
   *
   *   @exception ComparatorRelationUndefinedException if the
   *   parameter is not a valid relation.
   */
  public StringComparator(final int c) {
    if ((c < lessThan) || (c > greaterThanOrEqualTo))
      throw new ComparatorRelationUndefinedException() ;
    theRelation = c ;
  }
  /**
   *   The relation that this <CODE>Comparator</CODE> represents.
   *   Compares the two parameters according to the relation.
   *
   *   @exception ComparatorParameterException if the parameters
   *   are not both <CODE>String</CODE>.
   *
   *   @exception ComparatorRelationUndefinedException if there is an
   *   attempt to compare with a relation whose index is out of
```

```
 *  range.  (This can never happen!)
 */
public final boolean relation(final Object a, final Object b) {
  if (! (a instanceof String) || ! (b instanceof String))
    throw new ComparatorParameterException() ;
  switch (theRelation) {
  case lessThan:
    return lessThan(a, b) ;
  case lessThanOrEqualTo:
    return lessThanOrEqualTo(a, b) ;
  case equalTo:
    return equalTo(a, b) ;
  case notEqualTo:
    return notEqualTo(a, b) ;
  case greaterThan:
    return greaterThan(a, b) ;
  case greaterThanOrEqualTo:
    return greaterThanOrEqualTo(a, b) ;
  default: // This cannot happen!
    throw new ComparatorRelationUndefinedException() ;
  }
}
/**
 *  The less than relation that this <CODE>Comparator</CODE> can
 *  test for.
 */
public static boolean lessThan(final String a, final String b) {
  return a.compareTo(b) < 0 ;
}
/**
 *  The less than or equal relation that this
 *  <CODE>Comparator</CODE> can test for.
 */
public static boolean lessThanOrEqualTo(final String a,
                                        final String b) {
  return a.compareTo(b) <= 0 ;
}
/**
 *  The equal to relation that this <CODE>Comparator</CODE> can
 *  test for.
 */
public static boolean equalTo(final String a, final String b) {
  return a.equals(b) ;
}
/**
 *  The not equal to relation that this <CODE>Comparator</CODE>
 *  can test for.
 */
public static boolean notEqualTo(final String a, final String b) {
  return ! a.equals(b) ;
}
/**
 *  The greater than relation that this <CODE>Comparator</CODE>
 *  can test for.
 */
public static boolean greaterThan(final String a, final String b) {
  return a.compareTo(b) > 0 ;
}
/**
 *  The greater than or equal to relation that this
 *  <CODE>Comparator</CODE> can test for.
 */
public static boolean greaterThanOrEqualTo(final String a,
                                           final String b) {
  return a.compareTo(b) >= 0 ;
}
```

```
/**
 *   The equals method for this <CODE>Comparator</CODE>.  This method
 *   is overridden in order to ensure that
 *   <CODE>StringComparator</CODE> equality is a semantic operation,
 *   i.e. the operation represented is the same, rather than an
 *   object equality operation.
 *
 *   @param o The object to compare ourself with.
 */
public synchronized boolean equals(final Object o) {
  return (o != null) && (o instanceof StringComparator) &&
    (theRelation == ((StringComparator)o).theRelation) ;
}
}
```

The original way of using these order relation objects, calling the `relation` method, is still possible with this definition but we have restored the ability to use static methods to access the relations (although it should be noted that the static methods do not throw a `ComparatorParameterErrorException` if the argument objects are not `Strings`) :

```
import ADS.Comparator ;
import ADS.StringComparator ;
class testStringComparator {
  public static void main(final String[] args) {
    //
    //  Create a couple of Strings to show the Comparator at
    //  work.
    //
    String a = new String ("Hello") ;
    String b = new String ("World") ;
    //
    //  Create a Comparator representing the < relation.
    //
    Comparator tester = new StringComparator (Comparator.lessThan);
    //
    //  Show the Comparator being used to compare two String
    //  values.  Nothing different here from previously.
    //
    boolean testResult = tester.relation(a, b) ;
    System.out.println(testResult) ;
    //
    //  We can also use the relations without reference to an
    //  object.
    //
    testResult = StringComparator.lessThanOrEqualTo(a, b) ;
    System.out.println(testResult) ;
    //
    //  The following statement would not work because tester is a
    //  Comparator and Comparators do not have the appropriate
    //  methods.
    //
    //    testResult = tester.lessThanOrEqualTo(a, b) ;
    //
    //  If we want to do this sort of thing we must use a variable
    //  of the type and not the interface.
    //
    StringComparator anotherTester
      = new StringComparator (Comparator.lessThan) ;
    testResult = anotherTester.lessThanOrEqualTo(a, b) ;
    System.out.println(testResult) ;
  }
}
```

Objects of this class can act not just as servers of a remembered relation but as servers of any named relation. The fractional loss of efficiency (having to make an extra method call) when executing the `relation` method is really not worth worrying about.

12.7.4 Which Design is Best?

The question is, of course: Which is really the better design, the 'multi-class' or 'single class' one?

We could argue that the implementations of `IntegerComparator` and `String-Comparator` are not good ones in comparison to the 'multi-class' implementation of the `Integer` order relations because they involve code that requires careful editing if changes are made: care must be taken to get the order relation selection labels correct and synchronized in `Comparator`, `IntegerComparator` and `StringComparator`. In effect, this argument is saying that the 'single class' design does not have good maintainability since these files need to be edited in order to provide new relations. In the 'multi-class' design, new relations can be added simply by creating a new class, no other code needs editing: there are no variables in the class and no `switch` statements and 'constants' that have to be kept in synchronization should any changes be made. However, we should note that whilst this is a good argument in general, it is weak in this particular case since there are only six possible order relations.

The apparent disadvantage of the 'multi-class' way of doing things is that a good class naming strategy is required since the number of classes and the number of source files can get quite large. Having said this, the name problem also exists for the 'single class' design since there must be selector labels for each relation. It seems, then, that the big benefit for the 'single class' design is only that a relation testing service independent of an object can be set up. Hence, the 'many class' design might be the only sensible architecture.

Many present what is effectively the same argument as above by saying that using a `switch` statement in this situation is not the 'object-oriented way', inheritance is the object-oriented way of handling these situations and therefore the 'multi-class' solution is better. This could, however, be labelled the 'religious dogma' argument since it does not explain why the design choice is being made.

As noted earlier, in the JGL, there are types `UnaryPredicate` and `BinaryPredicate` from which `Comparators` are built. So for example, if we were using the JGL as our base library, and the 'many classes' architecture, `IntegerLessThanComparator` would look like:

```
package ADS ;
import com.objectspace.jgl.BinaryPredicate ;
/**
 *   A class to represent the less than order relation between
 *   <CODE>Integer</CODE> types.
 *
 *   @version 1.0 1997.07.02
 *   @author Russel Winder
 */
public class IntegerLessThanComparator implements BinaryPredicate {
  /**
```

```
    *   The relation that this <CODE>Comparator</CODE> represents.
    *   Compares the two parameters according to the relation.
    *
    *   @exception ComparatorParameterException if the type of
    *   the data is not <CODE>Integer</CODE>.
    */
   public final boolean execute(final Object a, final Object b) {
     if (! (a instanceof Integer) || ! (b instanceof Integer))
       throw new ComparatorParameterException() ;
     return ((Integer)a).intValue() < ((Integer)b).intValue() ;
   }
   /**
    *   The static form of the relation that this
    *   <CODE>Comparator</CODE> represents.  Compares the two
    *   parameters according to the relation.
    */
   public static boolean execute(final Integer a, final Integer b) {
     IntegerLessThanComparator c = new IntegerLessThanComparator();
     return c.execute(a, b) ;
   }
 }
```

At this point, we could argue that because JGL has chosen the 'multi class' way of doing things, it must be the right way but that would be abdicating our responsibility of understanding why. Knowing that the JGL has chosen this design, and also that they have the more general binary predicates rather than just comparators, does give us some more information. With a class as general as `BinaryPredicate`, it is impossible to imagine enumerating all possible predicates in a single class. We would be mixing very different sorts of predicate into the same class simply because the architecture said we had to. Also, the `switch` statement would become massive. In this circumstance the 'multi-class' solution is the only feasible one.

Thus, the 'multi-class' approach turns out to be the only sensible library architecture.

12.8   The Biggest Question of All

In the previous section we addressed the issue of comparing data values in the package and came up with a component of the library architecture. Whether it was apparent or not, the issue that was being addressed was one of abstraction and representation. This is, of course, a core issue for all packages: what are the abstractions and how are the abstractions to be represented in concrete forms? For a package such as this one, providing as it does container classes that are intended to implement ADTs, this is a more than usually important question!

The core of the problem is that there are three ways that we could present the abstraction and provide concrete representations. Let us label these: abstraction by conformance, abstraction by inheritance and abstraction by association.

Abstraction by Conformance: The ADT is represented by an interface and the concrete representations are separate classes which conform to the interface.

Abstraction by Inheritance: The ADT is represented by an abstract class and the concrete representations are subclasses of the abstract class.

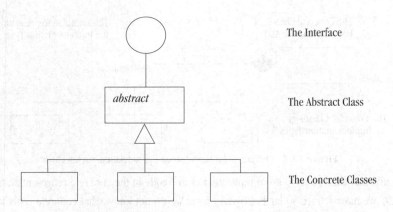

The Interface

The Abstract Class

The Concrete Classes

Figure 12.1 A paradigm for a package architecture, merging the 'abstraction by conformance' and 'abstraction by inheritance' ideas

Abstraction by Association: The ADT is represented by a class (the ADT class) and the concrete representations are separate classes managed by the ADT class.

The conformance and inheritance mechanisms are, in principle, the same basic architecture. They both have the ADT represented by a interface or class that cannot be instantiated and the concrete representations as separate classes. The difference is that with the conformance mechanism, the ADT, being represented by an interface, contains no implementation information whatsoever. In comparison, the inheritance model is used where the abstract class holds some of the implementation information — where the algorithms are identical no matter what the actual concrete representation. In fact, the most usual way to proceed using these architectures is to use an hybrid. This is exactly what Collections does. Interfaces are used to represent the abstract ADTs and then abstract classes that conform to the interface collect together all the implementation that is common to all variations of the abstraction. Finally there are the concrete classes which inherit from the abstract class and provide the final representation of the ADT. The J2SDK documentation on Collections presents the details. Figure 12.1 presents an UML diagram showing the basic architectural structure used by Collections.

This point about commonality of algorithms for the ADTs is central to the third architectural mechanism, abstraction by association: the ADT class is concrete, can be instantiated and contains all the algorithms that are identical no matter what the representation of storage is. The different concrete representations are handled by separate storage classes all conforming to a common interface which is used by the ADT class. Figure 12.2 presents an UML diagram showing this architectural structure.

All this is relatively abstract in itself, which actually is exactly as it should be since we are trying to define the architecture of the package. However, without examples, it can be difficult to appreciate what is really being said here. We can present one example at this point. ADS will be following the Collections style (Figure 12.1) of using abstract classes to support code reuse. The principle here is that the code common to all concrete representations of an ADT can be gathered together into a

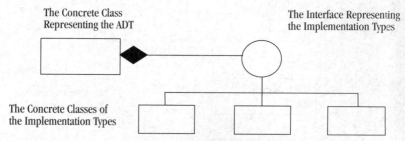

The Concrete Class
Representing the ADT

The Interface Representing
the Implementation Types

The Concrete Classes of
the Implementation Types

Figure 12.2 A Paradigm for the 'abstract by association' architecture.

single abstract class so as to avoid replication of this code in the concrete representation classes.
The ADT we have defined so far is Container. We do not know what concrete representations
there are as yet but we can already define some common and default code. We define the
AbstractContainer as follows:

```
package ADS ;
/**
 *  An abstract <CODE>Container</CODE>.
 *
 *  @version 1.1 1999.08.23
 *  @author Russel Winder
 */
public abstract class AbstractContainer implements Container {
  /**
   *  Remove the entire contents of the <CODE>Container</CODE>.
   */
  public abstract void makeEmpty() ;
  /**
   *  Determine whether the <CODE>Container</CODE> is an empty one.
   */
  public boolean isEmpty() {
    return size() <= 0 ;
  }
  /**
   *  Return the number of items in the <CODE>Container</CODE>.
   */
  public int size() {
    int count = 0 ;
    for (Iterator i = iterator() ; !i.atEnd() ; i.advance(), ++count)
      ;
    return count ;
  } ;
  /**
   *  Compare this <CODE>Container</CODE> with another and determine
   *  whether they represent the same value, i.e. have the same item
   *  values in the <CODE>Container</CODE>.
   *
   *  <P> <CODE>equals</CODE> is made into semantic equality
   *  rather than an object identity equality.  Equality for
   *  <CODE>Object</CODE>s is defined to be that the two
   *  <CODE>Object</CODE>s are the same <CODE>Object</CODE>.  For
   *  <CODE>Container</CODE>s, we want to define equality to be that
   *  they contain exactly the same elements.
   */
  public boolean equals(Object o) {
    //  We are always equal to ourself!
    if (this == o)
      return true ;
    //  If o is null or it is not some form of Container or if it is a
    //  Container but it's size is different from ourselves then it
```

```
      //  cannot be equal to us.  Rely on left to right evaluation of
      //  the or expression.
      if ((o == null) ||
          ! (o instanceof Container) ||
          (size() != ((Container)o).size()))
        return false ;
      //  We know that we are both Containers of the same size, so check
      //  whether our elements are all the same.  By iterating over
      //  them.
      Iterator i1 = iterator() ;
      Iterator i2 = ((Container)o).iterator() ;
      for ( ; !i1.atEnd() && !i2.atEnd() ; i1.advance(), i2.advance()) {
        Object o1 = i1.get() ;
        Object o2 = i2.get() ;
        if ((o1 == null) || (o2 == null) || !o1.equals(o2))
          return false ;
      }
      return i1.atEnd() && i2.atEnd() ;
  } ;
  /**
   *  Determine whether we have the value represented by the
   *  parameter <CODE>Object</CODE> in us.  Uses linear search.
   *
   *  @exception AccessEmptyContainerException if there are no
   *  items in the <CODE>Container</CODE>.
   */
  public boolean contains(Object o) {
    if (o == null)
      return false ;
    for (Iterator i = iterator() ; !i.atEnd() ; i.advance()) {
      if (i.get().equals(o))
        return true ;
    }
    return false ;
  } ;
  /**
   *  Add an element to the <CODE>Container</CODE>.
   */
  public abstract void add(Object o) ;
  /**
   *  Remove an element of a given value from the
   *  <CODE>Container</CODE> if it is in the <CODE>Container</CODE>.
   *
   *  @return whether the item was actually in the
   *  <CODE>Container</CODE>.
   *
   *  @exception AccessEmptyContainerException if there are no
   *  items in the <CODE>Container</CODE>.
   */
  public abstract boolean remove(Object o) ;
  /**
   *  Deliver up a complete shallow copy of the
   *  <CODE>Container</CODE>.
   */
  public abstract Object clone() ;
  /**
   *  Deliver up a <CODE>String</CODE> representation of the
   *  <CODE>Container</CODE>.
   */
  public String toString() {
    StringBuffer sb = new StringBuffer () ;
    sb.append("[ ") ;
    for (Iterator i = iterator() ; !i.atEnd() ; i.advance()) {
      sb.append(i.get().toString() + ' ') ;
    }
    sb.append(']') ;
```

```
    return sb.toString() ;
  }
  /**
   * Deliver up an iterator over all the items in the
   * <CODE>Container</CODE>.
   */
  public abstract Iterator iterator() ;
}
```

Probably the most important thing to observe from this is how much we can define in terms of the, as yet undefined, iterators. We have defined a number of methods in very general terms that will apply to many of the concrete representations thereby removing the need for them to define these methods. Concrete representation classes are free to override any of the definitions so we have lost no freedom of expression.

It may not be obvious but it is a sensible requirement that we allow the contents of any container to be compared with the contents of any other container even if they are of different concrete classes. The rationale here is that as far as an application is concerned, it should not have to care whether or not two containers have the same representation in order to be able to see whether they contain the same elements. This means we must ensure that equality testing is implemented between two `Containers`. This immediately means that equality testing has to be undertaken using iterators to avoid any connection with explicit representation. Again, it may not be obvious but the strategy of using iterators to implement equality testing means that the implementation of the equals method will be the same for all concrete container classes. Fortunately, all `Containers` must have iterators.

12.9 More Exceptional Material

Containers of all types have a size and, in particular, they can sometimes be empty. What happens if we try and remove something from an empty container? Also, some containers are of fixed size; what happens if we try and add more data to a 'full' container? Finally, what happens if someone tries to retrieve an element not actually present in the container. All of these situations are errors that require the application to be properly informed. As always, exceptions are the vehicle for doing this informing. Thus, three more exceptions are declared for the classes in the package to make use of when a container is used when it is an inappropriate state:

```
AccessEmptyContainerException
ContainerCapacityExceededException
IndexOutOfBoundsException.
```

All three have identical structure to `ComparatorParameterErrorException` shown earlier so there is no point in showing what is essentially identical code here (the names of the class change of course). In fact all the exception classes introduced within ADS are essentially identical but with different names. There is, therefore, no point in presenting the implementations of all of them. So whilst we will be introducing new exceptions to the ADS package as we introduce new classes but will not be presenting the source code for them explicitly.

We make all of three of the above exceptions `RuntimeExceptions` rather than `Exceptions`, so they are unchecked exceptions (ones that do not have to be explicitly caught by the application code) rather than checked exceptions. This has been done for a number of reasons, the basic argument is: Control over the use of the containers is entirely within the application, there is no outside agency that can affect the behaviour of the container. The algorithms within the application should never allow the attempt to access an empty container so exceptions of this sort should never, ever happen. It would be messy and irritating to have to protect against an exception for each and every access to any of the containers.

We could have chosen to use the standard `java.util.NoSuchElement` exception to represent the exception of attempting to remove data from an empty container, instead of declaring `AccessEmptyContainerException`, but we have not, we have chosen to declare the new exception. In part this is an arbitrary decision but the guide used was consistency: this package declares some exceptions to handle improper behaviour and so should declare its own exceptions for *all* the improper behaviours that can be generated within the package.

2.10 Documentation and Style

It is probably obvious to you (but looking at some packages and libraries some people do not believe this) that a package should be coded with a single code layout style. The major elements of the style include:

Where should { and } be placed?

What are the indentation rules?

There is no one correct style of code layout. There are just good styles (ones that are consistent and used consistently throughout) and bad styles (inconsistent and used inconsistently). We believe that the style we have used throughout this book is a paradigm of *a* good style.

Another element of style is commenting. Many programmers think that commenting is for wimps, they often argue that source code is self-explanatory. Fortunately, such attitudes amongst programmers are getting outdated, outmoded, unfashionable and rarer. Source code should be well documented and this is especially true for libraries.

As well as commenting source code, there should be user manuals, or in the case of libraries, programmer manuals. In the past, it has always been a problem maintaining code and manuals separately. People are increasingly believing that user/programmer documentation and source code should be the same document, so that text that is the manual should be in the file that contains the source code. This is exemplified by the Literate Programming community, who championed the idea of having coding comments and manual comments in the source code and then generating the executable and the documentation from the same source code. The Java approach follows exactly this principle.

As introduced in Section 2.7, Page 33, source code comments use the `//` or `/*...*/` type comments and `/**...*/` indicates a documentation comment. As we have already seen above, these different types of comments are used in different places for different purposes.

When the code is finished, the JDK utility program `javadoc` is used to generate, automatically, a set of Web pages that are the manual. This technique is not wholly useful for user manuals and such-like documents; they still need to be written separately since they must be written for the users from their perspective, not from the perspective of the code. However, for system manuals and maintenance manuals, particularly for libraries, this system for automatically generating manual pages is an enormous improvement over what many people are used to.

In this book, we have tried to show our code as a paradigm of an appropriate programming style. This is only one of many appropriate styles. The rule is to follow one appropriate style throughout a project — there is no problem changing from one style to another when moving between applications or libraries but for a given project a standard and uniform style should be used.

The HTML documentation for the ADS library is as http:// www.dcs.kcl.ac.uk/ DevJavaSoft/ ADS_Manual/.

12.11 Summary

This chapter has set the ground work for the design and implementation of the ADS package. A core architecture has been defined, emphasizing the need to avoid making assumptions about how clients of the package will want to use the components of the package. A core part of this package is the mechanism to be used for comparing objects stored in containers. The discussion of different ways of implementing comparators has highlighted the kinds of issues and trade-offs that the package designer confronts. The issue of how to use inheritance and association to handle the relationships between the classes in the package turns out to be the cornerstone of the architecture.

The lesson to be learnt is that the effort in carefully thinking through the possible design options and considering the consequences of each alternative, will be repaid in the future by identifying the most robust design for your code.

The chapter emphasized yet again the need for good layout style and documentation. If you expect others to use your library you must get the documentation right or you will fail to gain the trust of your users.

Having covered the architecture 'rules', the following chapters get on with the contents of the package. A summary diagram of the ADS package can be found in Appendix K, Page 979.

Self-review Questions

Self-review 12.1 Why should we construct libraries?

Self-review 12.2 What is the relationship between class, package and library?

Self-review 12.3 Why is the environment variable CLASSPATH important?

Self-review 12.4 What is an architecture?

Self-review 12.5 Why is it important to avoid assumptions in the implementation of a library?

Self-review 12.6 Why is it important to make assumptions in the implementation of a library?

Self-review 12.7 What is an iterator? Why are they important?

Self-review 12.8 What is an order relation? Why are they important?

Self-review 12.9 What are the three ways of implementing order relations?

Self-review 12.10 Does Collections use 'abstraction by association'?

Self-review 12.11 Does JGL use 'abstraction by inheritance'?

Self-review 12.12 When is it appropriate for a method in a library class to throw an exception?

Self-review 12.13 What kinds of exception should a client of a library class be expected to deal with?

Self-review 12.14 How are Java documentation comments used?

Programming Exercises

Exercise 12.1 Write a full test plan and test programs for the six Integer comparators and the six String comparators.

Exercise 12.2 Extend the program developed in Exercise 12.1 to work with the comparators from JGL rather than ADS.

Exercise 12.3 Using each of the 3 architectures proposed in Section 12.7.1, Section 12.7.2 and Section 12.7.3, write a Date Comparator for class Date in package java.util.

Challenges

Challenge 12.1 Evolve the `IntegerLessThanComparator` and its five colleagues into comparator that work with numbers, i.e `NumberLessThanComparator`.

13

Sequences, Arrays and Lists

Objectives

In this chapter we look at the linear containers, their abstractions and their implementations. As well as looking at implementations and properties we look at usage of these containers.

Keywords

sequence

array

list

linked list

singly-linked list

doubly-linked list

13.1   Introduction

We are all very familiar with the concept of a list in our daily lives. Examples of lists are: a shopping list — a list of items we need to purchase; a recipe — a list of instructions to convert ingredients into something edible; a timetable — a list of times and places someone or something has to be. These lists are containers of items, any of which can be accessed at any time — they are open containers. We can insert new items anywhere in the list and we can delete items from anywhere in the list. In the usual conception of a list, when an item is removed, the positions of all the other items are changed so that there is no gap; if we delete the second item of the list, what was the third item becomes the second item, what was the fourth item becomes the third item, and so on. Conversely, when an item is inserted all the items further down the list move down one in the list; if we insert a new second item, the old second becomes the third, the old third becomes the fourth, and the process repeats until the end of the list.

Contrast this with the properties of arrays. An array certainly has many of the same properties: it is a container and there is a sequential linearity to the way the elements are organized. Arrays and lists are clearly related in some ways. However, an array doesn't have the easy flexibility of insertion and deletion that we are asking for from lists: when we insert or remove an item from an array, the other items do not change their position automatically as they do with a list. Of course we have already seen an argument of this sort regarding the flexibility of arrays. It was in Section 5.3, Page 126 and forced us to make use of the class `ArrayList` from the J2SDK. Notice how the name of this class has both array and list in it, indicating that it is both an array and a list in some way. `ArrayList` is actually a part of Collections, so we must research this library in order to discover why the name.

Collections has the abstract idea of a container, which it calls a `Collection`, and then the abstract idea of a linear container which it calls a `List`. Being abstract these concepts are realized using interfaces. `ArrayList` is a class that conforms to `List`, is a subclass of `AbstractList` and has an array as an implementation representation: an `ArrayList` is an array-based implementation of a `List`. `AbstractList` is an abstract class that conforms to `List` and is a subclass of `AbstractCollection`. `AbstractCollection` is an abstract class that conforms to `Collection` (see Figure 13.1). Here we see the hybrid 'abstraction by conformance/abstraction by inheritance' approach that characterizes the architecture of Collections.

JGL does something very similar, it has interfaces `Container` and `Sequence` which describe collections and linear collections respectively. There are then classes like `Array` which conform to `Sequence` (see Figure 13.2). JGL uses a simpler architecture than Collections, using only 'abstraction by conformance'. However, conceptually both are essentially identical, the ADTs are represented by interfaces and concrete representations of the ADTs are implemented by classes.

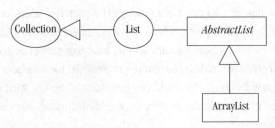

Figure 13.1 The relationship between `Collection`, `List`, `AbstractList` and `ArrayList` in Collections.

Figure 13.2 The relationship between `Container`, `Sequence` and `Array` in JGL.

The crucial point in the case of both libraries is that the commonality between array and list is being formalized into an explicit relationship. Indeed, both libraries are formalizing things using the same 'abstraction by conformance' approach, the ADTs being interfaces and the concrete representations being classes.

There is, unfortunately, quite a lot of confusion surrounding the term list in computing. A few people describe an ADT, which is a container of objects that has a basically sequential structure, and call it a list (this is, in effect, the meaning that Collections uses). Some people describe a data structure with *nodes* and *links,* and call this a *linked list* (or just a list — this is the meaning we will attach to the term list later in the chapter). Far too many books describe an ADT that is a container of objects with the ability to insert and remove objects only at the ends, and call this a list.

The first meaning of list given above is a very reasonable definition of list but we eschew it in favour of the term sequence (as used by JGL) to avoid confusion. The second definition of list, that of linked list, is the description of some programming technology rather than an ADT per se. However, it is important since it is exactly the technology required to implement not just the flexible array-like ADT we need to handle containers such as the shopping list, but also a number of other very interesting ADTs, as we shall see in subsequent chapters. The last meaning, a kind of closed container, is more properly called a *queue* and we will describe this in Chapter 14, Page 407.

Returning to ADS, the position we are in is that we have concluded that arrays and lists have commonalities as well as differences and we want to formalize this in our library. However, we now have something of a problem. Although we are presenting things in something of a top-down manner with the abstractions clear, packages are never actually developed in this way. Whilst the core abstraction may be obvious, for example that we are going to have a sequence concept in ADS, the details of what methods should be in the interface are far from clear. Without having built a set of ADTs we cannot know the full details of the abstractions we need and what the details of the architecture will be. At the same time we need to fully define the abstractions and architecture before we can be certain what the concrete representations need to be. Clearly there is a strong need for iteration in the construction of a library. Library design is a matter of taking on board as much previous work as possible and then doing iterative development until it all fits. In the construction of ADS, we had Collections and JGL plus a wealth of other knowledge about design to draw on and have then designed, programmed, redesigned and re-programmed the interfaces and classes until we got to point presented in this book. The work is far from finished though. What we are presenting here could be seen as the third iteration cycle of the package development. Much is now decided but there is more work to be done.

13.2   Sequence

A `Sequence` is any container that defines a definite ordering on the elements. This means that for each element we can associate a definite position in the sequence. Clearly an array is a sequence since each element is associated with an index which defines the ordering of elements. As we shall see shortly, linked lists are very definitely sequences since they enforce a serial ordering to the elements contained. Thus it seems that some form of access/update by position in the sequence is a property of a sequence. However, beyond this, it is difficult to come up with the set of operations that characterize a sequence (over and above those from `Container`). The definition of `List` in Collections and `Sequence` in JGL show no real commonality beyond the essential nature of a sequence as being a container. The following interface represents our current thinking about the methods common to all sequence-like containers in the ADS library:

```
package ADS ;
/**
 *  This interface is the general abstraction of a sequential
 *  container.
 *
 *  @version 1.1 1999.09.11
 *  @author Russel Winder
 */
public interface Sequence extends Container {
  /**
   *  Return the first item in the <CODE>Sequence</CODE>.
   *
   *  @exception AccessEmptyContainerException if there are no
   *  items in the <CODE>Sequence</CODE>.
   */
  Object first() ;
  /**
   *  Return the last element in the <CODE>Sequence</CODE>.
   *
   *  @exception AccessEmptyContainerException if there are no
   *  items in the <CODE>Sequence</CODE>.
   */
  Object last() ;
  /**
   *  Return the element at a given position in the
   *  <CODE>Sequence</CODE>.
   *
   *  @exception AccessEmptyContainerException if there are no
   *  items in the <CODE>Sequence</CODE>.
   *
   *  @exception IndexOutOfBoundsException if the requested
```

```
 *   <CODE>index</CODE> is not valid due to the size of the
 *   <CODE>Sequence</CODE>.
 */
Object get(int index) ;
/**
 *   Assign a value to a position in the <CODE>Sequence</CODE>.
 *   This overwrites whatever value was there.
 *
 *   @exception AccessEmptyContainerException if there are no
 *   items in the <CODE>Sequence</CODE>.
 *
 *   @exception IndexOutOfBoundsException if the requested
 *   <CODE>index</CODE> is not valid due to the size of the
 *   <CODE>Sequence</CODE>.
 */
void set(int index, Object o) ;
/**
 *   Excise an element from the <CODE>Sequence</CODE>.
 *
 *   @exception AccessEmptyContainerException if there are no
 *   items in the <CODE>Sequence</CODE>.
 *
 *   @exception IndexOutOfBoundsException if the requested
 *   <CODE>index</CODE> is not valid due to the size of the
 *   <CODE>Sequence</CODE>.
 */
void remove(int index) ;
/**
 *   Insert a new item in the <CODE>Sequence</CODE>.  Insertion
 *   happens before, i.e. the new item becomes the index'th item
 *   with the old index'th item becoming the index+1'th item, etc.
 *
 *   @exception AccessEmptyContainerException if there are no
 *   items in the <CODE>Sequence</CODE>.
 *
 *   @exception IndexOutOfBoundsException if the requested
 *   <CODE>index</CODE> is not valid due to the size of the
 *   <CODE>Sequence</CODE>.
 */
void insert(int index, Object o) ;
/**
 *   Find out the position of an <CODE>Object</CODE> in the
 *   <CODE>Sequence</CODE>.
 *
 *   @return the "index" of the sought item.  Return
 *   <CODE>-1</CODE> (which being negative is an illegal index) if
 *   the value <CODE>o</CODE> is not part of the
 *   <CODE>Sequence</CODE>.
 *
 *   @exception AccessEmptyContainerException if there are no
 *   items in the <CODE>Sequence</CODE>.
 */
int indexOf(Object o) ;
/**
 *   Deliver up an iterator positioned at the beginning of the
 *   <CODE>Sequence</CODE>.
 */
ForwardIterator begin() ;
/**
 *   Deliver up an iterator positioned at the end of the
 *   <CODE>Sequence</CODE>.
 */
ForwardIterator end() ;
/**
 *   The class that provides a synchronized interface for use in
 *   multi-threaded applications.
```

```java
    */
    public static class Synchronized
      extends Container.Synchronized implements Sequence {
      /**
       *   The default constructor.
       */
      public Synchronized(final Sequence s) {
        super(s) ;
      }
      /**
       *   The constructor that supplies an object to synchronize on.
       */
      public Synchronized(final Sequence s, final Object o) {
        super(s, o) ;
      }
      /**
       *   Return the first item in the <CODE>Sequence</CODE>.
       *
       *   @exception AccessEmptyContainerException if there are no
       *   items in the <CODE>Sequence</CODE>.
       */
      public final Object first() {
        synchronized (theLock) {
          return ((Sequence)theContainer).first() ;
        }
      }
      /**
       *   Return the last element in the <CODE>Sequence</CODE>.
       *
       *   @exception AccessEmptyContainerException if there are no
       *   items in the <CODE>Sequence</CODE>.
       */
      public final Object last() {
        synchronized (theLock) {
          return ((Sequence)theContainer).last() ;
        }
      }
      /**
       *   Return the element at a given position in the
       *   <CODE>Sequence</CODE>.
       *
       *   @exception AccessEmptyContainerException if there are no
       *   items in the <CODE>Sequence</CODE>.
       *
       *   @exception IndexOutOfBoundsException if the requested
       *   <CODE>index</CODE> is not valid due to the size of the
       *   <CODE>Sequence</CODE>.
       */
      public final Object get(final int index) {
        synchronized (theLock) {
          return ((Sequence)theContainer).get(index) ;
        }
      }
      /**
       *   Assign a value to a position in the <CODE>Sequence</CODE>.
       *   This overwrites whatever value was there.
       *
       *   @exception AccessEmptyContainerException if there are no
       *   items in the <CODE>Sequence</CODE>.
       *
       *   @exception IndexOutOfBoundsException if the requested
       *   <CODE>index</CODE> is not valid due to the size of the
       *   <CODE>Sequence</CODE>.
       */
      public final void set(final int index, final Object o) {
        synchronized (theLock) {
```

```
      ((Sequence)theContainer).set(index, o) ;
    }
  }
  /**
   *  Excise an element from the <CODE>Sequence</CODE>.
   *
   *  @exception AccessEmptyContainerException if there are no
   *  items in the <CODE>Sequence</CODE>.
   *
   *  @exception IndexOutOfBoundsException if the requested
   *  <CODE>index</CODE> is not valid due to the size of the
   *  <CODE>Sequence</CODE>.
   */
  public final void remove(final int index) {
    synchronized (theLock) {
      ((Sequence)theContainer).remove(index) ;
    }
  }
  /**
   *  Insert a new item in the <CODE>Sequence</CODE>.  Insertion
   *  happens before, i.e. the new item becomes the index'th item
   *  with the old index'th item becoming the index+1'th item, etc.
   *
   *  @exception AccessEmptyContainerException if there are no
   *  items in the <CODE>Sequence</CODE>.
   *
   *  @exception IndexOutOfBoundsException if the requested
   *  <CODE>index</CODE> is not valid due to the size of the
   *  <CODE>Sequence</CODE>.
   */
  public final void insert(final int index, final Object o) {
    synchronized (theLock) {
      ((Sequence)theContainer).insert(index, o) ;
    }
  }
  /**
   *  Find out the position of an <CODE>Object</CODE> in the
   *  <CODE>Sequence</CODE>.  Uses linear search.
   *
   *  @return the "index" of the sought item.  Return
   *  <CODE>-1</CODE> (which being negative is an illegal index) if
   *  the value <CODE>o</CODE> is not part of the
   *  <CODE>Sequence</CODE>.
   *
   *  @exception AccessEmptyContainerException if there are no
   *  items in the <CODE>Sequence</CODE>.
   */
  public final int indexOf(final Object o) {
    synchronized (theLock) {
      return ((Sequence)theContainer).indexOf(o) ;
    }
  }
  /**
   *  Deliver up an iterator positioned at the beginning of the
   *  <CODE>Sequence</CODE>.
   */
  public final ForwardIterator begin() {
    synchronized (theLock) {
      return ((Sequence)theContainer).begin() ;
    }
  }
  /**
   *  Deliver up an iterator positioned at the end of the
   *  <CODE>Sequence</CODE>.
   */
  public final ForwardIterator end() {
```

```
            synchronized (theLock) {
              return ((Sequence)theContainer).end() ;
            }
          }
        }
      }
```

Notice that not only do we inherit `Sequence` from `Container` but we also inherit `Sequence.Synchronized` from `Container.Synchronized`. This parallel inheritance ensures that we provide the necessary support tools for managing synchronization protection. Remember the package architecture is to keep objects as lightweight as possible, avoiding unnecessary synchronization protection. Defining things in the way we have here achieves this and also localizes everything to help the programmer in getting it right. For every new method provided by `Sequence` there is a new method provided by `Sequence.Synchronized`.

13.3   AbstractSequence

One of the reasons for the hybrid 'abstraction by conformance/abstraction by inheritance' architecture used by ADS and Collections is that it allows for easy code reuse. Method implementations that are independent of the underlying representation are likely to be the same in all implementations. It seems wasteful to have to replicate the code, which is what we would have to do if we used only the simple version of 'abstraction by conformance'. The way to avoid code replication is to introduce an abstract superclass of the concrete classes. This superclass can then hold the methods that are identical in all subclasses. This is use of inheritance for code reuse. So by introducing `AbstractSequence` between `Sequence` and any particular representation, we can provide common and default implementations of methods as required. Particular representations can always override the methods should the need arise, usually to provide a more efficient implementation.

We can go further with this. Since we already have `AbstractContainer`, we can make `AbstractSequence` a subclass of that and remove the need to redefine the default definitions of the methods inherited from `Container`. Of course, this does not stop us overriding methods should the subclass abstraction admit a more suitable semantics.

Here then is the implementation of `AbstractSequence`:

```
package ADS ;
/**
 *  An abstract sequence to act as a superclass for all the concrete
 *  sequences.  Provides all the default implementations that are
 *  representation independent.
 *
 *  @version 1.0 1999.09.18
 *  @author Russel Winder
 */
public abstract class AbstractSequence
  extends AbstractContainer implements Sequence {
    /**
     *  Return the first item in the <CODE>Sequence</CODE>.
```

```
 *
 *   @exception AccessEmptyContainerException if there are no
 *   items in the <CODE>Sequence</CODE>.
 */
public Object first() {
   return get(0) ;
}
/**
 *   Return the last element in the <CODE>Sequence</CODE>.
 *
 *   @exception AccessEmptyContainerException if there are no
 *   items in the <CODE>Sequence</CODE>.
 */
public Object last() {
   return get(size()-1) ;
}
/**
 *   Return the element at a given position in the
 *   <CODE>Sequence</CODE>.
 */
public abstract Object get(final int index) ;
/**
 *   Assign a value to a position in the <CODE>Sequence</CODE>.
 *   This overwrites whatever value was there.
 */
public abstract void set(final int index, final Object o) ;
/**
 *   Excise an element from the <CODE>Sequence</CODE>.
 */
public abstract void remove(final int index) ;
/**
 *   Insert a new item in the <CODE>Sequence</CODE>.  Insertion
 *   happens before, i.e. the new item becomes the index'th item
 *   with the old index'th item becoming the index+1'th item, etc.
 */
public abstract void insert(final int index, final Object o) ;
/**
 *   Find out the position of an <CODE>Object</CODE> in the
 *   <CODE>Sequence</CODE>.  Uses linear search.
 */
public int indexOf(final Object o) {
   sanityCheck() ;
   int count = 0 ;
   for (Iterator i = iterator() ;
        !i.atEnd() ;
        i.advance(), ++count) {
     if (i.get().equals(o))
       return count ;
   }
   return -1 ;
}
/**
 *   Remove the entire contents of the <CODE>Sequence</CODE>.
 *
 *   This does not affect the size of the underlying array, it only
 *   removes the elements.
 */
public void makeEmpty() {
   for (Iterator i = iterator() ; !i.atEnd() ; i.advance()) {
     remove(0) ;
   }
}
/**
 *   Compare this <CODE>Sequence</CODE> with another
 *   <CODE>Sequence</CODE> and determine whether they represent the
 *   same value, i.e. have the same item values in the same order
```

```
 *   in the <CODE>Sequence</CODE>.
 */
public boolean equals(final Object o) {
  if (! (o instanceof Sequence))
    return false ;
  return super.equals(o) ;
}
/**
 *  Determine whether we have the value represented by the
 *  parameter <CODE>Object</CODE> in us.
 *
 *  @exception AccessEmptyContainerException if there are no
 *  items in the <CODE>Sequence</CODE>.
 */
public boolean contains(final Object o) {
  sanityCheck() ;
  return indexOf(o) >= 0 ;
}
/**
 *  Deliver up an input iterator over the
 *  <CODE>Container</CODE>.
 */
public Iterator iterator() {
  return begin() ;
}
/**
 *  Copy from a sub-sequence defined by indexes into a
 *  <CODE>Sequence</CODE> into the current <CODE>Sequence</CODE>
 */
public final void copy(final Sequence s, final int b, final int e) {
  //  Don't use indexing, use an iterator since indexing into a list
  //  is horrendously inefficient.
  Iterator iter = s.iterator() ;
  int i = 0 ;
  for (; i < b ; ++i, iter.advance())
    ;
  for (; i < e; ++i, iter.advance()) {
    add(iter.get()) ;
  }
}
/**
 *  Copy from the sequence defined by two <CODE>Iterator</CODE>s.
 *
 *  @exception InvalidIteratorException if the two
 *  <CODE>Iterator</CODE>s are not working the same
 *  <CODE>SLList</CODE>.
 */
public final void copy(final Iterator b, final Iterator e) {
  if (b.myObject() != e.myObject())
    throw new InvalidIteratorException () ;
  for (Iterator i = (Iterator)b.clone() ;
       ! i.equals(e) ;
       i.advance()) {
    add(i.get()) ;
  }
}
/**
 *  Check for the correctness of the state.  This just check that
 *  the <CODE>Sequence</CODE> actually has elements.
 */
protected void sanityCheck() {
  if (size() == 0)
    throw new AccessEmptyContainerException () ;
}
/**
 *  Check for the correctness of the state.  This checks both that
```

```
 *   the <CODE>Sequence</CODE> actually has elements and that the
 *   proferred index is a legal one.
 */
protected void sanityCheck(final int index) {
  if (size() == 0)
    throw new AccessEmptyContainerException () ;
  if ((index < 0) || (index >= size()))
    throw new IndexOutOfBoundsException () ;
}
}
```

13.4 Array

Having defined the abstract concept of sequence, we need a concrete representation. A primitive array is very sequence-like but cannot be a `Sequence` since it is not a class. We need, as a minimum, a wrapper around a primitive array to provide an array-based representation of a sequence. In doing this, of course, we have the ability to add functionality to make the container more flexible than a primitive array.

This is obvious from what has gone before. We know that Collections has the `ArrayList` class and that JGL has the `Array` class that do exactly this. For the ADS package, we introduce the `Array` class.

ADS's `Array` will show the basic approach to the provision of primitive array wrappers, illustrating how we can create flexibility from a relatively inflexible base. `Array` encapsulates and abstracts all the code needed to provide the desired flexibility of usage. The core to the design is that we create new primitive arrays of appropriate size and copy the data whenever the primitive array is full, such as when more elements are added to the `Array`. This is handled simply by putting the appropriate tests into the appropriate methods. The other feature we can note before presenting the code is that we must be careful to enforce bounds checking and other sanity features before acting on the underlying array.

Here then is the code:

```
package ADS ;
/**
 *   Implementation of an array-like <CODE>Sequence</CODE> of
 *   <CODE>Object</CODE>s.  The underlying container is a primitive
 *   array.  The size of this underlying data structure grows as the
 *   need arises.  It never shrinks.
 *
 *   @version 1.0 1999.09.18
 *   @author Russel Winder
 */
public class Array extends AbstractSequence {
  /**
   *   The array that holds the data.
   */
  private Object[] datum ;
  /**
   *   The value of the initial size.  The smallest size of the
   *   underlying array for creating new <CODE>Array</CODE>s.
```

```
    */
  private final int initialSize ;
  /**
   *  The value of the size increment.  Whenever we need more array
   *  space we increment the size of the array by this amount.
   */
  private final int incrementSize ;
  /**
   *  This is the current size of the filled portion of the array.
   *  Any space in the array above this is not actually there as far
   *  as the application is concerned.
   */
  private int theSize = 0 ;
  /**
   *  The default constructor.  Gives an <CODE>Array</CODE> with
   *  default initial size and increment.
   */
  public Array() {
    this(10, 10) ;
  }
  /**
   *  The constructor which specifies the initial size of the
   *  <CODE>Array</CODE> using the default increment size.
   */
  public Array(final int initialSizeValue) {
    this(initialSizeValue, 10) ;
  }
  /**
   *  The constructor that specifies both the initial size and the
   *  increment size.
   */
  public Array(final int initialSizeValue,
               final int incrementSizeValue) {
    initialSize = initialSizeValue ;
    incrementSize = incrementSizeValue ;
    datum = new Object [initialSizeValue] ;
  }
  /**
   *  Construct an <CODE>Array</CODE> by copying the
   *  <CODE>Sequence</CODE>.
   */
  public Array(final Sequence s) {
    this(s.size(), 10) ;
    copy(s, 0, s.size()) ;
  }
  /**
   *  Construct an <CODE>Array</CODE> by copying the sub-sequence
   *  defined by two indexes into a <CODE>Sequence</CODE>s.
   */
  public Array(final Sequence s, final int b, final int e) {
    this(e-b+1, 10) ;
    copy(s, b, e) ;
  }
  /**
   *  Construct an <CODE>Array</CODE> by copying the sequence defined
   *  by two <CODE>Iterator</CODE>s.
   *
   *  @exception InvalidIteratorException if the two
   *  <CODE>Iterator</CODE>s are not working the same
   *  <CODE>SLList</CODE>.
   */
  public Array(final Iterator b, final Iterator e) {
    this(10, 10) ;
    copy(b, e) ;
  }
  /**
```

```
 *   Return the element at a given position in the
 *   <CODE>Array</CODE>.
 *
 *   @exception AccessEmptyContainerException if there are no
 *   items in the <CODE>Array</CODE>.
 *   @exception IndexOutOfBoundsException if the requested
 *   <CODE>index</CODE> is not valid due to the size of the
 *   <CODE>Array</CODE>.
 */
public final Object get(final int index) {
  sanityCheck(index) ;
  return datum[index] ;
}
/**
 *   Assign a value to a position in the <CODE>Array</CODE>.
 *   This overwrites whatever value was there.
 *
 *   @exception AccessEmptyContainerException if there are no
 *   items in the <CODE>Array</CODE> and the index is not 0.
 *   @exception IndexOutOfBoundsException if the requested
 *   <CODE>index</CODE> is not valid due to the size of the
 *   <CODE>Array</CODE>.
 */
public final void set(final int index, final Object o) {
  try {
    sanityCheck(index) ;
  }
  catch (AccessEmptyContainerException e) {
    if (index == 0) {
      add(o) ;
      return ;
    } else {
      throw e ;
    }
  }
  catch (IndexOutOfBoundsException f) {
    if (index == 0) {
      add(o) ;
      return ;
    } else {
      throw f ;
    }
  }
  datum[index] = o ;
}
/**
 *   Excise an element from the <CODE>Array</CODE>.
 *
 *   @exception AccessEmptyContainerException if there are no
 *   items in the <CODE>Sequence</CODE>.
 *   @exception IndexOutOfBoundsException if the requested
 *   <CODE>index</CODE> is not valid due to the size of the
 *   <CODE>Array</CODE>.
 */
public final void remove(final int index) {
  sanityCheck(index) ;
  for (int i = index ; i < theSize - 1 ; ++i) {
    datum[i] = datum[i+1] ;
  :
  --theSize ;
}
/**
 *   Insert a new item in the <CODE>Array</CODE>.  Insertion
 *   happens before, i.e. the new item becomes the index'th item
 *   with the old index'th item becoming the index+1'th item, etc.
 *
```

```
 *    @exception AccessEmptyContainerException if there are no
 *    items in the <CODE>Sequence</CODE> and index is not 0.
 *    @exception IndexOutOfBoundsException if the requested
 *    <CODE>index</CODE> is not valid due to the size of the
 *    <CODE>Array</CODE>.
 */
public final void insert(final int index, final Object o) {
  try {
    sanityCheck(index) ;
  }
  catch (AccessEmptyContainerException e) {
    if (index == 0) {
      add(o) ;
      return ;
    } else {
      throw e ;
    }
  }
  if (theSize == datum.length) {
    // The array must be extended.  Create a new larger one.  Copy
    // up to the insertion point insert the new element, copy the
    // rest of the array.
    Object[] newDatum = new Object [datum.length + incrementSize] ;
    System.arraycopy(datum, 0, newDatum, 0, index) ;
    newDatum[index] = o ;
    System.arraycopy(datum, index,
                     newDatum, index + 1,
                     datum.length - index) ;
    datum = newDatum ;
  } else {
    for (int i = theSize ; i > index ; --i) {
      datum[i] = datum[i-1] ;
    }
    datum[index] = o ;
  }
  ++theSize ;
}
/**
 *  Remove the entire contents of the <CODE>Array</CODE>.  This does
 *  not affect the size of the underlying array, it only removes the
 *  elements.
 */
public final void makeEmpty() {
  theSize = 0 ;
}
/**
 *  Determine whether the <CODE>Array</CODE> is an empty one.
 */
public final boolean isEmpty() {
  return theSize == 0 ;
}
/**
 *  Return the number of items in the <CODE>Array</CODE>.
 */
public final int size() {
  return theSize ;
}
/**
 *  Append an element to the end of the <CODE>Array</CODE>.
 */
public final void add(final Object o) {
  if (theSize == datum.length) {
    Object[] newDatum = new Object [datum.length + incrementSize] ;
    System.arraycopy(datum, 0, newDatum, 0, datum.length) ;
    datum = newDatum ;
  }
```

```
    datum[theSize++] = o ;
}
/**
 *  Remove an element of a given value from the
 *  <CODE>Array</CODE> if it is in the <CODE>Array</CODE>.
 *
 *  @return whether the item was actually in the <CODE>Array</CODE>.
 *  @exception AccessEmptyContainerException if there are no
 *  items in the <CODE>Sequence</CODE>.
 */
public final boolean remove(final Object o) {
  sanityCheck() ;
  int i = indexOf(o) ;
  if (i < 0)
    return false ;
  remove(i) ;
  return true ;
}
/**
 *  Deliver up a complete shallow copy of the
 *  <CODE>Array</CODE>.
 */
public final Object clone() {
  Array a =
   new Array (theSize < initialSize ? initialSize : theSize,
             incrementSize) ;
  a.theSize = theSize ;
  for (int i = 0 ; i < theSize ; ++i) {
    a.datum[i] = datum[i] ;
  }
  return a ;
}
/**
 *  Deliver up an iterator positioned at the beginning of the
 *  <CODE>Array</CODE>.
 */
public final ForwardIterator begin() {
  return new Iterator () ;
}
/**
 *  Deliver up an iterator positioned at the end of the
 *  <CODE>Array</CODE>.
 */
public final ForwardIterator end() {
  Iterator i = new Iterator () ;
  i.position = size() - 1 ;
  return i ;
}
/**
 *  The iterator over <CODE>Array</CODE>s.  This is an inner class
 *  (as opposed to being a nested top-level class) so that it
 *  automatically has a reference to it's parent object, i.e. the
 *  object it is an iterator for.
 */
public class Iterator implements RandomAccessIterator {
  /**
   *  The current location of the iterator.  Since indexing is
   *  efficient for this data structure, we keep only the current
   *  index position.
   */
  private int position = 0 ;
  /**
   *  Deliver the value we are currently referring to.
   *
   *  @exception AccessEmptyContainerException if there are no
   *  items in the <CODE>Sequence</CODE>.
```

```
 *   @exception InvalidIteratorException if the iterator is not
 *   referring to a valid element.
 */
public final Object get() {
  sanityCheck() ;
  return Array.this.datum[position] ;
}
/**
 *   Amend the value of the element we are currently referring to.
 *
 *   @exception AccessEmptyContainerException if there are no
 *   items in the <CODE>Sequence</CODE>.
 *   @exception InvalidIteratorException if the iterator is not
 *   referring to a valid element.
 */
public final void set(final Object o) {
  sanityCheck() ;
  Array.this.datum[position] = o ;
}
/**
 *   Move forward one element in the container.
 */
public final void advance() {
  if (position != theSize) {
    ++position ;
  }
}
/**
 *   Move forward <CODE>increment</CODE> elements in the container.
 */
public final void advance(final int increment) {
  if (position != theSize) {
    position += increment ;
  }
}
/**
 *   Move backward one element in the container.
 */
public final void retreat() {
  if (position != -1) {
    --position ;
  }
}
/**
 *   Move backward <CODE>increment</CODE> elements in the
 *   container.
 */
public final void retreat(final int increment) {
  if (position != -1) {
    position -= increment ;
  }
}
/**
 *   Have we reached the beginning of the iteration?
 */
public final boolean atBegin() {
  return position == 0 ;
}
/**
 *   Have we reached the end of the iteration?
 */
public final boolean atEnd() {
  return position == theSize ;
}
/**
 *   Are two iterators equal, i.e. do two iterators refer to the
```

```
 *   same item in the same data structure.
 */
public boolean equals(final ADS.Iterator i) {
  if (! (i instanceof Iterator))
    return false ;
  return (myObject() == i.myObject()) &&
    (position == ((Iterator)i).position) ;
}
/**
 *   Return the reference to the object I am working.
 */
public final Object myObject() {
  return Array.this ;
}
/**
 *   Clone this <CODE>Iterator</CODE>.
 */
public final Object clone() {
  Iterator i = new Iterator () ;
  i.position = position ;
  return i ;
}
/**
 *   The distance between two iterators.
 *
 *   The two iterators must clearly be working the same
 *   <CODE>Array</CODE>.
 */
public final int separation(final RandomAccessIterator i) {
  if (!(i instanceof Iterator) || (myObject() != i.myObject()))
    throw new RuntimeException ("Incompatible iterators.") ;
  return position - ((Iterator)i).position ;
}
/**
 *   Check for the correctness of the state.  This checks both that
 *   the <CODE>Array</CODE> actually has elements and that the
 *   preferred index is a legal one.
 */
private final void sanityCheck() {
  if (Array.this.theSize == 0)
    throw new AccessEmptyContainerException () ;
  if ((position < 0) || (position >= Array.this.size()))
    throw new InvalidIteratorException () ;
}
  }
 }
```

Looking at this implementation, all the indexing-oriented operations seem very efficient. All the methods required of the interfaces Sequence and Container that it was necessary to implement seemed straightforward to provided. The only semi-complex issues were the ones of resizing the underlying primitive array and making sure Array objects are in a sensible state when operations are undertaken on them. The difficulties, if they could be called that, were the iterator and the provision of thread safety.

We have chosen to implement an iterator which has more capability that the interface Iterator actually requires. The new type, Array.Iterator, has been declared as a member class. This means that any instance of an Array.Iterator class automatically knows which Array object it has been defined on. We do not need to provide a constructor parameter to make this happen. As a consequence an Array.Iterator object can only be created associated with a given `Array` and we cannot change the association. This is all very much as wanted and very harmonious with the factory method `iterator`. When `iterator` is called on an `Array` object it delivers up an `Array.Iterator` object rather than an `Iterator` object but since `Iterator` is the superclass of `Array.Iterator` that is fine. The code that called the `iterator` method can then choose whether to treat the returned object as an `Iterator` (the default) or as an `Array.Iterator` (by employing casting) depending on whether it wants to make use of the extra functionality. The extra functionality of the `Array.Iterator` is possible because `Iterator` is really only the specification of a forward iterator and yet an `Array` can support a random access iterator. Thus `Array.Iterator` adds movement in the reverse direction as well as the forward direction (the iterator is bi-directional), and also it allows movement by amounts other than one element (the iterator is random access).

The core methods in this class have no thread management at all. So whilst this means they are efficient for single-threaded applications, they are definitely not thread safe. Yet it was a part of the stated architecture that all classes be thread safe. So what are the tools at the programmer's disposal? There are in fact three approaches.

The architecturally supported method is to make use of the `Synchronized` class from the ADT that `Array` implements, namely `Sequence.Synchronized`, for example:

```
Sequence s = new Sequence.Synchronized(new Array ()) ;
```

After all, an `Array` is a `Sequence` and the philosophical approach is that we should be programming with type `Sequence` anyway with `Array` only mentioned as an implementation type.

The only difficulty would arise if `Array` had more functionality than `Sequence` and that extra functionality was required by the application. In this situation we could either build a special `ArraySynchronized` class as a proxy class to Array or we could just "cop out" and do something like:

```
Array a = new Array () ;
synchronized (a) {
   // code using the Array that requires a lock
}
```

If you look at the implementation of `ArrayList` in Collections or `Array` in JGL, you will find that they are implemented in a very similar way to `Array` above. There are more methods and there is more sophistication in the implementation of the methods but that is really because they are production code whereas the ADS implementation is more to show the techniques and to try and draw out the properties of the representation. Clearly, access to a given item in an `Array` is quick, almost as quick as for a primitive array. Inserting and deleting items in the middle of the sequence is, however, slow since items must be rearranged within the array implementing the container. Adding or removing the item at the very end is, however, efficient. `Array` is very definitely optimized for access.

The following program shows better than any textual presentation could how the features of this class can be used. This program is the very beginnings of a test program for the `Array` class. It was written with the intention of trying to show that the class worked at all. Clearly a proper test program needs writing.

```java
import ADS.AccessEmptyContainerException ;
import ADS.Array ;
import ADS.IndexOutOfBoundsException ;
import ADS.Sequence ;
/**
 *  A program to partially test the <code>Array</code>.
 *
 *  <P> Exercises some but not all of the methods in some but not all
 *  of the situations.  This is certainly not exhaustive and very
 *  definitely needs to be extended to provide anything like a
 *  sensible test for the <CODE>Array</CODE> class. The result should
 *  be:
 *
 *  <PRE>
 *     a = [ ]
 *     a = [ 1 2 2 ]
 *     a = [ 4 2 2 3 ]
 *     Caught IndexOutOfBoundsException.
 *     a = [ 3 2 1 3 ]
 *     Removing an element...successful.
 *     a = [ 3 1 3 ]
 *     a == b is true
 *     a = [ 3 1 3 ], b = [ 3 4 3 ]
 *  </PRE>
 */
public class testArray {
  public static void main(final String[] args) {
    //Array a = new Array () ;
    Sequence a = new Sequence.Synchronized (new Array ()) ;
    System.out.println("a = " + a) ;
    a.set(0, new Integer (1)) ;
    a.add(new Integer (2)) ;
    a.add(new Integer (2)) ;
    System.out.println("a = " + a) ;
    //  Change the value of a specific element.
    a.set(0, new Integer (4)) ;
    a.add(new Integer (3)) ;
    System.out.println("a = " + a) ;
    //  Test an exception.
    try {
      a.set(10, new Integer (1)) ;
    }
    catch (AccessEmptyContainerException aece) {
      System.out.println("Caught AccessEmptyContainerException.") ;
    }
    catch (IndexOutOfBoundsException ioobe) {
      System.out.println("Caught IndexOutOfBoundsException.") ;
    }
    //  See if an iterator works.
    Array.Iterator ai = (Array.Iterator)a.iterator() ;
    ai.set(new Integer (3)) ;
    ai.advance(2) ;
    ai.set(new Integer (1)) ;
    System.out.println("a = " + a) ;
    //  See if removal by content works.
    if (a.contains(new Integer (2))) {
      System.out.println("Removing an element..." +
                      (a.remove(new Integer (2))
                       ? "successful." : "failed.")) ;
```

```
    }
    System.out.println("a = " + a) ;
    // Try cloning.  Make sure they are different.
    Array b = (Array)a.clone() ;
    System.out.println("a == b is " +
                        (a.equals(b) ? "true" : "false")) ;
    b.set(1, new Integer (4)) ;
    System.out.println("a = " + a + ", b = " + b) ;
  }
}
```

We are now in a position to return to the question this chapter opened with: What can we do if we need a sequence optimized for editing? What we need is a sequence where the relationships between the elements is more flexible than that provided by an array or an `Array`.

13.5 Linked Lists

In order to construct a sequence optimized for editing, we need an underlying data structure which is not like an array at all. We need one that maintains the sequence of elements in a way that means the relationships between elements is not rigid thereby allowing quick and easy editing. The necessary trick is to put the organization of the data as part of the data itself. Such a data structure is called a *linked list*. A basic *singly-linked list* is a list of nodes linked together. Diagrammatically:

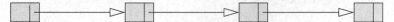

Instead of storing just the data we store a management unit, usually called a *node*. A node comprises some data item(s) and a field that holds a link to the next node. We can construct a class to represent such a node in a linked list; the following is a skeleton:

```
class Node {
  . . . ;
  Node next ;
}
```

Looking at this skeleton class, it is very important to remember that variables of class type do not contain representations of values of that type but are references to objects of that type. If this was not the case the above skeleton class would describe an infinitely recursive data structure. Instead, the variable `next` holds a reference to another `Node` object. This is, of course, exactly what is needed to implement singly-linked list.

Associated with such a data structure is the notion of traversing the list. The way of accessing an item in the list is to have a variable that is a reference to one of these nodes. We can then move down the list using the expressions as in:

```
Node current ...
current = current.next ;
```

Here the variable `current`, which is assumed to refer to a `Node` in the list, can be made to refer to the next item in the list with the expression `current = current.next`.

For historical reasons, it is common to use the term *pointer* when discussing reference variables such as `next` and `current`: we can say that the variables `next` and `current` are pointers to objects. With objects such as instances of `Node`, it is often stated that one object points at (or points to) another. There is nothing wrong with using this sort of terminology as long as everyone is using the same meanings for the words. People with a knowledge of other programming languages (e.g. Pascal, Modula-2, Ada, C, C++) will be used to using such terminology. However, particularly with respect to C and C++, there is a danger of confusion: pointers in C and C++ are rather different things to object references in Java. The way object references behave in Java is just one of the ways that pointers can be used in C and C++. In fact, the generality and flexibility of C and C++ pointers is one of the reasons that Java is the way it is. C and C++ pointers are so flexible that, not only are they very powerful tools, they can be positively dangerous. Certainly they are the cause of vastly more faults than any other language feature. UNIX people are used to the error messages:

```
Bus error -- core dumped
Segmentation violation -- core dumped
```

and Windows programmers are used to:

```
General Protection Fault
```

The majority of these faults are caused by pointer errors in C and C++ programs. The inventors of Java decided to completely remove this category of problem (and hence a large number of errors) by restricting these things to be object references.

Thus, this apparent pedantry over terms is entirely intentional and to be promoted; it is sticking to a precise terminology so that people understand the concepts in the same way the compiler does and to reinforce the fact that Java object references cannot be used in the same way that C and C++ pointers can.

13.6 Using A Singly-linked List

Having the skeleton of linked list technology is a good start but what we really need to do is encapsulate the linked list idea into a class, let us call it `SLList`, that can be added to the ADS package.

We know that `SLList` is going to conform to `Sequence` and inherit from `AbstractSequence` so we know what the core methods are going to be. The question is how is the list to be represented. We know what the basic sequence representation is going to be, it is a singly-linked list. The issue is how the methods are going to access the list structure. One common technique is to provide head and tail references, as shown in Figure 13.3. This gives all methods a fixed starting point for manipulating the list.

The operations of inserting an element into and deleting an element from a `SLList` are achieved by manipulating the references held by the nodes forming the `SLList`. There is no need

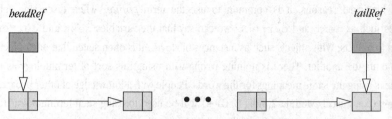

Figure 13.3 The basic structure for an `SLList`.

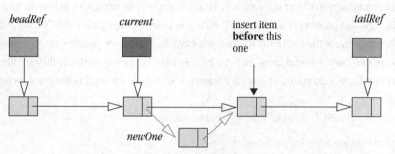

Figure 13.4 Inserting a new item into a `SLList`.

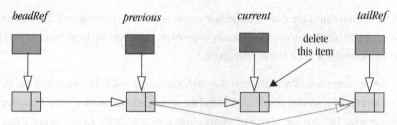

Figure 13.5 Deleting an item from a `SLList`.

to move data to complete insertion and deletion as was the case with arrays. Possibly the best way of conceptualizing these operations is in terms of diagrams. In Figure 13.4 we show how an element is inserted into the middle of a list whereas Figure 13.5 shows deletion from the middle of the list. Dealing with insertion at the head of the list or deletion from either end of the list requires extra care. As always, it is the edge cases that cause the most difficulty. Perhaps the best way of appreciating the details of the operations is to study example code very carefully and be really certain that you understand what is happening.

Here then is an implementation:

```
package ADS ;
/**
 *  This class implements a singly-linked list as a concrete
 *  representation of the <CODE>Sequence</CODE> abstraction.
 *
 *  <P> This implementation uses a head and tail reference with the
 *  singly-linked list strung between them.
 *
 *  @see Container
 *  @version 2.2 1999.12.26
 *  @author Russel Winder
 */
```

```java
public class SLList extends AbstractSequence {
  /**
   *  This is the class from which linked-list nodes are
   *  instantiated.
   */
  //  This is a very passive sort of Node so it is a nested top-level
  //  class and not an inner class since it has no need to ever know
  //  who its parent is.
  private static class Node {
    /**
     *  A <CODE>Node</CODE> has some datum that it is storing.
     */
    protected Object datum ;
    /**
     *  A <CODE>Node</CODE> has a tail, a reference to another
     *  <CODE>Node</CODE>.
     */
    protected Node next ;
    /**
     *  Constructor for an unconnected <CODE>Node</CODE>.
     *
     *  @param o The datum for this <CODE>Node</CODE>.
     */
    public Node(final Object o) {
      this(o, null) ;
    }
    /**
     *  Constructor for a <CODE>Node</CODE> with a given list of
     *  <CODE>Node</CODE>s to become the head of.
     *
     *  @param o The datum for this <CODE>Node</CODE>.
     *  @param n The <CODE>Node</CODE> to be the tail of this one.
     */
    public Node(final Object o, final Node n) {
      datum = o ;
      next = n ;
    }
  }
  /**
   *  The head of the <CODE>SLList</CODE>.  This is the first
   *  <CODE>Node</CODE> in the list.
   */
  private Node head = null ;
  /**
   *  The last <CODE>Node</CODE> in the list.  This is not
   *  absolutely necessary but having it makes appending
   *  <CODE>Node</CODE>s at the end of the list a lot easier.
   */
  private Node tail = null ;
  /**
   *  The count of the number of elements in the <CODE>SLList</CODE>.
   *  This is not absolutely necessary but having it makes a lot of
   *  operations a lot easier.  A good efficiency measure.
   */
  private int elementCount = 0 ;
  /**
   *  Default constructor.  Only needed since we need to define the
   *  constructors that follow.
   */
  public SLList() {}
  /**
   *  Construct an <CODE>SLList</CODE> by copying
   *  <CODE>Sequence</CODE>.
   */
  public SLList(final Sequence s) {
    copy(s, 0, s.size()) ;
```

```
  }
  /**
   * Construct an <CODE>SLList</CODE> by copying the sub-sequence
   * defined by two indexes into a <CODE>Sequence</CODE>.
   */
  public SLList(final Sequence s, final int b, final int e) {
    copy(s, b, e) ;
  }
  /**
   * Construct an <CODE>SLList</CODE> by copying the sequence defined
   * by two <CODE>Iterator</CODE>s.
   *
   * @exception InvalidIteratorException if the two
   * <CODE>Iterator</CODE>s are not working the same
   * <CODE>SLList</CODE>.
   */
  public SLList(final Iterator b, final Iterator e) {
    copy(b, e) ;
  }
  /**
   * Return the first item in the <CODE>SLList</CODE>.
   *
   * @exception AccessEmptyContainerException if there are no
   * items in the <CODE>SLList</CODE>.
   */
  public final Object first() {
    sanityCheck() ;
    return head.datum ;
  }
  /**
   * Return the last element in the <CODE>SLList</CODE>.
   *
   * @exception AccessEmptyContainerException if there are no
   * items in the <CODE>SLList</CODE>.
   */
  public final Object last() {
    sanityCheck() ;
    return tail.datum ;
  }
  /**
   * Return the element at a given position in the
   * <CODE>SLList</CODE>.
   *
   * @exception AccessEmptyContainerException if there are no
   * items in the <CODE>SLList</CODE>.
   * @exception IndexOutOfBoundsException if the requested
   * <CODE>index</CODE> is not valid due to the size of the
   * <CODE>SLList</CODE>.
   */
  public final Object get(final int index) {
    sanityCheck(index) ;
    return nodeAt(index).datum ;
  }
  /**
   * Assign a value to a position in the <CODE>SLList</CODE>.
   * This overwrites whatever value was there.
   *
   * @exception AccessEmptyContainerException if there are no
   * items in the <CODE>SLList</CODE> and the index is not 0.
   * @exception IndexOutOfBoundsException if the requested
   * <CODE>index</CODE> is not valid due to the size of the
   * <CODE>SLList</CODE>.
   */
  public final void set(final int index, final Object o) {
    try {
      sanityCheck(index) ;
```

```
    }
    catch (AccessEmptyContainerException e) {
      if (index == 0) {
        add(o) ;
        return ;
      } else {
        throw e ;
      }
    }
    catch (IndexOutOfBoundsException f) {
      if (index == 0) {
        add(o) ;
        return ;
      } else {
        throw f ;
      }
    }
    nodeAt(index).datum = o ;
  }
  /**
   *  Excise an element from the <CODE>SLList</CODE>.
   *
   *  @exception AccessEmptyContainerException if there are no
   *  items in the <CODE>Sequence</CODE>.
   *  @exception IndexOutOfBoundsException if the requested
   *  <CODE>index</CODE> is not valid due to the size of the
   *  <CODE>SLList</CODE>.
   */
  public final void remove(final int index) {
    sanityCheck(index) ;
    Node toGo = head ;
    if (index == 0) {
      //  Deal with the case where it is the first Node in the list
      //  that has to go as a special case.  If we removed the last
      //  item, make tail sensible.
      head = head.next ;
      if (head == null) {
        tail = null ;
      }
    } else {
      //  It is not the first item in the list that has to go and the
      //  index is known to be valid.  Find the element before the one
      //  we need to remove so that we can excise the one that has to
      //  go.
      Node previous = nodeAt(index - 1) ;
      toGo = previous.next ;
      previous.next = toGo.next ;
      //  If we are removing the last element, we need to reset the
      //  tail.
      if (toGo == tail) {
        tail = previous ;
      }
    }
    //  Nullify the next of the garbage item just in case.  This is
    //  probably not required since the garbage collector will get
    //  things right but as a safety measure let's just do it.  Also
    //  ensure we decrement the element count to the proper value.
    toGo.next = null ;
    elementCount-- ;
  }
  /**
   *  Insert a new item at the given index.  Insertion happens before,
   *  i.e. the new item becomes the index'th item with the old
   *  index'th item becoming the index+1'th item, etc.
   *
   *  @exception AccessEmptyContainerException if there are no items
```

```java
 *    in the <CODE>Sequence</CODE> and the index is not 0.
 *    @exception IndexOutOfBoundsException if the requested
 *    <CODE>index</CODE> is not valid due to the size of the
 *    <CODE>SLList</CODE>.
 */
public final void insert(final int index, final Object o) {
  try {
    sanityCheck(index) ;
  }
  catch (AccessEmptyContainerException e) {
    if (index == 0) {
      add(o) ;
      return ;
    } else {
      throw e ;
    }
  }
  Node n = new Node (o) ;
  if (index == 0) {
    //  Handle insertion at the head of the SLList as a special
    //  case: make the new item's next refer to the same object that
    //  head used to and then make head refer to the new item.
    n.next = head ;
    head = n ;
  } else {
    //  Find the correct place in the SLList to do the insertion and
    //  then do the insertion.
    Node current = nodeAt(index - 1) ;
    n.next = current.next ;
    current.next = n ;
  }
  elementCount++;
}
/**
 *  Remove the entire contents of the <CODE>SLList</CODE>.  This
 *  does not affect the size of the underlying array, it only
 *  removes the elements.
 */
public final void makeEmpty() {
  head = null ;
  tail = null ;
  elementCount = 0 ;
}
/**
 *  Return the number of items in the <CODE>SLList</CODE>.
 */
public final int size() {
  return elementCount ;
}
/**
 *  Append an element to the end of the <CODE>SLList</CODE>.
 */
public final void add(final Object o) {
  Node n = new Node (o) ;
  if (isEmpty()) {
    head = n ;
    tail = n ;
  } else {
    tail.next = n;
    tail = n ;
  }
  elementCount++ ;
}
/**
 *  Remove an element of a given value from the
 *  <CODE>SLList</CODE> if it is in the <CODE>SLList</CODE>.
```

```
 *
 *   @return whether the item was actually in the
 *   <CODE>SLList</CODE>.
 *   @exception AccessEmptyContainerException if there are no
 *   items in the <CODE>Sequence</CODE>.
 */
public final boolean remove(final Object o) {
  sanityCheck() ;
  Node toGo = head ;
  if (head.datum.equals(o)) {
    // Get rid of the head element.  Also if this was the last
    // element make sure that tail gets reset.
    head = head.next ;
    if (head == null) {
      tail = null ;
    }
  } else {
    //
    // Walk down the list looking for the item to remove.
    // Cut it out only if it was found! Can do this
    // in two ways:
    //
    // 1.  Use two references, one referring to the element being
    // tested (current) and one to the previous element.  Previous
    // is used to actually do the editing once current refers to
    // the right Node.
    //
    // 2.  Use a single reference to do the walking, performing all
    // activities from the "previous" Node so that we do not go
    // past the place at which the editing has to be done.
    //
    // The following is an implementation of algorithm 1 using two
    // references.
    //
    //   Node previous = head ;
    //   toGo = toGo.next ;
    //   while ((toGo != null) && ! toGo.datum.equals(o)) {
    //       previous = toGo ;
    //       toGo = toGo.next ;
    //   }
    //   if (toGo == null)
    //       return false ;
    //   previous.next = toGo.next ;
    //   if (toGo == tail) {
    //       tail = previous ;
    //   }
    //
    // The following is an implementation of algorithm 2 using the
    // previous reference for everything:
    //
    Node previous = head ;
    while ((previous.next != null) &&
           ! previous.next.datum.equals(o)) {
      previous = previous.next ;
    }
    if (previous.next == null)
      return false ;
    toGo = previous.next ;
    previous.next = toGo.next ;
    if (toGo == tail) {
      tail = previous ;
    }
  }
  toGo.next = null ;
  elementCount-- ;
  return true ;
```

```
    }
    /**
     *  Deliver up a complete shallow copy of the
     *  <CODE>SLList</CODE>.
     */
    public final Object clone() {
      SLList l = new SLList () ;
      for (ADS.Iterator i = iterator() ; !i.atEnd() ; i.advance()) {
        l.add(i.get()) ;
      }
      return l ;
    }
    /**
     *  Deliver up an iterator positioned at the beginning of the
     *  <CODE>SLList</CODE>.
     */
    public final ForwardIterator begin() {
      return new Iterator () ;
    }
    /**
     *  Deliver up an iterator positioned at the end of the
     *  <CODE>SLList</CODE>.
     */
    public final ForwardIterator end() {
      Iterator i = new Iterator () ;
      i.current = tail ;
      return i ;
    }
    /**
     *  Merge a <CODE>SLList</CODE> after a given index.  The moves (not
     *  copies) all the <CODE>Nodes</CODE> from the <CODE>SLList</CODE>
     *  that is the parameter into us.
     */
    public final void merge(final int index, final SLList l) {
      if (isEmpty() && (index == 0)) {
        head = l.head ;
        tail = l.tail ;
      } else {
        sanityCheck(index) ;
        if (index == elementCount - 1) {
          merge(l) ;
          return ;
        } else {
          Node n = nodeAt(index) ;
          l.tail.next = n.next ;
          n.next = l.head ;
        }
      }
      elementCount += l.elementCount ;
      l.makeEmpty() ;
    }
    /**
     *  Append a <CODE>SLList</CODE> to ourself.  The moves (not copies)
     *  all the <CODE>Nodes</CODE> from the <CODE>SLList</CODE> that is
     *  the parameter into us.
     */
    public final void merge(final SLList l) {
      if (isEmpty()) {
        head = l.head ;
      } else {
        tail.next = l.head ;
      }
      tail = l.tail ;
      elementCount += l.elementCount ;
      l.makeEmpty() ;
    }
```

```
/**
 *  Find a <CODE>Node</CODE> given an index.
 *
 *  @exception IndexOutOfBoundsException if the requested
 *  <CODE>index</CODE> is not valid due to the size of the
 *  <CODE>SLList</CODE>.
 */
private final Node nodeAt(final int index) {
  //  A little optimization for access at the tail.
  if (index == size() - 1)
    return tail ;
  //  We know that the index is valid so walk the SLList until we
  //  get to the right place and then return the value at that
  //  place.
  Node n = head ;
  for (int i = 0 ; i < index ; i++) {
    n = n.next ;
  }
  return n ;
}
/**
 *  The iterator over <CODE>SLList</CODE>s.  This is an inner class
 *  (as opposed to being a nested top-level class) so that it
 *  automatically has a reference to its parent object, i.e. the
 *  cbject it is an iterator for.
 */
public class Iterator implements ForwardIterator {
  /**
   *  The current location of the iterator.
   */
  private Node current = head ;
  /**
   *  Deliver the value we are currently referring to.
   *
   *  @exception InvalidIteratorException if the iterator is nct
   *  valid.
   */
  public final Object get() {
    validityCheck() ;
    return current.datum;
  }
  /**
   *  Amend the value of the element we are currentl referring to.
   *
   *  @exception InvalidIteratorException if the iterator is not
   *  valid.
   */
  public final void set(final Object o) {
    validityCheck() ;
    current.datum = o ;
  }
  /**
   *  Move on to the next element in the container.
   *
   *  @exception InvalidIteratorException if the iterator is not
   *  valid.
   */
  public final void advance() {
    validityCheck() ;
    current = current.next ;
  }
  /**
   *  Have we reached the end of the iteration?
   */
  public final boolean atEnd() {
    return current == null ;
```

```
      }
      /**
       *  Are two iterators equal, i.e. do two iterators refer to the
       *  same item in the same data structure.
       */
      public boolean equals(final ADS.Iterator i) {
        if (! (i instanceof Iterator))
          return false ;
        return current == ((Iterator)i).current ;
      }
      /**
       *  Return a reference to the object the iterator is working.
       */
      public final Object myObject() {
        return SLList.this ;
      }
      /**
       *  Clone this <CODE>Iterator</CODE>.
       */
      public final Object clone() {
        Iterator i = new Iterator () ;
        i.current = current ;
        return i ;
      }
      /**
       *  Append a new item after the current one.
       *
       *  @exception InvalidIteratorException if the iterator is not
       *  valid.
       */
      public final void add(final Object o) {
        validityCheck() ;
        Node n = new Node(o, current.next) ;
        current.next = n ;
        if (tail == current) {
          tail = n ;
        }
        elementCount++ ;
      }
      /**
       *  Merge an <CODE>SLList</CODE> after the current item.
       *
       *  @exception InvalidIteratorException if the iterator is not
       *  valid.
       */
      public final void merge(final SLList l) {
        validityCheck() ;
        if (l.isEmpty())
          return ;
        l.tail.next = current.next ;
        current.next = l.head ;
        elementCount += l.elementCount ;
        l.makeEmpty() ;
      }
      /**
       *  Check to see if the iterator is valid.
       */
      private void validityCheck() {
        if (current == null)
          throw new InvalidIteratorException () ;
      }
    }
  }
}
```

There are many things to note about this implementation of a sequence. Perhaps the most obvious issue is that unlike the array-based implementation, indexing is not efficient. Every time we want to go to a particular place in the list, we have to start from the head and move past each entry in the list until we arrive at the point in the list we were aiming for. Whereas arrays are random access, lists are very definitely sequential access. Of course this was rather to be expected. In gaining the ease and simplicity of editing, we were bound to lose something.

Actually, this is not a negative thing. Different representations of an abstraction must have different properties and appear natural when used in different situations. The whole point of having different representations is that they are matched to and suited to different tasks. It was, after all, the issue of the separation of easy access and easy insertion/deletion that led to this situation. The question is not how to get round what appears to be a problem but how the representation should be used to its best ability. With the array concept, we are thinking of indexing as an important property of sequences and for problems driven by random access this is the case. The linked list representation, however, emphasizes the sequential nature of sequences. Indexing is not an important concept, but iteration and iterators are: Arrays promote indexing and random access, linked lists promote sequential approaches and iterators. The key to effective and efficient use of linked lists is the proper use of iterators with appropriate functionality.

Looking at the definition of `SLList.Iterator`, we see that it is a forward iterator. Unlike in the case of `Array` we cannot move in both directions on a single-linked list, at least not without starting from the head again. Two methods are added to the forward iterator interface, one to add an item and one to merge in a complete `SLList`. Here we see the real capability of singly-linked lists and of iterators. Not only are these operations natural, they are easy to program and efficient at execution time.

However, there is one obvious lack, we cannot remove an item using the iterator. Why is this? The problem is that we need access to the node before the item that is to be removed in order to link around the removed item. There is no problem with the remove operations in the `SLList` class itself since we can do the checks necessary to ensure we have access to all necessary nodes. It appears that removal via an iterator requires a bi-directional capability in the underlying data structure.

13.7   Using A Doubly-linked List

It seems then that to allow easy removal of items we need to support a bidirectional capability in our list: We need to have bi-directional links between all nodes of the linked list. This requires us to have two links in each node and to make them point in such a way as to make the bi-directional linear structure. Diagrammatically, we need:

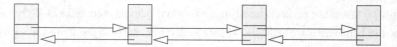

Using this doubly-linked list data structure as the basis for our list abstraction should give us all the editing capabilities that we need.

So how should we implement this doubly linked list? (Let us call it DLList). First let us notice that a DLList 'is-a' SLList, the relationship is relatively apparent from the diagram. Moreover, a node for this list definitely looks like, indeed 'is-a', Node. It seems that we are being drawn into two sorts of inheritance relationship. DLList should inherit from SLList and then, because we have this relationship, we can use inheritance between the node classes. This direction is quite seductive but … following this route means we end up overriding a large number (possibly too many) of the methods in order to take care of the extra reference that is the extension to the node. Certainly this is what happened when we experimented with this approach. Also militating against this approach is the fact that there are a number of efficiencies we can introduce into the standard list manipulation methods knowing that the list is doubly rather than singly linked — not declaring methods in DLList because they are already available in SLList actually hinders efficiency (a run time rather than implementation time efficiency, of course).

Thus, it seems that whilst it is true that a DLList is an SLList, it is not appropriate to use inheritance to implement DLList. Actually this is not unreasonable: SLList and DLList are both Sequences and this is the important abstraction. It is unlikely that SLList and DLList will be used on their own by applications programmers, they are most likely to be used in their status as Sequences. Used in this way, any inheritance relationship between SLList and DLList is just redundant, unused, information; the inheritance relationship does not really impinge on the programmer's use. It would not hurt, therefore, if it were not present. In effect it is just forcing the use of inheritance when it is not actually needed. It is much better to treat them as different representations of a sequence.

Whilst we are reviewing things we should note that there is a major problem with the SLList implementation and that is that there appears to be a necessity for extra code to handle the end cases. In the list with head and tail approach, the way of editing the list in the middle is different from either end, which are different from each other. Clearly it would be much better if there was some way we could increase the symmetry of the various situations so as to cut down the number of special cases and hence code.

So, we are being led to think about implementing DLList from scratch as an independent representation with a data structure that has a different mechanism of dealing with the two ends. The different design for handling the end points that we are looking for centres on what may seem like a 'trick' but it simplifies most of the code quite significantly. The insight is that instead of using head and tail references as has been used for the SLList implementation, we can make use of a dummy doubly-linked list node to manage the ends of the list. Figure 13.6 shows the situation

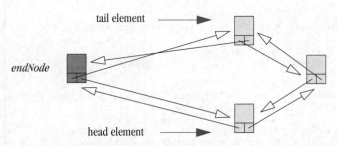

Figure 13.6 A linked list using a node as the control point.

diagrammatically. Changing to this sort of data structure leads to a symmetry of cases and hence to a significant reduction in the amount of code we have to write. Of course we should note immediately that this altered design could be applied to the case of the singly-linked list just as much as to the doubly-linked list. In fact, we could (perhaps should) go back and re-factor the `SLList` implementation.

The following class is an implementation, of `DLList`, based on being completely separate from `SLList`:

```java
package ADS ;
/**
 *  This class implements a doubly-linked list as a concrete
 *  representation of the <CODE>Sequence</CODE> abstraction.
 *
 *  <P> This implementation uses a dummy <CODE>Node</CODE> to act as
 *  both ends of the list of doubly-linked elements. For each
 *  <CODE>Node</CODE>, previous points from the tail to the head and
 *  next points from the head to the tail.
 *
 *  @see Container
 *  @version 2.2 1999.12.26
 *  @author Russel Winder
 */
public class DLList extends AbstractSequence {
  /**
   *  This is the class from which linked-list nodes are
   *  instantiated.
   */
  // This node knows how to undertake various editing
  // operations. This is possible because the doubly linked nature of
  // the list means that any node has all the information to do the
  // editing.
  protected static class Node {
    /**
     *  A <CODE>Node</CODE> has some datum that it is storing.
     */
    protected Object datum ;
    /**
     *  A <CODE>Node</CODE> has a next, a reference to another
     *  <CODE>Node</CODE>.
     */
    protected Node next ;
    /**
     *  A <CODE>Node</CODE> has a previous, a reference to
     *  another <CODE>Node</CODE>.
     */
    protected Node previous ;
    /**
     *  Constructor for an unconnected <CODE>Node</CODE>.
```

```
 *
 *   @param o The datum for this <CODE>Node</CODE>.
 */
public Node(final Object o) {
  this(o, null, null) ;
}
/**
 *   Constructor for a <CODE>Node</CODE> with a given list of
 *   <CODE>Node</CODE>s to become the head of.
 *
 *   @param o The datum for this <CODE>Node</CODE>.
 *   @param n The <CODE>Node</CODE> to be the tail of this one.
 *   @param p The <CODE>Node</CODE> to be the previous of this
 *   one.
 */
public Node(final Object o, final Node n, final Node p) {
  datum = o ;
  next = n ;
  previous = p ;
}
/**
 *   Append an element after ourself.
 */
public void add(final Node n) {
  n.previous = this ;
  n.next = next ;
  next.previous = n ;
  next = n ;
}
/**
 *   Excise ourself from the <CODE>DLList</CODE>.
 */
public final void remove() {
  next.previous = previous ;
  previous.next = next ;
  next = null ;
  previous = null ;
}
/**
 *   Insert an element before ourself.
 */
public void insert(final Node n) {
  n.next = this ;
  n.previous = previous ;
  previous.next = n ;
  previous = n ;
}
/**
 *   Merge a <CODE>DLList</CODE> after ourself.
 */
public void merge(final DLList l) {
  next.previous = l.endNode.previous ;
  l.endNode.previous.next = next ;
  next = l.endNode.next ;
  l.endNode.next.previous = this ;
}
}
/**
 *   The <CODE>Node</CODE> that does not have any data but acts as
 *   both the head and the tail of the list of element.
 */
protected final Node endNode = new Node (null) ; {
  makeEmpty() ;
}
/**
 *   The count of the number of elements in the <CODE>DLList</CODE>.
```

```
 *   This is not absolutely necessary but having it makes a lot of
 *   operations a lot easier.  A good efficiency measure.
 */
protected int elementCount = 0 ;
/**
 *   Default constructor.  Only needed since we need to define the
 *   following constructors.
 */
public DLList() {}
/**
 *   Construct a <CODE>DLList</CODE> by copying the
 *   <CODE>Sequence</CODE>.
 */
public DLList(final Sequence s) {
  copy(s, 0, s.size()) ;
}
/**
 *   Construct a <CODE>DLList</CODE> by copying the sub-sequence
 *   defined by two indexes into a <CODE>Sequence</CODE>.
 */
public DLList(final Sequence s, final int b, final int e) {
  copy(s, b, e) ;
}
/**
 *   Construct an <CODE>DLList</CODE> by copying the sequence defined
 *   by two <CODE>Iterator</CODE>s.
 *
 *   @exception InvalidIteratorException if the two
 *   <CODE>Iterator</CODE>s are not working the same
 *   <CODE>DLList</CODE>.
 */
public DLList(final ADS.Iterator b, final ADS.Iterator e) {
  copy(b, e) ;
}
/**
 *   Return the first item in the <CODE>DLList</CODE>.
 *
 *   @exception AccessEmptyContainerException if there are no
 *   items in the <CODE>DLList</CODE>.
 */
public final Object first() {
  sanityCheck() ;
  return endNode.next.datum ;
}
/**
 *   Return the last element in the <CODE>DLList</CODE>.
 *
 *   @exception AccessEmptyContainerException if there are no
 *   items in the <CODE>DLList</CODE>.
 */
public final Object last() {
  sanityCheck() ;
  return endNode.previous.datum ;
}
/**
 *   Return the element at a given position in the
 *   <CODE>DLList</CODE>.
 *
 *   @exception AccessEmptyContainerException if there are no
 *   items in the <CODE>DLList</CODE>.
 *   @exception IndexOutOfBoundsException if the requested
 *   <CODE>index</CODE> is not valid due to the size of the
 *   <CODE>DLList</CODE>.
 */
public final Object get(final int index) {
  sanityCheck(index) ;
```

```
      return nodeAt(index).datum ;
    }
    /**
     *  Assign a value to a position in the <CODE>DLList</CODE>.
     *  This overwrites whatever value was there.
     *
     *  @exception AccessEmptyContainerException if there are no
     *  items in the <CODE>DLList</CODE>.
     *  @exception IndexOutOfBoundsException if the requested
     *  <CODE>index</CODE> is not valid due to the size of the
     *  <CODE>DLList</CODE>.
     */
    public void set(final int index, final Object o) {
      try {
        sanityCheck(index) ;
      }
      catch (AccessEmptyContainerException e) {
        if (index == 0) {
          add(o) ;
          return ;
        } else {
          throw e ;
        }
      }
      catch (IndexOutOfBoundsException f) {
        if (index == 0) {
          add(o) ;
          return ;
        } else {
          throw f ;
        }
      }
      nodeAt(index).datum = o ;
    }
    /**
     *  Excise an element from the <CODE>DLList</CODE>.
     *
     *  @exception AccessEmptyContainerException if there are no
     *  items in the <CODE>DLList</CODE>.
     *  @exception IndexOutOfBoundsException if the requested
     *  <CODE>index</CODE> is not valid due to the size of the
     *  <CODE>DLList</CODE>.
     */
    public final void remove(final int index) {
      sanityCheck(index) ;
      nodeAt(index).remove() ;
      elementCount-- ;
    }
    /**
     *  Insert a new item in the <CODE>DLList</CODE>.  Insertion
     *  happens before, i.e. the new item becomes the index'th item
     *  with the old index'th item becoming the index+1'th item, etc.
     *
     *  @exception AccessEmptyContainerException if there are no
     *  items in the <CODE>DLList</CODE> and the index is not 0.
     *  @exception IndexOutOfBoundsException if the requested
     *  <CODE>index</CODE> is not valid due to the size of the
     *  <CODE>DLList</CODE>.
     */
    public final void insert(final int index, final Object o) {
      try {
        sanityCheck(index) ;
      }
      catch (AccessEmptyContainerException e) {
        if (index == 0) {
          add(o) ;
```

```
        return ;
      } else {
        throw e ;
      }
  }
  nodeAt(index).insert(new Node (o)) ;
  elementCount++;
}
/**
 *  Remove the entire contents of the <CODE>DLList</CODE>.
 *
 *  This does not affect the size of the underlying array, it only
 *  removes the elements.
 */
public final void makeEmpty() {
  endNode.next = endNode ;
  endNode.previous =  endNode;
  elementCount = 0 ;
}
/**
 *  Return the number of items in the <CODE>DLList</CODE>.
 */
public int size() {
  return elementCount ;
}
/**
 *  Append an element to the end of the <CODE>DLList</CODE>.
 */
public void add(final Object o) {
  endNode.previous.add(new Node (o)) ;
  elementCount++ ;
}
/**
 *  Remove an element of a given value from the
 *  <CODE>DLList</CODE> if it is in the <CODE>DLList</CODE>.
 *
 *  @return whether the item was actually in the
 *  <CODE>DLList</CODE>.
 *  @exception AccessEmptyContainerException if there are no
 *  items in the <CODE>DLList</CODE>.
 */
public final boolean remove(final Object o) {
  sanityCheck() ;
  for (Iterator i = (Iterator)iterator() ;
       ! i .atEnd() ;
       i.advance()) {
    if (i.get().equals(o)) {
      i.remove() ;
      return true ;
    }
  }
  return false ;
}
/**
 *  Deliver up a complete shallow copy of the
 *  <CODE>DLList</CODE>.
 */
public Object clone() {
  DLList l = new DLList () ;
  for (ADS.Iterator i = iterator() ; !i.atEnd() ; i.advance()) {
    l.add(i.get()) ;
  }
  return l ;
}
/**
 *  Deliver up an iterator positioned at the beginning of the
```

```
 *    <CODE>DLList</CODE>.
 */
public final ForwardIterator begin() {
  return new Iterator () ;
}
/**
 *   Deliver up an iterator positioned at the end of the
 *   <CODE>DLList</CODE>.
 */
public final ForwardIterator end() {
  Iterator i = new Iterator () ;
  i.current = endNode.previous ;
  return i ;
}
/**
 *   Merge a <CODE>DLList</CODE> after a given index.  This moves
 *   (not copies) all the <CODE>Nodes</CODE> from the
 *   <CODE>DLList</CODE> that is the parameter into us.
 */
public final void merge(final int index, final DLList l) {
  nodeAt(index).merge(l) ;
  elementCount += l.elementCount ;
  l.makeEmpty() ;
}
/**
 *   Append a <CODE>DLList</CODE> to ourself.  The moves (not copies)
 *   all the <CODE>Nodes</CODE> from the <CODE>DLList</CODE> that is
 *   the parameter into us.
 */
public final void merge(final DLList l) {
  endNode.previous.merge(l) ;
  elementCount += l.elementCount ;
  l.makeEmpty() ;
}
/**
 *   Find a <CODE>Node</CODE> given an index.
 *
 *   @exception IndexOutOfBoundsException if the requested
 *   <CODE>index</CODE> is not valid due to the size of the
 *   <CODE>DLList</CODE>.
 */
private final Node nodeAt(final int index) {
  //  The index is already known to be reasonable, choose the end
  //  which is nearest the node we want and then walk the list to
  //  the appropriate Node.
  Node current = endNode.next ;
  if (index >= size() / 2) {
    current = endNode.previous ;
    for (int i = size() - 1 ; i > index ; i--) {
      current = current.previous ;
    }
  } else {
    for (int i = 0 ; i < index ; i++) {
      current = current.next ;
    }
  }
  return current ;
}
/**
 *   The iterator over <CODE>DLList</CODE>s.
 *
 *   This is an inner class (as opposed to being a nested top-level
 *   class) so that it automatically has a reference to it's parent
 *   object, i.e. the object it is an iterator for.
 */
public class Iterator implements BiDirectionalIterator {
```

```
/**
 *   The current location of the iterator.
 */
private Node current = endNode.next ;
/**
 *   Deliver the value we are currently referring to.
 *
 *   @exception InvalidIteratorException if the iterator is
 *   invalid.
 */
public final Object get() {
  validityCheck() ;
  return  current.datum;
}
/**
 *   Amend the value of the element we are currently referring to.
 *
 *   @exception InvalidIteratorException if the iterator is
 *   invalid.
 */
public final void set(final Object o) {
  validityCheck() ;
  current.datum = o ;
}
/**
 *   Move on to the next element in the container.
 *
 *   @exception InvalidIteratorException if the iterator is
 *   invalid.
 */
public final void advance() {
  validityCheck() ;
  current = current.next ;
}
/**
 *   Have we reached the beginning of the iteration?
 */
public final boolean atBegin() {
  return current == endNode.next ;
}
/**
 *   Have we reached the end of the iteration?
 */
public final boolean atEnd() {
  return current == endNode ;
}
/**
 *   Are two iterators equal, i.e. do two iterators refer to the
 *   same item in the same data structure.
 */
public boolean equals(final ADS.Iterator i) {
  if (! (i instanceof Iterator))
    return false ;
  return current == ((Iterator)i).current ;
}
/**
 *   Return the reference to the object I am working.
 */
public final Object myObject() {
  return DLList.this ;
}
/**
 *   Clone this <CODE>Iterator</CODE>.
 */
public final Object clone() {
  Iterator i = new Iterator () ;
```

```java
    i.current = current ;
    return i ;
}
/**
 *   Move on to the next element in the container.
 *
 *   @exception InvalidIteratorException if the iterator is
 *   invalid.
 */
public final void retreat() {
  validityCheck() ;
  current = current.previous ;
}
/**
 *   Insert a new item.
 *
 *   @exception InvalidIteratorException if the iterator is
 *   invalid.
 */
public final void insert(final Object o) {
  validityCheck() ;
  current.insert(new Node (o)) ;
  elementCount++ ;
}
/**
 *   Insert a new item.
 *
 *   @exception InvalidIteratorException if the iterator is
 *   invalid.
 */
public final void add(final Object o) {
  validityCheck() ;
  current.add(new Node (o)) ;
  elementCount++ ;
}
/**
 *   Remove this item move the iterator on one so that it is still
 *   valid.
 *
 *   @exception InvalidIteratorException if the iterator is
 *   invalid.
 */
public final void remove() {
  validityCheck() ;
  Node n = current ;
  current = current.next ;
  n.remove() ;
  elementCount-- ;
}
/**
 *   Can do merging of <CODE>DLList</CODE>s easily.
 *
 *   @exception InvalidIteratorException if the iterator is
 *   invalid.
 */
public final void merge(final DLList l) {
  validityCheck() ;
  current.merge(l) ;
  elementCount += l.elementCount ;
  l.makeEmpty() ;
}
/**
 *   Check to see if the iterator is valid.
 */
private final void validityCheck() {
  if (current == null)
```

```
                throw new InvalidIteratorException () ;
        }
    }
  }
```

The most obvious thing to note about this implementation is that we have put significant functionality into the `Nodes` themselves. Each node knows how to:

- remove itself from a list;
- insert a new `Node` before itself;
- add a new `Node` after itself; and
- add a complete `DLList` after itself.

Adding the methods to the `Node` class has meant a significant simplification of the `DLList` class itself. Insertion and deletion of items in the list is conceptually exactly as it was with the singly-linked list but is now expressed in a much cleaner way. The complication is the extra reference but the complexity has all been moved into the `Node` class. At the same time, this extra state in the list nodes has allowed us to extend the functionality of the iterator further: `DLList.Iterator` is a bi-directional iterator that can insert before as well as add after.

It seems then that `DLList` might be just much better than `SLList`, in effect making `SLList` redundant. The overhead of an extra object reference for each node in the `DLList` is just not a significant penalty at all. So whilst JGL has both singly-linked and doubly-linked list implementation of sequence, Collections has not bothered with the singly-linked list abstraction and just uses a doubly linked list. Singly-linked list technology is not actually redundant though as we shall see, although it has no real use as a representation of an ADT it still has use as part of an implementation of other data structures.

A final thing to point out here is that a number of the methods in `Array`, `SLList` and `DLList` are actually the same. This is the observation that drives the decision in Collection to introduce the abstract classes sitting between the interfaces and the concrete classes. These abstract classes are just there to hold the common methods and hence avoid code replication.

13.8 But Which to Use When?

We have three implementations of `Sequence` (`Array`, `SLList` and `DLList`) and need to have some heuristics and guidelines to support us knowing when to use which. Abstraction by conformance is all very well but we still have to decide which representation to use in given situations.

Actually in this situation, the issue is apparently straightforward. We can argue on an informal basis that if we need to access elements randomly and there is little updating then, clearly, we should use a `Array` to implement a `Sequence`. If there is significant editing of the elements, and especially if the number of elements is large, then we should use the `DLList` rather than either the

`Array` or `SLList` since it has better insertion characteristics. Of course, this argument is trivially obvious because it is the argument we used to justify the different representations in the first place.

We can put the debate on a slightly more formal basis using a notation called 'Big O' notation along with the idea of measuring time and space resources of the actions involved in the algorithms implemented by the methods.

Thinking about the memory required to store the data in a `DLList`, we see that in order to store n items in the list, we need n linked list nodes. Each of these nodes takes up some memory space. The actual amount of space is not of concern; the important thing is that it is a constant amount of space for each node. We can also ignore the two object references and the `int` storing the element count since only a small and constant amount of space is needed for them. Putting all this together we say that the space usage, which will be denoted by $S(n)$, is $O(n)$ — spoken as 'order n'. If we are writing it down we would write:

$$S(n) = O(n)$$

showing the space requirement of the data structure is linear in the variable which defines the size of the problem.

Ferreting around the source code of the `Array` implementation, we see that we cannot be quite as exact about knowing the exact space usage of `Array` at any given moment. What we can say is that the underlying data structure is an array of some constant size larger than the largest number needed at any one time. This however is near enough for our purposes. If n is the size of the problem then the array is of size $n+c$ with c constant so:

$$S(n) = O(n)$$

just the same as for `DLList`.

This clearly doesn't actually help us make any decisions. Both types use the same (indeed effectively the minimal) amount of storage.

What about getting the value of an element in the `Sequence`?

For the `DLList`, we have to follow object references down the list from the `headPtr` to the object that has the data we are trying to get hold of. On average this will be half way down the linked list which means $n/2$ moves. So the time taken to access a value in a `DLList` is $O(n)$. The time taken is usually denoted $T(n)$, so we would say that element access in `DLList` is:

$$T(n) = O(n)$$

For an `Array`, indexing an element is simply a matter of calculating the offset of the required item from the beginning of the Array. The time taken by this computation is essentially constant, certainly it is not dependent on the size of the array. So the time complexity of array access is:

$$T(n) = O(1)$$

We can do the same performance estimation for insertion into and removal from the sequence.

T(n) for	Array	SLList	SLList. Iterator[†]	DLList	DLList. Iterator[†]
Access at start	O(1)	O(1)	O(1)	O(1)	O(1)
Access in middle	O(1)	O(n)	O(1)	O(n)	O(1)
Access at end	O(1)	O(1)	O(1)	O(1)	O(1)
Insert at start	O(n)	O(1)	O(1)	O(1)	O(1)
Insert in middle	O(n)	O(n)	O(1)	O(n)	O(1)
Insert at end	O(1)	O(1)	O(1)	O(1)	O(1)
Delete at start	O(n)	O(1)	O(1)	O(1)	O(1)
Delete in middle	O(n)	O(n)	O(n)	O(n)	O(1)
Delete at end	O(1)	O(n)	O(n)	O(1)	O(1)
Insert sequence at start	O(n)	O(n)	O(n)	O(n)	O(n)
Insert sequence in middle	O(n)	O(n)	O(n)	O(n)	O(n)
Insert sequence at end	O(n)	O(n)	O(n)	O(n)	O(n)
Insert list at start	O(n)	O(1)	O(1)	O(1)	O(1)
Insert list in middle	O(n)	O(n)	O(1)	O(n)	O(1)
Insert list at end	O(n)	O(1)	O(1)	O(1)	O(1)

Table 13.1 Time complexity of operations of the sequence related data structures.
[†] The iterator estimates assume that the iterator is already in the required position.

For the DLList, insertion using the indexing access mode or removal using the search method is a matter of finding the item (an O(n) operation since we move down the list searching for the correct place) and then doing a few (constant number) of operations to either insert or remove an item. These are therefore O(n) operations. Inserting or removing at either end of the DLList is, however, very fast since no search along the linked list is needed; these algorithms are O(1). Moreover insertion and removal using an iterator is O(1).

For the Array, both insertion and deletion require significant movement of data, either to make space for the new element or to close up the space created by the removal of the new element. On average, $n/2$ moves will take place so the algorithms are O(n). This looks the same as for the DLList but this is slightly misleading. Although we ignore constants in deciding on the algorithmic complexity of the operations, in this situation we need to take note of them. The time taken to change the value of a pointer is significantly less than the time taken to move data in memory. The effect may be trivial for small n but as n gets very large then large constants become important. For this reason the O(n) for Array is qualitatively poorer than the O(n) for DLList. Also of course if we do the insertion or removal as an integral part of iterator activity then we can get as good as O(1) for the DLList. All this can be made clearer by tabulating the time complexities of all the operations for the data structures, as shown in Table 13.1.

Thus, we are lead to the same conclusions we had previously about the concrete representations of sequence (which is a good thing!) but now we can give arguments based less on hand waving and more on estimates of the performance of the algorithms used. This is a far more objective way of reasoning about these issues.

13.9   Summary

In this chapter, we have introduced the concepts of array, singly-linked list and doubly-linked list as data structures (i.e. data storage mechanisms) with associated bits of programming technology that can be harnessed as concrete representations of the abstraction sequence.

Some interesting Java programming techniques are embedded in the code. In particular, we showed how you can make code simpler by assigning the right responsibilities and functionality to the right part of the implementation of the classes.

The performance properties of the implementations were investigated to provide a framework to support the ability to reason about which representation to use when.

Self-review Questions

Self-review 13.1 What is the argument for introducing the class `Sequence`?

Self-review 13.2 Why has the abstract class `AbstractSequence` been introduced?

Self-review 13.3 Why do we need both `Array` and `DLList` in the ADS package?

Self-review 13.4 What are the necessary differences between `SLList` and `DLList`?

Self-review 13.5 Draw the UML diagram that describes the relationships between `Container`, `Sequence`, `AbstractSequence`, `Array`, `SLList` and `DLList`

Self-review 13.6 How is the necessity for thread safety supported for sequences in ADS?

Self-review 13.7 How does the Big-O notation help programmers?

Programming Exercises

Exercise 13.1 Devise and run a test program for the `Array` class.

Exercise 13.2 Implement a singly-linked list using the 'circular list' singly-linked data structure. (i.e. re-implement `SLList` using the type of underlying data structure used in `DLList`.)

Exercise 13.3 Devise and run a program to test both `SLList` and `DLList` to see (roughly) how much slower the doubly-linked is than the singly-linked list.

Exercise 13.4 Develop an implementation of SLList using the "dummy node" approach rather than the "head and tail reference" approach.

Exercise 13.5 Implement the version of DLList which is based on inheritance from SLList (it is almost certainly better to use the "dummy node" approach version) and compare and contrast the implementation with the one given in this chapter.

Exercise 13.6 Write a test program to allow comparison of performance of the Array class in ADS, the Array class in JGL and the ArrayList class in Collections.

Exercise 13.7 Write a test program to allow comparison of performance of the DLList class in ADS, the DList class in JGL and the LinkedList class in Collections.

Challenges

Challenge 13.1 Undertake a more in depth study of the sequence related classes in Collections and JGL and write an essay setting out the similarities and differences between the packages. Consider issues of architecture and programming style as well as of differences in particular classes.

Challenge 13.2 Compare and contrast the different ways in which ADS, Collections and JGL support thread safety.

Queues and Stacks

Objectives

This chapter introduces the `Queue`, `Dequeue` and `Stack` abstractions. A number of different implementation techniques are introduced along with a few architectural issues.

Keywords

data structure

queue

double-ended queue

stack

circular array

abstraction

conformance

association

wrapper

adapter

14.1   Introduction

We are all too familiar with queues, they exist throughout our lives. For example, if we want to fly from London, UK to Washington, USA then when we have arrived at the airport, we have to join a queue to be checked in for the flight, we then have to join a queue to get into the international departure lounge, then we have to join a queue for the security check (X-ray machine, etc.) then we join a queue for passport control in order to get into the departure lounge. The operators of the airport then hope we spend lots of money in the departure lounge before finally joining the queue to get into the waiting lounge so that we can wait to join the queue to board the plane. Queues are so important in our lives that we have not only a noun describing the behaviour but also a verb describing that behaviour — to queue.

We first saw queues in Section 7.3, Page 185.

The term 'last in, last out' (LILO) is equivalent but is not used to avoid confusion with a make of airbed.

Queues like those at airports are used to hold people in a waiting area in such a way that the first person to join the queue is the first person to be dealt with; a queue is a 'first in, first out' (FIFO) structure (indeed, queues are sometimes referred to as FIFO lists). In the same way that an airport needs to store people awaiting processing in a fair way, computer-based systems often need to store data in analogous ways. Diagrammatically, an abstract Queue is like a tube in which items enter at one end and exit through the other:

As the queue concept is going to be used by our programs, we must create an abstraction for it. The abstraction can be described in words:

> A queue is a container of objects into which we can add and remove elements with a FIFO policy and which is a closed container, such that there should be no direct access to an element in the queue unless the element is the next to be removed.

Our next problem is to decide which of the many, many different possible implementations of a queue is the one we want to put into our package. We can start the solution finding process by asking a slightly different question: Which of the three architectures (abstraction by conformance, inheritance or association) is the one we want? We need to look at all of them, constructing sample solutions using all three architectures to allow us to experiment and investigate the issues, before arriving at a solution.

14.2   Using the Abstraction by Conformance Architecture

In this approach to implementing an ADT, we define an interface declaring the methods that must be provided by any class (and hence object) that claims to implement the ADT. Following this lead, we will define a Queue interface to represent the Queue ADT, so that we provide a type that objects can conform to. There then need to be concrete classes that provide particular implementations. Each different concrete class will provide different performance characteristics. So first the interface declaration:

```java
package ADS ;
/**
 *  An interface defining the necessary properties to be deemed
 *  to be a <CODE>Queue</CODE> type <CODE>Container</CODE>.
 *
 *  <P> We define a queue to be any data structure that can have items
 *  inserted and removed and which guarantees a First in -- First out
 *  ordering policy.
 *
 *  @version 1.1 1999.09.17
 *  @author Russel Winder
 */
public interface Queue extends Container {
  /**
   *  Remove an item from the <CODE>Queue</CODE>.
   */
  Object remove() ;
  /**
   *  The class that provides a synchronized interface for use in
   *  multi-threaded applications.
   */
  public static class Synchronized
    extends Container.Synchronized implements Queue {
    /**
     *  The default constructor.  Gives an <CODE>Queue</CODE> with
     *  default initial size and increment.
     */
    public Synchronized(final Queue q) {
      super(q) ;
    }
    /**
     *  The constructor that supplies an object to synchronize on.
     */
    public Synchronized(final Queue q, final Object o) {
      super(q, o) ;
    }
    /**
     *  Remove an item from the <CODE>Queue</CODE>.
     */
    public final Object remove() {
      synchronized (theLock) {
        return ((Queue)theContainer).remove() ;
      }
    }
  }
}
```

The issue now is to decide how we are going to actually store the data in the queue, as we need to answer the question: which data structure are we going to use as a representation of the queue? Only then can we construct concrete classes that conform to the Queue interface. The obvious choices are that we could use any of the sequence classes (array based or linked list based) we have available or we could make direct use of array or linked list technology to implement a special data structure uniquely for the queue.

Using a ready-made class is the easiest way of doing the implementation since it builds on proven abstractions. It is very definitely the implementation strategy of choice. However, there are times when the overheads associated with a previously defined abstraction can be too high; sometimes we need to use optimized, more efficient implementation techniques. The architecture we are following does not disallow providing any number of implementations — in some senses it encourages providing multiple implementations. In the following subsections we present a number of different implementations to show not only the package architecture at work but also these variations on the array and linked list data storage techniques.

14.2.1   Sequence-based Implementation

This is, perhaps, the most straightforward of the implementation approaches. We are going to make explicit use of the already implemented sequence types. We have three classes that conform to Sequence: Array, SLList and DLList all of which will make reasonable representations of the queue — though, as we will find out two of them are far better than the other. Can you guess which is the odd one out?

Using the 'abstraction by conformance' architecture we end up with three new types one for each of the concrete sequence types. Let us call these ArrayQueue, SLListQueue, DLListQueue. It is conventional when using this architecture to construct names using this approach of concatenating the name of the concrete type and the name of the interface. It means that programmers have some of the information they need encoded in the name of the class.

Exactly as with Container and Sequence, it is a sensible requirement that we allow any queue to be compared with any other queue even if they are of different classes. Clearly we have to be able to test for equality between two ArrayQueues, two SLListQueues or two DLListQueues but it also makes sense for equality testing to work between an ArrayQueue and an SLListQueue or indeed any combination. This means we must ensure that equality testing is implemented between two Queues and not specifically for a queue of a given representation. This immediately means use of iterators but as all Containers must have iterators this is hardly a problem. Again, as with the Sequence implementation, the equals methods in ArrayQueue, SLListQueue and DLListQueue will be identical. This means they can and should be gathered together in an AbstractQueue class, which also provides an abstract type conforming to Queue, with the three concrete queue classes as subclasses, see Figure 12.1, Page 353.

Here then is the abstract queue that holds all the representation independent methods:

```
package ADS ;
/**
 *  An abstract <CODE>Queue</CODE> to act as a superclass for all the
 *  concrete queues.  Provides all the default implementations that
 *  are representation independent.
 *
 *  @version 1.0 1999.09.18
 *  @author Russel Winder
 */
public abstract class AbstractQueue
  extends AbstractContainer implements Queue {
  /**
```

```
 *   Remove a datum from ourself.
 *
 *   @exception AccessEmptyContainerException if we attempt to
 *   remove from an empty <CODE>Queue</CODE>.
 */
public abstract Object remove() ;
/**
 *   Cause ourself to be emptied.
 */
public void makeEmpty() {
  for (Iterator i = iterator() ; !i.atEnd() ; i.advance()) {
    remove() ;
  }
}
/**
 *   Test something against ourself for equality.
 */
public boolean equals(final Object o) {
  if (! (o instanceof Queue))
    return false ;
  return super.equals(o) ;
}
/**
 *   Always causes and exception since it is a nonsense operation.
 *
 *   @exception InvalidOperationException always thrown since this is
 *   not a valid operation.  <CODE>Queue</CODE>s are closed
 *   containers.
 */
public boolean remove(Object o) {
  throw new InvalidOperationException () ;
}
}
```

Now we are in a position to declare a concrete class that is a queue. Firstly, one implemented using an Array:

```
package ADS ;
/**
 *   A <CODE>Queue</CODE> implemented using an associated
 *   <CODE>Array</CODE>.
 *
 *   <P> The head (the place from which items will be withdrawn) of the
 *   <CODE>Queue</CODE> is position 0 in the <CODE>Array</CODE>, the
 *   tail (the place to which new items will be appended) is the last
 *   element.
 *
 *   @version 1.0 1999.09.17
 *   @author Russel Winder
 */
public class ArrayQueue extends AbstractQueue {
  /**
   *   The underlying representation.
   */
  private final Array storage ;
  //
  //   Arrays can be constructed in three ways, specifying the base
  //   size and the extension size, just the base size using the
  //   default extension size or using the defaults for both. Reflect
  //   this in our constructors.
  /**
   *   Default constructor.
   */
  public ArrayQueue() {
    this(10, 10) ;
  }
```

```
/**
 *   Constructor defining the initial size of the
 *   <CODE>Array</CODE> we are using to actually implement
 *   this form of <CODE>Queue</CODE>.
 *
 *   @param initialSize The initial size of the <CODE>Queue</CODE>.
 */
public ArrayQueue(final int initialSize) {
  this(initialSize, 10) ;
}
/**
 *   Constructor defining the initial size of the
 *   <CODE>Array</CODE> we are using to actually implement
 *   this form of <CODE>Queue</CODE> and also the increment
 *   whenever the <CODE>Array</CODE> needs extending.
 *
 *   @param initialSize The initial size of the <CODE>Queue</CODE>.
 *
 *   @param incrementSize The size of the <CODE>Queue</CODE> space
 *   increment.
 */
public ArrayQueue(final int initialSize, final int incrementSize) {
  storage = new Array(initialSize, incrementSize) ;
}
/**
 *   Constructor that forces a <CODE>Queue</CODE> onto the backing
 *   <CODE>Array</CODE>.
 */
public ArrayQueue(final Array a) {
  storage = a ;
}
/**
 *   Remove a datum from ourself.
 *
 *   @exception AccessEmptyContainerException if we attempt to
 *   remove from an empty <CODE>Queue</CODE>.
 */
public final Object remove() {
  if (isEmpty())
    throw new AccessEmptyContainerException () ;
  Object o = storage.first() ;
  storage.remove(0) ;
  return o ;
}
/**
 *   Cause ourself to be emptied.
 */
public final void makeEmpty() {
  storage.makeEmpty() ;
}
/**
 *   Tell the world what size we are, i.e. how many
 *   <CODE>Object</CODE>s we have stored in ourself.
 */
public final int size() {
  return storage.size() ;
}
/**
 *   Insert a datum into ourself.
 */
public final void add(final Object o) {
  storage.add(o) ;
}
/**
 *   We have to clone ourself properly as a
 *   <CODE>ArrayQueue</CODE>.
```

```
  */
public final Object clone() {
  return new ArrayQueue ((Array)storage.clone()) ;
}
/**
 *  Even though we are a closed container, conforming to
 *  <CODE>Container</CODE> requires that we provide a public
 *  iterator.  However, we do ensure that there is no possibility of
 *  updates.
 */
public final ADS.Iterator iterator() {
  return storage.iterator () ;
}
/**
 *  An iterator over <CODE>ArrayQueue</code>s.
 *
 *  This is just a proxy for an iterator from the underlying
 *  representation so as to stop the ability to write.  Implement
 *  only a forward iterator.
 */
public class Iterator implements ADS.Iterator {
  /**
   *  We just need to act as a proxy for an iterator from the
   *  underlying representation.
   */
  private ADS.Iterator current = storage.iterator() ;
  /**
   *  Deliver the value we are currently referring to.
   */
  public final Object get() {
    return current.get() ;
  }
  /**
   *  Move on to the next element in the container.
   */
  public final void advance() {
    current.advance() ;
  }
  /**
   *  Have we reached the end of the iteration?
   */
  public final boolean atEnd() {
    return current.atEnd() ;
  }
  /**
   *  Are two iterators equal, i.e. do two iterators refer to the
   *  same item in the same data structure.
   */
  public boolean equals(final ADS.Iterator i) {
    if (!(i instanceof Iterator))
      return false ;
    return current.equals(((Iterator)i).current) ;
  }
  /**
   *  Return the reference to the object I am working.
   */
  public final Object myObject() {
    return current.myObject() ;
  }
  /**
   *  Clone this <CODE>Iterator</CODE>.
   */
  public final Object clone() {
    Iterator i = new Iterator () ;
    i.current = (Iterator)current.clone() ;
    return i ;
```

```
        }
      }
    }
```

and now one implemented using an `SLList`:

```
    package ADS ;
    /**
     *   A <CODE>Queue</CODE> implemented using an associated
     *   <CODE>SLList</CODE>.
     *
     *   <P> The head (the place from which items will be withdrawn) of the
     *   <CODE>Queue</CODE> is position 0 in the <CODE>SLList</CODE>, the
     *   tail (the place to which new items will be appended) is the last
     *   element.
     *
     *   @version 1.0 1999.09.17
     *   @author Russel Winder
     */
    public class SLListQueue extends AbstractQueue {
      /**
       *   The underlying representation.
       */
      private final SLList storage ;
      /**
       *   Constructor.
       */
      public SLListQueue() {
        storage = new SLList () ;
      }
      /**
       *   Constructor that forces a <CODE>Queue</CODE> onto the backing
       *   <CODE>SLList</CODE>.
       */
      public SLListQueue(final SLList l) {
        storage = l ;
      }
      /**
       *   Remove a datum from ourself.
       *
       *   @exception AccessEmptyContainerException if we attempt to
       *   remove from an empty <CODE>Queue</CODE>.
       */
      public final Object remove() {
        if (isEmpty())
          throw new AccessEmptyContainerException () ;
        Object o = storage.first() ;
        storage.remove(0) ;
        return o ;
      }
      /**
       *   Cause ourself to be emptied.
       */
      public final void makeEmpty() {
        storage.makeEmpty() ;
      }
      /**
       *   Tell the world what size we are, i.e. how many
       *   <CODE>Object</CODE>s we have stored in ourself.
       */
      public final int size() {
        return storage.size() ;
      }
      /**
       *   Insert a datum into ourself.
       */
```

```
public final void add(final Object o) {
  storage.add(o) ;
}
/**
 *  We have to clone ourself properly as a
 *  <CODE>SLListQueue</CODE>.
 */
public final Object clone() {
  return new SLListQueue ((SLList)storage.clone()) ;
}
/**
 *  Even though we are a closed container, conforming to
 *  <CODE>Container</CODE> requires that we provide a public
 *  iterator.  However, we do ensure that there is no possibility of
 *  updates.
 */
public final ADS.Iterator iterator() {
  return storage.iterator () ;
}
/**
 *  An iterator over <CODE>ArrayQueue</code>s.
 *
 *  This is just a proxy for an iterator from the underlying
 *  representation so as to stop the ability to write.  Implement
 *  only a forward iterator.
 */
public class Iterator implements ADS.Iterator {
  /**
   *  We just need to act as a proxy for an iterator from the
   *  underlying representation.
   */
  private ADS.Iterator current = storage.iterator() ;
  /**
   *  Deliver the value we are currently referring to.
   */
  public final Object get() {
    return current.get() ;
  }
  /**
   *  Move on to the next element in the container.
   */
  public final void advance() {
    current.advance() ;
  }
  /**
   *  Have we reached the end of the iteration?
   */
  public final boolean atEnd() {
    return current.atEnd() ;
  }
  /**
   *  Are two iterators equal, i.e. do two iterators refer to the
   *  same item in the same data structure.
   */
  public boolean equals(final ADS.Iterator i) {
    if (!(i instanceof Iterator))
      return false ;
    return current.equals(((Iterator)i).current) ;
  }
  /**
   *  Return the reference to the object I am working.
   */
  public final Object myObject() {
    return current.myObject() ;
  }
  /**
```

```
     *   Clone this <CODE>Iterator</CODE>.
     */
    public final Object clone() {
      Iterator i = new Iterator () ;
      i.current = (Iterator)current.clone() ;
      return i ;
    }
  }
}
```

The version using a DLList is essentially identical to that for the SLList so we will not show it here. Interestingly, this solution of having completely separate classes for each concrete representation is not actually the best in the case of classes that conform to Sequence. As we shall see in Section 14.6, there is a better, hybrid, alternative.

Although the code is short and much the same for both the Array and SLList implementation (also the DLList implementation), the implementations have very different performance properties. In particular, whilst insertion is $O(1)$ for all implementations, removal of items is $O(n)$ for the Array-based implementation and $O(1)$ for the linked list implementations. This slow behaviour of the Array-based implementation is due to the $O(n)$ behaviour of removal from an array that happens due to all the shuffling up of values that happens.

14.2.2   Circular Array Implementation

As mentioned in the introduction to this section, there are some very rare occasions on which it is not entirely appropriate to use a pre-defined abstraction to implement an ADT. Invariably such occasions arise when extremely high levels of efficiency are required. In such circumstances we need to be able to provide highly optimized versions of the ADT that is to be used. Primitive array based implementations tend to be preferred over class based implementations in these sorts of situation since they are more efficient (but less flexible remember).

Clearly, we cannot just translate from the Array-based implementation given in the previous subsection since we would end up with $O(n)$ behaviour for removal. We need to find a way of using primitive arrays in a way that results in $O(1)$ insertion and deletion.

The problem for the Array-based implementation was that removal of an item meant that the items had to be moved since the removal point was always at index 0. The insight we need is that we should move the insertion and removal points in the array leaving the data stationary. This is not quite enough, however. If we just move the insertion point down the array for each item inserted we will only be able to accept as many data items as there are elements in the array. We need a further insight and that is that as long as we have removed items from the queue as well as inserted them then the removal point has moved up and element 0 is free. We can re-use this location for further storage. By treating the array as though it were circular, such that element 0 follows immediately after element size-1, we can continue accepting data for as long as we only have less data to store than we have locations in the array. Thus, we make the insertion and removal points wrap around in the array, making it appear circular and constructing a Queue that can have as many insertions as

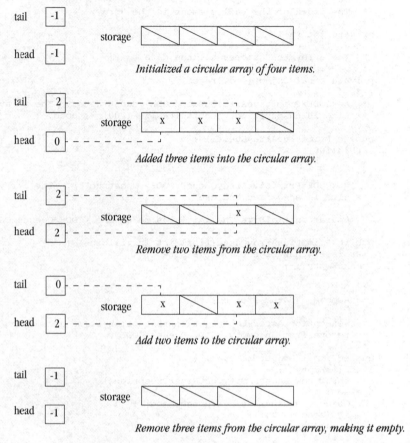

Figure 14.1 A circular array of four elements.

required as long as the total number of elements in the Queue is less that the size of the array.
Figure 14.1 shows how these circular buffers work in terms of an example.

We can implement class PrimitiveArrayQueue using these circular arrays:

```
package ADS ;
/**
 *  A <CODE>Queue</CODE> implemented using a circular array of
 *  <CODE>Object</CODE>s.
 *
 *  <P> The head (which is the "smaller" index trailing behind the
 *  tail!)  and tail (which is the "larger" index leading the head!)
 *  locations are wrapped around in the array as needed creating a
 *  circular array.  Use the index value -1 (which is illegal of
 *  course) to represent an empty <CODE>Queue</CODE>.
 *
 *  @version 1.1 1999.09.17
 *  @author Russel Winder
 */
public class PrimitiveArrayQueue extends AbstractQueue {
  /**
   *  The index of the head element in the array.
   */
  private int head ;
  /**
```

```
 *    The index of the tail element in the array.
 */
private int tail ;
/**
 *    The array that stores all the data.
 */
private final Object[] storage ;
/**
 *    A <CODE>PrimitiveArrayQueue</CODE> constructor.  The array
 *    size is unspecified, a default size (100) is used.
 */
public PrimitiveArrayQueue() {
  this(100) ;
}
/**
 *    A <CODE>PrimitiveArrayQueue</CODE> constructor.  The array
 *    size is specified and used.
 *
 *    @param initialSize The initial size of the <CODE>Queue</CODE>.
 */
public PrimitiveArrayQueue(final int initialSize) {
  storage = new Object [initialSize] ;
  makeEmpty() ;
}
/**
 *    Remove a datum from ourself.
 *
 *    @exception AccessEmptyContainerException if we attempt to
 *    remove from an empty <CODE>Queue</CODE>.
 */
public final Object remove() {
  if (isEmpty())
    throw new AccessEmptyContainerException() ;
  else {
    Object returnValue = storage[head] ;
    if (head == tail) {
      makeEmpty() ;
    } else {
      //
      //  We must ensure proper wrap around of the index when we do
      //  the increment hence the use of "modulo arithmetic".
      //
      head = (head + 1) % storage.length ;
    }
    return returnValue ;
  }
}
/**
 *    Cause ourself to be emptied.
 */
public final void makeEmpty() {
  head = -1 ;
  tail = -1 ;
  for (int i = 0 ; i < storage.length ; i++) {
    storage[i] = null ;
  }
}
/**
 *    Check to see whether we are empty or not.
 */
public final boolean isEmpty() {
  return head == -1 ;
}
/**
 *    Tell the world what size we are, i.e. how many
 *    <CODE>Object</CODE>s we have stored in ourself.
```

```
  */
public final int size() {
  if (isEmpty())
    return 0 ;
  if (head > tail)
    return storage.length - head + tail + 1 ;
  else
    return tail - head + 1 ;
}
/**
 *  Insert a datum into ourself.
 *
 *  @exception ContainerCapacityExceededException if we attempt to
 *  insert into the <CODE>Queue</CODE> more elements that it can
 *  take.
 */
public final void add(final Object o) {
  if (isEmpty()) {
    head = 0 ;
    tail = 0 ;
  } else {
    //
    //  We must ensure proper wrap around of the index when we do
    //  the increment hence the use of "modulo arithmetic".  We must
    //  also check to see if we actually have space to enter the new
    //  item.  So as to have a sensible state if the exception does
    //  occur, do not update tail until we are certain that
    //  everything is hunky dory.
    //
    int temp = (tail + 1) % storage.length ;
    if (head == temp)
      throw new ContainerCapacityExceededException() ;
    tail = temp ;
  }
  storage[tail] = o ;
}
/**
 *  We have to clone ourself properly as an
 *  <CODE>PrimitiveArrayQueue</CODE>.
 */
public final Object clone() {
  PrimitiveArrayQueue q = new PrimitiveArrayQueue (storage.length) ;
  q.head = head ;
  q.tail = tail ;
  //
  //  Copy the data array.  Could do:
  //    for (int i = 0 ; i < storage.length ; i++) {
  //        q.storage[i] = storage[i] ;
  //    }
  //  but can do the following instead:
  //
  System.arraycopy(storage, 0, q.storage, 0, storage.length) ;
  return q ;
}
/**
 *  Even though we are a closed container, conforming to
 *  <CODE>Container</CODE> requires that we provide a public
 *  iterator.  However, we do ensure that there is no possibility of
 *  updates.
 */
public final ADS.Iterator iterator() {
  return new Iterator () ;
}
/**
 *  An iterator over <CODE>PrimitiveArrayQueue</code>s.
 *
```

```
    *  This is just a proxy for an iterator from the underlying
    *  representation so as to stop the ability to write.  Implement
    *  only a forward iterator.
    */
  public class Iterator implements ADS.Iterator {
    /**
      *  We just need to have an index as a cursor.
      */
    private int current = head ;
    /**
      *  Deliver the value we are currently referring to.
      *
      *  @exception InvalidIteratorException if the iterator is not
      *  referring to a valid element.
      */
    public final Object get() {
      if (atEnd())
        throw new InvalidIteratorException () ;
      return storage[current] ;
    }
    /**
      *  Move on to the next element in the container.
      */
    public final void advance() {
      current = (current == tail)
        ? -1
        : (current == storage.length - 1)
           ? 0
           : current + 1 ;
    }
    /**
      *  Have we reached the end of the iteration?
      */
    public final boolean atEnd() {
      return current == -1 ;
    }
    /**
      *  Are two iterators equal, i.e. do two iterators refer to the
      *  same item in the same data structure.
      */
    public boolean equals(final ADS.Iterator i) {
      if (!(i instanceof Iterator))
        return false ;
      return current == ((Iterator)i).current ;
    }
    /**
      *  Return the reference to the object I am working.
      */
    public final Object myObject() {
      return PrimitiveArrayQueue.this ;
    }
    /**
      *  Clone this <CODE>Iterator</CODE>.
      */
    public final Object clone() {
      Iterator i = new Iterator () ;
      i.current = current ;
      return i ;
    }
  }
}
```

The only real limitation here is the maximum size of the queue that we can hold. Assuming we can guarantee that we can know the upper bound on the array size at the moment the queue gets created, then this implementation is probably the most efficient. It was, however, far harder to program and is prone to more errors. This implementation requires far more rigorous testing.

14.2.3 Linked List Implementation

Traditionally, queues have not been treated as ways of managing sequences (as was done in Section 14.2.1, Page 410) but have been treated as closed containers that needed to be implemented directly (as with the circular array implementation in the previous section). The circular array technology is complex to program compared to using linked list technology, but it turns out to be very easy to construct a queue using a custom linked list implementation (rather than using SLLIST or DLLIST). However, since the circular array implementation is probably the most efficient, and the queue implemented directly using a linked list has no real benefit over the implementation using a SLLIST by association, we are not entirely convinced that the custom linked list implementation of queue has any actual merit at all, since it achieves nothing new and has no real performance benefit over using versions employing sequences. We therefore mention such an implementation but do not present it.

14.2.4 An Example of Use

There are many uses of queues but most of the realistic examples involve quite large programs: small realistic examples of the use of queues are actually few and far between. Below we present one of the programs that forms part of the test suite for the various Queue types. It shows some of the ways that Queues can be used.

```
import ADS.Queue ;
import ADS.ArrayQueue ;
import ADS.SLListQueue ;
import ADS.DLListQueue ;
import ADS.PrimitiveArrayQueue ;
import ADS.LinkedListQueue ;
/**
 *  A program to test the various <CODE>Queue</CODE> implementations.
 */
public class testQueue {
  public static void main(final String[] args) {
    //
    //  Create one of each sort of Queue for this architecture and
    //  fill it with something -- test out the insert and delete
    //  amongst other things.
    //
    Queue a = new ArrayQueue () ;
    Queue b = new SLListQueue () ;
    Queue c = new Queue.Synchronized (new DLListQueue ()) ;
    Queue d = new PrimitiveArrayQueue () ;
    Queue e = new Queue.Synchronized (new LinkedListQueue ()) ;
    fillOut(a) ;
    fillOut(b) ;
    fillOut(c) ;
    fillOut(d) ;
    fillOut(e) ;
    checkout(a, a) ;
    checkout(a, b) ;
    checkout(a, c) ;
    checkout(a, d) ;
```

```
      checkout(a, e) ;
      checkout(b, b) ;
      checkout(b, c) ;
      checkout(b, d) ;
      checkout(b, e) ;
      checkout(c, c) ;
      checkout(c, d) ;
      checkout(c, e) ;
      checkout(d, d) ;
      checkout(d, e) ;
      checkout(e, e) ;
      System.out.println("===============================") ;
      //
      //  Clone all the Queues and then check whether various
      //  combinations are equal.
      //
      Queue aa = (Queue)a.clone() ;
      Queue bb = (Queue)b.clone() ;
      Queue cc = (Queue)c.clone() ;
      Queue dd = (Queue)d.clone() ;
      Queue ee = (Queue)e.clone() ;
      checkout(a, aa) ;
      checkout(b, bb) ;
      checkout(c, cc) ;
      checkout(d, dd) ;
      checkout(e, ee) ;
    }
    /**
     *  Perform various <code>Queue</code> actions to test them out.
     */
    private static void fillOut(Queue q) {
      checkEmpty(q) ;
      printIt(q) ;
      q.add(new Integer (15)) ;
      q.add(new Character ('a')) ;
      q.add(new Integer (30)) ;
      checkEmpty(q) ;
      printIt(q) ;
      q.remove() ;
      printIt(q) ;
      System.out.println("----------------------------------") ;
    }
    /**
     *  Check for emptiness.
     */
    private static void checkEmpty(Queue q) {
      System.out.println("The Queue is " +
                         (q.isEmpty() ? "" : "not ") + "empty") ;
    }
    /**
     *  Print the datum and its size.
     */
    private static void printIt(Queue q) {
      System.out.println(q + " of size " + q.size()) ;
    }
    /**
     *  Perform various equality tests on the parameters.
     */
    private static void checkout(Queue a, Queue b) {
      System.out.println(a.toString()) ;
      System.out.println(b.toString()) ;
      System.out.println("Pointer " +
                         ((a == b) ? "equivalent"
                          : "different")) ;
      System.out.println("a.b: Value " +
                         (a.equals(b) ? "equal"
```

```
                              : "different")) ;
        System.out.println("b.a: Value " +
                              (b.equals(a) ? "equal"
                              : "different")) ;
        System.out.println("--------------------------------") ;
    }
}
```

14.3 Using the Abstraction by Inheritance Architecture

Whereas with 'abstraction by conformance' the ADT is represented by an interface, with 'abstraction by inheritance', the ADT is represented with an abstract class. Instead of using an interface to represent the ADT and an abstract class to hold representation independent code, everything is bundled into a single abstract class. In essence, the basic approach is the same.

It is really a moot point as to which of these two very similar architectures is preferred. The previous architecture separates specification and implementation of defaults and so separates responsibilities more cleanly. The latter architecture requires less classes and possibly seems somehow less messy. Most people seem to be favouring the previous architecture despite the extra class involved. Collections, for example, uses the previous, mixed 'abstraction by conformance'/ 'abstraction by inheritance' architecture. For this reason we do not present a particular example of this approach.

14.4 Using the Abstraction by Association Architecture

In Section 14.2.1, Page 410, when we introduced the `ArrayQueue` and `SLListQueue` implementations of queue, we didn't really pick up on the point that these classes were just providing a data representation and that essentially all the methods were either implemented in `AbstractQueue` (in which case they are identical) or they were in the separate classes but were nonetheless almost identical. It seems that almost all the algorithms associated with `Queue` were actually independent of the data representation. In fact this is not quite true. The commonality was caused because `ArrayQueue` and `SLListQueue` are both instances of `Sequence` and all the algorithms could be expressed in terms of `Sequence`.

Figure 12.2, Page 354 showed the basic structure of 'abstraction by association'. Translating the general design to this particular situation, we have a concrete class `Queue` which has as a data member a `Sequence` that we can make concrete by providing a particular representation of a `Sequence`. This architecture works on the premise that the queue algorithms are identical whenever a `Sequence` is used as data storage, which is always.

```
package ADS ;
/**
 * A <CODE>Queue</CODE>.  The default storage mechanism is using a
 * <CODE>SLList</CODE> but any <CODE>Sequence</CODE> may be used.
```

```
    *   The choice is made a creation time.
    *
    *   @see Sequence
    *   @version 1.1 1999.09.17
    *   @author Russel Winder
    */
public class Queue implements Container {
  /**
   *   The place to store some data.
   */
  protected final Sequence storage ;
  /**
   *   Default constructor.
   */
  public Queue() {
    storage = new SLList () ;
  }
  /**
   *   Constructor allowing a choice of storage representation.
   *
   *   <P> The parameter is shallow copied so as to avoid potential
   *   sharing problems.
   *
   *   @param sequence The <CODE>Sequence</CODE> object to be used to
   *   store data.
   */
  public Queue(final Sequence sequence) {
    storage = (Sequence)sequence.clone() ;
  }
  /**
   *   Remove a datum from ourself.
   *
   *   @exception AccessEmptyContainerException if we attempt to
   *   remove from an empty <CODE>Queue</CODE>.
   */
  public Object remove() {
    if (isEmpty())
      throw new AccessEmptyContainerException() ;
    else {
      Object o = storage.get(0) ;
      storage.remove(0) ;
      return o ;
    }
  }
  /**
   *   Cause ourself to be emptied.
   */
  public void makeEmpty() {
    storage.makeEmpty() ;
  }
  /**
   *   Check to see whether we are empty or not.
   */
  public boolean isEmpty() {
    return storage.isEmpty() ;
  }
  /**
   *   Tell the world what size we are, i.e. how many
   *   <CODE>Object</CODE>s we have stored in ourself.
   */
  public int size() {
    return storage.size() ;
  }
  /**
   *   Test something against ourself for equality.
   */
```

```java
public boolean equals(final Object o) {
  if (this == o)
    return true ;
  if ((o == null) ||
      ! (o instanceof Queue) ||
      size() != ((Queue)o).size())
    return false ;
  return storage.equals(((Queue)o).storage) ;
}
/**
 *  Determine whether we have the value represented by the
 *  parameter <CODE>Object</CODE> in us.
 *
 *  @exception AccessEmptyContainerException if there are no
 *  items in the <CODE>Container</CODE>.
 */
public boolean contains(Object o) {
  return storage.contains(o) ;
}
/**
 *  Add an element to the <CODE>Container</CODE>.
 */
public void add(Object o) {
  storage.add(o) ;
}
/**
 *  Remove an element of a given value from the
 *  <CODE>Container</CODE> if it is in the <CODE>Container</CODE>.
 *
 *  @exception InvlaidOperationException is always thrown since this
 *  is an invalid operation, <CODE>Queue</CODE>s are closed
 *  containers.
 */
public boolean remove(Object o) {
  throw new InvalidOperationException () ;
}
/**
 *  We have to clone ourself properly as a <CODE>Queue</CODE>.
 */
public Object clone() {
  Queue q = new Queue ((Sequence)storage.clone()) ;
  return q ;
}
/**
 *  It is always useful to be able to print out the
 *  <CODE>Queue</CODE>, mostly to make debugging easy.
 */
public String toString() {
  return storage.toString() ;
}
/**
 *  Even though we are a closed container, conforming to
 *  <CODE>Container</CODE> requires that we provide a public
 *  iterator.  However, we do ensure that there is no possibility of
 *  updates.
 */
public ADS.Iterator iterator() {
  return iterator () ;
}
/**
 *  An iterator over <CODE>ArrayQueue</code>s.
 *
 *  This is just a proxy for an iterator from the underlying
 *  representation so as to stop the ability to write.  Implement
 *  only a forward iterator.
 */
```

```java
public class Iterator implements ADS.Iterator {
  /**
   *  We just need to act as a proxy for an iterator from the
   *  underlying representation.
   */
  private ADS.Iterator cursor = storage.iterator() ;
  /**
   *  Deliver the value we are currently referring to.
   */
  public final Object get() {
    return cursor.get() ;
  }
  /**
   *  Move on to the next element in the container.
   */
  public final void advance() {
    cursor.advance() ;
  }
  /**
   *  Have we reached the end of the iteration?
   */
  public final boolean atEnd() {
    return cursor.atEnd() ;
  }
  /**
   *  Are two iterators equal, i.e. do two iterators refer to the
   *  same item in the same data structure.
   */
  public boolean equals(final ADS.Iterator i) {
    if (! (i instanceof Iterator))
      return false ;
    return (myObject() == i.myObject()) &&
      cursor.equals(((Iterator)i).cursor) ;
  }
  /**
   *  Return the reference to the object I am working.
   */
  public final Object myObject() {
    return Queue.this ;
  }
  /**
   *  Clone this <CODE>Iterator</CODE>.
   */
  public final Object clone() {
    Iterator i = new Iterator () ;
    i.cursor = (Iterator)cursor.clone() ;
    return i ;
  }
}
/**
 *  The class that provides a synchronized interface for use in
 *  multi-threaded applications.
 */
public static class Synchronized extends Queue {
  /**
   *  The <CODE>Object</CODE> on which to do all locking.
   */
  private final Object theLock;
  /**
   *  The default constructor.  Gives an <CODE>Queue</CODE> with
   *  default initial size and increment.
   */
  public Synchronized() {
    theLock = this ;
  }
  /**
```

```
 *   The constructor that supplies an object to synchronize on.
 */
public Synchronized(final Object o) {
  theLock = o ;
}
/**
 *   Remove an item from the <CODE>Queue</CODE>.
 */
public final Object remove() {
  synchronized (theLock) { return super.remove() ; }
}
/**
 *   Remove the entire contents of the <CODE>Queue</CODE>.
 *
 *   This does not affect the size of the underlying array, it only
 *   removes the elements.
 */
public final void makeEmpty() {
  synchronized (theLock) { super.makeEmpty() ; }
}
/**
 *   Determine whether the <CODE>Queue</CODE> is an empty one.
 */
public final boolean isEmpty() {
  synchronized (theLock) { return super.isEmpty() ; }
}
/**
 *   Return the number of items in the <CODE>Queue</CODE>.
 */
public final int size() {
  synchronized (theLock) { return super.size() ; }
}
/**
 *   Compare this <CODE>Queue</CODE> with another and determine
 *   whether they represent the same value, i.e. have the same item
 *   values in the same order in the <CODE>Queue</CODE>.
 */
public final boolean equals(final Object o) {
  synchronized (theLock) { return super.equals(o) ; }
}
/**
 *   Determine whether we have the value represented by the
 *   parameter <CODE>Object</CODE> in us.
 *
 *   @exception AccessEmptyContainerException if there are no
 *   items in the <CODE>Queue</CODE>.
 */
public final boolean contains(final Object o) {
  synchronized (theLock) { return super.contains(o) ; }
}
/**
 *   Append an element to the end of the <CODE>Queue</CODE>.
 *
 *   @exception AccessEmptyContainerException if there are no
 *   items in the <CODE>Queue</CODE>.
 */
public final void add(final Object o) {
  synchronized (theLock) { super.add(o) ; }
}
/**
 *   Remove an element of a given value from the
 *   <CODE>Queue</CODE> if it is in the <CODE>Queue</CODE>.
 *
 *   @return whether the item was actually in the
 *   <CODE>Queue</CODE>.
 *
```

```
 *   @exception AccessEmptyContainerException if there are nc
 *   items in the <CODE>Queue</CODE>.
 */
public final boolean remove(final Object o) {
  synchronized (theLock) { return super.remove(o) ; }
}
/**
 *   Deliver up a complete shallow copy of the
 *   <CODE>Queue</CODE>.
 */
public final Object clone() {
  synchronized (theLock) { return super.clone() ; }
}
/**
 *   Deliver up a <CODE>String</CODE> representation the
 *   <CODE>Queue</CODE>.
 */
public final String toString() {
  synchronized (theLock) { return super.toString() ; }
}
  }
}
```

Note that as the nested class `Synchronized` can no longer conform to `Queue` it must be a subclass. Since we are inheriting from a `Queue` there is no need to store a `Queue` item and we can forward requests to super instead. Note also that we chose `SLList` as the default representation since it has the best resource usage characteristics of all the `Sequences`.

This implementation does have a massive benefit over the earlier one, though. We need only one class and it will work for all `Sequences`. There is no need for elaborate naming schemes and extra classes in order to provide new representations: the choice of representation is a matter of choosing a parameter rather than choosing a class name. However, this implementation would need amendment to deal with non-`Sequence` representations, (e.g. circular array).

So which of the two architectures, 'abstraction by conformance' and 'abstraction by association', is better? Whilst, for ADS, we have implemented both approaches as an experiment, JGL chooses 'abstraction by association'. Collections doesn't address this problem as it doesn't support an implementation of the queue abstraction. If it did, it would surely have to use 'abstraction by conformance' in order to present a consistent architecture — all other ADTs in Collections use this model. The only thing that is certain is that the two architectures cannot be mixed in the same library, one has to make a choice. At its crudest the choice is ease of naming and use ('abstraction by association') versus extensibility ('abstraction by conformance'). On balance, the conformance architecture probably wins on the grounds of extensibility, an important property for a library. We will therefore be concentrating on 'abstraction by conformance' from now on.

!

Extensibility means that 'abstraction by conformance' wins over 'abstraction by association' for library ADT design.

14.5   A Typesafe Queue

In Section 12.4, Page 330, we said that fully typesafe containers could be constructed. By this we meant containers that would only accept a certain type of data for storage and that would be fully typechecked at compile-time. In this section, we offer an example of such a container type.

This container will deal only with `int`s. All the methods are constrained to work only with `int` parameters and they deliver `int` data. Thus no casts are required in the application code when removing data from this sort of `Queue`.

```
package ADS ;
/**
 *  A class to implement a queue of <CODE>int</CODE>s with strong type
 *  checking of the data items put into and taken out of the queue.  A
 *  <CODE>DLListQueue</CODE> is used as representation.
 *
 *  <P> NB We cannot actually conform to <CODE>Queue</CODE> as the
 *  signatures of the methods that are appropriate for this class are
 *  not consistent with those of <CODE>Queue</CODE>.
 *
 *  @see DLListQueue
 *  @version 1.1 1999.09.17
 *  @author Russel Winder
 */
public class IntDLListQueue {
  /**
   *  The place to store some data.
   */
  private DLListQueue storage  = new DLListQueue () ;
  /**
   *  Insert a datum into ourself.  We only deal with
   *  <CODE>int</CODE>s.
   */
  public final void add(final int i) {
    storage.add(new Integer (i)) ;
  }
  /**
   *  Remove a datum from ourself ensuring that it is returned as an
   *  <CODE>int</CODE>.
   */
  public final int remove() {
    return ((Integer)storage.remove()).intValue() ;
  }
  /**
   *  Cause ourself to be emptied.
   */
  public final void makeEmpty() {
    storage.makeEmpty() ;
  }
  /**
   *  Check to see whether we are empty or not.
   */
  public final boolean isEmpty() {
    return storage.isEmpty() ;
  }
  /**
   *  Tell the world what size we are, i.e. how many
   *  <CODE>int</CODE>s we have stored in ourself.
   */
  public final int size() {
```

```
            return storage.size() ;
        }
        /**
         *  Test something against ourself for equality.
         *
         *  @param o The <CODE>Object</CODE> to compare ourself against.
         */
        public final boolean equals(final Object o) {
          if (this == o)
            return true ;
          if ((o == null) ||
              ! (o instanceof IntDLListQueue) ||
              (size() != ((IntDLListQueue)o).size())))
            return false ;
          return storage.equals((((IntDLListQueue)o).storage) ;
        }
        /**
         *  Do we contain a value?
         */
        public final boolean contains(final int i) {
          return storage.contains(new Integer (i)) ;
        }
        /**
         *  We have to clone ourself properly as an
         *  <CODE>IntQueue</CODE>.
         */
        public final Object clone() {
          IntDLListQueue q = new IntDLListQueue () ;
          q.storage = (DLListQueue)storage.clone() ;
          return q ;
        }
        /**
         *  It is always useful to be able to print out the
         *  <CODE>Queue</CODE>, mostly to make debugging easy.
         */
        public final String toString() {
          return storage.toString() ;
        }
      }
```

The good aspects of an ADT such as this are that no casting is necessary and we are not relying on run-time type checking; any application that compiles without error using this type is guaranteed to be typesafe. The problem is that we have to undertake such an implementation explicitly for each type. This leads to a maintenance nightmare. As referred to in Section 12.4, Page 330, it is for this reason that some other object-oriented programming languages support parameterized types. For those Java programmers who are happy with casting and run-time type checking there is no problem. For those who want or need full compile-time type safety in Java, some form of parameterized type mechanism is essential. Moreover, experience with other programming languages shows that this must not be left to library designers but must be a part of the standard language.

This sort of use of the 'abstraction by association' approach is usually called a wrapper or now, more commonly, an *adapter*. The class IntDLListQueue provides no functionality per se, its purpose is to change the public interface of another class: IntDLListQueue wraps DLListQueue altering its public interface, thereby providing an adapter between two similar but different public interfaces.

14.6 Double-ended Queues

The `Queue` ADT developed in the previous section only allows insertion of data at the head of the queue and removal of data from the tail of the queue. Sometimes it turns out to be very useful to have a double-ended queue or `Dequeue`, which is an ADT (a closed container) that allows insertion and removal at both the head and the tail of the queue. Diagrammatically, we are looking for the following sort of thing:

tail remove   *head add*

tail add   *head remove*

Using the 'abstraction by conformance' architecture, we could work analogously to the way we did with `Queue`, creating an interface, an abstract class and then concrete classes for each of the representations we want to provide implementations for. This is not restrictive since the architecture is a very flexible one and new representations can be added as required. Moreover, there is no need for the representation to inherit from or conform to a specific type as is true for the 'abstraction by association' architecture.

However, it is clear from comparing the above diagram and the diagram on Page 408 that a `Dequeue` is some form of extension of a `Queue`: A `Dequeue` is a specialization of a `Queue`. This is very indicative that there should be an inheritance relationship between them. It is also clear from the diagrams that wherever a `Queue` is required in a piece of code, it should be possible to use a `Dequeue`. It seems that the following relationship needs to be embodied in our code:

Using the 'abstraction by conformance' approach, this relationship is handled at the interface level, the `Dequeue` interface is a subinterface of the `Queue` interface and this completes the necessary details to allow concrete `Dequeues` to be used whenever a `Queue` is required. Here then is the interface:

```
package ADS ;
/**
 *  An interface defining the necessary properties to be deemed to be
 *  a <CODE>Dequeue</CODE> a type of <CODE>Queue</CODE>. Do not
 *  confuse this with <CODE>Deque</CODE> in the <small>JGL</small>.
 *
 *  <P> We define a dequeue to be any data structure that can have
 *  items inserted and removed from either end and which guarantees a
 *  First in -- First out ordering policy if items are only inserted
 *  at the tail and removed at the head.
 *
 *  @version 1.1 1999.09.17
 *  @author Russel Winder
 */
```

```java
public interface Dequeue extends Queue {
  /**
   *  Insert an item into the <CODE>Dequeue</CODE> at the head.
   */
  void headAdd(Object o) ;
  /**
   *  Insert an item into the <CODE>Dequeue</CODE> at the tail.
   */
  void tailAdd(Object o) ;
  /**
   *  Remove an item from the head of the <CODE>Dequeue</CODE>.
   */
  Object headRemove() ;
  /**
   *  Remove an item from the tail of the <CODE>Dqueue</CODE>.
   */
  Object tailRemove() ;
  /**
   *  Remove an item from the head of the <CODE>Dequeue</CODE>.
   */
  Object remove() ;
  /**
   *  The class that provides a synchronized interface for use in
   *  multi-threaded applications.
   */
  public static class Synchronized
    extends Container.Synchronized implements Dequeue{
    /**
     *  The default constructor.  Gives a <CODE>Dequeue</CODE> with
     *  default initial size and increment.
     */
    public Synchronized(final Dequeue q) {
      super(q) ;
    }
    /**
     *  The constructor that supplies an object to synchronize on.
     */
    public Synchronized(final Dequeue q, final Object o) {
      super(q, o) ;
    }
    /**
     *  Insert an item into the head of the <CODE>Dequeue</CODE>.
     */
    public final void headAdd(Object o) {
      synchronized (theLock) {
        ((Dequeue)theContainer).headAdd(o) ;
      }
    }
    /**
     *  Insert an item into the tail of the <CODE>Dequeue</CODE>.
     */
    public final void tailAdd(Object o) {
      synchronized (theLock) {
        ((Dequeue)theContainer).tailAdd(o) ;
      }
    }
    /**
     *  Remove an item from the head of the <CODE>Dequeue</CODE>.
     */
    public final Object headRemove() {
      synchronized (theLock) {
        return ((Dequeue)theContainer).headRemove() ;
      }
    }
    /**
     *  Remove an item from the tail of the <CODE>Dequeue</CODE>.
```

```
     */
   public final Object tailRemove() {
     synchronized (theLock) {
       return ((Dequeue)theContainer).tailRemove() ;
     }
   }
   /**
    *  Remove an item from the head of the <CODE>Dequeue</CODE>.
    */
   public final Object remove() {
     synchronized (theLock) {
       return ((Dequeue)theContainer).remove() ;
     }
   }
 }
}
```

Following the 'abstraction by conformance' architecture we have chosen for the package, we now introduce an `AbstractDequeue` class to hold all the code shared by all the concrete classes implementing double-ended queues. Actually we can use inheritance again here since much of the code we need is already in `AbstractQueue`. Thus, `AbstractDequeue` inherits from `AbstractQueue`:

```
package ADS ;
/**
 *  An abstract <CODE>Dequeue</CODE> to act as a superclass for all
 *  the concrete sequences.  Provides all the default implementations
 *  that are representation independent.
 *
 *  @version 1.0 1999.09.18
 *  @author Russel Winder
 */
public abstract class AbstractDequeue
   extends AbstractQueue implements Dequeue {
   /**
    *  Insert an item into the <CODE>Dequeue</CODE> at the head.
    */
   public abstract void headAdd(Object o) ;
   /**
    *  Insert an item into the <CODE>Dequeue</CODE> at the tail.
    */
   public abstract void tailAdd(Object o) ;
   /**
    *  Insert an item into the <CODE>Dequeue</CODE> at the head.
    */
   public void add(Object o) {
     tailAdd(o) ;
   }
   /**
    *  Remove an item from the head of the <CODE>Dequeue</CODE>.
    */
   public abstract Object headRemove() ;
   /**
    *  Remove an item from the tail of the <CODE>Dequeue</CODE>.
    */
   public abstract Object tailRemove() ;
   /**
    *  Remove an item from the tail of the <CODE>Dequeue</CODE>.
    *
    *  @exception AccessEmptyContainerException if we attempt to
    *  remove from an empty <CODE>Dequeue</CODE>.
    */
   public Object remove() {
     return headRemove() ;
```

```
      }
      /**
       *  Test something against ourself for equality.
       */
      public boolean equals(final Object o) {
        if (! (o instanceof Dequeue))
          return false ;
        return super.equals(o) ;
      }
    }
```

We are now in a position to write the code for the concrete implementations. For the circular array or directly coded doubly-linked list implementations we would just go ahead and code up a solution. For the implementations using Sequence, however, we can make use of the lessons from the 'abstraction by association' version of Queue. When looking at Queue we separated 'abstraction by conformance' and 'abstraction by association' as two separate approaches. We decided to work with the 'abstraction by association' model since it provided for greater flexibility. However, the 'abstraction by association' approach had some major benefits regarding the handling of Sequences as representations. For this implementation of a double-ended queue we make use of this experience to come up with an hybrid approach. For types that are not Sequences, we work as before with a separate concrete class for each type. For Sequences, however we make use of an 'abstraction by association' approach to create a SequenceDequeue avoiding the need for separate ArrayQueue, SLListDequeue and DLListDequeue classes:

```
      package ADS ;
      /**
       *  A <CODE>Dequeue</CODE> implemented using an <CODE>Sequence</CODE>.
       *  The particular <CODE>Sequence</CODE> is chosen at creation time,
       *  with <CODE>DLList</CODE> being the default.
       *
       *  <P> The head of the <CODE>Dequeue</CODE> is position 0 in the
       *  <CODE>Sequence</CODE>, the tail is the last element -- use the
       *  size() method to discover this: the <CODE>Sequence</CODE> is
       *  always exactly the size of the <CODE>Dequeue</CODE>.
       *  <CODE>Sequence</CODE> itself keeps track of the distinction
       *  between the number of items in the <CODE>Sequence</CODE> and the
       *  storage used to store it.
       *
       *  @version 1.0 1999.09.17
       *  @author Russel Winder
       */
      public class SequenceDequeue extends AbstractDequeue {
        /**
         *  The underlying representation.
         */
        private final Sequence storage ;
        /**
         *  Default constructor.
         */
        public SequenceDequeue() {
          storage = new DLList () ;
        }
        /**
         *  Constructor defining the <CODE>Sequence</CODE> we are using to
         *  actually implement this form of <CODE>Dequeue</CODE>.
         */
        public SequenceDequeue(final Sequence s) {
          storage = s ;
        }
```

```
/**
 *  Head insert a datum into ourself.
 */
public final void headAdd(final Object o) {
  storage.insert(0, o) ;
}
/**
 *  Tail insert a datum into ourself.
 */
public final void tailAdd(final Object o) {
  storage.add(o) ;
}
/**
 *  Head remove a datum from ourself.
 *
 *  @exception AccessEmptyContainerException if we attempt to
 *  remove from an empty <CODE>Queue</CODE>.
 */
public final Object headRemove() {
  if (isEmpty())
    throw new AccessEmptyContainerException () ;
  else {
    Object o = storage.get(0) ;
    storage.remove(0) ;
    return o ;
  }
}
/**
 *  Tail remove a datum from ourself.
 *
 *  @exception AccessEmptyContainerException if we attempt to
 *  remove from an empty <CODE>Queue</CODE>.
 */
public final Object tailRemove() {
  if (isEmpty())
    throw new AccessEmptyContainerException () ;
  else {
    int i = storage.size() - 1 ;
    Object o = storage.get(i) ;
    storage.remove(i) ;
    return o ;
  }
}
/**
 *  Cause ourself to be emptied.
 */
public final void makeEmpty() {
  storage.makeEmpty() ;
}
/**
 *  Tell the world what size we are, i.e. how many
 *  <CODE>Object</CODE>s we have stored in ourself.
 */
public final  int size() {
  return storage.size() ;
}
/**
 *  We have to clone ourself properly as a
 *  <CODE>SequenceQueue</CODE>.
 */
public final Object clone() {
  return new SequenceDequeue ((Sequence)storage.clone()) ;
}
/**
 *  Even though we are a closed container, conforming to
 *  <CODE>Container</CODE> requires that we provide a public
```

```
 *   iterator.  However, we do ensure that there is no possibility of
 *   updates.
 */
public final ADS.Iterator iterator() {
  return storage.iterator () ;
}
/**
 *   An iterator over <CODE>SequenceQueue</code>s.
 *
 *   This is just a proxy for an iterator from the underlying
 *   representation so as to stop the ability to write.  Implement
 *   only a forward iterator.
 */
public class Iterator implements ADS.Iterator {
  /**
   *   We just need to act as a proxy for an iterator from the
   *   underlying representation.
   */
  private ADS.Iterator current = storage.iterator() ;
  /**
   *   Deliver the value we are currently referring to.
   */
  public final Object get() {
    return current.get() ;
  }
  /**
   *   Move on to the next element in the container.
   */
  public final void advance() {
    current.advance() ;
  }
  /**
   *   Have we reached the end of the iteration?
   */
  public final boolean atEnd() {
    return current.atEnd() ;
  }
  /**
   *   Are two iterators equal, i.e. do two iterators refer to the
   *   same item in the same data structure.
   */
  public boolean equals(final ADS.Iterator i) {
    if (!(i instanceof Iterator))
      return false ;
    return current == ((Iterator)i).current ;
  }
  /**
   *   Return the reference to the current object.
   */
  public final Object myObject() {
    return SequenceDequeue.this ;
  }
  /**
   *   Clone this <CODE>Iterator</CODE>.
   */
  public final Object clone() {
    Iterator i = new Iterator () ;
    i.current = (Iterator)current.clone() ;
    return i ;
  }
}
}
```

If ADS were a production library, we would now go back to the `Queue` implementation and alter that to make use of this design strategy. This is just iterative development at work. As we gain more knowledge about how to implement features of the library we must make the changes to the library.

Iterative development is even more important for packages than for applications.

14.7 A Short Digression on Design Philosophy

Actually there is another potential solution which we ought to consider to the design approach for the `Dequeue`. It turns out we will reject it but we should at least consider it.

We can exemplify this alternate design by posing the question: Is `Queue` a restriction of a `Dequeue` rather than a generalization of a `Dequeue`, as suggested above? Rephrasing this: Should we, in fact, implement `Dequeue` from scratch so as to base the `Queue` implementation on it rather than have `Dequeue` be a subclass of `Queue`? The answer is no but it is, nonetheless, a sensible and valid question. We need cogent reasoning as to why it is not the right approach.

First, though, here is an argument *for* creating `Dequeue` and restricting it to get a `Queue`: A `Dequeue` contains all the capabilities needed by a `Queue` but can do more than a `Queue`. A `Queue` is, therefore, a restriction on the behaviour of a `Dequeue`. Thus we can implement a `Queue` by using 'abstraction by association': a `Queue` uses a `Dequeue`, restricting its interface. By carefully implementing the type with the greater functionality we can trivially create types with less functionality.

What about the argument against? The first step is to accede the validity of the above argument as put forward. However, there are two principal reasons for not accepting it as the way forward.

The first point is that with the '`Queue` as restriction on `Dequeue`' approach we first have to build the more general, and hence more complex, class. This means that no matter how much complexity we actually need in the implementation of an application, we will make use of larger, more complex software components to build it. This is a bad idea by corollary of Ockham's Razor which in effect, in this situation, says: only use sufficient sophistication to achieve the desired goal. Of course, we must never go too far, we must always be prepared to use more sophisticated subsystems if they make the overall system easier and quicker to construct.

The second point relates to the question "What is the most general case?" The advantage of constructing complexity on top of simplicity using inheritance or association is that we can generate the complexity we need, when we need it and when we understand it. If we are going to construct a more complex solution and then restrict it, we need to know what purpose the complexity is ultimately meant to address. Unfortunately, it is only very rarely that we can predict all possible future requirements of the complex solution from which to make our restrictions. Also, identifying the general case is hard enough already without having to merge all possible cases together so that restriction can take place.

What the restriction argument fails to treat as core is that Queues are simpler than Dequeues, they are more basic. Furthermore, a Dequeue 'is-a' Queue but a Queue is not a Dequeue and cannot, in general, be substituted for one. Thus, inheritance is, in fact, the right road to follow in implementing Dequeues.

A final point to note while considering restriction, is that trying to create Queue as a subclass of Dequeue and somehow 'removing' the unwanted pieces that Queue doesn't need is not feasible at all. Not only are there no language mechanisms to do this but it would also violate the principle of substitutability that comes with inheritance. We cannot substitute provide a Queue when a Dequeue is expected, as sooner or later an attempt will be made to perform a Dequeue operation that Queue cannot support.

14.8 Stacks

We first saw stacks in Section 6.2, Page 146.

The Queue and Dequeue are 'first in, first out' (FIFO) data structures. This immediately opens up the question of whether there is a 'first in, last out' (FILO) structure. Clearly the answer is yes and indeed such a thing is called a *stack*. Like queues, stacks are around us in the real world as well as in programming. An in-tray is a form of stack, the item on top is the one that can easily be got at. If you want to get any other item you have to search from the top. Finally, it is easiest to put a new item on top. An in-tray is not always a stack; some people put new items at the bottom so that it is really a queue and some people insert items at random places in the pile!

A plate stacker in a canteen is a true stack; only the top plate is accessible and the first plate put on the stack is the last plate taken off. Diagrammatically a stack is like a box into which we can put things with the first-in, last-out protocol enforced:

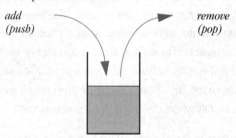

Traditionally, the operation of putting an item on a stack is called *pushing* and taking an item off the stack is called *popping*. To use these names would, however, conflict with the naming scheme we have been developing for the ADS package. Indeed to be a Container, the class must implement the add and remove methods. We therefore must implement these two methods as the data storage operations. This gives us our required consistency package-wide. However, we can also provide the methods push and pop as aliases so that people can use the more traditional names should they wish.

It seems quite perverse that add/remove (or sometimes insert/remove or even enqueue/dequeue) has been the terminology for queues whereas push/pop has been the terminology for stacks. After all they have essentially the same behaviour with just a different ordering property. While that is an important difference, nonetheless queues and stacks have more similarities than differences. It is entirely possible that the divergence of terminology stems from the fact that stacks were in heavy use in the processor hardware design and implementation arena whereas queues grew up principally in the areas of operating systems and simulation programs. The different domains having different people and different concerns developed different jargon.

Actually, stacks are so much like queues in terms of implementation, that we are not going to present a full implementation. Instead we shall leave this as an exercise for the reader. What we will say is that whilst we could implement a stack using either 'abstraction by conformance' or 'abstraction by association', 'abstraction by conformance' is really the mechanism of choice due to the flexibility in being able to add additional representations without alteration of existing code.

Both JGL and J2SDK implement a stack abstraction. The JGL implements its stack ADT using 'abstraction by association' on the premise that in reality flexibility is not a serious issue since all sensible implementations are already available. There is an implementation of `Stack` in the standard Java library, though it is somewhat different. In J2SDK, `Stack` is implemented as a subclass of `Vector`, `Vector` being a class very much like `ArrayList`. This has many consequences, the two major ones of which are:

- Only `Vector`s can be used as the storage type for the `Stack`. This is actually not a poor deal since the implementation is an efficient one, $O(1)$ in fact.
- All of the public methods of `Vector` are available to be used on a `Stack` even though they may be wholly inappropriate for the stack abstraction. This is *very* bad.

Basically, inheritance is completely the wrong relationship, conceptually, between `Vector` and `Stack` since there is no way of retracting methods (i.e. not allowing certain public methods of the superclass to be public methods of the subclass). The only way of restricting the set of public methods is to use association and not inheritance. Also a `Stack` is not a `Vector`, it is only true that a `Stack` can be implemented using a `Vector`. This is another indication that association and not inheritance is the appropriate relationship between `Stack` and `Vector`. It seems that method code reuse, that is not having to duplicate method bodies, rather than the construction of a proper ADT has driven the design of this implementation of `Stack`. It really ought to be replaced. The JGL implementation and the one presented above are far better designs.

14.9   An Example of Using a Stack

Whilst it appears to be an artificial example, let us consider reversing a string as an application that uses a stack.

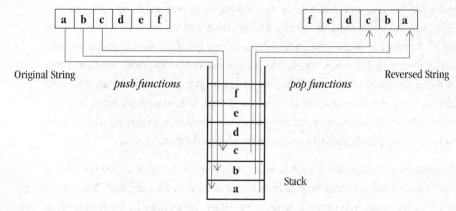

Figure 14.2 Reversing a string using a stack.

We can reverse a string by reading a character at a time from the string, storing it in the stack and then, once all the characters are on the stack, taking them out of the stack. Because of the last-in, first-out nature of a stack the characters come out in reverse order. The algorithm is shown diagrammatically in Figure 14.2.

The characters are read in order from the string, starting from index 0 and going to maximum index and inserted onto the stack. They are then removed from the stack and put, using the same index order, back into the same array.

```
import ADS.Stack ;
import ADS.SequenceStack ;
//
// Would need (one of) these if we used anything other than the
// default storage types when constructing the Stack.
//
//    import ADS.Array ;
//    import ADS.SLList ;
//    import ADS.DLList ;
//
class StringReverser {
  public static String reverse(final String s) {
    StringBuffer sb = new StringBuffer (s) ;
    Stack st = new SequenceStack () ;
    //
    // Could also use any of these but make sure the correct import
    // is included:
    //
    //    Stack st = new SequenceStack(new Array ()) ;
    //    Stack st = new SequenceStack(new SLList ()) ;
    //    Stack st = new SequenceStack(new DLList ()) ;
    //
    for (int i = 0 ; i < sb.length() ; i++) {
      st.add(new Character (sb.charAt(i))) ;
    }
    //
    // Setting the StringBuffer length to zero essentially removes
    // the previous string creating an empty string ready for more
    // operations.
    //
    sb.setLength(0) ;
    while (! st.isEmpty()) {
      sb.append(st.remove()) ;
```

```
      }
    return sb.toString() ;
  }
}
```

Whilst this shows a reasonable algorithm for string reversal and a very nice example of how a stack can be used, it is not actually the best way of solving this particular problem in Java. The observation to be made is that, searching through the manual pages for `StringBuffer`, it transpires that `StringBuffer` has a method `reverse`. This can best be discovered by using the full index of the online documentation and looking up 'reverse'. Thus, the following is actually a much better solution to the string reversal problem:

```
class StringReverser {
  public static String reverse(final String s) {
    StringBuffer sb = new StringBuffer (s) ;
    return sb.reverse().toString() ;
  }
}
```

As a matter of interest, the algorithm in the `reverser` method is not a stack-based one but instead does pair-wise swapping. The following is not the actual code used in `java.lang.StringBuffer` but presents the identical algorithm:

```
class StringReverser {
  public static String reverse(final String s) {
    int n = s.length() ;
    char[] datum = new char[n] ;
    s.getChars(0, n, datum, 0) ;
    n-- ;
    for (int i = (n-1)/2 ; i >= 0 ; i--) {
      char temp = datum[i] ;
      datum[i] = datum[n-i] ;
      datum[n-i] = temp ;
    }
    return new String (datum) ;
  }
}
```

The algorithm being used here is that elements are pair-wise swapped starting with the two elements in the middle. There are clearly two cases to worry about: when there are an even number of entries and when there are an odd number of entries. In the case of an even number we have the following sort of situation:

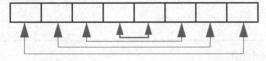

In the case of an odd number of entries, we do not need to move the middle element so we end up with:

This 'pair swapping' algorithm is used since it is the most efficient one, $O(n)$ in fact. Of course the stack algorithm is also $O(n)$ so, in theoretical terms, they are of identical performance. We actually need to look in a little more detail to determine why the 'pair swapping' algorithm is considered to be the more efficient. The stack algorithm is actually $O(2n)$ whereas the 'pair swapping' algorithm is $O(n/2)$. Constants are normally ignored in Big-O notation but in this case we need to take this factor of 4 into account. Another factor which is at the level of a constant and therefore normally ignored is that the stack algorithm uses method calls whereas the 'pair swapping' algorithm uses primitive operations on arrays. Since primitive operations are faster that method calls, this is a constant factor of performance in favour of the 'pair swapping algorithm'. The 'pair swapping' algorithm is therefore a constant factor of 4 faster in execution. In terms of storage, the 'pair swapping algorithm' is also at an advantage as it is possible for the string to be reversed 'in-place' without allocating any new data structure. Using a stack always requires the use of an additional data structure.

14.10 Summary

We have developed a number of implementations of `Queue`, `Dequeue` and `Stack`. This shows a number of things:

- There are many possible implementations of an abstraction/ADT, indeed many architectures of implementation.
- ADTs can be represented by interfaces or classes in Java.
- Different implementations of ADTs have different performance properties.
- A good package architecture is needed to properly support ADTs and their multiple implementations.
- The appropriate choice of ADT implementation depends on use.
- A library needs to specify not just the ADTs, their implementations and the semantics of the available methods but also the performance properties of the methods.

Essentially we have discovered that whilst 'abstraction by inheritance' is useful for open containers, 'abstraction by association' is probably more useful for closed containers.

Self-review Question

Self-review 14.1 Describe the abstractions of queue, double-ended queue and stack.

Self-review 14.2 Why do we favour the 'abstraction by conformance' architecture for the ADS package?

Self-review 14.3 How do JGL and Collections handle the queue, double-ended queue and stack abstractions?

Self-review 14.4 Why does using the 'abstraction by association' `Stack` implementation lead to O(n) behaviour when using Array as the representation?

Exercises

Exercise 14.1 Create a implementation of `Dequeue` using the 'abstraction by association' architecture.

Exercise 14.2 The claim was made earlier in this chapter that a singly linked list implementation of a `Dequeue` would have tail removal that had O(n) time properties. Show that this is so by constructing a `LinkedListDequeue` which implements the `Dequeue` interface given earlier using a singly linked list data structure. (The obvious approach is to take the `LinkedListQueue` class amend it.)

Exercise 14.3 Create an implementation of `Stack` using the 'abstraction by conformance' architecture, that could be inserted into the ADS package.

Challenges

Challenge 14.1 What modification would be required of the 'abstraction by conformance' implementations of the queue, double-ended queue and stack abstractions in order to be inserted into Collections.

Challenge 14.2 What modification would be required of the 'abstraction by conformance' implementations of the queue, double-ended queue and stack abstractions in order to be inserted into JGL.

Trees

Objectives

This chapter introduces a non-linear abstraction, the tree, and in particular the binary tree. There are a number of different forms of binary tree, so we do not cover the details of all of them but introduce the basics so that you are in a position to understand how other types of tree might be added to ADS.

Keywords

tree
binary tree
graph
traversal
iterators

15.1 Introduction

All the linked list based data structures considered previously have been very linear. The data structures with a single linkage must clearly be linear:

but even the doubly linked list data structures built with more than one link are linear, since the forward and backward references simply collaborated to provided a bi-directional linkage between nodes:

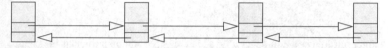

However, having more than one link in a node opens up a number of very interesting possibilities.

Each of the links for a given node could be part of completely independent linear sequence in which case we would have what is called a *multi-list*: this is a set of data items which are given more than one sequencing, with the sequences embedded in the data. A doubly-linked list is a multi-list with a forward ordering and a reverse ordering. Such multi-linear data structures (except doubly-linked list) are difficult to maintain and are therefore little used. It is much easier to maintain multiple separate linear lists referencing the same data when such multiple sequencing of data is required.

Although multi-lists are not interesting (except for doubly-linked list), using multiple links to construct a single non-linear data structure is *very* important and very frequently used. Instead of constraining the links in such a way as to join the nodes in a linear fashion, we can allow the links to connect to any other node in the data structure. We can go further, we can construct data structures where each node has any number of links to any other node. Such a data structure implements a thing called a *graph*. Figure 15.1 shows an example of a graph data structure. Because each link has a definite direction, such a structure is called a *directed graph* or sometimes *digraph*. Moreover, the link structure is such that there are loops or *cycles* (sometimes also called *circuits*) in the structure: the *paths* (1, 2, 5, 1), (1, 2, 4, 5, 1), (1, 3, 6, 2, 5, 1) and (1, 3, 6, 2, 4, 5, 1) are four cycles in the example of Figure 15.1. If a graph has no cycles it is called an *acyclic graph*.

Graphs and graph data structures tend to be quite complicated things and the algorithms (and their implementations) associated with them complex and not always very efficient. Thus, whilst graphs are important, they are only used where they are necessary. In fact, most of the situations where we might use a graph need only a restricted form of graph and these restricted graphs can have efficient implementations. Such restricted forms of graph are interesting and important data structures in their own right.

In fact, we have met two such restricted forms of graph already. First, a linked list is an acyclic directed graph with each node having only one link. Note, though, that the circular linked list is

note

In graph theory, a branch of mathematics, a graph comprises vertices and edges with the edges connecting vertices. Some people call the edges arcs. To be awkward, some people call the vertices nodes, giving fours variants of terminology.

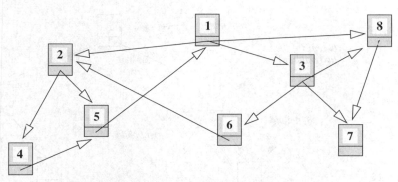

Figure 15.1 A non-linear data structure — a graph.

definitely not acyclic even though it is a very restricted form of graph. Second, the doubly-linked list can be considered either cyclic or acyclic but normally the latter, with the pairs of links effectively providing a bi-directional connection between nodes, giving what is essentially an *un-directed graph*.

Acyclic directed graphs have the property that there is a unique identifiable node that is called the *root* node, which has no links pointing at it from any other node. Moreover, each node can be classified according to the number of nodes between the root node and it, providing an hierarchical structure.

A *tree* is a restricted form of acyclic directed graph but not all acyclic directed graphs are trees. The extra property separating a tree from other acyclic directed graphs is that each node has only a single node linking to it. This property means that there can be no links from lower level nodes to higher level nodes and no links between nodes at the same level. This enforces an absolute hierarchy of nodes (a partial order) based on the distance from the root node, with distance being measured by the number of nodes between a selected node and the root. For any given node, the nodes it provides links to are called the *children* of the node, while the single node that links to it is called the *parent*. Each node has one and only one parent, except for the root node (the node at level 0) which has no parent, and each node stores a single data value.

In general, any node in the tree can have as many links to children as it wants. However, to allow such a situation leads to complex algorithms and hence complex code and so is only used where essential. Usually it is the case that all nodes in the tree have the same maximum number of links to children (although some links may not be used). The number of potential children at each node is often called the *branching factor* but is more usually called the *order* of the tree.

A tree of order 1 turns out to be nothing more that the singly-linked list. However, we have already covered linked lists so we are not going to re-examine order 1 here. The most important kind of tree we can investigate is the one of order 2, more usually called a *binary tree*. The diagram in Figure 15.2 presents an example binary tree, showing the hierarchical structure of the tree, along with annotations introducing some of the jargon used to talk about binary trees. Nodes can have 0,

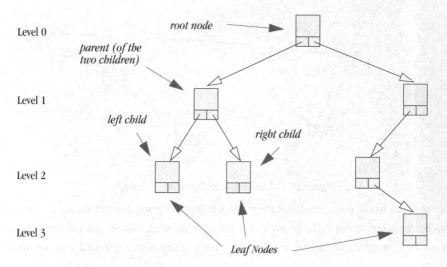

Figure 15.2 A binary tree and some of the jargon used.

1 or 2 children and the nodes at the edge of the tree, usually with no children, are called the *leaf nodes* of the tree.

Why do we say that a binary tree is the most important of the tree data structures? There are three basic reasons:

1. In going from order 1 to order 2, we introduce all the most important algorithm issues.

2. Moving from order 2 to order 3 or higher introduces some efficiency at the expense of some complexity but doesn't change the core nature of the algorithms.

3. Trees of order 2 are the simplest non-linear structures.

For these reasons we will focus our attention on binary trees. We will look at the basic algorithms of binary tree manipulation and then an example of a binary tree to put into the ADS package. Whilst we introduce the techniques in the context of a binary tree, almost all apply equally well to other forms of tree: AVL Trees, 2–3 Trees, Red–Black Trees, B-trees and B*-trees. We will not be giving detailed information about these different sorts of tree, this is not a book on algorithms and data structures. Instead we ask you to investigate the books that specialize in covering this material. We note here though that Red–Black Trees are perhaps the most important for memory-resident data whereas B-Trees and B*-Trees are the most important for use within databases. It is certainly the case that both Collections and JGL use Red-Black Trees as part of their implementation.

15.2   Manipulating Trees

It is all very well describing what a tree looks like, in a declarative sort of way, but the most important things are really how to observe and change the state of the tree. The issues we have to tackle with a

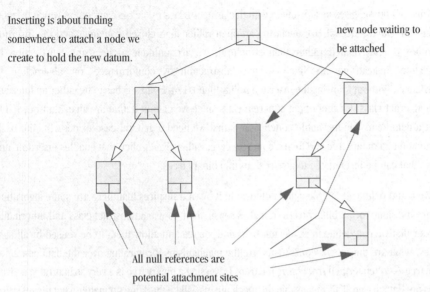

Inserting is about finding somewhere to attach a node we create to hold the new datum.

new node waiting to be attached

All null references are potential attachment sites

Figure 15.3 Inserting an item into a `BinaryTree`.

tree are: how to insert elements, how to remove elements and how to iterate over the elements in the tree.

Insertion of a new item into a tree is essentially straightforward. It is a matter of creating a new node to hold the datum that is to be inserted and then finding an unused reference to allow the new node to be attached to the tree. Figure 15.3 shows diagrammatically the issues involved.

Although, conceptually at least, inserting seems straightforward, the difficulty is: Where do we put a new datum? What is the organizational property that the data in the tree obey? It could be that a new datum is attached at a certain place in the tree. This is a structural relationship not a relationship based on properties of the data. Closed container types such as `Queue` and `Stack` are usually associated with structural relationships, data is added and removed according to a positional algorithm not according to any relationship between the data values. We shall see in Chapter 16, Page 477 one use of a structuralist approach with trees to create the closed container `Heap`. In this chapter we focus on using trees as open containers, more akin to `Array` and `DLList`. The analogy with the linear data structures is clear, there are open containers from which closed containers can be constructed. Whilst this gives us a direction, it doesn't quite solve the problem: How do we insert a new datum?

Having rejected a structural approach to insertion of data, insertion must be driven by a relationship between the data values stored in the binary tree. It seems likely that the relationship will be a *parameterized property* of the binary tree — that is, the relationship can be set independently of the rest of the implementation of the tree. Choosing different values for the relationship gives us different sorts of tree. In summary, the insertion algorithm is "Find the right point and attach a new node containing the new datum at the appropriate point" is as far as we can go until we define a data relationship: binary trees need a policy before they can be instantiated.

note

Binary tree is an abstract concept. Concrete tree types must have an insertion policy.

This, of course, gives us a problem with declaring a `BinaryTree` class out of which to make objects; we can't. Since we are declaring an open rather than closed container and the insertion algorithm is data related rather than structural, we are unlikely to be using 'abstraction by association' instead we are likely to use 'abstraction by conformance' or 'abstraction by inheritance'. Without knowing the insertion policy then `BinaryTree` has to be either an interface or an abstract class, it cannot be a concrete class since we cannot define the algorithm needed to insert a data item. The inevitable conclusion is that we need a general case to describe the basic abstraction of a binary tree and then a concrete case, with a given policy, that enables insertion, and so on., that can be instantiated to give real, usable binary trees.

We could define an interface and conform to it but it transpires that there are some algorithms that are the same for all binary trees. It makes sense, then, to use an abstract class and inheritance in order that we can define these default behaviours once and allow them to be reused by all sub-classes. What are these behaviours? They are the mechanisms for iterating over the data contained in the tree — often termed *traversing* the tree. Traversing a binary tree is a very structuralist activity, as it is not data driven. This means that the mechanisms will be the same no matter what the insertion policy is for the particular binary tree. This is the reason for putting the implementations of the algorithms into a single place rather than repeating them in different binary trees.

Unlike linked lists, there is no one obvious way of visiting every node during a traversal of a tree. In fact, there are four different possible traversals stemming from the different orders in which the current node and the child sub-trees are visited:

Post-order: left child, right child, current node.

Pre-order: current node, left child, right child.

In-order: left child, current node, right child.

Level-order: all nodes on the current level, all child nodes of each node left to right.

note

Post-order, pre-order and in-order traversals are depth-first traversals whilst level-order is a breadth-first traversal.

Traversing the tree is essentially 'flattening' the data into a sequence form with the four different traversals delivering up different orderings of that data. It is always easiest to get a feel for what these different traversal orders mean by using a diagram. Figure 15.4 shows the four different traversals around an example binary tree.

Note the very left–right orientation to the traversals. This is standard. It is axiomatic and not a thing to be challenged. In fact, it doesn't actually matter since, if we were to reverse the treatment of right and left, we would just reverse the resultant traversal list according to the following symmetry properties:

- a right–left in-order traversal generates the reverse list to a left–right in-order traversal.
- a right–left post-order traversal generates the reverse of a left–right pre-order traversal.
- a right–left pre-order traversal generates the reverse of a left–right post-order traversal.

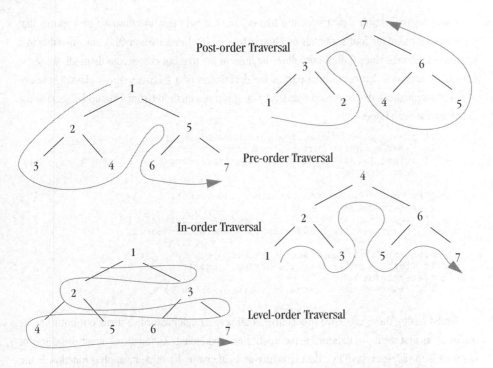

Figure 15.4 The different traversals over an example binary tree. The numbers indicate the position in the list that the datum will appear.

note

Level-order is qualitatively different to the other traversals.

The right–left level-order traversal is different from the left–right level-order traversal but for all known algorithms that use level-order traversal, the permutation of the nodes at each level is irrelevant; what is important is that all the nodes at each level are visited before moving to the next level. Thus, although there are actually eight different interesting traversals of a binary tree we only need to worry about four of them.

Before we go any further we need to introduce a little lower-level code so that we can think about how traversal designs might be implemented: we need to introduce something of the code level implementation of a tree, in particular the nodes. Working by analogy with the diagrams and the node class declarations from the various linked list based classes, we are probably going to be making use of a class looking something like:

```
class Node {
  Node left ;
  Node right ;
  Object datum ;
  ...
}
```

as the Java code description of the nodes of the binary tree. This relies, of course, on the fact that a variable of type `Node` holds a *reference* to an object of type `Node`, not the object itself. We are now able to continue discussing traversals.

Using recursion with a data structure like `Node`, it is very easy to construct procedures that implement three of the four traversals of a binary tree — level-order traversal is not amenable to a recursive treatment since it does not follow the links in the tree but cuts across them all. We show here three methods that could be a part of the declaration of a `BinaryTree` class. These are *applicators*, methods that traverse a data structure applying a method (from a method object) to the data found at each node:

```
public void postorderApplicator(MethodObject f) {
    if (left != null) left.postorderApplicator(f) ;
    if (right != null) right.postorderApplicator(f) ;
    f.execute(datum) ;
}
public void preorderApplicator(MethodObject f) {
    f.execute(datum) ;
    if (left.next != null) left.preorderApplicator(f) ;
    if (right.next != null) right.preorderApplicator(f) ;
}
public void inorderApplicator(MethodObject f) {
    if (left != null) left.inorderApplicator(f) ;
    f.execute(datum) ;
    if (right != null) right.inorderApplicator(f) ;
}
```

Whilst having these recursive procedures is all very straightforward, it turns out not to be as useful as at first sight — iterators make applicators redundant. Although the most usual use of iterators is to visit each item in a data structure and either use the value or apply a function to the value, it is not always convenient to encapsulate the action in a single method object. Also, the entire data structure has to be locked against alteration for the entirety of the traversal which in a multi-threading environment is not always convenient. The most telling issue though is that once an iterator mechanism is provided that is within the architecture, the applicators provide no extra functionality. Thus, by Ockham's Razor they will not go into the class declarations. They do, however, present a very simple conceptualization of the notions of traversal and are therefore useful for that.

So what is the architecture of traversal that we need to implement? The standard way of implementing iteration is for the iterator type to store the minimum information about the data structure in question so that it can deliver each of the values one-by-one. With the linear data structures all we had to remember was the current node of interest which meant the iterator state was simply a reference to a item in the sequence. This was possible since there was only a single 'next' item for each item in the data structure, making the iteration algorithm essentially trivial.

The problem with trees is that, because the data structure is not a linear one, it is not trivial to decide where to go next since the history of where you have already been is needed to make this decision. With the recursive applicators, the necessary state information is implicitly maintained by the chain of recursive calls. What we need to do then, it seems, is to use the recursive algorithms in some way. There is, however, a difficulty marrying together of the recursive approach with the `Iterator` interface, the issue being control. In a recursive method, the method is in total control at all times until the evaluation is complete. The `Iterator` interface requires much more of a client–server approach, the iterator moves from one item to the next at the behest of the client. We have a problem then: How to make use of recursion?

?

Applicators are rarely actually used since use of iterators and the Visitor pattern is much more flexible.

One clue to the way forward is to re-visit the issue introduced earlier where we claimed that a recursive implementation of level-order iteration was not feasible. If this is indeed the case, how do we construct a level-order iteration? It is clear that it is not possible to follow links around to implement the iterator (this is why a recursive implementation is not feasible). Furthermore, we need a mechanism to remember where we have been in the tree. We could extend the node with a node marking mechanism to support the traversals but this would not be acceptable as it would force nodes to take part in the mechanism of iteration when they should be completely independent from it.

The question is then: Can we construct algorithms to enable an iterator to implement the various traversals, without having to mark the tree structure?

The required insight is to note that the traversal is a flattening, the creation of a queue from a tree. Indeed, we can actually use a `Queue` for this. Delivering up the next item of the iterator is simply removing an item from the `Queue`. When do we put things into the `Queue` in order to construct a level-order traversal? The insight we need here is that the moment to insert an item into the `Queue` is when its parent is being removed: as an item is being delivered by the iterator, all its children are inserted into the `Queue`. This gives us the side-to-side behaviour. So the `LevelorderIterator` class is going to include something along the lines of the following skeleton:

```
private Queue q ;
. . .
public void advance() {
  q.remove() ;
  if (returnValue.left != null)
    q.insert(returnValue.left) ;
  if (returnValue.right != null)
    q.insert(returnValue.right) ;
}
```

In effect we are storing part of the total sequence of items in a `Queue` and leaving the rest to be processed. Of course, this leaves us with a minor problem in a multi-threading environment. Unless we lock the data structure, other threads could amend it or the tree could simply be altered by a method called as each item is visited (although that can be considered a programming error). These amendments may or may not cause the iterator problems, indeed may or may not be observed by the iterator. If amendment is in a part of the tree already processed, the amendments will definitely not be seen by the iterator. If the amendments are in parts of the tree yet to be processed they will probably be seen by the iterator. In fact, removals from the tree, particularly of whole sub-trees, can cause serious problems. This sort of non-determinism of behaviour can be seen as either desirable or undesirable but it is not often disastrous — though it can be catastrophically so! The moral is that there is no complete solution to the problem other than locking the data structure no matter whether recursive or imperative techniques are used. Actually, because of this lack of knowledge regarding the locking requirements of the data structure during iteration, the iterator implementation cannot decide on the locking strategy, it must be left to the application code.

note

It is not sensible to have to mark the tree itself in order to perform iteration.

!

Applications must decide whether a data structure being iterated over must be locked or not. Single-threaded ones need not providing the tree is not mistakenly modified during traversal.

Returning to the other iterators, the use of a `Queue` gives us the technology we need to marry up the `Iterator` interface with the recursive methods. We can use the recursive methods to traverse the tree when the iterator is initialized and store the items in a `Queue` ready for removal as and when the application needs them. That is, we take a snapshot of the tree at the time that we create the iterator, storing the values in the `Queue`. Taking the pre-order traversal as an example:

```
protected Queue q = new SLListQueue () ;
protected void preOrder() {
  if (root != null) {
    queueItem(root) ;
  }
}
protected void queueItem(final Node n) {
  q.add(n) ;
  if (n.left != null) {
    queueItem(n.left) ;
  }
  if (n.right != null) {
    queueItem(n.right) ;
  }
}
```

However, it turns out that this is a poor solution to the problem: using recursion in this way could be problematic since it could lead to potentially large use of space resources, mostly to store references to all the objects in the data structure rather than the resource issues regarding recursion itself. To require such resource usage is, in fact, an excessively dictatorial position to take. As library developers we have a responsibility to deliver robust classes but they must also be flexible and efficient. We are therefore drawn to the conclusion that we should try and find a mechanism that does not store everything at the outset. Essentially, we want to implement the post-order, pre-order and in-order iterators more in the style of the level-order iterator, with only minimal numbers of nodes being entered into the supporting data structure. In effect, we need to manually manage the 'recursion' of traversing the tree, storing as little control information as possible. This implies not taking a snapshot of the data structure at the moment of creating the iterator. As noted earlier this has dangers in a multi-threaded system since the data structure can be altered during the iteration. We nonetheless accept this 'slightly dangerous' approach to iteration so that the resource usage is as low as possible. In doing this, though, the application developer must clearly understand that they must use the iterator in certain ways. The rules are simple:

> *Either*: Use the iterator in one go without the possibility of update.

> *Or*: Lock the data structure before starting the iteration.

This seems like a reasonable compromise so it is the one we will follow. The problem then is what infrastructure do we need in order not to use recursion. The insight here is that recursion is implemented using a stack. What we need to do then is to make explicit use of a `Stack` to simulate just enough of the way in which recursion works to properly traverse the tree.

Weiss (1996) presents an interesting algorithm which stems from an observation about traversing trees. Whenever we need to, we insert into a stack a record comprising a reference to a tree node and a counter counting how many times we have removed the record from the stack —

!

Library developers must ensure best efficiency of their implementations.

we call this observing the node. Whenever the iterator is asked to deliver the next value, it removes the top element from the stack and determines what the 'observed count' is (i.e. how many times the item has been removed from the stack). The rest of the behaviour depends on which iterator is being used:

Post-order: We need to find the first element with observed count 3 since we have to deal with both children first (i.e. an item gets observed three times before it becomes the item to be returned). If the node on top of the stack is not the one we want, we insert it back into the stack. If the observed count was 1, we need to stack the left child, if it exists. If the observed count was 2, we need to stack the right child, if it exists. We then try again looking at the top item on the stack to see if we have found the element to be returned. At any moment in the iteration, the stack holds a list of nodes from root to the current node being processed.

Pre-order: We use the element that is on top of the stack immediately since we only need the first item with observed count 1. We then insert the left child, if it exists, and then the right child, if it exists, into the stack. At any moment, the stack holds a sub-set of the nodes yet to be processed. This is a very thin slice across the tree.

In-order: We find the first item with observed count of 2. If the observed count is only 1 then re-insert the item and then insert the left child if it exists. If the count is 2 then we have found the item but we must then insert the right child. Like the post-order iteration, the stack, at any moment holds a list of nodes from the root to the current node.

This seems like a splendid way forward: we have the lightweightness of not using actually using recursion with the basic algorithms, albeit partially executed, of a recursive traversal. We could now assemble a full implementation … except that we can have another 'ah ha' step.

The above algorithms, and their use of a supporting stack, are only needed because the links between nodes are only from parent to child. When we were working with linked lists we saw that when we went from uni-directional (`SLList`) to bi-directional (`DLList`) links between nodes we dramatically increased the editing capability and flexibility of the data structure. What happens if we do the same here? By introducing a parent pointer, giving a link from the child to its parent, we make all the links in the tree bi-directional. This allows much easier editing of the tree and it means we can implement the various traversals without any supporting data structures. Actually, while this is true of the depth-first traversals (pre-order, post-order and in-order), level-order always needs the support of a queue since the ordering of nodes does not follow the link structure.

So, for the expense of introducing an extra variable into our nodes, we can make the traversal algorithms and editing very much more straightforward. This is a big win so we will take this line for our implementation. The architecture of ADS requires us to create an interface to represent the abstraction of being a binary tree and then put the default implementation code into an abstract class. The following is the interface.

```
package ADS ;
/**
 *  The abstracion of a binary tree.
 *
```

```
     *  <P> A <CODE>BinaryTree</CODE> is not a closed abstract data type
     *  but, like a linked list, is really more of a data structure
     *  implementation mechanism.  We do not make this an interface but we
     *  make it an abstract class: there are some methods that can only be
     *  added by subclasses of <CODE>BinaryTree</CODE>.  In effect this is
     *  just a class containing default definitions awaiting completion by
     *  inheritance.
     *
     *  @version 1.1 1999.10.24
     *  @author Russel Winder
     */
    public interface BinaryTree extends Container {
      /**
       *  The method to deliver a post-order traversal iterator.
       *  Post-order traversal of the <CODE>BinaryTree</CODE> visits the
       *  nodes in the order: left child, right child, current node.
       */
      Iterator postorderTraversal() ;
      /**
       *  The method to deliver a pre-order traversal.  Preorder traversal
       *  means visit nodes in the order: current node, left child, right
       *  child.
       */
      Iterator preorderTraversal() ;
      /**
       *  The method to deliver a in-order traversal In-order traversal
       *  visits the nodes in the order: left child, current node, right
       *  child.
       */
      Iterator inorderTraversal() ;
      /**
       *  The method to deliver a level-order traversal. Level-order
       *  traversal visits the nodes left-to-right, level-by-level.  It is
       *  a breadth-first traversal rather than the depth-first traversal
       *  that the others basically are.
       */
      Iterator levelorderTraversal() ;
      /**
       *  The synchronized version of a <CODE>BinaryTree</CODE>.
       */
      public static class Synchronized
        extends Container.Synchronized implements BinaryTree {
        /**
         *  The standard constructor.
         */
        public Synchronized(final BinaryTree t) {
          super(t) ;
        }
        /**
         *  The constructor that supplies an object to synchronize on.
         */
        public Synchronized(final BinaryTree t, final Object o) {
          super(t, o) ;
        }
        /**
         *  The method to deliver a post-order traversal iterator.
         *
         *  <P> Post-order traversal of the <CODE>BinaryTree</CODE> visits
         *  the nodes in the order: left child, right child, current node.
         *
         *  <P> NB The user is responsible for all synchronization issues
         *  associated with iterators.
         */
        public final Iterator postorderTraversal() {
          return ((BinaryTree)theContainer).postorderTraversal() ;
        }
```

```
/**
 *  The method to deliver a pre-order traversal iterator.
 *
 *  <P> Preorder traversal means visit nodes in the order: current
 *  node, left child, right child.
 *
 *  <P> NB The user is responsible for all synchronization issues
 *  associated with iterators.
 */
public final Iterator preorderTraversal() {
  return ((BinaryTree)theContainer).preorderTraversal() ;
}
/**
 *  The method to deliver a in-order traversal iterator.
 *
 *  <P> In-order traversal visits the nodes in the order: left
 *  child, current node, right child.
 *
 *  <P> NB The user is responsible for all synchronization issues
 *  associated with iterators.
 */
public final Iterator inorderTraversal() {
  return ((BinaryTree)theContainer).inorderTraversal() ;
}
/**
 *  The method to deliver a level-order traversal iterator.
 *
 *  <P> Level-order traversal visits the nodes left-to-right,
 *  level-by-level.  It is a breadth-first traversal rather than
 *  the depth-first traversal that the others basically are.
 *
 *  <P> NB The user is responsible for all synchronization issues
 *  associated with iterators.
 */
public final Iterator levelorderTraversal() {
  return ((BinaryTree)theContainer).levelorderTraversal() ;
}
}
```

The following is the abstract class, it has a few interesting additions to what you might have expected:

```
package ADS ;
/**
 *  The abstract class representing a binary tree.
 *
 *  @version 1.0 1999.10.25
 *  @author Russel Winder
 */
public abstract class AbstractBinaryTree
  extends AbstractContainer implements BinaryTree {
  /**
   *  The datum that is the root for the <CODE>BinaryTree</CODE>.
   *  Employ a dummy item rather than a null reference since it make
   *  many of the algorithms a easier.
   *
   *  <P>NB root.left refers to the tree itself.
   */
  protected final Node root = new Node (null) ;
  /**
   *  The <CODE>Node</CODE> of a <CODE>BinaryTree</CODE>.  This may
   *  well be sub-classed in sub-classes of <CODE>BinaryTree</CODE>.
   *
   *  <P> <CODE>Node</CODE>s know who their parent is as well as who
   *  their children are in order to make editing and traversal
   *  easier.
```

note

In the same way that introducing a dummy node as the root rather than using a reference assisted in the case of linked lists, it helps here as well. We use root.left as the reference to the tree.

```
      */
// Nodes do not need to know which their containing BinaryTree is
//  so we make them nested top-level classes rather than inner
//  classes.
protected static class Node implements Cloneable {
  /**
   *  The datum that is stored in this <CODE>Node</CODE>.
   */
  protected Object datum ;
  /**
   *  The left sub-tree of this <CODE>Node</CODE>.
   */
  protected Node left ;
  /**
   *  The right sub-tree of this <CODE>Node</CODE>.
   */
  protected Node right ;
  /**
   *  The parent of this <CODE>Node</CODE>.
   */
  protected Node parent ;
  /**
   *  Default constructor of a <CODE>Node</CODE> where we only
   *  know the datum that is to be stored.
   */
  public Node (final Object o) {
    this(o, null, null, null) ;
  }
  /**
   *  Constructor of a <CODE>Node</CODE> where we know not only the
   *  datum that is to be stored but also the child
   *  <CODE>Node</CODE>s and the parent.
   */
  public Node (final Object o,
               final Node l,
               final Node r,
               final Node p) {

    datum = o ;
    left = l ;
    right = r ;
    parent = p ;
  }
  /**
   *  Remove ourself from the tree.
   */
  protected void remove() {
    final Node newThis = mergeChildren() ;
    if (newThis != null) {
      newThis.parent = parent ;
    }
    if (parent.left == this) {
      parent.left = newThis ;
    } else if (parent.right == this) {
      parent.right = newThis ;
    } else
      throw new InvalidOperationException () ;
  }
  /**
   *  Support method for the tree editing.  Usual algorithm: If
   *  there is only one sub-tree then deliver it up.  If there are
   *  two sub-trees but the right sub-tree has no left sub-tree,
   *  link the left sub-tree as the left child of the right sub-tree
   *  and deliver it up.  Otherwise find the left-most node of the
   *  right sub-tree and cut it out to replace the current node.
   */
```

note

Each node has a reference to it's parent as well as left and right children. In the same way that moving from singly to doubly linked lists aided editability, so adding the parent reference makes each link bidirectional and makes editing and traversal much easier.

note

Each node knows how to remove itself from the tree. This is possible only because of the double linking.

```java
  private final Node mergeChildren() {
    if (left == null)
      return right ;
    if (right == null)
      return left ;
    if (right.left == null) {
      right.left = left ;
      left.parent = right ;
      return right ;
    }
    Node newRootParent = right ;
    Node newRoot = newRootParent.left ;
    while (newRoot.left != null) {
      newRootParent = newRoot ;
      newRoot = newRoot.left ;
    }
    newRootParent.left = newRoot.right ;
    if (newRoot.right != null) {
      newRoot.right.parent = newRootParent ;
    }
    newRoot.right = right ;
    newRoot.left = left ;
    left.parent = newRoot ;
    right.parent = newRoot ;
    return newRoot ;
  }
  /**
   * Cloning means copying not just this item but both sub-trees
   * rooted here.
   */
  protected Object clone() {
    return clone(null) ;
  }
  /**
   * Cloning means copying not just this item but both sub-trees
   * rooted here.
   */
  protected Object clone(final Node parent) {
    Node n = new Node (datum, null, null, parent) ;
    if (left != null){
      n.left = (Node)left.clone(n) ;
    }
    if (right != null) {
      n.right = (Node)right.clone(n) ;
    }
    return n ;
  }
  /**
   * Print out the tree.  This is simply a debug routine.  Leave it
   * in since it doesn't hurt and it may again prove useful.
   */
  public void printTree(final int level) {
    if (right != null) right.printTree(level + 1) ;
    for (int i = 0 ; i <= level ; ++i) System.out.print("\t") ;
    System.out.println(datum) ;
    if (left != null) left.printTree(level + 1) ;
  }
}
/**
 * Remove all the elements from the <CODE>BinaryTree</CODE>.
 */
public void makeEmpty() {
  root.left = null ;
}
/**
 * Check the <CODE>BinaryTree</CODE> for emptiness.
```

```
  */
public boolean isEmpty() {
  return root.left == null ;
}
/**
 *  Equality means equality of the values in this
 *  <CODE>BinaryTree</CODE>.
 */
public boolean equals(final Object o) {
  if ((o == null) || ! (o instanceof BinaryTree))
    return false ;
  return super.equals(o) ;
}
//
//  There are a number of different ways of traversing a BinaryTree,
//  provide an Iterator for each of them.  Initial inspiration for
//  these algorithms from the the C++ code to be found in:
//
//    Budd T (1998) Data Structures in C++: Using the Standard
//    Template Library , Addison Wesley.
/**
 *  Deliver an iterator over the elements contained in the
 *  <CODE>BinaryTree</CODE>.  Provides in-order traversal.
 */
public Iterator iterator() {
  return inorderTraversal() ;
}
/**
 *  The basic iterator template for post-order, pre-order and
 *  in-order traversals.  This is an abstract class defining the
 *  common elements.  The parameter is the queueing method.
 */
protected abstract class AbstractIterator implements Iterator {
  /**
   *  The item to be delivered up by the iterator.
   */
  protected Node theItem = root.left ;
  /**
   *  Deliver up the next item in the iteration.
   */
  public Object get() {
    if (atEnd())
      throw new InvalidIteratorException () ;
    return theItem.datum ;
  }
  /**
   *  Move the iterator on one.
   */
  public abstract void advance() ;
  /**
   *  Determine whether we have iterated over all the elements.
   *  This is when we have arrived back at the dummy root node since
   *  this is when we have been around all elements.
   */
  public boolean atEnd() {
    return isEmpty() || theItem == root ;
  }
  /**
   *  Are two iterators equal, i.e. do two iterators refer to the
   *  same item in the same data structure.
   */
  public abstract boolean equals(final ADS.Iterator i) ;
  /**
   *  Return the reference to the current object.
   */
  public Object myObject() {
```

```
    return AbstractBinaryTree.this ;
  }
  /**
   *  Clone this <CODE>Iterator</CODE>.
   */
  public abstract Object clone() ;
}
/**
 *  Post-order traversal iterator.  Post-order traversal of the
 *  <CODE>BinaryTree</CODE> visits the nodes in the order: left
 *  child, right child, current node.
 */
public final Iterator postorderTraversal() {
  class PostOrderIterator extends AbstractIterator {
    public PostOrderIterator() {
      slideLeftGoRightRepeatedly() ;
    }
    public void advance() {
      Node child = theItem ;
      theItem = theItem.parent ;
      if ((theItem != null) && !atEnd() &&
          (theItem.right != null) &&
          (theItem.right != child)) {
        theItem = theItem.right ;
        slideLeftGoRightRepeatedly() ;
      }
    }
    public boolean equals(final ADS.Iterator i) {
      if (!(i instanceof PostOrderIterator))
        return false ;
      return theItem == ((PostOrderIterator)i).theItem ;
    }
    private void slideLeftGoRightRepeatedly() {
      while ((theItem != null) &&
              ((theItem.left != null) || (theItem.right != null))) {
        while ((theItem != null) && (theItem.left != null)) {
          theItem = theItem.left ;
        }
        if ((theItem != null) && (theItem.right != null)) {
          theItem = theItem.right ;
        }
      }
    }
    public final Object clone() {
      PostOrderIterator i = new PostOrderIterator () ;
      i.theItem = theItem ;
      return i ;
    }
  }
  return new PostOrderIterator () ;
}
/**
 *  Pre-order traversal iterator.  Preorder traversal means visit
 *  nodes in the order: current node, left child, right child.
 */
public final Iterator preorderTraversal() {
  class PreOrderIterator extends AbstractIterator {
    public void advance() {
      if (theItem.left != null) {
        theItem = theItem.left ;
      } else if (theItem.right != null) {
        theItem = theItem.right ;
      } else {
        Node child = theItem ;
        theItem = theItem.parent ;
        while ((theItem != null) && !atEnd() &&
```

note

Using the parent reference we can calculate which child has just been processed and so there is no need for a stack to hold that information. The algorithms for post-, pre- and in-order traversal remain the same, it is only the decision making that has changed. This code is more efficient since there is no use of a stack.

```
                        ((theItem.right == child) ||
                         (theItem.right == null))) {
              child = theItem ;
              theItem = theItem.parent ;
            }
            if ((theItem != null) && !atEnd() &&
                (theItem.right != null)) {
              theItem = theItem.right ;
            }
          }
        }
    public boolean equals(final ADS.Iterator i) {
      if (!(i instanceof PreOrderIterator))
        return false ;
      return theItem == ((PreOrderIterator)i).theItem ;
    }
    public final Object clone() {
      PreOrderIterator i = new PreOrderIterator () ;
      i.theItem = theItem ;
      return i ;
    }
  }
  return new PreOrderIterator () ;
}
/**
 *  In-order traversal iterator.  In-order traversal visits the
 *  nodes in the order: left child, current node, right child.
 */
public final Iterator inorderTraversal() {
  class InOrderIterator extends AbstractIterator {
    public InOrderIterator() {
      while ((theItem != null) && (theItem.left != null)) {
        theItem = theItem.left ;
      }
    }
    public void advance() {
      if (theItem.right != null) {
        theItem = theItem.right ;
        while ((theItem != null) && (theItem.left != null)) {
          theItem = theItem.left ;
        }
      } else {
        Node child = theItem ;
        theItem = theItem.parent ;
        while ((theItem != null) && !atEnd() &&
               (theItem.right == child)) {
          child = theItem ;
          theItem = theItem.parent ;
        }
      }
    }
    public boolean equals(final ADS.Iterator i) {
      if (!(i instanceof InOrderIterator))
        return false ;
      return theItem == ((InOrderIterator)i).theItem ;
    }
    public final Object clone() {
      InOrderIterator i = new InOrderIterator () ;
      i.theItem = theItem ;
      return i ;
    }
  }
  return new InOrderIterator () ;
}
/**
 *  Level-order traversal iterator. Level-order traversal visits the
```

```
        *  nodes left-to-right, level-by-level.  It is a breadth-first
        *  traversal rather than the depth-first traversal that the other
        *  basically are.  For this reason we need the support of a queue.
        */
    public final Iterator levelorderTraversal() {
      class LevelOrderIterator extends AbstractIterator {
        public void advance() {
          if (itemQueue.isEmpty()){
            theItem = root ;
          } else {
            theItem = ((Node)itemQueue.remove()) ;
            if (theItem != null) {
              if (theItem.left != null) {
                itemQueue.add(theItem.left) ;
              }
              if (theItem.right != null) {
                itemQueue.add(theItem.right) ;
              }
            }
          }
        }
        public boolean equals(final ADS.Iterator i) {
          if (!(i instanceof LevelOrderIterator))
            return false ;
          return theItem == ((LevelOrderIterator)i).theItem ;
        }
        protected Queue itemQueue = new SLListQueue () ; {
          theItem = root.left ;
          if (theItem != null)  {
            if (theItem.left != null) {
              itemQueue.add(theItem.left) ;
            }
            if (theItem.right != null) {
              itemQueue.add(theItem.right) ;
            }
          }
        }
        public final Object clone() {
          LevelOrderIterator i = new LevelOrderIterator () ;
          i.theItem = theItem ;
          return i ;
        }
      }
      return new LevelOrderIterator () ;
    }
    /**
     *  The method to find a particular node in the tree.  Each binary
     *  tree has to provide a mechanism for searching to allow the
     *  O(log(n)) searching behaviour to be accessed.  If this mechanism
     *  is not made available then all searching is linear since only
     *  the traversal iterators are available.  Unlike the other four
     *  iterators, this one is really intended for internal purposes
     *  since it has to provide access to the internal representation.
     */
    protected abstract Iterator searchFor(Object o) ;
    /**
     *  There are time during debugging when you have to print the tree
     *  out to see what is going on.  Don't really need it after the
     *  class is built but leave it here just in case.
     */
    public void printTree() {
      root.left.printTree(0) ;
    }
  }
```

note

Level-order traversal cuts across the links in the tree so there is no option but to use a supporting queue.

15.3 Ordered Binary Tree

The `BinaryTree` class defined above is just an abstract class, the missing items of information are the insertion and removal policies. We need to make a sub-class of `BinaryTree` to construct a concrete class that supplies these policies and which we can instantiate to create binary tree objects. The first, simplest and most usual subclass of `BinaryTree` is the `OrderedBinaryTree`. Many people call this a *binary search tree* for reasons that, if not immediately apparent in this chapter, certainly will be when we look at searching in Section 19.6, Page 564.

An `OrderedBinaryTree` is simply a `BinaryTree` with a specific insertion and removal policy defined on it: in particular, the insertion policy is such as to guarantee that an in-order traversal of the tree will visit all the elements in a defined data-related ordering. In creating `OrderedBinaryTree` using inheritance from `BinaryTree`, we will make use of the `Comparator` interface defining order relations (see Section 12.7, Page 339) to define an insertion policy so that the methods `insert`, `remove` and `clone` can be defined. This will define the sort of element that it is acceptable to insert into a given binary tree, as well as enabling discovery of the correct place to insert the new element.

Insertion into the tree is a relatively easy process as we have defined a policy: associate the order relation being true with left links so that the order relation is true on the in-order traversal. As with applicators/iterators, conceptualizing the algorithm is best done using a recursive method. Using the same design structure as we have used for clone, we can describe insertion in terms of an operation on the `Node` class (indeed, we could implement things like this):

```
private class Node {
  public Object datum ;
  public Node left ;
  public Node right ;
  public Node parent ;
  ...
  public void insert(Object value) {
    if (datum.equals(value)) {
      // Do whatever when the value is already in the tree.
    }
    if (order.relation(datum, value)) {
      if (left == null) {
        left = new Node(value) ;
      } else {
        left.insert(value) ;
      }
    } else {
      if (right == null) {
        right = new Node(value) ;
      } else {
        right.insert(value) ;
      }
    }
  }
}
```

Inserting is finding the Node to attach the new node to, such that the in-order iterator gives the order determined by the Comparator.

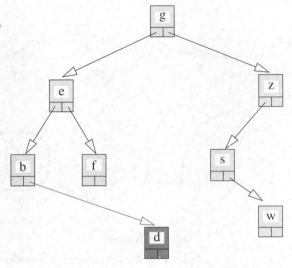

Figure 15.5 Inserting an item into a `BinaryTree`.

Here the variable `order` is a `Comparator` maintained in the enclosing class. An example of an insertion into a tree is given in Figure 15.5. Note the arrangement of the nodes and values in the tree.

As with tree traversal, recursive algorithms such as the above are not usually used in production code exactly because of the recursion. Whilst the design is neat, it has an overhead which can easily and simply be removed. Because the recursion is actually tail recursion, it can be transformed out to leave an identically structured iterative algorithm and it is this that is usually used. What is usually done these days is to encapsulate the search algorithm in an iterator. This is the right technology because not only do we need to search to insert we also need to search to find if an element is in the tree and also to remove elements from the tree.

In fact, removing a datum from the tree turns out to be quite complicated. Finding the item involves the same search through the tree that was required when inserting. Well not quite. With insert, we were searching for the node that was going to be the parent of the new datum, the iterator looks for the node with the correct relationship to the datum to be entered. With removal we are searching for the parent of the datum to be removed, the iterator looks for the datum to be removed but it is the parent of that node that we need to work with. We need this distinction for exactly the same reason we did with linked lists, we can only edit the links from the parent node. As long as the search iterator keeps track of parents as well as target nodes then we have a suitably functional iterator for all searching tasks.

So what is the complexity of removal from a tree? Well, unlike linked lists where it is just a question of re-linking the linear structure, each node in a tree has two sub-trees and these must be merged together. The brute force way of doing this would be to remove the whole sub-tree rooted at the node we need to remove, set up iterators over the two sub-trees of that node and then use the `insert` method to allow the tree to re-position the data that is to remain in the tree. This, however,

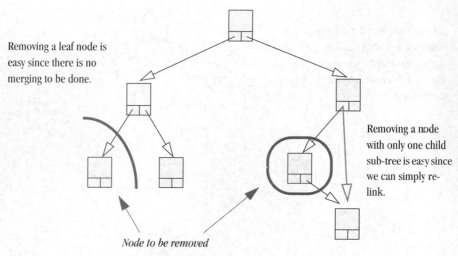

Removing a leaf node is easy since there is no merging to be done.

Removing a node with only one child sub-tree is easy since we can simply re-link.

Node to be removed

Figure 15.6 Removing a node with zero or one child.

would be an $O(n)$ way of doing the merge and we really need an $O(1)$ algorithm. Brute force is clearly not the right way.

Fortunately, there is an (obvious) observation about ordered trees that we can make use of that makes things relatively straightforward for most cases:

Any sub-tree of an ordered tree is itself ordered.

Let us consider the different cases:

- *The node to be removed is a leaf node having no children.* (See Figure 15.6.) This case is easy as we can simply remove the node by overwriting the parent reference to it with `null`. Overall this is $O(\log(n))$ since we have to undertake $\log(n)$ comparisons to find the datum with the editing itself being $O(1)$.

- *The node has only either a left sub-tree or a right sub-tree.* (See Figure 15.6.) Here we have what is essentially a linear situation and can just do the obvious re-linking. The sub-tree ordering rule guarantees that any sub-tree of the node to be removed is in the right relationship with the parent of the node to be removed so that we can just make the simple link. As above this is an $O(\log(n))$ activity overall which is fine.

- *The node has two sub-trees but the right sub-tree has no left sub-tree.* Because of the sub-tree ordering rule we can avoid the full generality in this case. In this situation, a simple re-link is possible. As above this is an $O(\log(n))$ activity overall. (See Figure 15.7.)

- *The general case.* In fact it is possible to use a re-linking algorithm even in the most general case — which is all cases not mentioned so far. The initial observation is a generalization of the above case: the left-most node of the right sub-tree of the node that is to be removed has an empty left node where the left sub-tree of the removed node could be placed. This simple algorithm leads, however, to a potentially massive increase in the depth of the tree — which is not a good idea. So in the general case what we do is find the left-most node of

Node to be removed

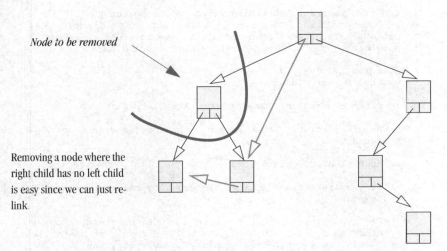

Removing a node where the right child has no left child is easy since we can just re-link

Figure 15.7 Removing a node with two children but where the right child has no left child.

Node to be removed

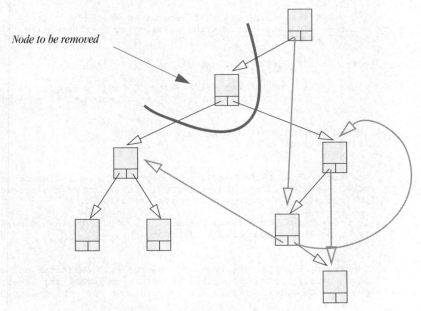

Figure 15.8 The most general case of removing a node.

the right child sub-tree of the node that is to be removed and cut it out of the tree and use it as a replacement for the node that is actually to be removed. Here the search for the datum is $O(\log(n))$ and the search for the item to be relocated is $O(\log(m))$ with $m < n$. This means that, formally, this is a $O(\log(n) + \log(m))$ algorithm, which is bounded above by $O(\log(n))$ so that is fine. (See Figure 15.8.)

This gives us all the information we need to declare the class:

```
package ADS ;
/**
 *  The simplest instantiatable <CODE>BinaryTree</CODE>.  We inherit
```

```
 *    from the abstract <CODE>BinaryTree</CODE> adding the
 *    <CODE>add</CODE>, <CODE>remove</CODE> and <CODE>clone</CODE>
 *    methods.  The insertion policy is to use an order relation
 *    provided by the <CODE>Comparator</CODE> method objects.
 *
 *    @version 1.2 1999.10.25
 *    @author Russel Winder
 */
public class OrderedBinaryTree extends AbstractBinaryTree {
  /**
   *  The order relation that augments the root reference as the state
   *  of the tree.
   */
  protected final Comparator order ;
  /**
   *  The Comparator that defines the equality relation between data
   *  items.
   *
   *  <P> We use this technique (using a <CODE>Comparator</CODE>)
   *  rather than using <CODE>equals</CODE> directly so that clients
   *  of this class can define equality however they want.
   */
  protected final Comparator equal ;
  /**
   *  The <CODE>boolean</CODE> that determines whether the tree
   *  accepts duplicate entries (the default) or whether duplicates
   *  are forbidden.
   */
  protected final boolean duplicatesAllowed ;
  /**
   *  Construct an <CODE>OrderedBinaryTree</CODE>.  We insist on being
   *  given a valid <CODE>Comparator</CODE> to implement the insertion
   *  policy.  Duplicate entries are allowed.
   */
  public OrderedBinaryTree(final Comparator o) {
    this(o, new EqualToComparator (), true) ;
  }
  /**
   *  Construct an <CODE>OrderedBinaryTree</CODE>.  We insist on being
   *  given a valid <CODE>Comparator</CODE> to implement the insertion
   *  policy.  Specify whether duplicates are allowed.
   */
  public OrderedBinaryTree(final Comparator o, final boolean dups) {
    this(o, new EqualToComparator (), dups) ;
  }
  /**
   *  Construct an <CODE>OrderedBinaryTree</CODE>.  We insist on being
   *  given a valid <CODE>Comparator</CODE> to implement the insertion
   *  policy.  Duplicate entries are allowed.  Specify an equality
   *  relation.
   */
  public OrderedBinaryTree(final Comparator o, final Comparator e) {
    this(o, e, true) ;
  }
  /**
   *  Construct an <CODE>OrderedBinaryTree</CODE>.  We insist on being
   *  given a valid <CODE>Comparator</CODE> to implement the insertion
   *  policy.  Specify whether duplicates are allowed.  Specify an
   *  equality relation.
   */
  public OrderedBinaryTree(final Comparator o,
                           final Comparator e,
                           final boolean dups) {
    order = o ;
    equal = e ;
    duplicatesAllowed = dups ;
```

```
}
/**
 *  Insert a value into the <CODE>OrderedBinaryTree</CODE>.
 */
public void add(final Object o) {
  SearchIterator si = new SearchIterator (o) ;
  if (si.atEnd()) {
    si.set(o) ;
  } else {
    if (duplicatesAllowed) {
      si.add(o) ;
    }
  }
}
/**
 *  Remove an item from the <CODE>OrderedBinaryTree</CODE>.
 */
public boolean remove(final Object o) {
  SearchIterator si = new SearchIterator (o) ;
  if (!si.atEnd()) {
    si.remove() ;
    return true ;
  }
  return false ;
}
/**
 *  Search the tree looking for a given element.
 */
public final boolean contains(final Object o) {
  return ! new SearchIterator (o).atEnd() ;
}
/**
 *  Cloning is actually easy since everything has been prepared for
 *  in <CODE>BinaryTree</CODE>, in particular the <CODE>Node</CODE>s
 *  know how to recursively clone themselves.
 */
public Object clone() {
  OrderedBinaryTree t = new OrderedBinaryTree (order,
                                               equal,
                                               duplicatesAllowed) ;
  if (! isEmpty()) {
    t.root.left = (Node)root.left.clone(t.root) ;
  }
  return t ;
}
/**
 *  A special iterator to handle the searching (usually for adding
 *  or removing an item).  NB This is not a subclass of
 *  <CODE>AbstractIterator</CODE> since that iterator was about
 *  iterating over the values in the data structure whereas this
 *  iterator is about iterating over the <CODE>Node</CODE>s of the
 *  data structure.
 */
protected class SearchIterator implements Iterator {
  /**
   *  The item to be delivered up by the iterator.
   */
  protected Node theItem = root.left ;
  /**
   *  The parent of the item to be delivered up by the iterator.
   */
  protected Node theParent = root ;
  /**
   *  A variable to keep track of whether the child is the left or
   *  right child of the parent.  Cannot avoid use of this variable
   *  since an integral part of the algorithm is ending up with the
```

note

We define a special iterator for searching through the tree to find a node. This iterator encapsulates the O(log(n)) search algorithm and can be used by all methods that need to search for a given place in the tree. In partivcular the add, remove and contains methods employ the search iterator.

```
   *   child reference being null at which point left and right can
   *   be indistinguishable.
   *
   *   <P> The default stems from the root node of the tree being the
   *   left child of the dummy root hook.
   */
  protected boolean isLeft = true ;
  /**
   *   The value we are given at the outset.
   */
  protected final Object theValue ;
  /**
   *   The constructor.  We must have an item to search for.  This
   *   constructor allows us to use an alternate equality relation.
   *
   *   @return a reference to the node that has the given value or
   *   null if it is not in the tree.
   */
  public SearchIterator(final Object o) {
    theValue = o ;
    search(theValue) ;
  }
  /**
   *   Deliver up the next <CODE>Node</CODE> in the iteration.  NB
   *   This is a different approach to the normal iterators since it
   *   may, correctly, deliver null.
   */
  public Object get() {
    if (theParent == null)
      throw new InvalidIteratorOperationException() ;
    return theItem ;
  }
  /**
   *   Set the datum of the current <CODE>Node</CODE> to be the
   *   proferred object.  If <CODE>theItem</CODE> is null then attach
   *   to the parent as a new <CODE>Node</CODE>.
   */
  public void set(final Object o) {
    if (theParent == null)
      throw new InvalidIteratorOperationException() ;
    if (theItem == null) {
      Node n = new Node (o, null, null, theParent) ;
      if (isLeft) {
        theParent.left = n ;
      } else {
        theParent.right = n ;
      }
    } else {
      theItem.datum = o ;
    }
  }
  /**
   *   Move the iterator on one.
   */
  public void advance()
  {
    if (theParent == null)
      throw new InvalidIteratorOperationException() ;
    theParent = theItem ;
    if (theItem != null) {
      //  If there are duplicates then they are to be found in the
      //  left child.  See add.
      theItem = theItem.left ;
      isLeft = true ;
      search(theValue) ;
    }
```

```
}
/**
 *  Determine whether we have iterated over all the elements.
 */
public boolean atEnd() {
  return theItem == null ;
}
/**
 *  Are two iterators equal, i.e. do two iterators refer to the
 *  same item in the same data structure.
 */
public boolean equals(final ADS.Iterator i) {
  if (!(i instanceof SearchIterator))
    return false ;
  return theItem == ((SearchIterator)i).theItem ;
}
/**
 *  Return the reference to the current object.
 */
public Object myObject() {
  return OrderedBinaryTree.this ;
}
/**
 *  Clone this <CODE>Iterator</CODE>.
 */
public final Object clone() {
  return new SearchIterator (theItem,theParent,isLeft,theValue) ;
}
/**
 *  Add an item.
 */
public void add(final Object o)
{
  while (theItem != null) {
    search(o) ;
    if ((theItem != null) && ! duplicatesAllowed)
      throw new InvalidIteratorOperationException () ;
    if (theItem == null)
      break ;
    //  If there are duplicates then they are to be found in the
    //  left child.  See advance.
    theParent = theItem ;
    theItem = theItem.left ;
    isLeft = true ;
  }
  set(o) ;
}
/**
 *  Remove this item.  Advance the iterator first.
 */
public void remove() {
  if (theItem != null) {
    Node toGo = theItem ;
    advance() ;
    toGo.remove() ;
  }
}
/**
 *  Go searching for an item.
 */
private void search(final Object o)
{
  while (theItem != null) {
    if (equal.relation(o, theItem.datum))
      return ;
    theParent = theItem ;
```

```
        if (order.relation(o, theItem.datum)) {
          theItem = theItem.left ;
          isLeft = true ;
        } else {
          theItem = theItem.right ;
          isLeft = false ;
        }
      }
    }
    /**
     *  An internal only constructor for cloning.
     */
    private SearchIterator(final Node nI,
                           final Node nP,
                           final boolean b,
                           final Object o) {
      theItem = nI ;
      theParent = nP ;
      isLeft = b ;
      theValue = o ;
    }
  }
  /**
   *  The method to find a particular node in the tree.
   */
  protected Iterator searchFor(final Object o) {
    return new SearchIterator (o) ;
  }
}
```

The most obvious applications of this class are presented in Section 19.6, Page 564 and Section 20.7, Page 584.

15.4 Other Binary Trees

In the normal course of events, the `OrderedBinaryTree` presented in the previous section provides a reasonable implementation of a binary tree since it is simple and straightforward. However, there are circumstances where the behaviour is 'pathological'. In particular, if you insert already sorted data into an `OrderedBinaryTree` then the tree structure degenerates into a linear list; clearly this is not very efficient since all the $O(\log(n))$ behaviour degenerates to $O(n)$ behaviour which is what we were trying to get away from.

!

Ordered binary trees have some serious deficiencies and are not good for use in real systems. Red–Black trees are the current basic tree for general use.

This sort of problem was recognized as early as the early 1960s by Adel'son-Vel'skii and Landis, who developed an algorithm that led to an ADT that has been named after them: the AVL Tree. AVL trees are ordered binary trees that are self-modifying so that they are as balanced as possible at all times (i.e. AVL trees are self-balancing). Balanced here means that for each node the left and the right sub-trees have equal or almost equal depth (differ by depth of at most one, in fact).

Whenever an insertion into or removal from an AVL tree occurs, a check is made throughout the affected part of the tree to determine whether the tree needs re-balancing (has one of the two children become deeper than the other by more than one) and takes action if it does. Thus, an AVL tree is guaranteed to be as balanced as it is possible to be. This means that the AVL tree is an ordered binary tree that efficiently supports searching and sorting. In particular, an AVL tree, unlike the `OrderedBinaryTree` cannot suffer pathological situations. However, the complexity of the AVL tree means that it is rarely used.

A later variation on the self-balancing binary tree theme is the Red–Black Tree. The same principles of ensuring that the tree remains balanced for all insertions and removals is followed but the algorithms for performing the re-balancing are more efficient than that for the AVL tree. Moreover, because the Red–Black tree has references from children to parents (making the parent–child relationship bi-directional) it is possible to implement all the depth first iterators using very lightweight iterative algorithms, without the need for stacks. This makes the Red–Black tree the best (i.e. having the best balance of flexibility and efficiency) binary tree implementation known so far and so it is the one that is used in most libraries. However, if you look for an implementation in the public interface, you will not find one: Collections and JGL do not offer any tree at the public interface. Red–Black trees are present but they are there only to support other containers, in particular maps and sets. The philosophy is that trees are an implementation tool not an ADT in exactly the same way that linked lists are.

Earlier in the chapter, we stated that dealing with trees that had an arbitrary branching factor at each node was not to be considered since the trees were too complex, and instead we should stick to trees with a fixed branching factor and indeed stick to branching factor two (i.e. binary trees). For teaching and learning this is a fair statement but for real situations, it is not. Although for memory-based data structures it is normal to use binary trees (usually Red–Black trees these days), databases have traditionally used more complicated trees: B-Trees and B*-Trees. These are trees with arbitrary branching factors at each node, B*-Tree being an efficiency variation on the B-Tree. They turn out to be crucial data structures for the implementation of efficient databases exactly because the branching factor is not fixed.

We are not going to present implementations of AVL tree, Red–Black tree or B-Tree here but leave it as a challenge for the reader to find the definitions in the algorithms and data structures literature and program them. Our rationale is that to look at these data structures will add nothing new to understanding how to program with Java which is the primary purpose of this book. Only time, and you the reader, will tell if this was the correct decision!

note

Both Collections and JGL employ Red–Black trees internally.

15.5 Summary

In this chapter we have introduced non-linearity into our data structures. We have argued that binary trees are the most important and have developed an implementation of the various basic algorithms in an abstract class.

A concrete ordered binary tree has been introduced and at the same time various issues in the manipulation of binary trees have been covered. Various algorithm performance issues have been addressed as part of the justification for using binary trees.

Self-review Questions

Self-review 15.1 Why is recursion avoided where possible in implementing the algorithms over trees?

Self-review 15.2 Why is there more than one iterator for a tree?

Self-review 15.3 Why separate out so many different ways of removing a node from a tree?

Self-review 15.4 The equals and clone methods in the AbstractBinaryTree.Node are recursive. Is this a good decision?

Self-review 15.5 Why is it a poor design that requires the tree to be marked to support iterators?

Self-review 15.6 Why a tree not be changed during iteration of the elements stored in it?

Self-review 15.7 Why is it necessary to redefine clone in OrderedBinaryTree when there is an implementation in AbstractBinaryTree?

Self-review 15.8 Why is OrderedBinaryTree (aka binary search tree) not the standard tree implementation?

Programming Exercises

Exercise 15.1 Re-implement the equals and clone methods in AbstractBinaryTree and AbstractBinaryTree.Node so as to remove the use of recursion.

Exercise 15.2 There are number of algorithms for implementing the depth first iterators that do not require a special count to be kept of the number of times a node has been visited (and hence the type StackUnit). Find a presentation of these algorithms and implement them replacing the current algorithms in AbstractBinaryTree.

Exercise 15.3 Add implementations of reverse iterators to the OrderedBinaryTree. A reverse iterator is an iterator that works from the end and finishes at the beginning of the specified traversal.

Challenges

Challenge 15.1 Implement an AVLBinaryTree class to fit into the ADS library.

Challenge 15.2 Implement a RedBlackBinaryTree class to fit into the ADS library.

Challenge 15.3 Implement a BTree class to fit into the ADS library.

16

Heap

Objectives

A heap is a form of binary tree that has some very special properties. This chapter introduces the heap so that we can make use of it in later chapters.

Keywords

representation

binary tree

complete tree

array

association

conformance

16.1 Introduction

In the previous chapter, we investigated the notion of binary tree as a non-linear dynamic data structure and the ordered binary tree (or binary search tree) as a particular instance of a binary tree. Also, we mentioned the AVL tree and the Red–Black tree as specialized ordered binary trees, optimized to ensure that the tree was balanced in height. The implementation technique was always in terms of nodes, references and dynamic object allocation.

In older books on algorithms and data structures, considerable time and effort goes into showing various different ways of implementing lists and trees using array-based storage. Most of this programming technology is now generally forgotten since the responsibility for managing dynamic allocation is now seen as the task of the run-time system. Even the programming languages FORTRAN (as of FORTRAN90) has introduced pointers and managed dynamic allocation, relieving the programmer of the need to manipulate arrays to create dynamic storage.

In general, this is progress: making the language, rather than the programmer, do as much of the housekeeping as possible seems a very sensible thing to do. Interestingly, though, there is a restricted set of dynamic data structures that are represented and manipulated far more efficiently using array technology than using dynamic allocation — index manipulation and array access is faster than moving through a data structure built of nodes and references.

Where there is no predictable arrangement of data in a data structure, such as with an ordered binary tree (the arrangement is entirely data determined) then using dynamic allocation technology is the only sensible way forward. Where, however, the arrangement of the data structure is predictable, a mapping can be set up between the nodes of the data structure and indexes into an array, and array technology may be more efficient.

The classic data structure that fits into this category is the *heap*. Whether this is a data structure used in day-to-day systems development is open to question but authors of academic textbooks certainly think it is important and all courses on algorithms and data structures introduce it.

So what is a heap? A heap is a complete binary tree with the heap order property. Two bits of jargon here: *complete binary tree* and *heap order property*.

A complete binary tree, as illustrated in Figure 16.1, is one which is fully balanced and only has 'gaps' on the right-hand side of the lowest level (again we make use of the left–right symmetry to concern ourselves with only one ordering).

All these structuring properties mean that the level-order traversal is guaranteed to provide a consistent, essentially static, labelling of the nodes as well as a traversal since there can be no gaps in the data structure except at the end of the level-order traversal. If this was not the case, it would not be a heap. What we mean by a consistent, static labelling is that a given node is always in the

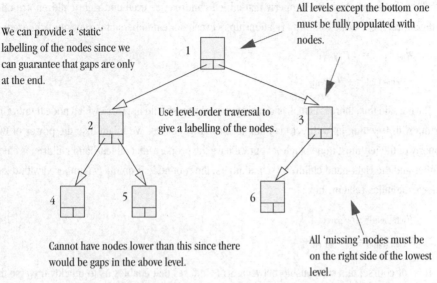

We can provide a 'static' labelling of the nodes since we can guarantee that gaps are only at the end.

All levels except the bottom one must be fully populated with nodes.

Use level-order traversal to give a labelling of the nodes.

Cannot have nodes lower than this since there would be gaps in the above level.

All 'missing' nodes must be on the right side of the lowest level.

Figure 16.1 A complete binary tree.

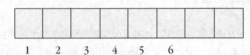

Figure 16.2 Mapping of node to array elements for a tree structure.

same position in the list given by the level-order iteration ordering unless it has been removed from the heap.

This structural property of the heap is why we can introduce the array representation. The fact that we have a consistent, static labelling of the nodes means we can use the label as an index into an array and hence we can store the node in an array and it will never need to move as long as the item is in the heap. By restricting the sort of dynamism that is possible we have allowed the possibility of representation by means other than nodes and references. Some people call this array-based representation of a list or tree structure an *implicit representation* since nowhere do we have explicit references; they are implicit in the indexing of the array. Figure 16.2 shows the mapping of nodes to slots in an array for the above tree structure.

Unfortunately, the node number is not actually the index since Java arrays start with index 0 — Java arrays are 0-origin not 1-origin (the first element having index 1). We could actually ignore the element at index 0 and start with index 1, setting up a direct mapping between index and node number. Indeed, a number of textbook authors do exactly this and show very reasonable implementations. For fairly arbitrary reasons, including that the JGL does not do this, we will not follow this route here.

Why do we not change the node numbering to start with 0, you ask? Starting with 1 sets up some very useful properties founded on the fact that the left-most node on a given level has node number

$2^{\text{level-number}}$. Also we have the property that all left children are even and right children are odd. Furthermore, there is the following relationship between node numbers of parents and children:

$$n_{\text{left-child}} = 2\, n_{\text{parent}}$$
$$n_{\text{right-child}} = 2\, n_{\text{parent}} + 1$$

Having said this, there is actually no real reason why we should not work with a node numbering starting with 0 setting up a direct mapping to the array indexes. We might lose the power of two property of the left-most node of a level but we have the property that all left-hand children are odd number and the right-hand children even numbers, the root node is uniquely numbered with 0 and we have the index relationships:

$$n_{\text{left-child}} = 2\, n_{\text{parent}} + 1$$
$$n_{\text{right-child}} = 2\, n_{\text{parent}} + 2$$

It is, of course, this relationship between array indexes that enables us to quickly traverse the complete binary tree and hence not have to use nodes and pointers: it is this relationship that is core to the implicit representation of the heap.

So far so good but we haven't defined the heap order property yet. Actually, the definition of this property is a matter of debate. Some books will decisively tell you:

> The heap order property *is that each node in the heap must have a value less than or equal to that of both its children.*

whereas some will, just as decisively, say:

> The heap order property *is that each node in the heap must have a value greater than or equal to that of both its children.*

In fact, of course, both are entirely reasonable, neither is wrong. The important point is that there is no total ordering on the tree as there was with the ordered binary tree, there is just a partial ordering and that ordering is either 'less than or equal to' or 'greater than or equal to'. In the following declaration of a `Heap` class, we take account of this possibility of having a 'less than heap' or a 'greater than heap' by parameterizing the relation using a `Comparator`.

Things are looking good so far but trees, including heaps are dynamically sized while arrays are statically sized. What happens when we want to introduce a node and we have insufficient space in the array? Simple: we don't use an array, we use an `Array` (`ArrayList` in Collections or `Array` in JGL) to store things. Because this class implements a dynamic array, extending itself as necessary, it provides the ideal representation for the heap.

Having decided the representation, all we now need to do before actually declaring the `Heap` class is to decide how insertion of data into and deletion of data from the `Heap` actually works.

!

Heaps are complete binary trees that impose a partial order on the data (cf. ordered binary tree which was not complete and imposed a total order).

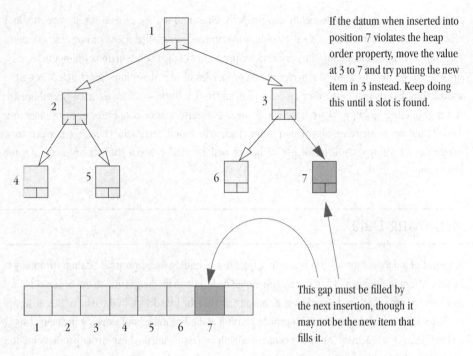

If the datum when inserted into position 7 violates the heap order property, move the value at 3 to 7 and try putting the new item in 3 instead. Keep doing this until a slot is found.

This gap must be filled by the next insertion, though it may not be the new item that fills it.

Figure 16.3 Inserting a new datum into a heap.

16.2 Inserting Data

From the rule that a heap is a complete binary tree, any insertion must cause the next available 'gap' to be filled. It is not certain though whether the new value will be the one to fill the 'gap'. The determinant is whether inserting the new datum at that point in the tree preserves the heap order property. If it does then we just put it in — an $O(1)$ activity. If the heap order property would be violated then we move the value contained in the parent node into the 'gap' and see if we can insert the new datum into the 'gap' provided by this move without violating the heap order property. This activity is continued until an appropriate 'gap' is found into which to place the new datum. If the worst comes to the worst, we put the new datum as the root node of the tree which means having travelled all the way up the tree — an $O(\log(n))$ activity. This process is often referred to as *percolating up*. Figure 16.3 shows how it works on a particular example.

It seems we have $O(\log(n))$ as the performance of insertion into a heap which is exactly the same as for the ordered binary tree. Unfortunately, there is a factor we have ignored. In using `Array` rather than a primitive array as the storage medium, we have hidden away some performance issues. If we had been using primitive arrays explicitly, we would have discovered that if inserting the new datum would require extending the array, we would have to have created a new array and copied all the data into it from the original array before deleting the original array — arrays are of fixed size so to extend them we must create a new one and copy it. This is an $O(n)$

note

Heap insertion requires a structural approach to insertion to preserve the completeness and then data manipulation to preserve the heap property. This mix of structural and data-related activity is a direct analogy with that of balanced binary trees like AVL trees and Red–Black trees.

activity. We have though, quite rightly and properly, chosen to use `Array` as the storage medium since it abstracts away all the nitty-gritty of how to construct arrays that appear to be able to extend themselves. But, we must know the performance properties of the various actions within the `Array` in order to be able to know the performance properties of our algorithms constructed using the abstraction. In this case, extending an `Array` is an $O(n)$ activity — whilst we have gained in ease of programming (a big win) we have not changed the performance properties of heap insertion. This should not surprise us, abstraction is not magic. The moral here is the check the performance properties of the types you make use of before making claims about the performance of your algorithms.

16.3 Removing Data

Removal of a datum from a heap is mostly a question of finding the appropriate datum or finding it is not present in the heap. Since there is no global ordering on the heap (unlike the ordered binary tree) we cannot search in the same way by moving around the tree driven by the data values. It seems we have no way of doing anything other than starting at the beginning and working through. This is a very linear, $O(n)$, activity. We can optimize it slightly by employing the heap order property but the algorithm tends to be more complicated than most people think worth it so it is never done. Once the relevant item is found, it can be removed. However, this is not trivial since it leaves a 'gap' and hence destroys the heap property.

Having removed the datum, we must fill the 'gap' so as to preserve the heap status. Since we know that the heap is going to decrease in size by one, we take the last element and 'insert' it in the 'gap' created by removing the datum. This attempt at insertion of an element may not restore the heap order property. However, it is not a question of percolating up the element since we know, from the heap order property, that its actual place is down the heap. So instead of working the 'gap' up the heap to find the right place to put the new element, we work the inserted item down the heap; we *percolate down* the new datum. We may end up percolating the datum down from the root element to a leaf position in order to restore the heap order so this is an $O(\log(n))$. Overall though, because we have undertaken a search as well as the percolation down, the performance is $O(n)$ for datum removal. Figure 16.4 shows how removal works on a particular example.

Having handled the general case, it transpires that the most usual remove operation is not to find a particular value in the heap but is to simply remove the datum in the root node. Given that this is a structural rather than data related removal, we do not have to go looking for an element, we only have to perform the percolation down. We apply the percolate down algorithm to the gap at the root. We have to percolate down the 'last' element to ensure that we do not end up with any 'gaps' in the tree, violating the heap properties. So this removal operation is $O(\log(n))$.

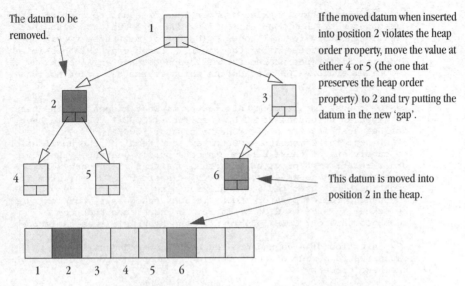

The datum to be removed.

If the moved datum when inserted into position 2 violates the heap order property, move the value at either 4 or 5 (the one that preserves the heap order property) to 2 and try putting the datum in the new 'gap'.

This datum is moved into position 2 in the heap.

Figure 16.4 Removing an item from a heap.

16.4   The Declaration of the Class

Having outlined all the core design decisions, we now have to get down to the details of programming. The principle decision to be made is: Is an heap a kind of tree (as AVL tree and Red–Black tree are) or is it an abstraction that uses a tree as a representation (cf. queues and stacks)? The question is somewhat moot because although we have talked about heap as being a tree with very definite properties, we are also talking about array representations of an heap. Whilst the solution is not entirely clear, we take the view that heap is an abstraction with a representation. We shall see later that this decision is confirmed as a strategy in other libraries.

Having made the policy decision, the structure of the code is now clear: abstraction with representation is the 'abstraction by association' architecture as was used with queues and stacks. This leads us quite directly to the following code by direct analogy with the way that the queue and stack code was constructed. Here though, because there is only a single representation that it is sensible to use, there is no need for the interface/abstract class/class approach, we can encapsulate everything within a single class. Clearly this is taking a very strong line on future expansion, as we are saying there is none. In general this is a bad choice. However, in this case the knowledge that we have about heaps and their representation, make this a valid decision.

```
package ADS ;
/**
 *   An implementation of heap as a data structure.
 *
 *   <P> A heap is a complete binary tree data structure in which there
 *   is no order relation between nodes at the same level but there is
 *   a rigorously controlled relationship between nodes at different
 *   levels, i.e. the heap implements a partial order.  There are two
 *   possibilities for the heap ordering relation: either all children
```

```
 *  of a node must have a value greater than or equal to that of the
 *  parent node or they must all be less than or equal to, with this
 *  relation holding for all nodes.  (NB Cannot mix these two in any
 *  given heap, must be one or the other!)  Because of this possible
 *  ordering difference we require all heaps to have an associated
 *  <CODE>Comparator</CODE> to define which of the two orderings a
 *  heap maintains.
 *
 *  <P> Of course the problem this leaves is what happens if the heap
 *  is given an unreasonable <CODE>Comparator</CODE>?  We could have
 *  defined a subinterface of <CODE>Comparator</CODE>,
 *  <CODE>HeapOrderComparator</CODE> say, and required the application
 *  to supply one of these but we cannot actually guarantee that the
 *  order relation so provided is actually either "less than" or
 *  "greater than" so we are back where we started.  So, whilst it
 *  might help the user get it right providing
 *  <CODE>HeapOrderComparator</CODE> it adds unnecessary complexity so
 *  by Ockham's Razor we did not do it.  We hope then that the
 *  <CODE>Comparator</CODE> provided to the heap is a reasonable one!
 *
 *  <P> Insertion of a value into the heap can, and usually does,
 *  cause rearrangement of the nodes in the heap in order to preserve
 *  the heap property.
 *
 *  <P> A heap could be implemented as a tree with nodes and links but
 *  because of the heap property the tree is always maximally complete
 *  for the number of nodes and is therefore not only as shallow as it
 *  is possible to make the tree for the number of elements, it can be
 *  represented very efficiently in an array.  In fact, we use a
 *  <CODE>Array</CODE>, making use of it's dynamic extensibility (as
 *  compared to a primitive array), so that we do not need to manage
 *  the changing size of the heap in our code.
 *
 *  @see Comparator
 *  @see Array
 *  @version 2.0 1999.10.23
 *  @author Russel Winder
 */
public class Heap implements Container {
  /**
   *  The constructor that requires only the order relation,
   *  everything else is defaulted.
   *
   *  @param c must be a <CODE>Comparator</CODE> implementing either
   *  "less than" or "greater than".  Any other sort of relation will
   *  mean that the data structure is not necessarily a heap!
   */
  public Heap(final Comparator c) {
    storage = new Array () ;
    order = c ;
  }
  /**
   *  The constructor that defines the initial size and the order
   *  relation, but defaults the amount by which the
   *  <CODE>Array</CODE> is extended when required to do so.
   *
   *  @param initialSize the initial size of the <CODE>Array</CODE>
   *  that implements the <CODE>Heap</CODE>
   *  @param c must be a <CODE>Comparator</CODE> implementing either
   *  "less than" or "greater that".  Any other sort of relation will
   *  mean that the data structure is not necessarily a heap!
   */
  public Heap(final int initialSize, final Comparator c) {
    storage = new Array (initialSize) ;
    order = c ;
  }
```

```java
/**
 *  The constructor that defines all aspects of the behaviour, the
 *  initial size and expansion amount of the <CODE>Array</CODE> and
 *  the order relation.
 *
 *  @param initialSize the initial size of the <CODE>Array</CODE>
 *  that implements the <CODE>Heap</CODE>.
 *  @param resizeSize the size by which the <CODE>Array</CODE> is
 *  incremented when it is grown.
 *  @param c must be a <CODE>Comparator</CODE> implementing either
 *  "less than" or "greater than".  Any other sort of relation will
 *  mean that the data structure is not necessarily a heap!
 */
public Heap(final int initialSize,
            final int resizeSize,
            final Comparator c) {
  storage = new Array (initialSize, resizeSize) ;
  order = c ;
}
/**
 *  Create an <CODE>Heap</CODE> from the array provided.
 *
 *  @param s the array that is used to initialize the
 *  <CODE>Heap</CODE>.
 *  @param c must be a <CODE>Comparator</CODE> implementing either
 *  "less than" or "greater than".  Any other sort of relation will
 *  mean that the data structure is not necessarily a heap!
 */
public Heap(final Object[] v, final Comparator c) {
  storage = new Array (v.length) ;
  for (int i = 0 ; i < v.length ; i++) {
    storage.add(v[i]) ;
  }
  order = c ;
  if (!storage.isEmpty()) {
    makeHeap(storage, order) ;
  }
}
/**
 *  Create an <CODE>Heap</CODE> using the <CODE>Sequence</CODE>
 *  provided.
 *
 *  @param s the <CODE>Sequence</CODE> providing the data for the
 *  <CODE>Heap</CODE>.
 *  @param c must be a <CODE>Comparator</CODE> implementing either
 *  "less than" or "greater than".  Any other sort of relation will
 *  mean that the data structure is not necessarily a heap!
 */
public Heap(final Sequence s, final Comparator c) {
  storage = new Array (s.size()) ;
  for (Iterator i = s.iterator() ; !i.atEnd() ; i.advance()) {
    storage.add(i.get()) ;
  }
  order = c ;
  if (!storage.isEmpty()) {
    makeHeap(storage, order) ;
  }
}
/**
 *  The method for inserting new items into the heap.
 *
 *  @param o the <CODE>Object</CODE> to be inserted.  It is assumed
 *  that the actual type of the object is compatible with all those
 *  in the <CODE>Heap</CODE> and with the <CODE>Comparator</CODE>.
 */
public void add(final Object o) {
```

```
      // Add the item to the end ready for percolation.  Actually this
      // is here just to make sure the Array is the right size, where
      // we have put the datum is actually treated as a gap.  Position
      // is the imdex of this gap.
      int position = storage.size() ;
      storage.add(o) ;
      // Check to see that if the new element were really put in the
      // empty slot it would be in a place that preserves the heap
      // property.  If it is then there is nothing to do.  If it is
      // not, then move the parent to the empty space and see if we can
      // put the value in the space opened up.
      int parent = (position-1)/2 ;
      while (position > 0 &&
              order.relation(o, storage.get(parent))) {
        storage.set(position, storage.get(parent)) ;
        position = parent ;
        parent = (position-1)/2 ;
      }
      // At this point we know that the empty space is a valid space in
      // which to put the new element ensuring preservation of the heap
      // property.
      storage.set(position, o) ;
  }
  /**
   * Remove the item that is at the top of the heap.
   *
   * @exception AccessEmptyContainerException if there are no
   * items in the <CODE>Array</CODE>.
   */
  public Object remove() {
    Object returnValue = storage.get(0) ;
    remove(0) ;
    return returnValue ;
  }
  /**
   * Remove a specified value from the <CODE>Heap</CODE>.  Requires
   * <CODE>equals</CODE> to be defined appropriately for all obejcts
   * in the <CODE>Heap</CODE>.  Uses a linear search to find the
   * element.
   *
   * @param o the value to be searched for.  Assumed to be compatible
   * with the objects in the <CODE>Heap</CODE>
   */
  public boolean remove(final Object o) {
    for (int i = 0 ; i < storage.size() ; i++) {
      if (storage.get(i).equals(o)) {
        remove(i) ;
        return true ;
      }
    }
    return false ;
  }
  /**
   * Remove a specified value from the <CODE>Heap</CODE>.  Uses
   * <CODE>equality.relation</CODE> to compare items for equality.
   * Uses a linear search to find the element.
   *
   * @param o the value to be searched for.
   * @param equality a <CODE>Comparator</CODE> to test for equality
   * of <CODE>o</CODE> with the items in the <CODE>Heap</CODE>.
   */
  public boolean
  remove(final Object o, final Comparator equality) {
    for (int i = 0 ; i < storage.size() ; i++) {
      if (equality.relation(o, storage.get(i))) {
        remove(i) ;
```

```
        return true ;
      }
    }
    return false ;
  }
/**
 *  Ask whether the <CODE>Heap</CODE> contains a specific value.
 *  Requires <CODE>equals</CODE> to be defined appropriately for all
 *  objects in the <CODE>Heap</CODE>.
 *
 *  @param o the value to be searched for.  Assumed to be compatible
 *  with the <CODE>Object</CODE>s in the <CODE>Heap</CODE>
 */
public boolean contains(final Object o) {
  for (int i = 0 ; i < storage.size() ; i++) {
    if (storage.get(i).equals(o))
      return true ;
  }
  return false ;
}
/**
 *  Ask whether the <CODE>Heap</CODE> contains a specific value.
 *  Uses <CODE>equality.relation</CODE> to compare items for
 *  equality.
 *
 *  @param o the value to be searched for.
 *  @param equality a <CODE>Comparator</CODE> to test for equality
 *  of <CODE>o</CODE> with the items in the <CODE>Heap</CODE>.
 */
public boolean
contains(final Object o, final Comparator equality) {
  for (int i = 0 ; i < storage.size() ; i++) {
    if (equality.relation(o, storage.get(i)))
      return true ;
  }
  return false ;
}
/**
 *  Determine the size of the <CODE>Heap</CODE>.
 */
public int size() {
  return storage.size() ;
}
/**
 *  Empty out the heap.
 */
public void makeEmpty() {
  storage.makeEmpty() ;
}
/**
 *  Determine whether the heap is empty or not.
 */
public boolean isEmpty() {
  return size() == 0 ;
}
/**
 *  Redefine <CODE>equals</CODE> so that it is a semantic equality,
 *  i.e. the two <CODE>Heap</CODE>s contain the same values in the
 *  same heap ordering, rather than being object equality.
 */
public boolean equals(final Object o) {
  if ((o == null) ||
      ! (o instanceof Heap) ||
      (size() != ((Heap)o).size()))
      return false ;
  return storage.equals(((Heap)o).storage) ;
```

```
}
/**
 *  Cloning is not only allowed it is required.
 */
public Object clone() {
  Heap h = new Heap (order) ;
  h.storage = (Array)storage.clone() ;
  return h ;
}
/**
 *  Create a string representation of the <CODE>Heap</CODE>.
 */
public String toString() {
  return storage.toString() ;
}
/**
 *  Deliver up an iterator over all the values in the
 *  <CODE>Heap</CODE>.
 *
 *  <P> There is an assumption that the heap remains unaltered
 *  during use of the iterator.  If changes are made then there
 *  are no gurantees as to what the iterator will do.
 *
 *  @exception InvalidIteratorException if an attempt is made to
 *  access outside the proper bounds of the underlying data
 *  structure.
 */
public Iterator iterator() {
  class Iterator implements ADS.Iterator {
    /**
     *  The current cursor is represented by an index into the
     *  <CODE>Array</CODE>.
     */
    private int currentIndex = 0 ;
    /**
     *  Deliver the value we are currently referring to.
     */
    public Object get() {
      if (atEnd())
        throw new InvalidIteratorException () ;
      return storage.get(currentIndex) ;
    }
    /**
     *  Move on to the next element in the container.
     */
    public void advance() {
      ++currentIndex ;
    }
    /**
     *  Have we reached the end of the iteration?
     */
    public boolean atEnd() {
      return (currentIndex < 0) || (currentIndex >= storage.size());
    }
    /**
     *  Are two iterators equal, i.e. do two iterators refer to the
     *  same item in the same data structure.
     */
    public boolean equals(final ADS.Iterator i) {
      if (!(i instanceof Iterator))
        return false ;
      return currentIndex == ((Iterator)i).currentIndex ;
    }
    /**
     *  Return the reference to the current object.
     */
```

```
      public Object myObject() {
        return Heap.this ;
      }
      /**
       *  Clone this <CODE>Iterator</CODE>.
       */
      public final Object clone() {
        Iterator i = new Iterator () ;
        i.currentIndex = currentIndex ;
        return i ;
      }
    }
    return new Iterator () ;
  }
/**
 *  Heaps come in a synchronized form.
 */
public static class Synchronized extends Heap {
  /**
   *  The default constructor.  Gives an <CODE>Heap</CODE> with
   *  default initial size and increment.
   */
  public Synchronized(final Heap h) {
    super(h.order) ;
    storage = h.storage ;
    theLock = this ;
  }
  /**
   *  The constructor that supplies an object to synchronize on.
   */
  public Synchronized(final Heap h, final Object o) {
    super(h.order) ;
    storage = h.storage ;
    theLock = o ;
  }
  /**
   *  Remove an item from the <CODE>Heap</CODE>.
   */
  public final Object remove() {
    synchronized (theLock) { return super.remove() ; }
  }
  /**
   *  Remove the entire contents of the <CODE>Heap</CODE>.
   *  This does not affect the size of the underlying Array, it only
   *  removes the elements.
   */
  public final void makeEmpty() {
    synchronized (theLock) { super.makeEmpty() ; }
  }
  /**
   *  Determine whether the <CODE>Heap</CODE> is an empty one.
   */
  public final boolean isEmpty() {
    synchronized (theLock) { return super.isEmpty() ; }
  }
  /**
   *  Return the number of items in the <CODE>Heap</CODE>.
   */
  public final int size() {
    synchronized (theLock) { return super.size() ; }
  }
  /**
   *  Compare this <CODE>Heap</CODE> with another and determine
   *  whether they represent the same value, i.e. have the same item
   *  values in the same order in the <CODE>Heap</CODE>.
   */
```

```java
  public final boolean equals(final Object o) {
    synchronized (theLock) { return super.equals(o) ; }
  }
  /**
   *  Determine whether we have the value represented by the
   *  parameter <CODE>Object</CODE> in us.
   *
   *  @exception AccessEmptyContainerException if there are no
   *  items in the <CODE>Heap</CODE>.
   */
  public final boolean contains(final Object o) {
    synchronized (theLock) { return super.contains(o) ; }
  }
/**
 *  Ask whether the <CODE>Heap</CODE> contains a specific value.
 *  Uses <CODE>equality.relation</CODE> to compare items for
 *  equality.
 *
 *  @param o the value to be searched for.
 *  @param equality a <CODE>Comparator</CODE> to test for equality
 *  of <CODE>o</CODE> with the items in the <CODE>Heap</CODE>.
 */
  public final boolean contains(final Object o, final Comparator c){
    synchronized (theLock) { return super.contains(o, c) ; }
  }
  /**
   *  Append an element to the end of the <CODE>Heap</CODE>.
   *
   *  @exception AccessEmptyContainerException if there are no
   *  items in the <CODE>Heap</CODE>.
   */
  public final void add(final Object o) {
    synchronized (theLock) {  super.add(o) ; }
  }
  /**
   *  Remove an element of a given value from the
   *  <CODE>Heap</CODE> if it is in the <CODE>Heap</CODE>.
   *
   *  @return whether the item was actually in the
   *  <CODE>Heap</CODE>.
   *  @exception AccessEmptyContainerException if there are no
   *  items in the <CODE>Heap</CODE>.
   */
  public final boolean remove(final Object o) {
    synchronized (theLock) { return super.remove(o) ; }
  }
/**
 *  Remove a specified value from the <CODE>Heap</CODE>.  Uses
 *  <CODE>equality.relation</CODE> to compare items for equality.
 *  Uses a linear search to find the element.
 *
 *  @param o the value to be searched for.
 *  @param equality a <CODE>Comparator</CODE> to test for equality
 *  of <CODE>o</CODE> with the items in the <CODE>Heap</CODE>.
 */
  public final boolean remove(final Object o, final Comparator c) {
    synchronized (theLock) { return super.remove(o, c) ; }
  }
  /**
   *  Deliver up a complete shallow copy of the
   *  <CODE>Heap</CODE>.
   */
  public final Object clone() {
    synchronized (theLock) { return super.clone() ; }
  }
  /**
```

```
    *   Deliver up a <CODE>String</CODE> representation the
    *   <CODE>Heap</CODE>.
    */
  public final String toString() {
    synchronized (theLock) { return super.toString() ; }
  }
  /**
    *   The <CODE>Object</CODE> on which to do all locking.
    */
  private final Object theLock;
}
/**
  *   The <CODE>Array</CODE> which actually stores all the values.
  *   Initialize it in the constructors rather than here in case the
  *   user provides initialization arguments.
  */
protected Array storage ;
/**
  *   The <CODE>Comparator</CODE> which determines whether the heap
  *   property relation is "greater than" or "less than".
  */
protected Comparator order ;
/**
  *   Make a <CODE>Array</CODE> into one that has the heap
  *   properties.
  *
  *   <P> This is static simply so that we can make use of it in
  *   <CODE>HeapSortArray</CODE> so that we can heap sort a
  *   <CODE>Array</CODE> without creating a copy of the data in a
  *   <CODE>Heap</CODE>.
  *
  *   @see HeapSortArray
  */
public static void makeHeap(final Array a, final Comparator c) {
  int length = a.size() ;
  if (length > 1) {
    for (int i = length/2 ; i >= 0 ; i--) {
      percolateDown(a, length, i, c) ;
    }
  }
}
/**
  *   Enforce the heap properties on the not-necessarily-an-heap
  *   rooted at start index <CODE>index</CODE>.
  *
  *   <P> The sub-trees of the root are both <CODE>Heap</CODE>s but
  *   the root node may break the heap properties.  Percolate the
  *   datum down the tree until heapness is restored.
  *
  *   <P> This is protected static simply so that we can make use of
  *   it in <CODE>HeapSortArray</CODE> so that we can heap sort a
  *   <CODE>Array</CODE> without creating a copy of the data in a
  *   <CODE>Heap</CODE>.
  *
  *   @param v the <CODE>Array</CODE> that is to have heap properties
  *   re-imposed on it.
  *   @param maximum defines the end of the sub-<CODE>Heap</CODE> to
  *   be manipulated.
  *   @param index the index of the root of a sub-<CODE>Heap</CODE>
  *   which is potentially violating the heap order property.
  *   @param c the <CODE>Comparator</CODE> defining the order relation
  *   imposing heap order.
  *   @exception IndexOutOfBoundsException when either the desired
  *   maximum range or the desired index are larger that the size of
  *   the <CODE>Array</CODE>.
  *   @see HeapSortArray
```

```
       */
      protected static void percolateDown(final Array a,
                                          final int maximum,
                                          int index,
                                          final Comparator c) {
    int length = a.size() ;
    if (maximum > length)
      throw new IndexOutOfBoundsException("maximum > length") ;
    if (index > length)
      throw new IndexOutOfBoundsException("index > length") ;
    if (length <= 1)
      return ;
    // Take the root value, creating the 'gap' at the root.
    Object o = a.get(index) ;
    // Loop, moving the 'gap' until we find the right situation for
    // the value.
    for (int child =  2 * index + 1 ;
         child < maximum ;
         index = child, child = 2 * child + 1) {
      // We have assumed that it is the left child that we need to
      // deal with.  Check to see if it is actually the right child
      // that we need.  We must ensure we preserve the heap
      // properties whenever an item is moved!
      int right = child + 1 ;
      if ((right < maximum) &&
           c.relation(a.get(right), a.get(child))) {
        child = right ;
      }
      // Check to see if the current position is the place we need to
      // put the item to create the heap.  If it is finish iterating,
      // otherwise set up the next iteration by moving the child
      // value to the current node.
      if (c.relation(o, a.get(child)))
        break ;
      else {
        a.set(index, a.get(child)) ;
      }
    }
    // The 'gap' is now in the right place so fill it.  Of course, if
    // the gap was already in the right place we are just reassigning
    // but this is probably very rare.
    a.set(index, o) ;
  }
  /**
   * Remove the item at the index given.
   */
  private void remove(final int index) {
    int newSize = storage.size() - 1 ;
    storage.set(index, storage.get(newSize)) ;
    storage.remove(newSize) ;
    if (newSize > 1) {
      percolateDown(storage, newSize, index, order) ;
    }
  }
}
```

16.5   A Note on Using Heaps

Inserting a new datum into an heap is actually a relatively expensive activity, $O(\log(n))$ in fact. This means that code such as:

```
Heap h = new Heap() ;
for (int i = 0 ; i < 10 ; i++) {
  h.insert(i) ;
}
```

is relatively expensive. Many authors when describing heaps argue that this is such a problem that they introduce a method, let us call it `insertUnHeapify`, which simply adds the node at the end of the heap but does not percolate up the value; this then is an $O(1)$ activity. This may of course destroy the heap property and so they introduce a flag to state whether the complete binary tree is known to be a heap. Use is made of the `makeHeap` method at any point at which it has to be true that the data structure is a heap. They work on the, correct, premise that the heap property is only important at the moment that a non-insert action is taken on the heap. These actions can then check to see if the 'heap' needs heapifying whenever they are called.

We believe, however, that most applications of a heap are such that the above 'problem' of insertion performance is not a problem since either insertions are relatively rare or they are done in bulk at the beginning of the life of the heap. If true, this would mean that preserving the heap properties at all times is actually more efficient. We have therefore provided two constructors for creating heaps from arrays or from `Sequences`, so that bulk initialization can be done by entering values into an array or `Sequence` and then making the `Heap`, for example:

```
import ADS.DLList ;
import ADS.Comparator ;
import ADS.IntegerLessThanComparator ;
import ADS.Heap ;
public class testHeapInitialization {
  public static void main(final String[] args) {
    Comparator c = new IntegerLessThanComparator () ;
    DLList d = new DLList () ;
    d.add(new Integer(3)) ;
    d.add(new Integer(56)) ;
    d.add(new Integer(2)) ;
    d.add(new Integer(33)) ;
    d.add(new Integer(38)) ;
    d.add(new Integer(23)) ;
    Object[] a = {
      new Integer(3) ,
      new Integer(56) ,
      new Integer(2) ,
      new Integer(33) ,
      new Integer(38) ,
      new Integer(23)
    } ;
    Heap x = new Heap(d, c) ;
    Heap y = new Heap(a, c) ;
    System.out.println("x = " + x) ;
    System.out.println("y = " + y) ;
    System.out.println("Pointers " +
                       ((x == y) ? "equivalent" : "different")) ;
    System.out.println("x.y: Value "
                       + (x.equals(y) ? "equal" : "different")) ;
    System.out.println("y.x: Value " +
                       (y.equals(x) ? "equal" : "different")) ;
  }
}
```

16.6   Heaps Elsewhere

Notably, whilst JGL implements the concept of an heap it doesn't provide a type `Heap` in the same way we have here. Within JGL, the idea of heap is simply a property of any container that supports a bi-directional iterator. So whereas we have decided for ADS that `Array` will be the representation of the heap, JGL has parameterized this so that all the base data structures can be used to represent heap. We should note that whilst this is very different from the design choice within ADS, it confirms our decision that heap is an abstraction independent of binary tree.

The choice made in JGL to make heapness a property of any sequence preserves generality but introduces complexity. Whilst generality is something to be aimed for in constructing a library of algorithms and data structures, it is not entirely clear that being able to apply the heap property over many different representations is actually a major benefit. The complexity introduced may reduce the cost–benefit below that which is sensible. However, it is now done and available.

What about Collections? All that is needed is to note that Collections and J2SDK seem to ignore the whole issue of heaps completely. This may be an omission but is more likely a comment on their perceived usefulness.

16.7   Summary

In this chapter we have presented the heap data structure. We shall see uses of this class in the next chapter and also in Section 20.8, Page 585. We have seen that in making use of array-like storage for certain very restricted sorts of binary trees, we can achieve significant performance benefits compared with node/pointer/dynamic allocation implementation strategies.

Although we have implemented `Heap` as a `Container` here, it is worth noting that JGL does not do this. It sees 'heapness' as a property of a `Sequence` and therefore, while there is a class `com.objectspace.jgl.algorithms.Heap`, it is not a data structure, it is a collection of static methods for imposing the heap property on the data structure defined by two bi-directional iterators: it is a non-instantiable method server object.

Although we have presented `Heap` as a container, we have seen hints of why JGL has chosen to see it as an algorithm in the way that we implemented `makeHeap` and `percolateDown`.

Self-review Questions

Self-review 16.1 What is the heap property?

Self-review 16.2 Why is it that we can store a tree in an array?

Self-review 16.3 What are the benefits of using an array representation of an heap?

Programming Exercises

Exercise 16.1 Given that an heap imposes a partial order on the contained items, it must be possible to write a sort using an heap. Write a program to sort values using an heap.

Priority Queue

Objectives

This chapter introduces the concept of a priority queue along with some possible implementations: array of queues, sorted list and heap. Priority queues are one of the important uses of a heap.

Keywords

array

queue

sorted list

heap

representation

association

conformance

17.1   Introduction

We explored the notion of a queue in Chapter 14, Page 407. There we highlighted how important queues were in our lives and hence any simulations of the world that we construct with our programs. A thought though: Have you ever wanted to live in a world where when you had to join a queue, your status in the world was such that you joined half-way down or even right at the front — perhaps even interrupting the individual at the front of the queue to gain immediate attention? Such a world would be much less hassle, as long, of course, as only very few people had this status in the world. If everyone had it, life would really be chaotic. In effect, people who break certain rules of behaviour gain great benefit as long as they only do it rarely and there are only a few people doing it.

note

Batch processing is a style of computing where non-interactive programs are run in a sequence, one after another, attempting to make the most efficient use of the computer.

It turns out that such queues as implied above are actually very useful in computing. When dealing with batch processing, programs are run in an order determined by their resource requirements, in particular, how long they are expected to run as the principle determinant, with memory and file usage also taken into account. The jobs are given a priority and queued awaiting execution according to their priority. Print servers often have this sort of queue sorting behaviour, though many stick with the rigid 'first-in, first-out' (FIFO) behaviour for ease and simplicity, if not user satisfaction. Operating systems like UNIX and WindowsNT make use of these sort of queues in managing the programs we are running on them. Each program has a priority associated with it and is run more often if the priority is high.

It seems then that we can see a need for a special sort of queue which is not simply FIFO but has a partial sorting behaviour. Such a data structure is termed a *priority queue*.

17.2   Priority Queue as Array of Queues

One way of thinking of the desired behaviour is as being an array of queues each one labelled with a priority (see Figure 17.1). If we insert a datum, we either associate it with a given priority and it is inserted into the queue with that priority, or it is given a default priority and then it is inserted in exactly the same way. Removal is a question of deciding which priority to choose and grabbing an item from that queue. The default removal policy is to take from the highest priority queue.

Of course, the client of the priority queue, because of abstraction, has no idea how the items are stored in the queue. All it knows is that priority queues allow an extra argument (the priority) to be specified when inserting into and removing from the queue. Also, the queue is not a 'first in, first out' data structure, as the use of priorities amends the sequencing of data. However, a priority queue is a queue — if the priorities are all the same, we do get full and proper queue behaviour. A priority queue is an extension of a queue, so it seems that using inheritance looks like the right sort of way to tackle the implementation.

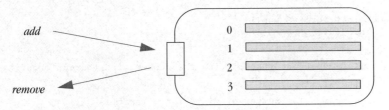

Figure 17.1 Conceptual model of a priority queue.

Having decided that a `PriorityQueue` 'is-a' `Queue` then using the 'abstraction by conformance' architecture we have chosen for the ADS package, we simply inherit from `AbstractQueue` exactly as was done for all the other queue implementations. The only non-trivial aspect of this implementation is to decide what representation to use for the container and what it means to iterate over the values in the `PriorityQueue`. Making use of our existing classes, we employ an `Array` of `SLListQueues` as the representation. We use `SLListQueue` for the individual priority queues since these seem the least resource intensive.

The only other minor issue related to this is that, whilst we can extend the number of queues, and hence the number of priorities, as and when we want, it makes a great deal of sense to ask the client to supply the expected number of different priorities at queue creation time. During the lifetime of a `PriorityQueue` object we allow an increase in the number of priorities but not a decrease.

The declaration of the `PriorityQueue` turns out to be relatively straightforward now that we have a set of abstractions to use as tools for construction:

```
package ADS ;
/**
 *  A <CODE>PriorityQueue</CODE>.  This is a <CODE>Sequence</CODE> of
 *  <CODE>Queue</CODE>s implementation allowing the priority
 *  management strategy to be determined by the application.
 *
 *  <P> Priorities are integers but since the priority management
 *  strategy is application determined we have very little to do.  It
 *  is assumed that smaller numbers are higher priority.  Default
 *  insert is at lowest priority and default remove is at the highest
 *  priority.
 *
 *  <P> The application is expected to supply the minimum number of
 *  different priority level at creation time.  We allow a default of
 *  10 though.  New lower priority levels can be added as required.
 *
 *  @version 1.1 1999.10.23
 *  @author Russel Winder
 */
public class PriorityQueue extends AbstractQueue {
  /**
   *  The underlying representation.
   */
  private final Array storage ;
  /**
   *  The constructor defaulting the number of different priority
   *  levels to 10.
   *
   *  @exception AccessEmptyContainerException if an attempt is made
   *  to start with 0 or less priority levels.
```

```
   */
  public PriorityQueue() {
    this(10) ;
  }
  /**
   *  The constructor specifying the number of different priority
   *  levels.
   *
   *  @param n The number of different priorities.
   */
  public PriorityQueue(final int n) {
    storage = new Array (n) ;
    for (int i = 0 ; i < n ; i++) {
      storage.add(new SLListQueue ()) ;
    }
  }
  /**
   *  Add one new priority level.
   */
  public final void addPriorityLevel() {
    storage.add(new SLListQueue ()) ;
  }
  /**
   *  Insert a datum into ourself.  This happens at lowest priority.
   */
  public final void add(final Object o) {
    add(o, storage.size()-1) ;
  }
  /**
   *  Insert a datum into ourself specifying a priority.  If the
   *  priority is outside the range of possibilities it is assigned to
   *  the appropriate bound.
   */
  public final void add(final Object o, int priority) {
    priority = (priority < 0) ? 0 :
      (priority >= storage.size()) ? storage.size() -1 : priority ;
    ((Queue)storage.get(priority)).add(o) ;
  }
  /**
   *  Remove a datum from ourself.  Use the highest priority.
   *
   *  @return a reference to the first item at the highest priority
   *  or null if there is no item anywhere.
   */
  public final Object remove() {
    for (int i = 0 ; i < storage.size() ; i++) {
      Queue q = (Queue)storage.get(i) ;
      if (! q.isEmpty())
        return q.remove() ;
    }
    return null ;
  }
  /**
   *  Remove a datum from ourself.
   *
   *  @return a reference to the first item at that priority or null
   *  if there is no such item.
   */
  public final Object remove(final int priority) {
    Queue q = (Queue)storage.get(priority) ;
    return q.isEmpty() ? null : q.remove() ;
  }
  /**
   *  Cause ourself to be emptied.
   */
  public final void makeEmpty() {
```

```
    for (int i = 0 ; i < storage.size() ; i++) {
      ((Queue)storage.get(i)).makeEmpty() ;
    }
  }
  /**
   *  Check to see whether we are empty or not.
   */
  public final boolean isEmpty() {
    for (int i = 0 ; i < storage.size() ; i++) {
      if (! ((Queue)storage.get(i).isEmpty())
        return false ;
    }
    return true ;
  }
  /**
   *  Check to see whether we are empty or not at a given priority.
   */
  public final boolean isEmpty(final int priority) {
    return ((Queue)storage.get(priority)).isEmpty() ;
  }
  /**
   *  Tell the world what size we are, i.e. how many
   *  <CODE>Object</CODE>s we have stored in ourself.
   */
  public final int size() {
    int count = 0 ;
    for (int i = 0 ; i < storage.size() ; i++) {
      count += ((Queue)storage.get(i)).size() ;
    }
    return count ;
  }
  /**
   *  Tell the world what size we are, i.e. how many
   *  <CODE>Object</CODE>s we have stored in ourself.
   */
  public final int size(final int priority) {
    return ((Queue)storage.get(priority)).size() ;
  }
  /**
   *  Test something against ourself for equality.
   *
   *  @param o The <CODE>Object</CODE> to compare ourself against.
   */
  public final boolean equals(final Object o) {
    if ((o == null) || ! (o instanceof PriorityQueue))
      return false ;
    for (int i = 0 ; i < storage.size() ; i++) {
      if (!((Queue)storage.get(i)).equals(
          ((PriorityQueue)o).storage.get(i)))
        return false ;
    }
    return true ;
  }
  /**
   *  We have to clone ourself properly as a
   *  <CODE>PriorityQueue</CODE>.
   */
  public final Object clone() {
    PriorityQueue p = new PriorityQueue (storage.size()) ;
    for (int i = 0 ; i < storage.size() ; i++) {
      p.storage.set(i, ((Queue)storage.get(i)).clone()) ;
    }
    return p ;
  }
  /**
   *  It is always useful to be able to print out the
```

```
 *   <CODE>Queue</CODE>, mostly to make debugging easy.
 */
public final String toString() {
  StringBuffer sb = new StringBuffer () ;
  sb.append("<<\n") ;
  for (int i = 0 ; i < storage.size() ; i++) {
    sb.append('\t' + ((Queue)storage.get(i)).toString() + '\n') ;
  }
  sb.append(">>") ;
  return sb.toString() ;
}
/**
 *  Allow iteration over elements in the <CODE>PriorityQueue</CODE>.
 *  Should only really be available to <CODE>PriorityQueue</CODE>
 *  but we can only have public methods in interfaces so we have to
 *  put up with the publicness of the method.  This is not too bad
 *  since it does not allow update of the
 *  <CODE>PriorityQueue</CODE>.
 */
public final Iterator iterator() {
  class Iterator implements ADS.Iterator {
    //
    //  Represent this iterator by an iterator over the contained
    //  queues and an iterator into a given queue.
    /**
     *  The iterator over the contained <CODE>Queue</CODE>s.
     */
    private ADS.Iterator currentQueue = storage.iterator() ;
    /**
     *  The iterator over the referred to <CODE>Queue</CODE>.
     */
    private ADS.Iterator currentItem ; {
      if (! currentQueue.atEnd()) {
        currentItem = ((Queue)currentQueue.get()).iterator() ;
      }
    }
    /**
     *  Deliver the value we are currently referring to.
     */
    public final Object get() {
      if (atEnd())
        throw new InvalidIteratorException () ;
      return currentItem.get() ;
    }
    /**
     *  Move on to the next element in the container.
     */
    public final void advance() {
      currentItem.advance() ;
      if (currentItem.atEnd()) {
        currentQueue.advance() ;
        if (! currentQueue.atEnd()) {
          currentItem =
            ((PriorityQueue)currentQueue.get()).iterator() ;
        }
      }
    }
    /**
     *  Have we reached the end of the iteration?
     */
    public final boolean atEnd() {
      return currentQueue.atEnd() ;
    }
    /**
     *  Are two iterators equal, i.e. do two iterators refer to the
     *  same item in the same data structure.
```

```
    */
    public boolean equals(final ADS.Iterator i) {
      if (!(i instanceof Iterator))
        throw new InvalidOperationException () ;
      return currentItem.equals(((Iterator)i).currentItem) &&
       currentQueue.equals(((Iterator)i).currentQueue) ;
    }
    /**
     *   Return the reference to the current object.
     */
    public final Object myObject() {
      return PriorityQueue.this ;
    }
    /**
     *   Clone this <CODE>Iterator</CODE>.
     */
    public final Object clone() {
      Iterator i = new Iterator () ;
      i.currentQueue = (ADS.Iterator)currentQueue.clone() ;
      i.currentItem = (ADS.Iterator)currentItem.clone() ;
      return i ;
    }
  }
  return new Iterator () ;
  }
}
```

The only real complexity in this implementation is the iterator. But even this is actually quite straightforward with all the supporting abstractions that have been constructed and placed within the ADS package. The algorithm is conceptually simple: we iterate over the queues and then over each of the elements in the queue. The use of iterators has, in fact, made this very easy to implement.

It is an indicator that things might be right when it is easy to build new bits of the library on top of existing bits (i.e. that reuses is easy and natural).

17.3 Priority Queue as a Single List

Another way of thinking about a priority queue is as a single queue with partitions (possibly empty) representing each of the possible priority levels.

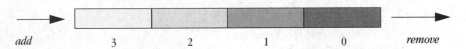

add   3   2   1   0   *remove*

The queue has, as ever, a single insertion point and a single removal point but now instead of the sub-queues being in parallel, they are in series. When an item is inserted into the queue, the item doesn't necessarily stay put. The queue checks on the priority associated with the just inserted item and percolates it through the queue until it reaches the end of the sub-queue associated with its priority. Removal is no different from a queue; we take the element at the head of the queue, which will always be the element in the queue with the highest priority due to the ordering property of the queue.

How to implement this design? There are three observations to be made immediately:

1. The arguments made in the previous section about 'is-a' relationships and inheritance between `PriorityQueue` and `Queue` still hold so there is every reason to believe that `PriorityQueue` implements `Queue` and inherits from `AbstractQueue`.

2. The `PriorityQueue` is being represented by a list that sorts itself.

3. Each datum in the list is not simply the item input into the queue but is a pair being the datum itself with its associated priority.

Dealing with Item 3 first, we need to construct a class to represent the (priority, datum) pair. `Pair` is a straightforward class encapsulating the idea of an immutable pair of values:

```
package ADS ;
/**
 *  A class representing a pair of <CODE>Objects</CODE>.
 *  <CODE>Pair</CODE>s are immutable.
 *
 *  @version 1.1 1999.10.24
 *  @author Russel Winder
 */
public class Pair implements Cloneable {
  /**
   *  Construct a <CODE>Pair</CODE>.
   */
  public Pair(final Object aI, final Object bI) {
    a = aI ;
    b = bI ;
  }
  /**
   *  Accessor for a.
   */
  public final Object getA() {
    return a ;
  }
  /**
   *  Accessor for b.
   */
  public final Object getB() {
    return b ;
  }
  /**
   *  Two <CODE>Pair</CODE>s are equal if their a and b values are
   *  the same.
   */
  public boolean equals(Object o) {
    if ((o == null) || ! (o instanceof Pair))
      return false ;
    Object oa = ((Pair)o).getA() ;
    Object ob = ((Pair)o).getB() ;
    if (((a == null) && (oa != null)) ||
        ((oa == null) && (a != null)))
      return false ;
    if (((b == null) && (ob != null)) ||
        ((ob == null) && (b != null)))
      return false ;
    if ((a != null) && ! a.equals(oa))
      return false ;
    if ((b != null) && ! b.equals(ob))
      return false ;
    return true ;
  }
  /**
   *  Clone ourself.
```

```
     */
  public Object clone() {
    return new Pair(a, b) ;
  }
  /**
   *  Create a <CODE>String</CODE> representation (for debugging).
   */
  public String toString() {
    return "(" + a + ", " + b + ")" ;
  }
  /**
   *  The first of the <CODE>Pair</CODE>
   */
  private final Object a ;
  /**
   *  The second of the <CODE>Pair</CODE>.
   */
  private final Object b ;
}
```

Attacking the issue of Item 2, we clearly need a new kind of `Sequence` which is a list that is self sorting, let us call it a `SortedList`. Since significant quantities of editing of the list are possible we need to use a representation that is optimized for editing. The best candidate is clearly the `DLList` since it is a doubly-linked list. The following is a minimalistic extension of the `DLList` to provide the sorting behaviour we require:

```
package ADS ;
/**
 *  This class encapsulates a doubly-linked list which orders entries
 *  according to a key field.
 *
 *  <P> The list is always in sorted order, adding an item causes the
 *  list to shuffle the new item to the correct place.  The
 *  application must provide a <CODE>Comparator</CODE> to handle the
 *  ordering.
 *
 *  <P> The semantics of the insertion functions have been changed
 *  over those of the superclass <CODE>DLList</CODE>.  In particular,
 *  attempting to insert at a given point in the list will not
 *  succeed, insertion is always by appending at the end and then
 *  percolating up, no matter what the interface is!  Some might
 *  consider this bad form.
 *
 *  @version 1.1 1999.10.23
 *  @author Russel Winder
 */
public class SortedList extends DLList {
  /**
   *  The <CODE>Comparator</CODE> that defines the sort order.
   */
  private Comparator order ;
  /**
   *  The constructor forces the application to define a
   *  <coce>Comparator</CODE>
   */
  public SortedList(final Comparator c) {
    order = c ;
  }
  /**
   *  We have to define <CODE>clone</CODE> since we implement
   *  <CODE>Cloneable</CODE>.
   */
  public final Object clone() {
    SortedList d = new SortedList (order) ;
```

```
      for (ADS.Iterator i = iterator() ; !i.atEnd() ; i.advance()) {
        //  No worries about efficiency here since the iterator sees
        //   things in priority sorted order anyway.
        d.add(i.get()) ;
      }
      return d ;
    }
    /**
     *  Assign a value to a position in the <CODE>SortedList</CODE>.
     *  Actually does not do this at all.  It simply appends at the
     *  end and lets the percolation find the right spot.
     */
    public final void set(final int index, final Object o) {
      add(o) ;
    }
    /**
     *  Insert a new item in the <CODE>SortedList</CODE>.  Actually
     *  does not do this at all.  It simply appends at the end and
     *  lets the percolation find the right spot.
     */
    public final void add(final int index, final Object o) {
      add(o) ;
    }
    /**
     *  Append an element to the end of the <CODE>SortedList</CODE>.
     *  It then percolates up the list to the right place as defined
     *  by the sort order.
     */
    public final void add(final Object o) {
      //  Insert the new item: Because we are using a
      //  Node as the end point the algorithms is always the same,
      //  we never worry about an empty list!
      Node n = new Node(o, endNode, endNode.previous) ;
      endNode.previous.next = n ;
      endNode.previous = n ;
      elementCount++ ;
      //  Now we must swap this element we have just inserted with the
      //  one before it in the list until either it is at the end of the
      //  sub-list it is supposed to arrive at according to the
      //  Comparator or until it reaches the head of the entire list.
      //  We have reached the head of the queue if previous refers to
      //  the dummy node used to hold the list together.
      while (n.previous != endNode) {
        if (order.relation(n.datum, n.previous.datum)) {
          //  The sort order was violated so we need to edit.  Because
          //  the list is doubly linked we can do all the necessary
          //  editing from the node that needs to be moved one space
          //  forward.
          n.next.previous = n.previous ;
          n.previous.next = n.next ;
          n.next = n.previous ;
          n.previous = n.previous.previous ;
          n.next.previous = n ;
          n.previous.next = n ;
        } else
          //  The order is now as we need it so we have
          //  finished.
          break ;
      }
    }
  }
```

This has actually broken the back of the problem since the hard part of priority queues is the ordering of the data. All we now need to do is provide the access control and create the `PriorityQueue` class. As argued earlier, this is just a relatively trivial extension of

AbstractQueue. As ever, we are employing 'abstraction by conformance' to define the type
structure and 'abstraction by association' to manage the representation. Clearly we have said this a
number of times already about a number of the classes we have developed for the ADS package. This
is partly because we made an explicit choice to use this architecture as the way of building ADS and
partly as this is the only sensible way of handling the situation. Here then is this version of the
PriorityQueue type:

```
package ADS ;
/**
 *  A <CODE>PriorityQueue</CODE> represented as a
 *  <CODE>SortedList</CODE> of <CODE>Pair</CODE>s (datum, priority).
 *
 *  Priorities are integers.  It is assumed that smaller numbers are
 *  higher priority.  Default insert is at priority 10.  Removal
 *  always takes the highest priority item. Because priorities are
 *  integers the application has no need to determine the number of
 *  different priorities at creation time.
 *
 *  @version 1.1 1999.10.23
 *  @author Russel Winder
 */
public class PriorityQueue extends AbstractQueue {
  /**
   *  The <CODE>SortedList</CODE> which is the representation.
   */
  // We sort on the priority, which is the second item of the Pair
  // which is an Integer, into the order where the lower the
  // priority is the closer the item is to the head of the queue.
  //
  private SortedList storage = new SortedList (
    new PairBComparator (new IntegerLessThanComparator ()));
  /**
   *  Insert a datum into ourself.  This happens at the default
   *  priority of 10.
   */
  public final void add(final Object o) {
    add(o, 10) ;
  }
  /**
   *  Insert a datum into ourself specifying a priority.
   */
  public final void add(final Object o, final int priority) {
    storage.add(new Pair (o, new Integer (priority))) ;
  }
  /**
   *  Remove a datum from ourself.  Use the highest priority.
   */
  public final Object remove() {
    Pair p = (Pair)storage.first() ;
    storage.remove(0) ;
    return p.getA() ;
  }
  /**
   *  Cause ourself to be emptied.
   */
  public final void makeEmpty() {
    storage.makeEmpty() ;
  }
  /**
   *  Check to see whether we are empty or not.
   */
  public final boolean isEmpty() {
    return storage.isEmpty() ;
```

```
}
/**
 *  Tell the world what size we are, i.e. how many
 *  <CODE>Object</CODE>s we have stored in ourself.
 */
public final int size() {
  return storage.size() ;
}
/**
 *  Test something against ourself for equality.
 *
 *  @param o The <CODE>Object</CODE> to compare ourself against.
 */
public final boolean equals(final Object o) {
  if ((o == null) || ! (o instanceof PriorityQueue))
    return false ;
  return storage.equals(((PriorityQueue)o).storage) ;
}
/**
 *  We have to clone ourself properly as a <CODE>Queue</CODE>.
 */
public final Object clone() {
  PriorityQueue p = new PriorityQueue() ;
  p.storage = (SortedList)storage.clone() ;
  return p ;
}
/**
 *  Allow iteration over elements in the <CODE>PriorityQueue</CODE>.
 *  This should only really available to <CODE>PriorityQueue</CODE>
 *  but we can only have public methods in interfaces so we have to
 *  put up with the publicness of the method.  This is not too bad
 *  since it does not allow update of the
 *  <CODE>PriorityQueue</CODE>.
 */
public final Iterator iterator() {
  class Iterator implements ADS.Iterator {
    /**
     *  The iterator cursor.
     */
    private ADS.Iterator currentItem = storage.iterator() ;
    /**
     *  Deliver the value we are currently referring to.
     */
    public final Object get() {
      if (atEnd())
        throw new InvalidIteratorException () ;
      return currentItem.get() ;
    }
    /**
     *  Move on to the next element in the container.
     */
    public final void advance() {
      currentItem.advance() ;
    }
    /**
     *  Have we reached the end of the iteration?
     */
    public final boolean atEnd() {
      return currentItem.atEnd() ;
    }
    /**
     *  Are two iterators equal, i.e. do two iterators refer to the
     *  same item in the same data structure.
     */
    public boolean equals(final ADS.Iterator i) {
      if (!(i instanceof Iterator))
```

```
          return false ;
        return currentItem.equals(((Iterator)i).currentItem) ;
      }
      /**
       *  Return the reference to the current object.
       */
      public final Object myObject() {
        return PriorityQueue.this ;
      }
      /**
       *  Clone this <CODE>Iterator</CODE>.
       */
      public final Object clone() {
        Iterator i = new Iterator () ;
        i.currentItem = (ADS.Iterator)currentItem.clone() ;
        return i ;
      }
    }
    return new Iterator () ;
  }
}
```

Although we have not implemented it above, we could implement the concept of getting the first datum of a given priority from the queue in addition to getting the highest priority item. This would simply involve searching from the head of the queue to find the appropriate item.

So far so good, but … there is something distinctly unsatisfactory about this solution.

17.4 Priority Queue as Heap

While developing the solution in the last section, something should have been saying to us "not the best way of doing this". The issue is performance — as always with algorithms. The above priority queue implementation relies on linear insertion of a new item into the sorted list. This is an $O(n)$ activity and as such should be seen as not good enough.

We have already seen examples of $O(\log(n))$ insertion. The ordered binary tree has this property — except for the pathological case, of course. Apart from having given the game away with the section title, we can now have an 'ah ha' step; the moment of blinding inspiration that makes everything obvious and clear. The architecture derived from the previous section is essentially the right one but the data structure used as the representation was not the best one. We need to replace the insertion algorithm with a tree based one. We could go ahead and construct a priority queue using an `Item` of some sort and an `OrderedBinaryTree` but there is a better way: we can use an heap. Using an heap gives us guaranteed $O(\log(n))$ insertion behaviour and also the guarantee that items will be removed in sorted order. This is about the closest to magic we are likely to get!

There is no need to show the full implementation here since it is exactly the same as the version using `SortedList` except that we need to replace `SortedList` with `Heap` throughout (which is not very many places) and we can make the `remove` method more efficient by replacing what was in the `SortedList` version with:

```
      public final Object remove() {
        storage.remove() ;
```

tip

When you have an 'ah ha' moment during programming do not immediately rush to code. Step back and assess the consequences of any change.

```
}
```

This essentially trivial implementation has shown that the architecture we are employing appears to be right.

17.5   A Note on the Implementations

We have presented, in this chapter, three possible solutions to the construction of a priority queue each of which has its own interesting and useful properties.

The 'array of queues' solution has a flexibility not present in the other solutions in that there is a choice of priority of removal — the other two designs only allow removal of the currently highest priority item. This algorithm has an insertion performance $O(1)$ and a removal performance $O(k)$ where k is the number of priorities, essentially this is $O(1)$.

The sorted list based solution is probably best remembered as a stepping stone to the heap-based solution; it has useful architectural messages for us but is probably not useful for real systems. Removal is $O(1)$ but insertion is $O(n)$ where n is the number of stored entries.

The heap-based solution is a very interesting application of heaps and appears to be the standard choice for an implementation of a priority queue. Insertion is $O(\log(n))$ and removal $O(1)$. The advantage of this design over the 'array of queues' is the massive flexibility over what constitutes acceptable priorities. The sorted list solution also has this property but we have already rejected it as a viable implementation on other grounds.

In Section 21.3, Page 594, we will bring to light that the 'array of queues' solution is analogous to a Count Sort, with Section 20.5, Page 575, showing that the sorted list solution is, in fact, an implementation of an Insertion Sort and Section 20.8, Page 585, showing that the heap-based solution is a Heap Sort. The essence of the problem of building a priority queue type is the need to sort and the performance of the different sorting techniques.

We have been relating the ADS architecture and implementation to that of the JGL and Collections all the way through the description of the types and classes comprising ADS — ADS is after all a pedagogical device whereas the JGL and Collections are packages for day-to-day use. It is appropriate, therefore, to explain a little of how JGL and Collections handle `PriorityQueues`.

In essence, JGL follows exactly the heap-based solution outline earlier. The JGL has a container type `PriorityQueue` that uses, by association, a `Sequence` that has the heap properties enforced on it. Remember that the JGL treats 'heapness' as an algorithmic property of a `Sequence`, it does not have a separate heap abstraction. As far as there can be, ADS and JGL are unanimous in their choice of approach to provision of priority queues.

Collections ducks the whole issue by not dealing with queues at all.

17.6 Summary

This chapter has presented three different implementations of a priority queue. This was as much to show how types such as this are developed in the context of being constituent members of a package as it was to introduce the concept of a priority queue. We have reinforced our belief that the chosen hybrid of 'abstraction by conformance' for types and 'abstraction by association' for representations is the right one and have shown how easy it can be to produce new abstractions if the architecture of the package and the core abstractions of the package are well designed and implemented.

Self-review Questions

Self-review 17.1 What is the only design difference between the 'array of queue' approach and the `SortedList` approach to the implementation of `PriorityQueue`?

Self-review 17.2 Why can `SortedList` be replaced by `Heap` as a representation of `PriorityQueue`?

Self-review 17.3 Why was the `SortedList` representation rejected?

Self-review 17.4 Why can't the heap-based `PriorityQueue` support a remove method that removes a given priority datum.

Self-review 17.5 Why might the 'array of queue' design be chosen in preference to the heap-based design?

Programming Exercises

Exercise 17.1 An assertion was made that `SLListQueue` was the best representation of `Queue` in the 'array of queues' implementation. Implement versions of `PriorityQueue` using `Array` of `DLListQueue` and `Array` of `ArrayQueue` and then test the assertion by experimentation.
Hint: Create a driver program and then a (very large) data set to exercise the classes, measuring the space and time resources.

Exercise 17.2 Develop a version of `SortedList` that allows the operation of getting an item of a given priority from the `PriorityQueue`.

Exercise 17.3 Develop an implementation of `PriorityQueue` using an `Heap`.

Exercise 17.4 Develop a test program to see whether the heap-based `PriorityQueue` really is better than the `SortedList`-based implementation as has been asserted in the text.

Exercise 17.5 Develop a test program to compare the heap-based version of `PriorityQueue` and the "array of queues" version of `PriorityQueue` to see if there is a significant difference in performance.

Sets, Relations and Mappings

Objectives

In this chapter we investigate how to work with data items that are represented as pairs of values. This requires us to investigate the ideas of sets, relations and mappings. The concept of a mapping is also known as associative array, dictionary or sometimes table. We investigate several design and implementation possibilities for sets, relations and mappings and, in particular, introduce the hash table as a new data structure that is often the most efficient implementation technique.

Keywords

set

relations

mapping

associative array

trees

hash table

open hashing

chaining

18.1   Introduction

So far in our investigation of data structures and their implementation as ADTs, we have been concerned only with data that we thought of as single 'atomic' values, values without internal structure. With classes such as `Array`, `SLList`, `DLList` and `OrderedBinaryTree` we were interested in the variety of different structures we could use to store data. With classes such as `Queue`, `Stack` and `Heap`, we were interested in the variety of different protocols we could superimpose on top of the storage strategies to create useful closed container types. In all the discussion, the nature of the data itself was not really of concern.

We now want to turn our attention to the situation where the data is a pair of values and not just a single value. The classic example of the sort of data we are thinking of here is a dictionary, for example the *Oxford English Dictionary*. A dictionary is a (usually sorted) collection of pairs, a word and its meaning. Of course there are foreign language dictionaries which are slightly different, they are (usually sorted) collections of pairs, a word (or phrase) in one language and a word (or phrase) in another language. In fact, most foreign language dictionaries are actually pairs of dictionaries; the first is a dictionary of pairs with one language first and then the other dictionary has the other language first.

If we wanted to implement the concept of a dictionary of this sort, we could think of using either a sequence or a tree to store pairs of items. In fact, the tree wins over the sequence since searching is $O(\log(n))$ rather than $O(n)$. However, this is far too low a level to be thinking about the problem, we really should be thinking in terms of: What is the correct abstraction that describes a dictionary?

A dictionary is an instance of what is usually called a *mapping*. Mathematics has a lot to say about mappings. In thinking about mappings for implementation as classes for use in our applications, it behoves us to make use of this knowledge. We will not go into great detail here but leave it instead to the many excellent books on discrete mathematics. Having said this, we do need to introduce a little bit of the jargon so that we may use it freely. We introduce the terms quite informally, though, so as to avoid becoming a mathematics text.

18.2   Mathematical Prelude

A *mapping* is a *relation* between *sets* which has certain, special properties. For the example of the dictionaries mentioned above, one set is the set of words in a natural language and the other is the set of sentences describing meaning, or for foreign language dictionaries one set is the set of words in one language and the other is the set of words in the other language. The mapping in these cases is the set of associations between elements from one set and elements from the other set. Diagrammatically, a mapping can be drawn as illustrated in Figure 18.1.

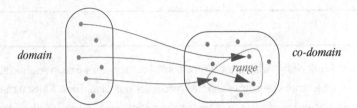

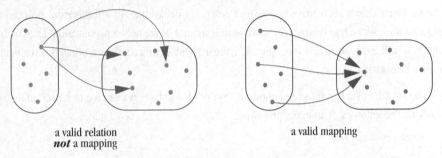

Figure 18.1 A mapping from one set to another.

a valid relation
not a mapping

a valid mapping

Figure 18.2 Valid and invalid mappings.

A relation is a set of *ordered pairs*, (a, b), where a is a member of the set that is the *domain*, and b is a member of the set that is the *co-domain*. These pairs are ordered pairs because (b, a) may be different from (a, b), the ordering of the values in the pair matters. The *range* is the sub-set of the co-domain which comprises only values which are related to data in the domain.

A mapping is a relation where there are no two elements that have the same value in the first position, so if (a, b) is in the mapping then there is no distinct element (a, c) no matter what the value of c (see Figure 18.2). In some places (including within JGL) the term *multi-mapping* is used to label the relation where (a, c) is allowed to co-exist with (a, b).

Thinking in terms of our example application, dictionaries are, of course, relations and not mappings since each word may have more than one meaning or translation. It seems therefore that we need to construct `Relation` as an abstraction from which we can construct `Mapping` by specialization. Traditionally in computing, mapping and not relation has been treated as the core abstraction. The issue here is determinacy. In a relation, given a value from the domain, there is not necessarily an unique value from the range. Without the concept of iterator, this non-determinacy can be very difficult to handle. With iterators, it becomes relatively straightforward: In effect, iterators define sets of values which makes handling multiple return values from an operation straightforward. There is, however, potentially a small loss of efficiency but initially it is the definition of the abstractions and not efficiency that is critical. Only when the abstractions are in place can we sensibly consider optimization. We will therefore treat `Relation` as the principal abstraction. Of course, we need to deal with `Set` first since a relation is a set and we should model this with our abstractions.

?

We are assuming that readers know about the concept of set. If this is not the case you may want to quickly read up about it in a mathematics text.

tip

Construct the abstractions first and be concerned about optimization once the abstraction are in place.

18.3   Set

The issue here is not really "What is the abstraction?" but "How do we represent the abstraction?" So far we have seen various sequences and trees which are our candidates. Whilst it can be done, it is basically horrendously inefficient to represent abstractions such as sets, relations and mappings using a sequence. It is immediately clear that a tree, with its $O(\log(n))$ searching behaviour is going to be far better than a sequence with its $O(n)$ searching behaviour. We will therefore proceed to build a set abstraction based on a tree. However, this will not be the only representation. Later in this chapter we will introduce a new representation, the hash table, which will turn out to be even better for most circumstances.

Following the usual architectural approach, we need to define an interface to represent the set as an ADT. The following is an initial prototype:

```
package ADS ;
/**
 *   The interface describing a set.
 *
 *   @version 1.2 1999.10.30
 *   @author Russel Winder
 */
public interface Set extends Container {
  /**
   *  Set union.
   */
  Set union(Set s) ;
  /**
   *  Set intersection.
   */
  Set intersection(Set s) ;
  /**
   *  Set difference.
   */
  Set difference(Set s) ;
  /**
   *  The synchronized version.
   */
  public static class Synchronized
    extends Container.Synchronized implements Set {
    /**
     *  The default constructor.
     */
    public Synchronized(final Set s) {
      super(s) ;
    }
    /**
     *  The constructor that supplies an object to synchronize on.
     */
    public Synchronized(final Set s, final Object o) {
      super(s, o) ;
    }
    /**
     *  Set union.
     */
    public final Set union(final Set s) {
      synchronized (theLock) {
        return ((Set)theContainer).union(s) ;
      }
```

```
      }
    /**
      *  Set intersection.
      */
    public final Set intersection(final Set s) {
      synchronized (theLock) {
        return ((Set)theContainer).intersection(s) ;
      }
    }
    /**
      *  Set difference.
      */
    public final Set difference(final Set s) {
      synchronized (theLock) {
        return ((Set)theContainer).difference(s) ;
      }
    }
  }
}
```

As ever, we make use of an abstract set to encapsulate all the representation independent methods that are part of the implementation:

```
package ADS ;
/**
  *  An abstract set.
  *
  *  @version 1.0 1999.10.30
  *  @author Russel Winder
  */
public abstract class AbstractSet
  extends AbstractContainer implements Set {
  /**
    *  Compare this <CODE>Set</CODE> with another and determine
    *  whether they represent the same value, i.e. have the same item
    *  values in the <CODE>Set</CODE>.
    *
    *  <P> Since we are not defining the basic iterator to be one which
    *  guarantees to work in-order over the domain, this method uses
    *  the most general algorithm.  This may be inefficient for
    *  particular representations and should be overridden whenever
    *  possible.
    */
  public boolean equals(final Object o) {
    if (! (o instanceof Set))
      return false ;
    for (Iterator i = iterator() ; !i.atEnd() ; i.advance()) {
      if (! ((Set)o).contains(i.get()))
        return false ;
    }
    for (Iterator i = ((Set)o).iterator() ; !i.atEnd() ; i.advance()){
      if (! contains(i.get()))
        return false ;
    }
    return true ;
  }
  /**
    *  Set union.
    */
  public Set union(final Set s) {
    Set newSet = (Set)clone() ;
    for (Iterator i = s.iterator() ; !i.atEnd() ; i.advance()) {
      newSet.add(i.get()) ;
    }
    return newSet ;
  }
```

As always, we provide very general algorithms using iterators in the abstract class expecting the methods to be overridden in concrete sub-classes where a more efficient algorithms can be constructed using specific information about the representations.

```
/**
 *  Set intersection.
 */
public Set intersection(final Set s) {
  Set newSet = (Set)clone() ;
  for (Iterator i = s.iterator() ; !i.atEnd() ; i.advance()) {
    Object o = i.get() ;
    if (! s.contains(o)) {
      newSet.remove(o) ;
    }
  }
  return newSet ;
}
/**
 *  Set difference.
 */
public Set difference(final Set s) {
  Set newSet = (Set)clone() ;
  for (Iterator i = s.iterator() ; !i.atEnd() ; i.advance()) {
    //  We can try removing every element since nothing happens if
    //  it is not there.  This save traversing the underlying data
    //  structure twice.
    newSet.remove(i.get()) ;
  }
  return newSet ;
}
}
```

Finally, we can introduce the representation to create the concrete class from which objects can be instantiated:

?

*We use
OrderedBinaryTree
here because that is the
tree type we have in ADS.
In a production library
we would use a Red–
Black tree since it is
essential to use a self-
balancing tree.*

```
package ADS ;
/**
 *  A set implemented using an <CODE>OrderedBinaryTree</CODE>.
 *
 *  @version 1.1 1999.10.30
 *  @author Russel Winder
 */
public class OrderedBinaryTreeSet extends AbstractSet {
  /**
   *  The OrderedBinaryTree that acts as our storage.
   */
  protected OrderedBinaryTree storage ;
  /**
   *  Construct an <CODE>OrderedBinaryTreeSet</CODE> using the
   *  equality relation (<CODE>EqualToComparator</CODE>) as a method
   *  object encapsulating the <CODE>equals</CODE> method.  The less
   *  than order relation must be provided by the caller.  NB Must
   *  ensure that the <CODE>OrderedBinaryTree</CODE> does not allow
   *  duplicates.
   */
  public OrderedBinaryTreeSet(final Comparator c) {
    storage =
      new OrderedBinaryTree (c, new EqualToComparator (), false) ;
  }
  /**
   *  Remove the entire contents of the
   *  <CODE>OrderedBinaryTreeSet</CODE>.
   */
  public void makeEmpty() {
    storage.makeEmpty() ;
  }
  /**
   *  Return the number of items in the
   *  <CODE>OrderedBinaryTreeSet</CODE>.
   */
```

```java
public int size() {
  return storage.size() ;
}
/**
 *  Add an item.
 */
public void add(final Object o) {
  storage.add(o) ;
}
/**
 *  Remove the pair with given key.
 */
public boolean remove(final Object o) {
  return storage.remove(o) ;
}
/**
 *  Cloning is actually easy.
 */
public Object clone() {
  OrderedBinaryTreeSet t =
   new OrderedBinaryTreeSet(storage.order) ;
  if (! isEmpty()) {
    t.storage = (OrderedBinaryTree)storage.clone() ;
  }
  return t ;
}
/**
 *  Determine whether we have the value represented by the
 *  parameter <CODE>Object</CODE> in us.  Uses linear search.
 */
public boolean contains(Object o) {
  return storage.contains(o) ;
}
/**
 *  Deliver up an iteration over all the items in the
 *  <CODE>OrderedBinaryTreeSet</CODE>.
 */
public ADS.Iterator iterator() {
  return new Iterator () ;
}
/**
 *  Define the iterator over <CODE>OrderedBinaryTreeSet</CODE>s.
 */
public class Iterator implements ADS.Iterator {
  /**
   *  The cursor is just an iterator over the
   *  <CODE>SetTree</CODE>. Use the default of in-order
   *  traversal.
   */
  protected ADS.Iterator cursor = storage.iterator() ;
  /**
   *  Deliver the value we are currently referring to.
   */
  public Object get() {
    return cursor.get() ;
  }
  /**
   *  Move on to the next element in the container.
   */
  public void advance() {
    cursor.advance() ;
  }
  /**
   *  Have we reached the end of the iteration?
   */
  public boolean atEnd() {
```

```
      return cursor.atEnd() ;
    }
    /**
     *  Are two iterators equal, i.e. do two iterators refer to the
     *  same item in the same data structure.
     */
    public boolean equals(final ADS.Iterator i) {
      if (!(i instanceof Iterator))
        return false ;
      return cursor.equals(((Iterator)i).cursor) ;
    }
    /**
     *  Return the reference to the current object.
     */
    public Object myObject() {
      return OrderedBinaryTreeSet.this ;
    }
    /**
     *  Clone this <CODE>Iterator</CODE>.
     */
    public final Object clone() {
      Iterator i = new Iterator () ;
      i.cursor = (Iterator)cursor.clone() ;
      return i ;
    }
  }
}
```

Clearly this is only the beginnings of a full set implementation, there are a number of other methods that need implementing since there are other set operations that are possible. However, it is a good start and for the purposes of our presentation here to go further would just be "filling in the details" providing no extra issues relating to programming.

It is worth noting at this point that whilst Collections take essentially the above approach to its set abstraction, JGL takes a very different viewpoint. JGL provides a tree-based set abstraction but it assumes that all entities that support iterators can supply input to set operation (i.e. that all containers are effectively sets). JGL defines all the set operations as static methods using iterators as parameters. This is taking the view of iterators as defining sets to its logical conclusion. It is not a question of one of these architectures being right and the other wrong, it is a question of two very different architectures.

Looking at the JGL documentation regarding set, we see that one of the parameters to the set constructors is a Boolean to specify whether or not duplicate entries are allowed. JGL introduces the term *multi-set* for a set which permits duplicate values to be in the container — sets of course do not allow duplicate entries — such a container is often called a *bag*. Whilst JGL supports bags as fully as it supports sets, Collections appears to ignore bags completely.

So how to introduce bags into ADS? We don't use quite the same architecture for ADTs and their representation as we have previously (i.e. using an abstract class). We still need the interface Bag which is a subinterface of Set:

```
package ADS ;
/**
 *  The interface describing a bag.
 *
```

```
 *   @version 1.2 1999.10.30
 *   @author Russel Winder
 */
public interface Bag extends Set {
  /**
   *  Determine the number of times an item appears in the
   *  <CODE>Bag</CODE>.
   */
  int countOf(Object o) ;
  /**
   *  The synchronized version.
   */
  public static class Synchronized
    extends Set.Synchronized implements Bag {
    /**
     *  The default constructor.
     */
    public Synchronized(final Bag b) {
      super(b) ;
    }
    /**
     *  The constructor that supplies an object to synchronize on.
     */
    public Synchronized(final Bag b, final Object o) {
      super(b, o) ;
    }
    /**
     *  Determine the number of times an item appears in the
     *  <CODE>Bag</CODE>.
     */
    public int countOf(final Object o) {
      synchronized (theLock) {
        return ((Bag)theContainer).countOf(o) ;
      }
    }
  }
}
```

We can dispense with the abstract bag class since we can simply inherit OrderedBag from OrderedSet directly:

```
package ADS ;
/**
 *  A bag implemented using an <CODE>OrderedBinaryTree</CODE>.
 *
 *   @version 1.1 1999.10.30
 *   @author Russel Winder
 */
public class OrderedBinaryTreeBag
  extends OrderedBinaryTreeSet implements Bag {
  /**
   *  Construct an <CODE>OrderedBag</CODE> using the equality relation
   *  <CODE>EqualToComparator</CODE> as a method object encapsulating
   *  the <CODE>equals</CODE> method.  The less than order relation
   *  must be provided by the called.
   */
  public OrderedBinaryTreeBag(final Comparator c) {
    //  The superclass uses an ordered binary tree without duplicates
    //  all we need to do is to replace the representation.
    super(c) ;
    storage =
     new OrderedBinaryTree (c, new EqualToComparator (), true) ;
  }
  /**
   *  Clone a <CODE>Bag</CODE>.
   */
```

```
public Object clone() {
  OrderedBinaryTreeBag b =
   new OrderedBinaryTreeBag (storage.order) ;
  b.storage = (OrderedBinaryTree)storage.clone() ;
  return b ;
}
/**
 *  Determine the number of times an item appears in the
 *  <CODE>Bag</CODE>.  This implements an O(log(n)) linear search.
 */
public int countOf(Object o) {
  int count = 0 ;
  for (OrderedBinaryTree.SearchIterator si =
        (OrderedBinaryTree.SearchIterator)storage.searchFor(o) ;
       ! si.atEnd() ;
       si.advance()) {
    ++count ;
  }
  return count ;
}
}
```

The point here is that we guarantee that not only is a `Bag` a subclass of `Set` — which is the necessary relationship between types to model the mathematics correctly — but the representation is (unusually) identical so that using inheritance between `OrderedBag` and `OrderedSet` is the best code reuse scheme: there is no new representation independent code for the bag.

18.4 Relation

Returning to the issue of creating relations. Mathematically, a relation is a set of ordered pairs. It seems sensible, therefore, to investigate whether this is the right way of implementing the abstraction. We certainly need to create a `Relation` interface:

```
package ADS ;
/**
 *  The interface describing a relation.
 *
 *  @version 1.0 1999.10.30
 *  @author Russel Winder
 */
public interface Relation extends Set {
  /**
   *  Insert a (key, value) pair into the <CODE>Relation</CODE>.
   */
  void add(Object d, Object c) ;
  /**
   *  Remove the (key, value) pair.
   *
   *  @return whether the element was found and deleted.
   */
  boolean remove(Object d, Object c) ;
  /**
   *  Create an iterator over all the sub-set of the domain that is
   *  used in this relation..
   */
  Iterator domain() ;
  /**
   *  Create an iterator over the sub-set of the domain that is
   *  used in this relation which relate to a given value in the
```

```
 *   co-domain.
 */
Iterator domain(Object value) ;
/**
 *  Create an iterator over all the values range.
 */
Iterator range() ;
/**
 *  Create an iterator over the sub-set of the range that relate to
 *  a given item from the domain.
 */
Iterator range(Object key) ;
/**
 *  We have to provide a class to support synchronization of
 *  <CODE>Relation</CODE>s.
 */
public static class Synchronized
  extends Set.Synchronized implements Relation {
  /**
   *  The default constructor.  Gives an <CODE>Relation</CODE> with
   *  default initial size and increment.
   */
  public Synchronized(final Relation m) {
    super(m) ;
  }
  /**
   *  The constructor that supplies an object to synchronize on.
   */
  public Synchronized(final Relation m, final Object o) {
    super(m, o) ;
  }
  /**
   *  Insert a (key, value) pair into the <CODE>Relation</CODE>.
   */
  public final void add(final Object key, final Object value) {
    synchronized (theLock) {
      ((Relation)theContainer).add(key, value) ;
    }
  }
  /**
   *  Remove the (key, value) pair.
   *
   *  @return whether the element was found and deleted.
   */
  public final boolean remove(final Object key, final Object value){
    synchronized (theLock) {
      return ((Relation)theContainer).remove(key, value) ;
    }
  }
  /**
   *  Create an iterator over all the sub-set of the domain that is
   *  used in this relation.
   */
  public final Iterator domain() {
    return ((Relation)theContainer).domain() ;
  }
  /**
   *  Create an iterator over the sub-set of the domain that is used
   *  in this relation which relate to a given value in the
   *  co-domain.
   */
  public final Iterator domain(Object c) {
    return ((Relation)theContainer).domain(c) ;
  }
  /**
   *  Create an iterator over all the values range.
```

```
    */
  public final Iterator range() {
    return ((Relation)theContainer).range() ;
  }
  /**
   *  Create an iterator over the sub-set of the range that relate
   *  to a given item from the domain.
   */
  public final Iterator range(Object d) {
    return ((Relation)theContainer).range(d) ;
  }
  }
}
```

We have introduced a number of methods for `Relation` that are easily and sensibly implemented using iterators and are hence independent of representation. As ever, we put these into an abstract class:

```
package ADS ;
/**
 *  An abstract relation.
 *
 *  @version 1.0 1999.01.30
 *  @author Russel Winder
 */
public abstract class AbstractRelation
  extends AbstractSet implements Relation {
  /**
   *  Remove the entire contents of the <CODE>Relation</CODE>.
   */
  public abstract void makeEmpty() ;
  /**
   *  Compare this <CODE>Relation</CODE> with another and determine
   *  whether they represent the same value, i.e. have the same item
   *  values in the <CODE>Relation</CODE>.
   */
  public boolean equals(Object o) {
    if (! (o instanceof Relation))
      return false ;
    for (Iterator i = iterator() ; !i.atEnd() ; i.advance()) {
      if (! ((Relation)o).contains(i.get()))
        return false ;
    }
    for (Iterator i = ((Relation)o).iterator() ;
         !i.atEnd() ;
         i.advance()) {
      if (! contains(i.get()))
        return false ;
    }
    return true ;
  }
  /**
   *  Insert a (key, value) pair into the <CODE>Relation</CODE>.
   */
  public void add(Object d, Object c) {
    add(new Pair(d, c)) ;
  }
  /**
   *  Remove the (key, value) pair.
   *
   *  @return whether the element was found and deleted.
   */
  public boolean remove(Object d, Object c) {
    return remove(new Pair(d, c)) ;
  }
```

```
/**
 * Create an iterator over all the sub-set of the domain that is
 * used in this relation.
 */
public abstract  Iterator domain() ;
/**
 * Create an iterator over the sub-set of the domain that is
 * used in this relation which relate to a given value in the
 * co-domain.
 */
public abstract  Iterator domain(final Object c) ;
/**
 * Create an iterator over all the values range.
 */
public abstract  Iterator range() ;
/**
 * Create an iterator over the sub-set of the range that relate to
 * a given item from the domain.
 */
public abstract  Iterator range(final Object d) ;
}
```

As normal we now move on to constructing the concrete class. In this case, we are going to represent
the relation with an ordered binary tree. Given that we have already implemented a set with an
ordered binary tree and a `Relation` is a `Set` and an `OrderedBinaryTreeRelation` is
an `OrderedBinaryTreeSet`, we might consider inheriting `OrderedBinaryTree-`
`Relation` from `OrderedBinaryTreeSet` in the same sort of way we organized things with
the `Bag` class in the previous section. However, we also have `AbstractRelation` which we
want to be the superclass of `OrderedBinaryTreeRelation`. With these ideas, we have a
problem. Java does not allow a class to have two superclasses; Java is a single inheritance language.
What to do? Clearly we can only inherit from one of the classes, the question is which? First we must
understand why we are using inheritance. In both cases it is not really to do with the ADT (the ADTs
are represented by the `Set` and `Bag` interfaces which already have an inheritance relationship), it
is essentially just code re-use. So it is really down to which does more code re-use. In fact there is
another issue: consistency of architecture. At all times we should maintain consistency of the
package architecture. Using this point we decide in favour of inheriting from the abstract class:

tip

*Do not use inheritance
for code re-use if there is
a type relationship to be
modelled — with only
single inheritance, type
relationships take
precedence over re-use.*

```
package ADS ;
/**
 * A relation implemented using an <CODE>OrderedBinaryTree</CODE>.
 *
 * @version 1.0 1999.10.30
 * @author Russel Winder
 */
public class OrderedBinaryTreeRelation extends AbstractRelation {
  /**
   * The <CODE>OrderedBinaryTree</CODE> that acts as our storage.
   */
  protected OrderedBinaryTree storage ;
  /**
   * Construct an <CODE>OrdereBinaryTreeRelation</CODE> using the
   * default equality relation (<CODE>Function</CODE>.  We must
   * insist on being given a valid <CODE>Comparator</CODE> defining
   * the order relation to implement the insertion policy.
   */
  public OrderedBinaryTreeRelation(final Comparator c) {
    storage = new OrderedBinaryTree (new PairAComparator(c),
                                     new EqualToComparator ()) ;
```

```
  }
  /**
   *  Remove the entire contents of the
   *  <CODE>OrdereBinaryTreeRelation</CODE>.
   */
  public void makeEmpty() {
    storage.makeEmpty() ;
  }
  /**
   *  Return the number of items in the
   *  <CODE>OrdereBinaryTreeRelation</CODE>.
   */
  public int size() {
    return storage.size() ;
  }
  /**
   *  Insert a (key, value) <CODE>Pair</CODE> into the
   *  <CODE>OrdereBinaryTreeRelation</CODE>.
   */
  public void add(final Object o) {
    if (! (o instanceof Pair))
      throw new InvalidOperationException () ;
    storage.add(o) ;
  }
  /**
   *  Remove an <CODE>Object</CODE>.
   *
   *  @exception InvalidOperationException if the parameter is
   *  anything other than a <CODE>Pair</CODE>.
   */
  public boolean remove(final Object o) {
    if (! (o instanceof Pair))
      throw new InvalidOperationException () ;
    return storage.remove(o) ;
  }
  /**
   *  Cloning is actually easy.
   */
  public Object clone() {
    OrderedBinaryTreeRelation t =
     new OrderedBinaryTreeRelation(storage.order) ;
    if (! isEmpty()) {
      t.storage = (OrderedBinaryTree)storage.clone() ;
    }
    return t ;
  }
  /**
   *  Determine whether we have the value represented by the
   *  parameter <CODE>Object</CODE> in us.  Uses linear search.
   */
  public boolean contains(Object o) {
    return storage.contains(o) ;
  }
  /**
   *  Deliver up an iteration over all the items in the
   *  <CODE>OrdereBinaryTreeRelation</CODE>.
   */
  public ADS.Iterator iterator() {
    return new Iterator () ;
  }
  /**
   *  Define the iterator over <CODE>OrdereBinaryTreeRelation</CODE>s.
   */
  public class Iterator implements ADS.Iterator {
    /**
     *  The cursor is just an iterator over the
```

```
 *    <CODE>RelationTree</CODE>. Use the default of in-order
 *    traversal.
 */
protected ADS.Iterator cursor = storage.iterator() ;
/**
 *  Deliver the value we are currently referring to.
 */
public Object get() {
  return cursor.get() ;
}
/**
 *  Amend the value of the element we are currently referring to.
 *  Usage invalidates the iterator.
 */
public void set(final Object o) {
  if (!(o instanceof Pair))
    throw new InvalidIteratorOperationException () ;
    //  This looks horrendously inefficient even though it is safe.
    //  There must be a better way.  This issue is that the in-order
    //   traversal iterator is not an editing iterator so we can edit
    //   using it.
    storage.remove(cursor.get()) ;
    storage.add(o) ;
    cursor = null ;
}
/**
 *  Move on to the next element in the container.
 */
public void advance() {
  cursor.advance() ;
}
/**
 *  Have we reached the end of the iteration?
 */
public boolean atEnd() {
  return cursor.atEnd() ;
}
/**
 *  Are two iterators equal, i.e. do two iterators refer to the
 *  same item in the same data structure.
 */
public boolean equals(final ADS.Iterator i) {
  if (!(i instanceof Iterator))
    return false ;
  return cursor.equals(((Iterator)i).cursor) ;
}
/**
 *  Return the reference to the current object.
 */
public Object myObject() {
  return OrderedBinaryTreeRelation.this ;
}
/**
 *  Clone this <CODE>Iterator</CODE>.
 */
public final Object clone() {
  Iterator i = new Iterator () ;
  i.cursor = (Iterator)cursor.clone() ;
  return i ;
}
}
/**
 *  Create an iterator over all the sub-set of the domain that is
 *  used in this relation.
 */
public ADS.Iterator domain() {
```

528

```
      return new Iterator () {
        public Object get() {
          return ((Pair)cursor.get()).getA() ;
        }
      } ;
    }
    /**
     * Create an iterator over the sub-set of the domain that is
     * used in this relation which relate to a given value in the
     * co-domain.
     */
    public ADS.Iterator domain(final Object c) {
      class DomainIterator extends Iterator {
        public DomainIterator() {
          if (! ((Pair)cursor.get()).getB().equals(c)) {
            moveOn() ;
          }
        }
        public Object get() {
          return ((Pair)cursor.get()).getA() ;
        }
        public void advance() {
          moveOn() ;
        }
        private void moveOn() {
          while (!atEnd()) {
            super.advance() ;
            if (atEnd() || ((Pair)cursor.get()).getB().equals(c))
              break ;
          }
        }
      }
      return new DomainIterator () ;
    }
    /**
     * Create an iterator over all the values range.
     */
    public ADS.Iterator range() {
      return new Iterator() {
        public Object get() {
          return ((Pair)cursor.get()).getB() ;
        }
      } ;
    }
    /**
     * Create an iterator over the sub-set of the range that relate to
     * a given item from the domain.
     */
    public ADS.Iterator range(final Object d) {
      class RangeIterator extends Iterator {
        public RangeIterator() {
          if (! ((Pair)cursor.get()).getA().equals(d)) {
            moveOn() ;
          }
        }
        public Object get() {
          return ((Pair)cursor.get()).getB() ;
        }
        public void advance() {
          moveOn() ;
        }
        private void moveOn() {
          while (!atEnd()) {
            super.advance() ;
            if (atEnd() || ((Pair)cursor.get()).getA().equals(d))
              break ;
```

!

Note the use of local classes here rather than anonymous classes so as to be able to use constructors. Anonymous classes cannot have explicit constructors.

```
         }
       }
     }
     return new RangeIterator () ;
   }
 }
```

Comparing the above with the implementation of `OrderedBinaryTreeSet` earlier, we see that the concrete classes are more or less just wrappers to the underlying representation — the classes use 'abstraction by association' for dealing with the underlying representation and the methods are just forwarding queries and state changes to the representation. So whilst there is a little code replication, there is actually very little of it. The decision not to have an inheritance relationship between `OrderedBinaryTreeRelation` and `OrderedBinaryTreeSet` has therefore not been any trouble.

18.5 Mapping

Since a mapping is just a relation which requires uniqueness of the values used in the first position of the ordered pair, then `Mapping` must clearly be a subinterface of `Relation`:

```
package ADS ;
/**
 *  The interface describing a mapping.  A mapping is a relation in
 *  which there are no duplicate keys.
 *
 *  @version 1.2 1999.10.30
 *  @author Russel Winder
 */
public interface Mapping extends Relation {
   /**
    *  Find the value for a given key.
    *
    *  @return value from (key, value) pair given a key or null if the
    *  key is not present in the <CODE>Mapping</CODE>.
    */
   Object getValue(Object key) ;
   /**
    *  The synchronized form.
    */
   public static class Synchronized
     extends Relation.Synchronized implements Mapping {
     /**
      *  The default constructor.  Gives an <CODE>Mapping</CODE> with
      *  default initial size and increment.
      */
     public Synchronized(final Mapping m) {
       super(m) ;
     }
     /**
      *  The constructor that supplies an object to synchronize on.
      */
     public Synchronized(final Mapping m, final Object o) {
       super(m, o) ;
     }
     /**
      *  Find the value for a given key.
      *
```

```
     *  @return value from (key, value) pair given a key or null if
     *  the key is not present in the <CODE>Mapping</CODE>.
     */
    public final Object getValue(final Object key) {
      synchronized (theLock) {
        return ((Mapping)theContainer).getValue(key) ;
      }
    }
  }
}
```

Immediately we can create a concrete type since we have already implemented the relation with an ordered binary tree. As we did with bags and sets, we inherit `OrderedBinaryTreeMapping` directly from `OrderedBinaryTreeRelation` without having an abstract class as a code reuse repository. Essentially we are saying there will be no implementation independent code for a mapping that is not already available for a relation:

```
package ADS ;
/**
 *  A mapping which is a <CODE>Relation</CODE> where it is not allcwed
 *  to have two elements that both have the same value from the
 *  domain.  This is the version implemented using an
 *  <CODE>OrderedBinaryTree</CODE>.
 *
 *  @version 2.0 1999.10.30
 *  @author Russel Winder
 */
public class OrderedBinaryTreeMapping
  extends OrderedBinaryTreeRelation implements Mapping {
  /**
   *  Construct an <CODE>OrderedBinaryTreeMapping</CODE> using the
   *  default equality relation (<CODE>Function</CODE>).  We must
   *  insist on being given a valid <CODE>Comparator</CODE> defining
   *  the order relation to implement the insertion policy.
   */
  public OrderedBinaryTreeMapping(final Comparator c) {
    super(c) ;
    storage = new OrderedBinaryTree (
      new PairAComparator(c),
      new PairAComparator(new EqualToComparator ())) ;
  }
  /**
   *  Insert a (key, value) <CODE>Pair</CODE> into the
   *  <CODE>OrdereBinaryTreeRelation</CODE>.  If there is an element
   *  (key, xxx) then xxx is overwritten with value.
   */
  public void add(final Object o) {
    if (! (o instanceof Pair))
      throw new InvalidOperationException () ;
    OrderedBinaryTree.SearchIterator si =
      (OrderedBinaryTree.SearchIterator)storage.searchFor(o) ;
    if (si.atEnd()) {
      si.set(o) ;
    } else {
      si.remove() ;
      storage.add(o) ;
    }
  }
  /**
   *  Remove an <CODE>Object</CODE>.  This can either be a
   *  <CODE>Pair</CODE> in which case only the item that matches the
   *  pair is removed, if it is in the <CODE>Mapping</CODE> or the
   *  parameter is assumed to be from the domain and the element with
   *  this value is found and removed.
```

```
        */
    public boolean remove(final Object o) {
      Pair p = null ;
      if (o instanceof Pair) {
        p = (Pair)o ;
      } else {
        p = new Pair (o, null) ;
      }
      return storage.remove(p) ;
    }
    /**
     *  Cloning is actually easy.
     */
    public Object clone() {
      OrderedBinaryTreeMapping t =
       new OrderedBinaryTreeMapping(storage.order) ;
      if (! isEmpty()) {
        t.storage = (OrderedBinaryTree)storage.clone() ;
      }
      return t ;
    }
    /**
     *  Determine whether we have the value represented by the
     *  parameter <CODE>Object</CODE> in us.  Uses linear search.
     */
    public boolean contains(Object o) {
      return storage.contains(o) ;
    }
    /**
     *  Find the value from the range associated with a given value from
     *  the domain.
     *
     *  @return value from (key, value) pair given a key or null if the
     *  key is not present in the <CODE>Mapping</CODE>.
     */
    public final Object getValue(final Object o) {
      ADS.Iterator i = range(o) ;
      return i.atEnd() ? null : i.get() ;
    }
  }
```

18.6   Mappings, Procedures and Arrays

Of course, using sets of ordered pairs is not the only way of representing mappings. We are used to representing many of the mappings we use as algebraic expressions. So for example the mapping 'square' is usually represented as:

$$\text{square}(x) = x^2$$

rather than enumerating all the ordered pairs comprising the mapping. This is particularly helpful where the domain of the mapping is infinite, it avoids trying to list an infinite number of ordered pairs! Obviously, the expression is not all the information we need to give, we also need to specify the domain and co-domain, for 'square':

$$\text{square}: R \rightarrow R$$

where R stands for the set of real numbers. 'square' is a mapping from the real numbers to the real numbers, where each value x is mapped to the value x^2. If we restrict the domain and co-domain to the positive real numbers, then there is an inverse mapping, usually called 'square root':

$$squareRoot: R^+ \rightarrow R^+$$

$$squareRoot(x) = \sqrt{x}$$

This terminological problem with the word function in computing is a good reason for not using it with the meaning of procedural abstraction. As we use the term method for a procedural abstraction we can, and do, reserve the term function for a mathematical function.

Mappings such as this are often termed *functions* in mathematics. The term 'function' has also been used to refer to a procedural abstraction that accepts input arguments and calculates a value that is returned (in Java terms, a non-void method). This is very different from the notion of a function in mathematics though there is, obviously, a direct relationship. The notion of constructing a value having been presented with a value is clearly a mapping of some sort, a mapping represented as an algorithm for transformation of values. However, except where a method is actually implementing a mathematical function, there is no guarantee that it actually is a function.

Where a function can be represented using an algebraic expression, as with 'square' above, we can and should implement it using a method which encapsulates an algorithm that implements the expression. Doing this means that we do not have to be concerned with predetermining which of the infinite number of values to have in a data structure representation of a mapping. So, for example, we can represent the 'square' function using a method:

```
public static double square(final double x) {
   return x * x ;
}
```

We use multiplication here since, unlike some programming languages, the exponentiation operator does not exist in Java.

Of course, there are mappings that are almost impossible to represent as an expression and hence impossible to represent directly as an algorithm. These are the ones that we use the classes implementing the interface Mapping for. So, for example, the following mapping is easily represented using the class OrderedBinaryTreeMapping:

$$f: Z \rightarrow Z$$

$$f = \{(1, 3), (2, 3), (3,7), (4, 5), (5, 2)\}$$

where Z is the set of integers. The domain and range of this mapping are:

$$dom f = \{1, 2, 3, 4, 5\}$$

$$ran f = \{2, 3, 5, 7\}$$

However, some people might say that "Isn't the use of a class here using too much resource?" These people might consider implementing the mapping with a switch statement most likely encapsulated in a method as in:

```
public int f(final int i) {
   switch (i) {
   case 1 :
      return 3 ;
   case 2 :
```

```
    return 3 ;
  case 3 :
    return 7 ;
  case 4 :
    return 5 ;
  case 5 :
    return 2 ;
  default :
    throw new IllegalArgumentException () ;
  }
}
```

Alternatively we could use an array to directly represent the mapping:

```
int[] f_1 = {0, 3, 3, 7, 5, 2} ;
```

Here we are making use of the fact that the domain of the mapping is $\{1, 2, 3, 4, 5\}$ and can be used directly as indexes into an array. Clearly an array is an implementation mechanism for a mapping between the integers that are the array indexes and the data in the array, in the above example also integers. Of course, there is one very serious problem with the above: we have had to introduce a dummy datum at index 0 to properly establish the domain. This is a show stopping problem since it is valid to use the expression f[0] and yet 0 is not in the domain of the mapping. Arrays only directly implement mappings where the domain is $0..n$. A way of resolving this issue is to wrap the array in a method which manages the domain range. So we could construct:

```
private static final int[] map = {3, 3, 7, 5, 2} ;
public int f(int i) {
  //  Set the offset of the beginning of the domain from zero.
  int offset = 1 ;
  if ((i < offset) || (i >= (map.length + offset)))
    throw new IllegalArgumentException () ;
  return map[i - offset] ;
}
```

employing a translation of index values and also bounds checking. This means we store the values for the co-domain apparently associated with the indexes $0..n$ and programmatically map the domain to the desired range from the integers. On an implementation note, see that we 'parameterize' the offset so that if it changes we only need to change one value — more defensive programming.

Thus, procedural abstraction has made the switch statement representation and the array representation indistinguishable as far as the application is concerned: we can change the representation of the mapping within the procedural abstraction with no-one being the wiser. Using procedural abstraction, rather than just an array representation, also brings extra functionality to controlling access to the representation. This is, of course, the whole point of procedural abstractions.

Using arrays and procedural abstraction to implement representations of mappings is only useful where the domain is some sub-range of the integers and the domain values used in the mapping are contiguous. so, for example, it would not be sensible to use the procedural abstraction ideas presented above in the case of the mapping:

$$f = \{(100, 3), (200, 3), (300, 7), (400, 5), (500, 2)\}$$

note

Arrays implement mappings.

!

Note how we use map.length as the upper bound mechanism. This allows us to extend the function simply by adding new items into the array initializer; none of the statements in the method needs amending.

tip

Always program defensively. We have said this before but it bears repetition.

since we would have to have an array of 501 elements to hold five values. Not very efficient at all, to say the least. In this sort of situation we could revert to the switch statement approach and, indeed, this would probably be the solution of choice in this case. Alternatively we could employ a class implementing the interface `Mapping`.

The problem we have from the above can be characterized as 'the mapping is sparse': what we mean here is that the values in the domain are widely scattered values. There are few values from the host domain (the integers in the cases we are discussing at present) used in the domain of the mapping and they are far from contiguous. This is ideal territory for the `OrderedBinary-TreeMapping`. It represents the general case of being able to store a mapping whether it be sparse or not.

In the case where the domain of the mapping is the integers, we have what is called a *sparse array*. A sparse array is an array where most of the elements are null. If the array is large and mostly holding null elements then using an actual array as the representation means that significant space resource is being wasted. Using the `OrderedBinaryTreeMapping` is clearly sensible since we store only the non-null values using a tree. To look up a value, we have to look through the tree for the required index and then we can return the desired value. So instead of using array technology:

```
int[] array = new int [45] ;
array[4] = 25 ;
```

we have a sparse array concept, constructed as a sub-class of the `OrderedBinaryTree-Mapping`, the use of which might look like:

```
SparseArray array = new SparseArray () ;
array.set(4, new Integer(25)) ;
```

It is assumed that `SparseArray` implements the `Sequence` interface so that it looks as much as possible like an `Array`. Like all the other ADT classes we have been looking at, `SparseArray` stores objects (via object references) rather than primitive types such as `int`, so we need to create an `Integer` object in the case above.

Of course, there is a trade-off; in lowering the space usage we increase the time of access. If there are n items of data and k is the range of values used from the domain then, using an array directly, space usage is $O(k)$ and look-up is an $O(1)$ activity. Using the tree-based implementation, space usage is $O(n)$ and look-up is $O(\log(n))$. The tree implementation uses less space but has slower insert, look-up and delete.

The `SparseArray` class is an interesting application of a `Mapping`, particularly for mathematical software. If we were building mathematically oriented packages, we could construct sparse matrices using this technology and then go on to construct a representation of matrix algebra. A number of people have done exactly this sort of thing and some of them are very good indeed. Some of them (even some of the good ones) are freeware available on the Web. Our interest in this book, though, is in the construction of the ADS library rather than the contents per se. We therefore leave the sparse array and sparse matrix ideas for elsewhere, since looking at their construction would not add anything particularly new.

We finish this section by noting that we have used integers as the domain for the examples in this section: for primitive arrays, `Arrays` and `SparseArrays` the indexes all had to be integers. However, the representation of mapping using a tree does not demand this constraint — this is, of course, why it can be used as a representation of a general mapping. The term *associative array* has been used to label array-like constructs where the array "index" is something other than an integer, a string for example. Anyone who has used the Perl programming language or one like it will be used to expressions such as:

```
people["russel"] = 36 ;
```

Clearly we can't write this sort of expression directly with Java syntax but with the technology we have from `Mapping` there is nothing to stop us writing things like:

```
Mapping m = new OrderedBinaryTreeMapping (someSensibleComparator) ;
m.insert("russel", new Integer(36)) ;
```

which is, to all intents and purposes, exactly the same. An associative array really is just another name for a mapping.

18.7 Hashing

Arrays (primitive and classes) and `OrderedBinaryTreeMapping` appear to provide all we need for all our set, relation and mapping related needs. Well almost. `Arrays` have $O(1)$ access to the data given an index whereas `OrderedBinaryTreeMapping` has $O(\log(n))$ access. The question is: Can we find a data structure that gives us the ability to handle sets, relations and mappings and give us access more like $O(1)$ than $O(\log(n))$? It turns out that the answer is yes.

The 'ah ha' insight we need here is that the tree implementation solves the problem by mapping the data using a completely different structure to an array and then providing the access interface by employing appropriate algorithms. Why is this an insight that moves us forward? It is that we must avoid this structural mapping if we are to preserve $O(1)$ access performance, so we must keep the array structure in some way.

We appear to be back where we started; we need to have `int`s to use as array indexes. This is not, however, a 'Catch-22'. In the previous section, we mapped the domain values to array indexes using either an identity mapping or a simple translation but there is no reason why we cannot have a non-trivial mapping: all we need is a transformation of domain data into positive `int`s suitable to be indexes in an actual array. So whilst the tree-based solution was a direct solution to the mapping problem, we appear to be arguing our way into the position where we have a two-stage mechanism to implementing the mapping. The first stage is to construct an array index using the value from the domain and the second stage is to have an array in which to hold the value from the range of the mapping and hence be able to map array indexes into data values. As long as we can construct a

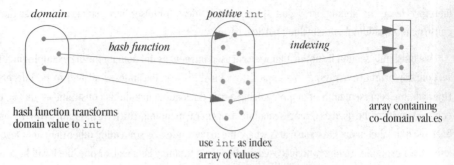

Figure 18.3 Using a hash function.

transformation from domain values to array indexes which is O(1) then we have found the necessary data structure.

So, what we are looking for is a function that we can calculate easily. Such a function is usually called an *hash function* (see Figure 18.3). Given that the `int`s generated by the hash function are used as indexes into an array of definite size, we have a constraint on the hash function, it must create `int`s in the range: [0, array_size - 1]. Also, these generated `int`s need to be as evenly distributed across this range as possible. We do not intend to go into the theory behind good quality hash functions in this book, any book on algorithmics is the place to go for this. We do, however, give some example hash functions for transforming strings into indexes:

- "*add together all the Unicode values of the characters of the string and take the modulus of the resultant number with the table size*".

```
public int hash(final String s, final int tableSize) {
  int result = 0 ;
  for (int i = 0 ; i < s.length() ; ++i) {
    result += s.charAt(i) ;
  }
  return result % tableSize ;
}
```

Note here that `s.charAt(i)` returns a `char` (a 16-bit value) which has an automatic conversion into an `int`. Also, we use the modulus function to guarantee that the range of the returned hash value is a valid index.

This actually turns out to be a poor hash function. Its limiting property is that typically only a small range of characters are used for a given language, less than 127 for standard English for example. As English characters are encoded in the range 0 to 127, the maximum value the hash function can generate is 127 × `stringLength` which is very rarely a particularly large number. This means that if the table is actually quite large, 100,000 items say, then the hash function will cluster all the elements at the beginning of the table which is not a good thing.

- "*multiply the Unicode values of all the characters together and then take the modulus of the resultant number with the size of the array*".

```
public int hash(final String s, final int tableSize) {
  int result = 0 ;
  for (int i = 0 ; i < s.length() ; ++i) {
```

```
      result *= s.charAt(i) ;
  }
  return result % tableSize ;
}
```

This tries to solve the spacing problem by multiplication rather than addition of the values, but this turns out to be a bad idea as well, since the result can become far too large and can start overflowing the `int` variable, which will again lead to clustering.

- The following is the algorithm (though not the actual code) used in `java.lang.String` in JDK1.1 to create a hash value for a `String`:

```
public int hash(final String s, final int tableSize) {
  int result = 0 ;
  int length = s.length() ;
  if (length < 16) {
    // For short strings use all the characters.
    for (int i = 0 ; i < length ; ++i) {
      result = (result * 37) + s.charAt(i) ;
    }
  } else {
    // For longer strings use only some of the characters.
    int skip = length / 8 ;
    for (int i = 0 ; i < length ; i += skip) {
      result = (result * 39) + s.charAt(i) ;
    }
  }
  return result % tableSize ;
}
```

Here short and long strings are separated, using all characters for short strings and a sample of the characters for longer strings. This is a 'multiply and add algorithm' where we multiply the current result by a number and then add the next character value from the string.

- The following is the algorithm (though not the actual code) used in `java.lang.String` in J2SDK v1.2.2 to create a hash value for a `String`:

```
public int hash(final String s, final int tableSize) {
  int result = 0 ;
  for (int i = 0 ; i < s.length() ; ++i) {
    result = (result * 31) + s.charAt(i) ;
  }
  return result % tableSize ;
}
```

This algorithm is again a 'multiply and add' algorithm but ensuring that all characters of the string are always used and hence without the selection on the length of the string. The rationale for the change of algorithm between JDK1.1 and J2SDK v1.2.2 is not documented in the source code (which is a bad thing) so it is difficult to understand why the authors of the `String` class decided to change algorithm. It may be significant that 39 is not a prime whereas 37 and 31 are and also that all Java integers are 32 bits long. However, without studying the theoretical detail of the algorithm it is impossible to actually say anything constructive.

By partitioning the problem into two using the intermediate representation of array indexes we have given ourselves the opportunity of performing lookup in constant time. The foundation is that we use an array structure as the actual mapping which is $O(1)$ and that we map the domain not directly to the co-domain but to the set of array indexes using a method representing a hash function, which we ensure runs in $O(1)$ time. Well actually $O(l)$ where l is the length of the string but this is likely to be very small in comparison to n the number of items. Since it is likely that $O(1) \approx O(l) \ll O(\log(n))$, hashing will be much quicker that using a binary tree.

It is important to note that Java takes hashing very seriously. So seriously, in fact, that every class has a hash method, `hashCode`. Class `Object` defines a default `hashCode` method which delivers an unique `int` for each object in the system. This actually makes our programming problem a lot easier since all we have to do is ensure that we map the hash code into an array index, taking into account that the array we use to hold the co-domain values of the mapping is going to be of finite size (the modulus operator comes in very handy in this situation). We could of course generate a completely new hash function, and in certain circumstances that is very appropriate, but in the main this generic hash function will suffice. In the Java system itself, as we noted above, `String` overrides the `hashCode` function explicitly so as to produce more appropriate hash values than the default method can do.

We now have all we need to make use of hash functions and arrays to create mappings. Implemented in this fashion we usually call them *hash tables*.

Actually there is one more problem that we have not investigated: What happens if two domain values deliver the same has value? We have to define a *collision algorithm*. There are two basic algorithms that are used, open hashing and chaining, defining two sorts of hash table.

A short note before delving in: when dealing with hash tables it is usual to say that the pair that is the datum is a pair (*key, value*) where the *key* is a value from the domain and *value* is a value from the co-domain of the mapping being implemented. We use this nomenclature here since we feel it make the explanations clearer.

18.8   Open Hash Table

The collision algorithm employed in *open hashing* is to move from the index calculated by the hash function by incrementing the index by one, until we find the array entry we need. The needed entry differs depending on whether we are looking up a key that should already be in the table or trying to enter a new (key, value) pair into the table. In the former case we look for a given key. If we find it we can access the associated value. If we find a null entry, the domain value is not in the table. For entering a new pair we look for the key, which if found indicates we have already entered it and we must act accordingly, or we find the first available null entry into which can put the new datum. Normally, if we are entering a new pair and the key is already in the table then we update the value of that pair with the new entry preserving the uniqueness of the key in the table. This algorithm is known as *linear probing*.

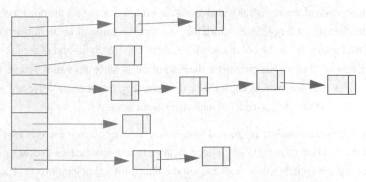

Figure 18.4 A chained hash table.

If the hash function is only partially successful at spreading the resultant indexes from the presented domain values, there will be clustering using this linear probing. There is a technique called *quadratic probing* that some people employ. This uses the square of the number of attempts to probe as the distance jumped to try the next. The linear probing collision algorithm checks the sequence are array cells indexed by:

$$h, h+1, h+2, h+3, h+4, \ldots$$

where h is the index calculated by the hash function. Quadratic probing uses the sequence:

$$h, h+1, h+4, h+9, h+16, \ldots$$

Hopefully it is obvious that the size of the array used to store the values from the range must be quite a lot larger that the number of values in the range in order for hashing to be useful. For a really good hash table we need to make sure that a significant number of elements in the array are empty. This is usually done by setting an upper limit on the number of used slots, based on a percentage of the size of the table, so that there is always a certain ratio of empty slots in the array. Less obviously, making the size of the hash table be a prime number invariably helps with the spread of the data through the hash table.

You may have noticed that we have not presented an implementation here. For good or bad, open hash tables appear to be rarely used in practice. Instead, most hash tables implement an algorithm called chaining. Much of the code of the two implementations is essentially the same so it is not particularly useful to present both in this book. Since we are definitely going to present the chained hash table implementation, we do not present the open hash table implementation.

18.9   Chained Hash Table

The chaining collision algorithm is based on not having a collision at all! When this algorithm is used, by a *chained hash table*, the array does not hold the values from the co-domain but instead holds a linked list of values from the co-domain (see Figure 18.4).

The hash code of the key is calculated giving the array index as with the open hash table. This array index identifies a list of values, which may of course be empty. If we are looking up a key we walk the list looking for the key — the key is not there if we reach the end of the list — if we are entering a new key then we add the entry at the head of the list since this avoids walking the list at all and also hides any pre-existing entries with the same key. Whether we leave any inaccessible duplicate entries in the list is a matter of implementation choice.

Many people who implement chained hash tables, use singly-linked list technology directly to deal with the collision chains. However, since we already have abstractions to deal with these data structures, we really ought to use them and not use linked-list technology directly. The question is which of our `Sequence` implementations to use?

`Array`: We could use an `Array` rather than a linked list as the representation but we would have to make very certain that we added new entries on the end and not the front and that we searched from the end towards the beginning. We could leave all entries in and not delete them so as to avoid the $O(n)$ shuffling that has to take place when data is removed from the middle of an `Array`. *n* here should always be very small.

`SLList`: Using a `SLList` we could use head insertion and searching from the head to the tail.

`DLList`: Using a `DLList` we could use either the algorithm for `Array` or the algorithm for `SLList`. Editing of the lists is easier than either `Array` or `SLList`.

The behaviour for chain management is not the same for all `Sequence`s, tail insert is used for `Array` representation and head insert for `SLList` — `DLList` can do either. Thus, we can decide that either `Array`s and `DLList`s are possible representations and use an appropriate interface or we can decide that `SLList`s and `DLList`s are possible representations and use an appropriate and different interface. Given that we have to search the list, the benefit of arrays over lists — $O(1)$ rather than $O(n)$ access time is not relevant — linear searching is essentially as efficient on lists as it is on arrays. This situation is not entirely dissimilar to that we find when implementing stacks. Creating an algorithm that worked for all `Sequence`s means that the algorithms for one of `Array` or `SLList` are moderately inefficient.

For this implementation, we shall ignore all the `Sequence`-related issues and just use a `DLList`. As with all the abstractions in ADS, we use the mixed 'abstraction by conformance' and 'abstraction by inheritance' approach. We define an interface so that we can deal with the abstraction of Hash Table independent of whether we use open hashing or chained hashing or even something else:

```
package ADS ;
/**
 *  An hash table abstraction. This is intended to be an
 *  implementation tool for <CODE>Set</CODE>, <CODE>Relation</CODE>
 *  and <CODE>Mapping</CODE> rather than a publically used ADT.
 *
 *  @version 1.0 1999.10.31
 *  @author Russel Winder
 */
public interface HashTable extends Container {
```

```
/**
 *  Add a (key, value) pair.
 */
void add(Object key, Object value) ;
/**
 *  Find a key for a given value.
 */
Object getValue(Object key) ;
/**
 *  This is the synchronized form.
 */
public static class Synchronized
  extends Container.Synchronized implements HashTable {
  /**
   *  The default constructor.  Gives an <CODE>HashTable</CODE> with
   *  default initial size and increment.
   */
  public Synchronized(final HashTable h) {
    super(h) ;
  }
  /**
   *  The constructor that supplies an object to synchronize on.
   */
  public Synchronized(final HashTable h, final Object o) {
    super(h, o) ;
  }
  /**
   *  Add a (key, value) pair.
   */
  public final void add(final Object key, final Object value) {
    synchronized (theLock) {
      ((HashTable)theContainer).add(key, value) ;
    }
  }
  /**
   *  Return the number of items in the <CODE>Container</CODE>.
   */
  public final Object getValue(final Object o) {
    synchronized (theLock) {
      return ((HashTable)theContainer).getValue(o) ;
    }
  }
}
}
```

The we have the abstract class that holds all the representation independent parts of the implementation:

```
package ADS ;
/**
 *  An abstract hash table.
 *
 *  @version 1.0 1999.10.31
 *  @author Russel Winder
 */
public abstract class AbstractHashTable
  extends AbstractContainer implements HashTable {
  /**
   *  The storage for the hash table.
   */
  protected Object[] table ;
  /**
   *  Keep a count of the number of items to make things more
   *  efficient.
   */
  protected int pairCount ;
```

```java
/**
 *  The hash function method object defining our hash function.  The
 *  hash function guarantees to deliver a positive integer.  The
 *  table indexing operations are responsible for ensuring that the
 *  integer is a valid index.  On most occassions this simply means
 *  taking the modulus of the hash value against the size of the
 *  array being used as representation.
 */
protected HashFunction hf ;
/**
 *  The default size of the hash table.  Best if this is a prime
 *  number.
 */
protected final static int DEFAULT_SIZE = 511 ;
/**
 *  Remove the entire contents of the
 *  <CODE>ChainedHashMapping</CODE>.
 */
public void makeEmpty() {
  //  We contemptuously (!) leave the garbage collector to handle
  //  all the clean up by just releasing all the DLLists to be
  //  garbage.  This is quicker than calling makeEmpty on each one.
  for (int i = 0 ; i < table.length ; i++) {
    table[i] = null ;
  }
  pairCount = 0 ;
}
/**
 *  Determine whether the <CODE>ChainedHashMapping</CODE> is an
 *  empty one.
 */
public final boolean isEmpty() {
  return pairCount <= 0 ;
}
/**
 *  Return the number of items in the
 *  <CODE>ChainedHashMapping</CODE>.
 */
public final int size() {
  return pairCount ;
}
/**
 *  Compare <CODE>HashTable</CODE>s of any representation.
 */
public boolean equals(final Object o) {
  if ((o == null) ||
      ! (o instanceof HashTable) ||
      (size() != ((HashTable)o).size()))
    return false ;
  for (Iterator i = iterator() ; !i.atEnd() ; i.advance()) {
    if (! ((HashTable)o).contains(i.get()))
      return false ;
  }
  for (Iterator i = ((HashTable)o).iterator() ;
       !i.atEnd() ;
       i.advance()) {
    if (! contains(i.get()))
      return false ;
  }
  return true ;
}
/**
 *  Add a (key, value) pair.
 */
public void add(final Object key, final Object value) {
  add(new Pair(key, value)) ;
```

```
    }
    /**
     *   Find a value for a given key.
     */
    public abstract Object getValue(Object key) ;
}
```

We have decided that the hash function used should be a parameter of the hash table and have
decided to realize this by using method objects. The default is:

```
package ADS ;
/**
 *   A class to act as a definer of hash function method objects.
 *   An hash value is a positive integer.
 *
 *   @version 1.0 1999.10.30
 *   @author Russel Winder
 */
public class HashFunction {
    /**
     *   The hash algorithm encapsulated as a method.
     */
    public int hash(final Object o) {
        //
        //   It is interesting that in the Java library there is a function
        //   in the package java.lang.Math called abs which ensures that a
        //   value is positive and yet it is unused in the types
        //   java.util.Hashtable and com.objectspace.jgl.HashMap.   abs is
        //   basically programmed as:
        //
        //       public int abs(int a) {
        //           return a < 0 ? -a : a ;
        //       }
        //
        //   which is deemed to be inefficient and hence not usable:
        //   everyone assumes 2's complement 32-bit ints (which is fair
        //   since that is what the JVM defines int to be) and simply masks
        //   out the sign bit.  Essentially an efficiency measure since no
        //   selection is needed.
        //
        return (o.hashCode() & 0x7FFFFFFF) ;
    }
}
```

Finally, we can have the chained hash table itself:

```
package ADS ;
/**
 *   An hash table that uses chaining.  In this implementation, the
 *   chains of the hash table are <CODE>DLList</CODE>s.  Use this
 *   rather than the simpler <CODE>SLList</CODE> so that editing the
 *   list in the middle is easier.  We need this capability only to
 *   support removal of an item.
 *
 *   @version 2.0 1999.10.29
 *   @author Russel Winder
 */
public class ChainedHashTable extends AbstractHashTable {
    /**
     *   The default constructor. Use the default size of 511 and the
     *   default hash function as supplied by the class
     *   <CODE>HashFunction</CODE>.
     */
    public ChainedHashTable() {
        this(DEFAULT_SIZE, new HashFunction ()) ;
    }
```

note

Note the definition of the hash function. We take the hash code of the object and ensure it is a positive number by masking out the sign bit. This is JVM specific coding. We know that an `int` is a 32 bit number with the top bit being the sign.

```
/**
 *  The constructor specifying the size of the table but using the
 *  default hash function as supplied by the class
 *  <CODE>HashFunction</CODE>.
 */
public ChainedHashTable(final int tableSize) {
  this(tableSize, new HashFunction ()) ;
}
/**
 *  The constructor that assumes the default size but provides an
 *  hash function..
 */
public ChainedHashTable(final HashFunction f) {
  this(DEFAULT_SIZE, f) ;
}
/**
 *  The constructor specifying the size of the table and the hash
 *  function.
 */
public ChainedHashTable(final int tableSize, final HashFunction f) {
  table = new DLList [tableSize] ;
  hf = f ;
}
/**
 *  Deliver up a complete shallow copy of the
 *  <CODE>ChainedHashTable</CODE>.
 */
public Object clone() {
  ChainedHashTable h = new ChainedHashTable (table.length) ;
  for (int i = 0 ; i < table.length ; i++) {
    if (table[i] != null) {
      h.table[i] = ((DLList)table[i]).clone() ;
    }
  }
  h.pairCount = pairCount ;
  return h ;
}
/**
 *  Insert a (key, value) pair into the
 *  <CODE>ChainedHashTable</CODE>.  Since removal of items is
 *  allowed we do not just add the new item, we remove the old item
 *  associated with key -- or (key, value), depending on whether
 *  equality is key equality or <CODE>Pair</CODE> equality --
 *  i.e. we do not use shadowing.
 */
public void add(final Object o) {
  if (!(o instanceof Pair))
    throw new InvalidOperationException () ;
  int index = findIndex(((Pair)o).getA()) ;
  if (table[index] == null) {
    table[index] = new DLList () ;
  }
  for (DLList.Iterator i =
         (DLList.Iterator)((DLList)table[index]).iterator() ;
       !i.atEnd() ;
       i.advance()) {
    if (i.get().equals(o)) {
      i.remove() ;
      --pairCount ;
      break ;
    }
  }
  ((DLList)table[index]).add(o) ;
  ++pairCount ;
}
/**
```

```java
 *   Find a value for a given key.
 *
 *   @return value from (key, value) pair given a key or null if
 *   the key is not present in the <CODE>Table</CODE>.
 */
public Object getValue(final Object key) {
  for (ADS.Iterator i =
         ((DLList)table[findIndex(key)]).iterator();
       !i.atEnd() ;
       i.advance()) {
    Pair p = (Pair)i.get() ;
    if (p.getA().equals(key))
      return p.getB() ;
  }
  return null ;
}
/**
 *   Remove the pair with key key.
 */
public boolean remove(final Object o) {
  for (DLList.Iterator i =
         (DLList.Iterator)((DLList)table[findIndex(o)]).iterator() ;
       !i.atEnd() ;
       i.advance()) {
    if (((Pair)i.get()).getA().equals(o)) {
      i.remove() ;
      --pairCount ;
      return true ;
    }
  }
  return false ;
}
/**
 *   Remove the (key, value) pair.
 */
public boolean remove(final Pair p) {
  DLList d = (DLList)table[findIndex(p.getA())] ;
  if (d != null && ! d.isEmpty()) {
    if (d.remove(p)) {
      --pairCount ;
      return true ;
    }
  }
  return false ;
}
/**
 *   Deliver up an iterator over all the items in the
 *   <CODE>ChainedHashMapping</CODE>.
 */
public ADS.Iterator iterator () {
  return new Iterator () ;
}
/**
 *   The basic iterator.  Subclass this to get different behaviours
 *   as needed.
 */
protected  class Iterator implements ADS.Iterator {
  //
  //   Start the index at -1 since the first action of the instance
  //   initializer of cursor is to call the method to set up the
  //   iterator and its first action is to increment this index.
  //   The first used value must be 0 so we initialize to -1.  NB
  //   This declaration must come before the setting up of cursor so
  //   that things get properly initialized: it is important that
  //   index has the value -1 before setUpNextIterator is called.  We
  //   need to remember that the initializations happen in the order
```

```
  //   they are written down!
  /**
   *   Keep note of which DLList we are working on.
   */
  protected int index = -1 ;
  /**
   *    A cursor is a DLList.Iterator.
   */
  protected DLList.Iterator cursor = null ; {
    setUpNextIterator() ;
  }
  /**
   *   Deliver the value we are currently referring to.
   */
  public Object get() {
    if (atEnd())
      throw new InvalidIteratorOperationException () ;
    return cursor.get() ;
  }
  /**
   *   Move on to the next element in the container.
   */
  public void advance() {
    if (!atEnd()) {
      if (! cursor.atEnd()) {
        cursor.advance() ;
        if (cursor.atEnd()) {
          setUpNextIterator() ;
        }
      } else {
        setUpNextIterator() ;
      }
    }
  } ;
  /**
   *   Have we reached the end of the iteration?
   */
  public boolean atEnd() {
    return index == -1 || cursor == null ;
  } ;
  /**
   *   Are two iterators equal, i.e. do two iterators refer to the
   *   same item in the same data structure.
   */
  public boolean equals(final ADS.Iterator i) {
    if (!(i instanceof Iterator))
      return false ;
    return (index == ((Iterator)i).index) &&
      cursor.equals(((Iterator)i).cursor) ;
  }
  /**
   *   Return the reference to the current object.
   */
  public Object myObject() {
    return ChainedHashTable.this ;
  }
  /**
   *   Clone this <CODE>Iterator</CODE>.
   */
  public final Object clone() {
    Iterator i = new Iterator () ;
    i.index = index ;
    i.cursor = (DLList.Iterator)cursor.clone() ;
    return i ;
  }
  /**
```

```
   *   This is an editing iterator so we allow removal.
   */
  public void remove() {
    if (!atEnd()) {
      cursor.remove() ;
      --pairCount ;
    }
  }
  /**
   *   Set up the cursor to refer to a valid DLList.  Utility method
   *   used in the constructor and in advance.
   */
  protected void setUpNextIterator() {
    while(++index < table.length) {
      if (table[index] != null) {
        if (((DLList)table[index]).size() > 0) {
          cursor =
            (DLList.Iterator)((DLList)table[index]).iterator() ;
          return ;
        }
      }
    }
    cursor = null ;
    index = -1 ;
  }
}
/**
 *   Find the index of a given key, i.e. the position in the table
 *   of an entry with this key or to the first null entry.
 *
 *   <P> This is as near O(1) as we can get.
 *
 *   @return the index into table of the value the entry is null is
 *   key is not in the table.
 */
private int findIndex(final Object o) {
  return hf.hash(o) % table.length ;
}
}
```

The most difficult part of this implementation is really the iterator, this is far more complicated than would be required for open hashing.

In the same way that it is important that there is always a certain amount of space in the open hash table, we must ensure that there is space in the chained hash table. On average, we will need to re-size a chained hash table less often since collisions cause lists to be lengthened rather than array slots to be filled. However, the ideal of having evenly spaced entries still applies: we want the lists in a chained hash table to be as short as possible, preferably of length one. So exactly as with the open hash table, we want a production version of this class to ensure that there is always space available.

As with the open hash table, having a table size for the chained hash table that is a prime number helps distribute the data evenly throughout the table.

18.10　Set, Relations and Mappings using Hash Tables

Having defined implementations of hash tables we can make use of them to implement the set, bag, relation and mapping abstractions. We have all the infrastructure, as it was defined when the implementations using ordered binary tree were constructed. Therefore we can just do the implementation of the concrete classes. We show here the implementations of relation and mapping. The implementations of set and bag can be deduced easily. First the `Relation`:

```
package ADS ;
/**
 *  A mapping implemented using an <CODE>ChainedHashTable</CODE>.
 *
 *  @version 1.0 1999.10.30
 *  @author Russel Winder
 */
public class ChainedHashTableRelation extends AbstractRelation {
  /**
   *  The <CODE>ChainedHashTable</CODE> that acts as our storage.
   */
  protected ChainedHashTable storage ;
  /**
   *  Construct an <CODE>OrderedBinaryTreeRelation</CODE>.
   */
  public ChainedHashTableRelation() {
    storage = new ChainedHashTable () ;
  }
  /**
   *  Remove the entire contents of the
   *  <CODE>OrdereBinaryTreeRelation</CODE>.
   */
  public void makeEmpty() {
    storage.makeEmpty() ;
  }
  /**
   *  Return the number of items in the
   *  <CODE>OrdereBinaryTreeRelation</CODE>.
   */
  public int size() {
    return storage.size() ;
  }
  /**
   *  Insert a (key, value) <CODE>Pair</CODE> into the
   *  <CODE>OrdereBinaryTreeRelation</CODE>.
   */
  public void add(final Object o) {
    if (! (o instanceof Pair))
      throw new InvalidOperationException () ;
    storage.add(o) ;
  }
  /**
   *  Remove an <CODE>Object</CODE>.
   *
   *  @exception InvalidOperationException if the parameter is
   *  anything other than a <CODE>Pair</CODE>.
   */
  public boolean remove(final Object o) {
    if (! (o instanceof Pair))
      throw new InvalidOperationException () ;
    return storage.remove(o) ;
  }
  /**
```

```
 *   Cloning is actually easy.
 */
public Object clone() {
  ChainedHashTableRelation t =
   new ChainedHashTableRelation() ;
  if (! isEmpty()) {
    t.storage = (ChainedHashTable)storage.clone() ;
  }
  return t ;
}
/**
 *  Deliver up an iteration over all the items in the
 *  <CODE>OrdereBinaryTreeRelation</CODE>.
 */
public ADS.Iterator iterator() {
  return new Iterator () ;
}
/**
 *   Define the iterator over <CODE>OrdereBinaryTreeRelation</CODE>s.
 */
public class Iterator implements ADS.Iterator {
  /**
   *  The cursor is just an iterator over the
   *  <CODE>RelationTree</CODE>. Use the default of in-order
   *  traversal.
   */
  protected ADS.Iterator cursor = storage.iterator() ;
  /**
   *  Deliver the value we are currently referring to.
   */
  public Object get() {
    return cursor.get() ;
  }
  /**
   *  Amend the value of the element we are currently referring to.
   *  Usage invalidates the iterator.
   */
  public void set(final Object o) {
    if (!(o instanceof Pair))
      throw new InvalidIteratorOperationException () ;
    //  This looks horrendously inefficient even though it is safe.
    //  There must be a better way.  This issue is that the in-order
    //  traversal iterator is not an editing iterator so we can edit
    //  using it.
    storage.remove(cursor.get()) ;
    storage.add(o) ;
    cursor = null ;
  }
  /**
   *  Move on to the next element in the container.
   */
  public void advance() {
    cursor.advance() ;
  }
  /**
   *  Have we reached the end of the iteration?
   */
  public boolean atEnd() {
    return cursor.atEnd() ;
  }
  /**
   *  Are two iterators equal, i.e. do two iterators refer to the
   *  same item in the same data structure.
   */
  public boolean equals(final ADS.Iterator i) {
    if (!(i instanceof Iterator))
```

```
        return false ;
      return cursor.equals(((Iterator)i).cursor) ;
    }
    /**
     *  Return the reference to the current object.
     */
    public Object myObject() {
      return ChainedHashTableRelation.this ;
    }
    /**
     *  Clone this <CODE>Iterator</CODE>.
     */
    public final Object clone() {
      Iterator i = new Iterator () ;
      i.cursor = (Iterator)cursor.clone() ;
      return i ;
    }
  }
  /**
   *  Create an iterator over all the sub-set of the domain that is
   *  used in this relation.
   */
  public ADS.Iterator domain() {
    return new Iterator () {
      public Object get() {
        return ((Pair)cursor.get()).getA() ;
      }
    } ;
  }
  /**
   *  Create an iterator over the sub-set of the domain that is
   *  used in this relation which relate to a given value in the
   *  co-domain.
   */
  public ADS.Iterator domain(final Object c) {
    class DomainIterator extends Iterator {
      public DomainIterator() {
        if (! ((Pair)cursor.get()).getB().equals(c)) {
          moveOn() ;
        }
      }
      public Object get() {
        return ((Pair)cursor.get()).getA() ;
      }
      public void advance() {
        moveOn() ;
      }
      private void moveOn() {
        while (!atEnd()) {
          super.advance() ;
          if (atEnd() || ((Pair)cursor.get()).getB().equals(c))
            break ;
        }
      }
    }
    return new DomainIterator () ;
  }
  /**
   *  Create an iterator over all the values range.
   */
  public ADS.Iterator range() {
    return new Iterator() {
      public Object get() {
        return ((Pair)cursor.get()).getB() ;
      }
    } ;
```

```
    }
    /**
     *  Create an iterator over the sub-set of the range that relate to
     *  a given item from the domain.
     */
    public ADS.Iterator range(final Object d) {
      class RangeIterator extends Iterator {
        public RangeIterator() {
          if (! ((Pair)cursor.get()).getA().equals(d)) {
            moveOn() ;
          }
        }
        public Object get() {
          return ((Pair)cursor.get()).getB() ;
        }
        public void advance() {
          moveOn() ;
        }
        private void moveOn() {
          while (!atEnd()) {
            super.advance() ;
            if (atEnd() || ((Pair)cursor.get()).getA().equals(d))
              break ;
          }
        }
      }
      return new RangeIterator () ;
    }
}
```

And now the version of mapping:

```
package ADS ;
/**
 *  A mapping which is a <CODE>Relation</CODE> where it is not allowed
 *  to have two elements that both have the same value from the
 *  domain.  This is the version implemented using an
 *  <CODE>ChainedHashTable</CODE>.
 *
 *  @version 2.0 1999.10.31
 *  @author Russel Winder
 */
public class ChainedHashTableMapping
  extends ChainedHashTableRelation implements Mapping {
  /**
   *  Construct a <CODE>ChainedHashTableMapping</CODE>.
   */
  public ChainedHashTableMapping() {
    storage = new ChainedHashTable () ;
  }
  /**
   *  Insert a (key, value) <CODE>Pair</CODE> into the
   *  <CODE>ChainedHashTableRelation</CODE>.  If there is an element
   *  (key, xxx) then xxx is overwritten with value.
   */
  public void add(final Object o) {
    if (! (o instanceof Pair))
      throw new InvalidOperationException () ;
    storage.add(o) ;
  }
  /**
   *  Remove an <CODE>Object</CODE>.  This can either be a
   *  <CODE>Pair</CODE> in which case only the item that matches the
   *  pair is removed, if it is in the <CODE>Mapping</CODE> or the
   *  parameter is assumed to be from the domain and the element with
   *  this value is found and removed.
```

```
     */
    public boolean remove(final Object o) {
      Pair p = null ;
      if (o instanceof Pair) {
        p = (Pair)o ;
      } else {
        p = new Pair (o, null) ;
      }
      return storage.remove(p) ;
    }
    /**
     *  Cloning is actually easy.
     */
    public Object clone() {
      ChainedHashTableMapping t =
       new ChainedHashTableMapping () ;
      if (! isEmpty()) {
        t.storage = (ChainedHashTable)storage.clone() ;
      }
      return t ;
    }
    /**
     *  Find the value from the range associated with a given value from
     *  the domain.
     *
     *  @return value from (key, value) pair given a key or null if the
     *  key is not present in the <CODE>Mapping</CODE>.
     */
    public final Object getValue(final Object o) {
      return storage.getValue(o) ;
    }
  }
```

18.11 Summary

In this chapter we have investigated the concepts of set, relation and mapping, implementing them with arrays, binary trees and the new data structure of hash table. The tree-based implementations were investigated first but resulted in $O(\log(n))$ performance for most actions. Via arrays, with their $O(1)$ access, we investigated hashing (open hashing and chained hashing) and hash tables as an $O(1)$ approach to solving the problem of efficiently storing and using sparse data structures.

Hashing is an extremely important activity because of this $O(1)$ lookup property and the ability to handle non-integer domains. Collections implements HashSet, HashMap, TreeSet and TreeMap very much along the lines we have shown here. A Red–Black tree is used for the tree representations and a chained hash table is used for the hash table representations. JGL offers the same functionality and the same basic structuring, HashSet and HashMap are implemented using a chained hash table with OrderedSet and OrderedMap implemented using a Red–Black tree. As noted earlier Collections does not address the issue of bag or relation whereas JGL uses the terms multi-set and multi-map to refer to these concepts.

We note that Collections does not actually implement set as a superclass of relations and then mapping as we have done here. Instead, Collection implements mapping as a base type and then implements set as an identity mapping. The design difference here probably relates to the different viewpoints of the authors and is indicative not of right and wrong but of mindset of the programmers involved.

There is a technique, which we have not addressed here, called *dynamic hashing* (aka *perfect hashing*) which is a technique often used in database systems where a hash table is restructured on every insertion to ensure that there are no collisions at all. This is a very important technique but we do not address it here as it is a more advanced technique than we should be addressing in this book.

We have throughout the chapter been skating around the fact that everything we have been doing is searching and to some extent sorting. It is time to address these issues from another perspective, algorithm rather than data structure.

Self-review Questions

Self-review 18.1 For Set, Relation and Mapping, it is critical that if the representation is a tree then it be a self-balancing one. Why is this?

Self-review 18.2 Why is there no AbstractBag nor AbstractMapping?

Self-review 18.3 Under what circumstances might a tree-based representation of the set, relation and mapping abstractions be preferred over an hash table representation?

Self-review 18.4 What properties should a good hashing function possess?

Programming Exercises

Exercise 18.1 Implement and test an OpenHashTable class.

Exercise 18.2 Using the OpenHashTable, implement OpenHashTableSet, Open-HashTableRelation and OpenHashTableMapping.

Exercise 18.3 Write a test program to test the performance of OpenHashTableSet, ChainedHashTableSet, OrderedBinaryTreeSet, HashSet from JGL and HashSet from Collections for inserting accessing and removing data.

Exercise 18.4 Implement and test ChainedHashTableBag and ChainedHashTable-Bag.

Exercise 18.5 Implement and test a SparseArray class. Which data structure is the best for the underlying representation of SparseArray?

Exercise 18.6 Extend the `OpenHashTable` and `ChainedHashTable` so that if too many entries are put into the table then the array is extended and all the entries re-hashed. Too many here means that more entries than some percentage of the total size of the array are entered into the hash table.

Challenges

Challenge 18.1 Investigate how you might provide a perfect hashing hash table based on the ADS architecture.

Searching

Objectives

The previous chapters have relied on the ability to search for items within a data structure. This chapter summarizes the issues raised in those chapters.

Keywords

linear search

logarithmic search

primitive array

sequence

ordered binary tree

hash table

19.1   Introduction

Throughout the last few chapters, we have had to consider searching as an algorithm. In particular, in trying to find data items in a data structure, we have had to search. Searching is probably one of the most common activities in the universe: Pre-historic people in hunter–gatherer mode searched for food; modern people in hunter–gatherer mode search for good restaurants for dinner after a hard days shopping; media moguls search for new depths of sensationalism to plumb in their ratings war; detectives search for clues to solve crimes, many of them committed by the aforementioned media moguls. Also, of course, computers do a lot of searching: database systems get searched for items of data they contain; chess computers search for moves to play whilst beating grandmasters; Web browsers search for pages to display in the never ending search for new ways to entertain people.

Many of the issues relating to searching as an activity for a computer to undertake, controlled by the programs we write, have already been uncovered, albeit implicitly, in earlier chapters. In this chapter, we bring together the threads and make the issues explicit.

19.2   Some Constraints

In order to undertake any search, a level of structure must be imposed. If we are searching for the pen that is supposed to be by the phone at home when we need it to take a message, it is not appropriate to get in a car and drive to a field in the countryside and look there. We impose the structure of asking two questions:

1. Is the pen still by the phone but just hidden from view?
2. Has the pen been used and put somewhere else?

Whilst (2) happens frequently, (1) is much more likely. Already we have constrained the search. For all locations in the universe, we have structured the problem and rejected almost all possible solutions in favour of the most likely. We then turn the papers on the telephone table over one by one until we find the pen. Then, of course, just as we are about to write the message, we discover the pen has run out of ink and we need to search for another pen — but that is another story.

Just as we constrain our searches by structuring and applying algorithms guided by what are likely solutions, so must the computer. In order to search at all, the data must be in a data structure that permits searching. If we ask the computer to "find the number 10", there is not enough contextual information in which to work. We need to ask questions like "find the number 10 in this data structure", with the program having a data structure as context in which the search can occur. We have seen sequences (arrays and lists), binary trees and hash tables as data structures so far and it turns out that these are the important data structures. Of course these are all 'in memory' data structures and, as we know, databases use disk files to store data, so searching using files is clearly very important. This book is not the place to address the issues of algorithms and data structures for supporting databases, we leave that to the books on databases. We simply note here that B-Trees (a variation of binary trees) are the most important data structures for database indexes.

Whilst having a data structure is necessary it is not sufficient; we need algorithms. In fact, unless we know something about the data there is only one way of searching — linear search.

19.3 Linear Search (aka Sequential Search)

Perhaps the simplest and most obvious way of searching is to line up all the items to be searched and then work through them, one at a time, until the correct one is found. In terms of computer actions, we put all the data in sequence and search it. Here is an encapsulation of linear search of a primitive array of `int`s as a method object class:

```
package ADS ;
/**
 *   Search a primitive array of <CODE>int</CODE>s using linear search,
 *   an O(n) search.
 *
 *   @version 1.0 1999.11.27
 *   @author Russel Winder
 */
public final class LinearSearch {
  /**
   *   The search operation.
   *
   *   @param a the array to be searched.
   *   @param i the <CODE>int</CODE> to be searched for.
   *   @return index of the item or -1 if it is not there.
   */
  public static int search(final int[] a, final int i) {
    for (int index = 0 ; index < a.length ; ++index) {
      if (a[i] == i)
        return index ;
    }
    return -1 ;
  }
}
```

The core of the algorithm is that of a simple iteration over indexes into the array to access each element of the array in turn, `==` being used to test for value equality. Whilst this is fine for `int`s (and analogously for other primitive types), this does not help us with searching arrays of objects which is likely to be the more usual case. We could contemplate amending the above by changing `int` to `Object` and replacing the `==` test with a call to the `equals` method but this turns out to be the wrong thing to do. Altering `int` to `Object` is fine but we cannot use the `equals` method. Although we can guarantee that the `equals` method is defined for all classes, (as it is inherited from class `Object`) we cannot be certain of its semantics. We know that the default semantics for `equals` is identity equality but we do not know if any particular class has overridden this to value equality. So for example if we were searching an array of objects whose class did not override `equals`, then that `equals` would determine only if the item in the array was the same object as the searched for item. `Integer` however, overrides `equals` to be value equality, so if we were searching an array of `Integers`, we would be searching to see if the value of the object being searched for exists as the value of one of the objects in the array. We cannot progress using `equals` in the presence of this uncertainty so we need to impose a mechanism which provides more certainty. The solution is quite straightforward since the ADS package architecture is designed to encompass this sort of situation: we make use of order relation method objects. This leads to:

```
package ADS ;
/**
 *   Search a primitive array using linear search, an O(n) search.
 *
 *   @version 1.0 1999.11.27
 *   @author Russel Winder
 */
public final class LinearSearch {
  /**
   *   The search operation.
   *
   *   @param a the array to be searched.
   *   @param o the <CODE>Object</CODE> to be searched for.
   *   @param c the <CODE>Comparator</CODE> defining value equality.
   *   @return index of the item or -1 if it is not there.
   */
  public static int search(final Object[] a,
                           final Object o,
                           final Comparator c) {
    for (int i = 0 ; i < a.length ; ++i) {
      if (c.relation(a[i], o))
        return i ;
    }
    return -1 ;
  }
}
```

There is still uncertainty here: we are reliant on the caller of the method providing a `Comparator` which is testing value equality. However, because this mechanism is more explicit than relying on correct overriding of `equals`, it is more likely to be done correctly. Moreover, it might be the case that we are not in a position to be able to override `equals` in which case this mechanism of using `Comparators` is the only feasible one.

There is another issue relating to searching arrays of `Objects` that we have already solved by using this `Comparator` approach. When manipulating objects with internal structure, it might be that we do not want to search for the value as a whole but to search based on a particular field. The object we are given as the value to look for, the search key, could be of the same type as the data in the array or it could be of the type of the field to be searched. As long as the `Comparator` object properly selects fields from objects for testing and then does a value-based equality check, we can search data structures based on a field and not the whole value. The method object class given above permits this to be done without any change to the code.

Thus, we have a relatively general solution to linear searching in a primitive array. What about our constructed sequence types? We could use the same algorithm for the class `Array` since it has the same indexing properties (index access is $O(1)$). However, an `Array` is a type of `Sequence` and we ought to be able to search all forms of `Sequence` using the same code — and not have to have different code for each type of `Sequence`. Using indexing with `SLList` and `DLList` is a very bad idea since this is an $O(n)$ operation. Of course we have the necessary tool, the forward iterator: linear search is essentially an application of a forward iterator. Putting all this together we come up with the following method object class:

```
package ADS ;
/**
 *   Search a <CODE>Sequence</CODE> using linear search, an O(n)
 *   search.
 *
 *   @version 1.0 1999.11.27
 *   @author Russel Winder
 */
public final class LinearSearchSequence {
  /**
   *   The search operation.
   *
   *   @param s the <CODE>Sequence</CODE> to be searched.
   *   @param o the <CODE>Object</CODE> to be searched for.
   *   @param c the <CODE>Comparator</CODE> defining value equality.
   *   @return index of the item or -1 if it is not there.
   */
  public static int search(final Sequence s,
                           final Object o,
                           final Comparator c) {
    int position = 0 ;
    for (Iterator i = s.iterator() ;
         !i.atEnd() ;
         i.advance(), ++position) {
      if (c.relation(i.get(), o))
        return position ;
    }
    return -1 ;
  }
}
```

As with the earlier code for primitives arrays, the core of the algorithm is a for loop with a test for equality. Pretty obvious and in both cases deeply inefficient. On average, we will have to test half of all the items in the sequence using a search like this, which makes it an $O(n)$ activity. This is slow, we really must be able to do better than this. What is the problem here? Well, although the data is in a sequence, there is no internal structure to the data to help guide the search.

What we need to do to improve the search performance is to impose more structure on the data: there needs to be a data-oriented relationship between the items of data. There are two ways of doing this:

1. ensure that the data is pre-sorted in the sequence; or
2. use a data structure other than a sequence that has some sort of ordering property defined, for example an `OrderedBinaryTree` or `HashTable`.

19.4 Logarithmic Search (aka Binary Chop Search)

If the data is sorted in the sequence before we start looking then we can perform what is called a *binary chop search*. Instead of looking through the data from one end of the sequence we look at the item in the middle of the sequence. If it is the item we are looking for then we have found it and the search is over. Otherwise we ask the question: "Is the item being searched for less than or greater than the value we are currently comparing against?" One of these two must be true since the data is already sorted into an order. We then perform the search in the appropriate half of the remaining data, discarding the other half from the search.

Here is the crucial difference as compared to linear search. With linear search we simply ask the "Is this the one?" question and then move on if it isn't, and because we had started at one end, there was only one datum that could be considered the next datum to check. With binary chop search we ask the "Is this the one?" question but then, if the answer is no, ask the subsidiary question "Which of the two halves does not contain the data?" in order to choose which of the two halves of the data to search. This reduces the search space by half. By choosing the middle item of the current range at each stage, we have given ourselves two possible next datum to consider.

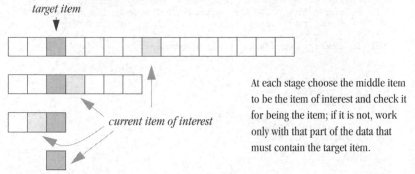

target item

current item of interest

At each stage choose the middle item to be the item of interest and check it for being the item; if it is not, work only with that part of the data that must contain the target item.

Introducing this choice and discrimination, enabled by the ordering of the data, has enabled us to exclude, at each stage, not just one element from the search but half the remaining elements. This is a ***serious*** win. Why? Let us ask the question "How many times can you half a number before you end up with 1". The answer is $\log(n)$. This means that this search algorithm is a $O(\log(n))$ one.

Binary chop search on primitive arrays can be programmed very quickly using recursion since the partitioning can easily be described as a very recursive activity: make a check at the centre element and then do the same on that half of the data that contains the target item:

```
package ADS ;
/**
 *  Search a sorted array using binary chop search.  This is
 *  an O(log(n)) search.
 *
 *  @version 1.1 1999.11.27
 *  @author Russel Winder
 */
public final class BinaryChopSearch {
    /**
     *  The search operation.
     *
     *  @param a the sorted array to be searched.
     *  @param o the <CODE>Object</CODE> to be searched for.
     *  @param ce the <CODE>Comparator</CODE> defining value equality.
     *  @param cr this <CODE>Comparator</CODE> must either be
     *  "less than" or "greater than" and the same comparator that
```

```
   *   defines the order on the array.
   *   @return index of the item or -1 if it is not there.
   */
  public static int search(final Object[] a,
                           final Object o,
                           final Comparator ce,
                           final Comparator cr) {
    return binaryChop(a, 0, a.length-1, o, ce, cr) ;
  }
  /**
   *   The recursive support function that actually does the hard
   *   work.
   */
  private static int binaryChop(final Object[] a,
                                final int lo,
                                final int hi,
                                final Object o,
                                final Comparator ce,
                                final Comparator cr) {
    if (hi == lo)
      return  ce.relation(a[hi], o) ? hi : -1 ;
    int centre = (hi + lo) / 2 ;
    if (cr.relation(a[centre], o))
      return binaryChop(a, centre, hi, o, c) ;
    else if (cr.relation(o, v[centre]))
      return binaryChop(a, lo, centre, o, c) ;
    else
      return centre ;
  }
}
```

Of course, whilst this may be neat and conceptually expressive, it is relatively inefficient and transforming the recursive algorithm into an iterative algorithm is very much worth doing:

```
package ADS ;
/**
 *   Search a sorted primitive array using binary chop search.  This is
 *   an O(log(n)) search.
 *
 *   @version 1.1 1999.11.27
 *   @author Russel Winder
 */
public final class BinaryChopSearch {
  /**
   *   The search operation.
   *
   *   @param a the sorted array to be searched.
   *   @param o the <CODE>Object</CODE> to be searched for.
   *   @param ce the <CODE>Comparator</CODE> defining value equality.
   *   @param cr this <CODE>Comparator</CODE> must either be
   *   "less than" or "greater than" and the same comparator that
   *   defines the order on the array.
   *
   *   @return index of the item or -1 if it is not there.
   */
  public static int search(final Object[] a,
                           final Object o,
                           final Comparator ce,
                           final Comparator cr) {
    int hi = a.length ;
    int lo = 0 ;
    while (true) {
      int centre = (hi + lo) / 2 ;
      if (centre == lo) {
        return ( ce.relation(a[centre], o)
                 ? centre
```

```
                                   : ( ce.relation(a[centre+1], o)
                                       ? centre+1
                                       : -1)) ;
             }
             if (cr.relation(a[centre], o)) {
               lo = centre ;
             } else if (cr.relation(o, a[centre])) {
               hi = centre ;
             } else
               return centre ;
           }
         }
       }
```

We can extend the iterative algorithm to work with Sequences but it becomes much more complicated than was the case with linear search. As before we will have to move from using indexes into arrays to using iterators into Sequences. However, instead of using a forward iterator, we need to use a bidirectional iterator so as to be able to jump around in the underlying Sequence. Unfortunately, only Array and DLList support bidirectional iterators, SLList only supports a forward iterator. There are many, many ways of implementing the necessary algorithms. In the following example we have chose to separate the Array and DLList implementation completely so as to be able to use the most efficient algorithm for the given data structure:

```
package ADS ;
/**
 *   Search a sorted <CODE>Sequence</CODE> using binary chop search.
 *   This is an O(log(n)) search.
 *
 *   <P> Only support <CODE>Array</CODE> and <CODE>DLList</CODE> since
 *   <CODE>SLList</CODE> cannot support a sensible bidirectional
 *   iterator.
 *
 *   @version 1.0 1999.11.27
 *   @author Russel Winder
 */
public final class BinaryChopSearchSequence {
  /**
   *   The search operation for <CODE>Array</CODE>.
   *
   *   @param a the sorted <CODE>Array</CODE> of to be searched.
   *   @param o the <CODE>Object</CODE> to be searched for.
   *   @param ce the <CODE>Comparator</CODE> defining value equality.
   *   @param cr this <CODE>Comparator</CODE> must either be
   *   "less than" or "greater than" and the same comparator that
   *   defines the order on the array.
   *   @return index of the item or -1 if it is not there.
   */
  public static int search(final Array a,
                           final Object o,
                           final Comparator ce,
                           final Comparator cr) {
    int hi = a.size() ;
    int lo = 0 ;
    while (true) {
      int centre = (hi + lo) / 2 ;
      if (centre == lo) {
        return (ce.relation(a.get(centre), o)
                 ? centre
                 : ( ce.relation(a.get(centre+1), o)
                     ? centre+1
                     : -1)) ;
      }
```

```java
      if (cr.relation(a.get(centre), o)) {
        lo = centre ;
      } else if (cr.relation(o, a.get(centre))) {
        hi = centre ;
      } else
        return centre ;
    }
  }
  /**
   *  The search operation for <CODE>DLLList</CODE>.
   *
   *  @param d the sorted <CODE>DLLList</CODE> of to be searched.
   *  @param o the <CODE>Object</CODE> to be searched for.
   *  @param ce the <CODE>Comparator</CODE> defining value equality.
   *  @param cr this <CODE>Comparator</CODE> must either be
   *  "less than" or "greater than" and the same comparator that
   *  defines the order on the array.
   *  @return index of the item or -1 if it is not there.
   */
  public static int search(final DLLList d,
                           final Object o,
                           final Comparator ce,
                           final Comparator cr) {
    int hi = d.size() ;
    int lo = 0 ;
    boolean goUp = true ;
    BiDirectionalIterator i = (BiDirectionalIterator)d.iterator() ;
    while (true) {
      int centre = (hi + lo) / 2 ;
      if (centre == lo) {
        if (ce.relation(i.get(), o))
          return centre ;
        i.advance() ;
        if (ce.relation(i.get(), o))
          return centre + 1 ;
        return -1 ;
      }
      if (goUp) {
        for (int j = lo ; j < centre ; ++j) {
          i.advance() ;
        }
      } else {
        for (int j = hi ; j > centre ; --j) {
          i.retreat() ;
        }
      }
      if (cr.relation(i.get(), o)) {
        lo = centre ;
        goUp = true ;
      } else if (cr.relation(o, i.get())) {
        hi = centre ;
        goUp = false ;
      } else
        return centre ;
    }
  }
}
```

! *For the case of an* `Array`, *use indexing. Indexing is a random access mechanism and is therefore more efficient that using bidirectional iterators.*

! *For the case of a* `DLLList`, *we have to use a bidirectional iterator since no random access iterator is defined.*

19.5   Searching in Collections and JGL

Collections and JGL take very different approaches to searching that are, in effect, two different responses to the issues of complexity brought about by trying to support sequences that are not arrays.

Collections takes the 'ignore the problem' approach. It assumes there is no need to deal with linear search since the application programmer can deal with this trivially using indexing (for arrays) or a forward iterator (for non-array sequences). Support is, therefore, only provided for binary chop search. Collections also makes the assumption that only primitive arrays will ever be searched in this way. The class `Arrays` provides static methods, `binarySearch`, for undertaking binary chop searching on primitive arrays of all types of data. Other `Collection` types are searched by requiring objects of such type to create a primitive array using the `toArray` method. Real care needs taking using this approach since the `toArray` method could be $O(n)$ which ruins the whole point of using a $O(\log(n))$ search.

JGL takes a very different approach. It makes use of its very powerful iterator-based architecture to enable linear searching to be undertaken on any `Container` or any sequence defined by two iterators (the iterators must be working the same `Container`, of course). The class `Finding` contains a number of static methods that perform the linear searches. JGL does not provide any mechanism for doing binary chop search. The assumption being made that if efficient searching is required then the application will be designed to use maps (implemented as binary trees or hash tables) or some other data structure so that searching through a sequence does not actually occur.

The difficulty with binary chop search causing JGL to ignore the algorithm is that:

1. The data has to be sorted before we start. If we start with unsorted data then it needs to be sorted before we can undertake this form of search. As we shall see in the next chapter the best we can do for sorting data tends to be $O(n.\log(n))$. So to sort then search would be an $O(n.\log(n))$ activity. This makes linear search look far more appealing than might have been thought at first.

2. $O(\log(n))$ isn't really fast enough, $O(1)$ is required.

We must therefore look at other forms of structuring the data so that faster searching is possible.

19.6   Binary Tree Search

Instead of putting values into an sequence, we can always put them into a binary tree and, if we put them into an ordered binary tree, the data gets sorted as it is entered — which, given the arguments above, could be a very good idea. There is a very straightforward algorithm for discovering whether an item is in an ordered binary tree. We can express this very easily as an algorithm implemented as a recursive method in the tree nodes:

```
public boolean isIn(final Object o) {
  if (datum.equals(o))
    return true ;
  if (order.relation(o, datum)) {
    return left == null ? false : left.isIn(o) ;
  } else {
    return right == null ? false : right.isIn(o) ;
  }
}
```

with the following method being in the ADT class:

```
public boolean isIn(final Object o) {
  if (root == null)
    return false ;
  else
    return root.isIn(o) ;
}
```

Whilst this is straightforward, this is another situation where recursion is useful for dealing with the concepts but is not generally the way people actually implement things. The observant reader will have already spotted that the OrderedBinaryTree class has a search algorithm. Three in fact. Inserting a new item requires a search, removing an item requires a search and there is a contains method as well. To avoid inefficiency of algorithm and replication of code, a special iterator for performing the search exists. The contains method is coded trivially in terms of this search iterator:

```
public final boolean contains(final Object o) {
  return ! new SearchIterator (o).atEnd() ;
}
```

which is a predicate determining whether an element is in the tree: exactly the same function as the isIn method above but with the recursion being replaced by use of the search iterator. The searching is done by the search method of the SearchIterator:

```
private void search(final Object o) {
  while (theItem != null) {
    if (equal.relation(o, theItem.datum))
      return ;
    theParent = theItem ;
    if (order.relation(o, theItem.datum)) {
      theItem = theItem.left ;
      isLeft = true ;
    } else {
      theItem = theItem.right ;
      isLeft = false ;
    }
  }
}
```

This is just an iterative coding of the recursive algorithm introduced above.

In fact, because an OrderedBinaryTree is a data structure with a data-oriented relation superimposed, every operation on items in the tree involves a search. This is, obviously, why many people call an ordered binary tree a binary search tree!

What about performance? We know that traversing the tree from the root to a leaf is the worst case path. The depth of the tree can be between $O(\log(n))$, best case for a fully balanced tree, and

$O(n)$, worst case for a tree that has degenerated to a singly linked list. Search in a binary tree is therefore $O(\log(n))$ in the best case and $O(n)$ in the worst case.

19.7 Searching using Hash Tables

So it seems that $O(\log(n))$ is the best search algorithm we have so far. What about the goal of $O(1)$? This is actually achievable, making the foregoing redundant of course. How can we achieve an $O(1)$ lookup? Anyone who has read the last chapter will know the answer immediately: Use an hash table. Assuming that we have chosen a reasonable size of table and hash function to minimize collisions, and assuming that the hash function is an $O(1)$ computation, hash table lookup is a search that is $O(1)$.

Because the last chapter was, in fact, all about searching but presented in terms of the data structure rather than the process of searching, all that we need to do is ask you to re-read that chapter with this different perspective — there is no point in replicating the material!

There is one extra point to be made though: The collision algorithm used in both open hashing and chained hashing is a linear search. This is seen as acceptable as long as the main hash creates few collisions, since it is linearity in the number of entries that have collided and not the number of data items being stored that matters. Also the complexity of introducing more efficient algorithms to handle the clashing is not appropriate. If there is a problem, make the initial hashing more efficient!

There is another point worth repeating as well: Every object in a Java program can generate an hash value using the method `hashCode`. Thus very little preparation needs to be undertaken in order to create and therefore use hash tables in Java programs.

Although hash tables give us $O(1)$ look up of values, it is not necessarily the case that we will use such a structure. Hash tables can take up an enormous amount of space and this may be inappropriate. It may be more appropriate to use a tree-based representation of a mapping since, although it is slower, it takes up much less space. It is really a question of what the application requires. This fact is recognized in the ADS, Collections and JGL libraries — all provide both tree-based and hash table-based classes for all sets, relations and mappings so that the application may choose the most appropriate representation with respect to itself. The libraries do not make dictatorial decisions where they do not have all the necessary information.

19.8 Summary

In this chapter, we have pulled together material that we had already presented but using a different viewpoint. By taking a look at the material on searching from a different perspective, we have gained an insight into when some of the data structures are useful. This is supporting the goal of being problem driven: if we can define the requirements of the problem, we can then determine the required properties of the implementation which can then drive the choice of representation. Just because we have a tree type doesn't mean it is appropriate to use it. Likewise, having an $O(1)$ search algorithm doesn't mean we necessarily have to use it. Choosing the appropriate type and algorithm is a matter of satisfying as many of the application problem requirements as possible.

Self-review Exercises

Self-review 19.1 Why does the data have to be sorted to undertake binary chop search?

Self-review 19.2 Why might linear search be chosen over logarithmic search?

Self-review 19.3 How do linear search and binary chop search differ in their handling of duplicate values in the data structure?

Self-review 19.4 Binary chop search and ordered binary tree search can be said to be two representations of the same algorithm. Explain this claim.

Programming Exercises

Exercise 19.1 Develop a version of `BinaryChopSearchSequence` that uses only a single method to support searching an `Array` and a `DLList`.

Challenges

Challenge 19.1 Develop binary chop search implementations that could be added to the JGL library.

Sorting — Comparative Methods

Objectives

This chapter introduces a number of algorithms for sorting data that work by comparing the values of data items with each other and then performing some action.

Keywords

Selection sort

Bubble sort

Insertion sort

Sifting

Quicksort

Binary tree sort

Heap sort

20.1   Introduction

In the previous chapter, various searching algorithms were presented. Searching is an important factor in many applications and therefore making it efficient for the particular context and task is essential. To make searching efficient the data had to be stored in some sorted way. This leads to the obvious question: "If we have the data unsorted in a data structure then how do we sort it?"

In this chapter, we introduce a number of sorting algorithms. Why are there so many? Well different data sets have different properties and hence different needs from sorting algorithms. As we shall see, the best general sorting algorithms are $O(n.\log(n))$ but because data is sometimes almost sorted we make use of some algorithms whose general performance is $O(n^2)$ since they turn out to be more efficient in some contexts.

Before looking at the various algorithms and their implementations, we must point out that there are two principle varieties of sorting algorithms: *comparison sorts* and *distributive sorts*. What distinguishes them is whether or not the values of the data are compared with each other during the sort. There is also a categorization of sorting algorithms as either *internal sorts* or *external sorts*. Here, the split is between whether the data is held in main memory or secondary storage (disks, tapes, etc.) during the sort. In fact, all external sorts are distributive sorts, since it is only sensible to do comparison sorts as internal sorts (we need the data in memory to perform a comparison). Internal, distributive sorts are possible and we shall see a couple of these in the next chapter. In this chapter we will deal with comparison sorts, leaving distributive and external sorts for subsequent chapters.

20.2   Comparison Sorts

For any data to be sorted, there must be an order relation on the data values; it must be possible to define an ordering of the values in a data set. So for example, the integer numbers, the real numbers, the complex numbers, and so on, all have an ordering and we can test whether one element is less than ($<$), less than or equal to ($\leq$), equal to ($=$), not equal to ($\neq$), greater than ($>$) or greater than or equal to ($\geq$) another element. The `char`, `int`, `long`, `float` and `double` primitive data types in Java are ordered types and have the operations `<`, `<=`, `==`, `!=`, `>`, `>=` defined, with the necessary order relation semantics. However, sorting primitive data is not the usual task. Sorting records (data items with internal structure) is much more usual. Just as with searching, where, if we were searching amongst a collection of records, a search key would be defined, with sorting we define an order relation on the records by defining a sort key: the data is sorted only on one (or sometimes more) of the fields rather than the whole record. Given that records are invariably implemented as objects of some class, we need to define the order relation operations based on those objects. As Java does not allow overloading of the operator symbols in the way that some other languages do (for example, languages like Algol68 and C++ allow operators such as > to be overloaded by the programmer), we must define a set of methods that need to be provided by a class which implements a type with an order relation. As was introduced in Section 12.7, Page 339, there are two ways of implementing such order relations on objects:

1. Ensure that the class implementing the type supplies the appropriate methods; or

2. Ensure that helper method objects are available.

Java has a good mechanism for supporting (1), the interface. All classes that define an order relation implement the interface `Comparable`. The sorting methods than manipulate the data using the order relation defined by the `compareTo` method. (2) uses method objects instantiated from method object classes implementing the `Comparator` interface. (1) is perhaps the easiest and simplest way forward but only as long as all types that define an order relation properly conform to `Comparable`. However, this does not help in the situation where the sort key is not the whole datum. In this situation (2) is the only way forward. This is therefore the way that ADS will handle all the cases for the various sorting algorithms.

In order to fit with the ADS package architecture, each sorting algorithm is implemented as a method object providing a sorting service. As with the searching method objects, each sorting algorithm class provides a public static method which can be called to sort a sequence given a `Comparator`. This allows the sort to be called from any location within a program without actually having to use a function object.

Invariably, sorting takes place on sequences. Historically, only primitive arrays were used. This was partly because arrays were the only data structure available and partly because the abstraction of iterator was not yet fully established. As JGL shows, having bidirectional iterators means that sorting can easily be undertaken on any sequence or even any sub-sequence defined by two iterators. Collections has chosen to eschew the use of iterators for sorting; the Collections sorting methods work only using primitive arrays and indexing. To sort other sequences in Collections requires the production of a primitive array using the `toArray` method.

20.3   Selection Sort

This is perhaps the conceptually simplest of the sorting algorithms. Expressed informally, the algorithm is "for each location in the sequence, find the appropriate datum by searching the rest of the sequence for that datum" (see Figure 20.1). Since the data is unsorted, we must use a linear search for this. For use with primitive arrays of objects, we have:

```
package ADS ;
/**
 *  Sort an array of <CODE>Object</CODE>s using Selection Sort.   This
 *  is an O(n^2) sort.
 *
 *  @version 1.1 1999.11.27
 *  @author Russel Winder
```

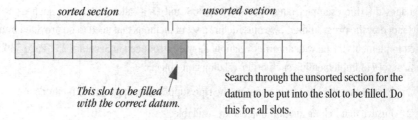

sorted section   *unsorted section*

This slot to be filled with the correct datum.

Search through the unsorted section for the datum to be put into the slot to be filled. Do this for all slots.

Figure 20.1 Selection Sort.

```java
*/
public class SelectionSort {
  /**
   *   The sort operation.
   *
   *   @param a the array to be sorted.
   *   @param c the <CODE>Comparator</CODE> used to compare the
   *   <CODE>Object</CODE>s during the sort process.
   */
  public static void sort(final Object[] a, final Comparator c) {
    for (int i = a.length-1 ; i > 0 ; --i) {
      //  Find the next (maximum or minimum depending on the order
      //  relation) value from that part of the array that is as yet
      //  unsorted.  This is the value to put in the current location
      //  of interest.
      int indexOfValue = 0 ;
      Object value = a[indexOfValue] ;
      for (int j = 1 ; j <= i ; ++j) {
        if (c.relation(value, a[j])) {
          value = a[j] ;
          indexOfValue = j ;
        }
      }
      //  Exchange the value in the current location of interest with
      //  the "maximum" value from the rest of the unsorted array.
      //  This increases by one the part of the array that is now
      //  fully sorted.
      if (indexOfValue != i) {
        a[indexOfValue] = a[i] ;
        a[i] = value ;
      }
    }
  }
}
```

whereas for use with `Sequences` we have:

```java
package ADS ;
/**
 *   Sort a <CODE>Sequence</CODE> of <CODE>Object</CODE>s using
 *   selection sort.  This is an O(n^2) sort.
 *
 *   @version 1.1 1999.11.27
 *   @author Russel Winder
 */
public class SelectionSortSequence {
  /**
   *   The sort operation.
   *
   *   @param s the <CODE>Sequence</CODE> to be sorted.
   *   @param c the <CODE>Comparator</CODE> used to compare the
   *   <CODE>Object</CODE> during the sort process.
   */
  public static void sort(final Sequence s, final Comparator c) {
```

```
            if ((s instanceof SLList) || (s.size() <= 1))
              throw new InvalidOperationException () ;
            for (BiDirectionalIterator i = (BiDirectionalIterator)s.end() ;
                 ! i.atBegin() ;
                 i.retreat()) {
              Object value = s.first() ;
              Iterator j = s.iterator() ;
              ForwardIterator swapItem = (ForwardIterator)j.clone() ;
              while (true) {
                if (c.relation(value, j.get())) {
                  value = j.get() ;
                  swapItem = (ForwardIterator)j.clone() ;
                }
                if (j.equals(i))
                  break ;
                j.advance() ;
              }
              if (! swapItem.equals(i)) {
                swapItem.set(i.get()) ;
                i.set(value) ;
              }
            }
          }
        }
```

!

Note that we exclude
SLList *since it does not*
support a bidirectional
iterator.

This algorithm is guaranteed to sort the data but it is also guaranteed to be somewhat inefficient. We have to work through each location in the sequence, an $O(n)$ activity, and for each location search the rest of the sequence, which is effectively an $O(n)$ activity as well. So overall the performance is $O(n^2)$ in terms of the number of comparisons. The only saving grace of this algorithm is that it works with the data *in situ* and only performs $O(n)$ movements of data.

20.4   Bubble Sort

As a step to becoming more efficient we introduce Bubble Sort. Instead of searching the sequence globally for the next value to put into the correct place to create a sorted sequence, as is done in Selection Sort, Bubble Sort simply compares adjacent values in such a way as to create a sorted sequence. Bubble Sort is all about using local activity in such a way as to create a global effect.

For each location in the sequence, we start at the opposite end of the sequence and pair-wise compare values putting them in the correct order, moving down the sequence until we reach the location of interest (see Figure 20.2). Effectively this picks up the largest value locally, or smallest depending on the order relation, and moves it as far into the correct place as it can. The overall affect is to pick up the next appropriate value and put it in the right place in the sequence. This algorithm is still an $O(n^2)$ in the number of comparisons and actually does more data moving than Selection Sort. So why is it interesting?

The Bubble Sort algorithm automatically performs local optimizations of the data for each pass, which means that we may reach the goal of sorting the sequence long before all the for loops have been executed. This allows us to put into the basic algorithm an optimization that means Bubble Sort

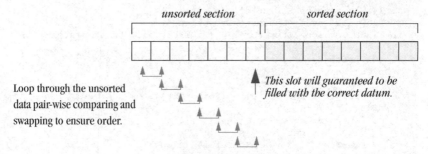

unsorted section   *sorted section*

Loop through the unsorted
data pair-wise comparing and
swapping to ensure order.

*This slot will guaranteed to be
filled with the correct datum.*

Figure 20.2 Bubble Sort.

can be very efficient on almost sorted data. For primitive arrays Bubble Sort can be implemented as
follows:

```
package ADS ;
/**
 *  Sort an array of <CODE>Object</CODE>s using Bubble Sort.  This is
 *  an O(n^2) sort in general but, due to optimization, is extremely
 *  efficient on almost sorted data.
 *
 *  @version 1.1 1999.11.27
 *  @author Russel Winder
 */
public class BubbleSort {
  /**
   *  The sort operation.
   *
   *  @param a the array to be sorted.
   *  @param c the <CODE>Comparator</CODE> used to compare the
   *  <CODE>Object</CODE>s during the sort process.
   */
  public static void sort(final Object[] a, final Comparator c) {
    for (int i = a.length-1 ; i > 0 ; --i) {
      //  Iterate from the beginning of the array to the location of
      //   interest.  Keep track of whether we make any swaps.
      boolean swapped = false ;
      for (int j = 0 ; j < i ; ++j) {
        //  Check to see if this pair of elements is in the right
        //   order.  If they are not then swap them.
        if (c.relation(a[j+1], a[j])) {
          Object temp = a[j] ;
          a[j] = a[j+1] ;
          a[j+1] = temp ;
          swapped = true ;
        }
      }
      //  If we made no swaps then the data is already sorted so
      //   terminate.
      if (! swapped)
        break ;
    }
  }
}
```

whereas for `Sequences`:

```
package ADS ;
/**
 *  Sort a <CODE>Sequence</CODE> using Bubble Sort. This is an O(n^2)
 *  sort in general but, due to optimization, is extremely efficient
 *  on almost sorted data.
```

```
 *
 *   @version 1.1 1999.11.27
 *   @author Russel Winder
 */
public class BubbleSortSequence {
  /**
   *   The sort operation.
   *
   *   @param s the <CODE>Sequence</CODE> to be sorted.
   *   @param c the <CODE>Comparator</CODE> used to compare the
   *   <CODE>Object</CODE> during the sort process.
   */
  public static void sort(final Sequence s, final Comparator c) {
    if ((s instanceof SLList) || (s.size() <= 1))
      throw new InvalidOperationException () ;
    for (BiDirectionalIterator i = (BiDirectionalIterator)s.end() ;
         ! i.atBegin() ;
         i.retreat()) {
      boolean swapped = false ;
      Object value = s.first() ;
      ForwardIterator j = s.begin() ;
      while(! j.equals(i)) {
        //  The iterator j must be of type Iterator to be cloned.
        //  This seems like a fault in Java to me but...
        ForwardIterator k = (ForwardIterator)((Iterator)j).clone() ;
        j.advance() ;
        Object a = j.get() ;
        Object b = k.get() ;
        if (c.relation(a, b)) {
          Object temp = a ;
          j.set(b) ;
          k.set(temp) ;
          swapped = true ;
        }
      }
      if (! swapped)
        break ;
    }
  }
}
```

20.5   Insertion Sort (aka Sifting)

Unlike Selection Sort and Bubble Sort, which make *n* passes through the data, Insertion Sort only performs one main pass through the data. Selection Sort and Bubble Sort ensure that one datum is in its correct position in the final sorted sequence in each pass. Insertion Sort dispenses with the need for multiple passes by only ensuring that each item is placed correctly with respect to the other data and not with respect to the containing data structure. The Insertion Sort algorithm works through each element of the sequence but instead of percolating values through the unsorted part of the sequence to put the correct value into the correct location, as we did with Selection Sort and Bubble Sort, we percolate the next unsorted value from its current location through the sorted part of the sequence to leave it in the right place with respect to the other sorted items (see Figure 20.3). This algorithm requires removal and insertion of items in the sequence as opposed to the swapping of elements as was true for Selection Sort and Bubble Sort. This means that, when used with array-

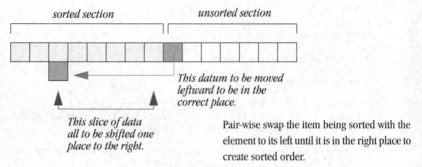

Figure 20.3 Selection Sort.

like sequences, a lot of shuffling of elements is required. List-like data structures, on the other hand, do not have this problem. Thus, because this sort involves editing rather than swapping, it is far more efficient with list-like sequences than array-like sequences. Overall the algorithm is $O(n^2)$ in the number of comparisons and $O(n^2)$ in the number of data moves for array-like sequences and $O(n)$ in the number of data moves for list-like sequences. However, the single pass nature of this algorithm makes it very efficient for almost sorted data. Indeed of the three sort algorithms seen so far, it is agreed to be the most efficient and hence generally useful.

For the case of primitive arrays we have this method object class:

```
package ADS ;
/**
 *  Sort an array of <CODE>Object</CODE>s using Insertion Sort.  This
 *  is an O(n^2) sort in general.  This version is optimized to cut
 *  down the number of assignments.
 *
 *  @version 1.1 1999.11.27
 *  @author Russel Winder
 */
public class InsertionSort {
  /**
   *  The sort operation.
   *
   *  @param a the array of <CODE>Object</CODE>s to be sorted.
   *  @param c the <CODE>Comparator</CODE> used to compare the
   *  <CODE>Object</CODE>s during the sort process.
   */
  public static void sort(final Object[] a, final Comparator c) {
    for (int i = 0 ; i < a.length-1 ; ++i) {
      //  If the current item is in the right place, do nothing,
      //  otherwise percolate it to the right place.
      if (c.relation(a[i+1], a[i])) {
        //  Remember the current value, and percolate the 'gap' to the
        //  right place in the sorted part of the array.
        Object temp = a[i+1] ;
        int j = i ;
        while (true) {
          //  Move the space back down the sorted part of the array by
          //  one, by copying values.  If we reach the end of the
          //  array or find the right place, stop the loop.
          a[j+1] = a[j] ;
          if ((j == 0) || c.relation(a[j-1], temp))
            break ;
          --j ;
        }
```

```
                   //  We have got the 'gap' to the right place so drop in the
                   //  value.
                   a[j] = temp ;
                 }
              }
           }
        }
```

For `Sequences` we have the following method object class. Notice that we separate the cases of `Array` and `DLList` so as to optimize each as much as possible for the underlying data structures. Doing this, we can obtain $O(n)$ data moves for `DLList` even though we have to suffer $O(n^2)$ moves for `Array`. We are not sacrificing abstraction here since the caller of the `sort` method in `InsertionSortSequence` is not able to observe this separation, it is just an implementation decision for optimization purposes.

```
package ADS ;
/**
 *  Sort a <CODE>Sequence</CODE> using Insertion Sort.  This is an
 *  O(n^2) sort in general.
 *
 *  @version 1.1 1999.11.27
 *  @author Russel Winder
 */
public class InsertionSortSequence {
  /**
   *  The sort operation for an <CODE>Array</CODE>.
   *
   *  @param a the <CODE>Array</CODE> to be sorted.
   *  @param c the <CODE>Comparator</CODE> used to compare the
   *  <CODE>Object</CODE> during the sort process.
   */
  public static void sort(final Array a, final Comparator c) {
    if (a.size() <= 1)
      throw new InvalidOperationException () ;
    for (int i = 0 ; i < a.size()-1 ; ++i) {
      if (c.relation(a.get(i+1), a.get(i))) {
        Object temp = a.get(i+1) ;
        int j = i ;
        while (true) {
          a.set(j+1, a.get(j)) ;
          if ((j == 0) || c.relation(a.get(j-1), temp))
            break ;
          --j ;
        }
        a.set(j, temp) ;
      }
    }
  }
  /**
   *  The sort operation for a <CODE>DLList</CODE>.
   *
   *  @param d the <CODE>DLList</CODE> to be sorted.
   *  @param c the <CODE>Comparator</CODE> used to compare the
   *  <CODE>Object</CODE> during the sort process.
   */
  public static void sort(final DLList d, final Comparator c) {
    if (d.size() <= 1)
      throw new InvalidOperationException () ;
    DLList.Iterator i = (DLList.Iterator)d.begin() ;
    while (true) {
      DLList.Iterator j = (DLList.Iterator)i.clone() ;
      i.advance() ;
      if (i.atEnd())
```

note

No sort method for SLList *is provided so the compiler will catch any attempt to sort* SLList*s using* InsertionSort- Sequence*. Previously we had to rely on run- time type checking and throwing exceptions to deal with this situation.*

```
              break ;
          if (c.relation(i.get(), j.get())) {
            Object temp = i.get() ;
            i.remove() ;  // This moves the iterator on one which we...
            i.retreat() ; // ...have to undo.
            while (true) {
              if (j.atBegin()) {
                j.insert(temp) ;
                break ;
              }
              j.retreat() ;
              if (c.relation(j.get(), temp)) {
                j.add(temp) ;
                break ;
              }
            }
          }
        }
      }
    }
```

20.6   Quicksort

All the previous algorithms have been O(n^2) sorts. In general, this is just not good enough, we need more efficient algorithms. Perhaps the most famous and most used sorting algorithm is Quicksort. Whilst this algorithm can be coded iteratively, it is best described and implemented using recursion.

The core of the algorithm (see Figure 20.4) is to partition the data into two roughly equal parts such that all data in one partition is less than (or greater than if that is the order relation chosen) all the data in the other partition. The sort method is then called recursively on the two unsorted partitions. This continues until each partition has only one datum, which is by definition a sorted partition. At this point the whole array is sorted.

The complexity here is really in the partitioning algorithm. There are a large number of different ways of programming the partitioning. In the following we show two. The first algorithm implemented here (for primitive arrays) requires only the order relation (either 'less than' or 'greater than') as a method object. The second algorithm (for `Sequences`) requires not only the order relation but also a value equality method object since it needs to test for both order and equality of values.

The only other issue is that we must ensure that we never copy the data. This leads to making use of indexes, in the case of primitive arrays, or iterators, in the case of `Sequences`, to define upper and lower bounds of the slices being manipulated by each of the (recursive) calls of the sorting method.

Here then is the version for sorting primitive arrays:

```
package ADS ;
/**
 *  Sort an array of <CODE>Object</CODE>s using Quicksort.  This is an
 *  O(n.log(n)) sort except when the data is almost sorted in which
```

pivot value

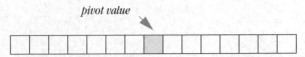

Search from the beginning of the array for the first item not 'less than' (or 'greater than' if that is the relation) the pivot value.

Search from the end of the array for the first item that is 'less than' (or 'greater than' if that is the relation) the pivot value.

Swap these two data items so that they are in the appropriate half of the array and then carry on until the index moving up the array meets the index moving down the array. This is the split point.

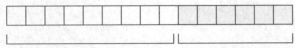

All values in this part of the array are 'less than or equal to' (or 'greater than' if that is the relation) the pivot value.

All values in this part of the array are not 'less than' (or 'greater than' if that is the relation) the pivot value.

Having partitioned the array we know that all items are in the correct part according to the order relations. Now apply the algorithms recursively to the two halves of the array.

pivot value   *pivot value*

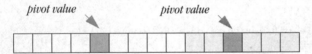

Having partitioned in two we apply the algorithm to both halves and create four partitions; each partition is unsorted but the order of partitions is correct according to the order relation. Carry on doing this recursively and eventually we have partitions that are pairs or singletons, which can be sorted trivially. Voila a sorted array!

Figure 20.4 QuickSort.

```
 *   case it O(n^2).
 *
 *   @version 1.1 1999.11.27
 *   @author Russel Winder
 */
public class Quicksort {
  /**
   *  The sort operation.
   *
   *  @param a the array to be sorted.
   *  @param c the <CODE>Comparator</CODE> used to compare the
   *  <CODE>Object</CODE>s during the sort process.
   */
  public static void sort(final Object[] a, final Comparator c) {
    quicksort(a, 0, a.length-1, c) ;
  }
  /**
   *  Given the array and two indices, swap the two items in the
   *  array.
   */
  private static void swap(final Object[] a,
                           final int x,
```

```
                                final int y) {
      Object temp = a[x] ;
      a[x] = a[y] ;
      a[y] = temp ;
  }
  /**
   *  Partition an array in two using the pivot value that is at the
   *  centre of the array being partitioned.
   *
   *  <P> This partition implementation based on that in Winder, F
   *  (1993) "Developing C++ Software", Wiley, p.395.  NB. This
   *  implementation (unlike most others) does not guarantee that
   *  the split point contains the pivot value.  Unlike other
   *  implementations, it requires only < (or >) relation and not
   *  both < and <= (or > and >=).  Also, it seems easier to program
   *  and to comprehend.
   *
   *  @param a the array out of which to take a slice.
   *  @param lower the lower bound of this slice.
   *  @param upper the upper bound of this slice.
   *  @param c the <CODE>Comparator</CODE> to be used to define the
   *  order.
   */
  private static int partition(final Object[] a,
                               int lower,
                               int upper,
                               final Comparator c) {
    Object pivotValue = a[(upper+lower+1)/2] ;
    while (lower <= upper) {
      while (c.relation(a[lower], pivotValue)) {
        lower++ ;
      }
      while (c.relation(pivotValue, a[upper])) {
        upper-- ;
      }
      if (lower <= upper) {
        if (lower < upper) {
          swap(a, lower, upper) ;
        }
        lower++ ;
        upper-- ;
      }
    }
    return upper ;
  }
  /**
   *  The recursive Quicksort function.
   *
   *  @param a the array out of which to take a slice.
   *  @param lower the lower bound of this slice.
   *  @param upper the upper bound of this slice.
   *  @param c the <CODE>Comparator</CODE> to be used to define the
   *  order.
   */
  private static void quicksort(final Object[] a,
                                final int lower,
                                final int upper,
                                final Comparator c) {
    int sliceLength = upper-lower+1 ;
    if (sliceLength > 1) {
      if (sliceLength == 2) {
        if (c.relation(a[upper], a[lower])) {
          swap (a, lower, upper) ;
        }
      } else {
        //  This partition implementation does not guarantee that the
```

```
                // split point contains the pivot value so we cannot assume
                //  that the pivot is between the two slices.
                int pivotIndex = partition(a, lower, upper, c) ;
                quicksort(a, lower, pivotIndex, c) ;
                quicksort(a, pivotIndex+1, upper, c) ;
            }
        }
    }
}
```

The following is the version of Quicksort for Sequences. Note that we have provided the capability to sort whole Arrays, whole DLLists and also any sub-sequence defined by an Array and two indexes or two bidirectional iterators.

```
package ADS ;
/**
 *  Sort a <CODE>Sequence</CODE> or a sub-sequence defined by two
 *  <CODE>BiDirectionalIterator</CODE>s using Quicksort.  This is an
 *  O(n.log(n)) sort except when the data is almost sorted in which
 *  case it O(n^2).
 *
 *  @version 1.2 1999.12.26
 *  @author Russel Winder
 */
public class QuicksortSequence {
    /**
     *  The sort operation on <CODE>Array</CODE>s.
     *
     *  @param a the <CODE>Array</CODE> to be sorted.
     *  @param cr the <CODE>Comparator</CODE> used to compare the
     *  <CODE>Object</CODE>s during the sort process.
     *  @param ce the <CODE>Comparator</CODE> defining value equality.
     */
    public static void sort(final Array a,
                            final Comparator cr,
                            final Comparator ce) {
      sort(a, 0, a.size()-1, cr) ;
    }
    /**
     *  The sort operation on <CODE>DLList</CODE>s.
     *
     *  @param d the <CODE>DLList</CODE> to be sorted.
     *  @param cr the <CODE>Comparator</CODE> used to compare the
     *  <CODE>Object</CODE>s during the sort process.
     *  @param ce the <CODE>Comparator</CODE> defining value equality.
     */
    public static void sort(final DLList d,
                            final Comparator cr,
                            final Comparator ce) {
      sort((BiDirectionalIterator)d.begin(),
          (BiDirectionalIterator)d.end(),
          cr,
          ce) ;
    }
    /**
     *  The sort operation for handling a slice of an
     *  <CODE>Array</CODE>.
     *
     *  @param a the <CODE>Array</CODE> out of which to take a slice.
     *  @param lower the lower bound of this slice.
     *  @param upper the upper bound of this slice.
     *  @param c the <CODE>Comparator</CODE> to be used to define the
     *  order.
     */
    private static void sort(final Array a,
```

Although it is not used, we require a value equality method object to be supplied for the Array sort method (in addition to the required order relation) so that the parameter list is the same as for the DLList sort method. This is to support polymorphism (i.e. hiding differences in implementation from the caller). Also, of course, we might wish to change the implementation of the method to one that does require both Comparators at some time in the future.

```
                                final int lower,
                                final int upper,
                                final Comparator c) {
      int sliceLength = upper-lower+1 ;
      if (sliceLength > 1) {
        if (sliceLength == 2) {
          if (c.relation(a.get(upper), a.get(lower))) {
            swap (a, lower, upper) ;
          }
        } else {
          //  This partition implementation does not guarantee that the
          //  split point contains the pivot value so we cannot assume
          //  that the pivot is between the two slices.
          int pivotIndex = partition(a, lower, upper, c) ;
          sort(a, lower, pivotIndex, c) ;
          sort(a, pivotIndex+1, upper, c) ;
        }
      }
    }
    /**
     *  The sort operation for <CODE>BiDirectionalIterator</CODE>s.
     *
     *  @param b iterator positioned at the bottom of the slice.
     *  @param t iterator positioned at the top of the slice.
     *  @param cr the <CODE>Comparator</CODE> to be used to define the
     *  order.
     *  @param ce the <CODE>Comparator</CODE> defining value equality.
     */
    private static void sort(final BiDirectionalIterator b,
                             final BiDirectionalIterator t,
                             final Comparator cr,
                             final Comparator ce) {
      if (! b.equals(t)) {
        BiDirectionalIterator pivot = partition(b, t, cr, ce) ;
        if (! pivot.equals(b)) {
          pivot.retreat() ;
          sort(b, pivot, cr, ce) ;
          pivot.advance() ;
        }
        if (! pivot.equals(t)) {
          pivot.advance() ;
          sort(pivot, t, cr, ce) ;
        }
      }
    }
    /**
     *  Given the array and two indices, swap the two items in the
     *  array.
     */
    private static void swap(final Array a,
                             final int x,
                             final int y) {
      Object temp = a.get(x) ;
      a.set(x, a.get(y)) ;
      a.set(y, temp) ;
    }
    /**
     *  Given two iterators swap the two items.
     */
    private static void swap(final BiDirectionalIterator a,
                             final BiDirectionalIterator b) {
      Object temp = a.get() ;
      a.set(b.get()) ;
      b.set(temp) ;
    }
    /**
```

```
 *   Partition an <CODE>Array</CODE> in two using the pivot value
 *   that is at the centre of the array being partitioned.
 *
 *   <P> This partition implementation based on that in Winder, R
 *   (1993) "Developing C++ Software", Wiley, p.395.  NB. This
 *   implementation (unlike most others) does not guarantee that
 *   the split point contains the pivot value.  Unlike other
 *   implementations, it requires only < (or >) relation and not
 *   both < and <= (or > and >=).  Also, it seems easier to program
 *   and to comprehend.
 *
 *   @param a the <CODE>Array</CODE> out of which to take a slice.
 *   @param lower the lower bound of this slice.
 *   @param upper the upper bound of this slice.
 *   @param c the <CODE>Comparator</CODE> to be used to define the
 *   order.
 */
private static int partition(final Array a,
                             int lower,
                             int upper,
                             final Comparator c) {
  Object pivotValue = a.get((upper+lower+1)/2) ;
  while (lower <= upper) {
    while (c.relation(a.get(lower), pivotValue)) {
      lower++ ;
    }
    while (c.relation(pivotValue, a.get(upper))) {
      upper-- ;
    }
    if (lower <= upper) {
      if (lower < upper) {
        swap(a, lower, upper) ;
      }
      lower++ ;
      upper-- ;
    }
  }
  return upper ;
}
/**
 *   Partition an array in two using the pivot value that is at the
 *   beginning of the array being partitioned.
 *
 *   @param b iterator positioned at the bottom of the slice.
 *   @param t iterator positioned at the top of the slice.
 *   @param cr the <CODE>Comparator</CODE> to be used to define the
 *   order.
 *   @param ce the <CODE>Comparator</CODE> defining value equality.
 */
private static BiDirectionalIterator partition(
    final BiDirectionalIterator lower,
    final BiDirectionalIterator upper,
    final Comparator cr,
    final Comparator ce) {
  // **MUST** treat the parameters as immutable so make clones.
  // This has the advantage of preparing the object that we will
  // return.  For some bizarre reason only Iterators and not
  // subinterfaces can be cloned.  Is this a bug in Java or just in
  // the interface inheritance hierarchy?
  final BiDirectionalIterator b =
    (BiDirectionalIterator)((Iterator)lower).clone() ;
  final BiDirectionalIterator t =
    (BiDirectionalIterator)((Iterator)upper).clone() ;
  final BiDirectionalIterator pivot =
    (BiDirectionalIterator)((Iterator)b).clone() ;
  final Object pivotValue = pivot.get() ;
```

```
            while (true) {
              while ((cr.relation(b.get(), pivotValue) ||
                      ce.relation(b.get(), pivotValue)) &&
                     ! b.equals(t)) {
                b.advance() ;
              }
              while (cr.relation(pivotValue, t.get()) && !t.equals(b)) {
                t.retreat() ;
              }
              if (! b.equals(t)) {
                swap(b, t) ;
              } else {
                while (cr.relation(pivotValue, t.get())) {
                  t.retreat() ;
                }
                break ;
              }
            }
            swap(pivot, t) ;
            return t ;
          }
        }
```

To, informally at least, determine the performance of this algorithm, we observe that there are $O(\log(n))$ partitionings (since you can only divide a sequence of length n in half $\log(n)$ times) with each partitioning comparing each item in the array, an $O(n)$ activity. It seems then that Quicksort is $O(n.\log(n))$.

This is not the whole story though. The implementation for DLLists suffers from one difficulty. If the data is almost sorted then the partitioning algorithm, instead of creating partitions that are slices of almost equal length, creates one partition that is a slice with just one element in it and the other partition being a slice with all the rest of the elements. This means that instead of halving the problem at each partition, we simply remove one data item from the problem. Now instead of $O(\log(n))$ performance of the partitioning we get $O(n)$, leading to an $O(n^2)$ performance overall rather than the $O(n.\log(n))$ performance that is normal. The other algorithm (used for Arrays and previously for primitive arrays) did not suffer this problem since it took the middle value of the sub-sequence being sorted and not the left-most value as the pivot value. The reason for not using this algorithm for the DLlist version of the code is the problem of finding the middle value of a sequence using bidirectional iterators, it is an $O(m)$ problem — something not an issue using indexing since that is a random access mechanism, $O(1)$.

20.7   Binary Tree Sort

When considering searching in the last chapter, we saw that $O(\log(n))$ performance was obtained when, instead of asking a binary question, we were able to ask a ternary question and halve the size of the data set to be considered at each stage. We raised the analogy of partitioning a sequence with a binary tree. In the previous section, we saw an analogous "partitioning in half" effect with the Quicksort algorithm. It seems likely then that there is a tree-based sort which has the same performance properties as Quicksort.

Actually, we have already seen binary tree sort: it is impossible to construct an `OrderedBinaryTree` that is not sorted — this was an integral part of the reason why binary trees are good for searching.

This, of course, leads directly to an algorithm for sorting. We take all the data out of the sequence and put it into an `OrderedBinaryTree`. We then undertake an in-order traversal and put the, now sorted, data back into the sequence:

```
package ADS ;
/**
 *   Sort an array of <CODE>Object</CODE>s using Binary Search Tree
 *   Sort.  This is an O(n.log(n)) sort in general but if the data is
 *   nearly sorted can be as bad as O(n^2).  This problem would be
 *   cured by using a Red-Black Tree or AVL Tree (i.e. a self-balancing
 *   tree) instead of the <CODE>OrderBinaryTree</CODE>.
 *
 *   @version 1.1 1999.11.29
 *   @author Russel Winder
 */
public class BinaryTreeSort {
  /**
   *   The sort operation.
   *
   *   @param a the primitive array to be sorted.
   *   @param c the <CODE>Comparator</CODE> used to compare the
   *   <CODE>Object</CODE> during the sort process.
   */
  public static void execute(final Object[] a, final Comparator c) {
    BinaryTree tree = new OrderedBinaryTree (c) ;
    for (int i = 0 ; i < a.length ; i++) {
      tree.add(a[i]) ;
    }
    int index = 0 ;
    for (Iterator i = tree.inorderTraversal() ;
         ! i.atEnd() ;
         i.advance()) {
      a[index++] = i.get() ;
    }
  }
}
```

To determine the performance of this algorithm we see that we have two loops that run over all the data. This is $O(n)$ since $O(2n) = O(n)$. The second loop is simply data copying which is $O(1)$. The first, though, is binary tree insertion and is $O(\log(n))$. The whole Binary Tree Sort algorithm is therefore $O(n.\log(n))$.

20.8 Heap Sort

The implementation of Binary Tree Sort above has the same pathology as some of the variations of Quicksort — it becomes list-based rather than tree-based, and hence $O(n^2)$, for almost sorted data. The problem is that the `OrderedBinaryTree` is not self-balancing. Of course, we could make use of a Red–Black Tree or an AVL Tree which are, but that would be inefficient exactly because they are self-balancing. There is a type of binary tree that leads to a sort with no known pathologies and which stays efficient: the Heap. This leads to the following sort implementation:

```
package ADS ;
/**
 *  Sort an array of <CODE>Object</CODE>s using Heap Sort.  This
 *  is guaranteed to be an O(n.log(n)) sort.
 *
 *  @see Comparator
 *  @see Heap
 *  @version 1.1 1999.11.27
 *  @author Russel Winder
 */
public class HeapSort {
    /**
     *  The sort operation.
     *
     *  @param a the array to be sorted.
     *  @param c the <CODE>Comparator</CODE> used to compare the
     *  <CODE>Object</CODE> during the sort process.
     */
    public static void sort(final Object[] a, final Comparator c) {
      Heap heap = new Heap (a.length, c) ;
      for (int i = 0 ; i < a.length ; ++i) {
        heap.add(a[i]) ;
      }
      for (int i = 0 ; i < a.length ; ++i) {
        a[i] = heap.remove() ;
      }
    }
}
```

Note that we ensure that the `Heap` *is the right size from the outset so as to avoid resizing and copying of the underlying data structures.*

This algorithm is guaranteed to be $O(n.\log(n))$ with no pathologies. It therefore seems that this is the best sorting algorithm we have. Well, except that the above algorithm makes a copy of the data which the Quicksort algorithm did not. This can, however, be circumvented. If we are working with an `Array` as the sequence to be sorted, we can apply the heap property directly to the `Array` and then sort within the `Array`:

```
package ADS ;
/**
 *  Sort a <CODE>Array</CODE> using Heap Sort.  This is guaranteed to
 *  be an O(n.log(n)) sort.
 *
 *  <P> NB This produces a result in reverse order to all the other
 *  sort algorithms given the same Comparator!
 *
 *  @version 1.1 1999.11.29
 *  @author Russel Winder
 */
public class HeapSortArray {
    /**
     *  The sort operation.
     *
     *  @param a the <CODE>Array</CODE> to be sorted.
     *  @param c the <CODE>Comparator</CODE> used to compare the
     *  <CODE>Object</CODE> during the sort process.
     */
    public static void sort(final Array a, final Comparator c) {
      // Apply the heap ordering property to the Array.
      Heap.makeHeap(a, c) ;
      // For each item in the Array, move the top value on the Heap to
      //  the end position and percolate the value we swapped down the
      //  heap.  This guarantees that the appropriate value is at the
      //  very end of the heap so we can ignore it in the next
      //  iteration.
      for (int i = a.size()-1 ; i > 0 ; i--) {
```

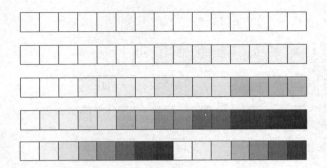

Recursively partition the array into two at each stage until all the partitions are of length one.

Pair-wise merge the sub-arrays together at each stage causing half the number of slices to exist, each twice the length it was with all slices always sorted.

Figure 20.5 Merge Sort.

```
        Object o = a.get(0) ;
        a.set(0, a.get(i)) ;
        a.set(i, o) ;
        Heap.percolateDown(a, i, 0, c) ;
      }
    }
  }
```

So the initial barrier to using Heap Sort, the fact that it makes a copy of the data, is not in fact a barrier in many circumstances. Heap Sort can be applied directly on an `Array` so that its performance in space terms, is as good as Quicksort. Although Heap Sort does not have the pathologies that Quicksort has, its performance in terms of the number of copy operations turns out to be worse that Quicksort, making Quicksort the preferred choice between the two.

20.9 Merge Sort

The final sort that we will consider in this chapter is not dissimilar to Quicksort in that there is a recursive splitting of a sequence into two parts (see Figure 20.5). However, there is no sorting during the partitioning phase as there is with Quicksort, the partition is literally by position. In Merge Sort, the sorting action is undertaken by merging, pair-wise, the slices. This merging is where the comparison is undertaken, creating a larger sorted sequence from two smaller sorted sequences. Merge Sort puts the effort into the recombination whereas Quicksort puts its effort into careful partitioning. Unlike Quicksort, Merge Sort must make many copies of the data. Despite this it turns out to be an important sort since it is guaranteed not to have pathologies. An example sort is illustrated in Figure 20.6. Here is an implementation for use with primitive arrays of objects:

```
package ADS ;
import ADS.Comparator ;
/**
 *  Sort an array using Merge Sort.  This is an O(n.log(n)) sort.
 *
 *  @version 1.1 1999.11.27
 *  @author Russel Winder
```

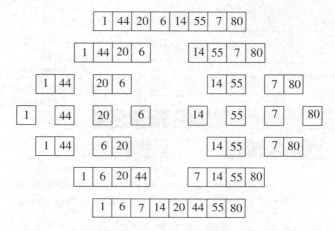

Figure 20.6   An example Merge Sort. This shows how the array is partitioned into slices until each slice is of length one and then the slices are merged to form longer sorted slices eventually resulting in a fully sorted array.

```
*/
public class MergeSort {
  /**
   *   The sort operation.
   *
   *   @param a the array to be sorted.
   *   @param c the <CODE>Comparator</CODE> used to compare the
   *   <CODE>Object</CODE> during the sort process.
   */
  public static void sort(final Object[] a, final Comparator c) {
    if (a.length > 1) {
      //  Find the length of the data.  Arbitrarily split the data
      //  into two arrays by simply splitting in two.  Then
      //  recursively sort the two arrays and when that has happened
      //  merge the two arrays into a single result array.
      int xLength = (a.length-1)/2 + 1 ;
      int yLength = a.length - xLength ;
      Object[] x = new Object[xLength] ;
      Object[] y = new Object[yLength] ;
      System.arraycopy(a, 0, x, 0, xLength) ;
      System.arraycopy(a, xLength, y, 0, yLength) ;
      sort(x, c) ;
      sort(y, c) ;
      merge(a, x, y, c) ;
    }
  }
  /**
   *   Merge two source arrays which are pre-sorted to a target
   *   array.  The <CODE>Comparator</CODE> is used to select which
   *   element from the two queues to take next.
   *
   *   @param target the array into which to copy things.
   *   @param a one of the two source arrays.
   *   @param b the second of the two source arrays.
   *   @param c the <CODE>Comparator</CODE> used to compare the
   *   objects to determine the correct selection policy.
   */
  private static void merge(Object[] target,
                            Object[] a,
                            Object[] b,
                            Comparator c) {
    int t_index = 0 ;
```

```
        int a_index = 0 ;
        int b_index = 0 ;
        while (true) {
          //  The a array is used up so just copy the b array and
          //  finish.
          if (a_index >= a.length) {
            System.arraycopy(b,b_index,target,t_index,b.length-b_index) ;
            break ;
          }
          //  The b array is used up so just copy the a array and
          //  finish.
          if (b_index >= b.length) {
            System.arraycopy(a,a_index,target,t_index,a.length-a_index) ;
            break ;
          }
          //  Select the appropriate element from the two arrays and
          //  go to the next iteration.
          target[t_index++] = c.relation(a[a_index], b[b_index])
           ? a[a_index++]
           : b[b_index++] ;
        }
      }
    }
```

and an implementation for use with Sequences:

```
    package ADS ;
    /**
     *  Sort a <CODE>Sequence</CODE> using Merge Sort.  This is an
     *  O(n.log(n)) sort.
     *
     *  @version 1.2 1999.12.26
     *  @author Russel Winder
     */
    public class MergeSortSequence {
      /**
       *  The sort operation for <CODE>SLList</CODE>s.
       *
       *  @param s the <CODE>SLList</CODE> to be sorted.
       *  @param c the <CODE>Comparator</CODE> used to compare the
       *  <CODE>Object</CODE> during the sort process.
       */
      public static void sort(final SLList s, final Comparator c) {
        if (s.size() > 1) {
          int splitIndex = (s.size()-1)/2 + 1 ;
          SLList s1 = new SLList (s, 0, splitIndex) ;
          SLList s2 = new SLList (s, splitIndex, s.size()) ;
          sort(s1, c) ;
          sort(s2, c) ;
          s.makeEmpty() ;
          merge(s, s1, s2, c) ;
        }
      }
      /**
       *  The sort operation for <CODE>Sequences</CODE>s other than
       *  <CODE>SLList</CODE>s.  Copies the elements into an
       *  <CODE>SLList</CODE>, does the sort and then copies things back.
       *  The extra copying is a little inefficient but we make savings
       *  during the actual sorting working with <CODE>SLList</CODE>s.
       *
       *  @param s the <CODE>Sequence</CODE> to be sorted.
       *  @param c the <CODE>Comparator</CODE> used to compare the
       *  <CODE>Object</CODE>s during the sort process.
       */
      public static void sort(final Sequence s, final Comparator c) {
        SLList sl = new SLList (s) ;
```

```
                       sort(sl, c) ;
                       s.makeEmpty() ;
                       for (Iterator i = sl.iterator() ; ! i.atEnd() ; i.advance()) {
                         s.add(i.get()) ;
                       }
                     }
                     /**
                      *  Merge two source lists which are pre-sorted to a target
                      *  list.  The <CODE>Comparator</CODE> is used to select which
                      *  element from the two queues to take next.
                      *
                      *  @param target the <CODE>SLList</CODE> into which to copy
                      *  things.
                      *  @param a one of the two source <CODE>SLList</CODE>s.
                      *  @param b the second of the two source <CODE>SLList</CODE>s.
                      *  @param c the <CODE>Comparator</CODE> used to compare the
                      *  objects to determine the correct selection policy.
                      */
                     private static void merge(final SLList target,
                                               final SLList a,
                                               final SLList b,
                                               Comparator c) {
                       while (true) {
                         if (a.isEmpty()) {
                           target.merge(b) ;
                           break ;
                         }
                         if (b.isEmpty()) {
                           target.merge(a) ;
                           break ;
                         }
                         Object o_a = a.get(0) ;
                         Object o_b = b.get(0) ;
                         if (c.relation(o_a, o_b)) {
                           target.add(o_a) ;
                           a.remove(0) ;
                         } else {
                           target.add(o_b) ;
                           b.remove(0) ;
                         }
                       }
                     }
                   }
```

Like Quicksort, Merge Sort is $O(n.\log(n))$. Unlike Quicksort, Merge Sort has to make copies of the data. Although the space usage is only $O(n.\log(n))$ rather than the $O(n)$ of Quicksort, some people consider that this space usage limits the usefulness of Merge Sort.

20.10   Sorting in JGL and Collections

Both JGL and Collections have ready-made methods for sorting sequences. As might be expected, JGL emphasized support for sub-sequences defined by iterators as well as whole sequence-like data structures. Collections on the other hand, assumes that only primitive arrays will be sorted and that if other sequence-like data structures need to be sorted then they can be copied to primitive arrays (using the `toArray` method), sorted and then copied back into the original data structure.

Both libraries support the Quicksort algorithm but this is modified by using Insertion Sort when the sequence slices get sufficiently small (7 for Collections and 16 for JGL). The comments in the source code for Collections cite Jon L. Bentley & M. Douglas McIlroy (1993) "Engineering a Sort Function", *Software — Practice and Experience*, **23**(11), 1249-1265 for the theory behind the mix of Quicksort and Insertion Sort. Interestingly whilst JGL uses its mix of Quicksort and Insertion Sort for all sorting, Collections only uses its mix of Quicksort and Insertion Sort for primitive arrays of primitive types. For primitive arrays of objects, Collections uses a variation of Merge Sort. It is not entirely clear from the source code comments what the rationale is for this choice but there definitely is one. We will not delve into this issue here but instead point you towards the specialist books on algorithms and algorithmics to investigate.

JGL provides its sorting methods in the class `Sorting` which is in the package `com.objectspace.jgl.algorithms`. Collections provides its sorting methods in the class `Arrays` which is in package `java.utils`. Like the implementations we have presented for the ADS library, JGL makes use of order relation method objects. Collections on the other hand relies on the data type being sorted implementing the `Comparable` interface (i.e. providing a method `compareTo` to provide the order relation). There are benefits to both decisions: relying on the existence of the `compareTo` means that the caller of the `sort` method is not required to think about order relations. On the other hand, employing caller provided order relation method objects is more flexible since types that do not implement `compareTo` can still be sorted.

The principle issue is, of course, consistency of library architecture. Both JGL and Collections are consistent in their use and application of the two approaches.

20.11   Summary

In this chapter we have investigated a number of different data sorting methods: Selection Sort, Bubble Sort, Insertion Sort, Quicksort, Tree Sort, Heap Sort and Merge Sort. All of these are comparative sorts in that the core of the algorithms are comparisons and movements of data. We have left the details of the theory behind the various algorithms for other texts, concentrating instead on their implementation in Java as method objects.

The sorting methods are categorized in terms of their run-time performance and whether or not they copy the data. This leaves us with Merge Sort and Quicksort as the techniques of choice, with Quicksort preferred by most people, possibly only for historical rather than theoretical reasons.

Self-review Exercises

Self-review 20.1 Of the $O(n^2)$ sorts (Selection Sort, Bubble Sort, Insertion Sort) why is Insertion Sort the preferred one?

Self-review 20.2 Of the $O(n.\log(n))$ sorts (Tree Sort, Heap Sort, Quicksort, Merge Sort) why is Quicksort generally the preferred one?

Self-review 20.3 Why are the cases of `Array` and `DLList` separated out in the implementations of Insertion Sort and QuickSort?

Self-review 20.4 Why are the cases of `Array` and `DLList` not separated out in the implementations of Selection Sort, Bubble Sort, Tree Sort, Heap Sort and Merge Sort?

Programming Exercises

Exercise 20.1 Write a program to test the correctness of the various sorting implementations presented here and implemented in the ADS library. (If you find any real bugs, please let us know.)

Exercise 20.2 Write a program to test the correctness of the various sorting methods found in the JGL and Collections libraries.

Exercise 20.3 Write a program to test the relative performance of all the different algorithms implemented in ADS, JGL and Collections.

Hint: Create a `Stopwatch` class that can measure elapse time in milliseconds (the best mechanism is to wrap up calls to `System.currentTimeMillis`). Create a program that runs some data through all the algorithms measuring the sorting time in each case using the stopwatch mechanism previously created. Run this for several sizes of data set (from small, c.10, to large, c.100,000) and plot the results on a graph.

Challenges

Challenge 20.1 None of the sorting method object classes presented are actually "production versions". Implement a production version for insertion into the ADS library.

Sorting — Distributive Methods

Objectives

The previous chapter investigated a number of sorting algorithms that used a comparative approach. This chapter introduces an alternative approach, 'distributive sorting' which is usually far more efficient. However, the data has to have very specific structure for these sorts to be applicable, so the sorts of the last chapter are still often used.

Keywords

Count Sort

Pigeonhole Sort

Bucket Sort

Radix Sort

Digit Sort

21.1   Introduction

In the last chapter, we investigated various sorting techniques that relied on comparing the values of data items. We found that $O(n.\log(n))$ seemed to be the best performance we could get, at least in the general case.

Sometimes there is structure to the data to be sorted that can be exploited so as to achieve sorting performance of $O(n)$. Clearly, such situations need to be exploited as much as possible because of this better performance. The sorting techniques that achieve this sort of performance are not comparison sorts but use a very different approach.

21.2   Distributive Sorts

When we were dealing with the various data structures and searching algorithms, we noted that direct use of indexing into array-like data structure always led to the fastest performance. This motivated the use of array storage for trees (heaps) and array-based hash tables for indexed data storage. The core point behind all that thinking was that indexing is the fastest way of implementing mapping of data. We now want to make use of this observation with sorting algorithms.

The two sorts we present in this chapter are very different in nature and yet they use the same core idea: instead of comparing values and swapping as necessary, as is done in comparison sorts, data is distributed into arrays using indexing techniques without there being any comparisons.

In order to employ such *distributive sorts*, the data must be such that they can be used directly, at least one way or another, as array indexes. It is this use of direct access via array indexing that allows us the $O(n)$ performance of these distributive sorts — whereas the tree-structured comparative sorts could only manage $O(n.\log(n))$ at best.

The restrictions on the data set necessary to be able to use distributive sorts are usually seen as too restrictive for general usage, which is probably why these sorts are rarely a core part of most packages. As noted earlier, JGL provides only Quicksort (with some use of Insertion Sort) and Collections only provides Quicksort (with some use of Insertion Sort) and Merge Sort, neither libraries bothering about any other sort technique. It is, nonetheless, wise to have the technique in the armoury in case the data fits the requirements — and we can harness the significantly better performance

21.3   Count Sort (aka Pigeonhole Sort or Bucket Sort)

The principle used for this sort is that, if the data is a set of integers of some variety, then we do not need to sort the data at all; we can simply note each datum's existence in such a way that the list of sorted values can be generated. What we do is to use an array to keep a frequency table. That is, we set up a mapping from data values to occurrence count in the data set. This can then be used to generate the sorted list without actually sorting the data using a comparative method.

As each datum is some variety of integer value, it can be used directly as an index into an array (i.e. the array holds the data value implicitly rather than explicitly). The content of an array element is the number of times the value represented by the index of that element occurs in the data set, the data value being the index of the array element.

The sorting technique is then quite straightforward. We run through the original data creating the frequency table — an $O(n)$ activity — and then we run through the frequency table outputting the relevant number of data items of the value that is the array index of that array element — another $O(n)$ activity. At no stage are we comparing values and because of this we have ended up with an $O(n)$ sorting technique. Of course, we have placed a very rigid requirement on the data set.

In fact, we must put a further restriction on the data set. This relates to the use of memory: if the range of integer values is very large then we will need a large amount of memory to store the array. As long as we actually have enough address space to do this, it can be worth it, particularly when there is a very large amount of data to be sorted. However, if there are a large number of values from the range which do not occur in the data set (if the occurrence of a value is sparse with respect to the data), then this can be very poor use of memory. The point at which to change to a comparative sort is not determinable a priori since the permitted liberal use of memory is very much application dependent.

So to put it another way, if the range of values that actually occurs is not much less than the range of values that could possibly occur then Count Sort may be a good choice of sorting algorithm, if sufficient memory is available. On the other hand, if only a small proportion of the values that could occur do actually occur then the initialization routine will spend a long time setting to zero array elements that will not be used and the final output routine will spend a long time visiting array elements that contain zero. This destroys the $O(n)$ property that would otherwise be the case.

The most obvious way to implement this sort is by using a primitive array. We could use `Array` but since primitive arrays provide all the facilities we need, and they offer much faster performance, there seems no need to do so. Assuming the data set is presented as an array of `Number` values, the following implements Count Sort:

```
package ADS ;
/**
 *   Sort a primitive array of <CODE>int</CODE>s using Count Sort
 *   (also occasionally heard of as Pigeonhole Sort or even Bucket
 *   Sort).  This is an O(n) sort.
 *
 *   <P> This implementation is very simple and straighforward (it
 *   could do with being made more sophisticated).  It assumes that the
 *   data are always positive integers.
 *
 *   @version 1.1 1999.11.27
 *   @author Russel Winder
 */
```

```java
public final class CountSort {
  /**
   *   The sort operation.
   *
   *   @param a the array to be sorted.
   */
  public static void sort(final Integer[] a) {
    //   Set up the counters.
    int n = findMaximum(a) ;
    int[] counts = new int[n + 1] ;
    //   For each datum in the array increment the frequency count in
    //   the counter.
    for (int i = 0 ; i < a.length ; i++) {
      counts[a[i].intValue()]++ ;
    }
    //   Create the sorted list by working through each counter and
    //   outputting into the array the number of of items of that
    //   value.
    int dataIndex = 0 ;
    for (int i = 0 ; i < counts.length ; i++) {
      for (int j = 0 ; j < counts[i] ; j++) {
        a[dataIndex++] = new Integer (i) ;
      }
    }
  }
  /**
   *   Find the maximum value in the array.
   */
  private static int findMaximum(final Integer[] a) {
    int max = 0 ;
    for (int i = 0 ; i < a.length ; i++) {
      int testValue = a[i].intValue() ;
      if (testValue > max) {
        max = testValue ;
      }
    }
    return max ;
  }
}
```

Since we can convert all the primitive integral data types into Integers, there is no real need to have a version specially designed for use with `ints`. However, if absolute performance were essential we might consider doing this since there is some overhead to using objects to represent integer values compared to using `int`. It is unlikely that such a sort would ever be used for `long` data since it is more than likely that the 'density of occurring values' property required to make this sort useful. That and the fact that it is probably impossible for any computer today to actually construct the necessary array!

We saw when investigating how to implement mappings (Section 18.5, Page 529) that by translating the domain, it is possible to handle negative data values. Of course, the total range of possible values must admit the mapping of the whole domain onto array indexes for this to work.

What happens if we want to deal with data that are `Objects` and not `Numbers`. Well, as long as the data has an isomorphism to the set of array indexes, we can set up a transformation. This should be left to the application(i.e. the application must be responsible for generating the primitive array of `Numbers` that represent the data to be sorted). The method object class presented above can then be used. The alternative, which is useful in a few circumstances, is to have a version of the method object class that handles part of the transformation itself.

21.4 Radix Sort (aka Digit Sort)

Sometimes, we find that the data to be sorted is actually a set of values that can be treated as though each value is a sequence of digits. The following integers have this property:

> 243, 567, 101, 999

Each value comprises three digits in the range $[0, 9]$. The following set of values has identical structure:

> the, cat, sat, mat

Each word comprises three letters. Note that although the term digit is used associated with descriptions of this sort, we don't mean digit in the sense $[0, 9]$ as is usual. For Radix Sort, as long as the digits have a mapping to the integers they can be used. Letters are digits in the range $[0, 25]$ in this context. The crucial factor is not the values of the digits but is that the data is structured as a sequence of m digits. We do not have to have exactly the same number of digits in each datum. Where an integer does not have quite the appropriate number of digits, we can prefix 0s without changing the value. For words, we can postfix spaces to pad out the word to the required length without changing its value. Thus the following data sets are valid inputs to a Radix Sort:

> 001, 243, 567, 101, 999, 012, 005

> the , cat , sat , on , the , brown, mat

With data structured in this way we can make use of the array-based technology that characterizes distributive sorts but in a very different way to that used in Count Sort. Instead of an array element for each element, we have an array element for each possible digit and make multiple passes through the data. This will require us to store and move around the data values which we didn't have to do in Count Sort since the array index was the value. This means that whilst we can use primitive arrays for the core set of 'bins' into which we will put values, they do not provide an appropriate data structure for the bins themselves. A more dynamic data structure such as `Array` will be far more appropriate. In fact, we will use `Queues` but we need to look at the algorithm in more detail before we can justify this design decision.

The basic algorithm can be represented by saying:

> For each digit place in the datum starting with the least significant and working towards the most significant:

>> Take each datum from the data array and place it in the sequence of the sorting array element indexed by that digit.

Starting with the array element of the smallest digit and working towards the array element of the largest digit, copy the sequence of values in the order they appear into the original data array.

An example of applying Radix Sort can be seen in Figure 21.1.

As noted above, we use a primitive array of bins since this is the most efficient of the array-like data structures and we require no other facilities than those provided by primitive arrays. In the implementation we present here, we use a primitive array of Queues to provide the bins into which the values will be placed during the sorting. We choose this representation since this hides all the manipulations associated with the flexible length storage required to actually store the data values. Moreover, it provides the right abstraction to enforce the preservation of order of the data values within the bins. For the case where the data are Numbers held in a primitive array we have the following method object class:

```
package ADS ;
/**
 *  Sort a primitive array of items where each item is a sequence of n
 *  digits where there are m possibilities for each digit.  It is
 *  assumed that digits have a mapping to <CODE>int</CODE>s.  Use
 *  Radix Sort (also has been referred to as Digit Sort).  This is an
 *  O(q) sort, where q is the number of data items.
 *
 *  @version 1.1 1999.11.29
 *  @author Russel Winder
 */
public final class RadixSort {
  /**
   *  The sort operation.
   *
   *  @param a the array to be sorted.
   *  @param n the number of digits in each sort key.
   *  @param m the number of different possible digits.
   */
  public static void sort(final Integer[] a,
                          final int n,
                          final int m) {
    // Set up the pigeonholes into which we will put numbers.  It is
    // important that we treat the pigeonholes as FIFO data
    // structures so we make them Queues.
    final Queue[] holes = new SLListQueue [m] ;
    for (int i = 0 ; i < m ; ++i) {
      holes[i] = new SLListQueue () ;
    }
    // For each digit in the sort key do a pigeonhole stuffing
    // exercise.
    for (int i = 0 ; i < n ; ++i) {
      int divisor = (int)Math.pow(m, i) ;
      for (int j = 0 ; j < a.length ; ++j) {
        // Put the number in a pigeonhole determined by the value of
        // the digit in the slot we are currently sorting on.
        holes[(a[j].intValue() / divisor) % m].add(a[j]) ;
      }
      // Merge all the entries in the pigeonholes in order into a
      // single list ready for the next pass.  Reset the pigeonholes
      // ready for the next pass as well.
      int index = 0 ;
      for (int j = 0 ; j < m ; ++j) {
        while (! holes[j].isEmpty()) {
          a[index++] = (Integer)holes[j].remove() ;
```

Original sequence with
data to be sorted.

001	243	567	101	012	005

Put items from the sequence into appropriate bins
by least significant digit.

0	1	2	3	4	5	6	7	8	9
	001	012	243		005		567		
	101								

Take items from the bins and put them back into the
sequence, in their new, partially sorted order.

001	101	012	243	005	567

Put items from the sequence into appropriate bins
by middle digit.

0	1	2	3	4	5	6	7	8	9
001	012			243	567				
101									
005									

*It is critically important
that the order of items is
preserved when in the
bins.*

Take items from the bins and put them back into the
sequence, in their new, partially sorted order.

001	101	005	012	243	567

Put items from the sequence into appropriate bins
by middle digit.

0	1	2	3	4	5	6	7	8	9
001	101	243			567				
005									
012									

Take items from the bins and put them back into the
sequence, in their new, totally sorted order.

001	005	012	101	243	567

Figure 21.1 An example of a Radix Sort.

```
          }
          holes[j].makeEmpty() ;
        }
      }
    }
  }
```

Analysing the performance of the algorithm: If there a k digits and n data values then there are $2kn$ copying actions. This makes this an $O(n)$ sort — assuming that k does not depend on n and that k is small compared to n. If these assumptions are not true then we would have to call this an $O(kn)$ sort.

21.5   Summary

In this short chapter we have looked at a couple of internal distributive sorts. Whilst their use is rare, due to the restrictions on the data required for them to be applicable, they are very useful when they are applicable because of their $O(n)$ performance. So whilst they are rarely in the libraries that come with development environments, they are important techniques for those occasions on which the data meets the requirements of these sorts.

Self-review Exercises

Self-review 21.1 What distinguishes comparative and distributive sorts?

Self-review 21.2   Why are the distributive sorts $O(n)$ whilst the comparative sorts are $O(n.\log(n))$?

Self-review 21.3 Why are Queues used for the Radix Sort implementation?

Programming Exercises

Exercise 21.1 Implement a version of the Count Sort for use with primitive arrays of ints. Compare the performance of this with the performance of the version for use with Numbers.

Exercise 21.2 Write the version of Count Sort and Radix Sort to work with ADS Sequences.

Exercise 21.3 Amend the performance measurement program of the previous chapter to include Count Sort and Radix Sort so that you can put the performance of these two sorts onto the graph and compare their real performance against the comparative sorts.

Challenges

Challenge 21.1 Develop versions of Count Sort and Radix Sort that could be added to the JGL and Collections libraries.

22

Sorting — External Methods

Objectives

The previous two chapters introduced a number of sorting algorithms that required the data to be held in memory. This chapter introduces sorting techniques where there is so much data to be sorted that it must be stored on disk rather than in memory.

Keywords

files

records

factory objects

Balanced Multi-way Merge Sort

Polyphase Merge Sort

22.1   Introduction

In days long gone, computers had so little memory that to sort *any* data set required secondary storage such as disks and tapes. Indeed, disks were something of a luxury in the for some time! Despite these slight problems, sorting was still important and undertaken frequently. Techniques and algorithms were devised to employ some number of secondary storage devices, usually tape drives, to sort the data sets. Because of the nature of the storage medium (a tape drive is a linear sequence of data held in blocks) the algorithms were all based on data streaming and merging.

Today, where memory is plentiful — assuming the operating system and user interface software have not expanded to fill all the space available — attention is invariably focused almost exclusively on sorting techniques that require all the data to reside in memory, the internal sorts. The various algorithms of sorting internally, both comparative and distributive, have been analysed and optimized though Quicksort allied with Insertion Sort (Section 20.6, Page 578) still remains the solution of choice for most people. The last two chapters have summarized the issues and presented implementations, as method objects within the ADS package, of the various algorithms.

There are still times, however, when there is more data than can be comfortably managed by an internal sort. In such circumstances we can either not do the job or resurrect the old-fashioned external sorts. Well not necessarily. Many books describe these external sorts and, indeed, discuss their performance properties but they rarely discuss their implementation. The underlying assumption seems to be that any problem that requires this sort of data manipulation will actually be handled using a database management system.

This may well be true, and in fact we believe it to be so. Why then are we discussing the issue at all? There are a number of reasons:

- Discussing these external sorting algorithms allows us to discuss some aspects of managing secondary storage and in particular disk files.

- There are a few package architecture issues that arise in implementing these algorithms.

- There might be a problem you come across when there is a problem that is too big for an internal sort that is not really a database problem.

- The algorithms show how the technique underlying the internal Merge Sort (Section 20.9, Page 587) can be applied to an external sort.

- The algorithms bring out very neatly how the properties of the underlying infrastructure affect the algorithms that we use.

So, in this chapter, we present a couple of external sorting algorithms to try and bring out the above points. Interestingly, both of these sorts rely on the ability to do an internal sort, used effectively as a bootstrap to the external algorithm.

Whereas in an internal algorithm it is entirely reasonable to manipulate individual data items, external algorithms have to take into account the fact that such operations are effectively impossible on secondary storage, the properties of secondary storage just do not permit such activities. The internal algorithms have, in fact, made use of the properties of main memory already so there is nothing essentially new going on here. The properties we are talking of here are:

- Main memory gives access to individual data items in constant time.
- Main memory access time is fast.
- Secondary memory stores data in blocks, so access to an individual data item requires fetching the whole block in which it resides.
- Secondary storage is slow.
- Secondary storage is much better manipulated by obtaining block of data in sequence. (This is especially true of tapes, of whatever sort, since access is very linear).
- Data values can only be compared in main memory.

Thus, the very nature of secondary storage is such that only merging-oriented algorithms based on streams of data make any sense whatsoever. No amount of clever caching techniques in the operating system or I/O library are going to obviate this fact.

All merging algorithms require an element of comparison, at any moment there must be a comparison of values to determine which one to take next. This can only happen in main memory. So our external sorting algorithms are actually going to be a combined use of primary and secondary storage. Merging also implies streams of pre-sorted data to merge. In Merge Sort (Section 20.9, Page 587) this was achieved by splitting the array down to individual elements which are, by definition, sorted. Because of blocking this is not an appropriate strategy for external sorts. Instead we need to construct initial blocks of sorted data another way. This is the bootstrap that requires the internal sorting.

The initial step in any external sort is to create some basic sorted blocks of data by using an internal sort, more often that not using Quicksort. The external sort then manages the merging of these basic blocks using secondary storage. It is how the merging is managed that distinguishes the various external sorts. All the external sorts do, however, provide the same functionality.

22.2 Architectural Issues

In the implementation of the two external sorts we will look at, a new structural problem appears for the ADS package. With the internal sort algorithms, we were able to 'parameterize' the source code, using `Comparators` and `Objects`, so that the same methods could be used for all data without having to know about the data beforehand — we were able to create an architecture for the method objects that enabled them to handle any data type at all. The equivalent problem for the external sorts is that the method objects must be parameterized in terms of the file structures: we must construct the external sort method object so that it can handle any and all file structures without having to have knowledge of the exact structure.

The first step in achieving this generalization is actually to impose a little structure The structuring tool is to state that all files are sequences of records. This imposition gives great freedom since we can write the method object code in terms of a type, let us call it `SortableRecord`, which we effectively leave as undefined (i.e. we make it an interface). The only assumption we need to make about a `SortableRecord` is that it has some key that can be used as a sorting key — after all each record needs some value on which an order relation is defined so that it can be sorted on. By parameterizing the method object in this way, we are basically leaving all definition of what a `SortableRecord` actually is to the application code. This is, in effect, a direct analogue of using `Object` as the data item in the internal sorts.

For the ADS package, we use the following interface for the `SortableRecord`:

```
package ADS ;
/**
 *  An interface defining the concept of a record, the sort of thing
 *  written to and read from a file.
 *
 *  @see SortableRecordReader
 *  @see SortableRecordWriter
 *  @version 1.0 1997.05.19
 *  @author Russel Winder
 */
public interface SortableRecord {
    /**
     *  A <CODE>SortableRecord</CODE> must have a key that the records
     *  can be ordered on.
     */
    int key() ;
    /**
     *  A <CODE>SortableRecord</CODE> must have a printed form.
     */
    String toString() ;
}
```

The obvious difficulty this leaves us with is how to actually do input–output of these records. We clearly need to use the `java.io` package and in particular the types `FileReader`, `FileWriter`, `BufferedReader`, `BufferedWriter`, but we do not know (and are requiring not to know) the structure of a `SortableRecord` so we do not know how to actually read and write the `SortableRecord`s. Again we must parameterize by introducing a type, or two in this case. We introduce `SortableRecordReader` and `SortableRecordWriter` as place holders in the package code for application supplied classes since it is only when the application is constructed that the nature of a `SortableRecord` is known and the actual reading and writing semantics are known.

Again we use interfaces as these placeholders:

```
package ADS ;
import java.io.File ;
import java.io.IOException ;
/**
```

```
 *   An interface defining the concept of a record reader, the sort of
 *   thing capable of reading a <CODE>SortableRecord</CODE> from a
 *   file.
 *
 *   @see SortableRecord
 *   @see SortableRecordWriter
 *   @version 1.0 1997.05.19
 *   @author Russel Winder
 */
public interface SortableRecordReader {
  /**
   *   A <CODE>SortableRecord</CODE> must be readable.
   */
  SortableRecord readSortableRecord() throws IOException ;
  /**
   *   A <CODE>SortableRecordReader</CODE> must be closeable.
   */
  void close() throws IOException ;
  /**
   *   A <CODE>SortableRecordReader</CODE> must have a finalizer to
   *   clean up on being garbage collected.
   */
  void finalize() throws IOException ;
  /**
   *   Mark an input stream.
   *
   *   @see java.io.BufferedReader#mark
   */
  void mark(int lookAheadLimit) throws IOException ;
  /**
   *   Move back to the mark.
   *
   *   @see java.io.BufferedReader#reset
   */
  void reset() throws IOException ;
}


package ADS ;
import java.io.File ;
import java.io.IOException ;
/**
 *   An interface defining the concept of a record writer, the sort of
 *   thing capable of writing a <CODE>SortableRecord</CODE> to a file.
 *
 *   @see SortableRecord
 *   @see SortableRecordReader
 *   @version 1.0 1997.05.19
 *   @author Russel Winder
 */
public interface SortableRecordWriter {
  /**
   *   A <CODE>SortableRecord</CODE> must be writeable.
   */
  void writeSortableRecord(SortableRecord r) throws IOException ;
  /**
   *   A <CODE>SortableRecordWriter</CODE> must be closeable.
   */
  void close() throws IOException ;
  /**
   *   A <CODE>SortableRecordWriter</CODE> must have a finalizer to
   *   clean up on being garbage collected.
   */
  void finalize() throws IOException ;
}
```

So far, so good. Unfortunately, there is one more difficulty before we can actually sort anything. In order to undertake any reading and writing of `SortableRecords`, we need to construct `SortableRecordReader` and `SortableRecordWriter` objects. However, two points:

1. We cannot actually instantiate interfaces.

2. We appear to have no way of knowing what the application classes conforming to these interfaces are at package compile-time.

We are clearly in need of a new technique of implementation. The 'trick' that we need is to define one last class. Again this class is a place holder, another interface. The application is required to construct an object conforming to this interface. The task of this object is to supply application specific `SortableRecordReader` and `SortableRecordWriter` conformant objects on demand to the sort function object, this class is a *factory class*. We call this interface `SortableRecordInformation`:

```
package ADS ;
import java.io.File ;
import java.io.IOException ;
/**
 *  An interface defining a factory object encapsulating
 *  <CODE>SortableRecord</CODE> management information.  Necessary for
 *  using any <CODE>FileSort</CODE> classes.
 *
 *  <P> When dealing with files, there have to be records. This
 *  interface defines that which needs to be known in order to use any
 *  <CODE>FileSort</CODE> function objects.  The user must supply a
 *  <CODE>SortableRecordInformation</CODE> conformant object in order
 *  to provide all the tools needed.
 *
 *  @see FileSort
 *  @see SortableRecord
 *  @see SortableRecordReader
 *  @see SortableRecordWriter
 *  @version 1.0 1997.05.19
 *  @author Russel Winder
 */
public interface SortableRecordInformation {
  /**
   *  Deliver up an order relation <CODE>Comparator</CODE> so that we
   *  can test the order of records.  Usually this will be an ordering
   *  defined by some key in the record.
   */
  Comparator getComparator() ;
  /**
   *  Deliver up a Comparator that can test for value equality of the
   *  sort key.
   */
  Comparator getEqualToComparator() ;
  /**
   *  We must be able to get a <CODE>BufferedReader</CODE> so that
   *  we can read records from a file.
   */
  SortableRecordReader newSortableRecordReader(File f)
    throws IOException ;
  /**
   *  We must be able to get a <CODE>BufferedWriter</CODE> so that
   *  we can write records to a file.
   */
  SortableRecordWriter newSortableRecordWriter(File f)
    throws IOException ;
```

}

The four interfaces we have described define all the infrastructure that the application must provide in order for generic external sorting algorithms to work. The application has the responsibility of providing objects conforming to these interfaces. With this imposition on the application, which is relatively minimalistic, we are able to make sufficient assumptions in the implementation of the sorting algorithms that general external sorting is achievable.

We are now in a position to discuss the two particular algorithms.

22.3   Balanced Multi-way Merge Sort

In this approach to external sorting we have two sets of files, the A files and the B files. There can be any number of pairs of these files, the condition being that there are the same number of A files as B files. We then use these files to create longer and more sorted sequences of data values until we end up with a single file containing all the data in sorted order.

There are no X-files in these sort algorithms!

The first step is to perform the bootstrapping, the creation of the initial set of sorted blocks. The original data is taken a block at a time, each block containing some number of records. Each of these blocks is sorted using an internal sorting algorithm and the sorted block written to one of the A files. These initial sorted blocks are distributed as evenly as possible amongst all the A files so that the result is that each A file has an equal number of sorted blocks. There may, of course, be an imbalance by one for some of the A files. This stage is sometimes termed *dispersion*.

We then take one block from each A file and merge them together writing the result to the first B file. Another block is taken from each of the A files, merged and put into the next B file, this process continues until the A files are empty. The resulting, much longer but still sorted, blocks are distributed evenly through the B files.

The process is then reversed: a block is taken from each B file, merged and the result placed in the first A file. Another block is taken from each B file, merged and the result placed in the next A file. Again we continue, evenly spreading amongst the A files until the B files are empty.

Eventually, rather than putting more than one block in each file, there comes a time when there is only one (probably quite long) block in each of the files — we cannot decide whether this will be A files or B files, of course, so we will need to be careful of this. At this point of course, we are about to create a single block with all the data, fully sorted, in one file. This is the end of the algorithm so we then copy the data back to the original file.

We can express this algorithm in psuedocode:

```
dispersion:
    fileIndex = 1
    while (there are blocks in data file)
        sort block
```

> *write block to A file fileIndex*
> *fileIndex = (fileIndex + 1) modulus numberOfAFiles*

> *sorting:*
>   *while (more than one file is not empty)*
>   *while there are blocks in A file 1*
>   *foreach (B file)*
>   *merge 1 block from each A file to this B file*
>   *if (only 1 B file has data)*
>   *exit*
>   *while there are blocks in Bfile 1*
>   *foreach (A file)*
>   *merge 1 block from each A file to this B file*

The fact that we always distributed blocks as evenly as possible is where the name of this sort comes from: Balance Multiway Merge Sort. The following implements this algorithm:

```
package ADS ;
import java.io.File ;
import java.io.FileNotFoundException ;
import java.io.FileWriter ;
import java.io.IOException ;
/**
 *  A function object delivering a balanced merge sort of a file on
 *  the filestore.
 *
 *  @see SortableRecord
 *  @see SortableRecordReader
 *  @see SortableRecordWriter
 *  @see SortableRecordInformation
 *  @see SortableRecordCopyFile
 *  @version 1.1 1999.11.29
 *  @author Russel Winder
 */
public final class BalancedMultiwayMergeSort {
  /**
   *  A sort operation with some defaults.
   *
   *  @param fileName the <CODE>String</CODE> giving the name of the
   *  file to be sorted.
   *  @param r the <CODE>SortableRecordInformation</CODE> factory
   *  object for creating <CODE>SortableRecordReader</CODE>s and
   *  <CODE>SortableRecordWriters</CODE>s and able to deliver a
   *  <CODE>Comparator</CODE>.
   */
  public static void sort(final String fileName,
                          final SortableRecordInformation r)
    throws FileNotFoundException, IOException {
    sort(fileName, 20, 2, r) ;
  }
  /**
   *  A sort operation.
   *
   *  @param fileName the <CODE>String</CODE> giving the name of the
   *  file to be sorted.
   *  @param blockSize the number of data items in the initial sorted
   *  blocks.
   *  @param numberOfFiles the number of files to use for initial
   *  dispersion.
   *  @param r the <CODE>SortableRecordInformation</CODE> factory
   *  object for creating <CODE>SortableRecordReader</CODE>s and
   *  <CODE>SortableRecordWriters</CODE>s and able to deliver a
   *  <CODE>Comparator</CODE>.
   */
```

```
public static void sort(final String fileName,
                        final int blockSize,
                        final int numberOfFiles,
                        final SortableRecordInformation rInfo)
  throws FileNotFoundException, IOException {
  // Create all the files needed for the sorting.
  File file = new File (fileName) ;
  File[] f_A = new File [numberOfFiles] ;
  File[] f_B = new File [numberOfFiles] ;
  for (int i = 0 ; i < numberOfFiles ; i++) {
    f_A[i] = new File ("tmp_A_"+i) ;
    f_B[i] = new File ("tmp_B_"+i) ;
  }
  // Perform the initial dispersion into the A files.
  distributeSortedBlocks(file, f_A, blockSize, rInfo) ;
  // Undertake the number of merge loops required to guarantee that
  // everything is sorted.  Remember whether we ended up with A_0
  // or B_0 containing the final sorted data.
  File[] from = f_A ;
  File[] to = f_B ;
  boolean B_isFinal = true ;
  for (int i = 0 ;
       merge(from, to, (int)Math.pow(2, i)*blockSize, rInfo) ;
       i++) {
    File[] temp = from ;
    from = to ;
    to = temp ;
    B_isFinal = ! B_isFinal ;
  }
  // Copy the data to the final destination.
  File fileToCopy = B_isFinal ? f_B[0] : f_A[0] ;
  SortableRecordCopyFile.copy(fileToCopy, file, rInfo) ;
  // Delete all the files.
  for (int i = 0 ; i < numberOfFiles ; i++) {
    f_A[i].delete() ;
    f_B[i].delete() ;
  }
}
/**
 *  Perform the initial dispersion of the data.
 */
private static void distributeSortedBlocks(
    final File from,
    final File[] to,
    final int blockSize,
    final SortableRecordInformation rInfo)
  throws FileNotFoundException, IOException {
  // Create a Reader for the original data and a set of Writers for
  //  the A files.
  SortableRecordReader reader =
   rInfo.newSortableRecordReader(from) ;
  SortableRecordWriter[] writers =
   new SortableRecordWriter[to.length] ;
  for (int i = 0 ; i < to.length ; i++) {
    writers[i] = rInfo.newSortableRecordWriter(to[i]) ;
  }
  boolean allDone = false ;
  while(! allDone) {
    for (int i = 0 ; ! allDone && (i < writers.length) ; i++) {
      // Pull in a few records, put them into an Array that is
      //  where we are performing the internal sort that creates us
      //  the sorted block.  Do the sort then write out the block.
      Array a = new Array () ;
      for (int k = 0 ; k < blockSize ; k++) {
        SortableRecord r = reader.readSortableRecord() ;
        if (r == null) {
```

```
          allDone = true ;
          break ;
        }
        a.add(r) ;
      }
      QuicksortSequence.sort(a,
                             rInfo.getComparator(),
                             rInfo.getEqualToComparator()) ;
      for (Iterator iter = a.iterator() ;
             ! iter.atEnd() ;
             iter.advance()) {
        writers[i].writeSortableRecord((SortableRecord)iter.get()) ;
      }
    }
  }
  //  Be tidy and close all the files.  Actually this is
  //  essential to ensure we get a flush.
  for (int i = 0 ; i < writers.length ; i++) {
    writers[i].close() ;
  }
  reader.close() ;
}
/**
 *  Undertake a round of merging.
 */
private static boolean merge(final File[] from,
                             final File[] to,
                             final int currentBlockSize,
                             final SortableRecordInformation rInfo)
  throws FileNotFoundException, IOException {
  //  Open up the set of Readers and the set of Writers.
  SortableRecordReader[] readers =
   new SortableRecordReader[from.length] ;
  for (int i = 0 ; i < readers.length ; i++) {
    readers[i] = rInfo.newSortableRecordReader(from[i]) ;
  }
  SortableRecordWriter[] writers =
   new SortableRecordWriter [to.length] ;
  for (int i = 0 ; i < writers.length ; i++) {
    writers[i] = rInfo.newSortableRecordWriter(to[i]) ;
  }
  //  We make us of an array which holds the next Record for each of
  //  the files -- we need to have the record in memory in order to
  //  compare the keys and so decide which Record to write to the
  //  output file.  Have another array which is keeping count of how
  //  many Records we take from each of the files so that we can
  //  cease drawing from a given file when we have taken the
  //  appropriate number yet there are still records left.
  boolean returnValue = false ;
  boolean allDone = false ;
  SortableRecord[] items = new SortableRecord[readers.length] ;
  int[] counts = new int[readers.length] ;
  while (! allDone) {
    for (int i = 0 ; i < writers.length ; i++) {
      //  Initialize the array holding the next record from each of
      //  the files.  Determine whether we are finished or not by
      //  whether there are any records left or not.
      allDone = true ;
      for (int j = 0 ; j < readers.length ; j++) {
        counts[j] = 0 ;
        items[j] = readers[j].readSortableRecord() ;
        if (items[j] != null) {
          counts[j] = 1 ;
          allDone = false ;
        }
      }
```

```
        if (allDone)
          break ;
        while (true) {
          //  Determine which is the next Record to add to the output
          //  stream.  If there isn't one then we get a negative index
          //  and we can terminate the loop.  If we do not terminate
          //  then there was a Record and we must write it out.
          int index = findAppropriate(items,
                                    rInfo.getComparator()) ;
          if (index < 0)
            break ;
          writers[i].writeSortableRecord(items[index]) ;
          if (i > 0) {
            //  We have not yet reduced the problem to only a single
            //  file so there must be at least one more iteration --
            //  we know when we are finished when everything goes into
            //  a single file.
            returnValue = true ;
          }
          //  Draw a new Record from the file whose Record was chosen
          //  -- unless of course we have finished our quota from that
          //  file.
          if (counts[index] < currentBlockSize) {
            items[index] = readers[index].readSortableRecord() ;
            if (items[index] != null) {
              counts[index]++ ;
            }
          } else  {
            items[index] = null ;
          }
        }
      }
    }
    //  Be tidy, close all the files.  Actually this is essential to
    //  ensure there is a flush.
    for (int i = 0 ; i < writers.length ; i++) {
      writers[i].close() ;
    }
    for (int i = 0 ; i < readers.length ; i++) {
      readers[i].close() ;
    }
    return returnValue ;
  }
/**
 *  Determine which Record is the one to be output next.
 *
 *  @param items the array of <CODE>SortableRecords</CODE> from
 *  which to select the next according to the order relation defined
 *  by <CODE>c</CODE>.
 *  @param c the <CODE>Comparator</CODE> defining the required order
 *  relation on the <CODE>SortableRecord</CODE>s.
 *  @return the index in the array of the item that should be
 *  chosen next.
 */
private static int findAppropriate(final SortableRecord[] items,
                                   final Comparator c) {
  //  Assume no output is to be done and then find the first
  //  non-empty entry.
  int index = -1 ;
  for (int i = 0 ; i < items.length ; i++) {
    if (items[i] != null) {
      index = i ;
      break ;
    }
  }
  //  If there were no non-empty entries then do nothing, we are
```

```
    //  finshied.  Otherwise...
    if (index >= 0)  {
      //  ...do a linear search through the items to see which is the
      //  next one to select.
      SortableRecord value = items[index] ;
      for (int i = index+1 ; i < items.length ; i++) {
        if (items[i] != null) {
          if (c.relation(items[i], value)) {
            index = i ;
            value = items[i] ;
          }
        }
      }
    }
    return index ;
  }
}
```

Since we knew that copying a file from one place to another was going to be a facility required by any external sort method object, this action has been extracted from the sorting method object and turned into a method object in itself:

```
package ADS ;
import java.io.File ;
import java.io.FileNotFoundException ;
import java.io.IOException ;
/**
 *  A method object to copy a file containing <CODE>Record</CODE>s.
 *
 *  @see SortableRecord
 *  @see SortableRecordReader
 *  @see SortableRecordWriter
 *  @see SortableRecordInformation
 *  @see BalancedMergeSort
 *  @see PolyPhaseMergeSort
 *  @version 1.1 1999.11.27
 *  @author Russel Winder
 */
public final class SortableRecordCopyFile {
  /**
   *  The copying method.
   *
   *  @param from the file to read <CODE>SortableRecord</CODE>s from.
   *  @param to the file to write <CODE>SortableRecord</CODE>s from.
   *  @param rInfo the factory object (builder?) required to be able
   *  to construct the <CODE>Reader</CODE> and <CODE>Writer</CODE> of
   *  <CODE>SortableRecord</CODE>s.
   *  @return the number of records copied.
   */
  public static int copy(final File from,
                         final File to,
                         final SortableRecordInformation rInfo)
    throws FileNotFoundException, IOException {
    //  Set up the Reader and the Writer.
    SortableRecordReader source = rInfo.newSortableRecordReader(from);
    SortableRecordWriter target = rInfo.newSortableRecordWriter(to) ;
    //  Copy all the SortableRecords from the Reader to the Writer.
    int count = 0 ;
    while (true) {
      SortableRecord r = source.readSortableRecord() ;
      if (r == null)
        break ;
      target.writeSortableRecord(r) ;
      count++ ;
    }
```

```
        // Close the files and ensure the flush.
    source.close() ;
    target.close() ;
    return count ;
    }
    }
```

The performance of this algorithm, being a merge sort, is likely to have some sort of logarithmic performance but it is not entirely obvious how this relates to n, the number of data items. If we have k files (leading to many people calling this a k-way Balanced Merge Sort) and we construct b initial sorted blocks each containing m data items (where $(b-1)m \leq n \leq bm$) we can construct the following table showing how the blocks are distributed amongst the files in each pass:

Pass	Number of block in each file	Length of each block
1	b/k	m
2	b/k^2	km
3	b/k^3	k^2m
t	b/k^t	$k^{t-1}m$

This gives us a handle of a performance measure since the sort finishes when the number of blocks is one and the length of the block is n:

$$\frac{b}{k^t} = 1 \quad \Rightarrow \quad t = \log_k b$$

$$k^{t-1}m = n \quad \Rightarrow \quad t = \log_k\left(\frac{n}{m}\right) - 1$$

which is not entirely unreasonable since we know that $n \approx bm$. So the best measure of performance for this sort is the number of passes that the sort takes and this is effectively $O(\log(n/m))$.

22.4 Polyphase Merge Sort

Many books present the argument that (paraphrasing a mixture of the various arguments seen):

> "Balanced Multi-way Merge Sort requires $2k$ files which can be prohibitively expensive and is therefore not a solution of choice. Polyphase Merge Sort uses only $k+1$ files and is therefore far more preferable."

The term sophistry springs to mind. Clearly if k is large, then the argument is entirely valid but most people use $k = 2$, 3 or 4 for Balanced Multi-way Merge Sort and $k = 2$ for Polyphase Merge Sort. The resource usage in these circumstances is basically minimal.

Having said this, Polyphase Merge Sort is another external sort algorithm and, worth looking at because it is there. As implied above, this sort can be used with $k > 2$ but it is invariably presented with $k = 2$.

So what is the algorithm? It is a way of managing the blocks of sorted data and the merging of files founded on the properties of the Fibonacci numbers. The standard Fibonacci sequence is:

$$1, 1, 2, 3, 5, 8, 13, 21, \ldots$$

The importance of these numbers is that they are generated by the recurrence relation:

$$f_n = f_{n-1} + f_{n-2}$$

We can tell that you are asking the question: Huh?

The importance of this recurrence relation is that at each pass in a Polyphase Merge Sort (with $k = 2$) we are merging from two files into the third until we completely empty one of the sources, leaving ourselves two files with blocks and one empty ready to be a target. Now comes the other major difference with Balanced Multi-way Merge Sort: The block lengths can be different in each of the files with Polyphase Merge Sort whereas they were always the same length in each of the files during a given pass of Balanced Multi-way Merge Sort. The best way of seeing this is to use an example. In the following table, the columns F_0, F_1, F_2 specify properties of the content of the respective file, the number before the parentheses is the number of sorted blocks with the number in parentheses indicating the length of the sorted blocks:

Pass	F_0	F_1	F_2	Number of blocks	Blocks moved
0	–	13 (m)	8 (m)	21	–
1	8 ($2m$)	5 (m)	–	13	16
2	3 ($2m$)	–	5 ($3m$)	8	15
3	–	3 ($5m$)	2 ($3m$)	5	15
4	2 ($8m$)	1 ($5m$)	–	3	16
5	1 ($8m$)	–	1 ($13m$)	2	13
6	–	1 ($21m$)	–	1	21
Total					**96**

We take the data (n items) and construct blocks of sorted data just as we did for the Balanced Multi-way Merge Sort. This time however, we force the size of the blocks (m) to be a number such that (n/m) is a number from the Fibonacci series. We then disperse the blocks into two of the three files ensuring that the number of items in the two files fits with the Fibonacci series. So, in the above example, we have ended up with 21 blocks which we partition 13 to F_1 and 8 to F_2. We then merge 8 blocks from F_1 with 8 from F_2 into F_0, which was originally empty — each of these blocks is of length $2m$. This empties F_2 ready to be the target on the next pass. We now take 5 blocks from F_0 and F_1 (it matters not that the blocks from F_0 are longer than the block from F_1) and merge them into F_2. This empties F_1 ready to be the next target. Note that each file is taking its turn, in rotation, at being the emptied file ready to be the next target. This merging back and forth, taking just enough blocks to empty one of the files, continues until there is only a single file with any blocks in. It is this shuffling backward and forward between the files that makes the Fibonacci numbers so important, the recurrence relation models exactly the number of blocks in the files that contain blocks.

Remember, though, that the argument as presented (using the Fibonacci numbers) works only with $k = 2$, for $k > 2$ there are the Generalized Fibonacci numbers that must be used. Returning to $k = 2$, the following is an implementation. There has been some attempt to prepare the ground for $k > 2$ in this implementation but it is fundamentally a $k = 2$ solution.

```java
package ADS ;
import java.io.File ;
import java.io.FileNotFoundException ;
import java.io.FileWriter ;
import java.io.IOException ;
/**
 *  A function object delivering a polyphase merge sort of a file on
 *  the filestore.
 *
 *  @see SortableRecord
 *  @see SortableRecordReader
 *  @see SortableRecordWriter
 *  @see SortableRecordInformation
 *  @see SortableRecordCopyFile
 *  @version 1.1 1999.11.29
 *  @author Russel Winder
 */
public final class PolyphaseMergeSort {
  /**
   *  The sort operation with some defaults.
   *
   *  @param fileName the <CODE>String</CODE> giving the name of the
   *  file to be sorted.
   *  @param r the <CODE>SortableRecordInformation</CODE> factory
   *  object for creating <CODE>SortableRecordReader</CODE>s and
   *  <CODE>SortableRecordWriters</CODE>s and able to deliver a
   *  <CODE>Comparator</CODE>.
   */
  public static void sort(final String fileName,
                          final SortableRecordInformation r)
    throws FileNotFoundException, IOException {
    sort(fileName, 20, 2, r) ;
  }
  /**
   *  The sort operation.
   *
   *  @param fileName the <CODE>String</CODE> giving the name of the
   *  file to be sorted.
   *  @param blockSize the number of data items in the initial sorted
   *  blocks.
   *  @param numberOfFiles the number of files to use for initial
   *  dispersion.
   *  @param r the <CODE>SortableRecordInformation</CODE> factory
   *  object for creating <CODE>SortableRecordReader</CODE>s and
   *  <CODE>SortableRecordWriters</CODE>s and able to deliver a
   *  <CODE>Comparator</CODE>.
   */
  public static void sort(final String fileName,
                          final int approximateBlockSize,
                          int numberOfFiles,
                          final SortableRecordInformation rInfo)
    throws FileNotFoundException, IOException {
    //  Forceably stick to 3 files for now instead of just having one
    //  more than the number of input files.
    //numberOfFiles++ ;
    numberOfFiles = 3 ;
    //  Create all the files needed for the sorting.
    File file = new File (fileName) ;
    File[] temp = new File [numberOfFiles] ;
```

```
for (int i = 0 ; i < numberOfFiles ; i++) {
  temp[i] = new File ("tmp_"+i) ;
}
// Calculate the block size.  Must get things into the Fibonacci
// series for it to work properly.  Have to run through the file
// to find the number of records.  We need to copy the file
// anyway so this is not a wasted activity.  We use the array F
// to calculate the Fibonacci numbers as we go, calculating the
// initialBlockSize to best fit the nearest Fibonacci number.
int indexOfNumberOfBlocks = 1 ;
int initialBlockSize = 1 ;
int numberOfRecords =
 SortableRecordCopyFile.copy(file, temp[0], rInfo) ;
int[] F = new int [numberOfRecords] ;
for (int i = 0 ; i < numberOfFiles ; i++) {
  F[i] = 1 ;
}
for (int i = numberOfFiles ; i < numberOfRecords ; i++) {
  F[i] = 0 ;
  for (int j = i-1 ; j > i-numberOfFiles ; j--) {
    F[i] += F[j] ;
  }
  initialBlockSize = numberOfRecords / F[i] ;
  if (initialBlockSize < approximateBlockSize) {
    indexOfNumberOfBlocks = i-1 ;
    break ;
  }
}
while (true) {
  if (++initialBlockSize * F[indexOfNumberOfBlocks] >
      numberOfRecords)
    break ;
}
// Ceate the support arrays containing current block size and
// block count in the various files.
int[] blockSizes = new int [numberOfFiles] ;
int[] blockCounts = new int [numberOfFiles] ;
blockSizes[0] = 0 ;
blockCounts[0] = 0 ;
for (int i = 1, j = indexOfNumberOfBlocks-1 ;
     i < numberOfFiles ;
     i++, j--) {
  blockSizes[i] = initialBlockSize ;
  blockCounts[i] = F[j] ;
}
// Create the files of blocks of sorted records.
distributeSortedBlocks(temp,0,initialBlockSize,blockCounts,rInfo);
// Set up the file readers for all the files.
SortableRecordReader[] readers =
 new SortableRecordReader[numberOfFiles] ;
for (int i = 0 ; i < numberOfFiles ; i++) {
  readers[i] = rInfo.newSortableRecordReader(temp[i]) ;
}
while (true) {
  // Check what work there is to do.  If there is, find out which
  // is the empty file.
  int toIndex = -1 ;
  int numberOfNonEmptyFiles = 0 ;
  int indexOfNonEmptyFile = -1 ;
  for (int i = 0 ; i < numberOfFiles ; i++) {
    if (blockCounts[i] == 0) {
      toIndex = i ;
    } else {
      indexOfNonEmptyFile = i ;
      numberOfNonEmptyFiles++ ;
    }
```

```
      }
      //  Exit if everthing is done but close all the files
      //  and copy the result back before exiting.
      if (numberOfNonEmptyFiles <= 1) {
        for (int i = 0 ; i < numberOfFiles ; i++) {
          readers[i].close() ;
        }
        SortableRecordCopyFile.copy(temp[indexOfNonEmptyFile],
                                    file,
                                    rInfo) ;
        for (int i = 0 ; i < numberOfFiles ; i++) {
          temp[i].delete() ;
        }
        break ;
      }
      //  Perform the next round of merging.
      readers[toIndex].close() ;
      SortableRecordWriter writer =
       rInfo.newSortableRecordWriter(temp[toIndex]) ;
      merge(readers,writer,toIndex,blockSizes,blockCounts,rInfo) ;
      writer.close() ;
      readers[toIndex] = rInfo.newSortableRecordReader(temp[toIndex]);
    }
}
/**
 *  Perform the initial dispersion of the data.
 */
private static void distributeSortedBlocks(
    final File[] files,
    final int fromIndex,
    final int blockSize,
    final int[] blockCounts,
    final SortableRecordInformation rInfo)
  throws FileNotFoundException, IOException {
  //  Create a Reader for the original data and a set of Writers
  //  for the output files.
  SortableRecordReader reader =
   rInfo.newSortableRecordReader(files[fromIndex]);
  SortableRecordWriter[] writers =
   new SortableRecordWriter[files.length] ;
  for (int i = 0 ; i < files.length ; i++) {
    writers[i] = i == fromIndex
      ? null
      : rInfo.newSortableRecordWriter(files[i]) ;
  }
  for (int i = 0 ; i < writers.length ; i++) {
    if (i != fromIndex) {
      for (int j = 0 ; j < blockCounts[i] ; j++) {
        //  Pull in a few records, put them into an Array that is
        //  where we are performing the internal sort that creates
        //  us the sorted block.  Do the sort then write out the
        //  block.
        Array a = new Array () ;
        for (int k = 0 ; k < blockSize ; k++) {
          SortableRecord r = reader.readSortableRecord() ;
          if (r == null)
            break ;
          a.add(r) ;
        }
        QuicksortSequence.sort(a,
                               rInfo.getComparator(),
                               rInfo.getEqualToComparator());
        for (Iterator iter = a.iterator() ;
             ! iter.atEnd() ;
             iter.advance()) {
          writers[i].writeSortableRecord((SortableRecord)iter.get());
```

```
            }
          }
        }
      }
      // Be tidy and close all the files.  Actually this is
      // essential to ensure we get a flush.
      for (int i = 0 ; i < writers.length ; i++) {
        if (i != fromIndex) {
          writers[i].close() ;
        }
      }
      reader.close() ;
    }
    /**
     * Undertake a round of merging.
     */
    private static void merge(final SortableRecordReader[] readers,
                              final SortableRecordWriter writer,
                              final int toIndex,
                              final int[] blockSizes,
                              final int[] blockCounts,
                              final SortableRecordInformation rInfo)
      throws FileNotFoundException, IOException {
      SortableRecord[] items = new SortableRecord[readers.length] ;
      int[] counts = new int[readers.length] ;
      int numberOfBlocksMerged = 0 ;
      while (true) {
        boolean allDone = false ;
        for (int i = 0 ; i < readers.length ; i++) {
          counts[i] = 0 ;
          if (i == toIndex) {
            items[i] = null ;
          } else {
            readers[i].mark(64) ;
            items[i] = readers[i].readSortableRecord() ;
            if (items[i] == null) {
              for (int j = 0 ; j < i ; j++) {
                if (j != toIndex) {
                  readers[j].reset() ;
                }
              }
              allDone = true ;
              break ;
            } else {
              counts[i] = 1 ;
            }
          }
        }
        if (allDone)
          break ;
        numberOfBlocksMerged++ ;
        while (true) {
          int i = findAppropriate(items,toIndex,rInfo.getComparator()) ;
          if (i < 0)
            break ;
          writer.writeSortableRecord(items[i]) ;
          if (counts[i] < blockSizes[i]) {
            items[i] = readers[i].readSortableRecord() ;
            if (items[i] != null) {
              counts[i]++ ;
            }
          } else {
            items[i] = null ;
          }
        }
      }
    }
```

```
      blockSizes[toIndex] = 0 ;
      for (int i = 0 ; i < readers.length ; i++) {
        if (i != toIndex) {
          blockSizes[toIndex] += blockSizes[i] ;
        }
      }
      for (int i = 0 ; i < readers.length ; i++) {
        blockCounts[i] -= numberOfBlocksMerged ;
      }
      blockCounts[toIndex] = numberOfBlocksMerged ;
    }
    /**
     *  Determine which <CODE>SortableRecord</CODE> is the one to be
     *  output next.
     *
     *  @param items the array of <CODE>SortableRecords</CODE> from
     *  which to select the next according to the order relation defined
     *  by <CODE>c</CODE>.
     *  @param toIndex the index into the array of the target.  The
     *  others are assumed to be sources.
     *  @param c the <CODE>Comparator</CODE> defining the required order
     *  relation on the <CODE>SortableRecord</CODE>s.
     *  @return the index in the array of the item that should be chosen
     *  next.
     */
    private static int findAppropriate(final SortableRecord[] items,
                                       final int toIndex,
                                       final Comparator c) {
      //  Assume no output is to be done and then find the first
      //  non-empty entry.
      int index = -1 ;
      for (int i = 0 ; i < items.length ; i++) {
        if (i != toIndex) {
          if (items[i] != null) {
            index = i ;
            break ;
          }
        }
      }
      //  If there were no non-empty entries then do nothing, we are
      //  finshied.  Otherwise...
      if (index >= 0)  {
        //  ...do a linear search through the items to see which is the
        //  next one to select.
        SortableRecord value = items[index] ;
        for (int i = index+1 ; i < items.length ; i++) {
          if (i != toIndex) {
            if (items[i] != null) {
              if (c.relation(items[i], value)) {
                index = i ;
                value = items[i] ;
              }
            }
          }
        }
      }
      return index ;
    }
  }
```

Estimating performance efficiency for Polyphase Merge Sort is perhaps even more difficult that for Balance Multi-way Merge Sort. Again the number of passes is a relatively good measure but the problem is that a pass for Polyphase Merge Sort is a somewhat different sort of thing from a pass in Balanced Multi-way Merge Sort.

The solution usually employed is to drop passes as the measure of efficiency and, instead, use the number block movements:

$$merge\ efficiency\ =\ \frac{number\ of\ blocks\ moved}{number\ of\ initial\ blocks}$$

For the above Polyphase Merge Sort example this efficiency works out to be 96/21 = 4.6. In comparison, a Balanced Multiway Merge Sort with 32 initial blocks has an efficiency of log(32) = 5.

22.5   Summary

In this chapter, we have introduced the idea of an external sort, being a sort of data held, not in main memory, but on disk or tape. We have presented two sorting algorithms along with the file handling infrastructure needed to manoeuvre the data and hence achieve the sorting. A number of major issues affecting the architecture of the ADS package were raised and the notion of a factory object was employed as a solution to the most significant problem.

The introduction of the `Record` interface shows how to solve various problems arising from using files on secondary storage. This solution is, however, only a part of the total solution that would be used in a production package. The concepts are correct and appropriate ones but for a production package the concepts of *persistent objects* and *Serialization* would have to be introduced. It is outside the scope of this book to address this complexity, we leave this point as a 'dangling reference' for you to follow up.

Self-review Exercises

Self-review 22.1 When might you consider using an external sort?

Self-review 22.2 Why are external sorts all distributive sorts?

Self-review 22.3 Why are the Fibonacci numbers important for Polyphase Merge Sort?

Programming Exercises

Exercise 22.1 Write a test program to show that the two sort implementations presented in this chapter work as expected and also compare their performance.

Exercise 22.2 Compare the performance of these external sorts with the internal sorts from the previous chapter. (This is really to see how much slower disk and tape activity really is compared to memory activity.)

Challenges

Challenge 22.1 Evolve the Polyphase Merge Sort implementation to use more than two files. NB This will necessitate finding out about Generalized Fibonacci Numbers.

3

Case Studies in Developing Programs

Part 3

Objectives

This part presents a selection of complete example applications to show how real programs are constructed

Contents

Introducing the Case Studies

Objectives

There are a few introductory remarks to this part of the book which we give in this chapter. The following chapters present some case studies of Java program design and development.

Keywords

case studies

23.1 Introduction

!

The use of mathematics should not be ignored. The design of algorithms and data structures often benefits from a careful mathematical analysis.

Programming is, mainly, a practical skill, based primarily on computing technology with some science and mathematics included. Experience and familiarity with tools and programming languages matters a great deal. The design of a program, rather than the programming of it, is even more important and is similarly dependent on skill and experience. A professional developer using a professional approach to systems development will know about, and know how to exploit, good design as well as sophisticated programming technology, whereas amateurs and hackers tend to just 'throw software together'. The aim of this book is to put the reader firmly on the road to becoming a professional, so this part of the book looks at how some example, non-trivial, programs were designed and developed.

Good programmers need to be properly trained, but with the recognition that programming is not something that can be taught, it can only be learnt. Fortunately, design and programming are skills that people can, and do, learn. The best way to learn these skills is to actually design programs and do plenty of programming with feedback from an already learned and sophisticated practitioner. There is some theory around to give support to the programmer but this amounts to facts about what can and can't be done, what are good and bad ways to do certain programming things, and so on; the keywords to look out for are algorithmics, patterns, and programming plans.

While learning how to program is best done by doing, it must also include looking at examples of good and bad programming completed by other people, so that the novice can learn to distinguish the good from the bad. Far too many people think that programming is simply a matter of learning the syntax and semantics of the programming language and then just doing. People who do this invariably end up constructing very simplistic, certainly not sophisticated, programs and do an awful lot of re-inventing of bits of code: we have been advocating abstraction and reuse as fundamental principles behind making programs sophisticated but also as a way of avoiding re-inventing wheels. An useful analogy here is to the skill of making pottery; you can learn all about the equipment but until you have tried and learnt how to make your own pot you do not have the skill. Moreover, learning to make pottery guided by an expert makes things easier as they can help you learn techniques that are well known and avoid equally well known mistakes.

Not all useful sophistications in programming are abstractions embedded in classes and packages, some are ways and approaches to using features of the language to achieve certain ends. These components of the skill of programming, some would call them programming plans, programming idioms or patterns, can only be learnt by looking at other people's code and observing them in use. Programmers in general do not spend nearly enough time reading other people's code to see how they have approached things, what they have done well and what they have done badly. This is surprising for many reasons. Most people involved in systems development are using pre-existing systems and evolving them, they are not building systems from scratch. This requires people to read and understand software so as to make the changes that evolve it. Some people find themselves involved in code inspections (aka walk-throughs) and these are indeed reflections on people's code. However, such inspections do not have the aim of allowing people to learn, they are concerned with improving the code itself. Employers tend to want programmers to produce new or amended code and tend not to think of code inspection as an employee learning and self-improvement activity: code inspection is not seen as a staff development activity. This is a shame but understandable. It means, though, that the system does not really support programmer learning, the programmer has to make use of what they are asked to do to support their learning.

However it is achieved, the reading and reflection on other people's code is an extremely important activity in learning to program. The whole of this book supports this, we think. We hope that so far we have presented examples of good practice in Java programming. We believe, however, that there is nothing like studying the development of complete systems to support the learning of the programming skill. Thus we have set aside this complete part of the book to present some complete developments.

23.1.1 Testing

Another element of good development practice is testing. Code that doesn't produce the right answer is essentially useless (although there are many cases where such code is naively relied on as producing the correct answer — such mistakes are frequently very costly). Code that cannot be tested reliably and repeatedly is highly suspect. Testing is all too often left to be done after the programming has been more or less completed. There is a frantic testing phase in which to find as many bugs as possible, while at the same time trying to ship code before an approaching deadline.

It is far better to test code continually as it is being written. Ideally the testing should be automated, so that testing becomes second nature and not a chore. The use of test harness code and test classes provides a mechanism for doing this. Some would go further and advocate writing the testy code *before* the code to be tested — if you don't know how to test the code you plan to write, how do you know what code you actually need to write?

To test effectively you need to know what to test, how to do the test and what the correct answer is. Thinking through these questions often highlights the crucial design issues, putting you on the right track to develop correct and efficient code.

23.2 The Case Studies

We are not claiming that these examples are massively sophisticated (but they are definitely not simplistic), nor that they give a complete view of developing a system. What we believe they achieve is to be examples of developments to indicate how things proceed. We think they provide a starting point for people to then carry on the process of studying and learning.

So, in this part we have constructed three systems to present as case studies of Java developments:

1. A Mail Merge Program.
2. A Traffic Light Simulation.
3. An Ant Simulation.

We chose these as examples because they already existed, they were systems developed by us for a purpose other than being presented in a book. Thus, in some sense they are real programs. Clearly, though, we have had to restrict ourselves to a summary of all the issues rather than delving deep into all the detail on all three: each of these case studies could be a 500 page book in it's own right!

Although each of the case studies are intended to stand alone, there is a flow to them: In the mail merge program, we are building a basic, traditional 'data-in / data-process / data-out' computation. This is implementation of essentially straightforward algorithms usually thought of as being exemplars of procedural abstraction. Here we show one way of constructing this application in an object-oriented language using all the building blocks provided by that language's library in order to avoid reinventing low-level abstractions.

The second example, the traffic light simulation, shows how to construct new class-based abstractions using a prototyping approach and addresses an architecture issue raised as a consequence of construct generic abstractions — factory objects.

The third example, the ant simulation, extends the use of a prototyping approach to development by considering how reusable classes to be made a part of an application framework can be identified and put into a package.

All three examples address some of the basic issues of how to construct user-interfaces but the issue of user interface design itself is not addressed. We have just put together the interfaces based on our own thoughts. For a real development, we would undertake task analyses, user interface prototyping, user interface evaluations, and so on, in order to support the development of a usable and efficient user interface. This is not the book in which to address these issues; the human–computer interaction books listed in the bibliography are the place to go to get this material.

23.3   The Presentations of the Case Studies

Each of the case studies is presented in something of a *post facto* way: the studies do perhaps suffer a little from being rationalizations after the fact. It would, perhaps, have been better to have presented the case studies more as a complete blow-by-blow account of exactly what happened when we undertook the development but space does not allow this. Nor would it have been, in our view, quite as useful as this summary, exactly because each individual has a different way of developing software. Also, it is very difficult to present all the intermediate stages in the development. Thus we present only the final version of the program but with commentary on how and why each part is there to indicate how the development actually occurred. We believe that by focusing on the core decisions in building and the end structure of the systems, we are presenting the most crucial elements of the development.

As with all the code presented so far, a lot of detail is actually presented as comments in the source code: not all the important information appears in the narrative.

A Mail Merge System

Objectives

This chapter presents the development of a small mail merge program. Initially, a command-line version is constructed then a version with a graphical user interface is evolved from this initial version.

Keywords

T_EX

L^AT_EX

mail merge

batch processing

files

streams

Swing

AWT

24.1　Introduction

Most word processing systems (e.g. Word, WordPerfect, etc.) incorporate a mail merge facility: a mail merge being where the system takes a template letter file and a file of names and addresses (the mailing list) and prints out a copy of the letter which is personalized for each entry in the address file. We are all too familiar with the fact that a number of companies use this sort of feature all too extensively for marketing purposes.

One of the authors (RW) uses the L^AT_EX2ε system quite a lot and, in the past, wrote a C program to implement a mail merge facility for L^AT_EX2ε documents which was then turned into a C++ program. As an example of a Java development, we re-implement the program in Java.

We do not need a great deal of information about L^AT_EX2ε in order to develop the mail merge system but a certain amount must be known about how L^AT_EX2ε is used in order to design the mail merge process and also what has to be true about the template file for things to work.

L^AT_EX2ε is a tool for turning documents represented in an ASCII text file form (the L^AT_EX2ε source) into typeset documents. It is normally used for documents where there is a significant amount of complex mathematics to be typeset since it is quite easy to typeset mathematics with L^AT_EX2ε. Word processing systems still have great difficulty with mathematics and desk top publishing (DTP) systems can still be very awkward to use to set large amounts of mathematics.

To employ L^AT_EX2ε, the user constructs a L^AT_EX2ε source file using any text editor and then, from a command line, causes the L^AT_EX2ε tool to process the source and construct a representation of the typeset form (called the DVI file). This representation requires further processing by another tool to create a representation that can be printed. For example, the dvips tool transforms DVI representations into PostScript representations. There is much more to the complete system — tools for handling bibliographies (BibT_EX), for creating indexes (makeindex), for creating new fonts (METAFONT), and so on — but for this problem, the basic tools are all we need.

Below is a sample L^AT_EX2ε document, a trivial letter which is a complete source file that can successfully be processed:

```
\documentclass{rlw_letter}

\begin{document}
\begin{letter}{A Person\\
1 Some Street\\
A City\\
UK}
\opening{Dear A Person,}

This is just some text to show where the text of the letter would be.

\closing{Yours sincerely,}
\end{letter}
\end{document}
```

note

L^AT_EX2ε *is pronounced something like "lay-techs" or "lah-techs" (ch as in Scottish loch or technology).*

The text of the letter is 'marked-up' with formatting control information (the bits starting with '\'). When the letter is processed by L^AT_EX2ε, the formatting control information is used to direct the appearance of the letter on the printed page. When processed the result looks like:

One final point to note: the L^AT_EX2ε system exists on UNIX, Windows95/98/NT and MacOS machines, so we will want our mail merge program to run on all these systems. In addition, we would ideally like the *same* program to work on all three systems, avoiding the need to create and maintain three or more versions.

Immediately we can see that this is where Java has a strong advantage due to its ability to support platform independent programs. It should be possible to design and write the program once and then use it on all the platforms we want to support. Moreover, because of the way Java is executed, we can run the *same* executable program on each platform, without needing to re-compile all the code. Later in the chapter, when we add a graphical user interface (GUI) to the program, the platform independence will become even more valuable as the Java libraries give us a standard set of classes for constructing user interfaces. This will avoid all the problems that programmers have had to struggle with in the past when working with incompatible platform dependent GUIs.

Overall, the Java mail merge program promises to give us some critical advantages over the C and C++ versions.

24.2 Understanding the Problem

First and foremost, we need to understand the problem as fully as we can before trying to construct an implementation: we need to understand the basic requirements of the system as an initial step in creating the solution.

24.2.1   An Initial Analysis

There will be two files that the user must create prior to running the mail merge program: the *letter file* and the *address file*. We assume that the user employs some text editor or other (we use emacs, for example) to create these files. The letter file is a L\(^A\)T\(_E\)X2ε document which contains tags (place holders) instead of a particular person's contact details. The address file contains data in the form of contact details for everyone on the mailing list, organized such that we can associate this data to the tags in the letter file.

note

emacs is a text editor that is part of the GNU toolset produced by the Free Software Foundation. Whilst originally developed as a UNIX application, it has been ported to Windows95/98/NT.

The basic mail merge process can be described by the following pseudocode:

> *foreach entry in address-file {*
>   *edit a copy of letter-file replacing tags with data*
>   *process edited letter-file with LaTeX2e*
>   *print merged letter-file*
> *}*

This is all very satisfactory; the fact that we can express the core process as a single piece of pseudocode in this way implies the application is actually going to be quite straightforward. However, there are more questions that need to be answered before we can move forward in the design of the program. In particular, there are two obvious ones:

1. What is the set of contact information?

2. How do we represent this information in:

    a. the letter file; and

    b. the address file.

We can answer (1) fairly straightforwardly. A person's contact information is usually understood as being:

> Name
>
> Postal address
>
> Telephone number
>
> Fax number
>
> Email address

Knowing a person's email address is not useful for this exercise since we are using paper-based communication. However, we include it since, in the future, we may want to use the address file for doing electronic mailshots.

To proceed further, we must move to the initial design phase of the development since, in order to specify how the information is to be stored in the address file and what the tags are that appear in the letter file, we must know what we can and can't do with Java code.

24.2.2 An Initial Design

The basic architecture of the system is a classic 'batch processing', data processing system. There is an input, some processing and an output.

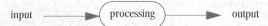

This leads us to reason that the basic design clearly has two aspects, one dealing with the file handling and the other with string manipulation. The data files can be managed by stream classes from the Java libraries but what else is there? It seems that everything else is just methods. We highlight this fact by refining the pseudocode of the core algorithm a little more:

> *set up address file*
> *set up tag strings*
> *foreach entry in address-file {*
> *   set up replacement strings*
> *   set up letter file*
> *   foreach line of text in letter file {*
> *   edit occurrences of a tag string with replacement string*
> *   }*
> *   process edited letter-file with LaTeX2e*
> *   print merged letter-file*
> *}*

This feels almost detailed enough to be able to write source code. We are just left with the questions left over from the previous sub-section. What are the tags in the letter file and what is the structure of the address file?

Now that we are clear that this is a string processing problem, it is clear that a tag must be a string that is easily recognizable and which will never occur in a letter file except as a mail merge tag. This then is something of an arbitrary design decision, we just need to be decisive. We choose the following as tags for the letter file:

> <NAME>
> <ADDRESS>
> <TELEPHONE>
> <FAX>
> <EMAIL>

We do not believe that these strings are ever likely to occur naturally in a letter and they are very easy to recognize. To make it obvious what this means, the following is the previous L^AT_EX2ε source file amended to make it a mail merge letter file:

```
\documentclass{rlw_letter}

\begin{document}
\begin{letter}{<NAME>\\
<ADDRESS>}
\opening{Dear <NAME>,}

This is just some text to show where the text of the letter would be.

\closing{Yours sincerely,}
```

```
\end{letter}
\end{document}
```

The fact that only the `<NAME>` and `<ADDRESS>` tags have been used is a choice made by the writer of the letter and that is as it should be; the mail merge program is providing a service and should impose as few restrictions as possible.

That seems to take care of the letter file, now we must turn our attention to the address file and this is slightly more complicated. The most important issue for the address file is being able to match the contents with the tags. The contents will be organized as lines of text that can be read in and stored as a string. It is convenient to think about the file in terms of text lines, since this is easy to process as the end of line acts as the end of string, making it very easy to recognize. The problem with this is recognizing which string is which. We could define an absolute ordering for the strings, called *fields*, within each person's entry or *record*, with records having fields in the order `<NAME>`, `<ADDRESS>`, `<TELEPHONE>`, `<FAX>`, `<EMAIL>`. Using such a design, we would have an address file something like:

```
A Person
1 Some Street, Sometown, Somecountry
+1 345 567 2345
+44 1234 345 4567
a.person@somehost.or.other
A Bod
1 Astreet, Atown, Acountry
+33 1 23 34 45 56
+49 12 345 4567
a.bod@somehost.or.other
```

We could implement the program with such a design for the address file. However, it has a several problems that mean we do not proceed quite yet:

1. There is no separator between records. Actually this is easily soluble: we define any line containing only zero or more whitespace (space or tab) characters between the `<EMAIL>` field of one record and the `<NAME>` field of the next record to be non-significant.

2. We cannot immediately tell which is the telephone field and which is the fax field, we have to rely on the ordering being correct. For other fields this is not a problem since the data itself tells the reader (though not the computer) which field is which. For telephone numbers and fax numbers, since they are from the same domain, there is a real problem.

3. Fields may be missing completely, due to mistakes being made when creating the file contents. This would most likely result in the program matching the wrong fields with the wrong tag (for example supplying an address instead of a person's name). We definitely want to avoid this happening before all the letters are printed out.

4. There is no way of formatting (i.e. using line breaks in), the address. This is a show-stopping problem.

(1) is simply a requirement on the final implementation, it is not a problem for the design. (2) and (3) can be solved by simply changing the specification slightly and putting tags at the beginning of each line in the address file:

```
<NAME> A Person
<ADDRESS> 1 Some Street, Sometown, Somecountry
<TELEPHONE> +1 345 567 2345
<FAX> +44 1234 345 4567
<EMAIL> a.person@somehost.or.other

<NAME> A Bod
<FAX> +49 12 345 4567
<EMAIL> a.bod@somehost.or.other
<ADDRESS> 1 Astreet, Atown, Acountry
<TELEPHONE> +33 1 23 34 45 56
```

A number of points to note about this. We are now freed of the ordering requirement, we can have the fields in any order since the lines are self-tagging. We can determine if any field is missing and know exactly which field data belongs in. We can have any amount of non-significant whitespace between the tag and the replacement string, the first non-whitespace character defines the start of the string. We can choose to have, or not, blank lines between records.

The problem that is left is the ability to format the address. We solve this by re-imposing a little bit of a field ordering. We require the address to be the last entry and require the address string terminator to be a line containing only whitespace, with all other newline characters being part of the address string. Note how this affects our thinking about blank lines between records, we are now forcing there to be at least one! The following is an example of this new file format:

```
<NAME> A Person
<TELEPHONE> +1 345 567 2345
<FAX> +44 1234 345 4567
<EMAIL> a.person@somehost.or.other
<ADDRESS> 1 Some Street,
Sometown,
Somecountry

<NAME> A Bod
<FAX> +49 12 345 4567
<EMAIL> a.bod@somehost.or.other
<TELEPHONE> +33 1 23 34 45 56
<ADDRESS> 1 Astreet,
Atown,
Acountry
```

There is now no ordering requirement on any of the fields other than the address field. As a subsidiary point we note that if any tag is repeated in a record then it is the last occurrence of the tag that defines the replacement string.

There do not seem to be any outstanding problems with this address file structure that are immediately apparent so we will proceed with this specification.

24.2.3 Objects?

Interestingly, what we have examined so far has had very little, if anything, to say about objects and classes. Indeed, we have not really exploited any of the object-oriented design techniques outlined in Chapter 9. Nonetheless, we will be writing an object-oriented program. What is going on?

Firstly, our design discussion has focused on the algorithm and the format of data files, not on the structure of the program as a whole. The algorithm will end up being implemented as a collection of methods belonging to a single class, while the format of the files is external to the program structure.

Secondly, we are taking for granted the existence of library classes that provide strings, streams for accessing the files and any other supporting roles needed. We don't need to design any of these, just use them. But that is the whole point: build your low level abstractions once and repeatedly reuse them.

Thirdly, we always want to simplify and the mail merge turns out to be nice and simple. Additional infrastructure and complexity can be introduced in the future if found to be needed but let's concentrate on getting a clean simple version working first. Don't forget, however, to check the need for and exploit the strengths of object-oriented design. Be on the look-out for the key abstractions and think about the problem domain.

That said, what we have here is an algorithm that can be inserted into a mail merge class, which can in turn be inserted into the standard (and object-oriented) Java application infrastructure, all of which can make use of standard library classes. Java gives us all the basic material, we just add the extra bits to create our specific application.

24.2.4   A More Detailed Design

There is actually very little left to be decided before getting down to writing source code. We need to prototype from what we have in order to find out what the unresolved problems are: it is almost impossible to try and predict all the problems before we begin to implement so we don't even try.

However, we can, indeed should, think about the basic set of methods that we will declare in the mail merge class needed by this program. From what we have said above the following seem obvious candidates:

- getting a person record from the address file, `getPerson`;
- executing an operating system command, `executeCommand`; and
- editing the markers in a line of text, `editMarkers`.

So we are going to work with the basic code outline of:

```
public class MergeApplication {
   // Set up any variables and constant strings needed.
   // The main method drives the merge.
   public static void main(final String[] args) {
     // process all the command line arguments
     // open address file
     while (getPerson()) {
       // open letter file
       // open temporary file
       while (true) {
         // read a line from letter file into currentLine
         if (no_input)
           break ;
         currentLine = editMarkers(currentLine) ;
         // write line to temporary file
       }
       // close temporary file
```

```
            // close letter file
            // execute LaTeX2e command to create DVI file
            // execute dvips command to create PostScript file
            // execute print command
      }
    // close address file
    }
    private static boolean getPerson() {
      do {
        // Get fields other than address field.
        // Get address field
      } while (input_to_be_had) ;
      return true ;
    }
    private static String editMarkers(String s) {
      // copy characters from String s to output catching
      // any instances of tags and not outputting them but
      // outputting the replacement text instead.
    }
    private static void executeCommand(String c) {
      // Execute String c as an operating system command,
      // handling all exceptions
    }
  }
```

Most of the rest of the design decisions are low level and are best appreciated by reading the commentary in the comments of the source code shown in Section 24.3, Page 643. The methods have all been declared `static` as, following the keep things simple approach, the `MergeApplication` class will not have instance objects.

24.2.5 Streams and Files

Before moving on to the implementation of the mail merge program, we need to have a quick look at how data files can be handled within a Java program. Data files are, of course, stored as disk files managed by whatever operating system is running on the current machine. The Java class libraries provide a number of classes to allow disk files to be used in a platform independent way. While we don't need to worry about all the details of how this is done, we do need to be familiar with the basic use of these classes in order to understand the program code in the next section.

Data files are managed using two abstractions:

- The basic file abstraction provided by the library class `File` in the package `java.io`. This encapsulates all the details of what a file is and how it is named.

- The stream abstraction which provides a way of reading and writing data to and from a file.

A stream is essentially a sequence of values of some type acting very much like a queue. For reader streams, one end of the queue is connected to a source of data (such as a disk file) while data values are read from the other end. Writer streams are connected to a data sink at one end with data values being written into the other end.

A basic stream is no more than a sequence of bytes, or 8-bit values, with a set of methods for reading or writing bytes, and performing general stream management. In order to allow values of types such as the primitive types or Unicode characters to be read and written in a convenient way, a variety of higher level stream abstractions are provided. These different streams can be chained together, such that higher level streams are connected together using lower level streams: the output of one stream is connected the input of another. This, for example, allows a stream capable of reading integers to be connected to a stream of raw bytes which in turn can be connected to a disk file. This highly flexible arrangement allows streams to be customized to provide whatever client interface is desired while being easy to connect to sources or sinks of data.

The Java libraries actually provide two principal kinds of stream; byte streams and character streams. Byte streams work with 8-bit values, which can be used to represent data of any type. Character streams work with 16-bit Unicode character values and are used for reading and writing strings and text. The name of a stream class indicates what kind of stream it is; any class with a name including the word `Stream` is a byte stream, any class with a name including `Reader` or `Writer` (but not `Stream`) is a character stream.

In the mail merge program, character streams and files are used in the following way:

1. Create a `File` object for the file to be accessed:

    ```
    File aFile = new File (fileName) ;
    ```

    The `File` constructor takes a file name string as its argument.

2. Create a `FileReader` or `FileWriter` stream connected to the `File` object:

    ```
    FileReader reader = new FileReader (aFile) ;
    ```

    or

    ```
    FileWriter writer = new FileWriter (aFile) ;
    ```

    These statements need to be in try blocks as failure to open the file or connect the stream will cause an exception to be thrown.

3. Chain on additional stream objects to provide the appropriate interface to the file data, for example buffering:

    ```
    BufferedReader in = new BufferedReader (reader) ;
    ```

    or

    ```
    BufferedWriter out = new BufferedWriter (writer) ;
    ```

    Again these statements need to be in try blocks. Diagrammatically, the situation looks like:

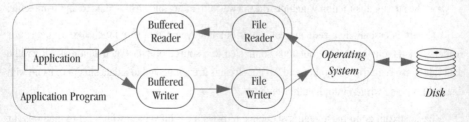

For more information about these classes browse the J2SDK documentation for the package `java.io`.

24.3   A Command Line Implementation

In the traditional spirit of the use of L^{A}T$_E$X2ε being a command line activity, we first implemented the mail merge application as a command line tool. There were many iterations in moving from initial code outline to working code. We are not going to provide a complete blow by blow account but here is an informal, notebook style, history of the code:

- Constructed the command line arguments processing code. Tested this by using the program as an echo program (i.e. a program to simply echo the command line arguments).

- Constructed the file opening and closing code. Discovered that there were exceptions to handle. Created the messaging functions to encapsulate error message reporting, both terminal and non-terminal. Didn't actually test this separately on the claim that it was trivial code. This was undoubtedly an overly arrogant and unsafe position to take but…

- Wrote the `getPerson` function. Originally forgot to reset the class variables holding the name, telephone, fax, email and address information to the empty string. This came to light when testing the program and discovered carry over of information from one record to the next when a record did not define one of the fields. Easily fixed though. Also initially did not have the `trim` method called on the string. The effect appeared when all the data had extra space and newlines. Pleasantly surprised at how easy all the sub-string manipulation turned out to be.

- Wrote the `editMarkers` method. Did three or four versions of this. The early attempts were too embarrassingly unsophisticated to remember. The sub-string method of `String` makes this function actually very neat.

- Wrote the `executeCommand` method. Discovered more exceptions that needed to be taken care of. Decided to 'cheat' and simply propagate these up to the top level. This method turned out to be an easy one in the end but the stumbling block initially was not being able to simply call `Process.exec` — the `exec` method of `Process` requires an object. Discovering the ability to get a reference to the `Runtime` object solved the problem. A big issue here was that the first version of this method did not block waiting for the command to complete. This led to interesting behaviour of the command pipeline. Another major problem was thinking C++ when conceptualizing what was happening with the command execution — this relates to the deletion command. Command interpreters (aka shells) have wildcard expansion of files names (globbing). The C++ `system` function starts a command interpreter to deal with the operating system commands and so wild card expansion is available. Java does not start a command interpreter and so there is no wildcard expansion. This resulted in changing the delete command string to start a command interpreter so that it could use wildcard expansion.

- Discovered problem with L^{A}T$_E$X2ε processing, the program seemed to hang in some circumstances. Found that the problem occurred when there was a fault in the letter file —

tip

Test ALL the code you write. The most embarrassing and difficult to find bugs invariably occur in code you thought unnecessary to test.

had forgotten that L^AT_EX2ε enters an interactive mode when it sees an error in the source file. Added code to insert the relevant command to perform processing in batch mode.

- Found another problem deleting files, the delete command didn't.

This was the point at which the first edition of the book was published. Since then the following development happened:

- Sorted out the temporary file deletion problem by creating the `deleteTemporary-File` method. The problem was to do with string processing in the `Process.exec` method. The strings that comprise the operating system command must be provided separately not as a single string.

- Reassessed the decision to propagate the exceptions and caught them all locally.

- Realized the program was very UNIX oriented. In fact, this is not really a problem since the Windows95/98/NT based L^AT_EX2ε systems are UNIX style. By making sure that the UNIX tools are available on the Windows95/98/NT platform, everything works fine. Ensured that the Cygnus tools existed on the test Windows95/98/NT platform. WindowsNT has support for the lpd protocol so the lpr command should work — except that it doesn't appear to for us. This is still an unsolved bug but appears to be an issue with WindowsNT and not this program. Treat this as a working hypothesis and wait for Windows2000.

- Realized that all the comments were not `javadoc` type comments so changed all the appropriate ones so that HTML documentation could be produced.

- Fixed a few bugs associated with email information. This information was provided in a hurry just prior to the publication of the first edition and a few bugs were left in. These are corrected in this edition.

There are some further changes that it would have been sensible to make but we leave discussion of these issues until discussion of the GUI version. In essence we treat this command-line version of the system as an initial prototype and do not develop it any further.

Whilst we could present the code for the command line version here (as we did in the first edition), so much of it is replicated in the GUI version that we feel it is not appropriate. Instead we talk a little bit about how this version of the code was tested and then move directly into the next iteration of the prototype.

24.3.1 Testing

As ever, no program can be claimed to be a release until it has been tested. What then is the testing strategy for this program? There are two basic components:

1. testing the handling of the command line; and
2. testing the actual mail merge functionality.

The first of these is relatively easy. We need to start the application with zero, one, two and three parameters and check the behaviour. With zero or one parameters, the program should inform us

note

The Cygnus tools can be obtained from http://www.cygnus.com/.

correctly that there is a problem that means it cannot execute. Two parameters should lead to a run of the mail merge but see below. Three parameters means there are more parameters than needed. The mail merge should run but this is just to ensure nothing untoward happens if we supply extra information. In the case of two and three parameters we must check using both valid and invalid file names with one, two and three parameters so as to check the file accessing code and error handling. In effect this is an exhaustive test.

The second test is far more complex and certainly not exhaustive. We should check with a letter file that has no markers to check that there are no changes made to such a document. We then need to check a number of different letter files with a number of different usages of tags to see if we can find any bugs. We need to check with an address file with no records, with one incomplete record, with one complete record and with many records of mixed completeness. As noted earlier in having data entries in the address file that did not specify all possible contact details we found a bug in the code!

Actually, it is difficult to know what constitutes a truly sufficient test data set here. We just need to try as many different situations as we can and see if we find any bugs. Our confidence in the program increases with each test that does not highlight a bug — assuming it is different from all the other tests carried out. We just have to decide when there is no longer a cost benefit to continuing.

24.4 A Version with a Graphical User Interface

24.4.1 Introduction

Command line interfaces are all very well and good, relatively easy to design and implement, and so on, but the world these days demands graphical user interfaces (GUIs) — often even when such a thing is not appropriate! In the case of this mail merge system, there is a strong case for a more interactive user interface and hence a GUI — based mainly on the issue of file selection. It seems eminently reasonable to allow the user the opportunity of selecting from a set of choices rather than requiring the files to be specified exactly by typing.

We therefore want to evolve the program to add a new user interface. We do not simply dive in and add code but step back first and reassess our analysis and design. In effect we must ask the question: Is there anything about the original program that would be done differently now that we are seeking to use a GUI? Unsurprisingly, the answer is a solid, yes.

The core analysis and basic structure of the program do, in fact, remain unchanged. There is nothing about them that related to the interaction with the user or the issuing of commands for processing: the file handling remains the same, the processing algorithms remain the same, and so on.

So what does change?

The command line parameter handling for one thing and the way of outputting messages to the user for another. In fact, we need to design the interaction first and then see how to amend the application code. Also there is an issue about portability (or rather lack of it) which leads to a significant change in how the command strings are dealt with.

24.4.2   The User Interface

We think it is patently obvious that, if we are to construct a graphical user interface, we need a set of graphical user interface construction components: buttons, sliders, scroll bars, selection boxes, and the rest — all the components that everyone knows and expects. An ideal candidate for a package! Indeed, so important and so basic is such a package that there should be, must be, indeed is, a standard package to deal with all this — or at least the basic level. The J2SDK distribution provides two packages that between them provide all the facilities: the Abstract Window Toolkit (AWT) and Swing. An introduction to Swing was provided in Chapter 11 but we will include sufficient information about Swing in this chapter to allow it to be read independently of Chapter 11.

AWT and Swing together are the standard packages for developing GUIs using Java; they are the building kits providing components to construct GUIs. Swing comprises a set of abstractions, for example `JFrame`, `JButton`, `JMenu`, `JCheckBox`, `JPanel`, and others, which are platform independent graphical interface components. Some of the classes are concrete and can be used in our program directly, some are abstract and are provided to be inherited from by classes declared in applications in order to create concrete classes. Swing, internally, has a structure that allows these abstractions to work with a number of different 'look and feel' styles. Fortunately, it provides a default 'look and feel' that is the same on all platforms. We believe that considering details of how to work with the 'programmable look and feel' (PLAF) is beyond the scope of this book so we stick with the default 'look and feel'.

Find out what facilities are available in Swing and AWT before trying to design and implement a user interface.

We are not going to present here a description of the whole of Swing or the AWT; there is the online material that comes with the J2SDK and there are also tomes enough already entirely devoted to this topic and we refer you to one of those. Here we will introduce just enough to be able to follow the development of the applications we develop here. The moral here though is: If you intend to write any user interface code learn about Swing and AWT before you start.

*Read and learn about human–computer interaction **before** trying to design and implement user interfaces.*

The most important fact about any GUI programming, and Swing and AWT are no exception, is that any such program is event driven rather than application driven. We have to construct our application code as a system that creates a state and then awaits outside intervention to cause a change of state. Any application that does input–output using a multi-tasking windowing system, such as the X-Window system on UNIX or Windows95/98/NT, has to be written in the knowledge that it can never have absolute control. The user is always in control. The application is driven by the events that the user generates using the window manager and the hardware (mouse and keyboard).

AWT defines an event management system (the `java.awt.event` package). The original Java (JDK1.0) event handling model was very different to the current Java event handling model (introduced in JDK1.1 and kept 'as is' in Java 2). We will only concern ourselves here with the current model since the earlier model is deprecated and will disappear as soon as vendors complete the move to the Java 2 model in their products.

What we have to know to build any application using Swing and AWT is that events are managed by setting up *listeners*. An AWT-based user interface component organizes itself, sets up event listeners and awaits events. The Java runtime system organizes all the events that happen in the system, including all the window system events, and informs all listeners when an event they are listening for happens. So an application component setting up a listener is effectively registering the component that created it with the runtime system as a component that is wanting to be told about a given event. The events that can be listened for are abstract and related to the component. Thus, an action event on a mouse button is the button being clicked. The AWT itself manages the lower level events of mouse clicking or keystrokes

Events are basically of two sorts, low-level and high-level. Low-level events are things such as mouse clicks or keystrokes and whilst these can be handled directly by the application programmer, they tend to be left to the AWT to manage. High-level events are ones generated within the AWT and are caused by low-level events. The AWT interprets low-level events in terms of the type of the component that the state of the interface implies is the target of the low-level event, and generates an appropriate high-level event for that component. Each component has a type and a set of events that are appropriate for that component. Applications programmers make life easy for themselves by worrying only about high-level events and leaving the rest to the AWT — abstraction wins again!

In this mail merge application, we are going to be interested in button clicking events and some window management events.

In a high-level sense the only thing that can happen to a button is that it can be pressed — it cannot be adjusted in the sense of having it represent a new value in the way a slider or scroll bar can — though it can be resized. The obvious sort of event that it can have then is an `ActionEvent`. This is usually by mouse click, though it can be by pressing return if we have set the button up properly. The point is that we do not care how the event is generated at the low-level since the abstraction provided by the AWT means that we are listening for the high-level `ActionEvent`.

Windows are a little more complicated and have the `WindowEvent` event to describe events generated by the window manager.

There are two listeners that we will be interested in; `ActionListener` and `Window-Adapter`. All `...Listener` types are interfaces whereas all `...Adapter` types are concrete classes providing a 'no-op' implementation of the associated `...Listener`. So `Window-Adapter` is an implementation of the `WindowListener` interface. `WindowAdapter` is also the base class that is used (by inheritance) to create listeners for events generated by the window

tip

Avoid working with low-level events unless it is absolutely essential.

manager (X-Window System, Windows95/98/NT, etc.). Each and every `Window` can listen for events generated by the window manager.

Other classes from Swing and AWT that we will use are: `JButton`, `JDialog`, `FlowLayout`, `JFrame`, `GridBagConstraints`, `GridBagLayout`, `GridLayout`, `JLabel`, `JPanel`, `JTextField`. We leave the online manuals and other books to give you the details of these classes and explain here how and why we use them in this application:

`JButton` — A button with a label that causes some action. Each button has an appropriate listener defined (using the `addActionListener` method), often using anonymous classes (where the required actions are unique) or with top-level or member classes (where a listener is the same in a number of cases).

`JDialog` — All the windows we construct are actually dialogue boxes so we use this class as the superclass.

`FlowLayout` — The left–right flow manager for automatically packing the user interface elements into `JPanels`.

`JFrame` — All the windows that will be displayed are `JDialogs` but each `JDialog` needs a parent. We make the application an undisplayed `JFrame` to act as the parent.

`GridBagConstraints` — Used to hold various layout parameters when using the `GridBagLayout` to pack interface elements.

`GridBagLayout` — The most general and therefore most powerful of the various layout managers. Used only where the simpler ones will not suffice. Must use `GridBagConstraints` to define the layout parameters.

`GridLayout` — A layout manager that puts things on a rectangular grid.

`JLabel` — A container for a `String` that appears on a window.

`JPanel` — A container to support the required layout. Used to manage the different layers of layout manager actions required to achieve the desired layout. Actually we could do without many of the instances of `JPanel` in this program. They are used to control the resizing behaviour of the other components such as `JButton` and `JTextField`. If the user resizes any window, we want to ensure that the buttons and things do not get resized. Do this by employing a `JPanel` to act as the re-sizable entity.

`JTextField` — An input mechanism to enable the user to enter a `String`.

In composing GUI components to form a particular window, the components have to be laid out in the window. This can be done manually by specifying a definite location but this can get very tedious indeed. It is far more usual to employ some element of automatic layout managers and this is where `FlowLayout`, `GridBagConstraints`, `GridBagLayout`, `GridLayout` come in: they provide specific algorithms for semi-automated layout. For further details see your favourite AWT reference manual.

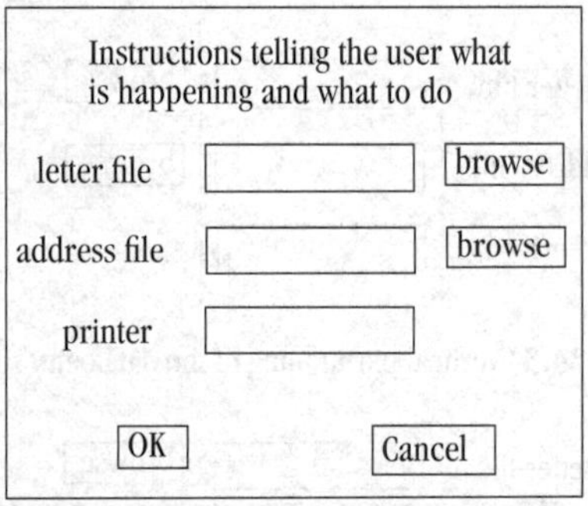

Figure 24.1 Initial mock-up of the opening window.

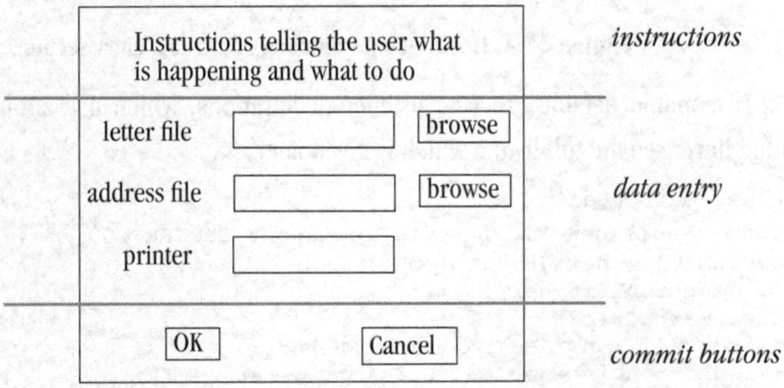

Figure 24.2 Structure of the opening window.

To realize the window design, we first drew the design out on paper. We then imposed a structure hierarchy on this to determine which elements of the design were associated with which so as to define the packing order using JPanels and the layout managers. Taking the opening window that enables the user to specify the letter file, address file and printer options to the execution of the program, the initial design mock-up is shown in Figure 24.1.

We then looked at the alignment of the elements to determine the structure. The first step is to observe that there are three parts to the window stacked vertically: the instruction, the data entry and the commit buttons, as shown in Figure 24.2.

The instructions are just a couple of vertically stacked labels which can be created using the following code:

```
JPanel label = new JPanel(new GridLayout(2, 1)) ;
label.add(new JLabel("Instructions telling the user what")) ;
label.add(new JLabel("is happening and what to do")) ;
```

The JPanel is used as the container into which we add user interface elements guided by the layout manager. In this case we are asking for 2 rows of 1 column using the GridLayout.

The commit buttons are, analogously, JButtons laid out in a JPanel but this time using the left–right flow layout manager. We could also have chosen to use a 1 row of 2 column GridLayout but we choose to use the more flexible FlowLayout, which also tries to keep the

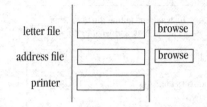

Figure 24.3 Vertical partitioning of the data entry section.

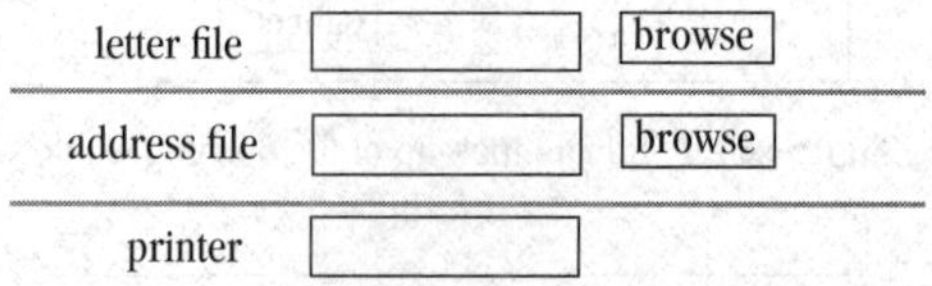

Figure 24.4 Horizontal partitioning of the data entry section.

buttons a reasonable default size (the listener declarations, which use anonymous classes, have been elided here; see the full listing which is given later):

```
JPanel buttonBar =
  new JPanel(new FlowLayout(FlowLayout.CENTER, 50, 5)) ;
JButton b3 = new JButton("OK") ;
b3.addActionListener(...) ;
buttonBar.add(b3) ;
JButton b4 = new JButton("Cancel") ;
b4.addActionListener(new ExitActionListener()) ;
buttonBar.add(b4) ;
JButton b5 = new JButton("Clear") ;
b5.addActionListener(...)
buttonBar.add(b5) ;
```

As you can see, we added a new button labelled 'Clear' — during implementation we realized that we needed a 'reset' button, to clear the current data and restart data entry. With the `FlowLayout` the only change required was to add the button. If we had used the `GridLayout`, we would have had to additionally change the number of columns from 2 to 3 when the layout object was created. Trivial but indicative.

The hard part of all this user interface component layout is the data entry section. There are two ways of partitioning the elements of this section, either vertically where we have a 1 row by 3 column layout of components, each of which is a vertical stack (see Figure 24.3); or horizontally, where we have a vertical stack components, each of which is a left–right flow of elements (see Figure 24.4). The choice is determined by whether we want vertical alignment of the elements or not. In this case we have chosen not to worry about vertical alignment and laid out things as in the latter layout.

The code for doing the layout is as follows (`BrowseButtonActionListener` is an event listener defined in our program; see the full listing later):

```
JPanel letterSelector =
  new JPanel(new FlowLayout(FlowLayout.LEFT)) ;
letterSelector.add(new JLabel("Letter file")) ;
letterSelector.add(letterField) ;
JButton b1 = new JButton("Browse") ;
b1.addActionListener(
```

```
    new BrowseButtonActionListener(letterField)) ;
letterSelector.add(b1) ;
JPanel addressSelector =
    new Panel(new FlowLayout(FlowLayout.LEFT)) ;
addressSelector.add(new JLabel("Address file")) ;
addressSelector.add(addressField) ;
JButton b2 = new JButton("Browse") ;
b2.addActionListener(
    new BrowseButtonActionListener(addressField)) ;
addressSelector.add(b2) ;
JPanel printerSelector =
    new JPanel(new FlowLayout(FlowLayout.LEFT)) ;
printerSelector.add(new JLabel("Printer name")) ;
printerSelector.add(printerField) ;
JPanel editFields = new JPanel(new GridLayout(3, 1, 0, 10)) ;
editFields.add(letterSelector) ;
editFields.add(addressSelector) ;
editFields.add(printerSelector) ;
```

Having created the various sub-components, we are now in a position to put them all together. The complexity introduced here, and hence the reason for using the `GridBagLayout`, is that we want to centre the three elements (instructions, data entry and commit buttons) in the window:

```
setLayout(new GridBagLayout()) ;
GridBagConstraints gbc = new GridBagConstraints() ;
gbc.gridx = 0 ;
gbc.gridy = GridBagConstraints.RELATIVE ;
add(label, gbc) ;
add(new JLabel(), gbc) ;
add(editFields, gbc) ;
add(new JLabel(), gbc) ;
add(buttonBar, gbc) ;
addWindowListener(new ExitWindowAdapter()) ;
```

note

`GridBagLayout` *works by laying out components on a flexible grid specified by the* `GridBagConstraint` *objects provided.*

The two blank labels are added to act as spacing between the three centred, vertically stacked items.

The final phase of activity is to force the size of the window to be exactly the right size to contain all the elements we have laid out into it. This is achieved by 'packing' the elements in the window. Then we ensure the user cannot resize the window, give the window an initial location, and finally, actually put the window up on the screen:

```
pack() ;
setResizable(false) ;
setLocation(50, 50) ;
setVisible(true) ;
```

When the `setVisible(true)` method is executed, because the dialogue box has been declared to be 'modal', the program blocks awaiting the completion of activity of the `FilesSelector` window; control is passed to the user and our program awaits the event of the `FilesSelector` window returning.

So as we can see, laying out a window is a question of understanding the vertical and horizontal relationships between the elements to appear in the window and, in particular, choosing an hierarchical structuring of relationships that allows easy laying out. Anyone used to manipulating boxes in $\text{L\kern-.36em\raise.3ex\hbox{A}\kern-.15em TEX}2\varepsilon$ or TEX, will be very comfortable with these ideas already, as will anyone familiar with the InterViews user interface programming system. The alternative is to try and associate each element individually with a given position on the window. This is a dangerous approach since it is

tip

Avoid explicit positioning of components, use layout managers.

requires great care should the size of the dialogue box, or any component of it, change. The big advantage of the box packing approach is that because much of the window size computation is automatic it is far easier to maintain. Hopefully you will agree that whilst using the hierarchy of automatic layout may seem harder at first but is easier in the end.

The other windows that are part of this application were designed using the same algorithm:

1. draw a design for the window on paper;

2. analyse the box and packing structure;

3. implement the design in Java;

4. test the implementation;

5. reflect on the design and implementation;

6. if satisfied declare a release

7. goto 1

note

This algorithm is an infinite loop. A system is never finished. The only question is how long to wait between stages 6 and 7.

Of course, the design and implementation is never truly finished, just delivered in the current version. We must always be prepared to evolve things further. Indeed, in this application a number of the dialogue boxes were re-worked a number of times during the development.

24.4.3   A Portability Issue

As noted earlier, the 'freezing' of the command-line version of the code and the starting of a version of the code with a GUI is an opportunity to reassess other parts of the system as well as the user interface. We noted earlier that there was an issue about portability, or rather a lack of it: Under testing, the command line version of the application worked fine under UNIX but failed in various places under Windows95/98/NT. Since the author uses the system only on UNIX it could be argued that portability doesn't matter. This may work (just) for amateur personal software but it is a very weak, lame excuse that cannot hold for professionally produced software.

What then were the issues?

Principally it was that the commands issued by the mail merge application to the operating system were hard-wired into the application in a way that militates against portability: there was no 'parameterization' of the command strings. The solution strategy was clear, we introduced the ability to select the commands issued depending on the execution environment. So how did we do this?

The 'obvious' (hackers) way to do this is to have variables for each of the command strings and then select between them at the point of execution. For anyone at all skilled and professional in programming this is so obviously the wrong thing to do that we immediately stop thinking along these lines.

There are in fact a number of different ways of solving this properly depending on which programming language is being used. Since we are looking at Java and object-oriented programming, we take an object-oriented approach. The following is still only one possible solution but it strikes us as being the neatest of those we have thought of.

The core of this solution is to remove responsibility for calling the operating system commands from the application itself and give it to a server object. When the application needs to initiate a command it requests the server object to do it on its behalf. The application has of course set this server up at initialization time at which point it knows which operating system it is working on and therefore which actual server object to instantiate. This server object parameterizes the commands since the actual object is operating system dependent and enables us to be operating system independent within the application code. The following class diagram shows the situation we need to construct:

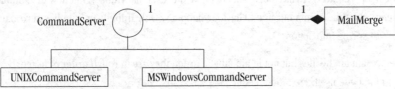

The application constructs one and only one `CommandServer` of the appropriate type that it then uses to service requests for command execution. In fact, there is sufficient commonality between the UNIX and Windows95/98/NT versions of the class that instead of using an interface, we use an abstract class so that there can be code sharing. This avoids replication of code. The actual situation will therefore look like:

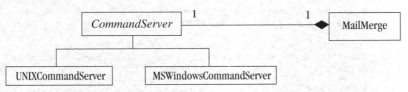

This leaves, of course, the question as to how to select between the two server classes at run-time. This turns out to be very easy since the Java run-time system knows exactly which operating system it is running on and can tell us the required information on demand. The `System` class has a method `getProperty` which delivers up strings that are the values of various system properties. One of those properties is `os.name`, the name of the operating system. Experimentation shows that `SunOS`, `Linux`, `Windows 95` and `Windows NT` are the strings delivered on the systems we have tested.

Thus, at initialization time, we can code things so that we dynamically determine the operating system hosting the application and create an instance of the correct `CommandServer` subclass to service all the requests for command execution.

What we have here, in fact, is a small version of the classic client–server architecture. The mail merge applications is the client and the provider of operating system commands is the server.

note

We are using here features of the design patterns called Abstract Factory and Singleton.

24.4.4   The Source Code

The source code is split into a number of files. They are, in alphabetic order:

```
CommandServer.java, ExitActionListener.java,
ExitWindowAdapter.java, FailedCommandException.java,
FilesSelector.java, MSWindowsCommandServer.java,
MailMerge.java, MessageBox.java, Report.java,
UNIXCommandServer.java
```

Only `MailMerge.java` contains code from the command line version of the program, all other files are associated with the GUI. In perusing this code, you will see that the command line system has not been replaced, it has been added to. If the user uses this version with command line parameters then the command line behaviour happens. Only if the user supplies zero parameters will the GUI spring into action.

We present all the files but not in alphabetic order, they are in rough order of usage, both by the user and the code itself. First then the file `Mailmerge.java`:

Can't use < in documentation comments to get < in the HTML file, must use < instead.

```
import java.io.BufferedReader ;
import java.io.BufferedWriter ;
import java.io.File ;
import java.io.FileReader ;
import java.io.FileWriter ;
import java.io.FileNotFoundException ;
import java.io.IOException ;
import javax.swing.JFrame ;
import javax.swing.JOptionPane ;
//   NB In the following comments use &lt; to represent < so that
//   things work properly in the HTML files generated by javadoc.
/**
 *   A program to do a mail merge of a L<SUP>A</SUP>T<FONT
 *   SIZE=+1><SUB>E</SUB></FONT>X2e letter class template with an
 *   address file.
 *
 *   <P> The address file contains records which contain fields for
 *   name, telephone, fax, email and address.  For each record, the
 *   L<SUP>A</SUP>T<FONT SIZE=+1><SUB>E</SUB></FONT>X2e letter file
 *   (which has been copied into memory) is edited and this edited
 *   letter file "compiled" to DVI, processed to produce PostScript and
 *   then the PostScript file spooled for printing.
 *
 *   <P> The L<SUP>A</SUP>T<FONT SIZE=+1><SUB>E</SUB></FONT>X2e
 *   template is a standard L<SUP>A</SUP>T<FONT
 *   SIZE=+1><SUB>E</SUB></FONT>X2e letter class file but with the
 *   markers &lt;NAME>, &lt;TELEPHONE>, &lt;FAX>, &lt;EMAIL>,
 *   &lt;ADDRESS> replacing actual data.  The address file contains
 *   entries using these markers as introducers, for example:
 *
 *   <PRE>
 *       &lt;NAME> A Person
 *       &lt;TELEPHONE> 0999 1234 1234
 *       &lt;FAX> 0999 4321 4321
 *       &lt;EMAIL> A.Person@somehost.or.other
 *       &lt;ADDRESS> 1 Some Street
 *       A City
 *       CountryX
 *   </PRE>
 *
```

```
 *   <P> Each record in the address file is terminated by a blank line.
 *   The address must be the last field of the record but the others
 *   can appear in any order.  Indeed they can appear many times but
 *   the last entry for each field is the one used.
 *
 *   <P> This program was developed and has been tested with the Live4
 *   distribution under Solaris, the standard installation under Red
 *   Hat Linux 5.2 and MikTeX 1.20 under WindowsNT and Windows95.
 *   Currently it seems to work fine in all three contexts.
 *
 *   <P> There is an interesting issue regarding dvips and printing.
 *   dvips can output directly to a printer or it can output to a file.
 *   To avoid obtaining either no or duplicate printouts we must ensure
 *   that dvips ignores any individual user's setting for dvips and
 *   forces output to a file so that we can be certain that we need to
 *   spool it out explicitly.
 *
 *   <P> In C and C++, the <CODE>system(char*)</CODE> function can be
 *   used to handle the execution of the commands.  This procedure
 *   invokes a shell to interpret the string as a shell command.  This
 *   allows pipelining to be used.  <CODE>Runtime.exec(string)</CODE>
 *   is the obvious analogue in Java but this does not use a shell to
 *   interpret commands.  This has severe consequences as to how
 *   commands are managed: it means no pipelining and no globbing.
 *
 *   <P> NB The print command has to be constructed at run time since
 *   the user may want to specify a particular printer on the command
 *   line.
 *
 *   <P> NB Although this class is a subclass of <CODE>JFrame</CODE> it
 *   is never displayed.  The purpose of it being a <CODE>JFrame</CODE>
 *   is so that it can be the parent of all the dialogue boxes that get
 *   displayed.
 *
 *   @version 1.3  1999.08.07
 *   @author Russel Winder
 */
public class MailMerge extends JFrame {
  /**
   *   The name of this command.  Used for the frame titles in GUI
   *   mode.
   */
  public final static String commandName = "MailMerge" ;
  /**
   *   The string constituting the summary of how to use the command if
   *   you want to use command line arguments.
   */
  private final static String usageString =
    "Usage: MailMerge [[-P...] <letter file> <addresses file>]" ;
  //
  //////////////////////////////////////////////////////////////////////
  //
  //   The global strings relating to the file handling and command
  //   processing.
  /**
   *   The option string for explicitly setting the printer name for
   *   the print spool command.
   */
  private final static String printerParameterPrefix = "-P" ;
  /**
   *   The base name for all the temporary files that will be created
   *   by the L<SUP>A</SUP>T<FONT SIZE=+1><SUB>E</SUB></FONT>X2e
   *   command.
   */
  private final static String tempFileRoot = "temp" ;
  /**
```

The application is an undisplayed JFrame to provide a parent for all the dialogue boxes.

```
    *   The name of the L<SUP>A</SUP>T<FONT
    *   SIZE=+1><SUB>E</SUB></FONT>X2e file that will be constructed
    *   during the mail merge.
    */
private final static String latexFileName = tempFileRoot + ".ltx" ;
/**
    *   The name of the PostScript file.
    */
private final static String psFileName = tempFileRoot + ".ps" ;
//
////////////////////////////////////////////////////////////////////
//
//   The strings to do with template file processing.
/**
    *   The character that starts a merge replacement tag.
    */
private final static char markerStartCharacter = '<' ;
/**
    *   The character that ends a merge replacement tag.
    */
private final static char markerEndCharacter = '>' ;
/**
    *   The name merge replacement tag.
    */
private final static String nameMarker =
    markerStartCharacter + "NAME" + markerEndCharacter ;
/**
    *   The telephone number merge replacement tag.
    */
private final static String telephoneMarker =
    markerStartCharacter + "TELEPHONE" + markerEndCharacter ;
/**
    *   The fax number merge replacement tag.
    */
private final static String faxMarker =
    markerStartCharacter + "FAX" + markerEndCharacter ;
/**
    *   The email address merge replacement tag.
    */
private final static String emailMarker =
    markerStartCharacter + "EMAIL" + markerEndCharacter ;
/**
    *   The postal address merge replacement tag.
    */
private final static String addressMarker =
    markerStartCharacter + "ADDRESS" + markerEndCharacter ;
//
////////////////////////////////////////////////////////////////////
//
//   There are some class scope data items.  This sort of data
//   (accessible to all methods in the class) is usually considered a
//   really bad idea but the justification here is as follows: To
//   create an object (and hence class) to wrap these 4 data items
//   seems like unecessary overkill but we cannot ask a method to
//   return more than one item, thus the data items must be external
//   to the method.  The data items are static since the methods are
//   static and to do otherwise causes error messages from the
//   compiler.
/**
    *   The name in the current record being processed.
    */
private static String name ;
/**
    *   The telephone number in the current record being processed.
    */
private static String telephone ;
```

```
/**
 *  The fax number in the current record being processed.
 */
private static String fax ;
/**
 *  The email address in the current record being processed.
 */
private static String email ;
/**
 *  The postal address in the current record being processed.
 */
private static String address ;
//
////////////////////////////////////////////////////////////////
//
//   The locations for the file names that are extracted from the
//   user.  These have package scope since there are various distinct
//   objects (of differing classes), that need to access them.
/**
 *  The name of the letter template file.
 */
static String letterFileName ;
/**
 *  The name of the addresses file.
 */
static String addressFileName ;
/**
 *  The name of the printer to print to.
 */
static String printerName = "" ;
/**
 *  A boolean to determine whether input output should be done using
 *  a GUI or just on the command console.
 */
private static boolean isGUI = false ;
/**
 *  The root frame of the application.  Only instantiate an object
 *  if we go into GUI mode.
 */
private static MailMerge mm = null ;
/**
 *  The message list object.
 *
 *  Don't show it until it has some output.  Indeed, only
 *  instantiate an object if we go into GUI mode.
 */
private static MessageBox mb = null ;
/**
 *  There has to be a command server to handle all the operating
 *  system specific managing of external programs.
 */
private static CommandServer commandServer =
  CommandServer.getInstance();
//
////////////////////////////////////////////////////////////////
/**
 *  The program start point.
 *
 *  The mail merge action consists of getting the relevant filename
 *  information from the user and then causing the actions to
 *  happen.  The information can be garnered in two ways from the
 *  command line or via a GUI if no command line arguments are given
 *  by the user.
 */
public static void main(final String[] args) {
  // Check for command line arguments.
```

```
if (args.length == 0) {
  //  The user has given no command line parameters so go into GUI
  //  mode to get the filename and printer information from the
  //  user.  In order to proceed beyond this point, we really need
  //  to guarantee that we have non-empty Strings for the
  //  letterFileName and addressFileName variables.  The question
  //  is: Is it the responsibility of the FilesSelector dialogue
  //  box to ensure that this is the case or should the guarantee
  //  be satisfied by a code/loop at this point?  For the moment
  //  we put the responsibility with the dialogue box.
  isGUI = true ;
  mm = new MailMerge() ;
  mb = new MessageBox(commandName + " Messages") ;
  FilesSelector fs = new FilesSelector(mm) ;
} else {
  //  Process the parameters.  Need to keep track of which
  //  parameter is the letter file and which the address file
  //  since we may have a printer specification as one of the
  //  parameters.  NB Unlike C++, the parameter list does not
  //  include the name of the command, just the parameters to it
  //  so the first parameter is in position 0 of the array.
  int letterFileIndex = 0 ;
  //  See if the first parameter starts with
  //  printerParameterPrefix.  If it does then the user has
  //  requested a specific printer so ensure we use it!  We do not
  //  include the printerParameterPrefix in the printerName.
  if (args[0].length() > 2) {
    if (args[0].substring(0, 2).
        compareTo(printerParameterPrefix) == 0) {
      printerName = args[0].substring(2) ;
      letterFileIndex++ ;
    }
  }
  int addressFileIndex = letterFileIndex + 1 ;
  //  Check to make sure we have a viable set of parameters.
  if (addressFileIndex >= args.length) {
    terminate(1, "Too few parameters given.\n" + usageString) ;
  }
  if (addressFileIndex < args.length - 1) {
    information("Excess parameter(s) ignored.") ;
  }
  //  Set up the filenames and the file handles.
  letterFileName = args[letterFileIndex] ;
  addressFileName = args[addressFileIndex] ;
}
//  If we are a GUI then report back to the user, via a pop-up
//  window, the values of the parameters that are being used in
//  this run.  This is a confirmation dialogue, the program blocks
//  until it returns.
if (isGUI) {
  Report r = new Report(mm) ;
}
//  Set up the file handles.
File letterFile = new File(letterFileName) ;
File addressFile = new File(addressFileName) ;
File latexFile = new File(latexFileName) ;
//  Read the letter file into a String so that we need only read
//  the letter file once.  We can use an 'in memory' copy during
//  the processing.
BufferedReader letterReader = null ;
try {
  letterReader = new BufferedReader(new FileReader(letterFile)) ;
}
catch (FileNotFoundException e) {
  terminate(2, "Could not open letter file " +
            letterFileName + ".") ;
```

```
}
StringBuffer letterText = new StringBuffer () ;
while (true) {
  // Get a line from the letter file and enter it into the
  // String. Since readLine removes the newline from the data
  // and we require it to remain since the line structure is
  // important to LaTeX2e, add the newlines back in.
  String currentLine = null;
  try {
    currentLine = letterReader.readLine() ;
  }
  catch (IOException e) {
    terminate(3, "Problem reading letter file.") ;
  }
  if (currentLine == null)
    break ;
  letterText.append(currentLine) ;
  letterText.append('\n') ;
}
// Open the address file and process all the people that the
// address file contains details about.
BufferedReader addressReader = null ;
try {
  addressReader = new BufferedReader(new FileReader(addressFile));
}
catch (FileNotFoundException e) {
  terminate(2, "Could not open address file " +
            addressFileName + ".") ;
}
while (getPerson(addressReader)) {
  // Let the user know the information about this round of
  // merging.
  information("\n    Name: " + name +
             "\n    Telephone: " + telephone +
             "\n    Fax: " + fax +
             "\n    Email: " + email +
             "\n    Address: " + address) ;
  // Open the file to write the amended letter to.
  BufferedWriter latexWriter = null ;
  try {
    latexWriter = new BufferedWriter(new FileWriter(latexFile)) ;
  }
  catch (FileNotFoundException e) {
    terminate(2, "Could not open temporary file " +
              latexFileName + ".") ;
  }
  catch (IOException e) {
    terminate(3, "Problem with input-output on temporary file.") ;
  }
  // We must ensure that LaTeX2e works in batch mode so that if
  // it comes across an error in the processing it does not enter
  // interactive mode. Then we can output the amended letter.
  try {
    latexWriter.write("\\batchmode") ;
    latexWriter.newLine() ;
    latexWriter.write(editMarkers(letterText.toString()));
  }
  catch (IOException e) {
    terminate(4, "Error writing LaTeX2e file.") ;
  }
  // Finished this merge so close things up.
  try {
    latexWriter.close() ;
  }
  catch (IOException e) {
    terminate(3, "Error closing LaTeX2e file.") ;
```

```
    }
    //  Run the latex command, and the printing command then delete
    //  all the temporary files ready for the next letter.
    commandServer.latexToDVI(latexFileName) ;
    commandServer.dviToPostscript(tempFileRoot) ;
    if (printerName.equals("")) {
      commandServer.printFile(psFileName) ;
    } else {
      commandServer.printFile(psFileName, printerName) ;
    }
    commandServer.deleteFiles(tempFileRoot) ;
  }
  try {
    addressReader.close() ;
  }
  catch (IOException e) {
    terminate(5, "Error closing addres file.") ;
  }
  //  Interestingly (!) although the main method is about to
  //  finish, simply returning will not terminate execution since
  //  there are window objects still in existance, in particular the
  //  MessageBox.  We need to terminate some other way.  The
  //  following is inelegant but effective.
  System.exit(0) ;
}
/**
 *  Output a message to the user.  Add this message to the messages
 *  list.
 */
public static void information(final String s) {
  if (isGUI) {
    mb.append(s + '\n') ;
  } else {
    System.out.println(s) ;
  }
}
/**
 *  Output a message to the user and then stop execution.
 */
public static void terminate(final int code, final String s) {
  if (isGUI) {
    //  We have to pass a reference to a Container to act as the
    //  parent of the dialogue.  Pass the (undisplayed) main object.
    JOptionPane.showMessageDialog(mm,
                                  s,
                                  mm.commandName + " Error",
                                  JOptionPane.ERROR_MESSAGE) ;
  } else {
    information(s) ;
  }
  commandServer.deleteFiles(tempFileRoot) ;
  System.exit(code) ;
}
/**
 *  Get the details for the next person.  Can have any number of
 *  lines with any number of markers other than the address marker,
 *  followed by an address the end of which is the end of the
 *  record.  Obviously the last of any duplicates wins.
 */
private static boolean
getPerson(final BufferedReader addressReader) {
  //  Ensure that there is no carry over of information from one
  //  record to the next.
  name = "" ;
  telephone = "" ;
  fax = "" ;
```

```
            email = "" ;
            address = "" ;
            //  Do things until we get to the end of the record.
            boolean completed = false ;
            while (! completed) {
              //  Read a line.  Trim whitespace from both ends, then check to
              //  see which marker the line has.  Store the information to the
              //  appropriate buffer.
              String s = null ;
              try {
                s = addressReader.readLine() ;
              }
              catch (IOException e) {
                terminate(3, "Problem reading address file.") ;
              }
              if (s == null)
                return false ;
              s.trim() ;
              if (s.startsWith(nameMarker)) {
                name =
                 s.substring(s.indexOf(markerEndCharacter)+1).trim();
              } else if (s.startsWith(telephoneMarker)) {
                telephone =
                 s.substring(s.indexOf(markerEndCharacter)+1).trim();
              } else if (s.startsWith(faxMarker)) {
                fax =
                 s.substring(s.indexOf(markerEndCharacter)+1).trim();
              } else if (s.startsWith(emailMarker)) {
                email =
                 s.substring(s.indexOf(markerEndCharacter)+1).trim();
              } else if (s.startsWith(addressMarker)) {
                //  Reached an address.  Get all the lines to the next totally
                //  blank line and treat them as the address.
                StringBuffer sb = new StringBuffer(s.substring(
                  s.indexOf(markerEndCharacter)+1).trim()) ;
                //  Pick up all the rest of the lines of the address up to the
                //  first fully blank line.  This ends the record.
                while(true) {
                  try {
                    s = addressReader.readLine() ;
                  }
                  catch (IOException e) {
                    terminate(3, "Problem reading address file.");
                  }
                  if (s == null)
                    break ;
                  s.trim() ;
                  if (s.length() == 0)
                    break ;
                  //  Add the end of line marker (\\) and a newline to the
                  //  previous line before adding the next one!  NB Must use
                  //  \\ for each \ in \\!
                  sb.append("\\\\\n" + s) ;
                }
                address = sb.toString() ;
                completed = true ;
              } else {
                terminate(3, "Malformed address file.") ;
              }
            }
          }
          return true ;
        }
        /**
         *  Copy the source string to the returned string removing all
         *  markers and replacing them with the appropriate value.
         */
```

```
      private static String editMarkers(String s) {
        StringBuffer sb = new StringBuffer() ;
        while (s.length() != 0) {
          // See if the string actually has any possibility of a marker
          // in it and if not simply copy the line and finish.  If there
          // is the possibility of a marker copy the substring up to that
          // point to the return value and remove it from the string.
          int index = s.indexOf(markerStartCharacter) ;
          if (index < 0) {
            sb.append(s) ;
            break ;
          }
          sb.append(s.substring(0, index)) ;
          s = s.substring(index) ;
          // Check to see if this was entirely spurious, i.e. check to
          // see if there if the potential marker has a proper closing
          // character. If it was spurious simply copy the rest of the
          // line and return.
          index = s.indexOf(markerEndCharacter) ;
          if (index < 0) {
            sb.append(s) ;
            break ;
          }
          // See if the potential marker was in fact a valid marker.  If
          // it was then do the necessary output to the return value,
          // otherwise copy and move on as ever.
          if (s.startsWith(nameMarker)) {
            sb.append(name) ;
          } else if (s.startsWith(telephoneMarker)) {
            sb.append(telephone) ;
          } else if (s.startsWith(faxMarker)) {
            sb.append(fax) ;
          } else if (s.startsWith(emailMarker)) {
            sb.append(email) ;
          } else if (s.startsWith(addressMarker)) {
            sb.append(address) ;
          } else {
            sb.append(s.substring(index)) ;
          }
          // Remove everything we have dealt with from the source string.
          s = s.substring(index+1) ;
        }
        return sb.toString() ;
      }
    }
```

The following is the file `FilesSelector.java`:

```
import java.awt.Container ;
import java.awt.FlowLayout ;
import java.awt.GridBagConstraints ;
import java.awt.GridBagLayout ;
import java.awt.GridLayout ;
import java.awt.event.ActionEvent ;
import java.awt.event.ActionListener ;
import javax.swing.JButton ;
import javax.swing.JDialog ;
import javax.swing.JFileChooser ;
import javax.swing.JLabel ;
import javax.swing.JOptionPane ;
import javax.swing.JPanel ;
import javax.swing.JTextField ;
/**
 *  The way of selecting the letter file name, the address file name
 *  and the printer name.
 *
```

```
 *   @version 1.1 1998.08.29
 *   @author Russel Winder
 */
class FilesSelector extends JDialog {
  /**
   *  The place for the user to enter the string that is the name of
   *  the file containing the template letter.
   */
  private final JTextField letterField = new JTextField(20) ;
  /**
   *  The place for the user to enter the string that is the name of
   *  the file containing the addresses.
   */
  private final JTextField addressField = new JTextField(20) ;
  /**
   *  The place for the user to enter the string that is the name of
   *  the printer to be used for printing.
   */
  private final JTextField printerField = new JTextField(20) ;
  /**
   *  The constructor.  In fact, this does all the work; once the
   *  constructor terminates the dialog has completed.
   *
   *  <P> NB The parameter MUST be final since it is used by spawned
   *  listeners of inner class type.
   */
  public FilesSelector(final MailMerge mm) {
    // Set up the Window itself with the Window title.  This has to
    // done here as calls to super have to be the first action in the
    // constructor.  Make the dialogue modal.
    super(mm, mm.commandName + " Files Selection", true) ;
    // Set up the JPanel with the instructions to the user.  The text
    // is formatted using JLabels and a simple vertical layout policy
    // for ease and simplicity.  NB The strings used in each JLabel
    // have been partitioned for no other reason than that we need to
    // make the code fit onto a printed page and still be a
    // completely compilable program.  THIS IS A COMPLETE HACK AND
    // SHOULD NEVER BE DONE IN A REAL PROGRAM.
    JPanel label = new JPanel(new GridLayout(4, 1)) ;
    label.add(new JLabel("")) ;
    label.add(new JLabel("Please enter the names of the " +
                         "letter file, the address file")) ;
    label.add(new JLabel("and, if the default is not to be " +
                         "used, the printer name.")) ;
    label.add(new JLabel("")) ;
    // Set up the letter file name, address file name and printer
    // name interaction boxes.  Wrap each component in a JPanel so
    // that the elements do not themselves get re-sized if the user
    // re-sizes the FilesSelector box.  Associate a listener with
    // each button to provide the necessary actions when the user
    // presses the button.  NB BrowseButtonActionListener is an inner
    // class of this one and hence has a parent reference to its
    // instantiating parent.  Every listener has to know who its
    // parent is after all!
    JPanel letterSelector =
     new JPanel(new FlowLayout(FlowLayout.LEFT)) ;
    letterSelector.add(new JLabel("Letter file")) ;
    letterSelector.add(letterField) ;
    JButton letterBrowseButton = new JButton("Browse") ;
    letterBrowseButton.addActionListener(
      new BrowseButtonActionListener(letterField)) ;
    letterSelector.add(letterBrowseButton) ;
    JPanel addressSelector =
     new JPanel(new FlowLayout(FlowLayout.LEFT)) ;
    addressSelector.add(new JLabel("Address file")) ;
    addressSelector.add(addressField) ;
```

```
JButton addressBrowseButton = new JButton("Browse") ;
addressBrowseButton.addActionListener(
  new BrowseButtonActionListener(addressField)) ;
addressSelector.add(addressBrowseButton) ;
JPanel printerSelector =
 new JPanel(new FlowLayout(FlowLayout.LEFT)) ;
printerSelector.add(new JLabel("Printer name")) ;
printerSelector.add(printerField) ;
// Arrange the interaction JPanels into a nice layout in a
// JPanel.
JPanel editFields = new JPanel(new GridLayout(3, 1)) ;
editFields.add(letterSelector) ;
editFields.add(addressSelector) ;
editFields.add(printerSelector) ;
// Set up a button bar.  The OK button causes the FilesSelector
// to be terminated but execution to continue. The Clear button
// causes the field to be reset to the empty string but the
// dialogue to remain the current focus.  The Cancel button is an
// exit button and causes execution of the command to terminate.
// NB Anonymous classes are used here to save on the number of
// defined classes.  It allows the action declaration to be close
// to where the action is.  Remember that these are inner classes
// and therefore keep a reference to their parent.  Any variable
// usage or associated method calls not understandable in the
// current object are assumed to be for the parent, cf. use of
// parent variable and dispose and repaint method calls.
JPanel buttonBar =
 new JPanel(new FlowLayout(FlowLayout.CENTER, 50, 5)) ;
JButton okButton = new JButton("OK") ;
okButton.addActionListener(
  new ActionListener() {
    // The action of this listener.  We have the responsibility
    // of ensuring that letterField and addressField are non-null
    // Strings so we test for this and if either are null we do
    // not exit the dialogue.  If the user is getting frustrated
    // they can always terminate the program.  Since this is a
    // modal dialogue, we have this power.  We set the data
    // fields in the parent MailMerge object from the data
    // entered into the various fields of the dialogue box.  We
    // then dispose of ourself since we have served our purpose.
    public void actionPerformed(ActionEvent event) {
      // Get the strings from our dialogue and behave in the
      // right way depending on non-emptiness.
      String letterString = letterField.getText() ;
      String addressString = addressField.getText() ;
      if (letterString.equals("") || addressString.equals("")) {
        // At least on of the string was empty. Give
        // appropriate error messages and then make the user
        // continue filling in the dialogue.
        String message = "" ;
        if (letterString.equals("")) {
          message += "Must specify a letter file name. " ;
        }
        if (addressString.equals("")) {
          message += "Must specify an address file name.";
        }
        JOptionPane.showMessageDialog(FilesSelector.this,
                                      message) ;
        repaint() ;
      } else {
        // The strings were non-empty so fill the appropriate
        // variable in our dialogue's parent (remember we are
        // the listener).
        mm.letterFileName = letterString ;
        mm.addressFileName = addressString ;
        mm.printerName = printerField.getText() ;
```

```
                    dispose() ;
                }
            }
        }
        ) ;
    buttonBar.add(okButton) ;
    JButton clearButton = new JButton("Clear") ;
    clearButton.addActionListener(
        new ActionListener() {
            // The action of this listener.  When this button is pushed,
            //  the user has asked us to clear all the fields in our
            //  parent dialogue, so do it and refresh the window.  Since
            //  we are an inner class we have a reference to our
            //  containing parent.
            public void actionPerformed(ActionEvent event) {
                letterField.setText("") ;
                addressField.setText("") ;
                printerField.setText("") ;
                repaint() ;
            }
        }
        ) ;
    buttonBar.add(clearButton) ;
    JButton cancelButton = new JButton("Cancel") ;
    cancelButton.addActionListener(new ExitActionListener()) ;
    buttonBar.add(cancelButton) ;
    // Now add the three elements (the user instructions, the three
    //  interaction boxes with their buttons, and the button bar) to
    //  the main FilesSelector window.  To get the look we want, we
    //  use a full GridBagLayout.  Do things to the contentPane not
    //  the Window.
    Container myPane = getContentPane() ;
    myPane.setLayout(new GridBagLayout()) ;
    // We want the items in the container to appear one under the
    //  other.
    GridBagConstraints gbc = new GridBagConstraints() ;
    gbc.gridx = 0 ;
    gbc.gridy = GridBagConstraints.RELATIVE ;
    // Actually add things in.  Use a blank JLabel as padding.
    myPane.add(label, gbc) ;
    myPane.add(editFields, gbc) ;
    myPane.add(buttonBar, gbc) ;
    // Ensure that the window listens to the events the window
    //  manager sends us.  In fact we only listen out for termination
    //  events, we ignore all the others.
    addWindowListener(new ExitWindowAdapter()) ;
    // Set the size by packing, mark the window as not re-sizable and
    //  then show the window.
    pack() ;
    setResizable(false) ;
    setLocation(50, 50) ;
    setVisible(true) ;
}
/**
 * The action for all browse buttons is the same so we have a
 * common class from which to instantiate the various listener
 * objects.
 *
 * <P> This is an inner class and therefore objects of this class
 * have access to their instLantiating parent's state.  Every
 * listener does have to know who its parent is after all!
 */
private class BrowseButtonActionListener
    implements ActionListener {
    /**
     * Have to remember which field we have been asked to fill.
```

```
         */
        private final JTextField fieldToSet ;
        /**
         * The constructor.  The listener has to know which field it is
         * being asked to fill when it is put into action.  We have to
         * remember which one it is when we are set up so that we can
         * access it when called upon to do so.
         */
        public BrowseButtonActionListener(final JTextField field) {
          fieldToSet = field ;
        }
        /**
         * The listener's action.  When the button is pressed, set off a
         * JFileChooser and await its completion.  When we are in charge
         * again grab the information and put it into the field we were
         * asked to fill and refresh the FilesSelector so that the new
         * information appears on the user's screen.
         */
        public void actionPerformed(final ActionEvent event) {
          JFileChooser jfc =
           new JFileChooser(System.getProperty("user.dir", "user.home")) ;
          jfc.setLocation(25, 25) ;
          // The parent of the JFileChooser is the FilesSelector (which
          // is a JDialog) which we can access since we are an inner
          // class of it and therefore have a containment relationship
          // with our parent.  JFileChoosers disappear automatically when
          // the showDialog method returns.
          if (jfc.showDialog(FilesSelector.this, "File Select") ==
              JFileChooser.APPROVE_OPTION) {
            fieldToSet.setText(jfc.getSelectedFile().getName()) ;
          }
          repaint() ;
        }
      }
    }
  }
```

The file Report.java:

```
    import java.awt.Container ;
    import java.awt.FlowLayout;
    import java.awt.GridBagLayout;
    import java.awt.GridBagConstraints;
    import java.awt.GridLayout;
    import java.awt.event.ActionEvent ;
    import java.awt.event.ActionListener ;
    import javax.swing.JButton ;
    import javax.swing.JDialog ;
    import javax.swing.JLabel ;
    import javax.swing.JPanel ;
    /**
     * A brief report to tell the user what is happening.
     *
     * @version 1.1 1998.08.29
     * @author Russel Winder
     */
    class Report extends JDialog {
      /**
       * The constructor.
       */
      public Report(final MailMerge mm) {
        // Even though this is a dialogue just for information, we make
        // it blocking (i.e. modal) so that the user has the opportunity
        // to crash out if they got it wrong.  Put everything, especially
        // JButtons, into JPanels so that they are easily packable and
        // don't have unexpected re-sizing behaviour.
        super(mm, mm.commandName + " Confirmation", true) ;
```

```
       Container myPane = getContentPane() ;
       //  The three items of information that we are giving the user.
       JPanel infoPanel = new JPanel(new GridLayout(3, 1)) ;
       JPanel letterPanel =
        new JPanel(new FlowLayout(FlowLayout.LEFT)) ;
       letterPanel.add(new JLabel("Letter file:")) ;
       letterPanel.add(new JLabel(mm.letterFileName)) ;
       JPanel addressPanel =
        new JPanel(new FlowLayout(FlowLayout.LEFT)) ;
       addressPanel.add(new JLabel("Address file:")) ;
       addressPanel.add(new JLabel(mm.addressFileName)) ;
       JPanel printerPanel =
        new JPanel(new FlowLayout(FlowLayout.LEFT)) ;
       printerPanel.add(new JLabel("Printer:")) ;
       printerPanel.add(new JLabel(mm.printerName)) ;
       infoPanel.add(letterPanel) ;
       infoPanel.add(addressPanel) ;
       infoPanel.add(printerPanel) ;
       //  We pause the activity by requiring OK button to be pressed to
       //  continue.  As ever the Cancel button causes program
       //  termination.
       JPanel buttonPanel = new JPanel(new FlowLayout()) ;
       JButton okButton = new JButton("OK") ;
       okButton.addActionListener(
         new ActionListener() {
           public void actionPerformed(ActionEvent event) {
               //  All we have to do is let things continue so we dispose
               //  of ourself and just let it all happen.
               dispose() ;
            }
         }
         ) ;
       buttonPanel.add(okButton) ;
       JButton cancelButton = new JButton("Cancel") ;
       cancelButton.addActionListener(new ExitActionListener()) ;
       buttonPanel.add(cancelButton) ;
       //  We want the items in the Frame to appear centred one under the
       //  other with the two panels of different heights.
       myPane.setLayout(new GridBagLayout()) ;
       GridBagConstraints gbc = new GridBagConstraints() ;
       gbc.gridx = 0 ;
       gbc.gridy = GridBagConstraints.RELATIVE ;
       myPane.add(infoPanel, gbc) ;
       myPane.add(buttonPanel, gbc) ;
       //  Ensure that the window listens to the events the window
       //  manager sends us.  In fact we only listen out for termination
       //  events, we ignore all the others.
       addWindowListener(new ExitWindowAdapter()) ;
       //  Set the size by packing, attempt to mark the window as not
       //  re-sizable and then show the window.
       pack() ;
       setResizable(false) ;
       setLocation(50, 50) ;
       setVisible(true) ;
    }
 }
```

The file MessageBox.java:

```
  import java.awt.BorderLayout ;
  import java.awt.Container ;
  import java.awt.event.ActionEvent ;
  import java.awt.event.ActionListener ;
  import javax.swing.JButton ;
  import javax.swing.JFrame ;
  import javax.swing.JPanel ;
```

```java
import javax.swing.JTextArea ;
/**
 *  The text area into which all the information messages are put.
 *
 *  @version 1.1 1998.08.29
 *  @author Russel Winder
 */
class MessageBox extends JFrame {
  /**
   *  The JTextArea that will actually hold the messages.
   */
  private JTextArea ta = new JTextArea(20, 25) ;
  /**
   *  The constructor.
   */
  public MessageBox(final String s) {
    //  Set up a read-only text area to hold the messages.
    //  Have a Hide button that simply hides the window.  Put the
    //  button into a JPanel so that it doesn't start changing its
    //  size and shape.  Add the necessary listener.
    super(s) ;
    ta.setEditable(false) ;
    Container myPane = getContentPane() ;
    myPane.setLayout(new BorderLayout()) ;
    myPane.add(BorderLayout.CENTER, ta) ;
    JPanel buttonPanel = new JPanel() ;
    JButton hide = new JButton("Hide") ;
    hide.addActionListener(
      new ActionListener() {
        public void actionPerformed(ActionEvent event) {
          setVisible(false) ;
        }
      }
      ) ;
    buttonPanel.add(hide) ;
    myPane.add(BorderLayout.SOUTH, buttonPanel) ;
    //  Set the size by packing, mark the window as re-sizable.  Do
    //  not show this window at this time.  The window is constructed
    //  at load time and we need to wait to show it until the
    //  application needs it.
    pack() ;
    setResizable(true) ;
    setLocation(50, 250) ;
  }
  /**
   *  Add a new message to the message window.
   */
  public void append(final String s) {
    //  Add the message to the text area and then show the window to
    //  let the user know that something has happened.
    ta.append(s) ;
    setVisible(true) ;
  }
}
```

The file `ExitWindowAdapter.java`:

```java
import java.awt.event.WindowAdapter ;
import java.awt.event.WindowEvent ;
/**
 *  The class for constructing listeners for window closing events.
 *
 *  <P> The behaviour implemented here is to ignore all events other
 *  than close events and to terminate the application immediately and
 *  with severe prejudice when a close event is received.
 *
```

```
 *   <P> A listener of this sort must conform to the
 *   <CODE>WindowListener</CODE> interface.  Fortunately, we do not
 *   have to implement all the necessary methods since there is a
 *   class, <CODE>WindowAdapter</CODE>, which conforms to
 *   <CODE>WindowListener</CODE> and provides the default of ignore for
 *   all events.  By inheriting from <CODE>WindowAdapter</CODE> we need
 *   only override the method for handling close events.
 *
 *   @version 1.0 1998.10.09
 *   @author Russel Winder
 */
public class ExitWindowAdapter extends WindowAdapter {
  /**
   *   Process a close event by terminating the application.
   */
  public void windowClosing(final WindowEvent event) {
    System.exit(0) ;
  }
}
```

The file `ExitActionListener.java`:

```
import java.awt.event.ActionEvent ;
import java.awt.event.ActionListener ;
/**
 *   The class for creating listeners for quit button action signals.
 *
 *   The action performed by a listener of this class is to terminate
 *   the application immediately and with severe prejudice.
 *
 *   @version 1.0 1998.10.09
 *   @author Russel Winder
 */
public class ExitActionListener implements ActionListener {
  /**
   *   Button was pressed, terminate the application.
   */
  public void actionPerformed(final ActionEvent event) {
    System.exit(0) ;
  }
}
```

The file `CommandServer.java`:

```
import java.io.IOException ;
/**
 *   An abstract class that acts as the superclass of all actual
 *   <CODE>CommandServer</CODE> types.  We choose to implement
 *   <CODE>CommandServer</CODE> as a Singleton since there is no point
 *   in having multiple copies: There can only be one!  All defaults
 *   are defined here.
 *
 *   <P> For more details of design patterns (Singleton, etc.) see one
 *   of: Roberts & Winder (forthcoming) Java: Idioms, Patterns and
 *   Architectures, Wiley; Gamma et al. (1995) Design Patterns, Addison
 *   Wesley; Buschmann et al. (1996) Pattern-oriented Software
 *   Architecture, Wiley; Grand (1999) Patterns in Java, vol 1, Wiley.
 *
 *   @version 1.0  1999.08.05
 *   @author Russel Winder
 */
abstract class CommandServer {
  /**
   *   The L<SUP>A</SUP>T<FONT SIZE=+1><SUB>E</SUB></FONT>X2e command.
   *   Assumed to take a single parameter, the L<SUP>A</SUP>T<FONT
   *   SIZE=+1><SUB>E</SUB></FONT>X2e source file and to deliver up a
```

```
 *   DVI file with the same root as the source file and a dvi
 *   extension.
 */
protected String latexCommand = "latex" ;
/**
 *   The dvips command for transforming a DVI file into a PostScript
 *   file.  Assumes that a -o option is available to name the output
 *   file.
 */
protected String dvipsCommand = "dvips" ;
/**
 *   The reference to the actual object that is the server.
 */
private static CommandServer instance = null ;
/**
 *   Provide an accessor method for the Singleton object that is the
 *   server of coommands to the mail merge application.
 *
 *   <P> It is here that the decision is made as to which operating
 *   system the application is running on and hence which actual type
 *   we need an instance of for the command processor.  Clearly there
 *   is coupling here between the strings returned by the runtime
 *   system and the types we require.  We could get very
 *   sophisticated here to remove the coupling but it is probably not
 *   really justified.  If there was great dynamism in terms of the
 *   number of options, it would be worth the effort.  However, since
 *   the number of different operating systems is small and slowly
 *   changing, it does not seem worth the extra effort to obtain the
 *   greater protection for portability.
 *
 *   @exception RuntimeException when the operating system name
 *   string (the os.name property) is not one that is known about.
 */
public static CommandServer getInstance() {
  if (instance == null) {
    String osName = System.getProperty("os.name") ;
    if (osName.equals("SunOS") ||
        osName.equals("Linux")) {
      instance = new UNIXCommandServer () ;
    } else if (osName.equals("Windows NT") ||
          osName.equals("Windows 95")) {
      instance = new MSWindowsCommandServer () ;
    } else
      throw new RuntimeException ("Unrecognized OS name.") ;
  }
  return instance ;
}
/**
 *   Perform the act of creating the DVI file from a
 *   L<SUP>A</SUP>T<FONT SIZE=+1><SUB>E</SUB></FONT>X2e source file.
 *
 *   <P> This method produces a DVI file with the same file name root
 *   as the file name provided as parameter.
 *
 *   @exception FailedCommandException when there is any error
 *   starting or executing the latexCommand command.
 */
public void latexToDVI(final String latexFileName)
  throws FailedCommandException {
  executeCommand(latexCommand + "  " + latexFileName) ;
}
/**
 *   Perform the act of creating the PostScript file from the DVI
 *   file.
 *
 *   <P> The parameter is the root name.  The DVI file will be
```

```
 *   root.dvi and the PostScript file will be root.ps.
 *
 *   @exception FailedCommandException when there is any error
 *   starting or executing the dviPSCommand command.
 */
public void dviToPostscript(final String fileNameRoot)
  throws FailedCommandException {
  executeCommand(dvipsCommand + " -o " + fileNameRoot + ".ps " +
                 fileNameRoot + ".dvi") ;
}
/**
 *   Perform the act of printing a file to the default printer.
 *
 *   @exception FailedCommandException when there is any error
 *   starting or executing the print command.
 */
public abstract void printFile(final String fileName)
  throws FailedCommandException ;
/**
 *   Perform the act of printing a file to a specified printer.
 *
 *   @exception FailedCommandException when there is any error
 *   starting or executing the print command.
 */
public abstract void printFile(final String fileName,
                               final String printerName)
  throws FailedCommandException ;
/**
 *   Perform the act of deleting all files with a given file name
 *   root.  All files with this root, no matter what the extension,
 *   will be deleted.
 *
 *   @exception FailedCommandException when there is any error
 *   starting or executing the remove command.
 */
public abstract void deleteFiles(final String fileNameRoot)
  throws FailedCommandException ;
/**
 *   Set off an external command supplied as a <CODE>String</CODE>.
 *   Having spawned the process, wait for it to terminate, check the
 *   return code and terminate if there was a problem.
 *
 *   <P> The command is executed directly as is by the operating
 *   system.
 *
 *   <P> NB MUST ensure that the commands terminate before the next
 *   begins hence the <CODE>waitFor()</CODE>.
 *
 *   @exception FailedCommandException when there is any error
 *   starting or executing the command.
 */
protected void executeCommand(final String command)
  throws FailedCommandException {
  //  Inform the user about what is happening.
  MailMerge.information(command) ;
  //  Initiate a sub-process to execute the command.
  Process process = null ;
  try {
    process = Runtime.getRuntime().exec(command) ;
  }
  catch (IOException e) {
    MailMerge.information("Problem starting execution of \"" +
                         command + "\".") ;
    throw new FailedCommandException () ;
  }
  //  Wait for the process to finish, i.e. for the command to
```

```java
    //  complete.
    try {
      process.waitFor() ;
    }
    catch (InterruptedException e) {
      MailMerge.information(
        "Waiting on command execution interrupted.") ;
    }
    //  Check the return value from the process to see if the command
    //  completed in what it thinks was a satisfactory manner.
    if (process.exitValue() != 0) {
      MailMerge.information("Execution of \"" +
                            command + "\" failed.") ;
      throw new FailedCommandException () ;
    }
  }
  /**
   *  Execute a command supplied as an array of <CODE>String</CODE>s.
   *  Having spawned the process, wait for it to terminate, check the
   *  return code and terminate if there was a problem.
   *
   *  @exception FailedCommandException when there is any error
   *  starting or executing the command.
   */
  protected void executeCommand(final String[] commandArray)
    throws FailedCommandException {
    //  Construct a String representation of the command by
    //  flattening, i.e. concatenate all the strings in the array.
    StringBuffer temp = new StringBuffer () ;
    for (int i = 0 ; i < commandArray.length ; i++) {
      temp.append(commandArray[i] + " ") ;
    }
    String command = temp.toString() ;
    //  Inform the user about what is happening.
    MailMerge.information(command) ;
    //  Initiate a sub-process to execute the command
    Process process = null ;
    try {
      process = Runtime.getRuntime().exec(commandArray) ;
    }
    catch (IOException e) {
      MailMerge.information("Problem starting execution of \"" +
                            command + "\".") ;
      throw new FailedCommandException () ;
    }
    //  Wait for the process to finish, i.e. for the command to
    //  complete.
    try {
      process.waitFor() ;
    }
    catch (InterruptedException e) {
      MailMerge.information(
        "Waiting on command execution interrupted.") ;
    }
    //  Check the return value from the process to see if the command
    //  completed in what it thinks was a satisfactory manner
    if (process.exitValue() != 0) {
      MailMerge.information("Execution of \"" +
                            command + "\" failed.") ;
      throw new FailedCommandException () ;
    }
  }
}
```

The file `UNIXCommandServer.java`:

```
/**
 *   A class to implement the services required for the mail merge
 *   system for a UNIX machine.
 *
 *   @version 1.0  1999.08.07
 *   @author Russel Winder
 */
class UNIXCommandServer extends CommandServer {
  /**
   *   Instances of this class can only be constructed by the abstract
   *   superclass so as to support the Singleton nature of the command
   *   server.  Cannot make this constructor private or there could be
   *   no instances at all!
   */
  protected UNIXCommandServer() { }
  /**
   *   The command for actually printing out a file.
   *
   *   <P> NB It is assumed that the printer is a PostScript printer
   *   and/or that all the usual printer spooler transformation filters
   *   to transform PostScript into printer language are in place and
   *   active.
   */
  protected String printCommand = "lpr  -h" ;
  /**
   *   Perform the act of printing a file to the default printer.
   *
   *   @exception FailedCommandException when there is any error
   *   starting or executing the print command.
   */
  public void printFile(final String fileName)
    throws FailedCommandException {
    executeCommand(printCommand + " " + fileName) ;
  }
  /**
   *   Perform the act of printing a file to a specified printer.
   *
   *   @exception FailedCommandException when there is any error
   *   starting or executing the print command.
   */
  public void printFile(final String fileName,
                        final String printerName)
    throws FailedCommandException {
    executeCommand(printCommand + " -P" + printerName +
                " " + fileName) ;
  }
  /**
   *   Perform the act of deleting all files with a given file name
   *   root.  All files with this root, no matter what the extension,
   *   will be deleted.  Need to use a shell for this one to get the
   *   globbing.
   *
   *   @exception FailedCommandException when there is any error
   *   starting or executing the remove command.
   */
  public void deleteFiles(final String fileNameRoot)
    throws FailedCommandException {
    String[] commandArray =  {
      "sh", "-c", "rm -f " + fileNameRoot + ".*"
    };
    executeCommand(commandArray) ;
  }
}
```

The file MSWindowsCommandServer.java:

```java
/**
 * An class to implement the services required for the mail merge
 * system for a Windows machine.
 *
 * @version 1.0  1999.08.07
 * @author Russel Winder
 */
class MSWindowsCommandServer extends CommandServer {
  /**
   * Instances of this class can only be constructed by the abstract
   * superclass so as to support the Singleton nature of the command
   * server.  Cannot make this constructor private or there could be
   * no instances at all!
   */
  protected MSWindowsCommandServer() { }
  /**
   * The command for actually printing out a file.
   *
   * <P> Most Windows printers are not PostScript printers so we have
   * to use a mechanism that not only allows spooling but also
   * transformation of PostScript into the printer language.  There
   * is no standard way in Windows of doing this so we must employ an
   * imported mechanism.  GhostScript and its wrapper Ghostview
   * provide such a facility.
   */
  protected String printCommand = "C:/GSTools/GSView/gsview32.exe" ;
  /**
   * Perform the act of printing a file to the default printer.
   *
   * @exception FailedCommandException when there is any error
   * starting or executing the print command.
   */
  public void printFile(final String fileName)
    throws FailedCommandException {
    executeCommand(printCommand + " /F " + fileName) ;
  }
  /**
   * Perform the act of printing a file to a specified printer.
   *
   * @exception FailedCommandException when there is any error
   * starting or executing the print command.
   */
  public void printFile(final String fileName,
                        final String printerName)
    throws FailedCommandException {
    executeCommand(printCommand + " /S\"" + printerName + "\" " +
                   fileName) ;
  }
  /**
   * Perform the act of deleting all files with a given file name
   * root.  All files with this root, no matter what the extension,
   * will be deleted. Need to use a shell for this one to get the
   * globbing.
   *
   * @exception FailedCommandException when there is any error
   * starting or executing the remove command.
   */
  public void deleteFiles(final String fileNameRoot)
    throws FailedCommandException {
    String[] commandArray =  {
      "command.com", "/c", "del", fileNameRoot + ".*"
    };
    executeCommand(commandArray) ;
  }
}
```

The file `FailedCommandExcpetion.java`:

```
/**
 *   A class to represent the exception of attempting to start a
 *   command via the operating system.
 *
 *   @version 1.0 1998.08.04
 *   @author Russel Winder
 */
class FailedCommandException extends RuntimeException {
  /**
   *   The exception without a message.
   */
  public FailedCommandException() {
    super() ;
  }
  /**
   *   The exception with a message.
   */
  public FailedCommandException(final String s) {
    super(s) ;
  }
}
```

To show how this application's user interface looks, we present two sets of screen dumps, one of a Solaris 2.6 invocation (Figure 24.5) and one of a WindowsNT invocation (Figure 24.6) of the same program. It is important to bear in mind that the mail merge program that was run when the images where captured on the two different systems, was not only created from the same source code (`.java` files) but used the same compiled code (`.class` files). The different window systems and operating systems lead to different window decoration but the contents of the windows are the same.

24.4.5 Testing

The test strategy for this version of the application is very much the same as for the previous one. We test the user interface components and then the mail merge functionality. Since the mail merge code is essentially identical to the previous version it should work exactly as the previous version did. But we must not make the assumption that it does. We must actually run all the tests so that we have confidence in the program.

Testing the user interface is a little more complicated than previously but follows the same approach. We must test all the command line configurations exactly as before. Except for the case of zero parameters we should get the same behaviour as before. With zero parameters of course we get the GUI appearing. We need to test all possible types of user input following the same principle of exhaustively trying all possibilities. This is not actually hard but it must be done. If we do not we can have no confidence in the program.

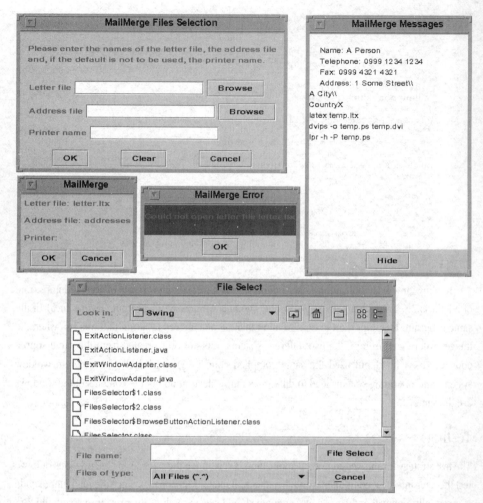

Figure 24.5 Screen dumps of the `MailMerge` windows as appear under Solaris2.5.1. These are the images of the classes `FilesSelection`, `Report`, `MessageBox` and `TerminatingDialog`.

24.5 Summary

In this chapter we have investigated a straightforward complete application. From a brief analysis of the problem via a rough design, we prototyped a command line based version of the application. This showed how command line arguments can be managed and how files can be manipulated. The core algorithms also showed how some simple string manipulation can be achieved. The mechanism for calling upon other commands at the operating system level was also shown.

The simplicity and lack of GUIness of the interface was then addressed and an evolution of the application undertaken by adding a windows-based user interface to the application. This showed the use of the Java AWT and Swing for creating graphical user interfaces in a platform independent

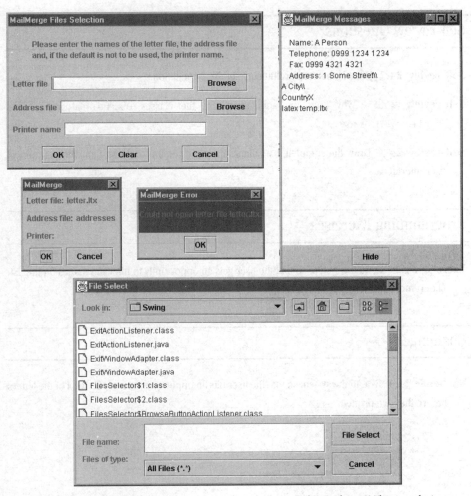

Figure 24.6 Screen dumps of the `MailMerge` windows as appear under WindowsNT. These are the images of the classes `FileSelection`, `Report`, `MessageBox` and `TerminatingDialog`.

manner — the same code runs on a Solaris/X-Windows platform and a Windows95/98/NT platform completely unchanged.

This portability of user interface code in itself makes Java, with AWT and Swing, the language of choice for developing applications with a user interface.

Having developed this prototype, we really ought now to carry out a user interface evaluation in order to determine any required changes and continue the evolution of the application. Evaluations are not that difficult, simply involving asking a set of users to make use of the product in a way that enables data concerning use of the application to be obtained. Describing the various techniques is outside the scope of this book but any good book on human–computer interaction will describe them or give pointers to descriptions of the techniques. Some such books are listed in the bibliography.

Self-review Questions

Self-review 24.1 What is the core architecture of this application?

Self-review 24.2 Why does the application use the classes `BufferedReader` and `BufferedWriter`?

Self-review 24.3 Draw the complete UML diagram for the version of the system with a graphical user interface.

Programming Exercises

Exercise 24.1 Extend the system so that the user gets an opportunity to filter the names on the list, (i.e. remove individual potential recipients, before the mail merge is done).

Challenges

Challenge 24.1 Extend the system so that the user has an opportunity to see previews of the letters before they are printed.

Pedestrian Crossing Simulation

25

Objectives

This chapter presents a small case study of the first few stages of the development of a program to simulate a pedestrian crossing. The intention is to expose some of the processes of systems development as much as illustrating how to write Java programs.

Keywords

Swing

AWT

simulation

traffic flow

modelling

thread

25.1   Introduction

The problem that will be tackled in this chapter is, perhaps, not an everyday one. In fact, one of the authors started it simply as an exercise in Java programming, an exercise guaranteed to make use of almost all the principal features of the Java language. It has developed into, what we think is, a fun tutorial case study.

The background rationale to the problem is that transport studies people need to be able to experiment with models of traffic systems to try and assess the effects of various parameters on traffic and people flow in a traffic system. For example, these people use sophisticated simulators backed by sophisticated statistical models to predict the effects that different timings of traffic lights have on expected flows in a given system. We are not about to try and build a complete simulator but we have identified a small sub-problem that could contribute to an overall system.

The problem tackled here is to simulate, on the computer, a single light-controlled pedestrian crossing across a single carriageway road, with a single lane in each direction. As you can see we are specifying and constraining the problem so that it is as simple as it can be.

To start, we give a rough specification of the problem. This specification contains enough to begin developing the program but it is not entirely complete. Furthermore, there are aspects of the problem and the solution which are not immediately apparent. These are the indicators, in a relatively small problem like this anyway, that an exploratory approach would be appropriate. Another term might be *evolutionary prototyping*. The aim is to quickly develop some part of the solution that works and then to evolve that, all the time having something that works, until sufficient of the solution is developed to deem the problem solved. In a way, we saw aspects of this in the previous study.

Following this approach, we do a rough top-down analysis and design sufficient to highlight the major components that will be needed in the final system. We then construct some of the components and ensure they work as required. We next plug the components together to make the first full prototype. This is then developed somewhat, showing how to proceed further.

25.2   The Initial Problem Specification

Figure 25.1 shows the layout of the sort of light-controlled pedestrian crossing that is to be simulated. The traffic lights normally allow the vehicles to flow (i.e. the traffic lights are on green). When a pedestrian button is pressed, there is some delay and then a sequencing of the lights occurs. First the traffic lights halt the traffic, then the pedestrian lights allow pedestrians priority on the crossing for a period. Then the traffic is allowed to flow again. The problem is to provide a simulation of this with the crossing displayed on the screen as an animated image.

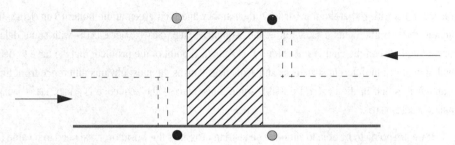

Figure 25.1 A light-controlled pedestrian crossing on a right-hand drive road. The pedestrian crossing itself is the hatched area. The solid circles represent the lights controlling the traffic. The grey-shaded circles represent the pedestrian lights. The dashed lines represent the standard road markings, with the arrows indicating the source and direction of travel of the traffic.

25.3 The Initial Thinking

Finding the basic objects and hence classes for this problem is relatively straightforward: the 'things' in the problem are traffic lights, pedestrian lights, vehicles, pedestrians and the crossing. These are clearly the components we need to build: we need to develop classes for each of these types so that we can build a simulation model by instantiating objects from them. The lights seem to be the easiest so lets start by considering them.

25.3.1 Lights

The first and most obvious observation we can make about the control lights we have in this problem (i.e. both traffic and pedestrian lights) is that the same basic technology underlies both. Each type of light is a collection of light bulbs placed in some arrangement, each having a different colour and/or display shape. At any one time one or more of the lights will be either full on or flashing. Although there are separate light bulbs for each of the colours, people generally talk of the traffic light as a whole, saying things like "the light has changed colour". The collection of bulbs is being seen as an abstraction as though it were a single bulb that changed its output — an interesting analogy with the notion of abstraction we have been discussing all the way through this book!

This is leading us to the conclusion that there is a base concept 'control light' and then variations of it like 'traffic light' and 'pedestrian light'. We can either model this using inheritance; treat it as some form of conformance; or choose to ignore it and model traffic and pedestrian lights separately. It is impossible to choose at this time as we have insufficient information to actually make a choice. We need to probe the problem further.

25.3.2 Traffic Lights

Traffic lights around the world are all very different, there is no absolute commonality of structure or behaviour. However, perhaps the most common sort of traffic light, at least those controlling traffic at junctions and pedestrian crossings, is a trio of vertically (or occasionally horizontally) placed lights with red at the top (or left), then amber and then green at the bottom (or right). In action, these traffic lights usually follow the sequence <RED, GREEN, AMBER, RED> with some delay occurring between the changes of colour. It is actually a point of the problem that we have to deal with a plethora of different structures and sequences. For us the most obvious difference from this 'standard' is that in the UK (and possibly some other places) the sequence is <RED, RED+AMBER, GREEN, AMBER, RED>.

If we are going to be able to simulate pedestrian crossings the world over, we need to be able to simulate any sort of traffic light. This could be a job either for an interface with a number of classes that conform to it or it could be a job for inheritance, where a default light is provided which gives the functionality of the most usual case and different lights are subclasses, modifying the behaviour as needed. Consider the following points:

- A large number of countries have basically the same structure and sequencing to their traffic lights; this can be captured in a standard traffic light class from which all country specific lights could be inherited.

- Using USA and UK as examples, a traffic light in the USA is a form of traffic light as is a traffic light in the UK. A UK traffic light is not, however, a form of USA traffic light, nor vice versa, they are just different. Thus, it is not appropriate to relate UK and USA traffic lights directly by inheritance but they are both forms of traffic light so it is appropriate to define a generic interface that they both conform to or inherit both from a common abstract superclass.

- A traffic light with a filter (left and/or right filter that allows green for certain lanes of traffic when the main traffic is halted at red) is a traffic light and hence it is appropriate to make the traffic light with a filter a subclass of the traffic light.

This seems to lead us to a design using either an interface `TrafficLight` that a collection of country specific lights will conform to or a class `StandardTrafficLight` which acts as a superclass for all the traffic light classes. Special traffic lights, such as ones with filters, will be subclassed from a more general traffic light.

The next decision that needs to be considered before we can think about prototyping is: Should the traffic lights be totally self-contained sub-systems or should they be sub-systems reacting to an outside agency? Let us investigate some of the issues.

We start with the observation that there appear to be two varieties of traffic lights. There are those that you find at traffic junctions that sequence from red through their colours back to red, wait a while and then do it again. Then there are those that are used at pedestrian lights which are green until told to sequence, at which time they sequence to red, wait a while whilst the pedestrian lights sequence to green for a while and then sequence back to green to stay there until another event happens. This implies there needs to be some direct action on the light from outside agencies.

The next observation to make is that any traffic system controlled by lights must be controlled by a central sequencer which knows about which light is where at the junction of crossing: it is not possible to allow the lights to run totally independently — the whole point of the light system is to provide coordinated behaviour. The sequencer provides the central knowledge of the junction or crossing and the coordination and management of the lights' behaviour. Hence, it is not appropriate to try and make the traffic lights entirely self-contained. However, it is right and proper, and very much the object-oriented way, that we try and encapsulate as much as possible.

We could make the traffic light be a relatively passive object (simply a set of light bulbs) manipulated directly by a sequencer or we could make the light be an active thing that has its own active behaviour managed by the sequencer — the details of the behaviour are encapsulated in the traffic light, the sequencer does not need knowledge of the internal structure of the light. The former approach does not really encapsulate in the way we have come to believe is appropriate but it is probably easier to envision and initially implement such a system. With the latter approach, the traffic light maintains its own state, and is in control of the actual sequencing, a nice encapsulation. The sequencer will, however, need to program the sequence (essentially state the timings of the various changes of state) and then initiate it, so the lights must have an element of programmable behaviour; there needs to be an element of openness (or "unencapsulatedness") to the traffic light. The point is that there is coupling between lights and sequencer that no amount of encapsulation can remove. The final comment to make here is that the number of light states and changes is not the same for all lights. By encapsulating this within an active light, we remove some of the detail that the sequencer needs to know about the light. In effect this approach modularizes responsibility which is a good thing in improving comprehensibility and hence maintainability and evolvability of the system.

If we follow this 'active light' approach then for safety reasons, essentially to ensure that the lights do not get out of synchronization, the lights must not sequence entirely independently but must sequence between synchronization points managed by the sequencer. At each synchronization point the sequencer has total control and no light is active. Following this line is not only a good safety measure but gives the added benefit that we can change behaviours of all the lights at this point, for example to implement different timing behaviour at different times of day.

25.3.3 Pedestrian Lights

Pedestrian lights are both very much the same as traffic lights and very different from traffic lights. The similarities are such that it is likely that some behaviours will be the same for all lights. It therefore makes sense to introduce a common super-type (probably an interface), let us call it ControlLight. Pedestrian lights are different from traffic lights in that they usually have only two lights with either the sequence <RED, GREEN> (or in the UK <RED, GREEN, *flashing*GREEN>) — sometimes what is labelled as green here is physically white but green is a reasonable abstraction.

There is (at first sight) another fundamental difference between traffic lights and pedestrian lights: traffic lights are sequenced continuously whereas pedestrian lights are only sequenced when a request button is pressed. This is specific to pedestrian crossings, of course. Pedestrian crossing lights at a major traffic junction are sequenced with the rest of the traffic lights. Well, except that sometimes (late at night usually) they are not, the traffic lights sequence ignores the pedestrian lights unless the button is pressed.

Observation indicates that this sort of 'sequence on request' behaviour is also exhibited by some traffic lights — for some major/minor road junctions, the major road is normally green and the minor road red with the sequencing happening only when a vehicle on the minor road approaches the junction. Sensors under the road act as the 'button press' requesting a sequencing.

What we are leading up to here is a common architecture for all lights and junctions: lights sit waiting in a state until told to sequence by the sequencer. The sequencer may receive input events from buttons, or other sensors, requesting sequencing action. We have achieved a level of generality in this architecture that it may well be appropriate for all control lights not just the pedestrian light we are trying to control. Clearly this is a good thing. The extra time taken to create the generic architecture will definitely be rewarded as we try and tackle more and more complex situations. To solve only the pedestrian crossing problem is to leave a collection of difficulties for later.

25.4 A First Pass

As with any problem solving, there is the temptation to try and solve the whole problem before beginning implementation ('paralysis by analysis') or, conversely, to wade into implementation before enough thinking has been done ('hacking'). We need some middle ground. We have tried to think about most of the major issues in an attempt to make sure we have a sufficiently general architecture that reuse and extension will be possible but we have to recognize that not all issues can be tackled or even known about before we start designing and implementing the system components. We have to recognize that sometimes, particularly with the exploratory approach we are following here, that we will come to points at which we need to throw away the current implementation and start again. The point here is that the implementation is a codification of knowledge about the solution to the problem and that as more information and knowledge is obtained we might have to completely redesign the code.

With this in mind we start on an implementation, as much to gain more information and knowledge than anything else. Figure 25.2 tries to capture the knowledge gained so far by indicating the class structure that we are about to implement, which is a text-based version (the program will display text messages in the console to show its progress) to see if the structure is viable — also to see if we forgot anything.

First we declare the ControlLight interface:

```
/**
 *  Any variety of control light (traffic lights, pedestrian lights,
 *  etc.) must conform to this interface.
 *
 *  @version 1.1 1997.08.14
 *  @author Russel Winder
 */
```

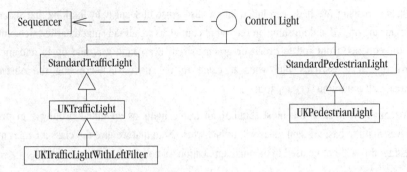

Figure 25.2 An initial class diagram.

```
public interface ControlLight {
  /**
   *  Set the wait periods between colour changes.  Units are
   *  seconds.
   *
   *  <P> It is assumed that the user of this method on a given object
   *  knows what sequence that particular light follows, i.e. what
   *  type of light this is, in order to know what waits to set.  This
   *  violates encapsulation is some sense but is sensible, indeed
   *  necessary.
   */
  void setWaits(int[] waits) ;
  /**
   *  Initiate a sequencing of the light according to the currently
   *  set wait periods from the colour it is now back to the same
   *  colour.
   */
  void sequence() ;
  /**
   *  Initiate a sequencing of the light terminating with the
   *  specified colour according to the currently set wait periods.
   */
  void sequenceTo(int colour) ;
  /**
   *  An exception for when there is problem with the wait time
   *  initialization.
   */
  static class WaitsInitializationException
    extends RuntimeException {
    public WaitsInitializationException() { super() ; }
    public WaitsInitializationException(final String s) { super(s) ; }
  }
  /**
   *  An exception for when there is an attempt to use an illegal
   *  colour.
   *
   *  <P> We need this since colours are represented by
   *  <CODE>int</CODE> values, Java does not have enumerated types or
   *  sub-range types.
   */
  static class IllegalColourException
    extends RuntimeException {
    public IllegalColourException() { super() ; }
    public IllegalColourException(final String s) { super(s) ; }
  }
}
```

Notice that this is version 1.1 of the interface: Version 1.0 did not have the `sequenceTo` method. It became painfully obvious that this had been missed out when we came to build the initial

pedestrian crossing. We had been lulled into a false sense of security by thinking that sequencing
meant starting on red and finishing on red but of course, as we already noted earlier, we sometimes
need to sequence from red to green or green to red. Everything was fine up to and including
constructing a crossroads but when it came to the pedestrian crossing the absence of
sequenceTo became very apparent.

We can now declare the most standard of traffic lights as an initial prototype to prove to
ourselves that the basic design ideas will in fact work. Note that we give the class a main method
for testing; this will not be used in the final application, of course.

```
/**
 *  Perhaps the most common traffic light, certainly used in USA,
 *  Canada, France, Germany.
 *
 *  @version 1.1 1999.08.09
 *  @author Russel Winder
 */
public class StandardTrafficLight implements ControlLight {
    //  We don't need to define all the possible colours here, we can
    //  add more as we subclass.  It's a pity Java doesn't have
    //  enumerated types, it would save a lot of hassle in checking the
    //  colour representations were legal if it did.  We should perhaps
    //  construct a generic sub-range type in order to enforce the limit
    //  on the number of values in the type, however, this has not been
    //  done.
    /**
     *  The constant representing the state RED.
     */
    public final static int RED = 0 ;
    /**
     *  The constant representing the state GREEN.
     */
    public final static int GREEN = 1 ;
    /**
     *  The constant representing the state AMBER.
     */
    public final static int AMBER = 2 ;
    /**
     *  The current state of this light.  Default to RED for safety.
     */
    protected int currentState = RED ;
    /**
     *  The array of seconds to wait on a given colour before moving
     *  to the next colour.
     */
    protected int[] delay = new int[3] ;
    /**
     *  The default constructor.  This is only here to support the
     *  inheritance hierarchy it must never be called explicitly.
     *
     *  <P> Because <CODE>setWaits</CODE> is dynamically bound, we
     *  cannot afford to call it in superclass constructors when
     *  constructing subclasses only in that subclass constructor --
     *  otherwise there will be attempts to construct the wrong size of
     *  array for <CODE>delay</CODE>.  This means that subclasses must
     *  not call their superclass constructor but Java insists that we
     *  do.  We therefore provide this constructor as a null
     *  constructor.
     */
    protected StandardTrafficLight() { }
    /**
     *  The constructor that takes an array of waits.  The array must
```

```java
 *   contain 3 entries.
 */
public StandardTrafficLight(final int[] waits) {
  setWaits(waits) ;
}
/**
 *   The constructor that requires the creating code to specify the
 *   initial state.
 *
 *   @param r_w the RED wait time.
 *   @param g_w the GREEN wait time.
 *   @param a_w the AMBER wait time.
 */
public StandardTrafficLight(final int r_w,
                            final int g_w,
                            final int a_w) {
  this(new int[] {r_w, g_w, a_w}) ;
}
/**
 *   Set the wait periods between colour changes.  Units are
 *   seconds.
 *
 *   @param waits contains the waits for the different colours in
 *   the order RED, GREEN, AMBER.
 *   @exception ControlLight.WaitsInitializationException if the
 *   number of items in the array is not correct for this light or if
 *   any of the entries are negative.
 */
public void setWaits(final int[] waits) {
  if (waits.length != 3) {
    throw new ControlLight.WaitsInitializationException
      ("Array size was " + waits.length + " not 3.") ;
  }
  for (int i = 0 ; i < waits.length ; i++) {
    if (waits[i] < 0)
      throw new ControlLight.WaitsInitializationException
        ("Wait value was negative.") ;
  }
  System.arraycopy(waits, 0, delay, 0, 3) ;
}
/**
 *   Initiate a sequencing of the light according to the currently
 *   set wait periods from the colour it is now back to the same
 *   colour.
 */
public void sequence() {
  sequenceTo(currentState) ;
}
/**
 *   Initiate a sequencing of the light terminating with the
 *   specified colour according to the currently set wait periods.
 *
 *   @exception ControlLight.IllegalColourException if ever we are in
 *   a state with a colour we did not think possible.
 */
public void sequenceTo(final int colour) {
  System.out.print(toString() + "...") ;
  do {
    switch (currentState)  {
    case RED:
      waitAWhile(delay[RED]) ;
      currentState = GREEN ;
      break ;
    case GREEN:
      waitAWhile(delay[GREEN]) ;
      currentState = AMBER ;
```

```
      break ;
    case AMBER:
      waitAWhile(delay[AMBER]) ;
      currentState = RED ;
      break ;
    default:
      //  This cannot happen.
      throw new ControlLight.IllegalColourException () ;
    }
    System.out.print(toString() + "...") ;
  } while (colour != currentState) ;
  System.out.println() ;
}
/**
 *  Print out the value of the light.  Need this in this
 *  implementation in order to do the i/o of the example!
 *
 *  @exception ControlLight.IllegalColourException if ever we are in
 *  a state with a colour we did not think possible.
 */
public String toString() {
  String returnValue  = null ;
  switch (currentState)  {
  case RED:
    returnValue = "red" ;
    break ;
  case GREEN:
    returnValue = "green" ;
    break ;
  case AMBER:
    returnValue = "amber" ;
    break ;
  default:
    //  This should not happen.
    throw new ControlLight.IllegalColourException () ;
  }
  return returnValue ;
}
/**
 *  We need to wait a while on many occasions.
 */
public void waitAWhile(final int delay) {
  //  The sequencing requires that we can wait for a given period.
  //  The Thread class provides a static method to do this so just
  //  use it.  We catch the exception that might be thrown.  Units
  //  must be transformed from seconds to milliseconds.
  try {
    Thread.sleep(1000*delay) ;
  }
  catch (InterruptedException e) {
    System.out.println("Interrupted Exception") ;
  }
}
/**
 *  Force the light to a given colour.  A very dangerous
 *  activity this so don't allow general use.
 *
 *  @param colour the colour to set the state of the light to.
 *  @exception ControlLight.IllegalColourException if the argument
 *  does not represent a legal colour.
 */
private void setState(final int colour) {
  if ((colour < 0) || (colour > 2)) {
    throw new ControlLight.IllegalColourException () ;
  }
  currentState = colour ;
```

```
    }
    /**
     *  For testing this class we provide a main method.
     */
    public static void main(final String[] args) {
        StandardTrafficLight l = new StandardTrafficLight (4, 4, 2) ;
        l.sequence() ;
    }
}
```

We can use the code we have so far to model a crossroads, basically as a test that we are getting things essentially correct. This is, in effect, a sequencer but one with a very trivial algorithm.

```
/**
 *  Simulate a very trivial crossroads using the standard traffic
 *  lights.
 *
 *  @version 1.1 1999.08.09
 *  @author Russel Winder
 */
public class CrossroadsStandard {
    public static void main(final String args[]) {
        int[] sequenceWaits = {2, 5, 2};
        StandardTrafficLight leftright =
         new StandardTrafficLight (sequenceWaits) ;
        StandardTrafficLight updown =
         new StandardTrafficLight (sequenceWaits) ;
        while (true) {
            System.out.print("LeftRight: ") ;
            leftright.sequence() ;
            System.out.print("UpDown: ") ;
            updown.sequence() ;
        }
    }
}
```

The above crossroads simulation will probably be recognizable to readers in USA, Canada, France, Germany and many other countries. UK citizens, and possibly many others, on the other hand, may not recognize such a junction. To show that the architecture and design will work, we show how a general UK traffic light can be constructed in this text-based implementation.

```
/**
 *  A basic UK traffic light.
 *
 *  @version 1.1 1999.08.09
 *  @author Russel Winder
 */
public class UKTrafficLight extends StandardTrafficLight {
    // The possible colour states are amended by one.  Note that the
    // integers representing the colours are not the order in which the
    // colours occur, unlike in StandardTrafficLight.
    /**
     *  RED+AMBER to be added to the possible states of the traffic
     *  light.
     */
    public final static int REDAMBER = 3 ;
    /**
     *  The default constructor.  This is only here to support the
     *  inheritance hierarchy it must never be called explicitly.
     *
     *  <P> Because <CODE>setWaits</CODE> is dynamically bound, we
     *  cannot afford to call it in superclass constructors when
     *  constructing subclasses only in that subclass constructor --
```

```
   *  otherwise there will be attempts to construct the wrong size of
   *  array for <CODE>delay</CODE>.  This means that subclasses must
   *  not call their superclass constructor but Java insists that we
   *  do.  We therefore provide this constructor as a null
   *  constructor.
   */
  protected UKTrafficLight() { }
  /**
   *  The constructor that takes an array of waits.  The array must
   *  contain 4 entries.
   */
  public UKTrafficLight(final int[] waits) {
    delay = new int[4] ;
    setWaits(waits) ;
  }
  /**
   *  The constructor that requires the creating code to specify the
   *  initial state.
   *
   *  @param r_w the RED wait time.
   *  @param ra_w the RED+AMBER wait time.
   *  @param g_w the GREEN wait time.
   *  @param a_w the AMBER wait time.
   */
  public UKTrafficLight(final int r_w,
                        final int ra_w,
                        final int g_w,
                        final int a_w) {
    this(new int[] {r_w, ra_w, g_w, a_w}) ;
  }
  /**
   *  Set the wait periods between colour changes.  Units are
   *  seconds.
   *
   *  @param waits contains the waits for the different colours in the
   *  order RED, REDAMBER, GREEN, AMBER.
   *  @exception ControlLight.WaitsInitializationException if the
   *  number of items in the array is not correct for this light or if
   *  any of the entries are negative.
   */
  public void setWaits(final int[] waits) {
    if (waits.length != 4) {
      throw new ControlLight.WaitsInitializationException
        ("Array size was " + waits.length + " not 4.") ;
    }
    for (int i = 0 ; i < waits.length ; i++) {
      if (waits[i] < 0)
        throw new ControlLight.WaitsInitializationException
          ("Wait value was negative.") ;
    }
    //  The user gives the waits in sequence order which is not
    //  actually the order of the elements in the array.  We therefore
    //  have to be careful when we copy the values.
    delay[RED] = waits[0] ;
    delay[REDAMBER] = waits[1] ;
    delay[GREEN] = waits[2] ;
    delay[AMBER] = waits[3] ;
  }
  /**
   *  Initiate a sequencing of the light terminating with the
   *  specified colour according to the currently set wait periods.
   *
   *  @exception ControlLight.IllegalColourException if ever we are in
   *  a state with a colour we did not think possible.
   */
  public void sequenceTo(final int colour) {
```

```
      System.out.print(toString() + "...") ;
      do {
        switch (currentState)  {
        case RED:
          waitAWhile(delay[RED]) ;
          currentState = REDAMBER ;
          break ;
        case REDAMBER:
          waitAWhile(delay[REDAMBER]) ;
          currentState = GREEN ;
          break ;
        case GREEN:
          waitAWhile(delay[GREEN]) ;
          currentState = AMBER ;
          break ;
        case AMBER:
          waitAWhile(delay[AMBER]) ;
          currentState = RED ;
          break ;
        default:
          // This cannot happen.
          throw new ControlLight.IllegalColourException () ;
        }
        System.out.print(toString() + "...") ;
      } while (colour != currentState) ;
      System.out.println() ;
    }
    /**
     * Print out the value of the light.  Need this in this
     * implementation in order to do the i/o of the example!
     *
     * @exception ControlLight.IllegalColourException if ever we are in
     * a state with a colour we did not think possible.
     */
    public String toString() {
      String returnValue = null ;
      switch (currentState)  {
      case RED:
        returnValue = "red" ;
        break ;
      case REDAMBER:
        returnValue = "redamber" ;
        break ;
      case GREEN:
        returnValue = "green" ;
        break ;
      case AMBER:
        returnValue = "amber" ;
        break ;
      default:
        // This should not happen.
        throw new ControlLight.IllegalColourException () ;
      }
      return returnValue ;
    }
    /**
     * Force the light to a given colour.  A very dangerous
     * activity this so don't allow general use.
     *
     * @param colour the colour to set the state of the light to.
     * @exception ControlLight.IllegalColourException if the argument
     * does not represent a legal colour.
     */
    private void setState(final int colour) {
      if ((colour < 0) || (colour > 3)) {
        throw new ControlLight.IllegalColourException () ;
```

```
      }
      currentState = colour ;
    }
    /**
     *  For testing this class we provide a main method.
     */
    public static void main(final String[] args) {
      UKTrafficLight l = new UKTrafficLight (4, 2, 4, 2) ;
      l.sequence() ;
    }
  }
```

Not all traffic lights are this straightforward; many throughout the world have extra bulbs in filters. The modelling mechanism is exactly as for the UKTrafficLight. We make use of inheritance to extend the capabilities of the light. As an example, we show here UKTrafficLightWithFilter:

```
  /**
   *  A basic UK traffic light but with a single filter as well.
   *
   *  @version 1.1 1999.08.09
   *  @author Russel Winder
   */
  public class UKTrafficLightWithFilter extends UKTrafficLight {
    /**
     *  The current state of this light.  Default to RED for safety.
     */
    public final static int REDWITHFILTER = 4 ;
    /**
     *  The current state of this light.  Default to RED for safety.
     */
    public final static int REDAMBERWITHFILTER = 5 ;
    /**
     *  The default constructor.  This is only here to support the
     *  inheritance hierarchy it must never be called explicitly.
     *
     *  <P> Because <CODE>setWaits</CODE> is dynamically bound, we
     *  cannot afford to call it in superclass constructors when
     *  constructing subclasses only in that subclass constructor --
     *  otherwise there will be attempts to construct the wrong size of
     *  array for <CODE>delay</CODE>.  This means that subclasses must
     *  not call their superclass constructor but Java insists that we
     *  do.  We therefore provide this constructor as a null
     *  constructor.
     */
    protected UKTrafficLightWithFilter() { }
    /**
     *  The constructor that takes an array of waits.  The array must
     *  contain 5 entries.
     */
    public UKTrafficLightWithFilter(final int[] waits) {
      // NB We must make this the size of the possible number of
      //  colours even though some are impossible states (REDAMBER in
      //  this case).
      delay = new int[6] ;
      setWaits(waits) ;
    }
    /**
     *  The constructor that takes the waits individually.
     *
     *  @param r_w the RED wait time.
     *  @param rwf_w the RED with filter GREEN wait time.
     *  @param rawf_w the RED+AMBER with filter GREEN wait time.
     *  @param g_w the GREEN wait time.
```

```
 *   @param a_w the AMBER wait time.
 */
public UKTrafficLightWithFilter(final int r_w,
                                final int rwf_w,
                                final int rawf_w,
                                final int g_w,
                                final int a_w) {
  this(new int[] {r_w, rwf_w, rawf_w, g_w, a_w}) ;
}
/**
 *   Set the wait periods between colour changes.  Units are
 *   seconds.
 *
 *   @param waits contains the waits for the different colours in the
 *   order RED, REDWITHFILTER, AMBERWITHFILTER, GREEN, AMBER.
 *   @exception ControlLight.WaitsInitializationException if the
 *   number of items in the array is not correct for this light or if
 *   any of the entries are negative.
 */
public void setWaits(final int[] waits) {
  if (waits.length != 5) {
    throw new ControlLight.WaitsInitializationException
      ("Array size was " + waits.length + " not 5.") ;
  }
  for (int i = 0 ; i < waits.length ; i++) {
    if (waits[i] < 0)
      throw new ControlLight.WaitsInitializationException
        ("Wait value  was negative.") ;
  }
  //  The user gives the waits in sequence order which is not
  //  actually the order of the elements in the array.  We therefore
  //  have to carefully copy the values.  Although we have only 5
  //  possible states our superclass has a state that we do not use.
  //  We must take it into account.
  delay[RED] = waits[0] ;
  delay[REDAMBER] = 0 ;
  delay[REDWITHFILTER] = waits[1] ;
  delay[REDAMBERWITHFILTER] = waits[2] ;
  delay[GREEN] = waits[3] ;
  delay[AMBER] = waits[4] ;
}
/**
 *   Initiate a sequencing of the light terminating with the
 *   specified colour according to the currently set wait periods.
 *
 *   @exception ControlLight.IllegalColourException if ever we are in
 *   a state with a colour we did not think possible.
 */
public void sequenceTo(final int colour) {
  System.out.print(toString() + "...") ;
  do {
    switch (currentState)  {
    case RED:
      waitAWhile(delay[RED]) ;
      currentState = REDWITHFILTER ;
      break ;
    case REDWITHFILTER:
      waitAWhile(delay[REDWITHFILTER]) ;
      currentState = REDAMBERWITHFILTER ;
      break ;
    case REDAMBERWITHFILTER:
      waitAWhile(delay[REDAMBERWITHFILTER]) ;
      currentState = GREEN ;
      break ;
    case GREEN:
      waitAWhile(delay[GREEN]) ;
```

```
                      currentState = AMBER ;
                      break ;
                    case AMBER:
                      waitAWhile(delay[AMBER]) ;
                      currentState = RED ;
                      break ;
                    default:
                      // This cannot happen.
                      throw new ControlLight.IllegalColourException () ;
                    }
                    System.out.print(toString() + "...") ;
                  } while (colour != currentState) ;
                  System.out.println() ;
                }
                /**
                 * Print out the value of the light. Need this in this
                 * implementation in order to do the i/o of the example!
                 *
                 * @exception ControlLight.IllegalColourException if ever we are in
                 * a state with a colour we did not think possible.
                 */
                public String toString() {
                  String returnValue = null ;
                  switch (currentState)  {
                  case RED:
                    returnValue = "red" ;
                    break ;
                  case REDWITHFILTER:
                    returnValue = "redwithfilter" ;
                    break ;
                  case REDAMBERWITHFILTER:
                    returnValue = "redamberwithfilter" ;
                    break ;
                  case GREEN:
                    returnValue = "green" ;
                    break ;
                  case AMBER:
                    returnValue = "amber" ;
                    break ;
                  default:
                    // This should not happen.
                    throw new ControlLight.IllegalColourException () ;
                  }
                  return returnValue ;
                }
                /**
                 * Force the light to a given colour. A very dangerous
                 * activity to use this method though.
                 *
                 * @param colour the colour to set the state of the light to.
                 * @exception ControlLight.IllegalColourException if the argument
                 * does not represent a legal colour.
                 */
                private void setState(final int colour) {
                  if ((colour < 0) || (colour > 5)) {
                    throw new ControlLight.IllegalColourException () ;
                  }
                  currentState = colour ;
                }
                /**
                 * For testing this class we provide a main method.
                 */
                public static void main(final String[] args) {
                  UKTrafficLightWithFilter l =
                   new UKTrafficLightWithFilter (4, 2, 2, 4, 2) ;
                  l.sequence() ;
```

```
        }
    }
```

All very satisfactory. But what about some pedestrian lights? The implementation of these are essentially identical to the traffic lights but forming a separate type hierarchy. We believe the code is so similar to that for the traffic lights that it would serve no useful purpose to present the code here. We leave it as an 'exercise for the student' to construct the relevant classes that are needed for the following, which is our first pedestrian crossing simulation:

```java
import java.io.IOException ;
/**
 *  Simulate a very trivial pedestrian crossing using the standard
 *  traffic lights.
 *
 *  @version 1.1 1999.08.09
 *  @author Russel Winder
 */
public class CrossingStandard {
  public static void main(final String args[])
    throws IOException {
    StandardTrafficLight traffic =
     new StandardTrafficLight (2, 5, 2 ) ;
    StandardPedestrianLight pedestrian =
     new StandardPedestrianLight (2, 4 ) ;
    while (true) {
      System.out.print("Traffic: ") ;
      traffic.sequenceTo(StandardTrafficLight.GREEN) ;
      System.out.print(
"Awaiting keystroke to represent pedestrian light button push.") ;
      System.in.read() ;
      traffic.sequenceTo(StandardTrafficLight.RED) ;
      System.out.print("Pedestrian: ") ;
      pedestrian.sequenceTo(StandardPedestrianLight.RED) ;
    }
  }
}
```

This looks like a reasonable state for the end of this round of evolution. Unfortunately, on testing the system, it appears to suffer from an item of bizarre behaviour when running under Windows95/ NT. The lights sequence and wait for a keystroke as the pedestrian request button exactly as expected but when the return key is pressed the lights perform two cycles — it appears to the program that the single keystroke is in fact two. This does not happen running the same compiled code under Solaris 2.6. Under that operating system, pressing the return key causes a single cycling exactly as expected. This difference in behaviour is caused by a difference in the way that Windows and UNIX represent the end of a line of text. Windows uses two characters whereas UNIX uses only one. Since the operating systems convert a stroke of the return key into the end of line sequence before giving it to the program, it actually gets two keystrokes for single key press under Windows. It is small differences like this that make thorough testing essential if a Java application is going to reliably run on a number of different platforms. True platform independence is not here yet!

We could progress this textual version of the system, making the simulation more detailed, but we choose instead to look at making things graphical first.

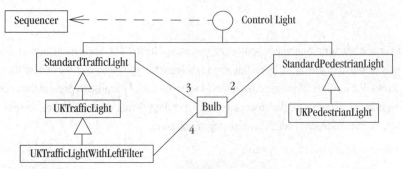

Figure 25.3 An evolved class diagram to take account of the graphical representation.

25.5   A Second Round

The problem we tackle next is to construct a graphical rather than text-based implementation. As the first step, we create (using the AWT and Swing packages) a representation of the traffic lights and pedestrian button as independent windows. Figure 25.3 shows the evolution of the class diagram to incorporate the notion of a control light being comprised of bulbs.

We achieve the graphics for the lights by creating light bulbs with the ability to be switched on and off plus some colouring determined at creation time, and then creating some number of them in some arrangement (usually just a vertical order) exactly as the real lights are. The `Bulb` type is:

```java
import java.awt.Canvas ;
import java.awt.Color ;
import java.awt.Graphics ;
/**
 *  A light bulb is a circle of colour on a square <CODE>Canvas</CODE>
 *  background.  Each bulb has an on colour and an off colour and can
 *  be switched on and off.
 *
 *  @version 1.0 1997.08.15
 *  @author Russel Winder
 */
class Bulb extends Canvas {
  /**
   *  The <CODE>Color</CODE> representing on.
   */
  private final Color onColour ;
  /**
   *  The <CODE>Color</CODE> representing off.
   */
  private final Color offColour ;
  /**
   *  The current state of the <CODE>Bulb</CODE>.
   */
  private Color colour ;
  /**
   *  The constructor of a <CODE>Bulb</CODE>.  Remember the on and
   *  off colours, set the size of the <CODE>Canvas</CODE> and the
   *  background colour for the square space that the circle is
   *  drawn on.
   */
  public Bulb(final Color on_c, final Color off_c) {
    onColour = on_c ;
```

```
      offColour = off_c ;
      //  Must force the size of a Bulb so that the light units get
      //  sensibly sized.
      setSize(50, 50) ;
      setBackground(new Color (163, 163, 163)) ;
    }
    /**
     *  The <CODE>Canvas</CODE> redraw method.  We do not call this
     *  directly, it gets called by the runtime system as part of the
     *  repaint method call.
     */
    public void paint(final Graphics g) {
      g.setColor(colour) ;
      //  For some reason 5+5+40 (=50) does not centre the circular blob
      //  of colour on the size 50 background.  Experimentally it is
      //  determined that 35 is the appropriate size for a 5 offset.
      g.fillOval(5, 5, 35, 35) ;
    }
    /**
     *  Switch the bulb on.  Set the state then ask the
     *  <CODE>Canvas</CODE> that we are to redraw ourself.
     */
    public void on() {
      colour = onColour ;
      repaint() ;
    }
    /**
     *  Switch the bulb off.  Set the state then ask the
     *  <CODE>Canvas</CODE> that we are to redraw ourself.
     */
    public void off() {
      colour = offColour ;
      repaint() ;
    }
  }
```

Of course we have to change all the traffic light and pedestrian light classes to encompass the new, graphical representation rather than the old textual one. In doing this we must remember to expunge all terminal based input–output. As an example of this transformation, we show just the StandardTrafficLight:

```
import java.awt.Color ;
import java.awt.Container ;
import java.awt.GridLayout ;
import javax.swing.JFrame ;
/**
 *  Perhaps the most common traffic light, certainly used in USA,
 *  Canada, France, Germany.
 *
 *  @version 1.2 1999.08.09
 *  @author Russel Winder
 */
public class StandardTrafficLight
  extends JFrame implements ControlLight {
  /**
   *  The top, red, bulb.
   */
  protected final Bulb upper = new Bulb (Color.red, Color.black) ;
  /**
   *  The middle, amber, bulb.
   */
  protected final Bulb middle = new Bulb (Color.yellow, Color.black) ;
  /**
   *  The lower, green, bulb.
```

```
  */
protected final Bulb lower = new Bulb (Color.green, Color.black) ;
/**
 *  The current state of this light.  Default to RED for safety.
 */
protected Color currentState  = Color.red ;
/**
 *  The delay between red and green.
 */
protected int redToGreenDelay = -1 ;
/**
 *  The delay between green and amber.
 */
protected int greenToAmberDelay = -1 ;
/**
 *  The delay between amber and red.
 */
protected int amberToRedDelay = -1 ;
/**
 *  Construct the graphical representation ONLY.  Since this only
 *  does partial construction make it protected so that it must be
 *  called by another constructor.
 *
 *  <P> The issue is the initialization of the waits and the fact
 *  that there is an inheritance hierarchy built on this class --
 *  <CODE>setWaits</CODE> is dynamically bound and we have to ensure
 *  that the correct version is called so we have to `hack' a little
 *  with the construction system.
 */
protected StandardTrafficLight(final String s) {
   //  Decide on the packing model, set the appropriate size, put the
   //  bulbs into the container, set the default colour of the light
   //  and then show it all.
   super(s) ;
   Container myPane = getContentPane() ;
   myPane.setLayout(new GridLayout (3, 1)) ;
   myPane.add(upper) ;
   myPane.add(middle) ;
   myPane.add(lower) ;
   pack() ;
   setRed() ;
   setVisible(true) ;
}
/**
 *  The constructor that takes a <CODE>String</CODE> to be the
 *  window name and an array of waits.  The array must contain 3
 *  entries.
 */
public StandardTrafficLight(final String s, final int[] waits) {
   super(s) ;
   setWaits(waits) ;
}
/**
 *  The constructor that requires the creating code to specify the
 *  initial state.
 *
 *  @param s the <CODE>String</CODE> that becomes the label for
 *  the window
 *  @param r_w the RED wait time.
 *  @param g_w the GREEN wait time.
 *  @param a_w the AMBER wait time.
 */
public StandardTrafficLight(final String s,
                            final int r_w,
                            final int g_w,
                            final int a_w) {
```

```
      this(s, new int[] {r_w, g_w, a_w}) ;
   }
   /**
    *   Set the wait periods between colour changes.  Units are
    *   seconds.
    *
    *   @param waits contains the waits for the different colours in the
    *   order RED, GREEN, AMBER.
    *   @exception ControlLight.WaitsInitializationException if the
    *   number of items in the array is not correct for this light.
    */
   public void setWaits(final int[] waits) {
      if (waits.length != 3) {
        throw new ControlLight.WaitsInitializationException
          ("Array size was " + waits.length + " not 3.") ;
      }
      for (int i = 0 ; i < waits.length ; i++) {
        if (waits[i] < 0)
          throw new ControlLight.WaitsInitializationException
            ("Wait value was negative.") ;
      }
      redToGreenDelay = waits[0] ;
      greenToAmberDelay = waits[1] ;
      amberToRedDelay = waits[2] ;
   }
   /**
    *   Initiate a sequencing of the light according to the currently
    *   set wait periods from the colour it is now back to the same
    *   colour.
    */
   public void sequence() {
      sequenceTo(currentState) ;
   }
   /**
    *   Initiate a sequencing of the light terminating with the
    *   specified colour according to the currently set wait periods.
    *
    *   @exception ControlLight.IllegalColourException if ever we are in
    *   a state with a colour we did not think possible.
    */
   public void sequenceTo(final Color colour) {
      do {
        if (currentState == Color.red)  {
          WaitAWhile.seconds(redToGreenDelay) ;
          setGreen() ;
        } else if (currentState == Color.green) {
          WaitAWhile.seconds(greenToAmberDelay) ;
          setAmber() ;
        } else if (currentState == Color.yellow) {
          WaitAWhile.seconds(amberToRedDelay) ;
          setRed() ;
        } else {
          throw new ControlLight.IllegalColourException () ;
        }
      } while (colour != currentState) ;
   }
   /**
    *   Set the red bulb on and the other two off.
    */
   protected void setRed() {
      currentState = Color.red ;
      upper.on() ;
      middle.off() ;
      lower.off() ;
   }
   /**
```

```
    *   Set the green bulb on and the other two off.
    */
   protected void setGreen() {
     currentState = Color.green ;
     upper.off() ;
     middle.off() ;
     lower.on() ;
   }
   /**
    *   Set the amber bulb on and the other two off.
    */
   protected void setAmber() {
     currentState = Color.yellow ;
     upper.off() ;
     middle.on() ;
     lower.off() ;
   }
   /**
    *   For testing this class we provide a main method.
    */
   public static void main(final String[] args) {
     StandardTrafficLight l =
      new StandardTrafficLight ("Test Light", 4, 4, 2) ;
     l.sequence() ;
   }
 }
```

The creation of a `UKTrafficLight` follows exactly the same inheritance route as was followed for the text-only version and is therefore not presented here. With these tools, though, we can construct the basic crossroads simulation:

```
/**
 *   A crossroads simulation using UK traffic lights.
 *
 *   @version 1.1 1999.08.09
 *   @author Russel Winder
 */
public class CrossroadsUK {
  public static void main(final String[] args) {
    int[] sequenceWaits = {2, 2, 5, 2} ;
    UKTrafficLight leftright =
     new UKTrafficLight ("Left--Right", sequenceWaits) ;
    leftright.setLocation(100,100) ;
    leftright.addWindowListener(new ExitWindowAdapter ()) ;
    UKTrafficLight updown =
     new UKTrafficLight ("Up--Down", sequenceWaits) ;
    updown.setLocation(200,100) ;
    updown.addWindowListener(new ExitWindowAdapter ()) ;
    while (true) {
      leftright.sequence() ;
      updown.sequence() ;
    }
  }
}
```

The pedestrian crossing itself seems very straightforward as well, if we use the `StandardPedestrianLight`. There are no new issues, it is simply a question of making the appropriate changes to the sequencer code. There is clearly something different, though, about the `UKPedestrianLight` and that is that it requires a flashing green light. This is a major new problem. Behaviour of this sort (flashing things) is a time related behaviour that is almost certainly best handled by a new thread.

It would be feasible for the main thread to handle the flashing. It would have to be responsible for timing the starting and stopping of the flashing green and also the switching on and off of the light. This overlapping timing activity would require the system to calculate the flashing on/off timing so as to fit exactly within the start/stop time of the light. This is relatively straightforward but leads to a lot of data coupling. So although this could be done, it seems conceptually easier to have one thread responsible for timing the starting and stopping of the flashing behaviour and another responsible for the switching on/off of the light. This allows the flashing period and the flashing light on period to be completely decoupled. This partitioning of responsibility is easily implemented in a language such as Java which has integral support for threads and aids maintainability since the concepts as well as the data are decoupled. Here then is the `UKPedestrianLight` that uses this two thread approach:

```
import java.awt.Color ;
/**
 *  Perhaps the most usual of pedestrian lights.
 *
 *  @version 1.3 1999.08.11
 *  @author Russel Winder
 */
public class UKPedestrianLight extends StandardPedestrianLight {
  /**
   *  The `handle' for the thread that is used to create flashing
   *  green.
   *
   *  <P> This is an object variable rather than being a local
   *  variable since we must ensure access to the same variable
   *  between two different methods, notably
   *  <CODE>setFlashingGreen</CODE> and
   *  <CODE>unsetFlashingGreen</CODE>.
   */
  protected SuspendableThread flashingGreenThread = null ;
  /**
   *  The delay between red and redamber.
   */
  protected int greenToFlashingGreenDelay = -1 ;
  /**
   *  The delay between redamber and green.
   */
  protected int flashingGreenToRedDelay = -1 ;
  /**
   *  This constructor is only here to support the inheritance
   *  hierarchy it must never be called explicitly.
   *
   *  <P> Because <CODE>setWaits</CODE> is dynamically bound, we
   *  cannot afford to call it in superclass constructors when
   *  constructing subclasses only in that subclass constructor --
   *  otherwise there will be attempts to construct the wrong size of
   *  array for <CODE>delay</CODE>.  This means that subclasses must
   *  not call their superclass constructor but Java insists that we
   *  do.  We therefore provide this constructor as a null
   *  constructor.
   */
  protected UKPedestrianLight(final String s) {
    super(s) ;
  }
  /**
   *  The constructor that takes a <CODE>String</CODE> to be the
   *  window name and an array of waits.  The array must contain 3
   *  entries.
   */
```

```
public UKPedestrianLight(final String s, final int[] waits) {
  super(s) ;
  setWaits(waits) ;
}
/**
 *   The constructor that requires the creating code to specify the
 *   initial state.
 *
 *   @param s the <CODE>String</CODE> that becomes the label for
 *   the window
 *   @param r_w the RED wait time.
 *   @param g_w the GREEN wait time.
 *   @param a_w the FLASHINGGREEN wait time.
 */
public UKPedestrianLight(final String s,
                           final int r_w,
                           final int g_w,
                           final int fg_w) {
  this(s, new int[] {r_w, g_w, fg_w}) ;
}
/**
 *   Set the wait periods between colour changes.  Units are
 *   seconds.
 *
 *   @param waits contains the waits for the different colours in the
 *   order RED, GREEN, FLASHINGGREEN.
 *   @exception ControlLight.WaitsInitializationException if the
 *   number of items in the array is not correct for this light or if
 *   any of the entries are negative.
 */
public void setWaits(final int[] waits) {
  if (waits.length != 3) {
    throw new ControlLight.WaitsInitializationException
      ("Array size was " + waits.length + " not 3.") ;
  }
  for (int i = 0 ; i < waits.length ; i++) {
    if (waits[i] < 0)
      throw new ControlLight.WaitsInitializationException
        ("Wait value was negative.") ;
  }
  redToGreenDelay = waits[0] ;
  greenToFlashingGreenDelay = waits[1] ;
  flashingGreenToRedDelay = waits[2] ;
}
/**
 *   Initiate a sequencing of the light terminating with the
 *   specified colour according to the currently set wait periods.
 *
 *   @exception ControlLight.IllegalColourException if ever we are in
 *   a state with a colour we did not think possible.
 */
public void sequenceTo(final Color colour) {
  do {
    if (currentState == Color.red) {
      WaitAWhile.seconds(redToGreenDelay) ;
      setGreen() ;
    } else if (currentState == Color.green) {
      //  NB We use Color.orange to represent flashing green.
      WaitAWhile.seconds(greenToFlashingGreenDelay) ;
      currentState = Color.orange ;
      setFlashingGreen() ;
    } else if (currentState == Color.orange) {
      //  Setting to red also requires that flashing green is turned
      //  off.
      WaitAWhile.seconds(flashingGreenToRedDelay) ;
      unsetFlashingGreen() ;
```

```
          setRed() ;
        } else  {
          throw new ControlLight.IllegalColourException () ;
        }
    } while (colour != currentState) ;
}
/**
 *  Set the flashing green state.
 */
protected void setFlashingGreen() {
    flashingGreenThread = new SuspendableThread () {
      public void run() {
          // The action of this thread is to implement flashing
          // green.  To do this, switch the light on, wait half a
          // second, switch it off, wait half a second and repeat
          // until the thread is terminated. After each action check
          // to see what the current state is.  The only object lock
          // we can ever own is our own since none of the actions
          // require any locking so the potential suspension implied
          // by the checkState call is safe.
          while (true) {
            if (! checkState()) break ;
            setGreen() ;
            if (! checkState()) break ;
            WaitAWhile.tenths(5) ;
            if (! checkState()) break ;
            lower.off() ;
            if (! checkState()) break ;
            WaitAWhile.tenths(5) ;
          }
      }
    } ;
    flashingGreenThread.start() ;
}
/**
 *  Cease the flashing green.  Need this switch off mechanism for
 *  flashing green because a thread is involved.
 */
protected void unsetFlashingGreen() {
    if (flashingGreenThread != null) {
      flashingGreenThread.setState(SuspendableThread.STOPPED) ;
      flashingGreenThread = null ;
    }
}
/**
 *  For testing this class we provide a main method.
 */
public static void main(final String[] args) {
    UKPedestrianLight l =
     new UKPedestrianLight ("UKPedestrianLight", 2, 2, 4) ;
    l.sequence() ;
}
}
```

In the above code, the flashing behaviour is implemented by creating and starting a new thread immediately the light changes to FLASHINGGREEN state. The thread is stopped as soon as the light changes to RED.

In general, stopping or suspending a thread in a system such as Java is an unsafe activity, it can lead to system deadlock in various situations. There are conditions that need to be met by an application before suspension is safe. If a stopped or suspended thread does not hold any object locks that will be needed by other threads after it is stopped or whilst it is suspended then it is safe to suspend it. This is a stronger condition than is actually required for safety but to describe the weakest condition that ensures safety would be very lengthy and would require many different cases. Because of this inherent lack of safety of stopping and suspending threads all the methods that were available in the `Thread` class for doing this sort of thing have been deprecated in Java 2 (i.e. they are being removed in future versions and their use is strongly discouraged). In fact, it was an error for them to be there in the first place since it allowed people to think that they could use them safely, which is not true — in general. As noted above, in specific cases, everything is fine. So the Java policy is to not provide these methods in the base `Thread` class but to require applications developers to build subclasses of `Thread` in those cases where stopping or suspending a thread are valid activities. With the situation we have here, flashing a light, it turns out that the algorithm employed by the thread implementing the flashing will not obtain object locks and so it will always be safe to stop it. Hence, we need to construct a subclass of `Thread` to provide the `terminate` method since there is no equivalent method in `Thread`.

The following class, `SuspendableThread`, is a subclass of `Thread` which supports the 'stop', 'suspend', and 'resume' operations that `Thread` does not. We have constructed this class very much as one that could be put into a library (i.e. it is general rather than being application specific). This does not mean that it can be used generally though. The application developer must be clear about the use of object locks before employing this class.

```
/**
 *   This class supports the stopping, suspending and resuming of
 *   threads.  These are inherently unsafe operations in general which
 *   is why the methods are not available in <CODE>Thread</CODE>.  In
 *   JDK 1.1 the <CODE>Thread</CODE> class had methods
 *   <CODE>stop</CODE>, <CODE>suspend</CODE> and <CODE>resume</CODE>.
 *   However, for various sensible reasons, these methods have been
 *   deprecated in Java 2.  Hence this class.
 *
 *   <P> This class should only be used where the logic of the
 *   application ensures that blocking does not occur.  This basically
 *   means that a thread that is stopped or suspended must not hold any
 *   object locks required by other threads when it is stopped or
 *   suspended.  Resumption is always safe but is not provided by
 *   <CODE>Thread</CODE> since there is no suspend.
 *
 *   <P> As a design decision this class is not instantiable.  Only
 *   subclasses, which must override the <CODE>run</CODE> method
 *   including suitable calls to <CODE>checkState</CODE>, can be
 *   instantiated since the <CODE>run</CODE> method of this class is
 *   the default <CODE>Thread</CODE> which does nothing and returns
 *   immediately.  Since the <CODE>checkState</CODE> method is
 *   protected so that it can only be used by subclasses, it is not
 *   possible to use this class in tandem with <CODE>Runnable</CODE>
 *   objects in the way that <CODE>Thread</CODE> could be used.
 *
 *   <P> This technique was presented by Scott Oaks in the article
 *   "Programming with thread in Java 1.2", Java Report, December 1997.
 *
 *   @version 1.1  1999.08.11
 *   @author  Russel Winder
 */
public class SuspendableThread extends Thread {
    /**
     *   The thread is in running state.
```

```
      */
     public final static int RUNNING = 0 ;
     /**
      *  The thread is in suspended state.
      */
     public final static int SUSPENDED = 1 ;
     /**
      *  The thread is in stopped state and will be destroyed at the next
      *  possible safe opportunity.
      */
     public final static int STOPPED = 2 ;
     /**
      *  The current state of the thread.  A newly created thread should
      *  attempt to run as its default action.
      */
     private int state = RUNNING ;
     /**
      *  Do not permit general instantiation.
      */
     protected SuspendableThread() { }
     /**
      *  Change the state of the thread.  Having set the state, notify
      *  the thread waiting on the object lock so that it can proceed to
      *  recheck the state and act accordingly.
      */
     public synchronized void setState(final int newState) {
       if ((state < 0) || (state > 2))
         throw new RuntimeException
           ("Illegal SuspendableThread state.") ;
       state  = newState ;
       notify() ;
     }
     /**
      *  Check the state of the thread and act accordingly.  If the state
      *  in RUNNING then return immediately with the value true.  If the
      *  state is supposed to be STOPPED then return immediately with the
      *  value false.  If the state is SUSPENDED then <CODE>wait</CODE>
      *  until a <CODE>notify</CODE> occurs at which point re-check the
      *  state and act accordingly.
      *
      *  <P> NB <CODE>wait</CODE>ing release the object lock that was
      *  obtained to make the call.
      *
      *  <P> This method must only be called from the <CODE>run</CODE>
      *  method defined in subclasses of this one.
      *
      *  @return true => running, false => stopping
      */
     protected synchronized boolean checkState() {
       while (state == SUSPENDED) {
         try {
           wait() ;
         }
         catch (Exception e) { }
       }
       return state == RUNNING ;
     }
   }
```

The above is not the whole story, it is just a support class. The actual algorithm for flashing was implemented in the class UKPedestrianLight where an anonymous subclass of SuspendableThread was created, which defined the run method that the second thread executed.

There has been one other change in the implementation that is worthy of note: The mechanisms for waiting have been extracted out from the main class and a new class created with a set of static methods enabling waiting for some number of different units. In the context of this example, this change could be considered a little gratuitous but it is justified in that the new class can go into a local library of such utility classes and be reused in a number of different applications.

```
/**
 *   A class to support delays in execution.
 *
 *   <P> The class <CODE>Thread</CODE> provides a static method
 *   <CODE>sleep</CODE> that delays execution for a number of
 *   milliseconds.  It throws exceptions that must be caught.  This
 *   class provides a set of methods to wrap up the exception handling
 *   and to provide a set of second related timings.
 *
 *   <P> This class assumes that there are not multiple interacting
 *   threads using the class.  In particular, it assumes that the
 *   method <CODE>Thread.interrupt()</CODE> is never used on any thread
 *   using this class.
 *
 *   @version 1.0 1998.12.06
 *   @author Russel Winder
 */
public class WaitAWhile {
  /**
   *  Delay for a given number of minutes.
   */
  public static void minutes(final int delay) {
    thousandths(60000*delay) ;
  }
  /**
   *  Delay for a given number of seconds.
   */
  public static void seconds(final int delay) {
    thousandths(1000*delay) ;
  }
  /**
   *  Delay for a given number of tenths of seconds.
   */
  public static void tenths(final int delay) {
    thousandths(100*delay) ;
  }
  /**
   *  Delay for a given number of milliseconds.
   */
  public static void thousandths(final int delay) {
    try {
      Thread.sleep(delay) ;
    }
    catch (InterruptedException ie) {
      //  In the applications using this class, there will never be a
      //  case where another thread sends a waiting thread the
      //  interrupt method.  We therefore assume that this exception
      //  can never happen.
    }
  }
}
```

With all these alterations we are now in a position to create an evolved version of the pedestrian crossing simulation:

```
import java.awt.Color ;
/**
```

```
 *   Simulate a very trivial pedestrian crossing using the UK
 *   lights.
 *
 *   @version 1.0 1997.08.15
 *   @author Russel Winder
 */
public class CrossingUK {
  public static void main(final String args[]) {
    UKTrafficLight traffic = new UKTrafficLight ("Traffic") ;
    traffic.setWaits(new int[] { 2, 2, 6, 2 }) ;
    traffic.setLocation(100, 100) ;
    traffic.addWindowListener(new ExitWindowAdapter ()) ;
    UKPedestrianLight pedestrian =
     new UKPedestrianLight ("Pedestrian") ;
    pedestrian.setWaits(new int[] { 2, 4, 6 }) ;
    pedestrian.setLocation(200,100) ;
    pedestrian.addWindowListener(new ExitWindowAdapter ()) ;
    ButtonPush b = new ButtonPush ("Pedestrian") ;
    b.setLocation(300, 100) ;
    while (true) {
      traffic.sequenceTo(Color.green) ;
      b.waitOn() ;
      traffic.sequenceTo(Color.red) ;
      b.setButtonState(false) ;
      pedestrian.sequenceTo(Color.red) ;
    }
  }
}
```

The pedestrian button push class, `ButtonPush`, is the one thing not already presented. It is:

```
import java.awt.Color ;
import java.awt.Container ;
import java.awt.event.ActionEvent ;
import java.awt.event.ActionListener ;
import javax.swing.JButton ;
import javax.swing.JFrame ;
/**
 *   A button to press to request the lights to change to allow
 *   pedestrians to cross.
 *
 *   @version 1.2 1999.01.09
 *   @author Russel Winder
 */
public class ButtonPush extends JFrame {
  /**
   *   The state of the push button.
   */
  private boolean buttonState = false ;
  /**
   *   The button to push to request pedestrian crossing time.
   */
  private final JButton button = new JButton("Press") ; {
    //  Add a listener defined using an anonymous class to the button
    //  to add the semantics of requesting a sequencing.
    button.addActionListener(
      new ActionListener() {
        public void actionPerformed(final ActionEvent event) {
          setButtonState(true) ;
        }
      }
      ) ;
    setButtonState(false) ;
  }
  /**
   *   The constructor.
```

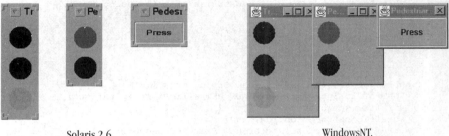

Solaris 2.6.   WindowsNT.

Figure 25.4 Screen dumps from the second round version of the traffic light simulation. The Windows version windows are 'bizarrely' wide since there is a minimum width for windows due to the decorations in the top window bar.

```java
     */
    public ButtonPush(final String s) {
      super(s) ;
      getContentPane().add(button) ;
      addWindowListener(new ExitWindowAdapter ()) ;
      setSize(90,70) ;
      setResizable(false) ;
      setVisible(true) ;
    }
    /**
     *  Wait for the button to be pressed.  This is a polling wait (aka
     *  busy wait) which is horrendously inefficient.  There must be a
     *  more interrupt-based mechanism that could be used.
     */
    public void waitOn() {
      while (buttonState == false) {
        WaitAWhile.seconds(1) ;
      }
    }
    /**
     *  Set the state of the button to a given boolean value.  The
     *  colour should be white if the boolean is true, grey if it is
     *  false.
     */
    public void setButtonState(final boolean b) {
      buttonState = b ;
      button.setBackground(buttonState
                           ? Color.white
                           : new Color(163, 163, 163)) ;
      button.setText(buttonState ? "WAIT" : "Press") ;
    }
    /**
     *  For testing this class we provide a main method.
     */
    public static void main(final String[] args) {
      ButtonPush b = new ButtonPush ("Test Button") ;
    }
  }
```

A screen image of this version of the simulation is shown in Figure 25.4. The Solaris 2.6 run of the program behaves exactly as expected. The WindowsNT run of the same program shows different and unexpected behaviour. The problem is clear from the figure, the windows are wider than they should be. We believe that this is because there is a minimum window width in WindowsNT.

This is effectively the culmination of this round of activity. It does, however, leave two problems to be solved in the next round of evolution.

One of the problem with this solution is that the button changes its state as soon as the pedestrian light starts its sequencing. This is not how most button feedback lights actually work. Normally the button changes its state as the pedestrian light changes from red to green (i.e. the feedback light indicates a light change is pending until the moment that the pedestrians are given a green and can proceed). This highlights the fact that the button is actually in the wrong place. `CrossingUK` does not have the responsibility of controlling the feedback status displayed by the button. The button is really an integral part of the pedestrian light and should be controlled by it. The feedback status can then be controlled in the right place in the code. The issue that making this change would leave is how to create the coupling between the `CrossingUK` and the button that is required to actually start the sequencing.

There is another, very serious, problem which may have got lost in amongst all the source code: The lights are of fixed size — the bulbs are 50×50 and the lights the appropriate multiples of this. This is clearly not good enough, we really need to have a scaling mechanism within the traffic lights so that we can specify an overall size from the sequencer when it sets up the lights.

25.6 A Third Round

In the next round of development we need to solve the above problems but more important than that even, we need to address the representation of the pedestrian crossing. So far we have been developing the overall architecture and some of the components but we have not addressed the issue of the graphical representation of the problem. So in this round, we need to stop putting each element in a separate window and put all the elements into a single window. This is relatively straightforward if non-trivial, being mainly an exercise in using the AWT and Swing rather than anything else.

In fact, the fixed sized problem highlighted in the previous section is just one of the many sub-problems of this larger problem.

The basic strategy adopted here is to:

1. Parameterize the size of `Bulbs` using parameters to the constructor.

2. Parameterize all the control light classes with the required bulb size, achieved using a constructor parameter. These classes also become `JPanels` rather than being `JFrames`.

3. The subclasses of `StandardTrafficLight` and `StandardPedestrianLight` require almost no changes at all.

4. Some small rearrangements of the `StandardTrafficLight` mostly in the constructor.

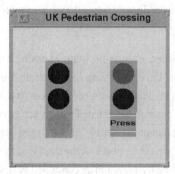
Solaris 2.6.

WindowsNT.

Figure 25.5 Screen dumps from the third round version of the traffic light simulation.

5. Merge the facilities of the `ButtonPush` class directly into `StandardPedestrianLight` and then delete the `ButtonPush` class completely.

6. Arrange for the button to communicate with the sequencer.

7. Make some amendments to the sequencer itself.

The biggest difficulty we experienced when doing this was getting the packing of the bulbs and the button correct. This took roughly 60% of the total time for two reasons:

1. At first we overlooked a faulty amendment of the `Bulb` class which caused some seriously bizarre behaviours that had us foxed for ages.

2. We spent a long time experimenting with different ways of packing the elements of the `StandardPedestrianLight` together.

After what turned out to be an unexpectedly short time, we ended up with a version of the system that met the third round objectives very well. The result of this round of development is shown in the screen dumps in Figure 25.5.

25.7   Oh Dear… Round Four is Round Three Re-visited

Anyone who has lived in or travelled in UK will probably already have realized that there is a fundamental bug in all that has gone before. Real UK pedestrian signals, when the pedestrian light is flashing green, present a flashing amber to the traffic. In the above we have, erroneously, made the assumption that all traffic lights are the same. Unfortunately they are not!

We could claim that this 'error' was purposefully done, on pedagogical grounds, in order to make a point. Unfortunately, the situation is far more realistic: our analysis was done from memory of observation and not direct observation and essentially we got it wrong. This, perhaps, makes it all more worth the telling because the situation really arose and is therefore an analogue of real systems development. Of course, we could have reworked the whole of this chapter to try and avoid this embarrassment but we thought it more instructive to expose the error.

All this means, of course, that we must put further development on hold and revisit everything we have done to date. What are the issues? Clearly there is more than one sort of traffic light in the UK. Moreover, there is significant coupling that occurs between the pedestrian light sequence and the traffic light sequence at a pedestrian crossing, something that is not true of a traffic crossroads. Our drive for encapsulation has given us an architecture that does not really allow for the required coupling. The most obvious solution then is to un-encapsulate everything, that is making the traffic lights passive abstractions of light bulbs that offer the sequencer the ability to set any light to any value at any time. Certainly, this solution is likely to work since the sequencer is in command of all things at all times — in fact, this is just the solution we rejected at the very outset (Page 683). It could be said that this was a big error.

As you may be aware, a large number of people in this situation would try and patch the existing system rather than being prepared to completely rework things. Let us then investigate a solution that preserves the full sequencing encapsulation and yet gives us the relevant synchronization facility. Actually, we have a responsibility to investigate this design approach before falling back on the 'no encapsulation' approach, it is a matter of knowledge. The metric for rejection of the evolved encapsulated approach will be if serious contortions and/or tortuous rationale are required to keep the encapsulation solution alive.

The basic problem we have is that the behaviours of the lights overlap whereas previously we had assumed that sequencing was a completely independent sequential activity. In this situation we need to synchronously initiate flashing green of the pedestrian light with the flashing amber of the traffic light and then synchronously change the pedestrian light to red and the traffic light to green.

The following is one strategy we could follow to solve the problem. We would create a version of the traffic light, `UKTrafficPedestrian` say, which had a flashing amber rather than a red and amber state (note that this would be a sibling to `UKTrafficLight` rather than a subclass). We would then alter the `CrossingUK` sequencer so that instead of sequencing the pedestrian light all the way through, it only sequenced it to flashing green. It would then sequence the traffic light to flashing amber and wait for the requisite period before sequencing the pedestrian light to red and the traffic light to green. The sequencing code might look something like:

```
while (true) {
  traffic.sequenceTo(Color.green) ;
  while (! pedestrian.getButtonState()) {
    //
    //  Don't want to check the state of the button too
    //  often, this is a busy wait polling loop after all.
    //
    WaitAWhile.seconds(1) ;
  }
  traffic.sequenceTo(Color.red) ;
  pedestrian.sequenceTo(Color.orange) ;
  traffic.sequenceTo(Color.orange) ;
  WaitAWhile.seconds(2) ;
  pedestrian.sequenceTo(Color.red) ;
}
```

This seems like a reasonable solution so why any hesitancy? The principal problem is that we have distributed responsibility. The lights are no longer totally responsible for their own behaviour, the sequencer is now responsible for the timing of the flashing phase, replicating information and behaviour that is already in the light. The cross-coupling and algorithm and data replication is indicative of pending maintainability problems and an inappropriate architecture.

So, this cross-coupling of behaviours is somewhat at variance with the basic architecture that we have, which seeks to completely encapsulate sequencing behaviour within the light class. The problem we have here is responsibility: who is responsible for which aspects of the behaviour? In the solution we are currently working with we have distributed responsibility, the lights are responsible for their own sequencing behaviour and the sequencer is responsible for initiating and synchronizing slices of that behaviour. To lay across this mechanism another to allow cross-coupling of responsibility for behaviour between different sorts of light rings warning bells: Wrong architecture. Maybe the decision to attempt to encapsulate state change within the traffic light was the wrong one? Clearly we could continue but are things getting over complicated, is there a simpler way?

Here we arrive at what could be an example of the single biggest problem in almost all system development. Can an individual or organization admit that they got it wrong initially and restart effectively from scratch. Well, not quite from scratch, we have generated a great deal of knowledge, *all* of which is reusable. The issue is the architecture, design and source code. All too often, psychological, sociological and political barriers get in the way of making the right technical decision. All too often, systems are hacked about, forcing them to work simply because individuals or organizations feel that they cannot afford to admit, even internally, that they got it wrong. The culture of 'success is all that is allowed, failure is always punished' really does not help here.

Returning to the problem at hand, we seemed to have argued our way to a fundamental architecture change. This is not to say we have to change it but we must investigate the new architecture implied from the reasoning. This is particularly true in this case as we are using exploratory prototyping as our development methodology. Trying new architectures, designs and code is an integral part of this methodology: nothing must be considered sacred, we cannot afford not to be able to admit error!

The basic required feature is that light sequencing can happen in parallel but in a highly synchronized manner. This is an indicator of the need of a far more centralized approach. The implied architecture is then that the lights are passive with all actions issued by a central sequencer. The architecture we rejected on encapsulation grounds (Page 683) is exactly the one we are now proposing to work with. The issue here is what is being encapsulated; earlier we were trying to encapsulate abstraction, presentation and behaviour. With the centralized behaviour architecture we are encapsulating only the abstraction and the presentation. The encapsulation of the light is being opened out so that behaviour is a completely different dimension of design. Thus, we are still encapsulating but in a less all encompassing way.

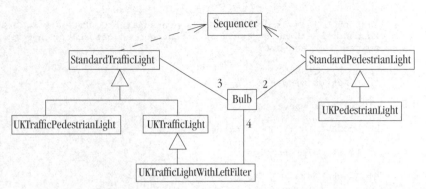

Figure 25.6 A further evolved class diagram to take account of the new architecture.

In the new architecture, each light is responsible for implementing only state change, providing an abstract light changing interface to the sequencer. The sequencer is responsible for knowing exactly the type of light at each place and for properly sequencing it through all state changes.

A hidden problem that we had not dealt with until now, which goes away completely with the new architecture of course, is that of how do we have multiple copies of lights which are wired together? In the previous architecture this would have been hard. An observation here: We are leading ourselves to a software architecture that is basically isomorphic to the hardware architecture of real light systems. Lights are wired together and the sequencer switches given bulbs on and off at a given time. Perhaps we should have taken more notice of this in the beginning? Perhaps we should have modelled the physical system more closely rather than trying to be abstract about it all. Well maybe in this case but beware, simulation (modelling the world as it behaves) and emulation (modelling the world as it exists) are different modelling activities. The fact that for this simulation we are being drawn to a more emulation-oriented architecture is due to the problem at hand, it is not a general property of simulation. Some people tend to forget this and end up using emulation architectures for all their simulations when there are far simpler and more efficient ways of simulating.

To go with the new architecture, we need a new set of classes. Because there is no a priori knowledge about lights in this new architecture, the `ControlLight` interface is basically a null interface. We might perhaps even consider abandoning it since it does not seem likely that it will serve a useful purpose in the code. For this round we do exactly this. We also need to bring in the new variety of traffic light. Figure 25.6 shows the new class hierarchy.

In fact, a surprisingly short time was required to create the new system. The transformation of the various types was relatively speedy because the appropriate knowledge for both architectures was already embedded in the code. We didn't have to throw much away at all; the ideas and concepts were all there, they just needed rearrangement and redistribution.

The light bulb is only slightly changed from the Round 2 version and is identical to the Round 3 version:

```
import java.awt.Canvas ;
import java.awt.Color ;
import java.awt.Graphics ;
```

```java
/**
 *  A light bulb is a circle of colour on a square <CODE>Canvas</CODE>
 *  background.  Each bulb has an on colour and an off colour and can
 *  be switched on and off.
 *
 *  @version 2.1 1998.12.07
 *  @author Russel Winder
 */
class Bulb extends Canvas {
  /**
   *  The <CODE>Color</CODE> representing on.
   */
  private final Color onColour ;
  /**
   *  The <CODE>Color</CODE> representing off.
   */
  private final Color offColour ;
  /**
   *  The current state of the <CODE>Bulb</CODE>.
   */
  private Color colour ;
  /**
   *  The current size of the <CODE>Bulb</CODE>.
   */
  private int size ;
  /**
   *  The constructor of a <CODE>Bulb</CODE>.  Remember the on and
   *  off colours, set the size of the <CODE>Canvas</CODE> and the
   *  background colour for the square space that the circle is
   *  drawn on.
   */
  public Bulb(final Color on_c,
              final Color off_c,
              final Color background,
              final int radius) {
    onColour = on_c ;
    offColour = off_c ;
    size = radius ;
    setSize(size, size) ;
    setBackground(background) ;
  }
  /**
   *  The <CODE>Canvas</CODE> redraw method.  We do not call this
   *  directly, it gets called by the runtime system as part of the
   *  repaint method call.
   */
  public final void paint(final Graphics g) {
    //  The sizing and relationship between the numbers is determined
    //  entirely by experiment.
    int offset = 2 ;
    int radius = size - 3 * offset ;
    g.setColor(colour) ;
    g.fillOval(offset, offset,  radius, radius) ;
  }
  /**
   *  Switch the bulb on.
   */
  public final void on() {
    colour = onColour ;
    repaint() ;
  }
  /**
   *  Switch the bulb off.
   */
  public final void off() {
    colour = offColour ;
```

```
          repaint() ;
      }
  }
```

The standard traffic light now looks like:

```java
import java.awt.Color ;
import java.awt.GridLayout ;
import javax.swing.JFrame ;
import javax.swing.JPanel ;
/**
 *  Perhaps the most common traffic light, certainly used in USA,
 *  Canada, France, Germany.
 *
 *  @version 3.1 1998.12.07
 *  @author Russel Winder
 */
public class StandardTrafficLight
  extends JPanel {
  /**
   *  The background colour used for the light.
   */
  public final static Color greyBackground =
    new Color (163, 163, 163) ;
  /**
   *  The top, red, bulb.
   */
  protected final Bulb upper ;
  /**
   *  The middle, amber, bulb.
   */
  protected final Bulb middle ;
  /**
   *  The lower, green, bulb.
   */
  protected final Bulb lower ;
  /**
   *  The constructor for the traffic lights which are to be of the
   *  size given.  Forces the state to be RED.
   */
  public StandardTrafficLight(final int bs) {
    upper =
     new Bulb (Color.red, Color.black, greyBackground,bs) ;
    middle =
     new Bulb (Color.yellow, Color.black, greyBackground, bs) ;
    lower =
     new Bulb (Color.green, Color.black, greyBackground, bs) ;
    setLayout(new GridLayout (3, 1)) ;
    add(upper) ;
    add(middle) ;
    add(lower) ;
    setSize(bs, 3 * bs) ;
    setRed() ;
    setVisible(true) ;
  }
  /**
   *  Set the red bulb on and the other two off.
   */
  protected void setRed() {
    upper.on() ;
    middle.off() ;
    lower.off() ;
  }
  /**
   *  Set the green bulb on and the other two off.
   */
```

```
    protected void setGreen() {
      upper.off() ;
      middle.off() ;
      lower.on() ;
    }
    /**
     *  Set the amber bulb on and the other two off.
     */
    protected void setAmber() {
      upper.off() ;
      middle.on() ;
      lower.off() ;
    }
    /**
     *  For testing this class we provide a main method.
     */
    public static void main(final String[] args) {
      JFrame f = new JFrame ("Test Standard Traffic Light") ;
      StandardTrafficLight l = new StandardTrafficLight (30) ;
      f.add(l) ;
      f.pack() ;
      f.setLocation(100,100) ;
      f.setVisible(true) ;
    }
  }
```

This is effectively considerably simplified compared to the previous round's version, needing only to deal with the representation of the traffic light and not with its usage. The standard pedestrian light is similarly simplified but it retains the complexity of managing the button.

```
import java.awt.Color ;
import java.awt.GridLayout ;
import java.awt.event.ActionEvent ;
import java.awt.event.ActionListener ;
import javax.swing.JButton ;
import javax.swing.JFrame ;
import javax.swing.JPanel ;
/**
 *  Perhaps the most basic of pedestrian lights.
 *
 *  <P>Such a light has two bulbs and a button to request a
 *  sequencing.  This class manages the presentation of the light, the
 *  sequencing is managed elsewhere.
 *
 *  @version 3.1 1998.12.07
 *  @author Russel Winder
 */
public class StandardPedestrianLight extends JPanel {
  /**
   *  The background colour used for the light.
   */
  public final static Color greyBackground =
    new Color (163, 163, 163) ;
  /**
   *  The top, red, bulb.
   */
  protected final Bulb upper ;
  /**
   *  The lower, green (or white) bulb.
   */
  protected final Bulb lower ;
  /**
   *  The button to push to request pedestrian crossing time.
   */
  protected final JButton button = new JButton () ; {
```

```java
    button.addActionListener(
      new ActionListener () {
        /**
         *  Whenever the button is pressed set the button
         *  state to true, i.e. pressed.
         */
        public void actionPerformed(final ActionEvent event) {
          setButtonState(true) ;
        }
      }
    ) ;
  setButtonState(false) ;
}
/**
 *  The state of the light.
 */
protected Color currentState = Color.red ;
/**
 *  The state of the push button.
 */
protected boolean buttonState = false ;
 /**
  *  The constructor for the traffic lights which are to be of the
  *  size given.  Forces the state to be RED.
  */
public StandardPedestrianLight(final int bs) {
  upper =
   new Bulb (Color.red, Color.black, greyBackground,bs) ;
  lower =
   new Bulb (Color.green, Color.black, greyBackground, bs) ;
  setLayout(new GridLayout (3, 1)) ;
  add(upper) ;
  add(lower) ;
  add(buttonPanel) ;
  setSize(bs, 3 * bs) ;
  setRed() ;
  setVisible(true) ;
}
/**
 *  Set the red bulb on and the other off.
 */
protected void setRed() {
  currentState = Color.red ;
  upper.on() ;
  lower.off() ;
}
/**
 *  Set the green bulb on and the other off.
 */
protected void setGreen() {
  currentState = Color.green ;
  upper.off() ;
  lower.on() ;
}
/**
 *  Set the state of the button to a given boolean value.  The
 *  colour should be white if the boolean is true, grey if it is
 *  false.
 */
protected final void setButtonState(final boolean b) {
  buttonState = currentState == Color.green ? false : b ;
  button.setBackground(buttonState
                          ? Color.white
                          : greyBackground) ;
  button.setText(buttonState ? "WAIT" : "Press") ;
}
```

```
/**
 *  Return the value of the button state for this pedestrian
 *  light.
 */
public final boolean getButtonState() {
  return buttonState ;
}
/**
 *  The <CODE>Panel</CODE> to hold the <CODE>Button</CODE> to stop
 *  it getting resized.
 */
private final JPanel buttonPanel = new JPanel () ; {
  buttonPanel.add(button) ;
  buttonPanel.setBackground(greyBackground) ;
}
/**
 *  For testing this class we provide a main method.
 */
public static void main(final String[] args) {
  JFrame f = new JFrame ("Test Standard Pedestrian Light") ;
  StandardPedestrianLight l = new StandardPedestrianLight (30) ;
  f.add(l) ;
  f.pack() ;
  f.setLocation(100,100) ;
  f.setVisible(true) ;
}
}
```

From these we use inheritance exactly as before to create the UK traffic light as used at a pedestrian crossing (which is the sibling of the UK traffic light as used at a crossroads — there is nothing difficult in that type so we do not show it here):

```
import javax.swing.JFrame ;
/**
 *  A traffic light as used for a pedestrian crossing in the UK.
 *
 *  @version 3.2 1999.08.11
 *  @author Russel Winder
 */
public class UKTrafficPedestrianLight extends StandardTrafficLight {
  /**
   *  The thread variable controlling the flashing amber behaviour.
   */
  private final SuspendableThread flashingAmberThread =
    new SuspendableThread () {
    /**
     *  The purpose of this (anonymous) subclass of
     *  <CODE>SuspendableThread</CODE> is to flash the green
     *  light.  Set up an infinite loop to do exactly this.
     */
    public void run() {
        // Switch the light on wait half a second switch it off wait
        // half a second and repeat ad infinitum.  The starting and
        // stopping of the behaviour is not handled here but by
        // suspending and resuming the entire thread.  The only object
        // lock we can ever own is our own since none of the actions
        // require any locking so the potential suspension implied by
        // the checkState call is safe.
        while (true) {
          if (! checkState())  break ;
          setAmber() ;
          if (! checkState())  break ;
          WaitAWhile.tenths(5) ;
          if (! checkState())  break ;
          middle.off() ;
```

```
          if (! checkState())  break ;
          WaitAWhile.tenths(5) ;
      }
    }
} ;
//  Set up the necessary behaviour and suspend the thread.  When we
//  need flashing green we just resume the thread.  Stopping the
//  behaviour is suspending the thread again.
{
  flashingAmberThread.setState(SuspendableThread.SUSPENDED) ;
  flashingAmberThread.start() ;
}
/**
 *  The constructor for the traffic lights.  Forces the
 *  state to be RED.
 */
public UKTrafficPedestrianLight(final int bs) {
  super(bs) ;
}
//  We have to override all the bulb setting methods in order to
//  ensure proper operation of the thread.
/**
 *  Set the red bulb on and the other two off.
 */
protected void setRed() {
  //  Make sure we deal with the switching off of flashing amber.
  //  This method gets called as part of the superclass constructor
  //  (as well as at other times) and hence before all the
  //  construction of this class is done.  In particular, we know
  //  that the thread for dealing with flashing green will not have
  //  been established when this call is made so we must protect
  //  against using a null reference.
  if (flashingAmberThread != null) {
    flashingAmberThread.setState(SuspendableThread.SUSPENDED);
  }
  upper.on() ;
  middle.off() ;
  lower.off() ;
}
/**
 *  Set the green bulb on and the other two off.
 */
protected void setGreen() {
  flashingAmberThread.setState(SuspendableThread.SUSPENDED) ;
  upper.off() ;
  middle.off() ;
  lower.on() ;
}
/**
 *  Set the red and green bulbs off and the amber flashing.
 */
protected void setFlashingAmber() {
  upper.off() ;
  lower.off() ;
  flashingAmberThread.setState(SuspendableThread.RUNNING) ;
}
/**
 *  For testing this class we provide a main method.
 */
public static void main(final String[] args) {
  JFrame f =
   new JFrame ("Test UK Pedestrian Crossing Traffic Light") ;
  UKTrafficPedestrianLight l =
   new UKTrafficPedestrianLight (50) ;
  f.add(l) ;
  f.pack() ;
```

```
          f.setLocation(100,100) ;
          f.setVisible(true) ;
      }
  }
```

The UK pedestrian light itself is a very similarly structured subclass of StandardPedestrianLight, so much so that there is no need to show it here. With all this in place we can construct the new sequencer:

```java
import java.awt.Color ;
import java.awt.Container ;
import javax.swing.JFrame ;
/**
 *  Simulate a very trivial pedestrian crossing using the UK
 *  lights.
 *
 *  @version 3.1 1998.12.07
 *  @author Russel Winder
 */
class CrossingUK extends JFrame {
  private UKTrafficPedestrianLight traffic =
    new UKTrafficPedestrianLight (40) ;
  private UKPedestrianLight pedestrian =
    new UKPedestrianLight (40) ;
  public CrossingUK(final String s) {
    super(s) ;
    Container myPane = getContentPane() ;
    myPane.setLayout(null) ;
    myPane.add(traffic) ;
    myPane.add(pedestrian) ;
    myPane.setBackground(new Color (215, 215, 215)) ;
    traffic.setLocation(50, 50) ;
    pedestrian.setLocation(150, 50) ;
    setSize(250, 250) ;
    setLocation(100, 100) ;
    addWindowListener(new ExitWindowAdapter ()) ;
    setVisible(true) ;
  }
  public void runSimulation() {
    WaitAWhile.seconds(2) ;
    traffic.setAmber() ;
    WaitAWhile.seconds(2) ;
    traffic.setGreen() ;
    while (true) {
      while (! pedestrian.getButtonState()) {
        WaitAWhile.seconds(1) ;
      }
      WaitAWhile.seconds(2) ;
      traffic.setAmber() ;
      WaitAWhile.seconds(2) ;
      traffic.setRed() ;
      WaitAWhile.seconds(2) ;
      pedestrian.setGreen() ;
      WaitAWhile.seconds(4) ;
      pedestrian.setFlashingGreen() ;
      traffic.setFlashingAmber() ;
      WaitAWhile.seconds(4) ;
      pedestrian.setRed() ;
      traffic.setGreen() ;
    }
  }
  public static void main(final String[] args) {
    CrossingUK junction =
     new CrossingUK ("UK Pedestrian Crossing") ;
    junction.runSimulation() ;
```

```
        }
      }
```

The necessity to initialize the sequencing waits in the lights has gone away at the expense of having to manage all the waits in the sequencer. Some of the need to manage state in the lights has gone away, of course, which has simplified them enormously. This includes not having to use colours such as orange to represent the red+amber or flashing green state. The main thing we have lost in order to gain the ability to interleave managing the behaviour of different lights is the encapsulation of the behaviour of a light. This has been an explicit design decision, though.

Note also that we can now confirm that there seems little point in having a common supertype for the light classes since there are no common methods, a least a priori. In fact, to have a common supertype and use it would actually increase the complexity of the code since we would need to keep downcasting.

In fact, what we now have is a most flexible architecture. The moral of the story is that you really have to be very flexible and prepared to consign code and/or designs and/or whole architectures to the bin, even if they did take hours and/or days to produce.

There is no need to show images here since they are exactly the same as those shown at the end of the previous section. In order to tell the difference between these two implementations, you need to see the dynamic behaviour. We could present a sequence of images to show this but it is probably a lot easier for you to run the code on your machine. Perhaps you would like to treat this as an exercise?

25.8 A Fifth Round

The fifth round of development is clearly to put the rest of the graphics together to create a representation of the image we presented right at the beginning of this chapter (Figure 25.1, Page 681). This is a further exercise in AWT and Swing programming. To show more here would, we feel, add little to the presentation we are making. It would be far more useful to you to actually try to build the extensions yourself. Programming is a practical activity and is best learned by doing.

Beyond the basic simulation, there is something very different that we also need to look at and that is the issue of having traffic and pedestrians. At this point things get both interesting and far more tricky. The field of Discrete Event Simulation becomes important and the problem becomes one far bigger than can or should be tackled in an introductory book on programming! So, unfortunately we must leave this problem now for you to either forget about or research more deeply.

25.9   Summary

In this chapter we have investigated the beginnings of a simulation of a pedestrian crossing. Because of our drive for abstraction and seeking out generalization, we have actually laid the foundations for a complete library that enables all forms of traffic and pedestrian control. In particular, the architecture we have finally arrived at allows us to look at modelling not just the standard three light traffic light and two light pedestrian lights but also the single red or single amber traffic control lights that are used in a number of countries.

Self-review Questions

Self-review 25.1 Why was the sequence of development the way it was?

Self-review 25.2 Describe the basic architecture of the system and how it has developed during the various iterations.

Self-review 25.3 What are the dangers of doing too little analysis?

Self-review 25.4 What are the dangers of doing too much analysis?

Programming Exercises

Exercise 25.1 Undertake the fifth round of development implementing the graphical representation of the crossing.

Exercise 25.2 Undertake the development of a simple crossroads simulation.

Challenges

Challenge 25.1 Investigate the subject of Discrete Event Simulation and do the initial design of a full simulation with animation of the crossing simulation.

Simulating Ants

Objectives

This chapter presents a study of the development of a prototype program to simulate emergent behaviour based on ant foraging. An interesting aspect of the study is the identification of a core set of classes that can be formed into a simple framework and reused for other similar simulations.

Keywords

emergent
framework

26.1   Introduction

The underlying ideas presented in this chapter were very much inspired by reading the book *Turtles, Termites, and Traffic Jams — Explorations in Massively Parallel Microworlds* by Mitchel Resnick. The book describes the use of a parallel programming language called StarLogo, derived from the language Logo, to build simulations of systems such as ant or termite colonies and traffic jams.

Many systems, especially biological systems, exhibit complex behaviour. Interestingly, it turns out that such systems are often composed of large numbers of *simple* components with no overall central control to coordinate them. The components are all autonomous and follow a small set of behavioural rules. The random interaction of the components results in a complex behaviour pattern, referred to as *emergent behaviour* or *self-organizing behaviour*. The system of components is decentralized and, in the real world, is massively parallel.

As a familiar example of emergent behaviour, consider a flock of birds. When in motion, the birds in a flock will fly in formation, twisting and turning together, giving the appearance of a single coordinated entity. How does this happen? Does the flock have a leader that every other bird follows? Is there a sophisticated system of central control that instructs every bird where to be and when to turn?

The answer to these questions is no. Each bird is an autonomous, self-contained, free *agent*, there is no central control and no flock leader. Instead, each bird follows a set of behaviour rules for flying in a flock — something along the lines of trying to keep a safe distance from any surrounding birds, turning as necessary to avoid collisions. When a group of hundreds or thousands of birds comes together, with each bird following the rules, the cumulative effect of all the local interactions between birds gives rise to the flock and its motion.

Individual birds don't know the shape or form of the flock as a whole, just their small part of it. They don't have control over the flock but just follow the simple rules for being in a flock. And yet the result of all the individual behaviours is the coordinated behaviour of the flock, which to the casual observer seems to be a single entity that 'knows' where it is going and behaves in a sophisticated way.

It turns out that a surprising number of systems both in the natural world and human constructed exhibit emergent behaviour caused by the interactions between many simple (relatively speaking) components. Researchers have been studying such behaviour with the aid of computer simulations. A good source of example simulations comes from the study of insect colonies, in particular ant or termite colonies. This chapter will look at the features such simulations in order to identify a core set of classes, or *framework*, to represent the basic infrastructure of a simulation application. The framework will then be specialized to represent a particular simulation based on ants and ant foraging. In the longer run, it is intended that the framework will be used to build a

!

We work with ants and not termites, as the authors live in a (more or less) termite-free region of the world!

range of simulations based on the same underlying ideas, hence, the framework should be reusable and not specific to any particular ant simulation.

The simulation idea and the design to be presented here have evolved over several years, and were first implemented using the C++ programming language. The move to a Java implementation turned out to be straightforward as the object-oriented design mapped directly to the facilities provided by Java. An advantage of using Java is the ease with which the graphical interface can be implemented. Along the way, the design idea has been used as the basis for student coursework and projects, where it works very well and always generates a lot of interest. A version of the program has also been written using a parallel version of C++ called UC++.

UC++ (University College C++) was developed over several years to provide a version of C++ supporting parallel programming on high-performance computers. It has now evolved in KC++ (King's College C++).

26.2　The Simulation Model

The basic problem specification is derived from Resnick's book. A simulation is based on the following features:

- A **Grid** divided into patches (grid squares), to represent the simulated world or environment.

- **Patches** to represent the grid squares within the world. A patch can hold values representing the state of the patch (the amount of food present, for example) and can be the location of zero or more turtles. The state of a patch changes over time (more food grows, perhaps).

- **Turtles** to represent the mobile entities that live within the world. A turtle holds values to represent its state (e.g. whether it is hungry or carrying something) and can move around the patches. A turtle can interact with the patch it is standing on (for example, by eating or picking up an item). The name 'turtle' is used as the Logo programming language, and hence Starlogo, has the idea of an entity that can be controlled, moved around and used to draw shapes — the Turtle!

Each turtle *and* patch represents an agent which follows its own set of behaviour rules and changes over time. Moreover, when a simulation is running they are all assumed to be updated in parallel, so all turtles and patches are simultaneously active (just as every component within a real world system is simultaneously active). On a parallel computer system, it is possible to run a simulation where the simultaneous activity is actually achieved. Our Java simulations won't be running on a parallel machine so we are going to have to *serialize* the activity of turtles and patches and assume this won't make too much difference.

A simulation is set up by creating a grid and randomly allocating a number turtles to patches. The patch values are initialized, perhaps to indicate whether there is a piece of food or nest building material on the patch (see Figure 26.1).

note

Serialize means to make sequential, so that, for example, the state of each turtle is updated one after the other, rather than potentially all at the same time.

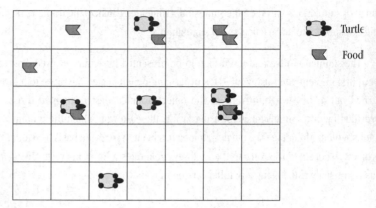

Figure 26.1 A simulation grid.

When the simulation is started the turtles begin wandering around the grid following their movement rule which could be as simple as 'choose a random direction and move one square forward if possible'. When a turtle moves to a new patch it has a rule about what to do, such as eat some food, or pick up the item on the patch. Patches are in fixed positions and don't move but their state can change over time, independently of whether they are visited by a turtle or not. For example, the amount of food on a patch can grow or shrink according to the overall state of the patch

If a simulation is set up with the right initial conditions, each patch and turtle given an appropriate set of behaviour rules and the simulation is left running long enough, then emergent behaviour may become apparent. For example, if turtles are specialized to behave as termites and patches specialized to behave as different pieces of terrain, some containing food sources, some containing termite nests, then 'organized' food foraging emerges. Of course, the organization of foraging is actually the result of the interaction of large numbers of termites and patches all following their rules. Nonetheless, the net effect of foraging is there to be observed.

With a basic simulation running, attention can then turn to varying the parameters to find out what is required for the foraging behaviour to appear. For example, what is the minimum number of termites needed before foraging occurs? What if there are more termite nests? What if termites from different nests are allowed to fight for food? The overall aim is to gain insight into how the behaviour in real systems actually comes about and under what conditions.

26.3 The Program Specification

The core aim is to get a basic simulation up and running. From the start we have recognized that all simulations have the same basic infrastructure (turtles and patches on a grid.), so there is scope for the reuse of this core infrastructure from one specific simulation to the next. To the object-oriented designer this immediately suggests a class framework, where a set of probably abstract classes define the basic infrastructure and behaviour of a simulation, with inheritance used to specialize the classes for a particular application. However, this is running ahead of the game as we need to step back and determine a strategy for developing our application and decide on an example simulation to work with.

When starting from scratch, using a prototyping cycle seems by far the best bet. We want to explore the possible design solutions to the problem without initially being overloaded with a large amount of design work. Also, the problem isn't large and doesn't need a great deal of requirements gathering or analysis. The basic algorithms are pretty much fixed, although we have to remember that we are going to be implementing a sequential version of what would be a parallel simulation. It's also going to be a good idea to start with a nice simple simulation, at least for the first few prototypes. We don't want the complexities of a more sophisticated simulation to get in the way of getting the basic infrastructure right.

One of the simplest simulations is that of ants (or termites) foraging for nest building material in the form of wood chips. We want to demonstrate that, with the right numbers of ants and randomly scattered wood chips, the emergent behaviour of gathering the chips into piles takes place. Each chip pile represents a (very simplistic) ant nest.

In this simulation patches are passive and may hold zero or more wood chips.

Ants follow a few basic rules:

1. Move a random distance in a random direction to another grid square.
2. If a destination grid square contains any wood chips and the ant is not carrying anything, then the ant picks up a wood chip.
3. If a destination grid square contains any wood chips and the ant is carrying a wood chip, then the ant drops the wood chip.

And that's it. Ants move randomly and pick up or drop wood chips depending on the state of a patch and what an ant is or is not carrying. These simple rules are enough to demonstrate that the wood chips will be concentrated into a small number of piles given the right starting conditions and enough time for the behaviour to emerge.

26.4 Initial Analysis and Design

We have decided to follow a prototyping approach which will mean 'analyse a little, design a little, implement a bit, test everything and review'. The first step is to identify the key classes and think about how objects of those classes interact in order for a simulation to be run. Looking at the description of simulations above, three classes immediately suggest themselves: `Grid`, `Turtle` and `Patch`. A first pass at identifying their properties gives:

`Grid` — can be represented as a two-dimensional array of patches (although the word array is used it doesn't necessarily mean the class will be implemented using arrays) and needs

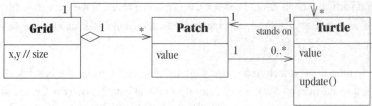

Figure 26.2 First class diagram.

to have a size. It also contains the complete collection of turtles, although patches could hold
turtles as well, so there are details that need to be thought about further.

`Turtle` — a turtle needs a way of moving about the grid and needs a value to indicate whether
or not it is carrying something. If a turtle is to be generic, the value will probably need to be
a collection of values but at this stage we go for the simplest option.

`Patch` — a patch needs to store a patch value and possibly a count or list of the number of
turtles standing on it. Again, we would like the patch to be as general as possible but as yet
are not sure how this will work out. For now we will work with a minimal representation
and assume a patch stores a single value. A general purpose patch would also need to be
updated as the simulation runs but for the moment we can simplify by assuming that patches
are passive and the patch value is only changed by the action of a turtle.

These classes and their relationships are documented by the first attempt UML class diagram
shown in Figure 26.2. This is read as "A grid consists of a collection of patches on which zero or
more turtles are located. The grid also holds a collection of turtles. A turtle stands on one patch".

While looking at a class diagram like that in Figure 26.2, you should remember that the classes
and their relationships describe the static structure of the program being designed, and that
structure will be directly reflected by the code that we write. When the program is run, instance
objects of the classes are created, which reference each other according to the class relationships.
This requires a certain amount of mental juggling as you try to think about both points of view while
looking at a single diagram. It also explains why we can talk about a grid consisting of a collection
of patches when there is only one patch class — we really mean that one grid object references a
collection of patch objects when the program is run. Note also, that the class associations have been
labelled with arrow heads (giving *navigability associations*) as we want to be quite specific about
which objects know about or contain references to other objects.

Next we want to think about how the objects might interact to actually run a simulation. The
basic idea is that each turtle is repeatedly moved according to the rules by which the turtle is
governed. This immediately raises the question of how to represent time. We can't represent time as
a continuous flow of events (i.e. in an analogue form), so instead time has to be represented as a
sequence of discrete steps. Each unit of time should move the simulation forward by one step, with
the hope that this is good enough to capture time in a reasonable way. Hence, the decision is made
that moving forward one time step is realised by calling a turtle's `update` method once, allowing it
to do one step of whatever it does (in the case of ants, moving to a new grid square and dealing with

wood chips). Using time steps also means calling an `update` method for each patch if we decide to make the patches active.

Filling in a some initialization details, the behaviour of the program so far looks like this:

> *Create a grid*
> *Initialize each patch in the grid*
> *Create a collection of turtles and spread them around the grid*
> *while (true) {*
>   *call the update method for each patch*
>   *call the update method for each turtle*
> *}*

26.5   A Second Pass

This looks reasonable so far but we want to push ahead to get a first prototype program working. As yet, however, we don't have enough specified to try that. A short review indicates that the initial three classes seem to be looking reasonable, but what else is needed?

First, we need something to display the state of a simulation. This will probably be some sort of graphical display but we don't want to commit to details just yet. For the moment a class `Display` will be introduced to encapsulate and separate the details of displaying a grid from the actual grid itself. We note, however, that somehow the information about what to display needs to be extracted from the grid but it's not yet clear how.

Second, we want to revisit how a turtle moves. If it is on one patch how does it get to another? The options seem to be:

1. A patch knows its neighbour in each direction, so the turtle asks the patch it is standing on for a reference to a neighbour and moves itself there.

2. The turtle examines the grid to find a neighbouring patch to move to and moves to it.

Option 2 perhaps seems obvious at first sight but has the disadvantage that turtles would have to know about the grid, know the position of their current patch in the grid and have a way of looking for neighbouring grid patches. This requires either the encapsulation of class `Grid` to be opened up to turtles, or a number of public (possibly protected) methods for general grid interrogation by turtles.

With option 1, the turtle only needs to know the patch it is on and that it can move to one of eight neighbouring patches (if available) by simply asking its patch for the neighbour in a particular direction. The turtle only needs to interact with its current patch and doesn't need to know anything about the grid as a whole. This looks like a more general approach, so we will go with this option.

A consequence of this decision is that a patch now needs to either know about its neighbours or be able to find out about them by accessing the grid. Following the same reasoning applied to the turtles it would be preferable for patches not to have to access the grid object, so a patch is given a

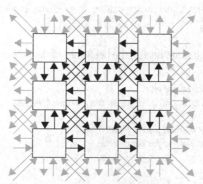

Figure 26.3 Connections between patches.

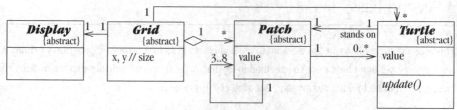

Figure 26.4 Second pass class diagram.

direct connection to each of its eight neighbours (giving a grid structure of the form seen in Figure 26.3). This decision can be further justified by calling on previous experience of developing true parallel versions of the simulation, where it is an advantage to minimize method calls on the grid object which will typically be located on a separate processor. While the version of the design presented here will not be parallel, we do want the design to be as reusable as possible so that future versions won't require unnecessary re-working. A disadvantage of the decision does mean that patches now have to hold an extra set of references but this addition is made in the belief that it will be useful in the long run (i.e. that keeping all information and actions as local as possible will outweigh the extra use of resources).

The result of this pass through the design has been to add one more class and an additional association from class Patch back to itself, giving the updated class diagram shown in Figure 26.4. A significant feature of Figure 26.4 is reflected in the additional decision to mark all the classes as *abstract*. Although the classes capture the basic structure and behaviour of a simulation, they do not represent any particular simulation. To do that a concrete subclass of each abstract class is required, filling in the details of what each class represents to create a specific simulation, such as the ant simulation.

26.6   The Abstract Class Framework

With the core simulation framework coming into place we want to spend a bit more time filling in the details of what each class does. We will do that by jotting down a short description of each class, thinking carefully about the set of methods needed and what behaviour should be supported. We also need to consider how the program as a whole works, in terms of the sequence of methods that need to called in order for things to happen. As this is going on, versions of the classes will be coded directly in Java, enabling us to verify that the design ideas can be sensibly realised in code, and also to press on with getting the code written.

In practice, this process relies on quite a lot of iteration and many adjustments to the design as issues are uncovered and addressed, perhaps making use of the techniques presented in Chapter 9 to help guide the process. Of course, we have the benefit of hindsight to allow a more straightforward and shorter presentation of the design here!

Note also that this chapter is intended to present an informal prototyping approach to program development, to discover how a simulation program might be structured. We can get away with this as the program being developed is relatively small. The development of larger programs, however, needs more order and discipline in order to keep track of the volume of detail that will be generated. With a small program it is possible to remember enough details of the design and implementation to (just about) avoid serious problems. With a larger program it isn't (unless you have an exceptional memory!).

The next decision to make is that all the classes within the core framework will be in their own Java package which will be called `SimFrameWork`. This will allow the framework classes to be neatly collected together for inclusion into an actual simulation application.

26.6.1 Class Grid

This class represents a generic grid of patches. It needs to be generic in the sense that it should provide a grid suitable for all simulations but not include anything specific to a particular simulation.

The methods implemented by the class should try to do as much generic work as possible but will rely on calls to abstract methods that must be overridden by a subclass. This is a commonly used technique in this kind of framework, as it allows a generic algorithm to be expressed in terms of control statements and calls to methods declared as abstract in the same class. Subclasses override the abstract methods to provide implementations which will be called using the dynamic binding mechanism when the superclass algorithm is executed.

The methods that can be directly identified are:

- A constructor, which will create the patches and then allocate a number of turtles around the patches.

- A method to step the simulation forward one or more time steps.

- An abstract method to output the grid to the display. This needs to be abstract as the grid class can't know anything about how a grid may be displayed, just that it can be.

Attempting to translate the design into Java code, however, reveals more details. First, the constructor needs to include a loop like the following:

```
for (int i = 0 ; i < sizey ; ++i) {
  for (int j = 0 ; j < sizex ; ++j) {
    patches[i][j] = ??? ;
  }
}
```

The problem here is that the constructor needs to construct a grid of *concrete* patch objects without knowing which concrete class to use, as this would violate the requirement of the grid class and its methods being generic. A convenient way to solve this problem is to use a *Factory* class. This class will provide an abstract create patch method that can be overridden by a concrete subclass to create patch objects for a specific simulation. The grid class is then written to use the abstract factory class without needing to know about any concrete subclasses even though it will actually be using a concrete subclass object. Thanks to inheritance and dynamic binding a concrete subclass object can be used wherever an object of the abstract superclass type has been specified. At runtime, the grid object is supplied with a concrete factory object and can go ahead and create the correct concrete patch objects.

This will result in the loop above looking like:

```
for (int i = 0 ; i < sizey ; ++i) {
  for (int j = 0 ; j < sizex ; ++j) {
    patches[i][j] = factory.createPatch() ;
  }
}
```

This technique will also be useful for creating turtles. Further consideration also reveals that the factory can be an interface rather than a class, as it won't need to provide any method bodies.

The code above also shows that another decision that has been made: the grid will be stored using a two dimensional array. The rationale for this is partly based on convenience (arrays and array indexing are convenient to use) and partly with some idea that arrays will allow efficient access to the grid, although there is no quantifiable evidence to back this up at this stage. Whether these assumptions will stand the test of time remains to be seen but decisions have to be made to make progress, and no compelling reason not to use arrays has so far been put forward.

We can now go ahead and present the actual Java code for the full version of class `Grid`, not forgetting that getting to this point has been the result of a number of iterations of design and coding. It is immediately noticeable that quite a bit of infrastructure has been added to the class beyond that discussed above.

```
package SimFrameWork ;
import java.util.List ;
import java.util.ArrayList ;
/**
 *  Abstract Grid class representing a generic world. This class is
 *  written so that it does not depend on any particular simulation.
 *  Note that the class is dependent on abstract methods that must be
 *  overridden by subclasses to plug in the specific behaviour for a
 *  particular simulation.
 *
 *  @version 2.0 March 1999
```

```
 *   @author Graham Roberts
 */
public abstract class Grid {
  /**
   * Create a grid of given size using patches
   * supplied by a factory object.
   *
   * @param x width of grid in patches
   * @param y height of grid in patches
   * @param f factory object to be used to create patches
   * @param d display object used to display grid.
   */
  public Grid(int x, int y, Factory f, Display d) {
    sizex = x ;
    sizey = y ;
    factory = f ;
    display = d ;
    turtles = new ArrayList() ;
    patches = new Patch[y][x] ;
    // Create all the patches
    for (int i = 0 ; i < sizey ; ++i) {
       for (int j = 0 ; j < sizex ; ++j) {
         // Use the factory to create patches without
         // having to specify the concrete patch type
         // used.
         patches[i][j] = factory.createPatch() ;
       }
    }
    // Connect all the patches together.
    linkPatches() ;
    // Now add turtles to grid.
    createTurtles() ;
  }
  /**
   *  Move the simulated world through 100 time steps, to allow the
   *  simulation to move forward at a reasonable speed. At some
   *  point this should be modified to allow the number of steps to
   *  be changed by the users.
   */
  public final void step() {
    for (int i = 0 ; i < 100 ; ++i) {
      count++ ;
      update() ;
    }
    // When the update is completed, redisplay the grid.
    output() ;
  }
  /**
   *  Return number of timesteps completed.
   */
  public int getTimeCount() {
    return count ;
  }
  /**
   *  Output grid representation to display.  Must be
   *  overridden as this class has no knowledge of how grids are
   *  actually displayed.
   */
  public abstract void output() ;
  /**
   *  Update grid one time step.
   */
  public abstract void update() ;
  /**
   *  Create turtles and add to patches on grid.  This version
   *  completely delegates to a subclass.
```

```java
    */
  public abstract void createTurtles() ;
  /**
   * Link patches to their neighbours.
   */
  private void linkPatches() {
    for (int i = 0 ; i < sizey ; ++i) {
      for (int j = 0 ; j < sizex ; ++j) {
        Patch patch = patches[i][j] ;
        if (i > 0) {
          patch.setNeighbour(Patch.S,patches[i-1][j]) ;
          if (j > 0) {
            patch.setNeighbour(Patch.SW,patches[i-1][j-1]) ;
          }
          if (j < (sizex-1)) {
            patch.setNeighbour(Patch.SE,patches[i-1][j+1]) ;
          }
        }
        if (j > 0) {
          patch.setNeighbour(Patch.W,patches[i][j-1]) ;
        }
        if (j < (sizex-1)) {
          patch.setNeighbour(Patch.E,patches[i][j+1]) ;
        }
        if (i < (sizey-1)) {
          patch.setNeighbour(Patch.N,patches[i+1][j]) ;
          if (j > 0) {
            patch.setNeighbour(Patch.NW,patches[i+1][j-1]) ;
          }
          if (j < (sizex-1)) {
            patch.setNeighbour(Patch.NE,patches[i+1][j+1]) ;
          }
        }
      }
    }
  }
  /**
   *  Width of grid in patches.
   */
  protected int sizex ;
  /**
   *  Height of grid in patches.
   */
  protected int sizey ;
  /**
   * Count of the number of time steps.
   */
  protected int count = 0 ;
  /**
   *  Factory to be used to create turtles and patches.
   */
  protected Factory factory ;
  /**
   *  2D array of patches in the grid.  Using an array as once
   *  connected, patches remain fixed in position.
   */
  protected Patch[][] patches ;
  /**
   *  Collection of all turtles on the grid.
   */
  protected List turtles ;
  /**
   *  Display object used to render grid on.
   */
  protected Display display ;
}
```

The complete class sees the addition of a private helper method called `linkPatches` to link the patches together. The update method has been split into two, with the new method `step` providing the basic behaviour of iterating through time steps, and the abstract method `update` allowing a concrete subclass to provide specialised behaviour. As simulations require very large numbers of time steps (tens of thousands) to show results, the `step` method actually goes through one hundred single updates to speed things up. A counter is provided to keep track of how many time steps have been performed.

As decided earlier, the class uses a two-dimensional array to hold a reference to each patch in the grid. This is in addition to the references each patch holds to its neighbours. There is a bit of overhead in doing this but there are advantages when it comes to displaying the grid. The class also maintains a `List` of all the turtles as this will be needed when iterating through the set of turtles to update them for each time step. The rest of the declarations in the class provide the instance variables needed by all grid objects.

note

`List` *is a container interface from the Java Collections framework.*

26.6.2 The Factory Interface

The factory interface introduced in the previous sub-section is used to declare the methods needed for the creation of patches and turtles.

```
package SimFrameWork ;
/**
 *  Abstract Factory interface for creating turtles and patches.
 *  This provides an interface that allows other classes to
 *  create turtles and patches without needing to know
 *  the specific turtle and patch subclasses used.
 *
 *  @version 2.0 March 1999
 *  @author Graham Roberts
 */
public interface Factory {
  /**
   *  Create a new patch.
   */
  Patch createPatch() ;
  /**
   *  Create a new turtle on a given patch.
   *
   *  @param p patch turtle is created on.
   */
  Turtle createTurtle(Patch p) ;
}
```

26.6.3 Class Patch

The generic patch class requires methods to do the following:
- Construct patch objects.
- Add and remove turtles as they move around. This implies that a variable holding the collection of turtles currently on a patch is needed.
- To access the collection of turtles on the patch.

- To access and update the patch value.

- To get a reference to a neighbouring patch.

This results in the code listed below.

```java
package SimFrameWork ;
import java.util.List ;
import java.util.ArrayList ;
/**
 *  This class represents the abstract properties of a patch in a
 *  simulation.
 *
 *  @version 2.0 March 1999
 *  @author Graham Roberts
 */
public abstract class Patch {
  /**
   *  An array is used to store references to patch neighbours
   *  (for efficiency) and a List collection to store the turtles
   *  currently on the patch.
   *  The neighbours are fixed and once connected do not change.
   *  The turtles do change so an ArrayList is used for easy
   *  manipulation. Only this class should know the actual
   *  implementation type is ArrayList. All other class should
   *  use the List interface.
   */
  public Patch() {
    neighbours = new Patch[8] ;
    turtles = new ArrayList() ;
  }
  /**
   *  Update patch one time step.
   */
  public abstract void update() ;
  /**
   *  Add a turtle to the collection already on patch.
   *
   *  @param t turtle to be added to those on the patch.
   */
  public final void addTurtle(Turtle t) {
    turtles.add(t) ;
  }
  /**
   *  Return number of turtles on patch.
   *
   *  @return the number of turtles on the patch.
   */
  public final int turtleCount() {
    return turtles.size() ;
  }
  /**
   *  Remove turtle from patch.
   *
   *  @param t turtle to be removed from the patch,
   */
  public final void removeTurtle(Turtle t) {
    turtles.remove(t) ;
  }
  /**
   *  Return list of turtles on patch.
   *
   *  @return a List of the turtles on the patch.
   */
  public final List getTurtles() {
    return turtles ;
```

```
}
/**
 *  Return reference to selected neighbour patch.
 *
 *  @param i direction of neighbour.
 */
public final Patch getNeighbour(int i) {
  return neighbours[i] ;
}
/**
 *  Return patch value.  This can be overridden to provide a
 *  more sophisticated kind of value or values.
 *
 * @return integer value of patch.
 */
public int value() {
  return patchValue ;
}
/**
 *  Increment value of patch.
 */
public void incrValue() {
  patchValue += 1 ;
}
/**
 *  Decrement value of patch.
 */
public void decrValue() {
  patchValue -= 1 ;
}
/**
 *  Connect patch to a neighbour. Protected so that the method is
 *  only accessible inside package.
 *
 *  @param nbour direction of neighbour to connect.
 *  @param p reference to neighbouring patch.
 */
protected final void setNeighbour(int nbour, Patch p) {
  neighbours[nbour] = p ;
}
/* These constants are used to provide directions for neighbouring
 * patches.
 */
/**
 *  Constant to represent North
 */
public final static int  N = 0 ;
/**
 *  Constant to represent North East
 */
public final static int NE = 1 ;
/**
 *  Constant to represent East
 */
public final static int  E = 2 ;
/**
 *  Constant to represent South East
 */
public final static int SE = 3 ;
/**
 *  Constant to represent South
 */
public final static int  S = 4 ;
/**
 *  Constant to represent South West
 */
```

```
      public final static int SW = 5 ;
      /**
       *  Constant to represent West
       */
      public final static int  W = 6 ;
      /**
       *  Constant to represent North West
       */
      public final static int NW = 7 ;
      /**
       *  Generic value of patch, available to all patches.
       *  Subclasses can add more.
       */
      protected int patchValue;
      /**
       *  References to neighbouring patches
       */
      private Patch[] neighbours ;
      /**
       *  Collection of turtles currently on patch.
       */
      private List turtles ;
    }
```

The class defines a set of constants (static final variables) which are needed to encode the points of the compass when linking patches and when turtles move around the patches. These are used to index an array of references to the neighbouring patches.

An abstract `update` method has been provided to allow patches to be updated each time step (although this won't be used further in the ant simulation).

26.6.4   Class Turtle

The turtle class turns out to be simple as most of the behaviour, such as moving around, needs to be delegated to a concrete subclass. The basic turtle methods are:

- A constructor which places a turtle on a specific patch.
- An update method, to update the turtle each time step.

Although initially it was thought a turtle might need a value to indicate its state, this has been left out, as it seems to be a subclass responsibility.

```
    package SimFrameWork ;
    /**
     *  This class represents the basic properties of a turtle in a
     *  simulation.
     *
     *  @version 2.0 March 1999
     *  @author Graham Roberts
     */
    public abstract class Turtle {
      /**
       *  A turtle must be located on a patch when constructed.
       *
       *  @param p patch turtle is located on.
       */
      public Turtle(Patch p) {
        location = p ;
      }
      /**
```

```
        *   Update turtle state one time state.
        */
      public abstract void update() ;
      /**
        *   Patch where turtle is currently located.
        */
      protected Patch location ;
    }
```

A generic turtle has a reference to the patch it is located on. Any other state is added by subclasses.

26.6.5 Class Display

The display class connects the generic framework classes to concrete classes that actually display things. It can make no assumptions about how a simulation is displayed so relies on abstract methods to delegate behaviour to subclasses.

A grid will be displayed by calling a class `Display` method to output a value for each patch in turn. This implies that the display object must retain a complete displayable representation of a simulation grid, updated one patch at a time. Once the complete grid has been processed, the display object can be told to show the grid, so that the new grid representation appears on the screen. Hence, grid objects are responsible for iterating through the patches and drive the display process. An alternative implementation, worth exploring in future work, would be for the grid class to return a member class object that the display can use to access the grid. The display might then take over iterating the patches via the member object.

The methods needed by the display class are:

- A constructor that records the size of the grid to be displayed, allowing subclasses to directly access that information.
- A method to accept the value of a specified patch.
- A method to display the grid.

The full code for the class is:

```
package SimFrameWork ;
/**
  *   Abstract Display class for rendering grids.
  *
  *   @version 2.0 March 1999
  *   @author Graham Roberts
  */
public abstract class Display {
  /**
    *   Create new display for a grid of given grid size.  Use x,y
    *   coordinates to refer to patches.  In this abstract class the
    *   width and height are given in terms of the number of patches,
    *   not any graphics unit.
    *
    *   @param w width in patches of display.
    *   @param h height in patches of display.
    */
  public Display(int w, int h) {
    width = w ;
```

```
    height = h ;
  }
  /**
   *  Display patch at x,y with value c.
   *
   *  @param x patch x coordinate.
   *  @param y patch y coordinate.
   *  @param c value of patch to be displayed
   */
  public abstract void show(int x,int y,int c) ;
  // The following methods should be overridden by derived classes
  // but may be defined to do nothing, depending on the way the
  // actual display class works.
  /**
   *  Clear display area so it is blank.
   */
  public abstract void clear() ;
  /**
   *  Update display to show current grid.
   */
  public abstract void showGrid() ;
  /**
   *  Display width in patches.
   */
  protected int width ;
  /**
   *  Display height in patches.
   */
  protected int height ;
}
```

A method called `clear` has also been included as some displays may need to be cleared before each update of the full grid.

26.6.6   Class Control

We now have a collection of abstract classes that provide the components originally identified (`Patch`, `Turtle`, `Grid`). Class `Grid` provides a `step` method to move the simulation through one or more time steps but we are still missing an overall control component that drives a simulation. This is obviously going to include a loop that repeatedly calls the grid's `step` method but we need to consider some additional issues.

Running a simulation is going to be processor intensive, and it can be anticipated that sooner or later we will want several other distinct activities to be going on simultaneously (such as displaying status information, providing a control panel and so on). This strongly suggests that the main simulation loop runs within its own separate thread, with other activities also each having their own thread.

Further analysis reveals that each activity has the same basic control mechanism: keep looping while the thread is active, and provide a safe way of stopping the thread once it is no longer needed. This basic behaviour can be captured in an abstract class that can be added to the framework.

```
package SimFrameWork ;
/**
 *  This class provides a basic extension of class Thread, providing a
 *  control loop and a safe way of terminating the thread.
 *
```

```
 *   @version 2.0 March 1999
 *   @author Graham Roberts
 */
public abstract class Control extends Thread {
  /**
   * Default constructor is declared for completeness but doesn't
   * do anything
   */
  public Control() {
  }
  /**
   *  Default run policy is to loop while the thread is kept active,
   *  and defer all other behaviour to an abstract update method.
   */
  public void run() {
    active = true ;
    while (active) {
      update() ;
    }
  }
  /**
   *  Stop the thread by setting the active flag to false.
   */
  public void stopControl() {
    active = false ;
  }
  /**
   *  Do whatever the thread does.
   */
  public abstract void update() ;
  /**
   *  Flag used to store active state of simulation thread.
   *  Declared as volatile as its value can be changed by a thread
   *  other than the simulation thread, and we want to guarantee that
   *  the simulation thread always reads its current value.
   */
  private volatile boolean active = false ;
}
```

The most important thing about this class is the way it manages the thread, which is kept running in a while loop controlled by a boolean variable. Calling the stopControl method sets the boolean to false which causes the while loop and then the run method to terminate, resulting in the thread stopping safely.

This class is pretty basic and may well need extending as the framework is developed. In particular, synchronisation and thread priorities are not addressed and effectively delegated to subclasses. However, at this stage we don't have enough insight about what extensions may be desirable, so will go with this simple version.

26.6.7 Class MainLoop

To complete the SimFrameWork package it turns out to be useful to provide two non-abstract support classes. The first, a subclass of class Control seen in the last section, is class MainLoop which is responsible for running the main simulation. When constructed a MainLoop object is given a reference to a grid, representing a simulation world, that needs to be run.

```
package SimFrameWork ;
/**
```

```
     *   This class implements the main control loop of a simulation
     *   which is run in a separate thread.  This allows the simulation
     *   to run independently of whatever else the rest of the program
     *   is doing.
     *
     *   @version 2.0 March 1999
     *   @author Graham Roberts
     */
public class MainLoop extends Control {
    /**
     *   Need a world object to run.
     *
     *   @param g grid to be run.
     */
    public MainLoop(Grid g) {
      world = g ;
    }
    /**
     *   Move simulation through next time step.
     */
    public void update() {
      world.step() ;
    }
    /**
     *   Reference to world being run.
     */
    private Grid world ;
}
```

26.6.8   Class RandomGen

The final framework class is really no more than a re-packaging of class `java.util.Random` from the Java class libraries. Random numbers are used in simulations to give less predictable behaviour. Although the potential of the class is not exploited here, it serves to decouple the use of a random number generator from a specific (and unchangeable) library class. If changes are needed they can be made in this class without the rest of the code having to be modified to use a different methods.

```
    package SimFrameWork ;
    import java.util.Random ;
    /**
     *   This is a utility class providing a wrapper for the JDK class
     *   java.util.Random, giving a simple interface to random number
     *   generation used by simulations.
     *   A single instance of the class is created and initialised
     *   when the class is loaded (an example of the Singleton pattern).
     *   If a more sophisticated generator is needed, this class
     *   will localize the effects of any changes made.
     *
     *   @version 2.0 March 1999
     *   @author Graham Roberts
     */
    public class RandomGen {
      /**
       *   Do nothing constructor that is made private to prevent
       *   instance creation outside of the class scope.
       */
      private RandomGen() {}
      /**
       *   Generate a random integer in the range 0 to n-1 inclusive.
       *
```

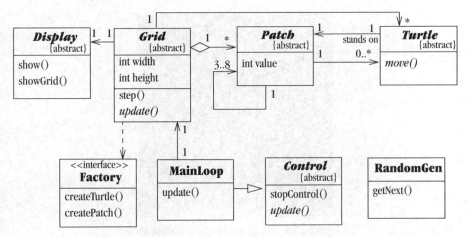

Figure 26.5 Final core framework class diagram.

```
 *   @param n the upper limit of the number generated.
 *   @return a random number in the range 0 to n-1.
 */
public static int getNext(int n) {
  return rand.nextInt(n) ;
}
/**
 *   Variable used to represent the single instance.
 *   The Random class constructor will seed the random number
 *   generator automatically using the current time.
 */
private static Random rand = new Random() ;
}
```

26.6.9 The Complete Framework

We have now defined all the classes in the `SimFrameWork` package. The class diagram shown in Figure 26.5 shows the final set of classes. The next step is to define concrete subclasses of the abstract classes, provide a class with the static `main` method, and implement a complete simulation application.

26.7 The Concrete Classes

The longer term aim is that each specific simulation will provide its own set of concrete subclasses but use the superclasses from the framework unchanged. To verify that the framework is adequate, and identify changes and extensions, we need to build applications using the framework. The concrete classes that follow will implement the simple ant nest material foraging simulation described earlier in the chapter.

The simulation will use a simple GUI built from Swing components, as shown in Figure 26.6. The display shows each patch as a small square coloured according to what is located on the patch. An empty patch has the default background colour of brown while patches containing piles of wood

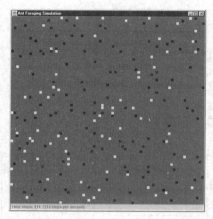

Figure 26.6 The ant simulation — near the start.

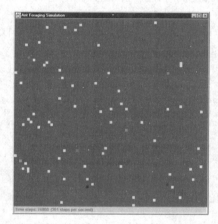

Figure 26.7 The ant simulation — after running some time.

chips but no ants are displayed in green, with the brightness of the green colour increasing as more chips are concentrated on the patch. A patch containing one or more loaded ants (i.e. ants carrying a wood chip) is coloured yellow, while one with unloaded ants is coloured red. The graphics on the screen are updated after every execution of the simulation's main loop, consisting of 100 time steps. Below the graphics display is a status bar which shows the number of time steps the simulation has run through.

Initially the display shows a number of wood chips scattered around the grid (see Figure 26.6). After the simulation has been running for a few minutes the number of patches containing wood chips has decreased to around ten (see Figure 26.7), with each of those being coloured bright green indicating that there are a large number of wood chips on the patch. As the simulation runs, the number of piles of wood chips can only decrease and never increase (as a wood chip cannot be dropped on an empty patch). The simulation is likely to reach a state of equilibrium with a stable number of 'nests'.

26.7.1 Class AntPatch

Class `AntPatch` inherits from class `Patch` and does no more than initialize a patch to contain one or zero wood chips.

```
import SimFrameWork.Patch ;
import SimFrameWork.RandomGen ;
/**
 *   Subclass of Patch specialising patches for the ant simulation.
 *
 *   @version 2.0 March 1999
 *   @author Graham Roberts
 */
class AntPatch extends Patch {
  /**
   *   Antpatches don't do much except use the patch value field as a
   *   count of the number of wood chips on the patch. Constructor
   *   initializes the count randomly.
   */
  public AntPatch() {
    int n = RandomGen.getNext(100) ;
    if (n > 90) {
      patchValue = 1 ;
    } else {
      patchValue = 0 ;
    }
  }
  /**
   *   Not required for this simulation but must be overridden to
   *   make this class concrete.
   */
  public void update() {}
}
```

The `update` method is not used by this simulation but must be overridden as it was declared as abstract in the superclass.

26.7.2 Class Ant

Class `Ant` is the specialization of `Turtle` and implements the ant rules described in Section 26.3.

```
import SimFrameWork.Patch ;
import SimFrameWork.Turtle ;
import SimFrameWork.RandomGen ;
/**
 *   This class provides Ant objects for the simple ant foraging
 *   simulation, by specializing the Turtle class.
 *
 *   @version 2.0 March 1999
 *   @author Graham Roberts
 */
class Ant extends Turtle {
  /**
   *   Ant creation. An ant does not initially carry a wood chip.
   *
   *   @param p patch ant is initially located on.
   */
  Ant(Patch p) {
    super(p) ;
    chip = false ;
  }
  /**
   *   Update ant by one time step.
```

```
     */
    public void update() {
      // Move ant a random distance.
      move() ;
      // If ant has a chip and if the current patch already has
      // at least one chip on it then assume it is a pile and
      // drop chip.
      int val = location.value() ;
      if (chip && (val > 0)) {
        location.incrValue() ;
        chip = false ;
        return ;
      }
      // If the ant is not carrying anything and there is a chip
      // available pick it up.
      if (!chip && (val > 0)) {
        location.decrValue() ;
        chip = true ;
      }
    }
    /**
     *   Test if ant is carrying a wood chip.
     *
     *   @return return true if the ant is carrying a wood chip.
     */
    public boolean isLoaded() {
      return chip ;
    }
    /**
     *   Move ant a random distance in a random direction.
     */
    private void move() {
      int distance = RandomGen.getNext(3) ;
      int direction = RandomGen.getNext(8) ;
      Patch p = location ;
      for (int i = 0 ; i < distance ; ++i) {
        Patch t = p.getNeighbour(direction) ;
        if (t != null) {
          p = t ;
        }
      }
      location.removeTurtle(this) ;
      location = p ;
      location.addTurtle(this) ;
    }
    /**
     *   Set to true when ant is carrying a woodchip.
     */
    private boolean chip ;
}
```

A private helper method called move has been added to deal with moving the ant a random distance in a random direction. This makes use of the network of connections between patches.

An extra public method called isLoaded has been added to return true if the ant is carrying a wood chip. This requires each ant to have a boolean variable called chip to record the carrying state (the fact that turtles have values, like patches, may be something which needs to be added back to the Turtle class in a future review).

26.7.3 Class AntWorld

AntWorld is the specialization of Grid and only needs to implement the abstract methods declared in Grid.

```java
import java.util.List ;
import java.util.Iterator ;
import SimFrameWork.* ;
/**
 *  AntWorld - a specialized grid representing an ant world.
 *
 *  @version 2.0 March 1999
 *  @author Graham Roberts
 */
class AntWorld extends Grid {
  /**
   *  Create a grid specialized for the ant simulation.
   *
   *  @param x width of display in patches.
   *  @param y height of display in patches.
   *  @param d display object to display simulation.
   */
  public AntWorld(int x, int y, Display d) {
    super(x,y,new AntFactory(),d) ;
  }
  /**
   *  Iterate through the grid of patches and output a value for
   *  each patch, using the display object.
   */
  public void output() {
    display.clear() ;
    for (int i = 0 ; i < sizey ; ++i) {
      for (int j = 0 ; j < sizex ; ++j) {
        // Generate a display value for each patch
        Patch patch = patches[i][j] ;
        int patchvalue = patch.value() ;
        List turtles = patch.getTurtles() ;
        int val = 0 ;
        if (patchvalue > 0) {
          val = patchvalue ;
        }
        if (turtles.size() > 0) {
          val = -1 ;
          for (Iterator iter = turtles.iterator() ;
               iter.hasNext() ; ) {
            Ant ant = (Ant)(iter.next()) ;
            if (ant.isLoaded()) {
              val = -2 ;
              break ;
            }
          }
        }
        // Send the coordinates and value of each patch to the
        // display object.
        display.show(j,i,val) ;
      }
    }
    // Tell the display object that the iteration is complete and
    // that it should go ahead and display the grid.
    display.showGrid() ;
  }
  /**
   *  Call update for one time step on all updatable objects. For
   *  this simulation, only the ants need to be updated.
   */
```

```
      public void update() {
        for (Iterator i = turtles.iterator() ; i.hasNext() ;) {
          ((Turtle)i.next()).update() ;
        }
      }
      /**
       *  Allocate ants at random around the grid.
       */
      public void createTurtles() {
        for (int i = 0 ; i < 150 ; ++i) {
          int px =  RandomGen.getNext(sizex) ;
          int py =  RandomGen.getNext(sizey) ;
          Patch p = patches[py][px] ;
          Turtle t = factory.createTurtle(p) ;
          turtles.add(t) ;
          p.addTurtle(t) ;
        }
      }
    }
```

The output method needs some attention in the future but has been left as it is pending development of the GUI in a future version of the simulation.

26.7.4   Class AntFactory

The `Factory` interface needs to be implemented by a factory class that will generate ants and ant patches. This results in class `AntFactory` which very simply implements the methods declared in `Factory`, returning appropriate new objects.

```
import SimFrameWork.Factory ;
import SimFrameWork.Patch ;
import SimFrameWork.Turtle ;
/**
 *  AntFactory for creating ants and ant patches. This specialises the
 *  framework factory class to create ant specific objects.
 *
 *  @version 2.0 March 1999
 *  @author Graham Roberts
 */
class AntFactory implements Factory {
  /**
   *  Create and return an ant.
   *
   *  @param p patch ant is located on.
   *  @return new ant.
   */
  public Turtle createTurtle(Patch p) {
    return new Ant(p) ;
  }
  /**
   *  Create and return an ant patch.
   *
   *  @return a new ant patch.
   */
  public Patch createPatch() {
    return new AntPatch() ;
  }
}
```

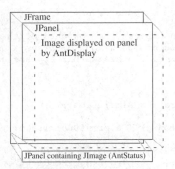

Figure 26.8 Structure of the GUI.

26.7.5 Class AntApp — The Application Class

A class is needed to contain the static `main` method and tie everything else together. Called class `AntApp`, it does not inherit from any of the framework classes as it will be specific to the ant simulation. `AntApp` is also responsible for constructing the user interface, or GUI, from Swing components.

The GUI is layered as shown in Figure 26.8. The window is built from a `JFrame` containing two `JPanel`s. The bottom `JPanel` contains a `JLabel` used to display status information. The top `JPanel`, which occupies most of the window area, displays an `Image` created by `AntDisplay` to graphically show the simulation world. The image object is generated off-screen and then copied onto the panel. This allows the display to be completely updated all at one go and is much quicker than trying to update the display one patch at a time.

When a world grid is displayed, each patch is displayed as a square block of pixels. Both the size of the grid in patches and the size of the displayed blocks in pixels are fixed by final instance variables. These can be changed by editing the class and re-compiling it. Ideally, however, it would be better to have controls or settings the user can interactively configure when the program is running.

The `AntApp` class constructor actually builds the user interface, adding an event handler to allow the user to quit the program. A separate method called `runSimulation` needs to be called to start a simulation. When the program terminates, the class also makes sure that any threads are properly stopped.

```
import java.awt.* ;
import javax.swing.* ;
import java.awt.event.* ;
import SimFrameWork.* ;
/**
 *  This class provides the application window that an ant
 *  simulation grid is displayed in. It also provides the static
 *  main method and declares variables to specify the size
 *  of the grid being used.
 *
 *  @version 2.0 March 1999
 *  @author Graham Roberts
 */
```

```java
public class AntApp extends JFrame {
  /**
   *  Construct and layout the contents of the display window.
   *  The main area of the window displays a graphical representation
   *  of the ant world. A status bar appears at the bottom of the
   *  window.
   */
  public AntApp() {
    super("Ant Foraging Simulation") ;
    try { jbInit(); }
    catch (Exception e) { e.printStackTrace(); }
  }
  private void jbInit() throws Exception {
    getContentPane().setLayout(new BorderLayout()) ;
    displayPanel = new JPanel() ;
    // Force the display panel to be the correct size to display
    // the simulation grid.
    displayPanel.setPreferredSize(
      new Dimension(WIDTH*BLOCKSIZE,HEIGHT*BLOCKSIZE)) ;
    getContentPane().add("Center",displayPanel) ;
    // Add a status panel at the bottom of the window
    JPanel statusPanel = new JPanel(new BorderLayout()) ;
    statusPanel.setBorder(BorderFactory.createLoweredBevelBorder()  ;
    getContentPane().add("South",statusPanel) ;
    statusLabel = new JLabel() ;
    statusPanel.add(statusLabel) ;
    // Add a listener for the window being closed.
    // This just exits the application.
    addWindowListener(new WindowAdapter () {
      public void windowClosing(WindowEvent e) {
        stopSimulation() ;
        System.exit(0) ;
      }
    }) ;
    pack() ;
    setVisible(true) ;
  }
  /**
   *  Create a new ant world and start the simulation.  The simulation
   *  itself is run as a separate thread, as is the routine to update
   *  the status bar at the bottom of the window.
   */
  public void runSimulation() {
    AntDisplay display =
      new AntDisplay(WIDTH,HEIGHT,BLOCKSIZE,displayPanel) ;
    AntWorld world = new AntWorld(WIDTH,HEIGHT,display) ;
    control = new MainLoop(world) ;
    control.start() ;
    status = new AntStatus(world,statusLabel) ;
    status.start() ;
  }
  /**
   *  Stop the simulation thread.
   */
  public void stopSimulation() {
    status.stopControl() ;
    control.stopControl() ;
  }
  /**
   *  Main method to start the application.
   */
  public static void main(String[] args) {
    AntApp app = new AntApp() ;
    app.runSimulation() ;
  }
  /**
```

```
     * Thread object used to run the simulation.
     *
     */
    private MainLoop control ;
    /**
     * Thread object used for the status thread.
     *
     */
    private AntStatus status ;
    /**
     * Panel used to display the simulation grid.
     */
    private JPanel displayPanel ;
    /**
     * Label used to display status information.
     */
    private JLabel statusLabel ;
    /**
     * Constants setting the simulation grid size in patches.
     */
    private final int WIDTH = 75 ;
    private final int HEIGHT = 75 ;
    /**
     * Constant setting display block size in pixels.
     */
    private final int BLOCKSIZE = 8 ;
}
```

26.7.6 Class AntDisplay

The `AntDisplay` class is the specialization of the generic `Display` class, and makes use of the AWT `Image` class to display a representation of the simulation world. When the value of each patch is set by a call to the `show` method, a coloured square block is drawn at the appropriate position on the image. When the `showGrid` method is called, indicating that the full grid has been output, the image is copied onto the display panel and appears on the screen.

```
import java.awt.* ;
import javax.swing.* ;
import SimFrameWork.Display ;
/**
 *  This class specializes Display to show an ant simulation display,
 *  using AWT/Swing graphics.
 *
 *  @version 2.0 March 1999
 *  @author Graham Roberts
 */
class AntDisplay extends Display {
    /**
     *  Initialize display. For better performance a grid is first
     *  drawn onto an off-screen image. When complete the image
     *  is copied onto the display panel in one operation.
     *
     *  @param x width of display in patches
     *  @param y height of display in patches
     *  @param size size of patch in pixels
     *  @param p JPanel used to display the graphics image
     */
    public AntDisplay(int w, int h, int size, JPanel p) {
        super(w,h) ;
        panel = p ;
        blocksize = size ;
        image = p.createImage(w*blocksize,h*blocksize) ;
```

```java
      imageGraphics = image.getGraphics() ;
    }
    /**
     *  Display patch at x,y with value val.  The value of val is
     *  mapped to a colour used to display the patch.
     *
     *  @param x x position of patch.
     *  @param y y position of patch.
     *  @param val value of patch.
     */
    public void show(int x, int y, int val) {
      x *= blocksize ;
      y *= blocksize ;
      // If val is greater than zero then it represents
      // the number of wood chips on a patch.
      // If -1 then an unloaded ant.
      // If -2 then a loaded ant.
      if (val > 0) {
        val = val * 5 ;
        val = (val > 255) ? 255 : val ;
        Color clr = new Color(0,val,0) ;
        imageGraphics.setColor(clr) ;
        imageGraphics.fillRect(x,y,blocksize,blocksize) ;
      } else if (val == -1) {
        imageGraphics.setColor(ANTCOLOR) ;
        imageGraphics.fillRect(x,y,blocksize,blocksize) ;
      } else if (val == -2) {
        imageGraphics.setColor(LOADEDANTCOLOR) ;
        imageGraphics.fillRect(x,y,blocksize,blocksize) ;
      }
    }
    /**
     *  Clear the display panel and display brown as the background
     *  color.
     */
    public void clear() {
      imageGraphics.setColor(new Color(128,64,0)) ;
      imageGraphics.fillRect(0,0,width*blocksize,height*blocksize) ;
    }
    /**
     *  Show the updated image by copying it onto the display panel.
     */
    public void showGrid() {
      panel.getGraphics().drawImage(image,0,0,panel) ;
    }
    // Variables to deal with graphics.
    private JPanel panel ;
    private Graphics imageGraphics ;
    private Image image ;
    private int blocksize ;
    // Colors of ants.
    private final Color ANTCOLOR = Color.red ;
    private final Color LOADEDANTCOLOR = Color.yellow ;
  }
```

26.8   Class AntStatus

As a simulation runs it is useful to be able to display status information, such as how many time steps have passed. The simulation window provides a status bar, containing a JLabel that can be used to display the status information and class `AntStatus` is responsible for generating and updating the information.

Although in the ant simulation we are only displaying information about the number of time steps completed, it can be anticipated that other, more detailed, information may be wanted in the future. Further, we can assume that updates will need to occur at fixed intervals, but not necessarily after every time step. In fact, time steps are likely to pass so quickly that far too many updates would occur otherwise. Given this, we need to update the status information using a separate thread that runs periodically, say every second, and this is what `AntStatus` provides.

The behaviour of an `AntStatus` object is to start a new thread, and then repeatedly fetch the number of time steps completed from the `Grid` object, update the status display and sleep for 1 second. As class `Control` in the framework already provides part of this behaviour (looping repeatedly with safe thread termination), `AntStatus` is made a subclass. This conveniently means that all threads used within the simulation program (excluding those used by the Java runtime system) are created by subclasses of `Control`. This may be important in the future if `Control` is modified to provide more sophisticated thread management, as we wouldn't have to separately modify `AntStatus`.

```java
import SimFrameWork.* ;
import javax.swing.* ;
/**
 *   This class displays basic status information for the
 *   ant simulation.
 *   By inheriting from Control, the status update is run
 *   as a separate thread.
 *
 *   @version 2.0 March 1999
 *   @author Graham Roberts
 */
public class AntStatus extends Control {
  /**
   *   Use the Grid object to obtain status information and the
   *   JLabel to display it.
   *
   *   @param g grid object providing status information
   *   @param l JLabel used to display information on screen
   */
  public AntStatus(Grid g, JLabel l) {
    grid = g ;
    label = l ;
  }
  /**
   *   Perform the status update. Use the sleep method to wait 1 second
   *   between each update.
   */
  public void update() {
    int count = grid.getTimeCount() ;
    label.setText(" Time steps: " +
                  new Integer(count).toString() +
                  " (" + (count-lastCount) + " steps per second)") ;
    lastCount = count ;
    try {
      sleep(1000) ;
    }
    catch (InterruptedException e) { }
  }
```

```
/**
 *  The priority of this thread is increased by one, so
 *  that the status thread is guaranteed priority
 *  over the simulation thread. This is needed to ensure
 *  that the status thread will be run on
 *  JVMs that don't support pre-emptive
 *  multi-tasking of threads with the
 *  same priority.
 */
public void run() {
  setPriority(getPriority()+1) ;
  super.run() ;
}
/**
 *  Reference to simulation object holding statistics
 */
protected Grid grid ;
/**
 *  Label used as status display.
 */
JLabel label ;
/**
 *  Record of number of time steps completed at last update.
 */
private int lastCount = 0 ;
}
```

note

Pre-emptive multi-tasking means that the JVM gives each thread its own chunk of processing time in turn, so that each thread is guaranteed a chance to run.

There is one complication with the implementation of AntStatus to do with thread scheduling. By default new threads are given the same thread priority and compete with threads at that priority for processing resources. If a JVM does not support pre-emptive multi-tasking of threads at the same priority, it is possible for one thread to hog the processor, starving all the other threads. This could mean that the simulation thread prevents the status thread from running on time or even from running at all.

If a JVM does support pre-emptive multi-tasking this would not be an issue as the status thread would be guaranteed processing time. However, we want simulation programs to work correctly with all JVMs, so need to provide a solution that is not dependant on the detailed behaviour of a JVM. The solution turns out to be simple — the thread priority of the status thread is increased by 1, so that it will interrupt the simulation thread and update the status display. This will not slow down the simulation thread significantly, as the status thread does little actual processing and spends most of its time sleeping. We should make a note, though, that future modifications to AntStatus must not significantly increase the amount of processing it does. In the longer term it may be better to incorporate a better thread scheduler into class Control, and keep all threads at the same priority.

Finally, class AntStatus need not be the only class displaying information that is periodically updated. Future developments could include a family of classes, all of which update at different intervals.

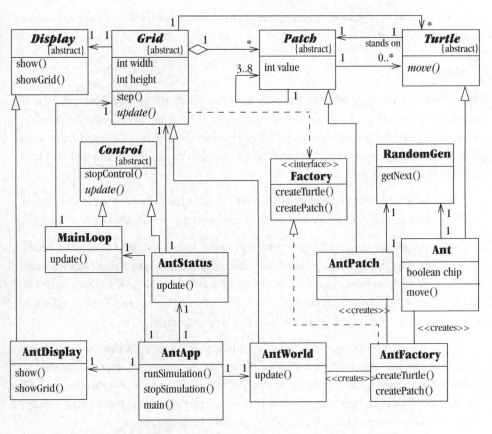

Figure 26.9 Class diagram for the complete program.(Java library classes are not shown.)

26.9 The Complete Program

The full set of classes has now been described resulting in the overall program structure shown in Figure 26.9.

Each class (and interface) presented in the chapter is stored in a separate `.java` file, named after the class (or interface). The classes in the `SimFrameWork` package must go into a subdirectory called `SimFrameWork`, following the rules for dealing with packages (see Section 30.5, Page 864).

Once each source file has been compiled, the program is run using the command:

```
java AntApp
```

from the command line (or using the development environment equivalent).

All the classes have been documented using documentation comments, meaning that it is possible to automatically generate WWW based documentation for them. This is very convenient and a big time saver when producing documentation for class libraries. Always be sure to document your code as you go along!

26.9.1 Testing

Before finishing we must consider the issue of testing. Although we have been following a prototyping approach this should not be used as an excuse to be sloppy. As each class is worked on it should be tested and re-tested continuously. Testing verifies that objects of the class behave in the way intended, while re-testing verifies that changes and additions not only work but don't break anything that previously worked.

Being disciplined about testing also leads to more disciplined thinking about what a class should do. If you don't know how to test a class, you don't know what the class should actually be doing.

In this prototyping context we can perform unit testing. Initially the unit is a class, so we test each class, relying on the assumption that if each class works, then the combination of them is more likely to also work. As more classes are developed it becomes possible to test groups of classes together. Distinct from the unit testing, there is also application testing, where the entire application is tested. This will come later when a useful prototype is up and running.

Unit testing involves writing a test harness class to test each application class. For an abstract class, the test harness will need be a subclass. The test harness class then creates instance objects, calls the object's methods and checks the result of the method call or the state of the object to see if the expected result or changes have occurred. Over time a collection of test classes will be built up, each performing a range of tests, which can be easily and repeatedly run.

There are packages that support and automate unit testing, one of the most useful and straightforward being JUnit developed by Erich Gamma and Kent Beck. This can be downloaded (free) from http://www.xprogramming.com/software.htm.

26.10 Summary

This chapter has presented a prototyping approach to the development of a simple simulation program. The main purpose has been the identification of a core framework of classes that can potentially be re-used for many simulations. The framework has been shown to be viable by the development of a simulation based on it.

At this stage we now have a much better idea of how our simulation programs might be designed and what classes are needed. This was the reason behind using the prototyping approach in the first place — explore the problem and identify a potential solution. The next stage in development is to try the framework with other simulations to see if it is adequate or if it requires further extensions. Once the framework and general program design have been proven, the code can be re-worked to production quality and put into use.

Self-review Questions

Self-review 26.1 Why is continuous testing important?

Self-review 26.2 What is a test harness?

Self-review 26.3 Think carefully about the update rules in the ant program. Why do piles of wood chips appear? Does it matter that ants could remove wood chips from a large pile?

Self-review 26.4 Consider the overall efficiency of the simulation framework. Are there alternative data structures for the grid, patches and turtles that might lead to much faster execution of the program?

Programming Exercises

Exercise 26.1 A thought exercise: The ant simulation program will be run as a sequential program. Will this give different results compared with a parallel version of the simulation run on a parallel machine?

Exercise 26.2 Classes `Patch` and `Turtle` seem to have a number of similarities. Can they be combined into a single abstract class? Try declaring such a class and verify that `Ant` and `AntPatch` can still be declared as subclasses of it.

Exercise 26.3 Draw an object diagram corresponding to the class diagram shown in Figure 26.9. The object diagram should show objects of the classes, rather than the classes themselves.

Exercise 26.4 Add start, stop and pause control buttons to the GUI of the ant application.

Exercise 26.5 Extend the GUI of the ant application so that the size of the grid, the initial number of ants and wood chips, and the colours used can all be set by the user.

Exercise 26.6 The core framework of classes is designed to be subclassed to provide different simulations. Select two or more additional simulations and add them to the framework (visit the StarLogo web site at http://starlogo.www.media.mit.edu/people/starlogo/index.html to find simulations).

Challenges

Challenge 26.1 The behaviour of ants in the simulation is hard-coded by methods in class `Ant` (and in `AntPatch`). To change the behaviour requires the code to be modified and re-compiled. To avoid this add the ability to specify ant behaviour using a mini-language, allowing the user of the program to interactively experiment with different behaviours without having to stop and recompile the program. A mini-language is a small, simple programming language. Each ant or ant patch could be controlled by a mini-language program.

Part 4

The Java Programming
Language in Detail

Objectives

This part provides a systematic description of the Java programming language. The aim is to provide a language reference for those learning Java which is supported by many small example programs showing how to use the language features.

Contents

A Java Language Reference

Objectives

This part of the book describes the Java language in detail, providing a language reference for those new to Java, along with many small example programs and advice on how to use the language effectively. This chapter gives a short introduction as to how the reference is structured.

Keywords

syntax
semantics
examples

27.1   Introduction

Parts 1 and 2 introduced the ideas and concepts underlying Java and object-oriented programming, giving examples of what Java programs look like. Part 3 investigated a few larger programs to show Java in action. In this part of the book we work systematically through a description of the Java programming language. The main purpose is to review and confirm knowledge of Java being as precise as possible about the semantics of the various components of the language so as to support construction of correct Java programs.

Whilst we will describe the language, we will not be describing the Java class libraries in any detail. There are several reasons for this. Firstly, the libraries contain many hundreds of classes, so there is a lot to write about and we don't have room in the book! Secondly, as noted a number of times already in this book, the J2SDK is accompanied by a complete set of library documentation in the form of Web pages. Much of the time, browsing these pages is more convenient that using a book-based reference. Thirdly, there are a number of good books and Web sites devoted to explanation of the Java libraries.

The documentation is currently distributed as a separate file to be included with the main J2SDK system. Make sure that this documentation has been installed on the machines you are using.

27.2   Syntax and Semantics

The Java language is described by its *syntax* and *semantics*. The syntax defines the structure and appearance of Java source code when it is written down. The semantics define what each piece of code means and how it will behave when executed.

The basic components of the syntax are *keywords* and *tokens*. A keyword is a word or *identifier* that has a specific meaning in the language. For example, the if keyword is used to introduce if statements. Words which are keywords may only be used in the way the language defines. Tokens include every other word, name, symbol or group of symbols that appear in the source code of the program. Names include class, method and variable names, while symbols include brackets ([], {}, ()) and operator symbols (+, −, *, /, &, =, ", ', etc.). Groups of symbols include numbers (123) and any other valid combination of characters.

A *grammar* is used to bring all the components of the syntax together and define the structure of syntactically correct units of Java code. The Java grammar specifies the precise order in which keywords and symbols can be written down and is used by the Java compiler to make sure the programmer has got things right! Any code that is not grammatically correct will cause the compiler to emit error messages and not construct an executable program.

The grammar only specifies the order in which things can be written down. To interpret the meaning of what has been written we need the language semantics. This defines the meaning of every properly constructed expression in a piece of program code, allowing us to reason about what the code does. Note, however, the semantics provide no guarantee that the code we write does anything useful or sensible! It only allows us to know what happens when the code is executed.

It is worth noting that the Java language has been defined using informal semantics which are described textually but hopefully correctly and unambiguously. Java does not have a formal semantics described using a formal or mathematical notation.

To be an effective Java programmer, both the syntax and the semantics of the language need to be understood. This enables the programmer to not only know how to express an idea in code but also how to interpret what the code will do.

27.3 The Presentation

The chapters in this part will describe the Java language by working through its features, starting with the basic building blocks (variables, types and expressions), then flow control (selection and iteration), then classes and finishing with exceptions and threads. As well as describing the syntax and semantics of each language feature, small example programs are provided to illustrate how the feature is used, accompanied by some advice about how to get the best from the feature.

To aid with the description of each feature a series of heading labels are used. These include *Purpose*, *Intention*, *Syntax*, *Description* and *Examples*.

Purpose gives a short description of what the feature is for.

Intention outlines what the intention is behind providing the feature.

Syntax outlines the keywords, symbols or structure of the feature using an informal notation.

Description provides a detailed description of the properties of the feature and how to use it.

Examples gives at least one example program that uses the feature along with advice about the style of use.

When first learning the language it is worth reading through the complete description of each feature and having a close look at the example programs. As experience is gained the syntax and example sections provide a reference, while the description can be used for more information when problems or issues arise.

27.4 The Example Programs

Many language features are illustrated with small example programs. All of these programs are Java *applications,* meaning that they are run from the command line prompt (or equivalent on your development environment). They are not Java applets and so cannot be run within Web browsers.

As a number of these programs are very short they consist only of a single class containing a single method. This method is the *static main* method that must be provided with an application in order to locate the starting point when the program is run. Every Java application must declare at least one class, as there is no way to define methods outside of a class. This gives the following basic outline for the examples:

```
public class Test {
  public static void main(String[] args) {
    // The example program code
  }
}
```

Additional methods and classes are added to this basic structure for the more advanced examples.

As many examples are short they may not exhibit much in the way of object-oriented design but all of them are implemented in an object-oriented way since Java supports only object-oriented programming. In order to provide sensible programs in the earlier sections of this part, some use will inevitably be made of features not yet presented.

Input and output (I/O) is done using the standard input and output streams, which by default are connected to the computer keyboard and terminal window. The Java Abstract Window Toolkit (AWT) and Swing are not used in this part.

Output to the screen is done using `System.out` which is the standard output stream, meaning that it is the default place to send output (`System` is a library class that maintains information about the program's environment, `out` is a public member variable of type `PrintStream`). Output will be done using statements like:

```
System.out.println("This is some output") ;
```

This calls the `println` method of the `PrintStream` object referenced by the public static data member `out` of class `System`. When the statement is executed, "This is some output" will appear in the initiating terminal window.

The `println` method is overloaded so there are actually versions that can take arguments of type `String` and of any primitive type (`int`, `double`, `char`, etc.). This allows statements such as the following to be written:

```
int i = 123 ;
System.out.println(i) ;
float f = 3.141 ;
System.out.println(f) ;
```

There is also a version that can take an argument of type `Object` allowing any object value to be printed. This works by automatically inserting a call to the `toString` method (inherited from `Object`) to generate a displayable string value.

It is also possible to output several values by concatenating their `String` representations using the '+' operator as follows:

```
System.out.println("The value of i is: " + i) ;
```

The argument to `println` will evaluate to the single string "The value of i is: 123" which is then output.

The `println` method always outputs a newline following the value displayed, meaning that the next piece of output will start on the next line. There is another method `print` which behaves exactly the same as `println` but does not output a newline.

While output is relatively straightforward, input is trickier. `System.in` is a public variable of type `InputStream` that is used to read input typed at the keyboard. All input is received as characters or strings of characters representing the value typed on the keyboard. These characters then have to be converted to the type of value that is actually wanted. For example, the integer 123 would be typed as three characters, '1' followed by '2' then '3' and finally the return key, requiring a conversion from the characters into an integer value; a process called *parsing*. While output can be done in one step, input often requires several steps. Input is further complicated by the need to deal with exceptions that can be thrown by input streams.

As it is useful to use input in the example programs without having to be concerned with the handling of exceptions, a supporting class called `KeyboardInput` is provided to package up the input operations. The following reads an integer value then a character value from the keyboard:

```
KeyboardInput in = new KeyboardInput() ;
int i = in.readInteger() ; // Read in an integer
char c = in.readCharacter() ; // Read in a character
```

The `KeyboardInput` implementation is shown in the appendix (see Appendix F, Page 963). If an error occurs during input, a default value will be returned and no exceptions will be propagated. For the example programs this is entirely sufficient but real applications will undoubtedly want to provide rather more robust input.

The example programs are written under the assumption that `KeyboardInput` will be in the same Default package as the application, so no import statements are needed.

To say that input is harder than output is a serious understatement. It is an unfortunate fact of life that input of any kind to a program is generally awkward, not least because you have to anticipate the strange things that users of your programs might try!

27.5 Summary

In this chapter, we have presented the required background information so that we are ready to move on to the description of the Java language.

Variables, Types and Expressions

Objectives

This chapter introduces the basic building blocks of variables, types and expressions and their supporting infrastructure.

Keywords

comments

documenation

variables

types

expressions

operators

28.1   Introduction

To start writing programs, we need to know how to express basic concepts such as variables and types. These need to be named, using a declaration, and written down in a syntactically correct way. Expressions then provide the means for combining types, variables and operators into meaningful combinations to create new values. In turn, expressions form the sub-structure of *statements* which comprise the code of a program.

Starting with a short description of source code comments, this chapter continues by defining what a name is and how names can be expressed. It then describes types and variables, both of which need names, before moving on to expressions and operators. The reader is assumed to be familiar with the material presented in Part 1 as, by necessity, explaining the basic features requires forward references to more advanced features.

28.2   Comments

Purpose

Comments allow the source code of a program to be annotated with textual notes which are ignored by the compiler.

Intention

In many cases the source code of a program needs additional descriptive comments in order to make clear to a human reader what sections of the code actually do. Such comments are made using a specific syntax and appear in the program text. Except in one case, all comments are ignored by the compiler.

Comments should be used to add information not obvious by a quick scan of the program code. Typically, each class and method has an introductory comment explaining its purpose, with comments being added for variables and algorithms as necessary. The programmer should strike a balance between providing too few comments, making the intent of the code hard to follow, and too many comments, burying the code in large amounts of text. Comments should not be used to state the obvious.

Syntax

Comments come in three forms:

```
// This is a single line comment
/* This is multi-line
   comment */
/** This is a documentation
    comment */
```

Description

The first kind of comment is marked by the use of `//` and can start anywhere on a line. The comment continues until the first newline (i.e. the end of the current line). The start of the next line is not within the comment. The comment can contain any character and all characters in the comment will be ignored by the compiler.

The start of the second kind of comment is marked by /* which can appear anywhere on a line. The comment continues on the current line and any subsequent lines until the end comment marker, */ is found (hence the name multi-line comment). The comment can contain any characters except the sequence */. Multi-line comments cannot be nested, as the first appearance of */ always marks the end of the comment regardless of how many times /* might have appeared.

The third kind of comment is the documentation comment. These are recognized by a JDK tool called `javadoc`, that will read documentation comments and automatically generate Web pages containing a neatly formatted version of the comment information. Each page documents one class and will list each instance variable and method along with any comment information provided. The Java libraries are documented using documentation comments and the `javadoc` tool.

Documentation comments start with the marker /** and end with */. They can span multiple lines but may not be nested. Only documentation comments that appear immediately before class declarations, interface declarations, instance variable declarations and method declarations are recognized by `javadoc` as documentation comments, any others are treated as though they were multi-line comment. Within a documentation comment, various *tags* can appear which allow comment information to be processed in specific ways by the `javadoc` tool. Each tag is marked by an @ symbol and should start on a new line. The following set of tags is a subset of all possible tags, these being the ones that are the most frequently used (see the Java 2 Platform documentation for the full set of tags):

`@author` — name the author(s) of the code being commented. The author's name is simply written as text:

```
@author Graham Roberts
```

Multiple author tags can appear or several names can be put into the same tag:

```
@author Graham Roberts, Russel Winder
```

`@deprecated` — used to indicate that the following class or method is left over from a previous version of the code and is to be removed in future versions. The tag can be followed by a short explanation:

```
@deprecated Will not be available in the next version
```

Ideally `@deprecated` should be followed by an `@see` tag directing the reader to the replacement feature. This tag is recognized by the Java compiler which will issue a warning message if the deprecated feature is used.

`@exception` — provide information on exceptions that may be thrown by a method. An exception name appears after the tag followed by a textual comment:

```
@exception IndexOutOfBoundsException an attempt was made to
    access an invalid element
```

A documentation comment can contain several `@exception` tags.

`@param` — provide information about method and constructor parameters. The tag is followed by a parameter name and then a comment:

```
@param size size of the data structure
```

These tags should only appear in comments preceding methods and constructors. Ideally, there should be one tag for each parameter, presented in the same order as the parameters.

`@return` — document the return value for non-void methods.

```
@return the index of the matching element
```

The comment is simply text. A documentation comment should only contain one `@return` tag since there can only be a single return value.

`@see` — provide a cross reference to another class, interface, method, variable or URL. The following are all valid cross references:

```
@see java.lang.Integer
@see Integer
@see Integer#intValue
@see Integer#getInteger(String)
@see <a href="info.html">See here for further information</a>
```

Classes and interfaces can be referenced by either their name or full package name. Instance variables and methods can be referenced by appending their name to the class name following a # symbol. URLs can appear if formatted using the HTML `<a>...</a>` tags. Multiple `@see` tags can appear in a single comment.

`@since` — used to state when a particular feature was included (i.e. since when it has been available). The tag is followed by text giving the required information:

```
@since JDK1.0
```

`@version` — used to give version information about the current revision of the code being commented. The format of the version information is not specified and is left to the programmer. An unofficial convention is growing in usage that the version number is followed by the release date

```
@version 1.2 2000.01.08
```

Only one version tag can appear within a single comment.

Text within a documentation comment can also marked with HTML tags used for controlling the appearance of text, including `<code>...</code>` (delimits text that should appear in the font used for program code) and `<p>` (indicates the start of a new paragraph, often used in delimiter form `<p>...</p>`). Books on HTML should be consulted for details of the HTML notation.

Examples   Single line comments are typically used either on the line preceding the statement being commented, or on the end of the same line.

```
// Height of the widget in centimetres.
float height = 2.54 ;
float width = 5.6 ; // Width of the widget in centimetres.
```

Multi-line comments can be placed as a block where needed:

```
/* This is a comment which is
   several lines long, and will explain
   what the following method is supposed
   to do.
*/
int f() { ... }
```

The following class declaration illustrates the use of documentation comments:

```
/**
   This is a test class to show the use of documentation
   comments.
   @author Graham Roberts
   @see java.lang.String
   @version 1.0 1997.08.10
*/
public class Comment1 {
   /**
      A string used by the <code>main</code> function.
   */
   static String s = "Hello" ;
   /**
      Return the argument times 2.
      @param x the integer value to be doubled.
      @return the method argument doubled.
      @deprecated will be removed in the next version of the class
      @see #multiplyByTwo
   */
   public int times2(final int x) {
     return x * 2 ;
   }
   /**
      Return the argument times 2.
      Replacement for the previous version of this method.
      @param x the integer value to be doubled.
      @return the method argument doubled.
   */
   public int multiplyByTwo(final int x) {
     return 2 * x ;
   }
   /**
      The main function used to test the class.
      @param args command line arguments (not used).
   */
   public static void main(final String[] args) {
     Comment1 test = new Comment1 () ;
     int n = test.times2(5) ;
     n = test.multiplyByTwo(10) ;
     System.out.println(s) ;
   }
}
```

When processed by the `javadoc` tool, this source code produces the Web page that is shown in Figure 28.1.

The classes comprising the ADS package developed in Part 2 contain many examples of the use of documentation comments. In using a slightly different layout style for the documentation comments to that shown above, the documentation comments in the ADS package classes show that the actual appearance of the comments is a matter of personal style. The important criteria is that the comment style be consistent, readable and obvious.

In the case of the multi-line comment, experience with C and C++ programming, from which Java inherits the feature, has found that the five styles shown in Figure 28.2 have emerged as the most favoured.

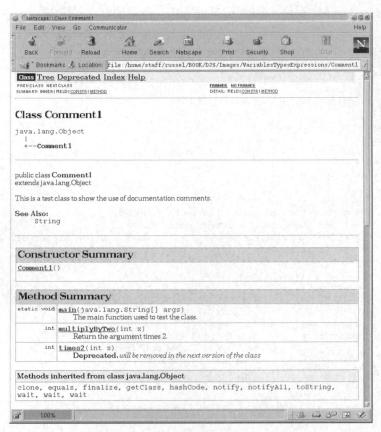

Figure 28.1 A Web page generated by `javadoc`.

```
/*                          /*                          /*some words
   some words                  some words                  comprising
   comprising                  comprising                  a comment */
   a comment                   a comment
*/                          */


          /*                          /*
          * some words                ** some words
          * comprising                ** comprising
          * a comment                 ** a comment
          */                          */
```

Figure 28.2 Various styles of multi-line comment.

28.3   Identifiers

Purpose   Variables, methods, classes and interfaces all need to be named, i.e. given an *identifier*. Rules are
             needed to tell us what the legal identifiers are and from what characters they can be constructed.

Intention   Identifiers allow the programmer to give variables, methods, classes and interfaces sensible names
             that reflect their purpose. Without this it would not be possible to write any form of human readable
             code.

An identifier is some sequence of characters that names something within a program. For example:

```
result, PI, today, xyz123, aVeryLongNameThatIsAwkwardToType
```

An identifier is basically formed from any sequence of alphabetic characters or digits that starts with an alphabetic character. To be absolutely correct, an identifier is any unlimited sequence of *Unicode* characters representing a letter or digit that starts with a *JavaLetter*. Names can also include the underscore (_) and $ (although $ shouldn't be used in normal code).

The Unicode Standard is an international standard that defines the representation of characters from a wide range of alphabets. Traditionally, programming languages have used the ASCII (American Standard Code for Information Interchange — ANSI is the American National Standards Institute) character set. This is limited to 127 (or 256 for extended ASCII) characters, stored in 7 (or 8) bits, which basically includes those characters that appear on a standard QWERTY keyboard. For programmers that use the English language this provides more or less all the characters that are needed. However, Java aims to be an international programming language and should be usable with the character sets required by as many languages as possible. This requires far more than 256 different characters. Representing characters using Unicode allows Java to do this. Unicode stores characters as 16-bit values so the basic Java character has a 16-bit representation.

Identifiers must start with a JavaLetter, which is any character for which the method `Character.isJavaIdentifierStart` returns true. Any Unicode character that does not represent a digit or punctuation character will be a Java Letter according to this method. In the English alphabet these are the characters `A-Z`, `a-z`, `_` (underscore) and `$`. A similar method called `isJavaIdentifierPart` will return true for any valid letter or digit in the Unicode character set that can be used for all other characters in a name except the first. These include the digits `0-9`.

Providing the restrictions in the last paragraph are met, an identifier can be of unlimited length. For practical reasons, it is best to keep identifiers to less than about twenty characters.

Identifiers cannot include spaces and cannot be any of the Java keywords or literals listed in Appendix D, Page 957.

Valid identifiers include:

```
answer, total, position, Person, distance, size
```

When choosing identifiers it is good practice to use those that give meaning to the thing being named. For example, a variable named 'result' is more meaningful than one named 'r'.

Identifiers can use any valid Unicode character, although you may find that your editor has trouble displaying and working with them; the following are valid Java names:

```
ανσωερ, τοταλ, ποσιτιον, Περσον, διστανχε, λαστ_τοταλ, σιζε
```

A common practice is to create an identifier as a concatenation of two or more words, separated by either underscore characters or by using capitalization of the first letter of words:

```
last_total, relativePostion, gridElement
```

By convention, identifiers that start with a capital letter are only used for class or interface names and identifiers that are all in upper case denote constants. Variable and method names start with a lower case character. Defining and following naming conventions like these aid the readability of code.

28.4   Unicode Escapes

Purpose

To provide a universal way of representing Unicode characters.

Intention

There are many thousands of potential characters, most of which it will not, in general, be possible to type directly in an editor. Unicode escapes allow them to be represented. Further, it allows programmers to use their own local character set for developing Java programs — assuming appropriate tools are available.

Description

A Unicode escape stands for a character and is represented using the `\u` escape sequence followed by the hexadecimal digits of the character code the escape represents.

A critical feature of Unicode escapes is that they are processed and converted into characters before anything else is done to the program text. Moreover, there is a standard way of translating from source text written using Unicode escapes into an ASCII based subset that can be worked on by tools such as the Java compiler. This allows the source code of a program to be written in any supported language.

Examples

The following are Unicode escapes:

```
\u0343, \u2f4, \uabcd
```

28.5   Literals

Purpose

Literals allow values of primitive types, the `String` type or `null`, to be written directly as part of a program text.

Intention

Values of some types need to be expressed directly in the source code of a program. Without this facility it would be difficult to write most of the programs we would want to. In particular, integer and `String` literals are widely used.

Description

Literals can be of the following types (see Section 28.6 for more information on types):

   `int` and `long` (integers)

   `float` and `double` (floating point numbers)

   `boolean`

   `char` (character)

   `String`

> `null` (the null reference)

A literal can be used in any expression where its use will be type correct.

Integer Literals

Examples

Decimal values of type `int` (32-bit) can be written as follows:

    0, 123, -456, 55665, 2354545, -3456345

Octal values of type `int` are preceded by a leading 0 followed by digits in the range 0–7:

    00, 0123, 0777, -045323, 023232, -01

Hexadecimal values of type `int` are preceded by 0x or 0X. Hexadecimal digits can be represented by a–f or A–F as well as 0–9:

    0x0, 0X12F, -0xffed, 0XFFFF, 0x12def1, 0xff342232

Literals of type `long` (64-bit) are denoted by appending L or l to any of the integer literal representations:

    0L, 0l, 1223434545L, 0xffeeL, 077L, -345435431, -045l, -0XC0B0L

Floating-point Literals

Basic floating point numbers include a decimal point. By default floating point numbers are of type `double`:

    1.2345, 1234.4323423, 0.1, 3.4, .3, 1., -23.456

If the floating point number is suffixed with f or F it will be of type `float`:

    1.23f, 2.34F, 0f, .2F, -4.5643F, -4434.223f

The suffix d or D can be similarly used to denote type `double`.

Floating point literals can also be written using exponent format with e or E with the same rules concerning the appending of f, F, d and D as applied above:

    4.54003e+24, 5.3453E-22, 1.2e5F, -1.978748E+33D, 2.54465e+9f

Floating point literals cannot be written using octal or hexadecimal notation.

Boolean Literals

There are, not surprisingly, two boolean literals:

    true, false

These are effectively treated as keywords and the names cannot be reused for anything else.

Character Literals

A character literal represents a single character and is bounded by single quotes:

    'a', 'A', '!', '3', '{', ' '

Characters that don't have a visible representation (e.g. newline or tab) require an escape sequence which is denoted by \ followed by a character:

    '\b' backspace
    '\f' formfeed

'\n' newline

'\r' carriage return

'\t' tab

Some punctuation characters also need the escape sequence:

'\\' backslash

'\'' single quote

Escape sequences can also be used to specify the octal code of a character directly. Valid codes are from 000 to 377 and no leading zero is needed:

\123, \167, \023

Unicode escapes can also be used as characters literals. Note that because Unicode escapes are processed first there can be a few surprises. For example, if the Unicode character representing linefeed appears in a character literal ('\u000a') it will be translated into an end of line in the program text, not a linefeed character literal.

String Literals

String literals are enclosed in double quotes and will be stored as String objects when the program is executed. String literals can include escape characters (most often newline):

"This is a string", "Hello World\n", "One\tTwo\tThree"

Null Literal

This simply appears as null and, like the boolean literals, is also effectively a keyword.

28.6   Types

The idea of type was introduced in Section 2.5.3, Page 28, so that we know a type has a name and represents a set of values. Java has two categories of types: primitive types and reference types. For each type there is a set of operators for operations on values of that type (e.g. +, -, *, etc.).

Java is a strongly typed language, meaning that all expressions, values and objects must have a type, and the use of the types must be consistent. The Java compiler will enforce the correct use of types through strong type checking.

28.6.1   Primitive Types

Purpose   To represent the fundamental, built-in types that are part of the Java language. All other types are constructed from the primitive types using classes, interfaces and arrays.

Intention   There must be a set of fundamental or primitive types on which to build everything else. They represent the lowest level of representation of values. Given these building blocks and mechanisms for combining them, we can create any other type we require.

The primitive types fall into the following categories:

Boolean — `boolean`

Numeric

Integral — `byte, short, int, long, char`

Floating point — `float, double`

These types are chosen as primitive as they reflect the basic types that are directly support by a typical machine processor, making them the most efficient types to use. Operations on these types usually map directly to processor instructions. Having said that, Java carefully defines a standard representation for each of these types, so they behave exactly the same on any machine supporting a Java Virtual Machine (JVM). Most current processors can actually support these representations directly.

The primitive types are represented as follows:

`boolean`

The `boolean` type simply has two values, `true` and `false`.

`byte`

8-bit signed 2's complement integers, range: -128 to 127

`short`

16-bit signed 2's complement integers, range: -32768 to 32767

`int`

32-bit signed 2's complement integers, range: -2147483648 to 2147483647

`long`

64-bit signed 2's complement integers, range: -9223372036854775808 to 9223372036854775807

`char`

16-bit unsigned values from 0 to 65535, representing Unicode characters.

`float`

Single-precision, 32-bit IEEE 754 format floating-point values, range: 1.40239846e-45 to 3.40282347e+38

`double`

Double-precision, 64-bit IEEE 754 format floating-point values, range: 4.9406564581246544e-324 to 1.79769313486231570e+308

There are three special floating point values: 'positive infinity', 'negative infinity' and 'not-a-number' (NaN). These are generated when floating point operations overflow or a division by zero occurs.

The operators defined for these types will be described in Section 28.9.2.

The Java class library provides (in the package `java.lang`) a class matching each of the primitive types above, allowing the values of these types to be represented as objects. These classes are `Boolean`, `Byte`, `Short`, `Integer`, `Long`, `Character`, `Float` and `Double`.

There is one further type which is built into the language like the primitive types. This is type `void` (`void` is a keyword). There are no values of type `void` so it has no representation. The only use of `void` is for declaring methods that return no result (or to be more accurate return a value of type `void` for which no representation and, hence, no storage is required).

28.6.2 Reference Types

Purpose   To represent types defined by classes, interfaces and arrays.

Intention   Classes, interfaces and arrays each allow new types to be constructed. Values of these types are always objects, so reference types are used to denote the type of an object being referenced by an expression.

Description There are three kinds of reference type: *class types, interface types and array types*. Every expression that references an object has a reference type. Objects themselves can *conform* to one or more reference types.

A *class type* is created when a new class is declared. The type name will be the same as the class name.

An *interface type* is created when a new interface is declared. The type name will be the same as the interface name.

An *array type* is specified whenever an array is declared. For example, `int[] i ;` has the type `array of int` (see Section 28.8.3 on array variables).

Type names are *identifiers* and follow the rules shown in Section 28.3.

The `String` reference type is given special recognition within the language due to the need to support string `String` literals, despite there being a class `String` in the class library.

28.6.3 Automatic Type Conversion

Java provides a variety of automatic conversions between types that allows greater flexibility in writing expressions. For example, it is possible to assign a value of type `int` to a variable of type `long`. This is allowed as `ints` can be converted to `longs` without loss of information. The opposite assignment, `long` to `int` is not allowed as it can potentially lose information — the range of `long` is larger than that of `int`. Conversions in the opposite direction can be forced using a cast expression, providing the programmer is prepared to potentially lose information (see Section 28.9.2).

The following types of automatic conversions are supported:

Widening Primitive Conversions — these convert from one primitive type to another providing there is no loss of information. The conversions allowed are:

byte to short, int, long, float or double

short to int, long, float or double

int to long, float or double

long to float or double

float to double

Widening Reference Conversions — these allow a reference of a subclass type to be treated as a reference of a superclass type.

String Conversion — when the + (string concatenation) operator has one argument of type String the other argument can be converted from any other type to type String.

Conversions like those above are performed during assignment and when values are passed as method parameters. This allows the programmer to write statements such as:

```
short a = 12 ;
long b = a ;
```

even though at first sight a and b are of different types. When such code is compiled, the compiler will insert the needed conversions automatically and without comment. Most of the time this will not cause any problems but occasionally it can cause surprises, particularly in the case of reference conversions.

The use of a conversion is often talked about using the phrase '*assignment compatible*', so for example ints are assignment compatible to longs.

28.7   Scope

A scope defines a region of a program within which a variable, method, class, interface or package can be declared (given a name and type) and be used. Outside of its scope, a named entity is not accessible and may not exist. Scope is used as the basis of encapsulation.

Purpose

We want to carefully define in which parts of a program a named entity can be accessed and used. By confining use to a specific region, we limit the accessibility of an entity to the minimum necessary, preventing other parts of the program from misusing it. We can also tie the lifetime of a variable to its scope, so it can be known when to create or destroy it.

Intention

A program can use the following scopes:

Description

Global Scope — names in this scope are accessible to any statement within the entire program. Only package names are global.

Package Scope — a package defines a scope and a unit of encapsulation. Names declared within the package can be global to the package and can also be made public so they are accessible to users of the package. Packages cannot be nested within one another but one package can use another.

Compilation Unit Scope — a compilation unit is, in effect, a synonym for a source file. Names can be global to the file. All contents of any file are always part of a package.

Class Scope — names declared within a class are accessible to *any* other part of the same class or of subclasses if public or protected. Names can also be made public so they are accessible to users of the class, or if not specified public, protected or private can be accessible to other classes within the same package (see Chapter 30).

Local Scope — a compound statement (a statement delimited by { and } and which can contain a sequence of other statements) defines a local scope. Method and control statement bodies are also both local scopes. Local scopes may be *nested* to as many levels as needed (i.e. one local scope can be declared within another local scope). Names declared in a local scope are only accessible within that scope or any nested scope. Moreover, the name is only usable from the textual point of declaration until the end of the scope, i.e. you can't use a name before it has been declared in the text (compare this with class scope).

Scopes are always nested within one another, with the global scope at the outermost level. A name declared in a nesting or containing scope is accessible to nested or contained scopes unless hidden by another declaration using the same name.

Examples

Examples of global, package compilation unit and class scope will appear when those features are discussed in detail.

A local scope is typically defined by a compound statement:

```
{
    int i ; // A variable local to this scope.
}
// i is not accessible here and does not exist
```

Any name declared in a local scope is not accessible outside the scope. Local variables declared within a local scope are created when the scope is entered and destroyed when the scope is left (we say the variable has gone out of scope). Once a local variable has gone out of scope it cannot be recovered. If the scope is re-entered a new local variable will be created.

Variables defined in a local scope cannot be redefined in a nested local scope:

```
{       // Nesting or outer local scope
  int i = 2 ;
  int j = 4 ;
  ...
  {    // Nested or inner local scope
   int i = 6 ; // ERROR -- redeclaring i from nesting local scope
   j = 8 ; // j from nesting scope is still accessible
  }
}
```

note

Overriding variable names defined in a nesting local scope within a nested local scopes is permitted in C++ but not in Java.

28.8 Variables

Variables are named containers that hold representations of values which can be changed by assignment. A variable has a type which dictates the kind of representation it can hold.

Java is an imperative language that relies on variables to hold the state of the computation. A program uses a collection of variables that can change their contents over time. Without the ability to store and manipulate the state held in its variables, a Java program would not be able to do anything that required remembering or storing values.

28.8.1 Declaring Variables

A variable must be given a name (which is an identifier) and type before it is used, using a declaration. The declaration also identifies the variable scope and the kind of variable it is meant to be.

Purpose

The rules of the language and the need to do strong type checking require that a variable is properly introduced. Allowing variables to be used without declaration would effectively make the compilation and execution model of Java programs impossible. It would also lead to programs that are much harder to understand, debug and maintain.

Intention

The basic syntax for declaring variables is:

Syntax

```
typename identifier ;
```
or
```
typename identifier = expression ;
```

The former is a variable with default initialization, the latter is an explicitly initialized variable. Depending on the scope, variable declarations can be preceded by one or more of the keywords:

```
public, protected, private, final, static, transient, volatile
```

It is possible to declare two or more variables of the same type in the same declaration statement:

```
typename id1, id2, ... ;
```

Individual variables within such a list can also be initialized.

There are two categories of variable:

Description

1. Variables of primitive type which directly contain a representation of a value of a primitive type.
2. Variables of reference type which hold a reference to an object *conforming* to the named type or the value `null` (which is the null reference).

A variable declaration introduces a variable into the current scope, giving the variable a name and type. All variables *must* be declared and declared before being used.

As well as the two categories, various kinds of variables can be identified based on where they are declared:

Class variables are declared as `static` within a class. These are shared between all instance objects of a class.

Instance variables are declared within a class. Each instance object of the class will have its own copy of each instance variable declared.

Method and Constructor parameters are declared within the parameter list of a method or constructor.

Exception-handler parameters are declared within the parameter list of a catch clause.

Local variables are declared within any local scope, usually a compound statement, including method bodies.

A variable is declared by specifying its type and name, where the name is an identifier, following the rules for constructing identifiers. The following are variables with default initialization:

```
int j ;
long d ;
```

In addition, in the correct circumstances a variable can be declared `public`, `protected`, `private final`, `static`, `transient` or `volatile`, with the following intention:

`public` — the class or instance variable is accessible from all scopes.

`protected` — the class or instance variable is accessible only in the current class scope, the current package scope and in all subclasses of the current class.

`private` — the class or instance variable is only accessible in the current class scope.

`final` — the variable is a constant, so its value cannot be changed.

`static` — the variable is a class variable, shared between all instance objects of a class

`transient` — an instance variable is declared to not be part of an objects persistent state (i.e. if the objects state is saved, the value of a transient variable is not included).

`volatile` — sometimes needed when an instance variable is used by threads to prevent the compiler optimizing access to it.

The first three of these relate to the declaration of classes and will be covered further in Section 30.2.2, Page 836. Of the other four, the `final` keyword is the most important as it gives Java a mechanism for declaring constants. As well as instance variables, local variables, method parameters and exception-handler parameters can be declared final.

It is possible to declare several variables in the same declaration using a comma separated list such as:

```
int a, b, c ;
```

A variable name is an identifier following the rules in Section 28.3. By convention, variables names usually start with a lower case letter and should reflect the purpose of the variable. Hence, variable names such as `position`, `weight` or `colour` are much more preferable than `p`, `w` or `c`.

28.8.2 Variable Initialization

Provide a mechanism for giving a variable a known initial value at the point at which it is declared.

To support the construction of correct programs, we want a mechanism to guarantee that a variable is given a known, valid value as soon as possible after it is declared. This will prevent uninitialized variables being created containing a random value. Java requires that *every* variable is always initialized.

Variable initialization requirements vary with the kind of variable.

Class and Instance Variables

The usual practice is to explicitly initialize these kinds of variables. However, to meet the requirement that all variables are always initialized, Java provides default values for the primitive and reference types when they are declared without explicit initialization. The programmer, therefore, has the choice of relying on the default or providing an explicit initialization expression.

The following default values are used:

```
byte — (byte)0
short — (short)0
int — 0
long — 0l
float — 0.0f
double — 0.0d
char — '\u0000' (the null character)
boolean — false
reference types — null
```

If a variable of reference type is initialized to `null` it holds the `null` value directly and does not reference an object.

Class and instance variables can be explicitly initialized in three ways (see also Section 6.5, Page 155):

1. By giving an *initialization expression* following an = sign after the variable name:

   ```
   int i = 100 ;
   char c = 'd' ;
   float f = 10.345 ;
   ```

2. By using an instance initializer which is a compound statement placed immediately after the variable declaration containing statements which initialize the variable:

   ```
   int i ;
   { i = 100 ; }
   ```

3.   By assignment within a constructor body.

Where a list of variables is given in the declaration, each variable in the list may be explicitly initialized using a separate initialization expression:

```
int a = 10, b, c = 5 ;
```

Parameter Variables

These variables are always initialized to be a copy of the value used in the call of the method or constructor. There is no programmer control over this mechanism. (Note that objects are passed by reference, so the object reference is copied, not the object itself.)

Exception-handler Parameters Variables

These variables are always initialized to a copy of the value thrown by an exception.

Local Variables

All local variables must, either directly or indirectly, be *explicitly* initialized before use. This must be done by an initialization expression or initializer:

```
{
  int i = 10 ;
  ...
}
```

or by an assignment made to the variable before it is used in any other expression:

```
{
  int i ;
  ...   // no statements here can use i
  i = 10 ;// assign value to i
  // i can now be used
  ...
}
```

The Java compiler will check that an appropriate initialization or assignment has been done, reporting an error if it has not been done.

Final Variables

Normally a final instance or local variable is initialized as part of the declaration, as seen above. However, *blank finals* are also allowed where the initialization is deferred. Before a blank final variable is used it must be initialized by assignment but after that it cannot be changed.

Example

The following simple program shows some local variables being initialized and then used. Note the use of the blank final.

```
import java.util.Date ;
import com.objectspace.jgl.Array ;
public class Var1 {
  public static void main(final String[] args) {
    //  Initialize variables with an expression
    int i = 1 ;
    String s = "Hello";
    Date d = new Date () ;
    final Array a = new Array () ; //  a always refers to this Array.
    int j ; //  j declared but not initialized here
```

```
            //  j cannot be used here
            j = 4 ; //  j assigned here before being used.
            //  j can now be used
            //  If j had not been assigned to, the compiler would
            //  report an error on this line
            System.out.println(j) ;
            final int q ;  //  Blank final declaration
            // Cannot use q yet
            q = 10 ;        //  q now initialized
            //  Now cannot change q by assignment
            // q = 20 ;     //  error! if uncommented
            //  Now declare and initialize 3 variables in the same statement.
            //  Note that to initialize floats the literals must include f or
            //  F otherwise the compiler assumes they are doubles and we have
            //  a type mismatch.
            float fa = 1.0f, fb = 2.0f, fc = 3.0f ;
        }
        //  class variable
        static int m = 10 ;
        //  instance variable initialized using initializer statement
        int n ; { n = m * 2 ; }
    }
```

28.8.3   Array Variables

To allow arrays to be declared, making use of a supporting syntax to denote array types.   **Purpose**

Arrays are a special case within the Java language, so we need to establish an extra set of rules to   **Intention**
deal with them. Arrays are represented by objects but there is no class that array objects are
instances of. Variables of array type are declared using bracket ([]) notation.

```
    typename[] varname ;
    typename[] varname = arrayInitializationExpression ;
    typename varname[] ;
    typename varname[] = arrayInitializationExpression ;
```
Syntax

Multi-dimension arrays can be declared by repeating pairs of brackets up to the required
dimension.

Array initializers are supported:

```
    typename[] varname = { initializerList } ;
```

and also for multi-dimension arrays. This syntax is really just a short form for:

```
    typename[] varname = new typename[] { initializerList } ;
```

Arrays are *container objects* that can hold a fixed number of array elements (values) which are   **Description**
accessed by array indexing (see Chapter 5.2, Page 114).

A variable of array type holds a reference to an array object which is created by an array
initialization expression. Brackets are used to denote array types, so the declaration:

```
    int[] x = ... ;
```

declares x to be a variable of type array of int. A variation on the declaration syntax (a result of
the C++ influence on Java) allows the brackets to appear after the variable name. The following
declaration is exactly equivalent to the last:

```
    int x[] = ... ;
```

but this could be considered to be poor style since it splits the name of the type which is `int[]`. The first style of array declaration is used throughout this book.

The size of the array is not specified in the array type but is required when the variable is initialized. The size must always be expressed as a value of type `int`:

```
int[] x = new int[10] ;
```

This will create an array object for holding 10 integer values. Once created, the size of the array cannot be changed but the array variable can be reassigned (unless it is a final variable) to reference an array of the same type but different size. The above example illustrates that declaring an array variable is distinct from actually creating the array object. Array variables must be initialized according to the rules listed in Section 28.8.2.

Arrays of any type can be declared and type checking will be performed to make sure that only values of the correct type are stored in the array:

```
String[] words = new String[100] ;
```

After an array has been created it is possible to determine the number of elements it can hold using an expression like:

```
int l = words.length ;
```

`length` is an instance variable (see Section 30.2.3, Page 837) of the array object which holds the size or length of the array.

Multi-dimensional arrays can be declared by simply adding on dimensions using extra sets of brackets. For example, the following declarations and initializations are for two, three and four dimensional arrays:

```
int[][] twoD = new int[10][10] ; // 10x10 array
float[][][] threeD = new float[8][10][12] ; // 8x10x12 array
boolean[][][][] fourD =
        new boolean[4][8][12][16] ; // 4x8x12x16 array
```

A multi-dimensional array is effectively an array of arrays (of arrays, etc.), so each dimension is actually represented by another array object.

The length of a multi-dimensional array can also be found using the `length` variable:

```
int l = twoD.length ;
```

In this case the number of elements of the first dimension is returned (which is 10 using the declaration and initialization above). The length of other dimensions, which are represented by array objects, can be found by using an index expression (see Section 28.9.2) to return an element array and asking for its length:

```
int len = twoD[1].length ; // Length of 2nd row
```

When declaring multi-dimensional arrays, thought should be given to the overall size and resulting memory usage of the array. It can be easy to declare an array that will use a very large amount of memory.

The above examples all define the array size using integer literals. In fact, an integer valued expression can be used to specify the array size:

```
double[][] d = new double[rows][columns] ;
```

Multi-dimensional arrays are stored 'row-wise'. For a two dimensional array this means that the first dimension indicates the number of rows and the second dimension the length of each row (the number of columns). For arrays with more dimensions the same basic principle applies.

In the same way that variables of primitive type can be directly initialized, it is also possible to do the same with array elements. The following example illustrates the syntax:

```
int[] n = {1,2,3,4,5} ;
```

An initializer list is delimited by braces, with each element separated by a comma. Note that the braces do not denote a compound statement when used in this way. The example will create an array of size five (determined by the length of the initializer list) and initialize each element following the written order of the initial values. When using an initializer list, the array creation using `new` is implicit, it does not need to be done by the programmer.

Multi-dimensional arrays can be initialized by nesting initializer lists:

```
int[][] m = { {1,2,3,4}, {4,5,6,7} } ;
```

This will create a 4×4 array with the first row initialized to 1, 2, 3, 4 and the second to 4, 5, 6, 7. If an incomplete set of elements is provided:

```
int[][] m = { {1,2}, {4,5,6,7} } ;
```

the array initialization will still be valid but will give an array of uneven size with only the initialized elements being accessible. An attempt to access any other element will result in an exception being thrown.

Based on the syntax above it is also possible to do *anonymous array* initializations, allowing an array to be declared and initialized outside of a variable declaration. For example, the following declares an anonymous array and displays it using an output statement:

```
System.out.println(new char[] {'h','e','l','l','o'}) ;
```

The word `hello` will appear on the computer screen. In general, an anonymous array declaration and initialization can appear wherever a reference to an array of the same type is allowed:

```
int[] n ; // Default initialization
...
n = new int[] {5,6,7} ; // Create anonymous array and assign
              // reference to n
```

If an array is not directly initialized each element will be initialized to the default value of its type.

Array indexing will be covered in the section on operators (Section 28.9.2).

The first example provides some further examples of array declaration and initialization:

Examples

```
public class Array1 {
  public static void main(final String[] args) {
    int[] i = new int[5] ;  // Array of 5 integers
```

```
                i = new int[10] ;           // Can assign new array to i
                // Initialized array of strings
                String[] words = {"Hello", "World1"} ;
                // Initialized 2D array of doubles
                double[][] matrix = { {1.2, 4.7, 3.4},
                                      {0.6, -4.5, 9.2},
                                      {10.9, 0.47, -0.98}} ;
        }
    }
```

The next example shows an uneven two dimensional array being used. Note the sections of code that are commented out. If they were not, the program would fail when run.

```
    public class Array2 {
      public static void main(final String[] args) {
        int[][] m = { {1,2}, {4,5,6,7} } ;
        // Error if executed, as element is out of bounds
        // m[0][2] = 4 ;
        // Display first row
        for (int a = 0 ; a < m[0].length ; a++) {
          System.out.print(m[0][a] + " ") ;
        }
        System.out.println("") ;
        // Display second row
        for (int a = 0 ; a < m[1].length ; a++) {
          System.out.print(m[1][a] + " ") ;
        }
        System.out.println("") ;
        /*
          Executing this would cause an exception
        for (int a = 0 ; a < 2 ; a++) {
          for (int b = 0 ; b < 4 ; b++) {
            System.out.print(m[a][b] + " ") ;
          }
          System.out.println("\n") ;
        }
        */
      }
    }
```

tip

Avoid using literals in loops iterating over arrays, use the actual length of the array as determined by the array.

28.9   Expressions and Operators

Expressions are used for fetching, computing and assigning values. Computing values makes use of a wide range of operators built in to the Java language. Except for a call to with a method with a void return type, all expressions return a value, allowing expressions to be combined into more complex expressions.

The evaluation of an expression can have a side-effect by changing the value of a variable, so applying operators is not a purely mathematical operation. Further, some expressions yield a variable as a result, rather than just an unchangeable value.

When discussing expressions using values, the value are representations of primitive or reference types.

28.9.1 Primary Expressions

Primary expressions fetch or create values. **Purpose**

These are the very basic building blocks that allow values to be fetched ready for manipulation by **Intention**
other expressions. The following are primary expressions:

- the keywords `this`, `super` (see Chapter 30 and Chapter 31) and `null`
- a literal value (see Section 28.5)
- a parenthesized expression
- a field expression, using '.'
- an array index expression, using '`[]`'
- a method call expression (see Chapter 31)
- an allocation expression

Parenthesized expression: **Syntax**

```
( expression )
```

Field expression:

```
identifier
primaryExpression . identifier
package . identifier
```

Array index expression:

```
term [ intvalueExpression ]
```

Method call expressions will be described in Chapter 31.

Allocation expression:

```
new typename ( argumentList )
new typename [ integerExpression ]
          (additional array dimensions added as required)
```

A `term` is any primary expression excluding an allocation expression.

The keywords `this` and `super` will be described in Chapter 30 and Chapter 31 respectively, **Description**
Chapter 31 will also cover method calls. Field expressions give access to the fields or instance
variables of objects, classes and packages, and will also be covered elsewhere. A field expression
can use '.', as in:

```
obj.varname ;
```

Here the left hand side is essentially an object reference and the '.' is used to select a named variable
belonging to that object (as defined by its class).

`null` evaluates to the null reference and can be used to test a variable of a reference type to see
if it has the value `null`:

```
if (aVar == null) ...
```

Parenthesized expressions allow expressions to be grouped together in the same way that
mathematical expressions are. Most importantly, this gives explicit control of the order in which sub-

expressions of a larger expression are evaluated. For example, normally the expression `a + b *` `c` would be evaluated by doing the multiplication first. Using parentheses, we can force the addition to be done first: `(a + b) * c`. The value of a parenthesized expression is the same as the value of the expression inside it, as is the type.

Array index expressions are used to perform array indexing using the bracket notation. When used with an expression that evaluates to an array object reference (usually a variable of an array type), the value returned is a *variable* that can be assigned to or have its value fetched. Typical array index expressions have the form:

```
a[1] = 10 ; // Assign to variable returned by indexing
x = a[2] ; // Fetch value of variable returned by indexing
```

To evaluate an index expression, first the expression or variable name to the left of the opening bracket, `[`, is evaluated to obtain a reference to an array object. If this returns `null` a `NullPointerException` is thrown. Otherwise the expression inside the brackets, which must evaluate to type `int`, is evaluated to return an integer index. The index value must be in the range zero to the length of the array minus one (array indexing starts from zero; arrays are 0-origin). If the index value is within the range the variable (i.e. array element) being indexed is returned otherwise the exception `ArrayIndexOutOfBoundsException` is thrown.

Indexing of multi-dimension arrays happens in the same way by repeatedly evaluating the index expressions from left to right. For example, given:

```
int[][][] a = ... ;
...
a[1][2][3] = 24 ;
```

The first index expression `a[1]` will yield an expression of type `int[][]` for which the second index expression can be evaluated. This will in turn yield an expression of type `int[]` which will return the variable required when the third array index expression is evaluated.

Allocation expressions use the `new` keyword to create an object or array. The `new` keyword is followed by a type name (either a reference or primitive type) and either a parameter list in parentheses (which may be empty) or an array creation using brackets (see Section 28.8.3) `new` will be covered further in Chapter 30.

28.9.2   Operators

Purpose

Operators allow expressions to be combined into more complex expressions. *Association* and *precedence* rules are used to determine how to evaluate expressions using operators.

Intention

Operators (for example +, =, ==, <) provide the core set of operations that are built into the Java language. They provide all the basic computational operations and also allow more complex expressions to be constructed.

As operators are primitive they are expressed using a range of symbols (many familiar from mathematics) rather than keywords.

Java provides a fixed set of operators to work with the various primitive types and on reference types. Operators can be broadly classified as either unary, binary or ternary, prefix, infix or postfix. Unary operators are applied to a single parameter or *operand*, with the operator symbol appearing before the operand (prefix) or after the operand (postfix); unary operators are usually prefix operators. Cast operators are prefix unary operators. Binary operators are applied to two operands with the operator symbol appearing between the operands (infix).

In nearly all expressions containing operators, operands are evaluated in a strictly left to right order before any operators are applied. So in the situation:

```
exp1 + exp2
```

Both `exp1` and `exp2` will be fully evaluated before the + operator is applied.

Operator precedence is used to determine the order in which operators are applied when several appear in the same expression. For example, given the expression:

```
b + c / d ;
```

the / (division) operator will be applied first as it has a higher precedence than +. Evaluation order due to precedence can be overridden using parentheses as shown in Section 28.9.1.

Operators with higher precedence in a given sub-expression are always applied first. The following list shows precedence of all operators, array indexing, field selection (using '.'), casting and `new`. The list goes from high to low precedence, also showing that some operators have the same precedence.

unary postfix	`[] . () ++ --`
unary prefix	`++ -- + - ~ !`
creation and cast	`new (type)`
multiplicative	`* / %`
additive	`+ -`
shift	`<< >> >>>`
relational	`< > >= <= instanceof`
equality	`== !=`
and	`&`
xor	`^`
or	`|`
boolean and	`&&`
boolean or	`||`
conditional	`?:`
assignment	`= += -= *= /= %= >>= <<= >>>=`
	`&= ^= |=`

Operator association is used to determine the order that operators with the same precedence are applied in an expression. With the exception of the assignment operators, all operators are *left-associative*. This means that they will be applied in left-to-right order. For example:

```
a + b + c - d - e
```

will be evaluated by applying the operators in the order they are written down, equivalent to parenthesizing in the following way:

```
(((a + b) + c) - d) - e
```

Assignment operators are *right-associative*, meaning that the expression to the right is evaluated first. The main practical consequence of this is that expressions like:

```
a = b = c ;
```

will be evaluated with `b = c` first. This is equivalent to parenthesizing in the following way:

```
a = (b = c)
```

An understanding of the precedence and association rules can be exploited to minimize the number of parentheses needed. For example an expression like:

```
if (i >= 0 && i < 100) ...
```

can be interpreted correctly by knowing that the `>=` and `>` operators will be applied before the `&&`. The expression is equivalent to:

```
if ( (i >= 0) && (i < 100) ) ...
```

However, while parenthesizing can become unwieldy it does make the precise intention of an expression clear. Particularly while learning Java, it is worthwhile putting the brackets in.

We will now examine each operator in turn.

Postfix Increment Operators

There are two postfix increment operators, `++` and `--`. Being postfix they appear after the operand and increment (`++`) or decrement (`--`) the operand by one. The operand must be a variable or array element. The operators can be used with integral and floating point variables or array elements. For example:

```
int i = 1 ;
double j = 10.4 ;
i++ ; j-- ; // increment i, decrement j
// here i == 2 and j == 9.4
```

However, what is not obvious from the initial explanation is that the value of the increment or decrement expression is the *original* value of the variable. The updated variable value will be available next time the variable is used. For example:

```
int i = 1 ;
int j = i++ ; // j is assigned the value 1
int k = i ; // k is assigned the value 2
```

Essentially, these two operators work by the side-effect of updating a variable value after returning the original variable value.

Unary Operators

These operators are:

- prefix increment and decrement, `++` and `--`
- unary `+` and `-`
- the bitwise complement operator, `~`
- the logical complement operator, `!`

The prefix ++ and -- operators can be used with integral and floating point types. The operand must be a variable or array element and of integral or floating point type. Like the postfix versions of these operators they have the side-effect of incrementing or decrementing the operand value by one. However, unlike the postfix operators the value of a prefix ++ or -- expression is the updated variable value. For example:

```
int i = 1 ;
int j = ++i ; // j is assigned the value 2
int k = i ; // k is assigned the value 2
```

Unary + is available for numeric types and returns the value of the expression it is applied to without doing any computation (like the mathematical operation). If the type of the operand is byte, short or char applying + will yield a value of type int after application of the appropriate conversion.

Unary - is also available for numeric types and its application results in arithmetic negation. For integral types, this is done by first converting the operand value to type int as necessary and then subtracting it from zero. Note, that because of the 2's complement representation of integers this operator cannot produce a positive value when negating the largest negative integer. For floating point types, unary - changes the sign of its operand.

The bitwise negation operator ~ (the character is a tilde), can be applied to integer data types, converting to type int if needed. The integer value is then treated as a collection of bits with each zero bit being changed to one and each one bit being changed to zero. For example:

```
Before: 10111001110010101110010101011101
After:  01000110001101010001101010100010
```

This operator is one of a number for doing so called 'bitwise' operations on binary numbers. It is useful whenever bit-level operations are needed — bit manipulation is usually a systems programming thing rather than an applications programming thing. For example the following method uses ~ and another bitwise operator, &, to return a bit-pattern with the low order (last) four bits of its argument forced to be 0:

```
int maskLastFourBits(int x) {
   return x & ~0xf ;
}
```

The boolean negation operator, !, is applied to boolean values and does a boolean negation: if the operand value is true the result is false, is the value is false the result is true. This operator is frequently used in boolean expressions associated with if statements and while loops, as for example in this code skeleton:

```
boolean ready = false ;
while (! ready) {
   ...
   if ( ... ) {
     ready = true ;
   ...
   }
}
```

This sort of programming approach is used by people who are not happy using explicit control flow statements as in the following code skeleton which has the same behaviour:

```
while (true) {
  ...
  if ( ... ) {
    break ;
    ...
  }
}
```

New

The new operator is used for creating new class objects and array objects. The parameter to new must be a type name. If a class type name is specified it can be followed by a constructor parameter list (see Chapter 30, Page 833). If an array type is specified, the array dimensions must be given. (new is discussed in detail in a number of other places so we shall not repeat things here.)

Cast

A cast allows the type of an expression to be changed, providing the change does not violate the type compatibility rules. The compatibility rules restrict the possible casts to those that preserve the meaning of a value, preventing any other sort of cast such as changing the type of a double into a boolean.

The following is an example if the use of a cast expression:

```
float f = 2.3 ;
int n = (int)f ;
```

The cast expression appears on the second line as (int)f. The operand is f, while the prefix operator consists of a type name in parentheses. The type name gives the type that the operand should be cast to. The example uses the cast to assign a float value to an int variable. Direct assignment of a float to an int is not possible but the cast forces it to be allowed. Note, however, that the cast results in a loss of information, all the decimal places are lost from the float: the cast causes truncation of the value. Thus, in the above example, n will be initialized with the value 2.

Where possible, the validity of a cast is checked at compile time, resulting in an error message if not valid. However, some casts require run-time checks as insufficient information is available at compile-time to determine if the cast will always be legal. If the run-time check fails an exception will be thrown.

The rules for when a cast is allowed or not can be summarized as follows:

- Any type can be cast to itself.
- Any primitive numeric type can be cast to any other primitive numeric type, but may result in the loss of information. Some of these casts are the same as the automatic conversions presented in Section 28.6.3.
- The boolean type cannot be cast to or from at all.
- Primitive types cannot be cast to reference types or vice versa.

- A reference to a subclass type can be cast to its superclass type (this is also an automatic conversion).

- A reference to a superclass type can be cast to a subclass type, with the cast result checked at run-time.

- A reference of a class type can be cast to an interface type providing the class implements the interface. In certain cases this is checked at run-time.

- A reference of type `Object` can be cast to an array type, providing the reference is to an array object of the correct type. The cast will be checked at run-time.

- A reference of an interface type can be cast to a class type providing the object referenced is an instance of the class or a subclass. The cast may need checking at run-time.

- A reference of an interface type can be cast to another interface type providing the class of the object referenced implements both interfaces. The cast needs to be checked at run-time.

- A reference to an array object can be cast to type `Object`.

- A reference to an array object can be cast to another array type if the array elements are of the same primitive type or the elements can be cast to the right type.

Of all these cast operations the ones that are most used are those that cast from a superclass (or interface) type to a subclass type — this is often called *downcasting*. In particular, many data structures store references of type `Object` so that any type of object can be stored (remember that any class type can automatically convert to type `Object`). In order to recover the actual type a cast is needed. So, for example:

```
Stack myStack = new Stack () ; // Stack of Object
myStack.push("Hello") ; // String object reference stored as Object
...
String s = (String)myStack.pop() ; // Cast to retrieve correct type.
```

Arithmetic Operators

The arithmetic operators are:

+ — addition

- — subtraction

* — multiplication

/ — division

% — remainder

These are all binary operators with +, -, * and / doing what are essentially the obvious mathematical operations. The % operator may be a little less familiar, it returns the remainder after division.

Actually this isn't quite the whole story. There are in fact 10 operators, a set for where both operands are `int`, giving an `int` result and a set for when both operands are `double` giving a `double` result, i.e. there are actually two binary + arithmetic operators, `int` + `int` and `double`

+ `double`, likewise for the other operators. For all practical purposes, this distinction is irrelevant for all the operators except division. The following are all true expressions:

```
3 + 4 == 7
3.0 + 4.0 == 7.0
3 - 4 == -1
3.0 - 4.0 == -1.0
3 * 4 == 12
3.0 * 4.0 == 12.0
3 / 4 == 0
3.0 / 4.0 == 0.75
3 % 4 == 3
3.0 % 4.0 == 3.0
```

This use of the same syntactic symbol in slightly different contexts and with appropriately different, but nonetheless appropriately similar, semantics is called overloading. + is a heavily overloaded symbol!

Although the representations are different, the abstract value represented by the calculation is the same for both operators of the given arithmetic operation — except for division. This example highlights what the remainder operation is useful for: when undertaking integer division you sometimes need to know what the remainder is as well as the value of the division.

Where a type that is not `int` or `double` is used in an arithmetic operator expression, the appropriate conversion is applied to construct an `int` or `double` value so that the operands are of the same type. The conversion rules mean, of course, that we can have any combination of primitive type in an arithmetic operator expression, e.g. `int / float`. In such a case, one or both of the operands will be converted to a type suitable for applying the arithmetic operation ensuring the operator is actually applied to operands of the same type. The conversion is done by converting to the most general type (i.e. the one that will not cause a loss of information). `double` is most general, followed by `float`, `long`, `int`, `short`, `char` and `byte`. For example:

```
short n = 1 ;
int i = 5 ;
double d= 3.0 ;
... n + i ...     // convert value of n to int and return an int
... i / d...      // convert value of i to double and return ...
                  // ... a double
... i / i ...     // no conversion until the type required of ...
                  // this sub-expression is known
```

Applying these operators can result in overflow or underflow (i.e. the result cannot be represented). If this happens a result is returned using as many bits as are available and no exception is thrown. This will result in a value that appears valid but is not the right result!

Floating point operations (i.e. ones involving `double`s) are a bit more complicated as they may involve the value NaN ('Not a Number') used when it is not possible to represent a number.

String Concatenation Operator

The symbol for the string concatenation operator is + (yet another overload of this symbol!). The operator is selected when one or both of the operands is of type `String`. If only one operand is of type `String` then the other operand will be converted to `String` if it is possible to do so, otherwise a compilation error will be thrown. For the primitive types conversion to `String` is done using an automatic conversion. For reference types the conversion is done by calling the referenced object's `toString` method. All classes inherit `toString` from class `Object` and usually specialize it to return an appropriate string representation for instances of the class.

The concatenation operator is often used with output statements, for example:

```
System.out.println("The value of i is: " + i) ;
```

This statement will work whatever the type of `i` actually is.

Shift Operators

The shift operators use the symbols:

> `<<` — left shift
>
> `>>` — right shift
>
> `>>>` — unsigned right shift

All three operators are binary and performing bit shifting operations on values of integral types. The left hand operand is the value to be shifted and will be converted to type `int` if it is of type `byte`, `short` or `char`. The right hand operand is the number of positions to shift.

The maximum number of positions to shift depends on whether the left hand operand is of type `int` or `long`. `ints` can be shifted from 0 to 31 positions and `longs` from 0 to 63 positions. The number of shifts is actually taken as the least significant five or six bits of the right hand operand.

Left shift shifts left the number of bits specified, shifting in zeros from the right:

```
0x01234567 << 4 == 0x12345670
```

Right shift shifts right the number of bits specified with the bits shifted in from the left being copies of the sign bit of the unshifted value (i.e. signed shift):

```
0x01234567 >> 4 == 0x00123456
0xF0123456 >> 4 == 0xFF012345
```

Unsigned right shift is the same as right shift except that zeros are always shifted in from the left:

```
0x01234567 >>> 4 == 0x00123456
0xF0123456 >>> 4 == 0x0F012345
```

Relational Operators

The following relational operators are available:

> `==` — equal to
>
> `!=` — not equal to
>
> `<` — less than
>
> `>` — greater than
>
> `>=` — greater than or equal to
>
> `<=` — less than or equal to
>
> `instanceof` — is an object an instance of a named type

All the relational operators are binary and return a `boolean` result. They are all used to compare two values, according to the obvious meanings of the operators:

a `==` b is true if a has the same value as b

a `!=` b is true if a has a different value from b

a `<` b is true if value of a is less than b

a `>` b is true if value of a is greater than b

a `>=` b is true if value of a is greater than or equal to b

a `<=` b is true if value of a is less than or equal to b

a `instanceof` b is true if the type of a is b (b is the name of a type)

Except for `instanceof`, all the operators are only supported for the primitive types. Like the arithmetic operators, operands are converted to the most general type before the comparison takes place.

The `==` operator may additionally be applied to reference types and will return `true` only if both references refer to the *same object*. Note that the value the object represents is not taken into account with this operator (to compare values the method `equals` must be used).

The `instanceof` operator is used to determine whether an object is an instance of a class or interface type. The left hand operand is an object reference while the right hand operand is a type name:

```
String s = "Hello" ;
if (s instanceof String)
   System.out.println("s is a String") ;
```

And, Or and Xor

These three operators are:

      `&` — bitwise or logical AND

      `|` — bitwise or logical OR

      `^` — bitwise or logical exclusive XOR

All three are binary operators returning a boolean value. If applied to integral operands they perform bitwise and, or and xor. If applied to boolean operands they perform logical operations. Bitwise operators work with either type `int` or `long` and will convert any operands to match.

Bitwise `&` performs the binary *and* operation on the matching bits of each operand. Bitwise `|` performs the binary *or* operation while `^` performs the binary *xor* operation.

The logical versions perform the corresponding boolean operations and always evaluate both operands before applying the operator (compare this behaviour with `&&` and `||`).

Boolean And and Or

These operators are:

&& — boolean conditional AND

|| — boolean conditional OR

These are both binary operators and may only be applied to operands of type `boolean`. They return a `boolean` result.

The crucial difference between these operators and `&` and `|` lies in the way they evaluate their operands. `&&` and `||` first evaluate their left hand operand. If the value of that operand is sufficient to determine the value of the entire boolean expression, the evaluation of the right hand operand is skipped.

This means that when `&&` is applied, the right hand operand is only evaluated when the left hand operand has the value `true`. If the left hand operand has the value `false`, the value of the entire `&&` expression must be `false` (`false` and anything is always `false`) and there is no need to evaluate the right hand side to determine the result (hence the label conditional).

A similar situation applies to the `||` operator. If the left hand operand evaluates to `true` then the value of the whole expression must be `true` and the right hand operand need not be evaluated.

These operators are normally used in boolean expressions in preference to `&` and `|`. The conditional evaluation can often be exploited. For example:

```
// o is an object reference than may have the value null
if ((o != null) && (! o.isEmpty())) {
  // do something
}
```

In this situation, we want to call a method given an object reference but the reference may be `null`. Using the `&&` operator a single boolean expression can be written that first tests that the reference is not `null` and then if it is referencing an object can call a method to get a boolean result. If the method had been called using a `null` reference an exception would have been thrown. The use of the conditional operators avoids calling a method on a null reference.

Conditional Operator

The conditional operator is unique in that it is the only ternary operator — one that takes three arguments. Essentially, it behaves in an analogous way to the if statement (see Section 29.2.1, Page 806), it allows a choice between the evaluation of one of two expressions.

The structure of the operator is as follows:

```
booleanExpression ? trueExp : falseExp
```

There are three operands. The first, in front of the `?`, is a boolean expression. The second and third, following the `?` and `:`, respectively, are expressions of the same or compatible types.

An expression using the operator is evaluated as follows. First the boolean expression is evaluated. If it has the value `true`, the expression immediately after the `?` is evaluated and its value returned as the result of the operator. If the boolean expression has the value `false`, the expression following the `:` is evaluated and its value returned as the result of the operator.

The advantage of using the operator is that it is compact and allows conditions to be made part of an expression rather than having to be expanded to make use of an if statement. For example:

```
int i = j < 0 ? 5 : 10 ;
```

This will assign 5 to i if j is less than 0, 10 otherwise.

Assignment Operators

The basic assignment operator is =. This is a binary operator that will assign the value of the right operand to the variable or array element which forms the left hand operand. Assignment is subject to the implicit type conversion and casting rules see in Section 28.6.3 and earlier in this section (Page 794).

The other assignment operators are all binary and combine assignment with various of the arithmetic and bitwise operators:

```
+=, -=, *=, /=, %=, |=, &=, ^=, <<=, >>=, >>>=
```

To illustrate the behaviour of these operators, consider +=. The expression:

```
int i = 5 ;
i += 10 ;
```

will leave i with the value 15. The += operator first of all evaluates the right hand operand, then adds the result to the value stored in i and finally assigns the result to i. Hence, the statement i += 10 is equivalent to i = i + 10. The other assignment operators all work in the same way, applying their own particular operator.

The main use of these operators is a convenient shorthand.

Operator Summary

The following operators can be applied to values of the primitive integral types (byte, short, int, long, char):

relational	`< > >= <= instanceof == !=`
unary	`+ -`
arithmetic	`+ - * / %`
increment	`++ -- (prefix and postfix)`
shift	`<< >> >>>`
bitwise	`~ &	^`
conditional	`?:`
cast	`()`
String	`+`

The following operators can be applied to values of floating point types (float and double):

relational	`< > >= <= == !=`
unary	`+ -`
arithmetic	`+ - * / %`
increment	`++ -- (prefix and postfix)`
conditional	`?:`
cast	`()`
String	`+`

The following operators can be applied to values of type `boolean`:

relational	`== !=`
logical	`! &	^`
conditional	`&& || ?:`
String	`+`

The following operators can be applied to values of reference types:

relational	`== !=`
conditional	`?:`
cast	`()`
String	`+`
other	`instanceof .`

The following program illustrates the use of the majority of the operators.   Examples

```
class Operators {
  public static void main(String[] args) {
    int j = 1 ;
    int k = 0 ;
    boolean b = true ;
    char c = 'a' ;
    double d = 3.141 ;
    k = j++ ;
    k = j-- ;
    k = ++j ;
    k = --j ;
    k = +(-1) ;
    k = -(+1) ;
    b = !true ;
    k = ~k ;
    k = (int)d ;
    j = 10 ;
    k = k + j * j - k / j  % k ;
    k = j << 3 ;
    k = j >> 4 ;
    k = j >>> 5 ;
    b = j < k ;
    b = j > k ;
    b = j <= k ;
    b = j >= k ;
    b = j != k ;
    b = j == k ;
    String s = "Hello", t = "World", u = s ;
    b = s == t ;
    b = s == u ;
    b = s instanceof String ;
    k = j | k ;
    k = j & k ;
    k = j ^ k ;
    b = (j < 0) && ((j % 3) == 3) ;
    k = (j < 0) ? -j : j ;
    k += j ;
    k -= j ;
    k ^= j ;
  }
}
```

28.10   Source Files

A Java program consists of a series of class and interface declarations, with each consisting of method and variable declarations. The text, or source code, of a class or interface declaration is stored in a *source file*. Although the declarations for several classes and/or interfaces can be put into the same source file, typically each declaration is stored in a separate file. This is not just due to preference but relates to the way Java classes are loaded when a program is run.

Source files always have names ending in .java. The first part of the file name is the class or interface name of the class or interface declared in the file. For example, class `Test` would be stored in the file Test.java. If a file contains more than one class or interface declaration, the file must still be named after one of them (which must be the only public class or interface in the file).

28.11   Summary

This chapter has worked through the details of how the Java language provides comments, identifiers, primitive and reference types, variables, expressions and operators. These provide all the basic infrastructure of Java code and will be used constantly when writing code. The programmer learning the language should spend time using all these features and put in plenty of programming practice!

Self-review Exercises

Self-review 28.1 Which of the following are illegal variable names and why?

```
aName, 2D, WIDTH, Position, HeIgHt, this, x&y,
whiletrue, name$, current_position, Float
```

Self-review 28.2 What is seen if the following string are displayed on the computer screen?

```
"Hello\nWorld\n!"
"\t\t\\tHello"
"\\\\\\nHello"
"1.23e+9f"
"Hello\b\bWorld"
\'\\Hello\'"
```

Self-review 28.3 Are any of the following expressions using ++ and -- legal? If not, why not?

```
int j = 5 ;
j++ ++ ;
j(++) ;
(j++)++ ;
j++-- ;
(j)++ ;
```

Self-review 28.4 What value is assigned to n in each of the following?

```
int n = 0 ;
int x = 1 ;
n = x++ + x++ ;
n = n++ - x++ ;
n = x-- + -x++ ;
```

Self-review 28.5 Why can't the largest integer be negated?

Self-review 28.6 What does the expression:

```
i < 0 ? 0 : i > 10 ? 1 : i >20 ? 2 : 3
```

evaluate to for values of i between -5 and 50?

Programming Exercises

Exercise 28.1 Write a program to use each kind of cast between primitive types. Which casts lose information and what is lost?

Exercise 28.2 Write a program to investigate the effects of overflow. What happens to the result when an overflow occurs when multiplying two integers or doubles?

Exercise 28.3 Write a program to illustrate how each primitive type is represented as a string. What happens to the value null?

Exercise 28.4 Write a program that demonstrates the effects of applying the shift operators.

Exercise 28.5 Write a program that inputs an integer value and uses the bitwise operators to print out the binary representation of the integer.

Flow Control

Objectives

This chapter presents flow control statements. These statements allow the programmer to control the order in which statements are executed. Each statements is presented by first giving a summary of its features and purpose, and then providing examples of it in use.

Keywords

selection

if

switch

iteration

while

do

for

flow control

break

continue

return

29.1   Introduction

Java provides a selection of *flow control* statements to control the order in which statements are executed. There are three categories of flow control statement:

- Selection statements: *if* and *switch*.
- Iteration (loop) statements: *while*, *do* and *for*.
- Transfer statements: *break*, *continue* and *return*.

29.2   Selection

Most algorithms depend on the ability to choose between different actions depending on some set of conditions (see Figure 29.1). Selection statements provide the mechanisms for making choices and come in two forms; binary selection and multi-way selection.

Binary selection allows a choice between two possible statement sequences, while multi-way selection allows a choice out of many statement sequences. Both rely on the idea of a *boolean condition*, an expression evaluating to `true` or `false`, to determine which sequence to choose.

29.2.1   The If Statement

Purpose

The *if statement* provides binary selection, allowing conditional execution of a statement depending on the value of a boolean expression.

Intention

It is frequently the case that a statement should be executed only if some condition is met, for example "if the value of x is less than 10 then add 1 to x". If the condition is not met then the statement should be bypassed and not executed. The condition is in the form of a boolean expression which evaluates to `true` or `false`, with a value of `true` resulting in the statement being executed.

Syntax

```
if ( booleanExpression )
   statement
```
or
```
if ( booleanExpression )
   statement
else
   statement
```

Description

An if statement allows a choice over which statement to execute next, based on a boolean condition. The statement has two variants, referred to as if-then and if-then-else.

The if-then variant has the form:

```
if (a == b)
   c = 10 ; // 'then' or body part
h = 1.2 ; // Next statement after the if
```

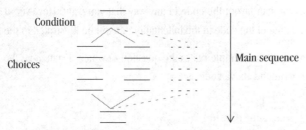

Figure 29.1 Selection.

The boolean expression, a == b, which must be in parentheses following the if keyword, is evaluated. If it has the value true, the 'then' part is executed. If it evaluates to false, the 'then' part is ignored and the statement following the if statement executed. The 'then' part is often referred to as the if statement body.

Notice that the 'then' part is actually just another statement and can, in fact, be any valid statement. Remembering that a compound statement is a kind of statement allows us to write:

```
if (a == b) {
  c = 10 ;
  d = 20 ;
  f() ;
}
h = 1.2 ; // Next statement after the if
```

allowing a sequence of statements to be executed rather than just one.

The second form of the if statement is:

```
if (a == b)
  c = 10 ; // 'then' part
else
  c = 20 ; // 'else' part
h = 1.2 ; // Next statement after the if
```

If the boolean expression evaluates to true the statement forming the 'then' part is executed, otherwise (else) the statement forming the 'else' part is executed. One and only one of the 'then' and 'else' parts will be executed, after which execution proceeds with the statement following the if statement. Again, note that compound statements can be used instead of single statements.

```
if (a == b) {
  c = 10 ;// 'then' part
  f() ;
} else {
  c = 20 ;// 'else' part
  g() ;
}
h = 1.2 ;// Next statement after the if
```

If statements can be nested which means that the body of an if statement can be another if statement:

```
if (a == b) {
  if (c == d) {
    System.out.println("c == d") ;
  } else {
    System.out.println("c != d") ;
  }
}
```

It is invariably better to use compound statements as then and else parts of an if statement.

Note that you can layout the code in any way that you want. However, it is always advisable to reflect the meaning of the code in the indentation, as will be illustrated in the following paragraphs.

The previous code example raises the question of which if statement the 'else' part belongs to. If we were to write the above code as:

```
if (a == b)
  if (c == d) {
    System.out.println("c == d") ;
  }
else {
  System.out.println("c != d") ;
}
```

we highlight the two principle issues. The first is that as far as the Java system is concerned, the 'else' part always belongs to the closest `if` keyword. So, these two segments of code have identical meaning. This brings up the second issue: indentation should always reflect meaning. The indentation immediately above is inappropriate; it should have been:

```
if (a == b)
  if (c == d) {
    System.out.println("c == d") ;
  } else {
    System.out.println("c != d") ;
  }
```

The useful guideline we can draw out from this is that making the if statement bodies into compound statements removes any ambiguity on the part of the programmer and should really always be done as a matter of good practice — another element of defensive programming.

Examples

The example below is a complete program that uses an if statement:

```
public class IfTest1 {
  public static void main(final String[] args) {
    int a = 1 ;
    int b = 2 ;
    if (a < b) {
      System.out.println("a < b") ;
    } else  {
      System.out.println("a >= b") ;
    }
  }
}
```

The style of indentation we have used here is the paradigm of what we consider to be good style — taking into account the points raised earlier. The body of the if statement is indented to give a visual cue of its role with the braces being on lines of their own at the level of the `if` keyword. All selection and iteration statements, not just if statements, should be properly and consistently indented to aid the readability of the program. The basic layout style introduced above is the same for all flow control statements in our style.

We should point out, of course, that there is more that one good style; there are a number of different layouts that are accepted as good: the principle properties of all of them is that they are clear and consistent. The style we will follow is, we believe, the best but this can be a matter of personal taste.

An if statement's condition can be any valid boolean expression and can include function calls.

```
public class IfTest2 {
  public static boolean f(final int x, final int y) {
    return (x < y) ;
  }
  public static void main(final String[] args) {
    int a = 1 ;
    int b = 2 ;
    if (f(a, b)) {
      System.out.println("f returned true") ;
    } else {
      System.out.println("f returned false") ;
    }
  }
}
```

In both of the examples above the 'then' and 'else' parts are both compound statements, even though the compound statements only contain one statement each. This is just following our defensive programming style of always using compound statements so as to prevent the following errors, such as:

```
public class IfTest3 {
  public static void main(final String[] args) {
    int a = 2 ;
    if (a == 1)
      System.out.println("a == 1") ;
      a = 0 ;  // Extra statement added here
    System.out.println("Value of a = " + a) ;
  }
}
```

The if statement was originally written without the assignment and without using a compound statement as its body. Subsequently the program is modified to make an assignment when a == 1. However, the programmer can easily forget to put in the braces denoting a compound statement when modifying the if statement and produce the code shown above. This is a correct program in that it will compile without error but, when executed, the variable a is always assigned zero, regardless of the presence of the if statement. Such errors as not only easy to make, they are hard to find and correct. It is better just to adopt 'defensive programming' and always use compound statements, thereby avoiding the whole problem.

Another common mistake is to include an extra semi-colon, as in:

```
public class IfTest4 {
  public static void main(final String[] args) {
    int a = 2 ;
    if (a == 1) ;  // Extra semi-colon
      a = 0 ;      // Statement following if, despite indentation!
    System.out.println("Value of a = " + a) ;
  }
}
```

This is again a valid program but the if statement body is empty (contains no statements) due to the erroneous semi-colon. In other words, this is another way of always assigning zero to a! The indentation means nothing here — it is the sequence of characters that matter not the column positioning. So whilst indentation should be indicative, there are still traps for the unwary. This is another argument for always being defensive, for always using compound statements.

29.2.2 Switch Statement

Purpose

The *switch statement* provides multi-way selection, allowing conditional execution of one or more out of many statements depending on the value of an expression.

Intention

We want to choose which statement sequence to execute depending on the value of an integer or character expression. For example, if we have a variable holding an `int` in the range 1–7 to represent the current day of the week, we want to be able to display the name of the current day. This could be done using a series of if statements but as this kind of situation occurs relatively frequently in programs, Java provides the switch statement to package up what we want in a more convenient way.

Syntax

```
switch ( expression ) {
  case char/byte/short/int constant : statementSequence
  ...
  default : statementSequence
}
```

Description

The switch statement provides another way of selecting between choices. In contrast to the if statement, the switch statement allows a choice to be made between any number of statement sequences, not just two statements. The body of the switch statement must be a compound statement (i.e. a sequence of statements enclosed in braces). This compound statement actually comprises a number of *labelled statement sequences*, where each labelled sequence represents one choice. A labelled sequence starts with the `case` keyword followed by a constant value (the label), a colon and then the sequence of statements to be executed (which as always may include a compound statement, this will again be important to our defensive style). One and only one of the labelled sequences may be labelled with the keyword `default` rather than a case label.

When a switch statement is evaluated, the expression following the `switch` keyword is evaluated first. Execution then jumps to the statement labelled by the case label which matches the value of the expression (the matching being the boolean expression). The statements following the matched case label are then executed. If there is a default label and the value does not match any of the case labels, then the statement sequence following the default label will be executed.

The type of the expression must be one of `byte`, `char`, `short` or `int`. Note that `long` is not permitted nor are any other types. All the case labels must be constants that are either the same type as the expression or of a type assignable to the type of the expression. Further, every case label must be distinct. Hence, a switch statement is restricted to working with only a small subset of types.

A properly constructed switch statement has a case label for each relevant value of the switch expression and includes a default label which matches any values not covered by the other case labels. If no labels are matched and no default is provided, no statements in the switch statement body are executed at all. This is allowed, it is not a run-time error, but we believe it is not good practice to use this.

Usually, the statements following a case label end with a *break statement*, giving the following structure for a typical switch statement:

```
int i = 3 ;
...
switch (i) {
 case 1 : f() ; break ;
 case 2 : g() ; break ;
 default : h() ; break ;
}
```

The break statement causes execution to jump to the statement following the switch statement. Interestingly, though, a break statement can be omitted and then execution will proceed on to the next statement inside the switch statement. This is known as *fall-through* and can be useful but can also cause problems if the programmer forgets to include a break statement. Switch statements can also be exited using a return statement.

Fall-through makes a switch statement a bit more complicated than just a re-packaged set of if statements. Effectively it allows a program to jump to a particular point in a statement sequence (those in the switch statement body), and execute statements until either the end of the enclosing switch statement or until some other statement like break causes a jump to somewhere else.

Another consequence of fall-through is that a statement can effectively have several case labels:

```
switch (i) {
 case 1 :
 case 2 :
 case 3 : f() ; break ; // Call f() if i has value 1, 2 or 3
 default : h() ; break ;
}
```

Any number of statements can be labelled by a single label; it is a labelled statement sequence, after all:

```
int z ;
switch (i) {
 case 1 : z = 1 ; f() ; break ;
 case 2 : z = 2 ; break ;
 case 3 : z = 3 ; f() ; g() ; break ;
 default : h() ; break ;
}
```

Again the question of coding style arises here. The above might better be laid out as:

```
int z ;
switch (i) {
 case 1 :
  z = 1 ;
  f() ;
  break ;
 case 2 :
  z = 2 ;
  break ;
 case 3 :
  z = 3 ;
  f() ;
  g() ;
  break ;
 default :
  h() ;
  break ;
```

```
    }
```

This style might create a lot of white space in a book but it is a good style (possibly even the standard style) to use when constructing files online where white space on a page is not an important issue. In fact, experience shows that this sort of layout is less prone to error. Defensive programming supports the use of such a style!

However, we can take being defensive further. As would be expected, a labelled statement can be a compound statement, which can be useful for defining a new local scope. There are many possible layouts of such statements. Here are four styles (from what is probably a much larger number):

```
switch (i) {
   case 1 : { int z = 1 ; m(z) ; break ; }
   case 2 : { int z = 2 ; m(z) ; g() ; break ; }
   default : { h() ; break ; }
}

switch (i) {
 case 1 :
   { int z = 1 ; m(z) ; break ; }
 case 2 :
   { int z = 2 ; m(z) ; g() ; break ; }
 default :
   { h() ; break ;}
}
```

```
  switch (i) {                      switch (i) {
   case 1 :                          case 1 :
     {                                 {
        int z = 1 ;                       int z = 1 ;
        m(z) ;                            m(z) ;
        break ;                         }
     }                                 break ;
   case 2 :                          case 2 :
     {                                 {
        int z = 2 ;                       int z = 2 ;
        m(z) ;                            m(z) ;
        g() ;                             g() ;
        break ;                         }
     }                                 break ;
   default :                         default :
     {                                 {
        h() ;                             h() ;
        break ;                         }
     }                                 break ;
  }                                 }
```

Note that the break statement can appear inside a nested compound statement and still results in the switch statement terminating.

On balance the last of these (bottom, right) is probably the most defensive coding style. The statement sequence for each option is enclosed in a compound statement which provides a scope unit for local variables and acts as a collecting together of statements to make them into a unit (at least visually and conceptually), with the control flow statement (a break or return statement) immediately after the compound statement so that it is clearly visible (or not if use is being made of fall-through).

Switch statements can always be rewritten as a series of nested if statements, but, we believe, this leads to a loss of clarity. Whenever appropriate, i.e. when a multi-way choice is being made with a discriminator of an acceptable type, switch statements are a better option that using if statements. Unfortunately, the switch statement only works with a very limited range of types. If we want a multi-way switch on a variable that is not of one of these types, we must descend to using nested if statements. This is a shame.

The following program inputs an integer and outputs the name of the day corresponding to the integer, if it is in the range 1–7 (and assuming day 1 is a Sunday).

Examples

```java
public class Switch1 {
  public static void main(final String[] args) {
    KeyboardInput input = new KeyboardInput() ;
    System.out.print("Enter a number between 1 and 7: ") ;
    int day = input.readInteger() ;
    switch (day) {
     case 1 : System.out.println("Sunday") ; break ;
     case 2 : System.out.println("Monday") ; break ;
     case 3 : System.out.println("Tuesday") ; break ;
     case 4 : System.out.println("Wednesday") ; break ;
     case 5 : System.out.println("Thursday") ; break ;
     case 6 : System.out.println("Friday") ; break ;
     case 7 : System.out.println("Saturday") ; break ;
     default : System.out.println("Not a day! " + day) ; break ;
    }
  }
}
```

If the integer is between 1 and 7, a day name will be displayed, using the switch to select the name. If the number is greater than 7 or less than 1, a default message is printed out. Whatever the input, only one message gets displayed as only one labelled statement is executed.

The type of the switch expression can also be `char`, `byte` or `short` as well as `int`. The following example works with `char`s:

```java
public class Switch2 {
  public static void main(final String[] args) {
    KeyboardInput input = new KeyboardInput () ;
    System.out.print("Type a character and press return: ") ;
    char c = input.readCharacter() ;
    switch (c) {
     case 'a' : System.out.println("You typed an 'a'") ; break ;
     case 'b' : System.out.println("You typed an 'b'") ; break ;
     case 'c' : System.out.println("You typed an 'c'") ; break ;
     case 100 : System.out.println("You typed an 'd'") ; break ;
     case 101 : System.out.println("You typed an 'e'") ; break ;
     default  :
       System.out.println("You didn't type an a,b,c,d or e!");
       break ;
    }
  }
}
```

Note that two of the case labels use integer constants rather than character constants. This is allowed as characters can be safely converted to integers (actually their Unicode value), allowing a valid comparison to be done. Of course, although it can be done, it should be avoided at all times.

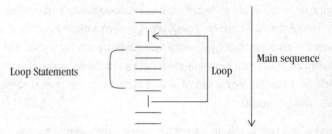

Figure 29.2 Iteration using loops.

Fall-through is sometimes useful but should be used with caution as it is easy to misunderstand what is meant:

```
public class Switch3 {
  public static void main(final String[] args) {
    KeyboardInput input = new KeyboardInput () ;
    System.out.print("Type command code: ") ;
    int n = input.readInteger() ;
    switch (n) {
      // Use fall through on cases 0 and 1 since case 0 is case
      // 1 with some extra, prior, processing.
      case 0  : System.out.println("Restart System") ;
      case 1  : System.out.println("Start System") ; break ;
      case 2  : System.out.println("Stop System")  ; break ;
      default : System.out.println("Unknown instruction") ; break
    }
  }
}
```

In this program the result of entering command code '0' is the same as entering code '1' but with an additional step preceding the statements executed for code '1'. The break statement is omitted to allow fall-through to occur. The comment here is absolutely essential to make sure that others don't try to 'fix' the omission of the break statement because they think it is an error.

29.3 Iteration

As well as selection, algorithms require the ability to execute a set of statements repeatedly inside a *loop* (see Figure 29.2). This allows the statements to be written once and executed as many times as needed.

There are two categories of loop statements available to express iteration. While loops and do loops provide unbounded iteration, where looping continues as long as a particular condition holds. For loops provide bounded or counted iteration, where (in principle) the execution of the loop is performed a pre-determined number of times using a counter to count the iterations.

Each kind of loop has the same basic form:

- a statement sequence forming the *loop body*;
- a boolean expression which is evaluated to decide whether to execute the loop body for another iteration;

- an *end condition* after which the loop terminates and execution continues with the statement following the loop; and
- usually, one or more statements or expressions within the loop that changes the state of the program in such a way to move closer to the end condition of the loop, ensuring that it terminates.

In addition, it may be necessary to initialize variables or establish other conditions before the loop statement is executed, so that the boolean expression initially evaluates to something sensible.

29.3.1 The While Loop

The while loop allows a statement sequence to be repeatedly executed while a boolean condition evaluates to `true`. | **Purpose**

Frequently an algorithm needs to express an action like "while a condition is true keep evaluating the following". The number of repetitions can vary each time the algorithm is applied, determined by the state on which the condition depends. Moreover, the number of iterations is typically only determined by the state of the program, rather than being known before the program is executed. | **Intention**

The loop condition is evaluated before the loop body is executed, so if the condition evaluates to `false` initially, the loop body is not executed at all. Hence, the while loop provides for zero or more executions of the loop body.

```
while ( booleanExpression )
  statement
```
Syntax

A while loop executes 'while' the loop condition is true. The loop executes by first evaluating the boolean expression. If it is true, the statements in the loop body are executed. Control then returns to the start of the loop and the boolean expression is evaluated again. If true, the body is executed again; if false the loop terminates and the statement following the loop is executed. | **Description**

Almost invariably, a loop is written such that the statements in the loop body eventually cause the value of the boolean expression to change to `false` in order for the loop to terminate. For example:

```
// Count from 0 to 9
int x = 0 ;
while (x < 10) {
  System.out.println(x) ;
  x++ ;
}
// x == 10 after the loop terminates
```

Here the boolean expression depends on the variable x which is incremented inside the loop body. Incrementing x satisfies the condition of moving closer to loop termination. Note that the variable x is left with the value 10 following execution of the loop. It is important to be clear about the state of variables after executing a loop as mistakes can easily be made.

A loop can also be terminated by executing a `break` or `return` statement (see Section 29.4.1, Page 824 and Section 29.4.3, Page 829) or when an exception is thrown.

The body of a while loop can be executed *zero* or more times, as the test expression is always evaluated before the body is executed. So, if the variable x in the example above is initialized to 20, the boolean expression x < 10 will immediately evaluate to false and the loop body is not executed at all.

A while loop may, deliberately or accidentally, execute forever; the boolean expression never evaluating to false. This is known as an *infinite loop*. It is up to the programmer to ensure that this doesn't happen when it shouldn't. However sometimes we get the boolean expression wrong or we have some other logic error and our programs run for an unexpectedly long time without doing anything. In such a circumstance, the program may be stuck in an infinite loop, though this is not necessarily so and there could be other reasons for the behaviour.

Sometimes, we genuinely want a while loop that never terminates, as we are deliberately creating an infinite loop:

```
while (true) {
    // statements, e.g. read data from the network
}
```

This can be useful, for example, in conjunction with threads, where a thread enters an infinite loop reading data from an input source and never needs to do anything else. In this case the loop will stop executing only when the thread is stopped.

What looks like an infinite loop may not actually be one, of course, since it is also possible to jump out of an infinite loop using a break or return statement. For example.

```
while (true) {
    ...
    if (x <= 1)
        break ;
    ...
}
```

We will explain this more fully in Section 29.4.1, Page 824.

It is possible to put state changing operations into the boolean expression itself, i.e. use a sub-expression of the boolean expression to change the values of variables in order to move towards loop termination. For example, the following kind of loop is often seen:

```
int x = 0 ;
while (x++ < 10) {
    System.out.println(x) ;
}
```

Here the postfix increment operator is used to increment the value of x within the boolean expression. Using boolean expressions like this can be quite complicated, even to the point where they can be confusing. It is often better to be a bit more verbose rather than end up with something likely to be misinterpreted!

Examples

The following program illustrates the basic use of while loops, showing two loops both using the variable n to determine when to terminate. The first loop increments n and counts upwards while the second loop decrements n and counts downwards.

```
public class While1 {
  public static void main(final String[] args) {
    int n = 0 ;
    while (n < 10) {
      System.out.println("Counting up " + n) ;
      n++ ;
    }
    while (n > 0) {
      System.out.println("Counting down " + n) ;
      n-- ;
    }
  }
}
```

We could write this program using increment operators within the boolean expression:

```
public class While1A {
  public static void main(final String[] args) {
    int n = 0 ;
    while (n++ < 10) {
      System.out.println("Counting up " + n) ;
    }
    while (n-- > 0) {
      System.out.println("Counting down " + n) ;
    }
  }
}
```

Unfortunately, in altering the program to the above, we have introduced a bug. We leave it as an exercise to find the bug and indicate how to fix it (Self-review 29.1).

The next example repeatedly loops until the user enters a 'y' or 'n'. If a valid character is entered initially, the loop body does not need to be executed. Notice the almost identical repetition of the two statements preceding the loop inside the loop body. This is an unfortunate side-effect of the test-first nature of while loops (compare this to the do loop example that follows).

```
public class While2 {
  public static void main(final String[] args) {
    KeyboardInput in = new KeyboardInput () ;
    System.out.print("Type y(es) or n(o): ") ;
    char c = Character.toLowerCase(in.readCharacter()) ;
    while (c != 'y' && c != 'n') {
      System.out.print("Type y(es) or n(o): ") ;
      c = Character.toLowerCase(in.readCharacter()) ;
    }
    System.out.println("You typed a " + c) ;
  }
}
```

There is an apparent bug in the above program. We leave finding the problem and fixing it as an exercise (Self-review 29.2).

29.3.2 The Do Loop

The do loop allows a statement sequence to be repeatedly executed while a boolean condition evaluates to `true`, with a guarantee that the loop body will be executed at least once.

Purpose

When using a while loop it is sometimes necessary to execute the loop body at least once which means, if we actually use a while loop, that there is repetition of code. Do loops obviate this

Intention

repetition by having the boolean condition come after the loop body. This is useful when the loop body can be used to set up the loop conditions and avoids having to duplicate code outside the loop.

Syntax

```
do
  statement
while ( booleanExpression ) ;
```

Description

The do loop is similar to the while loop except that the test to see whether the loop body should be executed again comes after the loop body, guaranteeing at least one execution of the loop body.

```
int x = 0 ;
do {
  System.out.println(x) ;
  x++ ;
} while (x < 10) ; // Note the semi-colon here
// x == 10 after the loop terminates
```

This loop will count from 0 to 9 (compare this to the similar while loop example earlier). Whatever value the variable x is initialized to, at least one number will always be printed out. Notice especially the semi-colon following the boolean expression. Also the fact that we put the `while` on the same line following the closing brace to ensure that it looks different from the start of a while loop. This is just a code layout style and therefore there are alternatives. We think this is the best, though.

Examples

The first example shows two typical do loops:

```
public class Do1 {
  public static void main(final String[] args) {
    int n = 0 ;
    do {
      System.out.println("Counting up") ;
      n++ ;
    } while (n < 10) ;
    do {
      System.out.println("Counting down") ;
      n-- ;
    } while (n > 0) ;
  }
}
```

The next example is the do loop version of the program to read input until the user types a 'y' or 'n'. This is cleaner than the while version in that there is no repetition of the input and case conversion statements.

```
public class Do2 {
  public static void main(final String[] args) {
    KeyboardInput in = new KeyboardInput () ;
    char c = ' ' ;
    do {
      System.out.print("Type y(es) or n(o): ") ;
      c = Character.toLowerCase(in.readCharacter()) ;
    while (in.readCharacter() != '\n')
      ;
    } while (c != 'y' && c != 'n') ;
    System.out.println("You typed a " + c) ;
  }
}
```

However, if the program is modified to print out an error message then the test has to be repeated inside the loop body:

```
public class Do3 {
  public static void main(final String[] args) {
    KeyboardInput in = new KeyboardInput () ;
    char c = ' ' ;
    do {
      System.out.print("Type y(es) or n(o): ") ;
      c = Character.toLowerCase(in.readCharacter()) ;
      while (in.readCharacter() != '\n')
        ;
      if (c != 'y' && c != 'n') {
        System.out.println("Error - please type y or n!") ;
      }
    } while (c != 'y' && c != 'n') ;
    System.out.println("You typed a " + c) ;
  }
}
```

Finding the program structure that avoids this repetition is left as an exercise (Self-review 29.3).

29.3.3   The For Loop

The for loop allows a statement sequence to be repeatedly executed with the number of repetitions controlled using a loop variable.

Purpose

In a number of situations a loop is required where control is made explicit using a loop variable. The loop variable is updated in a systematic way at the end of each iteration until a pre-defined limit is reached. The loop variable is typically used inside the loop body to perform operations such as array indexing. The use of the loop variable gives bounded iteration.

Intention

```
for ( initialExpression ; booleanExpression ; updateExpression )
   statement
```

Syntax

The for loop has a more complicated structure than while or do loops, although it doesn't actually give more functionality, just different packaging. In the parentheses following the for keyword are three expressions:

Description

initialExpression — this is used to initialize, and possibly also declare, the loop variable. For example:

```
for (int x = 1 ; ...
```

booleanExpression — this is used to test whether to continue with the loop. Usually this test involves the loop variable(s), for example:

```
for (... ; x < 10 ; ...
```

means the loop will execute while x is less than 10.

updateExpression — this expression is evaluated after every execution of the loop body. Usually, this updates the value of the loop variable(s), for example:

```
for (... ; ... ; x++)
```

The expression should move the loop control state one step closer to loop termination.

The loop body is a statement, though more defensively and hence usually a compound statement. The body can use the value of the loop variable but, for good practice, should not change its value by assignment, updating the loop variable should be left to the *updateExpression*. An interesting feature of the for loop is that the entire loop, including the loop body, even if it is a compound statement, defines a scope.

Putting this together gives a loop structure like the following which will count the loop variable x from 1 to 10.

```
for (int x = 1 ; x <= 10 ; x++) {
  // Loop body
}
```

The expression int x = 1 declares and initializes x before the loop body is executed. The expression x <= 10 is evaluated every time *before* the loop body is executed. The loop body is only executed if x <= 10 is true. The expression x++ is executed every time *after* the loop body is executed.

When this loop is executed, x counts through 1, 2, 3, 4, 5, 6, 7, 8, 9, 10 and so can be described as a *counted loop*. At the end of the last iteration x will be incremented to hold 11 but will go out of scope when the boolean test evaluates to false.

The semi-colons in the parenthesized section of the for loop are necessary and must be present.

It is very important to note and remember that the variable x in the above example is declared within the scope of the loop and is local to that scope. It will not be in scope in the statements following the loop. If it is necessary for the loop variable to exist in the scope surrounding the for loop, then it must be declared before the loop:

```
int x ; // declare loop variable outside loop scope
for (x = 1; x <= 10 ; x++) {
  // Loop body
}
// x is still in scope here
```

However, following good defensive practice, the scope of the loop variable should be minimized whenever possible to the loop itself.

The for loop initialization, boolean and update expressions can be any valid expression. Indeed, there is no requirement to use the for loop for counting, as seen above, and one or more of the expressions can even be left out. Neither is there is any requirement for the loop to use integer variables, so any type of variable can be used.

The following is a legal for loop:

```
int y = 0 ;
int z = 0 ;
for (; y < 100 ; z++) {
  y = z * 2 ;
}
```

An infinite loop can be written using a for loop:

```
for (;;) // No expressions at all! {
  System.out.println("Hello") ;
}
```

For loops come in extremely useful when dealing with arrays where counted loops tend to be a natural way of iterating over the array. They are not, however, essential. We noted earlier that we could construct counted loops with a while loop. Thus the for loop:

```
int i = 1 ;
for ( ; x <= 10 ; x++) {
  // Loop body
}
```

is equivalent to the while loop:

```
int x = 1 ;// Initialisation expression
while (x <= 10) { // Boolean test expression
  // Loop body
  ...
  x++ ;   // Update expression
}
```

though it would be far more usual to use:

```
for (int x = 1 ; x <= 10 ; x++) {
  // Loop body
}
```

which is different because of the scope of the variable x. Although for loops are really just a form of syntactic sugar, they are nonetheless invariably used where counted loops are required since they package up very nicely, and in a conceptually neat way, the necessary functionality.

The first example is equivalent to the first while and do loop examples.

Examples

```
public class For1 {
  public static void main(final String[] args) {
    for (int i = 0 ; i < 10 ; i++) {
      System.out.println("Counting up") ;
    }
    for (int i = 10 ; i > 0 ; i--) {
      System.out.println("Counting down") ;
    }
  }
}
```

As we indicated earlier, a typical use of a for loop is in conjunction with array (or ArrayList, Vector (Collections), or Array (ADS, JGL)) indexing. The loop variable is used to index the array.

```
public class For2 {
  public static void main(final String[] args) {
    int[] x = new int[10] ;
    for (int i = 0 ; i < 10 ; i++) {
      x[i] = i ;
    }
    for (int i = 0 ; i < 10 ; i++) {
      System.out.println(x[i]) ;
    }
  }
}
```

The final for loop example takes the strings given as arguments to the program and prints out a version of them with any upper case characters converted to lower case.

```
public class For3 {
  public static void main(final String[] args) {
    if (args.length == 0) {
      System.out.println("No strings to transform") ;
```

```
        } else {
          for (int i = 0 ; i < args.length ; i++) {
            String s = args[i] ;
            char[] result = new char[s.length()] ;
            for (int j = 0 ; j < s.length() ; j++) {
              result[j] = Character.toLowerCase(s.charAt(j)) ;
            }
            System.out.println(result) ;
          }
        }
      }
    }
```

Some people will argue (probably quite rightly) that the above program, which is good for showing the use of for loops and array indexing, is not actually a good one because it uses an array of `char` when it is really a `String` that is being manipulated. The following is an equivalent program that performs the transformation using a method from class `String`:

```
public class ToLower {
  public static void main(final String[] args) {
    if (args.length == 0) {
      System.out.println("No strings to transform") ;
    } else {
      for (int i = 0 ; i < args.length ; i++) {
        System.out.println(args[i].toLowerCase()) ;
      }
    }
  }
}
```

29.3.4   Checking Loop Behaviour

With all kinds of loop a common source of bugs occur when the loop executes the wrong number of iterations. We saw an instance of this with the program `While1A` (Page 817). Quite often these will take the form of *off-by-one* errors where the loop executes one too many or one too few iterations. This was exactly the problem with the `While1A` program. Another variety of the off-by-one error is that it is easy to forget that array indexing starts from zero with the final index being one less that the length of the array. So, for example:

```
for (int i = 1 ; i < anArray.length ; i++) {
  anArray[i] = 1 ;
}
```

will count from 1 through to the length of the array minus 1 (so if the array is of length 5, the loop will count through 1, 2, 3, 4). This is the correct place to stop the loop but almost certainly not what was wanted in terms of initializing every element. When executed no immediate run-time error will occur but element 0 of the array will not have been set to 1. Unpredictable errors could well occur in some other part of the program where element 0 is assumed to have a particular value

A related kind of error occurs when the boolean condition to detect loop termination is wrongly expressed. For example, in the code segment:

```
for (int i = 0 ; i <= anArray.length ; i++) {
  anArray[i] = 1 ;
}
```

if the array is of size five, then this loop will count through 0, 1, 2, 3, 4, 5 giving six iterations, as the termination condition uses the <= operator. When an attempt is made to access `anArray[5]` an exception will be thrown as this array element does not exist. In this case of an off-by-one error, at least, the error will be made visible immediately, although the program will terminate!

The boolean conditions in loops are often best expressed using the < or > operators. Using == or != can often result in the termination condition being missed. Say we had written:

```
for (int i = 0 ; i != size ; i++) {
    ...
}
```

and the code works fine. No problem. Suppose now we discover that the algorithm only ever needs to deal with even numbers. We immediately want to optimize the running of our program so we amend it:

```
for (int i = 0 ; i != size ; i += 2) {
    ...
}
```

We now discover, during testing, that sometimes the program goes into an infinite loop. Bizarre, it used to work. Very quickly if our testing strategy is at all reasonable, we discover that whenever `size` is an odd number, the program fails to terminate. Now we look at the code this is obvious but because we had not been as defensive about the boolean expression we had the little hiccup. We should have written:

```
for (int i = 0 ; i < size ; i++) {
    ...
}
```

in the first place in order to protect against those situations that are impossible.

Although the above examples use the for loop, the same sort of issues can arise using the while and do loops. In general, whenever any loop is written, the programmer needs to check the following:

- What are the initial values of all variables used by the loop? Do they need to be freshly initialized or have their existing values checked?
- What are the loop termination conditions?
- Does the loop move closer to termination after each iteration and can the termination condition actually be met?
- Will the correct number of iterations be performed?
- What is the state of variables after the loop has terminated?

Loops provide fertile ground for subtle errors in programs so the programmer needs to go through the checklist carefully whenever a loop is used.

This is just one more element of the defensive programming approach. The professional programmer takes a defensive approach now to avoid as many bugs as possible in the future, particularly the ones that arise later during maintenance.

29.4   Transfer Statements

29.4.1   Break

Purpose

It is often convenient to terminate a loop at an arbitrary place in its execution without waiting until the boolean expression evaluates to `false`. The break statement allows control to jump out of a loop and continue with the following statement. It is also used with switch statements and has the same effect of jumping out of the statement.

Intention

Although it should be possible to express all loops in such a way that the boolean test expression is used to determine when the loop terminates, in practice it is often convenient to 'break out' of a loop as a result of some test within the loop body.

It is also possible to jump out of not only the current statement but any enclosing statement. This latter is done by attaching a label to an enclosing statement and using the label with the break statement. This allows the execution of an arbitrary number of enclosing statements to be terminated.

The break statement should only be used in loops to simplify what would otherwise be overly complex boolean tests and loop bodies.

Syntax

```
break ;
```

or

```
break label ;
```

Description

The break statement can occur anywhere within a switch, for, while or do statement and causes execution to jump to the statement following the innermost applicable statement. An attempt to use the break statement not in one of these kinds of statement will cause a compile-time error.

We have already seen the break statement used to structure flow control in a switch statement (Page 811). We also (Page 816) saw an example of using a break statement to terminate an infinite loop. The loop need not be infinite if a break statement is to be used:

```
while (exp) {
   ...
   if (exp2)
     break ; // End the loop now
   ...
}
```

Here the basic loop will execute while `exp` evaluates to `true`. However, should `exp2` evaluate to `true` during an iteration, a break statement will be executed and the loop terminated, regardless of the value of `exp`. Executing a break statement can be seen as a jump to the statement following the loop, with the loop body going out of scope and any local variables declared within the body being destroyed.

The second form of the break statement is when it is used within the scope of any surrounding labelled statement:

```
for (int i = 0 ; i < size ; i++) {
 here: // <-- A label that labels the if statement.
  if(...) {
    while (exp) {
      ...
      if (exp2)
        break here ; // Exit from the labelled statement
                // not just the loop.
      ...
    }
    ... // rest of if statement.
  }
      // we start here immediately if the break is executed.
  ... // rest of for loop.
}
```

In this case, an enclosing if statement is labelled with the label `here:`. Labels are denoted using a name followed by a colon. The label must be attached to a statement like a loop, switch or if that has a body. When `break here ;` is executed both the loop containing the break statement and the enclosing if statement are terminated, so that execution jumps to the statement following the if statement (the rest of the for loop).

This can be a bit confusing at first (and also later on!) as the label is not at the point where execution continues but is used to denote which nesting statements will be terminated. You must never interpret a break statement that uses a label as a way of jumping to the labelled statement — that kind of jump is not possible with Java — the break statement is always a way of breaking out of statements.

The break statement, in either form, gives a safe way to use a limited version of what in older programming languages used to be provided with the infamous goto statement. The goto statement is considered bad in all good programming circles, and is not present in Java, as it allows control to jump anywhere within a procedure. Such behaviour undermines any structure the program might have, making it difficult, if not impossible, to understand it. Although the break (and continue and return) statements bring some structure to this unstructured flow control, and whilst infinitely better than using a goto statement, it can still be difficult to understand code that uses the break statement too liberally.

Our defensive programming philosophy dictates that we should use the break statement only if necessary and then only if *absolutely* necessary. Agreed, break statements are very common wherever switch statements are used, but they are rare with loops and extremely rare indeed in their label using form. Labels themselves should be almost never seen and when they are used must be commented to indicate why they are being used and what the control flow should be. It is also wise to present a justification of why more structured forms of flow control would not suffice. Then, if maintenance changes are being made, the maintainer can quickly and easily understand the thinking. With luck they may find an elegant way of avoiding the use of the break statement!

The first example shows the basic use of break to terminate a loop when a variable has a certain value. In this case the loop will continually ask the user to type a digit until a '5' is typed:

```
public class Break1 {
```

note

Some programming languages (C and C++ included) even have mechanisms for non-local gotos, i.e. for jumping from one procedure into another. For some languages, there are some circumstances where you do actually have to do this sort of thing even in a good, well-structured program. Fortunately, good exception handling systems, for example as in Java, mean the feature is never needed.

Examples

```
    public static void main(final String[] args) {
      KeyboardInput in = new KeyboardInput () ;
      while (true) {
        System.out.print("Type a digit:") ;
        int n = in.readInteger() ;
        if (n == 5) {
          System.out.println("You typed a 5 - I quit!") ;
          break ;
        }
      }
    }
  }
```

The while loop boolean expression is true, so the loop is potentially infinite. Using the break statement provides a convenient way of exiting the loop without introducing a boolean variable.

A similar strategy can be used to simplify the input 'y' or 'n' examples shown for the do and while loops. Here is the do loop modified to use a break statement:

```
public class Break2 {
  public static void main(final String[] args) {
    KeyboardInput in = new KeyboardInput () ;
    char c = ' ' ;
    while (true) {
      System.out.print("Type y(es) or n(o): ") ;
      c = Character.toLowerCase(in.readCharacter()) ;
      while (in.readCharacter() != '\n')
        ;
      if (c == 'y' || c == 'n') {
        break ;
      }
      System.out.println("Error - please type y or n!") ;
    }
    System.out.println("You typed a " + c) ;
  }
}
```

Notice the change to the expression testing the input character and that no code now needs to be duplicated.

The final example shows the use of break with a label:

```
public class Break3 {
  public static void main(final String[] args) {
    KeyboardInput in = new KeyboardInput () ;
    System.out.print("Type an integer less than 25: ") ;
    int i = in.readInteger() ;
  here:
    //  ^
    //  +--- The label labelling the statement we will be
    //       exiting from when we use a labelled break.
    if (i < 25) {
      System.out.println("Inside if") ;
      for (int n = 0 ; n < i ; n++) {
        System.out.println("Looping") ;
        if (i > 15)
          break ;
        i++ ;
        if (i > 8)
          break here ;
      }
      System.out.println("After for loop") ;
    } else {
```

```
        System.out.println("Input not less than 25") ;
      }
      System.out.println("Final statement") ;
    }
  }
```

The program asks the user to type an integer less than 25 and then does various things depending on what was input. In particular, if the input is greater than 8 but less than 16, the break statement with the label is executed causing both the loop to terminate (in its first iteration) and the enclosing if to terminate. If the input is less than 8 the for loop will iterate until the input is incremented so that the same condition applies. If the input is greater than 15 but less than 20, the unlabelled break is executed. Note that, whatever happens, the if statement is only executed once.

29.4.2 Continue

The continue statement allows the current iteration of a loop to be terminated and causes the next iteration to begin. In effect it causes a jump to the end of the loop body, so that the evaluation of the boolean expression happens next.

Purpose

If the loop body has done all that it needs to in the current iteration, the continue statement allows the iteration to be cleanly stopped and the next one started. This avoids having to use something like an if statement to achieve the same result. Like break, continue can also be used with a label, allowing any enclosing loop to be the target, with the nesting loops being terminated.

Intention

```
    continue ;
```
or
```
    continue label ;
```

Syntax

The continue statement can occur anywhere within a for, while or do loop statement and causes execution to jump to the end of the loop body, ready to start the next iteration. An attempt to use the continue statement anywhere else will cause a compile time error.

Description

The basic use of continue is as follows:

```
while (exp) {
  ...
  if (exp2)
    continue ; // Skip the rest of the loop for this iteration
  ...
}
```

Here the basic loop will execute while exp evaluates to true. If during execution of the loop body exp2 also evaluates to true then the rest of this execution of the body is skipped; in effect this is a jump to the end of the loop body. exp is re-evaluated to determine whether to continue with the next iteration, i.e. execution continues normally. The continue statement without a label will not, in itself, cause the loop to terminate.

The continue statement can also be used with a label attached to any enclosing loop (i.e. a loop within which the loop containing the continue statement is nested):

```
here:
for (int i = 0 ; i < size ; i++) {
  while (exp) {
```

```
      ...
      if (exp2)
        continue here ; // End the loop now
        ...
    }
    ... // rest of for loop
  }
```

In this case an enclosing for loop is labelled with `here:`. When the continue statement is executed, the nested while loop will be terminated and the enclosing for loop will immediately move onto its next iteration.

Examples

The first example of using the continue statement shows that part of a loop body can easily be skipped when needed:

```
public class Continue1 {
  public static void main(final String[] args) {
    KeyboardInput in = new KeyboardInput () ;
    for (int i = 0 ; i < 10 ; i++) {
      System.out.print("Type a digit between from 0 to 9:") ;
      int n = in.readInteger() ;
      if (n == 0) {
        System.out.println("Can't divide by zero") ;
        continue ;
      }
      System.out.println("100/" + n + " = " + 100.0/n) ;
    }
  }
}
```

As dividing by zero cannot produce a valid result, the continue statement is used to skip the statement containing the division (if the division by zero went ahead the result would be the place holder value Infinity). Notice how we have used the `double` constant `100.0` (rather than the `int` constant 100) to force the division to use floating point arithmetic.

The second example shows the use of the continue statement with a label:

```
public class Continue2 {
  public static void main(final String[] args) {
    here:
    for (int i = 0 ; i < 10 ; i++) {
      int n = 0 ;
      System.out.println("For loop, i = " + i) ;
      while (n < i) {
        System.out.println("While loop, n = " + n) ;
        n++ ;
        if (n == 5) {
          System.out.println("Continue here") ;
          continue here ;
        }
      }
    }
  }
}
```

Whenever the variable n has the value 5 inside the nested while loop, the continue statement will cause execution to jump to the next iteration of the enclosing for loop, terminating the while loop.

29.4.3 Return

The return statement terminates the execution of the current method, with control returning to the caller. All non-`void` methods *must* include a return statement as the last executed statement which includes the value to be returned by the method.

Return serves two purposes. The first is to terminate execution of a method, potentially at any point in the method body. The second is to specify the value to be returned by a non-`void` method.

```
return ;
```
or
```
return expression ;
```

return statements can appear anywhere within a method body and in multiple places. A non-`void` method must include at least one return statement. The following is a rather trivial method but does exhibit the use of the return statement:

```
int timesTwo(int n) {
  return n * 2 ;
}
```

The type of the value returned must be compatible with the return type specified in the method declaration. In the case of object references, a reference to a subclass object can be returned where a superclass type was expected.

Using return often avoids making the method body more complicated but has the side-effect of creating 'multiple exits' from the method, which can make it harder to understand.

The following example includes a method `min` to return the minimum of two arguments:

```
public class Return1 {
  private static int min(final int a, final int b) {
    if (a < b)
      return a ;
    else
      return b ;
  }
  public static void main(final String[] args) {
    System.out.println("Minimum of 5 and 8 is: " + min(5, 8)) ;
  }
}
```

In this case the method `min` must return an integer value as it has been declared to do so (the compiler would object if no value was returned at all). `min` actually has two return statements, one of which is executed to return the argument with the minimum value. We could have written the method as:

```
public class Return2 {
  private static int min(final int a, final int b) {
    if (a < b)
      return a ;
    return b ;
  }
  public static void main(final String[] args) {
    System.out.println("Minimum of 5 and 8 is: " + min(5, 8)) ;
  }
}
```

Here this version of `min` makes use of the fact that if $a < b$ then the 'then' part of the if statement is executed and the method returns; the rest of the method body can never be reached. If $a < b$ is false then the 'then' part of the if statement is ignored and the rest of the method body is executed, returning the value of b. Whilst we are happy with multi-exit methods, many people are not — some people really much prefer a single entry, single exit method construction style. For example:

```java
public class Return3 {
  private static int min(final int a, final int b) {
    int returnValue = a ;
    if (a > b) {
      returnValue = b ;
    }
    return returnValue ;
  }
  public static void main(final String[] args) {
    System.out.println("Minimum of 5 and 8 is: " + min(5, 8)) ;
  }
}
```

Which to use is really a matter of choice. All three versions are equally correct in that they deliver the same value given the same input. Again, consistency is everything in order to support predictability and hence comprehension when reading the code. Whichever style you choose for a particular program, use the same style throughout that program.

29.5   Recursion

Before moving on to look at classes, there is one more technique that we need to have a quick look at: *recursion*. We first mentioned recursion in Section 3.3.5, Page 59 describing how a method can call itself. Because recursion relates to the way a sequence of statements is called, it is a flow control mechanism even though it is not, strictly, a flow control statement as we have been dealing with in this chapter.

In mathematics, there are many functions which are defined in terms of themselves, i.e. using recurrence equations. The factorial function is one of them; it is usually defined:

$$\text{factorial}_n = \begin{cases} 1 & n = 0 \\ n \times \text{factorial}_{n-1} & n > 0 \end{cases}$$

This function, as with all recurrence equations, seems 'naturally' to indicate that a recursive method is required:

```java
public class Factorial {
  public static int factorial(final int i) {
    if (i > 0)  // termination condition
      return i * factorial(i - 1) ;  // recursive call
    else
      return 1 ; // base case
  }
  public static void main(final String[] args) {
    KeyboardInput in = new KeyboardInput() ;
    System.out.print("Enter an integer: ") ;
```

```
        final int i = in.readInteger() ;
        final int result = factorial(i) ;
        System.out.println(i +"! = " + result) ;
    }
  }
```

This recursive method, indeed any recursive method, calls itself in order to have the effect of repeatedly executing a method body. But 'repeatedly executing' is exactly what iteration is. Clearly, recursion is a method-based technique for implementing iteration.

It seems then that for those algorithms that are 'naturally' recursive, expressing them as a recursive method is the 'natural' way of writing them down using a programming language like Java, even though it is iteration that is the flow control technique.

Implementing mathematical functions is not the only place that recursive techniques are traditionally used. Operations on list-based data structures (see Part 2) are also often expressed using recursive operations. However, the disadvantage of using recursion lies in the need to do a method call for each iteration. This is not only time consuming but also uses up memory. If too many recursive calls are made, there is the risk of running out of memory. Loops, on the other hand, need no extra memory (subject to whatever the loop body does).

In general, recursion should only be used where the programmer is sure that the number of recursive calls will remain relatively small.

As a second example of this issue of loop versus recursion, the following example prints out the sequence of Fibonacci numbers less than 1000. The Fibonacci numbers are defined by the recurrence equation:

$$f_n = f_{n-1} + f_{n-2}$$

The following is a program that uses a while loop to perform the iteration:

```
public class Fibonacci {
  public static void printFibonacciSeriesUpTo(final int maximum) {
    int current = 1 ;
    int previous = 1 ;
    System.out.println(current) ;
    while (current < maximum) {
      System.out.println(current) ;
      int next = current + previous ;
      previous = current ;
      current = next ;
    }
  }
  public static void main(final String[] args) {
    printFibonacciSeriesUpTo(1000) ;
  }
}
```

29.6   Summary

This chapter has described the flow control statements in the Java language — if, switch, while, do, for, break, continue and return. Each of these statements is used to control the order in which other statements are executed, providing the basic control mechanisms of the language.

We have also had a quick look at recursion as a technique for implementing iteration.

Self-review Exercises

Self-review 29.1 Run the programs While1 and While1A and determine what the introduced bug is. Why do we get this behaviour? What can we do to fix it (apart from using the original, correctly behaved program)?

Self-review 29.2 What is the error associated with the program While2. How can it be fixed?

Self-review 29.3 The repetition of the boolean expression in Do3 can be avoided. How is this possible?

Self-review 29.4 Compare and contrast the four programs (iterative and recursive implementation of factorial numbers and Fibonacci series programs) using the factors of time to implement, execution speed and memory usage.

Programming Exercises

Exercise 29.1 Re-code the program Break1 without using the break statement. Which version of the program do you prefer? Why?

Exercise 29.2 Implement the factorial function without using recursion, i.e. implementing the iteration using iteration statements. Have you tested your factorial implementation? If you have, you will have noticed a serious flaw in the implementation. What is it and why is it there?

Exercise 29.3 Implement the Fibonacci function using recursion rather than implementing the iteration using iteration statements.

Classes and Packages

Objectives

This chapter first describes the basic features of classes and then focuses on the specific features of top-level classes and the various kinds of inner classes. Most of the detail about inheritance is left to the following chapter along with interfaces. Packages are introduced at the end of this chapter.

Keywords

class
top-level class
nested class
inner class
member class
local class
anonymous class
package

30.1   Introduction

Chapter 6 introduced classes as the major structuring and abstraction tool in Java. All objects are instances of a class and, hence, classes embody all the knowledge that an object needs in order to perform its duties as part of an application.

This chapter focuses on the core properties of classes excluding inheritance which is covered in detail in the following chapter along with the description of how method calls are performed. As there are various kinds of class, the common features are described first, followed by the specific features of *top-level* and then *inner classes*. Inner classes were introduced with Java 1 1 and provide an important extension to the class mechanism, requiring them to be distinguished from ordinary top-level classes.

Class declarations are closely connected with packages which are, therefore, described at the end of the chapter.

30.2   Classes

In this section, we will describe the basic features and properties of all classes. The additional or different features of *top-level* classes are described in Section 30.3, Page 851, while those of *inner* or *nested* classes, including *nested top-level classes*, are described in Section 30.4, Page 852.

30.2.1   The Class Declaration

Purpose

The class declaration introduces a new class and in doing so also introduces a new reference type of the same name. A class describes the structure and behaviour of its instance objects in terms of instance variables and methods. Accessibility to variables and methods can be explicitly controlled, allowing a class to act as a unit of encapsulation.

Intention

Object-oriented programming revolves around identifying and then using new types or abstractions. The implementation of a type or abstraction is described by a class and, as Java is an object-oriented programming language, it directly provides a class declaration mechanism to do just that.

Like variables, classes may be declared in various different scopes. The scope a class is declared in directly affects certain properties of the class, which is why top-level and inner classes are being described in separate sub-sections.

Syntax

```
class identifier
{
    constructor declarations
    method declarations
    static method declarations
    instance variable declarations
    static variable declarations
}
```

A class is introduced by the `class` keyword which is followed by an identifier giving the class name. By convention, a class name always starts with a capital letter. The class body is delimited by braces and may contain a series of variable, method, class or interface declarations. The `class` keyword can be preceded by modifiers, as will be seen in subsequent sections.

The class name introduces a new reference type name, allowing variables of the type to be declared (see Section 28.8.1, Page 781). A variable of reference type holds a reference to an *instance object* of a class. An instance object is created using the `new` operator in an allocation expression (see also Section 30.2.7, Page 845). For example:

```
Stack s = new Stack() ;
```

A class acts as a unit of encapsulation and creates a class scope (see Section 28.7, Page 779 and Section 30.2.2, Page 836). All classes are declared within a package, which may be the default anonymous package. In addition, a class is contained within a source file or compilation unit which is part of a package. Both the package and the file provide scopes. Normally, unless nested, each class is declared in a separate source file, but, subject to the rules about public top-level classes, it is possible to have several class declarations in the same file.

The name of a source file containing a class declaration should be the *same* as the name of the class it contains, with the extension `.java` added. For example, class `Stack` should be stored in a file called `Stack.java`. If there are several classes within the same source file, the file must be named after the sole public class in the file. If this is not done correctly the source file cannot be compiled.

Class scope allows any expression within the class declaration to use any instance variable or method declared by the class. The order of declarations does not matter, unlike the order in local scopes. A further and significant consequence of class scope is that the variables and methods of *any object of the class* are accessible to any method of the class (see the example below). This means that, although objects are generally strongly encapsulated, within their class encapsulation is based on class scope.

The following example illustrates a class declaration and highlights the effects of class scope:

```
class ClassScope {
  //  This method illustrates that the private variables of any
  //  ClassScope object can be accessed in a ClassScope method.
  public void alter(final ClassScope c) {
    //  c is the parameter, not the object the method was called for,
    //   but the private variable n can still be accessed.
    c.n = 123 ;
  }
  // Display the value of an instance object by using the value of the
  // private variable n.
  public String toString() {
    return new Integer(n).toString() ;
  }
  // A private variable only accessible with the scope of this class.
  private int n = 1 ;
}
// Use this class to test the behaviour of class scope.
public class ScopeTest {
```

```
        public static void main(final String[] args) {
          // OK to create ClassScope objects and use their public methods.
          ClassScope a = new ClassScope () ;
          ClassScope b = new ClassScope () ;
          // Note: The private variable n belonging to the object referenced
          // by b can be modified by a method called for an object of the
          // same class referenced by a.
          a.alter(b) ;
          System.out.println("Object a: " + a) ;
          System.out.println("Object b: " + b) ;
          // BUT cannot break encapsulation of a ClassScope object in this
          // class.  Uncommenting this line will lead to a compilation
          // error.  This will be true wherever it could be moved to within
          // additional methods added to this class.
          // a.n = 123 ;
        }
      }
```

Instance objects used outside the scope of their class are strictly encapsulated. However, within the methods of class ClassScope it is possible to access the private variables of any instance object of ClassScope, regardless of which instance object the method was called for.

Note that the example includes two classes. These could either be placed in separate source files called ClassScope.java and ScopeTest.java, or both placed in a single source file called ScopeTest.java with class ScopeTest being public (as is the case for this example).

Also note that it is very useful to use a consistent style of indentation when writing classes and to define and follow a convention for the order in which variables and methods appear. An example order is:

- Public static final variables.

- Public instance variables.

- Protected instance and static variables.

- Private instance and static variables.

- Constructors.

- Public methods.

- Protected and private methods.

- Public static methods.

- Protected and private static methods.

30.2.2   Public, Private and Protected

Purpose   The use of the keywords public, private and protected with a declaration allows the programmer to explicitly control accessibility to a variable, method, nested class or nested interface from outside the scope of a class.

Intention   To enable useful encapsulation we want some class members to be private and inaccessible to anything else, while others need to be public in order to provide the public interface of instance objects. This needs to be done on an individual basis, so that the programmer can carefully choose the level of accessibility granted to each member of a class. To provide a finer grain of encapsulation, it is also desirable to limit the accessibility of some class members to classes in the same package and to subclasses, leading to the use of protected members.

Any declaration at class scope may be preceded by *one* of the keywords (also known as *access modifiers*):

Syntax

```
public, protected, private
```

The use of an access modifier is optional and it can be omitted.

The keywords, have the following meaning:

Description

`public` — a declaration is accessible by any class.

`protected` — a declaration is accessible to any subclass of the declaring class, or to any class in the same package (see Section 31.2.2, Page 872).

`private` — a declaration is only accessible from within the class it is declared in.

If none of the three keywords are provided, the declaration has *default accessibility*, meaning that it is accessible to any other class in the same package. Note, however, such a declaration is not accessible to any subclass within a different package, default accessibility is controlled strictly by package scope.

Good programming practice dictates that, by default, any method or variable should be explicitly declared as private, to guarantee the maximum level of encapsulation. Further, only the minimum number of methods should be made public, while instance variables should never be made public unless absolutely necessary. Static variables should ideally only be made public if they are also final.

The set of public methods declared by a class defines the public interface of instance objects. Public methods should be chosen carefully and only provide operations that are appropriate to the abstraction the class represents. Care should also be taken not to over-expose the internal implementation of the class, such that clients (i.e. users) of the class become dependent on how the class is implemented rather than the services it provides.

tip

Never make variables that are not final public, always make them private and use accessor methods.

The following are all declarations that can appear within a class:

Examples

```
public void method1() { ... }
private int method2() { ... }
protected int x = 1 ;
private Stack s ;
float method3() { ... }
String t = "Hello" ;
```

30.2.3   Instance Variables

An instance variable forms part of the state of an instance object. Each object gets its own copy of the variables declared by its class.

Purpose

Objects use variables to store the state of the object. As computation proceeds the object changes state when the values of its variables change.

Intention

Syntax	The declaration and initialization of instance variables has been described in Section 28.8.1, Page 781 and Section 28.8.2, Page 783. Note that instance variable declarations can include the modifiers `public`, `private` or `protected`, and additionally the modifiers `final`, `transient` and `volatile`.
Description	Instance variables should be chosen so as to represent the state of instance objects of a class. They can be of any type, including that of the class they are declared in (so objects of the class can hold references to other objects of the same class). By convention, an instance variable name starts with a lowercase letter.
	The rules for initialization require instance variables to be initialized when declared or a default initialization will be made. Also, the programmer needs to decide whether a variable has public, private, protected or default access.
	An instance variable can be declared as `final`, meaning that it is a constant and cannot be changed by assignment. This is very useful if the variable has to be public and should also always be used if the initial value of the variable will not be changed.
Examples	The following class declares various variables:

```
class Blah
{
    public String hello = "hello" ;
    public final String world = "world" ;
    protected int count = 0 ;
    private float length = 2.345f ;
    long size = 123432L ;
}
```

In this case the class only consists of instance variable declarations. This is legal but normally only used if the instance objects are being used as simple data structures that are part of the infrastructure of another class.

30.2.4 Static or Class Variables

Purpose	A static variable belongs to a class and is not part of the state of individual instance objects. Only one copy of each static variable exists. Static variables are often called *class variables*.
Intention	It is frequently useful to have a variable that is shared by all instance objects of a class or, if public, can be used by any clients of a class. Static variables exist at class scope and support such behaviour.
Syntax	A class variable is declared using the `static` keyword and may be explicitly initialized (see Section 28.8.1, Page 781 and Section 28.8.2, Page 783).
Description	Class variables have several distinct uses:

- As variables shared by all instances of the class. As such they can be described as 'global' to the class scope and are typically declared as private.

- As variables accessible to any client of the class. As such they are effectively global to an entire program and would need to be declared as `public`. Such variables, being updatable from any piece of code, are seriously dangerous and hence extremely rare.

- As constants declared as `final`. Typically such constants are made `public` to be used anywhere within a program. Many Java library classes make use of such `public static final` variables. By convention their names are spelt using uppercase letters.

It should be noted that although class variables may exist for a particular class, there is no class object that they are part of (as might be the case in languages such as Smalltalk).

The variable initialization rules state that static variables must be initialized either explicitly or by taking the default value of the variable type. In addition, a static variable initialization cannot refer to any static variables declared after its own declaration. Hence, the following code is not allowed:

```
class Example {
  ...
  static int a = b * 10 ; // Error here
  static int b = 3 ;
  ...
}
```

though if the statements are reversed then all is fine.

A static variable can be accessed by any method or static method (see Section 30.2.6, Page 844) in the same class scope by simply using its name. Clients outside the scope of the class need to use a field expression (see Section 28.9.1, Page 789) using the class name, for example:

```
Integer.MAX_VALUE
```

will access the static variable `MAX_VALUE` declared in the library class `Integer`.

The following class declares and uses some static variables: **Examples**

```
import com.objectspace.jgl.Array ;
class Static1 {
  // Publically accessible constants
  public final static int UP = 1 ;
  public final static int DOWN = 2 ;
  // Publically accessible class variable that can be changed by
  // assignment.  DO NOT DO THIS IN A REAL PROGRAM UNLESS YOU
  // *REALLY* MUST
  public static String s = "default" ;
  // Private class variables
  private static float f = 3.141f ;
  private static Array a = new Array () ;
  // Static variables can be accessed from within a method.  Cannot
  // actually tell whether they are class or instance variables from
  // the usage.
  public void test() {
    int i = UP ;
    s = "hello" ;
    a.add(s) ;
  }
  public static void main(final String args[]) {
    // Static variables can be accessed from a static method
    s = "hello" ;
    a.add(s) ;
    Static1 s1 = new Static1 () ;
    s1.test() ;
```

```
    }
  }
```

This shows that static variables can be directly accessed within both normal and static methods.

30.2.5   Methods

Purpose A method serves as a procedure that is called for a specific object. A method has a body containing a statement sequence which is executed when the method is called. The method has access to all the instance variables of the object it is called for and all the class variables declared for the class of the object it is called for.

Intention Methods provide the implementation of the dynamic behaviour of objects and may change the state of the object they are called for.

Syntax The basic method declaration has the following form:

```
modifiers typeName methodName ( parameterList ) {
    statementSequence
}
```

The modifiers are optionally one of `public`, `protected` and `private`, with zero or more of `abstract` (see Section 31.2.10, Page 889), `final` (see Section 31.2.5, Page 877), `native` and `synchronized` (see Section 33.3, Page 929). The method body is a compound statement delimited by braces, containing a statement sequence.

A method may throw exceptions which are declared with a `throws` clause (see Chapter 32):

```
modifiers typeName methodName ( parameterList )
  throws typeNameList {
    statementSequence
}
```

The type name list following the `throws` keyword is a comma separated list of one or more type names of the exceptions that can be thrown.

Methods declared as `native` do not have a method body and a semi-colon is substituted:

```
modifiers native typeName methodName ( parameterList ) ;
modifiers native typeName methodName ( parameterList )
  throws typeName ;
```

This is also the case for methods declared `abstract`:

```
modifiers abstract typeName methodName ( parameterList ) ;
modifiers abstract typeName methodName ( parameterList )
  throws typeName ;
```

If a method returns an array type then the following variation on the syntax may be used:

```
modifiers typeName methodName ( parameterList ) [] {
    statementSequence
}
```

with a pair of square brackets appearing after the parameter list. Although the above is a legal syntax, it is much more usual to put the square brackets where they really belong following the return type name:

```
modifiers typeName[] methodName ( parameterList ) {
```

```
    statementSequence
  }
```

Arrays with more dimensions simply require extra sets of brackets, exactly as with a variable declaration.

Methods are procedures that are called for a specific object using a field or method call expression (see Section 31.2.6, Page 878). There are two kinds of method: void and value-returning.

A void method is declared with a return type of `void`. The body of a void method simply performs a computation, which may have the side-effect of changing the state of the object it was called for, and terminates without explicitly returning a value, although it can still use a `return` statement (see Section 29.4.3, Page 829) without an argument:

```
void f() {
  a = 4 ; // Assume a is an instance variable
}
```

A value returning (or non-`void`) method is declared with a non-`void` return type. The body of the method must contain at least one `return` statement, returning a value of a type that either matches or can be converted to the specified return type (see Section 28.6.3, Page 778 for information about conversions):

```
int f() {
  return a * 10 ; // Assume a is an accessible variable
}
```

As a value must be returned from a non-`void` method, the compiler will check that all possible exits from a method will result in a `return` statement being executed. In the example below, this is not the case as when `x` has a value greater than 9 control will reach the end of the method body without reaching a `return` statement. As a result, the compiler will not accept the method until another `return` statement is added.

```
int f() { // Warning - will not compile
  if (x < 10) // x is an instance variable
    return value ;
  // ERROR - Should be a return statement here
}
```

The modifiers `public`, `protected` and `private` can appear at the start of a method declaration, as noted in Section 30.2.2, Page 836. In addition the modifiers `abstract`, `final`, `native` and `synchronized` may be present. `Abstract` and `final` are both related to inheritance and are covered in Chapter 31. The others have the following meanings:

`native` — The method is a *native method,* implemented using a programming language other than Java (often C or C++) and is typically specific to a particular operating system or type of hardware. This provides a way of interfacing Java programs to the facilities of a machine that are otherwise inaccessible from standard Java. The Java libraries also use native methods to map operations, such as handling graphics and windows, to a particular operating system in such a way as to hide any details or differences from the Java program (and, hence, enable the platform independence of Java programs). A native method declaration specifies the name of the method, any method arguments and a result type but does not include a method body. Further discussion of native methods is outside the scope of this book.

`synchronized` — a *synchronized method* is one that can only be executed by one thread at a time for a specific object. The details are covered in Chapter 33.

A method name is an identifier (see Section 28.3, Page 772) and by convention starts with a lowercase letter. Following the method name is a parenthesized formal parameter list, which may be empty (but the brackets must still be present). If a method has several parameters they are specified as a comma separated formal parameter list. Each parameter consists of a type name followed by a parameter variable name. The following are examples:

```
int a() { ... } // No parameters
int b(int x) { ... } // One parameter called x of type int
int c(String s, float f) { ... } // Two parameters
int d(Array a, short[] b, char c) { ... } // Three parameters
```

The parameter variables are local variables within the scope of the method body and are initialized when the method is called (see Section 31.2.6, Page 878). Parameters can be declared as final (and will be treated as blank finals), indicating that their values cannot be changed in the method body (they are constants):

```
int e(final int a) { ... }
```

If a parameter variable will not be altered by a method body, it is good practice to make it final as this reminds the programmer that the variable should not be changed *and* allows the compiler to check that that is the case.

If a method can throw a type of exception that must be declared, the method declaration must include a `throws` clause following the parameter list. Chapter 33 describes this further.

Methods can be *overloaded*, meaning that two or more methods in the same class can have the same name provided they have different parameter lists. For example:

```
int f(int a) { ... }
char f(float g) { ... }
String f(String a, String b) { ... }
double f(int a, int b, int c, int d) { ... }
```

All these methods are called `f` but can be distinguished due to their differing parameter lists (in a method call the number and types of the arguments are used to determine which method to use). The return types are not taken into account and can differ as shown above.

Examples

The following program consists of a class declaring various methods:

```
public class Class1 {
  private String name = "hello" ;
  //  Fill all elements of an integer array with a given value
  public int[] fill(int[] array, final int value) {
    for (int i = 0 ; i < array.length ; i++) {
      array[i] = value ;
    }
    return array ;
  }
  //  Note the final parameter
  public int f(final int i) {
```

```
        if (i > 0)
           return i ;
        //  Trying to assign to i would be an error
        // i = 0 ; // Error!
        return 0 ;
     }
     //  Can only be used by one thread at a time for a given object
     public synchronized void assignString(final String s) {
        name = s ;
     }
     public static void main(final String[] args) {
        final Class1 c = new Class1 () ;
        int[] array = new int[10] ;
        array = c.fill(array, 5) ;
        c.assignString("world") ;
        final int n = c.f(-1) ;
     }
  }
```

The next example provides a series of overloaded `max` methods that return the maximum of two argument values. Each method works with a different primitive type.

```
  public class Class2 {
     public byte max(final byte a, final byte b) {
        return a > b ? a : b ;
     }
     public short max(final short a, final short b) {
        return a > b ? a : b ;
     }
     public int max(final int a, final int b) {
        return a > b ? a : b ;
     }
     public long max(final long a, final long b) {
        return a > b ? a : b ;
     }
     public float max(final float a, final float b) {
        return a > b ? a : b ;
     }
     public double max(final double a, final double b) {
        return a > b ? a : b ;
     }
     public char max(final char a, final char b) {
        return a > b ?  a : b ;
     }
     public static void main(final String args[]) {
        final Class2 maxObject = new Class2 () ;
        final byte a = maxObject.max((byte)3, (byte)5) ;
        final short b = maxObject.max((short)3, (short)5) ;
        final int c = maxObject.max(3, 5) ;
        final long d = maxObject.max(31, 51) ;
        final  float e = maxObject.max(3.4f, 5.6f) ;
        final double f = maxObject.max(3.4, 5.6) ;
        final char g = maxObject.max('a', 'z') ;
     }
  }
```

Notice that each `max` method has different parameter types and also each returns a different result type. This class only declares methods and effectively packages together a set of functions (value returning methods). This style of class is used to create *function objects*, which allow methods to be treated as objects and stored and passed as parameters.

30.2.6   Static or Class Methods

Purpose   A *static method* or *class method* belongs to a class and is not part of the implementation of individual instance objects. Such methods may be called directly rather than for a particular object.

Intention   It is useful to have methods which do not have to be called for an object but, instead, can be called whenever needed without having an object of a particular type available. Static methods are often used to provide general utility or helper methods which perform useful operations that don't really belong to any object.

Syntax   A static method declaration is similar to a standard method declaration. The basic method declaration has the following form:

```
modifiers static typeName methodName ( parameterList ) {
  statementSequence
}
```

The modifiers are optionally one of `public`, `protected` and `private` (as already described), and zero or more of `final` (see Section 31.2.5, Page 877), `native` and `synchronized` (see Section 33.3, Page 929). Static methods cannot be declared `abstract` and are actually `final` whether or not explicitly specified as such.

The method body is a compound statement delimited by braces and containing a statement sequence.

Static methods can throw exceptions and can therefore be declared with a `throws` clause:

```
modifiers static typeName methodName ( parameterList )
  throws typeNameList {
    statementSequence
}
```

The type name list following the `throws` keyword is a comma separated list of one or more type names of the exceptions that can be thrown.

Array types can be returned using both the syntax variations seen in Section 30.2.5, Page 840.

Description   Static methods are subject to largely the same rules as standard methods with the following exceptions:

- A static method belongs to a class not its instance objects.
- A static method can be called both directly and for an object of the same class.
- A static method cannot access any instance variables or methods (as it has no instance object) but can access any static variables or methods.
- The keyword `this` (see Section 30.2.9, Page 849) cannot be used.

Apart from these restrictions, a static method can be declared and used as required.

There is one special use of static methods in the form of `static main`. When a class declares a public static method called `main`, it provides a starting point for the execution of a program using that class. All the complete example programs seen so far have included such a static main method.

The static main method takes on the responsibility of establishing the initial state of the program, creating the initial set of objects and doing the appropriate method calls to continue execution.

Any class can have a static main method, with some or all of the classes in a single program each having one. When a program is executed using the `java` tool the name of the class containing the static main method to be executed is given:

```
java MyClass
```

so in this case the static main in class `MyClass` will be the first method to be executed.

A static main method takes one argument which is an array of `Strings` containing any command line arguments provided by the user as run-time.

The following class declares and uses static methods:

Examples

```
class Static2 {
  public static void g(final int i) {
    System.out.println("In static void g(i = " + i + ")") ;
  }
  public static void f() {
    System.out.println("In static void f()") ;
    g(10) ;
    // Cannot call an instance method here without an object
    // test() ;  // Error!
  }
  // instance method calling class method
  public void test() {
    g(5) ;
  }
  public static void main(final String args[]) {
    f() ;
    g(10) ;
    // Create an instance object
    Static2 s2 = new Static2() ;
    s2.f() ; // Note - can do this.
    s2.test() ;
  }
}
```

Notice the line `s2.f()` where a static method is called like an instance method. It seems indistinguishable from an instance methods but is, nonetheless, a static method call.

30.2.7 Constructors

All objects must be initialized when created, so that they start in a well defined state. A constructor is a special kind of method that is used to explicitly control initialization, and is guaranteed to be called when an object is created.

Purpose

The Java language will not allow an object to be created without being initialized, meaning that all its instance variables will be given a known value. Initialization of instance variables can be performed in various different ways (see Section 28.8.2, Page 783) with a assignment within a constructor method being one of them. In addition, constructors allow object initialization to be parameterized and are useful for any other kind of initialization an object may require, such as reading data from a file or opening a network connection.

Intention

Syntax

A constructor is declared like a method and has a parameter list. However, a constructor declaration has no return type and the constructor name must be the same as the class it is declared in (which is how constructors are identified):

```
constructorName ( parameterList ) {
    statementSequence
}
```

A constructor can optionally be declared `public`, `protected` or `private`. No other modifiers are allowed.

A constructor can also throw an exception, requiring a throws clause:

```
constructorName ( parameterList ) throws typeNameList {
    statementSequence
}
```

Description

Whenever an object is created a constructor method will be called automatically. This is always guaranteed to happen and cannot be avoided, regardless of how the instance variables may be initialized. A class may declare one or more constructor methods, with constructor overloading being allowed provided each has a different parameter list.

A constructor with an empty parameter list is known as a *default constructor*. If a class does not explicitly declare any constructors the Java compiler will automatically create a public default constructor — one that has any empty parameter list. If a class explicitly declares any constructor, with whatever parameters, then the compiler will not generate a default constructor automatically.

An object is created in an allocation expression using the `new` keyword, for example:

```
Array a1 = new Array () ;
Array a2 = new Array (10) ;
```

The `new` keyword is followed by a class name and a parenthesized actual parameter list. The parameter list is matched against those provided by the class constructors to determine which one to call. An empty parameter list matches the default constructor. Provided a match is found (see Section 31.2.6, Page 878), the constructor will be called. Before the constructor body is executed, any superclass constructors will be executed (see Section 31.2.8, Page 886), followed by any instance variable initializations for variables declared in the constructor's class. This allows the constructor body to be written in the knowledge that all other initializations will have been done before it is executed. Good practice dictates that the constructor body will only perform initialization relevant to its class and not attempt to initialize any superclass variables.

As instance and class variables can be initialized by initialization expressions or initializer blocks, there may not be any need to explicitly declare any constructor and the class can simply rely on the Java compiler generated default constructor. However, constructors provide the only generally effective way of parameterizing the creation of objects, so that creation and initialization can be tailored to each particular situation. For example, the `String` class in the package `java.lang` provides the following constructors, each one for creating a string object from a different set of arguments:

```
String()
String(byte[])
String(byte[], int)
String(byte[], int, int)
String(byte[], int, int, int)
String(byte[], int, int, String)
String(byte[], String)
String(char[])
String(char[], int, int)
String(String)
String(StringBuffer)
```

Public constructors, including the compiler generated public default constructor, allow instance objects of the class to be created anywhere within a program. Most, if not all, top-level classes will include a public constructor.

Constructors can also be protected and private, providing a way of limiting access to some or all constructors and, hence, controlling which other parts of a program can create instance objects of the class. In particular, if all constructors are made private, then only methods of the same class can create instance objects of the class. This can actually be quite useful; some classes may only declare static methods and need no instance objects, while other classes may want to prevent clients creating objects directly using new.

When an object is no longer referenced it is destroyed by the garbage collector within the Java run-time system. A method called finalize can be defined to be called just before destruction and is described in Section 31.2.12, Page 892.

This example has three overloaded constructors, each of which initializes the instance variables in a specific way. All the constructors are public so any of them can be used by any client code.

Examples

```
import com.objectspace.jgl.Array ;
class Constructor1 {
  //  Instance variables that will get default initialization unless
  //  assigned to in a constructor
  private final int initialSize ;
  private final Array a ;
  //  Default constructor
  public Constructor1() {
    //  The assignment to this variable is not actually needed as the
    //  default initialization is OK.
    initialSize = 0 ;
    a = new Array () ;
  }
  //  Create vector of a given size
  public Constructor1(final int size) {
    initialSize  = size ;
    a = new Array (size) ;
  }
  //  Create vector of given size and initialize all the elements to
  //  the string argument.
  public Constructor1(final int size, final String val) {
    initialSize  = size ;
    a = new Array (size, val) ;
  }
  public static void main(final String[] args) {
    //  Create object with default constructor.
    final Constructor1 c1 = new Constructor1 () ;
    //  Other constructors.
    final Constructor1 c2 = new Constructor1 (10) ;
```

```
        final Constructor1 c3 = new Constructor1 (10, "Hello") ;
    }
}
```

30.2.8   Static Initializers

Purpose

A *static initializer* is a statement sequence that is executed when a class is loaded. It can be used to initialize static variables and perform other initialization needed by a class rather than objects of the class.

Intention

Just as an object can be initialized in various ways (via direct initialization, instance initializers and constructors), a class also needs mechanisms to initialize itself, even though classes are not directly represented as objects. Static variables can be initialized directly but static initializers provide an alternative similar to instance variable initializers when more complicated initialization is needed.

Syntax

A class declaration can contain one or more initializers, consisting of a compound statement preceded by the keyword `static`:

```
static { statementSequence }
```

Only static variables declared before the initializer are in scope inside the compound statement.

Description

When a program is run, classes are loaded into memory as they are needed (rather than all at once before execution begins). Loading a class means fetching the `.class` file containing the method code and doing all the static initialization. Static variables and static initializers are initialized or executed in the order they are written down within the class declaration. Hence, in the following example:

```
class Example {
    ...
    static int i = 10 ;
    static int j ;
    static { j = i * 10 ; }
    static String h = "hello" ;
    static { h = h + "world" ; }
    ...
}
```

the variable `i` is initialized first, followed by a default initialization of `j` to 0 (as there is no direct initialization expression). Then `j` is assigned a value in a static initializer, followed by the initialization of `h`, and finally, the evaluation of another static initializer which assigns a new value to `h`. Note that a static initializer cannot refer to static variables declared after itself, so the following would generate an error:

```
class Example {
    ...
    static { j = i * 10 ; } // Error here, illegal forward reference
    static int i = 10 ;
    static int j ;
    ...
}
```

Examples

The following example demonstrates both the use of a static initializer and of a private constructor. The class `Constructor2` uses a static initializer to create a pool of ten instance objects which can be fetched one-by-one by calling a static method. The private constructor prevents any client from directly creating objects, and clients are only allowed to fetch objects in the pool using a static method. The ten objects are returned on a round-robin basis which wraps round to the beginning after every ten fetches. The second class provides a test routine.

```java
public class Constructor2 {
  private String name ;
  private static final int SIZE = 10 ;
  private static int next = 0 ;
  //  The next variable has an initializer block.  This is not a
  //  method!
  private static Constructor2[] objects = new Constructor2[SIZE] ;
  static {
    for (int i = 0 ; i < SIZE ; i++) {
      objects[i] = new Constructor2 (new Integer (i).toString()) ;
      System.out.println("here") ;
    }
  }
  //  The single private constructor prevents any client of the class
  //  creating instance objects directly using new.
  private Constructor2(String s) {
    name = s ;
  }
  public String toString() {
    return "Constructor2 object: " + name ;
  }
  // The factory method that delivers up an object of type
  // Constructor2
  public static Constructor2 getInstance() {
    if (next >= SIZE) {
      next = 0 ;
    }
    return objects[next++] ;
  }
}

public class Constructor2Test {
  public static void main(final String[] args) {
    //  Defense measure, use a constant rather than a literal
    //  as the number to protect against changing the number.
    final int numberOfItems = 25 ;
    final Constructor2[] obs = new Constructor2[numberOfItems] ;
    for (int i = 0 ; i < numberOfItems ; i++) {
      obs[i] = Constructor2.getInstance() ;
    }
    for (int i = 0 ; i < numberOfItems ; i++) {
      System.out.println(obs[i]) ;
    }
  }
}
```

Classes based on `Constructor2` have a practical application whenever the number of instance objects needs to be carefully controlled and initialized as a pool when a class is loaded. For example, each object could control access to a limited resource such as a specific printer.

30.2.9 This

`this` is a final variable that is automatically declared in constructors, instance methods and instance initializers, and is initialized to hold a reference to the object the constructor, method or initializer has been called for. The type of `this` is the reference type of the object.

Purpose

Intention

In a number of circumstances it is useful to explicitly refer to the current object using `this`, or to pass a reference to the current object as a parameter to another method. This is only made possible by having an automatically declared variable initialized to reference the current object.

Syntax

The name `this` is defined as a keyword in the Java language and is in scope within all constructors, instance methods and initializers.

Description

`this` can be used like any other variable of class reference type, not forgetting that it cannot be assigned to as it is final. This means that inside a method it is possible to write statements using the dot operator such as:

```
{
    ...
    this.x = 10 ;
    this.f() ;
    ...
}
```

where `x` is an instance variable and `f` a method, both declared within the same class. These have exactly the same result as simply writing the more familiar:

```
{
    ...
    x = 10 ;
    f() ;
    ...
}
```

and these statements are actually a shorthand for writing the longer version.

Sometimes using the long form can be useful, for example when an instance variable name gets hidden by a parameter name in a nested scope:

```
class Example {
    ...
    void f(int x) // parameter x hides the instance variable
    {
        this.x = x ;// this.x used to get access to the hidden
                // instance variable
    }
    ...
    private int x = 10 ;
}
```

Another common usage of `this` is to pass a reference to the current object to another method of another class:

```
{
    ...
    A a = new A() ;
    ...
    a.f(this) ; // pass this to method f of class A
    ...
}
```

`this` is also important when used in conjunction with constructors as it allows one constructor to call another. An expression consisting of `this` followed by a parameter list in parentheses will call the constructor with a matching parameter list. For example, if a class has two constructors, one default and one taking an `int` argument then the following is possible:

```
    public Test() {
      this(10) ; // Call another constructor
    }
```

Here the expression `this(10)` results in a call to the constructor taking the `int` argument. Note that the `this` expression must appear as the *first* statement in a constructor body and that such a call to a constructor can only be made from another constructor, not from instance or class methods.

Constructor calls using `this` cannot be recursive, the following constructor will not compile:

```
    public Test(int x) {
      this(10) ;// Error - recursive call to same constructor
    }
```

The following class uses `this` in various ways, including that of calling one constructor from another:

Examples

```
    class This {
      private int i = 10 ;
      private int j = this.i ;  //  same as private int j = i ;
      private int k ; { k = this.j ; }  // same as private int k = j ;
      public This() {
        this(10) ;  // call the other constructor
      }
      private This(int i) {
        this.i = i ;
      }
      public void f() {
        //  Illegal, cannot assign to this as the current object cannot be
        //  changed.
        // this = new Test() ;
        //  The following is also illegal, can only call constructors from
        //   a constructor
        // this(10) ;
      }
      public static void main(final String[] args) {
        final This t = new This () ;
        final This t2 = new This (10) ;
      }
    }
```

30.3 Top-Level Classes

A top-level class is an ordinary class declared at package scope level (the 'highest' level that a class can be declared at, hence top-level).

Purpose

Most classes are declared at package level and are not nested within another class. Top-level classes need to be distinguished as nested or inner classes are subject to additional rules.

Intention

Top-level classes follow the syntax seen in Section 30.2.1, Page 834. In addition, a class declaration may optionally be preceded by the keywords:

Syntax

```
    public, abstract, final
```

Description   Top-level classes can optionally be declared as `public`, `abstract` and/or `final` with the
following meanings:

> *public* — a public class is globally accessible and may be used by any other class. To be used
> by a class within another package an import statement must be present in the source file
> containing the other class, unless the class is within the default package. A single source file
> can only have *one* public class or interface.
>
> *abstract* — an abstract class can have no instance objects and is designed to be inherited from.
> Abstract classes are covered in Section 31.2.10, Page 889.
>
> *final* — a final class cannot be subclassed. Final classes are covered in Section 31.2.3,
> Page 874.

If a top-level class is not declared public it can only be accessed by other classes in the same
package.

Otherwise top-level classes behave as already described.

30.4   Nested Classes

A *nested* or *inner class* is declared within a nested or *enclosing* scope (a class declaring a nested
class is described as the enclosing class). There are different kinds of nested class; nested top-level
class, member class, local class and anonymous class. Inner classes cannot be declared as
`native`, `synchronized`, `transient` or `volatile`.

30.4.1   Nested Top-Level Classes

Purpose   A nested top-level class is a standard class declared within the scope of a standard top-level class.
This allows the class name to be subject to the scope and encapsulation rules of classes. In
particular, a nested class can be declared as private, so that it is only accessible within the enclosing
class.

Intention   Without nested classes, all classes would have to be declared at package level, which would conflict
with the convention of restricting declarations to the minimum scope. This is undesirable as it
increases the number of names at the package level and lets other class have access even if they are
not meant to. Using a nested class, implementation details of the enclosing class can be hidden away.

Syntax   Nested top-level classes are declared as `static` within a standard top-level class. Apart from the
restrictions of not being `native`, `synchronized`, `transient` or `volatile`, they follow
the same declaration rules as standard top-level classes.

Description   Nested top-level classes can be declared `public`, requiring that their name is qualified by the
name of the class they are nested in if used by other classes:

```
OuterClass.InnerClass c = new OuterClass.InnerClass () ;
```

This can be useful if the scope of the name of the nested class needs to be restricted.

However, more normally, nested top-level classes are protected or private and act as a building block of the internal data structure of the class they are nested in. For example, a linked list class might have an internal structure consisting of a chain of node objects. Each node object would be an instance of a private nested top-level class. The class is made private as there is no need for any clients of the list class to know about it or try to use it; it simply acts as a piece of internal infrastructure.

A nested top-level class can access the static variables declared in its enclosing class even if private, but does not have access to instance variables. Nested top-level classes can contain further nested top-level classes.

The following example program uses a nested top-level class called CountedString. Objects of the class associate a count with a string, such that class StringCounter can use them in order to count the number of times a string is added using the addString method. Notice that the instance variables of CountedString are not made private and can be directly accessed by the enclosing class. This decision was made as the nested class is used as a building block and does not need to be strongly encapsulated.

Examples

```
import com.objectspace.jgl.Array ;
import com.objectspace.jgl.ForwardIterator ;
public class Class3 {
  private Array items = new Array () ;
  private static class CountedString {
    String item ;
    int count = 1 ;
    public CountedString(final String s) {
      item = s ;
    }
  }
  //  If the String argument already exists, increment the
  //  count. Otherwise add a new CountedString with a count of 1
  public void addString(final String s) {
    final CountedString tmp = searchFor(s) ;
    if (tmp == null) {
      items.add(new CountedString (s)) ;
    } else  {
      tmp.count++ ;
    }
  }
  // Return the number of times a string has been added
  public int getCount(final String s) {
    final CountedString tmp = searchFor(s) ;
    return tmp == null ? 0 : tmp.count ;
  }
  // Private helper method.  If a string has already been added,
  // return its CountedString object, otherwise return null.
  private CountedString searchFor(final String s) {
    for (ForwardIterator i = items.begin() ;
          ! i.atEnd() ;
          i.advance()) {
      final CountedString tmp = (CountedString)i.get() ;
      if ((tmp.item).equals(s))
        return tmp ;
    }
    return null ;
```

```
    }
    public static void main(final String[] args) {
      final Class3 c3 = new Class3 () ;
      c3.addString("hello") ;
      c3.addString("world") ;
      c3.addString("world") ;
      c3.addString("hello") ;
      c3.addString("hello") ;
      c3.addString("world") ;
      c3.addString("hello") ;
      c3.addString("world") ;
      c3.addString("hello") ;
      c3.addString("hello") ;
      c3.addString("world") ;
      c3.addString("world") ;
      System.out.println("hello as been added " +
                         c3.getCount("hello") + " times") ;
      System.out.println("world as been added " +
                         c3.getCount("world") + " times") ;
      System.out.println("Hello as been added " +
                         c3.getCount("Hello") + " times") ;
    }
  }
```

The next example program illustrates that a nested top-level class can access the static variables of the enclosing class and also that a nested top-level class can contain a nested top-level class.

```
  public class Class4 {
    private static int x = 10 ;
    private static String h = "hello" ;
    private static class Nested {
      private static double d = 3.141 ;
      public static class InnerNested {
        public void f() {
          System.out.println(x) ;
          System.out.println(h) ;
          System.out.println(d) ;
        }
      }
      public void f() {
        System.out.println(x) ;
        System.out.println(h) ;
      }
    }
    public static void main(final String[] args) {
      final Nested n = new Nested () ;
      final Nested.InnerNested pn = new Nested.InnerNested () ;
      n.f();
      pn.f() ;
    }
  }
```

30.4.2   Member Classes

Purpose

A *member class* is a variety of nested or inner class that is *not* declared static. An object of a member class is directly associated with the object of the enclosing class that created it and automatically has an implicit reference to it. As a result, the member class object has direct access to the instance variables of the enclosing class object.

In effect, a member class object can be used as an extension of an enclosing class object. Normally the extension is temporary and is used to get direct access to the internal structure of the enclosing object, avoiding the need to create accessor methods which, if public, would seriously weaken the encapsulation.

Syntax

Member classes share the standard features of inner classes but cannot be declared static and cannot declare static variables, methods or nested top-level classes. A member class cannot have the same name as any enclosing class or package (which is different from the rules about variable and method naming).

this, new and super have an extended syntax for use with member classes:

```
className.this
objectReference.new
objectReference.super
```

Description

A *member class object* (or *member object*) has an implicit reference to the object of the enclosing class that created it which is automatically added by the Java compiler. This allows access to the enclosing class object state. Access in the other direction (from the enclosing class to the member class) respects the encapsulation of the member class object, so its private variables and methods cannot be accessed directly.

Member objects are typically used to create data structures whose objects need to know which object they are contained in, and also to aid in accessing the data structures. The prime example of this is when implementing iteratorse that iterate through private data structures. The classes developed in Part 2 contain many examples of this kind of usage.

To support member classes several extra kinds of expression are provided. The first is an extension to this expressions. An expression like:

```
x = this.y ;
```

will only be valid if y is an instance variable declared by the member class, not if y is declared by the enclosing class. If y does belong to the enclosing class, then it can be accessed using:

```
x = TestClass.this.y ;
```

where TestClass is the name of the enclosing class. This works by identifying which class an instance variable accessible to the member object is declared by.

Inner classes can be nested to any depth and the this mechanism can be used with the nesting. For example, if class C is nested in class B which is nested in class A:

```
class A {
  int a ;
  class B {
    int b ;
    class C {
      int c ;
      void f() {
        A.this.a // variable a declared in class A
        B.this.b // variable b declared in class B
        this.c // access the variable c in class C
      }
    }
```

```
       ...
     }
       ...
   }
```

then variables declared by each enclosing class can be accessed by naming the class in the `this` expression. Note that an expression like:

```
A.B.C.this.a
```

is not valid, as the enclosing class should be named directly.

The second additional kind of expression involves the `new` operator. Member class objects can only be created if they have access to an enclosing class object. This happens by default if the member class object is created by an instance method belonging to its enclosing class. Otherwise, it is possible to specify an enclosing class object using the `new` operator in the following way:

```
B b = a.new B() ; // note the objectReference.new syntax
```

where the `new` operator is preceded by an object reference and the dot operator. This means: create a new `B` member object using the object referenced by the variable `a` (which must be an instance of the correct enclosing class). The new member object will then have access to the state of the object referenced by `a`.

The syntax for this form of new expression can be surprising at first. If class `C` is nested in class `B` which is nested in class `A` then it is possible to write the following valid statement:

```
A.B.C c = b.new C () ; // b is reference to a B object
```

This means: declare a variable called `c` of type `C` which is nested in `B`, which is nested in `A` (i.e. the `A.B.C` part). Then create a new `C` given a reference to an object of type `B`. Notice that the expression `b.new C ()` is used and not something like `b.new A.B.C()`. This is because the class of the object to be created is given relative to the class of the enclosing object. The example in the examples section below further illustrates this syntax.

The third and final additional kind of expression concerns `super` and is outlined in Section 31.2.9, Page 888.

A consequence of member class' access to an enclosing class is that the scope rules become more complicated as there are now two ways to look up a name; using the inheritance hierarchy and using the enclosing object containment hierarchy. This is examined in Section 31.2.7, Page 884.

Examples   The first example shows the basic use of member classes and objects.

```
public class Class5 {
  private int i = 10 ;
  private String s = "hello" ;
  private class Member {
    //  This method demonstrates the the private instance variables of
    //  the enclosing class object can be accessed
    public void test() {
      i += 10 ;
      System.out.println(i) ;
      System.out.println(s) ;
    }
  }
```

```
     // This method creates a Member class object which has access to
     // the private state of the object it is called for.
     public void test() {
       final Member n = new Member() ;
       n.test() ;
     }
     public static void main(final String[] args) {
       final Class5 c5 = new Class5() ;
       c5.test() ;
     }
   }
```

The next example illustrates the use of the extended this syntax with a series of nested member classes.

```
     public class Class6 {
       private String name = "Class6" ;
       private class A {
         private String name = "A" ;
         private class B {
           private String name = "B" ;
           private class C {
             private String name = "C" ;
             public void test() {
               System.out.println(name) ;
               System.out.println(A.this.name) ;
               System.out.println(B.this.name) ;
               System.out.println(C.this.name) ;
             }
           }
           public void test() {
             final C c = new C () ;
             System.out.println(name) ;
             System.out.println(A.this.name) ;
             System.out.println(B.this.name) ;
             c.test() ;
           }
         }
         public void test() {
           final B b = new B () ;
           System.out.println(name) ;
           System.out.println(Class6.this.name) ;
           b.test() ;
         }
       }
       public void test() {
         final A a = new A () ;
         a.test() ;
       }
       public static void main(final String[] args) {
         final Class6 c6 = new Class6 () ;
         c6.test() ;
       }
     }
```

The next example program illustrates the use of the new operator with member classes.

```
     class A {
       private String name = "A" ;
       public class B {
         private String name = "B" ;
         public class C {
           private String name = "C" ;
           public void test() {
             System.out.println(name) ;
             System.out.println(B.this.name) ;
```

```
                            System.out.println(A.this.name) ;
                          }
                        }
                        public void test() {
                          System.out.println(name) ;
                          System.out.println(A.this.name) ;
                          final C c = new C () ;
                          c.test() ;
                          //  Can do this as method already has member object reference to
                          //  an A
                          final B b = new B () ;
                          // b.test() ; // Watch out infinite recursion!!
                        }
                      }
                      public void test() {
                        System.out.println(name) ;
                        final B b = new B () ;
                        b.test() ;
                        //  Can't do this (no B object specified)
                        // B.C c = new C () ; // Error
                        //  Can do this
                        final B.C c = b.new C () ;
                        c.test() ;
                      }
                    }
                    public class Class7 {
                      public static void main(String[] args) {
                        final A a = new A () ;
                        //  Cannot create a member class object without an A object
                        // A.B = new B () ; // Error
                        //  Can do this. Note the form of the new expression
                        final A.B b = a.new B () ;
                        b.test() ;
                        //  Can also do this to create a C object using a B object
                        final A.B.C c = b.new C () ;
                        c.test() ;
                        //  Cannot do this as a C object needs a B object
                        // A.B.C c1 = a.new C () ; // Error
                      }
                    }
```

30.4.3 Local Classes

Purpose

A *local class* is a class declared within the scope of a compound statement, i.e. local to a method body or instance initializer, like a local variable. With some restrictions, a local class is also a member class since it is created within an enclosing class object. As well as access to member data in any enclosing classes, a local class has access to any parameter variables or local variables (subject to declaration order) declared in the same scope as the local class, provided that they are final.

If a reference to a local class object remains after its creating scope has gone out of scope (e.g. as a reference returned from a method), then the local object remains in existence retaining access to the final parameters or final local variables of its creating scope.

Intention

It turns out to be quite useful to declare a class in a local scope, create instance objects and then use them after the scope has gone. This usually works in conjunction with an interface (see Section 31.3, Page 897) which is implemented by the local class. Objects of the class then conform to the interface type and can be used without needing their actual class, overcoming any problems with the class not being in scope when the object is used.

This is particularly used within the Swing and AWT classes where a local class object, conforming to an interface, is returned as an event 'listener'. When a relevant event occurs, a method on the local class object is invoked to respond to it. As all methods are called through the interface type specification it doesn't matter that the class of an object is not available. The advantage of doing this lies in the need to have many different listener classes, some of which need to be declared by the user of Swing and AWT. Local classes allow a listener class to be declared at the point it is used and avoids the need for large numbers of top-level classes.

Local classes follow the member class syntax but cannot include static variables, methods or classes. In addition, they cannot be declared public, protected, private or static.

Syntax

A local class is a form of member class and can use the extended `this` syntax but cannot use the extended `new` or `super` syntax.

A local class name cannot be the same as any enclosing class or package.

Local classes are essentially member classes that are declared in a local scope and, as a result, are subject to additional rules and restrictions. The most important new feature of a local class is its ability to access final variables and parameters in its declaring scope. This gives a limited ability for a local class object to retain the state of a local scope after it has gone out of scope.

Description

Typically, a local class is declared in a method as implementing an interface type and then an object of the class is returned from the method. This allows the scope of the class declaration to be limited to the minimum area but still allows usable objects.

The first example shows how a local class can access variables from the enclosing scope and the enclosing object.

Examples

```
class Class8 {
  private String name = "Class8" ;
  public void f(final String h, String w) {
    int j = 20 ;
    final int k = 30 ;
    class Local {
      public void test() {
        //  OK as h is final
        System.out.println(h) ;
        //  Cannot do this as w is not final
        // System.out.println(w) ; // Error
        //  Cannot do this as j is not final
        // System.out.println(j) ; // Error
        //  OK k is final
        System.out.println(k) ;
        //  Cannot do this as i is not yet declared
        // System.out.println(i) ; // Error
        //  Like a member class, instance variables of the enclosing
        //  object can be accessed.  They don't need to be final.
        System.out.println(name) ;
      }
    }
    final Local l = new Local () ;
```

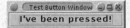

Before button press   After button press

Figure 30.1 Windows and buttons displayed by `Button1` example in Section 30.4.3

```
    l.test() ;
    final int i = 10 ;
  }
  public static void main(final String[] args) {
    final Class8 c8 = new Class8 () ;
    c8.f("hello", "world") ;
  }
}
```

The second example modifies the first to use an interface to which the local class conforms, allowing a reference to a local class object to be returned from the method declaring the class. A method is called for the local object after the scope in which it was created has gone out of scope.

```
interface Thing {
  void test() ;
}
class Class9 {
  private String name = "Class9" ;
  public Thing f(final String h, String w) {
    int j = 20 ;
    final int k = 30 ;
    class Local implements Thing {
      public void test() {
        //  OK as h is final
        System.out.println(h) ;
        //  Cannot do this as w is not final
        // System.out.println(w) ; // Error
        //  Cannot do this as j is not final
        // System.out.println(j) ; // Error
        //  OK k is final
        System.out.println(k) ;
        //  Cannot do this as i is not yet declared
        // System.out.println(i) ; // Error
        //  Like a member class, instance variables of the enclosing
        //  object can be accessed.  They don't need to be final.
        System.out.println(name) ;
      }
    }
    Local l = new Local() ;
    final int i = 10 ;
    return l ;
  }
  public static void main(final String[] args) {
    final Class9 c9 = new Class9 () ;
    //  Get a reference to a local class object conforming to type
    //  Thing
    final Thing t = c9.f("hello", "world") ;
    //  Call a method of the local class object to verify its state
    t.test() ;
  }
}
```

The next example shows a simple program that uses Swing and AWT to display a button in a window that changes its label when pressed (see Figure 30.1). Two local classes are defined. The first, called `MyExit`, implements a listener that waits for the event triggered when a window is closed. The second, called `MyEvent`, provides a listener for a button click event and responds by changing the button label. Please refer to the J2SDK documentation for information about what the various Swing and AWT classes and methods do.

```java
import java.awt.* ;
import java.awt.event.* ;
import javax.swing.* ;
class Button1 extends JFrame {
  private String label = "Press Me!" ;
  public Button1() {
    super("Test Button Window") ;
    class MyExit extends WindowAdapter {
      public void windowClosing(WindowEvent e) {
        System.exit(0) ;
      }
    }
    Container myPane = getContentPane() ;
    myPane.setLayout(new BorderLayout ()) ;
    final JButton b = new JButton (label) ;
    class MyEvent implements ActionListener {
      public void actionPerformed(ActionEvent e) {
        b.setLabel("I've been pressed!") ;
        pack() ;
      }
    }
    b.addActionListener(new MyEvent ()) ;
    add(b, BorderLayout.CENTER) ;
    pack() ;
    addWindowListener(new MyExit ()) ;
  }
  public static void main(final String[] args) {
    Button1 b = new Button1 () ;
    b.setVisible(true) ;
  }
}
```

30.4.4 Anonymous Classes

An *anonymous class* is a local class that has no name.

Purpose

An anonymous class allows an object to be created using an expression that combines object creation with the declaration of its class. This avoids the need to name a class, at the cost of only ever being able to create one instance of that anonymous class.

Intention

An anonymous class is declared as part of a `new` expression and must either be a subclass or implement an interface:

Syntax

```
new className ( argumentList ) { classBody }
new interfaceName () { classBody }
```

className is the name of the superclass of the anonymous class, while *interfaceName* is the name of the interface to which the anonymous class must conform. The *argumentList* is a parameter list that is used to call a matching constructor of the named superclass.

The class body can define methods but cannot define any constructors (as they cannot be named). The restrictions imposed on local classes also apply. Like local classes, anonymous classes also have the basic properties of member classes and have an implicit reference to the object they were created in.

Description

The principle use of an anonymous class is to directly define an object using an extension of the new syntax. This allows a single instance of a specific type of object to be created exactly where it is needed without declaring a full class for it. The anonymous class must, however, explicitly be a subclass or implement an interface. If it implements an interface the class will be a subclass of `Object`.

When an anonymous class is declared as a subclass the intention is that inherited methods will be overridden and specialized. There is little point in adding any other public methods as they cannot be called. Private methods can be added, however.

As an anonymous class has no constructors it relies on direct instance variable initialization and instance initializers to initialize instance variables.

Examples

The following program illustrates the use of anonymous classes.

```java
interface Thing {
  void test(final String s) ;
}
class Subclass {
  public void doSomething() {
    System.out.println("Doing Something") ;
  }
}
class Class10 {
  // Return an object created using an anonymous class implementing
  // an interface
  public Thing i1() {
    final Thing t = new Thing () {
      public void test(final String s) {
        System.out.println(s) ;
      }
    } ; // Note the semi-colon here
    return t ;
  }
  // A shorter version of the last method, eliminating the local
  // variable
  public Thing i2() {
    return new Thing () {
      public void test(final String s) {
        System.out.println(s) ;
      }
    } ; // Note the semi-colon here
  }
  // Return an object created using an anonymous class subclassing a
  // class
  public Subclass f1() {
    final Subclass t = new Subclass() {
      public void doSomething() {
        something() ;
      }
      private void something() {
        System.out.println(name) ;
      }
      String name = "Anonymous 1" ;
    } ;
    return t ;
  }
```

```
      // Simpler version of f1
      public Subclass f2() {
        return new Subclass() {
            public void doSomething() {
              something() ;
            }
            private void something() {
              System.out.println(name) ;
            }
            String name = "Anonymous 2" ;
          } ;
      }
      public static void main(final String[] args) {
        final Class10 c10 = new Class10 () ;
        final Thing t1 = c10.i1() ;
        t1.test("hello") ;
        final Thing t2 = c10.i2() ;
        t2.test("world") ;
        final Subclass t3 = c10.f1() ;
        t3.doSomething() ;
        final Subclass t4 = c10.f2() ;
        t4.doSomething() ;
      }
    }
```

The next program is a version of the button program seen in the previous section, modified to use anonymous classes. This version is actually more practical as there is no need to create any named classes, illustrating the usefulness of being able to create a specialized object on demand. (It also illustrates that anonymous classes can be awkward to indent and format on the page!)

```
import java.awt.* ;
import java.awt.event.* ;
import javax.swing.* ;
class Button1 extends JFrame {
  private String label = "Press Me!" ;
  public Button2() {
    super("Test Button Window") ;
    Container myPane = getContentPane() ;
    myPane.setLayout(new BorderLayout()) ;
    final JButton b = new JButton (label) ;
    b.addActionListener(new ActionListener() {
        public void actionPerformed(ActionEvent e) {
          b.setLabel("I've been pressed!") ;
          pack() ;
        }
      }) ;
    myPane.add(b, BorderLayout.CENTER) ;
    pack() ;
    addWindowListener(new WindowAdapter () {
        public void windowClosing(WindowEvent e) {
          System.exit(0) ;
        }
      }) ;
  }
  public static void main(final String[] args) {
    Button2 b = new Button2 () ;
    b.setVisible(true) ;
  }
}
```

30.5   Packages

Purpose

A *package* allows a collection of classes to be grouped together into a single named unit which also acts as a scope.

Intention

A mechanism is needed to provide a unit of grouping and scoping above that of classes. This allows a collection of classes providing a service, library or framework to be grouped into a single named unit or package. Classes in a package can then be used or *imported* into other packages that need access to the services of the package classes. Unless a class declared in another package is imported, it is not in scope and cannot be used.

Syntax

There are two parts to the package syntax, one for declaring packages and one for importing classes from another package.

A package is declared using a package statement that must appear before any other statement in a source file (also known as a compilation unit). It has the following form:

```
package packageName ;
```

The package name is an identifier or a series of dot separated identifiers (such as `java.awt.event`).

Classes are imported into a package from another package using an import statement. These come in two varieties:

```
import packageName.className ;
import packageName.* ;
```

The first form imports a specific, named class, while the second form is a convenient shorthand that allows all the classes in a single package to be imported at one go.

Description

To understand how packages are used it is necessary to realize that package names map to directory names within the local filestore. Each directory contains all the `.class` files for the classes in a given package. Tools such as the Java compiler locate these directories relative to a series of fixed points in the filestore which are stored as filestore path names in an environment variable called CLASSPATH.

The mapping from a package name to a specific directory is done by first taking each component of the package name and mapping it to a relative pathname appropriate for the filestore on the local machine. For example, a package called:

```
adts.containers.sorted
```

would map to the path:

```
adts\containers\sorted
```

under Windows95/98/NT or to:

```
adts/containers/sorted
```

under UNIX.

The relative pathname generated is then appended to each entry in the CLASSPATH environment variable to generate a full pathname. The full pathname is then used to search each directory for classes. For example, when using a Windows95/98/NT system and the CLASSPATH environment variable contains:

```
.;D:\myclasses
```

the following full directory names are generated:

```
.\adts\containers\sorted
D:\myclasses\adts\containers\sorted
C:\jdk1.2.2\lib\adts\containers\sorted
```

assuming that the Java system has been installed in C:\jdk1.2.2. If using an UNIX system, then the CLASSPATH:

```
.:$HOME/lib/Java
```

results in the following full directory names being generated:

```
./adts/containers/sorted
$HOME/lib/Java/adts/containers/sorted
/opt/jdk1.1.3/lib/adts/containers/sorted
```

assuming that the Java system has been installed in /opt/jdk1.2.2.

The file with the same name as the class being searched for should be found in one of these directories. If a .class file is found then it is used. If a .class file is not found but a .java file is then it is compiled to create a .class file which is then used.

Note that the syntax of the CLASSPATH environment variable follows the syntax of the operating system: under Windows95/98/NT, the path separator is a semi-colon (since colon is used as part of the disk specifier), whereas under UNIX the path separator is a colon.

It is also possible to specify the name of a .jar file (a Java archive format file containing a number of files) or a .zip file (a different format archive file containing a number of files) in the CLASSPATH as well as directories containing .class files. If such files do appear in the CLASSPATH then these files are searched for contained .class files analogously to the way directories are searched for .class files.

When a class is declared to be part of a package using a package statement, the expectation is that the matching .class file is located in the corresponding directory. During development of the class the .java file is usually kept in the same directory for convenience. Package names can have as many components as desired but the more there are, the deeper the directory structure is going to end up.

Import statements specify either a single class or all the classes in a package. The same mapping of package names to directory names is used to locate the class or classes being imported. If the mapping fails, compilation will fail as well.

If any class from another package is to be used in the current package it must be imported. For all classes and Java library classes this must be done explicitly, except for the classes in java.lang which are always imported implicitly.

In order to be imported into another package a class must be declared public (and remember that only one class in a source file can be public). Non-public classes are local to their package giving a degree of control over the visibility of classes.

The classes in a given package will be declared in a series of source files, so a package is in turn derived from that collection of files. A class can be added to a package by simply including a `package` statement at the start of the file. Note, however, that a class (and, hence, file) can only be part of a single package so there can only be one `package` statement in a source file.

`package` statements are treated in a fairly casual way so a class can actually be declared to be part of any package the programmer likes, even the Java library packages. The only restriction on this is that the directory matching the package name must be accessible and writable, so that the `.class` file can be put into it.

If a class is not declared to be within a package (as are all of the example programs seen so far), then it is part of the unnamed default package, so all classes are actually within a package. For learning and testing (and example!) purposes this is quite convenient as all the source files of a program can be placed in the current working directory and not cause any conflicts with the package to directory mapping process. As soon as the programmer starts using packages, however, the appropriate directory structure should be put into place.

Examples   Some of the example programs in earlier in the chapter use import statements. The library classes in Part 2 are all part of a package called ADS which provides many examples of use.

30.6   Summary

This chapter has covered the details of classes without dealing with inheritance. It turns out that there are a number of different kinds of class which all share the same basic properties and syntax but differ significantly in details.

Member classes are particularly significant as they have an extended scope with access to an enclosing class object. Local and anonymous classes extend this further by gaining access to a local scope.

Packages are closely associated with both classes and the computer filestore, making it important that the programmer understands how the relationship works.

In the next chapter the description of classes is completed with a full examination of inheritance and interfaces.

Self-review Exercises

Self-review 30.1 In the class `Blah`:

```
class Blah
{
  public String hello = "hello" ;
  public final String world = "world" ;
  protected int count = 0 ;
  private float length = 2.345f ;
  long size = 123432L ;
}
```

Why is the length variable completely redundant?

Self-review 30.2 Why are the cast expressions necessary in the first two calls of `max` in the `Class2` program?

Self-review 30.3 What happens if the following calls had existed in `Class2`?

```
maxObject.max(3.0, 5) ;
maxObject.max(3, 31) ;
maxObject.max(3.4f, 5.0) ;
```

Self-review 30.4 In program `Class2` each `max` method is identical except for the type name used. Is it possible to write a single `max` method that will work for any of the integral types? If it is possible, would you use the single method?

Self-review 30.5 Explain why the statement `s2.f()` in `Static2` is legal.

Self-review 30.6 Work through the execution of program `Class6` as a pencil and paper exercise to determine how it works. What does the program display?

Self-review 30.7 What does the `Class7` program display?

Programming Exercises

Exercise 30.1 Write a class to represent complex numbers, where the real and imaginary parts are represented by `double` values. Provide a least two constructors for creating complex number objects and implement the basic operations of addition and subtraction.

Inheritance and Interfaces

Objectives

This chapter continues the coverage of classes by examining inheritance and the various inheritance mechanisms. The chapter concludes with a description of interfaces.

Keywords

subclass

superclass

subinterface

superinterface

subtype

supertype

type conformance

abstract classes

abstract methods

31.1   Introduction

Inheritance is the key mechanism that turns class-based development into object-oriented development. The previous chapter has prepared the ground for describing inheritance in Java by outlining the basic details of how classes are constructed. This chapter will continue and conclude that description by describing how inheritance works.

Interfaces are closely associated with inheritance and so are also covered in this chapter.

31.2   Inheritance

Inheritance provides the mechanism for extending an existing class to create a new class. The new class has all the features of the class that is inherited from and also adds its own additional features. The class that inherits is known as the *subclass*, while the class that is inherited from is known as the *superclass*.

A crucial consequence of inheritance is the idea of *substitutability* — an instance object of the subclass may be substituted for an instance object of the superclass and still 'fit' as it has the correct public interface. At the programming language level this is implemented as the idea of *assignment compatibility* — it is possible to assign a reference to a subclass object to a variable of superclass type. The same mechanism also works for initialization and parameter passing.

This section describes the mechanisms available in the Java language to support inheritance. For a description of inheritance in general, please refer back to Section 7.3, Page 185.

31.2.1   Basic Inheritance

Purpose   A subclass can inherit from or *extend* a superclass. The subclass takes all the variable and method declarations of the superclass (although not all may be accessible) and can add new variables and methods or *override* existing ones.

Intention   Inheritance serves two purposes. The first is a way of sharing implementation, where a superclass provides a set of variables and methods that can be used by subclasses. The second is a way of achieving substitutability by allowing a set of classes to conform to an inherited shared common public interface. In both cases, type and class extension is taking place.

Syntax   A subclass inherits from a superclass using the extends keyword:

```
class subClassName extends superClassName {
   variable and method declarations
}
```

The class body containing variable and method declarations is as described in the previous chapter.

Inheritance is applicable to top-level classes, nested top-level classes, member classes, local classes and anonymous classes (which must either inherit or implement an interface).

A class can inherit from any other class that is not final (see Section 31.2.3). Objects of the subclass contain all the instance variables declared by the superclass. Also, all the methods declared by the superclass can be called on the subclass object — the fact that the subclass has copies of all the instance variables of the superclass makes this a reasonable thing to allow. Note, however, that the accessibility rules are respected so that private variables and methods are not accessible from subclass methods and initializers (see Section 31.2.2) — a class can comprise parts that some of its own methods cannot access!

Description

Subclassing can be repeated as many times, or to as many levels, as desired; a subclass can have a subclass and so on (referred to as an *inheritance chain*). However, it is good practice to limit the number of levels to less than about five, which in most cases is not an issue as a good design will avoid going deeper. A class can only have one superclass but can have as many subclasses as needed. A collection of classes in super/subclass relationships is often referred to as a *class hierarchy*. Because of the 'single superclass' rule, this hierarchy is a tree (see Section 15.1, Page 446).

All classes inherit *directly* or *indirectly* from class `Object` (i.e. they are either an immediate subclass of `Object` or at a lower level in an inheritance chain starting from `Object`). This is true even if a class has not been explicitly declared as a subclass of `Object` using the `extends` keyword. So, for example, all the classes seen in the last chapter were subclasses of `Object`.

The inheritance relation between classes also applies to the types that the classes define, so it is possible to talk about *supertypes* and *subtypes*. This enables assignment compatibility or conversions between reference types (see Chapter 28.6.3, Page 778), so that it is possible to assign a reference to an object of a subtype to a variable whose type is the supertype. This also works for parameter passing and returning the result from a method.

Inheritance has the effect of increasing the number of scopes that need to be searched in order to verify that a variable or method is in scope and accessible. Identifying and checking methods is quite complex and is described in Section 31.2.6.

For variables, the search proceeds by checking for a declaration of the variables identifier in various scopes. Both static and instance declarations are checked. The search order is as follows, with the search ending when the identifier is found:

1. Check the local scope and any nesting local scopes.

2. Check the class scope.

3. Check each superclass scope in turn up to the top of the inheritance chain.

If in any scope a declaration for the identifier is found but is not for a variable then an error is reported. If no declaration is found at all then an error is also reported (that the variable is not declared). If variables with the same identifier are declared in several scopes then the first variable declaration found is used (i.e. the one in the closest scope). Declarations in nesting scopes are then said to be *hidden* or *shadowed* from the nested scope.

If the variable name is part of a field expression with a type name on the left hand side (e.g. `Math.PI` — a static double declared in class `Math` from the package java.lang, its value is approximately π.), then the search starts in the scope of the named class (step 2).

Examples

The example below shows a very simple use of inheritance and illustrates that methods of both the subclass and the superclass can be called for subclass objects. Also note that a subclass reference is assigned to a variable of superclass type.

```
class Superclass {
  public void superMethod() {
    System.out.println("Superclass") ;
  }
}
//  This class inherits superMethod from Superclass so that it can be
//  called for Subclass objects
class Subclass extends Superclass {
  public void subMethod() {
    System.out.println("Subclass") ;
  }
}
public class Inherit1 {
  public static void main(final String[] args) {
    //  Create a superclass object and call a superclass method
    Superclass superclass = new Superclass () ;
    superclass.superMethod() ;
    //  Create a subclass object and call both a subclass and
    //  superclass method
    Subclass subclass = new Subclass () ;
    subclass.superMethod() ;
    subclass.subMethod() ;
    //  This assignment is valid, the reverse is not.
    superclass = subclass ;
  }
}
```

31.2.2 Private and Protected Keywords and Inheritance

Purpose

Private methods and variables are not accessible to a subclass, even though they are part of the infrastructure of subclass objects. Protected methods and variables are accessible to subclasses and provide a way of opening up the encapsulation provided by a class in a controlled way.

Intention

A subclass can be thought of as a client of its superclass and needs to respect the accessibility rules for inherited methods and variables. Some methods and variables may need to be only accessible by the class that declares them. These are declared `private` and allow the programmer to state that they are strongly encapsulated and should not be changed or used by anything else. Other methods and variables may be safely made accessible to subclasses but not to general clients of a class, and so are declared `protected`.

Syntax

Variables and methods may be declared with the modifier `public`, `protected` or `private`. See Chapter 30.2.2, Page 836.

The important issue for the programmer is whether to declare methods or variables `public`, `protected`, `private` or with default access (no modifier). All have some advantages and disadvantages.

Private declarations offer a guarantee that no other class, including subclasses, can access the method or variable. This avoids any direct dependency on the details of the declarations. Thus, if changes are made to private methods or variables in a class then no other classes need to be edited. However, this may require more accessor methods to be added to the superclass in order to indirectly access the private state or methods.

Protected declarations allow classes in the same package and any subclass, even if in a different package, direct and efficient access to the superclass which may be useful for instance variables whose state is needed by the subclass and for helper methods that should not be public. This allows a controlled form of sharing. However, this can lead to the subclass misusing the inherited features and becoming unnecessarily dependent on them.

Public declarations are accessible to subclasses and everything else. This is essential if a class is to have instance objects providing useful services but can be dangerous if too much is made public, especially in the case of instance variables.

Default access is the same as public if the subclass is in the same package and the same as private if it is not.

As a general rule of thumb, declarations should be public only if non-related clients need to use them, otherwise they should be made private by default unless it is clear that subclasses need direct access, in which case they may be protected. As a superclass may be written before a subclass has even been thought of, protected declarations do require some careful planning.

The following example illustrates the use of protected and private variables and methods.

```
class Superclass {
  public int i = 5 ;
  protected int j = 10 ;
  private int k = 20 ;
  // Method that will be inherited but not accessible in a subclass.
  private void f() {
    System.out.println("f") ;
    // Can call g and h
    // g() ;
    // h() ;
  }
  //  Method that be inherited and is accessible to a subclass and
  //  other classes in the same package.
  protected void g() {
    System.out.println("f") ;
    //  Can call f and h
    // f() ;
    // h() ;
  }
  //  Shared method that is not overridden in the subclass.
  public void h() {
    System.out.println("Shared") ;
    //  Can call f and g()
    // f() ;
```

```
                    // g() ;
                  }
                }
                class Subclass extends Superclass {
                  public void test() {
                    i = 10 ; // OK inherited public variable
                    j = 20 ; // OK inherited protected variable
                    // k = 30 ; // Error - cannot access inherited
                    // private variable
                    // f() ; // Error as f is private in superclass
                    g() ;
                    h() ;
                  }
                }
                public class Inherit2 {
                  public static void main(final String[] args) {
                    final Superclass superclass = new Superclass () ;
                    // superclass.f() ; // Error method f is private
                    //  Can call g as although the method is protected this class is
                    //   in the same package
                    superclass.g() ;
                    superclass.h() ;
                    final Subclass subclass = new Subclass () ;
                    subclass.test() ;
                    // Error method f is inherited but private
                    // subclass.f() ;
                    //  Can call g as although the method is protected this class is
                    //   in the same package
                    subclass.g() ;
                    subclass.h() ;
                  }
                }
```

31.2.3 Final Classes

Purpose   A *final class* cannot be subclassed.

Intention   Not all classes need to be or are designed to be subclassed. This intention can be made explicit and enforceable by declaring a class final.

Syntax   The class declaration has the modifier `final`.

Description A class should only be subclassed if the designer meant it to be and has checked that subclassing would make sense. If there is any doubt or subclassing is not wanted, a class should be declared final, allowing the compiler to check that subclassing is not done.

A consequence of declaring a final class is that the compiler can often optimize the code generated from it. In particular, there will be no overriding methods in subclasses so it becomes possible to perform static binding instead of the more expensive dynamic binding (Section 31 2.6).

Examples   The following is the outline of a simple final class.

```
                public final class Example {
                  // Usual method and variable declarations
                }
                // Error cannot declare the class below
                class Subclass extends Example {
                  ...
                }
```

31.2.4 Method Overriding

A subclass can *override* an inherited method by providing a new method declaration that has the same name, the same number and types of parameters and the same result type as the one inherited. The inherited method is hidden in the scope of the subclass (more on this in Section 31.2.9, Page 888). When the method is called for an object of the subclass, the overriding method is executed using dynamic binding.

Purpose

Subclasses extend and specialize superclasses. Specialization often requires that an inherited method body is re-written to work with the details of the new subclass. This is done by completely re-declaring the method in the subclass but recognizing that it is a new version of the inherited method, rather than just another method. Overriding should not be confused with overloading.

Intention

An overriding method is declared in a subclass as any other method but must have the same name, the same number of parameters of the same type and the same return type as the overridden method in the superclass.

Syntax

Private methods cannot be overridden, so a matching method declared in a subclass is considered completely separate.

Access to the overridden method using `public`, `protected` or the default if no modifier, must be either the same as that of the superclass method or made more accessible (e.g. from `protected` to `public`). An overriding method cannot be made less accessible (e.g. changed from `public` to `protected`).

Static methods cannot be overridden. Instance methods cannot be overridden by a static method.

Method overriding relies on *dynamic binding* (see Chapter 6.8, Page 176), so that the type of the object a method is called for determines which version of an overridden method gets called. Hence, in an expression like:

Description

```
x.f() ; // f is an overridden method
```

the version of `f` that is called depends on the class of the object that is referenced by `x` when the method call is evaluated at runtime, not on the type of the variable `x`. The major consequence of this is that a variable of superclass type can be assigned a reference to a subclass object but when methods are called, dynamic binding ensures that the overridden subclass methods are called. Hence, the same expression evaluated at different times during the execution of a program can result in different methods being called. Static methods cannot use dynamic binding.

It is important to remember that the *method signature* (the combination of name, parameter types and return type) of an overriding method must match exactly. If not then method overloading will occur, where the method is overloaded across two classes (see Section 31.2.6).

The rule that the accessibility of an overriding method must be the same or increased is needed to preserve substitutability. If a subclass object is to be used where a superclass type has been specified then it must support at least the same public (or protected or default) interface. Removing a method from the interface would prevent substitution.

Using dynamic binding is an essential part of object-oriented programming but can make it difficult to find out which method will be called when reading source code. Given an expression like `x.f()` or just `f()` (which is really `this.f()`), the programmer first has to determine the type of `x` or `this` and then inspect the corresponding class, superclass(es) and subclass(es) to find out what kind of method `f` is and whether it is overridden. The programmer also has to determine the types of the objects that may be referenced by `x`. This can be time consuming and confusing so good commenting is important. Of course, good development environments give support for this searching activity but this does not mean that the commenting should not be done.

Examples   The following program illustrates a variety of overridden methods and the use of dynamic binding.

```java
class Superclass {
  //  May be overridden
  public void f(final int x) {
    System.out.println("Superclass f: " + x) ;
    //  Always calls g declared by this class as g is private
    g() ;
  }
  //  Can't override this method
  private void g() {
    System.out.println("Superclass g") ;
  }
  //  May be overridden
  protected void h() {
    System.out.println("Superclass h") ;
  }
  public void k() {
    System.out.println("Superclass k") ;
    //  Always call superclass g as g cannot be overridden
    g() ;
    //  Call h depending on type of object (type of this) using
    //  dynamic binding
    h() ;
    //  Always call s in this class, as s is static
    s() ;
  }
  public static void s() {
    System.out.println("Superclass static s") ;
  }
}
class Subclass extends Superclass {
  //  Overriding method - must be public
  public void f(final int x) {
    System.out.println("Subclass f: " + x) ;
    //  Call g in this class
    g() ;
  }
  //  New version of g not overriding version in Superclass
  private void g() {
    System.out.println("Subclass g") ;
  }
  //  Overridding inherited h with increased access.  Making this
  //  private or default access would be an error
  public void h() {
    System.out.println("Subclass h") ;
  }
  public static void s() {
```

```
      System.out.println("Subclass static s") ;
    }
  }
  public class Override {
    public static void main(final String[] args) {
      Superclass superclass = new Superclass () ;
      //  Call superclass version of f
      superclass.f(1) ;
      superclass.h() ;
      superclass.k() ;
      superclass.s() ;
      Subclass subclass = new Subclass () ;
      //  Call overridden subclass version of f and h
      subclass.f(2) ;
      subclass.h() ;
      //  Call superclass k as it is not overridden
      subclass.k() ;
      //  Call subclass s
      subclass.s() ;
      //  Now set a variable of superclass type to reference a subclass
      //  object
      superclass = subclass ;
      //  Call *subclass* versions of f and h
      superclass.f(3) ;
      superclass.h() ;
      //  Call superclass k for a subclass object
      superclass.k() ;
      //  Call superclass s as it is static and not dynamically bound,
      //  so method called depends on type of reference.
      superclass.s() ;
    }
  }
```

31.2.5 Final Methods

A final instance method cannot be overridden (but can still be overloaded). A final static method cannot be re-declared in a subclass.

Purpose

It is useful to be able to prevent a subclass overriding an inherited method and in doing so changing the method behaviour when called for a subclass object. This lets the programmer guarantee that subclasses must use an inherited method as it stands.

Intention

A method declaration includes the modifier `final`.

Syntax

Final methods prevent a method that has the same name and parameter types from being declared in a subclass (the result type is ignored). This takes into account both static and instance variables. Final does not prevent methods being overloaded in a subclass.

Description

Like static classes, static methods potentially allow the compiler to do method call optimizations.

This example shows uses some final methods.

Examples

```
class Superclass {
  //  Cannot redeclare these methods with same name and argument
  //  types.
  public static final void f() {
    System.out.println("Superclass f") ;
  }
```

```
      public  final void g() {
        System.out.println("Superclass g") ;
      }
    }
    class Subclass extends Superclass {
      /*  Cannot declare any of these - to try would be an error
      public static void f() {
        System.out.println("Subclass f") ;
      }
      public void g() {
        System.out.println("Subclass g") ;
      }
      public int f() {
        System.out.println("Subclass f") ;
        return 1 ;
      }
      */
      // These overloaded methods are OK.
      public void f(final int x) {
        System.out.println("Subclass f") ;
      }
      public int f(final double x) {
        System.out.println("Subclass f") ;
        return 1 ;
      }
    }
    class Final1 {
      public static void main(final String[] args) {
        final Subclass sub = new Subclass () ;
        sub.f() ;
        sub.g() ;
        sub.f(1) ;
        sub.f(1.1) ;
      }
    }
```

31.2.6   Method Call Expressions

Purpose

A method call expression determines which method to be called based on the method name and parameters. A series of rules is used to determine exactly which method is called. The method called may be static.

Intention

A method obviously has to be called to be of any use. However, determining which method gets called turns out to be more complicated than might be expected once scope, method overloading and inheritance are taken into account. Every method call must be unambiguous, in that it has to identify exactly one method (which may be overridden). If the call turns out to be ambiguous it will be rejected and an error reported.

Syntax

A method or static method is called in an expression that consists of a method identification followed by an *parameter list*:

```
methodIdentifier ( parameterList )
```

The parameter list may be empty but the parentheses must be present.

The method to be called can be identified in a number of ways:

- Using the method or static method name directly, if the method is declared in the same class or superclass scope:

  ```
  identifier ( parameterList )
  ```

- Using a field expression (the dot operator) with an object reference:

  ```
  primaryExpression.identifier ( parameterList )
  ```

  The primary expression before the dot should evaluate to an object reference which can then be used to select the named method or static method to be called. The named method must be accessible which usually means it must be public or protected or declared in the current class. The method can be static.

- Using a field expression with a class or interface name:

  ```
  ClassOrInterfaceName.identifier ( parameterList )
  ```

  This allows both static and instance methods to be called by specifying which class or interface should be used to find the method.

In order to call a method a process called *method lookup* is used. This is used to determine exactly which method to call and that the call is unambiguous. In some cases a complete method lookup can be done by the compiler, allowing it to exactly determine which method to call at compile time. This is referred to as *static binding* — the method call is bound or associated with a method during compilation.

Description

In other cases, however, it is not possible for the compiler to do a complete lookup as the full information needed is not available until runtime, at the point where the method is called. To overcome this problem, dynamic binding is used, where the binding is completed just before the method call takes place and the exact type of the object the method is called for is known. Dynamic binding is particularly associated with reference types and inheritance, as a reference of superclass type may refer to an object of any one of a number of subclass types.

To understand how method lookup takes place the first issue to deal with is overloaded methods (introduced in Chapter 30.2.5, Page 840) *without* considering inherited methods. If a call is made to a collection of overloaded methods it must be possible to select the one that will be called. This is done by comparing the types of the parameter values (the expressions that appear in the method call expression, aka *actuals*) with the types of the parameter variables (aka *formal parameters* or *formals*) declared in the method declaration. Method declarations where there is a type mismatch between actuals and formals are eliminated from the search. If there is one method left after the elimination, the call is unambiguous and the call expression valid. If there is more than one valid method, the call is ambiguous and therefore an error.

Unfortunately, determining whether actual and formal types match is complicated by the various kinds of implicit conversion, referred to as assignment compatibilities (see Chapter 28.6.3, Page 778), between types. For example, a method taking a `double` argument can be called with an `int` argument as `int`s are assignment compatible to `double`s. Given this an explanation is needed of what the following calls to f do, as potentially when f is called with an integer argument either declared method could be called:

```
class Example {
  public f(int x) { ... }
  public f(double x) { ... }
  ...
  void test() {
    f(10) ; // int argument
    f(1.1) ;// double argument
  }
}
```

In such cases, an attempt is made to find the *most specific* match. The call f(10) is a direct match for f(int x) and so that method is called. Calling f(double x) would require an implicit conversion and is therefore less specific. The call f(1.1) is not an issue as there is only one match since doubles are not converted to ints automatically.

Next consider the following:

```
class Example {
  public f(int x, double y) { ... }
  public f(double x, int y) { ... }
  ...
  void test() {
    f(1.0, 1) ;
    f(1, 1) ;
    f(1, 1.0) ;
  }
}
```

Here the first call of f(1.0,1) is valid since f(int x, double y) will be rejected as doubles are not assignment compatible to ints, leaving only one other method which matches exactly. The call of f(1,1.0) is also valid for similar reason, resulting in a call to f(int x, double y). However, the call f(1,1) is invalid as either version of f could be called, both requiring one implicit conversion. Neither method can be found to be more specific with respect to the method call. To compile the above class the call f(1,1) would have to be removed or one of the parameters explicitly cast to double.

Note that it is quite possible to declare a set of overloaded methods that are potentially ambiguous with respect to method calls. The Java compiler will only complain if an ambiguous call expression is actually written. If not, the code will compile without any notification of potential ambiguity.

The examples above used the primitive types of int and double, exploiting the fact that ints are assignment compatible to doubles. Exactly analogous reasoning will apply to the use of any type and any of the assignment compatibilities between them. In particular, don't forget that when dealing with references, a subtype is assignment compatible with a supertype.

As calling an overloaded method is an extension of the behaviour of calling a non-overloaded method (a non-overloaded method can be thought of as an overloaded method with only one choice), the rules for compiling a method call *where no inherited methods are involved* can be summarized as:

1. Locate all the methods with the required name that are in scope, including both static and instance methods. If no methods are found report an error.

2. Match the actual parameter types to the formal parameter types and eliminate all the methods that have one or more completely mismatched parameter types (where no automatic conversion is possible). If one method is left then the call is valid and the method can be chosen. If no methods are left report an error.

3. Take the remaining methods and consider the automatic conversions for each parameter. If one method can be called with less conversions than another, the one with more conversions can be eliminated. If one method is left it is most specific, the call is valid and the method can be chosen. If two or more methods are left then the call is ambiguous so report an error.

So far, so good, but inheritance introduces an extra complication with respect to inherited overloaded methods and also brings in overridden methods. If a subclass declares one or more methods with the same name as one or more superclass methods, then, unless overriding is occurring, all the methods will be overloading the single method name. This means that attempting to resolve which overloaded method to call must take into account both inherited methods *and* subclass methods. Furthermore, the overloading of the method name in subclasses which may not even have been written yet has to be taken into account as well.

Lookup is modified to deal with these issues by changing the definition of *most specific method* when dealing with inherited and overloaded methods, and by relying on dynamic binding.

Given a method call expression that results in the identification of two potential methods overloading the same name, the *most specific method* is the one that:

1. is declared in the same class or a subclass of the class where the other is declared; and

2. has each parameter assignment compatible with the corresponding parameter of the other method.

To illustrate this, consider the following:

```
class A {
  void f(double d) { ... }
}

class B extends A {
  void f(int i) { ... }
}

...
  B b = new B() ;
  b.f(1) ; // what method gets called?
```

The method `f(int)` in class B overloads the inherited method `f(double)` in class A. The call of `b.f(1)` could potentially call either method. However, by the rules above `f(int)` is more specific as it is declared in the subclass. Hence, `f` declared by class B gets called, much as might be expected by casual inspection of the code.

However, if the example is changed to the following:

```
class A {
  void f(int d) { ... } // Note argument type
}
class B extends A {
  void f(double i) { ... } // Note argument type
}

...
  B b = new B() ;
  b.f(1) ; // ERROR -- ambiguous
```

The call to f is now *ambiguous*. Although it might seem that f(int) should match, it falls foul of rule 1 while f(double) fails on rule 2 and neither can be found to be most specific. Using javac, we end up with the error message:

```
Reference to f is ambiguous. It is defined in void f(double) and void
f(int).
```

whilst with jikes we get the rather more informative:

```
*** Error: Ambiguous invocation of method "f". At least two methods
are accessible from here. Method "void f(double i);" declared in type "B"
and method "void f(int d);" declared in type "A".
```

Looking at a method with two arguments, the application of the most specific rule can be seen again:

```
class A {
  void g(double d, int i) { ... }
}
class B extends A {
  void g(int i, double d) { ... }
}
...
  B b = new B() ;
  b.g(1,1.0) ; // OK
  b.g(1.0,1) ; // OK
  b.g(1,1) ; // ambiguous
```

Here the first two calls to g present no problem as only one overloaded method in each case can possibly match and there is no need to invoke the most specific rules (e.g. b.g(1,1.0) cannot match g(double,int) as doubles are not assignment compatible with ints). The third call, however, is ambiguous as both declarations of g could match but according to the rules neither is most specific. Swapping the two method declarations makes no difference in this case.

The same principles apply when the arguments are of reference types.

```
class X {...}
class Y extends X {...}
class A {
  void h(X x) { ... }
}
class B extends A {
  void h(Y y) { ... }
}

...
  B b = new B() ;
  X x = new X() ;
  Y y = new Y() ;
  b.h(x) ; // OK
```

```
    b.h(y) ; // OK
```

Here both calls to method h are valid. With the first there is only one method that could match, h(X) in class A. With the second, both h methods could match but the rules say that h(Y) in class B is most specific and is the one to be called.

If the declarations of h are swapped:

```
class X {...}
class Y extends X {...}
class A {
  void h(Y y) { ... }
}
class B extends A {
  void h(X x) { ... }
}


...
  B b = new B() ;
  X x = new X() ;
  Y y = new Y() ;
  b.h(x) ; // OK
  b.h(y) ; // ambiguous
```

the second call to h becomes ambiguous as both h methods could match but neither is most specific.

Once method overloading has been resolved, method overriding has to be considered. If the selected method can be overridden then the method call may need to be dynamic. Given that any non-private or non-static method can be overridden (unless the class or method is final, see Sections 31.2.3 and 31.2.5) then all other calls must be dynamic — it is also possible for a compiler to do what is called *data flow analysis* to determine that the type of any objects the method is called for is always the same, removing the need for a dynamic call. It should not be forgotten that subclasses overriding a method can be added to a program at any time without re-compiling its superclasses, so dynamic binding has to deal with objects of classes that may only exist in the future.

Dynamic binding works by using code to find the class of the object a method is called for, checking that the class declares an overriding method with the correct signature (name, parameter type and return type) and then calling the method. Although this sounds slow and expensive to execute, the information needed to do the matching is encoded so as to reduce the overhead to a minimum. .class files carry the information around with them so that the checking can be done once a class is loaded.

To summarize this section, the general process for compiling a method call is as follows:

1. Determine where to start the search for a method by finding the type of the expression denoting the object the method is called for and using the corresponding class.

2. Locate all the methods (instance and static) that are accessible (i.e. private, protected, public, etc. as appropriate) with a name matching that of the method being called. This involves searching the local scope and nesting local scopes (if any), the class scope and superclass scopes. If no declarations are found, report an error.

3. Eliminate all methods that have one or more parameters that cannot match the type of those given in the call. If there is one method left goto 5. If there are no methods left report an error.

4. Apply the most specific rules and determine if one method is more specific than the rest. If one method is left goto 5, otherwise the call is ambiguous so report an error.

5. Determine if the method call needs to be dynamic, if so generate a dynamic method call, otherwise a static call.

Examples

```
class Superclass {
  private static String name = "Superclass" ;
  public void test(final int i) {
    System.out.println("Superclass test(int): " + i) ;
  }
  public void test(final double i) {
    System.out.println("Superclass test(double): " + i) ;
  }
  public String getName() {
    return name ;
  }
}
class Subclass extends Superclass {
  private static String name = "Subclass" ;
  public void test(final float i) {
    System.out.println("Subclass test(float): " + i) ;
  }
  public void test(final int i) {
    System.out.println("Subclass test(int): " + i) ;
  }
  public String getName() {
    return name ;
  }
}
public class Call1 {
  public static void main(final String[] args) {
    final Superclass[] objs = new Superclass[5] ;
    objs[0] = new Superclass () ;
    objs[1] = new Subclass () ;
    objs[2] = new Superclass () ;
    objs[3] = new Subclass () ;
    objs[4] = new Subclass () ;
    for (int i = 0 ; i < 5 ; i++) {
      System.out.println(objs[i].getName()) ;
      objs[i].test(1) ;
      objs[i].test(1.0F) ;
    }
    ((Subclass)objs[1]).test(1.0F) ;
  }
}
```

31.2.7   Modified Name Lookup for Member Classes

Purpose

Member, local and anonymous class objects are contained within an enclosing class object or objects if the classes are nested deeper. This creates a *containment hierarchy* of objects which is separate from the inheritance hierarchy of classes. The containment hierarchy represents another set of scopes that need to be searched when variable or method lookup is taking place.

The existence of inheritance and containment hierarchies is a consequence of the way member classes are supported. When using member classes the programmer needs to be aware that an extra set of scopes exist when binding variable and method names.

The syntax for member, local and anonymous classes is described in Chapter 30. The extended `this` syntax can be used to explicitly access variables and methods in containing objects:

```
classname.this.variableName
classname.this.methodName
```

As there are two distinct hierarchies to search when looking for names, there is a potential problem if the name can be found in both. The inheritance hierarchy is searched first followed by the containment hierarchy. If the same name with the same type is found to be declared in both, and both declarations are accessible, then an error is reported. Such conflicts can be resolved by using the extended `this` syntax to explicitly name the class declaring the name to be used. For example, if both hierarchies declare an in-scope and accessible variable called x then an expression such:

```
A.this.x
```

can be used to access x, where A is the name of the class declaring the variable that needs to be accessed.

The following program illustrates the results of using member classes and inheritance. Note that the member class itself is a subclass of a non-member class, so that there are two inheritance hierarchies, one of which the member class is part, the other of which the containing class is part. The member class object will also be part of a containment hierarchy defined by the containing class and its superclass. Note the comment indicating the conflict that occurs between the member class inheritance hierarchy and the containment hierarchy.

```
class A {
  protected final static String name = "A" ;
  public void f() {
    System.out.println(name + " f") ;
  }
}
class Superclass {
  protected final static String name = "Superclass" ;
  protected String vname ="Superclass instance variable" ;
  public void name() {
    System.out.println(name) ;
  }
}
class Subclass extends Superclass {
  protected final static String name = "Subclass" ;
  protected String vname = "Subclass instance variable" ;
  private class Member extends A { // Member class can inherit.
    private final static String name = "Member" ;
    public void show() {
      // Instance variable OK as instance name hides any inherited or
      // contained name.
      System.out.println(name) ;
      // Variables in the containing object can be accessed by using
      // the extended this syntax.
      System.out.println(Subclass.this.name) ;
      System.out.println(Subclass.this.vname) ;
      // No conflict here as only containment hierarchy has a vname.
      System.out.println(vname) ;
```

```
                    //  Containing object methods can be called.
                    Subclass.this.name() ;
                    //  If this is omitted then methods in the containing object can
                    //  still be accessed. As no method name is inherited there is
                    //  also no conflict.
                    name() ;
                    //  The followng is ambiguous due to name conflict between
                    //  inheritance and containment.
                    //  f() ; // Error
                    this.f() ; // Finds the f in Member scope (actually in A).
                    Subclass.this.f() ;
                }
                public void test(final int x) {
                    System.out.println(name + " test") ;
                }
            }
            public void name() {
                System.out.println(name) ;
            }
            public void test() {
                Member m = new Member () ;
                m.show() ;
            }
            public void f() {
                System.out.println("Subclass:f") ;
            }
        }
        public class Lookup1 {
            public static void main(final String[] args) {
                final Subclass subclass = new Subclass () ;
                subclass.test() ;
            }
        }
```

31.2.8   Constructors and Inheritance

Purpose

All Java classes exist as part of an inheritance hierarchy, so a constructor must be called for each superclass as well as the subclass when an object is created. This will be enforced by the language rules and the compiler.

Intention

The guarantee of proper initialization must be maintained in the presence of inheritance, so the language rules force constructors for each superclass to be called and provide the programmer with some syntax for explicitly controlling which constructors are called.

Syntax

The keyword super can be used to explicitly call a superclass constructor:

super (*parameterList*) **;**

The argument list is used to select a superclass constructor. It may be empty in which case the default superclass constructor will be called.

Constructors are not inherited and cannot be overridden. Overloading is restricted to the set of constructors declared in any one class.

Description

Constructors were introduced in Chapter 30.2.7, Page 845 and this subsection completes their description. It should be noted that apart from the single constructor in class Object, which has no superclass, all constructors need to call a superclass constructor. (Class Object relies on the compiler generated default constructor rather than declaring one explicitly. Interestingly, the J2SDK documentation (and some other sources) show `Object` as having an explicit default constructor. In case of doubt, inspect the source code of class `Object`.)

When a subclass object is created, the following sequence of events takes place:

- The object is allocated memory and the subclass object constructor is called.
- Before any other statement in the constructor body is executed, a superclass constructor is called or if the first statement uses `this` (see below) then another constructor in the subclass is called, which repeats this step.
- When the superclass (or `this`) constructor call returns, instance variables are initialized and instance initializer blocks executed in the order they are written down.
- The constructor body is then executed.
- The constructor call returns leaving an initialized object.

Hence, creating an object results in a series of constructor calls and initializations. This will happen automatically and cannot be prevented. The programmer can, however, control which superclass method is called from a constructor using the `super` keyword followed by an argument list. If such a statement is used, it *must* appear as the first statement in a constructor body:

```
public Example(int a, String b) {
    super(a, 1, b) ; // call superclass constructor taking
                     // int, int, String
}
```

Any superclass constructor can be called, including the default. It doesn't matter if the number of parameters is different from those given to the subclass constructor. The appropriate superclass constructor must not be private, of course.

If `super` is not used explicitly then an implicit call to `super()` is inserted by the compiler as the first statement in a constructor body, unless an explicit call is made to another constructor in the same class using `this` (see Chapter 30.2.9, Page 849). Hence, all constructors (except that in `Object`) that don't explicitly use `super` or `this` actually consist of the following:

```
public A {
    super() ;
    // rest of constructor body
    ...
}
```

The following program uses `super` to select which superclass constructor is called. Note the use of `this`.

Examples

```
class Superclass {
    private int x ;
    // Contains implicit call to super() as first statement
    public Superclass(final int n) {
        x = n ;
    }
}
class Subclass extends Superclass {
    // Call the other constructor using this, no super call is done here
    public Subclass() {
```

```
        this(10) ;
      }
      // Explicitly call super
      public Subclass(final int x) {
        super(x) ;
      }
    }
    public class Super1 {
      public static void main(final String[] args) {
        final Subclass subclass = new Subclass () ;
      }
    }
```

31.2.9 Super and Hidden Names

Purpose

The super keyword can also be used to access variables or methods that have been *hidden* by a re-declaration in a subclass, or a superclass method that has been overridden in a subclass.

Intention

On occasions it is useful to access variables or methods from superclasses that have been hidden by re-declarations.

Syntax

super can be used in a constructor, instance method or instance initializer. It cannot be used with static methods or initializers.

Description

super is somewhat like this (see Chapter 30.2.9, Page 849) when used like a variable, and is also automatically declared. Its type is a reference to the type of the superclass of the class in which the keyword super is used. Hence, it allows access to the immediate superclass bypassing the scope of the subclass. The value of super cannot be changed by assignment, it is effectively final.

Super can be used as an object reference in expressions such as:

```
super.x ; // x is an hidden superclass instance variable
```

and

```
super.f() ; // f is an hidden superclass method
```

As seen in Section 31.2.8, super can also be used to explicitly call superclass constructors.

Examples

The following example program illustrate the use of super to access hidden names.

```
class Superclass {
  public int i = 5 ;
  protected int j = 10 ;
  private int k = 20 ;
  public void show() {
    System.out.println("Superclass " + i + " " + j + " " + k) ;
  }
}
class Subclass extends Superclass {
  // Instance variable that hide those inherited from Superclass
  public int i = 1 ;
  protected int j = 2 ;
  private int k = 3 ;
  public void test() {
    // Display initial values of instance variables
    show() ;
    // Call superclass show method using super
    super.show() ;
    // Access superclass variables that have been hidden
```

```
      super.i = 100 ;
      super.j = 200 ;
      // Can't access a private variable in the superclass
      // super.k = 30 ; // Error
      // Access this classes instance variables normally
      i = 1000 ;
      j = 2000 ;
      k = 3000 ; // No problem accessing private variable in this class
      // Show values of instance variables again
      show() ;
      super.show() ;
    }
    // Overridden method
    public void show() {
      System.out.println("Subclass " + i + " " + j + " " + k) :
    }
}
public class Super2 {
  public static void main(final String[] args) {
    final Subclass subclass = new Subclass () ;
    subclass.test() ;
  }
}
```

31.2.10   Abstract Classes

An abstract class is a place holder for declaring shared methods and variables for use by subclasses and for declaring a common interface of accessible methods and variables.

Purpose

An abstract class cannot have instance objects and so exists as a class that other classes inherit from in order to include the variables and methods declared in the abstract class. Although this provides a useful code sharing mechanism (subclasses inherit rather than declare their own duplicate copies), the more important use of abstract classes is that they can declare a standard set of public methods that all their subclasses either use directly or override. This means that any of this standard set of methods can be called for any subclass object.

Intention

The declaration of an abstract class includes the `abstract` modifier before the `class` keyword.

Syntax

A class declared `abstract` can include any standard variable and method declarations but cannot be used in a new expression. It can also include abstract method declarations (see Section 31.2.11). The class defines a type, so variables of the type may be declared and can hold references to subclass objects.

Description

A subclass of an abstract class may itself be abstract but more usually it is *concrete* (i.e. designed to have instance objects).

Examples

```
abstract class Superclass {
  protected int i = 10 ;
  protected int j = 20 ;
  //  Shared method not to be overridden
  public final void f() {
    System.out.println("Superclass:test") ;
  }
  //  Method intended to be overridden but including a default
  //  implementation.
  public void common() {
```

```
              System.out.println("Superclass:common") ;
          }
      }
      class Subclass extends Superclass {
        public void test() {
          //  Can call superclass method
          f() ;
          //  Can use superclass instance variables
          i = 20 ;
        }
      }
      class Subclass2 extends Superclass {
        public void common() {
          System.out.println("Subrclass2:test") ;
        }
      }
      public class Abstract1 {
        public static void main(final String[] args) {
          //  Can't create Superclass objects
          // Superclass superclass = new Superclass() ; // Error
          final Subclass subclass = new Subclass() ;
          subclass.test() ;
          //  Can do this assignment and call method in
          //  shared public interface
          Superclass superclass = subclass ;
          superclass.common() ;
          //  Can also create Subclass2 object and call common
          superclass = new Subclass2() ;
          superclass.common() ;
          //  Method f is also part of shared interface
          subclass.f() ;
          superclass.f() ;
        }
      }
```

31.2.11   Abstract Methods

Purpose   A method can be declared abstract so that it must be overridden by subclasses.

Intention   Abstract methods declarations do not include a method body and are declared in abstract classes when the method needs to be part of the common interface that is inherited but no default implementation can be provided. The language rules ensure that an abstract method must be overridden and implemented by a concrete subclass, which would not be the case if a normal method with an empty method body were declared in place of the abstract method.

Syntax   An abstract method does not have a method body; the declaration ends with a semi-colon not a compound statement:

modifiers **abstract** *typeName methodName (paramterList) ;*

The parameter list is a sequence of zero or more comma separated parameters. Each parameter consists of a type name followed by a parameter variable identifier (e.g `int x`). The identifier must be present even though it is not used. An overriding method does not need to use the same identifier names.

A class declaring one or more abstract methods must be declared as an abstract class.

Private and static methods cannot be abstract as there is no way of overriding them.

Abstract methods allow an abstract class to specify a complete public or protected method interface even when a method body cannot be provided. The language rules then make sure that concrete subclasses must end up with a complete implementation of each inherited abstract method.

Abstract subclasses of an abstract class can choose to implement an inherited abstract method or can add additional abstract methods.

The following program illustrates the use of both abstract classes and abstract methods.

Description

Examples

```java
abstract class Superclass {
  // Non-abstract classes must override and implement this method.
  public abstract void f() ;
  // Standard method - can be shared or overriden
  public void h() {
    System.out.println("Superclass:h") ;
  }
  // Can't declare static methods as class is abstract
  // public abstract static void x() ; // Error
}
class Subclass extends Superclass {
  // Overridden inherited abstract method.  This class can have
  // instances
  public void f() {
    System.out.println("Subclass") ;
  }
}
// This class does not override the inherited abstract method f and
// so must be abstract
abstract class Subclass2 extends Superclass {
  // Declare a new abstract method
  public abstract void g() ;
}
// This class implements both inherited abstract methods and can have
// instance objects
class Subclass3 extends Subclass2 {
  // Must override inherited abstract method f here
  public void f() {
    System.out.println("Subclass2:f") ;
  }
  // Must also override inherited abstract method g here
  public void g() {
    System.out.println("Subclass2:g") ;
  }
  // Overridden inherited method.  Didn't have to override this but
  // it is allowed
  public void h() {
    System.out.println("Superclass:h") ;
  }
}
public class Abstract2 {
  public static void main(final String[] args) {
    // Can't create Superclass objects
    // Superclass superclass = new Superclass (); // Error abstract
    // Can't create Subclass2 objects
    // Subclass subclass2 = new Subclass2 () ; // Error abstract
    final Subclass subclass = new Subclass () ;
    subclass.f() ;
    subclass.h() ;
    final Subclass3 subclass3 = new Subclass3 () ;
    subclass3.f() ;
    subclass3.g() ;
    subclass3.h() ;
  }
}
```

31.2.12 Methods Inherited from Class Object

Purpose

Class `Object` declares default implementations of a small number of methods that can be overridden by subclasses. In order for subclass objects to behave correctly, the programmer must ensure that either the default implementation is adequate or a suitable overridden version is provided.

Intention

When implementing any class the programmer needs to consider how instance objects should be copied (cloned), compared, disposed of, given a string representation and given a hash code value. Getting these right is considered to be sufficiently important that class `Object` declares default methods for all these operations which will be inherited by all other classes. Classes override these methods when the default behaviour is not correct. This is particularly an issue for classes representing ADTs and data structures, as was seen in Part 2.

Syntax

Class `Object` declares the following methods that can be overridden by subclasses:

```
public boolean equals(Object obj) ;
public String toString() ;
public native int hashCode() ;

protected native Object clone() ;
protected void finalize() ;
```

Array objects also support these methods.

Description

Of the five methods that may be overridden, three are public and may be called for any instance object of any class. The other two are protected and need to be overridden as public methods if they are to be called.

```
boolean equals(Object obj)
```

`equals` is used to compare the object the method is called for with the argument object. The default implementation returns true if the two objects are actually the same object, using the `==` operator. A subclass will override this method to compare the *values* of the two objects, usually by systematically comparing the values of the instance variables.

The `equals` method for a given subclass should focus on comparing the state added by that class and call `super.equals()` to get the superclass state compared. Note, however, that a direct subclass of `Object` won't need to call `Object.equals()`.

The programmer needs to decide how to compare two objects of the same class. It may be sufficient to just compare all the instance variables (especially if they are all of primitive type). However, variables referencing other objects may require that each of the referenced objects are compared in full, relying on their classes to have implemented an appropriate version of `equals`. Hence, a full comparison may result in a whole series of `equals` methods from a number of different classes being called. The programmer should be aware that this can be a time consuming operation at runtime.

The J2SDK documentation defines a rigorous set of rules for what object equality means which the programmer needs to take into account when overriding `equals`. To quote from the documentation, these rules are:

The equals method implements an equivalence relation:

It is reflexive: for any reference value x, x.equals(x) should return true.

It is symmetric: for any reference values x and y, x.equals(y) should return true if and only if y.equals(x) returns true.

It is transitive: for any reference values x, y, and z, if x.equals(y) returns true and y.equals(z) returns true, then x.equals(z) should return true.

It is consistent: for any reference values x and y, multiple invocations of x.equals(y) consistently return true or consistently return false.

For any reference value x, x.equals(null) should return false.

The equals method for class `Object` implements the most discriminating possible equivalence relation on objects; that is, for any reference values x and y, this method returns true if and only if x and y refer to the same object (x == y has the value true).

It is important to implement `equals` correctly if instances object are to be used by any other class or method that relies on the equality relation.

```
String toString()
```

This method is used to return a string representing the value of the object it is called for. By default the class `Object` method returns a `String` like:

```
ClassName@1cc7a0
```

This is the name of the object's class, followed by @, followed by the hexadecimal value of the object's hash code (see below). To generate a more useful string a subclass can override the method and return any string that is a reasonable representation of the objects value.

The `toString` method is widely used by other methods to convert from the reference type of the object to `String`, notably when using streams, so it should usually be overridden to do something useful.

```
int hashCode()
```

A hash code is a single integer value that represents the entire value of an object, such that the full object value can be *hashed* to an integer. Each distinct value that an object can represent should have a relatively unique hash code (relatively unique as the number of values will often be larger than can be represented by an `int`). Hash codes are used as key values in a hash table (such as implemented by the `HashMap` class in `java.util`).

The default version of `hashCode` attempts to generate a hash code for any object but may end up generating different hash codes for different objects representing the same value. If that is the case, then it needs to be overridden to implement a new *hash function* that will generate correct hash codes. The J2SDK documentation states:

The general contract of `hashCode` is:

Whenever it is invoked on the same object more than once during an execution of a Java application, the `hashCode` method must consistently return the same integer. This integer need not remain consistent from one execution of an application to another execution of the same application.

If two objects are equal according to the equals method, then calling the `hashCode` method on each of the two objects must produce the same integer result.

In practice, only objects that are likely to be stored in a hash table will need the `hashCode` method. Programmers usually rely on the default `hashCode` implementation, rather than try to implement a new version, which can be hard work.

`Object clone()`

The `clone` method creates a copy of an object. By default, only the object is copied and not any other objects it references, i.e. this is a *shallow copy*. Primitive values are always copied. The potential weakness of the default `clone` is that its use can result in two copies of an object both referencing or sharing a collection of other objects. If the state of one of the referenced objects changes then so, effectively, does the state of all the objects referencing it. To overcome this, `clone` can be overridden to perform a *deep copy*, where both the object and the objects it references get copied. The overridden `clone` also needs to be made public if it is to be generally used.

A full deep copy relies on `clone` or a similar copying operation being implemented correctly by each class of a referenced object. Like `equals`, calling `clone` can result in a long sequence of methods being called, which can use up a lot of time during execution of a program. As a result, it is important to carefully define what copying an object means and what it really has to do.

A `clone` method should be responsible for cloning the state (i.e variables) declared in its class and should call `super.clone()` to copy the superclass state, unless that class is `Object` as the default `clone` method may not be needed.

Every object has a `clone` method: `Object` has a `clone` method and all classes inherit from `Object`. However, `clone` is defined protected in `Object` and is therefore not callable by default. In order for the `clone` method to be accessible, a class must overide the method — note that the `clone` method in `Object` throws `CloneNotSupportedException` and so this must be managed. It is usual for classes tha support cloning to implement the interface `Cloneable`. If the `clone` method is called for an object that cannot be cloned, a `CloneNotSupportedException` is thrown.

A class may not override `clone`, choosing instead to provide other methods for copying or using constructors (e.g. see the `String` class in the J2SDK).

```
void finalize()
```

The `finalize` method is called automatically by the garbage collector when an object is no longer referenced and can be thrown away. The default version in class `Object` has an empty method body. The garbage collector can run at any time, so there is no reliable way to determine when `finalize` will be called for an object. Typically, though, the garbage collector is only invoked when memory available to the program is running low.

`finalize` only needs to be overridden if an object holds state that won't be correctly dealt with if it is simply thrown away. For example, data may need to be written (flushed) out to a file before it is lost, or a network connection may need to be properly closed down.

A `finalize` method should be responsible for finalizing the class it is declared in and should call `super.finalize()` to deal with its superclass. A `finalize` method can be declared to throw a `Throwable` exception if an error occurs. If an exception is thrown, it will be caught by the garbage collector and ignored, leaving the program to carry on.

Further information about these methods and class `Object` in general, can be found within the J2SDK documentation.

The following example illustrates `equals`, `toString`, `clone` and `finalize`. `hashCode` is not overridden as the default is considered sufficient.

Examples

```java
import java.util.Date ;
public class ObjectMethods implements Cloneable{
  private int i ;
  private Date d ;
  private String[] s ;
  public ObjectMethods(final int a, final Date b, final String[] c) {
    i = a ;
    d = b ;
    s = c ; // Array is not copied
  }
  //  A private default constructor used when cloning an object It
  //  does no initialization as cloning will overwrite any values.
  private ObjectMethods() { }
  //  Override equals to compare the value of the argument with this.
  public boolean equals(final Object obj) {
    //  Check for testing equality with self and shortcut everything
    //  else.
    if (this == obj)
      return true ;
    //  Check that the argument object is an instance of the same
    //  class, as the argument is given type object not the type of
    //  this class.  First check if the argument is null. Note the use
    //  of the || operator which only evaluates its right hand
    //  argument if the left is false.
    if ((obj == null) || ! (obj instanceof ObjectMethods))
      return false ; // Can't be equal!
    //  Cast argument back to correct type
    ObjectMethods tmp = (ObjectMethods)obj ;
    //  Next compare the value of each instance variable.  Primitive
    //  types can be compared using the boolean operators.
    if (i != tmp.i)
      return false ;
    //  Objects of class types need to be compared using equals unless
    //  it is sufficient that both references are referencing the same
    //  object.
```

```java
      if (! d.equals(tmp.d))
        return false ;
      //  An array is an object. == or equals will only check if two
      //  references reference the same object, so a loop is needed to
      //  iterate through each array comparing elements.  The arrays
      //  need to be the same length.
      if (s.length != tmp.s.length)
        return false ;
      for (int i = 0 ; i < s.length ; i++) {
        if (! s[i].equals(tmp.s[i]))
          return false ;
      }
      return true ; // Same value
   }
   //  Generate a String representation of an object
   public String toString() {
      //  Use a Stringbuffer to build the String
      StringBuffer sb = new StringBuffer () ;
      sb.append("i = " + i + ", ") ;
      sb.append("d = " + d + ", " ) ;
      sb.append("s = ") ;
      for (int i = 0 ; i < s.length ; i++) {
        sb.append(s[i] + " ") ;
      }
      return sb.toString() ;
   }
   //  Perform a deep copy, making sure that the necessary referenced
   //  objects are cloned. Due to the way string objects are managed,
   //  they don't need to be cloned, but the date and array do.
   //  Object.clone performs the creation and shallow copying of the
   //  ObjectMethods object. The new object should not be
   //  created using a constructor, expecially if ObjectMethods
   //  is subclassed (calling clone would end up creating a copy
   //  of the superclass not the new subclass).
   public Object clone() throws CloneNotSupportedException {
      ObjectMethods tmp = (ObjectMethods)super.clone() ;
      tmp.d = (Date)d.clone() ;
      //  Copy array element by element.
      tmp.s = new String[s.length] ;
      for (int i = 0 ; i < s.length ; i++) {
        tmp.s[i] = new String (s[i]) ;
      }
      return tmp ;
   }
   //  Don't need to override this as the default does the right
   //  thing. However, as an example we override it anyway.
   public void finalize() {
      // Null all the array elements
      for (int i = 0 ; i < s.length ; i++) {
        s[i] = null ;
      }
      System.out.println("Finalized") ;
   }
   public static void main(final String[] args) {
      final String[] upper = {"A", "B", "C", "D", "E"} ;
      final String[] lower = {"a", "b", "c", "d", "e"} ;
      final ObjectMethods a = new ObjectMethods (1, new Date (), upper);
      ObjectMethods b =
       new ObjectMethods(10, new Date (), lower) ;
      System.out.println(a.equals(a)) ;
      System.out.println(a.equals(b)) ;
      System.out.println(b.equals(a)) ;
      System.out.println(b.equals(b)) ;
      System.out.println(a) ;
      System.out.println(b) ;
      //  Object that was referenced by b is no longer referenced and
```

```
        //  may get garbage collected (although that is very unlikely
        //  during the running of this program as it uses little memory).
        b = null ;
        //  Clone object a and compare the clone with the original.
        //  Note use of cast when using clone as it returns a value of
        //  type Object.
        final ObjectMethods c ;
        try {
          c = (ObjectMethods)a.clone() ;
          System.out.println(a.equals(c)) ;
          System.out.println(c.equals(a)) ;
          System.out.println(a) ;
          System.out.println(c) ;
        }
        catch (CloneNotSupportedException e) {
          e.printStackTrace() ;
        }
    }
}
```

31.3 Interfaces

An interface declaration allows the specification of a reference type without providing an implementation of that type in the way that a class does. This provides a mechanism for declaring types that are distinct from classes, giving an important extension to the way that objects and inheritance can be used within Java.

Interfaces exploit the concept of *type conformance*. A type can be specified by a name and a set of methods, each of which has a name, a set of parameter types and a return type. A type can *conform* to another type if it specifies at least the same set of methods as the other type (and possibly more), and each method has the same name, parameter types and result type. Moreover, the two types do *not* have to be related by inheritance, giving greater freedom as to which types may conform to other types.

To illustrate the basic idea, if `Type1` specifies:

```
void f() ;
int g(String s) ;
```

and `Type2` specifies:

```
void f() ;
int g(String s) ;
double h(int x) ;
```

then `Type2` conforms to `Type1` as it has all the methods that `Type1` does. This is sometimes written as a relation of the form:

```
Type1 ≤ Type2
```

If `Type2` conforms to `Type1` then a value of `Type2` can be substituted for a value of `Type1`, as it will support all the methods that a `Type1` value does.

The idea of substitutability should be familiar from having seen the properties of classes and inheritance. The crucial feature that interfaces add is that they are *defined outside of the class*

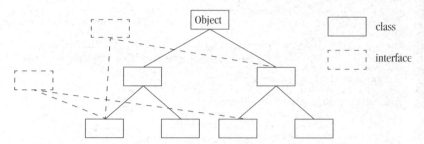

Figure 31.1 Classes and interfaces.

hierarchy (don't forget that all classes ultimately inherit from class Object, so all classes are within the same, single class hierarchy). Once defined, an interface can be *implemented* by a class which creates a new type conforming to the interface type. Further, any class can implement the same interface regardless of its position in the class hierarchy. Figure 31.1 illustrates the basic idea. It is then possible to declare a variable of the interface type and have that variable reference any object of any class that implements the interface. The object can be said to conform to the interface, or conform to the type. Moreover, a class can implement several interfaces so that objects of that class can be used wherever the interface types are specified.

This, in effect, provides a 'bolt-on plug' that allows a class to specify that its objects can be used wherever a matching interface 'socket' is provided, and it can do so without the class having to being in a particular place in the inheritance hierarchy. This has important consequences for program code as it can be written to use an interface type, in the knowledge that a class only has to implement the interface to allow its objects to be used with that code. If the same code has to be written using a class type then only objects of the corresponding class and its subclasses can be used. This would force the class of any other object that might be used in the future to be a subclass of a specific class, regardless of which class it actually needs to be a subclass of.

A common design issue that interfaces also address is the lack of multiple inheritance between classes. A class can only have one superclass but may need to inherit from two or more classes scattered around the class hierarchy. This would allow objects of the class to be substituted wherever objects of the multiple superclass types were specified. Adding interfaces solves the problem of substitutability as a class can implement several interfaces. The inheritance of variables and methods would have to be solved by changing class inheritance relationships to associations (not ideal but workable).

The Java class libraries make wide use of interfaces to specify a set of methods that a class must provide for its objects to be used in certain situations. An example, extensively used in Part 2, is that of the Iterator interface which specifies a type and a set of methods for iterating through a data structure. Different data structures require different classes to provide the iterators but all the classes can implement the same interface. Clients of iterators then only have to use the Iterator interface, without needing knowledge of how a particular iterator works or even what its real class is.

A final point about type conformance that is worth considering is that, in Java, it is based only on the syntactic matching of identifiers and type names. It does not specify the behaviour of interface methods and verify that implementations of the methods do the right thing. That is left to the programmer to check by hand.

31.3.1 Interface Declaration

An interface declaration specifies a reference type, consisting of a type name, a set of abstract method declarations and a set of final static (constant) variables.

Purpose

The declaration specifies a type that classes can implement (see above).

Intention

An interface is declared using the following *syntax:*

Syntax

```
interfaceModifier interface identifier {
   interfacemethodDeclarations
   interfaceVariableDeclarations
}
```

The optional interface modifier allows an interface to be declared `public`.

Interface variables may be declared using a standard static variable declaration and must be initialized. The only modifiers permitted are `public`, `static` and `private` but they are redundant and should not be used (see the description below). An interface variable may be initialized by an expression using another interface variable providing that variable has been declared textually before the one being initialized.

Interface methods are always abstract and are declared in the same way as abstract methods in classes (see Section 31.2.11) with no method body. The only modifiers permitted are `public` and `abstract` but they are also redundant and should not be used (see the description below).

An interface can extend *one or more* other interfaces (somewhat like inheritance) using the `extends` keyword.

```
interfaceModifier interface identifier extends interfaceNameList {
   interfacemethodDeclarations
   interfaceVariableDeclarations
}
```

The `interfaceNameList` is either a single interface name or a comma separated list of interface names. An interface cannot extend a class.

An interface can be nested within a top-level class or another interface and will implicitly be treated as static but may be declared `public`, `private` or `protected` like other declarations within classes.

An interface consists of a sequence of abstract method declarations and static, final variable declarations, e.g.:

Description

```
public interface X {
   int f(String s) ;
   boolean g(double d, long l) ;
   int SIZE = 10 ;
   String word = "hello" ;
```

```
    }
```

Any method declared will be implicitly abstract, and so does not need to be explicitly declared as such. Although current versions of Java still allow the `abstract` keyword to appear, this may not be the case in the future and so it should be omitted. Note that like abstract methods in classes, the parameter variables have to be named even though only their type is actually needed.

Any variables declared are implicitly constants and also static (i.e. they are loke class variables). Variables can be declared using the keywords `static` and `final`, but as with methods these should not be used.

An interface can be empty, so that it only declares a type name:

```
interface Empty {}
```

An interface is declared in a source file (compilation unit) like a class. It can be declared `public` in which case it can be used by classes in other packages. If an interface is declared public it must be the only public interface *or* class in the same source file. If not public an interface can only be used within the same package it is declared in.

If an interface is declared public then all the methods and variables it declares are also public. Otherwise, they all have default access and will only be accessible within the same package. This behaviour is different from that of classes so is worth noting.

An interface can extend or inherit one or more other interfaces (note the difference from classes):

```
interface C extends A, B { // Extend interfaces A and B
  // declarations
}
```

All the names declared in all the interfaces become part of the inheriting interface but variable names can be hidden by re-declarations in the inheriting interface. Field expressions can be used to access hidden variable names but only from within the same package, e.g.:

```
A.x ; // access variable x from interface A
```

This is not an issue with methods as they are only declared in order to be overridden and there are no method bodies.

An interface can be nested inside a top level class which allows the scope of its name to be controlled by the enclosing class. A nested interface is part of the enclosing class and is always treated as static and doesn't need to be explicitly declared as such (a non-static interface would make little sense as interfaces are not part of objects).

An interface can also be nested within another interface (as will be demonstrated in a later example). Whether there is much need to do this is not clear but it can be done.

Examples

The following files declare some interfaces. Note that they are made part of a package called ITest.

```
package ITest ;
interface X {
```

!

Interfaces and classes have different rules regarding scope of member variables and methods. The behaviour of the extends keyword is also different.

```
    int j = 1 ;
    String name = "X" ;
    int h(int x) ;
}

package ITest ;
interface Y {
  int p = 100 ;
  // X also declares variables with these names
  int j = 2 ;
  String name = "Y" ;
  int h(int x) ;
  void g() ;
}

package ITest ;
public interface Example extends X, Y {
  // Declare a nested interface
  interface Nested {
    void z() ;
  }
  // Can't do this initialization as m has not yet been declared in
  // the textual order the declarations have been written down.
  // int z = m ; // Error
  // Can initialize using a variable from extended interface.
  int f = p ; // Note variable name is same as method name
  // But this would be ambiguous
  // int m = j ; // Error
  // j has to be accessed in a field expression instead
  int m = X.j ;
  int n = Y.j ;
  void f(int x) ;
}
```

31.3.2   Implements

The `implements` keyword allows a class to implement (or conform to) one or more interfaces.

Purpose

The implements clause in a class declaration allows the connection to be made between a class and an interface. Once an interface is implemented by a class, references to objects of that class are assignment compatible with the interface type.

Intention

The class name in a class declaration is followed by the `implements` keyword and a list of one or more comma separated interface names:

Syntax

```
modifiers class identifier implements interfaceNameList {
  declarations
}
```

The rest of the class declaration is as normal. If the class does not override *all* the methods declared in the implemented interface(s) then the class must be declared abstract.

A class can implement any number of interfaces (and also extend a class at the same time). Any variables declared in the interfaces become static variables of the class. Any methods declared in the interfaces must either be overridden or the implementing class is abstract. Subclasses of the class must themselves either be abstract or override the rest of the methods.

Description

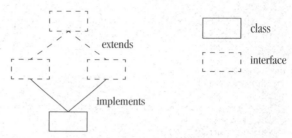

Figure 31.2 Interface implemented via two different routes.

When implementing two or more interfaces there may be problems with variables of the same name appearing in several interfaces, in which case an attempt to use them directly would be ambiguous. This can be resolved by using a field expression:

```
X.y ; // Use static interface variable y from interface X
```

Note, however, when interfaces are inherited by other interfaces there are limitations on accessing interface variables this way by classes in a different package to the interface (see example below).

There is no ambiguity with methods as the interfaces only contain abstract method declarations. However, if two interfaces declare the same method, with the same argument and result types, they probably both expect the method to be overridden differently. Hence, the overriding method in an implementing class will need to implement both sets of expectations in the same method.

A method declared in a public interface must be public in an implementing class, as accessibility cannot be decreased.

If a complicated set of inheriting interface declarations is implemented by a class, it is possible to implement the same interface by two or more different routes (see Figure 31.2). This is allowed and doesn't introduce any problems. Only one copy exists of any interface variable that is inherited by two or more routes.

Examples

The following two source files use the interfaces declared in the package ITest in the last section. The first declares a class in the same package which has access to hidden interface variables.

```
package ITest ;
//  This class is in the same package as all the interface
//  declarations
public class Thing implements Example {
  public void f(final int y) {
    System.out.println("Thing:f " + y) ;
    //  name is declared in an interface in the same package so is
    //  accessible but ambiguous unless used in a field expression
    //  naming the interface declaring the variable
    System.out.println(X.name) ;
    System.out.println(Y.name) ;
    //  The compiler may generate warning messages about the last two
    //  statements.  This following is ambiguous.
    // System.out.println(name) ; // Error
  }
  // Must override g and h as well
  public void g() {
```

```
      System.out.println("Thing:g ") ;
  }
  public int h(final int x) {
    System.out.println("Thing:h " + x) ;
    return x * 4 ;
  }
}
```

The next source file is a client of the package `ITest` and also contains the `main` method.

```
import ITest.* ;
class A implements Example {
  // Can have a nested interface
  private interface Local {}
  // Implementation of interface variable
  public void f(int x) {
    System.out.println("A:f " + x) ;
    // Use the interface variables
    System.out.println(f) ;
    System.out.println(Example.f) ; // Also allowed
    System.out.println(m) ;
    System.out.println(n) ;
    System.out.println(p) ;
    //  name is declared in a non public inherited interface and
    //  cannot be accessed outside the same package.
    // System.out.println(name) ; // Error
    // System.out.println(X.name) ;  // Error
    //  Interface variables are final so can't do this assignment.
    // m = 5 ; // Error
    //  This member class implements a nested interface declared in
    //  the InterfaceExample.  Why you would want to do this is
    //  another matter...
    class NestedClass implements Example.Nested {
      public void z() {
        System.out.println("NestedClass:z") ;
      }
    }
    final NestedClass nest = new NestedClass() ;
    nest.z() ;
  }
  // Must override g and h as well
  public void g() {
    System.out.println("A:g ") ;
  }
  public int h(int x) {
    System.out.println("A:h " + x) ;
    return x * 2 ;
  }
}
public class InterfaceTest {
  public static void main(final String[] args) {
    final A a = new A () ;
    a.f(10) ;
    final Thing t = new Thing () ;
    t.f(20) ;
    // Can't access a nested private interface
    // A.Local l ; // Error
  }
}
```

31.4   Summary

This chapter has covered details of the inheritance mechanisms provided by the Java language. These are powerful but relatively complex, and so need to be studied carefully. The chapter finished with a description of interfaces, which although less complex, form an important part of the Java language and have a very significant impact on the design of programs.

Self-review Exercises

Self-review 31.1 What is the output from running `Inherit1`? Why is this the output?

Self-review 31.2 What is the output from running `Inherit2`? `Why is` this the output?

Self-review 31.3 What is the output from running `Override`? Why is this the output?

Self-review 31.4 What is the output from running `Final1`? `Why is this` the output?

Self-review 31.5 Referring to the `classA`/`classB` example on Page 882, what happens with the following calls:

```
b.g(1.0, 1.0) ;
b.g(1.0f, 1) ;
b.g(1.0f, 1.0f) ;
b.g(1L, 1) ;
b.g(1L, 1L) ;
```

Self-review 31.6 Looking at the `Call1` program:

1. Which methods are overridden and which overloaded?

2. What does the program display?

3. What is the significance of the last statement?

Self-review 31.7 What does program `Lookup1` display? Why is this the output?

Self-review 31.8 What does program `Super2` display? Why is this the output?

Self-review 31.9 What does program `Abstract1` display? Why is this the output?

Programming Exercises

Exercise 31.1 Write a program incorporating all the different varieties of scope that displays the variable and method search algorithm. i.e. verifies the published variable and method lookup rules.

Exercise 31.2 Write a program based on the outline on Page 883 to verify that the most specific rules work when a method with two or more reference type parameters is used.

Exercise 31.3 Write a program to explore the interaction between member classes, containment and inheritance hierarchies, and overloaded methods and overridden methods.

Exception Handling

Objectives

This chapter describes the Java exception handling mechanism which allows errors that occur during the execution of a program to be dealt with in an effective and safe way. The proper use of exceptions allows the programmer to create robust programs that do not fail in an anti-social way.

Keywords

exception

exception handler

throws clause

throw

catch

try block

catch block

finally

32.1 Introduction

An *exception* is an event that occurs in a program whilst it is running. Exceptions are usually, but not always, deleterious to continued progress of the program. Some exceptions are generated by the JVM due to a problem with the state of the virtual machine whilst some are generated explicitly by the running program. Without explicit management, a program in which an exception occurs will terminate abruptly, losing the entire state of the computation, including any data not saved to file — this is clearly not a good state of affairs!

The Java exception handling mechanism allows exceptions to be caught and dealt with, ideally by correcting the problem that caused the exception and allowing the program to carry on without loss of data or to terminate gracefully saving all data that it is possible to save.

This chapter will describe the features of exception handling in Java.

32.1.1 Exception Classes

Purpose

Exception classes allow exceptions to be represented as objects. An *exception object* stores information about the cause of an exception and can be passed as a value to an *exception handler* implemented by a `catch` block.

Intention

When an exception occurs, it is important to capture the cause of the exception, along with any other information, such as the value of variables, that will help in dealing with it. To enable this, all exceptions are represented by objects, with the exception classes defining their representation.

Syntax

The full set of standard exception classes defined within the Java libraries is described in the J2SDK API documentation (see the index page for the package `java.lang`) and will not be repeated here.

All exception classes must be a direct or indirect subclass of class `Throwable`, which defines the default method interface of an exception class. `Throwable` also defines a private `String` variable that can be used to store a text message describing the cause of an exception. This variable can be initialized via a constructor and accessed via a public method.

The public method interface of `Throwable` is as follows:

```
// Default constructor
Throwable()
// Constructor with String argument describing the error.
// User defined subclasses should always provide a version
// of this constructor.
Throwable(String)
// Return the String describing the error.
String getMessage()
// Return a version of the error String in the local language.
// This method should be overridden by subclasses, as the
// default behaviour is to return the error String.
String getLocalizedMessage()
// Overridden version of class Object toString, returning
// information about the exception including the error String.
```

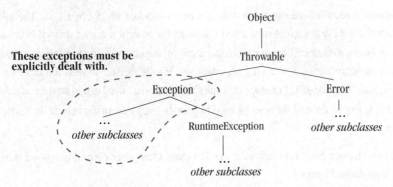

Figure 32.1 Outline of the exception class hierarchy.

```
// Can be overridden but Throwable version is quite useful
String toString()
// The following displays a stack trace (the method calls
// in progress when the exception occurred).
void printStackTrace() // Send to standard error stream
void printStackTrace(PrintStream) // Write to a print stream
void printStackTrace(PrintWriter) // Write to a print writer
// Adjust stack trace if the exception re-thrown
Throwable fillInStackTrace()
```

Subclasses can add as many variables and methods as needed to store further information about the exception their instances represent.

An exception class, despite the name, is an ordinary class defined in the normal way. All exception classes are either a direct or indirect subclass of the Java library class `Throwable` which is defined in the package `java.lang`. The same package defines a whole family of subclasses of `Throwable`, which are used throughout the library packages. The programmer can either use these directly to represent exceptions or, more usually, creates subclasses to represent user-defined exceptions.

Description

The basic exception hierarchy is shown in Figure 32.1. The library exception classes are split into two categories based on the library classes `Error`, `Exception` and `RuntimeException`:

- `Error`, `RuntimeException` and their subclasses represent serious errors usually caused by the JVM, the class loader or the run-time environment. These exceptions are mostly non-recoverable and will cause a program to terminate or fail in an un-recoverable way. Error exceptions indicate a failure of the system outside the control of the program. A Java program does not need to explicitly deal with any of these exceptions, providing abrupt termination is acceptable.

- Subclasses of `Exception`, except `RuntimeException` and its subclasses, represent errors caused by programmer initiated mistakes, omissions and logic failures. An exception represented by one of these classes must be explicitly dealt with by a Java program. User defined exceptions are almost always a subclass of `Exception`.

In most cases, a user-defined exception class is a direct subclass of `Exception`. The other exception classes are, in general, not subclassed (although they can be). A user defined exception class usually defines a default constructor including a call to `super` with an appropriate message `String`. A constructor taking a `String` argument which calls `super` to pass the String up to `Throwable`, also often appears. In many cases, the subclass doesn't need to add any new methods or variables but is free to do so if they can be used to provide extra information about the cause of the exception.

Examples

The first example shows a basic user defined exception class. Often, user defined exception classes are no more complicated than this.

```
class UserException extends Exception {
  public UserException() {
    super("A suitable message") ;
  }
  public UserException(String msg) {
    super(msg) ;
  }
}
```

The following class shows a slightly more complicated exception class that represents a failure of a search when given an invalid keyword string. The invalid keyword string is stored by objects of the class along with the default error string, and an accessor method is provided to return the keyword string when the exception is handled.

```
class SearchException extends Exception {
  // Storage for bad keyword string.
  private final String keyword ;
  // Construct object given invalid keyword string
  public SearchException(final String s) {
    super("Search failed using the invalid keyword") ;
    keyword = s ;
  }
  // Provide an accessor method to get the keyword string
  public String getKeyword() {
    return keyword ;
  }
}
```

32.1.2   Try, Catch and Finally

Purpose

The `try` and `catch` keywords provide the core syntax for handling exceptions. The `finally` keyword provides a mechanism for guaranteeing that a block of code will be executed regardless of what else happens.

Intention

If one or more statements are to be executed that may cause, or *throw*, an exception they can be put inside a *try block* which 'tries' to execute them. If an exception occurs as a result of executing one of the statements in the try block, it may caught by a corresponding *catch block* following the try block. The catch block can contain code to deal with the situation.

A *finally block* contains code that will be executed whether or not an exception occurs and provides a useful place to put statements that must be executed whatever happens.

A try block consists of the `try` keyword followed by a compound statement:

```
try {
    statementSequence
}
```

It can be followed by zero or more catch blocks:

```
catch ( parameter ) {
    statementSequence
}
```

Following the `catch` keyword is a parameter declaration that specifies the type of exception object the catch block will catch.

An optional finally block can follow after any catch blocks:

```
finally {
    statementSequence
}
```

The try block must be followed by at least one catch block or a finally block.

A basic try–catch block can be put together as follows:

```
try {
    f() ; // call a method that might through an exception
}
catch (Exception e) {
    System.out.println("Calling f failed") ;
    // print the exception message
    System.out.println(e.getMessage()) ;
}
```

The try block is a context in the method call `f` will be executed. If an exception occurs while executing `f` then an exception object will be created and *thrown*. The catch block following the try block then has an opportunity to *catch* the thrown exception. The exception is caught if the type of the exception object is assignment compatible with the type specified as parameter of the catch blocks. If the exception is caught, the statements in the catch block are executed and ethen xecution will proceed with the statement following the end of the try–catch block sequence. If the exception is not caught then the current method is terminated as though it had thrown the exception. If no exception occurs then the catch block is skipped and again execution proceeds with the statement following the end of the full try–catch block sequence. Hence, whatever happens the program has a chance to carry on running normally.

Matching an exception object to a catch block parameter is similar to a method call. If the object type is assignment compatible, the exception parameter variable is initialized to hold a reference to the exception object, allowing the object to be accessed within the scope of the catch block. In the example above the exception parameter is of type `Exception`, so will catch any instance of class `Exception` or any of its subclasses.

A try block can be followed by several catch blocks, each dealing with a different type of exception. For example:

```
try {
    f() ; // call a method that might throw an exception
}
```

```
catch (UserException e) {
  System.out.println("Calling f failed") ;
  System.out.println(e.getMessage()) ;
}
catch (Exception e) {
  System.out.println("Calling f failed") ;
  System.out.println(e.getMessage()) ;
}
```

When an exception is thrown, the type of the object is matched against each catch block parameter in the order they are written down. The first block to match is selected and executed, the rest are ignored. In the example, above this means that the exception object is first checked to see if it is an instance of `UserException` or one of its subclasses. If so, then the first catch block is executed, otherwise a match is made against the second catch block.

Note that the second catch block is more general and will catch more types of exceptions than the first. If the order of the catch blocks is reversed:

```
try {
  f() ; // call a method that might through an exception
}
catch (Exception e){
  System.out.println("Calling f failed") ;
  System.out.println(e.getMessage()) ;
}
// Compiler reports error here as this catch block
// is inaccessible
catch (UserException e) {
  System.out.println("Calling f failed") ;
  System.out.println(e.getMessage()) ;
}
```

then the second catch block can never be matched as the first will always succeed (`UserException` is assignment compatible with `Exception`). The Java compiler will detect this situation and report an error.

A finally block can follow a try–catch block:

```
try {
  f() ; // call a method that might through an exception
}
catch (Exception e) {
  System.out.println("Calling f failed") ;
  System.out.println(e.getMessage()) ;
}
finally {
  g() ; // Always call g whatever happens.
}
```

The finally block will always be executed regardless of what happens in the try block, even if an exception is thrown or a `return` statement is executed. This provides a place to put statements that will be guaranteed to be executed.

Normally, we use a catch block to recover the state of the program and let it proceed without terminating (by far the best option from the end user's point of view!). The catch block can use any variables and call any methods in scope, and may display a message informing the user there has been a problem. If another exception occurs within a catch block it will not be caught in the within the same try–catch block and will be propagated up (see Section 32.1.3).

When an exception object is caught by a catch block there is the option of calling one of the object's stack trace methods inherited from `Throwable`, as well as using the `getMessage` method to get the message string. This will show the chain of active method calls that have been made to reach the current point in the program. This information can be of use when debugging but, generally, doesn't want to be seen by the end user.

A stack trace looks like the following:

```
java.lang.NumberFormatException: abc
        at java.lang.Integer.parseInt(Integer.java:229)
        at java.lang.Integer.parseInt(Integer.java:276)
        at Exception1.convert(Exception1.java:14)
        at Exception1.main(Exception1.java:29)
```

The first line is the name of the class of the exception, followed by the message string. The following lines show each active method call up to the `main` method (or a `Thread` `run` method if the exception was thrown in a separate thread).

The following example shows a typical use of a try–catch block when converting a `String` representing an integer to an actual integer value. It calls a library method that throws an exception if the conversion can't be done.

Examples

```java
public class Exception1 {
  public int convert(final String s) {
    int result = 0 ;
    try {
      // Use a method from the library class Integer to convert a
      // string representing an integer to an integer value.  parseInt
      // will throw an exception if the String value is not
      // convertable to an integer.
      result = Integer.parseInt(s) ;
    }
    catch (NumberFormatException e) {
      System.out.println("String conversion failed: " + e) ;
      e.printStackTrace() ;
    }
    return result ;
  }
  final public static void main(final String[] args) {
    Exception1 e1 = new Exception1 () ;
    e1.convert("123") ;
    e1.convert("abc") ;
  }
}
```

The second example shows the use of multiple catch blocks and a finally block.

```java
class MyException extends Exception {
  MyException(final String s) {
    super(s) ;
  }
}
public class Exception2 {
  // This method deliberately throws an exception selected by the
  // argument. Note that NullPointerException and InterruptedException
  // are library exception classes.  InterruptedException is a direct
  // subclass of Exception NullPointerException is a subclass of
  // RuntimeException which is a subclass of Exception.
  public void g(final int x) throws Exception {
    switch (x) {
    case 1 :
```

```
                        throw new MyException ("Method g failed") ;
                    case 2 :
                        throw new NullPointerException ("Method g failed") ;
                    case 3 :
                        throw new InterruptedException ("Method g failed") ;
                    default :
                        throw new Exception ("Method g failed") ;
                }
            }
            public void f(final int x) {
                try {
                    if (x < 5) {
                        g(x) ;
                    }
                    System.out.println("Got past call to g without exception") ;
                    return ;
                }
                catch (MyException e) {
                    System.out.print("Caught MyException in Method f: ") ;
                    System.out.println(e.getMessage()) ;
                }
                catch (Exception e) {
                    System.out.print("Caught Exception in Method f: ") ;
                    System.out.println(e.getMessage()) ;
                }
                finally {
                    System.out.println("Done with f") ;
                }
            }
            public static void main(final String[] args) {
                final Exception2 e2 = new Exception2 () ;
                e2.f(1) ;
                e2.f(2) ;
                e2.f(3) ;
                e2.f(4) ;
                e2.f(5) ;
            }
        }
```

32.1.3   Exception Propagation

Purpose

If an exception is not caught within a method it must be *propagated* up the chain of active method calls until a catch block deals with it. Exceptions cannot be forgotten.

Intention

When a method throws an exception or any catch blocks are unable to catch an exception, the exception must be passed on somewhere for handling. This allows an exception to be dealt with in the most relevant place.

Description

Exceptions of classes Error, RuntimeException or their subclasses do not have to be explicitly dealt with and, if thrown, will simply be propagated up the chain of active method calls. Try–catch blocks or throws declarations (see Section 32.1.4) do not have to be used, although a method can catch the exception if required.

All other exceptions must always be explicitly dealt with using try–catch blocks and/or throws declarations. When using these exceptions, a method can return without the exception being caught if the method has a throws declaration and either has no catch blocks or none of the catch blocks following the relevant try block are able to catch the exception. The un-caught exception is then propagated back to the calling method. If there is a finally block present it will be executed before the exception is propagated.

When an exception is propagated, any catch blocks corresponding to an active try block in the calling method get a chance to catch the exception. If one of them does catch it, then the catch block is executed and execution continues with either the statement following the try–catch block or with the matching finally block and then the next statement. Otherwise, or if there are no catch blocks, the exception is propagated back up to the next calling method. As part of the propagation, a method goes out of scope so all local variables are destroyed.

When any exception (of whatever category) reaches the top of the active method chain (the main method or a Thread run method), a default handler will catch it and terminate the current thread. If that thread is the only thread or the thread that executed main, the program will terminate. If the main and other threads are still active then the program can continue execution but is likely to be seriously compromised.

Included as part of the next section.   Examples

32.1.4 Throws Declarations

A throws declaration is required by any method that either throws or propagates an exception that   Purpose
must be dealt with explicitly (i.e. a subclass of Exception, other than RuntimeException
and its subclasses). The declaration states the type or types of exception that can be thrown from the
method.

In order to ensure that all exceptions that must be dealt with actually are, a method declaration is   Intention
required to state explicitly what exceptions might be propagated from the method. The compiler will
use the information to verify that an exception will be caught or propagated to a method that will
catch it.

Any static method, instance method, abstract method or constructor declaration can include a   Syntax
throws declaration after the parameter list and before the method body (also see Section 30.2.5,
Page 840, Section 30.2.6, Page 844 and Section 30.2.7, Page 845):

```
modifiers typeName methodName ( parameterList ) throws typeNameList {
    statementSequence
}
```

The typeNameList specifies one or more comma separated type names (class or interface names). The type of every exception that can be thrown or propagated by the method must be included. Exceptions which are caught in the method body do not need to be listed.

When working with exceptions that must be handled explicitly, a method must either catch the   Description
exception or propagate it upwards. The throws declaration states which types of exception will be
propagated.

If a method calls another method with a throws declaration one of the following must be the
case:

- The method is called from a try block which has catch blocks capable of catching all the exception types that may be thrown by the called method. The calling method requires no throws declaration with respect to the call (but may require a declaration for other calls).
- The method is called from a try block with catch blocks which catch only some of the exceptions that may be thrown. The remaining exception types are propagated and must appear in the `throws` declaration of the calling method.
- The method is called outside of a try block and all the exception types that may be thrown must appear in the calling methods `throws` declaration.

Exceptions of class `Error`, `RuntimeException` and their subclasses do not need to be declared in a `throws` declaration. Any type specified in a throws declaration must be either `Throwable` or a subtype of it.

Constructors follow the rules above but `new` expressions creating objects of the constructors class do not have to appear in a try block. However, if exceptions thrown from a constructor are not caught they will cause the current thread and possibly the program to terminate.

Examples

The following program includes throws declarations and various examples of exception propagation.

```
//  Declare two subclass of Exception to provide user defined
//  exception classes. These exceptions must be dealt with explicitly.
class MyException extends Exception {
  MyException(final String s) {
    super(s) ;
  }
}
class YourException extends Exception {
  YourException(final String s) {
    super(s) ;
  }
}
public class Exception3 {
  public Exception3() throws MyException {
  }
  //  A constructor that throws an exception
  public Exception3(final int x) throws MyException {
    throw new MyException("Constructor failed") ;
  }
  //  A method that can throw two different exceptions, requiring the
  //  throws declaration to list both.
  public void h(final int x) throws YourException, MyException {
    if (x == 1)
      throw new YourException("Thrown in h") ;
    else
      throw new MyException("Thrown in h") ;
  }
  //  This method calls h and can handle any MyException exceptions it
  //  might throw. However, it cannot catch any YourException
  //  exceptions and they will be propagated upwards requiring a
  //  throws declaration
  public void g(final int x) throws YourException {
    try {
      h(x) ;
    }
    catch (MyException e) {
      System.out.println("Caught exception in g") ;
```

```
      System.out.println(e.getMessage()) ;
    }
    finally {
      System.out.println("g finally") ;
    }
  }
  //  This method will handle any exception thrown by the call to g
  //  and does not need a throws declaration.
  public void f(final int x) {
    try {
      g(x) ;
    }
    catch (Exception e) {
      System.out.println("Caught exception in f") ;
      System.out.println(e.getMessage()) ;
    }
  }
  //  The methods r,s and t below demonstrate that an exception or
  //  type Error does not need to be handled explicitly, so no throws
  //  declarations are provided.
  public void r() {
    throw new Error("Deliberate Error") ;
  }
  public void s() {
   r() ;
  }
  //  An Error exception can still be caught using a try-catch block.
  public void t() {
    try {
      s() ;
    }
    catch (Error e) {
      System.out.println("Caught exception in t") ;
      System.out.println(e.getMessage()) ;
    }
  }
  public static void main(final String[] args) throws Exception {
    // Test the exception handling
    final Exception3 e3 = new Exception3 () ;
    e3.f(1) ;
    e3.f(2) ;
    e3.t() ;
    //  The constructor taking an int argument will generate an
    //  exception that can be caught.
    try {
      final Exception3 e3b = new Exception3 (1) ;
    }
    catch (Exception e) {
      System.out.println(e.getMessage()) ;
    }
    //  However, the new expression does not need to appear in a try
    //  block. The exception thrown by the constructor will cause the
    //  program to terminate prematurely.
    final Exception3 e3c = new Exception3 () ;
  }
}
```

32.1.5 Throw

A throw statement causes an exception to be thrown.   Purpose

Some methods need to throw exceptions in response to an error condition. Usually these are newly   Intention
created exceptions that are instances of a user-defined exception class.

Syntax

The throw keyword is followed by an expression of type `Throwable` or a subtype.

```
throw typeThrowableExpression ;
```

Description

The `throw` statement will throw an exception following the rules outlined in earlier sections. Normally, the exception is expected to be propagated to the calling method, so the method containing the `throw` has a `throws` declaration. The exception can be thrown inside a try block and caught within the same method, if necessary.

Usually an exception is created using a `new` expression as part of the `throw` statement, e.g.:

```
throw new Exception("Gone wrong") ;
```

A `throw` statement can also be used to re-throw an exception that has already been caught. This allows more than one method in the active method chain to deal with the exception, perhaps with each doing its part to restore the state of the program so it can continue safely after the exception has been handled.

An exception can be re-thrown directly from a catch block:

```
try {
  f() ;
}
catch (Exception e) {
  throw e ; // re-throw exception
}
```

The principle use of `throw` is for methods in library and support classes to notify clients that a method call has failed, typically when a library class object has been misused by the client (for example, if the client tries to pop a value off an empty stack). The presence of the throw statement in the library method forces the programmer working on the client to consider the possibility of a call to the method failing and making provision for the failure using a try–catch block. Part 2 shows a number of data structure classes that use and throw exceptions.

Examples

The following example (and that in the last section) shows `throw` statements in use.

```
public class Exception4 {
  //  Throw an exception and catch it in the same method.  This may or
  //  may not be useful!
  public void f() {
    try {
      throw new Exception("thrown in f") ;
    }
    catch (Exception e) {
      System.out.println(e.getMessage()) ;
    }
  }
  //  Method just throws an exception that must be handled.  Do nct
  //  handle it here so must include a throws declaration.
  public void g() throws Exception {
    throw new Exception("thrown in g") ;
  }
  public void h() throws Exception {
    try {
      g() ;
    }
    catch (Exception e) {
      //  Print a stack trace to see the active method chain
      e.printStackTrace() ;
```

```
            // Reset stack trace so that it starts from here
            e. fillInStackTrace() ;
            // Re-throw the exception to let another method in the active
            // method chain handle it.
            throw e ;
        }
    }
    // Catch the exception and prevent further propagation.
    public void k() {
        try {
            h() ;
        }
        catch (Exception e) {
            e.printStackTrace() ;
        }
    }
    // Some extra methods to deepen the stack trace.
    public void x() {
        k() ;
    }
    public void y() {
        x() ;
    }
    public static void main(final String[] args) {
        final Exception4 e4 = new Exception4() ;
        e4.f() ;
        e4.y() ;
    }
}
```

The output from this program (providing the standard error stream is visible for the `printStackTrace` method) is:

```
thrown in f
java.lang.Exception: thrown in g
        at Exception4.g(Exception4.java:23)
        at Exception4.h(Exception4.java:30)
        at Exception4.k(Exception4.java:47)
        at Exception4.x(Exception4.java:58)
        at Exception4.y(Exception4.java:63)
        at Exception4.main(Exception4.java:70)
java.lang.Exception: thrown in g
        at Exception4.h(Exception4.java:38)
        at Exception4.k(Exception4.java:47)
        at Exception4.x(Exception4.java:58)
        at Exception4.y(Exception4.java:63)
        at Exception4.main(Exception4.java:70)
```

The `printStackTrace` method is called twice so there are two stack traces starting on the lines with `java.lang.Exception: thrown in g`. Each trace shows the chain of active method calls up to `main`. Notice that the first trace starts from method `g` while the second starts from method `h`, as a result of the call to the `fillInStackTrace` method which resets the start of the trace to the current method.

32.2 Summary

This chapter has outlined the statements and keywords in the Java language for dealing with exceptions. Certain kinds of exception must always be dealt with, providing guarantees about error handling that will be enforced by the Java compiler. It has also shown that exceptions are represented by objects which are instances of exception classes. All exception classes must be a direct or indirect subclass of the library class `Throwable`, demonstrating that there is a close link between the library and the features of the Java language — one cannot be used without the other.

Exceptions provide an important mechanism for creating robust programs and will be discussed further in the next part of the book.

Self-review Question

Self-review 32.1 What is the output of the Exception1 program? Why is this the output?

Self-review 32.2 Why does the default constructor of class `Exception3` appear with an empty body in the program above? Would it make any difference if it were deleted?

Threads and Concurrency

Objectives

his chapter describes the features that Java provides to support threads. Threads allow a program to have multiple flows of control active at the same time, opening up a wide range of programming and design possibilities.

Keywords

thread

synchronized methods

synchronized statement

deadlock

livelock

33.1   Introduction

A *thread* is a flow of control in a program, usually characterized as the sequence of method calls that is made when the thread is run. All simple programs assume there is a a single thread which starts executing with the `static main` method. However, a program can use *multiple threads* of control by having an existing thread start new threads (see the case studies in Part 3). This means that at any one time there can be a number of method call sequences in existence.

Using a computer that has a single processor, the execution of threads is *interleaved* so that several threads can *appear* to be running simultaneously, allowing a program to appear to do several things at once. This is not parallel processing as only one thread is actually active at any one moment — the Java Virtual Machine (JVM) is only working on one physical processor. However, the active thread may be swapped for another so that from moment to moment different threads may be active, creating the illusion of parallel processing. This is often called *concurrent processing* or *multi-tasking*. To have true parallel processing two or more threads would have to be *simultaneously* running which would require two or more physical processors in a machine. Interestingly, there is no reason why a JVM cannot support true parallel processing and such versions will almost certainly become widely available in the future.

In order to help manage multiple threads and to decide which one should be active, threads are given *priorities*. A thread with a higher priority gets precedence over a thread with lower priority and, therefore, gets the chance to run first. When a thread stops running, or is *suspended* (or sometimes 'goes to sleep'), another thread gets a chance to run. The selection and management of threads is handled by the *thread scheduler* which maintains a queue of threads at each priority and follows a set of rules to determine which thread to *schedule* or run next. The major rule is, as noted above, to choose the thread with the highest priority, noting that there may be more than one thread at this priority, in which case the one at the front of the queue is taken.

Some implementations of the JVM will interleave threads of the *same* priority automatically (using a mechanism such as global round-robin scheduling) so that each gets a roughly equal share of running time. However, other implementations will not, meaning that same priority threads don't get an equal chance to run. This, unfortunately, means that a program using certain aspects of threads can work properly on one system but not on another. As implementations of the JVM improve, this issue will hopefully disappear.

A consequence of this priority and scheduling mechanism is that threads with low priorities may never get the chance to run at all, as there may always be a thread with a higher priority waiting. This situation is usually termed *starvation*. The programmer has to be aware of this and take steps to ensure that all threads get a chance to run often enough to do their job.

Another feature of thread priorities is that a running thread can be interrupted, or *pre-empted*, by a thread with a higher priority which starts or wakes up (comes out of its suspended state) and

note

If you have a number of machines connected via a network then distributed (but not parallel) concurrency is possible by using Remote Method Invocation (RMI). We will not cover use of this part of the J2SDK in this book since the Java technology and the various programming techniques required are topics that require a significant sized book in their own right.

wants to run. This provides an important mechanism for quickly responding to the event that caused a higher priority thread to wake up but also requires the programmer to plan carefully which threads have which priority — this is usually termed *pre-emptive multi-tasking*.

All Java programs, whether applets or applications, are actually multi-threaded, even if the code the programmer writes uses only a single thread. This is because the JVM uses threads to provide and manage various internal housekeeping activities, for example garbage collection. The thread which runs the main method of a program is just another thread that is started by the JVM. The full set of threads that a program is using can be viewed using the JDK debugger tool, `jdb`, or the equivalent in commercial environments.

A program keeps running while its original thread or any threads it generates are still in existence, even if none of the threads can be scheduled because they are all blocked or suspended for one reason or another. When all the threads in the program have terminated so does the program; the state of the 'internal' threads maintained by the JVM for runtime system management purposes are not taken into account.

Threads are useful for many purposes including the support of concurrent programming techniques. A good many of the Java library classes use threads, typically to allow slow, infrequent or disjoint activities to take place without getting in the way of the main flow of the program. For example, the AWT uses threads to allow a program's GUI to be managed and updated while the program gets on with its main task. Threads also provide solutions to problems that are otherwise difficult or impossible to program. These include having to deal with multiple asynchronous events, such as reading data from several slow network sources, without the main program being halted waiting for data to arrive.

The case studies in Part 3 show a number of examples of threads being used for similar sorts of purposes.

33.2 Class Thread

Threads are represented by instances of class `Thread` found in the library package `java.lang`. `Thread` provides a variety of methods for creating and manipulating threads.

Purpose

A thread needs to be represented in a program so that it can be used and controlled. Java takes the approach of using objects to represent threads, providing a library class to define them. Whenever a new thread is required, a new instance of `Thread` is created.

Intention

Full documentation for class `Thread` can be found in the `java.lang` section of the JDK documentation. The more important features are summarized here.

Syntax

All threads have a name which if not set explicitly will be set to an automatically generated default. Each thread is member of a *thread group* (itself an instance of the library class `ThreadGroup`) which can also be set explicitly if the default is not wanted.

Class `Thread` defines three constants denoting the maximum, minimum and default priorities of threads:

```
public final static int MIN_PRIORITY = 1 ;
public final static int NORM_PRIORITY = 5 ;
public final static int MAX_PRIORITY = 10 ;
```

Threads always have the default priority of 5 when created.

The following public constructors and methods are those which are most often used with class `Thread`:

Thread(Runnable) — create a thread object given a reference to an instance of a class that implements the `Runnable` interface.

Thread(Runnable, String) — as above but give the thread an explicit name.

static native Thread **currentThread**() — return a reference to the thread object that controls the currently executing thread. This allows any piece of code to determine which thread is executing it.

static native void **yield**() — cause the thread to be re-scheduled in order to allow another thread to be scheduled. The yielding thread will not restart until the it gets scheduled according to the scheduler rules.

static native void **sleep**(long) throws InterruptedException — cause the thread to be marked as not re-schedulable for the number of milliseconds given in the argument. This will permit another thread to start running. There is no guarantee that the suspended thread will be able to continue immediately after it 'wakes up' as another thread of the same or higher priority may be running.

A sleeping thread may be interrupted by an active thread, which will cause an `InterruptedException` to be thrown. For this reason, sleep has to be called within a try-catch block. A sleeping thread also retains any locks that it holds on objects.

final String **getName**() — return the string name of the thread.

final String **getPriority**() — return the priority of the thread.

final native boolean **isAlive**() — return `true` if the thread has been started and has not yet terminated.

final void **join**() throws InterruptedException — when called for *another* thread object, the current thread will wait until the other thread terminates before continuing. This allows threads to join in the sense that one waits for another to finish. A waiting thread can be interrupted, in which case an `InterruptedException` is thrown.

void **run**() — starting a new thread results in a call to the run method which acts as the equivalent of a program's main function for a thread. To be of any use, subclasses of Thread must override this method, as the default does nothing. If the run method terminates, the thread terminates.

final void **setPriority**(int) — set the priority of the thread. The priority must not be less than MIN_PRIORITY or greater than MAX_PRIORITY.

native synchronized void **start**() — called to start a thread executing, making the thread alive and schedulable. A thread can only be started once, subsequent calls to start won't do anything.

In addition to the methods declared in class Thread, there are also thread related methods inherited from class Object that can be called for any object of any class. These methods are all public and also final, so cannot be overridden. They are used to allow simple communication between threads.

void **notify**() throws IllegalMonitorStateException — wake up one of the threads that is waiting to return from calling the wait method (see below) on the current object. The thread must obtain the object lock if necessary and be scheduled before continuing execution. The notify method can only be called by the thread that holds the object lock. If no threads are waiting then notify simply returns.

void **notifyAll**() throws IllegalMonitorStateException — wake up all the threads that are waiting to return from calling the wait method on the current object. A thread must obtain the object lock if necessary and be scheduled before continuing execution. The notifyAll method can only be called by the thread that holds the object lock. If no threads are waiting then notifyAll simply returns.

void **wait**() — cause the current thread to wait until notified by another thread to stop waiting using the notify or notifyAll methods. When the wait method is called, the calling thread releases its lock on the current object and has to re-obtain it to continue after being woken up.

Threads can be created using an instance of a class that implements the Runnable interface (see description below). This interface declares one abstract method:

```
public interface Runnable {
   public abstract void run();
}
```

Class Thread can be used in two ways:

Description

- By declaring a subclass of Thread that overrides the run method. When an instance of the subclass is created and the start method called, a new thread will begin running by first calling the run method.

```
class MyThread extends Thread {
  ...
  public void run() {
     ... // Code to implement whatever thread does
  }
```

```
      ...
    }
  ...
    MyThread t = new MyThread () ; // Create a new thread with ...
                                   // ... default priority.
    t.start() ; // Start the new thread by calling the run method.
```

- By declaring a class implementing the `Runnable` interface, so that it overrides the abstract `run` method declared in the interface. The class does not have to be a subclass of `Thread`. A new thread is started by first creating a new `Thread` object having passed an instance of the runnable class to the `Thread` constructor, and then calling the `start` method of the thread object. This results in thread creation, followed by a call to the `run` method of the runnable class. The thread terminates when `run` terminates.

```
  class MyThreadedClass implements Runnable {
  ...
    public void run() {
      ... // Code to implement whatever this thread is to do
    }
    ...
  }
  ...
    Thread t = new Thread (new MyThreadedClass ()) ;
    t.start() ;
```

In both cases, a new thread only actually begins executing when scheduled by the thread scheduler. This means that a new thread doesn't necessarily start executing immediately after creation and may never execute anything if poor design results in higher priority threads always grabbing all the processor time.

There is no difference between the runtime behaviour of threads whether using subclasses of `Thread` or instances of `Thread` holding an object implementing the `Runnable` interface The distinction is, however, important at design time. A subclass of `Thread` cannot be a subclass of any other class as Java only supports inheritance from a single superclass. This means that subclasses of `Thread` can only be used where no other class needs to be inherited from. Otherwise, a class needs to implement `Runnable`, allowing it to inherit as required.

Class `Thread` provides another example of the close integration between the Java language and its libraries. Threads require both library and language features to work correctly.

Examples

The first example illustrates a simple subclass of `Thread`, showing an overridden `run` method. A single thread is created and started which displays a sequence of 25 messages. The main control flow (executed by the default program thread) also displays a sequence of twenty five messages. Both the new thread and main program thread display their priorities which should be the same default of five. As both threads run at the same priority, the actual output from the program may vary depending on which JVM is used to run it. A JVM that supports pre-emptive multi-tasking of same priority threads will display both sets of messages interleaved with one another. Otherwise, one set of messages will appear before the other.

```
  public class ThreadTest1 extends Thread {
    //  Method to display a message 25 times.
    public void message(final String s) {
      for (int i = 0 ; i < 25 ; i++) {
```

```
      System.out.println(s + ": " + (i+1)) ;
    }
  }
  // Run method must be overridden and will be called when the thread
  // is started.
  public void run() {
    System.out.println("Thread priority is: " + getPriority()) ;
    message("Output from Thread") ;
  }
  public static void main(final String[] args) {
    // Create one object to run as a separate thread and one object
    // to be run by the main program (the default program thread).
    final Thread t = new ThreadTest1 () ;
    final ThreadTest1 test = new ThreadTest1 () ;
    // Note how a reference to the current thread is obtained using a
    // static method of class Thread.
    System.out.println("Main program thread priority is:" +
                        Thread.currentThread().getPriority()) ;
    // Start the new thread
    t.start() ;
    test.message("Output from main program") ;
  }
}
```

The interleaved output of this program may look like this (it will vary from system to system depending on the properties and speed of the JVM used):

```
Main program thread priority is:5
Output from main program: 1
Output from main program: 2
Output from main program: 3
Thread priority is: 5
Output from Thread: 1
Output from main program: 4
Output from main program: 5
Output from Thread: 2
Output from Thread: 3
Output from main program: 6
Output from main program: 7
Output from Thread: 4
Output from Thread: 5
Output from Thread: 6
Output from Thread: 7
...
```

The next example illustrates the use of the Runnable interface by passing an instance of a class that implements Runnable to a Thread constructor. The program acts as a very simple clock, printing out the time once per second. It also shows the use of the Thread class sleep method. Note that the program doesn't terminate when the end of the main method is reached as there is still a thread running.

```
import java.util.Date ;
public class ThreadTest2 implements Runnable {
  // Display the current time every second, repeating forever.
  public void run() {
    while (true) {
      System.out.println(new Date ()) ;
      // Wait 1 second by calling sleep, which has to be in a try
      // block. Any exception thrown is caught and ignored.
      try {
        Thread.currentThread().sleep(1000) ;
      }
      catch (InterruptedException e) { }
```

```
      }
    }
    public static void main(final String[] args) {
      final Thread t = new Thread (new ThreadTest2 ()) ;
      t.start() ;
      System.out.println("Main program done") ;
    }
  }
```

The clock could be stopped after 10 seconds by replacing the main method as is done in the program below which simply sleeps and then calls the stop method on the thread.

```
import java.util.Date ;
public class ThreadTest3 implements Runnable {
  // Control flag used to determine when to terminate the thread.
  private boolean done = false ;
  //  Display the current time every second, repeating forever.
  public void run() {
    while (! done) {
      System.out.println(new Date ()) ;
      //  Wait 1 second by calling sleep, which has to be in a try
      //  block. Any exception thrown is caught and ignored.
      try {
        Thread.currentThread().sleep(1000) ;
      }
      catch (InterruptedException e) { }
    }
  }
  // Method to call to terminate the thread.
  public void terminate() {
    done = true ;
  }
  public static void main(final String[] args) {
    ThreadTest3 thread = new ThreadTest3 () ;
    final Thread t = new Thread (thread) ;
    t.start() ;
    try {
      Thread.currentThread().sleep(10000) ;
    }
    catch (InterruptedException e) { }
    thread.terminate() ;
  }
}
```

The next program creates and starts an array of threads, and illustrates the use of join to enable the main program thread to wait until all the other threads finish.

```
class Calculate extends Thread {
  private int id ;
  public Calculate(final int i) {
    id = i ;
  }
  // Do some sort of calculation
  public void run() {
    System.out.println("Calculation "
                        + id + " started") ;
    int x = 2 ;
    for (int n = 0 ; n < 1000000 ; n++) {
      x = x * 2 / 2 ;
    }
    System.out.println("Calculation "
                        + id + " done") ;
  }
}
public class ThreadTest4 {
```

```
       public static void main(final String[] args) {
         //  Create an array of threads and start each one.
         final Thread t[] = new Thread[25] ;
         for (int i = 0 ; i < 25 ; i++) {
           t[i] = new Calculate (i) ;
           t[i].start() ;
         }
         //  Join to each thread in order, so that the main program thread
         //  does not terminate until all the threads have finished.
         for (int i = 0 ; i < 25 ; i++) {
           try {
             t[i].join() ;
             System.out.println("Calculate " + i
                                 + " joined") ;
           }
           catch (InterruptedException e) { }
         }
       }
     }
```

33.3 Synchronized Methods

Methods that change the state of an object need to be protected from two or more separate threads trying to execute the same method at the same time. A synchronized method can only be executed by a thread if the thread first obtains a lock on the object the method is called for.

Purpose

By default there is nothing to prevent two or more threads trying to assign a value to the same variable at the roughly same time (subject to the constraints of thread scheduling). The variable will be left holding the result of the assignment made by the *last* thread to complete, while the result of the other assignments will be over written and lost. Multiple threads calling a method that changes the state of an object magnify the problem, as often the statements in the method body will assign to more than one variable and call methods on other objects. If two or more threads are scheduled so that they are all executing the same method on the same object, the assignments made by each thread may become interleaved, resulting in the state of the object being corrupted.

Intention

Moreover, the same problem can occur if multiple threads call *different* methods on the same object at roughly the same time, as any one of the threads can perform an assignment that conflicts with the other threads. Worse still, a method call can be corrupted even if it doesn't change the state of an object when, while it is being executed, some other thread does change the state.

To overcome these problems a mechanism is needed to be able to guarantee that once a method is being executed by one thread, no other thread can also execute any method for the same object that might possibly cause a conflict. This guarantee is obtained by declaring all potentially conflicting methods of a class to be `synchronized`. Before a synchronized method can be executed, a thread first has to obtain permission in the form of a lock on the object the method is called for. Conflicts are then avoided as only one thread can be executing a synchronized method for the object while a lock is held.

Syntax

Instance and class methods can be declared with the `synchronized` modifier (see Section 30.2.5, Page 840 and Section 30.2.6, Page 844).

Description

Once created, all threads run within the same program and have access to any object a reference can be obtained for, leading to the likelihood of conflicts between threads as outlined above. The solution to the problem is based on the use of object locks. Each object has a *lock* (a token) that can be held by only one thread at any one time.

When a thread executes a call to a method that has been declared as `synchronized`, it first tries to obtain the lock for the object the method has been called for. If the lock is obtained, the thread goes ahead and executes the method, retaining the lock until the method call returns. If the lock cannot be obtained, the thread is blocked and will be suspended. When the lock is released, a blocked thread gets a chance to obtain the lock but only when the thread scheduler gives the thread another opportunity to run.

A thread that holds an object lock can call other `synchronized` methods on the same object without releasing and re-obtaining the lock.

Once a thread is holding an object lock it will only release it when either the execution of a synchronized methods ends and the caller was not itself a synchronized method called for the same object, or the `wait` method is called. Once the object lock has been claimed, no other thread can execute any synchronized methods for that object.

It is also possible to have synchronized static methods. As these methods are not called for a particular object, it is not possible to obtain an object lock. Instead, each class has a *class lock* which takes the place of an object lock. Before a synchronized static method is executed, the calling thread must first obtain the class lock. Apart from this, synchronized static methods behave in much the same as synchronized instance methods.

Care has to be taken that the use of synchronized methods does not lead to situations such as *deadlock* where all threads get blocked trying to obtain locks held by other threads. For example, consider the following two methods:

```
// Declared in class A
public synchronized void f(B b) {
  b.x() ;
}
// Declared in class B
public synchronized void g(A a) {
  a.y() ;
}
...
  A a = new A() ;
  B b = new B() ;
  ...
  //In thread 1
  a.f(b) ;
  ...
  // In thread 2
  b.g(a) ;
```

If a thread executes a call to method `f` for a class `A` object then first it must obtain the object lock. Once the method is being executed the same thread must obtain the lock on a class `B` object to make the call `b.x()` without releasing the lock it already holds. A similar situation applies to the call of `g` for a class `B` object. Both methods `f` and `g` require two locks to be obtained to successfully complete.

The problem arises if `f` and `g` are executed by two threads such that they are working with the same objects, as shown at the end of the example above. If the calls of `f` and `g` get interleaved then thread 1 could start executing method `f` and obtain a lock on `a`, while thread 2 could have already started executing method `g`, obtaining a lock on `b` but having been suspended before reaching the method call `a.y()`. At that point, neither thread can proceed as each is waiting for a lock held by another, and deadlock has occurred.

Deadlock can be hard to detect as there could be three or more threads involved and it may only occur when the thread scheduling happens to occur in a particular order and at a particular time relative to the method calls. In general, the only way to avoid deadlock is through careful design and avoiding method calls that might cause conflicts. Debugging programs where deadlock occurs is notoriously difficult, so it's best not to let the problem happen in the first place!

A class that is designed so that its objects work properly in the presence of multiple threads, is known as a *thread-safe class*. Typically, most, if not all, its public methods will be synchronized, unless a method is very simple and won't be affected by the object changing state due to another thread. If making a complete method synchronized is too unwieldy then a method can use synchronized statements, as described in the next sub-section.

Examples

The first example illustrates the difference between using synchronized methods and ordinary methods. The methods `f` and `g` both increment two instance variables which are both initialized to zero before each test the program performs is started. As `g` is synchronized it offers the guarantee that the instance variables will always hold the same value, as both start with the same value and are incremented together in the same method. The method `f`, however, is not synchronized and the thread executing it can be interrupted, allowing the values of the two instance variables to diverge. Note that this example uses member classes and priority 8 threads to guarantee that the lower priority thread gets pre-empted.

```
public class ThreadTest6 {
  private int i = 0 ;
  private int j = 0 ;
  //  Declare a set of member classes to create threads calling
  //  different test methods with different pauses.
  class MyThread1 extends Thread {
    public void run() {
      for (int i = 0 ; i < 10 ; i++) {
        g() ;
      }
    }
  }
  class MyThread2 extends Thread {
    public void run() {
      setPriority(8) ;
```

```
        for (int i = 0 ; i < 10 ; i++) {
          g() ;
          pause(700) ;
        }
    }
}
class MyThread3 extends Thread {
  public void run() {
    for (int i = 0 ; i < 100 ; i++) {
      f(500) ;
    }
  }
}
class MyThread4 extends Thread {
  public void run() {
    setPriority(8) ;
    for (int i = 0 ; i < 150 ; i++) {
      f(100) ;
      pause(200) ;
    }
  }
}
//  Package up call to sleep in an easier to use method.
public void pause(final int n) {
  //  Pause for a semi-random time
  int r = (int)(Math.random() * n) ;
  try {
    Thread.currentThread().sleep(r) ;
  }
  catch (InterruptedException e) {}
}
//  Unsynchronized method. Threads can be interleaved when running
//  this.
public void f(int p) {
  i++ ;
  pause(p) ;
  j++ ;
  System.out.println("method f: "
                      + ((i==j)? "Same" : "Different")) ;
}
//  Threads cannot be interleaved when executing this method.
public synchronized void g() {
  i++ ;
  j++ ;
  System.out.println("method g: "
                      + ((i==j)? "Same" : "Different")) ;
}
// Run the tests
public void go() {
  //  Call the synchronized method and note that the variables i and
  //  j never diverge.
  System.out.println("Calling method g") ;
  Thread t1 = new MyThread1() ;
  Thread t2 = new MyThread2() ;
  i = 0 ;
  j = 0 ;
  t1.start() ;
  t2.start() ;
  try {
    t1.join() ;
    t2.join() ;
  }
  catch (InterruptedException e) {}
  //  Call the unsynchronized method and note that i and j can
  // diverge.
  System.out.println("Calling method f") ;
```

```
        t1 = new MyThread3() ;
        t2 = new MyThread4() ;
        i = 0 ;
        j = 0 ;
        t1.start() ;
        t2.start() ;
    }
    public static void main(final String[] args) {
        final ThreadTest6 shared = new ThreadTest6() ;
        shared.go() ;
    }
}
```

The example below shows a very simple thread safe queue class with two synchronized methods. The `get` method uses the `wait` method inherited from object to cause a thread to wait if an attempt is made to read from an empty queue. The `put` method always calls `notify` when adding an element to a previously empty queue, so that a waiting method gets woken up to get the element. Notice that the call to `wait` is in a loop, as it is possible that before the waiting thread gets a lock on the queue object, another thread will do so and grab the waiting queue element. This is a side-effect of the `wait` method causing a thread to release its lock and is something that needs to be carefully planned for.

```
import com.objectspace.jgl.Array ;
public class SimpleQueue {
    private Array q = new Array () ;
    public synchronized void add(final Object o) {
        q.add(o) ;
        //  If queue was empty then let a waiting method know there is now
        //  something available.
        if (q.size() == 1) {
            notify() ;
        }
    }
    public synchronized Object get() {
        while (q.size() == 0) {
            try {
                wait() ;
            }
            catch (InterruptedException e) {}
        }
        Object o = q.get(0) ;
        q.remove(0) ;
        return o ;
    }
}
```

The classes developed in Part III provide many more examples of synchronized methods.

33.4 Synchronized Statement

A synchronized statement allows an individual statement (including a compound statement) to be protected by an object lock, which must be obtained before the statement is executed.

Purpose

Synchronized statements are similar in behaviour to synchronized methods, except they work at a finer grain by only locking a statement and not a full method, and also specify which object to obtain

Intention

the lock on rather than the object a method is called for. This allows additional flexibility and reduces the scope of an object lock which can be useful.

Syntax

The synchronized statement has the form:

synchronized (*objectReference* **)** *statement*

The statement can be a compound statement.

Description

The synchronized statement works by the thread first obtaining the lock on the object referenced by the value of the parenthesized expression. If the lock is obtained, the statement is executed and the lock released. Otherwise, the thread is blocked and forced to wait for the lock to become available again.

Examples

The program below uses a `synchronized` statement.

```
public class ThreadTest7 {
  private int[] vals = new int[100] ; {
    for (int i = 0 ; i < 100 ; i++) {
      vals[i] = i ;
    }
  }
  class MyThread extends Thread {
    public void run() {
      for (int i = 0 ; i < 99 ; i++) {
        synchronized (vals) { // ensure exclusive access to vals.
          vals[i] += vals[i+1] ;
        }
      }
    }
  }
  public void go() {
    Thread t1 = new MyThread() ;
    Thread t2 = new MyThread() ;
    t1.start() ;
    t2.start() ;
    try {
      t1.join() ;
      t2.join() ;
    }
    catch (InterruptedException e) {}
    for (int i = 0 ; i < 100 ; i++) {
      System.out.print(vals[i] + " ") ;
    }
  }
  public static void main(final String[] args) {
    final ThreadTest7 t7 = new ThreadTest7() ;
    t7.go() ;
  }
}
```

33.5 Summary

This chapter has covered the basic details of how threads work and how they are implemented by Java. The Java language provides two features, synchronized methods and synchronized statements, that need to be primitive to the language, while everything else comes from various classes in the Java class library, notably class `Thread`.

The use of threads is an important aspect of Java programming and many non-trivial programs can or need to make use of them. Java tries to make using threads as straightforward as possible but there is still a strong reliance on the programmer to carefully design programs so that they run correctly when using threads.

This chapter completes the detailed description of the Java programming language. Although Java is simpler than some languages, notably C++, it still has a large number of features and usage rules. Reading about the language can only take the learner so far; there is no substitute for real programming practice. It is often the case that particular language features and rules are really only understood after they have been used for real a few times.

Self-review Exercises

Exercise 33.1 Would removing the synchronized statement, and just leaving the statement body, ever make any difference to the execution of the program TestThread7?

Programming Exercises

Exercise 33.2 Re-write program TheadTest4 to include a thread running at a higher priority that periodically runs and displays the status of each `Calculate` thread.

Exercise 33.3 Rewrite the following program so that `PrimeFilter` extends `Thread` and each filter object runs as a separate thread. Think very carefully about how the filter objects have to communicate and how the run method might work.

```
// Class to represent a filter object.
class PrimeFilter {
  private final int prime ; // Prime number held by filter object.
  private PrimeFilter next ;  // Reference to next filter object.
  // Initializer new filter to hold given prime number.
  public PrimeFilter(final int i) {
    prime = i ;
    System.out.println(prime + " is prime") ;
  }
  //  Process the argument to see if it is divisible by the prime held
  //  by the current object. If it is then it can be rejected,
  //  otherwise it is passed on, creating a new filter if necessary.
  public void process(final int i) {
    if ((i % prime) != 0) {
      if (next != null) {
        next.process(i) ;
      } else  {
        next = new PrimeFilter (i) ;
      }
    }
  }
```

```
      }
    }
  public class Sieve {
    public static void main(final String[] args) {
      PrimeFilter two = new PrimeFilter (2) ;
      for (int i = 3 ; i < 10000 ; i += 2) {
        two.process(i) ;
      }
    }
  }
```

Exercise 33.4 Write a test program to test the `SimpleQueue` class and demonstrate that it works correctly.

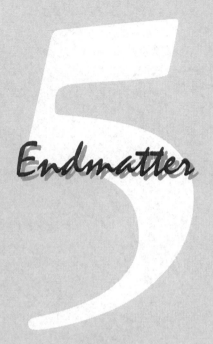

Endmatter

Objectives

This part of the book contains all the bits and pieces that were felt to be appropriate for the book but which did not fit elsewhere — the various appendices, the bibliography and the index.

Contents

Part 5

Glossary

We provide here short definitions of a number of the jargon terms used in object-oriented analysis, design and programming. Only a few of these terms are actually specific to Java, most being in general use.

Abstract Class — a class that partially implements a type by providing an incomplete set of declarations. An abstract class is designed to be inherited from and cannot have instance objects.

Abstract Method — a method declaration that acts as a place holder by declaring the method name, return type and argument types. No method body is specified.

Abstraction — a description of a concept that supplies the generalities but excludes the unnecessary detail.

Abstract Data Type or **ADT** — a formal or semi-formal specification of a type consisting of a name, a set of operations and an algebraic description of the behaviour of the operations.

Actual Parameter or **Actual** — an alternative term for method parameter value.

Abstract Window Toolkit or **AWT** — part of the Java class library that is used for implementing graphical user interfaces.

Aggregation — a design term meaning that an object is composed of or constructed from a group of some other objects such that the entire collection represents a whole. Aggregation relationships are specified between classes and reflected by their instance objects.

Algorithm — a step-by-step description of a method for solving a well defined problem.

Analysis — the process of identifying, modelling and describing what a system does and how it works.

Architecture Neutral — with respect to Java, the capability of running exactly the same Java executable program on different machines without needing to be aware of the hardware characteristics of any machine.

Argument — a value supplied to a method to initialize a parameter variable when the method is called.

Argument List — a list of values given to a method for it to initialize its parameters.

Array — a kind of container object consisting of a indexed sequence of values.

Assignment — storing a representation of a value into a variable.

Association — a relationship between two classes such that an instance of one class references an instance of the other class.

Associativity — see *Operator Associativity*.

Binary — a base 2 representation using 1s and 0s. Virtually all computers work with binary representations of values.

Binding — the activity of associating a name used in a program text with a specific variable or method. (See *Dynamic Binding*, *Static Binding*.)

Black Box Testing — testing of a class or component based only on its interface without knowing its internal structure.

Boolean — a value that is true or false.

Bytecode — a low level instruction or instruction argument used to represent Java code after it has been compiled. The JVM interprets bytecodes in order to run a Java program.

Call-by-Reference — a term sometimes used when an object reference is passed as a method parameter. The reference is copied (call by value) but the referenced object is not.

Call-by-Value — a method call where all parameter variables are initialized as copies of the actual parameter values supplied in the method call. All parameter passing in Java is by value.

Call Graph — a graph representing the flow of control through a program in terms of method calls.

Cast — explicitly change the type of an expression using a cast expression.

Class — an implementation of an abstract data type in terms of variables and methods. A class has instance objects which represented values of the type.

Class Diagram — a picture constructed using a semi-formal diagrammatic notation to visualize and document the relationships between classes in a system.

Class Hierarchy — a collection of classes organized in terms of superclass and subclass relationships.

Class Library — an organized collection of classes providing a set of reusable abstractions and components.

Client Class — a class that makes use of the services of another class.

Clone — make a copy of an object.

Cohesive — a way of describing a class that has tightly integrated parts, each of which contributes to describing the same abstraction.

Compile or **Compiling**— the name given to the process of translating source code into bytecodes.

Compiler — the tool that translates source code into bytecodes. The J2SDK compiler is called `javac`.

Compound Statement — a container statement consisting of a sequence of other statements and declarations. In Java, braces (i.e. { and }) are used to delimit a compound statement.

Conformance — see *Type Conformance*.

Concrete Class — a class designed to have instance objects.

Constructor — a method used to initialize the state of a new object.

Container — a class implementing a data structure that holds a collection of objects. Also used to denote a GUI component that contains a collection of other GUI components.

Coupling — a measure of the degree to which one object or component depends on another. Low coupling minimizes the dependencies and is an indication of good design.

Debugger — a tool to aid in locating errors in a program: `jdb` is supplied as part of the J2SDK. A debugger can set breakpoints, single step through a program and inspect the state of variables.

Debugging — the activity of locating and removing errors in a program, using tools such as a debugger.

Declaration — introduces a name into a program, along with its associated type. In Java, variables, methods and classes must all be declared.

Deep Copy — make a copy of an object and all the other objects it references, and all the objects they reference, and so on. A 'recursive' copy of an object.

Definition — alternative term for a declaration.

Design — the activity of defining how a program can be structured and implemented.

Design Pattern — a general description of the solution to a well established problem using an arrangement of classes and objects.

Dynamic Binding — binding of a method name to a method body performed while a program is running, as opposed to when the program is compiled.

Encapsulation — the localization and protection of the internal features and structure of an object.

Event — a trigger or signal indicating that some action has occurred. Usually associated with input events for graphical user interfaces (e.g., a mouse click).

Exception — an unexpected event indicating that a program has failed in some way. Exceptions are represented by exception objects.

Exception Handling — the activity of responding to an exception. Java provides `try` and `catch` blocks to handle events.

Execute — cause a program to be interpreted by loading it and stepping through the instruction sequence.

Expression — a sub-part of a statement that denotes a value. For example, the arithmetic expression '1+2' denotes the value 3. In Java, any legal syntactic construct that denotes a value is an expression.

Framework — the reusable and usually abstract core structure of an application, consisting of a number of classes and interfaces providing a partial implementation of the core features of a set of related programs.

Formal Parameter or **Formal** — a parameter variable declaration in a method parameter list.

Function — a mathematical construct that may be applied to values and returns a result. Non-void methods can implement functions.

Function Object — an object that packages a function, allowing the function to be both called and treated as though it were an object.

Garbage Collection — the process of going through the state of a running program and removing any objects that are no longer referenced from anywhere else.

Glass Box Testing — a strategy of testing which exercises all branches of the call graph of a method or program.

Graphical User Interface or **GUI** — an interface to a program that is implemented using graphics, windows, menus, and so on, that may be manipulated with a mouse.

Integer — a whole number (i.e. not a real number containing a decimal point), such as -3, 0, 2, 10, 2001. Integers can be represented in a Java program in two ways: using the primitive type `int` or using an instance of class `Integer`.

J2SDK — the Java 2 Software Development Kit distributed by Sun, providing the core set of tools for writing Java programs. It contains the Java class libraries, the Java compiler (`javac`) and a collection of other utilities. Versions are numbered in sequence with 1.2.2 and 1.3 being recent releases (both are implementations of the Java 2 Platform).

Java 2 Platform — the preferred name for the most recent version of the Java environment and libraries.

JDK — see J2SDK.

JVM — Java Virtual Machine. A software emulation of a machine that can execute Java bytecodes. It provides an implementation of the processor, memory system and interfaces to hardware devices. All Java programs are compiled to bytecodes which are executed by a `JVM`.

Keyword — in Java, a keyword (or reserved word) is a word defined as part of the programming language (see Appendix D, Page 957 for the full list). A keyword name may not be used for any other purpose.

Identifier — a name of a package, class, interface, method or variable.

Imperative Programming — programming based on the principles of instruction or command sequences, selection, repetition, variables and assignment. At its core, Java is an imperative language.

Implementation — the activity of writing, compiling, testing and debugging the code of a program.

Inheritance — a relationship between classes where a subclass extends a superclass.

Inner Class — a term used to describe a class declared within another class declaration.

Instance Object — an instance object is a representation of a value of the type implemented by its class. The class declares a set of instance variables that form the structure of an object and a set of methods that can be called on an object.

Instance Method — a method (or procedure) declared by a class to be called for its instance objects (or those of subclasses).

Instance Variable — a variable declared by a class to be part of every instance object of the class and its subclasses.

Interpreter — a software tool or program that reads a sequence of instructions and carries them out. The Java Virtual Machine (JVM) is an interpreter of java bytecodes, providing a software emulation of a machine processor.

Layout Manager — an object responsible for determining the size and position of GUI components within a GUI container.

Listener — an object providing one or more listener methods that respond to an event. Listeners are associated with (or registered with) components.

Member Class — the general term used to describe a class declared within another class declaration.

Message — a request sent to an object asking it to perform a named operation. The message includes a name and an optional parameter list.

Method — see *Instance Method* and *Static Method.*

Method Lookup — the activity of determining which method is executed when a method call is made. Lookup involves searching up through the current class and its superclasses until a match is found.

Method Object — an object that packages a method, allowing the method to be both called and treated as though it were an object.

Nested Class — a static class declared within another class. Also called a nested top level class in Java.

Network — the infrastructure that allows computers to communicate with each other.

Networking — the ability of computers and computer programs to communicate with one another across a network.

Object — see *Instance Object.*

Object-Oriented Analysis or **OOA** — analysis performed in terms of objects, classes and class relationships.

Object-Oriented Design or **OOD** — design performed in terms of objects, classes and class relationships.

Operator — a fundamental operation built into the Java language (for example, + and -).

Operator Associativity — the order in which to evaluate operators of equal precedence within an expression. Left associativity results in left-to-right evaluation, right associativity in right-to-left.

Operator Precedence — the priority of an operator within an expression used to determine in which order operators will be evaluated.

Overload — provide two or methods with the same name in the same scope, distinguished by having different parameter lists.

Override — where a subclass method redefines and specializes a method of the same type inherited from a superclass.

Package — a named unit of scope containing a set of class declarations. A package allows a collection of classes to be grouped together, providing a unit of encapsulation above that of classes.

Parameter — Formal parameters are specified in a method declaration, actual parameters are supplied in a method call.

Parameter List — the list of values given to a method for it to initialize its parameters or the list of parameter variable declarations .

Parameter Variable — a variable declared within a formal parameter list of a method and initialized when the method is called. Catch blocks also use parameter variables.

Pattern — see *Design Pattern*.

Precedence — see *Operator Precedence*.

Primitive Type — a type defined as part of the Java language, rather than one declared by a class or interface. Also called built-in types. Values of a primitive type have a direct binary representation.

Program — a series of instructions (or statements) that describe some application or activity run on a computer.

Programmer — a person who variously designs, writes, tests and debugs programs.

Programming Language — a notation used by programmers to write programs. A language has a syntax (the words and symbols used to write program code), a grammar (the rules which define a correct and meaningful sequence of words and symbols) and semantics (what code written with the language means). Java is a programming language.

Reference — a pointer to an object which is subject to strict controls on how it can be used to make sure that no unsafe operation is performed on it.

Requirements Gathering — the activity of discovering and describing what a proposed program should be required to do, particular from the program users point of view. Requirements gathering is the first stage of program development.

Run — see *Execute*.

Run-time System — the supporting code and infrastructure that a program needs in order to be run.

Scenario — an outline of a sequence of events used to describe part of the behaviour of a program.

Semantics — the set of rules that define the meaning of a syntactically valid program. Java takes an operational approach to semantics in that the behaviour and hence meaning of a program is defined by the machine the program is running on.

Shallow Copy — make a copy of an object but not of any objects that it may reference. The copy then shares references to the same objects as the original.

Software Engineering — the name given to the overall activity of gathering requirements, performing analysis and design, implementation, testing, delivery and maintenance of a program.

Source Code or **Source Text** — the text of a program before it has been compiled. The text is created and edited using an ordinary editor and contains normal, readable characters. Source code is primarily used by humans to describe programs and should therefore be made as readable and understandable as possible.

Specification — a description of the required structure and behaviour of a program.

SQL — Standard Query Language. A computer language for making queries and updates on a database.

Statement — a unit of code constructed from one or more expressions. In Java, the statement is the main building block from which code sequences are constructed. Statements are executed in the written order and are always terminated by a semicolon.

Static Binding — binding of a method name to a method body performed by the compiler by static analysis of a program text.

Static Method — a method declared by a class to be called directly without requiring an object to be called for.

Subclass — a class that inherits from or extends a superclass.

Substitutability — the ability to substitute one object for another without causing a program to fail. Substitutable objects must both implement the same type.

Subtype — a type that inherits from or extends a supertype.

Superclass — a class that is inherited from by a subclass.

Supertype — a type that is inherited from by a subtype.

Swing Set — the name of the Java library for constructing graphical user interfaces. It is a standard part of the Java 2 Platform.

Syntax — a set of rules that specify the composition of programs from keywords, symbols and characters. The syntax defines the structure of legal programs in terms of how the keywords and other characters may be written down and in what order.

Test or **Testing** — (verb) in programming terms, the activity of systematically checking that a program works correctly. A test (noun) is a description of how a specific function of a program can be checked to confirm it is working correctly. A test description should include: the purpose for doing the test, the data or initialisation required in order to perform the test, the test procedure (how the test is carried out) and the expected results. A test should always be repeatable so that it can be performed under the same conditions after a program has been modified.

Test Log — a description of the results of performing a test, typically realised as a log file (a text file containing messages generated by a program as it runs). The test log should be compared to the expected results described in a test plan to determine if a program performed as expected.

Test Plan — a complete collection of test descriptions used to test a program.

Thread — a sequence of method calls that may be run independently of other threads.

Type — denotes a set of values all sharing a representation and set of operations (such as type `int` or `String`).

Type Conformance — the relationship between types that allows a value of one type to be used where a value of another type was specified.

UML — the Unified Modeling Language, providing a standard visual notation for documenting the analysis and design of object-oriented systems.

Visual Component — an element of a GUI, such as a button or scroll-bar. Visual components have a graphical representation on a computer screen and can register listeners to respond to events.

The CRC Method

B

B.1 Introduction

This appendix outlines the CRC object-oriented analysis method. CRC is an informal object-oriented analysis and design process, principally aimed at small groups of developers (3–7 people). It works best with an incremental prototyping-based approach and emphasizes discovery by role playing and experimentation. CRC can be used for both analysis and design, and also for guiding implementation.

CRC assumes that analysis, or problem modelling, is where the problem is described and represented. Design, or solution modelling, is where a solution to the problem is discovered and represented. Implementation is where the code that makes up the working system is written and tested.

Using the CRC method is a very useful way for beginners to explore and become familiar with the basics of object-oriented development. Working through example problems in a small group provides an excellent shared learning experience, especially if the group includes a more experienced member to help guide the process and provide advice.

B.2 Basic Concepts

CRC stands for Class, Responsibility, Collaboration.

Responsibilities comprise the knowledge that a class maintains and the services it provides. For example, a bank class is responsible for maintaining a collection of bank accounts and providing a collection of access operations to use the accounts.

Collaborators are classes whose services are required to fulfil a responsibility. For example, a bank class collaborates with a bank account class in order to manipulate bank accounts. Each responsibility can be fulfilled by collaborating with zero or more collaborators.

The CRC method uses these basic ideas to find the set of classes needed to model a problem. As information about each class is discovered it is recorded on an index card as either a responsibility or collaboration. CRC information is found by the group of developers role-playing the interaction between objects and recording the results.

The method is deliberately informal and does not require computer-based tools (e.g. CASE tools) — indeed, it works best without them. The results, however, are not informal and when done well provide a good object-oriented description of the system being modelled.

As no computer-based tools are needed, the whole method is highly portable and can be used wherever the development group can meet together.

B.3 CRC Cards

CRC cards are simply $4" \times 6"$ (or metric equivalent!) index cards — the same cards that can be bought in any stationers. It is important to use cards rather than paper as they will be handled a lot as the method is applied and are more durable. It is also best to stick with the $4" \times 6"$ size as anything bigger gets too cumbersome and anything smaller tends not to have enough space to fit enough information on.

A card is laid out in the following way:

Class name:	
Superclasses:	
Subclasses:	
Responsibilities	Collaborators

The class name is at the top. The name should be chosen to accurately and unambiguously name the class. As the name could well be long lived (throughout the development process and lifetime of a program), it should be easily recognisable by whoever reads it. The names of any superclasses and subclasses are listed below the name.

The rest of the card is split into two columns, with responsibilities listed in the left-hand column and collaborators in the right-hand column.

Responsibilities are a list of knowledge the class maintains and services it provides. Each entry should be concise and descriptive, always containing an active verb. For example, a bank account class would maintain knowledge about the amount of money or balance held by the account. That responsibility would be listed as 'know balance' (i.e. the class is responsible for knowing the balance of a bank account). By convention, knowledge responsibilities are listed as 'know whatever', highlighting that the class will be responsible for maintaining that information. Services such as 'deposit money' or 'withdraw money' are also listed, corresponding to the messages that objects of the class will respond to.

A collaborator is a class whose services are needed to fulfil a responsibility. Collaborators are listed as class names and placed on the right-hand side of the card lining up with the corresponding responsibility. For example, a bank object collaborates with bank accounts objects to fulfil its deposit responsibility, so the bank account class name would appear opposite the deposit responsibility entry.

Collaborations exist only to fulfil responsibilities and should only be listed when one object of the class actually sends a message to its collaborator. Speculative collaborations are not listed. Collaborations are modelled as a one-way communication from initiator to collaborator (a message send) which may return a result.

The back of the CRC card may be used for two purposes. The first is a concise written description of the role of the class and the second is to list attributes (the front is only concerned with behaviour). Attributes represent state information stored by objects of the class. For example, a bank account may have name, account number and balance attributes.

B.4   CRC Method Process

The method focuses on creating and filling in CRC cards, each representing a class. Cards are created during informal brainstorming sessions, with the resulting set of cards forming an object model which can be documented using suitable notation (e.g. UML). This section outlines the method — a full description with examples can be found in the text book *Using CRC Cards* by Wilkinson (1995).

A session works best with around six participants. With more people the amount of communication gets too large and the process breaks down. Ideally, the group should include a combination of domain experts (i.e. users and customers) and developers, guided by an OO expert or mentor.

The general steps are as follows:

1. Create a user requirements document, including the problem statement, goals, description of operation of the system, constraints, and so on. This can be done using any appropriate method.

2. Build a preliminary list of classes. Hold a brainstorming session where everyone suggests classes based on the requirements. List potential classes on a large piece of paper or wallboard so everyone can see them. Add and remove class names as the brainstorming session evolves. As a general guide, look for names, roles, entities, abstractions and strategies. Actively filter classes, removing those which don't seem relevant. Try writing short

precise descriptions for the class abstractions to see if they are useful. Also look for class relationships.

3. Start to role play scenarios. Pick a subset of the system — typically one dealing with a specific interaction or activity, such as depositing money into a bank account. Create a CRC card for each potential class by writing the class name on the card and give each person in the group at least one card to manage. Try to allocate cards to the person who is most likely to understand the class abstraction but aim for an even distribution.

4. Next walk through a scenario verbalizing the message passing interactions that take place. As control passes from class to class, the person holding the card for the current class should be responsible for talking about the class and the behaviour of its objects, and writing on the card. As this is happening, responsibilities and collaborations will be identified and can be written on the cards. Only write down responsibilities and collaborations as they are discovered. Physically manipulate the cards to emphasize the sequence of interactions taking place (e.g. hold up cards, wave them around, put them in piles, arrange them on the table).

Other guidelines: avoid trying to work with a scenario that is too big or complicated. Choose a subset of a bigger scenario if necessary. Don't write down responsibilities or collaborations unless walking through the scenario actually identifies them. Avoid cluttering cards with assumptions and guesses or things that only might be needed. Attributes can be added but the real goal is to look for behaviour. This is responsibility driven design.

Don't be afraid to try alternatives.

If a scenario doesn't work out, back track and try again.

Write on cards using pencil so it is easy to erase what has been written when changes are made.

5. Keep walking through scenarios building up a complete class and responsibility model of the system. Larger scenarios can be built using smaller scenarios as building blocks.

6. Periodically review results and check that scenarios remain valid, especially if later scenarios make significant changes to existing classes. Always be prepared to consider alternatives and be prepared to make big changes if a better layout is found.

B.5 Problems

During this process there can be problems:

Deadlock — the group is unable to make a choice between two ways of modelling a situation. The solution is to arbitrarily pick one way (flip a coin if necessary) and see what happens. Make a record of the other approach and be prepared to return to it if the first choice doesn't work out.

Getting lost — a scenario gets too complicated. Keep scenarios specific, start with simpler (inner) scenarios and build outwards. Simple scenarios can become single steps within more complicated ones.

Procedural thinking and relapsing into data-flow mode — don't think of a class as a single thing that always exists. Classes are not transforms. Each class represents an abstraction over some kind of entity, thing or role, and may have many instances. Look for the abstractions over the system of interest — the structure, the domain, the strategy. Avoid using phrases such as 'send the message to the object' and instead talk about how 'instances of one class collaborate with instances of another class to achieve goal'.

B.6   Documentation

Once the set of class cards has been established and each card has been filled in, the result can be written up. Class, object and event diagrams can be created using an appropriate notations (such as UML). Cards can be turned into full class descriptions or directly coded.

B.7   Design

CRC design is really just a matter of continued refinement. During design the point of view moves to take into account implementation issues, such as detailed class structure (operations, member variables, and so on), GUI issues, data structure issues and overall system structure.

Further design can be done by annotating the CRC cards, by coding or by moving to a more formal OOD method. If CRC cards are used then the first design step is to take each responsibility and add to it the list of sub-responsibilities that make it up (i.e. expand the level of detail). Then methods can be derived from responsibilities and member variables from attributes.

The Online Documentation

From the very outset of the book, we refer to the J2SDK and its documentation. Without the documentation, in Section 2.10.2, Page 38, it would have been immensely difficult to discover that the class `String` had a method `compareTo` and, in Section 2.10.3, Page 41, it would have been difficult to know that method `sqrt` existed in the class `Math`. Making use of the online documentation is an integral part of programming as we keep saying regularly throughout this book. In fact, it is usually the case that all Java programmers have the documentation open alongside their program editor.

As noted in the main parts of the book, the J2SDK contains all the software and tools needed to develop and execute Java programs. In particular, it provides and documents the *class libraries*. The class libraries are organized into *packages*, each of which contains a number of classes. The classes provide a large number of pre-built components that are used when creating Java programs. This structuring is reflected in the documentation. The documentation for each J2SDK class is provided in the form of a Web page (using HTML format) that can be viewed on-screen using any Web browser.

For example, consider class `String`: This class belongs to the package `java.lang` that contains classes closely associated with the Java programming language. To find the documentation for class `String` you need to navigate through a number of Web links. If you open the browser starting with the documentation index you see the page shown in Figure C.1. Looking down the page you see a section with the title "API and Language Documentation", followed by a link labelled "Java 2 Platform API Specification". Following this link displays the page shown in Figure C.2.

note

API stands for 'Application Programmer's Interface'.

This page is split into several frames and provides access to all the packages and classes available (it is well worth bookmarking this location). Selecting the `java.lang` package link (top left frame) followed by the `String` link, or just using the `String` link directly (bottom left frame), gets to the page for the `String` class, as shown in Figure C.3.

This page gives us all the information we need about `String` to be able to use it effectively. The structure of this page is the same as for all the other pages describing classes in the J2SDK documentation. Initially there is some information about how the class fits into the overall system, then there is a summary overview of the class followed by a short-form index of all the variables and methods that can be employed on objects of type `String`. There is then a more detail listing of all the variables and methods. In this list we can find detailed information about the `compareTo` method, its parameters and its return value. The page also includes summaries of all the methods inherited from superclasses, which should not be ignored as many classes (particularly Swing classes) inherit a great deal of their implementation. Failure to check the inherited methods makes it easy to seriously underestimate what a class is capable of.

Figure C.1 Java 2 SDK documentation front page.

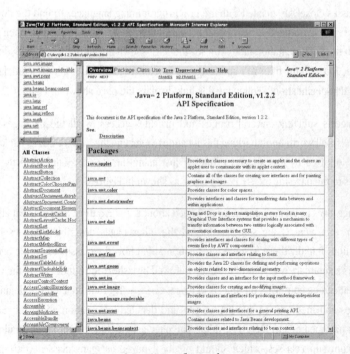

Figure C.2 API Specification front page.

Figure C.3 Class String documentation page.

At first sight the documentation can admittedly look quite intimidating, especially for beginners. However, don't be put-off and persevere. Over time, more and more will start to make sense and provide an invaluable and essential reference to Java. Skip over the parts you don't understand and come back to them later.

As well as documenting the J2SDK classes, the online documentation includes a wide range of other information, so devote time to browsing around to see what can be found — much of it is very useful at one time or another. Some links will take you to Sun's Java web site at http://java.sun.com, which contains a very extensive collection of document, tutorials and online help, as well as being the place to find out the latest news about Java and download the latest versions of the J2SDK and all its additional supporting libraries and tools. For those learning Java and how to use the Java libraries (especially Swing) the http://java.sun.com/ site has a very useful set of tutorials and tutorial trails, most of which can also be downloaded. The Swing tutorial is particularly recommended.

Java Keywords

These are the keywords used by the Java language:

abstract	default	implements	protected	throws
boolean	do	import	public	transient
break	double	instanceof	return	try
byte	else	int	short	void
case	extends	interface	static	volatile
catch	final	long	super	while
char	finally	native	switch	
class	float	new	synchronized	
const	for	package	this	
continue	if	private	throw	

In addition, some Java compilers also recognize `const` and `goto` as keywords. A few literal values have names which are also treated as keywords. These are `true`, `false` and `null`.

None of the keywords listed above can be used for any other purpose, such as naming a variable.

Writing Java Programs

E

E.1 Getting Started

The simplest and cheapest way to get started with Java is to use the free Java 2 Software Development Kit (J2SDK). This can be downloaded from http://java.sun.com/ or obtained from many other sources, often on CDROM. The J2SDK includes the `javac` compiler and the Java run-time environment that lets you run Java programs. Also included are a range of other tools, such as the `jdb` debugger, and the `javadoc` tool for generating Java documentation from documentation comments. In addition, a number of demonstration programs, complete with source code, come with the J2SDK.

As well as installing the J2SDK it is essential to install the matching documentation which comes as a separate file. Again this can be downloaded from http://java.sun.com/.

The J2SDK does not come with an editor, something which is essential if you want to type in and edit programs. Any editor capable of working with ASCII text files will do, but some are better than others. We strongly recommend the emacs editor, which can be downloaded for free from a number of GNU mirror sites.

The `javac` compiler works well but can be slow. An excellent, and much faster, alternative is the Jikes compiler available for free from IBM (see http://www.ibm.com/developerworks/opensource/). Jikes is very easy to install and its speed gives more or less instantaneous compilation of Java code. If you are working with a slow machine, then Jikes becomes essential.

Another way to get started with Java is to buy a commercial development tool or environment. One of the major advantages of such tools is that they typically include good support for code management, powerful debuggers and interactive visual GUI builders. However, for many people, especially those learning to program, the basic J2SDK tools combined with a good editor are more than sufficient and certainly a lot cheaper.

E.2 Compiling and Running a Program

This section gives an overview of how the command line tools of J2SDK are used to compile and run a Java program. This, assumes you are working with a command prompt like the one found in a UNIX terminal window or a DOS window. If you are using a programming environment, then follow the instructions for that environment.

Use your text editor to type in the source code of each class that comprises your program, not forgetting that each class is put into a separate file (unless the class is nested in another). Remember that your source code must be readable by people (especially yourself!) so use spaces to maintain the indentation, blank lines to avoid bunching too many lines of code together and comments to make clear what the code does. Properly used blank space has no affect on the speed of your program when run or the ability of the compiler to compile it.

Assuming you are creating a class called MyClass, its code would typed in and then saved to the file MyClass.java.

Next the program can be compiled by typing the command:

```
javac MyClass.java
```

Make sure that your command prompt is referring to the same directory that holds your source code file. If the compiler reports any errors then carefully check your source code, correct any mistakes and compile again. Successful compilation will result in the file MyClass.class being created, containing the compiled version of class MyClass.

If MyClass contains a main method, and you have a complete program, it can be run using the command:

```
java MyClass
```

Note that the class name only is given, with the .class extension omitted.

If you are using Jikes then you would use the command jikes *in place of* javac.

E.3   Using Classes KeyboardInput, FileInput and FileOutput

The three utility classes KeyboardInput, FileInput and FileOutput are used by a number of example programs within the book. The source code listing for the classes can be seen in Appendix F, Page 963, Appendix I, Page 971 and Appendix J, Page 975.

All three classes can be compiled and used in the same way. Taking KeyboardInput as an example, the simplest way to use the class with your programs is to do the following:

1. Copy the file KeyboardInput.java in your current working directory where your other source files are stored.

2. Compile KeyboardInput using the command:

```
javac KeyboardInput.java
```

(make sure you use the name KeyboardInput exactly, with the same upper and lower case letters). This creates a file called KeyboardInput.class. Do not delete this file until after you have finished running programs that make use of it. If you do delete it, just re-run the compilation to re-create the file.

Once KeyboardInput.class is created, it will be possible to use the class in the code you write. Create FileInput.class and FileOutput.class in the same way as above.

E.4 Using Classes DrawFrame and DrawPanel

The two utility classes DrawFrame and DrawPanel are used for the example drawing programs in Chapter 4. The source code listings can be seen in Appendix G, Page 967 and Appendix H, Page 969.

To create your own drawing program do the following:

1. Create a directory to hold your new drawing program.

2. Copy the files DrawFrame.java and DrawPanel.java into the directory.

3. Compile the files to create the .class files.

4. Write your drawing program and then run it.

tip

Keep the files for each program you write in a separate directory.

E.5 Using CLASSPATH

A better alternative to copying the utility classes .java or .class files, as described above, is to make use of the CLASSPATH environment variable or the equivalent -classpath flag (if you are using a development environment it will have its own way of managing its equivalent to CLASSPATH so check the documentation).

When a Java program is compiled or run, there needs to be access to all the .class or .jar files that contain all the classes used by the program. By default, those in the standard Java libraries or in the current directory will be found and used. Any other classes from .class or .jar files located elsewhere will be missed unless the compiler or runtime system are told where they are, and specifically what directory they are in.

It is possible to specify the locations of .class and .jar files in two ways: by listing the directories in the CLASSPATH environment variable or by using the -classpath flag in the javac or java command line. The exact syntax for specifying paths using either approach will depend on the operating system you are using, so you need to check your local documentation. When giving the path to a .jar file the name of the file should be included at the end of the path.

Using CLASSPATH or -classpath, the utility .class files can be located in a fixed directory located at some convenient place in your file store. Then the directory path name can be added to your CLASSPATH variable or given on the command line following the -classpath flag. The Java compiler or runtime system will then additionally look in the directory you specify for the .class files it needs. With this arrangement in place, you no longer need to make multiple copies of the .class files.

note

A .jar file is a Java Archive file, containing a collection of .class files. The standard Java library classes are contained in large .jar file called rt.jar.

Class KeyboardInput

This class is used by a number of the example programs to manage input from the keyboard. It encapsulates use of the standard Java input mechanisms hiding the management of exceptions: it packages the reading values of primitive types into methods, catching and dealing with any exceptions that may get thrown. If an error does occur then each method will return a default value so that no exceptions are propagated.

The reason for constructing and using this class is straightforward: Data input using the standard Java mechanisms requires the handling of exceptions but we want to get the reader of this book writing programs that input data from the user before we have covered this concept. The alternative of exposing sufficient of the exception mechanism very early on to be able to use the standard input mechanisms directly does not appeal to us. We feel that the disadvantages of introducing a class such as this to hide some of the complexity of input are far outweighed by allowing easy input early on in people's learning of Java. The tricky question is when to urge people to give up a class such as this in favour of using the standard mechanisms directly. We think the answer is as soon as exceptions have been covered.

As well as showing how to read values from the keyboard, the methods in this class also illustrate ways of converting from a string representation to values of the primitive types.

```java
import java.io.* ;
/**
 *  A simple input class to read values typed at the command line.  If
 *  an error occurs during input, any exceptions thrown are caught and
 *  a default value returned.
 *
 *  @version 1.1 1999.08.18
 *  @author Graham Roberts
 *  @author Russel Winder
 */
public class KeyboardInput {
  /**
   *  The buffered stream that works the keyboard so that we can read
   *  from it sensibly.
   */
  private final BufferedReader in =
    new BufferedReader(new InputStreamReader (System.in)) ;
  /**
   *  Read an <CODE>int</CODE> value from keyboard input.  The default
   *  return value is 0.
   */
  public final synchronized int readInteger() {
    String input = "" ;
    int value = 0 ;
    try {
      input = in.readLine() ;
    }
    catch (IOException e) { }
    if (input != null) {
      try {
        value = Integer.parseInt(input) ;
```

note

System.in *is the input stream defined by the Java run-time system. We wrap this up in a* BufferedReader *so as to be able to read a line of text easily all at once as a value of type* String.

note

Each of the classes for wrapping primitive values as objects has a method for parsing strings to construct values of the primitive type. Use these to do all the parsing.

```
    }
      catch (NumberFormatException e) { }
    }
    return value ;
  }
  /**
   *  Read a <CODE>long</CODE> value from keyboard input.  The default
   *  return value is 0L.
   */
  public final synchronized long readLong() {
    String input = "" ;
    long value = 0L ;
    try {
      input = in.readLine() ;
    }
    catch (IOException e) { }
    if (input != null) {
      try {
        value = Long.parseLong(input) ;
      }
      catch (NumberFormatException e) { }
    }
    return value ;
  }
  /**
   * Read a <CODE>double</CODE> value from keyboard input.  The
   *  default return value is 0.0.
   */
  public final synchronized double readDouble() {
    String input = "" ;
    double value = 0.0D ;
    try {
      input = in.readLine() ;
    }
    catch (IOException e) { }
    if (input != null) {
      try {
        value = Double.parseDouble(input) ;
      }
      catch (NumberFormatException e) { }
    }
    return value ;
  }
  /**
   *  Read a <CODE>float</CODE> value from keyboard input.  The
   *  default return value is 0.0F.
   */
  public final synchronized float readFloat() {
    String input = "" ;
    float value = 0.0F ;
    try {
      input = in.readLine() ;
    }
    catch (IOException e) { }
    if (input != null) {
      try {
        value = Float.parseFloat(input) ;
      }
      catch (NumberFormatException e) { }
    }
    return value ;
  }
  /**
   *  Read a <CODE>char</CODE> value from keyboard input.  The default
   *  return value is ' ' (space).
   */
```

```
      public final synchronized char readCharacter() {
        char c = ' ' ;
        try {
          c = (char)in.read() ;
        }
        catch (IOException e) {}
        return c ;
      }
      /**
       *  Read an <CODE>String</CODE> value from keyboard input.  The
       *  default return value is "" (the empty string).
       */
      public final synchronized String readString() {
        String s = "";
        try {
          s = in.readLine() ;
        }
        catch (IOException e) {}
        if (s == null) {
          s = "" ;
        }
        return s ;
      }
    }
```

The following program illustrates the class in use:

```
public class KeyboardInputTest {
  public static void main(final String[] args) {
    KeyboardInput in = new KeyboardInput() ;
    System.out.print("Type an integer: ") ;
    int n = in.readInteger() ;
    System.out.println("Integer was: " + n) ;
    System.out.print("Type a long: ") ;
    long l = in.readLong() ;
    System.out.println("Long was: " + l) ;
    System.out.print("Type a double: ") ;
    double d = in.readDouble() ;
    System.out.println("Double was: " + d) ;
    System.out.print("Type a float: ") ;
    float f = in.readFloat() ;
    System.out.println("float was: " + f) ;
    System.out.print("Type a char: ") ;
    char c = in.readCharacter() ;
    System.out.println("char was: " + c) ;
    System.out.print("Type a String: ") ;
    String s = in.readString() ;
    System.out.println("String was: " + s) ;
  }
}
```

Class DrawFrame

This class, which is used by all the example drawing programs in Chapter 4, subclasses a Swing JFrame adding some additional behaviour to provide a simple window for containing drawings. In particular, each DrawFrame has a quit button so that the application can be terminated using a mechanism independent of the window manager being used, by responding to the window closing event and quitting the application. Also, each DrawFrame has a method to enable the window it displays to be conveniently centred on the display screen.

The DrawFrame constructor is responsible for creating the basic window, making use of a Swing JPanel component as well as a JButton. The add method should be called to provide a JPanel responsible for actually drawing a picture. For the examples in the book, this is expected to be a subclass of DrawPanel (see Appendix H, Page 969), which is a subclass of JPanel.

```java
import java.awt.*;
import java.awt.event.*;
import javax.swing.*;
/**
 *  This class provides a basic window, with a quit button, that can
 *  be used to create simple GUIs.
 *
 *  @version 1.1 2000.01.07
 *  @author Graham Roberts
 *  @author Russel Winder
 */
public class DrawFrame extends JFrame {
  /**
   *  Override of the method to add a <CODE>JPanel</CODE> to the
   *  <CODE>DrawFrame</CODE> so that the <CODE>JPanel</CODE> is
   *  centred.
   */
  public void add(final JPanel panel) {
    getContentPane().add(panel, BorderLayout.CENTER) ;
  }
  /**
   *  Terminate the program when the user wants to quit.
   */
  private void quit() {
    System.exit(0) ;
  }
  /**
   *  Construct a <CODE>DrawFrame</CODE>.
   */
  public DrawFrame(final String title) {
    //  Initialize the JFrame ensuring the titlebar is set.
    super(title);
    //  Set up the quit button with it's listener.
    Button quitButton = new Button ("Quit") ;
    quitButton.addActionListener(new ActionListener () {
        public void actionPerformed(final ActionEvent e) {
          quit() ;
        }
      }) ;
    //  Put all the buttons into a JPanel.
    JPanel buttonPanel = new JPanel (new FlowLayout()) ;
```

note

JFrames *are different from other* Containers *in that each* JFrame *has an internal* Container *that holds the components. Get hold of this with the accessor* getContentPane.

```
        buttonPanel.add(quitButton) ;
        //  Create the contents of the frame. Use BorderLayout with the
        //  top (Center) part being the drawing area and the bottom
        //  (South) strip holding a quit button.
        getContentPane().setLayout(new BorderLayout()) ;
        getContentPane().add(buttonPanel, BorderLayout.SOUTH) ;
        //  Ensure that window close events from the window manager are
        //  caught and acted upon.
        addWindowListener(new WindowAdapter () {
            public void windowClosing(final WindowEvent evt) {
                quit() ;
            }
        }) ;
    }
    /**
     *  Position a window in the centre of the screen.
     */
    public void centreOnScreen() {
        Dimension displaySize = getToolkit().getScreenSize() ;
        Dimension windowSize = getSize() ;
        int x = (displaySize.width - windowSize.width) / 2 ;
        int y = (displaySize.height - windowSize.height) / 2 ;
        if (x < 0) {
            x = 0 ;
        }
        if (y < 0) {
            y = 0 ;
        }
        setLocation(x,y) ;
    }
}
```

note

In order to centre a window on the screen we ask the run-time system how big the screen is and the window how big it is so as to compute the correct positioning.

Class DrawPanel

This class, which is used in association with the `DrawFrame` class (see Appendix G, Page 967) in all the example drawing programs in Chapter 4, simply encapsulates a `JPanel` to ensure it has a default size. There are accessor methods for the size. `DrawPanel` should be subclassed to provide a panel with a `paint` method specialized to draw the picture desired. The `paint` method is inherited from a superclass of `JPanel` and is automatically called whenever the contents of the panel needs to be displayed.

The size of a drawing panel can be explicitly specified by making use of the second constructor method, which should be called using `super` from a subclass constructor (see Section 4.2, Page 92).

```
import java.awt.*;
import javax.swing.*;
/**
 *  A <CODE>JPanel</CODE> with a default size.  Subclasses must
 *  override the <CODE>paint</CODE> method which has signature:
 *
 * <PRE> public void paint(final Graphics g) </PRE>
 *
 *  @version 1.0  1999.09.04
 *  @author Graham Roberts
 *  @author Russel Winder
 */
public class DrawPanel extends JPanel {
  /**
   *  The width of the panel.
   */
  private int width = 300 ;
  /**
   *  The height of the panel.
   */
  private int height = 300 ;
  /**
   *  Default constructor, uses the default size.
   */
  protected DrawPanel() {
    setPreferredSize(new Dimension (width, height)) ;
  }
  /**
   *  Constructor for a size determined by the user.
   */
  protected DrawPanel(final int w, final int h) {
    width = w;
    height = h;
    setPreferredSize(new Dimension (width, height)) ;
  }
  /**
   *  Accessor for the width of the panel.
   */
  public int getWidth() {
    return width ;
  }
  /**
   *  Accessor for the height of the panel.
```

note

There is nothing special about 300×300 as the panel size, this was just a useful default for the examples we were constructing.

```
      */
    public int getHeight() {
      return height ;
    }
}
```

Class FileInput

I

This class is used by a number of the example programs to manage input from a file. There is a direct analogy with the `KeyboardInput` class in that the purpose of the class is to hide the exception handling required when using the standard Java file handling operations: the `FileInput` class packages reading values of the primitive types into methods, catching and dealing with any exceptions that may get thrown. If an file read error does occur then each method will return a default value, so no exceptions are propagated. Exceptions that occur when a file cannot be opened or closed, are also caught but will force a program to terminate displaying a suitable error message.

Exactly as with the `KeyboardInput` class the rationale for `FileInput` is to enable people to deal with input from a file before having dealt with exception handling. These classes are not intended for production software — the handling of exceptions in this way hides information usually needed in the application.

The class includes an end-of-file or *eof* flag that is set to true when an attempt is made to read a value after the end of file has been reached (note that eof is set after an attempt to read a value beyond the end of file has been made, not immediately the end of file is reached).

Chapter 5, Page 113 gives example programs showing how `FileInput` is used.

```
import java.io.* ;
/**
 *  A simple input class to read values from a file of characters.  If
 *  any file errors occur, methods in this class will display an error
 *  message and terminate the program.
 *
 *  @version 1.1 1999.09.10
 *  @author Graham Roberts
 *  @author Russel Winder
 */
public class FileInput {
  /**
   *  Instance variables to store the name of the file we are
   * associated with.
   */
  private String filename = "" ;
  /**
   *  Instance variables for the filestream associated with the file
   * that we are associated with..
   */
  private BufferedReader reader = null ;
  /**
   * Instance variables to store current state of EOF.
   */
  private boolean eof = false ;
  /**
   *  Construct <CODE>FileInput</CODE> object given a file name.
   */
  public FileInput(final String fname) {
    filename = fname ;
```

note

A `BufferedReader` connected to a file is the conduit for reading information from the file. We have to keep track of whether or not we have reached the end of file so that we can report this information correctly on demand.

```
    try {
      reader = new BufferedReader (new FileReader (filename)) ;
    }
    catch (FileNotFoundException e) {
      error("Can't open file: " + filename) ;
    }
  }
  /**
   *  Construct <CODE>FileInput</CODE> object given a
   *  <CODE>File</CODE> object.
   */
  public FileInput(final File file) {
    filename = file.getName() ;
    try {
      reader = new BufferedReader (new FileReader (file)) ;
    }
    catch (FileNotFoundException e) {
      error("Can't open file: " + filename) ;
    }
  }
  /**
   *  Close the file when finished
   */
  public final synchronized void close() {
    try {
      reader.close() ;
    }
    catch (IOException e) {
      error("Can't close file: " + filename) ;
    }
  }
  /**
   *  Return true if the end of file has been reached.
   */
  public boolean eof() {
    return eof ;
  }
  /**
   *  Read an <CODE>int</CODE> value from file.  The default
   *  return value is 0.
   */
  public final synchronized int readInteger() {
    String input = "" ;
    int value = 0 ;
    try {
      input = reader.readLine() ;
    }
    catch (IOException e)  {
      error("readInteger failed for file: " + filename) ;
    }
    if (input == null) {
      eof = true ;
    } else {
      try {
        value = Integer.parseInt(input) ;
      }
      catch (NumberFormatException e) {}
    }
    return value ;
  }
  /**
   *  Read a <CODE>long</CODE> value from file.  The default
   *  return value is 0L.
   */
  public final synchronized long readLong() {
    String input = "" ;
```

note

The algorithm for all the reading methods is essentially the same as is the same as for `KeyboardInput`: *Prepare a default value; read some data; parse the data if there was any to get; return a value. The main issues here are processing exceptions and dealing with end of file.*

```
    long value = 0L ;
    try {
      input = reader.readLine() ;
    }
    catch (IOException e)  {
      error("readLong failed for file: " + filename) ;
    }
    if (input == null) {
      eof = true ;
    } else {
      try {
        value = Long.parseLong(input) ;
      }
      catch (NumberFormatException e) {}
    }
    return value ;
}
/**
 *  Read a <CODE>double</CODE> value from file.  The
 *  default return value is 0.0.
 */
public final synchronized double readDouble() {
  String input = "" ;
  double value = 0.0D ;
  try {
    input = reader.readLine() ;
  }
  catch (IOException e)  {
    error("readDouble failed for file: " + filename) ;
  }
  if (input == null) {
    eof = true ;
  } else {
    try {
      value = Double.parseDouble(input) ;
    }
    catch (NumberFormatException e) {}
  }
  return value ;
}
/**
 *  Read a <CODE>float</CODE> value from file.  The
 *  default return value is 0.0F.
 */
public final synchronized float readFloat() {
  String input = "" ;
  float value = 0.0F ;
  try {
    input = reader.readLine() ;
  }
  catch (IOException e)  {
    error("readFloat failed for file: " + filename) ;
  }
  if (input == null) {
    eof = true ;
  } else {
    try {
      value = Float.parseFloat(input) ;
    }
    catch (NumberFormatException e) {}
  }
  return value ;
}
/**
 *  Read a <CODE>char</CODE> value from file.  The default
 *  return value is ' ' (space).
```

note

All the methods are synchronized to ensure that only one thread at a time can manipulate the input stream: the class is thread-safe.

```
    */
  public final synchronized char readCharacter() {
    char c = ' ' ;
    try {
      int n = reader.read() ;
      if (n == -1) {
        eof = true ;
      } else {
        c = (char)n ;
      }
    }
    catch (IOException e)  {
      error("readCharacter failed for file: " + filename) ;
    }
    return c ;
  }
  /**
   *  Read a <CODE>String</CODE> value from file.  The
   *  default return value is "" (the empty string).
   */
  public final synchronized String readString() {
    String s = "";
    try {
      s = reader.readLine() ;
    }
    catch (IOException e)  {
      error("readString failed for file: " + filename) ;
    }
    if (s == null) {
      eof = true ;
      s = "" ;
    }
    return s ;
  }
  /**
   * Deal with a file error, write a message and terminate.
   */
  private void error(String msg) {
    System.err.println(msg) ;
    System.err.println("Unable to continue executing program.") ;
    System.exit(0) ;
  }
}
```

Class FileOutput

Output, like input, is prone to error. The chances are significantly less since whilst input has to worry about input format error as well as equipment failure, output only has to worry about equipment failure. The probability of errors happening with output to the console is so small that there are no exceptions associated with output operations such as `System.out.println`. File output, however, is much more prone to error which means that the standard Java file output mechanisms make use of exceptions to handle any problems that do occur.

In order to make use of file output prior to knowing about exceptions, this class packages file output such that all file errors will result in the program being terminated. This is clearly not an appropriate strategy for production software — for that sort of software the standard Java mechanisms should be used and the exceptions handled explicitly. This class is just for teaching support until exceptions have been covered and understood.

Chapter 5, Page 113 gives example programs showing how `FileOutput` is used.

```java
import java.io.* ;
/**
 *  A simple output class to write values to a file of characters.
 *  If any file errors occur, methods in this class will display
 *  an error message and terminate the program.
 *
 *  @version 1.1 1999.09.10
 *  @author Graham Roberts
 *  @author Russel Winder
 */
public class FileOutput {
  /**
   * Instance variables to store file name.
   */
  private String filename = "" ;
  /**
   * Instance variables to store stream.
   */
  private BufferedWriter writer = null ;
  /**
   * Construct <CODE>FileOutput</CODE> object given a file name.
   */
  public FileOutput(final String name) {
    filename = name ;
    try {
      writer = new BufferedWriter (new FileWriter (filename)) ;
    }
    catch (IOException e) {
      error("Can't open file: " + filename) ;
    }
  }
  /**
   *  Construct <CODE>FileOutput</CODE> object given a
   * <CODE>File</CODE> object..
   */
  public FileOutput(final File file) {
    filename = file.getName() ;
```

note

A `BufferedWriter` connected to a file is the conduit for writing information to the file.

```
  try {
    writer = new BufferedWriter (new FileWriter (filename)) ;
  }
  catch (IOException e) {
    error("Can't open file: " + filename) ;
  }
}
/**
 *  Close the file when finished
 */
public final synchronized void close() {
  try {
    writer.close() ;
  }
  catch (IOException e) {
    error("Can't close file: " + filename) ;
  }
}
/**
 *  Write an <CODE>int</CODE> value to a file.
 */
public final synchronized void writeInteger(final int i) {
  try {
    writer.write(Integer.toString(i)) ;
  }
  catch (IOException e)  {
    error("writeInteger failed for file: " + filename) ;
  }
}
/**
 *  Write a <CODE>long</CODE> value to a file.
 */
public final synchronized void writeLong(final long l) {
  try {
    writer.write(Long.toString(l)) ;
  }
  catch (IOException e)  {
    error("writeLong failed for file: " + filename) ;
  }
}
/**
 *  Write a <CODE>double</CODE> value to a file.
 */
public final synchronized void writeDouble(final double d) {
  try {
    writer.write(Double.toString(d)) ;
  }
  catch (IOException e)  {
    error("writeDouble failed for file: " + filename) ;
  }
}
/**
 *  Write a <CODE>float</CODE> value to a file.
 */
public final synchronized void writeFloat(final float f) {
  try {
    writer.write(Float.toString(f)) ;
  }
  catch (IOException e)  {
    error("writeFloat failed for file: " + filename) ;
  }
}
/**
 *  Write a <CODE>char</CODE> value to a file.
 */
public final synchronized void writeCharacter(final char c) {
```

```
      try {
        writer.write(c) ;
      }
      catch (IOException e)  {
        error("writeCharacter failed for file: " + filename) ;
      }
    }
    /**
     *  Write a <CODE>String</CODE> value to a file.
     */
    public final synchronized void writeString(final String s) {
      try {
        writer.write(s) ;
      }
      catch (IOException e)  {
        error("writeString failed for file: " + filename) ;
      }
    }
    /**
     *  Write a newline to a file.
     */
    public final synchronized void writeNewline() {
      try {
        writer.write('\n') ;
      }
      catch (IOException e)  {
        error("writeNewline failed for file: " + filename) ;
      }
    }
    /**
     * Deal with a file error
     */
    private void error(final String msg) {
      System.err.println(msg) ;
      System.err.println("Unable to continue executing program.") ;
      System.exit(0) ;
    }
}
```

All the methods are synchronized to ensure that only one thread at a time can manipulate the output stream: the class is thread-safe.

The ADS Library

The ADS package developed in Part 2 really needs a complete UML diagram describing the design as well as having the HTML documentation generated using javadoc. Only with such a diagram can we get a real overview of the package.

Modern system development environments allow the development of packages such as ADS by using UML editors to create the design and using source code editors to flesh out the classes. In such environments, the UML diagram is automatically an integral part of the designed system and is automatically self-consistent with the source code.

The ADS package was, however, not developed this way, it was constructed directly via the source code. This means we need a mechanism for generating a correct UML diagram. There are three possibilities:

1. Move the source code into a suitable development environment so that it can be evolved using UML diagrams and source code.

2. Use a tool for reading source code and automatically generating the necessary UML diagram.

3. Construct the diagram by hand.

1. is clearly the most sensible option but we have not been able to find an environment which could import the extant package correctly. We have no doubt that very soon the environments will be able to do this but they cannot at the time of publication. A similar situation obtains for 2. the tool to automatically draw the diagram given the source code. In fact, this is not surprising since the systems needed for 1. and 2. are essentially the same. This appears to leave 3. as the only option at the time of publication at least.

The danger with 3. is that the diagram is likely not a completely correct representation of the source code. Moreover, if the source code is changed the UML diagram must be changed separately. This risks the source code and the diagram being different and diverging further with each change.

Given the above, we manually drew the diagram that follows. We believe it is correct as far as it goes but it is not complete. There are a number of associations that are not represented and there are some classes that are part of ADS that are not in the diagram. Any diagram such as this will be very complicated and it is very unlikely that it could ever be presented on a 2-dimensional page without some lines that are not related crossing each other. In the diagram following we have one such situation. Adding all the associations would lead to many more. So, for example, the association between `Array` and `ArrayQueue` is not notated. Whilst this is formally an error, we believe the class naming gives enough of a hint that we can get away with this.

Please note, we will be using a full environment to further evolve the ADS package just as soon as we can one that works.

tip

Developing systems using an environment that allows the design to be constructed using UML and then the classes to be completed using source code editors and which keeps the UML and source code in an integrated fashion is to be preferred.

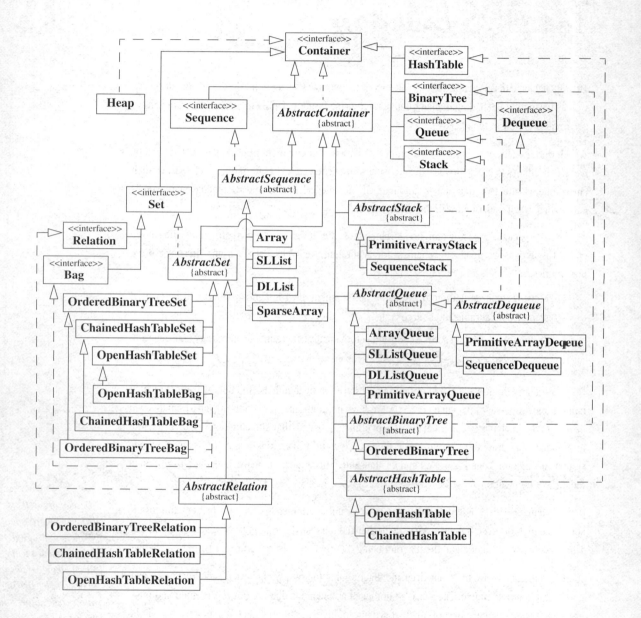

Bibliography

L

The following is a selection of the books available on object-oriented design and programming, algorithmics and algorithms, data structures and Java. Essentially this is a suggestion list for 'where to go next' in your study of systems development using Java. The list is based around those books we have found useful ourselves.

Aho, A V, Hopcroft, J E, Ullman, J D (1983) *Data Structures and Algorithms*, Addison–Wesley.

Beck, K (1999) *Extreme Programming Explained*, Addison Wesley.

Bentley, J (2000) *Programming Pearls — Second Edition*, Addison Wesley.

Booch, G, Rumbaugh, J and Jacobson, I (1999) *The Unified Modeling Language User Guide*, Addison Wesley.

Brassard, G and Bratley, P (1988) *Algorithmics —Theory & Practice*, Prentice–Hall.

Budd, T (1997) *An Introduction to Object-Oriented Programming*, second edition, Addison–Wesley.

Buschman, F, Meunier, R, Rohnert, H, Sommerland, P, and Stal, M (1996) *A System of Patterns — Pattern-Oriented Software Architecture*, John Wiley & Sons.

Campione, M, Walrath, K and Huml(1999) *The Java Tutorial Continued — The Rest of the JDK*, Addison Wesley.

Chan, P, Lee, R and Kramer, D (1998) *The Java Class Libraries Second Edition, Volume 1*, Addison–Wesley.

Chan, P, and Lee, R (1997) *The Java Class Libraries Second Edition Volume 2*, Addison–Wesley.

Chan, P, Lee, R and Kramer, D (1999) *The Java Class Libraries Second Edition, Volume 1, Supplement for the Java 2 Platform Standard Edition, v1.2*, Addison–Wesley.

Cook, S and Daniels, J (1994) *Designing Object Systems*, Prentice–Hall.

Dix, A, Finlay, J, Abowd, G and Beale, R (1993) *Human–Computer Interaction*, Prentice–Hall.

Firesmith, D, Henderson-Sellers, B and Graham, I (1997) *OPEN Modeling Language (OML) Reference Manual*, SIGS.

Flanagan, D (1999) *Java in a Nutshell*, third edition, O'Reilly.

Fowler, M with Beck, K, Brant, J, Opdyke, W, and Roberts, D (1999) *Refactoring — Improving the Design of Existing Code*, Addison Wesley.

Fowler, M with Scott, K (1997) *UML Distilled*, Addison–Wesley.

Gabriel, R P (1996) *Patterns of Software — Tales from the Software Community*, Oxford University Press.

Gamma, E, Helm, R, Johnson, R and Vlissides, J (1995) *Design Patterns: Elements of Reusable Object-Oriented Software*, Addison–Wesley.

Geary, D (1999) *Graphic Java Volume 1 AWT*, third edition, Prentice–Hall.

Geary, D (1999) *Graphic Java Volume 2 Swing*, third edition, Prentice–Hall.

Goodrich, M and Tamassia, R (1998) *Data Structures and Algorithms in Java*, John Wiley & Sons.

Goosens, M, Mittelbach, F and Samarin, A (1994) *The L^AT_EX Companion*, Addison–Wesley.

Gosling, J, Joy, W and Steele, G (1996) *The Java Language Specification*. Addison–Wesley.

Graham, I (1994) *Object-Oriented Methods*, second edition, Addison–Wesley.

Graham, I (1995) *Migrating to Object Technology*, Addison–Wesley.

Grand, M (1998) *Patterns in Java, Volume 1*, John Wiley & Sons.

Grand, M (1999) *Patterns in Java, Volume 2*, John Wiley & Sons.

Harold, E R (1999) *Java I/O*, O'Reilly.

Harold, E R (1997) *Java Network Programming*, O'Reilly.

Henderson-Sellers, B (1992) *Book of Object-Oriented Knowledge*, Prentice–Hall.

Henderson-Sellers, B and Edwards J M (1994) *Book Two of Object-Oriented Knowledge: The Working Object*, Prentice–Hall.

Hughes, M, Hughes, C, Shoffner, M and Winslow, M (1997) *Java Network Programming*, Prentice–Hall/Manning.

Jacobson, I, Booch, G and Rumbaugh, J (1999) *The Unified Software Development Process*, Addison–Wesley.

Jacobson, I, Christerson, M, Jonsson, P and Övergaard, G (1992) *Object-Oriented Software Engineering: A Use Case Driven Approach*, Addison–Wesley.

Kernighan, B and Pike, R (1999) *The Practice of Programming*, Addison–Wesley.

Knudsen, J (1999) *Java 2D Graphics*, O'Reilly.

Knuth, D E (1986) *The $T_EX$book*, Addison–Wesley.

Knuth, D E (1997) *The Art of Computer Programming Volume 1: Fundamental Algorithms*, third edition, Addison–Wesley.

Lamport, L (1994) *L^AT_EX A Document Preparation System User's Guide and Reference Manual*, second edition, Addison–Wesley.

Larman, C (1998) *Applying UML and Patterns: An Introduction to Object-oriented Analysis and Design*, Prentice–Hall.

Lea, D (1999) *Concurrent Programming in Java Second Edition — Design Principles and Patterns*, Addison–Wesley.

Magee, J and Kramer, J (1999) *Concurrency: State Models and Java Programs*, John Wiley & Sons.

Martin, J and Odell, J J (1995) *Object-Oriented Methods: A Foundation*, PTR Prentice Hall.

Muller, P-A (1997) *Instant UML*, Wrox Press.

Neapolitan, R and Naimipour, K (1996) *Foundation of Algorithms*, D C Heath.

Oaks, S and Wong, H (1999) *Java Threads 2nd edition, Java 2*, O'Reilly.

Pooley, R and Stevens, P (1999) *Using UML — Software Engineering with Objects and Components*, Addison–Wesley.

Preece, J, Benyon, D, Davies, G, Keller, L and Rogers, Y (1993) *A Guide to Usability: Human Factors in Computing*, Addison–Wesley.

Preiss, B (2000) *Data Structures and Algorithms with Object-oriented Design Patterns in Java*, John Wiley & Sons.

Resnick, M (1994) *Turtles, Termites, and Traffic Jams — Explorations in Massively Parallel Microworlds*, MIT Press.

Rumbaugh, J, Blaha, M, Premerlani, W, Eddy, F and Lorensen, W (1991) *Object-oriented Modelling and Design*, Prentice–Hall.

Rumbaugh, J, Jacobson, I and Booch, G (1999) *The Unified Modeling Language Reference Manual*, Addison Wesley.

Topley, K (1998) *Core Java Foundation Classes*, Prentice-Hall.

Vlissides, J (1998) *Pattern Hatching: Design Patterns Applied*, Addison–Wesley.

Walrath, K and Campione, M (1999) *The JFC Swing Tutorial — A Guide to Constructing GUIs*, Addison–Wesley.

Wilkinson, N M (1995) *Using CRC Cards*, SIGS Books.

Winder, R (1993) *Developing C++ Software*, second edition, John Wiley & Sons.

Winograd, T (1996) *Bringing Design to Software*, Addison–Wesley.

Zukowski, J (1997) *Java AWT Reference*, O'Reilly.